INTERNATIONAL ENCYCLOPEDIA OF
HOUSING AND HOME

INTERNATIONAL ENCYCLOPEDIA OF
HOUSING AND HOME

Editor-in-Chief

SUSAN J. SMITH
*Girton College and Cambridge University,
Cambridge, UK*

Associate Editors-in-Chief

MARJA ELSINGA
*Delft University of Technology,
Delft, The Netherlands*

ONG SEOW ENG
*National University of Singapore,
Singapore*

LORNA FOX O'MAHONY
*University of Durham,
Durham, UK*

SUSAN WACHTER
*University of Pennsylvania,
Philadelphia, PA, USA*

ELSEVIER

AMSTERDAM BOSTON HEIDELBERG LONDON NEW YORK OXFORD
PARIS SAN DIEGO SAN FRANCISCO SINGAPORE SYDNEY TOKYO

Elsevier
Radarweg 29, PO Box 211, 1000 AE Amsterdam, Netherlands
The Boulevard, Langford Lane, Kidlington, Oxford OX5 1GB, UK
225 Wyman Street, Waltham, MA 02451, USA

Copyright © 2012 Elsevier Ltd. All rights reserved

The following articles are US Government works in the public domain and not subject to copyright.
Housing Subsidies and Work Incentives
Mortgage Choice: Behavioural Finance
Mortgage Default: Determinants

No part of this publication may be reproduced, stored in a retrieval system or transmitted in any form or by any means electronic, mechanical, photocopying, recording or otherwise without the prior written permission of the publisher

Permissions may be sought directly from Elsevier's Science & Technology Rights Department in Oxford, UK: phone (+44) (0) 1865 843830; fax (+44) (0) 1865 853333; email: permissions@elsevier.com. Alternatively you can submit your request online by visiting the Elsevier web site at http://elsevier.com/locate/permissions, and selecting *Obtaining permission to use Elsevier material*

Notice
No responsibility is assumed by the publisher for any injury and/or damage to persons or property as a matter of products liability, negligence or otherwise, or from any use or operation of any methods, products, instructions or ideas contained in the material herein, Because of rapid advances in the medical sciences, in particular, independent verification of diagnoses and drug dosages should be made

British Library Cataloguing in Publication Data
A catalogue record for this book is available from the British Library

Library of Congress Catalog Number: 2012935706

ISBN (print): 978-0-08-047163-1

For information on all Elsevier publications
visit our website at books.elsevier.com

Printed and bound in Spain

12 11 10 9 8 7 6 5 4 3 2 1

Working together to grow
libraries in developing countries

www.elsevier.com | www.bookaid.org | www.sabre.org

ELSEVIER   BOOK AID   Sabre Foundation
             International

Editorial: Richard Berryman, Scott Bentley
Production: Mike Nicholls

EDITORS

EDITOR-IN-CHIEF
Susan J. Smith
Cambridge University
Cambridge
UK

ASSOCIATE EDITORS-IN-CHIEF
Marja Elsinga
Delft University of Technology
Delft
The Netherlands

Ong Seow Eng
National University of Singapore
Singapore

Lorna Fox O'Mahony
Durham Law School
Durham
UK

Susan Wachter
University of Pennsylvania
Philadelphia, PA
USA

SECTION EDITORS
David Clapham (Approaches)
Cardiff University
Cardiff
UK

Kavita Datta (Policy)
Queen Mary University of London
London
UK

Robyn Dowling (Home/Homelessness)
Macquarie University
Sydney, NSW
Australia

Suzanne Fitzpatrick (Home/Homelessness)
Heriot-Watt University
Edinburgh
UK

Kenneth Gibb (Approaches)
University of Glasgow
Glasgow
UK

Richard K. Green (Economics/Finance)
University of Southern California
Los Angeles, CA
USA

Chris Hamnett (Welfare/Well-Being)
Kings College London
London
UK

Kyung-Hwan Kim (Economics/Finance)
Sogang University
Republic of Korea
and
Singapore Management University
Singapore

Heather Lovell (Environment)
University of Edinburgh
Edinburgh
UK

Montserrat Pareja Eastaway (Environment)
University of Barcelona
Barcelona
Spain

Richard Ronald (Institutions)
Delft University of Technology
Delft
The Netherlands

Anthony B. Sanders (Economics/Finance)
George Mason University
Fairfax, AZ
USA

Sasha Tsenkova (Institutions)
University of Calgary
Calgary, AB
Canada

Peter M. Ward (Welfare/Well-Being)
University of Texas at Austin
Austin, TX
USA

Gavin Wood (Policy)
RMIT University
Melbourne, VIC
Australia

EDITORIAL ADVISORY BOARD

Antonio Azuela
National Autonomous University of Mexico
Mexico

Robert Buckley
The New School
New York, NY
USA

Karl E Case
Wellesley College
Wellesley, MA
USA

Rebecca L H Chiu
University of Hong Kong
Hong Kong

Alan Gilbert
University College London
London
UK

Deniz O Igan
International Monetary Fund
Washington
USA

Hugo Priemus
Delft University of Technology
Delft
The Netherlands

Freek Spinnewijn
FEANTSA
Brussels
Belgium

Judith Yates
University of Sydney
Sydney, NSW
Australia

GUIDE TO USING THE ENCYCLOPEDIA

STRUCTURE OF THE ENCYCLOPEDIA

The encyclopedia contains 521 entries, arranged in alphabetical order, and split across 7 volumes. There are five features to help you either browse the contents or to access specific topics which interest you.

1. ALPHABETICAL CONTENTS LIST

The full alphabetical contents list follows the editorial introductions. Titles, authors, volume and page numbers are provided.

2. SECTION IDENTIFIERS

The encyclopedia was developed around 7 thematic Sections, each with its own commissioning and editorial team. A list of entries organised by Section appears next. This is useful in providing a conceptual map of the contents, as well as for making quick connections between entries.

Most entries are around 4000 words. However, in every Section there are up to seven rather longer scene setting or 'overview' articles. These are identified in the main contents list.

On an entry by entry basis, a Section identifier is listed at the foot of the opening page, where there is also an indicator to identify Overview articles.

3. CROSS REFERENCES

Most entries in the encyclopedia are cross-referenced. The cross references, which appear at the end of an entry as a 'See also' list, serve four different functions:

  i. To draw the reader's attention to related material in other entries
  ii. To indicate material that broadens and extends the scope of the article
  iii. To indicate material that covers a topic in more depth
  iv. To direct readers to other articles by the same author(s)

4. CONTRIBUTORS

In addition to the comprehensive contents and author list, each of the seven alphabetical volumes includes a list of the specific authors whose entries appear in its pages.

5. INDEX

There is a comprehensive index for the whole work provided at the back of Volume 7. This index includes page numbers for quick reference to the information you are looking for. The index differentiates between references to a whole entry, a part of an entry, and a table or figure.

LIST OF ARTICLES BY SECTION

APPROACHES

Actor–Network Theory
Appraisal and Cost-Benefit Analysis
Austrian Economics
Behavioural Economics
Case Studies
Comparative Housing Research
Complexity
Construction of Housing Knowledge
Critical Realism
Cultural Analysis of Housing and Space
Democracy and Accountability
Demographic Perspectives in Economic Housing Research
Difference
Discourse Analysis
Econometric Modeling
Economic Approaches to Housing Research
Ethnography
Evolutionary Economics
Filtering
Forecasting in Housing Research
Foucauldian Analysis
Game Theory
Gentrification
Globalisation
House Biographies
House Price Indexes: Methodologies
House Prices and Quality of Life: An Economic Analysis
Housing Careers
Housing Classes and Consumption Cleavages
Housing Indicators
Housing Market Search
Housing Preferences
Housing Statistics
Inequalities in European Cities
Institutional Economics: New
Institutional Economics: Traditional
Life Course
Neighbourhood Effects: Approaches
Neoclassical Models of the Housing Market
Neural Networks and Analytic Hierarchy Processes
New Urban Economics and Residential Location
Path Dependency
People and the Built Form
Political Ideologies
Post-Bubble Housing in Japan
Power
Property Rights Approaches
Qualitative Interviewing
Qualitative Methods in Housing Research
Regulation Theory
Residential Segregation: Measurement
Rurality and Housing
Simulation Models for Housing Analysis
Small-Area Spatial Statistics
Social Class and Housing
Social Construction
Social History
Social Policy Approaches
Social Theory and Housing
Socio-Legal Perspectives
Spatial Economics
Stakeholder Analysis for Housing
Structure and Agency
Sustainability
Systems Theory
Textual and Linguistic Analysis
Visual Research Methods
Welfare States and Housing

ECONOMICS/FINANCE

Covered Bonds
Credit Derivatives
Credit Derivatives and the Housing Market
Discrimination in Mortgage Markets
Economics of Housing Choice
Economics of Housing Externalities
Economics of Housing Market Segmentation
Economics of Social Housing
Financial Deregulation
Financial Regulation
Hedging Housing Risk
Home Ownership: Economic Benefits
Home Ownership: Non-Shelter Benefits
House Price Expectations
House Price Indexes
Housing and Wealth Portfolios
Housing Demand
Housing Equity Withdrawal in the United Kingdom
Housing Finance: Mexico
Housing Finance: Global South
Housing Markets and Macroeconomic Policy

Housing Subsidies in the Developing World
Housing Wealth and Consumption
Housing Wealth and Inheritance in the United Kingdom
Housing Wealth as Precautionary Savings
Housing Wealth Over the Life Course
Housing Wealth Distribution in the United Kingdom
Industrial Organisation of the US Residential Mortgage Market
Islamic Housing Finance
Microfinance for Housing
Mortgage Choice: Behavioural Finance
Mortgage Choice: Classical Economics
Mortgage Contracts: Flexible
Mortgage Contracts: Traditional
Mortgage Default: Consequences
Mortgage Default: Determinants
Mortgage Equity Withdrawal
Mortgage Innovation
Mortgage Insurance
Mortgage Market Functioning
Mortgage Market Regulation: Europe
Mortgage Market Regulation: North America
Mortgage Market, Character and Trends: Africa
Mortgage Market, Character and Trends: Brazil
Mortgage Market, Character and Trends: China
Mortgage Market, Character and Trends: France
Mortgage Market, Character and Trends: Germany
Mortgage Market, Character and Trends: India
Mortgage Market, Character and Trends: Italy
Mortgage Market, Character and Trends: Japan
Mortgage Market, Character and Trends: Korea
Mortgage Market, Character and Trends: Mexico
Mortgage Market, Character and Trends: United Kingdom
Mortgage Market, Character and Trends: United States
Mortgage Markets and Macro-Instability
Mortgage Payment Protection Insurance
Neighbourhood Effects
Price Determination in Housing Markets
Price Dynamics in Housing Markets
Residential Property Derivatives
Residential Real Estate Investment Trusts
Risk in Housing Markets
Simulation Models for Urban Economies
Social Housing: Finance
Spatial Mismatch
Submarkets
Subprime Mortgages
Supply Elasticity of Housing
Taxation and Subsidies: The US Case
Time and the Economic Analysis of Housing Systems

Transaction Costs in Housing Markets
User Cost, Home Ownership and Housing Prices: United States

ENVIRONMENT

Abandonment
Adaptable Housing
Building Regulations for Energy Conservation
Climate Change
Climate Change: Adaptations
Community Energy Systems
Construction and Demolition Waste
Construction Methods
Crime Prevention Through Environmental Design
Defensible Space
Demolition
Eco-Communities
Ecological Footprint
Eco-Renovation
Energy Saving
Environmental Consciousness
Environmental Risks: Earthquakes
Environmental Risks: Flooding
Ethnic Minorities and Housing
Eviction
Fuel Poverty
Gated Communities
Gender and Space
Gentrification and Neighbourhood Change
Ghetto
Gypsy/Roma Settlements
Health and Housing
Health Risks: Damp and Cold
Health Risks: Overcrowding
High Rise
Household Waste Recycling
Housing and Sustainable Transport
Housing Developers and Sustainability
Housing Dynamics: Environmental Aspects
Housing Estates
Housing Pathology
Maintenance and Repair
Modern Methods of Construction
Multiple Homes
Neighbourhood Design: Green Space and Parks
Neighbourhood Design: Public Spaces
Neighbourhood Design: Urban Outdoor Experience
Neighbourhood Disadvantage
Neighbourhood Governance
Neighbourhood Incivilities
Neighbourhood Planning
Neighbourhood Reputation

Neighbourhood Watch
NIMBYism
Peripheral Neighbourhoods
Place Attachment
Residential Segregation
Residential Urban Form and Transport
Restorative Housing Environments
Rural Communities
Rural Housing
Second Homes
Self-Build: Global North
Self-Build: Global South
Shanty Towns
Slums
Social Spaces and Urban Policies
Social Sustainability
Sustainable Communities
Sustainable Housing Cultures
Sustainable Lifestyles
Sustainable Regeneration
Sustainable Urban Development
Temporary Housing
Vacancy Chains
Vernacular Housing
Water Supply and Sanitation

HOME/HOMELESSNESS

Anthropological Perspectives on Home
Children and Parenting
Cost Analyses of Homelessness: Limits and Opportunities
Criminological Perspectives on Homelessness
Do-it-Yourself
Domestic Technologies and the Modern Home
Domestic Violence
Domesticity
Domestic Pets
Domicide
Economic Perspectives on Homelessness
Emotions at Home
Ethnographies of Home and Homelessness
Experiencing Home
Experiencing Home: Sexuality
Feminist Perspectives on Home
Feminist Perspectives on Homelessness
Gender Divisions in the Home
Hidden Homelessness
High-Rise Homes
Home and Homelessness
Home as a Space of Care
Home as Inheritance
Home as Investment
Home as Leisure Space

Home as Workplace
Home Environments: Aesthetics, Fashion, Status
Home in Temporary Dwellings
Home Objects
Home: Paid Domestic Labour
Home: Unpaid Domestic Labour
Homeless Families: United Kingdom
Homeless Families: United States
Homelessness: Causation
Homelessness: Definitions
Homelessness: Measurement Questions
Homelessness: Prevention in the United States
Homeless People in China/East Asia
Homeless People: African Americans in the United States
Homeless People: Care Leavers
Homeless People: Care Leavers in the United Kingdom
Homeless People: Disasters and Displacement
Homeless People: Economic Migrants in Southern Europe
Homeless People: Ex-Prisoners in England and Wales
Homeless People: Ex-Service Personnel/Veterans in the United Kingdom
Homeless People: Indigenous/Aboriginal
Homeless People: Older People
Homeless People: Polish Migrants in the United Kingdom
Homeless People: Refugees and Asylum Seekers
Homeless People: Single Men in Japan
Homeless People: Street Children in Africa
Homeless People: Street Children in Asia
Homeless People: Street Children in Mexico
Homeless People: Street Children in the United Kingdom
Homeless People: Youth in Australia
Homeless People: Youth in the United Kingdom
Homes as a Space of Worship
Homestead and Other Legal Protections
Ideal Homes
Illicit Drug Use and Homelessness
Impairment and Experience of Home
Kitchens
Living Rooms
Material Cultures of Domestic Interiors: Africa
Material Cultures of Domestic Interiors: India
Material Cultures of Domestic Interiors: Japan
Material Cultures of Domestic Interiors: Transnationalism
Material Cultures of Home
Meanings of Home
Meanings of Home for Moveable Habitats
Meanings of Home for Older People
Meanings of Home: Gender Dimensions

Meanings of Home in Popular Culture
Memory and Nostalgia at Home
Mental Health and Homelessness
Migration: Ethnicity, Race and Mobility
Nature in the Home
Ontological Security
Philosophical Perspectives on Home
Policies to Address Homelessness
Policies to Address Homelessness: Criminalisation and Control of Public Space
Policies to Address Homelessness: Housing First Approaches
Policies to Address Homelessness: Partnership-Based Approaches in Ireland
Policies to Address Homelessness: Prevention in the United Kingdom
Policies to Address Homelessness: Rights-Based Approaches
Policies to Address Homelessness: 'Staircase' Models
Privacy, Sanctuary and Privatism
Representations of Home: Literature and Language
Representations of Home: Painting
Representations of Home: Photos and Film
Representations of Homelessness
Rural Homelessness in India
Rural Homelessness: An International Perspective
Shelter and Development
Social Psychological Perspectives on Homelessness
Squatting: Developing World
Squatting: United Kingdom
Suburban Homes
Technology and Surveillance in the Home

INSTITUTIONS

Affordable Housing Strategies
Architects
Central Government Institutions
Civil Sector Institutions and Informal Settlements
Community- and Neighbourhood-Based Organisations in the United States
Cooperative Housing/Ownership
Demand Subsidies for Low-Income Households
Ethnicity and Housing Organisations
Government Mortgage Guarantee Institutions
Government/Public Lending Institutions: Asia-Pacific
Government Sponsored Enterprises in the United States
Homeowners' Associations in Post-Socialist Countries

House Building Industries: Africa
House Building Industries: Asia Pacific
House Building Industries: Latin America
House Building Industries: Post-Socialist
House Building Industries: Western Europe and North America
Households and Families
Housing Agents and Housing Submarkets
Housing Auctions
Housing Developers: Developed World
Housing Developers: Developing World
Housing Finance Institutions: Africa
Housing Finance Institutions: Asia
Housing Finance Institutions: Latin America
Housing Finance Institutions: Transition Societies
Housing Institutions in Developing Countries
Housing Market Institutions
Housing Paradigms
Housing Policy: Agents and Regulators
Human Rights and Housing
Informal Housing: Asia
Informal Housing: Latin America
Institutions and Governance Networks in Housing and Urban Regeneration
Institutions for Housing Supply
Institutions for Neighbourhood Renewal
Institutions that Represent Housing Professionals
Land Owners
Land Registration Institutions: Developed World
Master Plan Developers
Mortgage Lenders and Loans
Neighbourhood Improvement: The Role of Housing and Housing Institutions
New Urbanism and Smart Growth Movements
Notaries and Legal Professionals
Older People: Housing Institutions
Planning Institutions: Canada/United States
Planning Institutions: China
Planning Institutions: Post-Socialist
Post-Conflict Housing Restitutions
Private Protection and Housing Property Insurers in the United States
Private Rental Landlords: Developing Countries
Private Rental Landlords: Europe
Private Rental Landlords: North America
Private Sector Housing Management: Asia Pacific
Private Sector Housing Management: Europe
Private Sector Housing Management: North America
Private Sector Housing Management: Post-Socialist
Public-Private Partnerships
Real Estate Agents
Research Networks and Professional Institutions in Housing
Resident and Neighbourhood Movements

Rights to Housing Tenure
Rights to Housing: Developing Societies
Rights to Housing: International Instruments
Rights to Housing: Marginalised Housing Groups
Rights to Land Tenure
Security of Tenure in Muslim Communities
Self-Help Housing Organisations
Self-Provided Housing in Developed Societies
Social Housing Institutions in Europe
Social Housing Landlords: Asia Pacific
Social Housing Landlords: China
Social Housing Landlords: Europe
Social Housing Landlords: Latin America
Social Housing Landlords: North America
Social Housing Landlords: Post-Socialist
Subprime and Predatory Lending: Legal Regulation
Supply-Side Subsidies for Affordable Rental Housing
Taxation
Tenant Cooperatives, Shareholders' Housing Companies
Tenure as an Institution
Welfare Agencies and Assistance: United States
Women and Housing Organisations

POLICY

Access and Affordability: Homeowner Taxation
Access and Affordability: House Purchase Certificates
Access and Affordability: Housing Allowances
Access and Affordability: Housing Vouchers
Access and Affordability: Mortgage Guarantees
Access and Affordability: Rent Regulation
Brownfield Development and Housing Supply
Choice and Government Intervention in Housing Markets
Contract Saving Schemes
Deposit Assistance Schemes for Private Rental in the United Kingdom
Development Land Tax
Discrimination in Housing Markets
Education Programmes for Home Buyers and Tenants
Energy Consumption, Housing, and Urban Development Policy
Exclusionary Zoning
First Home Owner Grants
Foreclosure Prevention Measures
HOPE VI
Housing and Labour Markets
Housing and Neighbourhood Quality: Home Improvement Grants
Housing and Neighbourhood Quality: Urban Regeneration
Housing Construction Industry, Competition and Regulation
Housing Finance Deposit Guarantees
Housing Governance
Housing Markets and Macroeconomic Policy
Housing Policies in Developing Countries
Housing Policies in Developing Countries: Microfinance
Housing Policies in Developing Countries: Sites-and-Services and Aided Self-Help
Housing Policy and Regeneration
Housing Policy Trends
Housing Standards: Regulation
Housing Subsidies and Work Incentives
Housing Supply
Housing Supply: Green Belts
Housing Supply: Urban Growth Boundaries
Housing Trust Funds
Immigration and Housing Policy
Impact Fees
Inclusionary Zoning to Support Affordable Housing
Intermediate Housing Tenures
Key Worker Housing Policies
Local Government Property Taxes
Low-Income Housing Tax Credits
Mobility Programmes for Disadvantaged Populations: The Moving to Opportunity Programme
Monetary Policy, Wealth Effects and Housing
Mortgage Interest Rate Regulation
Mortgage Markets: Regulation and intervention
Policies to Address Redlining
Policies to Address Social Mix in Communities
Policies to Address Spatial Mismatch
Policies to Promote Housing Choice in Transition Countries
Policies to Promote the Environmental Efficiency of Housing
Policies to Support Access and Affordability of Housing
Policy Instruments that Support Housing Supply: Social Housing
Policy Instruments that Support Housing Supply: Supply-Side Subsidies
Privatisation of Social Housing
Rent Policies For Social Housing
Securing Land Rights and Housing Delivery
Security of Tenure Legislation in Private Rental Housing
Self-Help: Policy Assistance
Shared Equity
Social Housing and Employment
Social Housing: Measures to Attract Private Finance
Taxation Policy and Housing
Upgrading Informal Settlements

WELFARE/WELLBEING

Access and Affordability: Developed Countries
Asset-Based Welfare
Asset-Based Well-Being: Use Versus Exchange Value
Collective Ownership
Disability and Enablement
Foreclosure Vulnerability
Gated Communities: Developed Countries
Gated Communities: Global South
Gender and Urban Housing in the Global South
Gentrification and Well-Being
Health and Well-Being
Health and Well-Being: Vulnerable Populations
Household Organisation and Survival in Developing Countries
Housing and the State in Australasia
Housing and the State in China
Housing and the State in Latin America
Housing and the State in South Africa
Housing and the State in South Asia
Housing and the State in the Middle East
Housing and the State in the Soviet Union and Eastern Europe
Housing and the State in Western Europe
Housing Need in the United Kingdom
Housing Subsidies and Welfare
Immigration and Housing: North-Western Europe
Immigration and Housing: United States
Informal Housing: Colonias in the United States
Migration and Housing: Global South
Migration and Population Mobility
Migration and Urban Living in Less Developed Countries
Mobility and Community
Mortage Default and Well-Being in the United States
Older People: Well-Being
Older People: Well-Being, Housing and Neighbourhoods
Politics of Housing
Post-Disaster Housing and Reconstruction
Privatisation of Housing: Implications for Well-Being
Remittances and Well-Being
Rental Market and Rental Policies in Less Developed Countries
Residential Segregation and Education
Residential Segregation and Ethnic Diversity in US Housing
Residential Segregation: Apartheid
Residential Segregation: Experiences of African Americans
Residential Segregation: Race and Ethnicity
Rights, Citzenship, and Shelter
Rights to the City
Self-Build: Latin America
Self-Help: Land Development
Self-Help and Informal Sector Housing in the United States and Canada
Shelter and Settlement for Forcibly Displaced People
Slum Clearance
Social Exclusion and Housing
Social Housing and Social Problems
Social Housing in the United States: Overview
Social Housing: Allocation
Social Justice
Social Mix in Western Countries
Social Movements and Housing
Squatter Settlement Clearance
Supported Housing
Urbanisation and Housing the Poor: Overview
Urban Regeneration in Latin America
Well-Being and Housing in the Caribbean

CONTRIBUTORS TO VOLUME 5: M–P

Manuel Aalbers
University of Amsterdam, Amsterdam, The Netherlands

Irwin Altman
University of Utah, Salt Lake City, UT, USA

Isobel Anderson
University of Stirling, Stirling, UK

Mark Andrew
City University London, London, UK

Richard Arnott
University of California, Riverside, CA, USA

Bo Bengtsson
Uppsala University, Uppsala, Sweden

Mike Berry
RMIT University, Melbourne, VIC, Australia

Barbara Brown
University of Utah, Salt Lake City, UT, USA

Tim Brown
De Montfort University, Leicester, UK

Barbara Goličnik Marušić
Urban Planning Institute of the Republic of Slovenia, Ljubljana, Slovenia

Kate Burningham
University of Surrey, Guildford, UK

Antoine Buyse
Utrecht University, Utrecht, The Netherlands

Tom Carter
University of Winnipeg, Winnipeg, MB, Canada

Man Cho
The KDI School of Public Policy and Management, Seoul, South Korea

Melek Cigdem
RMIT University, Melbourne, VIC, Australia

Lindy Clemson
University of Sydney, Lidcombe, NSW, Australia

Maurizio d'Amato
Technical University Politecnico di Bari, Bari, Italy

Nestor Davidson
University of Colorado Law School, Boulder, CO, USA

Nicola Dempsey
University of Sheffield, Sheffield, UK

Robyn Dowling
Macquarie University, Sydney, NSW, Australia

Ann Dupuis
Massey University, Auckland, New Zealand

Paul Flatau
Murdoch University, Perth, WA, Australia

Alan Gilbert
University College London, London, UK

Rose Gilroy
Newcastle University, Newcastle upon Tyne, UK

Jill Grant
Dalhousie University, Halifax, NS, Canada

Marietta Haffner
Delft University of Technology, Delft, The Netherlands

Benjamin Henwood
New York University, New York, NY, USA

Yosuke Hirayama
Kobe University, Kobe, Japan

Joris Hoekstra
Delft University of Technology, Delft, The Netherlands

Ralph Horne
RMIT University, Melbourne, VIC, Australia

Donald Houston
University of St. Andrews, St. Andrews, UK

Eddie Hui
The Hong Kong Polytechnic University, Hong Kong SAR, P R China

Kirsten Jacobson
University of Maine, Orono, ME, USA

Cassidy Johnson
University College London, London, UK

Tom Kauko
Norwegian University of Science and Technology – NTNU, Trondheim, Norway

Hal Kendig
University of Sydney, Lidcombe, NSW, Australia

Tareef Khan
University Technology Malaysia (UTM), Skudai, Johor, Malaysia

Kyung-Hwan Kim
Sogang University, Seoul, The Republic of Korea, and Singapore Management University, Singapore

Peter King
De Montfort University, Leicester, UK

Robert Klein
Georgia State University, Atlanta, GA, USA

Roderick Lawrence
University of Geneva, Carouge, Switzerland

Gonzalo Lizarralde
Université de Montréal, Montréal, QC, Canada

Jane Londerville
University of Guelph, Guelph, ON, Canada

Martin Lux
The Institute of Sociology, Prague, Czech Republic

Lynette Mackenzie
University of Sydney, Lidcombe, NSW, Australia

Ali Madanipour
Newcastle University, Newcastle upon Tyne, UK

Alan Mallach
The Brookings Institution, Roosevelt, NJ, USA

Peter Malpass
University of the West of England, Bristol, UK

D Manley
University of St Andrews, St Andrews, UK

Geoffrey Meen
University of Reading, Reading, UK

Vivienne Milligan
University of New South Wales, Sydney, NSW, Australia

Silvia Mugnano
University of Milano-Bicocca, Milan, Italy

Zorica Nedović-Budić
University College Dublin, Dublin, Ireland

Nico Nieboer
Delft University of Technology, Delft, The Netherlands

Christian Nygaard
University of Reading, Reading, UK

Diana Olsberg
University of New South Wales, Sydney, NSW, Australia

Tomas Eoin O'Sullivan
Trinity College Dublin, Dublin, Ireland

Michael Oxley
Delft University of Technology, Delft, The Netherlands

Deborah Padgett
New York University, New York, NY, USA

Chris Paris
University of Ulster, City of Derry, Ireland

Hal Pawson
Heriot-Watt University, Edinburgh, UK

Matthieu Permentier
Netherlands Institute for Social Research/SCP, The Hague, The Netherlands

Simon Pinnegar
University of New South Wales, Sydney, NSW, Australia

Emma Power
University of Western Sydney, Sydney, NSW, Australia

Jason Prior
University of Technology, Sydney, NSW, Australia

Ingrid Sahlin
University of Gothenburg, Gothenburg, Sweden

Richard Sendi
Urban Planning Institute of the Republic of Slovenia, Ljubljana, Slovenia

Ian Skelton
University of Manitoba, Winnipeg, MB, Canada

Yan Song
University of North Carolina, Chapel Hill, NC, USA

Victoria Stanhope
New York University, New York, NY, USA

Ralph Taylor
Temple University, Philadelphia, PA, USA

Sasha Tsenkova
University of Calgary, Calgary, AB, Canada

Harry van der Heijden
Delft University of Technology, Delft, The Netherlands

Maarten van Ham
University of St Andrews, St Andrews, UK

Julia Wardhaugh
Bangor University, Bangor, UK

Carol Werner
University of Utah, Salt Lake City, UT, USA

Richard Yarwood
University of Plymouth, Plymouth, UK

Judy Yates
University of Sydney, Sydney, NSW, Australia

Nicola Yates
Kingston upon Hull City Council, Kingston upon Hull, UK

PREFACE AND ACKNOWLEDGEMENTS

The urge to collect and catalogue is as old as humanity itself. Perhaps there is something about being human that insists on scholars pausing from time to time to gather up everything they know and set it down en masse. Certainly, encyclopedias have existed, pretty much in the form we know them now, for at least two millennia. Furthermore, most dictionary definitions of the term 'encyclopedia' contain phrases like 'complete education', 'comprehensive', and 'covering all knowledge'. Roget's Thesaurus likewise directs those looking for synonyms and antonyms of 'encylopedical' to the headings 'generality' and 'knowledge'. In short, anyone with an encyclopedic knowledge of a subject simply knows it all.

It cannot be denied that there is something satisfying about the thought of coordinating a project designed to pull the housing world together in this way. Housing studies, after all, is a quintessentially interdisciplinary and international enterprise whose research and teaching spans a wide range of social science, health, and environmental disciplines. Its relevance ranges from sociology and geography to law, from politics to public health, from economics to accountancy, and from architecture to planning, engineering, and environmental science. The meaning and materiality of home has likewise moved to centre stage in a broad sweep of cultural studies, English, and humanities research. Housing and home together are hot media topics, the staple diet of dinner parties, the heart of practical politics, and very big business in the sale of financial services, do-it-yourself (DIY), home interiors, and garden design. The thought of gathering 'everything you ever wanted to know' about housing and home together into a single massive reference work is enticing.

The *International Encyclopedia of Housing and Home* is not, however, an oracle of this kind. To pretend that it is would be tantamount to claiming that a map of Spain were as complete as Spain itself. But if the map were that comprehensive, it would *be* Spain! Subjects as diverse, dynamic, lively, changeable, topical, and important as housing and home could never be crammed into, or pinned onto, the pages of a book, no matter how many volumes or innovative media platforms were brought to bear. So, in a sense, we have broken the encyclopedic mould. The aim was always to produce a work that is wide-ranging enough to embrace the cutting edges of research, to probe the inner core and outer limits of the worlds of housing and home, to capture the sheer colour and vibrancy wrapped into these subjects, and to recognise the critical importance they hold for economic management, social policy, and public well-being. At the same time, however, the enterprise is designed to set hares running: to identify, as much as to fill, key gaps in the literature; to point to new themes and research agendas which might, in time, make the current work redundant.

Cataloguing the spheres of housing and home is, then, a dynamic and open-ended project. It is a venture that began in earlier works, for example, in Willem van Vliet's (1998) single-volumed *Encyclopedia of Housing*, and its companion work, David Levinson's (1998) *Encyclopedia of Homelessness* (both published by Sage). It is a process extended into more specialised compilations, such Jack Guttentag's (2004) *Mortgage Encyclopedia* (McGraw-Hill) and Andrew Arden's (1997) *Encyclopedia of Housing Law and Practice* (Sweet and Maxwell). Then there are Jack Rostron and Michael Nutt's *Dictionary of Housing* and Jack Rostron, Robert Hardy-Pickering, Laura Tatham and Linda Wright's *Dictionary of Property and Construction Law* (published by Arena in 1997, and Routledge in 2001, respectively). And there are numerous single-volume collections, most notably and recently, the *Handbook of Housing Studies* (Sage, 2011), edited by David Clapham, William Clark and Kenneth Gibb. Who knows where it might end? Not here, and not yet; I am sure. But one other thing is certain: there is nothing published, in press, or yet planned, which offers the sheer scale, complexity, and range of content now packed into the *International Encyclopedia of Housing and Home*. This is a massive work, equivalent in size to around 25 standard edited collections. We offer it, therefore, notwithstanding its partial, uneven, and evolving character, as the major single reference work for housing professionals – for academics and practitioners – for all teaching, learning, and research needs.

It is probably clear, but the words should be said, that the encyclopedia is very much a collective enterprise and a labour of love. Academic authors get little credit for an undertaking like this in the counting and ranking exercises that so many governments now engage in. To be sure, small payments have been made, and the publisher no doubt seeks a profit. But you can be certain that those who brought this project to life did so, above all, as a service to colleagues, reflecting absolute passion for the subject. That sense of imagination and excitement is, I think, reflected in the quality of the articles and the coherence of the work.

The project has been ongoing since 2007; fully 20 senior scholars have spent, on and off, at least 5 years planning, commissioning, debating, and editing the 2 million words that are published herein. They have worked with over

350 authors, and been supported by an enthusiastic international advisory board drawn from all walks of life around housing and home. There is input from most world regions and from every key centre for housing research as well as from the non-university sector. The result is in every sense a collaborative work: it reflects the expertise of the authors, the insight and efficiency of the section editors, the vigilance of the associate editors-in-chief, and the good humoured energy of the entire scholarly team. That, I feel is the main strength of the work, and key to its endurance.

I am sure there are many acknowledgements to funding agencies, institutions, projects, colleagues, and friends that everyone involved with this work would wish to make. My personal debt is to the UK's Economic and Social Research Council, whose Professorial Fellowships scheme made time for the plot to be hatched (RES 051-27-0126); to the members of the first Think Tank on Housing Wealth who debated its feasibility; and to Elsevier's Mary Malin who turned a modest proposal into a Major Reference Work.

If I had enough space, and readers had the patience, I would wish at this point to mention every editor, and many authors, by name, and list the distinctive qualities that each has brought to this amazing collective work. It has been a privilege to be part of that team. The work of the authors is, I feel sure, clear from the content of the articles. The achievements of the section editors can been seen from the coherence of the thematic volumes and the energy in their introductory statements. The role of the associate editors-in-chief is perhaps less obvious, because they have worked between sections to explore synergies, look for overlap, encourage themes that cross section boundaries, and of course they have worked as a resource for the sections themselves. Marja Elsinga steered 'Environment' and 'Policy'; Lorna Fox O'Mahony anchored 'Home and Homelessness' and 'Institutions'; Susan Wachter and Ong Seow Eng kept an eye on 'Economics and Finance' across the board. The editors in turn owe special thanks to Jim Follain and Jim Shilling for their work as reviewers in 'Economics and Finance'. We are all grateful to Mike Nicholls for his meticulous coordination of the proofs. If, however, there is one person without whom the project would have foundered, it is Richard Berryman, development editor for Elsevier's Major Reference Works. He has far exceeded his brief, keeping track of all the articles, managing the process of electronic manuscript submission (circumventing it where necessary), and bringing unfailing energy, good humour, and consummate professionalism to an otherwise impossible task.

Susan J Smith
Cambridge, October 2011

INTRODUCTION

Housing has never been more squarely in the spotlight; homes have rarely been closer to people's hearts. For the first time ever, we appreciate the full extent to which housing market dynamics can challenge macroeconomic stability, and expose the fragility of households' primary asset base. Residential mortgage markets have proved sufficiently volatile to trigger a global credit crisis, and to bankrupt entire residential neighbourhoods; yet, they have also added unprecedented financial flexibility to home-occupiers' domestic accounts. Meanwhile, the social aspects of housing (including issues around exclusion, inequality, and identity) are under intense scrutiny by politicians and social researchers alike. Many governments have rekindled their in-house, and commissioned, housing research programmes and revitalised housing policy. The search is on for housing solutions to a wide range of enduring social problems and for ways to manage a new suite of financial and environmental risks. As a result, the inherently multidisciplinary field of housing studies is undergoing a major renaissance. The time seems right to publish a comprehensive *International Encyclopedia of Housing and Home* designed to meet a suite of teaching, research, practical, professional, and policy needs among a wide-ranging readership.

Encyclopedias come in many shapes and sizes: some are little more than elaborate dictionaries, full of long words and short definitions; others seem more like edited books, with extended manuscripts covering a few core themes. This encyclopedia occupies neither extreme. It is, well, 'encyclopedic' in every sense. It is based on over 500 substantial contributions, enough to touch practically every core theme relating to housing and home. Most articles run to at least 4000 words, sufficient for subject experts to address their topics in depth, without sacrificing accessibility. This melée is structured around a series of longer keynote or overview articles, which set the scene for the seven thematic volumes or sections comprising the larger work. The result is a comprehensive, authoritative source of facts, ideas, and concepts anchored on housing and home. The contents are international in scope, engaging with trends in every world region; the authors are drawn from a wide range of countries, and the work as a whole collates a mix of expertise from academics, policy-makers, professionals and practitioners.

There is an infinite number of ways to collect and organise the contents of a publication like this. In the end, the encyclopedic tradition is to list articles alphabetically, and we feel this works for housing and home. 'Housing studies' is, after all, a tradition founded on 'mix and match' across sectors and disciplines; the uneasy jostling of incongruous ideas has already proved to be an exciting route to new knowledge. With that in mind, why not experiment with the alphabet?

For those who seek more structure, there are other ways of navigating the text. For example, readers may wish to search by 'discipline' (there are contributions from housing economics, housing law, the sociology of housing, psychology and housing, housing and health, cultures of housing, and politics of housing), by 'world region' (coverage extends to Europe, Australasia, North and South America, Africa, and Asia), 'thematically' (through topics such as housing finance, housing policy, and housing management), 'sectorally' (owner-occupation, social renting, private renting, buy-to-let, co-operative housing, self-build, etc.), 'conceptually' (housing markets, price mechanisms, housing need, housing allocation, housing consumption, and meanings of home), 'theoretically' (housing and the macroeconomy, the microstructures of housing markets, social theory and housing), 'methodologically' (life-course approach, behavioural economics, hedonic analysis, microsociology, ethnography, and synoptic reading), and 'practically' (housing interventions, planning, buying and selling, professional training, needs assessment, price index construction, taxation, etc.).

Notwithstanding these multiple organisational possibilities, the main conceptual map of the encyclopedia is constructed from seven broad themes, each of which was commissioned, written, and edited as a separate volume or section. Other than an alphabetical list, section headings are the main way in which the work is structured. Introductions to each section, written by the editors who devised them, appear next. In brief, the sections are as follows. 'Approaches' contains articles on the main concepts and theories used in housing research, and on the methodologies commonly used to explore key themes around housing, home, and homelessness. 'Economics and Finance' engages with all aspects of housing and economy, including housing economics, housing market dynamics, housing wealth, and housing finance. 'Environment' includes articles on the physical and social environments, including environmental sustainability, energy efficiency, neighbourhood trajectories, and residential segregation. 'Home and Homelessness' addresses the full range of ideas about homemaking, home cultures, home values, domestic interiors, design, and meanings of home; it also considers the absence of home – the predicament of homelessness – in its many and varied forms. 'Institutions' documents all the main institutions of the housing system: legal frameworks, housing tenures, lenders, insurers, valuation, marketing, intermediation, and so on. 'Policy' is concerned with all aspects of housing governance and regulation: access and affordability of housing, housing production, tax policies, and links between housing, labour markets, and mortgage markets. 'Welfare and Well-Being' is concerned with the social aspects of housing. It examines the links between housing, welfare, and well-being; it considers housing needs, risks, and affordability; and it touches on health, safety, and security.

There are, of course, aspects of housing and home that this work does not cover. Some areas are simply not in the brief: they would have made the project too large, and in some important respects unbalanced. These include: commercial real estate; aspects of welfare, urban studies and planning that do not pertain to housing; technical building regulations; and aspects of home not relating to dwelling or residential property. Some topics cried out for attention, but simply refused to be attached to an author: maybe that will change next time round, as key themes blossom; perhaps it is already a pointer to topics that will in future fail to thrive. Some authors, bluntly put, did not submit their articles, despite extended deadlines. But that is the messy reality of creating a major reference work. Encyclopedias can no longer be produced by a single person; the shape they take is in every sense a reflection of the busy worlds they inhabit. One thing is clear, however: the encyclopedia is not only the print in your hands or the text on an electronic platform. It has created the community that made it and that network will hopefully widen as time goes on: connecting scholars across spaces, disciplines, and languages; sparking new alliances, friendships, and debates; indeed, giving shape to areas of scholarship that were overlooked or taken for granted before. In that sense, the encyclopedia can never be finished. It has a life of its own which has already burst free of its covers.

M Elsinga, L Fox O'Mahony, SE Ong, SJ Smith, and S Wachter

APPROACHES

Housing is a complex entity that has many different dimensions and impacts on many areas of private and public life. Housing is at the same time shelter, the scene of people's most emotional moments, the place we call home, an indicator of status, and a point of access to employment as well as to a range of public and private facilities. Housing is also the most expensive purchase the majority of households will make and a repository for the majority of personal wealth. The complexity of housing is fascinating, but this presents problems as well as opportunities for housing analysts.

The peculiarities of housing (as a locationally fixed commodity, a strangely indivisible investment, an object of consumption, and a crucible of housing services) demand special methodological and conceptual attention. That is one reason why we have devoted an entire section of the encyclopedia to it. Some aspects of housing can readily be explored using tried and tested tools borrowed from cognate areas of social and economic research. Others demand a more bespoke range of approaches. More than anything else, while acknowledging that certain elements of housing – one or two attributes at once, perhaps – can readily and productively be subject to discipline-specific analyses, the articles in this section of the encyclopedia point to the opportunity, and incentive, which housing studies provides to undertake comprehensive and transdisciplinary research.

There are 67 articles in this section. They provide both theoretical depth and methodological detail; they span qualitative and quantitative, as well as social and economic, approaches to housing research. They can therefore be used in conjunction with substantive articles in many other sections. For example, the article on the methodology of house price indexes in this section has a counterpart in the section 'Economics and Finance' on the uses and application of such indexes. Similarly, an article on neighbourhood effects in this section has a bearing on several substantive articles in the section 'Environment'. By way of a more systematic introduction to the diverse approaches collected here, we briefly consider theories, methods, and social and economic approaches as applied to housing studies.

Theory has become increasingly important in housing studies in recent years. Only two decades ago, Jim Kemeny (1992) made a haunting plea for more theoretically-aware housing research. He was critical of the then-dominant empirical paradigm for its excessively policy-driven approach, around an agenda shaped by government agencies. He argued that this style of housing studies lacked an explicit research epistemology or ontology and was isolated from the societal context within which specific problems were situated. Instead, most research addressed questions set and problems defined by powerful agents – most notably by governments. This made housing studies useful in an instrumental sense (and this is still the case), but limited its explanatory power and capacity to imagine change.

To an extent, Kemeny solved the problem himself, taking a lead role in establishing the journal *Housing and Social Theory*. However, the success of that journal is just one indicator of a steady increase in the amount of theoretically aware housing research now under way. Many articles in this section testify to this continuing trend, profiling the wide array of theoretical perspectives that are now used to illuminate housing and home. Some of those ideas are 'borrowed' – drawn from the wider social sciences, as epitomised in the application of the concept of ontological security, drawn from the work of the sociologist Anthony Giddens (1984), to research on owner-occupation. But others are, or have been made, very specific to housing research. The scene is set in Jago Dodson's overview article: Social Theory and Housing.

The 'theoretical' picture is fairly comprehensive. Articles range from actor–network theory through constructionism, critical realism, Foucauldian approaches, housing classes, and welfare regimes. There are, inevitably, gaps in this coverage, and it is important to be aware that new theoretical ideas are coming to light all the time. The articles in this section pick up on that dynamism. For example, there is no consensus on the nature of the microfoundations of housing market dynamics. Traditional neoclassical economic approaches have their place in this section, but they have been increasingly criticised by adherents of institutional economics, behavioural economics, and other approaches such as material sociology. Some of this jostling is apparent in the selection of articles herein.

Hence, one question that arises is whether there can, or should, be any comprehensive or all-embracing 'grand theory' to guide housing research. On the one hand, the lack of a 'general' theory of housing may be something to worry about. Some regard the absence of a coherent and comprehensive theoretical framework as a substantial weakness, making it impossible to transcend individual partial analyses. How do you put different insights together and understand how they relate or make up a larger whole? How do you devise a policy when all you have to go on are partial findings from varying approaches? On the other hand, the theoretical eclecticism that now exists is a fair reflection of the complexity of housing and of the many different analytical or policy questions that it poses. Even single issues, such as consumer market behaviour (e.g., the notion of housing choice), can be viewed in many different ways, and each can offer its own particular inspiration. The theoretical angle adopted in a specific piece of housing research may therefore rightly be adjusted to or dictated by the precise research question being addressed.

If the lack of a comprehensive theoretical framework in housing studies is problematic, it reflects a wider challenge for the social sciences more broadly. What is exciting, and to an extent reflected in the ideas in this section, is that housing is already the focus of transdisciplinary work in a variety of areas – for example, in behavioural and institutional economics – because of its unique features. Perhaps this is why King (2009) has argued that housing provides a good base from which to devise theory from a vantage point at the forefront of transdisciplinary research. Clearly, there is much work to be done before progress can be made in this direction, but the scope of this encyclopedia, if nothing else, provides a good testing ground for such endeavours.

Methods are as important to 'Approaches' as theories, and the articles in this section also illustrate the application of many different elements of the methodological toolkit to a range of housing topics. Reflecting a broad array of disciplines and approaches, these 'how-to' articles range widely, and they are not just about practicalities; they include some fundamental methodological concerns. For example, Flood's analysis of housing indicators reflects on their intrinsic meaningfulness as well as commenting on good and bad practice at a more prosaic level. Other articles relevant at this juncture include those on housing statistics, small area spatial statistics, forecasting, and econometric modelling. There are also reflections on comparative methods, qualitative methods, cultural analysis, visual methods, and so on. There is probably something here for everyone who is in search of a methodological starting point for research on housing and home.

There is insufficient space to profile all the 'how-to' articles, but it is perhaps worth taking one example from an overview article by Mike Oxley that provides a critique of comparative housing research. This article shows that an important development in housing research in the past 20 years has been an increase in international research, comparing housing systems for deeper insights about policy, process, and practice. While it is relatively easy to provide a superficial analysis of different national housing systems, going 'deep' into contexts, institutions, and markets requires ongoing commitment, as well as exceptional conceptual and methodological clarity. Such articles encourage commentators on housing research to recognise the scope for policy transfer and to be more willing to address the complexities of housing systems in other countries.

A sea change in the social sciences across the last decade has been the reconciliation between economics and other styles of social research. Some of this rapprochement is evident in articles of this section. However, 'housing economics' (like economics generally) addresses some very specific problems using some very distinctive tools, and this particularity is well-reflected among contributors to the encyclopedia. Approximately 17 articles are apposite here, spanning the neoclassical mainstream as well as the emerging heterodox panoply. Interestingly, while the section 'Economics and Finance' properly contains articles with a mainstream flavour, a large part of the discussion in 'Approaches' represents the heterodox challenge. At the very least, it grapples with the heterogeneity of housing research and aptly illustrates the wealth of alternative economics approaches now in play. There is, for example, discussion of institutions, property rights, Austrian economics, evolutionary perspectives, new institutional economics, behavioural economics, and neural networks. The sheer range of these ideas is pulled together in a compelling overview article by Alex Marsh on economic approaches.

More than any other applied area of economics, the housing and land market seems disposed to nonmainstream approaches, even if only a few such approaches are commonly published in key disciplinary journals (with the exception of behavioural economics which has taken the discipline by storm). Perhaps there are specific features of housing and human interactions with real estate that lend themselves to broader analyses of economics – analyses which take appropriate account of local context, bounded rationality, power over resources, the importance of the elapsing of real time, durability and spatial fixity, the joint nature of housing (with neighbourhoods, local government, and finance markets, to name three important links), and the way households, firms, and the state cope with decision-making in the face of this complexity. Other commodities have some of these attributes but, as has often been said, housing is unique in possessing them all. This, however, is not to deny the continuing importance of the insights of neoclassical economics and the evidence base built up around it, including in the sphere of housing economics. Regardless of philosophical and methodological disputes, the study of housing would be much poorer if we were to ignore the mainstream, just as housing research would be sorely limited if we only had 'orthodox' economics to rely on.

Social research in housing has a heterodox history and there is no parallel here to the challenge now facing orthodox housing economics. However, there is no shortage of articles illustrating the diversity of social approaches, and capturing the tensions, as well as opportunities, these engender. We have attempted to make it clear that the distinction between economic and social approaches is one of practicality rather than ontology. It is equally important to avoid characterising one as demanding quantitative methods and the other as more fitted to qualitative understandings. However, notwithstanding recent interests among economists in focus groups and related approaches, some of the major contributions to the development of qualitative methods have come from the sociological and anthropological disciplines. It is these cutting-edge approaches that are profiled herein. That is why there is an overview article on qualitative methods in housing research by Henry Coolen, providing context for other articles on ethnography, discourse, house biographies, life-course perspectives, and so on. There is also an emphasis in the social research articles on approaches relating to welfare, well-being, and the monitoring of inequality. While 'approaches' are not usually thought of in terms of normative theory, by sensitising readers to historical methods, matters of sustainability, and questions of power, political ideology, and policy futures, this section builds a platform for articles elsewhere in the encyclopedia to take on this broader mantle.

To return, in conclusion, to the start. Even given the extensive section that 'Approaches' has become, there is more to say, gaps to fill, and potential to realise. There is no objective sense of resolution to many key debates, and no conclusion to the various conversations the articles open up. And nor should there be. Housing studies has blossomed through diversity, and a diverse array of 'approaches' is key to this continuing. To be sure, such breadth may pose a challenge to readers and their disciplinary priors. However, the section editors, themselves coming from different disciplines, have shaped this volume with engagement and rapprochement firmly in mind.

D Clapham and K Gibb

References

Giddens A (1984) *The Constitution of Society*. Polity Press: Cambridge.
Kemeny J (1992) *Housing and Social Theory*. Routledge: London.
King P (2009) Using theory or making theory: Can there be theories of housing? *Housing, Theory and Society* 26.1: 41–52.

ECONOMICS AND FINANCE

Overview

Economics as a discipline has a long history of engagement with housing research. However, it is fair to say that, until the last decade, housing rarely took the centre stage. Now, however, it is clear how crucial housing, mortgage, and related capital markets are for the financial fortunes of whole economies and for individual households. This section consists of 72 articles, selected to illustrate this. The essays cover a wide range of topics concerning the real (physical) side of housing, as well as housing finance. They address microeconomic issues as well as macroeconomic concerns, and are complementary to articles in the sections 'Policy' (in areas such as housing supply, zoning and land-use regulation, and taxation), 'Institutions' (where there are common themes around taxes and subsidies), and 'Approaches' which, for example, contains methodological details on the calculation of housing price indexes, as well as an overview of institutional, behavioural, and neoclassical analyses of the housing economy). Although most of the articles in this section are based on the US and UK literature, reflecting the bulk of academic research, some articles cover both developed and developing countries, especially on the subject of mortgage markets and their regulations as well as housing subsidies.

This brief introduction is organised around the major themes addressed in the collection. These may be grouped into seven categories: housing demand, supply, and markets; house prices; government intervention in housing markets in the form of regulations and the direct provision of social housing; government intervention in the form of taxes and subsidies; housing wealth; housing and the macroeconomy; and housing finance (which has traditionally been jurisdiction-specific) together with an emerging international perspective on mortgage markets. Each is introduced below.

Thematic Review

Housing Demand, Supply, and Markets

Housing is not a simple commodity, like grains or metals. It is rather a complex, composite commodity, which is hard to price and whose supply is determined by policy and politics as much as markets. Moreover, housing is an investment asset as well as a consumption good. And when people discuss house 'prices', they often refer to an asset price, rather than a commodity price: the true 'price' of the commodity known as housing is rent.

Many of the articles in this section engage with this dilemma, recognising that when households demand housing, they are in fact demanding a bundle of services. Part of the bundle is physical: houses embody different quantities of interior space, exterior space, materials, plumbing, heating, and so on. Some part of the bundle is not physical. The location of a house, for example, determines the government services that it and its occupants receive. To give but one instance, it has been known that the demand for houses in 'good' school districts exceeds the demand for housing in less good school districts. Housing demand changes with price and income, just as with any other good, and in this, a remarkable similarity of housing demand is found across countries. But house price is also sensitive to household type, household tastes, and a host of other variables.

Housing demand also involves the choice of tenure, that is, whether to own or to rent, which is often made simultaneously with choices about the quantity of housing. The tenure decision is affected by the relative price of owning and renting, access to housing finance, and terms of mortgage loans. Homeownership is attractive to individual households because it generates private economic benefits. Social benefits emanating from homeownership form a basis for government support to it. Renting is more difficult in that landlords essentially serve as a financial intermediary between users of property and property itself. Rental housing therefore produces principal–agent issues that are solved via home-owning. Homeownership also allows the hedging of rent increases as the owner-occupant household is effectively renting to itself. All these themes are covered by the articles in this section.

Housing supply is more complicated. It includes new construction and alteration of the existing stock, and these two sources of supply are determined by two distinct sets of players, with different motivations: developers, on the one hand, and owner-occupiers, on the other hand. New homes are generally manufactured at the place where they are occupied, and the materials used for construction can vary from one part of the world to another. Even when manufactured homes and materials for home buildings are shipped around, the land component of supply is fixed locally. Natural barriers can also create impediments to housing supply. Bangladesh, for example, a country that is especially susceptible to flooding, faces supply challenges that are considerably greater than most other countries, and topography constrains housing supply in some coastal cities in the United States.

Political attitudes have, arguably, the greatest impact on housing supply. That is why there are synergies between the section economics and finance, on the one hand, and that on policy, on the other hand. The American city of Houston has virtually no limitations on housing construction, and as such, the supply curve for housing there is highly elastic. Mumbai, on the other hand, is among the densest large cities in the world, and yet has for many years imposed regulations and requirements that substantially limit its ability to supply housing. The elasticity of housing supply is affected by both natural constraints and regulatory barriers; the balance is weighed up by the relevant articles.

Finally, the articles in this section recognise that there is no single national housing market but a large number of local housing markets; such markets are also segmented. Identifying the submarkets is an important issue for both market analysis and policy formulation; a number of articles on housing supply, demand, and markets investigate the implications of such heterogeneity.

House Prices

The recent global financial crisis has shown that understanding house price fundamentals and dynamics has many important implications for wealth profiles, for lending and borrowing, and for policy. But understanding house price trends and volatilities is not a trivial matter. This is clear from the cluster of articles concerned with the measurement and determinants of house prices through time and spatially.

One can view house prices from several perspectives. Even terminology is not straightforward: from an economic perspective, the 'price' of a house is the rent one pays (or implicit rent in the case of owner-occupied housing) to receive the flow of housing services. To be precise, the term housing price or rent in its common use is in fact expenditure on housing and equals the unit price of housing multiplied by the quantity of housing consumed in a particular housing unit. Differentiating housing expenditure into price and quantity of housing is itself a challenge for housing researchers. The transaction price of a house is its asset value, which can be looked at as the present discounted value of its service flow.

Measuring discounted value is difficult, particularly for owner-occupied housing. In the first place, one would need to measure and forecast the rent that a particular owner-occupied house might fetch in the market; second, one would need to choose a correct discount rate. A further complication is the tendency for the market price of housing assets in any given point in time to deviate from what is explained by fundamental values. The discrepancy is called a bubble, which is often driven by expectations about future price appreciation. The difficulties in establishing fundamental values may explain why, at the time housing bubbles appeared to be developing around the world in the middle of the first decade of the twenty-first century, there was no consensus among economists as to whether this was, or was not, a departure from fundamentals.

Another method for determining fundamental house price is simply to sum the construction costs of improvements with land value. But getting construction costs right is difficult enough; getting land value right as well requires one to determine the fundamental value of land. This in turn depends on calculating land rent and a discount rate, which puts us in the same predicament mentioned in the previous paragraph. Residential property prices are, as a result, still one of the most researched, yet least understood, topics in housing economics.

Government Interventions: Regulations and Direct Provision of Social Housing

Government intervenes in the housing market in a variety of ways: land-use regulation and the provision of social housing are two of the most critical factors where economics and finance are concerned. Planning regulations, for example, directly affect how housing developers meet housing demand. It is almost certain that the demand for large blocks of flats in cities in India exceeds supply. Important reasons for the shortage are that regulations have made it difficult for developers to assemble parcels of vacant land and have produced binding limits on floor area ratios. Washington, DC, is a city whose housing supply is shaped in part by height limits, which in turn leaves demand unmet. Government regulation, in short, does much to shape both the price of housing and development densities in cities around the world.

The social housing sector is important because it effectively (to an extent) suspends the price mechanism in housing markets. The size and significance of this sector varies across countries, and is covered in most detail in other sections (see 'Institutions', 'Policy', and 'Home and Homelessness'). However, there are articles in this section on the economics and the financing of social housing which provide important points of contrast with a literature more generally focused on owner-occupation.

Government Interventions: Taxation and Subsidies

Taxation exerts a powerful effect on the shape of the world's housing systems. Most interest, in practice, centres on the implications of taxation for the role and relevance of owner-occupation. This in turn varies across countries. Many countries provide homeowners with a subsidy in the form of mortgage interest deduction; almost all countries give a tax break to owner-occupied housing by not taxing imputed rents, or capital gains, on primary residences. The mortgage interest deduction can affect the user cost of housing (i.e., the economic cost of owning a house) and make homeownership more attractive than it would otherwise be. However, it almost certainly will get capitalised into house prices to a varying extent depending on the supply elasticity. So it is not really clear how mortgage interest deductibility affects homeownership rates or home prices. Some argue that its impact is more on the size of properties than on whether they are purchased or not.

Many, if not most, countries provide some form of subsidy (other than tax breaks) to some households, and while the nature of the subsidy varies, generally the subsidy favours homeownership. This is done because homeownership is believed to generate social benefits. Some countries, such as Singapore, have a long history of directly subsidising owner-occupied housing, and this has helped drive ownership rates to high levels. Other countries also subsidise renters, through provision of social housing (supply-side subsidy), through vouchers (demand-side subsidy), or through tax incentives to landlords. Several such themes are aired in this section.

Housing Wealth

A number of articles address the various dimensions of housing wealth, the ways households can tap into it, and the impact of housing wealth on consumption. We now know with a great deal of confidence that housing wealth is important – it is the world's largest single asset class, it makes up an enormous share of global wealth, accounts for the bulk of personal wealth in most national economies, and for the majority of owner-occupiers, is by far their largest, sometimes their only, asset. We do not, on the other hand, have as much confidence in knowing the total value of individual, national, or global housing assets, not least because of uncertainty about the fundamental value of houses.

This section also reflects the fact that there is not yet any consensus concerning the implications of housing wealth for the broader economy. There is, to be sure, extensive debate on the link between home prices and consumption, and on what the causal mechanisms might be. There have also been a number of estimates of the marginal propensity to consume out of housing wealth (rather than other parts of the wealth portfolio), but these estimates have a wide range. Part of the difficulty is that the fungibility of housing wealth – the ability to mobilise or 'cash in' home equity – varies between jurisdictions, according to the 'completeness' of mortgage markets, and the transactions costs in housing markets. The means of extracting equity also varies across the life course. For example, for households attached to a job, it is difficult to cash in on house value by moving from an expensive city to an inexpensive city; retirees, conversely, do have that option. On the other hand, home-buyers in work have more opportunities to borrow-up against owned homes (to engage in mortgage equity withdrawal) than do older outright owners without an income stream. There is some agreement that the collateral channel has increased in importance; that increased leverage together with equity borrowing accounts for a significant proportion of housing's wealth effects. However, on the subject of tapping into home equity via loans, there is a mix of evidence, some of which suggests that the ability to use that mechanism can be fleeting.

That is, mortgage equity withdrawal may not improve the household balance sheet in the long run, because the asset extracted (cash) is offset by a new liability (a future stream of mortgage payments). Nevertheless, as the articles in this section show, mortgage equity withdrawal is one means by which some homeowners smooth both incomes and consumption across the life course.

Housing and the Macroeconomy

The interplay between the housing sector and the macroeconomy has attracted growing attention in recent years. Research indicates that the housing sector interacts with the macroeconomy through three major channels: the investment, consumption, and banking channels. Regarding the first channel, it is sometimes argued that housing 'is the business cycle'. Indeed, variations in housing construction explain a disproportionate amount of variation in the broader economy. The question is why. The second channel, the housing wealth effect, has been discussed above. As for the third channel, the performance of mortgage loans, conditioned by the fluctuation in housing price, influences the balance sheet of lending institutions. This affects their ability to expand new credit to households and businesses, and hence the level of consumption and investment activities. The housing–macroeconomy linkages operate in the other direction as well. For example, changes in the interest rate and the supply of credit have an impact on housing demand and the supply of new housing.

Mortgage Markets: Character and Trends

Because housing is a long-lived and 'lumpy' (indivisible) consumer durable, and because households generally wish to smooth consumption over the lifetime, it is only natural that mortgage markets have expanded hand in hand with housing markets. When housing finance is not available, households must save for many years before they have the opportunity to purchase a house. The behaviour of borrowers regarding the choice of mortgage products and repayment of mortgage debt (or default there on) and the factors that affect their behaviour are covered by several articles in this section.

The size of the housing finance sector varies considerably across countries. Some developed countries, particularly the United States, the United Kingdom, Denmark, and the Netherlands, have very large mortgage markets relative to their economies. Most emerging countries have relatively small mortgage markets, but some high-income countries, including Italy and France, have relatively small markets too. Mortgage products are highly heterogeneous across countries and jurisdictions vary in the 'completeness' of the mortgage markets they support. The United States features a large variety of mortgage products, even now, and is, like Denmark, unusual in that fixed-rate, long-term, freely-prepayable mortgages are common. In Canada mortgages generally have terms of medium length (5 years is usual). The UK and Australian mortgage markets, in contrast, where long-term fixes are less common, support a wide range of loan products in the amortising adjustable rate and equity borrowing ranges.

In short, and until recently, mortgage markets have been stubbornly national in character, notwithstanding an otherwise-globalising economy. To illustrate that diversity, there are several articles on mortgage markets, character, and trends in specific illustrative jurisdictions, from Germany (with notably low rates of homeownership) to the United Kingdom and the United States (with reasonably high rates of highly mortgaged owner-occupation) in the developed world, and spanning all other world regions, from Africa to China.

Mortgages, because they are secured debt, allow households with a relatively small asset base to borrow at narrow spreads over risk-free assets. This is because properly underwritten loans consider both the ability of the borrower to repay the loan and the quality of the collateral underpinning it. In recent years, many lenders departed from good underwriting practices, for reasons that are currently subject to debate. Nevertheless, during those years when mortgages were carefully underwritten, they were very safe investments for lenders.

This might explain why, to meet a growing demand for credit in some parts of the more developed world, mortgage-linked instruments emerged during the 2000s as an important financial market. Mortgage-linked securities helped lending institutions tap the capital market as well as contributing to the development of capital markets. Countries vary in how mortgage finance is sourced, the major division being between those that rely on capital markets for housing finance and those that rely on depositories. Germany, Denmark, and the United States tend to rely on capital markets, while Australia, the United Kingdom, and Canada rely more on depositories. These themes are taken up in the remaining articles for this section.

Research Agenda Going Forward

The articles collected here cover a wide range of subjects in the economics and finance of housing. Already, however, they point out new directions and identify areas in which further research is needed. For example, a clear and encouraging trend in housing research in recent years is increased interest in housing supply. Additional research on supply elasticity, the role of regulations on supply, and the impact of the supply elasticity on the volatility in housing price and quantity would be helpful. Second, the effects of ageing, and cohorts, on the place of housing and mortgage debt in the household portfolio, have important policy implications and merit greater attention. Third, the relationship between the structure of mortgage markets (funding mechanisms and mortgage products) and the stability of housing markets requires far more careful study. A related topic worth exploring is the role of macroprudential measures in promoting housing market stability. Finally, explaining the driving forces of the co-movement of housing prices in many developed countries during the latest housing boom, and the different pathways to unwinding the boom, is a pressing topic for research, which may be feasible once internationally comparable housing price data become more widely available.

RK Green, K-H Kim, AB Sanders, and S Wachter

ENVIRONMENT

Aims and Objectives

The broad aims of this section echo that of the overall encyclopedia, namely to provide an international perspective on housing and to engage with academic and practitioner audiences. The objective is to provide an insight into the main issues associated with housing and the environment. This section brings together the key environmental issues for housing globally, including those relating to the physical and the social spheres, and the interaction between them. The dynamic relationship established between space and society over time is explored, with many of the articles covering issues at the intersection of the social and the physical, and recognising that this relationship is multidirectional. How do individuals and communities affect the housing and wider environment? How do physical circumstances, including housing environments, influence behaviours and social relationships?

The section comprises 68 core articles written by recognised experts in the field and providing comprehensive overviews of a wide range of environmental topics from climate change to ghettos, and from health risks to household waste recycling. To provide orientation, we commissioned a small number of longer overview articles on Sustainable Communities by Alina Congreve, Climate Change by Tina Fawcett, Housing Dynamics: Environmental Aspects by Gareth Powells, and Social Spaces and Urban Policies by Wim Ostendorf. The breadth and depth of the articles in this section provide evidence of a growing interest in environmental issues for housing research and practice.

Structure and Organisation

The articles in this section are broadly divided into two categories: social and physical. The reciprocal influences created around the physical and social domains in housing are barely extricable; however, a distinction was made to facilitate the design of the section, the identification of authors, and the categorising of key concepts and issues covered by the term 'environment'. The articles were commissioned as being primarily about either the social environment or the physical environment, though in practice, of course, the two themes often overlap.

The more physical-oriented articles (encompassing both the dwelling and the built environment) cover topics about housing and environmental change, the impact of housing on the biosphere, and housing environmental sustainability issues as well as articles about the material infrastructure of housing: the bricks and mortar and its physical layout. The articles concentrate on either the dwelling or the neighbourhood/city scale, or undertake a more generic 'theory and approaches' review. Thus, for instance, we have an article by Erling Holden that is primarily about the dwelling (Ecological Footprint), Gordon Walker deals with the scale of the neighbourhood (Community Energy Systems), and Rajat Gupta deals with more general matters of theory and approaches (Climate Change: Adaptations). For essays concentrating on built environment issues, topics relating to the dwelling are explained and developed in articles on rural housing by Mark Shucksmith and on second homes by Fernando Diaz Orueta. Built environment concepts associated with the neighbourhood and the city are also discussed, for example in articles on Green Space and Parks by Nicola Dempsey and on Housing and Sustainable Transport by Erling Holden.

Essays addressing the social perspective are concerned with the interactions between housing and householders, and more broadly with environment and society. The social dimension comprises both the individual and the community, and includes topics and ideas that go from individual perceptions to collective actions related to the physical environment, embodying several scales like the dwelling, the neighbourhood, or the city. For instance, the scale of the dwelling and the role of householders are evidenced in a few articles (Place Attachment by Barbara Brown, Irwin Altman, and Carol Werner and Household Waste Recycling by Matt Watson), while others concentrate on a larger environmental scale (Neighbourhood Design: Urban Outdoor Experience by Nicola Dempsey, Neighbourhood Watch by Richard Yarwood, and Eco-Communities by Heather Lovell). This perspective also includes articles that are more conceptually focused on 'theories and approaches' (Sustainable Housing Cultures by Eli Støa).

Certain entries reflect more than others the difficulties associated with disentangling the predominance of one approach or another. Examples of this include essays on the undesired effects on the environment of negative behaviours like crime (see Neighbourhood Incivilities by Ralph Taylor), the individual health risks associated with poor environmental conditions (see Health Risks: Damp and Cold by Jeroen Douwes), and the particularities and specificities of the relationship established between groups or collectives and the environment (see Vernacular Housing by Laida Memba Ikuga or Gypsy/Roma Settlements by Teresa San Román).

Over time, housing research has changed its focus to embrace problems and issues in the real world. Until the mid- to late 1990s, the majority of the wider housing studies literature tended to concentrate on either social issues (such as low-income housing and welfare) or economic issues (notably housing finance and the operation of housing markets), and the physical environment was rather overlooked. But in the last few decades, this has begun to change with a growing body of work researching environmental issues, including householder studies (on energy and water consumption and waste management), the design and production of sustainable housing, and attitudes in the house building industry towards the environment. Exemplifying this, the articles broadly grouped as pertaining to the physical environment section consider both traditional research issues related to housing and urban studies (Maintenance and Repair by Ad Straub, Housing Estates by Frank Wassenberg, and Ethnic Minorities and Housing by Gideon Bolt) as well as newer more contemporary housing research topics (Defensible Space by Paul Cozen and David Hillier, Eco-Renovation by Gavin Killip, and Eco-Communities by Heather Lovell).

The physical environment articles address a wide range of international perspectives covering the environmental issues at stake not only in the rich and developed part of the world but also in poorer, developing countries. To this end, leading researchers from around the world discuss international debates and case studies which include examples of community planning in Vancouver, Canada, in Seattle, USA and in Brisbane, Australia (see Neighbourhood Planning by Simon Pinnegar). There is also a comparison of self-build techniques between the Gaza Strip (Autonomous Palestinian Territories), Khartoum (Sudan), Kigali (Rwanda), Rio de Janeiro (Brazil), and Buenos Aires (Argentina) (see the article on Self-Build: Global South by Fernando Murillo).

Several transversal concepts of paramount importance for the whole section feature as a *leitmotiv* across many of the articles. They are mainly related to the impact of recent changes and shifts in societal cultures and lifestyles and its relation to the environment. The three pillars of sustainability, for instance, have been acknowledged in many of the articles as has the growing attention researchers pay to safety-related issues and environmental impacts on health. Another topic that demands attention is the way deprivation and persistent inequalities at the social level are reflected in territorial outcomes.

This section deals explicitly with processes and dynamics over the territory inspired (or not) by certain attitudes and behaviours of the population and its evolution over time. In that sense, the section puts a particular emphasis on the preconditions, requirements, and determinants over time for processes to develop. A few articles (Temporary Housing by Claire Lévy-Vroelant, Gated Communities by Rowland Atkinson and Sarah Blandy, and Gentrification and Neighbourhood Change by Marco van der Land, Alexander Curley and G van Eijk) are key examples here relating to social issues, whilst others (Adaptable Housing by Eli Støa or Construction and Demolition Waste by Vivian Tam) show a certain degree of progression and development on the physical side.

More than just theoretical analysis, many of the articles in this section discuss and debate the impact of policies, programmes, and actions: that is, both analytic and normative approaches are incorporated within the section. This is perhaps most evident in a series of case studies: for instance, Amsterdam's pattern of social segregation (Social Spaces and Urban Policies by Wim Ostendorf and Sako Musterd), Danish practices related to energy consumption (Sustainable Lifestyles by Kirsten Gram-Hanssen), the design of teahouses in Shanghai or the *favelas* in Brazil (Vernacular Housing by Laida Memba Ikuga), and the evolution of second homes at the Spanish Mediterranean coast (Second Homes by Fernando Diaz Orueta).

Finally, a few umbrella concepts considered in this section are also reflected in other sections of the encyclopedia. This is the case, for instance, with neighbourhood governance (Ali Madanipour), social sustainability (Monterrat Pareja-Eastaway), and sustainabe housing cultures (Eli Støa). There are also essays on sustainable lifestyles (Kirsten Gram-Hanssen) and on gender and space (Irene Molina).

In summary, housing and the home cannot be seen, experienced, or studied apart from in their environmental contexts and effects. The physical and the social environment contribute to what housing and home represents for individuals; that wider environment is itself shaped by the practices associated with housing and home. This section aims to provide the reader with an overview of the many different international dimensions of this interplay. The hope is that it provides a way into these issues for the nonexpert, that it opens new dimensions for those already well-read in the field, and that it inspires the research community towards fresh ways of thinking.

H Lovell, M Pareja Eastaway, and M Elsinga

HOME AND HOMELESSNESS

'Home' is a concept found across the natural and social sciences, referring in its broadest sense to the habitats of animals and plants. In the context of housing, home denotes the feelings, values, cultures, and practices associated with the physical structures of human dwelling. This concept of home refers to the ways in which dwelling structures become sites of emotional, cultural, and personal significance; the ways in which a sense of belonging in the world is constructed in and through the residential environment. The articles in this section reflect and expand upon this conceptualisation of home, and on the impacts (largely in the material sense) of absence of home ('homelessness'). There are 98 articles in this section, spread more or less evenly across topics relating to home and to homelessness.

Home: A Multidisciplinary Affair

Reflecting on the multiple meanings and experiences of the term 'home', a hallmark of the scholarship in this section – perhaps more so than in any other part of the encyclopedia – is its multidisciplinary character. To illustrate this, particular editorial effort has been made to ensure that all principal disciplinary perspectives on home are elaborated to some extent, each taking different theoretical points and hence conceptualising home in subtly different ways. Philosophical perspectives, for example, are primarily concerned with the ways in which homes – material or imaginative – are connected with our sense of 'being-in-the-world', with personhood most generally. Anthropology is more focused on the collective, rather than the self, in its emphasis on the built forms of housing and different meanings of home associated with different cultures and, more recently, with its recognition of the importance of objects and material culture more generally in making home. In literature, film studies, and popular culture, the creation and maintenance of normative definitions of home is paramount, highlighting, for example, the omnipresence of representations of home across diverse forms like Flemish painting, American postwar television, and women's magazines. Feminist perspectives are critical in understanding the 'house-as-home', initially in refuting the overly romanticised and gender-blind perspectives that dominated early housing studies, and more recently in elaborating the complex links between home and both masculinity and femininity. Feminist frameworks in fact underpin a number of articles in this section, including those on sexuality, emotions, home and work, and meanings of home.

Although the individual lenses through which home is comprehended varies across these disciplines, collectively three key themes emerge.

The first, reflecting the importance of feminism in scholarship on home, is the centrality of gender when both experiencing and conceptualising home. Men and women experience home in different ways. Whether home is a place of relaxation or a place of unpaid (or paid) work, whether a safe haven or site of violence and antagonism, for example, are experiences strongly correlated with gender. While gender differences remain critical to understanding home, recent feminist scholarship has also turned attention to new types of relations between gender and home, such as through migration, temporary dwelling, and technology. Furthermore, gender is central to key concepts used to understand home. The chain of association linking home with the domestic sphere, and infusing the domestic sphere with connotations of privacy, for instance, can be traced back to the eighteenth-century notion of separate spheres in which it was presumed that the realms of daily life for men and women were, and should be, completely different. Feminist critiques of this public–private dichotomy, and the reformulation of this dualism to stress the necessary interconnections of public and private, drive contemporary feminist theorisations of house-as-home.

A second key theme concerns the ways in which experiences of home reflect and reproduce patterns of historical, geographical, and social differentiation. How home is understood, practiced, and represented varies considerably depending on age (compare the way home is imagined by a child and by an elderly person), race, religion, and sexuality, as many of the articles demonstrate. These socially differentiated experiences of home are critical in shaping both people's life chances and their senses of themselves. Historical variations are also implicit in this section, exemplified in the changing representations of home in literature and film, and the altering technological foundations of the modern house-as-home. Perhaps not surprisingly, given the volume's emphasis on houses, the importance of geographical context in shaping home underpins many of the articles. Geographical context is approached at a number of scales: national–regional differences as exemplified in the different material cultures of home and home objects; the common and varying elements of home found in high-rise and suburban housing; and the experiences of domestic workers across the global North and South. This section also advances scholarship on home through its emphasis on the importance of transnational movements of people and ideas in transforming home.

A final key theme concerns the strong linkages between home and the myriad economic, political, and legal institutions of housing. While home is a more cultural concept than house, and scholarship on home draws less on political science, law, and economics than other dimensions of housing studies, what home means remains strongly connected to socioeconomic, political, and legal differentiation. Homeownership is a critical investment and wealth-building activity across the Western world that underpins many national economies and has been linked to a sense of 'ontological security'. The legal protection of homeownership underpins the experience of homeownership, and may even be the basis for claiming new legal rights, for example, through 'defensive homeownership'. Finally, institutions such as planning and welfare systems silently support homeownership and middle-class definitions of home through their continuing preference for homeownership and nuclear family/individualised patterns of social life.

Future scholarship on home will probably be influenced by broader intellectual trends across the social sciences, in concert with the changing social, political, cultural, and economic context. Within this frame, a number of likely directions can be identified. Empirically, many of the recent trends identified in this section will endure impacts of transnational movements on housing and home, imprint of social constructions of home across diverse policy and institutional fields, and increasingly complex identity formation in and through home. The implications of climate change for experiences of home are likely to become a key issue, as scholars explore the links between carbon-intensive practices and meanings of home, on the one hand, and the meanings of home (shared living spaces, more high rises?) that could underpin a carbon-reduced future, on the other hand.

Theoretically, the trend towards more integrative approaches is also likely to continue. While much scholarship on home already draws upon diverse social science and humanities disciplines, the current moment sees increasing dialogue across natural and social sciences through perspectives such as 'science and technology' studies in which the processes of the natural and social worlds are considered simultaneously. In relation to home, it may be that existing scholarship on material cultures and pets, which draw from an understanding of the 'more-than-human' world and dispute the separation of nature and culture, will take housing studies in new directions, such as recent work on the ways in which social networks and technologies are assembled to constitute home in an increasingly technologically embedded world. These new frameworks will enable housing studies to address changing contours of home into the future.

Homelessness: A Multifaceted Condition

'Homelessness' can, conceptually, be understood as the absence of 'home', but practical definitions tend to prioritise the material aspects of inadequate housing conditions. Such definitions vary in breadth across the developed world, from the categorisation of 'literal homelessness' traditionally found in the United States and elsewhere, which is confined to those sleeping rough or in homeless shelters, to the much wider definition employed in the United Kingdom, for example, which covers all those without a legal right to occupy 'reasonable' accommodation, and the 'cultural' definition used in Australia. The European Federation of National Organisations Working with the Homeless (FEANTSA) 'ETHOS' typology, which offers a homelessness definition encompassing aspects of 'rooflessness', 'houselessness', 'insecure housing', and 'inadequate housing', has been increasingly influential in Europe and beyond. But such broad-ranging definitions are inappropriate in the developing world, where the imposition of such 'Western' notions of housing security and adequacy would label most of the population as homeless. In India, for example, reference is more often made to those who are 'houseless' or 'shelterless', emphasising the absence of any form of shelter.

Homelessness is recognised as a major social policy concern in many developed countries, and as a feature of extreme poverty throughout the developing world. Homelessness can also happen dramatically as the result of human conflicts or natural disasters, with the needs of refugees and internally displaced people representing a major humanitarian challenge in many parts of the world. The material circumstances giving rise to homelessness differ across the globe, and its manifestations differ too: street children, informal settlements, and large refugee camps are key concerns in Asia, Africa, and Central and South Americas, whereas single adults sleeping rough or in shelters, families living in temporary accommodation, and 'hidden' homeless groups 'doubling up' with friends and relatives are core issues in much of the developed world. While most identifiable homelessness is located within urban settings, there is a growing understanding of the particular dimensions of rural homelessness in countries as diverse as India, the United States, New Zealand, Spain, Ireland, and Finland.

There are clear patterns, at least within the developed world, of the characteristics of the people most vulnerable to 'literal homelessness'. This group tends to be male, single, middle-aged, unemployed, or disabled, with a strong overrepresentation of ethnic minorities and recent migrants. Men leaving institutional settings – such as prison and the armed forces – are often at particular risk of street homelessness. However, the broader one's definition of homelessness, the more 'feminised' it becomes, with women and children predominating among refugees and internally displaced people in the developing world.

Understandings of homelessness, like meanings of 'home', have benefited from multidisciplinary scholarship, though major challenges remain in integrating the varying perspectives that these different disciplines offer. Economists tend to focus on aggregates and macroexplanatory levels, often giving overwhelming importance to housing market conditions in explaining homelessness, whereas applied social psychologists, for example, focus on the ways in which homeless people's self-identity influences their propensity to engage with housing and support services. Added to this rich intellectual mix are distinctive theoretical and methodological approaches, which cut across disciplinary boundaries. Social constructionist perspectives have explored the meanings attached to homelessness by various actors, and the impacts that these representations can have on policy responses. Ethnographers provide rich and culturally sensitive details on the lives of marginalised people, such as homeless people, that enable their perspectives to be 'included' in debate and policy formulation. Explanatory frameworks have been offered from a 'critical realist' perspective, which contends that complex causal mechanisms operate across a wide range of social strata, and no single factor is likely to be 'necessary' or 'sufficient' for the generation of homelessness. As with scholarship on 'home', feminist perspectives have been influential, and have gained in sophistication and subtlety over time.

At its core, the study of homelessness reflects a concern with human suffering and exclusion and a desire to prevent and resolve it, with an increasing emphasis on commitments to 'end homelessness' by governments and NGOs across the developed world. Demands for 'rights-based' approaches have come to dominate political discourse in recent years, although there are also counter voices arguing for less adversarial 'social partnership' models. Another key schism is between those who advocate 'continuum of care' models, whereby homeless people move through a series of accommodation and support 'steps' to render them 'housing ready' before accessing mainstream accommodation, and the 'Housing First' model, rapidly gaining ground across the developed world, whereby ordinary housing is provided immediately with support services configured around this permanent accommodation. There is encouraging evidence from a range of countries on improved specialist responses to diverse homeless groups – including young people, older people, people with mental health, drug or alcohol problems, and women fleeing domestic violence – but these targeted programmes sometimes attempt to compensate for the absence, or retrenchment, of mainstream welfare protection. Another cause for concern in many quarters is the 'criminalisation' of homelessness in nations as diverse as India, Australia, Brazil, Japan, England, Hungary, and Rwanda.

Future scholarship on homelessness will doubtless be informed by intellectual trends across the academic world, as with other areas of study, but two important practical points stand out.

First, improved quantitative data on homelessness are required. The availability of robust statistical evidence on homelessness is extremely patchy, even if one confines oneself to the developed world. The United States has by far the best quantitative research, based on large sample sizes and robust methodologies, including the use of longitudinal and control/comparison group techniques to assess rigorously the effectiveness of specific homelessness programmes. Elsewhere, there is a dearth of quantitative research on homelessness, aside from basic, descriptive work on the characteristics of homeless people. Cost–benefit analysis and associated economic techniques designed to demonstrate the efficient use of public resources are a key concern in this regard. These types of economic analyses are relatively well developed within the homelessness sector in only Australia and the United States at the moment, but it seems inevitable that their importance will grow in the coming years, especially given ongoing downward pressures on public expenditure following the global economic crisis.

Second, there is a clear need for international comparative research on homelessness (both qualitative and quantitative). Key research questions on, for example, the impact of structural contexts on the scale and nature of homelessness cannot be answered without such evidence. Conducting cross-country empirical research on homelessness requires significant resources which are rarely made available, and there are also considerable methodological challenges to overcome with respect to conceptual equivalence, data harmonisation, and, perhaps most profoundly, institutional divergence in responses. However, there are many other areas of housing studies where such barriers are, if not overcome, at least worked around in order to deliver useful comparative findings. There is, in principle, no reason why similar progress cannot be made in the homelessness field.

R Dowling and S Fitzpatrick

INSTITUTIONS

The Purpose and Place of Housing Institutions

While housing is a basic human need that can be provided at a rudimentary level of shelter, and the home is a quintessentially personal realm where intimacy and privacy is realised, the provision and consumption of homes has become a highly regulated practice, mediated by various institutions and agencies. Housing agents and organisations are, especially in developed societies, regulated by the state or even civil sector organisations run on a nonprofit basis. At the same time, private enterprises concerned with housing have increasingly organised themselves into larger units in order to represent their own interests, often in tandem with the institutional and legislative mobilisation of governments. This section of the encyclopedia addresses the diversity and complexity of institutions and institutional relationships in the realisation of housing.

One conventional understanding of housing institutions is focused on the social organisations that support the specific housing and housing-related needs of society. Other approaches emphasise the need to see institutions more broadly as the norms, rules, and regulations – the entire body of mechanisms and structures of social order and cooperation – that govern the behaviour of a set of individuals. From this perspective, housing institutions encompass the norms and rules that enable a society to fulfil its need for adequate housing, including the complex interactions of housing supply and demand, and housing needs. 'Institutions' may thus refer to organisations that perform specific tasks within society, the laws and regulations formulated at different levels of government, and informal values and norms concerning how housing is used and circulated.

In order to be as inclusive and comprehensive as possible, we have assumed a broad definition of institutions in this volume. The literature on institutions within housing studies has usually taken the existence of 'typical' institutional entities and practices as givens, and thus become a normative force that has inadequately questioned the nature and role of housing institutions. Indeed, examples of housing practices in places like Africa, Latin America, and East Asia as set out in this section illustrate considerable complexity and diversity in institutional arrangements concerning the home and processes of housing.

Approaches

Understanding institutions in housing is a formidable task that requires, on the one hand, considerable sensitivity to social and cultural variations, and on the other hand, appreciation of the growing influence of global economic and regulatory forces. Recently, the changing institutional relationships around housing markets have heightened the 'interconnectedness' of households to an international institutional network, subjugating the 'micro' phenomenon of 'home', and the security and orientation of the family within the home, to the influence of multiscalar flows of capital and finance. This became particularly evident in the international property price bubble that emerged at the beginning of the twenty-first century, which helped to stimulate irresponsible lending and borrowing, especially in subprime mortgage sectors, and which was followed by the credit crunch and a global recession that has spread far beyond housing markets and mortgage finance. Housing institutions, regulators, and agencies not only triggered the unfolding of the latest financial crisis; their alignment around a particular mode of market housing provision, and commodity consumption, albeit manifest differently in each local context, helped reconfigure housing processes on a global scale while at the same time reconstituting the very meaning and experience of home at the individual level.

This is not to say that institutional relationships in each society have converged in line with neoliberal forms of capitalism. Indeed, the meaning and nature of housing and home in each culture or community reflects the complexity and idiosyncrasy of housing systems, which are locally and historically contingent and demonstrate considerable path dependency.

The articles collected in this volume attempt to capture the diversity of institutions that intersect with housing as well as differences in the formation and development of institutional constellations in different countries. As researches on, for example, welfare regimes and varieties of capitalism have demonstrated, institutions and institutional frameworks both shape the interaction of political, economic, and social dimensions and are shaped by the context with which they arise and evolve. Consequently, there is a particularly comparative focus to this volume with a number of articles and clusterings of articles that address comparable institutional phenomena in different societies and regions of the world. On the one hand, this helps demonstrate local institutional relations and their impact on housing markets, policies, and practices, as well as change and development over time. On the other hand, it illustrates how much the impact of individual agency, political intervention, and global forces is contingent on historic frameworks of organisational formations and relations. What is apparent across the articles here is how often relatively similar housing policy developments are mediated by different institutional structures and networks, leading to highly variegated social and market outcomes.

While the geographic separation of countries and regions provides one way to approach this text, it is also possible to consider different institutional dimensions. In terms of scale, the range runs from international and state agencies to neighbourhood associations to individual professionals. In terms of institutions as regulations, or rules of the game, there is also considerable variety, from the laws that define rights of ownership and access to housing, to the means by which management decisions are made, and to the cultural norms that regulate the exchange of shelter and housing wealth within the family or household unit. This volume also touches on important social issues such as ageing, gender, and race and how different institutional relations and practices affect these. There are also the more familiar topics concerning housing supply and demand, housing markets, and public policy.

Themes and Issues

More theoretically or conceptually driven approaches to scientific collections like this one can often impose frameworks for understanding the phenomena and the nature of relationships between them. However, in compiling this section we have considered eclecticism a merit, and the diversity of topics and approaches as an opportunity to re-engage with the dynamism and complexity of housing relations. One of the distinctive contributions offered by a focus on 'institutions' of housing and home within the framework of an encyclopedia is considerable freedom to move between topics and thereby make unanticipated connections and associations between ideas, practices, and places. It is useful, nonetheless, to highlight a number of key themes and issues, as well as make some illustrative links between topics.

The contributions in this section essentially explore differences in housing regimes and housing institutions. Housing institutions are viewed as culturally embedded in the overall process of economic, social, and political transformation, while recognising the power of specific local imperatives and market pressures to shape their response. The main argument is that housing institutions have differential capacities to direct these processes of change, leading to divergent responses in the housing provision system. The section explores these differences as well as the institutional relationships in four principal domains: (1) housing tenure and housing rights; (2) housing institutions providing affordable housing; (3) institutions for the supply of housing; and (4) housing markets and the myriad of formal and informal institutions involved in the provision of housing. While the articles themselves reveal the complexities of housing institutions, it is possible to identify some of the most significant issues addressed in relation to each of these domains. These issues are likely to dominate the discourse in the housing literature for years to come.

Institutional Perspectives on Housing Rights and Housing Tenure

Housing tenure is one of the central social institutions in the field of housing. Tenures provide users with rights and burden them with responsibilities related to the consumption of housing. Several articles provide comparative perspectives on a variety of housing tenures, their evolution, and specific forms. Types of tenure are constructed by abstracting from the variety of empirically and historically existing forms – owner-occupation and renting – with major differences in terms of user rights, control, and disposition provided to the resident. Tenure differences are qualified by specific institutional arrangements in different societies with a particular emphasis on provisions ensuring the right to housing for marginalised groups in society as well as housing challenges in postconflict situations.

Housing Institutions Providing Affordable Housing

Meeting the growing need for affordable housing is one of the biggest challenges in both developed and developing countries. A number of articles explore the institutional context and the myriad of arrangements to finance, provide, allocate, and manage affordable housing through public and nongovernment models. They review a variety of approaches that have been adopted as well as the roles and contributions of different institutions across the housing system – governments, private agencies, not-for-profit organisations, and market intermediaries. Characteristics of the historic and contemporary contributions of these institutions to the provision of affordable housing highlight divergent pathways in different countries and regions. The policy debate centres on policy instruments – fiscal, financial, and regulatory – supporting the production (supply side) or the consumption (demand side) of housing. Strategies to promote, produce, and manage affordable housing are also differentiated by tenure – renting versus homeownership – and classified by the degree of targeting and efficiency.

Institutions for Housing Supply

National systems of housing supply involve dynamic public, private, and not-for-profit institutions. Although their relationships are influenced by the country (or regional) context, historic tenure mix, the place of housing in the welfare system, and local structures of housing provision, converging trends are evident. Several articles highlight a broad shift away from direct provision of affordable housing by public agencies in favour of approaches involving the private and not-for-profit sectors, either separately or in partnership. This has resulted in a complex landscape of housing finance, ownership, and management. The growth of new institutions, coupled with the more general emphasis on competitive supply by market agents (landowners, developers, house-builders, managers), has led to new forms of housing provision and 'hybrid' organisations. The contributions explore several major forms of new housing supply, including public/private partnerships, speculative house building, self-help, and informal housing. They review regional patterns and country-specific trends and relationships among key institutions related to the promotion, production, allocation, and consumption of housing.

Housing Markets: Informal and Formal Institutions

Housing markets are culturally embedded in society and the efficiency of their institutions is critical for the provision of adequate and affordable housing. Several articles explore housing market institutions in developing countries, highlighting the importance of informality and difference. Major activities – access to housing, maintenance, services (water, sanitation, access roads), tenure security (to prevent eviction), finance for construction, purchase, or renting – occur through a combination of more or less formal processes. Depending on the social, economic, political, and legal context, some of these activities have been institutionalised over time into more permanent norms and rules implemented with varying degrees of formality by agencies or organisations of the state, market, or civil society. Such informality is very much part of the institutional transformation of post-socialist housing markets and is likely to distinguish them from some of their more mature, well-established European counterparts.

Concluding Remarks

Despite the common challenges facing housing systems in different countries, there are historical and deeply embedded differences in the nature of their housing institutions. There are also significant differences in the political, economic, and social drivers affecting housing policy reforms and the transformation of these institutions, which challenge the idea of convergence. The volume examines the range of strategies used in contemporary societies to protect housing rights, to improve housing quality and affordability, and to enhance the efficiency of housing markets through the lens of housing institutions. This approach brings into focus the role and respective contributions of government, private sectors, and not-for-profit agencies in the provision of housing. In 83 articles, this section addresses the diversity of institutions that have developed around the financing, production, and consumption of housing, accounting for differences between countries and institutional transformation. While capturing diversity is an exhaustive task beyond the scope of this work, this section, nonetheless, illustrates core differences in institutional configurations and relationships regarding housing markets, housing management, construction, planning, tenure, and housing rights.

R Ronald and S Tsenkova

POLICY

Aims and Structure

The aim of this section is to provide a global overview of housing policies and to engage with academic and practitioner audiences. A well-functioning housing market that provides shelter for all regardless of income is of key importance in societies all over the world, and therefore a primary objective of housing policy. During the global financial crisis, we learned that low incomes, subprime loans, and a global financial market proved to be an explosive combination. As a consequence, housing policies and financial policies are being reconsidered as is evident from several articles in this and in other sections. This section of the encyclopedia focuses upon various aspects of housing policy in developed, developing, and transitional economies, collectively reflecting the evolution of housing policy formulation and implementation in a variety of economic, political, and social contexts.

This section comprises 58 core articles and 7 longer overview essays written by recognised experts in the field, providing a comprehensive guide to a wide range of policy topics. Together, the articles are organised around the following seven key themes.

Housing Policy Development

Two essays by John Doling and Peter Ward provide a comprehensive overview of the evolution of housing policy in advanced, transitional and developing economies. Doling suggests a framework that emphasises processes of convergence and divergence with respect to broad historical trends in housing policy (Housing Policy Trends). He shows that over time, with economic development and urbanisation, countries' housing policies are characterised by increased state intervention in housing, but over the course of the last half century, they have relied more on market processes, with an increasing emphasis on homeownership. While Doling's primary focus is on the advanced economies, he also considers transition and developing countries.

Ward, in contrast, provides an overview of housing policies in developing countries. Detailing the evolution of housing policies from the 1950s onwards, Ward argues that housing policies and their implementation are shaped by broader economic and political ideologies, levels of development and urbanisation, and rates of urban growth. Exploring this in relation to changing development paradigms ranging from modernisation to neoliberalism, he charts the changing nature of state intervention in the housing arena from the very direct role played by governments in various sites and service schemes in the 1980s to the subsequent rolling back of the state associated with neoliberal economics and politics. The latter era has been marked by an emphasis on decentralisation, good governance, urban sustainability, and greater efficiency of urban management and city planning.

Self-Help

Articles by Richard Harris (Self-Help: Policy Assistance) and Diana Mitlin (Housing Policies in Developing Countries: Sites-and-Services and Aided Self-Help) both focus on one of the most prominent housing initiatives across the developing world, namely aided self-help or site and service schemes. Harris's article provides a rare insight into the evolution of self-help policies which he traces back to the early years of the twentieth century when a number of European nations (including Germany, Scandinavia, Austria, and Canada) began to help those on low incomes to construct their own housing. Articulated in the writings of Crane in the 1940s and Turner in the 1960s, the key principles of self-help were to afford poorer individuals and households the 'freedom to build' and for the state to facilitate this through the (varied) provision of serviced land, advice, finance, building materials, and training in management and construction.

These arguments are further developed in Mitlin's article which concentrates on the experience of developing countries from the 1970s onwards. She attributes the growing popularity of site and service programmes among both international agencies (such as the United Nations and the World Bank) and national governments to rapidly expanding urban populations as well as an urbanisation of poverty. Within this context, self-help housing initiatives provided a viable alternative in relation to previous (failed) interventions including squatter eviction and relocation as well as publically provided housing. This said, drawing upon a range of examples, both Harris and Mitlin identify the limitations of site and service programmes including the limited scale of many programmes, speculative investment, downward raiding by the rich and powerful, and demanding building standards. On a more ideological note, site and service programmes have also been criticised for shifting the responsibility of housing provision from the state to vulnerable individuals and households and for depressing wage levels. The article by David Satterthwaite on upgrading presents a type of self-help initiative undertaken by poor urban populations living in 'slum' or informal settlements to improve their housing.

Access and Affordability

Judith Yates and Vivienne Milligan provide an overview of policies that promote access to housing opportunities and the affordability of housing. They explain a rationale for policies that improve access and affordability, which highlights their impact on individual households and on the economy as a whole. A taxonomy of policies is proposed that gives insight into the diverse range of direct and indirect forms of assistance that can be provided. The authors highlight the importance of evaluating these policies against a broad rather than narrow range of objectives. The group of articles addressing access and affordability issues includes programmes that aim to directly alleviate housing costs burdens (Peter Kemp writes on housing allowances, and Marion Steele on housing vouchers). Marietta Haffner, Marja Elsinga and Jap Hockstra examine private renting, Hugo Priemus writes on administered rents in public housing, Jenny Schuetz and Rebecca Meltzer address inclusionary zones, and Hans Lint reviews the legislation on security of tenure. In more recent times, state intervention in the form of regulatory controls has been relaxed and direct provision via social housing has contracted. Innovative attempts to improve low-income households' access to housing opportunities are tackled in two articles (Intermediate Housing Tenures by Marja Elsinga and Social Housing: Measures to Attract Private Finance by Peter Phibbs). As John Doling, (mentioned above), points out, advanced countries have increasingly concentrated on expanding homeownership. Government policies to improve access for first-time home-buyers are reviewed in two articles (Contract Saving Schemes by Richard Ronald and First Home-Owner Grants by Tony Dalton), while measures to improve access to private rental housing are discussed in one article (Deposit Assistance Schemes for Private Rental in the United Kingdom by Julie Rugg). Finally, there is an article on schemes in developing countries that aim to improve access to housing loans. The programmes reviewed by Peer Smets (Housing Policies in Developing Countries: Microfinance) usually consist of small loans obtained for a short period of time and are suited to the ways in which poorer households manage their finances, as well as the ways in which they build their housing – incrementally and progressively.

Taxation and Housing

Housing and the land that housing is built on are an important source of tax revenue to most governments. A broad range of taxes are applied to housing and land. They can significantly shape how land is used, the structures that are built, and the cost of housing to the tenant or home-buyer. In most countries, the taxation of housing poses difficult challenges for policy-makers. The key policy issues are outlined by Miranda Stewart (Taxation Policy and Housing), an overview article that also describes the wide range of transaction, income, and wealth tax measures applied to housing. From this article, we learn that taxes can impact on market efficiency by influencing the allocation of resources between different housing tenures, as well as being an important determinant of housing affordability. A key feature of the taxation of housing is homeowner tax expenditures that are departures from the benchmark tax treatment of income, assets, or transactions benefiting homeowners. These have tended to attract critical attention from policy analysts (see Steven Bourassa's article on this theme). Local governments frequently derive much of their tax revenue from local government property taxes (see the article Local Government Property Taxes by Gavin Wood and Rachel Ong) that are commonly levied on the unimproved capital value of buildings, including housing. These taxes are the subject of a large literature that addresses a wide range of housing-related issues, but which also tackles impacts on neighbourhoods and residential segregation. Policy-makers have periodically considered the lift in land values accompanying changes in zoning or the grant of planning permission as an 'unearned' income that should be subject to tax. In some countries, they will be captured by a capital gains tax; but where this is not the case, a development land tax (as discussed by Michael Oxley) is commonly advocated.

Housing Supply and Neighbourhoods

Access to housing opportunities and the affordability of dwellings in market-driven housing systems will in part depend upon an ample supply of housing that is also responsive to changing market conditions. Policies that address these housing supply issues are overviewed in Kerry Vandell's article on housing supply. Extreme supply shortages that follow severely disruptive events such as wars commonly motivate programmes of investment in social housing to support housing supply (see Michael Berry's entry). But in more normal circumstances, supply responses from private developers and builders can be stimulated by supply-side subsidies (as discussed by Melek Cigdem); the competitiveness of the developer and construction industries will help shape the efficiency of housing supply, and this is addressed by governments through competition policy and regulation (as explained by David Hayward). Urban planning is a key influence on the size, location, and design of housing supply. Three articles by, respectively, Kyung-Hwan Kim, Michael Buxton and Lucy Groenhart, and Timothy Dixon, describe how governments use green belts, urban growth boundaries, and brownfield development to influence where housing is built and supplied. The location of housing and its size help shape a city's 'carbon footprint'; this important subject is explored in the article by Anthony Yezer. Finally, government approaches to the design and enforcement of residential building standards are described by Henk Visscher.

Housing also has a critically important role in driving neighbourhood dynamics, and, as a consequence, housing programmes are a component of policies addressing neighbourhood decline. Urban regeneration policies are reviewed by Ronan Paddison, while Reinout Kleinhans explains how housing programs are integrated into urban regeneration policies. There are also individual articles in this section that address issues with a strong neighbourhood dimension

(Exclusionary Zoning by Alan Mallach), and others that are focused on specific housing programmes with a strong spatial focus (HOPE VI by Diane Levy).

Labour Markets and Mortgage Markets

Housing systems are vital to the efficient functioning of economies, and the interrelationships between housing, labour markets, and the finance sector are vital in this respect. Labour market issues that have attracted concern among housing policy-makers are overviewed by Paul Flatau (in a piece on Housing and Labour Markets). Individual articles explore the following: policy responses to the efficiency and equity consequences of spatial mismatch between the residential location of workers and job sites: (Donald Houston considers the general policy response); policies that aim to retain key workers (e.g., teachers and firefighters) in regions where housing costs are high are set out by Nicola Morrison; housing subsidy programmes and incentives to work are discussed by Mark Shroder; the use of housing programmes to encourage mobility among disadvantaged subgroups are illustrated in the 'Moving to Opportunity' Programme introduced by William Clark; and finally, the relationship between social housing and employment outcomes is discussed by Kath Hulse.

Housing systems are a major sector of the national economy and are closely linked to the finance sector through mortgage markets. Housing and macroeconomic policy is discussed by Stephen Whelan and regulation and intervention in mortgage markets is addressed by Martin Flanagan; more specific regulatory instruments are described in articles dealing with mortgage guarantees by Robert Van Order, deposit guarantees for housing finance institutions by James Barth and Harris Hollans, and mortgage interest rate regulation by Ian Harper and Lachlan Smirl. The importance of housing finance and housing equity in personal wealth portfolios has meant that housing asset values and mortgage debt are an important consideration in the application of monetary policy, as discussed by John Muellbauer (Monetary Policy, Wealth Effects, and Housing).

Choice and Discrimination

We have witnessed a transformation in the role of governments in housing policy over the last few decades with an increasing emphasis on market-based solutions to housing problems. These trends and the policies that use market mechanisms to increase choice and promote individual responsibility are examined in Melek Cigdem and Gavin Wood's overview article (Choice and Government Intervention in Housing Markets). One of the first and most important policy initiatives of this kind was the sale and transfer of public housing (Privatisation of Social Housing by Manuel Aalbers); other market-based policy initiatives reviewed in this section include articles by Andrew Caplin (Shared Equity), Ray Struyk (Access and Affordability: House Purchase Certificates), and Freidman Roy and Richard Ronald (Contract Saving Schemes). Policies in transition countries are reviewed in Martin Lux's article (Policies to Promote Housing Choice in Transition Countries). The enthusiasm for neoliberal market-oriented housing policies is tempered by market imperfections that can impede choice among disadvantaged groups. Policies to address discrimination in housing markets, to tackle redlining, and to provide education programmes for home buyers and tenants have been motivated by these concerns. They are discussed here by Dag Einar Sommervoll, Manuel Aalberts, and Anitra Nelson, respectively. Finally, Val Colic-Peisker's article on immigration and housing policy is especially pertinent given the importance of migration in a globalising world.

The *International Encyclopedia of Housing and Home* has a separate section on 'Policy' because housing is a basic need and a substantial sector of the economy. Housing policy is therefore of a key concern for governments all over the world. The 65 articles in this section aim to provide the reader with an overview of the diverse housing policies in different parts of the world.

G Wood and K Datta

WELFARE AND WELL-BEING

Why Well-Being?

The *International Encyclopedia of Housing and Home* would not be complete without a set of articles which very directly tackles issues of human welfare and well-being. Of course, this theme appears, tacitly or more explicitly, in a very wide range of essays across all the main sections. Nevertheless, a central aim of very many areas of housing studies has been to engage with the importance of housing systems not only in reflecting wider patterns of exclusion and inequality but also as way of documenting and intervening in processes of discrimination, exclusion, and impoverishment. Many of the contributions in this section of the encyclopedia aim to profile such matters.

The entire encyclopedia, in its aim to appeal internationally, is challenged by the variety of meanings and implications attached in politics, policy, and practice to certain key words. There are, however, few concepts that introduce more confusion than those used to describe welfare and well-being. In the United Kingdom, and in many other European countries, for example, the term 'welfare' has a very broad meaning, which includes individuals' material conditions as well as the range of services and policy instruments that aim to secure certain levels of welfare across the population. In this sense, improving human welfare and securing well-being have very similar connotations. In addition, many, if not most, developed countries have forms of social welfare policy which commonly include housing policy, and there are extensive debates about the nature, variety, and direction of what are often termed 'welfare state regimes'. While the scope and scale of social housing provision and subsidy has frequently been scaled back or privatised in recent decades, the legacy and extent of social housing is still important in many countries; for example, see articles on social housing and the welfare state in Western Europe by Peter Boelhouwer, on social housing in the United States by Rachel Bratt, on housing finance and welfare by Peter King, and on privatization by Peter Malpass. Thus, welfare in this context is equally an individual or collective state, an ideal, and a set of policy instruments. In the United States and elsewhere, by contrast, the term 'welfare' carries the baggage of formal social welfare programmes which have in some contexts a variety of derogatory connotations, as well as limited applicability in many developing countries. Hence, our choice of the terms 'welfare' and 'well-being' to try to embrace the variety of different understandings involved.

The 62 articles in this section gathered under the collective heading of 'Welfare and Well-Being' make an important statement. Housing and home lie at the centre of many issues concerning individual and social welfare and well-being in the broadest sense, which impact on the quality of life that people experience through housing across the life course. So while some researchers and policy-makers examine housing in the context of structure, tenure, location, asset values, affordability, and accessibility, and while others consider patterns of residential and social segmentation, and the opportunities they contain for social and political mobilization, the articles in this section also look to other possibilities for the meanings of housing and home, in particular, their role in securing a better quality of life for individuals, households, and communities.

It is important, finally, to note that the section 'Welfare and Well-Being' for the purpose of the encyclopedia refers neither to the subjective measures that have become popular in health studies, nor to the 'happiness benchmark' that has come into vogue as a policy goal. It is a treated as material condition as well as a meaningful experience, and the articles are concerned as much with what produces its absence – what strips households of well-being – as with what guarantees its presence. So there are articles on housing and the state in a variety of countries, on housing wealth and quality of life, and on the reciprocal link between housing and health that is shaped by environments, policies, and institutions.

At Home with Well-Being

Several decades ago, Lee Rainwater (1966) wrote a paper entitled *Fear and the House-as-Haven in the Lower Class* in which he analysed the value and significance of the home as a refuge from human and non-human threats. Whether a single family dwelling, a self-built squatter home, a terraced cottage, or a high-rise flat, the idea is that home can be a haven – a space that is both defensible and secure. Although feminist scholarship over the years has questioned such visions (showing that for many women, home is anything but refuge (see Gender and Urban Housing in the Global South by Sylvia Chant)), the articles in this section do encourage us to think about the complex role of housing in relation to well-being: in terms of physical and economic security (or insecurity); a place to relax and have fun, or to simply get by and survive; a place of quiet and privacy (or noise and intrusion); and an asset that can be used to meet needs, now, in older age, or for children (see Asset-Based Well-Being: Use Versus Exchange Value by Beverley Searle). Housing generally, and the home in particular, has multiple significances at the individual level and this applies in both developed and less developed worlds.

In Latin American squatter and informal settlements, young households embrace the risks and social costs of living in neighbourhoods without services or secure tenure, and face having to self-build their homes, because such settlements offer a space for family life, a place to live hassle free (*vivir tranquilo*), and the eventual prospect of leaving a legacy to children (*tener un patrimonio para los hijos*). Several articles in this section examine these processes of settlement and home creation, and elsewhere there are reflections on the meanings of the home for those that live out that experience.

Interestingly, too, a high proportion of original homeowners who settled peripheral unserviced land informally some 30 or more years ago continue to live on those same lots, in dwellings that are today fully consolidated, serviced, and located in the intermediate ring of the city (see Urban Regeneration in Latin America by Peter Ward). Physical immobility appears to be the order of the day – at least among low-income homeowners. It seems likely that the meaning of those homes and the significance of their sacrifices have changed over time as people consolidated and expanded the physical space of their dwellings. For many of their (now adult) children, the home is already a patrimony, since they continue to live on the lot with their own families and fully expect to continue to do so once their parents die. How second and even third generations perceive and construct meanings about the family home is only now beginning to be researched.

In developed countries, housing markets operate to allow households to adjust home and housing to needs through residential mobility: moving out or moving inwards; building assets or drawing down on equity; upsizing or downsizing; moving into school catchment areas; and searching for amenity of one sort or other. Here the constraints are largely market based – affordability – although ethnicity and race may also be important, as are national and subnational housing policies. Nevertheless, the wider point is that housing is more than an artefact, or an asset, or a space in which to live; it carries meanings and significance which change in the life course and which are likely to be shaped or constructed by class, ethnicity, social trends and fads, advertising and real estate promotions, national ideology, and so forth. As the articles in this section show, this all has a bearing on both welfare and well-being.

Scales of Welfare and Well-Being

Whether in the developed or emerging world, the articles in this section identify a range of scales at which welfare and well-being can be considered, from the macro to the micro.

At the 'macroscale', as we have clearly seen with the recent financial crisis, housing is important in terms of the role it plays in the economy (especially in the developed world) through housing-related construction and spending, in the growth of mortgage debt, and in national economic policy. The inflation of a home price and mortgage lending bubble is implicated in the financial turmoil precipitated by subprime mortgage lending and by mortgage heavy-credit derivatives which proved unsustainable. The subsequent credit crisis, with sharp contractions in mortgage lending, sudden illiquidity in housing markets, dips in price, and a rise in repossessions, particularly in the United States, dealt a major blow to households who are vulnerable to the social and financial consequences of negative equity, bankruptcy, and homelessness. In a number of cities, particularly in the United States, the level of repossessions has led to stagnant or cratering housing markets, which are associated with high levels of vacancies and abandonment and a variety of consequent social and economic problems. While many of these issues are, appropriately, explored in the section 'Economics and Finance', their implications for the financial and wider welfare of home-buyers are drawn out in several of the articles of this section, including those of Lucy Delgadillo and Dan Immergluck.

As a result of recession, which has destabilised the economies and finances of a number of countries, including the United States, the United Kingdom, Spain, and Ireland, all of which had major housing booms, many governments have now embarked on austerity policies in order to try to rein in their national debt. This in turn has created problems in terms of rising unemployment and falling incomes and welfare cuts. There are also cuts in housing-related expenditures and subsidies which have increased housing costs and added to problems of affordability. And, as mentioned earlier, housing is also important as an asset whose erosion can undermine the well-being of homeowners, particularly older homeowners who may rely on live-in adult children to care for them in old age (as in Latin America) or who seek to trade down and release equity for retirement (increasingly the case in developed nations). These issues are explored in articles by Laurence Murphy (Asset-Based Welfare), Beverley Searle (Asset-Based Well-Being: Use Versus Exchange Value), and Hal Kendig (Older People: Well-Being, Housing and Neighbourhoods).

In short, at a macroeconomic level, housing is of importance for social well-being across the board. This is clear even when it is examined from a variety of perspectives, ranging from free-market economics to welfare state regime theory.

Moving to the 'urban scale', housing has a bearing on well-being, in particular, through its role in mediating the practice of segregation between different social and income groups. As is well known, this operates in a variety of different ways in both developed and developing countries. It includes the concentration of low-income groups into low-price, low-quality housing in inner cities or in peripheral social housing estates and irregular settlements; the flight of some higher-income households to suburban or periurban areas; and the creation of segregated housing in inner cities based upon race, class, and ethnicity. The concentration of different income and ethnic groups in different segments of the housing market can generate major differences in social conditions and quality of life: at one extreme, deprived groups are segregated within the poorest housing enclaves, and at the other extreme, highly privileged groups lock themselves away in gated communities. These themes are picked up in several articles, including those of James De Filippis (Social Movements and Housing), Anthony Lemon (Residential Segregation: Apartheid), William Wilson (Residential Segregation: Experiences of African Americans), Edward Geotz (Slum Clearance), Nora Libertun de Duren (Gated Communities: Global South), and Elena Vesselinov (Gated Communities: Developed Countries). These authors also indicate the extent to which such housing issues are tied to political struggles and campaigns. Examples include low-income self-builders mobilizing for legal recognition and for basic services, renters demonstrating to resist eviction, and sometimes – as in Mugabe's Zimbabwe – struggles over blatant ethnic cleansing. Commonplace, too, are protests to challenge rent hikes or threats of gentrification and displacement. In all of these cases, housing and neighbourhoods are the medium through which affected groups attempt to influence or change central or local government policy or to halt new developments which are seen as prejudicial to neighbourhood quality or residents rights (see the articles by Roger Zetter (Shelter and Settlement for Forcibly Displaced People), James DeFilippis (Social Movements and Housing) and others). All this engages with well-being in the broader sense.

At the 'neighbourhood level', processes such as housing abandonment, clearance and redevelopment, gentrification, condominium conversion, and the sale of social housing can contribute to changes in both the availability and the quality and affordability of the housing stock, in ways that adversely affect well-being (see articles by Alan Morris (Social Housing and Social Problems), Alan Smart (Squatter Settlement Clearance), Peter Malpass (Privatisation of Housing: Implications for Well-Being), and others). The form of housing and the environment in which it is located are also important for social interaction and quality of life. There are major differences between homes with gardens in green, communal areas, and life in high-rise blocks in a depressing environment where residents may live in fear or in a state of virtual imprisonment. Housing and home are also important for specific social groups in terms of availability, access, and exclusion. While some groups, particularly the more affluent and able bodied, have relatively few problems in finding appropriate housing, others, such as travellers, refugees, and asylum seekers in the United Kingdom, have difficulties in finding affordable homes that meet their needs. In developing countries, of course, the majority of city populations struggle to find affordable housing at all, and can only do so through informal mechanisms of self-help. It is sobering to note, nevertheless, that self-help and self-managed housing is increasingly observed as a means to homeownership among low-income groups in the United States (see articles by Richard Harris (Self-Help and Informal Sector Housing in the United States and Canada), and Vinit Mukhija (Informal Housing: Colonias in the United States)).

Everywhere there is evidence that older people, and those suffering from various health conditions and disabilities, experience difficulty in finding appropriate, accessible, enabling housing which enhances quality of life. The design and layout of housing, environmental quality, and other features of dwelling that are linked to physical and mental health are dealt with in the articles by Philippa Howden-Chapman (Health, Well-Being, and Housing), Mary Godfrey (Supported ousing), Rita Jacinto (Disability and Enablement), Diana Olsberg (Older People: Well-Being), Jason Prior (Health, Well-Being and Vulnerable Populations), and others. There are links here, too, to the articles in the section 'Environment'.

As mentioned at the outset, at the individual household level, housing is significant in terms of its role in social reproduction. Homes provide the locale for a great deal of day-to-day life, from cooking and eating to sleeping and a host of other activities, such as school homework, all of which require adequate and appropriate spaces. Some households are fortunate in having sufficient spaces for these activities, while others may be overcrowded and lack appropriate space or facilities. At the most basic level, homes are where occupants can express individuality in the way they personalise and use space. Some types of housing and environments permit this much more easily than others.

Similarly, the scope to remodel or revamp one's housing at the individual level varies. Renters, by and large, have little opportunity or incentive to undertake major remodels or retrofits (although some tenants in low-rent settings may find redecorating or housing improvement investment worthwhile). But most households do take the opportunity to redecorate, improve, or extend their homes, particularly where they have become invested in the neighbourhood, and where the home and actual dwelling itself is imbued with a special significance. Whether through contracting out, or through do-it-yourself (DIY), or through self-building and mutual aid, the housing stock generally, and the home specifically, may be refurbished over time.

Sustainable Well-Being?

'Greening' the home is a contemporary arena for physical improvements. Energy-efficient homes are on the increase and many householders are retrofitting their homes to add solar panels, improve insulation, install more energy-efficient appliances, and engage in rainwater harvesting, garbage, and other recycling, as well as undertaking garden/yard microenvironmental improvements and uses. While sustainable housing applications have traditionally been the preserve of middle-income and better-off groups, the challenge in developing countries especially will be to extend participation in sustainable housing practices to working and lower-income homeowners.

In the United States, 'weatherization' campaigns for homes using resources of the American Reinvestment and Recovery Act has targeted poorer and working-class households, and in countries such as Brazil and Mexico, one observes a quickening of interest in applying green technologies to new housing and to retrofitting older homes in working-class neighbourhoods. Indeed, the savings from making homes more energy efficient and sustainable form a much larger proportion of income among the poor than the rich. We expect interest in sustainable home buildings and retrofits to become more widespread in the future. As such, they are likely to add significant new (green) 'meanings' to housing and the home, especially among younger generations.

In the same vein, cutting across many of these scales are issues of housing rights and social justice. Such issues are rarely simple, as the current 'right to the city' debates illustrated in the article by Edesio Fernandes. While the 'right to the city' is a powerful political slogan, it tends to gloss over the crucial questions of rights for whom, and rights to what. Do landlords and developers have rights to the city or rights to housing, and if so, what form do they take and how are they to be evaluated against the rights of the overcrowded or the homeless? Equally, issues of rights for refugees or rights for travellers need to be evaluated against the rights of long-term residents in an area who may feel that their rights are being ignored or pushed to one side. In this respect, housing, whether viewed as an economic good, an individual possession, or a social right, is at the heart of wider economic, social, and political debates about the structure of society and the pursuit of social well-being.

C Hamnett and P Ward

References

Rainwater L (1966) Fear and the house-as-haven in the lower class. *Journal of the American Institute of Planners* 32: 23–31.

CONTENTS OF VOLUME 5

Multiple Homes	C Paris	1
Nature in the Home	ER Power	6
Neighbourhood Design: Green Space and Parks	N Dempsey	12
Neighbourhood Design: Public Spaces	R Sendi and B Goličnik Marušić	21
Neighbourhood Design: Urban Outdoor Experience	N Dempsey	29
Neighbourhood Disadvantage	J Prior	43
Neighbourhood Effects	T Kauko and M d'Amato	50
Neighbourhood Effects: Approaches	M van Ham and D Manley	55
Neighbourhood Governance	A Madanipour	61
Neighbourhood Improvement: The Role of Housing and Housing Institutions	T Carter	67
Neighbourhood Incivilities	RB Taylor	73
Neighbourhood Planning	S Pinnegar	78
Neighbourhood Reputation	M Permentier	85
Neighbourhood Watch	R Yarwood	90
Neoclassical Models of the Housing Market	M Andrew	96
Neural Networks and Analytic Hierarchy Processes	T Kauko	103
New Urban Economics and Residential Location	R Arnott	111
New Urbanism and Smart Growth Movements	JL Grant and S Tsenkova	120
NIMBYism	K Burningham	127
Notaries and Legal Professionals	NM Davidson	131
Older People: Housing Institutions	R Gilroy	136
Older People: Well-Being	D Olsberg	143
Older People: Well-Being, Housing and Neighbourhoods	H Kendig, L Clemson and L Mackenzie	150
Ontological Security	A Dupuis	156
Path Dependency	B Bengtsson	161
People and the Built Form	R Lawrence	167
Peripheral Neighbourhoods	S Mugnano	174
Philosophical Perspectives on Home	K Jacobson	178
Place Attachment	BB Brown, I Altman and CM Werner	183
Planning Institutions: Canada/United States	I Skelton	189
Planning Institutions: China	Y Song	196
Planning Institutions: Post-Socialist	Z Nedović-Budić	202
Policies to Address Homelessness	P Flatau	209

Policies to Address Homelessness: Criminalisation and Control of Public Space	J Wardhaugh	215
Policies to Address Homelessness: Housing First Approaches	V Stanhope, DK Padgett and BF Henwood	230
Policies to Address Homelessness: Partnership-Based Approaches in Ireland	E O'Sullivan	237
Policies to Address Homelessness: Prevention in the United Kingdom	H Pawson	243
Policies to Address Homelessness: Rights-Based Approaches	I Anderson	249
Policies to Address Homelessness: 'Staircase' Models	I Sahlin	255
Policies to Address Redlining	MB Aalbers	261
Policies to Address Social Mix in Communities	G Meen	268
Policies to Address Spatial Mismatch	D Houston	274
Policies to Promote Housing Choice in Transition Countries	M Lux	280
Policies to Promote the Environmental Efficiency of Housing	RE Horne	286

Overview Article

Policies to Support Access and Affordability of Housing	J Yates and V Milligan	293
Policy Instruments that Support Housing Supply: Social Housing	M Berry	306
Policy Instruments that Support Housing Supply: Supply-Side Subsidies	M Cigdem	311
Political Ideologies	P King	317
Politics of Housing	B Bengtsson	322
Post-Bubble Housing in Japan	Y Hirayama	328
Post-Conflict Housing Restitutions	A Buyse	336
Post-Disaster Housing and Reconstruction	C Johnson and G Lizarralde	340
Power	P King	347

Overview Article

Price Determination in Housing Markets	G Meen	352
Price Dynamics in Housing Markets	M Cho and K-H Kim	361
Privacy, Sanctuary and Privatism	R Dowling	367
Private Protection and Housing Property Insurers in the United States	RW Klein	372
Private Rental Landlords: Developing Countries	A Gilbert	381
Private Rental Landlords: Europe	J Hoekstra, M Haffner, H van der Heijden and M Oxley	387
Private Rental Landlords: North America	A Mallach	393
Private Sector Housing Management: Asia Pacific	EC-M Hui and TH Khan	401
Private Sector Housing Management: Europe	N Nieboer	407
Private Sector Housing Management: North America	J Londerville	414
Private Sector Housing Management: Post-Socialist	S Tsenkova	420
Privatisation of Housing: Implications for Well-Being	P Malpass	427
Privatisation of Social Housing	MB Aalbers	433
Property Rights Approaches	CA Nygaard	439
Public-Private Housing Partnerships	T Brown and N Yates	446

Multiple Homes

C Paris, University of Ulster, City of Derry, Ireland

© 2012 Elsevier Ltd. All rights reserved.

Glossary

Dwelling use How a dwelling is used at different times; thus a dwelling owned by one household could be used as a permanent residence, as a holiday home, or as one among many occasional residences.

Leisure studies An interdisciplinary academic specialism, mainly involving the social sciences, which focuses on recreation, leisure, and tourism.

Multiple homes The use by one household of three or more dwellings, none of which is occupied on a permanent basis by other users.

Pied-à-terre A dwelling used in addition to a primary residence, typically during the working week.

Primary residence Dwellings in which households are usually resident, often defined for official purposes including tax and census returns.

Second homes Dwellings owned by households for private use, most are owned rather than rented and in most cases the households only own one such dwelling.

Introduction and Definition of Multiple Homes

The concept of multiple homes refers primarily to the ownership by an individual or household of numerous dwellings purely for personal/household use and not let commercially to tenants, holidaymakers, or other fee-paying users. The idea of 'multiple' homes is a development from the idea of 'second' homes. Many scholars and media commentators have written about second homes, typically used for recreation, and conceptualised as being owned in addition to 'primary' residences where people spend most of their time.

In many instances, however, recent research has shown that households own at least two dwellings for personal use in addition to the primary home. One problem with the distinction between the 'primary' and 'second' homes is linguistic: it is clumsy to refer to more than one 'second' home and it becomes very ungainly to talk about 'third', 'fourth', or more homes: hence the use of the term 'multiple homes'. Another reason for referring to 'multiple homes' is that it has become apparent that a growing minority of highly mobile households in affluent countries own three or more 'homes' with *none* of them necessarily being the 'main' or 'primary residence'. Hence the concept of *multiple* homes can be used as an umbrella term to cover all instances of the ownership of two or more dwellings purely for private use.

Much of the work on second and multiple homes has been pioneered in leisure studies, especially the recent collection edited by McIntyre et al. (2006) (see also Gallent et al., 2005; Hall and Muller, 2004). In their introduction, McIntyre et al. (2006: 6) noted that "Frequent moves of short duration between home and one or more destinations for work or pleasure are a fact of life for a significant minority of people today." They suggested that second and other homes did not fall below 'primary' homes in households' esteem but are often more highly valued than the 'usual' residence. Growing affluence and mobility (Urry, 2007) are central features of these developments in the use of homes. In the United States and the United Kingdom, in particular, growing affluence and high levels of income and wealth polarisation have enabled a significant minority of households to purchase additional dwellings purely for personal and family use, both within their own countries and overseas.

It is not proposed that the terms primary residence and second homes should be abandoned. For the great majority of households, indeed, there is only one 'home' and most owners of second homes only own one such dwelling. The term multiple homes, however, enables us to capture the diversity of ways in which more affluent households own and use domestic residential properties. For example, in December 2006, *The Observer* journalist David Smith wrote about the 'hidden world' of Roman Abramovich:

> Abramovich is part of the rich Russian set that has colonised London's most exclusive neighbourhoods. He has a house in Belgravia worth an estimated £28m as well as an £18m estate in West Sussex. His wife, Irina, a former air stewardess, enjoys the city life and the couple's five children go to English schools. But Abramovich – who also owns a £10m St Tropez villa, two super yachts and a Boeing 767 – does not necessarily regard the British capital as home. 'I live on a plane. I like to visit London.

'If I had to think where I could live if not Moscow, London would be my first choice and second would be New York. In Moscow I feel most comfortable. I'm used to four different seasons; it's difficult for people in London to understand. People brought up in Russia like my kids want to play in the snow.'

Background

There is a large literature on second homes, deriving from many disciplines including urban and regional planning, leisure studies, and housing studies. A recent review of literature on second homes (Paris, 2008a) identified core issues and debates.

Firstly, the role of second home purchase and use was conceptualised as an important component within individuals' and households' life course investment and consumption strategies. Just as the purchase of one house or apartment is a key investment decision for most households, whether or not to purchase more dwellings for personal and household use typically also involves an assessment of the viability of these investments. Although investment is an important element in the ownership of more than one home, in a minority of cases, second and multiple dwellings are rented rather than owned. In these cases, the second or multiple homes are purely consumption items. For example, some affluent households take long-term leases on houses in London to use as their base during visits to the city from overseas or another part of the United Kingdom. Secondly, second homes and multiple homes are often implicated in the gentrification of high amenity coastal and countryside areas, especially in countries where planning regimes restrict new development in such areas. There have also been many reported conflicts of interest between 'locals' and second home owners, although the nature and extent of such conflicts has varied enormously between places and over time, with diverse patterns of cause and effect. Fourthly, the review of literature on second homes identified many variations between countries and over time, with differences in planning regimes constituting a key differentiating factor. Recent research, moreover, showed that there had been a significant growth of multiple home ownership, whereby households own more than two dwellings for their own use, rather than households simply owning one 'primary' and one 'second' home. Recent research has also demonstrated that there has been a growth in the ownership of transnational 'second' and multiple homes, with households from affluent countries purchasing dwellings in many other countries. On the basis of these observations and arguments, Paris (2008a) suggested that it is impossible to devise a single theoretical analysis or classificatory schema to describe second and multiple homes due to variations over time and between places.

A Typology of Dwelling Use

Many commentators have noted difficulties in attempting to define and count 'second' homes in various countries. These problems are due to varying official definitions, absence of interest in some jurisdictions and diverse legal and tenure systems, different statutory definitions and, in many cases, lack of official interest. Such difficulties would apply even more to any attempt to count the numbers of multiple homes, as in many cases they are spread across a number of different countries with diverse systems of recording ownership. In many cases, too, ownership status is masked by a variety of corporate arrangements designed to take benefit from taxation and other advantages that may be available.

In addition to problems with official statistics, it is impossible to give numbers of dwellings in each type of use precisely because the use of dwellings can and does change over the course of a year; for example, where a dwelling usually used as a pied-à-terre (see below) is let on a short-term basis during a period of peak demand, for example the Olympic Games. In practice, categories may be blurred, perhaps deliberately for tax avoidance; for example, where parents buy a dwelling for their student children but charge rent to other occupants even though they do not declare the rental income to the tax authorities.

The terms 'second home' and 'multiple homes' refer to how dwellings are *used* rather than to enduring physical characteristics or dwelling types as used, for example, in house condition surveys (e.g., detached houses and apartments). Dwellings that are identical in physical terms, for example adjacent apartments, can vary both in tenure *and* use. One apartment may be occupied by private tenants whereas an adjacent dwelling is owned by a household that uses it only occasionally for holidays.

It is thus helpful to employ a typology of dwelling use as follows: primary residences; second homes and multiple residences (including pieds-à-terre and other noncommercial family uses); investment properties (privately rented accommodation and holiday homes let on a short-term basis to holidaymakers) (Paris, 2008b). This typology attempts to cover all possible ways in which dwellings are used, from 'primary' homes, through 'second homes' and 'multiple residences', and various forms of investment.

The typology can include caravans, mobile homes and recreational vehicles, holiday lodges, houseboats or cruisers, or any others among a plethora of possible physical types of dwelling. Caravans and mobile homes are not included within counts of 'permanent dwellings' in many national official definitions, but they are often the only residence of households even in affluent societies. Many are also used periodically by owners of second and multiple homes; thus caravans, holiday lodges, mobile homes, and other forms of moveable dwellings can and do fit one or more of the types of dwelling use listed below.

Some of the examples of different types of use, below, are chosen to highlight how identical dwelling types next door to each other can fit into different types of use. Some types and subtypes overlap and owners and users in practice may often change the ways in which they use the dwellings. But that is precisely the point of using a typology: it helps to distinguish similarities, differences, regularities, and variations in the frequently fluid use of dwellings. There is also much blurring of categories due to many variations in legal and taxation arrangements across the globe; for example, time share ownership and use of apartments means quite different things in different contexts. This typology shows how 'leisure' and 'housing' markets overlap seamlessly so that analyses of one may often include large elements of the other; for example, average house prices within a country or region include the prices paid for second and other multiple homes, including those purchased by nonresident citizens of other countries. Thus regional variations in house prices reflect such factors but this is rarely if ever taken into account by studies of affordability.

1. *Primary residences*
   a. These are dwellings occupied by households for all or most of the year. In most cases, they are the *only* residence of the occupiers. In other cases, the occupants may own second or multiple homes. Just as tenure is irrelevant within this typology, so too is the question of whether or not such dwelling users own other properties that may be let to tenants or holidaymakers.
   b. One example is a house in North Belfast, owned outright and occupied all year by a household that has no other property investments.
   c. Another example is an apartment in a coastal town that is occupied permanently by a retired couple who own a house elsewhere that is let to tenants (that house is their primary residence for the tenants).
2. *Second homes*
   a. A 'second home' within this typology is defined as a single dwelling used by the household, other family members and/or friends purely for leisure use, typically at weekends and for holidays.
   b. One example is an apartment in the coastal town, next door to the permanent residence of the retired couple in 1c above, and used at weekends by a family from South Belfast.
   c. Another example is a small house in North Belfast, two doors away from the permanent residence of the family in 1b above: this is owned by a medical doctor who lives permanently in a rural community but enjoys using this house at weekends and holidays in the relative anonymity of a big city.
3. *Multiple homes*
   a. The term 'multiple homes' refers to the ownership of more than one 'second' home. It can be used as an umbrella term to include 'second homes' as in 2a but it also embraces the growing number of cases where affluent households own many dwellings in different places, including different countries, *none* of which are used to generate rental income. In many cases it may be impossible to specify a 'primary' residence as all may be used for varying periods of time that differ from year to year.
   b. One example would be the homes of a household that owns an apartment in Tuscany and a condominium in Florida in addition to their 'primary' residence in London.
   c. Another example concerns a household that owns and routinely moves between a Los Angeles apartment, a townhouse in Mayfair, London, a country estate in Kent, England, and a ski lodge in South Island, New Zealand; none of these, however, are 'primary'.
4. *'Pied-à-terre'*
   a. The term 'pied-à-terre' refers to dwellings owned in addition to primary residences and used mainly as a base for work distant from primary residences. The Survey of English Housing, conducted since the early 1990s, has shown a concentration of 'second homes' in London. It is generally assumed that most of these are owned by people who consider the primary residence to be outside of the metropolitan area but who retain a city base for use during the working week.
   b. One example would be the dwellings used by political representatives when their parliament or assembly is in session: such as an apartment in Brussels that is owned by a Member of the European Parliament (MEP) from another European Union (EU) country or a Washington apartment of a US Senator.
   c. Although they are typically in cities, another example of a pied-à-terre could be an apartment in Chesapeake Bay, Maryland, that is used by a fishing charter boat captain whose primary residence is in a city.
5. *Other noncommercial family uses*
   a. This type of use refers to dwellings used by family/household members for a variety of durations and reasons during temporary absences (though in practice some such absences may become extended over long periods).

b. One example is an apartment in London that is purchased by parents for the use of their student child during university study. (If rent is paid by the family member student and/or co-occupants, then this would be considered an investment property as in 6 below.)

c. With the growth in LAT ('living apart together') relationships, where two household spouses or partners work in spatially distant places, households may have two dwellings for use during periods of separation, typically during the working week. In some cases such households may have other dwellings for leisure and family use; this subtype overlaps with 'multiple homes'.

6. *Investment properties*

a. The term 'investment properties' refers to dwellings that are owned, but *not* occupied at all by the owners/purchasers, as an investment. The dwellings are *used* by other people, usually as primary residences or as holidaymakers (with a small minority being used as multiple homes by tenants).

b. One widespread type of investment property is houses or apartments that are rented to tenants: 'the private rental sector'. The legal and taxation contexts vary greatly between countries, but typically dwellings are let to tenants, or leased to licensees. The dwellings are thus used on a daily basis by their occupants but they are investments by their owners who seek rental income and, it is usually hoped, a longer-term capital gain. In most countries, the landlords of such dwellings receive tax relief against the cost of acquisition and/or running the investment.

c. One example of an investment property is a terraced house in North Belfast let to tenants on a 6-monthly tenancy; this property is identical to and set between the dwellings in 1b and 2c above, and is used as the primary residence of the tenants.

d. Another example, called 'holiday homes' in the United Kingdom and Ireland but often 'vacation rentals' in the United States or 'holiday rentals' in Australia (where the term 'holiday home' may be used interchangeably with the term 'second home'). These dwellings are let on short-term holiday/leisure basis to other users, often using an estate agent or management company. Thousands of cottages across the United Kingdom and Ireland are routinely let for short terms to visitors on holiday. Time-share accommodation and other forms of partial ownership and use of dwellings may fall into different types of use, though it can also be considered that such 'ownership' may constitute a form of leasehold tenancy.

Current Issues, Debates, and Scenarios for the Future of Multiple Homes

Many of the issues and debates relating to second homes also apply to multiple homes. I focus on three broad aspects: social, economic, and environmental impacts; the meaning of 'the home'; and uncertainties about the future of multiple homes.

Many social, economic, and environmental impacts have been attributed to second and multiple dwelling ownership. Critics of second homes often focus on growing social polarisation in high amenity areas as affluent outsiders push up land and house prices beyond the reach of most local working residents. This results in affluent enclaves and 'ghost towns' which remain barely inhabited for large parts of the year. Much development has taken place in areas of high ecological sensitivity and there are many reports of environmental damage. High proportions of nonpermanent residential use is related to housing market distortions, including price volatility and overproduction, noticed after 2007 in many coastal areas of Spain. The growth in transnational multiple home ownership, involving massive amounts of high-energy use travel, is often concentrated in many of the world's most expensive residential areas. Multimillionaires and billionaires with homes in many countries systematically select properties in the most expensive suburbs or ex-urban areas of the most expensive cities. Thus the prices of mansions in London or country estates in South East England reflect *global* fortunes rather than the UK economy as a whole. In October 2007, *The Sunday Times* reported that almost half of the country homes in South East England worth more than £5 million were bought by foreigners as "Russian oligarchs and tycoons from Asia and the Middle East...emulate the lifestyle of Britain's landed gentry" and that "[Up] to 75% of country homes worth more than £10 million have been snapped up by wealthy investors from abroad." Meanwhile, in the United Kingdom, the property pages of newspapers such as *The Times*, *The Telegraph*, or *The Observer* contain many pages devoted to luxury dwellings for leisure use in dozens of overseas countries. Completely new 'communities' have been developed to attract wealthy owners of multiple dwellings, whether in newly created islands in Dubai or gated and fortified American luxury resorts: new spaces for hyperconsumption.

The meaning of 'the home' becomes increasingly problematic once it is accepted that many households own more than one home for their own use, raising doubts about some arguments concerning the special nature of 'the home' as a special place of sanctuary, providing 'ontological security', and a haven from the world. Instead, homes may be conceived simply as investment items and optional dwelling spaces to be used as convenient more or less during any one year. Hall (2005) suggested that "because of advances in transportation and communication technology, for a substantial proportion of the population in developed countries or for elites in developing countries being able to travel long distances to engage in leisure behaviour...is now a part of their *routine* activities" (Hall, 2005: 24; emphasis added). Therefore, he suggested, as individuals "develop close relationships to multiple localities" this throws into question the very notion of a single "home" (Hall, 2005: 95–96). In some expensive London suburbs, numerous mansions belong to overseas owners who rarely, if ever, visit the houses (reported in the *Sunday Times* magazine section, 22 June 2008), but have purchased them as investments and in some cases as possible bolt-holes should political or other problems emerge in their own – typically oil-rich – counties. During the 2008 presidential campaign in the United States, the Republican candidate Senator John McCain was taken by surprise in an interview when asked "How many houses do you and Mrs McCain have?" (reported on CBS News, 21 August 2008). His reported answer was that he was not sure so "I'll have my staff get to you. I'll try to tell you about that." His staff subsequently said that the McCains owned "at least four [homes]" but a watchdog organisation, PolitiFact.com, claimed that the McCains owned at least seven (reported on 20 August 2008 by PolitiFact.com, from the *St. Petersburg Times*) or probably eight, including a high-rise condo in Arlington, Virginia, a 6-acre ranch in Arizona, as well as various condos in Colorado, Texas, and Oklahoma. Some may be rented to tenants, but the diversity of this property portfolio may well be typical of the multiple homes of very rich Americans.

The world of housing has been rocked since early 2007 by the so-called credit crunch following the collapse of the subprime mortgage market in the United States and a growing tide of failures and near-failures in financial services and banking sectors, especially in the United States and the United Kingdom. House prices have fallen savagely in many areas and housing construction has fallen, especially in regions with high concentrations of second homes, such as the Atlantic seaboard counties in the Republic of Ireland and the Spanish costas. What are the implications for multiple homes? There is little systematic evidence concerning patterns of multiple home ownership, especially when that ownership is spread across many countries, but most owners of many homes certainly have other assets over and above residential property: they are not marginal home buyers or workers likely to lose their jobs in economic restructuring. Some may experience massive losses in stocks and shares, but others will be able to take advantage of wider global slowdown to buy *additional* homes at lower prices than was the case 2 or 3 years ago. There is no reason for supposing that multiple home ownership involves equity withdrawal from a 'primary' home; rather, growing affluence and income polarisation has created a large category of very rich households for most of whom at least there are enormous ranges of consumption and investment options. Some may hold back from purchasing additional homes during the uncertainties during the recession of 2007–10. Such is their degree of wealth, however, that when the global economy recovers there will be a renewed surge of transnational multiple home ownership. With recovery, too, there will be growing interest among other affluent households in the purchase of additional properties for leisure use: as outright home ownership grows in many countries, increasing real incomes are likely to be used for additional consumption. Of course, other scenarios are possible: there could be growing movement towards less polarised societies and a return to more egalitarian philosophies; climate change, together with what may be a longer and deeper recession than optimists suppose, may lead to lower levels of luxury consumption and a move towards simpler patterns of leisure movement and activities. On balance, however, it seems likely that the recession will be followed by further growth of second homes and multiple homes, in many cases within 'secure' well-fortified developments denying access to other people.

See also: Home as Investment; Housing Wealth and Consumption; Housing Wealth and Inheritance in the United Kingdom; Meanings of Home; Second Homes.

References

Gallent N, Mace A, and Tewdwr-Jones M (2005) *Second Homes*. Aldershot, Hampshire: Ashgate.
Hall CM (2005) *Tourism: Rethinking the Social Science of Mobility*. Edinburgh: Pearson.
Hall CM and Muller DK (eds.) (2004) *Tourism, Mobility and Second Homes*. Clevedon, Buffalo, and Toronto: Channel View Publications.
McIntyre N, Williams D, and McHugh K (eds.) (2006) *Multiple Dwelling and Tourism*. Cambridge, MA: CABI.
Paris C (2008a) Re-positioning second homes within housing studies: household investment, gentrification, multiple residence, mobility and hyper-consumption. *Housing, Theory and Society*, 4(2): 1–19.
Paris C (2008b) Second homes in Northern Ireland: Growth, impact and policy implications. *Final Report*. Belfast: Northern Ireland Housing Executive.
Urry J (2007) *Mobilities*. Cambridge: Polity.

Further Reading

Paris C (2010) *Affluence, Mobility and Second Home Ownership*. London: Routledge.

Relevant Websites

http://www.cbsnews.com – CBS News
http://www.politifact.com – PolitiFact.com
http://property.timesonline.co.uk – TimesOnline

N

Nature in the Home

ER Power, University of Western Sydney, Sydney, NSW, Australia

© 2012 Elsevier Ltd. All rights reserved.

Glossary

Domestication The historical, biological, and cultural process through which wildness is brought into the sphere of human influence, such as within the home and through agriculture.

More-than-human homemaking A term capturing the idea that home is made through relations between human and nonhuman actors.

Culture–nature binary The separation of nature and culture in Western thought; a way of thinking that constructs nature as separate, passive, and distant from human activity.

Uncanny A feeling of discomfort, unfamiliarity, or alienation within a familiar space or space of belonging, such as the home; related to the Freudian concepts of *heimlich/unheimlich*.

Nature in the Home

The idea that home is a human place that excludes nature is foundational to Western conceptualisations of home and underpins a sense of home as a safe, comfortable, and secure space. This separation has been subject to research attention across diverse disciplines including archaeology (Hodder, 1990), anthropology (Ingold, 2000), and geography (Kaika, 2004). This literature examines the historical, practical, and symbolic processes through which home is created as a place that excludes nature; highlights ruptures to home as a bounded and exclusionary space; and demonstrates that home is a hybrid space of cohabitation with nature. Home as a place that excludes nature is also implicit in a much wider range of research that focuses exclusively on the role of the human agent in homemaking. In absenting nature and nonhumans this literature reinforces the assumed dominance of humans in understandings of home. The culture–nature binary that informs Western relations with nature is a critical framework for comprehending home–nature relations.

Understandings of nature in the home begin with the premise that home is a process and practice that has material and imaginative dimensions. Homemaking is an ongoing, relational process that takes place through relations with and around the material world. The denial and exclusion of nature and natural processes is a key way that home is imagined and made. Through the exclusion of nature, the material dwelling place is transformed into a home, a site that is shaped by feelings of belonging and security. This article focuses predominately on home–nature relations in the Western home, although constructions of home and nature in non-Western cultures are also considered.

The article is organised in three sections. The first section discusses the historical, practical, and ideological construction of home as a place that is separate from nature. This separation has been central to Western conceptions of home as a safe, comfortable, and secure space, and it underpins a sense of home as an autonomous space independent of nature and natural processes. Notions of home as a domesticated space have been influential in shaping this view. The second section examines the materiality and spatiality of home–nature relations. Despite home's appearance as a place that is separate from nature, it is materially dependent on nature. The third section extends the focus on nature in the home to discuss the place of natural agency in homemaking. Nature is not a passive object that is simply enrolled into human designs and conceptions of home, rather it brings particular affordances that shape, make, and disrupt home.

Home and Nature: Separate Spheres

Views of home as a place that is separate from nature have long been central to Western cultural understandings of home as a safe, secure, and comfortable space. Separations between home and nature do not simply exist but are made through conceptual, symbolic, and practical relations around nature and the material world. Historically they can be traced to the Neolithic period when home was first constituted as a place of culture in opposition to nature and wildness. These separate spheres are captured in the oppositional concepts *domus* and *agrios* (Hodder, 1990). *Domus* means literally the house-as-home, but also references the symbolic and material processes through which the wild was brought within the sphere of human influence through practices around pottery, plants, and animals. As a space and set of activities, *domus* was a strongly gendered concept that included "mothering (women and children), nurturing (providing food), and caring (storage)" (Hodder, 1990: 84). In contrast, *agrios* lay outside home and was associated with masculinity and practices around hunting, weapons, and death. Processes of domestication are central to *domus* and *agrios*, addressing the culturing of 'wildness' within and around the home. This includes the gradual domestication of plant and animal species through agriculture, as well as the domestication of Neolithic society through the establishment of more permanent and elaborate housing and of planned and bounded villages. Since the Neolithic, the production of home as a domesticated space has thus been bound up with the domestication of human society.

Conceptually, separations between home and nature are founded on a culture–nature binary that constructs nature, understood as the nonhuman world, as a passive 'other' to human culture and activity. These separations are founded in an Enlightenment logic that emphasises the triumph of (human) culture over (nonhuman) nature. This binary has been historically important in constructing nature as a passive object and resource that is available for human use. By contrast, humans, viewed as having crossed an evolutionary threshold through the development of sentience, sapience, and linguistic ability, appear as active agents and the "authors of their own designs" (Ingold, 2000: 175). From a culture–nature framework, human interactions with nature are thus characterised as a one-way relationship, a monologue, where humans design without input from the natural world. A second definition of nature as human nature has also been influential in understandings of home and nature. In this definition, the development of culture also signifies the domination and domestication of the internal, human nature. The improvement and domestication of external, nonhuman nature, such as through agriculture and as evidenced in the making of home, is an essential pathway that indicates the humanity and superiority of humans over nature. This definition has significantly defined Western perceptions of non-Western cultures, as discussed later.

Culture–nature binaries have three key implications for understandings of home and nature. First, culture–nature binaries support the idea of separate spheres: of home as a space of culture that lies in opposition to nature. Table 1 shows how the culture–nature binary maps onto other key dualisms, constructing home as a domesticated and human space that lies in opposition to nonhumans and wildness. The exclusion of nature, nonhumans, and wildness creates home as a familiar and secure space; by contrast, nature in the home is viewed as matter out of place, a contaminating and anxiety-provoking presence that challenges the safety, comfort, and security of home. However, designations of nature and culture, dirt and cleanliness are not fixed, but rather are situated culturally and historically. These distinctions are clearly illustrated in Pink's (2004) comparison of homemaking cultures in Spain and England. For Spanish homemakers dust was encountered as dirt and out of place because it was associated with nature and spaces outside home, whereas English homemakers saw dust as a product of the home and therefore as less troubling. Individuals further manipulated these designations to construct particular identities, for instance tolerating the presence of dust/dirt to establish a resistance to dominant versions of housewifely practice.

Separations between nature and culture are most strongly articulated within the modern home. Reflecting the modernist goal of separating spheres and functions, the idea of home as a place that is separate from nature has been progressively written into the city through planning processes such as land zoning, restrictions around the presence of livestock, and webs of infrastructure that regulate the flow and supply of natural resources such as energy and water. These networks and practices construct the house-as-home as a place that appears to operate autonomously of nature and natural processes. Electric lights, for example, allow the home to operate independently of diurnal rhythms of daylight and darkness; networks of taps, pipes, and pumps supply seemingly limitless volumes of water; and technologies such as air conditioning materially and imaginatively disembed home from its immediate climatic setting. Abstract systems of exchange, such as the exchange of money for energy and water, consolidate these separations by distancing use values from the environmental source and

Table 1 Culture–nature binaries

House-as-home	Nature/nonhumans/outside
Culture	Nature
Human	Nonhuman
Subject	Object
Active/agent/homemaker	Passive/object
Domesticated	Wild

implications surrounding the use of these resources. These symbolic and institutional practices around nature are supported by everyday practices such as cleaning that further strengthen home–nature separations through the localised exclusion of undesirables such as dirt, pests, and germs. In effecting this exclusion, the modern home is made to appear as a secure space separate from nature and the outside world.

A second implication of the culture–nature binary is the reification of human agency in homemaking. From a culture–nature perspective, homemaking is a process of domestication: an intentional activity undertaken by knowledgeable human agents who exert biological and social control over the nonhuman world, domesticating it and producing it in the image of human culture. These processes commenced with the domestication of plants and later animals during the Neolithic period. The emphasis on human agency transforming passive natures facilitates a view of domesticated spaces (e.g., home) and domesticated bodies (e.g., companion animals) as simple reflections of human culture and agency. This is the default way that home has been viewed and represented in the social sciences and is most clearly apparent in the absence of discussions of nature and natural agency in research about homemaking. As suggested in the introduction to this article, the absence of nature and nonhumans in literature about home implicitly reinforces the assumed dominance of humans and human agency in homemaking.

A third implication that culture–nature binaries have for understandings of home speaks to the second definition of nature as internal, human nature. This definition of nature has been instrumental in constructing difference along the lines of gender and race, with women and people from non-Western cultures viewed as closer to nature. The naturalised association between women and mothering/nurturing sees women relegated to the space of the home. These ideas are apparent in the gendering of Neolithic conceptualisations of *domus* and are bound up with more recent articulations of the domestic space as a feminine space. At the same time, female sexuality, or feminine nature, has been constructed as a threat to home that requires regulation, control, and domestication (Berner, 1998). Non-Western cultures are differently placed in this hierarchy, with ideas about home, nature, and domestication providing a foundation for racial hierarchies on the basis of culturally specific (Western) understandings of property, ownership, and possession. Indigenous Australians, for example, have been construed as inferior 'savages' because of their nomadic culture and lack of fixed housing and agriculture (as perceived from a Western colonial perspective), factors that suggest that they are part of nature (Anderson, 1997).

Nature as Part of Home

The previous section established the historical and contemporary significance of home–nature separations in constituting the Western home as a safe, secure, and comfortable space. These separations are produced conceptually and practically through symbolic and practical relations with and around the nonhuman world. They are consolidated through a focus on human agency in homemaking that downplays the presence and significance of nonhuman natures in home. However, despite the dominance of this view, home is a space that is materially connected to, and dependent on, nature and natural processes. It does not simply exclude nature, but is made through complex relations with the nonhuman world. Understandings of homemaking as an ongoing process where the material space of a house is transformed into home are important in conceptualising this connection.

The ideological and conceptual construction of home as a space that is separate from nature and the nonhuman world contrasts with its material dependence on nature and natural processes. Maria Kaika's (2004) work has been particularly influential in foregrounding these connections through the case study example of water, an element that is essential to the construction of home as a comfortable and clean space, but which is contrastingly also imagined as separate and part of nature. Water is enabled as part of home through its social and material production as a purified, domesticated commodity. It is "abstracted, dammed, channelled, stored, distilled and chlorinated" (Kaika, 2004: 274), shifting geographically and conceptually from the country (nature) to the city and ultimately the home. By contrast 'dirty' water is removed from home. These connections reveal that rather than simply excluding nature, home is characterised by a selective porosity where desired elements are "*selectively* allowed to enter after having undergone significant material and social transformations" (Kaika, 2004: 274). Water "(along with other forms of produced nature) becomes part and parcel of the *material* construction of the modern home" (Kaika, 2004: 267). The invisibility of infrastructures that supply home is essential to the maintenance of the illusion of home's separation from nature. Hidden within the walls and below the floors of the modern home these infrastructures facilitate and consolidate a sense of home as an autonomous space that functions independently of nature, despite its essential connectivity.

This simultaneous need and denial of nature is the paradox of the modern home. While fostering feelings of comfort and security, this paradox at the same time alienates human occupants from home because, "In a deceitful way, remaining unfamiliar with [these] socionatural networks is a prerequisite for feeling familiar [and at home] within one's own home" (Kaika, 2004: 275). Home's paradoxical dependence and denial of nature thus constitutes nature as the domestic 'uncanny'. Drawing on Freudian notions of *heimlich* and *unheimlich*, this term refers to a process where "things that ought to have remained hidden come to light" (Kaika, 2004: 277). For example, at times of crisis such as water shortages these networks malfunction and 'come to light', highlighting the essential role of nature in home and giving rise to uncanny and unhomey feelings. As Kaika explains,

> These occurrences put the normalized character of the control and commodification of nature into question, and threaten the smooth functioning of the domestic sphere. Such an exposure of the limits of domestic bliss, and a revelation of its dependency on social relations of production generates a feeling of "not being at home in one's own home".
>
> (Vidler, 1992: 4, in Kaika, 2004: 276)

Home is also connected to nonhuman nature in ways that exceed human agency, control, and design. Pest animals frequently cohabit the house-as-home, rupturing and disturbing views of home as simply a human place. Insects like cockroaches and flies enter through gaps around drains and cracks in brickwork, actively challenging home's selective porosity. They also flourish in spaces viewed as empty, dirty, and uninhabitable by humans, foregrounding a view of home as a place that supports the life opportunities of diverse bodies that are not always human. Germs, and insects such as dust mites, further destabilise home–nature separations through their assertive presence in home. These entities represent danger and disorder within the home, rupturing and emerging from ruptures in human homemaking activity and flourishing in spaces such as the kitchen and bedroom that are central to imaginaries of home and that are the locus of feelings of comfort and homeyness (Power, 2007). The presence of insects and germs highlights the limits of human control over home, challenging home's selective porosity and highlighting a much greater permeability and openness to the outside. At a much larger scale, the pervasive impact of climate change and the current emphasis on local and household scale sustainability measures points to a broader shift in which nature and connections to nature are not only recognised, but also practiced as part of everyday homemaking.

More than simply disrupting home and senses of home as a safe, secure space, challenges to home as a place of culture can also emancipate occupants by confronting them with their alienation and therefore offering the opportunity for reflection "on alternative ways of engaging with the world" (Kaika, 2004: 23). Analysis of Australian homes shows that in some cultural contexts a blurring of inside and outside is an important way that home is made. This is evidenced in the growing popularity of 'outdoor rooms' associated with outdoor eating and entertaining, as well as in the trend to informal living areas that are "physically (e.g., large sliding door) and visually (extensive use of glass)" opened to the outside (Head and Muir, 2006: 512). In this context, openness offers new possibilities for living that involve encounters with spaces and bodies outside home. These are not spaces of anxiety, but are conceived as facilitating a productive engagement between inside and outside. Unanticipated ruptures to home, such as by pest animals, also offer new ways of living home as a space that is connected to nature and home at other scales. For example, relations with native animals in the home can shape feelings of belonging at a national scale.

More-Than-Human Homemaking

Home is not only connected to nature, but also made through complex relations with and around active, creative natures. Understanding home as a process that is made and re-made through everyday practices that transform the material space of the house into a home is a critical first step in comprehending the significant ways that home reflects the presence of diverse, active nonhuman natures. Acknowledging the active presence of nature in the home means allocating agency away from the central figure of the human, towards a distributed and more-than-human understanding of agency that recognises and engages with the active and sometimes creative presence of nonhuman entities in home including, but not restricted to, animals.

Historic narratives that challenge the central notion of a knowledgeable, disembodied, and intentional human agent in homemaking provide an important foundation for a broadened more-than-human understanding of home. Most notably, anthropologist Helen Leach (2007) foregrounds the unintended consequences of domestication to demonstrate the limitations of human control over these processes. As Neolithic society moved into increasingly sedentary dwelling spaces, the human species underwent observable biological and physiological changes that are comparable to those experienced by nonhuman animals undergoing domestication, such as the development of an increasingly gracile skeletal form. This perspective unsettles the assumed dominance of human agency and intentionality in processes of domestication and hence homemaking. It also suggests the capacity of the material space of home to 'speak back' and influence the development of the human form.

Relational views of homemaking have expanded understandings of home in two key directions. First, through the notion of accommodation as articulated by Daniel Miller (2002), homemaking is highlighted as a multidirectional relation where the materiality of the house can challenge and disrupt residents' feelings of being-at-home in the house-as-home. Accommodation expands human-centred notions of home by explicitly speaking to the materiality of homemaking through three definitions: First, accommodation means the physical dwelling place where people live and make home. Second, it describes homemaking as a multidirectional relation where (1) people appropriate and change this dwelling place so that it suits their living patterns and (2) people change themselves and/or their living patterns to suit the house. A final definition "expresses a sense of willing, or benign agreement to compromise on behalf of the other" (Miller, 2002: 115). In processes of accommodation agency lies in current and previous human residents as well as in the materiality of the house-as-home.

These ideas are comprehensively explored in Nicky Gregson's (2007) publication *Living with Things*, which examines the ways that home–nature separations are located in and (re)produced through homemaking activities around plants and domestic pets in the house and garden. Cohabitation with pets, for example, is characterised by three dilemmas, "specifically: how to manage their cohabitation in the dwelling space, how to manage cohabitation in things and how to manage animal bodies" (Gregson, 2007: 152). Recognition of these processes challenges traditional views of domestication as a one-off event located in the historical biological domestication of plants and animals and instead situates domestication as an ongoing and essential part of everyday homemaking practice that is essential to the cultural accommodation of nature in home. The home–nature separation is thus not a natural or inevitable part of home, but is a dynamic and contingent achievement that is predicated on the ongoing, vigilant activity of the homemaker. Views of domestic animals and plants as simple reflections of human culture are also destabilised by this view, which foregrounds their capacity for independent and at times disruptive action. Thus homemaking becomes a story of containment and holding nature within the bounds of human culture and respectability.

Understandings of home and nature have also been expanded in a second direction that emphasises the essential embodiment of the human actor and that focuses on the specific relations between human and nonhuman actors in home. Much of this research examines the place of animals in homemaking. Home is a site of cohabitation between human and nonhuman animals, including companion species and pests. Companion animals affect a range of homemaking practices including "housing choice and design, furnishing and the internal configuration of space" (Franklin, 2006: 154). They actively co-define the nature of the companionate relation and the form of the house itself, not only disrupting home as intimated in Gregson's analysis but also opening up new ways of living home. Smith's (2003) reflection on her own experiences of cohabiting with rabbits is particularly illuminating. Smith seeks to reconceptualise the power dynamics that shape human–companion animal relations in the house-as-home. Challenging accounts that suggest people always dominate these relations (particularly Tuan, 1984), she describes her efforts to recognise and engage with the free agency of the rabbits that she cohabits with, focusing on the ways that they open up new ways of living home. Her experience of 'becoming animal' recounts a process of learning to cohabit with rabbit ways of living. It is equally a process that shapes the house itself, as rabbits participate in their own forms of spatial management. Through this process of intimate cohabitation, Smith and the house itself are recognised as 'becoming animal'.

Nonliving elements, objects, and materials are also active in homemaking. Human homemaking activity does not take place independently of these entities but is entwined with them and takes place through them. Home is thus a more-than-human achievement that reflects the qualities, capacities, and properties of diverse nonhuman entities. For example,

> Water flows. It reacts with certain chemicals and dissolves others. Often these dissolved chemicals are invisible, and diffuse rapidly and uncontrollably. Water evaporates when warmed, condenses when cooled, and, as any homeowner in Minneapolis knows, expands when it freezes. It obstructs movement and enables movement. It serves as a pathway for viruses and bacteria, but is also used to cleanse. It seeps into porous materials, but flows across those that are nonporous.
> (Braun, 2005: 645–646)

These properties are configured into the home. Views of home as a place that is separate from nature are therefore challenged, not simply because 'nature' is connected to and physically part of the home (as suggested in the section 'Nature as Part of Home' of this article) but because these elements shape and co-constitute the possibilities for what home can be.

Conclusion

The idea that home is a human place that is separate from nature is central to Western understandings of home and practices of homemaking. This separation is based in a culture–nature binary that constructs nature as passive and distant from human activity. However, as this article has explored, this is a limited view of home that fails to account for the multiple connections and continuities between home and nature. Feelings of safety, comfort, and security are enabled through these connections, rather than simply challenged by them. Finally the article has shown that nature is also active in home, making a distinct contribution to people's sense of home, and the ways that they make home. Home is not simply a human achievement, but rather is necessarily more-than-human.

See also: Domestic Pets; Material Cultures of Home.

References

Anderson K (1997) A walk on the wild side: A critical geography of domestication. *Progress in Human Geography* 21: 463–485.

Berner B (1998) The meaning of cleaning: The creation of harmony and hygiene in the home. *History and Technology* 14: 313–352.

Braun B (2005) Environmental issues: Writing a more-than-human geography. *Progress in Human Geography* 29: 635–650.

Franklin A (2006) 'Be[a]ware of the dog': A post-humanist approach to housing. *Housing Theory and Society* 23: 137–156.

Gregson N (2007) *Living with Things: Ridding, Accommodation, Dwelling*. Oxford: Sean Kingston Publishing.

Head L and Muir P (2006) Suburban life and the boundaries of nature: Resilience and rupture in Australian backyards. *Transactions of the Institute of British Geographers* 31: 505–524.

Hodder I (1990) *The Domestication of Europe: Structure and Contingency in Neolithic Societies*. Oxford; Cambridge, MA: Blackwell.

Ingold T (2000) *The Perception of the Environment: Essays in Livelihood, Dwelling and Skill*. London; New York: Routledge.

Kaika M (2004) Interrogating the geographies of the familiar: Domesticating nature and constructing the autonomy of the modern home. *International Journal of Urban and Regional Research* 28: 265–286.

Leach HM (2007) Selection and the unforseen consequences of domestication. In: Cassidy R and Mullin M (eds.) *Where the Wild Things Are Now: Domestication Reconsidered*, pp. 71–99. Oxford; New York: Berg.

Miller D (2002) Accommodating. In: Painter C (ed.) *Contemporary Art and the Home*, pp. 115–130. Oxford; New York: Berg.

Pink S (2004) *Home Truths: Gender, Domestic Objects and Everyday Life*. Oxford; New York: Berg.

Power ER (2007) Pests and home-making: Depictions of pests in homemaker magazines. *Home Cultures* 4: 213–236.

Smith JA (2003) Beyond dominance and affection: Living with rabbits in post-Humanist households. *Society and Animals* 11: 181–197.

Tuan Y-F (1984) *Dominance and Affection: The Making of Pets*. New Haven, CT; London: Yale University Press.

Vidler A (1992) *The Architectural Uncanny: Essays in the Modern Unhomely*. Cambridge: The MIT Press.

Neighbourhood Design: Green Space and Parks

N Dempsey, University of Sheffield, Sheffield, UK

© 2012 Elsevier Ltd. All rights reserved.

Glossary

Finger plan Copenhagen's 1947 urban plan which was based on access to open countryside: built-up areas were located in the form of fingers on a hand with open countryside between the fingers.

Green corridor Land which provides wildlife habitats within an urban environment and supports the movement of wildlife along it, such as railway embankments, river banks, and roadside grass verges.

Guerrilla gardening A form of direct action by activists where a piece of abandoned land is 'reclaimed' to grow crops and/or plants.

Modernism (in Scandinavia) This particular interpretation of Modernism is related to health and was championed by Finnish architect Alvar Aalto, who argued that close proximity to nature could satisfy human needs better than buildings alone, and so architects should incorporate nature into designs to ensure residents have access to fresh air and sunlight.

Municipal park A park which is fully open to the public, free of charge, and to which right of access is 'secured in perpetuity'.

Pictorial meadow Flower meadows created in urban areas using a mix of native and nonnative wild flowers from seed with a long-flowering period, attracting wildlife including bees, butterflies, birds, and invertebrates.

Rus in urbe (Latin) the country (or more generally, nature) in the city.

Volkspark Municipal or 'people's park' established in Germany in the early twentieth century, typically very large in size to support physical activity and exercise.

Historical Background of the Park

The provision of publicly accessible green space in urban areas has a long history. There are examples of enclosed gardens and private space dating back over 3000 years in Egypt, Babylon, and Persia designed for sitting, growing fruit and vegetables, and in the case of Persia, creating paradise within and keeping out the unpleasant world. The publicly accessible park as we recognise it today stems from the idea of the garden as a place of repose, a natural environment and is essentially a Victorian invention created as a reaction to the rapid industrialisation of the time. The need for parks came about from the rapid population growth in urban areas and the problems associated with this urban migration which saw the proportion of urban dwellers rise from 20% in the mid-1700s to 50% in 1851 (Conway, 1996). During this period, the only city with parks in the first half of the nineteenth century was London. The royal parks, open to the public to varying degrees, were designed to accommodate both passive and active uses from strolling and enjoying the greenery to public gatherings and mustering of military troops. During the reign of Charles II in the seventeenth century, walking became a fashionable pastime and as a result, walks, parades, and promenades were created in many English towns. However, walking in industrialising cities such as London and Paris during the era of industrialisation would not have been a pleasant or safe experience; walking for pleasure in Paris would only have been possible in the green spaces of les Jardins des Tuileries, Luxembourg, or in the grands boulevards (Olsen, 1986).

Walking in green spaces such as parks had long been identified as having health benefits and led to the assumption that the creation of more walks would help alleviate some of the problems (such as air pollution and overcrowding) that industrialisation brought. The necessity of green space in the urban setting was heralded by social reformers and the first municipal park, Birkenhead Park (Merseyside, UK), was opened in 1847. A large number of parks were created from the 1850s onwards; for example, in 1846, the city of Manchester had no publicly accessible parks. By the 1920s, the city had almost 60. An aim of the early park designers was to create the illusion of countryside in the city. This was an aim shared by Frederick Law Olmsted's Central Park in New York, which was also designed to alleviate overcrowding and the unsanitary conditions of working-class life in industrial areas. The early twentieth century Volksparks (or 'People's Parks') in Germany were not initially characterised by their aesthetic qualities, but provided users with large recreational spaces. In other parts of northern Europe, including Germany and Scandinavia, the influence of the Modernist movement with its focus on physical fitness and good health manifested itself through functional green spaces where people could be in the fresh air and engage in physical activity. Examples include the German Volksparks and the Faelledparken in Copenhagen, Denmark.

Municipal parks were designed as spaces within which users could engage in particular recreational and leisure activities that they could not do elsewhere such as walking, playing sports including cricket and cycling for men (women were not allowed to engage in sports in parks until the late 1800s), and listening to musical performances. These activities were, however, controlled. The aim of the public park was not only to provide urban residents with green space that was good for their health but also to help diffuse social tensions and improve residents' moral condition by providing a wholesome alternative to the public house and the pleasure garden. The parks were a means of "'civilising'... a society which was viewed as threateningly unstable in its diversity" due to the growth of an "uneducated, newly urban, working-class" (Taylor, 1994: 3–4). Such control can be seen today where users of green space are directed to behave in a particular way and refrain from certain activities (see Figure 23, article 'Neighbourhood Design: Urban Outdoor Experience').

Key Dimensions of Green Areas and Parks

There are several key dimensions of parks and green areas which may have an influence on one's experience of urban green space. The following sections will focus on a number of these: the accessibility, function, design, maintenance and management, ecological value, and users. There are other associated aspects which can have an important influence on one's experience, such as how the green space fits into the wider urban context, and whether it is well connected for both pedestrians and public transport users. The perceived safety of the green space will be particularly influential on one's experience and is a consideration within all of the key dimensions described below as is the inclusiveness of the space for different users. These are all discussed in the next sections.

Access to and within Green Space

The term 'park' is one with which we are all familiar and is used to describe different green spaces such as urban parks, country parks, nature reserves, children's play areas, 'pocket' or small local parks, and formal gardens. On the whole, such parks are publicly and freely accessible; however, this may vary depending on how one is using the park – for example, there may be costs incurred for car parking or the use of sports facilities, and private events such as pop concerts, or theatre productions may restrict access to certain parts of the open space. Accessibility will vary according to the type of urban green space and how it is managed. There is a wide variety of urban green space types including parks and gardens, natural and semi-natural urban green spaces (e.g., city forests), green corridors (e.g., waterways), outdoor sports facilities (e.g., sports pitches), allotments, recreational spaces, private/shared gardens, cemeteries and churchyards, and community gardens. For example, a passer-by does not usually have access to other people's private or shared garden space, nor is it usual for he or she to freely access allotments in the United Kingdom (or 'community gardens' in the USA) as these are usually rented from the local authority/council. One may have to pay to use certain outdoor sports facilities, such as tennis courts or lidos, and enter formal gardens while, on the whole, parks and some other urban green spaces are open to the public who do not have to pay to enter. However, this does not mean that they are open throughout the entire day as many parks close at a certain time of night (often at dusk), although this may not (or cannot) necessarily be enforced (**Figures 1** and **2**). Accessibility also relates to reaching the space, the public transport, and pedestrian infrastructure: a park which is set on a main road may attract passers-by and people using nearby services and facilities.

The density of the neighbourhood in which a park is situated may be influential on the form that the park takes and its accessibility. For example, generally speaking, parks and green spaces in city centres or downtown business districts tend to be smaller than those in lower-density areas and may often be unfenced or walled to maximise a sense of space (**Figure 3**); examples of large city centre parks include Central Park (**Figure 4**), Hyde Park (**Figure 5**), and Holyrood Park, Edinburgh. There will also tend to be a higher ratio of built (or hard) space to green space in higher-density neighbourhoods, which will have an impact on the extent of greenery in the space and an effect on the wildlife supported in such a space (**Figure 6**).

Function

Urban green space tends to support biodiversity and wildlife in some way, however, minor. For example, UK allotments are easily identifiable green spaces where the holder can cultivate fruit and vegetables, attracting bees, birds, and insects. While 'cemetery' or 'graveyard' describe green space set apart for the burial of the dead, it is also a setting where small birds and mammals might be found feeding on well-established trees and plants. The variety of functions that green space serve is particularly well illustrated by the park. A park may have a variety of natural elements from trees, grass, and flowers to man-made features such as tennis courts, farms, swimming pools, boating lakes, and children's playgrounds. It therefore follows that users would visit different parks for different reasons,

Figure 1 The Circus Maximus, Rome, Italy, is open 24 hours a day.

Figure 2 An example of a fenced children's playground in Oxford, UK, which is locked every evening.

depending on the features available. In Randers (Denmark), Doktorparken was designed with an emphasis on ice skating while in Vestparken, a principal activity was sledging. In the past, a wider range of physical activities were supported in parks than is the case today. Victorian parks provided facilities for quoits, skittles, archery, badminton, skipping and were also used for musical performances, agricultural shows, and marching. The infrastructure for such activities is largely not provided in today's parks – although parks continue to be a popular venue for music concerts, art fairs, and theatre performances (but they are not always free of charge). One is more likely to find such provision in sports centres or other indoor and outdoor venues. Increasingly, as the pressure on open space in urban areas mounts, it is critical for the existence of parks to be justified economically. Providing financially viable facilities within parks that users want such as swimming pools, tennis courts, and the aforementioned events can contribute to this. In addition, it can be shown that proximity to parks and green areas has a positive effect on house prices, as well as health and well-being in general. However, the financial value of urban green space is often underestimated. For example, most UK councils currently estimate the value of their parks at just £1, calling into question traditional valuation methods of green space.

Figure 3 Tanner Springs Park, downtown Portland, Oregon, USA, with direct on-street access.

Figure 4 Central Park, New York, USA.
Reproduced with permission of Nigel Francis.

Design

While the suggestion of 'designing' green space arguably negates the positive benefits that it has (particularly green space which is there to conserve nature and support *wild*life), it is widely argued that the design of green spaces can significantly influence the user's experience. This is not a new idea: parks and gardens have been designed for thousands of years all over the world including ancient Assyria, Persia, India, Greece, and Rome. The influential landscape designs of Capability Brown in the eighteenth century focused on the landscape and he idealised and tamed nature in his attempts to create the sublime in the landscape. Brown's popularity can be seen well into the nineteenth century (and beyond) with clear influences on public parks including the Derby Arboretum (UK). Visitors inspired by the new Birkenhead Park which was designed by Joseph Paxton include Frederick Law Olmsted in 1850 who co-designed New York's Central Park with Calvert Vaux (**Figure 4**).

Parks which were designed for public use supported a range of active physical activities. The design of parks in Manchester was particularly forward thinking in providing, for example, an outdoor gymnasium for girls in the 1850s (Peel Park). City planning incorporated park development elsewhere in Europe: in Stockholm, the Lindhagenplanen was developed in 1866 to create parks and other green areas as places for health, recreation, and fresh air. Modernist landscape architectural design moved away from creating parks in the city to building cities within parks. While the aesthetic attractiveness of parks has largely been achieved through greenery, trees, and flowers (particularly bedding plants in municipal parks), water has always been important with features ranging from lidos and swimming pools to the recent and

16 Neighbourhood Design: Green Space and Parks

Figure 5 Hyde Park, London, UK.

increasingly popular dancing water jets, sprays, and fountains (**Figure 7**). Innovations in landscape design include roof gardens and, more recently, 'pictorial meadows'. The latter provide urban settings such as parks, public gardens, and grass verges along highways with visually striking green spaces, which attract wildlife and require little maintenance (**Figure 8**).

Current policy and practice relating to urban design and planning increasingly identifies the design of green space as an important contributory factor to the 'success' of a neighbourhood. In the last decade in the United Kingdom there has been increased focus on the regeneration and 'revitalisation' of neighbourhoods through, among other strategies, improving green areas and parks. Parks such as Shoreditch Park in the east end of London have been redesigned with new paths and seating (**Figure 9**), which allow greater visibility across the park, and changes made to secluded spots near high hedges, which were a magnet for antisocial behaviour. However, designing out features which might contribute to a sense of insecurity or be vulnerable to misuse and vandalism can also take away the local distinctiveness of a space that made it appealing in the first place. Therefore, striking a balance between the 'controlled' and the 'natural' environment is critical.

Maintenance and Management

Maintenance is consistently cited as one of the most important ingredients of successful parks and public spaces. The maintenance of a green area or park is a multidimensional aspect which encompasses the cleanliness of a place (e.g., level of litter), the condition of the space (e.g., quality of paths and walkways), and the maintenance services provided in a space (e.g., frequency of refuse collection). A space which is not well maintained may put off potential users of green areas and parks because it can indicate that 'nobody cares', which can have knock-on effects on people's feelings of safety and levels of crime. This is identified as the 'broken window

Figure 6 Haggerston Park, London, UK.

Figure 7 The Goodwin Fountains installed in 1998, Sheffield Peace Gardens, UK.

Figure 8 Pictorial meadows, an innovative landscape management technique.

syndrome', where it is argued that cosmetic damage such as graffiti and litter in a space can incite more serious antisocial behaviour. There have been recent calls in the United Kingdom for the reinstatement of park staff whose numbers have declined since the early 1980s. This is not only because of the associated maintenance services but also because park wardens can contribute to users' feelings of safety. This link between maintenance and perceived safety has been found in other research into public neighbourhood space and is well illustrated when one considers the management of parks or green areas after dark. The extent to which parks and green areas are accessible after dark varies in different countries and depends on the management of the space (see **Figures 1** and **2**). For example, municipal parks have varied opening times: some have changing closing times in accordance with dusk while others are open 24 hours a day. While promenading in parks and other public spaces continue to be a popular pastime in European towns and cities, the use of parks and green spaces after dark can depend on the provision of lighting and park staff to instil a sense of safety for potential users. Other aspects of park management involve a range of other stakeholders, many of whom may be members of local communities. They may relate to informing users and potential users about park activities which may range from walking groups, organised picnics to concerts, and community festivals. In addition, the management of larger-scale events may involve other public bodies not normally associated with parks, such as the police.

Ecological Value

The greenery in a park or green area can often be the main attraction for users. Gaining access to nature in an urban area can be difficult; parks and other green areas have a critical role to play in the support of biodiversity and form an important part of the ecosystem in urban areas. At a regional scale this is illustrated in the concept of 'green corridors' and the 1947 'Green Finger' plan in Copenhagen which created green areas close to the city and made nature accessible. Green areas can contribute positively to climate change mitigation and vegetation can help to reduce solar heat gain in built-up areas. Having access to green space is also

Figure 9 Shoreditch Park, Hackney, London: An example of a regenerated park which has been redesigned and relandscaped.

beneficial for one's health and continues to give urban dwellers respite from noisy, polluted living and working conditions. Recently these well-established ideas of the benefits of urban green space have been revived and there has been considerable focus on the importance of access for residents and users to ecologically rich spaces in the urban environment. A growing body of research shows that spending time in green space can have beneficial effects on health and well-being. These include reducing stress levels, being able to get away from it all and clear one's head, and increased recovery from illness when exposed to green space – be it physical access, or having a view of such space. Recent experimental research shows that people carrying out physical activity when exposed to views of green rather than built-up space had reduced blood pressure and improved self-esteem. Living in areas with green environments has also been found to be related to health in more general terms: populations exposed to the greenest environments have lowest levels of health inequality related to income deprivation. The resurgence in interest in ecologically rich urban green space has resulted in increased numbers of allotment tenants, the creation of community gardens, and the active creation of green spaces through 'guerrilla gardening'. This stems from the ongoing debate about the need for greening any 'left-over' or residual urban space which serves no clear purpose as transformative spaces which may previously have had no greenery. The need for wilder landscapes in the urban context is also a current topic of debate in landscape design: there are increasing calls for a move away from the ever popular tamed landscapes first designed by Capability Brown with the continuing prevalence of bedding plants and clipped lawns (**Figure 10**), to

Figure 10 Japanese Gardens, Washington Park, Portland, Oregon, was opened to the public in 1967.

wilder twenty-first century landscapes such as 'pictorial meadows' (**Figure 8**).

Users

The park is a form that is entirely unique to towns and cities: without cities, there would be no need for parks. There are certain roles that parks and green spaces play in urban areas: they provide users with therapeutic and restorative benefits which positively influence mental health and well-being. Fundamentally, for such spaces to be used – and it cannot be assumed that simply because green space is provided it will be used – users need, first and foremost, to feel safe and secure. Such perceived safety can be engendered through the presence of park staff and other users, the space being well maintained and for all users to feel welcome and not excluded from using the space. The democratic right for all to use and share green space promotes sociability between groups and bridges divisions between people: Speakers' Corner in Hyde Park is an example of a well-used, social, and inclusive public space. Green spaces have been put to less democratic uses: the German Volksparks were the setting of Nazi party parades which eradicated the Volkspark movement once the spaces were used for political activity and stopped providing democratic spaces.

Parks and green areas can be multifunctional spaces serving a range of different users: how these users interact (or potentially conflict with one another) can have an impact on one's experience. For example, a variety of activities may be provided for in any one space, including walking, dog-walking, taking children to play, cycling, and playing football. Depending on where these uses occur in the space and how different users interact, one's experience in the park might not be entirely positive: the speed at which cyclists travel may frighten older pedestrians passing by. The park or green space should also be a comfortable one in which people enjoy spending time. It is therefore important for parks (and other green areas) to have certain features such as seating and toilets, the lack of which can deter potential users of all ages. The park or green area is part of a wider neighbourhood context and the ease with which people can access the space can depend on how well the space is connected for pedestrians and users of public and private transport. A green area which is part of a wider network of green spaces can not only support biodiversity and wildlife but also provide users with a well-connected series of spaces as part of a neighbourhood's infrastructure of recreational services. Such green areas are places for people to meet freely and socialise, and where they can engage in a range of passive and active activities from jogging and dog-walking to sitting and watching the wildlife.

It is useful to briefly examine the relevance of parks and green areas designed in the nineteenth century for today's twenty-first-century multicultural societies. Increasingly, recreational activities do not take place in parks and green areas but rather take place indoors: in gyms, sports centres, and the home. Furthermore, the types of uses now carried out in parks are not supported by Victorian parks and alternatives such as skate parks, wilderness, as well as indoor sports facilities are more relevant today. Furthermore, it is unclear whether the activities currently supported in parks and green areas are suitable for the range of cultural groups living in urban areas and what the potential barriers might be of using such spaces. This is an under-researched area which requires rapid attention. Having said this, it continues to be argued that parks and green areas can engender feelings of ownership and civic pride in one's neighbourhood:

Figure 11 Duisburg-Nord Landschaftspark, Germany, is an example of an industrial landscape park which incorporates industrial heritage within a green environment.
Reproduced with permission of Siegfried Dammrath.

this was one of the original aims of the Victorian creators of parks and continues to be identified today as a characteristic of a good or successful public space.

Conclusion

It has been argued that in Western culture, the park is deeply embedded not only in history but in the collective psyche with such green space providing much needed access to nature, resonating with the concept of the garden, one to which urban residents are particularly attached. In the light of growing concerns about environmental change, urban green space is increasingly highlighted as an asset for climate change mitigation and adaptation. There is also increased focus on the importance of urban green space for health, both mental and physical. More and more urban residents around the world are obese or overweight and neighbourhood green space is identified as a potential tool in national health strategies. Research shows that encouraging people to spend time in local green spaces can be used to target mental health problems such as depression and work-related stress. Finally, the form of green space may be changing. Rather than landscapes designed as *rus in urbe*, perhaps it is the time for a more functional urban green space which provides food and space for farming. It may also be the age of the industrial park where biodiversity and industry come together in recreational outdoor space (**Figure 11**). It is clear that urban green space can play a very important part in people's lives. While the extent to which it is valued varies for different stakeholders, research shows that there are considerable environmental, social, and economic benefits of urban green space. There is therefore a need to continue harnessing these benefits through a range of good quality parks and green areas in towns and cities around the world.

See also: Defensible Space; Gated Communities: Developed Countries; Gentrification and Well-Being; Health and Housing; High Rise; High-Rise Homes; Housing Estates; Neighbourhood Design: Public spaces; Neighbourhood Design: Urban Outdoor Experience; Neighbourhood Planning; People and the Built Form; Place Attachment.

References

Conway H (1996) *Public Parks*. Princes Risborough: Shire Garden History.
Olsen DJ (1986) *The City as a Work of Art: London, Paris, Vienna*. New Haven: Yale University Press.
Taylor HA (1994) *Age and Order: The Public Park as a Metaphor for a Civilised Society*. London: Comedia & Demos.

Further Reading

Barbosa O, Tratalos JA, Armsworth PR, et al. Who benefits from access to green space? A case study from Sheffield, UK. *Landscape and Urban Planning* 83: 187–195.
Clark P (ed.) (2006) *The European City and Green Space: London, Stockholm, Helsinki and St Petersburg, 1850–2000*. Aldershot: Ashgate.
Grahn P and Stigsdotter UA (2003) Landscape planning and stress. *Urban Forestry & Urban Greening* 2: 1–18.
Kaplan R, Kaplan S, and Ryan RL (1998) *With People in Mind: Design and Management of Everyday Nature*. Washington, DC: Island Press.
Lasdun S (1991) *The English Park: Royal, Private & Public*. London: Andre Deutsch Limited.
Lund A (1997) *Guide to Danish Architecture 1000–1996*. Copenhagen: Arkitektens Forlag.
Pregill P and Volkman N (1993) *Landscapes in history: Design and planning in the Western tradition*. New York: Van Nostrand Reinhold.
Woolley H (2003) *Urban Open Spaces*. London: Spon Press.
Worpole K (2000) *Here Comes the Sun: Architecture and Public Space in Twentieth-Century European Culture*. London: Reaktion Books.

Neighbourhood Design: Public Spaces

R Sendi and B Goličnik Marušić, Urban Planning Institute of the Republic of Slovenia, Ljubljana, Slovenia

© 2012 Elsevier Ltd. All rights reserved.

Glossary

Active in presence Long-stay active use refers to movement all the time within a place, for example, playing or ball games.
Active in transition Movement through a place, such as walking, cycling, or pushing a pram.
Neighbourhood spaces A collective term for all the public spaces within a neighbourhood.
Passive in presence Long-stay passive activity refers to posing all the time within a place, for example, sitting or lying down.
Publicspace The description of a public space as one word emphasises its very characteristic of being an inseparable entity of a two-way process between both the components: people and place. The final unit constituting the spatial component of public space is a place's form and its main articulation. A social component of that public space is understood as its daily dynamic pattern of uses.

Definition of Public Space

Public space is variously addressed in the literature. As such, the literature also includes a variety of definitions of public space. Generally, however, public space is defined as space to which people normally have unrestricted access and right of way. In other words, public places and spaces are public because anyone is entitled to be physically present in them. Focusing on the way of engagement in places, public space is open, publicly accessible space where people go for group or individual activities. Public space is thus a place outside the boundaries of individual or small-group control, used for a variety of often-overlapping functional and symbolic purposes. Accordingly, people have access to spaces, access to activities, access to information, and access to resources. Public spaces, therefore, are usually multipurpose spaces distinguishable from completely green, partly green, or nongreen to soft or hard areas between built structures that are accessible to the public in the same way. To sum up, public space is an inseparable entity of a two-way process between both the components: public (people) and space (place). Public space is then not just a spatial frame, a waiting scene where an event will occur; it is more – it is *publicspace*.

The Importance of Public Space within Residential Neighbourhoods

Public spaces in residential neighbourhoods play a variety of roles through their different uses. The major roles of public space may be identified as recreation, exposure of different residents to one another, facilitation of social cohesion and intergenerational interaction, contact with nature (especially green spaces), articulation of the built areas, legibility of the residential area, and means of orientation within it. Because of its design aspects, public space may also have an impact on the image of the particular neighbourhood. Appropriately designed public spaces (especially green spaces) contribute to the aesthetic quality and to greater satisfaction of the inhabitants with their residential environment, which is important also as a restorative environment, addressing health issues and well-being.

Public space often plays an important role in the definition of the neighbourhood. Definitions of neighbourhoods are often seemingly synonymous with the idea of community. Public space is seen as this component of a neighbourhood where the community has a chance to communicate and grow. Such neighbourhood space consists of public outdoor territory close to home, which, because of frequent shared use as well as the residents' collective responsibility and familiar association, is considered to be their own.

Each community has the means and the potential to create its own public places. Thriving public spaces reflect a strong sense of community, whereas a lack of such character of places may lead towards situations where the residents may feel less connected to each other. Hence, public spaces give identity to neighbourhoods. They benefit neighbourhoods economically and socially and provide settings for cultural exchange. Public places are to be successful if they are well accessible and well linked with each other as well as with the programmes in the adjacent buildings. They are successful, when they can provide a variety of activities for different users, when they are pleasing and offer comfort, and, above all, when they support socialisation of users.

Accessibility and linkage refers to convenience, connectedness, proximity, continuity, reliability, readability, and walkability. Variety of activities and uses should include homegrown quality, vitality, fun, uniqueness, specialness, realness, sustainability, affordability, usefulness, celebration, and indigenousness. Comfort and image covers cleanliness, greenness, walkability, sittability, spirituality, attractiveness, safety, charm, and historical aspects, while sociability refers to friendliness, storytelling, gossip, stewardship, neighbourliness, cooperation, diversity, welcomeness, and pride.

However, the aforementioned description is essentially a theoretical perception of what public space ought to be, its desired function, and the roles it is ideally expected to play. In practice, on the other hand, public spaces often fail to satisfy the needs of their users and may also be a cause of various undesirable, or even negative, effects in a residential environment.

One of the problems commonly associated with public spaces concerns the conflicts that sometimes arise due to intergenerational and cultural differences between the various users. Incompatible interests of different user groups can limit the freedom of the others. Young people, for example, are often referred to in the literature as the most aggressive public space user group. There are several reasons for these allegations. Young people usually gather in public spaces in large numbers so that the size of the group itself is often intimidating. They also often tend to dominate and appropriate certain public spaces to their own needs, forcefully excluding other weaker user groups (e.g., small children and the elderly). What is important to recognise, however, is that most young people gather in public spaces only to practice sociability with their counterparts. In the majority of cases, young people do not pose any threat to the rest of the community. A better understanding of cultural issues and intergenerational differences is crucial for the reduction of feelings of threatening behaviour of young people.

It is also important to note that practical experience does) not provide much evidence of the intergenerational interaction that (according to social theory) is so desirable and is expected to take place in public spaces. On the contrary, many residential environments experience intergenerational conflicts which, in most cases, appear to arise from the failure to provide appropriately for the various activities that take place in social spaces and to take into account the specific public space requirements of specific categories of users. Settings that attempt to enforce interaction have been found to be less successful than those that offer a sufficient level of autonomy between the various user groups. Intergenerational interaction may indeed be desirable but the underlying aim in planning public space should be to create a well-balanced system of social spaces that offers a great variety of choice and provides a wide range of recreational opportunities for the various categories of users.

Poor management and inappropriate maintenance of public space may also lead to negative consequences. Although the richness of open public green space is often described as the most attractive feature of some residential neighbourhoods, their poor management and maintenance may turn them into the neighbourhood's most resented and most undesired spaces. Inappropriate management and maintenance of public spaces may result in the creation of a negative image of the neighbourhood as seen by outsiders, and, as a result, this may lead to dissatisfaction among the residents. Furthermore, failure to maintain public spaces properly may lead to the degradation of the aesthetic quality of the neighbourhood and, in some cases, such places may even become a safety problem. Well-managed and well-maintained public spaces, on the other hand, play a vital role in the development of a pleasant residential environment and may contribute greatly to the creation of a sense of neighbourhood or community cohesiveness for the residents.

Categories of Public Space

Residential neighbourhoods include a whole spectrum of public open spaces of which **Figure 1** shows the most characteristic.

Neighbourhood park
Open space developed in residential environments; publicly developed and managed as part of the zoned open space of cities, or as part of new private residential development; may include playgrounds, sport facilities, and the like.

Figure 1 (Continued)

Playground
Play areas located in neighbourhoods frequently include traditional play equipment such as swings and slides; amenities for adults such as benches; and can also include innovative designs such as adventure playgrounds.

Schoolyard
Play area, developed also as community use space within a residential neighbourhood.

Everyday spaces
Publicly accessible open places such as street corners, steps to buildings, and the like, which people claim and use for various activities.

Figure 1 Examples of public open spaces.

Regarding the definition of typology and categorisation of places in neighbourhood public space design, one needs to be careful in searching for the (proto)types of public spaces, because differences in spatial as well as social contexts of places may often overwhelm some obvious typological similarities. It is of key importance to know users' (user groups') preferences and needs. When addressing categories of public spaces in a neighbourhood, it is crucial to address equally at least three aspects: physical attributes of places, activities or actual uses, and users' conceptions of places. From this point of view, a category of neighbourhood spaces can be recognised as a hypernym, a collective term for all the public spaces in the neighbourhood. At the same time, it is crucial to pay attention to the provision of private or semiprivate spaces in relation to public spaces. Such spaces are particularly relevant in settings where each household is entitled to its own outdoor space. In such cases, complete enclosure is desirable.

An interesting form of categorisation of public space is the home zone. The home zone concept (also referred to as *woonerf*), was pioneered in the 1970s in the Netherlands. Since then, many countries have successfully transferred the core concepts and created their own safe areas. Home zones are an attempt to strike a balance between vehicular traffic and everyone else who uses the street – the pedestrians, cyclists, business people, and residents. Some see home zones as a way of 'reclaiming' local streets from a traditional domination by cars. Others see it more modestly as a way of trying to restore safety and peace in neighbourhoods that are becoming overwhelmed with speeding traffic.

Home zones work through the physical alteration of streets and roads in a residential area. These alterations force motorists to drive with greater care and at lower speeds. Many countries support this with legislation allowing the home zones to enforce appropriately reduced speed limits. The benches, flower beds, play areas, lampposts, fences, and trees used to furnish the streets and roads offer many additional community benefits to the home zones and are considered to enhance the beauty of an area and increase the housing prices.

Different Patterns of Use of Public Space

Studies on the subject have described various patterns of use, whereby some households are accustomed to conducting various activities in public space more frequently than others, for example, young children and teenagers. Furthermore, different age groups tend to use public spaces at different times of the day and for different reasons. For example, older people and children in particular are normally absent from public places after dark.

Public space is particularly important for the daily lives of children. This is where young children establish first contact with other people outside their family. These contacts and the activities that take place in these areas may have a significant influence on their upbringing and mannerisms.

Public space is equally important for young people as it serves this category of users as a vital prerequisite for social interaction and the development of social identity. Teenagers hanging out in public spaces use them as spaces for communication and interaction, for exercise, and as a retreat.

Like small children, elderly residents constitute that category of users whose outdoor activities are mostly confined to public spaces within their residential neighbourhood. This is also the category of users that may be greatly hampered by inappropriate design. It is vital that public spaces are designed in such a way as to allow small children and the elderly easy access and peaceful use.

However, users and their activities in public space can be addressed from different viewpoints: either from the designers' perspective on the composition of a place or from the users' perspective on quality and quantity of programmes, amenities, and the like. Exploring behaviour in a built environment, seeing people's activities classified on the basis of the degree of compulsory or voluntary outdoor activities, the literature describes the following:

Necessary activities are those that are more or less compulsory. As participants have no choice, their incidence is only slightly influenced by the physical setting.
Optional activities are those that are undertaken voluntarily, if time and space allow, and weather and setting invite them.
Social activities depend on the presence of others in public space. They are supported and occur whenever necessary, and optional activities are given better environmental conditions.

However, occupation of a place always relates to time scale in terms of presence and duration of one's activity in a place and to the users themselves, in terms of the way they are engaged with the activity in a place. In terms of activity and time, three situations are usually significant: continuously present, temporarily present, and in transit through a place. In terms of activity engagement, three general situations are very common: passive, intermittently active/passive, and active. However, all the pairings cannot be represented with equal relevance, although theoretically all options are possible. The most often and most usual situations are passive in presence, active in presence, and active in transition.

Passive in presence is about a long-stay passive activity and refers to posing all the time within a place. This can be exemplified by elderly people sitting on a bench and observing the world go by and by teenagers or young adults lying down in grassed areas, to read or sunbathe.
Active in presence is about a long-stay active use in a place and refers to movement all the time within a place. In neighbourhood places, this can be exemplified by children at playgrounds playing freely on the grass, playing hide-and-seek, playing with a ball, and the like. Adults can also be involved in such type of activity by playing football or volleyball, for example.
Active in transition represents movement through a place. This is the most frequent type of activity in places as it represents the activities of a daily routine such as walking, cycling, or pushing a pram. Any user can be involved in it.

More examples of different situations regarding ways of involvement of users in places and time of their occupancies are summarised **Table 1**.

Behavioural maps, for example, are media that enable visualisation of any such occupancy in places. The following examples of behavioural maps (**Figures 2** and **3**) show daily behavioural patterns in public space (10 minutes of observation) with regard to activities and age groups.

Public Space Design

As has been stated earlier, appropriate public space design positively impacts on the neighbourhood and its residents in a variety of ways. In order to achieve this objective, there are several key questions that need to be asked during the planning process: What type of an environment are we aiming to create? What types of activities are expected to take place? What kinds of recreation activities are appropriate for the particular community? What type of social interactions are desirable and how can these be encouraged while avoiding approaches that suggest forceful interaction? As these questions suggest, planners need to have adequate prior knowledge about the environment and the needs of the potential residents of the neighbourhood.

There are, however, certain general characteristics that are widely recognised as constituting to good public space design. Public spaces must be attractive, safe, healthy, sociable, convenient, identifiable, personalisable, adaptable, and ecologically efficient (e.g., water-sensitive, energy-efficient, and biodiverse). Following are some important aspects that must be addressed when aiming to achieve good public space design.

Usability

Changes in public spaces can be permanent or temporary. The planning of activities and programmes of places is of key importance for directing changes and foreseeing their dynamics. Accordingly, the question is what a particular user can do with or in a place, how reversible the changes the user introduces into a place are, and how much they can influence the place's meaning for its users.

Besides spontaneous changes in public spaces, it is also important to consider possible changes due to some special occasions, such as the celebration of a certain public event. It is, as such, vital that the nature and role of public space is fully understood by public space designers in order to be able to correctly determine the types of changes that can be made to it occasionally.

Physical Structure

The attractiveness of public spaces depends very much on their aesthetic quality, the planned uses, and the sensory perception of these places by potential users. The specific relationship that the system of open spaces presents to its

Table 1

Activity	Time occupation in a place		
	Continuously present	Temporarily present	In transit
Way of involvement			
Active	Movement all the time within a place: • Playing hide-and-seek • Playing with a ball	Movement, break, continuation of the movement through a place: • Walking a child while he/she plays from time to time on the way	Movement through a place: • Walking • Cycling • Rollerblading • Using a wheelchair
Intermittent	Movement, break, coming back to the 'stage': • Flying a kite • Skateboarding • Joining a ball game from time to time	Repeated movement-break patterns (along the way) within a place: • Walking a dog	Repeated movement through a place: • Jogging in circles, visiting a particular part of neighbourhood place several times
Passive	Posing all the time within a place: • Sitting on a bench • Lying down on grass • Waiting and leaning against the fence	Reposing a certain time period within a place: • Sitting on a bench while being on a walk/jogging through a place	Being transported by somebody/something through a place: • Sleeping baby being transported in a pram through a place

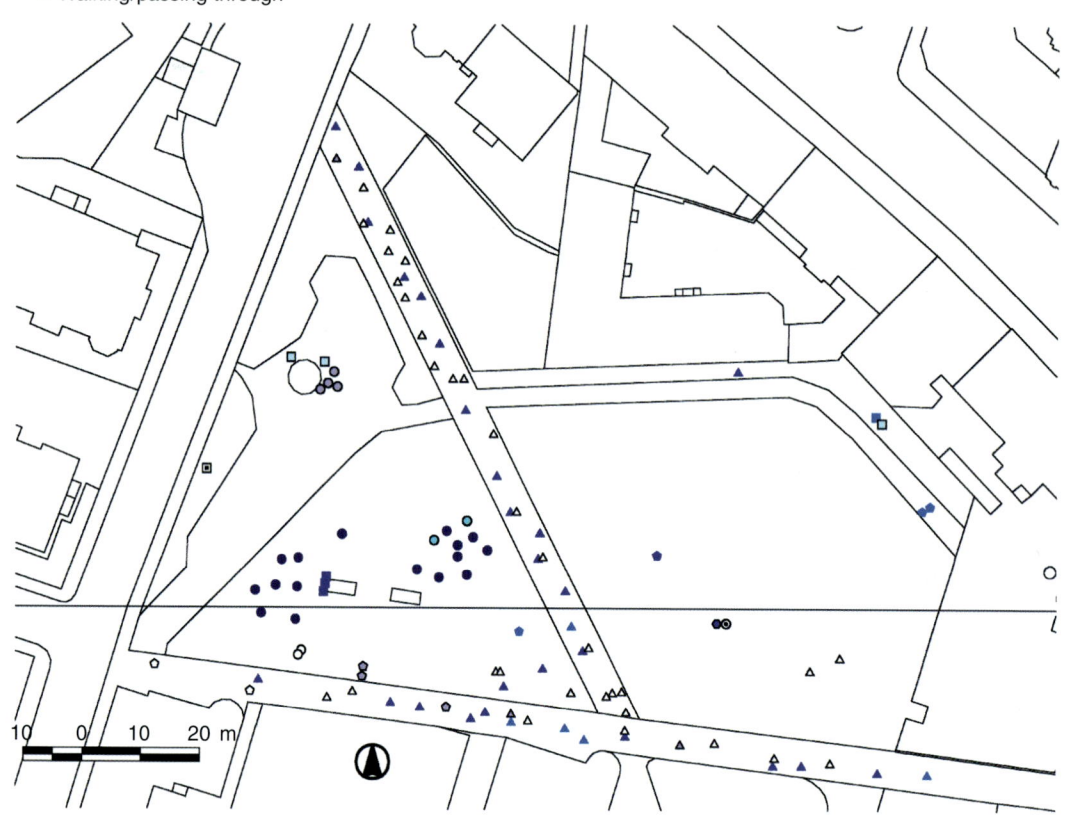

Figure 2 Argentinski Park, Ljubljana. A representative day showing usage of a neighbourhood park in Ljubljana. Reproduced from Goličnik B (2005) People in Place: A Configuration of Physical Form and the Dynamic Patterns of Spatial Occupancy in Urban Open Public Space, p. 222. PhD Thesis, Edinburgh College of Art, Heriot Watt University, Edinburgh.

users needs to be clearly defined and well laid out. Dwellings and other facilities within a residential neighbourhood should be designed to provide a pleasant external environment for the residents. The importance of physical structure, as a design aspect, is that it must promote a sense of place and provide an attractive and secure residential environment. Attempts to achieve an appropriate physical structure should be based on suitable answers to questions such as: For whom will the space be provided? What are the specific needs of the potential users of this space? How can the space itself be designed to meet these needs? Which shapes and sizes are most appropriate for the specific public spaces? And, how is access to the open space enabled for all potential users?

An important aspect of the physical structure of public space is the legibility of the residential environment as a whole. Legibility, in this case, refers to the ease with which individual neighbourhood elements or parts can be recognised as a consistent pattern. The characteristics of a legible environment have been described as well formed, distinct, remarkable, engaging the senses, and inviting participation. In addition to legibility, public space design must also ensure a certain degree of flexibility that allows residents to occasionally change or restructure sections of their environment. Physical structures that enable the users to actively participate in the alteration or adaptation of public spaces for special purposes or events, encourage socialisation, and provide conditions for the promotion of a sense of belonging among residents.

Safety Issues

Some public places in residential neighbourhoods are sometimes considered unsafe. Although most of these

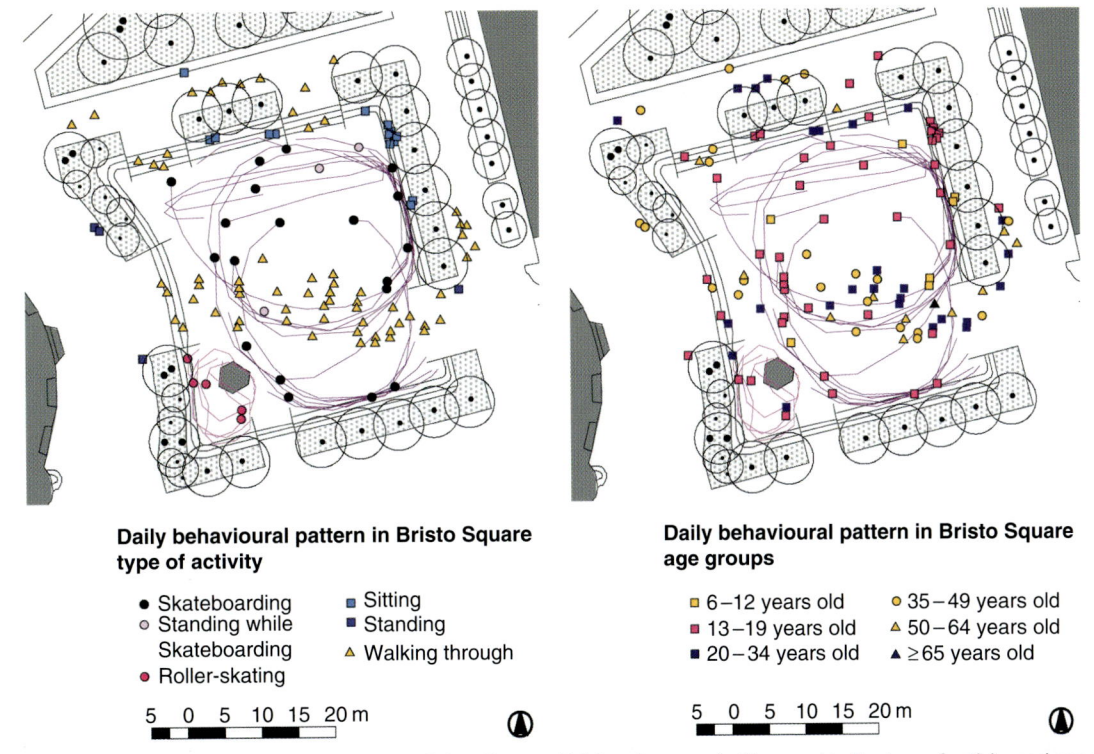

Figure 3 The usual example of a daily occupancy in Bristo Square, Edinburgh, ranged with regard to the type of activity and age group to which any participant belongs.
Reproduced from Goličnik B (2005) *People in Place: A Configuration of Physical Form and the Dynamic Patterns of Spatial Occupancy in Urban Open Public Space*, p. 86. PhD Thesis, Edinburgh College of Art, Heriot Watt University, Edinburgh.

fears are often unfounded, safety is not always an imaginary problem. Safety problems do exist in some residential areas and special attention needs to be paid to these issues during the designing process. Unsafe public spaces may, in the first place, pose serious danger to the lives of inhabitants and eventually lead to social and economic degradation of a particular residential area.

Where the safety and fear factors are real, designs aimed at guaranteeing safety must avoid creating unfriendly, alienating public spaces, for example, places with rigid restrictions on use. On the contrary, these may achieve the opposite, turning out to be scary or indeed unsafe. Practice shows that vibrant public places that allow a variety of activities at different times of the day are usually much safer than those that are less actively used. The principal objective must be to ensure safety throughout the entire neighbourhood and avoid inadequate solutions that displace crime from one area to another. The installation of a CCTV system, for example, in a particular spot may result in criminal activity relocating to other parts of the neighbourhood where there is no such surveillance.

Access

Accessibility is the dimension of public space most often linked with the definition of public space itself. Various authors give it different roles and meanings with regard to the definition of the term itself as well as with respect to its role in evaluating the successfulness of public spaces. In practice, three types of access are usually considered: physical, visual, and symbolic.

Physical access means absence of barriers and linkage with neighbouring spaces. Ease of access to public spaces is especially intended in the case of public space facilities for young children and the elderly. These areas should also be easily accessible in relation to the residential buildings.

Visual access refers to an appropriate visual contact between the user and the place towards which they are heading. Visibility, in this case, is a very important aspect of safety in public places. Being visible in a place is as important as the visibility of the place. Public places must appropriately offer both options.

Symbolic access is being increasingly recognised as important, too. It is often defined by the presence of signs or marks that show who is welcome and who is not in certain places or territories. These signs can be elements of physical structure and an articulation of a place such as landmarks (monuments, sculptures, etc.), significant programmes in a place such as pavilions, galleries, and other theme objects, as well as people – users themselves – such as user groups like teenagers or maintenance or security staff.

Comfort and Amenities

With regard to comfort and amenities in public space, one aspect predominates, and that is recreation. The recreational aspect refers to the relationship between the public space and its user and the impact of the use of public space on the personality of an individual. All the different interests and activities that are realised in public spaces by the various user groups with their various needs may be described simply as recreation.

Recreation facilities are increasingly being recognised as an urgent constituent part of residential neighbourhoods. Exterior recreation spaces are therefore a major factor that must be considered in the neighbourhood plan together with the residential buildings and other neighbourhood facilities. The location of recreation areas, such as open spaces, green areas, community facilities, and playgrounds, will be most effective if these are suitably considered and appropriately included in the neighbourhood plan at the beginning of the design process. The main objective is to provide areas and facilities that make possible a great variety of recreation activities serving a wide range of recreation interests for all residents, irrespective of age or economic status.

See also: Crime Prevention Through Environmental Design; Defensible Space; Housing Estates; Neighbourhood Design: Green Space and Parks; Neighbourhood Design: Urban Outdoor Experience.

Further Reading

Butler GD (1968) *Introduction to Community Recreation. Prepared for the National Recreation and Park Association*. New York: McGraw-Hill Book Company.
Carmona M (2001) *Housing Design Quality through Policy, Guidance and Review*. London: Spon Press.
Carr S, Francis M, Rivlin LG, and Stone AM (1992) *Public Space*. Cambridge: Cambridge University Press.
Elsley S (2004) Outsiders! Children and young people and their use of public space. *Paper Presented at the Conference Open Space-People Space*, Edinburgh, UK. http://www.openspace.eca.ac.uk/conference/proceedings/PDF/Elsley.pdf
Gehl J (1987) *Life between Buildings: Using Public Space*. New York: Van Nostrand Reinhold.
Goličnik B (2005) *People in Place: A Configuration of Physical Form and the Dynamic Patterns of Spatial Occupancy in Urban Open Public Space*. PhD Thesis, Edinburgh College of Art, Heriot Watt University, Edinburgh.
Goličnik B and Ward Thompson C (2010) Emerging relationships between design and use of urban park spaces. *Landscape and Urban Planning* 94(1): 38–53.
Hester R (1997) Neighbourhood space. In: Larice M and Macdonald E (eds.) *The Urban Design Reader*, pp. 376–387. London: Routledge: Taylor & Francis Group.
Lawson B (2001) *The Language of Space*. Oxford: Architectural Press.
Lynch K (1960) *The Image of the City*. Cambridge, MA: The Joint Centre for Urban Studies, MIT.
Lynch K (1981) *A Good City Form*. Cambridge, MA: MIT Press.
Madanipour A (2003) Why are the design and development of public spaces significant for cities? In: Cuthbert AR (ed.) *Designing Cities: Critical Readings in Urban Design*, pp. 139–152. Oxford: Blackwell Publishing.
Schwab E and Standler K (2004) Youth behaviour and young people's demands for open space: Teens_open_space. *Paper Presented at the Conference 'Open Space-People Space'*, Edinburgh, UK. http://www.openspace.eca.ac.uk/conference/proceedings/PDF/Standler.pdf
Sendi R, Aalbers BM, and Trigueiro M (2009) Public space in large housing estates. In: Rowlands R, Musterd S, and Van Kempen R (eds.) *Mass Housing in Europe: Multiple Faces of Development, Change and Response*, pp. 131–156. Basingstoke: Palgrave Macmillan.
Thiel P (1997) *People, Paths and Purposes: Notations for a Participatory Envirotecture*. Seattle and London: University of Washington Press.

Neighbourhood Design: Urban Outdoor Experience

N Dempsey, University of Sheffield, Sheffield, UK

© 2012 Elsevier Ltd. All rights reserved.

Glossary

Environmental determinism Theoretical view that the physical environment, rather than nonphysical conditions (e.g., social, economic), has a determining influence on human behaviour.

Environmental probabilism Theoretical view that some choices are more likely to be made than others in a particular physical setting. For example, when in a zoo, most visitors would not enter the animal enclosures even if the physical environment might allow access.

Garden City Internationally influential urban planning approach developed by Ebenezer Howard at the turn of the twentieth century. It was based on planned, self-contained communities surrounded by greenbelt land that contain carefully balanced residential, industrial, and agricultural areas.

'City Beautiful' movement Urban planning approach developed by Daniel Burnham in the early 1900s in the United States. The aim was to re-create the city as a visually beautiful and functional entity providing the setting for social order and economic progress.

'La Cité Radieuse' (the Radiant City) Le Corbusier's influential urban planning approach developed in the 1930s on the theoretical basis of providing high-density residential units according to his interpretation of residents' needs within green/open space, built in Marseilles and Chandigarh and adopted in many cities around the world.

Business improvement district (BID) A public–private partnership model that first emerged in Canada in the 1970s in which businesses and property owners pay an additional tax or fee to fund public realm improvements such as street cleaning and security services.

Theoretical Approaches of Examining the Urban Outdoor Experience

There is a plethora of literature examining the urban experience and different theoretical approaches have been adopted to explain the experience people have of the urban environment. Two of these theoretical standpoints, environmental determinism and environmental probabilism, are examined in more detail in this article.

Environment Determines Experience

It has long been claimed that the urban environment can have a significant effect on the experience of its residents. Historically, urban environments have enjoyed mixed reputations as places to live and work. Before industrialisation, the city was a place of culture and trade that the wealthy would visit before retreating to the country to recover. As cities industrialise, they become noisier, dirtier, and potentially dangerous places in which to live and work. For example, the living and working conditions in rapidly urbanising nineteenth-century Manchester had a very real and detrimental effect on one's health and life expectancy compared to rural workers. The rapid urbanisation associated with industrialisation can provide the impetus for architecture, planning, and urban design to provide high-quality environments in which people can live. The creation of green, low-density neighbourhoods with good-quality housing and open spaces was a reaction to industrialisation by the nineteenth-century philanthropists and influential urban planners, such as Ebenezer Howard in the United Kingdom and Daniel Burnham in the United States; the city was perceived to be unfit for human habitation. Around the same time in the United States, Daniel Burnham was developing the 'City Beautiful' movement to create the physical environment necessary for social order to prevail. The ideals of the utopian designs of the Garden City and the 'City Beautiful' and later Le Corbusier's 'La Cité Radieuse' reflected the underlying belief held by planners and architects that the physical environments in which people live shape and even determine their lives. It therefore follows this line of thought that the physical environment should be designed in such a way that it engenders social order and harmony in society. This underpinned the creation of parks in the nineteenth century, which were designed to promote civic pride and generally 'civilise' the newly urbanised working class (see article Neighbourhood Design: Green Space and Parks).

These tenets of environmental determinism were grounded in evolutionary biology and geography in the eighteenth to nineteenth century when it was claimed that the environment had an important influence on evolution, human settlement, and, ultimately, culture. However, it has been strongly contested largely because of the claimed lack of control that people have over their environments and the idea that human behaviour is dependent on the physical environment without any acknowledgement of the importance of nonphysical influences. This is demonstrated in Young and Willmott's classic work of the 1950s, which showed that re-location of slum dwellers to a physically higher-quality living environment failed residents because the social environment – the close-knit community – was lost and could not be recreated or improved unlike the physical environment.

Environment Influences Experience

While environmental determinism has been severely criticised, no theorist or practitioner would deny the influence, however small, that the environment has on human behaviour. A second theoretical approach has been proposed that suggests that humans do not simply respond directly to stimulus in a predictable way. A counter-alternative to environmental determinism, environmental probabilism is a theory adhered to by many built environment theorists. This posits the idea that "in a given physical setting some choices are more likely than others" (Carmona et al., 2003: 106); for example, most people choose to cross the road without walking directly in front of incoming cars. It has been described as a sliding scale indicating that the worse (the design of) the environment, the more likely it is to adversely affect users. This theory acknowledges the two-way relationship between user and environment: "what happens in any particular environment depends on those using it" (Carmona et al., 2003: 106–107). The dominant thinking however remains that successful spaces are ones in which people will want to spend time and behave in a socially acceptable way. It is therefore argued that such spaces can be designed and created which are safe, comfortable, and welcoming. This underpins current urban planning strategies for sustainable communities and neighbourhoods around the world that adhere to the tenet that good-quality spaces foster social inclusion and contribute to social cohesion (**Figure 1**), while poor-quality urban space is claimed to incite antisocial behaviour (**Figure 2**). Such underlying notions do not indicate a significant shift from environmental determinism. The act of interpreting 'good quality' into tangible features of the built environment exemplifies the deterministic predilection persistent in policy and practice. Bearing environmental determinism and probabilism in mind, some of the physical features are examined below that are claimed to influence human behaviour and the urban outdoor experience.

Physical Features of the Urban Outdoor Experience

It is useful to consider the urban outdoor experience at different scales as different features occur in different contexts at multiple scales. Relaxing in one's garden and running a marathon in and around a city centre are both examples of the urban outdoor experience. For example, public transport infrastructure and vehicular traffic will usually be more intense in city centres than in suburban areas. Housing tends to be of a lower residential density with more available open space the further one goes from the city, while generally more civic spaces occur in much more built-up areas in city centres (**Figures 3** and **4**).

Figure 1 Neighbourhood in Louisville, KY, USA, designed according to new urbanist principles, which use neo-traditional design to foster a sense of community and sense of place.

Figure 2 Fencing that has been vandalised with considerable litter – which came first?

Figure 3 Lower-density suburban housing, Sheffield, UK.

Land Use

Land use can have an influence on the urban outdoor experience (**Figure 5**). For example, walking after dark along wholly residential streets is a different experience compared to walking along bar-lined streets in a city centre. Both may engender some feeling of insecurity: the former because of the lack of other people on the streets and the latter because of the presence of people under the influence of alcohol. The services and facilities to which one has access also differ according to the extent of mixed land uses in a given neighbourhood. For example, recent planning policy in various countries including the United States and Australia promotes the creation of mixed-use, as opposed to wholly residential, housing developments claiming that mixing land uses will make neighbourhoods economically viable and ensure equitable access to services and facilities, depending on the affordability and suitability for a population. At a wider urban scale, it is common to find retail outlets and shopping centres on the outskirts of the towns, which are often aimed at car drivers rather than public transport users (**Figure 6**). It is claimed that if there are services, facilities, and green space in a neighbourhood, residents will use them. This direct and causal association can also be seen in the simplistic method of equating an economically viable 'high street' with the provision of a range of shops and services. While this may well be the case

Figure 4 Pioneer Square, Portland, OR, USA.

Figure 5 Retail-dominated city centre street, Oxford, UK.

for a neighbourhood with a limited number of services and facilities, a degree of choice is exercised in the use of such services, and it might be more convenient for a resident to use, for example, the supermarket en route to work than one closer to home. Similarly, if the quality of the service is perceived to be poor, the potential user may well travel further to access one that is considered to be of a higher standard. There are also wider contextual effects that may influence the availability of services and facilities. This can be seen in the current economic climate, which is adversely affecting the retail market (**Figure 7**). A further claim is made that where neighbourhood services and facilities are provided, users will interact socially with one another. This is likely to be the case for nurseries and primary schools where parents waiting for their children at the school gate may interact. However, it may not necessarily be the case in urban green space, which people may use to escape the day-to-day bustle of urban life and avoid other people altogether. The reason for one's use of a particular neighbourhood service or facility therefore has an important influence on one's experience in the environment.

Density

Density is a measure of population, in terms of the number of people living in a given area, and of physical form, in terms of how built-up an area is. The density of an urban settlement is closely related to its location: A neighbourhood that is closer to the city centre is likely to be of a higher density than a suburban neighbourhood. Density is also

Figure 6 Out-of-town retail park, which has several hundred car parking spaces and some cycle parking provision but has severely limited direct access via public transport.

Figure 7 Closed down retail outlets are a common sight on the high street during the current economic slowdown.

related to housing type: Flats are an example of high-density housing (**Figure 8**) while detached single houses tend to be found in lower-density settlements (**Figure 3**). The form that housing takes can have an impact on density. For example, a tower block with a large expanse of green space may have the same density as a housing development of two- or three-storey terraces with small gardens (**Figure 9**), but they will be perceived differently by passers-by, providing different backdrops. The lower-rise housing with limited setbacks provides more opportunities for social interaction between neighbours and passers-by, whereas the high-rise block's single entry point limits opportunities for bumping into neighbours and passers-by have no reason to approach the block of flats (set in its own green space) unless visiting them. Generally speaking, it is claimed that in compact, high-density neighbourhoods, people are more likely to socially interact with one another because there are more opportunities for social encounters. While different housing form can have an impact, the nature of the social interaction in high-density areas may well be of a passive and weak variety because of the sheer number of people encountered, the majority of whom are strangers to one another. Furthermore, one's desire to escape the hectic nature of urban life and retreat to parks, squares, and other public spaces may mean that social interaction is not always a priority of urban residents (**Figures 10** and **11**).

Density is however not simply a physical measure of people and place, but is also a subjective perception of the

Figure 8 Low- and high-density housing, Singapore. Reproduced with permission of Professor Mike Jenks.

Figure 9 Housing of different forms but similar densities.

physical environment. This perception is based on an interpretation of the number of people in a given place, how built-up the place is, and how the available space is organised. A city centre square serves a specific purpose when it is used as a market place, which is distinct from its use when the market is not on (**Figures 12** and **13**). The same space can therefore be used and perceived in different ways depending on how it is used.

The high-density compact city is heralded as an important model for sustainable city living. With commercial and retail land use on the ground floor and residential above, it is claimed that perceived safety is increased on the part of the pedestrian because the residents overlook the street and can engage in a kind of natural surveillance. The design of the built form will have a critical part to play in permitting this (**Figure 14**). For example, a gated community will provide few opportunities for interacting with the wider neighbourhood (**Figure 15**). Thinking about the finer grain urban scale of shared residential outdoor space which is increasingly provided for blocks of flats, overlooking can be both a positive and a negative aspect of high-density living (**Figure 16**). While it has the potential to help regulate and control antisocial behaviour, it can also have negative implications for the privacy of the legitimate user of that space.

Figure 10 Large numbers of people move around the compact high-density area of the Shinjuku district, Tokyo, Japan. Reproduced with permission of Professor Mike Jenks.

Figure 11 People sit out along the waterside, Bristol, UK. Reproduced with permission of Lynne Mitchell.

Urban Design and Layout

The important part that the configuration and design of the built environment have to play in one's urban outdoor experience has already been touched on. As a visitor to a new neighbourhood, the layout and design can have a very real impact on how easily one can navigate around the neighbourhood. Physical features designed into a neighbourhood can help orientation and make a place legible for the user, including landmarks, ornamentation and decoration, street furniture and planting, trees, and greenery (**Figures 17** and **18**). Such features are not only useful for visitors, but can also help older residents and people with dementia get around a neighbourhood more easily and independently. Ensuring that the neighbourhood is comfortable and inclusive for everyone to use is an objective of urban designers and can be seen in the provision of, for example, seating, litter bins (including specific bins for dog walkers), and cycle racks. It is not simply the provision of such features but also their design that can also influence one's experience in public spaces. For example, seating that is designed so that people do not linger not only puts off people described as 'undesirables' (e.g., homeless people) but all people as they are not comfortable or suitable for the purpose of sitting down (**Figure 19**).

Figure 12 Gloucester Green, Oxford, UK, on a typical weekday.

Figure 13 The weekly farmers' market, Gloucester Green, Oxford, UK.

At a broader scale, the connectedness of a neighbourhood relates directly to its design and how easy it is to navigate – providing a compact, permeable neighbourhood that connects the resident's home and other services and facilities they use within walking distance is another aim of urban designers and planners worldwide of new urbanist neighbourhoods, urban villages, and sustainable communities. The different kinds of legibility and permeability that can be achieved in the design of neighbourhood streets can be seen in **Figure 20**. The uniform grid pattern provides well-connected urban streets, while the 'lollipop' or cul-de-sac pattern restricts access between streets. The irregular grid pattern provides small perimeter blocks creating a range of block and street shapes.

Perceived safety can be directly influenced by the design of a neighbourhood's public spaces. Underpasses can be frightening spaces and people often avoid using them after dark (**Figure 21**). The level of maintenance can have a direct impact on one's urban outdoor experience and at worst may result in falls and injury. It is therefore argued that spaces should be designed not only with the user in mind, but also in a manner that nature and the built environment do not conflict with one another (**Figure 22**). While such features may not be important for able-bodied teenagers, the provision and

Figure 14 This housing does not permit 'natural surveillance' directly from residents' living space.

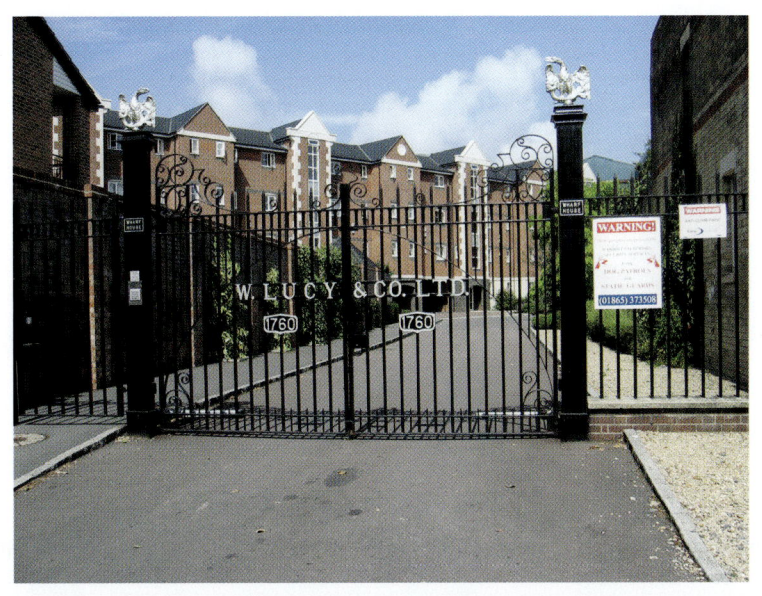

Figure 15 Gated communities are often not connected with the wider neighbourhood and opportunities for overlooking are therefore limited.

maintenance of facilities in different public spaces can be a concern for older people and people with disabilities and may restrict their use of neighbourhood spaces.

Nonphysical Aspects of the Urban Outdoor Experience

When describing the physical features of the environment in an examination of the urban outdoor experience, it is impossible to divorce the associated nonphysical aspects. Two examples that clearly illustrate this overlap are the quality of the environment and the nature of a space, public or private.

Quality of the Urban Environment

The quality of the urban environment can be described as the physical manifestation of a nonphysical concept. The physical form that a neighbourhood takes is a direct result of its quality. The term quality includes physical aspects such as the condition, maintenance, accessibility, and connectedness of the built form as well as nonphysical aspects including the character, perceived safety, and

Figure 16 High-density flats overlooking one of London's squares.

Figure 17 A neighbourhood street that is potentially difficult to navigate as there are few urban design features.

attractiveness. The level of maintenance of a street will be dependent on a number of things: the durability of the materials used, the extent and type of use it is subjected to (e.g., it might be a heavily used traffic route), the amount of litter that is left in bins and on the street by users, and the frequency with which bins are emptied and the street cleaned. Litter may be described by some as a superficial aspect of an environment, but it can have a real and detrimental effect on users' experience – for example, dog excrement found in parks and children's playgrounds can lead young families to take their children somewhere cleaner and safer to play. Litter, vandalism, and graffiti can be a sign that nobody cares about a street or neighbourhood and can also lead to more serious antisocial behaviour (see article Neighbourhood Design: Green Space and Parks). Recent research suggests that those aspects of quality that are based on one's subjective appraisal of a place (e.g., attractiveness and the perceived character) are closely associated with social cohesion, suggesting that the latter is more likely to occur in neighbourhoods that are perceived to be good quality (Dempsey, 2009).

Public and Private Spaces

Public and private spaces may not necessarily have different physical features, but the nature of the space will have an influence on one's experience. There may be rules and regulations to be obeyed; for example, in some London squares only accessible to key-holding residents, dogs must be registered and all ball games are prohibited. In other

Figure 18 A neighbourhood street with features including personalisation, planting, and different housing forms.

Figure 19 An example of seating that is not designed for lingering, Oxford, UK.

spaces, both public and private, activities such as dog-walking, cycling, and ball games are prohibited (**Figure 23**). There are growing numbers of examples of behaviour control and restriction in public spaces, such as the banning of leaflet distribution on streets and even the wearing of T-shirts with slogans that might be considered too political. European and American town centres are increasingly developed as business improvement districts (BIDs) where private companies are involved in the sanitation, maintenance, and management of streets and other public spaces because their premises adjoin the public space (**Figure 24**). BIDs have been described as management programmes that bring the rules of the shopping mall into the street, designating the public space private. Such newly privatised spaces may have security guards with powers to move along undesirables who are not using the space in the designated fashion, such as teenagers hanging around or people begging. Even though the impact of this particular management technique of public space on everyday users is unclear, there are thousands of BIDs around the world and new neighbourhood improvement districts have been developed in Hamburg, Germany.

Uses and Users of Space

A critical nonphysical aspect of one's outdoor experience is the underlying reason for being in the space, and the extent to which one is able to achieve this goal. For example, a family might want to go to their local park for a picnic and to play in the children's playground (**Figure 25**). To do this, they require an easily accessible park with clean, well-maintained green space, somewhere sheltered to sit such as a picnic table and in the shade if it is sunny. They also require well-maintained playground facilities in which the children can play, with somewhere for the parent(s) to sit and watch. To permit this, the park needs litter and dog bins as well as regular park maintenance through the presence of staff who regularly empty the bins and clear any debris such as fallen leaves, branches, and other litter. Factors that may hinder the family achieving this goal include other users of the park, such as teenagers using the playground if there are no other facilities in the park for them or dog-owners who do

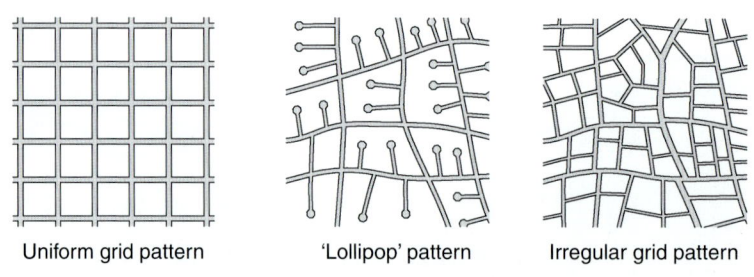

Figure 20 Different street layouts.
Reproduced with permission of Dr Daniel Kozak.

Uniform grid pattern   'Lollipop' pattern   Irregular grid pattern

Figure 21 Underpasses may be spaces that people avoid because of fears of safety.
Reproduced with permission of Daniel Saunders.

Figure 22 The root system of some trees can cause damage to walkways.

Figure 23 A London square, open to key holders only, prohibits a number of activities.

Neighbourhood Design: Urban Outdoor Experience 41

Figure 24 Louisville, KY, USA, has a Downtown Management District, which is an example of a BID.

Figure 25 This family brings a table and chairs to the park to have their picnic.
Reproduced with permission of Joost Bergers.

also bring their own personality to a space and attach significance and meaning to a space, both positive and negative. Children's points of reference when thinking about their neighbourhood are often very localised to home and enlarge geographically as they get older and are allowed to move more widely as they gain independence. A negative example of place attachment relates to gang territory which may emerge corresponding to postcodes, busy main roads, or other physical boundaries, which may prevent residents from going out after dark for fear of safety (**Figure 26**).

not keep the dog on the lead. These other users may pose a threat to the family through intimidation and fears for safety (particularly if the dogs are aggressive and running freely). Other users of that same space have their own uses and needs, which will differ according to, for example, age, gender, culture, and reason for using a space. The extent to which different groups can achieve their own goals in harmony or with conflict may have an important influence on any one of their urban experiences. Users

Figure 26 Graffiti denoting a particular territory, Oxford, UK.

Conclusion

It is clear that urban outdoor experiences differ from person to person, depending on both their characteristics and the characteristics of the urban outdoor space that they are using and the reasons for using the space. Environmental determinism and probabilism provide theoretical frameworks within which we can understand how the urban environment can have an influence on the user's experience. However, it is often a combination of factors, both physical and nonphysical, that can significantly influence the urban outdoor experience. The nature of space changes over time as do users' needs and demands. More recently, these needs and demands are changing our outdoor urban experience through increased regulation and managed public realms, such as the BID and gated housing. It is currently unclear to what extent such closely managed spaces impact on the outdoor experience of urban residents. To create good-quality neighbourhoods in which users feel safe and comfortable, it is therefore necessary to further develop our understanding of the combined influence of ever-changing physical and nonphysical features of the urban environment.

See also: Defensible Space; Gated Communities: Developed Countries; Gentrification and Well-Being; Health and Housing; High Rise; High-Rise Homes; Housing Estates; Neighbourhood Design: Green Space and Parks; Neighbourhood Design: Public Spaces; Neighbourhood Planning; People and the Built Form; Place Attachment.

References

Carmona M, Heath T, Oc T, and Tiesdell S (2003) *Public Places Urban Spaces: The Dimensions of Urban Design*. Oxford: Architectural Press.
Dempsey N (2009) Are good-quality environments socially cohesive? Measuring quality and cohesion in urban neighbourhoods. *Town Planning Review* 80: 315–345.
Young M and Willmott P (1957) *Family and Kinship in East London*. London: Routledge and Kegan Paul Ltd.

Further Reading

Broady M (1968) *Planning for People: Essays on the Social Context of Planning*. London: Bedford Square Press.
Burton E and Mitchell L (2006) *Inclusive Urban Design: Streets for Life*. Oxford: Architectural Press.
Carr S, Francis M, Rivlin LG, and Stone AM (1992) *Public Space*. Cambridge, New York: Cambridge University Press.
Churchman A (1999) Disentangling the concept of density. *Journal of Planning Literature* 13: 389–411.
Engels F (1845 [1987]) *The Condition of the Working Class in England*. London: Penguin.
Jacobs J (1961) *The Death and Life of Great American Cities*. Harmondsworth: Penguin Books.
Jenks M and Dempsey N (2005) The language and meaning of density. In: Jenks M and Dempsey N (eds.) *Future Forms and Design for Sustainable Cities*, pp 287–309. Oxford: Architectural Press.
Kohn M (2004) *Brave New Neighborhoods: The Privatization of Public Space*. New York: Routledge.
Madanipour A (2003) *Public and Private Spaces of the City*. London: Routledge.
Robbins E (2004) New urbanism. In: Robbins E and El-Khoury R (eds.) *Shaping the City: Studies in History, Theory and Urban Design*, pp. 212–230. London: Routledge.

Neighbourhood Disadvantage

J Prior, University of Technology, Sydney, NSW, Australia

© 2012 Elsevier Ltd. All rights reserved.

Glossary

Community renewal Programmes and initiatives that focus on particular social and economic dimensions of disadvantaged community.

Cultural exclusion Can be defined as a marginalisation from shared symbols, meaning, ritual, and discourse.

Economic exclusion Traditionally related to concepts such as poverty, underclass, and a lack of the economic resources normally secured through decent employment.

Neighbourhood effects The net change in the contribution to life-chances made by living in one neighbourhood rather than another. Neighbourhood effects can be positive and negative.

Neighbourhood renewal The physical rehabilitation of disadvantaged urban neighbourhoods by large-scale renovation or reconstruction of housing and public works.

Social capital Consists of the totality of resources an individual or group has by virtue of being enmeshed in networks of more or less institutionalised relationships of mutual acquaintance and recognition, or through membership in a group.

Social exclusion A complex and multidimensional process. It involves the lack or denial of resources, rights, goods, and services, and the inability to participate in the normal relationships and activities available to the majority of people in society, whether in economic, social, cultural, or political arenas.

Suburbanisation The process of population movement from within towns and cities to the rural–urban fringe. Suburbs are traditionally characterised by a low density, which provides a greater level of open space than that typically available within the urban contexts.

Disadvantages and Advantages of Neighbourhoods

Since the mid-nineteenth century the concentration of disadvantaged households within some and not other urban and suburban neighbourhoods has been a key concern in most cities across the globe. During this period diverse phrases have been used to describe these disadvantaged neighbourhoods, ranging from more emotive terms such as slums, through to more theoretical and policy-oriented descriptors such as localised disadvantage, neighbourhood deprivation, neighbourhood disadvantage, and neighbourhood exclusion amongst others. During this time there have been periods when the focus on neighbourhood disadvantage has intensified as a result of significant shifts such as the rapid appearance of slums and ghettos as industrial cities emerged in the late nineteenth century and again more recently as cities transitioned again into postindustrial urban centres. In its broadest sense neighbourhood disadvantage refers to the way in which living in one neighbourhood may limit the life-chances one might gain as compared to living in another neighbourhood. Such comparative disadvantage is diverse and can range from deficits of physical utility and amenity through to deficits in well-being and happiness within one neighbourhood when compared to another. Such comparative place-based disadvantage within human settlements can occur at a multitude of scales ranging from street to street through to between nations. Neighbourhood disadvantage is just one spatial descriptor that helps us to communicate the concept that some people in one place are less well off than others living within another similar scale of place.

In discussing disadvantage at the neighbourhood level, neighbourhood is generally used in countries as diverse as the United Kingdom, the People's Republic of China, South Africa, Australia, Japan, and the USA to refer to a physical place, that is a geographically delineated subunit of a district in a city, and to the group of people who occupy that place and share its accompanying circumstances. In general parlance neighbourhood is often used as a synonym for community but the terms are not entirely synonymous: while a neighbourhood may be a community, a community is not necessarily a neighbourhood.

The considerable attention that neighbourhood disadvantage has attracted throughout the past few centuries can be understood not only in terms of immediate needs but as part of a long history of analyses and understanding which has led to the belief that neighbourhoods play a key role in the formation of civilised life, and consequently neighbourhood disadvantage adversely affects the formation of civilised life. Since the time of the Greek philosophers, the neighbourhood has been extolled for the advantages it can provide both to inhabitants and to the broader urban settlements in which neighbourhoods are located. From the earliest time neighbourhoods have been understood to be one of the natural and necessary contexts for civilised life. Such positive sentiments extend through the history of medieval and renaissance cities in Europe through to the emergence of the industrial city in North America at the end of the nineteenth century when, spurred on by exponents of the Chicago School, there appeared a new, organic concept of American industrial cities, elevating the neighbourhood to iconic status. In the early twentieth century the influential work of Park described neighbourhoods as the basis of urban social organisation. While neighbourhoods have long been regarded as crucial elements of human settlement, concern has also arisen that they may not provide their inhabitants with adequate levels of opportunity thought to be appropriate within specific societies at specific times. Such focus goes beyond inhabitants of disadvantaged neighbourhoods to include their negative effects on the rest of the human settlement around their location.

The following overview of neighbourhood disadvantage traces its history since the mid-nineteenth century and explores how it has been understood and addressed, with particular attention given to its dependence on political agendas or ideology as well as the variations between how particular disciplines and professional groups define, approach, and understand the issue.

Early Approaches and Understandings of Neighbourhood Disadvantage

As Western cities made the transition from commercial centres to centres of industrial production in the later half of the nineteenth century, reorganisation took on a geographic dimension, apparent at the neighbourhood level, with neighbourhoods becoming more differentiated. As cities rapidly industrialised, some neighbourhoods within cities experienced overcrowded housing; noxious industrial, human, and animal wastes; and devastating outbreaks of infectious diseases. This period is marked by recurrent debates concerning the causes of the most severe concentrations of disadvantage in industrial cities' slums. Fundamental questions were raised about the appropriate role of planning and of governments in meeting the problems of these slums.

Neighbourhood Disadvantage, Environmental Determinism, and Human Nature

Throughout the later half of the nineteenth century, theories, driven partially by the ideas of sanitation and hygiene, argued that poor environmental conditions in slums generated social pathologies of urban life and acted as a breeding ground for violence, crime, poor morals, and bad habits. It was commonly feared that the instability slums posed for industrial nations and their cities might somehow capture their inhabitants in an ever-increasing downward spiral. Propelled by the idea that environment determines prosperity, those living in disadvantaged neighbourhoods became a key concern of governments and reformists who appealed for decent housing and neighbourhoods through the building of new urban sanitation infrastructure, parks, and playground planning, not just as a measure of humanity and justice for the poor, but as a matter of self-interest. Bad housing and neighbourhoods meant sick workers, and sick workers meant lower profits, higher relief outlays, and higher taxes. The idea was advanced that social, political, and economic problems could be best addressed by environmental interventions into urban slums.

Alternative theories argued that environmental approaches failed to acknowledge the role human nature played in forming concentrations of disadvantage in some urban neighbourhoods and not others. Eugenists, amongst others, sought to explain the emergence of urban slums in terms of human nature. They perceived the emergence of disadvantage within the neighbourhoods of industrial cities not as a symptom of the unfitness of housing or environments, but of the unfitness of the people themselves. Eugenists believed that the more traditional methods of environmental reform had to be supplemented by the new sciences of heredity and psychology. Many of the early eugenists were inclined to the view that the feeble-minded and destitute segments of society suffered above all from inherited defects that could only be corrected through breeding them out. By the outbreak of the First World War, eugenics theories were gaining popularity over the traditional environmental theories that had been used to address and understand concentrations of disadvantage within cities, although others suggested that such deprivation was a natural consequence of the type of social relations that industrial cities generated. The different internal logic of industrial cities, it was argued, undermined bonds that had been prevalent in earlier forms of human settlement, leading to a decline in neighbourliness and community. Such concentrated disadvantage could also be explained as a natural result of the density of city populations that concentrated physical and social problems, intensifying their effects and inflating pressures on mental health.

Suburbanisation, Urban Renewal, and the Residuum

Drawing predominantly on the view that the environment determines prosperity, early attempts to redress the lives of the disadvantaged within urban neighbourhoods was initiated through new building codes which sought to improve building conditions including ventilation, light, and water closet design. The Housing of the Working Classes Act (1890) in the United Kingdom reasserted local authorities' power to declare as unhealthy, urban areas where houses were unfit for human habitation, or where the conditions were thought to pose danger or risk of injury to inhabitants or to those in the area. Throughout the late nineteenth and early twentieth century planners sought to alleviate crowded living conditions in disadvantaged urban neighbourhoods by constructing so-called breathing spaces such as parks and outdoor recreation areas. For example the playground movement, building on the idea that fresh air and open space made better people, advocated for urban play spaces next to schools so that gymnasiums, reading rooms, and baths could all be used for children's recreation, literacy, and hygiene. Most reforms were grounded in the belief that advancements in science and technology could provide physical improvements that would make pathogenic urban environments and the immoral slum-dwellers more orderly and healthy. During this time governments sought to address disadvantage within urban neighbourhoods in cities such as London, Birmingham, Sydney, San Francisco, and New York.

The suburbanisation of industrial cities was garnered as a natural environmental remedy for the growing number of people living in cramped urban neighbourhoods in the late nineteenth century. From an environmentalist perspective, suburbanisation helped alleviate urban deprivation directly by emancipating those who left the physical degradation and were thus more greatly exposed to air and light, believed to enhance feelings and improve health. Meanwhile those left behind were thought to benefit from the better-quality lodgings released by those moving out. After 1900, concern over the growing disadvantage within particular urban areas of cities such as London, Sydney, and New York began to ease as a result of suburbanisation and decentralisation from urban centres, influenced through the emergence of planning acts.

Eugenists and others who approached neighbourhood disadvantage from the perspective of human nature regarded suburbanisation as only a partial solution to the emergent concentrations of disadvantage in particular urban neighbourhoods. They argued that a percentage of the population had particular innate tendencies and constituted a residuum unable to be helped by environmental improvements. Eugenists and many social reformers thought this residuum, as those left behind in urban slums came to be known, were unable, through weakness, to share in the improved living conditions offered by new suburbs. Radical socialists argued that environmental changes were insufficient in addressing such a residuum and that a more social engineering approach was needed. During the early twentieth century, especially during times of economic crisis such as the one that followed the Great War and took hold in the Great Depression, the idea of a residuum often provided policy-makers and governments with a rationale for diverting limited funding away from those it was thought could not be helped to those who could. Thus deliberate political decisions manifested in neglecting the slums and their residuum and instead focusing on new suburban housing estates based on such ideals as the garden city. During this period the attention of planners and others concerned with improving the environment was directed almost exclusively towards suburban development.

From the mid-1930s onwards, the chronic state of extensive areas of decaying neighbourhoods and overcrowded housing aroused considerable public comment and the housing policies hitherto pursued were questioned. A shift occurred in housing policies in countries such as the United Kingdom and Australia. Housing policy was redirected to clearance of disadvantaged urban areas and their rebuilding 'on cleared sites'. Based on emergent government directives through the following decades, planners advocated a coordinated approach to disadvantaged urban neighbourhoods, involving not only the creation of low-density, self-contained suburban settlements, but also the comprehensive redevelopment of the central areas of existing towns. This shift in focus was further supported through the middle decade of the twentieth century as a result of the emergence of progressive politicians and industrialists who sought to oppose diverse totalitarian, fascist, and communist ideologies that grew in strength during this period, and sought to demonstrate the vitality of a Western democratic system through raising the social and physical standards of the population as a whole. This new alignment excluded the ideals of the eugenists and others who sought to promote social engineering. In its place we see the emergence of notions of social justice and equity. These social and political concerns ultimately moved the housing debate away from the condition of individuals and their houses and towards the reconstruction of very large areas: away from purely physical solutions to social justice solutions manifested in a new orientation to the social system.

From the processes of suburbanisation and urban regeneration, social mixing was often promoted as a tool for addressing concentrations of disadvantage within urban neighbourhoods. Sarkissian has reviewed the history of arguments in favour of social mix, through the ideas of the social hygiene, eugenist, and garden city movements, to the desegregation and urban renewal strategies of the 1960s and 1970s. Early strategies to construct or redevelop urban neighbourhoods to diminish concentrations of poor households were based either on the theory that the presence of respectable hardworking neighbours would improve the socialisation, and hence the economic prospects, of poor households, or on often contradictory ideas about reducing class or racial tension by promoting either harmony or conflict at the local level. The most powerful and sustainable case for mandated deconcentration of poverty was that propounded in the 1950s by the US Supreme Court, which argued that separate amenities for an underprivileged minority were inherently inferior amenities. Throughout the second half of the twentieth century social mixing remained a key policy instrument for seeking to address concentrations of disadvantage within neighbourhoods, in particular attempts to disperse concentrations of disadvantage perceived to stem from public housing concentrations. Critical examination of the ideas underlying concern about concentration of disadvantage has revealed serious conceptual and methodological issues that call into question both the likelihood of success and the potential social utility of policy-makers' attempts to deconcentrate poor households. Some argue that social mixing, without other levels of support, tends to construct the concentration of poor people on housing estates as the problem, rather than poverty itself.

Contemporary Understandings and Approaches to Neighbourhood Disadvantage

The way in which neighbourhood disadvantage has been approached and understood within contemporary society has been influenced by the evaluation and experience of the effectiveness and appropriateness of ideas and approaches that were put forward as a means of understanding and addressing neighbourhood disadvantage over the previous century. Approaches based on principles of human nature as espoused by eugenists quickly fell into obscurity after the Second World War. Whilst eugenics was rapidly abandoned, research into the relationships between human nature and neighbourhood disadvantage nevertheless continues through studies that seek to differentiate and determine what role genetics, as opposed to environment, plays in the lives of those who live in disadvantaged neighbourhoods.

Attempts to address neighbourhood disadvantage through environmental initiatives such as the recreation of new parks and housing and suburbanisation through to the regeneration of urban centres also came into question. Almost at the same time that clearance and reconstruction were beginning to be implemented as a solution to extreme neighbourhood disadvantage within urban centres through the early twentieth century, the case for such environmental solutions began to be undermined by new evidence challenging the very basis of the argument that environmental improvement would bring better health and opportunity to those that lived in disadvantaged neighbourhoods. In 1937 two respected figures in the public health sphere, M'Gonigle and Kirby, published a book which indicated strongly that it was economic rather than environmental factors which controlled the level of public health. They reported a study of a population that had been transferred from slum dwellings to a modern self-contained housing estate and kept intact without a mixture of other populations, while a second comparable population continued to dwell in slum houses and served as a control for the study. The expenditure and health of these populations was carefully compared; results showed that although the estate to which the families moved was carefully planned and well-built, and the houses well equipped with the most modern sanitary arrangements, the death rate of the families increased over what it had previously been in the slum area they left behind. Even more startling was the observation that the death rate on the new estate exceeded that in the surviving slum area. Environmental improvement, the data seemed to suggest, could actually be injurious to health. The authors suggested that it is economical factors which control the situation since with incomes near the poverty level, wholly unavoidable expenditure on items other than food may inevitably lead to malnutrition. It left the clear impression that adequate nutrition was more important than good housing in promoting health: moreover, it made clear the importance of income levels in the nutrition of families.

The assumption that physical upgrading will eventually promote a nice living environment that fosters nice people came squarely into question throughout the later half of the twentieth century. Critics questioned the appropriateness of outcome-oriented physical planning, arguing that whilst physical renewal programmes address some of the symptoms of disadvantage, they do not address the underlying causes, such as the social and economic marginalisation of residents as revealed in research carried out by M'Gonigle and Kirby, for instance. Physical renewal schemes might bring improvements to the community but often at a cost. Consequently, it was argued that initiatives aimed at improving social and employment aspects of disadvantaged localities needed to become prominent in any programmes aimed at addressing such disadvantage. Frieden and Levin argued that slums and ghettos, whilst promoting some forms of disadvantage, did provide inhabitants with valuable social functions and that such factors were often jeopardised by social mixing and complete physical renewal.

Many of the physical renewal initiatives that were undertaken through the twentieth century were also increasingly questioned on the basis of the modernist-inspired, formalist physical solutions they used to redevelop disadvantaged neighbourhoods within urban centres. Mumford and Jacob argued that such formalist physical designs neglected to consider the way in which the physical form of cities and their neighbourhoods had merged over centuries so as to promote particular forms of social interaction that were important to the generation of an adequate neighbourhood life. Mumford insisted that the neighbourhood that he believed characterised the medieval city was vital to the regeneration of twentieth-century cities and the creation of a more caring society.

Social Capitals, Social Exclusion, and Neighbourhood Effects

Throughout the later decades of the twentieth century understanding of neighbourhood disadvantage was itself enhanced in social scientific and policy discourse by the emergence into broader discourse of the notions of social capital and social exclusion. People used these constructs in an attempt to explain and capture the complex and multiple factors theorised to maintain the relative socioeconomic disadvantage of individuals and families but which, particularly in policy discourse, quickly became associated with place-based concentrations of disadvantage and, in particular although not exclusively, with the sociocultural factors described above. The idea of socially excluded communities is commonly used to highlight an interactive relationship between, or compounding effects of, socioeconomic disadvantage and certain aspects of (usually urban) geography – including distance, infrastructure and services, built form, and land use. Social capital consists of the totality of resources an individual or group has by virtue of being enmeshed in networks of more or less institutionalised relationships of mutual acquaintance and recognition, or through membership in a group. The concept has attracted much interest towards understanding neighbourhood disadvantage, but is only half the story. Power and Wilson summarise social exclusion, also important, as the inability of our society to keep all groups and individuals within reach of what we expect as a society. The concept of social exclusion is often used uncritically to encompass economic and cultural exclusion. It is related to poverty, but makes sense only in the broader perspective of citizenship and integration into the social context.

Simultaneous with new theoretical lenses being developed, was the emergence of empirical research seeking to open up and explore the multiple social, economic, cultural, and physical dynamics that contribute to neighbourhood disadvantage. Sarkissian argued such research was often missing during early attempts to address neighbourhood disadvantage. For example, she notes, whilst many arguments were marshalled in favour of geographic mixing of households of varying socioeconomic status during the twentieth century, these rarely relied on research. Where attempted, the empirical evidence supporting intervention was scant and research designs were very simplistic. Generally speaking, this growing empirical evidence appears to validate the hypothesis that living in one neighbourhood rather than another can affect life-chances. In this sense neighbourhood effects can be positive and negative. In recent years researchers have accumulated a large and growing body of empirical evidence to test the hypothesis that living in a neighbourhood is likely to affect life-chances. For example the development of forms of social capital within a specific neighbourhood area may be constraining rather than enabling. This research into the effects of living in one neighbourhood as compared to another distinguishes between simple aggregations of characteristics found in the residents of a neighbourhood. For example, substantial evidence suggests that phenomena such as unemployment, educational underattainment, crime, and drug use are geographically concentrated. Over the past two decades one type of chronic stress that has been investigated in relation to children's development is neighbourhood disadvantage, as determined by the presence of a number of community-level stressors such as poverty, unemployment or underemployment, limited resources (service limitations), substandard housing, and high crime rates. These studies have found that children who face these high levels of hazardous environmental conditions are more likely than children growing up under more favourable circumstances to experience a variety of behavioural and emotional difficulties.

Whilst acknowledging the importance of the types of internal neighbourhood effects discussed above, Morris amongst other researchers has argued that neighbourhoods operate in wider contexts and that, for example, urban economic forces may ameliorate or exaggerate neighbourhood problems. They claim that public policies beyond the neighbourhood may have more influence on residents' lives than those effects that are generated within a neighbourhood. For example many researchers stress the overwhelming influence of structural macroeconomic factors in creating concentrations of poverty and argue that other factors are often much more important as sources of inequality. Some authors, notably Klienman, dismiss neighbourhood effects as much less important than inequalities arising from within the household, that is, what might be identified as the intergenerational transmission of poverty. However, most extended reviews of the effects of neighbourhoods conclude that there are causal associations between disadvantaged neighbourhoods and other social problems which are more than the consequences of macroeconomic forces and household characteristics, even if there is no agreement over exactly which social outcomes are the result of which factors.

Joined-up Solutions and Resident Participation

Whilst approaches to neighbourhood disadvantage have always been in the purview of government, towards the end of the twentieth century and into the early twenty-first century, a renewed concern for the sociospatial structure of contemporary cities and discussions relating to urban differentiation, segregation, social polarisation, and consequently social exclusion and inclusion have become central concerns in urban debates. New national and international socioeconomic forces have reshaped national geographies in general and the characteristics of cities in particular, resulting in a range of diverse social and spatial outcomes. Where once sociospatial outcomes may have been clearly defined in research focusing on cities of the industrial era, a new or different set of divisions has emerged in postindustrial or post-Fordist cities, often with a complex set of interlinked factors impacting on the social and economic processes under way in cities.

A key consequence of this emerging research and the complementary policy development in such locations as the United Kingdom and Australia is a growing awareness of a need to shift away from sectoral planning and service delivery towards more integrated governance of problems within disadvantaged areas to deal more effectively with the diverse aspects of exclusion they display. More integrated approaches are required to go beyond the sectoral solutions imposed by physical renewal and public intervention in the traditional sense (child support, social workers, and so forth). These new initiatives have been driven by a search for joined-up solutions based upon interdepartmental working and wide-ranging partnerships. This approach is based on a recognition that interconnected and intractable problems require interconnected policy solutions.

Such joined-up solutions were often first developed, and many still are, around attempts to bring together various departments, agencies, and community groups that had previously worked independently to address neighbourhood disadvantage. Over recent decades, as these joined-up approaches have evolved, there have been growing debates about the extent of partnerships and sources of data that should be considered when identifying and addressing neighbourhood disadvantage. Quantitative information is often perceived as providing the most objective and reliable basis for measuring programme effectiveness, as well as being the most easily understood, with outcomes that can be benchmarked and targets tested. Certainly statistical indicators can provide evidence that certain elements of disadvantage are spatially concentrated. However, it is increasingly being recognised and acknowledged that they do not in themselves imply a causal relationship between neighbourhood and concentrations of disadvantage within it, nor do they describe or account for the quality of life or relationships experienced by residents of these neighbourhoods, far less predict the likely impact of specific interventions on these aspects of neighbourhood life. Researchers claim that much can be gained from opening policy-making processes to participation by a wide range of stakeholders and citizens. As Randolph and Judd have highlighted, the limitations of using quantitative indicators in this context go to the epistemological questions of what constitutes exclusion and who defines disadvantage. The top-down, expert-driven approach, which forms the foundation of the traditional sectoral solution of welfare governance, reduces residents within disadvantaged areas to client-like and passive receivers of services. To foster self-esteem, an important prerequisite for social inclusion, residents must accept an obligation to take more responsibility and be given opportunities to be involved and empowered. This includes more collaborative approaches to planning which integrate economic, land use, and social planning, and embrace a bottom-up approach in which the starting point is to understand the local community rather than impose the ideals of experts from the top down. It is important to note that many of these initiatives face the problem of short-term funding, a barrier to the effective longer-term solutions that are required to address the complex and multifaceted problems faced by residents in disadvantaged localities. The growing emphasis on residents has often led to the term neighbourhood regeneration or neighbourhood renewal being associated with physical programmes and such terms as community renewal being adopted in recognition and as a point of emphasising that these initiatives are primarily based on addressing the broader concerns of residents, which may be social, economic, and cultural as much as they may be about the quality of their physical environment.

The emergence of programmes seeking to understand neighbourhood disadvantage from multiple perspectives is helping to dispel oversimplified views that have persisted, and often still persist, in the wider community and are expounded by policy-makers. It is important to understand the diverse reasons for localised disadvantages, the generation of diverse effects, and the combination of those effects at various geographic scales ranging from a neighbourhood, through to a city, regional, national, and international context, so that we are able to address and identify neighbourhood disadvantage. We need to also learn, from more participatory processes, that the lived experience of these neighbourhoods is just as important in modelling and in determining whether programmes are necessary.

See also: Crime Prevention Through Environmental Design; Ghetto; Health, Well-Being and Vulnerable

Populations; Housing and Neighbourhood Quality: Urban Regeneration; Neighbourhood Governance; Neighbourhood Incivilities; Neighbourhood Reputation; Power; Residential Segregation; Residential Segregation and Ethnic Diversity in the United States; Rights, Citzenship, and Shelter; Slums; Social Exclusion and Housing; Social Housing and Social Problems; Social Justice; Social Sustainability; Sustainable Regeneration; Urbanisation and Housing the Poor: Overview.

Further Reading

Alterman R and Cars G (1991) *Neighbourhood Regeneration: An International Perspective*. London: Mansell.

Baum S, Haynes M, Van Gellecum Y, and Han JH (2006) Advantage and disadvantage across Australia's extended metropolitan regions: A typology of socioeconomic outcomes. *Urban Studies* 43(9): 1549–1579.

Breetzke GD and Horn AC (2009) A geodemographic profiler for high offender propensity areas in the city of Tshwane, South Africa. *Environment and Planning A* 41(1): 112–127.

Buck N (2001) Identifying neighbourhood effects on social exclusion. *Urban Studies* 38(12): 2251–2275.

Fried M and Levin J (1968) Some social functions of the urban slum. In: Frieden BJ and Morris R (eds.) *Urban Planning and Social Policy*, pp. 60–83. New York: Basic Books.

Fulong W (2007) The poverty of transition: From industrial district to poor neighbourhood in the city of Nanjing, China. *Urban Studies* 44(13): 2673–2694.

Gale DE (1984) *Neighborhood Revitalization and the Postindustrial City: A Multinational Perspective*. Lexington, MA: Lexington Books.

Jacobs J (1961) *The Death and Life of Great American Cities*. New York: Vintage Books.

Kazepov Y (2005) *Cities of Europe: Changing Contexts, Local Arrangements, and the Challenge to Urban Cohesion*. Malden, MA: Blackwell Publications.

Klienman M (1999) There goes the neighbourhood: Area politics of place and poverty. *New Economy* 6(4): 188–192.

M'Gonigle GCM and Kirby J (1985) *Poverty and Public Health*. New York: Garland.

Morris L (1995) *Social Divisions: Economic Decline and Serial Structural Change*. London: UCL Press.

Mumford L (1945) *City Development: Studies in Disintegration and Renewal*. New York: Harcourt, Brace and Co.

Murie A and Musterd S (2004) Social exclusion and opportunity structures in European cities and neighbourhoods. *Urban Studies* 41(8): 1441–1459.

Oberwittler D (2007) The effects of neighbourhood poverty on adolescent problem behaviours: A multi-level analysis differentiated by gender and ethnicity. *Housing Studies* 22(5): 781–803.

Park RE (1915) The city: Suggestions for the investigation of human behavior in the city environment. *The American Journal of Sociology* 20(5): 577–612.

Power A and Wilson JW (2000) *Social Exclusion and the Future of Cities*. CASE papers, No. 35. London: Centre for Analysis of Social Exclusion, London School of Economics. See http://sticerd.lse.ac.uk/dps/case/cp/CASEpaper35.pdf (accessed 11 July 2010).

Prior J (2008) The role of local government in redressing neighbourhood disadvantage: A case study of Penrith City Council. *Commonwealth Journal of Local Government* 1(1): 1–22. See http://epress.lib.uts.edu.au/ojs/index.php/cjlg/article/viewArticle/767.

Randolph B and Judd B (2006) Qualitative methods and the evaluation of community renewal programs in Australia: Towards a national framework. *Urban Policy & Research* 24(1): 97–114.

Sarkissian W (1976) The idea of social mix in town planning: An historical review. *Urban Studies* 13(3): 231–246.

Wilkinson RG and Marmot MG (eds.) (2003) *Social Determinants of Health: The Solid Facts*, 2nd edn. Denmark: World Health Organization. See www.euro.who.int/document/e81384.pdf (accessed 11 July 2010).

Neighbourhood Effects

T Kauko, Norwegian University of Science and Technology – NTNU, Trondheim, Norway

M d'Amato, Technical University Politecnico di Bari, Bari, Italy

© 2012 Elsevier Ltd. All rights reserved.

Introduction

In the glossary of the recent book edited by Holt-Jensen and Pollock (2009), a neighbourhood is defined as follows:

> Diffuse concept, but often connected to physical planning traditions by which neighbourhoods are planned around the local services such as schools and shops, and delimited by traffic barriers or open space from other neighbourhoods. A more social definition is based on the idea that a neighbourhood is an area in which the inhabitants have a certain knowledge of each other or know that they live in the same area. One other definition is that neighbourhood is simply a place – it is purely a spatial definition and implies no particular community of interest among its inhabitants, other than that they live in that area.

Thus, we have physical, social, and spatial definitions of the neighbourhood. However, if one ties together and summarises the three kinds of definitions to a predominantly economic one – and this is not a too far-fetched assumption given the tendency of the factors above to generate externalities that are at least partially measurable in economic terms – then the issue of defining the concept becomes simplified: we should identify a score, or at least a categorisation of quality, for the desirability (i.e., ability to attract people and capital) of a given neighbourhood. In general, this measure is presented vis-à-vis other neighbourhoods, which, in principle, might be from the same city as well as from other cities. This is usually meaningful for residents, households, or (prospective) owner-occupant home-buyers, but in principle the same setting could be extended to include commercial actors such as investors, developers, and realtors as well as community activists and government actors. Various theoretical, methodological, and empirical facets of this issue have been discussed and analysed extensively in Kauko (2001, 2002, 2005).

Neighbourhoods, by means of their spatial confinement and concentration, induce positive and negative externalities that define the value of a neighbourhood. By influencing property values, neighbourhood effects created by these concentrations lead to the growth, stagnation, or decay of a given neighbourhood. For example, Rothenberg et al. (1991) show that low housing value in a given neighbourhood is often the result of concentration mechanisms that lead to the formation of housing submarkets with characteristics that then go on to negatively impact property values in those areas. In approaching and understanding neighbourhood effects, Rothenberg et al. (1991) argues that it is important to take into consideration the role of externalities on the formation of submarkets.

Neighbourhood effects comprise a vast research area and this article cannot deal responsibly with all sections of it. It is nevertheless necessary to give a general overview of the various lines of enquiry that are currently being applied for this research objective. It is important to be aware that the distinctions between different lines are both conceptual and methodological. The neighbourhood effect study traditions can be categorised in the following ways:

1. Conceptually, a distinction is made between two purposes of research on neighbourhood effects:

    (a) For moving behaviour, a tradition of residential choice studies made by urban geographers (e.g., Clark et al., 2006) is appropriate. This tradition could be traced back all the way to the Chicago School (1930s) or, in a more operative sense, to social area analysis and factor ecology (1950s).

    (b) For house buying, a tradition of urban (housing) economics and residential (property) valuation studies (e.g., Thériault et al., 2005) is relevant. This line of research could be said to stem from hedonic house price and housing market modelling (1970s) if not from earlier endeavours into multiple regression analysis (MRA)-based urban and housing economic analysis.

2. Methodologically, a distinction can be made between the following:

    (a) Two broad empirical (and mostly quantitative) approaches, insofar as they use stated preference/choice or revealed preference/choice modelling (see Timmermans et al., 1994).

    (b) Technically, a distinction as to how the 'neighbourhood' under study is operationalised as a distinct category from other 'neighbourhoods'. Drawing boundaries is difficult, since 'neighbourhood' is a bottom-up concept by definition whereby micro-location matters (Kauko, 2006a). However, it is often too difficult to find such data with location-specific information (but see Clapp and Wang, 2006), in which case administrative or ad hoc boundaries – or geographical information system (GIS) grid cells – are often used instead.

(c) Principally based on the definition of 'effect' (cf. the definition of Holt-Jensen and Pollock earlier):

- it is a composite effect of functional, physical, and socioeconomic factors (but usually not accessibility to the CBD (central business district) in the sense of a monocentric urban model a la Alonso-Muth-Mills) or
- it is an independent, residual effect pertaining to neighbourhood or location, when the abovementioned factors (i.e., the model variables) are controlled for; this could, for example, be an indicator constructed based on aggregated sales transaction prices (see Needham et al., 1998).

(d) Is it about linear/rational or nonlinear/nonrational effects, when the former are assumed to pertain to socioeconomics (e.g., poverty, see Cooke and Marchant, 2006) and the latter to sociocultural and behavioural factors (e.g., identity, see Hauge and Kolstad, 2007).

(e) The last methodological issue is about 'exactly how' to measure this effect most effectively (cf. Borst and McCluskey, 2008).

Of this smorgasbord of topics we discuss some elements from the categories 2(b)–(e) in more detail. As was mentioned above, we have selected a predominantly economic definition of the neighbourhood and, as a consequence, an economic treatment of neighbourhood effects. The novelty of such an approach is that it allows us to quantify the various indicators that characterise the neighbourhood and to understand the neighbourhood effect both in time and in relation to other neighbourhoods in an exact manner. The remainder of this chapter presents a selection of empirical findings and methodological aspects concerning the identification of neighbourhood effects.

Diagnosing the Neighbourhood Effects in the Literature

Based on a collection of papers presented for a special issue of *Housing Studies 9* (vol. 22, issue 5), Blasius et al. (2007) argue that research on neighbourhood effects was for a long time constrained by unsophisticated methodology despite the accumulation of a large body of literature that is truly interdisciplinary. While policy-relevant independent effects of neighbourhood on the well-being and life chances of their inhabitants have been identified widely since the early 1990s on both sides of the Atlantic, only recently have statistical methods been applied to fully verify the particularities of such phenomena using sophisticated techniques. The crucial methodological issue considers how to test whether perceived problem areas have certain features that only correlate with individual traits seen as problematic or this neighbourhood itself remains an independent and meaningful influence and determinant of the share of disadvantaged groups after the socioeconomic characteristics of the residents are controlled for and, thus indirectly, an indication of the negative state and worrying prospects of the residents of the neighbourhood under study. The key to appropriate policy implementation then is to pick the relevant particular dimension of the neighbourhood effect (schools, employment, race, etc.). If we assume the neighbourhood of the composite type (using the definitions 2(c) above), the right policy would be to encourage the moves of disadvantaged groups to affluent areas rather than dispersing rich households in to poor neighbourhoods.

This argument by Blasius et al. makes sense because it would be better to be poor in a rich neighbourhood than to be rich in a poor neighbourhood. In this regard, Koopman (2008) criticises the Dutch policy of mixing with this respect and favours the American voucher-based options as being more efficient (see also Fossett and Waren, 2005). Blasius et al., however, recognise that the country context potentially matters for the course of action to be taken in terms of mixing advantaged and disadvantaged populations.

Socioeconomic Effects

Cooke and Marchant (2006) analyse how poverty has shifted between central-city, inner-ring, and outer-ring areas in the US metropolitan areas. They use census data from two cross-sections of 1990 and 2000. Their results indicate that an increase in the number of urban core high-poverty neighbourhoods in the Northeast was associated with economic factors. However, a similar increase in the number of inner-ring neighbourhoods was found to be attributable to rapid population growth – like in Los Angeles and the Sunbelt regions.

The European experience is often presumed to be different from the American one while the British case perhaps lies in between. Rae (2009) brings up the following issues:

- In purporting a methodological revision, he applies an argument similar to that used by Kauko and Goetgeluk (2007) in their study on the Netherlands. However, unlike Kauko and Goetgeluk who selected and subsequently developed an approach based on administrative areas, Rae applies a wholly spatial approach. He also suggests areas of deprivation "... both in terms of internal characteristics and embedded in terms of spatial setting within larger concentrations of

disadvantage" rather than picking areas for special policy treatment, as Kauko and Goetgeluk did.
- Individual areas used as a basis for deprivation indices need to be related to wider spatial contexts, and such undertakings are possible using the nearest-neighbour technology and a method that allows for a varying influence of distance for different spatial structures.

Moving Behaviour

Do people move to a new home or to a new neighbourhood? And if the latter is true, which attributes of the neighbourhood are of interest? Clark and colleagues (2006) analyse residential mobility in the Netherlands using the Dutch housing demand survey (ca. 70 000 households, year 1998) as well as classifications of neighbourhood. They define neighbourhoods based on both socioeconomic status (postal codes) and environmental quality (grid based). They add to the moving behaviour literature by focusing on the role of neighbourhood quality which they find to be of substantial importance for the move. In doing so they note that there are many facets of a neighbourhood effect as the social and environmental factors impact the satisfaction, quality of life (QOL), and price, on one hand (which they refer to as the disequilibrium literature of economists), and moving propensity and housing choice on the other (the satisfaction/dissatisfaction literature). They find out that moving to a better neighbourhood without an improvement in housing quality is a relatively common path for the Dutch households. In other words, moving to a similar (or even worse) dwelling is possible. They furthermore find that the relevant household characteristics that matter for the neighbourhood choice go beyond income; as society ages, the age of the household head and the size of household become increasingly important in the moving process.

Sociocultural Factors

Hauge and Kolstad (2007) explore how the residents relate to their neighbourhood. They use a survey of 560 respondents and 18 qualitative interviews from two neighbourhoods with completely different house price ranges from Trondheim, Norway. They find out that the residents can be divided into three different groups depending on the way they express their identity via choice of neighbourhood (and indeed dwelling). One group had not thought much about the issue; another became aware of it when being prodded; and a third group was concerned about the way the neighbourhood (or dwelling) corresponds to one's taste and personality. As expected, it was the high-price neighbourhood that included residents of the third type. Interestingly, these residents had in fact lived a shorter period there, but still felt more like at home there than the ones in the cheaper neighbourhood. The differences in attitudes were, however, found to be larger between age groups than between neighbourhoods: older people showed less such perceptions than younger and middle-aged people. Overall, more than 50% of the respondents thought that identity is 'not' important.

The last sentence underlines some problematic assumptions in relation to the currently fashionable 'culturalist approach'. To claim that dwelling in general is perceived as a symbol of one's life is not entirely valid. Neighbourhood effect is a combination of many factors which may not necessary be related to identity or lifestyle choices but more to demographic, economic, financial, administrative, and political factors (see also Kauko, 2006b).

Methodological Issues

In the modelling literature, a neighbourhood is treated as an area in which the location variable (or variables, if several definitions are applied) can be assumed constant. The influence of the location variable can also be addressed as a neighbourhood influence variable and can be calculated in several ways.

Given that the neighbourhoods are reasonably homogeneous areas, the buildings in a given neighbourhood tend to be developed at the same time. Thus, one can expect properties in a neighbourhood to have similar structural characteristics such as dwelling size, vintage, and interior and exterior design features. Here we come to the topic of housing submarkets (i.e., housing market segments). Housing submarkets may, for instance, be defined by the physical characteristics of dwellings such as the number of rooms (Schnare and Struyk, 1976) or plot and floor area (Bajic, 1985). Typically, statistical techniques are used to define housing submarkets, and some heavily cited studies here are worth mentioning:

- Maclennan and Tu (1996) investigated the structure of housing submarkets in Glasgow using principal component analysis to identify the individual variables that explain the highest proportion of the variation within the data set. These variables are then used as the basis for cluster analysis, which in turn defines their submarkets.
- Goodman and Thibodeau (1998) used hierarchical methods to define submarkets in a study that focuses on the role of school districts in Dallas.
- Clapp and Wang (2006) used a classification and regression tree (CART) to construct the applicable 'neighbourhood'.
- Michaels and Smith (1990) investigated submarkets delineated by real estate agents.
- Housing market segmentation and neighbourhood effect can be analysed observing:

(a) preexisting geographic or political 'boundaries' (Goodman and Kawai, 1982, 1986; Schnare and Struyk, 1976) or
(b) 'spatial partitions' based on socioeconomic or environmental characteristics (Galster, 1987; Harsman and Quigley, 1995; Schnare, 1980).

- An operational definition based on household's utility maximisation function was offered by Vandell (1995). The work distinguished between 'homogeneous' and 'heterogeneous' neighbourhoods. In the former neighbourhood all the dwellings and the households have similar characteristics, whereas these characteristics vary in more than one dimension in the latter.

Regardless of the exact methodological approach being used, it is evident that two houses that are close substitutes may lie in the same neighbourhood. Neighbourhood residential properties share location amenities, too. For example, the same police and other local government departments protect area residents, and children in the neighbourhood have access to the same public schools. We emphasise here that the neighbourhood effect can be highlighted through market segmentation based either on property characteristics (location blind) or on spatial features. See, for example, Watkins (2001) and Wilhelmsson (2002) for specific market segmentation techniques.

Lastly, several studies have highlighted how a neighbourhood is embedded in housing prices (Goodman, 1978; Knaap, 1998). For this reason neighbourhood has become an important variable in mass appraisal and automated valuation modelling. A 'neighbourhood variable' can be included using a dummy variable indicating whether or not a property belongs to a given neighbourhood (Gloudemans, 1982). However, in doing so, the so-called dummy variable trap should be avoided. An alternative technique is the application of an 'adjustment grid' method to control such membership (Colwell et al., 1983). Finally it is possible to account for a given location influence using linearised variables such as location adjustment factors included in mass appraisal valuation process (d'Amato, 2011; McCluskey et al., 2000).

Summary and Conclusions

We have identified a number of diagnostic and methodological issues to take into account when analysing neighbourhood effects. The literature reviewed, while by no means comprehensive, offers some insight into the various facets of the complexity involved in the task of grasping neighbourhood effects. Here the literature has been evolving since the mid-1970s and already includes a sophisticated arsenal to determine neighbourhood effects with practical and political relevance. At least two issues seem to stand out in our view: that two houses that are close substitutes may lie in the same neighbourhood and that the neighbourhood effects can be an expression of house price levels. We have also shown that many of the arguments surrounding the existence, types, identification, and validity of neighbourhood effects are interlinked.

See also: Neighbourhood Effects: Approaches; Submarkets.

References

Bajic V (1985) Housing market segmentation and demand for housing attributes. *AREUEA Journal* 13(1): 58–75.

Blasius J, Friedrichs J, and Galster G (2007) Introduction: Frontiers of quantifying neighborhood effects. *Housing Studies* 22(5): 627–636.

Borst RA and McCluskey WJ (2008) The modified comparable sales method as the basis for a property tax valuations system and its relationship and comparison to spatially autoregressive valuation models. In: Kauko T and d'Amato M (eds.) *Mass Appraisal Methods – An International Perspective for Property Valuers*, pp. 49–69. RICS Series. Oxford, UK: Blackwell.

Clapp JM and Wang Y (2006) Defining neighborhood boundaries: Are census tracts obsolete? *Journal of Urban Economics* 59: 259–284.

Clark W, Deurloo M, and Dieleman F (2006) Residential mobility and neighbourhood outcomes. *Housing Studies* 21(3): 323–342.

Cooke Th and Marchant S (2006) The changing intrametropolitan location of high-poverty neighbourhoods in the US, 1990–2000. *Urban Studies* 43(11): 1971–1989.

Colwell PF, Cannady RE, and Wu C (1983) The analytical foundations of adjustment grid methods. *Journal of the American Real Estate and Urban Economics Association* 11(1): 11–29.

d'Amato M (2011) An application of location value response surface models for mass appraisal purposes in Italy. *Journal Terra Spectra* (2).

Fossett M and Waren W (2005) Overlooked implications of ethnic preferences for residential segregation in agent-based models. *Urban Studies* 42(11): 1893–1917.

Galster GC (1987) Residential segregation and interracial economic disparities: A simultaneous-equations approach. *Journal of Urban Economics* 21(1): 22–44.

Gloudemans RJ (1982) Simplified sales based models for condominium townhouse valuation. *First World Congress on Computer Assisted Valuation*. Cambridge, MA, USA.

Goodman AC (1978) Hedonic prices, price indexes and housing markets. *Journal of Urban Economics* 5: 471–484.

Goodman A and Kawai M (1982) Permanent income, hedonic prices, and demand for housing: New evidence. *Journal of Urban Economics* 12: 214–237.

Goodman AC and Masahiro K (1986) Functional form, sample selection, and housing demand. *Journal of Urban Economics* 20: 155–167.

Goodman AC and Thibodeau TG (1998) Housing market segmentation. *Journal of Housing Economics* 7: 121–143.

Harsman B and Quigley JM (1995) The spatial segregation of ethnic and demographic groups: Comparative evidence from Stockholm and San Francisco. *Journal of Urban Economics* 37: 1–16.

Hauge Å.L and Kolstad A (2007) Dwelling as an expression of identity. A comparative study among residents in high-priced and low-priced neighbourhoods in Norway. *Housing, Theory and Society* 24(4): 272–292.

Holt-Jensen A and Pollock E (eds.) (2009) *Urban Sustainability and Governance: New Challenges in Nordic-Baltic Housing Policies*. New York: Nova Science Publishers.

Kauko T (2001) Combining theoretical approaches: The case of urban land value and housing market dynamics, review article. *Housing, Theory and Society* 18(3/4): 167–173.

Kauko T (2002) *Modelling Locational Determinants of House Prices: Neural Network and Value Tree Approaches*. Doctoral dissertation, Utrecht. http://igitur-archive.library.uu.nl/dissertations/2002-1204-091756/inhoud.htm (accessed 30 October 2011).

Kauko T (2005) *Comparing Spatial Features of Urban Housing Markets: Recent Evidence of Submarket Formation in Metropolitan Helsinki and Amsterdam*. Delft, the Netherlands: DUP Science Publication.

Kauko T (2006a) What makes a location attractive for the housing consumer? Preliminary findings from metropolitan Helsinki and Randstad Holland using the analytical hierarchy process. *Journal of Housing and the Built Environment* 21: 159–176.

Kauko T (2006b) Expressions of housing consumer preferences – A proposition for a research agenda. *Housing, Theory and Society* 23(2): 92–108.

Kauko T and Goetgeluk R (2007) Analysing housing areas in the Netherlands with the Kohonen Map and GIS. *Presentation for the 2nd Nordic Geographers Meeting*. Bergen, Norway, 15–17 June 2007.

Knaap GJ (1998) The determinants of residential property values: Implications for regional planning. *Journal of Planning Literature* 12(3): 267–282.

Koopman M (2008) *The Spatial Foundations of the Housing Market*. Unpublished manuscript.

Maclennan D and Tu Y (1996) Economic perspectives on the structure of local housing system. *Housing Studies* 11(3): 387–406.

McCluskey WJ, Deddis WG, Lamont IG, and Borst RA (2000) The application of surface generated interpolation 3a models for the prediction of residential property values. *Journal of Property Investment and Finance* 18(2): 162–176.

Michaels RG and Smith VK (1990) Market segmentation and valuing amenities with hedonic models. The case of hazardous waste sites. *Journal of Urban Economics* 28: 223–242.

Needham B, Franke M, and Bosma P (1998) How the city of Amsterdam is using econometric modelling to value real estate. *Journal of Property Tax Assessment and Administration* 3(2): 25–46.

Rae A (2009) Isolated entities or integrated neighbourhoods? An alternative view of the measurement of deprivation. *Urban Studies* 46(9): 1859–1878.

Rothenberg J, Galster GC, Butler RV, and Pitkin R (1991) *The Maze of Urban Housing Markets: Theory, Evidence, and Policy*. Chicago, IL: University of Chicago Press.

Schnare AB (1980) Trends in residential segregation by race: 1960–1970. *Journal of Urban Economics* 7: 293–301.

Schnare AB and Struyk RJ (1976) Segmentation in urban housing markets. *Journal of Urban Economics* 3: 146–166.

Thériault M, Des Rosers F, and Joerin F (2005) Modelling accessibility to urban services using fuzzy logic. A comparative analysis of two methods. *Journal of Property Investment and Finance* 23(1): 22–54.

Timmermans H, Molin E, and Noortwijk L (1994) Stated versus revealed modelling approaches. *Netherlands Journal of Housing and the Built Environment* 9(3): 215–227.

Vandell KD (1995) Market factors affecting spatial heterogeneity among urban neighborhoods. *Housing Policy Debate* 6(1): 103–139.

Watkins CA (2001) The definition and identification of housing submarkets. *Environment and Planning A* 33: 2235–2253.

Wilhelmsson M (2002) Spatial models in real estate economics. *Housing Theory and Society* 19: 92–101.

Neighbourhood Effects: Approaches

M van Ham and D Manley, University of St Andrews, St Andrews, UK

© 2012 Elsevier Ltd. All rights reserved.

Glossary

Deprivation A multidimensional concept which overlaps with, but is not the same as, poverty. Concepts of deprivation include material (limited access to goods and resources) and social deprivation (limited social contacts, memberships, and power).

Experimental data Data produced by an experimental or quasi-experimental design in a controlled experiment. The data typically have a control group and a treatment group and assignment to groups is random.

Longitudinal data Data which consist of repeated observations of the same units (individuals) over time.

Neighbourhood A geographically localised community within a larger city or town. Neighbourhoods can exist at multiple spatial scales from a collection of a few houses to several streets or suburbs within a city.

Neighbourhood effect The idea that the social and physical environment of neighbourhoods can have an effect on residents' life chances over and above the effect of their individual characteristics.

Omitted-variable bias Statistical bias in estimates of parameters in a regression model as a result of omitted independent variables, often hard to measure variables not included in the data.

Reflection problem This problem occurs when the average behaviour in some group influences the behaviour of the individuals that make up the group. Problems with simultaneous causation may arise because the contextual conditions themselves may be caused by respondents' behaviour (also called the simultaneity problem).

Selection bias Statistical bias in the outcomes of a model as a result of a nonrandom sample. In studies of neighbourhood effects, selection bias can be caused by the selective mobility into and out of neighbourhoods (also called selection effects).

What Are Neighbourhood Effects?

It is widely believed by governments, policy-makers, and academics that living in deprived neighbourhoods can have a negative effect on residents' life chances over and above the effect of their individual characteristics – the so-called neighbourhood effects. An ever-increasing body of literature claims to have identified neighbourhood effects on a wide range of outcomes such as voting behaviour, educational attainment, school dropout rates, health, crime, unemployment, transitions from welfare to work, social mobility, earnings, and income. The vast majority of research on neighbourhood effects has concentrated on the assumed negative effects of living in deprived neighbourhoods. Research on the positive effects of living in wealthy neighbourhoods is rare.

The current interest in neighbourhood effects can be traced back to Wilson's (1987) book *The Truly Disadvantaged*. In this seminal work, Wilson identified an emerging group distinct from the urban poor whom he termed the underclass. Members of the underclass were predominantly ethnic minorities, experiencing severe social isolation and living in neighbourhoods with high concentrations of poverty. Wilson's thesis suggested that these individuals were worse off than would be expected based on their personal characteristics, as a result of the concentrations of poverty in which they lived.

The assumed existence of neighbourhood effects is one of the de-facto justifications behind many area-based (place) policies to tackle poverty. The idea is that if concentrations of poverty in neighbourhoods can have a negative effect on individual outcomes, then policies aimed at deconcentrating poverty, such as social mixing, could help to solve these problems. In many Western countries, mixed housing tenure policies are often used as a vehicle to create more socially mixed neighbourhoods. The idea is that mixing homeowners with social renters will create a more diverse socioeconomic mix in neighbourhoods, removing the potential of negative neighbourhood effects.

Theoretical Explanations of Neighbourhood Effects

There have been many suggestions of the potential causal connections between neighbourhood context and individual outcomes. There seems to be a broad consensus about how the underlying causal paths are thought to operate in theory. There is less consensus about which mechanisms, if any, are (the most) important. In any one neighbourhood it is likely that a wide range of mechanisms will be operating simultaneously as opposed to any single mechanism. This makes the empirical identification of neighbourhood effects highly challenging. It is debatable whether all potential causal mechanisms are relevant in all contexts. Small and Feldman (forthcoming) argue that many of the theories about neighbourhood effects have resulted from either ethnographies or case studies conducted in a small number of cities, most notably Chicago, which offer a selective reading of specific cityscapes. They demonstrate that poor neighbourhoods in Chicago are very different from poor neighbourhoods in other US cities in terms of the level of poverty, concentration of social housing, and the level of service provision. Hypotheses derived from these studies may therefore be less applicable to other cities in the United States or cities in other countries.

Galster (2012) has offered a comprehensive list of 15 potential causal pathways which may lead to neighbourhood effects, grouped into four categories: social-interactive mechanisms, environmental mechanisms, geographical mechanisms, and institutional mechanisms. Other categorisations are by Manski (1995): endogenous, exogenous, and correlated mechanisms; by Ellen and Turner (2003): concentration, location, socialisation, physical, and services; and by Leventhal and Brooks-Gunn (2000): institutional resources, relationships, and norms/collective efficacy. Here, we use the categorisation used by Galster (2012).

Social-Interactive Mechanisms

These mechanisms refer to social processes endogenous to neighbourhoods, which are generally seen as the core of the neighbourhood effects argument. Wilson's (1987) work focused largely on these mechanisms, identifying local cultures of poverty. Galster (forthcoming) identified the following mechanisms: social contagion, collective socialisation, social networks, social cohesion and control, competition, relative deprivation, and parental mediation. Socialisation is thought to take place through role models (or the lack of positive role models) encouraging individuals to conform to local social norms, such as relying on benefits. Social contagion is thought to take place through peer group effects where the behaviour of individuals is changed by contact with peers. It has been suggested that these mechanisms can lead to involvement in crime, long-term unemployment, and deviant behaviour.

Environmental Mechanisms

These mechanisms operate through natural and human-made attributes of neighbourhoods that may affect directly the mental and/or physical health of residents without affecting their behaviours. Galster (forthcoming) distinguishes these mechanisms as: exposure to violence; physical surroundings; and toxic exposure. High levels of crime may impact the well-being and functioning of individuals. Individuals may have a sense of powerlessness because of the poor state of the decayed physical conditions of their built environment. Health may also suffer because of exposure to pollutants.

Geographical Mechanisms

These mechanisms refer to the effects of the relative location of neighbourhoods. Galster (forthcoming) distinguishes spatial mismatch of jobs and workers and a lack of quality public services as important mechanisms. The spatial mismatch hypothesis (Kain, 1968) describes a broad set of geographical barriers to employment originating from the spatial separation of locations of residence and work, and a lack of transport between these locations.

Institutional Mechanisms

This category of mechanisms relates to the behaviour of actors external to neighbourhoods, who control the resources available and access to housing, services, and markets for neighbourhood residents. Galster (forthcoming) distinguishes stigmatisation, local institutional resources, and local market actors as important mechanisms. Neighbourhoods and the people within them may be stigmatised based on societal stereotypes, historical reputation, or other attributes, resulting in reduced access to, for example, jobs, mortgages (through redlining), or insurance policies. Institutions may limit access to services (such as schools or job agencies) in some neighbourhoods, adversely affecting the opportunities of residents. Commercial actors might avoid or target certain neighbourhoods resulting in negative effects on residents. Examples are the absence of local branches of banks, or the presence of liquor stores in deprived neighbourhoods. Institutional mechanisms can reinforce other mechanisms, for example, when social landlords allocate housing to vulnerable groups in the most deprived neighbourhoods, this can lead to isolation from labour markets (geographical mechanism) and expose individuals to negative role models (social-interactive mechanism).

Galster (forthcoming) used the pharmacological metaphor of 'dosage' to understand how the theoretical mechanisms identified above could be causally linked to individual outcomes. Neighbourhood residents can be exposed to a certain composition of mechanisms, over a certain time, with a certain frequency, and intensity. The relationship between the "dosage" of neighbourhood to an individual and certain outcomes may be nonlinear (thresholds), temporary or long-lasting, take time to have an effect, and only have an effect in combination with other factors. The understanding of the causal links between mechanisms and individual outcomes through empirical research is very limited.

Empirical Studies of Neighbourhood Effects

There is a vast body of literature on neighbourhood effects studying a variety of individual-level outcomes for different groups of residents (such as children, adults, men and women, and ethnic groups) in a large variety of local and national socioeconomic and political contexts. There are studies using qualitative or quantitative methods, cross-sectional or longitudinal data, and observational or (quasi-) experimental data. The current evidence base for neighbourhood effects is at best mixed and some go as far as arguing that there is little convincing evidence that living in deprived neighbourhoods really affects individual life chances (Cheshire, 2007). The variety of outcomes in studies makes it difficult to assess whether neighbourhood effects really exist. Indeed, since the literature has identified at least 15 types of effects and a range of exposure mechanisms such an assessment might even be impossible. Some types of effects might occur only in very specific neighbourhoods, in specific countries, and for specific categories of residents during one temporal period.

It is notable that studies using qualitative methods, focussing on the experiences of residents, tend to find stronger and more consistent evidence of neighbourhood effects than studies using quantitative methods. For example, using qualitative methods, neighbourhood effects have been identified in relation to neighbourhood reputation and employment outcomes (see Atkinson and Kintrea, 2001). Similarly, work investigating the social capital of residents has found ample evidence of neighbourhood effects occurring in deprived neighbourhoods. In comparison, studies using quantitative methods do not show such a consistent evidence base. Musterd and Andersson (2005) found evidence for neighbourhood effects on social mobility using Swedish longitudinal data. Oreopoulos (2003) using Canadian longitudinal data, and Van Ham and Manley (2010) using Scottish longitudinal data, found little evidence of neighbourhood effects on long-run labour market outcomes.

Studies using cross-sectional data often claim to have found evidence for neighbourhood effects, while the majority of studies using longitudinal data found no effects, although there are some important exceptions. Studies using cross-sectional data can only show correlations between neighbourhood characteristics and individual-level outcomes, but cannot show causal effects. Longitudinal data do allow the identification of cause and effect as these can be separated over time. Finally, there are different outcomes for (quasi-) experimental studies and studies using observational data. Durlauf (2004) reports that quasi-experimental studies, such as the Gautreaux and Moving to Opportunity programmes, find little impact of neighbourhood characteristics on adults' outcomes, while the bulk of nonexperimental observational studies do find effects. It has been argued that most existing 'evidence' from nonexperimental observational studies suffers from reverse causality (Cheshire, 2007; Durlauf, 2004).

Methodological Challenges in Measuring Neighbourhood Effects

Studies consistently find that people living in deprived neighbourhoods are less likely than people in affluent neighbourhoods to do well in life. However, this does not necessarily mean that living in deprived neighbourhoods causes people to do less well. A major challenge in the empirical investigation of neighbourhood effects is the (econometric) identification of causal relationships. Many studies which claim to have found causal neighbourhood effects are likely to have only found correlations between neighbourhood characteristics and individual outcomes, without clear evidence of the direction of causation. Moffitt (1998) distinguishes three general problems in the investigation of neighbourhood effects: the simultaneity problem; the omitted-context-variables problem; and the endogenous membership problem.

The simultaneity problem, also referred to as Manski's (1993) reflection problem, arises when a researcher tries to infer whether the average behaviour in some group influences the behaviour of the individuals that make up the group. Problems with simultaneous causation may arise because the contextual conditions themselves may be caused by respondents' behaviour (endogenous effect). For example, if we are interested in determining whether a high crime rate in a neighbourhood causes residents to be more likely to be involved in crime, an econometric problem arises because individuals committing crimes in the neighbourhood contribute to the neighbourhood crime rate. Partial solutions can be found in relating past crime rates to current criminal behaviour, which has the advantage that cause and effect are ordered in time.

A second problem is the omitted-context-variables problem, also called the correlated unobservables problem. This problem arises if important context characteristics are omitted from a regression model and these unobserved variables (at the neighbourhood level) are correlated with included variables. If important variables are omitted, researchers might draw the wrong conclusions from the estimated effects of context variables which are included. For instance, high concentrations of ethnic minorities in neighbourhoods have frequently been reported to be correlated with high crime rates. Concluding that high concentrations of ethnic minorities cause crime levels to be high is likely to be too simple. Ethnic concentration neighbourhoods are often also deprived neighbourhoods, and deprivation, and not ethnicity is likely to be the real causal explanation (this is known as the racial proxy hypothesis).

A third problem is the endogenous membership problem. This problem also involves omitted variables, but this time relating to the individual. The core of this problem is self-selection into neighbourhoods. Sorting into neighbourhoods is not based on a random process and if unobserved individual characteristics are correlated with both the location decision and the dependent variable, endogeneity occurs. In most studies, it is likely that selective mobility into neighbourhoods leads to biased estimates of neighbourhood effects. The key question is, "Do poor people live in poor neighbourhoods because living in affluent ones costs too much?" Or, "Does living in a poor neighbourhood make poor people significantly poorer?" (Cheshire, 2007). A model estimating the income effects of living in a deprived neighbourhood will show a high negative correlation between income and neighbourhood deprivation. The challenge is to separate the selection effect from any real neighbourhood effect.

An additional challenge in neighbourhood effects research is the identification of the appropriate spatial scale at which to measure neighbourhood characteristics. The issue of scale is frequently omitted from discussions in the empirical literature, but theoretical contributions highlight that the scale at which the neighbourhood is conceptualised is an important component of the neighbourhood effects thesis. Important questions relating to scale and neighbourhood boundaries are often not asked because administrative units are used as proxies for neighbourhoods driven by the availability of data. This is a problem because spatial scale should be driven by the mechanism and hypothesis under investigation. For example, testing hypotheses on the effect of neighbourhood reputation or neighbourhood stigma might require larger neighbourhood units than studies testing hypotheses on peer group effects.

Evidence from Studies using Experimental Data

The use of experimental data is generally regarded as the gold standard in neighbourhood effects research because it offers the potential to avoid problems with selection bias if the assignment to control group and treatment group is completely random. A range of studies using (quasi-) experimental data emerged from the United States through the Gautreux Project, Moving to Opportunity for Fair Housing programme (MTO), and HOPE VI programme. The idea behind these programmes was that households were randomly selected for 'treatment' (e.g., a move to a better neighbourhood), and their outcomes were compared to others who had not received the 'treatment' (remained in their neighbourhoods). Data generated by the programmes have been heavily researched using both qualitative and quantitative methodologies. Studies have found mixed evidence that individuals who participated in these programmes have experienced improved outcomes in labour market participation, youth school achievement, and health as a result of moving away from concentrated poverty into more affluent neighbourhoods. The evidence seems stronger for younger people than for adults.

The claim that the programmes randomly allocated individuals and households into various programme initiatives has been heavily criticised. For instance, in the Gautreux programme, individual households had to apply in order to participate and were only accepted under the conditions that they did not have a criminal record or had not previously defaulted on rental payments. As a result, around one-third of applicants deemed unsuitable for the programme were rejected. The route of entry and the conditions attached mean that selection into the programme was far from random. Another criticism made was that the improvements observed in individual outcomes were not gains from lower levels of poverty in the new neighbourhood per se but from the structural advantages of living in suburban areas, such as schools, public services, and job accessibility (Galster and Zobel, 1998).

In a study evaluating the claims made for the success of the MTO programme, Clark (2008) compared outcomes for residents who had been given vouchers and counselling prior to moving with residents who had only received housing vouchers. Clark did not identify any significant differences between the two populations and found that individuals who had not been given any assistance had still made gains through moving to neighbourhoods with lower levels of poverty. He concluded that many of the studies that had reported an advantage were poorly conceived or failed to take into account the appropriate populations for comparison. The gains reported were more likely to be the result of structural changes rather than effects directly relating to the neighbourhood and the social environment.

Developments in Neighbourhood Effects Research

Controlling for selection effects is one of the main challenges in neighbourhood effects research. People do not randomly select neighbourhoods and studies failing to control this are likely to show biased results. Large-scale experimental designs are the best way to avoid selection bias, but such studies are very expensive and there are practical and ethical issues regarding the selection of households into treatment and control groups. There are several alternatives to collecting experimental data. The first is to construct quasi-natural experiments. Several studies have investigated neighbourhood effects separately for social renters and homeowners. The argument was that social renters are allocated dwellings and neighbourhoods by social landlords, while homeowners have more freedom in choosing where to live. So to some extent it can be argued that the neighbourhood selection of social renters (before choice-based letting was introduced) was not driven by household preferences. Several studies have found 'neighbourhood effects' for homeowners, but not for social renters, suggesting that selection effects and not causal effects were responsible for the findings (see Oreopoulos, 2003; Van Ham and Manley, 2010).

Another way forward is the use of longitudinal data which allows researchers to follow people over time. This would, for example, allow researchers to include neighbourhood selection in models estimating neighbourhood effects. By using longitudinal data, it is possible to investigate the ordering of events that lead to certain outcomes, and thereby establishing causal pathways. Ideally, both qualitative and quantitative studies using longitudinal data should take people's histories into account and not only look at the effect of the current neighbourhood, but of all previous neighbourhoods. Longitudinal data also allow the study of duration effects. It can be expected that exposure to some neighbourhood attributes only has an effect on individual outcomes if residents are exposed over a longer period of time.

Several econometric solutions have been suggested to solve some of the problems discussed. One solution is to use an instrumental variable approach to overcome self-selection. This approach offers great potential, but requires the data to include the necessary instruments. A technique to get more insight into the effect of omitted-variable bias is the use of fixed effects models, which 'fix' all the individual-level characteristics, whether measured or unmeasured. Estimates of neighbourhood effects using such models are regarded as less biased than estimates from standard regression models.

Another development in neighbourhood effects research is the use of mixed-methods strategies, preferably incorporated within the same study design. Both qualitative and quantitative approaches have their strengths and weaknesses: Qualitative studies are better able to identify the specific mechanisms at play, while quantitative studies have the potential to produce more generalisable outcomes. Finally, researchers have called for a more careful approach to theory generation, based on a wider range of cities and neighbourhoods (Small and Feldman, forthcoming). It has been argued that much (quantitative) neighbourhood effects research does not test any specific hypotheses derived from specific theories. The literature has identified at least 15 causal pathways between neighbourhood context and individual outcomes, and studies should attempt to identify which causal pathway (if any) is at work and through what mechanisms neighbourhood characteristics identify individual outcomes. Especially the potential impact of threshold and duration effects should be investigated (Galster, forthcoming).

See also: Economics of Housing Choice; HOPE VI; Housing and Neighbourhood Quality: Urban Regeneration; Neighbourhood Disadvantage; Neighbourhood Effects; Neighbourhood Improvement: The Role of Housing and Housing Institutions; Neighbourhood Reputation; Policies to Address Social Mix in Communities; Residential Segregation and Ethnic Diversity in the United States; Residential Segregation: Race and Ethnicity; Social Housing and Social Problems; Social Housing: Allocation; Social Mix in Western Countries; Spatial Mismatch.

References

Atkinson R and Kintrea K (2001) Disentangling area effects: Evidence from deprived and non-deprived neighbourhoods. *Urban Studies* 38: 2277–2298.

Cheshire P (2007) *Segregated Neighbourhoods and Mixed Communities*. York, UK: Joseph Rowntree Foundation.

Clark WAV (2008) Re-examining the moving to opportunity study and its contribution to changing the distribution of poverty and ethnic concentration. *Demography* 45: 515–535.

Durlauf SN (2004) Neighbourhood effects. In: Henderson JV and Thisse JF (eds.) *Handbook of Regional and Urban Economics, Vol. 4: Cities and Geography*, pp. 2173–2242. Amsterdam: Elsevier.

Ellen IG and Turner MA (2003) Do neighborhoods matter and why? In: Goering J and Feins J (eds.) *Choosing a Better Life? Evaluating the Moving to Opportunity Experiment*, pp. 313–338. Washington, DC: Urban Institute Press.

Galster G (2012) The mechanism(s) of neighbourhood effects: Theory, evidence and policy implications. In: Van Ham M, Manley D, Bailey N, Simpson L, and Maclennan D (eds.) *Neighbourhood Effects Research: New Perspectives*, pp 23–36. Dordrecht: Springer.

Galster G and Zobel A (1998) Will dispersed housing programs reduce social problems in the US? *Housing Studies* 13: 605–622.

Kain J (1968) Housing segregation, Negro employment, and metroploitan decentralization. *Quarterly Journal of Economics* 82: 175–219.

Leventhal T and Brooks-Gunn J (2000) The neighborhoods they live in. *Psychological Bulletin* 126: 309–337.

Manski C (1993) Identification of endogenous social effects: The reflection problem. *Review of Economic Studies* 60: 531–542.

Manski CF (1995) *Identification Problems in the Social Sciences*. Cambridge, MA: Harvard University Press.

Moffitt R (1998) *Policy Interventions, Low-Level Equilibria, and Social Interactions*. WP 432. Baltimore, MD: Department of Economics, Johns Hopkins University.

Musterd S and Andersson R (2005) Housing mix, social mix and social opportunities. *Urban Affairs Review* 40: 761–790.

Oreopoulos P (2003) The long-run consequences of living in a poor neighborhood. *Quarterly Journal of Economics* 118: 1533–1575.

Small ML and Feldman J (forthcoming) Ethnographic evidence and neighborhood effects: Strong and weak approaches to testing propositions from the field. In: Van Ham M, Manley D, Bailey N, Simpson L, and Maclennan D (eds.) Neighbourhood Effects Research: New Perspectives. Dordrecht: Springer.

Van Ham M and Manley D (2010) The effect of neighbourhood housing tenure mix on labour market outcomes: A longitudinal investigation of neighbourhood effects. *Journal of Economic Geography* 10: 257–282.

Wilson WJ (1987) *The Truly Disadvantaged: The Inner City, the Underclass and Public Policy*. Chicago, IL: University of Chicago Press.

Further Reading

Dietz RD (2002) The estimation of neighborhood effects in the social sciences: An interdisciplinary approach. *Social Science Research* 31: 539–575.

Galster G (2001) On the nature of neighbourhood. *Urban Studies* 38: 2111–2124.

Ioannides Y and Zabel J (2002) Neighbourhood effects and housing demand. *Journal of Applied Econometrics* 18: 563–584.

Katz LF, Kling JR, and Liebman JB (2001) Moving to opportunity in Boston: Early results of a randomized mobility experiment. *Quarterly Journal of Economics* 116: 607–654.

Sarkissian S (1976) The idea of social mix in town planning: An historical overview. *Urban Studies* 13: 231–246.

Small ML and Stark L (2005) Are poor neighborhoods resource deprived? A case study of childcare centers in New York. *Social Science Quarterly* 86: 1013–1036.

Cisneros HG and Engdahl L (eds.) (2009) *From Despair to Hope: Hope VI and the Transformation of America's Public Housing*. Washington, DC: Brookings Institute Press.

Kling JR, Liebman JB, and Katz LF (2007) Experimental analysis of neighborhood effects. *Econometrica* 75: 83–119.

Pickett KE and Pearl M (2001) Multilevel analyses of neighbourhood socioeconomic context and health outcomes: A critical review. *Journal of Epidemiology and Community Health* 55: 111–122.

Sampson RJ (2008) Moving to inequality: Neighborhood effects and experiments meet social structure. *American Journal of Sociology* 114: 189–231.

Tunstall R and Fenton A (2006) *In the Mix: A Review of Mixed Income, Mixed Tenure and Mixed Communities*. York, UK: Joseph Rowntree Foundation, English Partnerships, and the Housing Corporation.

Van Ham M, Manley D, Bailey N, Simpson L, and Maclennan D (eds.) (forthcoming) *Neighbourhood Effects Research: New Perspectives*. Dordrecht: Springer

Wacquant L (1993) Urban outcasts: Stigma and division in the black American ghetto and the French periphery. *International Journal of Urban and Regional Research* 17: 366–383.

Relevant Websites

http://www.neighbourhoodeffects.org – CHR-led ESCR Seminar Series on Neighbourhood Effects

http://www.tc.umn.edu – University of Minnesota

Neighbourhood Governance

A Madanipour, Newcastle University, Newcastle upon Tyne, UK

© 2012 Elsevier Ltd. All rights reserved.

Glossary

Communitarian The idea that community has been under threat and needs to be given more priority as compared to individual self-interest or state control.

Comprehensive planning A method of planning for urban and regional development that aimed at addressing all the relevant issues with a long-term perspective.

Governance The set of actions and institutions that frame the life and material conditions of an organisation or a place; a map of how power is distributed within an organisation or a place.

Localism The opposite of centralism, the idea that economy, politics, and culture are best managed at the local level and under local control.

Neighbourhood charters The 2006 UK Local Government White Paper advocated setting up neighbourhood charters as formal agreements at the neighbourhood level, defining local standards and priorities.

Participatory budgeting Allocating a part of the city's revenues to the priorities set by citizen assemblies in local neighbourhoods.

Phenomenological value of place Attaching value to a place through subjective experience.

Social capital The strength of social relationships and networks.

Defining Neighbourhood Governance

Neighbourhoods are parts of towns and cities, as defined by their distinctive social and physical features, administrative subdivisions, or just perceived as a locality by their residents, and hence without any clear or fixed boundaries. Neighbourhoods' geographic boundaries, therefore, may or may not coincide with local government administrative boundaries. The first tier of local government in England and Wales is the parish, community, and town councils, with elected members and limited formal powers, which include planning, promoting tourism, licensing, representation, management of town and village centres, and providing community halls. The examples of the first tier in other countries are the communes in France and *Gemeinden* in Germany, where part of the political power resides with the local councils. The extent of power, population, and territory varies in these examples, nested as they are in higher levels of government and rooted in different histories and traditions. One of the most radical forms of local political power was advocated by Thomas Jefferson, the principal author of the American Declaration of Independence, who wanted wards to be the most powerful units of government, with other levels of county, state, and federal government having limited powers.

In addition to political boundaries, a host of other services subdivide an area in various ways and according to their own distribution of resources. Public and private organisations dealing with housing, health, education, police, water, electricity, gas, and so on may each have completely different territorial subdivisions. In a relatively small part of a town or city, therefore, there is always a variety of actors and institutions involved, with or without coordination with one another. This multiplicity and complexity entails attention to governance even at the neighbourhood level.

Neighbourhood associations are yet another level of organisation at the neighbourhood level. These are relatively formalised groups which work together on some local issue of common concern, such as housing and crime. These associations can act as a local forum for citizen participation, mobilising local actors, mediating between various stakeholders, including policy-makers and residents, and contributing to democratic governance. These associations can generate stronger connections between the residents and the neighbourhood and improve the quality of life in the neighbourhood.

The UN-HABITAT defines urban governance as the sum of the many ways individuals and institutions, public and private, plan and manage the common affairs of the city. It is a continuing process through which conflicting or diverse interests may be accommodated and cooperative action can be taken. It includes formal institutions as well as informal arrangements and the relationships between citizens. It acknowledges that people, community and voluntary organisations, private sector operators, as well as the local government all have a stake in the conditions of a locality. This would imply that nonstate actors are involved in the formulation, decision-making, and implementation of public policy. The concept of governance could be applied to different administrative levels and spatial scales. Neighbourhood governance refers to the range of actions and institutions that frame the life and material conditions of a neighbourhood.

The Context of Neighbourhood Governance

Concern with neighbourhood governance, and governance in general, has arisen as a result of major political and economic changes in recent decades. The changing relationship between the public and private sectors, as part of a larger strategy to reduce the size of the state and encourage private enterprise, has transformed the management and delivery of services in urban neighbourhoods. Whereas many services were once delivered by public agencies, there is now a multiplication of public and private agencies, at times with overlapping and competing roles. Concerns for coordinating these agencies and their actions within a particular area have given rise to the notion of governance.

Some analysts have called it a transition from government to governance: a transition from a situation in which most services are delivered or managed by the government, to a situation in which other agencies and people are also involved. In the United States and the United Kingdom, this transition started in the 1980s, when large-scale privatisation reduced the size of the government. During the period after the Second World War, governments had grown to manage many areas of activity, through nationalisation of industries, health care, and education, among others. In cities, this was reflected in comprehensive planning, development of large-scale public housing schemes, major road-building projects, and a range of subsidised public services. However, with the considerable economic difficulties of the 1970s, governments at national and local levels were not able or willing to fund these ambitious programmes any more. In response, a major ideological and policy shift privatised many of these activities, which energised the economy and gave the markets new powers, while reducing the government's sphere of activities and their costs. Transition from government to governance indicated a change in the relationship between the state and the economy.

The new governance ideas encourage all the stakeholders to work together. But this would be far easier if the agenda is clear and immediate. Focus on the neighbourhood would provide such an opportunity; it would allow the stakeholders to work together around a concrete agenda, set clear visions, and combine their forces to address specific problems. Furthermore, focus on place has helped some governments to restructure some of their functions, crossing the departmental boundaries for new forms of collaboration, and moving from functional to spatial division of labour. It has enabled establishing horizontal links between different agencies, as distinct from vertical and hierarchical functional organisations. In addressing the problems of social exclusion and poverty, it has been noticed that some neighbourhoods are concentrations of disadvantaged and vulnerable people. Attention to neighbourhood, it has been thought, would address the problems where they are most acute.

Social Diversity and Neighbourhood Governance

A neighbourhood is not a homogeneous environment; it is often formed of different people with different degrees of power and different identities. Focus on the neighbourhood does not necessarily provide equality of access to decision-making for people within that place. There will be differences of power and influence, and those who are politically and economically powerful are more likely to drive the agenda, while many other voices may remain on the margins.

In addition to differential access to resources, there is a diversity of identity. There is a general tendency by people outside an area to consider it as a uniform place, which could stigmatise people there en masse. The impact of trying to understand the conditions from within should give us a more nuanced sense of this diversity. There is much emphasis in the literature on the phenomenological value of place, without developing it any further to explore its implications for action. We need to distinguish the notion of place as held by individuals and households, from groups and communities. There are different dynamics involved at these different levels of analysis and intervention. Some localities have a more established sense of identity, especially if people have lived together long enough, while other places are formed of transient populations, and their place can easily become a site of tension and conflict. There is a difference between middle-class neighbourhoods, where the residents are mobilised and have membership of different social networks and are vocal in their demands and expectations, and the deprived neighbourhoods, where there is a feeling of powerlessness and inability to mobilise. There is also a difference between seeing neighbourhood governance as an empowering process or as coordination between outside and inside stakeholders. There is a difference between communitarian, republican, and liberal visions of neighbourhood governance, which advocate different forms of social life and power distribution at the local level.

Economic resources and political capacities are necessary for good governance, but not sufficient on their own. The experience of participatory budgeting in Latin America, for example, has been innovative, whereby a part of the city's revenues has been allocated to the priorities set by citizen assemblies in districts. This is a format that brings politics and economics together, and people can see that participation can lead to tangible results. Political and economic arenas, however, are often kept apart in most local areas. People have been mobilised in networks and organisations, but they are not given control over resources due to concerns about legitimacy; or resources are poured in, as in European urban regeneration schemes, but participatory networks are not in place. In both cases, the results can be ineffective, because of the lack of ability to attract or absorb resources. Also important are cultural resources, whereby individuals and groups can share experiences and express themselves, as part of the process of shaping their places.

Privatisation of Neighbourhood Governance

The trend of creating gated neighbourhoods has spread across the world, now evident in all continents. While the United States may have the largest number of such neighbourhoods, many other countries are reported to have set up walled and gated enclaves. The primary form of new residential development in China is a gated neighbourhood, where such gating has historic roots in the country. The reasons for gating are numerous, including the exclusive use of urban amenities, protection of property values, assertion of social status, and social control, but chief among these reasons has been the issue of safety and fear of crime. Gating is ultimately about control of space and management of strangers, with substantial implications for the governance of such places. The emergence of these often wealthy enclaves has been associated with an increase in social inequality, which has been experienced in much of the world in the past two decades. They have also been the result of urban regeneration processes that have gentrified parts of the cities, creating sharp divides between social groups within a locality. A gated community is a new development beyond the reach of the public, run by private property management and security companies, sometimes empowered to make demands on the residents that may not be possible in other parts of the city. In some countries, such as South Africa, gating has even been introduced in the existing parts of cities, so that a group of residents can set up fences and gates, blocking public roads and controlling access to the area. While those who are inside the walls may feel they are benefiting from added protection, the negative impacts on those who are outside the walls, that is, the majority of the population, are considerable, leading to fears of fragmentation and polarisation in cities.

The local governance in these cases resembles the organisation of a private club, in which the members may appoint a group to manage the place or hire management and security companies to do so on their behalf. The members may enter a contractual relationship, through which they agree to make payment and observe certain limitations. While there may be some similarities between this arrangement and other housing management systems, here the introduction of barriers and gates establishes visible boundaries and fortress governance, with negative impact on others outside.

Another example of an additional layer of private control in local governance is in the business improvement districts, where local businesses pay towards additional services, such as street cleaning and security as well as environmental improvement and marketing. Their boards work with the municipality, and as such are public–private partnerships with members from property owners, occupiers, and the local government. However, setting up a private club for the local businesses brings about higher demands on their members and the rest of the public. They improve but also place restrictions on public spaces, and go some way towards privatisation of neighbourhood governance. In both cases – gated neighbourhoods and improvement districts – a private layer is added to the local governance, justified by economic or security concerns, which renders it an exclusive part of the city, with reduced levels of public access and interest. It resembles the workings of a private shopping mall, as much as it is a semipermeable part of a city.

Features of Good Governance

Different organisations have developed key indicators for good governance. In the European Union (EU), to address the gap between people and the EU institutions, a programme of governance reform was introduced in 2001 in an EU white paper, which set out the principles of good governance as openness, participation, accountability, effectiveness, and coherence. These are principles operating at the national and international levels, encouraging the European member states to improve their practices at all levels, so that they can open their doors to engage their citizens in national and European affairs. We also see these principles in the UN-HABITAT's Urban Governance Index, which includes effectiveness, equity, participation, and accountability. The essential message in both the EU and UN principles is how to make the government more responsive as well as more effective. The key is how to strike a balance between effectiveness and accountability, while making sure that everyone is treated equally and has a chance to participate in the affairs of the city. If all the resources of individuals and institutions were used, the city could be more effective in solving its problems, but the challenge is to regulate this process, so that everyone can make a contribution without the fear of discrimination and corruption. At the neighbourhood level, where elected representation exists, these challenges would similarly apply. Even in neighbourhoods that lack such level of government, the issues surrounding urban governance are reflected clearly in the neighbourhood's everyday life.

Governance is the institutional framework within which economic pressures and political and cultural demands meet. We need to be clear that governance is not an opposite term to government, although some have tended to see this as such. Governance is the morphology of power, a map of where power lies and how it is distributed within an organisation or a place. It shows that power lies not only in the realm of the state and large private companies, but also in civil society groups and individuals. Democratic governance presents a normative agenda – that these other sources of power should be taken seriously. To do so, power should be distributed in new ways and mobilised to achieve local objectives. It involves discovering new sources of power and going beyond a zero-sum game. An optimistic reading of this transformation is that beyond global economics and national politics, there are local sources of power, and that an active and well-coordinated local population can take charge of its own destiny. However, this has failed to materialise for many places, either for the poor neighbourhoods in rich western cities or for many parts of the developing world, showing the limits of localism.

In addition to economic resources, there are at least two sets of resources that are necessary for effective governance: ideas and capacities. Ideas cover knowledge and skills, as well as imagination as to what can be done. Do people know what might be possible? Do they have access to information? This is hardly the case in many poor neighbourhoods, where low levels of education and absence of effective communication limit the prospect of even knowing what might be possible. The first step in solving a problem is defining it, which in many cases can be improved by a better knowledge of the world. Another question is: Do people know what their own capacities are? The impact of community development work has sometimes been very significant in showing to people that they can change things by working together. It has mobilised new sources of power that were not recognised before. A further question is: Do they know what external resources are available? The individuals and agencies involved need to be well supported.

The third set of resources belongs to capacities, including skills, social networks and institutional frameworks within which actions take place. Is the rule of law there in place? Is there sufficient freedom for people to work together? As Amartya Sen has argued, democracy is an important precondition for development. What is the shape of forums, networks, and institutions that enable people to work together? Are there leaders and network builders in the place? The strength of local networks and institutions that make up civil society is a necessary condition for a place to mobilise and use resources effectively. Where resources are scarce, populations fragmented and transient, and democratic institutions weak, conflict dominates the lives of people, making every incident a major battle to overcome. Forums and institutions in which people can negotiate their differences and solve their problems are often missing. Even when such forums are available, long-established, or new, their success depends on the existence of a number of other channels of communication, which are available in a functioning public sphere.

Public Services and Neighbourhood Governance

Emphasis on local participation, however, has sometimes led to a degree of localism that would even become more fragmentary than before. The spatial form of this localism has been the emphasis on urban development and management through neighbourhoods. One of the key features of focusing on neighbourhoods has been a pressure for engaging citizens in decision-making and service delivery. The Local Government White Paper by the British government in 2006 aimed to link citizen participation with public service delivery through neighbourhood arrangements. It outlined the challenges facing governments across Europe to be able to secure sustainable improvements in our public services and to reengage our citizens with the institutions of government. An important part of the answer, it was argued, lies at the neighbourhood level by promoting and developing activities that can harness people's interests in these local issues. The quality of services would improve by making them more responsive, enabling residents to be involved in making decisions that would affect their lives, enabling public service providers to work with community and voluntary groups to deliver better services, and building social capital and promoting social capacity and cohesion. The white paper proposed neighbourhood charters that would enable neighbourhoods to develop their own institutional arrangements, in which different stakeholders can work together to improve public services and enjoy a better quality of environment.

Focus on the neighbourhood is important, especially in deprived areas. These are places where many social problems come together due to a concentration of vulnerable populations, a phenomenon that is common across

Europe. It is essential that these neighbourhoods can benefit from some governance arrangements that would allow their residents to negotiate their differences and develop their capacities. Therefore, it is appropriate that some solutions be neighbourhood-based, integrating different activities and services. However, these problems are not all generated in these neighbourhoods; neighbourhoods are only spatial manifestations of these problems, which themselves lead to new problems for vulnerable populations. Furthermore, too much focus on the neighbourhood level would go against strategic thinking and equality of treatment across the city.

The method of representation in British democracy is geographical, and so there is already an institutional focus on neighbourhoods in the form of ward councillors. To improve citizen engagement, a theme-based, rather than space-based, approach may also be needed to ensure a more complete coverage of issues. Would creation of a multilevel governance hierarchy be a better solution than a crosscutting matrix of geographies and themes? The problem remains institutional design: Do we need particular organisations associated with particular areas? Research evidence suggests a forum is useful in negotiating different and competing needs, but also that it can turn into a bureaucratic and undemocratic exercise. Or, do we need reorganisation of the existing services on a spatial basis and encouraging them to network and collaborate? Experience in Denmark and the United Kingdom suggests moving away from local arrangements such as area committees, what some Danish politicians called 'little kingdoms'.

Focus on the neighbourhood can make joined up work possible, but it should take into account the diversity of a neighbourhood, rather than expecting it to be one homogeneous group having one voice. Therefore, the institutional design of a forum at the neighbourhood level needs to be sophisticated and flexible. The experience of European countries shows that even where democratic institutional arrangements have been in place at the neighbourhood level, they have not necessarily worked well with new immigrant populations, who may not share the norms and practices embedded in these institutions.

A major point is the distinction between deprived neighbourhoods and other urban areas, as their conditions, problems, and therefore solutions would be different. The key challenge is how to provide new neighbourhood arrangements that are universal enough to be fair, while helping those who need it the most. By their nature, the arrangements in deprived neighbourhoods will be different from the affluent ones. Even if legal and institutional provisions are the same, problems and solutions in these different neighbourhoods will be different. At the same time, in the interest of fairness and equality, when dealing with deprived neighbourhoods, we need to ask: Would we approach things in the same way for better-off neighbourhoods? All discussions of participation seem to focus on deprived neighbourhoods, to ensure better delivery of services. Do we expect middle-class neighbourhoods to participate in community affairs and take pride in their neighbourhood charter? Overall, they enjoy the freedom of getting involved if they want to, and they do so when they feel there are problems that are not being attended to by the authorities.

A key question is whether it is appropriate to relate citizen engagement to public services. This may reduce the relationship between citizens and the government to a narrow utilitarian one. However, if democracy is collective self-rule, then the relationship should be multidimensional. Middle-class citizens feel they are entitled to the services they pay for through their taxes, and do not want to have to be involved in matters that they consider to be in the domain of the relevant service providers. Should the residents of deprived neighbourhoods not be entitled to the same level of services without having to be involved? Maybe the link between active citizenry and good services lies in improving the mechanisms of accountability in local governance, as well as providing better resources for local service providers. While a degree of control over resources would encourage more participation, it should be remembered that the capacity for using these resources effectively depends on the area's strength of civil society, as evidence from Latin American cases shows. Evidence from the United Kingdom shows that without such capacities, local committees were unable even to spend their budgets.

Some neighbourhood arrangements are potentially positive in the enhancement of civil society. However, by definition, civil society falls outside the sphere of the state. The question is how far should (or could) the state intervene in the development of what lies outside its sphere of activity. Would it not lead to a degree of institutionalisation and bureaucratisation of civil society? By connecting civil society to state activities, there is a danger of making it dependent on, rather than independent of, the state. Investing in people's capacity to grow their own arrangements may have better, more democratic results. The UK experience has shown that investment in community empowerment can lead to a more active citizenry. However, local politicians are at times afraid of this challenging source of power, and are slow to learn how to work with it, rather than expecting it to be dragged into a long bureaucratic process.

See also: Community- and Neighbourhood-Based Organisations in the United States; Gated Communities; Ghetto; Homeowners' Associations in Post-Socialist Countries; Tenant Cooperatives, Shareholders' Housing Companies.

References

Department for Communities and Local Government (2006) Strong and Prosperous Communities: The Local Government White Paper, http://www.communities.gov.uk/publications/localgovernment/strongprosperous

Further Reading

Antalovsky E, Dangschat J, and Parkinson M (eds.) (2005) *European Metropolitan Governance: Cities in Europe – Europe in the Cities*. Vienna, Austria: Node.

Blakely E and Snyder MG (1999) *Fortress America: Gated Communities in the United States*. Washington, DC: Brookings Institution Press.

European Commission (2001) *European Governance: A White Paper*. Brussels, Belgium: Commission of the European Communities.

Glasze G, Webster C, and Frantz K (eds.) (2006) *Private Cities: Global and Local Perspectives*. London: Routledge.

Madanipour A, Hull A, and Healey P (eds.) (2001) *Governance of Place*. Aldershot, UK: Ashgate.

Madanipour A, Cars G, and Allen J (eds.) (2003) *Social Exclusion in European Cities: Processes, Experiences, Responses*. London: Routledge.

Mitchell J (2008) *Business Improvement Districts and the Shape of American Cities*. Albany, NY: Suny Press.

Office of the Deputy Prime Minister (ODPM) (2005) *Citizen Engagement and Public Services: Why Neighbourhoods Matter*. London: ODPM.

Sen A (1999) *Development as Freedom*. New York: Alfred Knopf.

Souza C (2001) Participatory budgeting in Brazilian cities: Limits and possibilities in building democratic institutions. *Environment and Urbanization* 13(1): 159–184.

Stoker G (2003) *Transforming Local Governance: From Thatcherism to New Labour*. Basingstoke, UK: Palgrave Macmillan.

Relevant Websites

www.infra.kth.se and www.dublinpact.ie. – Some of the author's research projects on neighbourhood governance, on which this article is based, can be found in these websites.

www.unhabitat.org – UN-HABITAT's indicators of good governance.

Neighbourhood Improvement: The Role of Housing and Housing Institutions

T Carter, University of Winnipeg, Winnipeg, MB, Canada

© 2012 Elsevier Ltd. All rights reserved.

Glossary

Affordable housing Adequate dwellings that cost low-income people less than, typically, 30% of their gross household income.

Asset-building programmes Programmes targeted at those with low income to teach skills in budgeting and money management and to save money for home purchases.

Housing institutions Public, private, or not-for-profit community-based organisations whose mandate is principally to provide new or renovated housing.

Neighbourhood Although not all neighbourhoods are homogeneous, they are generally areas containing people of broadly similar demographic, social, and economic characteristics where there may be elements of close community interaction.

Neighbourhood decline The concentration of multiple types of deprivation ranging from poverty to health problems, low levels of education and employment, to poor-quality housing in urban neighbourhoods.

Neighbourhood improvement The revitalisation of rundown neighbourhoods.

Social capital The shared knowledge, understanding, and patterns of interaction that people bring to initiatives such as neighbourhood improvement.

Introduction

Neighbourhood improvement is a programme-based approach to reduce deprivation in areas characterised by decline. Programmes generally have at least four dimensions: community capacity building to develop confident communities through educational initiatives and development of social capital; economic renewal to generate economic investment, job creation, and development of small businesses; social renewal to improve social conditions through better-coordinated public services, improving health and creating safer neighbourhoods; and physical renewal of housing and infrastructure to create more attractive environments and more affordable, quality housing. The following discussion highlights the prominent role that housing and housing institutions can play in facilitating successful neighbourhood improvement.

Neighbourhoods can be defined in many ways. Geographically, they are localised communities within an urban centre, often defined by specific boundaries such as streets and rivers. They normally contain people with similar demographic, economic, and social backgrounds. People may have a sense of belonging to the neighbourhood and there are areas where people share local facilities (education and recreation functions, for example) and belong to local organisations. Neighbourhoods become the geographic focus for the organisation and articulation of local issues. They may be the basis for social interaction and the development of social cohesion, or social exclusion. These characteristics make neighbourhoods the logical focus for housing initiatives and the actions of housing institutions to deliver neighbourhood improvement programmes.

Neighbourhood decline is characterised by the geographical concentration of multiple types of deprivation: declining population, departure of higher-income households, low levels of education, high poverty rates and welfare dependency, health problems, high crime rates and safety and security issues, family instability, and high proportions of single-parent households are common. Housing is usually in poor condition, often crowded, and maintenance and repairs are often neglected or makeshift, which only contributes to the spiral of decay. The level of ownership is usually low and mobility rates high. Local businesses attract little investment and often move or close. Institutions use housing as a basis for improving many of these problems so common in declining neighbourhoods.

Housing is a policy priority in neighbourhood improvement initiatives because it can play a role in at least four broad areas of people's lives: the physical, financial, locational/spatial, and psychological/social. The physical dimension includes the quality of the domestic environment, the condition and size of the home, number of bedrooms, and design features. Adequate physical features facilitate good health and educational outcomes. Financial aspects include purchase price or rent and operating costs which affect housing affordability, particularly for the poor. Those who pay too much of their income for housing have too little to spend on basic health, education, and nutrition needs. For owners, the equity in a home can be of significant financial benefit, particularly upon retirement. The locational aspects of the home intersect with neighbourhood characteristics. A location with isolation from many services can be a significant barrier for high-need households and those dependent on public transportation. Neighbourhood characteristics can also affect the way people feel about their home and their sense of safety and security. Homes also carry psychological meaning: a source of pride, status, the foundation of family life, a hub for social networking with family and friends, and the frontline in the social support system and the development of personal and cultural identity. Finally, constructing and renovating homes provide jobs, economic investment, and a focus for skills development in the community. Housing also has environmental importance as homes consume resources and generate waste and emissions.

Housing can be used as an effective tool in the hands of private, public, and community-based organisations for triggering a wider recovery process of neighbourhood improvement. Investment in housing has traditionally been used to trigger job growth in times of high unemployment and during recessionary times to stimulate the economy. Housing also has the capacity to play a multisectoral role by facilitating successful policy initiatives in other sectors. Building on its many attributes, institutions can use housing to facilitate positive education and health outcomes, reduce poverty, and build skills amongst community residents generating community economic development and positive social change. Frequently, poor housing conditions have been the spark around which groups coalesce and become a political force to bring pressure on government to support neighbourhood improvement. Governments, particularly local governments, have often been replaced by political coalitions that have developed around housing issues.

Role of Housing Institutions and Housing in Neighbourhood Improvement

There are many practical ways housing organisations have worked with housing to change neighbourhoods. Institutions working with housing can increase the potential for resident involvement and the opportunity for residents to work with community, government, and the private sector. Residents can get involved in identification of needs, priority setting, and planning and delivery of housing initiatives. This can spark wider participation and ownership of the renewal process and become the focus for collective action, social networking, and development of social capital, facilitating the 'bottom-up' approach to neighbourhood improvement.

Cooperative housing organisations, where residents have membership, voting rights, and a share of the legal entity (corporation), provide residents with greater potential for democratic engagement and collective action to improve housing, and also an opportunity to participate in action beyond housing. In Canada, for example, many co-ops make a special effort to educate their members. They offer a 'train the trainers' programme to certify people as adult educators. These people then deliver adult education courses to residents of the projects. This training often leads to paid employment or better employment and helps people break 'the cycle of poverty'. These organisations also generate progressive influence in other areas such as development of low-environmental-impact housing. In Ontario, co-op housing organisations have championed energy conservation and recycling programmes, and environmental education is provided to co-op members. Funding is also available to install low-water-use toilets and showerheads, energy-efficient refrigerators, washers, dryers and furnaces, and low-energy lighting. The democratic approach of the co-op housing models allows members to share knowledge and make collective decisions that benefit everyone while, at the same time, addressing environmental issues. Tenants First Housing Cooperative, Britain's largest mutual housing cooperative, is developing carbon-neutral housing. Housing initiatives such as these also help address the growing problem of energy poverty. The increasing price of energy is consuming a larger proportion of household income, creating ever-greater housing affordability problems for the poor. With these initiatives, built around housing, co-op housing institutions contribute to neighbourhood improvement.

Provision of housing and housing services can also help promote social inclusion. Residents in housing projects can participate in control of their own housing and living environment. The devolution of power to the user group builds social capital and skills. The Danish SAND project in homeless shelters in Denmark is a good example of using housing to promote inclusion. Under the Law of Social Services in Denmark, housing organisations have to establish user democracy in shelters for the homeless. Committees of project residents are established and, in regular meetings with administrators of the shelters, help set policy and establish programme features. Working with user councils, shelter organisations also offer skills-building courses for homeless people, for example, in financial management, accessing social services, and understanding social legislation. In this situation, housing organisations working with government funding provide improved housing and resident involvement, build skills, and strengthen social capital – key aspects of neighbourhood improvement.

Housing initiatives can also be exclusionary. Public or low-income housing projects often isolate and set residents apart from their neighbours. Pedestrian architectural design, income, ethnicity, and lifestyle differences segregate, as opposed to integrate, people in the projects from the surrounding neighbourhoods, often leading to discriminatory practices. NIMBY (not-in-my-backyard) reactions often prevent development of projects for low-income or racially different groups, excluding them from, as opposed to integrating them into, neighbourhood development projects.

Many housing initiatives have been strengthened when senior levels of government delegate authority for management of various aspects of the housing planning and delivery functions to neighbourhood organisations. This can enhance the sense of ownership and provide a better match between initiatives and neighbourhood needs. The Neighbourhoods Alive! Program administered by the province of Manitoba (Canada) in the city of Winnipeg delivers housing and other neighbourhood improvement initiatives through neighbourhood organisations. Funding is provided to support the formation, training, and operations of neighbourhood renewal corporations. These corporations play an active role in planning and delivering programmes that renovate existing units, provide new affordable accommodation, and increase the homeownership component of the housing stock in neighbourhoods. These community-based organisations, with help from government, work with other organisations (schools, local businesses, law enforcement agencies, and private housing companies) to deliver improved housing. However, these organisations have recognised that building healthy neighbourhoods is more than bricks and mortar so they use housing as a basis for initiatives in employment and training. The housing initiatives provide training for youth and ex-offenders during the construction and renovation programmes. The local input, skills development, and employment generation ideally strengthen local communities. The involvement of community organisations also improves governance, establishes new governance networks and partnerships, and improves the capacity to mobilise local communities. The institutional strengths developed under this approach bode well for long-term neighbourhood improvement.

The above discussion hints at the importance of the establishment of strategic partnerships in effecting positive neighbourhood outcomes. Many successful neighbourhood improvement projects owe their success to partnerships that successfully integrate housing initiatives with activities in other sectors. In the redevelopment of the Docklands area in Melbourne, Australia, for example, a partnership including the Victorian State Government; Housing Choices Australia, a community-based housing organisation; Lend Lease, a private developer; the National Australia Bank; and VicUrban, the State of Victoria's sustainable urban development agency, has worked on a project called The Merchant. It will provide more affordable housing in a mixed-income project that also incorporates ground floor retail to help revitalise the Docklands area. More than a third of the 133 apartments are available to low- and moderate-income tenants in inner-city Melbourne. The investment in this mixed-use project will also strengthen the business sector in the area. Without the partnership of private, public, and community-based organisations, which provide multiple sources of funding as well as different skill sets, this initiative would not succeed.

The importance of a mix of private and public sector housing initiatives in successful neighbourhood improvement initiatives is highlighted above. Creating this mix, many argue, requires an active role by the private sector. Housing activity in neighbourhood improvement areas, they suggest, should not be dominated by social housing initiatives. The activity of the Housing Opportunities Partnership (HOP) in Winnipeg provides a good example of building this mix with private sector involvement. HOP is a housing organisation established by the Winnipeg Real Estate Board. Its explicit objective has been to improve neighbourhoods by acquiring homes in need of repair, completely upgrading them, and then selling them to new moderate-income homeowners. The organisation was patterned after the Columbus Housing Partnership in the United States. Much of the funding comes from the Manitoba Securities Commission and represents interest earnings from the money realtors deposit in real estate broker trust accounts during sales transactions. HOP concentrates its revitalisation efforts within a few blocks to have a greater impact and, on the basis of what is perhaps an ideological position, believes that ownership brings stability to a neighbourhood as owners are keenly aware of their investment and want to ensure that it is maintained and appreciates over time. The evidence, they argue, suggests that the more owners in the area, the greater the likelihood of neighbourhood regeneration as all owners have a monetary incentive to protect the equity in their home. HOP has broadened its partnership to include Federal and Provincial Government departments and the city of Winnipeg and has increased its funding and activity levels as the partnership has broadened.

Mixing private and public sector initiatives may, on the other hand, generate a conflict of interest situation. The United Kingdom's Housing Market Renewal policy aimed at improving neighbourhoods by building market housing in declining areas may be a case in point. Some argued that the clearance and demolition of hundreds of houses, many of them repairable, has only served the interests of the private sector which benefits from the construction of new housing for middle-class homeowners as opposed to creating a mix that still provides housing options for the working class and the poor. Addressing neighbourhood decline has become the excuse to circumvent public policy objectives to the benefit of the private sector and higher-income households.

Often areas of neighbourhood decline are the location of high concentrations of social/public housing. However, social housing can also be used to create more socially diverse neighbourhoods. Social housing managers and organisations can play an active role in neighbourhood improvement by ensuring that publicly subsidised stock is in good repair and upgrades to energy efficiency incorporated. Work with community groups and local residents to organise renewal initiatives, lending their management and property development expertise, may help ensure the success of these initiatives.

The activity of social housing providers in Europe to renew large-scale housing estates in various countries is a good example of the active and positive role social housing organisations can play. Social housing, as a percentage of the total housing stock in Europe, ranges from a high of 32% in the Netherlands to a low of 4% in Hungary, so European social housing organisations are in a position to play a significant role in neighbourhood improvement in many countries. Although it is true to say that the social housing sector in Europe houses a disproportionate number of single-parent families, the elderly, and the poor in some countries, there has always been a mix of income groups and household types. In the renewal process, however, social housing organisations are introducing an even greater mix: moderate-income owners and renters, shared ownership, subsidised owner-occupation, housing for the minority ethnic low-income and middle class are all becoming more common. With a shift towards more local decision-making, social housing providers also have greater flexibility to use public assets in different ways and make them more of a focus for neighbourhood change. Public–private partnerships are being introduced which draw in funds from the private sector, and in some situations private developers are working with social housing providers in operating social housing. Although concerns have been raised about displacement of some of the most marginalised residents, the different ways the assets are being used in these socially creative strategies of integration are effective in creating mixed communities that have reduced levels of deprivation, more stability, and more commitment to community.

The advantages of neighbourhood mix in improving neighbourhoods cannot be overstated but housing policy and housing organisations are normally compelled to address affordability problems of the poor within declining neighbourhoods. Housing that low-income people can access without paying excessive amounts of their income can also be an effective poverty reduction tool. Protecting the poor is the focus of neighbourhood improvement in Vancouver's Downtown East Side in British Columbia (BC), Canada. The Downtown East Side epitomises the extreme of an area in need of affordable housing. It is an area of poverty, drugs, prostitution, gangs, and death, with the dubious distinction of being the poorest area in Canada and having the highest rate of HIV infection in the Western world. There is a chronic shortage of affordable housing. Single-room occupancy (SRO) units in old hotels represent the most common form of accommodation and the only type of accommodation that can be described as anywhere near affordable for the clientele of the area. These are small rooms, generally in privately owned and managed buildings, with shared bathrooms. For many, such units are the last step before homelessness. Intensifying development pressures, however, are threatening to reduce even this affordable option.

Preserving this stock for residents of the Downtown East Side has become the objective of a broad partnership of government, community housing, and service organisations, and private sector business and building groups. The government, working through BC Housing, the Provincial Housing Department, has purchased 24 hotels containing 1500 units to protect the affordable stock. Upgrades, including new electrical and plumbing fixtures, bathroom upgrading, elevator repair, installing sprinklers, and adding common kitchens, are part of the substantial repair programme following purchase. Programmes to address mental illness and addictions, including safe injection sites, are delivered to residents by community-based and government service agencies. Federal, provincial, and local governments, working with a private developer, are also renovating a large vacant department store in the area. This will provide 200 social housing units and 536 market units. A local Credit Union (Vancity) is also contributing funds and expertise to stimulate local businesses and social enterprises to provide employment in the area. A number of government departments have combined to provide employment training, training expenses, childcare, and wage subsidies to support employment strategies. Neighbourhood improvement in this area is a good example of how affordability can be attacked from two perspectives: protecting and improving the stock of affordable housing, and building on housing initiatives to improve the health and employability of the residents. Housing organisations, working with a range of partners, are attempting to build a better neighbourhood in the Downtown East Side.

As noted above, neighbourhood improvement programmes usually attack affordability from two perspectives, more affordable housing coupled with improved employability. Housing initiatives should be a platform for community economic development in neighbourhood improvement. Economic development initiatives focused around the delivery of new housing or the renovation of existing housing can help regenerate the local economy with employment opportunities, putting more cash into the system and stimulating local businesses. This approach is exemplified by Youth Builder Programs, a community-based service programme, in which young people employed by community-based housing organisations renovate local housing. It is a job training and preapprenticeship programme where youth work under the supervision of qualified carpenters. A variation of this programme is Winnipeg's Inner City Development, Inc., a social nonprofit focusing on renovations and repair of both residential and commercial property in Winnipeg's declining inner-city neighbourhoods. The organisation employs local residents, providing training and steady employment, and also employs ex-offenders just released from prison. Often this provides the ex-offenders with the training and stable employment to help prevent them from reoffending, and helps to improve safety and security in the neighbourhood.

SEED Winnipeg, a nonprofit, community-based economic development agency, uses housing as a basis for asset-building programmes. Their Individual Development Account (IDA) Program provides training and support for individuals trying to save towards buying or renovating a home. The programme provides education in household budgeting and money management. It also provides matching funds for low-income people who open accounts under the programme. Housing initiatives can be very effective 'enterprise' initiatives – a platform which enhances the skills, employment, wealth, long-term stability, and quality of life of residents in declining neighbourhoods.

In neighbourhood improvement initiatives, maintaining as much of the existing stock as possible helps protect the existing physical fabric and design of the neighbourhood. In Canada, the Neighbourhood Improvement Program of the 1970s focused on conservation, renovation, and upgrading of the existing housing stock. This programme followed on the heels of 20 years of policy that saw entire neighbourhoods demolished and ravaged and replaced by huge high-density projects that became concentrations of marginalised people. Under the programme, grants and low-interest loans were provided to low- and moderate-income homeowners and owners of rental properties to maintain and upgrade the existing stock. Local housing organisations worked with neighbourhood community organisations to assess needs, plan projects, and deliver and manage programmes. Vestiges of this programme remain today with funding for residential rehabilitation in both the ownership and rental sector and, in some provinces, funding for broader neighbourhood initiatives. The programme represented an era of neighbourhood building that has yet to be repeated in Canada.

Municipalities can play a major role in neighbourhood improvement through their responsibilities for the various regulations and by-laws designed to guarantee the quality and safety of the housing stock. Maintenance and occupancy standards, building codes, and health and safety regulations, if used effectively, can force property owners to improve and maintain the existing stock. Housing and neighbourhood renewal has to involve a combination of rehabilitation, enforcement action, and demolition, along with new building, and municipalities have a prominent role to play.

The discussion highlights the importance of integrating housing policy with policies in other sectors. Planning housing initiatives in isolation from initiatives in other policy sectors may result in failure to capitalise on other objectives that could have been achieved. Housing can make a contribution as a 'stand-alone' initiative, but it works best if there is integration with other policy sectors during the planning and implementation stage. The approach to neighbourhood improvement in Britain in recent years highlights such integration. A study carried out in 1988–89 indicated that as Britain moved into the 1990s it was faced with the situation where more than three million British homes (about one in seven) were lacking basic amenities or in need of urgent repair. Many of these homes were in neighbourhoods or on estates characterised by multiple deprivations. Housing initiatives had to be multisectoral and multiagency and had to relate to and support initiatives in other areas such as employment, training, environmental improvement, improved health, better social integration, and development of community confidence. Housing associations, residents groups, employment and training agencies, social services, schools, and private sector firms coalesced around the housing initiatives designed to trigger the revitalisation and neighbourhood improvement required to address multiple levels of deprivation. The initiative has been described as 'housing-led neighbourhood renewal'. It would not have been as effective, however, if the senior level of government and community-based organisations had not worked to establish effective linkages with other policy sectors to deliver positive nonhousing outcomes.

Conclusion

In distressed areas, providing affordable, quality housing can stimulate economic, physical, and social renewal. Decent affordable housing is essential to the development of strong, successful, and sustainable neighbourhoods. However, housing is more effective if it is not a 'stand-alone' initiative, but is closely integrated with initiatives in other policy sectors. Housing as a component of neighbourhood improvement has to be viewed in a holistic sense – not just for the shelter it provides, but for the benefits it can contribute to other sectors that must also play a role in improvement. A proactive role by housing organisations within the public, not-for-profit, and private sectors is crucial in ensuring that housing plays this broader role in neighbourhood improvement.

See also: Community- and Neighbourhood-Based Organisations in the United States; Housing and Neighbourhood Quality: Urban Regeneration; Social Housing and Social Problems; Upgrading Informal Settlements; Urbanisation and Housing the Poor: Overview.

Further Reading

Allen C (2008) *Housing Market Renewal and Social Class*. London: Routledge.

Alterman R and Cars G (eds.) (1991) *Neighbourhood Regeneration: An International Evaluation*. London: Mansell.

Drewe P, Klien J-L, and Husbergen E (eds.) (2008) *The Challenge of Social Innovation in Urban Revitalization*. Amsterdam: Techne Press.

Farnell R (2003) *'Faith' in Urban Regeneration? Engaging Faith Communities in Urban Regeneration*. Bristol, UK: Policy Press.

Joder E and Mumphrey J (2003) *Human Capital Investment for Central City Revitalization*. New York: Routledge.

Knox PL and McCarthy L (2005) *How Neighbourhoods Change in Urbanization*, 2nd edn., ch. 5. Upper Saddle River, NJ: Pearson/Prentice Hall.

Ley D and Frost H (2006) The inner city. In: Bunting T and Filion P (eds.) *Canadian Cities in Transition: Local Through Global Perspectives*, 3rd edn., ch. 11. Toronto, ON: Oxford University Press.

Maclennan D (2006) *Rethinking Neighbourhood Renewal: Towards Creative Neighbourhood Renewal Policies for Britain*. Ottawa, ON: The Caledon Institute of Social Policy.

Pierson J and Smith J (eds.) (2001) *Rebuilding Community: Policy and Practice in Urban Regeneration*. Basingstoke, UK: Palgrave.

Wood M, Randolph B, and Judd B (2002) *Resident Participation, Social Cohesion and Sustainability in Neighbourhood Renewal: Developing Best Practice Models*. Sydney, NSW: AHURI.

Zielenbach S (2000) *The Art of Revitalization: Improving Conditions in Distressed Inner-City Neighbourhoods*. New York: Garland.

Neighbourhood Incivilities

RB Taylor, Temple University, Philadelphia, PA, USA

© 2012 Elsevier Ltd. All rights reserved.

Introduction

The incivilities thesis refers to a set of theoretical models promoted over the last 35 years. The resemblance among all these models emerges from three core ideas. (1) Local behaviours that are discourteous, annoying, uncivil, negligent, socially inappropriate, harassing, or disrespectful can generate adverse local consequences. These behaviours are called social incivilities. These behaviours can be associated factually or in the minds of the local residents with the presence of unsupervised teen groups, drug users or sellers, street crazies, or homeless persons. (2) Local physical conditions including, but not limited to, vacant boarded-up houses; vacant houses open to the weather; extensive trash in vacant lots, in other open spaces like parks, on sidewalks, or in gutters; housing or commercial buildings in need of structural repair or which have not been properly maintained; abandoned or burned-out vehicles; and extensive litter, graffiti, or other similar defacement can also generate adverse local consequences. These conditions are called physical incivilities. (3) Both spatially and temporally, social and physical incivilities induce one another. In locations and at times when there are more physical incivilities, there are likely to be more social incivilities. The converse is also true.

Different sets of models vary in several key respects: the range of adverse consequences arising from these physical and social conditions, the dynamics by which these conditions link to adverse consequences, the presumed causes of these conditions, the relative weightings given to the presence of these conditions compared with locals' attitudes towards them, and the policy implications derived.

This set of models has historical roots and links to person–place transaction models. Observers of the poor of central London in the mid-nineteenth century decried housing conditions. In the mid-twentieth century in the United States, planners, researchers, observers, and policy makers expressed concern about the 'urban blight' in central city locations. Earlier work on territorial functioning and resident-generated signs of caring and upkeep in urban residential environments described how residents maintained local order – the opposite of incivilities. Some versions of the incivilities thesis consider the same dynamics as other closely related models, such as territorial functioning and attachment to place. However, they simply change the focus from one end of the continuum – caring and upkeep of properties, resident involvement, and supervision over nearby behaviours – to the opposite end. This set of models proves relevant to some current problems. Concerns about suburban deterioration were driven by the mortgage-housing crisis and the ensuing foreclosure processes and abandonment, which started in the United States in late 2007. This is just one example and will be elaborated later. The location has switched from poorer, central city locations – neighbourhoods that are oftentimes infested with drugs or gangs – to suburban locations. The same dynamics are invoked.

What are the different versions of the model, and how much support is there for these different versions?

Different Versions of the Incivilities Thesis

The earliest version of the incivilities thesis emerged in the early 1970s in response to the first results in the United States from the recently implemented US National Crime survey. Results showed fear of crime to be much more than proportionate to crime victimisation. Those who were the most fearful were the least likely to be victimised and vice versa. These questions arose therefore: 'Why are so many people fearful even though they have not been victimised?' 'Why are the wrong people fearful?' James Q. Wilson suggested that urban residents were concerned about daily hassles, stressors, disorderly conditions, and routinely experienced encounters. These matters became the social and physical incivilities described above. The focus shifted from crime to smaller, less serious matters, previously considered inconsequential.

In the early 1980s the thesis was made ecological and longitudinal. James Q. Wilson and George Kelling suggested in the now famous 'broken-windows' version of the incivilities thesis that unrepaired disorderly physical conditions spawned social incivilities: physical conditions emboldened local miscreants including unsupervised teen groups, local drunks, and streetwalkers; consequently, street regulars, residents, and business personnel alike, became intimidated and ceased attempting to regulate behaviour on the street.

The broken-windows version of the incivilities thesis has been enormously influential among policy-makers of many countries. In some places this interpretation has been invoked inappropriately as a justification for zero-tolerance policing policies. At the same time, key elements of the model have been ignored. The model laid emphasis on police learning about relevant incivilities from local residents and business personnel, and suggested that policing for incivility reduction should only be confined to 'teetering' neighbourhoods. The model has never received a scientifically rigorous, longitudinal, small area, face-to-face, group-level test to examine the proposed dynamics of physical changes and crime changes.

In 1990 another scholar more extensively ecologised the relevant processes, making the issue a neighbourhood or community-level one. Wes Skogan expanded it to a longer timeframe, suggesting that multiyear neighbourhood changes could be affected by incivilities. He added two important new outcomes: long-term changes in neighbourhood crime rates and neighbourhood structural decline. Neighbourhood structural decline might be evidenced by declining house values, conversions of owner-occupied housing to rental housing, residents living in the locale for shorter periods, and declining socioeconomic statuses of residents. Initial cross-sectional analyses purportedly supporting the model were later heavily criticised. Other empirical work examining crime and structural changes over a decade found some support for this version, although the support was not as strong or as consistent as the theory would lead one to expect.

The last model was first formulated in 1978 by Al Hunter, an extremely well-known urban sociologist. He suggested a symbolic interactionist approach to understanding the impacts of incivilities. His paper, presented at the annual meetings of the American Society of Criminology and widely read and shared among researchers, made two key arguments. The first was that crime and incivilities were linked because they both shared a common origin: disorder. The second was that the impact of incivilities depended on how they were interpreted by local residents or proprietors. Incivilities troubled local residents because they suggested either that (1) local neighbourhood leaders and stakeholders were unable or unwilling to improve conditions or that (2) key public agencies outside the neighbourhood were either unwilling or unable to devote attention or resources to improving conditions.

In the last decade two other scholars, Bernard Harcourt and Michael Innes, have both continued in this symbolic interactionist vein. They have emphasised that the impact of incivilities cannot be understood without an appreciation of how people perceive them. Literally, they both argue, the meaning of a house in disrepair depended on the viewer. Michael Innes introduced the idea of signal crimes and signal disorders: a small number of crime events or a small number of disorders that can have an extremely sizable impact on the safety concerns of local residents and users. Such events signal to locals that they are living in a dangerous or potentially dangerous setting.

The fundamental premise of all scholars working in a symbolic interactionist framework – for example, Hunter, Harcourt, and Innes – is absolutely unassailable. Reactions and impacts depend on meanings assigned. Over a century of psychology tells us that different people see the same thing differently. Look at **Figure 1**, for example. Is this an example of gang graffiti? Does this suggest a deteriorating neighbourhood? Or instead, is this artwork thoughtfully decorating and masking a pull-down grate over a small store on a clean, narrow street in the upscale and stable Gracia neighbourhood in Barcelona?

Challenges to Theory, Evidence, and Policy

Over the years, accolades have turned to acrimony and accusations. Let us start with Wilson's simple idea – it is the daily small stuff that worries people. This has been amply supported. Volumes of research from the 1980s, 1990s, and the current decade amply support the idea that those individuals with stronger concerns for personal safety also perceive more problems in their locale. Further, it is true that those perceiving more incivilities at an earlier point in time will have elevated fear at a later point in time. More complexities have arisen in this theory. Are all the effects of perceived incivilities channelled through perceptions of risk? Are both safety concerns and perceptions of risk each driven by a third more fundamental individual attribute such as anxiety or depression? Are the impacts of incivilities different for different people, depending on their vulnerabilities?

Skogan's ecological version has received some solid empirical support. Despite this, fundamental questions have once again arisen. Different types of incivilities have different types of longitudinal impacts. Various incivility indicators failed to show the close covariance that was anticipated, suggesting that they may not be capturing the underlying disorder. The community's initial socioeconomic status has a stronger impact on later changes both in incivilities and in outcomes of interest – structural decline, increasing concerns for personal safety, and increasing crime. These delayed impacts argue that this version needs stronger integration with work in urban political economy.

The symbolic interactionist view has received strong empirical support. Challenges for work in this vein, however, are considerable. It is easy to recover and document post hoc the differential impacts of particular crimes or particular incivilities, that is, to recover signal events. It is important to explore the range of factors shaping safety concerns, whether those originate from incivility or 'non-incivility' causes. More difficult, however, is predicting

Figure 1 Decorated storefront protective rolldown, relatively upscale Gracia district, Barcelona. Photo by author.

beforehand which particular incivilities will have substantial impacts on which perceivers, and why. For contextual non-incivilities also, impact prediction is similarly difficult. Until that is accomplished, the policy utility of symbolic interactionism is questionable.

The broken-windows version has received the strongest criticism and has simultaneously generated the strongest policy activity. The controversy seems unlikely to abate anytime soon. On the theory side, rigorous longitudinal multimethod studies of naturalistic face-to-face residential groupings – such as can be found on urban streetblocks – are needed. These studies need to extend for several years, need to be sensitive to the surrounding context, preferably be conducted in multiple cities, and should include crime, resident surveys, onsite assessments of behavioural and physical conditions, delinquency data, and removed and returning offender information. On the policy side, numerous studies purport to test this model but have really not done so. Perhaps most troubling has been the perceived scholarly imprimatur bestowed on zero-tolerance policing policies by the broken-windows theoretical foundation. Zero-tolerance policing and incivilities policing involve markedly different activities.

Closely Related Conceptual Models

In a version of human territorial functioning that was previously developed in the 1980s by this author, several connections with incivilities ideas can be seen. First, signs of social caring and physical caring are both relevant. Social caring means monitoring activities taking place nearby and being willing to intervene or at least do something if a disorderly situation emerges. Social caring is reflected in territorial cognitions about control, distinctions between insiders and outsiders, and responsibility. Physical caring means resident-generated signs of investment and involvement in upkeep. Discretionary gardening, sidewalk sweeping, and personal decorations are all signs of physical caring. In the same way that incivilities are interpreted in different ways by different people, so also are territorial behaviours and physical signs of territorial functioning interpreted. In the same way that physical incivilities' emergence and impacts are context-dependent, so also is it with territorial functioning. Impacts of neighbourhood contexts such as differences in status or stability have been established; so also impacts of how individual residents view their broader residential contexts should be acknowledged.

Policy Implications

The policy implications of territorial functioning are somewhat different from the policy implications of incivilities ideas. However, both sets of policy implications end up at the same place, although by different means. Territorial functioning ideas promote policies facilitating or encouraging enhanced resident involvement, investment, and beautification. Over time these actions will result in fewer social incivilities and fewer small-scale physical incivilities because territorial actions derive from and develop underlying person–place connections between residents and their immediate environment. Those underlying connections have the potential to create stronger advocacy and move resident groups toward coproducing community safety in concert with local police, and improving local conditions in concert with other local agencies.

Clearly, larger-scale physical incivilities such as abandoned houses cannot be controlled by residents. However, in suburban settings residents can contribute to the upkeep around abandoned or foreclosed properties, and in urban settings residents can exert pressure on local officials to keep vacant properties securely boarded up.

As of this writing in early 2010, the United States is in its third year of a large-scale mortgage crisis precipitated by subprime mortgage-lending practices and mortgage fraud. Numerous suburban counties in the United States are experiencing unprecedentedly high or dramatically increasing rates of home-abandonment and mortgage foreclosure. The volume of mortgage defaults, foreclosures, bank possessions, and resales has skyrocketed. It is a complex and locally textured crisis.

Two of the most widely used, assessed and perceived incivility indicators have been vacant houses and graffiti. In short, this model has identified abandoned or undermaintained houses and properties as key reflections on the quality of neighbourhood life and as key determinants of perceived and unfolding neighbourhood futures. Therefore, in a time of dramatically increasing unoccupied houses, this model seems well positioned to help us understand the community dynamics and crime consequences that may emerge as part of the mortgage-foreclosure crisis.

Several key policy prescriptions follow for preventing increasing local property and violent crime in suburban communities suffering from the mortgage crisis. (1) Keep houses occupied even if the original owners walk away, or if the houses are in foreclosure proceedings. (2) If houses cannot be kept occupied, then encourage local community groups to make the house *look* occupied by keeping up with exterior maintenance of the structure and maintaining the grounds. (3) Direct the community's attention to preventing increasing vacancies, especially in communities with historically low vacancy rates. It is in those locations that the increasing vacancies will be most noticeable to potential offenders. All of these policy approaches will require financial and governmental support, and resident-based groups need to think together with local government agencies about how this can be achieved.

Challenges

Initially, the incivilities thesis generated considerable excitement. It pinpointed a clear cause of a recognised urban malady, fear, and later crime, while offering a straightforward policy prescription. Now, almost three decades later, the model seeks to explain long-term neighbourhood crime changes as well as patterns of neighbourhood structural decline. Intricate patterns of small-group-based, streetblock-level informal control, physical deterioration, disorderly social behaviour, and also fear of crime are facets of these long-term changes.

However, there are points of confusion and challenges. Some of the research blurs distinctions between incivilities and minor crimes. Further, no one has established the construct validity of key incivility indicators at the community level. Significant questions have not yet been answered about the conceptual referent of incivilities indicators; the meaning of these variables remains quite unclear. It is interesting to compare the arc of this theory with urban-planning ideas about urban blight from the 1950s and 1960s. Both are evaluative terms making for measurement difficulties. Further, both the incivilities and the urban blight concepts have been linked to controversial policy solutions. Widespread urban renewal and redevelopment was the cure for blight in the mid-twentieth century. Zero-tolerance policing in the United States and reassurance policing in the United Kingdom were the cures for incivilities at the beginning of the twenty-first century. All these policy initiatives have been dogged by controversy while at the same time the proponents claim success.

See also: Crime Prevention Through Environmental Design; Gentrification.

Further Reading

Bottoms AE (2007) Place, space, crime and disorder. In: Maguire M, Morgan R, and Reiner R (eds.) *The Oxford Handbook of Criminology*, 4th edn., pp. 528–574. New York: Oxford University Press.

Gau JM and Pratt TC (2008) Broken windows or window dressing? Citizens' (in)ability to tell the difference between disorder and crime. *Criminology & Public Policy* 7(2): 163–194.

Harcourt BE (2001) *Illusion of Order: The False Promise of Broken Windows Policing*. Cambridge, MA: Harvard University Press.

Hawley AH (1971) *Urban Society: An Ecological Approach*. New York: The Ronald Press.

Innes M (2004) Signal crimes and signal disorders: Notes on deviance as communicative action. *British Journal of Sociology* 55(3): 335–355.

Perkins D and Taylor RB (1996) Ecological assessments of disorder: Their relationship to fear of crime and theoretical implications. *American Journal of Community Psychology* 24: 63–107.

Robinson J, Lawton B, Taylor RB, and Perkins DD (2003) Longitudinal impacts of incivilities: A multilevel analysis of reactions to crime and block satisfaction. *Journal of Quantitative Criminology* 19: 237–274.

Ross CE and Mirowsky J (1999) Disorder and decay: The concept and measurement of perceived neighborhood disorder. *Urban Affairs Review* 34(3): 412–432.

Skogan W (1990) *Disorder and Decline: Crime and the Spiral of Decay in American Cities*. New York: Free Press.

Taylor RB (1988) *Human Territorial Functioning*. Cambridge, UK: Cambridge University Press.

Taylor RB (1997) Social order and disorder of streetblocks and neighborhoods: Ecology, microecology and the systemic model of social disorganization. *Journal of Research in Crime and Delinquency* 33: 113–155.

Taylor RB (2001) *Breaking Away from Broken Windows: Evidence from Baltimore Neighborhoods and the Nationwide Fight against Crime, Grime, Fear and Decline*. New York: Westview Press.

Taylor RB (2007) Zeroing in on zero tolerance policing in the American context: Conceptual moorings, current limited evidence, and comparative quandaries. *Fourth Annual SCoPiC Conference. Cambridge University, Institute of Criminology.* Cambridge, UK: Cambridge University Press.

Wilson JQ and Kelling G (1982) Broken windows. *Atlantic Monthly* 211(March): 29–38.

Wyant BR (2008) Multilevel impacts of perceived incivilities and perceptions of crime risk on fear of crime. *Journal of Research in Crime and Delinquency* 45(1): 39–64.

Neighbourhood Planning

S Pinnegar, University of New South Wales, Sydney, NSW, Australia

© 2012 Elsevier Ltd. All rights reserved.

Glossary

Collaborative planning A communicative approach to planning that recognises a range of 'stakes' or interests in any given context, and which provides frameworks for negotiation and consensus building between communities, organisations, and institutions.

Community development corporation (CDC) Typically associated with the United States, CDCs are not-for-profit organisations supporting activities that promote and facilitate community development. Many have a geographical focus in inner-city neighbourhoods assisting lower-income residents.

Neighbourhood unit Often associated with neighbourhood design principles advocated by Clarence Perry in the 1920s, where the neighbourhood is seen as a bounded, self-contained district within which most day-to-day activities are available to residents within walking distance.

NIMBYism A pejorative term used to capture individual or community opposition to change in their locality, for example, affordable housing or infrastructure development. Resistance is often expressed in terms of not being anti-change, just not wanting it to affect them.

Urban consolidation Policy- and market-led activities that promote residential and employment densification in existing suburbs, particularly around well-serviced transport infrastructure nodes.

Urban governance The frameworks, processes, and institutions through which residents and groups organise economic, social, cultural, and environmental decision-making in the city.

A Design-Led Blueprint for Community Living

In planning terms, the neighbourhood concept is commonly traced back to the turn of the last century, when reform agendas tied to urban and suburban living influenced approaches to building new communities and renewing established ones. Although planning the ideal neighbourhood primarily manifests itself as a design-led response to preceding urban disorder, physical organisation and layout were also tied to a consideration of social order and everyday social needs. A focus on planning at the neighbourhood scale is most closely associated with the American Clarence Perry and his concept of the 'Neighborhood Unit', most clearly articulated in the 1929 Regional Plan of New York and its Environs (see **Figure 1**). It also accommodated the ecological organic principles of writers, such as Lewis Mumford, and Ernest Park and Robert Burgess from the Chicago School, shaping urban thinking at that time. Perry's concept was structured around six fundamental planning principles: (1) scale, determined by the population required to support a primary school; (2) identifiable boundaries, ideally carrying through traffic around the neighbourhood; (3) the provision of open space; (4) positioning of the school and a range of institutional buildings at its heart; (5) provision of a retail district, typically towards the edges of the neighbourhood; and (6) an internal layout that facilitated safe, local mobility.

The extent to which the concept sought to invest physical planning attributes with wider social goals has been widely debated, and as Herbert Gans noted, the physical form proposed was 'not neutral'. Concerns focused on the discriminatory and antiurban implications of a model which encapsulated a degree of social homogeneity within self-contained and bounded geographies. Initially, application of the Neighborhood Unit was primarily associated with the design of new residential areas, for example, in the collaboration of Clarence Stein and Henry Wright at Radburn, New Jersey, although its use as a template for comprehensive redevelopment of existing neighbourhoods suffering from blight was also acknowledged early on. It was not, however, until the late 1930s and post-Second World War that the neighbourhood consolidated its role as the core building block in both the redevelopment of old and planning for new urban environments.

In the United Kingdom, Abercrombie and Forshaw's plan for the County of London (1943), preparing for postwar reconstruction, envisaged the Capital reconstituting its myriad villages and towns into a series of cellular, stable communities in distinct neighbourhoods (see **Figure 2**). Reconstruction was to be both physical and social, with a strong emphasis on reestablishing a network of sustainable neighbourhoods structured around

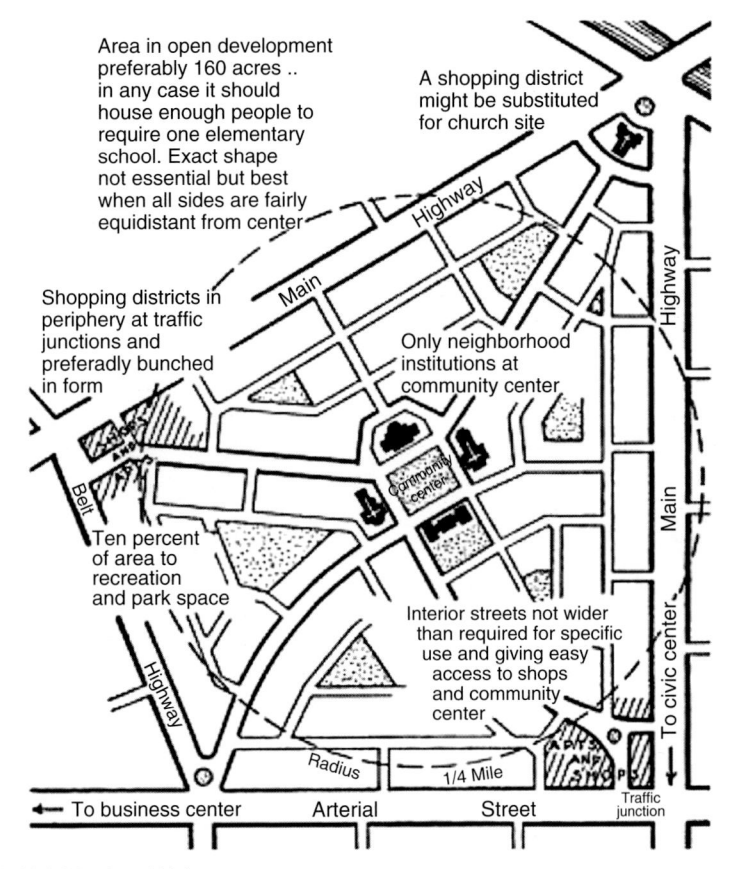

Figure 1 Clarence Perry's Neighborhood Unit.
Source: Perry CA (1929) The neighborhood unit: A scheme for the family-life community, Monograph One. In: *Regional Plan of New York and its Environs*, p. 88. New York: Committee on Regional Plan of New York and its Environs. Reproduced with permission from the Regional Plan Association, New York.

the organisation of everyday activities and enabling a local focus for civic pride. The neighbourhood was seen as an appropriate scale to provide centres of community life serving residents day-to-day social, retail, cultural, and educational needs. However, in contrast to the perceived homogeneity associated with Perry's Neighborhood Unit, Abercrombie and Forshaw's vision sought to foster mingling across classes within 'balanced' neighbourhood communities. In part, this reflected the broader desire to take the opportunity to establish greater order in the fragmented urban form and function of the city, but also acted as an important precursor to more contemporary arguments regarding the benefits of mixed-income, mixed-tenure communities.

Parallel to reconstruction of existing urban areas, the UK's New Towns programme presented neighbourhood planning principles with a significant test bed. Optimal neighbourhood size was, as with Perry's model, predicated on the population required to support a primary school and a layout that enabled day-to-day activities to be reached, safely, on foot. For particular population sizes and densities, guidelines for the appropriate number of shops (and mix), and the proportion of land to be given over to open and green space were identified. The transfer of best practice internationally saw neighbourhood planning principles enshrined far and wide. In Australia, a faithful application of New Town ideals can be seen in Kwinana, near Perth, and Elizabeth, near Adelaide. However, it is perhaps in the nation's capital, Canberra, that the clearest articulation of neighbourhood planning – and its evolution in the postwar decades – is seen.

As a model for setting out the design of new communities, the neighbourhood unit, and by extension neighbourhood planning, inevitably had its critics. Concerns were raised that a focus on the neighbourhood detracted from facilitating wider connectivity across, and functionality of, the urban area as a whole and recognition of the overlapping nature of everyday life lived at a variety of spatial scales. Indeed, a number of the later new towns, most notably Cumbernauld in Scotland (designated 1955), breached the model and through greater densities and concentration of urban form sought to focus activity on the town centre. Nevertheless, the neighbourhood as a building block – albeit more outward looking and connected – returned to provide the platform for the United Kingdom's most significant new town at Milton Keynes (designated 1967). Indeed, neighbourhood planning principles seen here – with grid roads carrying through traffic

Figure 2 London social and functional analysis, County of London plan, 1943.
Source: Abercrombie P and Forshaw JH (19434) London: social and functional analysis. In: *The County of London Plan*, p.21. London: London County Council. Reproduced with permission from City of London, London Metropolitan Archives.

and local centres located on the edge of residential areas – return faithfully to Perry's original articulation.

Many of the physical design imperatives shaping neighbourhood planning have remained pretty intact in their latest incarnation, whether in the form of Transit Oriented Development (TOD) or New Urbanism, where mixed use, accessibility, and a focus on scales conducive to walking are promoted. Although the sociospatial principles remain, rather than conceptualising neighbourhoods as cells within a larger whole, sustainable neighbourhoods are now structured as 'beads on a string' along transit corridors. Considerable faith remains in expectations that getting physical form and design right at the local level will translate into better social, economic, and environmental outcomes.

From Plans to Collaborative Process

The application of neighbourhood planning principles within existing areas has exposed substantive tensions. With neighbourhood redevelopment picking up pace in the 1950s, concerns arising from the impacts of top-down planning approaches determined by professional and expert authority soon followed. In the United States, aspects of the neighbourhood planning approach had become increasingly associated with the negative impacts of slum clearance, particularly following the redevelopment provisions of the 1949 Housing Act and greater emphasis placed upon private investment interests in the urban renewal process. Grassroots activity escalated as neighbourhoods, and the established social networks within localities, experienced the realities of progress. Jane Jacobs' seminal text *The Death and Life of Great American Cities* captured the challenges of neighbourhood change in the early 1960s. As US cities burned and the Civil Rights Movement challenged deep-seated and structural injustice, the essentially physical nature of the neighbourhood planning process transitioned to a more grounded focus on community development interested in stemming the flow of assets and resources from deprived neighbourhoods.

Community Development Corporations (CDCs) provided a basis for locally determined and locally driven responses to the broader social and economic shifts impacting on those communities, and a greater degree of local determinism through a redistribution of power was advocated as a means of rebuilding the sense of community that commentators felt was being eroded in pursuit of centralised goals. For example, New York City introduced 'Little City Halls' during Mayor Lindsay's tenure from 1965; and in 1974, Atlanta established its Neighborhood Planning Unit (NPU) which divided the city into 25 local districts. Such arrangements aimed to provide improved communication, connection, and accountability between government and local residents, with communities encouraged to engage in identifying issues, in visioning and the plan-making process itself, and (to a greater or lesser extent) the frameworks that deliver against identified actions. From being the subject of plans, residents become 'citizen planners' involved in a transactional process with a say in decisions affecting their neighbourhoods.

Although neighbourhood planning's design-led associations retain saliency, as seen in many aspects of New Urbanism and TOD, it is this more collaborative, deliberative application of the term that is prominent in recent debate and practice. In this regard, the need to establish frameworks to work through the often-perceived competing objectives of community and citywide interests across the range of urban spatial scales – what Patsy Healey has described as relating the 'whole to the parts, and the parts to the whole' – is seen as central. The conflicts, but also the opportunities for collaboration and improved consensus, capture why neighbourhood planning processes have been increasingly seen as central to more effective forms of urban governance. In addition, facilitating communication between city/local government and local communities, neighbourhood planning is seen to provide a focus for coordinating strategies and government and agency service provision impacting upon those localities. It provides a platform for different stakeholders to align arrangements, establish partnerships, and improve connections.

While urban renewal continues to underscore the importance of neighbourhood engagement, arguably the more substantive enrolment of neighbourhood planning initiatives can recently be seen in cities facing planning conflicts arising from growth management strategies. As cities seek to accommodate a significant proportion of future population growth in existing areas, pressures of urban consolidation present a challenge to the status quo and existing interests. Successful neighbourhoods – and in particular the middle-class property owners who have enjoyed much of that success – inevitably have a strong interest in maintaining the perceived quality of life encapsulated in the current urban form. Conflict is seen where Not-in-My-Backyard (NIMBY) tendencies arise. The prospect of change, or at least change perceived as undesirable, mobilises the more powerful within the community who invoke local hegemony as a means to resist those changes. Policies and initiatives emanating from town and city halls risk being characterised as imposed, external interests, for example, driven by developer or investor imperatives.

There are a number of approaches taken in the face of this disjuncture. One simple response is to constrain debate through limited engagement at the neighbourhood level in the preparation of broader strategic blueprints for cities. Alternatively, local determination can be advocated. Here, strategic citywide considerations cede interest to communities on the basis that they are best positioned to identify the appropriate direction for their localities. Neighbourhood planning aims to negotiate these two tendencies by building deliberative frameworks that move beyond top-down political lip service on the one hand and potentially parochial interests on the other hand. It does not, and cannot, resolve these tensions; rather, governance at the level of 'place' acts as the framework around which the nature and future direction of those places is negotiated on an ongoing basis.

Four case studies where neighbourhood planning principles have played a high-profile role in recent years are highlighted below. While placing a spotlight on these cities, many large urban areas have, and continue to, grapple with the challenges of accommodating a diversity of interests across a range of urban scales; a tension that lies at the heart of neighbourhood planning. A strong historical trajectory can be seen in the United States. Canadian cities also demonstrate a robust tradition, with cities including Victoria, Winnipeg, and more recently Ottawa establishing neighbourhood planning approaches alongside the high-profile activities of Vancouver. In the United Kingdom, interest in promoting local input into planning considerations is often driven by engagement as part of neighbourhood renewal activity, and has been consolidated through interest in neighbourhood governance and, more recently, the localism agenda.

CityPlan and the Community Visions Program, Vancouver, BC

Vancouver in British Columbia, Canada, is often lauded as one of the world's most liveable cities and one that has been successful in introducing higher urban densities in established neighbourhoods. The city benefits from a degree of legal and administrative autonomy from the Provincial government, which has made feasible meaningful, place-based input into the broader strategic planning process for the city. CityPlan, adopted in 1995, provides a citywide framework for shaping and determining core programmes, directions, and actions for Vancouver over 20 years, covering a broad range of issues such as services provision, housing, culture, and transportation. In 1996, the Community Visions Program was initiated in order to take CityPlan's strategic directions down to the neighbourhood level.

The roll out of the Community Visions Program was initiated and coordinated by planners at City Hall, although accompanied by the objective of residents taking ownership of their visions. The city's 13 neighbourhoods were consolidated into nine areas – which were therefore quite large, comprising 12–45 000 residents. Not all areas were tackled at the same time with a number prioritised for early consideration. The model used in the Community Visions exercise has been structured around four steps. The first involved outreach activities to encourage participation. The second stage was to hold a series of festivals and workshops, identifying the key issues to be explored in a 'choices' survey delivered to all households and businesses in the area. The survey provided a means where different directions and priorities in each neighbourhood could be explored. For example, if provision of more affordable housing was seen as a priority, the options process then explored how this provision could be met, such as increasing densities or different house-type options. The fourth stage was to finalise the community vision in the light of the survey responses for endorsement by the City Council.

The resulting Community Visions represent agreed frameworks to steer planning directions rather than detailed plans and funding arrangements. They help identify future housing needs, options for major redevelopment sites, potential improvements to shopping and service areas, to community facilities, and public and green space provision. Local review and determination of zoning policies is possible. The Vision Implementation Program has aimed to provide a collaborative structure between Council staff and the community to address the Vision Directions. Recommendations are then acted upon either through existing Council programmes and operational structures or through bespoke initiatives. Citywide 'Pan Visions' meetings have provided a forum whereby areas with completed Visions can get together, share best practice, discuss challenges, and identify opportunities for collaboration. Further support and oversight across levels of governance and stakeholders has been offered by an independent community-based committee.

In a 2009 evaluation, successes are identified in reengaging communities, building capacity to engage in both local and citywide issues, and rearticulating links between the Council and all stakeholders. Challenges identified point to the difficulty of translating plans into practice, mechanisms for prioritisation, and lack of clarity regarding responsibilities across different teams and departments. Nevertheless, the approach – despite these shortcomings – can be seen to have played its role in helping frame local issues and considerations within the big, strategic issues facing the city.

Neighborhood Planning Program, Seattle, WA

Across the border in the United States, Seattle – like Vancouver, a city seeking to manage much of its anticipated population growth and housing needs within the existing urban footprint – established the Neighborhood Planning Program (NPP) in the mid-1990s. The NPP emerged as a response to significant initial opposition to the 1994 strategic plan, *Towards A Sustainable Seattle*. This had been prepared with muted community engagement and had identified a hierarchy of nodes supporting different densities, including 'urban villages' that raised the spectre of significant neighbourhood change. The Neighborhood Planning Office (NPO) was created in 1995 to help neighbourhoods shape their future and with a stated purpose to 'enable the City and community to work in partnership'.

Each of Seattle's neighbourhoods was given the option of developing their own neighbourhood plans to determine 'the best ways to achieve established citywide goals'. Facilitated by staff and seed funding from the NPO but nonetheless community-led, each group was given flexibility to identify and define issues of core interest to their communities in the context of the broader citywide strategy. Establishing an evidence base was seen as vital, and groups were provided with a 'neighbourhood planning toolbox' comprising local-level data, financial tools, and process guidelines to assist. Organising committees were established to drive community engagement, prepare work plans, and set about putting together a draft plan. Plans typically took between 1 and 2 years to prepare, and once complete, were shared through a community-wide mail out. The final stage involved plan adoption, and a certain degree of iteration was required at this time in order to ensure all plans were robust and local considerations were reconciled with citywide goals. To a degree, this was a two-way process, where recommendations arising that had citywide implications were reflected within those strategies and dealt with on a citywide basis.

The resulting plans have given communities a voice in development issues, zoning changes, urban design guidelines, green space, and streetscape issues. Commentators have identified the vital role played by the designated project managers in acting as 'translators' between the varied stakeholders, different languages of policy, and competing interests across different spatial levels of urban governance. This not only helped in ensuring communities' needs to be effectively channelled, but also provided a basis for trust and alignment across government departments and delivery bodies. This has led to some restructuring of departmental functions and budgets into geographical sectors to facilitate collaboration at the local level. A further success identified was the degree of transparency enabled by relinquishing control, and therefore ownership, to the neighbourhood level. For example, by building a shared understanding of issues, there is also a greater awareness of cost and benefit considerations tied to the decision-making process, between City Hall and communities. Criticisms of NPP have, as with CityPlan in Vancouver, focused on the challenge of implementation, and questions of whether the voices of all community stakeholders, and particularly marginalised groups, across the city can be adequately captured and addressed.

CityShape 2026 and Neighbourhood Planning, Brisbane, QLD

Across the Pacific in Australia, the South East Queensland 2026 Regional Plan required Brisbane City Council to develop a Local Growth Management Strategy. The resulting *CityShape 2026* puts in place a structure for community consultation and development of neighbourhood plans. As in Vancouver and Seattle, a core driver has been the need to steward discussion, debate, and develop some consensus regarding neighbourhood change. The approach builds on initial consultation through 14 workshops across the city aimed at capturing a range of views and identifying priorities to be built into the planning process. Five large Home and Neighbourhood fairs were also held, where residents' views on different options for Brisbane's future urban form and function were explored: did they prefer a multi-centre, compact, corridor or dispersed city approach to meeting anticipated growth?

Following this citywide process, detailed neighbourhood planning has commenced in a number of suburbs. Council decides which areas need a Neighbourhood Plan and when, and those earmarked for high residential or employment growth are typically prioritised. Plans are developed through a staged framework, starting with a Council-led review of existing neighbourhood profiles, strategies and studies, and initial local community engagement. A community planning team, comprising 15–20 local residents, businesses, and other key stakeholders is established to provide support to the Council in preparation of the plan. The draft goes through a series of iterations as a result of feedback from both government and the local community and a second draft agreed. The plan is then finalised by the Council and an implementation framework put in place.

Typically, plans have addressed issues including affordable housing and infrastructure provision, transport, community and shopping facilities, public and green space, and environmental issues. With the Council retaining control of the process, the degree to which the initial level of community engagement has followed through in subsequent plan development and implementation has arguably been more top-down than seen in Seattle. Whether the approach has helped mitigate NIMBY interests or provided a platform for those most vocal with interests to preserve can be questioned. Nevertheless, a survey conducted in 2007 found that residents had become more aware of a range of neighbourhood planning issues and demonstrated a greater acceptance of the need to provide a range of housing types across the city.

Neighbors Building Neighborhoods, Rochester, New York

The final case study returns us to the United States, but to a city where the difficulties of reconciling strategic planning issues at neighbourhood level are often grounded in the challenges of managing decline and fostering renewal, rather than pressures arising from population growth. Initiated in the early 1990s, and a flagship initiative of Mayor Bill Johnson (1994–2005), the Neighbors Building Neighborhoods (NBN) programme in Rochester, New York sought to reconnect city government with its citizens by offering a basis for community empowerment and a framework within which identified actions could be implemented at the neighbourhood level. NBN organised the city into geographical sectors, and communities and stakeholders in each sector have worked together to put together strategies, leading to 10 Action Plans that between them identified 1450 action steps.

While participants were encouraged to be ambitious, the need to tie ideas to plans for actual implementation – with citizen planners having to identify partners and resources to make those actions happen – helped foster an approach focused on viable outcomes rather than simple wish lists. Implementation of those actions remained largely in the hands of communities themselves and the partnerships forged. City Hall's interest focused on ensuring a good degree of consensus in the community around priorities identified, and providing supporting arrangements to help facilitate their delivery. Local government operational structures or regulations could be reshaped in the light of plan recommendations, and residents have a say in establishing city budget priorities.

Neighbourhood Planning: An Ongoing Process Reconciling Interests across Spatial Scales

The concept, process, and outcomes of neighbourhood planning capture some of the core challenges at the heart of planning our cities, and in particular, the localities in which we live. Our understanding as to what neighbourhood planning constitutes remains a mix of ideas regarding the ideal physical (and through this, social) form of a neighbourhood and the processes involved in shaping such outcomes. In recent years, the latter has gained preeminence and is principally used to describe processes used in promoting greater collaboration and deliberation in local planning considerations.

Crucially, it seeks to reconcile interests across spatial scales of influence and activity. Although grounded in the desire for voices to be heard from the bottom-up, effective neighbourhood planning is not about simple devolution. At its most effective, it is a two-way process, providing communities with a say on future growth or renewal trajectories in their neighbourhoods on the one hand, and a basis for citywide strategic matters to be better understood, negotiated, and if necessary, trade-offs agreed, on the other hand. The desired outcome is a community with the necessary tools and outlets to engage in ensuring the vitality of both their own localities but also the wider city.

In seeking more collaborative frameworks, emphasis gets placed on relation building, fostering trust, integrating existing structures, and providing effective means of translating plans into practice. This encompasses building better connections between government, institutions, and communities, but also within the structures of government and service providers. Critics highlight the difficulties involved in actual implementation: often in reality, these transactional frameworks hold limited legislative powers. They also point to the challenges of actively engaging those less powerful, and whether frameworks act to simply consolidate relative advantage rather than provide a means for addressing structural disadvantage and social equity issues across the city.

Neighbourhood planning models around the world reflect strong similarities in terms of the core stages and processes undertaken in putting together and subsequently implementing local-level plans. However, they equally demonstrate diversity reflective of different cities' governance structures, preexisting networks of community engagement, and above all, degree of commitment to follow through resulting plans in implementation. Good neighbourhood planning does not manifest itself in seamless accord: indeed, effective frameworks are those that promote and channel argument, debate and discord as much as agreement. Mobilising such processes is hard work, ongoing, and requires long-standing commitment from inception through to implementation. Those frameworks need to be sufficiently flexible to accommodate changing priorities, interests and challenges, and to offer 'place governance' arrangements where these shifting forces can be responded to.

See also: Community- and Neighbourhood-Based Organisations in the United States; Democracy and Accountability; Neighbourhood Governance; NIMBYism.

Further Reading

City of Vancouver (2009) *Community Visions: Vision Implementation Program Review. Issues and Opportunities Paper (Revised)*. Vancouver: City of Vancouver.

Gans H (1972) *People and Plans: Essays on Urban Problems and Solutions*. London: Pelican.

Gillette H (1983) The evolution of neighborhood planning: From the progressive era to the 1949 Housing Act. *Journal of Urban History* 9(4): 421–444.

Healey P (2007) *Urban Complexity and Spatial Strategies: Towards a Relational Planning for our Times*, 2nd edn. London: Routledge.

Healey P (2010) *Making Better Places: The Planning Project in the Twenty-First Century*. Basingstoke, UK: Palgrave Macmillan.

Jacobs J (1961) *The Death and Life of Great American Cities*. New York: Random House.

Kotler M (1969) *Neighborhood Government: The Local Foundations of Political Life*. New York: Bobbs-Merrill.

Purcell M (2006) Urban democracy and the local trap. *Urban Studies* 43(11): 1921–1941.

Rasmussen SE (1957) Neighborhood planning. *The Town Planning Review* 27(4): 197–218.

Rohe W (2009) From local to global: One hundred years of neighborhood planning. *Journal of the American Planning Association* 75(2): 209–230.

Silver C (1985) Neighborhood planning in historical perspective. *Journal of the American Planning Association* 51(2): 162–174.

Sirianni C (2007) Neighborhood planning as collaborative democratic design. *Journal of the American Planning Association* 73(4): 373–387.

Stoney C and Elgersma S (2007) Neighbourhood planning through community engagement: The implications for place based governance and outcomes. *Paper Presented at Canadian Political Science Association Conference*, Saskatoon, Canada, May/June 2007.

Neighbourhood Reputation

M Permentier, Netherlands Institute for Social Research/SCP, The Hague, The Netherlands

© 2012 Elsevier Ltd. All rights reserved.

Glossary

Behaviour Purposeful actions taken by self-interested individuals to improve or maintain the quality of their lives.
Status The subjective evaluations of positions in a system of social stratification. Although status can also refer to the neighbourhood level, it is more often used at the individual level.
Urban neighbourhood hierarchy The general ranking of urban neighbourhoods by different groups (city residents, professionals, media).

The Name of the Neighbourhood: Defining Reputation

People constantly form opinions without always being aware of it. Places are no exception to the labelling process: people attach a reputation to most countries, states, cities, or neighbourhoods. Neighbourhoods too have a certain reputation, which can range from very negative to very positive. Areas like SoHo (New York), Holland Park in London, and Oud-Zuid in Amsterdam hold (mostly) a very positive connotation, whereas areas like South-Central (Los Angeles), La Courneuve (Paris), and Spangen (Rotterdam) have a more negative connotation. Scholars from the Chicago School of Sociology were already interested in the symbolic functioning of neighbourhoods. On this interest, Firey (1945) expanded further by acknowledging and studying the symbolic and sentimental dimension of the Bostonian neighbourhood Beacon Hill. He recognised that a spatial area can act as "a symbol for certain cultural values that have become associated with it" (Firey, 1945: 140). Firey's example of Beacon Hill, a residential area near the centre of Boston, illustrates that neighbourhoods can retain their position in the urban neighbourhood hierarchy by operating as a symbol for certain (as in the case of Beacon Hill, historic and aesthetic) values: in other words, the area has a certain reputation.

Although the concept of reputation has been applied to neighbourhoods, very few academics give insights into the theoretical construction of this concept. In this article, three elements of neighbourhood reputation are central: (1) the collective nature of it, (2) the difference between neighbourhood residents and other city residents, and (3) the element of stratification.

First, in line with other authors, it is argued that the collective shared view is an important feature of the concept of reputation. The individual views of only one or a few people do not constitute a reputation. A reputation is an image shared by a significant number of individuals. Consequently, the same neighbourhood may have multiple reputations: certain groups (with different sociodemographic characteristics) may see it as a highly impoverished no-go area, whereas others would assess it as a place full of potential.

Second, reputations are thought to differ between residents and nonresidents. The internal reputation – the reputation held among the neighbourhood residents – is often thought to be rated higher than the external reputation, the reputation among other city residents. The former type consists generally of a more detailed view based on the physical and social attributes of the neighbourhood. Residents often employ a microhierarchy of areas in the neighbourhood of good and bad parts. Compared with internal reputation, external reputation is based on lesser information and personal experience and consists of simplified images shaped by exaggerated differences between neighbourhoods. In **Figure 1** the reputation of 24 urban neighbourhoods in the Dutch city of Utrecht is shown among residents of the neighbourhoods, among other city residents, and among professionals (estate agents). **Figure 1** indicates that hierarchies among different groups are very similar. The three groups show generally the same ranking of neighbourhoods. At the same time, one can see that residents rate their own neighbourhood's reputation significantly higher than other city residents do, and in most cases, higher than estate agents do, thus supporting the conceptual difference between internal and external reputation.

Third, the reputation of a neighbourhood contains a stratification element: the reputation reflects the individual status of the residents. In other words, the neighbourhood can be used as an indicator and a symbol of residents' sociocultural and/or socioeconomic position in society and their preferences. The residential location is frequently used as an indicator of a person's sociocultural and socioeconomic position. The urban population assesses neighbourhoods and their residential

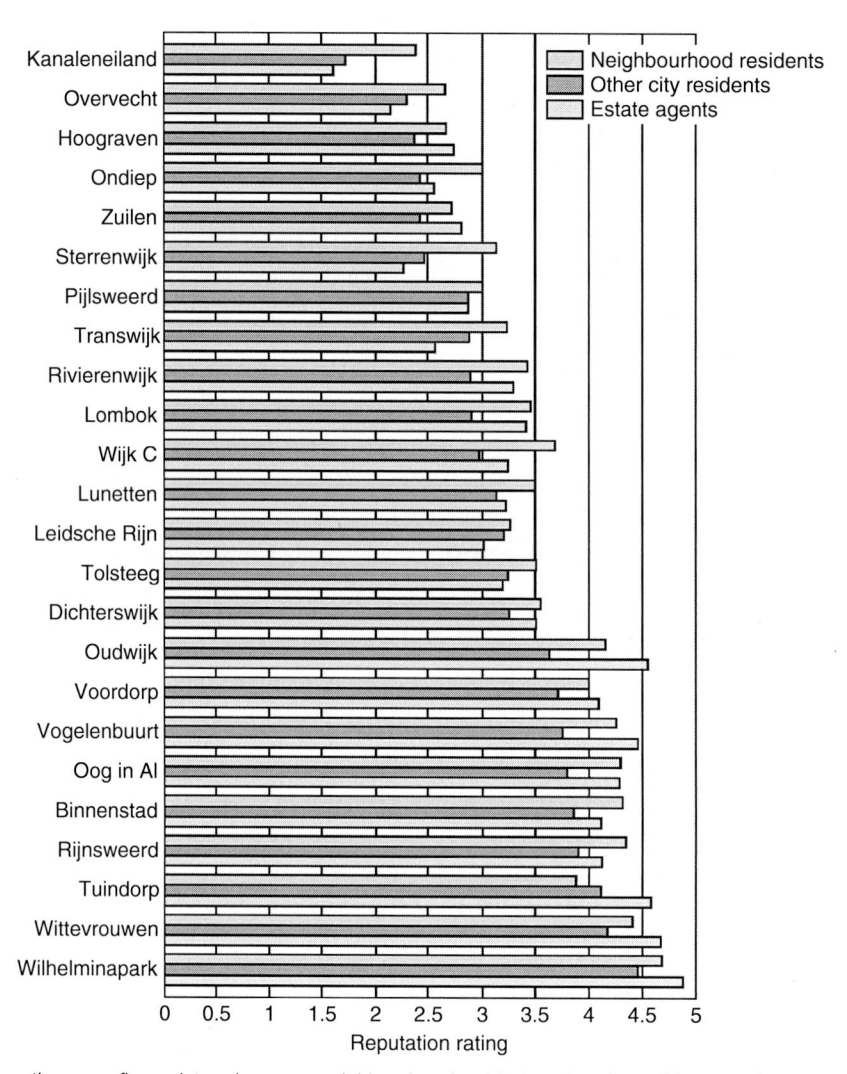

Figure 1 Reputation ratings on a five-point scale among neighbourhood residents, other city residents, and estate agents in Utrecht, 2006. Reproduced with permission from Figure 1 in Permentier MG (2009) *Reputation, Neighbourhoods and Behaviour*. Utrecht: Utrecht University/Faculty of Geosciences.

groups in a contrastive way in which each neighbourhood is seen as a counterpart to some of the others. This positioning leads to a hierarchy in which different neighbourhoods are positioned in relation to one another. Not the absolute, but the relative differences are thought to be relevant in the comparisons between neighbourhoods. The identification with a specific place automatically means identification *against* another place. The positioning of neighbourhoods in contrast to each other leads to a hierarchy in which the different neighbourhoods are positioned in relation to one another: the urban neighbourhood hierarchy. The reputation of a neighbourhood can be deduced from its position in this hierarchy.

Most of these previously discussed elements can be found in the following definition of neighbourhood reputation: "refers to the meaning and esteem that residents and other involved parties attribute to a neighbourhood. Reputation also refers to the relatively stable image a neighbourhood has among city residents and to its place in the urban neighbourhood hierarchy" [author's translation from Dutch] (Hortulanus, 1995). In contrast with the concept of stigma, reputation is more neutral. Stigma indicates an anomaly, something that society considers unacceptable. Reputation, on the other hand, can have either a negative or a positive connotation.

Reputation and Its Consequences

Outsiders Responses to Reputations

There is ample evidence available in the literature of the impact of reputations on the behaviour of other city residents. Avoidance not only of moving into, but also of visiting disreputable neighbourhoods has been documented. Especially about the role of institutions and other city residents quite a bit of evidence is available. For example, on the basis of the reputation of (bad) neighbourhoods, institutions and private companies may develop strategies to deal with such neighbourhoods and their residents. A clear example is 'blocking strategies' by which actors try to prevent certain groups from stigmatised neighbourhoods entering (highly regarded upmarket) urban neighbourhoods, thus avoiding changes in the neighbourhood features. Realtors are known to serve as gatekeepers, seeking to 'preserve' white neighbourhoods from an influx of people from stigmatised areas by steering individuals from these areas to certain other parts of the city. As a result, these blocking strategies can influence the attitudes and behaviour of the residents of stigmatised neighbourhoods. For example, these residents may develop antagonistic feelings towards society and may lose trust in institutions.

White avoidance is an example of how other city residents react to the reputation of neighbourhoods. The decision of city residents not to move into (predominantly nonwhite) urban neighbourhoods with a notorious reputation is a process that has been extensively studied in the American context. The racial composition of neighbourhoods is known to be affected by this process. Studies have shown the preference of white Americans for predominantly white neighbourhood and the impact this preference has on the racial composition of neighbourhoods. Another form of outsider's behaviour is the disinclination to visit certain neighbourhoods. In this respect, the attitudes and behaviour of nonresidents towards inner-city districts in the United States are a prime example. Because of the extremely negative reputations of these inner cities, nonresidents shun these districts for fear of the local (minority) community.

Consequences and Responses of Neighbourhood Residents

On the one hand, the reputation of a good/bad neighbourhood may have consequences for the lives of its residents. People might have trouble in obtaining work because their area is infamous. It is about what happens to residents. On the other hand, reputation may lead to purposeful (re)actions in response to the area's name. Most research has concentrated on either the material consequences, such as being denied work on the basis of the neighbourhood, or the psychological consequences, for example, the impact of living in stigmatised areas on self-esteem and feelings of happiness. Airey (2003) reports that long-term residents believe their personal identities are stigmatised through a negative reputation. People feel ashamed, and the neighbourhood stigma can lead to psychosocial stress. It is argued that the chances for social participation of people residing in neighbourhoods with a poor reputation are limited because of the bad name their neighbourhood has. Jobs are not offered to them (Wilson, 1996); people do not receive mortgages from banks, or do so only under disadvantageous conditions; and people's self-esteem can be damaged by living in a notorious area (Wacquant, 1993).

Recently some research has tried to address the question of how the residents' behaviour is impacted by neighbourhood reputations. It is thus not about what *happens* to residents, but about what *actions* neighbourhood residents take. Those living in a neighbourhood with a poor (perceived) reputation can make plans of moving out in an attempt to dissociate from the associated stigma. When people believe that their status suffers from a certain group membership, one way for them to react is to distance themselves from that group. This might be the case even when the people concerned are perfectly well satisfied with their neighbourhood. Different studies in Denmark and the Netherlands have found how reputation exerts an independent effect on the chance of intending to leave the neighbourhood. Residents who hold a negative perception of their neighbourhood's reputation are more likely to plan to leave the neighbourhood than those who hold a positive view. That this effect exists can be explained by pointing to the importance of neighbourhood status for the personal identity and self-worth of individuals.

If people believe that their individual status suffers from membership of a group (in this case based on their residential neighbourhood), they may decide to disassociate themselves from this group by moving out of the neighbourhood. The neighbourhood is thus found to be as important as a status object for not only the other city residents but also the residents of the studied neighbourhoods. To understand spatial differentiation of people into different neighbourhoods, neighbourhood reputations are not to be ignored by researchers and policymakers alike.

Other resident behaviour connected to the study of responses to reputations concerns resident participation. Again, different European studies suggest that reputations may have an effect on people's participation in local activities, such as city-initiated neighbourhood meetings and social contacts within the neighbourhood. Some qualitative studies argue that the residents' self-image is negatively impacted by a negative reputation and that they will therefore retreat from participation within the neighbourhood. When people believe that belonging to a certain group is detrimental to their status, they will try to disassociate themselves from that group. Nonparticipation allows them to mediate and escape the perceived negative reputation: residents distance themselves from an area with a disreputable name. Another reason for diminished participation in city-based meetings may be more related to the fact that neighbourhood residents do not expect that the authorities would take them (residents of stigmatised neighbourhoods) seriously. The perception of the neighbourhood's reputation can thus limit civic action at the neighbourhood level. Conversely, some researchers argue that residents of infamous neighbourhoods will not necessarily react to the stigma in this way, observing instead an energising effect on participation. The negative view that outsiders were believed to have of their neighbourhood might result in an adversarial stance towards the outside world and to a stronger in-group loyalty towards fellow residents. A quantitative study in the Netherlands concluded that people who hold a negative reputation perception are less likely to attend city-initiated meetings concerning the neighbourhood.

The reason those holding a negative reputation perception are less likely to participate could be that they do not expect voicing to help resolve the problem of the neighbourhood's reputation because many actors (other city residents, the media) are involved in the construction of this reputation.

Reputations and Policy

Professionals consider that the reputations of the most disreputable neighbourhoods need to be improved, for example, to improve their relative position in the urban housing market and to prevent possible negative effects of the reputation on the residents' life chances. Changing a reputation, however, is a complicated matter. Although different studies show that the socioeconomic and ethnic status of neighbourhoods and their reputations are related, improving reputations by changing the social composition of neighbourhoods is unlikely to succeed. Policies aimed at creating a social mix are often controversial (social engineering) because they appear to be at odds with ideas of social equity and individual choice. Displacement of residents can also lead to the breakdown of important social structures in neighbourhoods because many existing residents are not able to return to their neighbourhood. A new mix may result in tension between old and new residents and a decline of social cohesion. Other studies have also made clear that reputations are connected to the history of the neighbourhoods. A Scottish study of a neighbourhood in Northeast England showed that the current reputation was mainly related to the social class of its original (slum-clearance) residents of many years ago. Apparently, changing the history of a neighbourhood is very difficult; therefore, changing the reputation of an area may be a great challenge. Furthermore, artificially created socially mixed neighbourhoods will likely see a relative quick change of the population composition because of selective mobility in and out of neighbourhoods. Residents move away from neighbourhoods if a socioeconomic mix does not match their own characteristics. It seems paradoxical that creating sustainable mixed neighbourhoods might require substantial policy intervention to keep neighbourhoods mixed. Finally, nonresidents appear to be unwilling to accept that infamous neighbourhoods could change for the better. This creates another difficulty in overcoming negative images of neighbourhoods.

What are the alternative policy measures to improve neighbourhood reputations without explicitly changing the social mix of neighbourhoods? On the basis of the aforementioned discussion, the argument is that expected results of policy will be rather limited. One possibility is to try to weaken the link made by the general urban population between neighbourhood reputations and socioeconomic neighbourhood characteristics. A possible strategy to achieve this is by implementing reputation management as an integral part of neighbourhood renewal policy (branding). Stakeholders such as residents, welfare organisations, councils, and prospective residents should together create a vision of the desired neighbourhood image. Public relations are a significant part of this strategy: neighbourhood transformations (physical, functional, and social) should be widely publicised in local media and on signs along main arteries in the neighbourhood. Further, to attract nonresidents to the neighbourhood, positive pull factors should be used such as shopping, entertainment facilities, and street festivals, concentrating on the positive aspects of the neighbourhoods concerned. Finally, building landmarks on passageways may provide outsiders with a positive view of the neighbourhood.

The lack of evidence of the success of dealing with negative reputations through urban regeneration indicates that reputations are not easily changed and that labels do not simply alter even after intensive physical renewal. In this regard, systematic study that investigates the extent to which policy efforts have been successful in improving the reputations of residential areas is inadequate.

See also: Housing Policy and Regeneration; Neighbourhood Disadvantage; Neighbourhood Effects.

References

Airey L (2003) 'Nae as nice as scheme as it used to be': Lay accounts of neighbourhood incivilities and well-being. *Health & Place* 9: 129–137.
Firey W (1945) Sentiment and symbolism as ecological variables. *American Sociological Review* 10: 140–148.
Hortulanus R (1995) *Stadsbuurten – bewoners en beheerders in buurten met uiteenlopende reputatioes [Urban neighbourhoods – residents and managers in neighbourhoods with diverging reputations]*. Den Haag: VUGA.
Suttles GD (1972) *The Social Construction of Communities*. Chicago, IL; London: The University of Chicago Press.

Wacquant LJD (1993) Urban outcasts: Stigma and division in the black American ghetto and the French periphery. *International Journal of Urban and Regional Research* 17: 366–383.

Wilson WJ (1996) *When work disappears*. Chicago, IL: The University of Chicago Press.

Further Reading

Bauder H (2001) 'You're good with your hands, why don't you become an auto mechanic': Neighborhood context, institutions and career development. *International Journal of Urban and Regional Research* 25: 593–608.

Blokland T (2008) 'You got to remember you live in public housing': Place-making in an American housing project. *Housing, Theory and Society* 25: 31–46.

Bourdieu P (1984) *Distinction: A Social Critique of the Judgment of Taste*. Cambridge, MA: Harvard University Press.

Hastings A (2004) Stigma and social housing estates: Beyond pathological explanations. *Journal of Housing and the Built Environment* 19: 233–254.

Hastings A and Dean J (2003) Challenging images: Tackling stigma through estate regeneration. *Policy & Politics* 31: 171–184.

Permentier M, Van Ham M, and Bolt G (2007) Behavioural responses to neighbourhood reputations. *Journal of Housing and the Built Environment* 22: 199–213.

Permentier M, Van Ham M, and Bolt G (2008) Same neighbourhood...different views? A confrontation of internal and external neighbourhood reputations. *Housing Studies* 23: 833–855.

Permentier M, Van Ham M, and Bolt G (2009) Neighbourhood reputation and the intention to leave the neighbourhood. *Environment and Planning A* 41: 2162–2180.

Permentier MG (2009) *Reputation, Neighbourhoods and Behaviour*. Utrecht: Utrecht University/Faculty of Geosciences.

Semyonov M and Kraus V (1982) The social hierarchies of communities and neighborhoods. *Social Science Quarterly* 63: 780–789.

Skifter Andersen H (2008) Why do residents want to leave deprived neighbourhoods? The importance of residents' subjective evaluations of their neighbourhood and its reputation. *Journal of Housing and the Built Environment* 23: 79–101.

Neighbourhood Watch

R Yarwood, University of Plymouth, Plymouth, UK

© 2012 Elsevier Ltd. All rights reserved.

Glossary

Neighbourhood watch A community-based crime prevention scheme that encourages vigilance amongst residents.
Policing The maintenance of hegemonic behaviour, moral codes, and values beyond those defined by the law. Policing is undertaken by a range of voluntary public and private agencies as well as the police.
Social control The conscious or unconscious coercion of people to behave in ways deemed to be acceptable.
Surveillance A means of social control based on watching or appearing to watch subjects.
The police A state agency tasked with enforcing the law and maintaining social order.

What Is Neighbourhood Watch?

Neighbourhood watch (NW), also known as block watch, community watch, or home watch, is a community-based crime prevention scheme that relies on residents acting together to reduce or prevent crime through surveillance of their neighbourhood. It aims to:

1. cut crime and the opportunities for crime and anti-social behaviour;
2. provide reassurance to local residents and reduce the fear of crime and anti-social behaviour;
3. encourage neighbourliness and closer communities; and
4. improve the quality of life for local residents and tenants.

(Moley and Budd, 2008: 56)

Neighbourhood watch schemes (NWSs) operate in a specific area that can vary in size from a few houses to a large town. Most schemes, as the name suggests, cover several streets that are recognised by local residents as 'their neighbourhood'. The boundaries of a scheme are usually marked with street signs (**Figure 1**) and participating households display their involvement with notices on their properties.

The daily operation of an NWS relies on members simply being 'good neighbours' and keeping an eye out for suspicious activity or persons. Should participants view behaviour that they regard as criminal, antisocial, or simply 'out of place', they are encouraged to phone a local coordinator, who, in turn, liaises with police officers for information and advice. If a crime is witnessed in progress, residents call the police through the usual emergency number. Other than reporting crimes or incidents, members are told specifically not to involve themselves in direct or vigilante action: it remains the job of the police to deal with any trouble and, if necessary, make arrests.

Schemes are organised by local residents who act as coordinators. These coordinators organise the daily operation of the scheme by, for example, providing information, circulating newsletters, acting as a contact point for other members, and liaising with the police.

Support for NW varied between police forces when it was first introduced (Bennett, 1990) but the programme has now been incorporated into community policing strategies of most first-world forces, largely because it has helped to improve public relations (Yarwood and Edwards, 1995). Schemes are often supported by police officers or auxiliaries that have a dedicated community or 'beat management' remit. These officers are often instrumental in the establishment of schemes and work with community groups, such as parish councils, to initiate new ones. On a day-to-day basis, meetings with NW members contribute to proactive, community-based policing and can help to improve the visibility of the police in local areas. The cost of running a scheme may be borne by the public and/or the police, although, recently, there has also been evidence of private sponsorship (**Figure 2**). Insurance companies may also offer participating households a discount from their home insurance premiums.

Operationally, NWSs draw upon two theories of crime prevention (Bennett, 1990) that rely on the definition, communication, and enforcement of a specified territory (Yarwood and Edwards, 1995).

First, schemes use a situational approach by reducing opportunities for crime in a particular area. Thus, NW schemes can be used to disseminate information and resources on 'target hardening' (the often visible strengthening of building's properties and contents to deter or

Figure 1 The boundaries of a neighbourhood watch scheme indicated by a street sign.

resist crime). This might include advice on how to install window locks or the use of property-marking pens to identify processions. Increased vigilance may also lead to more crimes being reported or cleared up. Some NW schemes have evolved to incorporate more active forms of surveillance, such as 'citizen patrols' where members walk the streets.

Second, NW attempts to reduce criminal or undesirable behaviour by using surveillance to increase social control. Those entering an NW area are made aware, through signs and symbols (**Figure 1**), that they are being watched and, as Foucault (1975) argues, are disciplined to conduct themselves in ways that are deemed acceptable. Although at any particular time NW members may or may not be watching their street, the threat of increased surveillance thus serves as a deterrent to criminal behaviour. However, it is unclear whether either of these approaches is effective as there has been limited research on how NWS actually works (or not) (Bennett et al., 2008).

NW has proved to be a remarkably popular scheme that has been adopted by many households, governments, and police forces in many countries. Its advocates note, with some justification, that "Neighborhood Watch is undoubtedly one of the oldest and most well-known crime prevention programs in history" (USAonWatch, 2009). However, its impact on crime rates is unclear and NW has been criticised for its social bias towards middle-class, owner-occupied housing in low-crime areas. The following sections explore these issues in more detail.

Histories and Geographies of Neighbourhood Watch

A key distinction between NW and other more autonomous forms of policing is its support from the police and state. NW emerged in response to changes in state policing in many first-world countries. From the 1960s onwards, policing became increasingly driven by the demands of efficiency (Fyfe, 1995). Reactive, 'fire-brigade' policing became the norm, with less emphasis placed on proactive, community-based methods that were viewed as inefficient in time, money, and organisation. Consequently, the police were withdrawn from many community roles and, in effect, from low-crime areas, often middle-class suburbs or rural communities. Thus, following the 1964 Police Act, 158 local area police forces in the United Kingdom were replaced by only 43 with centralised headquarters. This drive for efficiency, today evidenced by performance targets and league tables, reflected increasingly pervasive neoliberal policy-making by successive western governments (Yarwood, 2007). The proverbial 'bobby on the beat' (an officer patrolling on foot who is known by the community), in itself steeped in myth and nostalgia, became a mourned figure in the eyes of the public.

Despite drives for greater police efficiency, increasing crime rates, coupled with a seemingly distant police force, reduced public confidence in the police and led to increasing demands for greater police visibility. NW offered a way of increasing police contact with some, and often the most vociferous, members of the public without onerous cost, time, or staff commitments.

A further impetus to NW was given by the 'active citizenship' policies of the late 1980s and the early 1990s that encourage members of the public to involve themselves more closely in the running and management of their own localities, including policing (Fyfe, 1995). Public agencies, including local governments and police forces, were obliged to work with and encourage local actors to improve the quality of life in local neighbourhoods. Such policy implies a shifting of blame for social

Figure 2 Neighbourhood watch is a partnership between the public, the police, and private companies in Western Australia.

problems from government to community, as the following example implies:

> crime is higher in 'socially disorganized areas' marked by weakened informal control due to an erosion of shared norms. Since formal control organizations (specifically law enforcement) cannot be in all areas at one time, informal control of residents is necessary if that community is to experience low crime rates. When neighborhoods become disorganized, the people and institutions that once assisted in maintaining standards of behavior no longer hold such status, resulting in a breakdown in informal control. This, in turn, produces high crime rates. (USAonWatch, 2009)

Given that NW had the potential to meet the demands of the public, government, and police, it is perhaps of little surprise that NW developed so quickly. The first formal NWSs were established in Seattle in 1972 by The National Sheriffs' Association in the United States (Bennet et al., 2008). By 1981, it was estimated that 12% of the US urban population was involved in a scheme, which had risen to as high as 20% by 1988 (USAonWatch,

2009). The first scheme in the United Kingdom was established in Mollington, Cheshire, in 1982. Membership increased dramatically during the 1990s and the British Crime Survey (BCS) estimated that 27% of households in the United Kingdom were members of a scheme in 2000 (Moley and Budd, 2008). According to Home Office data based on registrations for public liability insurance, there are 129 357 active schemes covering over 9 million households in the United Kingdom.

Although NWSs are now a presence in most first-world countries, they reflect spatial and social differences in society. Numerous studies have confirmed that NW schemes are favoured in middle-class, owner-occupied, low-crime areas (Hourihan, 1987; Hussain, 1988; Moley and Budd, 2008; Yarwood and Edwards, 1995) and that there is "less support for NW in those areas where the need for it is greatest" (Hough and Mayhew, 1985: 42). This is because schemes rely on existing community ties rather than creating them (Fyfe, 1995). Schemes are likely to flourish in places with high numbers of middle-aged, middle-class residents with the skills, time, confidence, and opportunity to run schemes. Conversely, 'socially disorganised areas' (to borrow the terminology of USAonWatch) with high levels of mistrust between neighbours, poor police relations, and few community groups are less likely to possess the social capital needed to establish and maintain a scheme. The location of an NWS tends to reflect rather than affect community relations and the fear of crime. Despite the need for more vertical integration across society, generics such as 'horse watch', 'marina watch', and 'vehicle watch' have emerged to protect different types of property rather than a wider range of people.

Like any form of policing, NW has the potential to enforce dominant codes, standards, and ideals held by society and, in doing so, to exclude certain social groups from space. In some cases, residents are seeking more direct control of public spaces and there is clearly a danger that NW can be used to police behaviour that is 'out of place' rather than criminal, such as young people 'hanging around' street corners. This said, experienced police officers may be able to distinguish more clearly between these behaviours and be capable of mediating and diffusing some of the more outrageous demands made by some NW members. But certainly NW, like the twitching of net-curtains, has become a metaphor for an ordered, heterogeneous suburbia.

Yet, if NW enforces and re-produces suburban norms, then it is of little surprise that it has not spread widely out of these places. It also raises important questions about its remit and the extent to which it could or should be used to enforce certain norms. Both of these premises, however, assume that NW is effective in its operation and, as the next section discusses, this is far from assured.

The Effectiveness of Neighbourhood Watch

The effectiveness of NW at reducing or preventing crime has been difficult to evaluate (Bennett, 1990; Bennett et al., 2008). Many schemes operate in areas where crime rates are already low and so it is hard to gauge with any statistical significance their impact on relatively minor fluctuations in crime. As NW encourages the reporting of crime, recorded crime rates may actually increase when a scheme is implemented reflecting increases in vigilance rather than in offences. Furthermore, schemes cannot be considered in isolation. Thus, changes in crime rates may reflect wider changes in local, regional, or national crime rates rather than the action of a scheme in a specific locality. It has also been suggested that the 'target hardening' associated with NWSs may lead to the displacement of crime to other 'softer' targets in other areas, making it hard to assess the overall impact of these schemes on crime rates.

Given these difficulties, there has been no academic consensus on the effectiveness of NW. Some studies have suggested that NW can reduce crime, especially low-level offences and antisocial behaviour (Hussain, 1988); others, that NW has made little difference (McConville and Shepherd, 1992); and still others, that it can lead to apparent increases in crime (Bennett, 1990). In an effort to draw these disparate threads together, Bennett et al. concluded after a review of selected literature that "Neighbourhood Watch is effective in reducing crime" (2008: 34). They note, though, that little is known about why schemes are effective and how NW works. Closer research on the mechanisms of NW may help to answer questions about its effectiveness but, until then, academics, policy-makers, and the police are likely to remain divided about its impact on crime.

It seems that NW's main contribution is to increase the feelings of security and improve relations between the police and the public (Bennett, 1990; Moley and Budd, 2008; Yarwood and Edwards, 1995). Given that NW is cheap and easy to implement, it is therefore of little surprise that so many forces have adopted and promoted schemes in order to gain from these benefits.

What is clear is that although NW can work in particular circumstances (Hock and Kosfeld, 2007), its success is far from guaranteed. Many schemes fall on stony ground: they are warmly received by residents but this initial enthusiasm often wanes. McConville and Shepperd (1992: 114) suggest that "crime is not a salient feature issue in most people's lives. It is not for the most part central enough to drive communities together". Thus, schemes in low-crime areas are liable to cease operation; become dormant until awakened by a real or perceived crime; or experience sporadic activity through occasional meetings, newsletters, and the actions of key individuals. Like any community-based organisation, NWS relies on strong social capital and key local stakeholders, such as local residents or police officers, to maintain operational schemes. By way of example, a scheme in Plymouth, UK, recently ceased operation after its coordinator left the neighbourhood and, despite police requests, nobody volunteered to replace him.

When evaluating NW it is also important to note the relation of NW with other forms of policing and security. Thus, Putnam (2000) notes that while 11% of US residents have attended an NW meeting, many more (43%) have invested in extra locks to secure their home according to some surveys. He argues that individual rather than community-based actions are of greater significance to most people (although the two are not mutually exclusive as NW schemes encourage greater personal security). Gated communities, private security, and closed circuit television (CCTV) surveillance now play a more active role in the policing of space, including certain residential areas, than NW does. In South Africa, for example, private security companies are a more significant feature of the policing landscape than voluntary schemes (or indeed state patrols). Paying rather than volunteering may provide a more convenient and effective form of security for those with the means to do so, reflecting the social and geographical inequalities of policing in a neoliberal society. Other forms of neighbourhood policing, such as community support officers and local policing teams in the United Kingdom, are also emerging to reassert the value of professional policing in residential areas. These new forms of policing are attracting academic interest (Yarwood, 2007), and, since the 1990s, research into NW has waned (Bennett et al., 2008).

Future

The twenty-first century has been a moribund period for NW. Schemes remain active in many areas and have become an established part of the 'community policing' strategies of most police forces. Yet numbers are static or in decline: reaching saturation point in middle-class communities but with little osmosis into more needy areas. Numbers of schemes in the United Kingdom are generally declining: according to the 2006–07 BCS only 16% of households were members compared to a peak of 27% in 2000 (Moley and Budd, 2008). Policy-makers too are less concerned with NW, evidenced by the dropping of questions about NW from the BCS.

Efforts have therefore been made to relaunch, rebrand, and expand the role of NW. By 1999, NW in New Zealand developed into neighbourhood support, with, as the name suggests, a broader civic remit. Besides preventing crime, members are encouraged to work together and with other community groups to 'solve local problems' and to 'identify the needs of neighbours and ways to assist each other'. Neighbourhood support groups have also been trained to work with civil defence teams during local or national emergencies by, for example, checking neighbours following an earthquake or flood event. In the wake of the 9/11 attacks in 2001, NW in the United States was relaunched as 'USAonWatch' with a remit to defend homes against not only crime but also terrorist threats. The aim is to "empower citizens to become active in homeland security" (USAonWatch, 2009). Scheme members have been encouraged to retrain as 'community emergency response teams' (CERTs) capable of providing first response and assistance at a time of civic emergency.

NW is set to remain a visible presence in the suburban landscape of most first-world countries. It offers a sticking-plaster approach to crime, dealing with the symptoms of insecurity but doing little to deal with the underlying causes of crime. Although doubts remain about its effectiveness in reducing crime, its convenience and low cost continue to make it an attractive if token element of community-based policing. The scheme will continue to benefit and reflect the values of elite social groups and areas, rather than people and places more in need of better security. Consequently, the location of NW reveals more about the spatialities of community, home, and policing than it does about crime.

See also: Crime Prevention Through Environmental Design; Defensible Space; Gated Communities; Neighbourhood Governance; Neighbourhood Incivilities; Resident and Neighbourhood Movements.

References

Bennett T (1990) *Evaluating Neighbourhood Watch*. Aldershot, UK: Gower.
Bennett T, Holloway K, and Farrington D (2008) *The Effectiveness of Neighbourhood Watch*. Oslo, Norway: The Campbell Collaboration.
Foucault M (1975) *Discipline and Punish: The Birth of the Prison*. New York: Random House.
Fyfe N (1995) Law and order policy and the spaces of citizenship in contemporary Britain. *Political Geography* 14: 177–189.
Hock S and Kosfeld M (2007) The dynamics of neighbourhood watch and norm enforcement. *The Economic Journal* 117: 270–286.
Hough M and Mayhew P (1985) *Taking Account of Crime: Key Findings of the Second British Crime Survey*. London: HMSO.
Hourihan K (1987) Local community development and participation in NW: A case study of Cork, Ireland. *Urban Studies* 24: 129–136.
Hussain S (1988) *Neighbourhood Watch in England and Wales: A Locational Analysis*. London: HMSO.

McConville M and Shepperd D (1992) *Watching Police, Watching Communities*. London: Routledge.

Moley S and Budd S (2008) Neighbourhood watch membership. In: Nicholas S, Flatley J, Hoare J, Patterson A, Southcott C, Moley S, and Jansson K (eds.) *Circumstances of Crime, Neighbourhood Watch Membership and Perceptions of Policing: Supplementary Vol. 3 to Crime in England and Wales 2006/07 Findings from the 2006/07 British Crime Survey*, pp. 55–67. London: Home Office.

Putnam D (2000) *Bowling Alone: The Collapse and Revival of American Community*. New York: Simon and Schuster.

USAonWatch (2009) About USAonWatch. http://www.usaonwatch.org/about/default.aspx (accessed 5 October).

Yarwood R (2007) The geographies of policing. *Progress in Human Geography* 31: 447–466.

Yarwood R and Edwards W (1995) Voluntary action in rural areas: The case of neighbourhood watch. *Journal of Rural Studies* 11: 447–460.

Further Reading

Neighbourhood and Home Watch Network (2009) http://www.mynhw.co.uk/about.php (accessed 8 October).

Neoclassical Models of the Housing Market

M Andrew, City University London, London, UK

© 2012 Elsevier Ltd. All rights reserved.

Glossary

Intertemporal optimisation Maximising an objective function over time.

Marginal rate of substitution The rate at which a consumer is ready to give up a unit of a good in exchange for another good while maintaining the same level of utility.

Methodological individualism A proposition that economic phenomena can be adequately explained by studying the behaviour of an individual. It is assumed that social interactions between individuals due to interdependent preferences and the process by which individuals organise themselves into groups/create institutions may be ignored.

Mix-adjusted house price A weighted average of the prices of different dwelling types and is constructed to account for the heterogeneous nature of houses.

Net saving The difference between saving and borrowing.

Nonhousing composite good A composite good is an abstraction and in this article is used to represent all nonhousing goods and services.

Perfect credit markets No restrictions on borrowing and lending.

Representative agent A term describing a typical decision-maker (consumer or firm) in an economic model. It is assumed that the choices of individuals can be aggregated together to represent the decision of one individual or that there are many identical individuals in the market.

Shadow price A price that eliminates excess demand in the market if the product was not rationed using nonprice criteria. It represents the marginal utility of relaxing the credit constraint, and provides an indication of how much a consumer would be willing to pay in order to obtain an extra unit of a mortgage loan.

Neoclassical Economic Models

Neoclassical economics attempts to explain the determination of equilibrium prices, outputs, and incomes and the distribution of economic activity using demand and supply analysis. It is based on micro-foundations or methodological individualism. Demand and supply interaction establishes a unique equilibrium price and output level, which reflects the solution to a representative agent's constrained optimisation problem. On the demand side, an individual is assumed to maximise utility by consuming goods and services, but is restricted in the amount consumed by available income and wealth and relative prices. On the supply side, it is assumed that a firm attempts to maximise profits but is constrained by market demand and factor costs. Prices act as signals informing agents on the course of actions to take. The paradigm assumes that agents (1) are rational and have preferences for identifiable outcomes which can be ranked, (2) attempt to maximise their objectives, and (3) act independently with access to full and relevant information.

Market supply and demand for final goods and services is obtained by aggregating across firms and individuals, and analogously, the market supply and demand for each factor of production. Factor demand is linked to market output through its marginal productivity and cost. Neoclassical economics is 'positive' in the sense that it can describe and explain why events occur, but unlike 'normative economics', does not provide an indication of what ought to have happened or what polices ought to be promoted. But 'positive' economic analysis is frequently necessary for ranking economic policies or outcomes to help in judging their acceptability.

The assumption of agents acting rationally is frequently criticised as it ignores important aspects of human behaviour. Behavioural economists argue that social, cognitive, and emotional factors should be taken into consideration. Agents are likely to have limited information, cognitive ability, and time in which to decide, and may be influenced by social pressures. Furthermore, it is argued that rational decision-making only occurs after the choices available have been reduced. Neoclassical economic models, on the other hand, assume that people are on average rational, and can in large enough numbers be approximated to act according to their preferences. For further discussion on this topic, see article Behavioural Economics.

Neoclassical economic analysis relies on mathematical and statistical models to explain economic phenomena, which tend to involve simplifying assumptions. Critics argue that this is often undertaken without sufficient consideration about whether the model specified actually describes a market. On the other hand, Friedman, an influential economist, asserts that theories should be judged by their ability to predict and explain events rather than by the realism of their assumptions. Neoclassical economic models are also criticised because they can neglect the role of institutions, which can condition individual behaviour. For more detail on this topic within the encyclopaedia, please see article Housing Policy: Agents and Regulators. But it is sometimes possible to adapt the standard neoclassical model to account for institutional features of a particular market.

The Special Characteristics of Housing

In this section, the main distinguishing characteristics of housing are highlighted as it helps in judging the extent to which neoclassical housing models are successful as an analytical tool.

1. Housing provides shelter and access to amenities. Housing is also a durable good and can be resold in the future. Therefore, it is both a consumption good and an asset.
2. Housing is indivisible, making it lumpy to purchase. Many households require finance to purchase a house, implying that mortgage markets play an important role.
3. Housing is multidimensional, comprising of physical and location attributes. No two houses are alike. It is not a homogeneous good.
4. There are significant frictions in the market which give rise to search costs. In addition, there are large transactions costs in the owner-occupied sector.
5. Housing is subject to large numbers of market imperfections and nonneutralities. Many arise from the social aspect of housing.

The Standard Neoclassical Model: The Housing User Cost of Capital

Early models of the housing market often neglected the investment dimension as demand and supply equations were specified in an ad hoc manner. The standard neoclassical model of the housing market is rigorously derived, based on the solution of a constrained intertemporal optimisation problem (Dougherty and Van Order, 1982). The representative agent has to decide on the amount of housing services and a nonhousing composite good to consume, subject to an income, wealth, and technical constraint. The flow of housing services is assumed to be directly proportional to the housing stock. Credit markets are assumed to be perfect. Formally, the lifetime utility function is as follows:

$$\int_0^\infty e^{-rt} U(C_t, H_t) dt \qquad [1]$$

where C = nonhousing composite good, H = housing stock/housing services, and r = real discount rate.

Using the price of nonhousing goods and services as a numéraire, the household budget constraint describing the relationship between real spending on housing and the nonhousing composite good, real income, and saving is as follows:

$$P_{ht} X_t + C_t + S_t = (1-\theta) Y_t + (1-\theta) i_t A_t \qquad [2]$$

where P_{ht} = real price of a dwelling, X_t = new purchases of dwellings, $P_{ht} X_t$ = real spending on new housing purchases, C_t = real spending on nonhousing consumption, S_t = real savings net of new loans, θ = marginal household tax rate, Y_t = real gross disposable income, $(1-\theta) Y_t$ = post-tax income, i_t = nominal mortgage interest rate, and A_t = real net nonhousing assets (net of new loans).

The right-hand side of eqn [2] represents the sources of household income and the left-hand side on how this income is spent.

The wealth constraint, describing how real financial wealth can change through net saving and asset value depreciation from inflation, is as follows:

$$\dot{A}_t = S_t - \pi A_t \qquad [3]$$

where ($\cdot$) represents the time derivative and π = general rate of inflation.

There is an equivalent constraint to account for the physical depreciation to housing:

$$\dot{H}_t = X_t - \delta H_t \qquad [4]$$

where δ is the depreciation rate.

Maximisation of the lifetime utility function subject to these constraints yields the first-order conditions. In particular, the marginal rate of substitution between housing and the composite nonhousing consumption good is as follows:

$$\mu_h / \mu_c = P_{ht} UCC_t \qquad [5]$$

where μ_h = the marginal utility of consuming housing services, μ_c = the marginal utility of consuming the composite nonhousing good, μ_h/μ_c = the marginal rate of substitution, and UCC_t = the housing user cost of capital.

The marginal rate of substitution depicts the trade-off between consuming housing services by forgoing the nonhousing composite good. The term to the right of the equals sign is made up of the housing user cost of capital multiplied by the real dwelling price and measures all the elements of owner-occupied housing costs. The house price is the price of a standardised dwelling or a mix-adjusted price. The housing user cost of capital is a discount rate representing the opportunity cost to investing in housing. Lower values imply that housing is more attractive as an investment compared to nonhousing assets. Thus, both the investment and consumption aspects of housing decisions are captured.

The marginal rate of substitution reflects the consumption value or the imputed real rental price of owner-occupied housing services. Equation [5] may be reexpressed as follows:

$$R_t = P_{ht} UCC_t \qquad [6]$$

where R_t = imputed real rent.

Note that alternative approaches may be used to derive this arbitrage relationship. For example, it may be obtained by examining how much rent landlords with similar tax breaks to homeowners would charge in a competitive market. On the assumption that the landlord would wish to maximise the present value of his/her real cash flow from rent, the equilibrium price and the equilibrium rent will depend upon the housing user cost (Dougherty and Van Order, 1982).

The housing user cost of capital contains a number of elements. As the basic model assumes perfect credit markets and households can borrow and lend at the same nominal interest rates, it takes the simple form as follows:

$$UCC_t = (1-\theta)i_t - \dot{g}^e_{ht} + M + \delta + LPT_t \qquad [7]$$

where M = maintenance expenditure on the dwelling, expressed as a percentage of the house price; δ = rate of depreciation; $\dot{g}^e_{ht}$ = expected rate of nominal housing capital gain; and LPT_t = local property taxes, expressed as a percentage of the house price.

Higher maintenance and local tax expenditures and/or a higher rate of depreciation make housing less attractive as an investment. Tax relief and subsidies reduce the user cost. In eqn [7], the rate of tax relief on mortgage interest payments is assumed to be equal to the marginal tax rate (θ) – homeowners only pay a proportion of the mortgage interest charged, a feature of the UK taxation system in the 1970s and early 1980s. More generally, the housing user cost can be adapted to account for different taxation systems. For example, US households can claim tax relief at their marginal tax rate not only on mortgage interest payments, but also on expenditure on maintenance and local property taxes, and receive an allowance for depreciation.

The controversial term in the user cost is the expected rate of nominal capital gain. One issue concerns its measurement. Information about expectations is not generally available. Typically, it is assumed that there is an adaptive expectations process and it can be proxied using the previous rate of actual capital gains or a moving average of past actual rates. The second issue concerns the assumption that it is a point estimate. Nordvik (1995) derives a more general measure which captures a household's uncertainty over its price expectations. Measurement is a problem and he dropped this term in the empirical analysis.

The Housing User Cost: Real and Nominal Interest Rates

The third issue concerns the magnitude of the expected rate of capital gain's impact on the housing user cost. The standard model implies that only real interest rates matter, and the US empirical evidence supports this view (Haurin et al., 1994). However, there is a theoretical argument for nominal interest rates to be influential due to front-end loading. Front-end loading occurs because the typical mortgage contract specifies fixed nominal payments during the mortgage term. Real mortgage repayments are thus higher at the start of the mortgage and fall over time. The higher the inflation rate, the steeper the fall in the real repayment profile, ceteris paribus. Front-end loading can be considered to be an approximation of general liquidity constraints preventing households from realising their capital gains immediately. Thus, both real and nominal rates potentially play a role. The real post-tax interest rate is the term in square brackets in eqn [8]:

$$UCC_t = [(1-\theta)i_t - \beta(\pi + \dot{p}^e_b)_t] + M + \delta + LPT_t \qquad [8]$$

where $0 \leq (\beta) \leq 1$, π = general inflation rate, $\dot{p}^e_b$ = expected rate of real housing capital gain, and $\dot{g}^e_b = (\pi + \dot{p}^e_b)$, the nominal rate of housing capital gains.

Only real and only nominal interest rates matter if $\beta = 1$ and $\beta = 0$, respectively. Meen and Andrew (1998) find that the estimated value of $\beta = 0.3$, a value consistently obtained using a range of different measures of expected nominal capital gains. Note that it is also possible that β taking a value of less than 1 might be capturing measurement errors in expectations.

The Housing User Cost: Imperfect Credit Markets

Housing is indivisible. In many countries, households have to take out a mortgage to purchase a home. But capital markets are often not perfect. Relaxing the assumptions of unrestricted access to credit and being able to lend and borrow at the same interest rate yields a more general measure of the housing user cost:

$$\text{UCC}_t = \text{LVR}_t(1-\theta)i_t + (1-\text{LVR}_t)i_{dt} - \dot{g}^e_{ht} + M + \delta + \text{LPT}_t + (\lambda/\mu_c)_t \qquad [9]$$

where LVR_t = the extent of debt gearing as opposed to equity finance, i_t = nominal mortgage interest rate, i_{dt} = the nominal interest rate representing the cost to the homeowner of holding an equity stake in the housing asset, and $(\lambda/\mu_c)_t$ = credit rationing term.

The user cost now includes a term (λ/μ_c) capturing the impact of a tightening or relaxation of credit market restrictions, representing the ratio of the shadow price of rationing to the marginal utility of the composite nonhousing good, and distinguishes between different lending and borrowing interest rates. The combined nominal interest rate becomes a weighted average, the weight being the typical loan-to-value ratio (LVR). If the typical amount of gearing is high, say 70%, then mortgage interest rates will have a larger influence than interest rates available on alternative investments.

Credit rationing occurs when the effective demand for mortgage funds exceeds supply, which has the effect of raising the user cost. The user cost can account for disequilibrium and equilibrium credit rationing regimes. Disequilibrium credit rationing occurs when the mortgage interest rate is not at the market clearing level due to an imperfect market structure, government regulations, or usury laws, and often results in a queuing system to allocate funds, for example, the need to have a savings record with the lender. The UK mortgage market in the 1970s and early 1980s experienced such a regime. Equilibrium credit rationing occurs when the nonprice mortgage terms and mortgage interest rates are at market equilibrium. But because mortgage lenders face asymmetrical information and moral hazard problems, and cannot fully insure their mortgage default risks, they exclude some potential borrowers from obtaining loans and other borrowers from taking out their desired mortgage debt. Meen (1990) and Meen (2008) provide an insight into measuring rationing under each type of regime.

The Life-Cycle Housing Demand and House Price Model

The arbitrage condition can be rearranged to show that the real house price is determined by real rents discounted by the housing user cost of capital:

$$P_{ht} = R_t/\text{UCC}_t \qquad [10]$$

Equation [10] suggests that there is a long-run equilibrium relationship between real rents, real house prices, and real returns in asset markets. A stable relationship between real rents and real house prices only exists if conditions in the asset markets remain unchanged. Otherwise, the long-run relationship between real rents and real house prices will adjust accordingly.

Implicit in eqn [10] is the assumption that the market for housing services is in equilibrium. The unobserved rent measuring the benefit homeowners receive from living in a dwelling may be substituted for market rents observed in the private rented sector, provided its housing stock is similar in quality to that in owner-occupation. In the United Kingdom, this substitution is inappropriate as the private rented housing stock is inferior. This is a lesser problem in countries with a larger private rented sector, notably the United States. The social dimension of housing and the desire to provide decent affordable homes has led governments in many countries to impose rent controls, to grant tenants a high degree of security of tenure, and to provide public housing. Rent controls often force landlords to charge rents below market levels. Lease agreements guaranteeing tenants a high degree of security of tenure may prevent the market from clearing. Public housing is often subject to rent controls and rationing in access to it – households have to fulfil certain 'needs'-based criteria to qualify. Equation [10] can be estimated directly, but in many cases this is not feasible because of the absence of suitable data on real rents. Since the real rent represents the market clearing price of housing services, it can be replaced with variables determining its value, such as real personal disposable income per household, the stock of dwellings, the number of households, and real financial wealth per household.

It is possible to invert the relationship in eqn [10] to obtain the life-cycle housing demand and housing supply equations (Meen and Andrew, 1998). Thus, life-cycle housing demand depends upon the housing user cost, real house prices, real personal disposable income per household, the number of households, and real financial wealth per household. Equation [10] is an aggregate housing market relationship, implicitly summing across the individual agent housing demands. This summation is valid if the parameters of the housing demand functions do not vary across households or if as it is likely that they do, when the income distribution is unchanged over time. In the United Kingdom, there are indications that a shift has occurred, with younger households faring poorly during the first half of the 1990s. In such cases, the aggregate neoclassical housing demand model should include an income distribution variable (Meen and Andrew, 1998).

The House Price Model and Housing Market Frictions

Buying and selling a house incurs higher search and transactions costs compared with financial assets. Financial transactions costs include brokers' fees, stamp duty, and conveyancing costs. In addition, there are psychological costs attached to moving. An additional component can be added to the housing user cost term to account for this:

$$UCC_t = LVR_t(1-\theta)i_t + (1-LVR_t)i_{dt} - \dot{g}^e_{bt} + M + \delta + LPT_t + TC_t + (\lambda/\mu_c)_t \quad [11]$$

where TC_t = annualised transactions costs, expressed as a percentage of the house price.

Measuring annualised transactions costs is problematic and is discussed later when examining tenure choice models. The presence of transactions costs and credit restrictions leads to lagged house price adjustment, that is, housing demand does not respond immediately to changes in the economic environment. Hence, it is possible for there to be short-run deviations from the arbitrage relationship depicted in eqn [10] but for it to still hold in the long run, when transactions costs and financial constraints, are less binding. Efficiency tests suggest that the arbitrage relationship does not hold in the housing market in every time period (Englund and Ioannides, 1997). A number of empirical studies report that house prices exhibit short-run positive autocorrelation with reversion in the longer term to the mean. Consequently, modern macro time-series house price models adopt an error correction econometric framework, where house price changes occur when the actual real house price deviates from its equilibrium value (Malpezzi, 1999; Meen, 2008). Time-series studies find that real house price changes are dominated by changes in interest rates, capital gains, and real incomes. The relative importance of search and transactions costs has led to the extension of the neoclassical housing model to explicitly examine the short-run adjustment in prices by establishing linkages between the search process, housing demand, housing supply, vacancies, and house prices (Wheaton, 1990).

The Housing Tenure Choice and Housing Services Consumption Model

The neoclassical housing tenure choice model examines the decision to rent or to buy a home using separate indirect utility functions to represent each housing tenure. The representative household is predicted to purchase a home when the value of its indirect utility function for owner-occupation is higher than renting. Similarly to the life-cycle housing demand model, the focus is on the relative cost of renting and owning, conditional on a household's characteristics. The cost of homeownership can be considered to be the rental income foregone by living in a dwelling. The link between them can be seen by rewriting the standard arbitrage condition to:

$$R_t = P_{ht} UCC_r \quad [12]$$

The imputed rent is equal to the housing user cost multiplied by the real house price. Although derived from the same theoretical framework as the life-cycle housing demand macromodel, there is a difference as explaining the housing tenure choice involves a comparison of a package of housing services rather than incremental changes to levels. Hendershott and Slemrod (1983) show that the relevant tax variable in the tenure choice decision is the average tax saving per dollar of expense due to being a homeowner rather than a tenant, whereas the appropriate tax variable for the quantity of housing demanded is the tax saving from a marginal dollar of housing-related expenses. This means that rate θ should replace θ_{tenure}, a ratio of the total tax savings from the purchase of a house to the potential reduction in taxable income due to the purchase.

Empirical housing tenure choice studies tend to be conducted on micro-data and apply discrete choice econometric methods. The standard housing tenure choice model predicts that households are more likely to become homeowners when owner-occupation costs are lower compared to renting, and/or when their permanent incomes are higher, holding other household characteristics constant. Empirical studies report that household composition such as the presence of a partner and children are influential in explaining homeownership rates. Surprises and unanticipated events such as partner separation/divorce or unemployment are very influential in explaining transitions out of homeownership. The housing tenure choice models are often extended to consider the quantity of housing services demanded for a chosen tenure (King, 1980).

The Housing Tenure Choice Model: Imperfect Capital Markets

A key assumption in the standard model is that access to perfect credit markets permits households to borrow against expected higher levels of future incomes. Credit market constraints and their impact on housing decisions has been a major focus of US research (Jones, 1989; Linneman and Wachter, 1989; Linnenman et al., 1997). Studies using tenure choice models with credit constraint terms conclude that current incomes and current net wealth become important determinants. The US empirical literature reports that the wealth constraint tends to exert a larger effect than the income constraint in reducing the likelihood of homeownership, and that for younger households, the constraints tend to be more binding and the effects are larger. Obtaining credit rationing measures requires data on wealth, debt, and banks' lending preferences, and being able to distinguish between constrained and nonconstrained households, as well as modelling desired housing demand.

Housing Mobility, Housing Tenure, and Housing Consumption

As shown earlier, transactions costs can be incorporated explicitly into the housing user cost of capital. However, it is not transactions costs per se that are important, but annualised transactions costs as households may spread the costs of moving by staying longer in the new home. Empirical investigations on this topic have tended to be conducted on micro-data. Residence spell determines the rate transactions costs are annualised – a shorter planned stay implies a higher housing user cost of capital (Haurin and Gill, 2002). Two major problems have to be overcome when attempting to incorporate transactions costs. The first problem is that planned stays are simultaneously determined with the housing tenure choice and the quantity of housing demanded. The second problem concerns the measurement of a planned spell since not all observed spells are planned. Unanticipated events may lead to an unplanned termination or prolonged stay in a dwelling. Haurin and Gill (2002) exploit a data set with married military personnel assigned to an area for a specific period of time, and conclude that the expected length of stay is significant in determining the housing tenure choice. However, the largest transactions costs, the psychological costs of moving, are often ignored because they are difficult to measure. The neoclassical housing tenure choice model has been extended to include household mobility (Goodman, 2002), where the utility function now includes a term for immobility costs to capture forgone utility as a consequence of not moving and staying in a dwelling that is no longer appropriate. The added advantage is that such models make it possible to discern separable impacts of incomes and housing costs on mobility, housing tenure, and housing consumption.

The Puzzling Relationship: House Prices and Housing Transactions

Although the standard neoclassical model omits key features of a housing market, it can be modified to incorporate the 'special' characteristics of housing. Sometimes, empirical implementations of the theoretical improvements prove to be difficult due to data problems. Well-specified housing models can provide insights into functioning of the market, which is one way to judge their value. We end by illustrating how a neoclassical model can explain the puzzle of observed relationships between house price movements and housing transactions found in many countries. A conventional model predicts that any demand shock should be immediately reflected in a change to house prices without any effect on the volume of transactions. But a model incorporating credit rationing and search and transactions costs can explain such relationships. Price falls make it difficult for liquidity-constrained homeowners to repay their mortgage debt and, at the same time, transfer sufficient equity to meet the deposit on a new home (Stein, 1995). The likelihood of moving falls and partly explains the observed positive correlation. The search process in the market involves matching buyers to sellers, which becomes difficult when their valuations of properties are different. Sellers will adjust their reservation prices but only slowly in response to demand shocks, implying that the volume of transactions is affected before house prices. If time on the market, the inverse of transactions, increases, it persuades sellers to lower reservation prices, implying that, in the short run, prices and transactions will be positively correlated. In the longer term, prices will fall to a new permanently lower level, whereas transactions return to their original level (Berkovec and Goodman, 1996). Andrew and Meen (2003) use the life-cycle housing demand model to obtain a measure of market disequilibrium. They undertake a simulation analysis to show how an economic shock results in a positive correlation in prices and transactions in the short run, transactions changing before prices in response to a shock, and shocks inducing permanent changes in prices but only temporary changes in transactions.

Summary and Conclusion

This article reviewed the neoclassical economic model of the housing market. The model is based on an arbitrage relationship between the real house price and real rent appropriately discounted by the housing user cost of capital. In its basic form, it incorporates both the investment and consumption dimensions of housing, but can be extended to capture the 'other' special characteristics of housing. This flexibility makes it a powerful tool for examining different housing issues. With the increased availability of better-quality data, it is likely that its empirical application will be extended to other countries and to investigating housing topics pertinent at lower spatial scales, for example, the spatial diffusion of house prices across subregions/housing market areas. Perhaps the biggest challenge to the neoclassical housing model is its ability to explain the large house price boom and bust in the 2000s. Some people have questioned whether individuals and lending institutions behaved rationally, and/or whether their behaviour was directly influenced by the actions of fellow participants in the market, 'peer group pressure'. Both assertions are inconsistent with the fundamental precept of the neoclassical housing model. Further investigation into the contentious and under-researched term in the housing user cost of capital, the expected rate of capital gain, might shed some light on this issue. Explicitly examining how expectations are formed could help to distinguish between behaviour caused by irrational (unrealistic) expectations from that due to individuals using market information when forming expectations but consistently making mistakes in the short term.

See also: Behavioural Economics; Housing Demand; Housing Policy: Agents and Regulators.

References

Andrew M and Meen GP (2003) House price appreciation, transactions and structural change in the British housing market: A macroeconomic perspective. *Real Estate Economics* 31(1): 99–116.

Berkovec JA and Goodman JL (1996) Turnover as a measure of demand for existing homes. *Real Estate Economics* 24(4): 421–440.

Dougherty A and Van Order R (1982) Inflation, housing costs and the consumer price index. *American Economic Review* 72: 154–165.

Englund P and Ioannides Y (1997) House price dynamics: An international empirical perspective. *Journal of Housing Economics* 6(2): 119–136.

Goodman A (2002) Estimating equilibrium housing demand for stayers. *Journal of Urban Economics* 51: 1–24.

Haurin DR and Gill HL (2002) The impact of transactions costs and the expected length of stay on homeownership. *Journal of Urban Economics* 51: 563–584.

Haurin DR, Hendershott PH, and Kim D (1994) Housing decisions of American youth. *Journal of Urban Economics* 35: 28–44.

Hendershott PH and Slemrod J (1983) Taxes and the user cost of capital for owner-occupied housing. *AREUA Journal* 10: 375–393.

Jones LD (1989) Current wealth and tenure choice. *Journal of the American Real Estate and Urban Economics Association* 17: 17–40.

King M (1980) An econometric model of tenure choice and demand for housing as a joint decision. *Journal of Public Economics* 14: 137–159.

Linneman P and Wachter S (1989) The impacts of borrowing constraints on homeownership. *AREUEA Journal* 17: 389–402.

Linneman P, Megbolugbe IF, and Cho M (1997) Do borrowing constraints change in U.S. homeownership rates? *Journal of Housing Economics* 6: 318–333.

Malpezzi S (1999) A simple error correction model of house prices. *Journal of Housing Economics* 8(1): 27–62.

Meen G (1990) The measurement of rationing and treatment of structural change in the UK mortgage market. *Journal of Applied Econometrics* 5(2): 167–188.

Meen GP (2008) *A Simple Model of Housing and the Credit Crunch. Discussion Paper.* Reading, UK: International Centre for Housing and Urban Economics.

Meen GP and Andrew M (1998) On the aggregate housing market implications of labour market change. *Scottish Journal of Political Economy* 45(4): 393–419.

Nordvik V (1995) Prices and price expectations in the market for owner occupied housing. *Housing Studies* 10(3): 365–381.

Stein JC (1995) Prices and trading volume in the housing market: A model with downpayment effects. *The Quarterly Journal of Economics* 110(2): 379–405.

Wheaton WC (1990) Vacancy, search, and prices in a housing market matching model. *Journal of Political Economy* 98: 1270–1292.

Further Reading

Goodman A (2003) Following a panel of stayers: Length of stay, tenure choice and housing demand. *Journal of Housing Economics* 12: 106–133.

Haurin DR, Hendershott PH, and Wachter S (1997) Borrowing constraints and the tenure choice of young households. *Journal of Housing Research* 8(2): 137–154.

Meen GP (1990) The removal of mortgage market constraints and the implications for econometric modelling of UK house prices. *Oxford Bulletin of Economics and Statistics* 52(1): 1–24.

Neural Networks and Analytic Hierarchy Processes

T Kauko, Norwegian University of Science and Technology – NTNU, Trondheim, Norway

© 2012 Elsevier Ltd. All rights reserved.

Glossary

Analytic hierarchy process (AHP) A technique for eliciting relative weights for competing elements (attributes or alternatives). Based on pair-wise comparison of elements, it produces a comparison matrix in which the relative importance of each element is determined (the Saaty method of elicitation).

Fuzzy logic Derived from fuzzy set theory dealing with reasoning that is approximate rather than precise.

Geographical information system (GIS) A computer system for capturing, storing, checking, integrating, manipulating, analysing, and displaying data related to positions on the Earth's surface. Typically, a GIS (or Spatial Information System) is used for handling maps of one kind or another. These might be represented as several different layers where each layer holds data about a particular kind of feature. Each feature is linked to a position on the graphical image of a map.

Hedonic price modelling A theoretical–methodological framework for estimating the implicit prices of attributes pertaining to heterogeneous goods. Original contributions were in price index research. Today widely used in empirical property price studies and automated property valuation.

Market segment Clusters that are combinations of location (in administrative or geographic terms) and house type.

Mass appraisal A systematic appraisal of groups of properties using standardised procedures.

Multiple regression analysis A statistical technique that enables explanation of a phenomenon based on known independent variables. It is based on identifying correlations between two variables, when controlling for as much other influences as possible. It provides a solid basis for identifying drivers and forecasting.

Neural network A powerful data modelling tool that is able to capture and represent complex input/output relationships. The motivation for the development of neural network technology stemmed from the desire to develop an artificial system that could perform 'intelligent' tasks similar to those performed by the human brain. (Thus sometimes 'Artificial neural network' is applied as a synonym.)

Pattern recognition To classify data (patterns) based on either a priori knowledge or on statistical information extracted from the patterns. The patterns to be classified are usually groups of measurements or observations, defining points in an appropriate multidimensional space. A subtopic of machine learning.

Self-organising map (SOM) A type of supervised competitive neural network, and a type of flexible regression technique (the Kohonen map). Mapping from a high-dimensional data space onto a (usually) two-dimensional lattice of points.

Microlevel Analysis of Housing Markets and Property Values – Rationale for Alternative Methodology

Given the seriousness and longevity of financial problems globally, it is not unreasonable to argue for a more scientific basis or at least more justifiable arguments for setting house prices. In other words, the need for rigorous housing market analysis and its 'more practical' relative – mass appraisal for residential property valuation – is getting more and more important. Applying a scientific method for house price analysis concerns, on the one hand, the price-establishing process in relation to the development of affordability, and on the other hand, establishing the price in relation to more static price factors tied to fundamental quality variables such as the physical and social environment or transport infrastructure. While this topic is arguably exceptionally important in general socioeconomic terms, we may now speculate about a more particular issue: given the pivotal role of the housing bubble in the subsequent credit crunch, could the global financial crisis (that begun in year 2008) have been moderated or even avoided if prudent property valuations had been made at the time of issuing bank loans, and if governments and other institutions were concerned about raising the quality of property market information. The crux here is that the issue of creditworthiness arguably ought to be tied more with the property value used as collateral rather than the personal traits of the lender. This issue is also relevant in terms of better price information that could have assisted the development and monitoring of asset-backed securities and perhaps lessened the risk.

Hedonic housing market models comprise the standard quantitative approach to analysing residential value and housing prices. The hedonic approach, developed in the early 1970s by Sherwin Rosen, is an analytic tool based on the assumptions and formalism of neoclassical microeconomics and, among others, applied for empirical modelling of property prices in static equilibrium conditions in local housing markets (see, e.g., Watkins, 2001). Without going into the specifics of this methodology, suffice is to note that the neoclassical utility theories in general accommodate serious shortcomings that have been noted throughout the last three decades. According to more recent arguments, not only are the events unfolding in the world indeterminate, but our decision-making with regard to those events is inconsistent. Therefore, reductionist analyses of market processes are too strict given the complexity of these processes and our handicapped capability to deal with them. Within the applied realm of house price analysis, the situation is none too different – if anything, here the situation is particularly ripe for an alternative approach given the spatial fixity, durability, and heterogeneity of the product, which on a practical level manifests itself in more granular and idiosyncratic data sets. In house price analysis, hedonic multiple regression analysis (MRA) is a good case in point, as there is plenty of research carried out that highlights the shortcomings of this method (see Kauko and d'Amato, 2008). Because of the inability of the standard MRA-based hedonic price models to capture all the necessary information involved in the formation of value the literature on how to develop the market and price analysis tools further is evolving.

While it is true that recently the hedonic approach has experienced some notable improvements with regard to its spatial and functional properties, at a more conceptual level the approach still is found wanting, which is why some more alternative methodologies are currently being developed (see Kauko and d'Amato, 2008). Model-free estimation (i.e., semi-parametric or nonparametric, flexible regression) techniques such as neural networks and fuzzy logic have been introduced to bring some flexibility to the property value calculations, without neglecting the mathematical rigor (see Kauko and d'Amato, 2008). Pattern recognition is yet another relatively untried approach within this realm. Indeed, a number of contributions here offer ingenious and pragmatic, if not totally transparent, modelling methodology.

Alternative approaches allow researchers to capture the complex nature of the housing market relationships. The remainder of this contribution discusses two such methodological strands of inquiry – or more specifically, the applications of two groups of mathematical techniques: the neural network family of techniques from computer science and the analytic hierarchy process (AHP) from the subfield of applied mathematics known as modern decision analysis (see Saaty, 1990; Zahedi, 1986). Here a couple of definitional issues are noteworthy. First, due to the heterogeneity of the former category of techniques the focus will be on only one particular type of neural network: the self-organising map (SOM) – also known as the Kohonen Map, after its innovator Teuvo Kohonen – as it will be argued that this technique is suited for visual and multilayered analysis in a manner that enables building bridges between quantitative modelling and more qualitative approaches to market analysis (Kaski, 1997; Kohonen, 1995; see also Carlson, 1998, for property valuation application). Second, it needs to be stressed that while each of these approaches is considered exiting and therefore also to some extent controversial within this realm, the two techniques discussed have absolutely nothing else in common than their alternative and partly qualitative nature (see, e.g., Kauko, 2002; 2008).

The Neural Networks and the SOM

Housing market structures and price data availability tend to cause problems for linear modelling, which provides the rationale for applying nonlinear modelling such as neural network techniques. The basic idea of the (artificial) neural network can be traced back to the 1940s, when McCulloch and Pitts attempted to simulate human intelligence by studying how the brain functions (cited in Zahedi, 1991). It was not until four decades later, however, that computers became capable of handling the requirements of the complex computational processes. This is why the history of applied neural network research is merely going back to the late 1980s. The most commonly used neural network method is known as multilayer perceptron (MLP).

The neural network can be described as a sophisticated statistical method and an estimation method that through an iterative training process captures nonlinear, regular associations (i.e., patterns) within a data set that has no predefined model. The iterations in the training process can be based on observed input and expected response values (supervised learning), or on input values alone (unsupervised learning). There are three basic types of network architectures: feed-forward, feedback, and competitive networks, depending on the direction of the calculation process: input-hidden-output (the feed-forward network), input-output (the competitive network), or unspecified (the feedback process). The SOM represents a neural network based on unsupervised learning and competitive network architecture. (To compare, the MLP is a supervised feed-forward network.) It is also a kind of nonlinear combination of projection, clustering, and regression analysis. The SOM processes multidimensional data into a 2D projection as illustrated in **Figures 1** and **2**. The following demonstration within a housing

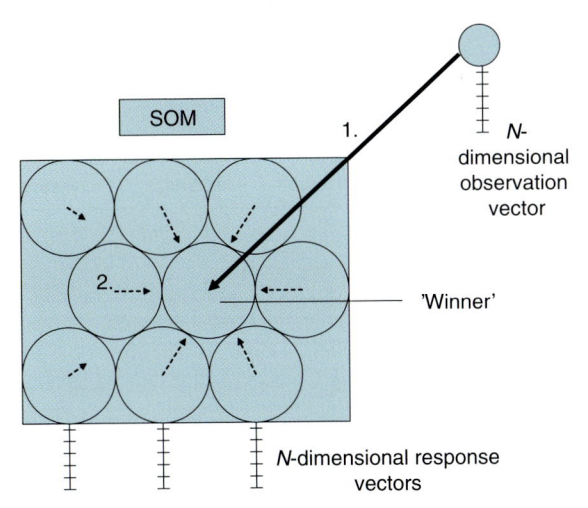

Figure 1 The two-stage training process in the SOM: (1) determine the 'winner' node and adjust its weights towards the weights of the observation; (2) similarly adjust the weights of adjacent nodes, but less the further they are situated from the 'winner'.

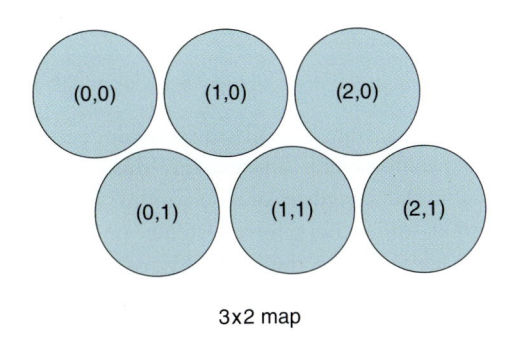

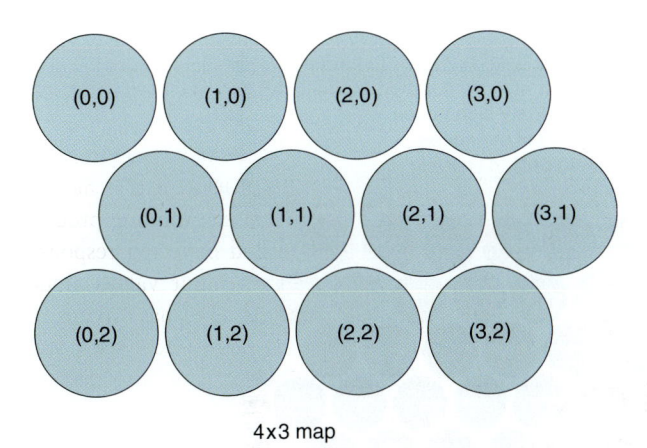

3x2 map

4x3 map

Figure 2 The ordering of the nodes in maps of hexagonal shape.

context shows the basic principles of the learning and organisation process.

Table 1 describes a sample of eight observation vectors with two measured attributes: the size of the house (sq.m. floor-space) and whether it has a garage or not (dummy). The first procedure concerns the imbalance in variable field ranges: 1 for garage and 194 for the size. Therefore, before running this sample with the SOM algorithm, we transform the garage variable by multiplying it by 200 in order to make the field range roughly comparable with the size variable. This is not compulsory, but unless we do it, the map will organise itself mainly based on the latter variable. Furthermore, this variable is discontinuous, but the algorithm deals with it as a continuous variable. We choose a 3 by 2 size network and suitable learning parameters.

Table 2 illustrates the SOM output after four stages of running the algorithm. In the first run each observation contributes to the learning process once. In the second run we increase the run to 8 + 80 (basic run plus fine-tuning), in the third to 80 + 800, and in the fourth to 300 + 3000, equalling 500 times the network size, following Kohonen's advice on the number of iterations. This illustrates the convergence from an arbitrary map towards a more stable map, with respect to clustering of observations and estimation of typical values (the last two runs). The output shows first which observations (1–8) are won by which node on the map and, second, the typical values of each node for having a garage (transformed back to a value between 0 and 1) and size, respectively. The latter are sophisticated averages (every observation on the map affects the value). The quantisation error (Q) is a measure denoting the goodness of the map: the smaller the Q, the better the map.

We note that similar observations are clustered together and that this clustering after the last two runs is identical. For the typical values, the map averages substantially; in other words, the value differences on the map are not as sharp as in reality. One can note that also the empty node obtains interpolated typical values but not a label which is determined based on the most frequent label among the observations won by that node (in case two or more labels have the same frequency the label is drawn). Thus, the output contains two kinds of information: (1) the similarity between units within the structure and (2) the typical properties of a given unit with respect to the input dimensions.

In the SOM, each node represents a specific multidimensional combination of numeric values depending on the input variable levels of the observations won by this node (and to a lesser extent, the corresponding mixes of the adjacent nodes). The variation in the numeric values of the neurons can be conveniently visualised either as a projection of the matrix of numeric values for one input variable at the time (normal method) or as a projection of the whole matrix of numeric values (alternative method). In the normal method the intensity with respect to the particular variable (i.e., map layer) under investigation is conveniently visualised in greyscales: the lighter the colour, the higher the value, and the darker the colour, the

Table 1 A sample of eight observations with two input variables for the demonstration

Observation ID	(1)	(2)	(3)	(4)	(5)	(6)	(7)	(8)
Garage	0	0	1	0	1	0	1	1
Size	150	62	240	90	46	180	170	90
Label	NoLarge	NoSmall	GaraLarge	NoSmall	GaraSmall	NoLarge	GaraLarge	GaraSmall

Table 2 The step-by-step process of organisation with the SOM

After 8 iterations			
(1), (2), (4), (8)	(6) (7)	(3) (5)	
After 8 + 80 iterations			
(1), (6) (2), (4)		(3), (7) (5), (8)	$Q = 63.02$
After 80 + 800 iterations			
(6) 0.239; 132.0 (2), (4) 0.223; 110.6	(1) 0.350; 141.6 0.333; 117.6	(3), (7) 0.450; 148.6 (5), (8) 0.435; 121.6	$Q = 55.58$
After 300 + 3000 iterations			
(6) 0.227; 132.0 (NoLarge) (2), (4) 0.210; 108.0 (NoSmall)	(1) 0.350; 143.0 (NoLarge) 0.331; 116.8	(3), (7) 0.455; 150.6 (GaraLarge) (5), (8) 0.440; 120.8 (GaraSmall)	$Q = 53.28$

lower the values for a given variable. Moreover, the nodes are conveniently identified based on a label, such as the district location in **Figure 3**. The alternative method of visualisation to the layer-specific variation is to visualise the Euclidean distances in the input dimensions between reference vectors of neighbouring map units using grey levels (Kohonen et al., 1996; see also Kauko, 2009). This is in a sense a measure of homogeneity of certain subsets within the total data structure.

Figure 3 shows how visually discernible patterns emerge in a specific layer – alternatively this occurs in all layers – as similar categories of observations, which are clearly different from others, form 'patches' on the map surface. Here we also note the possibility of using geographical information system (GIS) for visualising the numeric output. Thus, the SOM output can subsequently be plotted onto a geographical map, like the one of the Netherlands in **Figure 4**.

Light colour: neighbourhoods with relatively high house price level: the labels (e.g. 0910407) of the nodes (= circles) indicate location in Metropolitan Helsinki

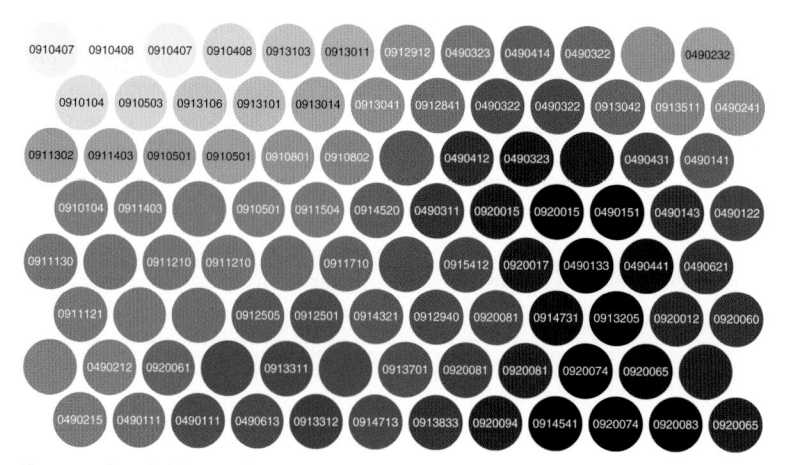

Figure 3 Feature map of house prices in Metropolitan Helsinki, this layer illustrates the variation in house prices across administrative districts and submarkets.

Results: SOM => GIS

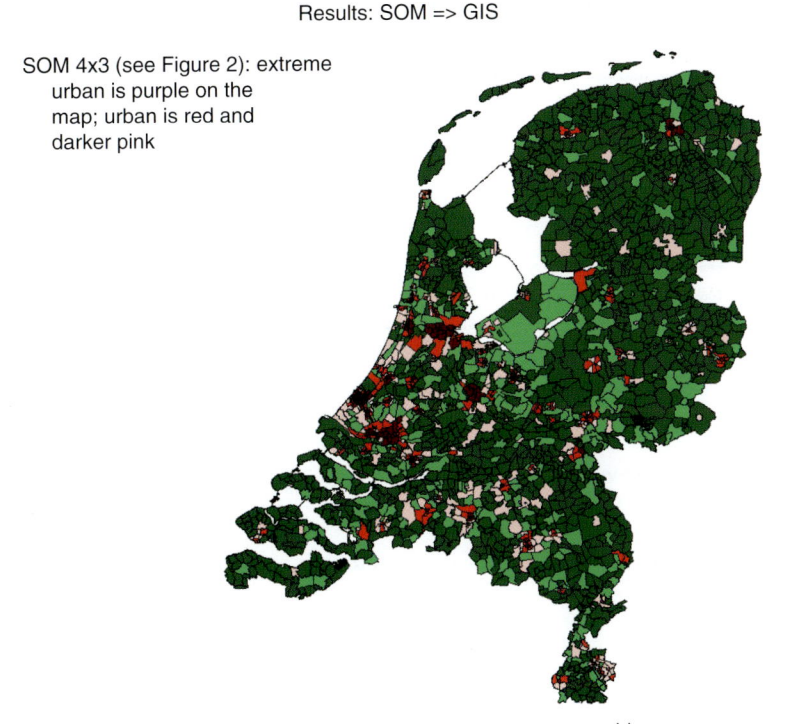

SOM 4x3 (see Figure 2): extreme urban is purple on the map; urban is red and darker pink

Figure 4 Example of how the output of the SOM analysis is transformed onto a geographic map.

How then to incorporate the dynamic dimension? If time is one variable among others, then the rigid map cannot adapt new observations. Carlson (1998) proposes two methods:

- Fixed time-windows, and
- Each new observation is compared with the values of the best-matching neuron.

The former method is illustrated in **Figure 5**. While this method is not dynamic in itself, the temporal dimension can be added by showing successive feature maps of cross sections over a sufficient time interval.

An additional benefit of the method is its capability to detect submarkets and the idiosyncratic aspect of spatial housing market structure (Kauko, 2002). Here particular similarities can be noted to *k*-means cluster analysis (e.g., Kaski, 1997; Openshaw et al., 1994). That the SOM generates fuzzy, partly qualitative outcomes is an additional advantage over hedonic regression with extensions. Despite the good qualitative results obtainable with the SOM, there are a variety of problems regarding the technical side of the analysis that must be considered when using the SOM. Above all, it is always important to code the sample feasibly and informatively, and attention should also be paid to adjusting the field ranges (scaling) and defining suitable network parameters, as the earlier simple example of a run with the SOM showed. It also needs to be acknowledged that testing for robustness of the result relative to enlargement of the sample size is possible only in terms of visual patterns, not in numeric terms (see Kauko, 2002, 2004).

To the extent that visual and qualitative properties are appreciated when building a method for housing market analysis, the SOM is definitely an improvement to traditional methods. This technique can be seen as both complement and substitute to hedonic modelling of house prices as the research questions to answer are the same (i.e., estimation of price/value, identification of market segments) or different ones (e.g., outlier analysis, pattern recognition). However, the issue of comparing different approaches is by no means unambiguous. The downside is that the estimates are sensitive to external assumptions, such as choice of particular algorithm and parameters. Furthermore, the results are strongly dependent on the data, as all necessary guidance to the analyses is obtained from the sample that is fed to the network together with the network parameters. Unfortunately, the lack of a straightforward functional relationship between input and output creates a problem of explicability: the classic 'black-box' argument. Therefore, expert info is necessary to validate the findings.

The Analytic Hierarchy Process

The AHP approach deals with judgements and choice. In sharp contrast to the classical multiattribute value-tree modelling approach, which is based on the assumption that utility functions can be explained, the AHP does not, however, assume that an individual has full information to formulate the goal and criteria for making a given

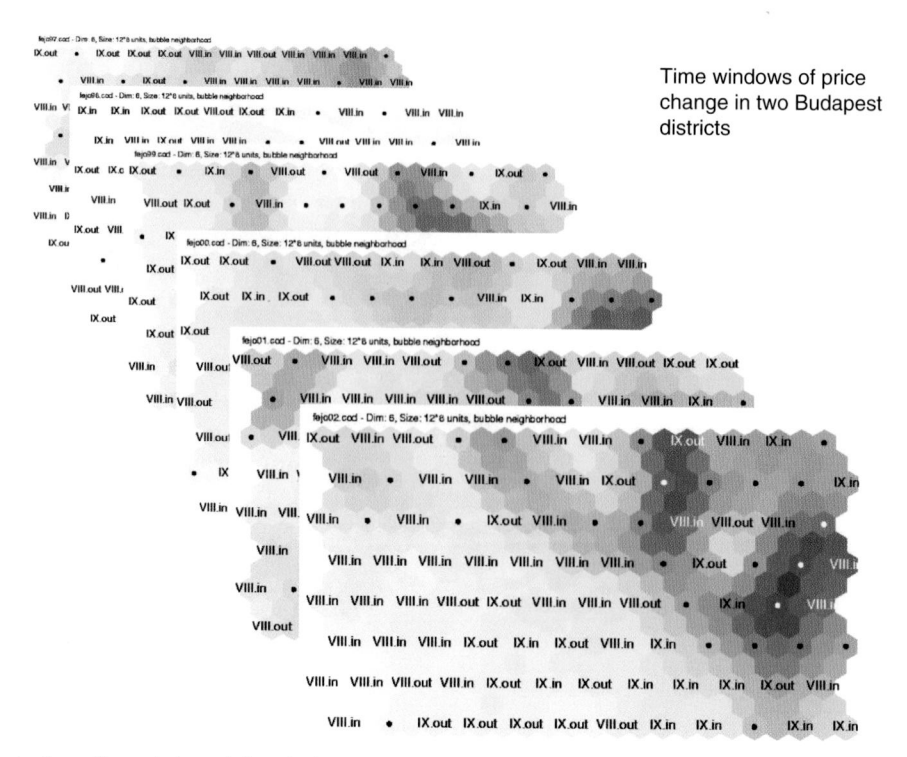

Figure 5 An illustration of 'quasi-dynamic' analysis using the method of fixed time-windows.

decision in a single procedure. Instead, the AHP is based on the assumption that the relevant dominance of one attribute over another can be measured with a systematic, pair-wise comparison of preferences at each level of a hierarchy of factors, presented as a value tree (e.g., Ball and Srinivasan, 1994). The overall objective of the decision stands at the top of the hierarchy, with lower-level objectives or attributes at the lower levels (e.g., Zahedi, 1986). A value tree of a house price modelling application is illustrated in **Figure 6**. Because of the problems of dealing with imperfect markets and the lack of adequate data, the AHP has been proposed to complement the more mainstream approaches – or indeed the SOM (see Kauko, 2008).

The starting point is to design a tree structure in relation to the specific problem. What is our goal? How do we arrive at the decision regarding this goal? This requires splitting the overall goal into partial goals which are then split further into even more specific partial goals. The tree is determined by the researcher, based on his/her specific knowledge of the problem setting. The crucial step is to acquire the necessary judgements and transform them to ordinal numerical inputs for each branch of the tree. Here often a small amount of expert interviews is more apt for the problem formulation than a large-scale questionnaire survey.

The comparison begins at the lowest level of the tree, where the elements (attributes or alternatives) are usually elicited with an ordinal scale from 1 to 9, with the values corresponding to verbal expressions. A value of 1 means that 'both are of equal importance', and a value of 9 means that '*A* has an extreme importance over *B*'. The comparisons are then converted into cardinal rankings. Balancing the pair-wise ranks in this way involves the use

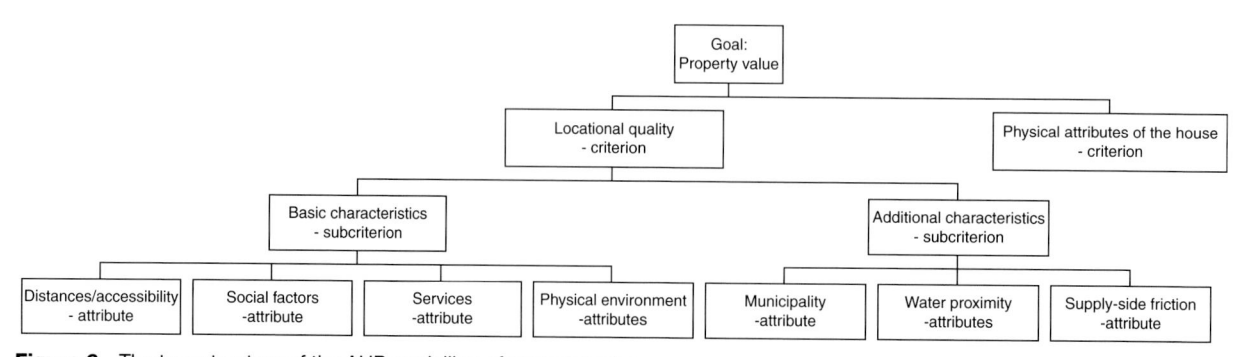

Figure 6 The tree structure of the AHP modelling of property value.

of measurement theory, as pair-wise judgements cannot be assumed consistent across the entire set of comparisons (e.g., Ball and Srinivasan, 1994). The weights are defined to sum up to 1 under each higher-level element (local weights) and also for the overall goal (global weights). In the final procedure, local weights are transformed into global weights by relating lower-level weights to the whole tree. In this way the most attractive element is determined by aggregating the local priorities into global priorities. This process quantifies the relative contribution of each element to the overall goal.

Following Thomas Saaty, who innovated the AHP in the late 1970s, the functioning of the AHP technique is explained in terms of a matrix equation. Consider the elements $A_1, A_2, \ldots, A_n$ within one level of the tree hierarchy. In practice, the maximum number of elements to compare within a single comparison matrix is nine, although there is theoretically no upper limit to the number of elements to compare. The comparisons among all of the elements $(A_1:A_2, \ldots, A_{n-1}:A_n)$ then generate a matrix, where the total number of comparisons is $(A_{n-1} \times A_n)/2$. Each comparison generates a pair-wise ratio (e.g., w_1/w_2, w_2/w_1). All of the ratios along the diagonal are obviously equal to 1, as it is not necessary to compare elements with themselves (Saaty, 1990).

The most common way to estimate the relative weights from the matrix of pair-wise comparisons is the eigenvalue method (see, e.g., Zahedi, 1986, for a full discussion).

The matrix formula $Aw = nw$ applies only for the theoretical ideal situation in which the comparison is fully consistent. This is usually not the case in observed pair-wise comparisons (unless the comparison is unambiguous and the matrix is very small, e.g., three elements that compare 2:1, 2:1, and 4:1), and the estimate λ_{max} is therefore used instead of the exact n. To enable approximation of a less than fully consistent comparison matrix, there must be more observations than weights. In fact, as Saaty (1990) demonstrated, λ_{max} is always greater than or equal to n and, as it approaches n, the values of A become more consistent. This property has led to the construction of the consistency index (CI) as follows:

$$CI = (\lambda_{max} - n)/(n-1)$$

The consistency of the comparisons is measured with the consistency ratio (CR), which is calculated according to the expected results of consistent pair-wise comparisons across the matrix, as follows:

$$CR = (CI/ACI) \times 100$$

The ACI is the average index of randomly generated weights (cited in Zahedi, 1986). While the CR should be very small, several opinions exist as to the exact treatment of the CR in a modelling exercise; for example, it may be used as a filter or disregarded altogether.

When compared with standard market analysis techniques, the strength of the AHP relies on the ability to combine judgements with numerical assessment, the incorporation of a qualitative dimension sensitive to nuances, and the problem-oriented approach. However, as the analysis is not based on actual but rather hypothetical data, lots of doubts have been raised about this kind of methods. While the interview-based methods may be suited for recording environmental info, the problem is that the preferences and choices evoke under hypothetical conditions that do not necessarily represent the actual choices made in the real world. Besides this problem, uncertainties related to the feasibility of the study and its costs are yet to be solved. The question is: Do we need all that extra context-specific and actor-centred information that is time consuming to get, for tasks such as housing market analysis and property valuation, which hitherto have been deemed relatively straightforward? However, the most important concern is how to perform an objective comparison between estimates based on market data and those based on hypothetical values.

Some Last Comments

Market valuations of houses vary between individuals due to imperfect markets and the lack of availability of transparent and frequent data. Two different modelling techniques, the SOM and the AHP, have now been proposed. The SOM deals with market patterns; pattern recognition, clustering, and nonlinear, flexible regression, and organisation of large – usually messy and noisy – data sets. The AHP deals with judgements and the buyer's choice, and generates expert-elicited preference models suited for making monetary values (i.e., transaction prices) commensurable with nonmonetary.

The discussion above has raised some key issues concerning the relative merits of each approach. However, the space available did not allow detailed descriptions of each method; neither did it allow delving into some of the intriguing issues involved. (For presentations of a recent event organised in Delft, the Netherlands, see http://www.otb.tudelft.nl/live/pagina.jsp?id=ac23443b-6d94-4513-a9ea-d312362c0b8b&lang=en. See also the following link: http://www.noaves.com/index.php.)

See also: Econometric Modeling; Economics of Housing Choice; House Price Indexes; Neighbourhood Effects; Price Determination in Housing Markets; Price Dynamics in Housing Markets.

References

Kaski S (1997) Data exploration using self-organizing maps. *Acta Polytechnica Scandinavica, Mathematics, Computing and Management in Engineering Series No. 82*, Espoo, Finland: Helsinki University of Technology.

Kauko T (2002) *Modelling the Locational Determinants of House Prices: Neural Network and Value Tree Approaches*. PhD Thesis, Utrecht: Labor Grafimedia. http://igitur-archive.library.uu.nl/dissertations/2002-1204-091756/inhoud.htm (accessed 24 August 2011)

Kohonen T (1995) *Self-Organizing Maps. Springer Series in Information Sciences*. Germany: Springer-Verlag.

Kohonen T, Hynninen J, Kangas J, and Laaksonen J (1996) SOM_PAK: The self-organizing map program package. *Helsinki University of Technology, Faculty of Information Technology, Laboratory of Computer and Information Science. Report A31*. Espoo, Finland: Helsinki University of Technology.

Openshaw S, Blake M, and Wymer C (1994) *Using Neurocomputing Methods to Classify Britain's Residential Areas. Working Paper 94/17*. Leeds, UK: School of Geography, University of Leeds.

Carlson E (1998) Real estate investment appraisal of land properties using SOM. In: Deboeck G and Kohonen T (eds.) *Visual Explorations in Finance with Self-Organizing Maps*, pp. 117–127. New York: Springer.

Kauko (2008) Utterly unorthodox modelling for the purposes of mass appraisal: An approach based on patterns and judgments. In: Kauko T and d'Amato M (eds.) *Mass Appraisal Methods – An International Perspective for Property Valuers. RICS Series*, pp. 203–219. Oxford, UK: Blackwells.

Kauko T and d'Amato M (2008) Introduction: Suitability issues in mass appraisal methodology. In: Kauko T and d'Amato M (eds.) *Mass Appraisal Methods – An International Perspective for Property Valuers. RICS Series*, pp. 1–19. Oxford, UK: Blackwells.

Ball J and Srinivasan VC (1994) Using the analytic hierarchy process in house selection. *Journal of Real Estate Finance and Economics* 9: 69–85.

Kauko T (2004) Towards the 4th generation – An essay on innovations in residential property value modelling expertise. *Journal of Property Research* 21(1): 75–97.

Kauko T (2009) Classification of residential areas in the three largest Dutch cities, using multidimensional data. *Urban Studies* 46(8): 1639–1663.

Saaty TL (1990) How to make a decision: The analytic hierarchy process. *European Journal of Operational Research* 48: 9–26.

Watkins CA (2001) The definition and identification of housing submarkets. *Environment and Planning A* 33: 2235–2253.

Zahedi F (1986) The analytic hierarchy process – A survey of the method and its applications. *Interfaces* 16(4) July–August: 96–100.

Zahedi F (1991) An introduction to neural networks and a comparison with artificial intelligence and expert systems. *Interfaces* 21: 25–38.

New Urban Economics and Residential Location

R Arnott, University of California, Riverside, CA, USA

© 2012 Elsevier Ltd. All rights reserved.

Glossary

Agglomeration economies Economic forces that encourage the spatial concentration of economic activity.

Agricultural bid rent (at location x in use i) The maximum amount a farmer is able to pay in land rent per unit area at location x, conditional on farming it in use i.

Closed city A city with a fixed population, with no in- or out-migration.

Muth rule A class of formulae expressing that the difference in rent (housing or land) between two locations reflects the difference in their accessibilities.

Open city A city in which households migrate freely in and out, so as to equalise the utility between the city and the rest of the world.

Residential bid rent (at location x by group i conditional on u) The maximum amount a household in group i is able to pay in land rent per unit area at location x, conditional on receiving utility u.

Von Thünen rings Rings of different agricultural land uses surrounding a central market, reflecting differences by land use in the costs of transporting a unit area's output to market.

Introduction

What determines the pattern of land use within a city? How is the city divided spatially between residential and nonresidential land uses? And what determines the residential locations of different income-demographic groups? These are the basic questions of the new urban economics. (Note that throughout the article, 'city' denotes the entire metropolitan area.)

The 1950s and 1960s saw a general equilibrium revolution in applied microeconomics. Prior to that, most applied microeconomics was partial equilibrium analysis – the single market, diagrammatic analysis encountered in today's economic principles courses. General equilibrium analysis, in contrast, focuses on the interrelation between different markets. The (now not so) new urban economics is the manifestation of this general equilibrium revolution in the context of urban economics. Prior to the 1960s, urban economics was largely discursive, demonstrating considerable accumulated wisdom but containing little systematic theory. The new urban economics was born in the 1960s, came of age in the 1970s, and reached maturity in the 1980s. Even though there has been little theoretical development since then, the new urban economic theory remains the foundation of modern urban economics.

The method of modern applied microeconomics puzzles many noneconomists. The method is model-based. A naively simple model is constructed that focuses on the behaviour of rational and typically self-interested economic agents in a particular economic context, and that elucidates some basic economic principles. That model is then gradually extended in the direction of realism in many different ways, and is added to the kitbag of models that the applied microeconomist employs in his policy analysis. The naively simple model that provides the foundation of the new urban economics is the basic monocentric (city) model, which describes the equilibrium of residential land use around a point central business district (CBD), where all nonresidential activity occurs. The basic principle it elucidates is how land rents at different locations adjust to offset differences in transport costs. Thus, the basic monocentric model links the land market and the transport market. Augmenting the basic monocentric city model to include production, labour, housing, and local public services financed by taxes yields a self-contained urban economy, in which all its markets are interrelated.

In Europe, location theory, housing economics, transport economics, and local public finance are separate fields with separate specialists. In North America, those parts of these fields that apply to cities have been integrated under the umbrella of urban economics. This integration has been achieved through the new urban economics, with its conception of a self-contained urban economy with interrelated markets.

Intellectual Antecedents

Historically, Anglo-Saxon economics deemphasised space, and its agricultural land rent theory followed David Ricardo in focusing on differences in fertility in explaining differences in land rent and land use. Continental economics, in contrast, paid considerable attention to space, and focused on differences in accessibility in explaining differences in land rent. Almost all the major contributors to spatial economic theory were trained in the German economic tradition, and the spatial economic theory taught today in English-language universities was introduced to Britain and the United States by German émigré economists.

Johannes von Thünen is the giant among spatial economic theorists. In *The Isolated State*, he developed a general equilibrium model of an agricultural economy organised around a central marketplace. Since his work provides the foundation of residential location theory, a simplified version of his model is now presented.

Imagine a large homogeneous plain (there are no mountains or rivers, and the fertility of land and the climate are the same everywhere) populated by farmers. The plain is divided up into market areas. Each of these market areas is self-sufficient, and contains a central marketplace, perhaps a town, surrounded by agricultural land. To sell his produce, a farmer has to transport it to the closest marketplace. A farmer whose land is located closer to the central marketplace incurs less in transport costs, and is therefore willing to pay more in land rent. To start with, consider a very simple agricultural economy with a single crop and a classical technology, in which a unit of land requires a fixed number of labourers to plant and harvest the crop. The following notation is employed:

p price per unit of agricultural output
θ yield per unit area
w the agricultural wage
n the number of labourers required per unit area of land
x distance to the closest central market
e cost of transporting one unit of the agricultural good a unit distance
$\pi(x)$ economic profit per unit area of land at x
$R(x)$ agricultural land rent per unit area at x

The economic profit per unit area of land at a distance x away from the central market is

$$\pi(x) = p\theta - wn - \theta xe - R(x). \quad (1)$$

The farmer receives $p\theta$ in revenue per unit area of land from the sale of his produce. He incurs three costs per unit area of land: labour costs (the wage rate times the number of labourers per unit area of land, wn); transport costs (output per unit area of land times the distance shipped times the cost of transporting a unit of output a unit distance, θxe); and land rent ($R(x)$). His profit per unit area of land equals his revenue minus his costs.

The market for land is assumed to be competitive. As a result, farmers bid up the rent on land at each location until the profit from farming a unit area of land at that location equals zero. Thus,

$$\pi(x) = 0 \text{ for all } x. \quad (2)$$

Combining [1] and [2] yields the equilibrium land rent at x:

$$R(x) = p\theta - wn - xe. \quad (3)$$

Thus, the land rent per unit area of land at x equals the revenue it generates minus the nonrent costs incurred in farming it, the labour costs, and the costs of transporting the output to the central market. Land rent is therefore determined as a residual.

Figure 1 displays the determination of land rent per unit area at x graphically.

Examine [3]. Suppose that the price of the agricultural good increases by one unit, all else being equal. The farmer's revenue per unit area of land increases by θ, so he is willing to bid θ more to farm a unit area of land. Suppose that the agricultural wage increases by one unit. The farmer's costs per unit area of land increase by n, so he is willing to bid n less to farm the unit area of land. Suppose that the cost of transporting a unit of output a unit distance increases by one unit. As, for every unit area of land, the farmer has to transport θ units of output of land x units of distance, the transport costs he incurs per unit area of land increase by θx, so he is willing to pay θx less to farm a unit area of land at that location.

Now extend the model by considering the same economy but with two agricultural goods, wheat (W) and tomatoes (T). Tomatoes are more perishable and so their transport costs per unit distance are higher. To deal with this extension, a new concept is introduced that is used extensively in land rent theory.

Define the bid rent on land at location x in use i, $b^i(x)$, to be the maximum amount that a farmer at location x is willing to pay in rent per unit area of land to farm the land in use i. The graph of the function is called a bid-rent curve in use i.

The maximum amount a farmer is willing to pay in rent per unit area of land to farm the land in a particular use is that amount which drives his profit down to zero. Thus,

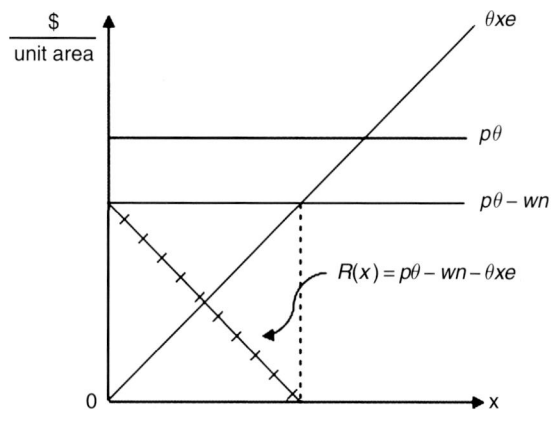

Figure 1 Determination of land rent per unit area at x.

$$b^i(x) = p^i\theta^i - wn^i - \theta^i x e^i, \quad i = W, \ T. \tag{4}$$

The absolute value of the slope of the bid-rent curve for product i is $\theta^i e^i$. This is how much a farmer would save in transport costs on product i per unit area of land if he were located a unit distance closer to the central market, and therefore the premium he would be willing to bid for a unit area of land in that use at the closer location.

Figure 2 plots the two bid-rent curves. The bid-rent curve for tomatoes is drawn as steeper than that for wheat as tomato production is more intensive than wheat production and as tomatoes are more easily damaged or spoiled in transportation.

The stage is now set to determine the equilibrium pattern of land use. The guiding principle is

Principle 1: Land goes to that use which bids the most for it.

In **Figure 2**, tomato farmers bid more for land between the central market and x' than wheat farmers, and therefore the land goes to tomato farmers. Between x' and x'', wheat farmers bid a positive amount, and more than tomato farmers, so that the land goes to wheat farmers. Beyond x'', neither wheat nor tomato farmers are willing to bid a positive amount to rent the land, so the land there is unfarmed. Viewed from the air, the land planted in tomatoes is a circle of radius x' and the land planted in wheat is a ring (or annulus) with inner radius x' and outer radius x''; hence, the term von Thünen rings.

Land rent as a function of distance to the central market is determined by another principle

Principle 2: The land rent at some location equals the maximum of the bid rents at that location and zero.

Geometrically, the rent curve is obtained as the upper envelope of the bid-rent curves and the zero line. Suppose that the cost of shipping tomatoes falls. This has no effect on the amount a tomato farmer at the central market is willing to pay in rent and reduces the premium tomato farmers are willing to pay for a more central location. Thus, the bid-rent curve for tomatoes pivots counterclockwise around the initial tomato bid rent at the central market. Tomato farming becomes more profitable, so that some land that was previously planted in wheat is planted in tomatoes. It is straightforward to determine the effects of other changes on the equilibrium pattern of land use and rent.

Residential Location Theory

In the 1960s, the von Thünen theory of agricultural land use and land rent was adapted to develop an accessibility-based theory of urban residential location and rent – residential location theory. A point CBD, where all nonresidential activity takes place, replaces the central market; residential land takes the place of agricultural land; different household groups take the place of different agricultural goods; and commuting costs take the place of agricultural goods' shipping costs to the central market. The adaptation of the von Thünen model to develop a theory of residential location involves more than a relabelling of variables, however. The von Thünen model derives the agricultural bid rents from the assumption that farmers bid up rents to the point where zero profit is made in equilibrium. But this condition does not apply to household choice of residential location, and needs to be replaced by some other condition.

Two types of cities are distinguished. In an open city, households migrate freely between the city and the rest of the world, so that in equilibrium each household is indifferent between living in the city and living in the rest of the world. The population of the various household groups adjusts so that this condition is satisfied. In a closed city, in contrast, the population of the various household groups is fixed, and the residential rent function adjusts such that the supply of land equals the demand for land at all locations. Open city analysis is typically more relevant in examining the long-run effects of a change in a particular city, and closed city analysis is more relevant for examining either the short-run (before migration has occurred) effects of a change in a particular city or the effects of a change that occurs in all cities together.

Let us start with the simplest case of an open city and a single household group. To further simplify, assume that lot size is fixed at T. Households derive utility from lot size and other goods, whose price is set equal to 1. As lot size is fixed, a household's utility can be measured by the quantity of other goods it consumes, C. Now consider a household that lives a distance x away from the CBD. It faces the budget constraint

$$Y = C + R(x)T + ex, \tag{5}$$

where Y is the household's income, which is fixed, $R(x)$ is the equilibrium land rent per unit area at x, and e is the

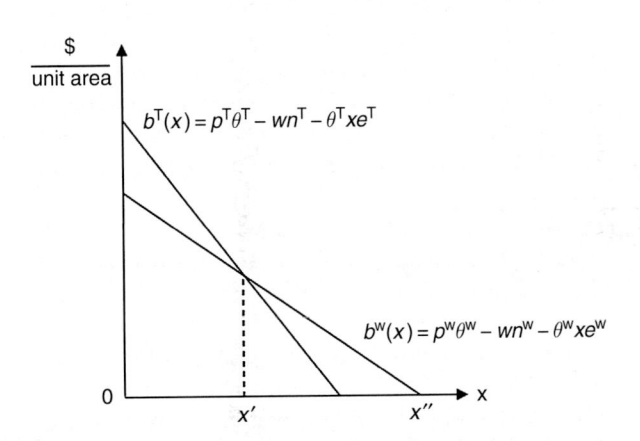

Figure 2 Two agricultural bid-rent curves.

commuting cost per unit distance, so that ex is the commuting cost incurred by the household. Thus, the budget constraint specifies that the household spends its income on other goods, lot rent $(R(x)T)$, and commuting costs. Let C^* be the quantity of other goods that the household can consume if it lives in the rest of the world. If the quantity of other goods a household can consume if it lives in the city is higher (lower) than this, households migrate into (out of) the city. Equilibrium is achieved only when the maximum level of other goods a household can consume – that amount that exhausts its budget – if it lives in the city is the same that it would obtain in the rest of the world. Thus, solving [5] with $C = C^*$ yields the equilibrium rent function:

$$R(x) = \frac{(Y - C^* - ex)}{T}. \quad (6)$$

As a household saves e in commuting costs if it lives a unit distance closer to the CBD, it is willing to pay e more in lot rent. And as lot size is T, it is willing to pay a premium of e/T in land rent per unit area. Thus, the absolute value of the slope of the rent function is

$$|R'(x)| = \frac{e}{T}. \quad (7)$$

This is the Muth rule, in this context. Now determine the equilibrium population. As a landowner is willing to rent out his land at a positive rent but not at a negative rent, land rent is zero at the boundary of the city, x^*. Thus, $x^* = (Y - C^*)/e$. As the city is on a homogeneous plain, the residential area is circular. Thus, the area of the city is $\pi(x^*)^2$, and as all the city's area is used for residences, and as lot size is T, the equilibrium population is $N^* = \pi(Y - C^*)^2/(e^2 T)$. How the equilibrium changes as parameters change can easily be calculated. Suppose, for example, that income increases. Lot rent rises by the full amount of the income increase, so that the city boundary shifts out and population increases.

Now consider a closed city with a single household group. As the population is fixed at N, the residential area is NT. As the city is circular, the radius of the city is $x^* = (NT/\pi)^{1/2}$. As rent at the urban boundary is zero and as the Muth rule continues to apply,

$$R(x) = \left(\frac{e}{T}\right)(x^* - x). \quad (8)$$

The equilibrium of the closed city responds differently to parameter changes than the equilibrium of an open city. For example, in the closed city, an increase in income has no effect on the rent function.

The closed city analysis is now generalised to two household groups, using **Figure 3**. Each group has an equilibrium bid-rent curve, which indicates how much households in that group are willing to pay per unit area of land as a function of x in order to achieve the equilibrium level of utility for that group. Each group's equilibrium bid-rent curve satisfies the Muth rule for that group. In equilibrium, the group that is willing to pay the higher premium per unit area of land to live closer to the city centre lives closer to the city centre. For purposes of illustration, suppose that the two groups are rich (R) and poor (P), with N^R rich households and N^P poor households, and that the equilibrium bid-rent curve of the poor is steeper than that of the rich: $e^P/T^P > e^R/T^R$. Then the poor live in a circle of area $N^P T^P$ around the city centre and the rich in a ring of area $N^R T^R$ surrounding them. The rent function is the upper envelope of the equilibrium bid-rent curves. At the urban boundary, the equilibrium bid rent of the rich equals zero, and at the boundary between rich and poor, the equilibrium bid rents of the rich and poor are equal.

The above analysis presented an especially simple variant of the model. The standard model treats variable lot size and housing.

Application to Suburbanisation

With the development of geographical information systems (GIS), vast increases in computing power, and the increased availability of spatial microdata, urban economics has become increasingly empirical. The United States has been in the vanguard of this development, as a result of which American cities have been studied considerably more intensively than cities in other countries.

One of the most studied applications of the monocentric model is suburbanisation in the United States. In the late nineteenth century, US cities were CBD-oriented. The CBD was the dominant employment and commercial centre, and was connected to residential areas by radial transit lines. By the end of the twentieth century, the average US city had grown considerably in population and even more in area, and the CBD had lost its dominance as an employment centre (though still remaining the most important centre), except in the FIRE (finance, insurance, and real estate) industries, and provided a narrower range of retail and entertainment services. Residential suburbanisation started in the mid-1800s with the commuter rail suburbs, increased in the 1920s, slowed down during the period from the Great Depression to the end of the Second World War, and then exploded during the 1950s and 1960s. The suburbanisation of jobs lagged the suburbanisation of residences, but now jobs are almost as suburbanised as residences. Currently, in major US metropolitan areas, the median residence is 8 miles from the CBD and the median job 7 miles.

How successful is the monocentric model in providing an explanation of US suburbanisation consistent in the two decades following the Second World War? The earliest explanation that gained currency was that, in the

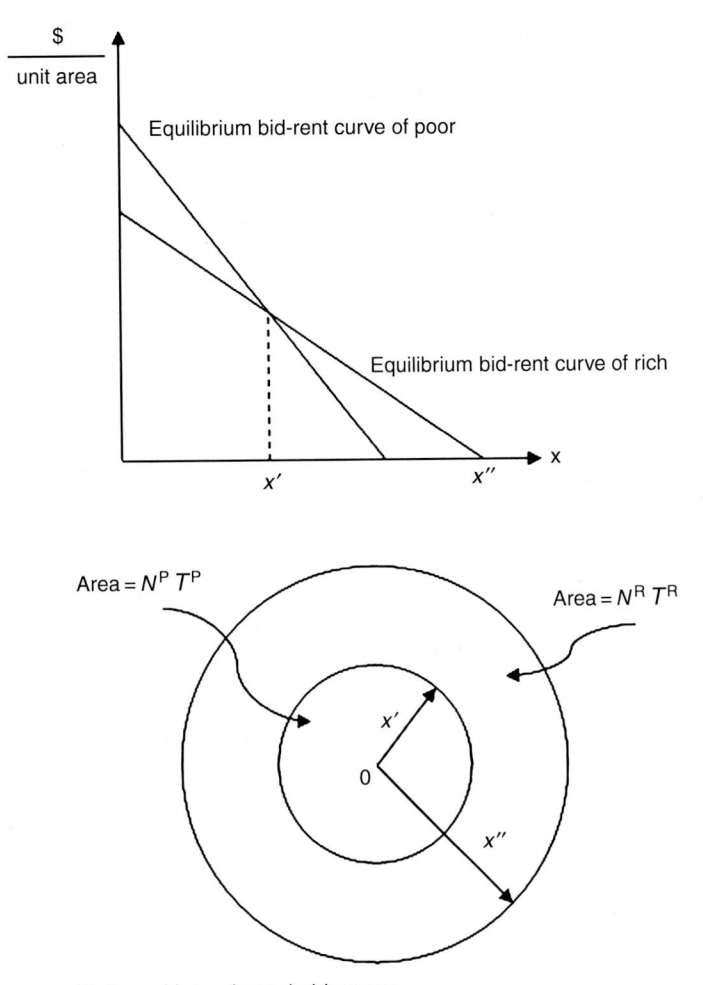

Figure 3 Residential land use equilibrium with two household groups.

1950s and 1960s, the poor lived downtown and the rich in the suburbs because the income elasticity of marginal commuting costs (the cost of travelling an extra unit distance) was less than the income elasticity of lot size, which would imply that the equilibrium bid-rent curve of the poor was steeper than that of the rich. In the late 1970s, this explanation was shown to be empirically weak. The relative size of the two income elasticities was found to be inconclusive, and average commuting distance was shown to be several times that predicted by the monocentric model, indicating the importance of other factors in residential location. An alternative explanation put forward at that time was white, middle-class flight to the suburbs, induced by not only racism (the massive migration of blacks from the rural south to cities in the north, combined with racial discrimination in the suburbs, had caused rapid expansion of the downtown black ghettos, especially in the 1950s) but also the deterioration of central city public services and high tax rates. An argument against this explanation was that the postwar suburban explosion happened not only in the northern US cities but also in Canadian cities, which had only small black populations. The next explanation that gained currency was the motorisation of commuting. As travel by car is considerably faster than travel by mass transit and as the time costs of commuting dominate the money costs, marginal auto commuting costs are considerably lower than marginal mass transit commuting costs. In terms of the model, the bid-rent curve of auto commuters is flatter than that of transit commuters. Car-owning households chose to live in the suburbs, while non-car-owning households downtown. The improvement of urban highways, especially in the 1960s, strengthens this explanation. The current view is that the motorisation of commuting was the primary cause of residential suburbanisation but that other factors were important too.

Suburbanisation has been occurring in cities around the world, though it started later and has proceeded less rapidly than in the United States. Reasons include car ownership and gasoline being more heavily taxed, urban highway and freeway systems being less developed, suburban land-use controls being stricter, and urban mass transit travel exhibiting greater service frequency, density, and reliability.

Through its assumptions, the monocentric model is intrinsically unsuccessful in explaining the suburbanisation of jobs over the last half century. Polycentric extensions of the monocentric model have however been successful.

Extensions

The monocentric model remains the core model of urban economics 50 years after its conception because it permits an integrated, general equilibrium treatment of the various components of the urban economy: land use, transportation, housing, local public finance, crime, environmental quality, and so on. It has the simplicity to admit numerous extensions and the breadth of conceptualisation to accommodate them.

Land Use

The theory has been extended to treat multiple land uses, employment dispersion, subcentring, and zoning. Conceptually only one of these extensions is difficult – the treatment of subcentring. The treatment of subcentring is important as cities around the world have been becoming increasingly polycentric. (Defining an employment subcentre to be a set of contiguous zones with an employment density exceeding 10 employees per acre and overall employment exceeding 10 000, there are now well over 20 subcentres in the Los Angeles Metropolitan Area.) The monocentric model can readily be extended to treat exogenous subcentres. The difficulty arises in extending the model to treat endogenous subcentres, as it is then necessary to determine the simultaneous locational equilibrium of firms and households.

Extended to treat exogenous subcentres, the monocentric model solves for the locational equilibrium of households, given the location of firms. To solve for the simultaneous locational equilibrium of firms and households, an additional set of equations is needed that describes the locational equilibrium of firms, given the location of households. In the theory, the trade-off a firm faces in deciding where to locate within a metropolitan area is between wages and factor productivity. Due to agglomeration economies, a firm is more productive when it is closer to other firms in the same and related industries. A firm may choose to locate right next to its workers; it can then pay them less as they do not incur commuting costs. Or it can locate close to other firms, which increases its workers' productivity, but it then has to pay its workers more. In a small city, the commuting cost of a worker travelling from the urban boundary to the CBD is modest; with even mild agglomeration economies, a monocentric urban structure is an equilibrium. As the city grows, commuting costs from the urban boundary to the CBD increase until at some point it becomes profitable for a firm in an industry that benefits little from agglomeration economies to relocate from the CBD to the urban boundary. Its location there makes it more attractive to other firms in the CBD to relocate to the urban boundary. Thus the process of subcentring begins. There are typically multiple equilibrium location patterns of firms and households, which occurs depending on the historical evolution of the city's spatial structure.

Transportation

Defining mode-specific bid-rent curves, multiple transport modes can be incorporated. Traffic congestion can be treated by allocating land to roads and assuming that travel speed on a road segment depends on traffic volume relative to the road capacity there, and the effects of transport policies (e.g., congestion pricing, investment in mass transit vs. freeways) can be analysed. Current urban simulation models built on the new urban economics employ the actual road and mass transit networks.

Housing

In the first generation of monocentric models, landowners/developers chose the profit-maximising floor–area ratio, taking as given land rent and other factor prices. Housing is built at that density such that it is equally expensive to add floor space horizontally as it is vertically. The next generation of models treated the durability of housing and other structures. As a city grows, development typically proceeds from the city centre outwards, and, when rents have grown sufficiently, downtown redevelopment becomes profitable, initiating a wave of redevelopment from the city centre outwards. The durability of structures is clearly important, creating a history-dependent spatial structure that is evident in all but new cities. Treating durable housing in a sound way is analytically difficult as a developer's choice of floor–area ratio depends on her expectations concerning the future growth rate of rents, which makes the model essentially intertemporal. As a result of these analytical difficulties, simulation models (models that are solved numerically rather than analytically) are needed to solve for equilibria in realistic cities. Land and property values are the present values of net rents.

Local Public Finance

The monocentric city model can be extended straightforwardly to include taxes and public services. An important feature of US cities especially is that different jurisdictions within the city offer different tax/public service packages. Household sorting across jurisdictions on this basis is the focus of the literature on the Tiebout hypothesis. The Tiebout and monocentric literatures have not yet been well integrated.

Environmental Quality

Emissions come from point sources and mobile sources. Point sources include power plants, factories, ports, as well as the heating and air conditioning of buildings. Mobile sources include cars, trucks, and mass transit vehicles. Urban spatial structure determines the pattern of travel and hence the spatial pattern of emissions. Then, based on topological and meteorological conditions, the spatial pattern of emissions maps into a spatial pattern of concentrations. In recent years, there has been considerable policy discussion of the potential environmental benefits of altering urban spatial structure in various ways – reducing sprawl, mixing land uses, and densifying – as well as of introducing greener technologies.

Dynamics

Apart from the work on the dynamics of urban spatial structure in a monocentric city with durable housing, disappointingly little work on urban dynamics has evolved from the new urban economics. In contrast, dynamics are central to work in the new economic geography, which looks at the evolution of urban structure at a regional, national, or international scale. Some work has been done aimed at synthesising the new urban economics and the new economic geography, but the literature is in its infancy.

Examining average commuting time across metropolitan areas provides an interesting perspective on the dynamics of urban spatial structure. One empirical regularity is that the elasticity of average commuting time with respect to metropolitan population is low. Another is that average commuting times are several times longer than would be the case if workers were matched with jobs to minimise aggregate commuting time, which indicates that factors other than accessibility to jobs are important in household residential location decisions. As no model has been developed that fully explains these empirical regularities, it is hard to say whether the population of metropolitan areas can just keep increasing.

Uncertainty

Some work has been done extending the monocentric model to treat uncertainty but the literature is underdeveloped.

Optimum and Equilibrium City Size

Urban spatial structure is determined by a balancing of dispersive and agglomerative forces. The primary dispersive force is people transport costs (if people transport cost were prohibitive, people would live and work at the same location and economic activity would be uniformly distributed over space). Agglomerative forces include agglomeration economies in production, and the greater variety of consumer goods, entertainment, and social interaction that larger cities provide. The Henry George theorem indicates that the first-best optimal distribution of population within and across cities can be decentralised under marginal cost pricing, with aggregate land rents covering the losses incurred by increasing returns to scale activities. But in reality there are important externalities, both positive (e.g., external economies of scale in production) and negative (e.g., unpriced congestion and crime), as well as the exercise of market power and failures in collective decision-making. The interaction between these market failures is complex, so that no generalisations can be made about how the equilibrium and optimal distributions of population differ within and across cities.

Simulation Modelling

Urban economic simulation modelling – simulation modelling that builds on the new urban economics – is discussed at some length in see article Simulation Models for Urban Economies. Because of its importance, however, a brief discussion is provided here. The power of the monocentric city model lies in its simplicity without triviality, which permits numerous extensions. Analytically, however, only one or two of these extensions can be treated simultaneously. Any variant of the model that attempts to capture real cities rather than to illustrate basic principles is sufficiently complex that it needs to be solved numerically – via an urban economic simulation model. With the huge increases in computing power, the development of geographic information systems, and the increase in publicly available spatial microdata, it is now possible to develop and solve urban simulation models, with fine spatial resolution and considerable disaggregation by household and industry group, that nevertheless are solidly grounded in new urban economic and more generally microeconomic theory. A state-of-the-art urban simulation model of the Los Angeles Metropolitan Area is under development that solves for the perfect foresight (by assumption agents know the future) intertemporal general equilibrium of the economy, with durable structures, a detailed production structure with multiple factors of production and multiple industries, the actual transport networks and zoning regulations, and a sophisticated treatment of pollution emissions and concentrations, which combines data from over a hundred sources. Such simulation models can forecast the effects of policy changes in considerable detail, and are likely the wave of the future in urban land use, transport, and environmental policy analysis.

No simulation model, however detailed, can fully capture the complexity of the real world. Being solidly based in the theory of competitive general equilibrium, urban economic simulation models assume away most sources of macroeconomic instability evident in the recent financial crisis, the exercise of market power, and the frictions that give rise to unemployment. At least in their current form, they take future population and incomes as exogenous. They also pay no attention to the politics of public policy. Finally, there is the problem of validation. If an urban economic simulation model produces an inaccurate forecast, it is all too easy to ascribe the inaccuracy to changes in the macroeconomic environment, which the model ignores. These problems notwithstanding, urban economic simulation models are potentially very valuable tools in policy analysis, as they quantify the importance of the various channels through which a policy operates and provide conceptual structure to the policy debate.

Omissions

Each urban specialty has it own, and perhaps many different, perspectives on the city. Urban economics naturally focuses on the economic aspects of cities, and pays little attention to urban politics, urban aesthetics, community development, and so on.

The new urban economics looks at the city from a general equilibrium economic perspective. Its approach is unapologetically neoclassical, individualistic, microeconomic, and market-based; the equilibria it describes are the outcome of atomistic individuals' self-interested behaviour, taking prices as given. It also looks at cities at the spatial resolution of the metropolitan area. Specialists from some other disciplines look at the city at a finer level – the neighbourhood or even the individual block. New economic geographers and regional economists look at the city as part of a system of cities or as part of one of many regions.

The most egregious oversights in the new urban economics derive from its particular perspective. But even within its narrow perspective, there have been some curious omissions in what it has studied. It has paid little attention to urban growth, perhaps because many of the determinants of a particular city's growth are external to the city; it has virtually ignored cyclical fluctuations, both internal dynamics (such as local real estate cycles) and the response of the urban economy to external shocks; its tools, while eminently suitable, have been little applied to the study of urban history; and, perhaps principally because of poor data, it has paid little attention to intercity trade and specialisation. Also, looking at cities through the lens of the monocentric city model has biased perspective. New urban economists were late in recognising the polycentricity of the modern city and in investigating the sources of agglomerative economies of scale. Finally, the central model's assumption that sites differ only in accessibility has resulted in insufficient attention being paid to Ricardian determinants of land use, such as microclimate and geology.

Concluding Remarks

The world is bewilderingly complex. To make some sense of it requires a conceptualisation that provides structure to some of what we see and filters out the rest. The new urban economics looks at the city from the perspective of competitive general equilibrium theory, adapted to incorporate urban space. Its signal success has been in providing a conceptualisation of the city that integrates its various economic components, which is needed for examining such issues as how the construction of a new transit line will affect housing prices in different neighbourhoods. It has a single core economic model, the monocentric model. The monocentric model has generated important and robust insights into the effects of accessibility on urban spatial structure, and its simplicity has admitted numerous extensions. While the perspective it provides is narrowly economic, its success is indicated by its having remained the central model in urban economics for almost 50 years and by the wealth of literature that draws on it.

See also: Economic Approaches to Housing Research; Economics of Housing Choice; Housing and Sustainable Transport; Simulation Models for Urban Economies; Spatial Economics.

Further Reading

Alonso W (1964) *Location and Land Use: Toward a General Theory of Land Rent*. Cambridge, MA: Harvard University Press.

Anas A and Liu Y (2007) A regional economy, land use and transportation model (RELU-TRAN): Formulation, algorithm design and testing. *Journal of Regional Science* 47: 415–455.

Anas A, Arnott R, and Small K (1998) Urban spatial structure. *Journal of Economic Literature* 36: 1426–1464.

Brueckner JK (1987) The structure of urban equilibria: A unified treatment of the Mills–Muth model. In: Mills ES (ed.) *Handbook of Urban and Regional Economics, Vol. 2: Urban Economics*, pp. 351–345. Amsterdam: North-Holland.

Brueckner JK (2000) Urban growth models with durable housing: An overview. In: Huriot J-M and Thisse J-F (eds.) *Economics of*

Cities, pp. 263–289. Cambridge, UK: Cambridge University Press.

Fujita M (1989) *Urban Economic Theory*. Cambridge, UK: Cambridge University Press.

Fujita M and Ogawa H (1982) Multiple equilibria and structural transition of non-monocentric urban configurations. *Regional Science and Urban Economics* 12: 161–196.

Hamilton BW (1982) Wasteful commuting. *Journal of Political Economy* 90: 1035–1053.

Mills ES (1967) An aggregative model of resource allocation in a metropolitan area. *American Economic Review* 57: 197–210.

Muth RF (1969) *Cities and Housing*. Chicago, IL: The University of Chicago Press.

Ponsard C (1983) *History of Spatial Economic Theory*. Berlin: Springer-Verlag.

Tiebout CM (1956) A pure theory of local public goods. *Journal of Political Economy* 64: 416–424.

Wheaton WC (1974) A comparative static analysis of urban spatial structure. *Journal of Economic Theory* 9: 223–237.

Wheaton WC (1977) Income and urban residence: An analysis of consumer demand for location. *American Economic Association* 67: 620–631.

von Thünen JH (1827) *Der Isolierte Staadt in Beziehung auf Landwirtschaft and Nationalöconomie*. Translated in English as von Thünen's isolated state by Wartenberg CW (1966). Oxford, UK: Pergamon Press.

New Urbanism and Smart Growth Movements

JL Grant, Dalhousie University, Halifax, NS, Canada
S Tsenkova, University of Calgary, Calgary, AB, Canada

© 2012 Elsevier Ltd. All rights reserved.

Glossary

New Urbanism A design and planning movement that advocates building complete communities with a mix of uses, pedestrian scale, and compact form. It is commonly associated with architect/planners like Andres Duany, Peter Calthorpe, and Leon Krier.

Smart Growth A movement that promotes urban growth in dense, compact, and transit-oriented forms. Governments across North America have widely adopted its principles to inform urban policy and development.

Sprawl A common term used to describe growth on the edges of cities that is haphazard, disorganised, poorly serviced, and largely unplanned. It refers to new suburban development with low-density, segregated land uses leading to traffic congestion, high infrastructure costs, and environmental degradation.

Sustainability A concept that originated in the environmental movement to connote development patterns that meet human needs while protecting natural systems, reducing resource demands, and minimising waste outputs.

Sustainable communities Places that can persist successfully over long periods of time because they have an aggregate of characteristics including economic security, environmental quality and integrity, social cohesion and quality of life, and community empowerment.

Introduction

The decades after the Second World War brought a period of affluence and rapid urban growth guided by faith in progress and a commitment to modernism. As car ownership proliferated, an increasing proportion of North Americans began to realise 'the American Dream': a home in the suburbs. Urban growth patterns changed, with new rings of suburbs housing commuters travelling to jobs reached by highways. Harvey Molotch described the postwar city as a growth machine abetted by coalitions of developers and political leaders pushing growth at every opportunity. Inner cities faced decline, historic buildings fell to bulldozers, and look-alike suburbs appeared across the continent.

By the mid-1960s people had begun to react to unrelenting growth. Neighbourhoods fought back against urban renewal and expressways that would destroy communities. In the early 1970s environmentalists demanded action on air and water protection, and sought to contain the loss of agricultural land. Organisations like the Club of Rome contributed to the public perception that endless growth had to be curbed to safeguard mankind. In this context, many states and cities began to institutionalise efforts to stop or slow down growth. Boulder, Colorado, established a greenbelt in 1967 to control the outward expansion of the city: In 1976 it imposed a height cap and limits on the number of building permits it would issue annually. State legislation in Oregon in 1973 required cities to develop land conservation plans: In 1979 Portland adopted an urban growth boundary to contain development. During the 1970s Canadian cities like Toronto and Vancouver began promoting intensification in the urban core to reduce the need to build highways for commuting. Their efforts to maintain densities and services within the city and to limit outward expansion experienced considerable success.

Despite planners' efforts, cities continued to experience problems of traffic congestion, urban sprawl, increasing housing costs, and environmental degradation into the 1980s. The conservative political agenda of the era created something of a backlash against land-use planning, with new interest in strategic planning and in physical design. Architect/planners like Leon Krier and Andres Duany began experimenting with a new model of neotraditional town planning. In 1982 Duany and his partner Elizabeth Plater-Zyberk designed the new town of Seaside, Florida, for developer Robert Davis. Rather than building placeless suburbs, these designers created compact, walkable, mixed-use, small towns. Their plan for The Kentlands (**Box 1**) in Gaithersburg, Maryland, became a model of how cities could build attractive new areas that might make growth acceptable to the public and profitable to developers.

> **Box 1: Case study of neotraditional planning**
> *The Kentlands (Gaithersburg, Maryland)*
> Developer Joe Alfandre hired the design firm Duany Plater-Zyberk (DPZ) Associates in the late 1980s to develop a plan for a farm in the Metro Washington area. DPZ created a concept for a mixed community with a range of housing types, a main street commercial area, a regional shopping centre, and an open-space system protecting sensitive areas. The resulting development has beautiful architecture and urban design and was widely seen as a model of what good design can produce (**Figure 1**).
>
> Despite its successes, however, Kentlands has not achieved some of the aims of its designers. While the main street commercial district is attractive, it contains mostly services rather than retail vendors. The town is primarily inhabited by commuters working in the Washington Metro area, not by people who work locally. Its residents are affluent and mostly white, rather than the mix of classes and races found in an urban context. To a significant extent, Kentlands was a victim of its own success: Its popularity drove up housing prices to a point that made it an exclusive enclave.

Designers on the West Coast also developed new urban/suburban models to deal with the challenges of coping with growth during the 1980s. Peter Calthorpe and Doug Kelbaugh experimented with pedestrian pockets – areas of high density and transit-oriented development. Their interest in using public transportation strategically to reshape growth patterns led these designers to develop a commitment to sustainability and regional planning. With the release of the report of the World Commission on Environment and Development, planners in North America began to use the language of sustainable development to advocate new kinds of urban growth that would change the character of the city and promote more sustainable communities.

During the 1990s many of the principles of these movements were blended first into New Urbanism and then, with an infusion of progrowth neoliberalism, into Smart Growth. A range of popular, professional, and political movements grew around the philosophies. Although New Urbanism and Smart Growth began with somewhat different priorities, by the 2000s they shared most principles in common (**Box 2**) and increasingly suggested that they could produce sustainability.

> **Box 2: Principles shared by New Urbanism and Smart Growth**
>
> - Mix land uses.
> - Take advantage of compact building design.
> - Create a range of housing opportunities and choices.
> - Create walkable communities.
> - Foster distinctive, attractive communities with a strong sense of place.
> - Preserve open space, farmland, natural beauty, and critical environmental areas.
> - Strengthen and direct development towards existing communities.
> - Provide a variety of transport choices.
> - Make development decisions predictable, fair, and cost-effective.
> - Encourage community and stakeholder collaboration in development decisions.
> - Provide a variety of transport choices.

Figure 1 The Kentlands: Elegant homes contribute to the sense of place.

New Urbanism

The Congress for the New Urbanism (CNU) was formed in 1993, bringing together the proponents of neotraditional town planning with the advocates of transit-oriented design. As an institution the CNU grew rapidly, holding annual conferences and producing materials about New Urbanism that created a community of professionals, educators, developers, and private citizens committed to the principles of the movement. State and local chapters provided a way of spreading the message and increasing the influence of New Urbanism in local practice. The profile of urban design and physical planning grew significantly in North American cities in the 1990s and 2000s. Hundreds of New Urbanism developments began construction (e.g., **Box 3**), and government programmes for rehabilitating public housing projects implemented the movement's principles.

Box 3: Case study of New Urbanism
Garrison Woods, Calgary, Alberta

The City of Calgary took an early interest in New Urbanism principles, publishing a *Sustainable Suburbs Study* in 1995 and other plans that promoted the idea. Garrison Woods in the city is a redeveloped army base of 1600 residential units about 10 minutes' drive from the main employment district in the city centre. It is one of the most successful examples of New Urbanism on the continent, with a mix of housing types and uses, well served by public transportation (see **Figure 2**). The developer, Canada Lands Corporation, refurbished old military housing and added new units on a reorganised street pattern. Site plans protected mature vegetation and many former military buildings reinvented as community amenities. The commercial district abuts and supports a preexisting shopping area. The project built out 2 years ahead of schedule and is being followed up with development on neighbouring properties. With an overall density of 25 units per hectare, Garrison Woods demonstrated the potential for accommodating considerable population growth without expanding urban boundaries. In the context of Calgary's over-heated housing market, however, the area did not prove affordable to the average household.

New Urbanism emphasises urban form, quality, and structure. It promotes a mix of uses and housing types, fine-grained design, compactness, connectivity, order, and sense of place. *The Charter of the New Urbanism* proposes high quality urban design, pedestrian-friendly environments, attractive streets, parks, and squares.

> We advocate the restructuring of public policy and development practices to support the following principles: neighborhoods should be diverse in use and population; communities should be designed for the pedestrian and transit as well as the car; cities and towns should be shaped by physically defined and universally accessible public spaces and community institutions; urban places should be framed by architecture and landscape design that celebrate local history, climate, ecology, and building practice. (Congress for the New Urbanism 1996: 1)

The movement seeks to integrate design with planning at distinct scales: large scale (region, metropolis, city, and town); medium scale (neighbourhood, district, and corridor); and small scale (block, street, and building). While New Urbanism initially focussed principally on design strategies and physical planning, in the last decade its advocates recognised the significance of policy and planning, and developed tools and institutions to advance the agenda.

Smart Growth

During the 1990s, decision makers in many regions faced calls from their constituents for ways to manage or stop growth. While they worked with policies and strategies to promote growth management, many showed considerable interest in the ideas for new development and redevelopment being promoted within New Urbanism. Governor Parris Glendening of Maryland and his colleagues in the National Governors Association coined the term Smart Growth in the mid-1990s to argue that properly managed growth could make places better. States like Maryland implemented a package of government incentives and policies to shape development by encouraging local governments to encourage intensification.

Central to the philosophy of Smart Growth is the premise that growth is inevitable but needs to be managed within the context of long-term regional planning to produce a sustainable future. In 1996 the newly formed Smart Growth Network of the United States, an institution with members from government, real estate, advocacy, and policy-making circles, adopted ten Smart Growth principles (see **Box 2**). The principles are complementary and interdependent. For example, compact and mixed-use land development strengthens the walkability of communities; the proximity of services to residential areas, along with a distinctive urban form, enlivens neighbourhoods and helps to create a sense of place. Compact development promotes high land-use intensity, while reducing development pressure on sensitive environmental areas preserves the natural amenity provided by the landscape. The mix of uses requires accessible transportation connections to help ensure multiple transportation options for all residents. Smart Growth absorbed the principles of New Urbanism while adding concerns about environmental protection and

Figure 2 Garrison Woods: Medium density housing on an urban green.

developing a suite of policy tools to encourage developers and governments to accept the new direction.

Smart Growth proved enormously popular in political and economic circles. State and provincial governments developed programmes and policies to implement the ideas. Governments created task forces, networks, departments, and plans to promote the agenda. Local development agencies and business organisations typically supported Smart Growth and used its principles for a range of redevelopment projects (see **Box 4**). Smart Growth has been widely institutionalised as an urban planning and development philosophy in the last decade.

Box 4: Case study of Smart Growth
High Point, Seattle, Washington

In 2007, the Seattle Housing Authority was awarded the National Award for Smart Growth Achievement for its High Point redevelopment project. High Point was formerly a run-down neighbourhood of 120 acres accommodating public housing in West Seattle. The redeveloped neighbourhood includes 1700 new units in a mixed-use, mixed-income environment planned in an environmentally friendly manner. High Point has many qualities of a Smart Growth community demonstrated in its application of a progressive strategy for citizen involvement, certified green building design, and environmental measures. Residents live in a mixed-use, pedestrian-friendly, and high-density redeveloped neighbourhood within the heart of West Seattle. The Seattle Housing Authority doubled the number of residential units for families in an existing urban area and also increased the supply of quality social housing.

The design emphasises connections to surrounding neighbourhoods, mixed land uses, diversity of built forms, higher-density housing, and a mix of homes for a variety of incomes. Public buildings in the neighbourhood include a community library, a health clinic, and community recreation centre. The development preserved mature trees, provided energy-efficient homes, and used a natural drainage system to collect and filter the water before it enters the nearby stream. Streets have storm-water infiltration swales, and green spaces are planted with low-water-usage native plant species.

Institutionalising the Concepts

In recent decades, designers and planners promoting the principles of New Urbanism and Smart Growth have improved some old tools and developed some original mechanisms to help institutionalise the new ideas. Where useful, they have worked with engineers to refashion rules and protocols that affect the shape and growth of the city. For instance, while developers have used restrictive codes and covenants for generations to control uses and users of private residential environments, the New Urbanism designers created new kinds of comprehensive design codes to shape and manage the public realm. Drawing on ecosystem analogies, Andres Duany and Emily Talen developed the concept of the urban-to-rural transect, used to inform a set of design-code requirements which DPZ Associates patented as the Smart Code in 2003. By 2000, hundreds of cities across North America had adopted urban design and planning codes that owed a debt to New Urbanism. The Congress for the New Urbanism also worked with the Institute of Transportation Engineers to develop revised standards to facilitate a transition to new principles of street design.

Some states and provincial governments moved the New Urbanism and Smart Growth agendas ahead through changes to legislation and policy. Among the most aggressive programmes is the growth plan and greenbelt legislation passed in the Canadian province of Ontario. In 2006 the province adopted a growth plan for the region around Toronto. The law required designated municipalities to develop long-term plans implementing many Smart Growth principles, such as promoting infill development, increasing densities, and encouraging mixed use. The province's ability to entrench Smart Growth through these initiatives may depend on the effectiveness of infrastructure investments and other incentives to local governments and to developers.

A new voluntary certification system of Leadership in Energy and Environmental Design (LEED) for Neighbourhood Development (ND) takes the approaches of Smart Growth and New Urbanism further. The US Green Building Council (USGBC), in partnership with the Congress for the New Urbanism and the Natural Resources Defense Council, released the Pilot Version of LEED-ND Rating System in 2007 (**Box 5**). Administered by the USGBC, the system evaluates the design and construction procedures of new development on infill and greenfield sites. LEED-ND hopes to encourage developers to create new development that will "revitalize existing urban areas, reduce land consumption, reduce automobile dependence, promote pedestrian activity, improve air quality, decrease polluted storm water runoff, and build more liveable, sustainable, communities for people of all income levels" (USGBC, 2007: 1). Once the 238 pilot projects are evaluated, the USGBC expects to launch the programme.

Box 5: LEED-ND rating system
The rating system sets credits in the following areas:

- Location efficiency: encouraging new development to occur in places where there is already access to services and amenities such as transit, walkable commercial development, existing municipal services, and so on.
- Environmental preservation: protecting wetlands and watercourses, wildlife habitats and endangered species, and sensitive or valuable agricultural lands.
- Design and construction elements: utilising technologies and design to improve the human experience of the urban environment.
- Resource efficiency: increasing efficiencies in the materials used for construction, as well as efficient electricity generation, water treatment, and waste management.

Implementation Trajectories

While governments have increasingly institutionalised the principles and tools of New Urbanism and Smart Growth, and many organisations and institutions promote the philosophies (see **Table 1**), critics suggest that building and planning practices reveal the challenge of changing development paradigms. Implementation has proven difficult in the United States. Recent studies have shown that despite popular praise and political support, Smart Growth and New Urbanism principles have had a limited effect on plans and planning implementation. While plans contain vision statements and objectives that conform to the intent of Smart Growth or New Urbanism, practice offers little evidence of change in the patterns of new development. Ye, Mandpe, and Meyer found principles such as limiting outward expansion, increasing densities, providing mixed-use developments, and emphasising public transit appeared more commonly in plans than did other Smart Growth elements. Anthony Downs outlined formidable obstacles to implementing Smart Growth goals and objectives, including resistance to policy shifts, hostility to high-density developments, inefficient public-transit policies, and lack of regional planning. While New Urbanism projects continue to be built and to win design awards, few have achieved the full suite of principles of the movement.

New Urbanism and Smart Growth have faced similar challenges in Canada. A recent survey of New Urbanism developments noted that the Canadian movement had produced beautiful suburbs but had not successfully implemented principles such as mixed-use, mixed-housing types at the block level, affordable housing, or urban densities. Canadians remain reliant on their cars and continue to prefer to live on cul-de-sacs. Canadian studies on Smart

Table 1 Examples of institutions promoting New Urbanism and Smart Growth

New Urbanism	Smart Growth
• Congress for the New Urbanism	• Smart Growth Network
• Center for Livable Communities	• Smart Growth America
• American Planning Association, NU Division	• Ontario Smart Growth Network
• Livable Streets Initiative	• Smart Growth BC
• The Seaside Institute	• National Center for Smart Growth Research and Education
• New Urbanism & Sustainable Development Meetup Groups	• Delaware Valley Smart Growth Alliance
• The Preservation Institute	• Minnesota Smart Growth Network
• Institute of Classical Architecture & Classical America	• Montana Smart Growth Coalition
• International Network for Traditional Building, Architecture & Urbanism	• Smart Growth Leadership Institute
• Center for Applied Transect Studies	• Sustainable Communities Network

Growth attributed the implementation gap to the lack of political will, resistance from the development community, and consumer preference for low-density residential suburbs. Case studies have illustrated the shortcomings of plans designed to mix uses, create affordable housing, reduce automobile use, or increase densities.

Conclusion

Do New Urbanism and Smart Growth provide the tools and institutions to direct growth on a more sustainable path? Experience to date offers limited evidence to suggest that they can dramatically alter development patterns away from car-oriented, low-density forms. Nevertheless, these movements have promoted a growing commitment to a new pattern of development that protects open space and farmland, revitalises communities, keeps housing more affordable, and provides transportation choices. Policies and plans increasingly advocate preserving ecologically sensitive areas, floodplains, and agricultural land, and promote compact development with a diversity of uses and housing types served by public transit.

The new planning approaches are guided by the vision for sustainable cities as places that build on their assets and have a strong sense of place. The planning policy framework advocates integrating land uses, clustering neighbourhood activities, and implementing an environmentally sensitive approach to development. It articulates the need to create a strong sense of place and neighbourhood identity through preserving cultural and environmental heritage. Residential communities built on these principles often challenge regulatory practices and city standards for planning approval and infrastructure provision; they require higher development costs and risks. The significant attention that urban growth management receives in different cities today highlights an ongoing debate, which questions the ability of Smart Growth and New Urbanism to produce more sustainable communities. The struggle to implement these principles in practice is likely to persist for planners, developers, local politicians, and city residents, particularly in the context of highly skewed growth patterns in North America. The next decade will offer new challenges and tests for the New Urbanism and Smart Growth movements to navigate as their proponents continue to advocate for effective growth management.

See also: HOPE VI; Housing Supply: Urban Growth Boundaries; Sustainable Urban Development.

Further Reading

Bruegmann R (2005) *A Compact History of Sprawl*. Chicago: University of Chicago Press.

Calthorpe P and Fulton W (2001) *The Regional City: Planning for the End of Sprawl*. Washington: Island Press.

Congress for the New Urbanism. (2006) The Charter of New Urbanism. http://www.cnu.org/charter, accessed on 23 June 2009.

Downs A (2005) Smart growth: Why we discuss it more than we do it. *Journal of the American Planning Association* 71(4): 457–479.

Duany A and Talen E (2002). Transect planning. *Journal of the American Planning Association* 68(3): 245–266.

Filion P (2003) Towards smart growth: The difficult implementation of alternatives to urban dispersion. *Canadian Journal of Urban Research (Supplement): Canadian Planning and Policy* 12(1): 48–70.

Grant J (2009) Theory and practice in planning the suburbs: Challenges to implementing new urbanism, smart growth, and sustainability principles. *Planning Theory and Practice* 10(1): 11–33.

Grant J (2006) *Planning the Good Community: New Urbanism in Theory and Practice*. London: Routledge.

Grant J and Bohdanow S (2008) New urbanism in Canada: A survey. *Journal of Urbanism* 1(2): 111–130.

Krieger A (ed.) (1991) *Andres Duany and Elizabeth Plater-Zyberk: Towns and Town-Making Principles*. New York: Rizzoli.

Molotch H (1976) The city as a growth machine: Towards a political economy of place. *American Journal of Sociology* 82(2): 309–332.

Porter D (2008) *Managing Growth in America's Communities*, 2nd edn. Washington: Island Press.

Tsenkova S (ed.) (2009) *Cities, Policy and Planning Research Series. Planning Sustainable Communities: Diversity of Approaches and Implementation Challenges*. Calgary: Faculty of Environmental Design, University of Calgary.

Tsenkova S and Damiani R (2009) Urban sustainability: Learning from evaluation of community plans in Calgary. *Canadian Journal of Urban Research* 18(1): 82–105.

Ye L, Mandpe P, and Meyer P (2005) What is 'smart growth' – really? *Journal of Planning Literature* 19(3): 301–315.

Relevant Websites

www.cnu.org/ – Congress for New Urbanism
www.garrisonwoods.com/ – Garrison Woods
www.smartgrowth.on.ca/ – Ontario Smart Growth Network
www.placestogrow.ca/index.php – Places to Grow
www.smartgrowth.org/ – Smart Growth
www.smartcodecentral.org/ – SmartCode Central
www.usgbc.org/ – U.S. Green Building Council

NIMBYism

K Burningham, University of Surrey, Guildford, UK

© 2012 Elsevier Ltd. All rights reserved.

Glossary
NIMBY An acronym from N(ot) I(n) M(y) B(ack) Y(ard). Used to describe opponents of new developments who recognise that a facility or technology is needed but are opposed to its siting within their locality.

What is NIMBYism?

NIMBY is an acronym from N(ot) I(n) M(y) B(ack) Y(ard). It is used to describe opponents of new developments who recognise that a facility or technology is needed but are opposed to its siting within their locality. The term dates from the 1980s although its exact origin is unclear: Some claim that it was first coined by Nicholas Ridley, a British Conservative MP, while others trace it to Walter Rodgers of the American Nuclear Society.

In everyday use, the term is often pejorative and is used as a convenient shorthand to denote irrational, selfish, and obstructive individuals who fear change and stand in the way of essential developments. NIMBYs are considered parochial individuals who place the protection of their individual interests above the common good. Thus, the concept of NIMBYism is popular with politicians and journalists and is frequently evoked in planning disputes.

Use of the concept of NIMBYism is also culture-specific. It is used to describe opponents to developments in relatively rich communities and 'developed' countries but is much less likely to be used of opponents in poorer communities or 'developing' countries. This may be because poor communities and 'developing' countries are keener to embrace the development of new infrastructure as a sign of investment and progress, and thus opposition is less prevalent. It may also reflect a tendency of authors to characterise opposition from poorer sectors of society or in poorer societies as struggles for environmental justice rather than examples of selfish attempts to protect local interests.

Most of the literature in the area concentrates on the siting of social facilities (e.g., prisons, homes for the mentally ill, etc.) or of waste or industrial facilities; however, the term is also used to describe opponents to new housing developments, particularly in rural locations. Recently, a number of studies have emerged focusing on responses to the siting of renewable energy technologies (notably wind farms).

The literature on NIMBYism is complex in a variety of ways: the types of facilities considered are varied; the research has its origins in a variety of different disciplines (notably planning, sociology, psychology, economics), and some studies focus on individual attitudes and beliefs while others explore collective action. The situation is further complicated by the fact that authors do not define the term in the same way. Some authors veer from the equation of NIMBYism with self-interest and instead use it as shorthand for local opposition, regardless of what seems to motivate it (i.e., NIMBY responses are regularly described as based on environmental or health concerns).

While some of the early US literature uncritically labeled project opponents as NIMBYs, as research in the fields has grown so critiques of the concept have mounted. Those seeking to avoid using the NIMBY label often refer instead to LULUs (locally unwanted land uses). While this has the advantage of suggesting that the problem lies with the land use, rather than with project opponents, it also suggests that proposed developments are uniformly viewed as 'unwanted' rather than recognising the diversity of local responses. Despite these complexities, the literature is unified by an interest in understanding opposition to proposed local developments.

What follows is a critical summary of attempts to understand local opposition and corresponding ways of responding to it. It begins by engaging with constructions of opponents as ignorant and selfish individuals and then aims to demonstrate how understandings have increasingly moved away from a focus on the negative attributes of opponents to understand the broader motivations and contexts of local opposition. It concludes by documenting recent calls for an end to using the language of NIMBYism.

Are Project Opponents Ignorant and Selfish?

Freudenberg and Pastor (1992) provide a useful review of the NIMBY literature and suggest that it can be characterised as falling into three distinct perspectives. The first is of NIMBY as an ignorant or irrational response. This perspective, which is particularly apparent in some early American studies, draws a clear distinction between the real risks or impacts associated with new developments and the public's assessment of these risks.

If opposition is understood as an ignorant response to essential developments, the appropriate response might be to educate people in order to improve their understanding of the benefits of the project or to allay their fears about the negative impacts. This perspective utilises a deficit model of public understanding in which the public are seen as having too little or incorrect knowledge. This position has been roundly criticised by sociological studies that have demonstrated that far from being passive vessels, which simply need to be filled with more or better information, members of the public are active in weighing up the usefulness and relevance of information. Lay people are able to assimilate even complex information if they can see practical gains from doing so and if they trust the sources. Indeed assumptions of public ignorance are undermined by empirical studies, which reveal that active project opponents are often more knowledgeable about the proposed development than are passive supporters.

Clearly, if opponents feel that they are being treated as ignorant, this is likely to exacerbate planning disputes. Thus, while supplying clear information from trustworthy sources is important, strategies for overcoming opposition that rely on educating ignorant opponents are unlikely to succeed. If project opponents are conceptualised as ignorant, an alternative response may simply be to ignore or overrule them. Experiments with this approach suggest, however, that such authoritarian 'solutions' may also be more likely to exacerbate than to solve the problem.

The second perspective on NIMBY identified by Freudenberg and Pastor is that it is a selfish response, based on limited self-interest. Some researchers who equate NIMBY with selfishness assume that this means that such protest is less important than that based on wider social and environmental concerns; others, however, note that actions taken in an individual's self-interest are considered to be rational within the free market systems and so can hardly be condemned.

While selfish NIMBYism is routinely used as an explanation for opposition to local developments, in practice empirical research finds little support for the idea that people adhere to the rational choice models of narrowly self-interested actors.

In addition, opponents are not alone in seeking to defend their own interests; project proponents too clearly have interests of their own. Land-use controversies are more complex than suggested by the simple dichotomy between local self-interest and the general interest/national interest/greater good.

If opposition is conceived as motivated by self-interest, then the solutions considered appropriate rely on trade-offs, compensation, or community benefits. While it is important for developers to consider how projects might deliver local benefit, monetary strategies are often interpreted as a form of bribery and as such can exacerbate opposition.

Concern about Local Impacts

Concerns about the impact of new developments clearly play a role in fostering local opposition. Common concerns are that the facility is wrong for the area; will have negative social, environmental, or health impacts; and may not be managed responsibly or efficiently. An obvious assumption is that the closer an individual lives to a proposed development, the more likely they are to oppose it, both because of the effect on property prices and because of any attendant impacts. Research on the effect of proximity shows mixed results, however. One problem in unpicking the effect of proximity is that studies of proposed and actual developments are sometimes conflated. Thus studies suggest that those residents closest to a 'proposed' development may be those most likely to object on the basis that they are most likely to experience any adverse impacts. On the other hand, studies of responses to 'actual' installations (such as wind farms) indicate that those living closest tend to be more positive about them than those who live further away and lack direct experience of the technology. It is difficult to generalise about the impact of new developments on property prices as the characteristics of the development, the perceived risks and impacts associated with it, and features of the local housing market will all play a role.

Concerns about noise and visual impacts are common in relation to proposals for industrial, waste, and energy developments. Kempton et al. (2005) analysis of public responses to a proposed off-shore wind farm makes the important point that expressed concerns about impact on 'the view' are often not only about visual or aesthetic considerations but may act as a proxy for more fundamental values.

If opposition is understood as motivated by concerns about local impacts, then responses may involve modifying aspects of the design of the development to ameliorate impacts or considering ways in which community benefit packages may offset the negative impacts. While concern about the impacts of the material features of proposed developments goes some way to explaining opposition, social assessments about management of the facility and particularly the extent to which local people trust those responsible for ensuring that it is run safely and without adverse impacts are fundamental.

Wexler (1996) provides a thought-provoking critique of the assumption that siting disputes are simply about 'local' impacts. He objects to simplistic spatial notions of 'backyard', noting the assumption that:

> backyards are small and that they 'belong' to the local community (while)...the central or higher interests, those equated in the conventional NIMBY perspective with the public good, seemingly do not have a turf or backyard to protect. This, in a nutshell, is why the centre is not biased or preoccupied with its own self-interest. But this is wrong. (1996: 96)

This is wrong not only because the idea of NIMBYism can be applied to whole countries or trading blocs who want to avoid the negative impacts of polluting industry (backyards are not always small), but also because it assumes that there is only one 'centre'. He draws attention here to the way in which disputes are often not simply 'local' but involve wider coalitions and social movements.

Broader Values and Motivations

Empirical studies of land-use disputes tend to reveal a wide range of motivations and explanations for opposition, which cannot be adequately characterised as NIMBYism. Project opponents typically draw on a range of social, environmental, and moral values and concerns as the bases for their position, and opposition is often informed by a lack of trust in those responsible for planning or managing developments. This understanding takes us far from the characterisation of opponents as ignorant and selfish NIMBYs.

If project opponents are viewed as having valid concerns and interests, then the focus shifts to consider ways of building trust between the parties involved and engaging with them to take their views into account in the decision-making process.

The motivations for public engagement in decision-making have been categorised by Fiorino (1990) as instrumental, substantive, and normative. The instrumental motivation expects public engagement to reduce conflict and promote learning and understanding among stakeholders, thus easing planning disputes and enabling development. From a normative perspective, participation is simply the right thing to do; the public have a right to have a say in decisions that will affect their lives. The substantive rationale holds that participatory processes are valuable as they yield better results.

A variety of methods of participatory decision-making have been mooted, which allow for greater dialogue and potential consensus building than the limited public information and consultation exercises typically employed by developers. These include such things as citizen's juries or panels, consensus conferences, and stakeholder workshops.

Features of the Planning Process

Calls for greater public participation also chime with studies that understand 'NIMBY' responses as to some extent produced by the features of decision-making processes that preclude consideration of local peoples' concerns and priorities.

For example, in the United Kingdom there are rarely opportunities for members of the public to be involved in general discussion of project options before developers apply for planning permission for specific developments, and subsequent engagement processes tend to rely on providing information and limited consultation on pre-determined options. In this context it is not surprising that local groups often adopt an obstructive stance. In addition the restrictions of the UK Public Inquiry process lead to particular kinds of issues and concerns being raised during the inquiry. Thus the form of the decision-making process may encourage responses that can easily be characterised as NIMBY as it is often only legitimate for objectors to draw attention to specific local and often personal economic impacts.

From this perspective limited or self-interested opposition may be seen as contextually generated. This approach leads away from seeking individual-level explanations for opposition to siting in favour of exploring the circumstances in which alternative problem framings might emerge.

Not only may decision-making processes generate NIMBY-style responses, assessments of the process itself (rather than of the proposed development per se) may play a role in generating local opposition. A number of authors have illustrated how individuals' perceptions of the fairness of the process play a key role in explaining opposition.

If local resistance to the siting of developments is understood as partly a product of the planning and decision-making system, then the responses considered appropriate involve changing the system to make it more fair and inclusive and able to engage with diverse concerns as outlined previously. It is important that changing aspects of the process is not simply seen as a way of overcoming opposition: "the fundamental issue is not how to persuade the public to accept an unwanted facility but how to structure the process in order to arrive at publicly acceptable decisions" (Armour, 1992: 32).

'Essential' Developments?

By this point, a shift may be detected in conceptualisations of local opposition. While the explanations outlined at the start focused on (negative) individual attributes, subsequent research has indicated that there are often broader social reasons for opposition whether these focus on the local, social, environmental, or health impacts of the project or are rooted in assessments of the credibility of those developing or managing the project. We then moved on to consider how the form of the decision-making process itself may foster oppositional responses. Perhaps the furthest step away from understanding opposition in terms of negative individual attributes is taken by authors who challenge some of the underlying premises about 'essential' developments.

For example, using the example of siting hazardous waste incinerators, Lake (1993) questions the premise inherent to the NIMBY concept that facilities are needed to provide societal benefits. He points out that building incinerators is only one of a variety of possible solutions to the problem of hazardous waste generation and one that "concentrates costs on local communities, as compared to the alternative strategy of restructuring production so as to produce less waste" (Lake 1993: 88).

Characterising siting disputes as examples of NIMBYism suggests that the only issue at stake is about location and marginalises questions about alternative means of providing the outcomes sought. It is a strategy which Lake suggests:

> places the onus for policy failure entirely on selfish local communities, obfuscates the interests of capital, and deflects attention away from the fundamental causes of societal problems. (1993: 88)

Beyond NIMBY

While the term NIMBY continues to be widespread in popular use, the cumulative message of social science research is that its use is problematic as ignorant and selfish NIMBYs prove hard to find and responding to opponents as such is often counterproductive. If project opposition is understood to be motivated by place attachment, concern about local impacts, or broader political, social, or environmental values, the epithet NIMBY with its pejorative connotations is inadequate; opposition may be motivated by the features of decision-making processes and the relationships between those responsible for planning, building, and managing developments; and the public and 'local' planning disputes may provide a forum for playing out deeper conflicts within the society.

Such considerations have led a number of authors to call for an end to the academic use of the term. NIMBYism is an inaccurate, offensive, and unhelpful way of characterising local opposition to new developments. An emergent research agenda focuses instead on how the language of NIMBYism is used and with what effect. The use of the term is understood as an intrinsic part of development disputes rather than an analytically adequate concept for understanding the complex reasons for local opposition. From this perspective there is a need for more research that focuses on ascriptions of NIMBYism and their consequences.

See also: Neighbourhood Effects; Neighbourhood Planning; Price Determination in Housing Markets.

References

Armour A (1992) The co-operative process: Facility siting the democratic way. *Plan Canada* March: 29–34.
Fiorino DJ (1990) Citizen participation and environmental risk: A survey of institutional mechanisms. *Science, Technology and Human Values* 15: 226–243.
Freudenberg W and Pastor S (1992) NIMBYs and LULUs: Stalking the syndromes. *Journal of Social Issues* 48(4): 39–61.
Kempton W, Firestone J, Lilley J, Rouleau T, and Whitaker P (2005) The offshore wind power debate: Views from Cape Cod. *Coastal Management* 33: 119–149.
Lake R (1993) Rethinking NIMBY. *Journal of the American Planning Association* 59(1): 87–93.
Wexler M (1996) A sociological framing of the NIMBY (Not-in-my-backyard) syndrome. *International Review of Modern Sociology* 26(1): 91–110.

Further Reading

Burningham K (2000) Using the language of NIMBY: A topic for research not an activity for researchers. *Local Environment* 5(1): 55–67.
Bell D, Gray T, and Haggett C (2005) Policy, participation and the 'social gap' in wind farm siting decisions. *Environmental Politics* 14(4): 460–477.
Dear M (1992) Understanding and overcoming the NIMBY syndrome. *Journal of the American Planning Association* 58(3): 288–300.
Devine-Wright P (2005) Beyond NIMBYism: Towards an integrated framework for understanding public perceptions of wind energy. *Wind Energy* 8: 125–139.
Futrell R (2003) Framing processes, cognitive liberation, and NIMBY protest in the U.S. chemical weapons disposal conflict. *Sociological Inquiry* 73(3): 359–386.
Gibson TA (2005) NIMBY and the civic good. *City and Community* 4(4): 381–401.
Hunter S and Leyden K (1995) Beyond NIMBY: Explaining opposition to hazardous waste facilities. *Policy Studies Journal* 23(4): 601–619.
Schiveley C (2007) Understanding the NIMBY and LULU phenomena: Reassessing our knowledge base and informing future research. *Journal of Planning Literature* 21: 255–266.
Wolsink M (2006) Invalid theory impedes our understanding: A critique on the persistence of the language of NIMBY. *Transactions of the Institute of British Geographers* 31: 85–91.

Notaries and Legal Professionals

NM Davidson, University of Colorado Law School, Boulder, CO, USA

© 2012 Elsevier Ltd. All rights reserved.

Glossary

Civil law notary Also known as a latin notary, a legal professional recognised by law to authenticate documents and advise parties.

Commonhold, condominium, cooperative Forms of shared individual and common ownership.

Covenants, conditions, and restrictions A common form of private property governance that binds owners in a common interest community.

Executory contract A contract involving unperformed obligations, in the housing context usually related to closing a sale or loan.

Legal professional A category of professionals trained and licensed to represent clients in legal matters.

Introduction

Almost every aspect of housing and home can raise legal issues that require the involvement of legal professionals. These professionals – including lawyers, civil law notaries, and paralegals, as well as legally trained individuals who work in fields related to housing, such as title insurance and lending – assist clients in transactions that undergird the housing market. Their roles include negotiating and documenting transactions, investigating legal risks, and ensuring regulatory compliance. Legal professionals likewise help clients navigate the myriad of legal questions that arise during the lifecycle of a home, including relations with stakeholders that include family members, neighbours, and the community, and questions related to security of tenure and nondiscrimination.

Legal Professionals in Housing-Market Transactions

Residential markets require the production of new housing stock as well as an active trade in existing housing. Legal professionals play an active and often central role in the transactions that drive every segment and phase of these markets, which can be divided into sectors such as single family or multifamily, for sale or for rent. In order to produce housing, market participants acquire land and other inputs, secure financing primarily in the form of equity and debt, and then oversee development. Transactions take place at critical junctures in this market cycle, and legal professionals represent a variety of clients in the design, production, and delivery of housing.

In the United States and many other jurisdictions, for transactions of any significance or complexity, legal professionals act for owners, developers, investors, lenders, architects, construction firms, and others. This area of legal practice has traditionally been local in scope, but in recent years has grown in many countries to be national and now even has a global dimension, particularly with capital–market integration.

For housing consumers, both purchasers and tenants, the market for legal representation has largely come to depend on the value and complexity of the transaction. Although the practice varies from jurisdiction to jurisdiction, in many markets single-family home sales take place without legal representation, with the parties using standard-form purchase-and-sale agreements only lightly negotiated, often with the help of real estate agents. Similarly, landlords and tenants in many residential tenancies eschew the involvement of lawyers, relying instead on readily available standard-form leases or even informal agreements. Nonetheless, high-end residential purchases, long-term residential leases, and sale or lease transactions with unusual legal aspects – such as unresolved regulatory issues, novel financing structures, and the like – tend more often to involve legal professionals.

Understanding the Work of Legal Professionals in Transactions

In all of these transactions, lawyers play a number of different, although overlapping, roles. It is common in complex transactions to have attorneys and other legal professionals guide precontracting negotiations, manage the executory contracting period, and take responsibility for closing. Legal professionals are involved in negotiating legal terms as well as many of the underlying business terms involved in housing transactions. Lawyers also take responsibility for memorialising the terms of agreement, often leveraging their control of what to nonlegal professionals might seem like technical language or even 'boiler plate' to act as the primary conduit for drafting. Negotiating and drafting roles then reinforce each other, placing legal professionals at the centre of the transactional dynamic.

In terms of the underlying function behind negotiation and drafting, much of what lawyers do in transactional work involves the assessment and management of risk. Risk can be primarily legal in origin, such as what encumbrances are there on title, how an ambiguous contract provision is likely to be interpreted by a court in the event of litigation, or how a regulatory body might respond to an unusual deal structure. In housing transactions and transactional practice, more broadly, risk can also relate to a variety of endemic information challenges. One party may have better information about, for example, the environmental history of a parcel of land. The other party may have better access to capital-market data necessary to evaluate future market trends. And both parties may have disparate perspectives on how to assess the same information.

Legal professionals have developed a number of tools to identify, reduce, and ultimately allocate risks associated with the imperfect information that in almost every transaction leads the parties to differential valuation. Disclosures, as well as representations and warranties, for example, contractually obligate parties to reveal information and then define the extent to which the party receiving that information should be able to rely on it. Similarly, due diligence rights – such as rights of access to inspect a property and the right to rescind a contract for a negotiated period of time based on disclosures and investigation – allow for further production and assessment of information about relevant risks and the corresponding reward that such risks entail. And closing conditions, which provide a mechanism to update information and often the right to rescind if requirements are not met, carry these risk-management tools forward to the completion of the transaction. Contracts and background legal rules thus assign risks to various parties and specify the consequences if those risks materialise.

Transactional Specialties

As with many professions, lawyers have developed transactional specialties reflecting particularly complex housing-market niches. Land use or planning law as a legal specialty, for example, serves single-family subdivision developers and lenders. In this specialty, a legal professional's stock in trade includes entitling – working through and at times seeking local government modification of land-use or planning requirements – as well as environmental law, complex title review, and other aspects of large-scale development. Multifamily housing development, whether in the rental apartment or for-sale multifamily context, is a similar niche. Both of these areas of practice often entail the creation of complex private governance regimes, whether through covenants, conditions and restrictions, and homeowners' associations for single-family developments, or through commonhold, condominium, or cooperative forms for multifamily developments.

Another niche for housing lawyers is affordable housing. This area of practice is increasingly important given the perennial failure of housing markets to produce sufficient stock of acceptable quality housing for all income levels. Although some subsidised housing is produced entirely by the state, as with traditional public housing in the United States or the United Kingdom, the prevailing model for this sector in a number of countries involves public–private partnerships. In this model, private entities – either for-profit or nonprofit – draw on public subsidies to construct and operate housing. Subsidies can come in a variety of forms, including tax credits for equity investments, direct grants or tenant vouchers for rental subsidies, below-market-interest-rate loans, and other techniques. Each of these subsidy sources carries its own regulatory requirements and policy objectives, and affordable housing developments often require multiple subsidies. This regulatory layering creates significant legal complexity, which in turn requires attorneys and related legal professionals to translate public law requirements into the fabric of private deal structuring.

Thus far, this description of the role of legal professionals in the transactional practice of housing has largely involved at least a nominal adversarialism, with each party represented by counsel ethically charged to represent their client zealously. This is generally how housing transactions of any significance play out in the common law jurisdictions of the United States and the United Kingdom. In civil law countries, however, this adversarial structure is moderated in some contexts by the requirement that conveyances occur through a civil law notary. These notaries take on slightly different functions from country to country, but in general share distinguishing features unfamiliar in most common law housing-related transactions. Notaries serve as neutral legal advisors, not representing the seller, buyer, lender, or other party. Notaries, rather, are charged with responsibility for managing regulatory requirements related to the conveyance, documenting of transaction, and in some instances advising all parties on transactional risks. Contrary to 'deal lawyers' in more adversarial systems, civil law notaries have an obligation to facilitate agreements in more of an arbitral role.

Legal Professionals in the Regulation of Housing Markets

Housing markets do not operate in a vacuum, as national legal systems create and channel market conditions. Legal professionals play a variety of roles in this public law infrastructure as well, as legislators, regulators, administrators, and enforcement officials. Because housing is a heavily regulated sector in most market economies, legal professionals assist the state – at various levels of government – in implementing the regulatory regimes in which development and housing finance take place. Legal professionals, for example, advise local governments about zoning and other land use regulations, counsel federal agencies on the acceptable terms of secondary mortgage market securities and lending practices, and work to enforce housing rights, including fair housing, fair credit, and related laws where these exist. Legal professionals are also involved in housing as community organisers, lobbyists, and even simply active, well-informed, concerned citizens.

Legal Professionals in the Lifecycle of Home

Because an individual or a family's tenure in a home often raises legal questions, lawyers and other legal professionals can play an important role in managing the nature of that tenancy. In the legal construction of home, not just economic value, but a range of meanings of home – shelter, source of identity, locus of community, and others – require some measure of conflict resolution and counsel, with legal professionals often involved.

Mediating Claims to Home

To begin, the day-to-day experience of most residents, whether homeowners or renters, requires ongoing interaction with a variety of stakeholders that can include landlords, neighbours, lenders, and others who have ongoing relationships with an individual or family's home. Covenants and easements, for example, require ongoing interpretation, leases raise disputes, and local land-use or planning regulations impact whether and how a home can be redeveloped. Many of these interactions are relatively informal, resolved less through legal means than through social norms and common understandings. But these relationships, which provide so much of the context of home, can also require more formal dispute resolution, which in turn implicate legal professionals. Case reports are accordingly populated by litigation related to landlord–tenant disputes, easements, adverse possession, property borders, nuisance, and many other residues of the failure of those with long-term interests in the home to resolve their conflicts informally.

Advising Owners and Renters

In the lifecycle of home, the economic value of the property to the owner or renter likewise raises important legal questions. As noted, many conveyances and even some financing for individuals and families occurs without counsel, but legal professionals nonetheless take part in some aspects of using the home to build equity and provide collateral. Legal professionals counsel on complex sales, subleases, home equity loans, and other transactions through which owners and, to some extent, renters realise the economic value of the asset.

Securing Housing Rights

Perhaps the most critical function that legal professionals play in the lifecycle of home involves questions about security of tenure. Despite popular conceptions of home as a font of stability, involuntary loss of home can create significant disruptions, and disputes about dispossession, which are particularly acute in times of economic crisis, can entail significant emotional and financial repercussions. For renters, involuntary loss of home can result from failure to pay rent or other default, or conversion of rental housing to condominiums or cooperatives, particularly housing that was affordable at below-market rents. For those who own their home, dispossession can come through foreclosure or other involuntary debt-related action, including repossession and sale, deeds in lieu of foreclosure, short sales, and other workout measures. Loss of home can also come through the state's exercise of its power of eminent domain or compulsory purchase, a practice that has raised significant political concerns in the United States, but remains a relatively rare occurrence. Given the contentious nature of many instances of dispossession, legal professionals can be called upon to represent all of the parties involved, including lenders, borrowers, landlords, tenants, and others.

Another critical aspect of the security of tenure involves housing laws that protect against discrimination. In the United States, for example, the federal Fair Housing Act protects against discrimination in housing based on race, colour, national origin, religion, sex, familial status, and disability, while the Equal Credit Opportunity Act protects against discrimination by creditors on the basis of race, colour, religion, national origin, sex, marital status, age, or certain sources of income. In helping to enforce these and similar rights grounded in local law or international agreement in other countries, legal professionals are called upon to defend borrowers, tenants, and other housing consumers when lenders, landlords, and other market participants violate legal requirements for fair housing and fair lending.

Evaluating the Legal Profession in Housing and Home

The ubiquitous presence of legal professionals in the production and management of housing and home raises concerns. Legal scholars, for example, have questioned the efficiency of legal professionals in various transactional settings. A second equally fundamental concern involves unequal access to counsel and the question whether particularly low-income and minority homeowners, tenants, and other potentially vulnerable parties face systematic disadvantage when they are in conflict with other market participants who do have legal representation.

From a transactional perspective, the basic question raised by the role that lawyers play in the housing market is whether their involvement is efficient – worth the fees that legal professionals command – or whether clients continue to involve these professionals so heavily because of unequal power, path dependency, and legalistic cultural norms. One school of thought has identified the lawyer's risk-management function as central to evaluating this question, placing emphasis on the legal professional's ability to advocate for clients facing transactional uncertainty. The limitation to this view is that it risks obscuring the potential for lawyers to add to the costs of transactions in a way that is not cost-justified. Where lawyers too zealously seek to gain advantage for their clients, transactions may be blocked or the overall value of a transaction may be undermined in the race for relative advantage.

Legal scholar Ronald Gilson has offered a distinct conception of the role of the attorney as transaction-cost engineer. In this vision, the lawyer's task is to identify and structure deals to minimise a variety of transaction-cost barriers that include information asymmetries, differential valuations, disparate time scales for transactional objectives, and even strategic bargaining. In acting as a transaction-cost engineer, the deal lawyer has the potential to add to the overall value of a transaction, rather than focusing on dividing static value more favourably for one or another party. Empirically, it is difficult to establish whether the benefits that legal professionals bring to transactions in housing and other markets are, in fact, cost-justified, but a value-creation perspective at least provides a way to approach this question.

An equally important normative issue concerning the role of legal professionals in housing and home arises from the reality of unequal access to counsel. Access to housing is primarily a function of market forces and social policy, but lawyers are imbedded in those determinants. In many important housing contexts, including single-family home sales between sophisticated developers and individual purchasers, home finance and refinance, and many residential landlord–tenant settings, there is not only disparate bargaining power but also disparate access to legal counsel. Similarly, in the realm of affordable housing, whether state-subsidised or not, tenants are often underrepresented, exacerbating the underlying market imbalances and insecurity that housing programmes are targeted at remedying. Indeed, it has been argued, by the American economist Robert Shiller and others that one lesson of the recent global economic downturn, which had its roots in the subprime mortgage market in the United States, is that advocates perhaps modelled on the civil law notary should be introduced to moderate the vulnerability to abuse that some borrowers in that market face.

Unequal access thus implicates legal professionals in power dynamics that disfavour vulnerable populations. The legal system in the United States and in some other jurisdictions has reacted to this dynamic by providing legal protections for owners and renters, particularly for habitability and security of tenure, but this protection is uneven at best and can require access to counsel to realise. This has made housing rights a part of the movement for access to counsel and an ongoing focus of advocacy.

See also: Access and Affordability: Rent Regulation; Cooperative Housing/Ownership; Economics of Housing Choice; Home as Investment; House Building Industries: Western Europe and North America; Housing Careers; Housing Developers: Developed World; Housing Governance; Housing Policy: Agents and Regulators; Institutions and Governance Networks in Housing and Urban Regeneration; Institutions that Represent Housing Professionals; Land Registration Institutions: Developed World; Mortgage Default: Well-Being in the United States; Mortgage Innovation; Private Rental Landlords: North America; Public-Private Housing Partnerships; Real Estate Agents; Residential Segregation: Race and Ethnicity; Rights to Housing Tenure; Securing Land Rights and Housing Delivery; Supported Housing; Transaction Costs in Housing Markets; Urbanisation and Housing the Poor: Overview.

Further Reading

Daye CE, et al. (1999) *Housing and Community Development*, 3rd edn. Durham, NC: Carolina Academic Press.
Ellickson RC (1991) *Order Without Law: How Neighbors Settle Disputes*. Cambridge, MA: Harvard University Press.

Fox L (2007) *Conceptualizing Home: Theories, Laws and Policies*. Oxford, UK: Hart Publishing Ltd.

Gilson RJ (1984) Value creation by business lawyers: Legal skills and asset pricing. *Yale Law Journal* 94: 239.

Iglesias T and Lento RE (eds.) (2006) *The Legal Guide to Affordable Housing Development*. Chicago, IL: American Bar Association.

Malloy RP and Smith JC (2007) *Real Estate Transactions: Problems, Cases, and Materials*, 3rd edn. New York: Aspen Publishers.

Murray PL (2007) *Real Estate Conveyancing in Five European Member States: A Comparative Study*. Brussels, Belgium: Council of the Notariats of the European Union.

Shiller RJ (2008) *The Subprime Solution: How Today's Global Financial Crisis Happened, and What to do About it*. Princeton, NJ: Princeton University Press.

Stein J (2001) *A Practical Guide to Real Estate Practice*. Philadelphia, PA: American Law Institute–American Bar Association.

Older People: Housing Institutions

R Gilroy, Newcastle University, Newcastle upon Tyne, UK

© 2012 Elsevier Ltd. All rights reserved.

The Centrality of Housing to a Good Life

It is undisputed that housing is a critical domain of concern for older people. Time studies reveal that older people spend more of their time in the home than people of other age groups. Quality-of-life research undertaken with older people reinforces the message that a safe and comfortable home is a dominant factor in determining a good life in old age. However, the ability of older people to live in settings that meet their needs in ways that they prefer has often been constrained by the attitudes and actions of institutional players. In the earlier centuries, older people of the working class (who were also inevitably poor) were stereotyped as frail inmates dependent upon the charitable support of almshouses or – in the harsher industrialised Victorian era – of workhouses. In the modern age, older people's needs have been met by specialist housing types, such as grouped bungalows and apartments with support facilities. For those with greater physical and cognitive frailties, there are residential and nursing homes. Choices about suitability are made by experts. The growing numbers of older people and their expanding proportion in the population have created anxiety about the affordability of services. Meanwhile, changes within the older group – increased wealth, the desire to age in place rather than in special settings, and the desire to break the mould – have all pushed institutional actors to find a range of new high-quality options for older people.

The Role of Institutions in Providing Housing and Welfare Services

Across the world, institutional actors are engaged in developing models of housing and care that meet the rising needs and aspirations of older people (**Table 1**). In Singapore, the Housing Development Board is the government agency charged with providing housing for rent for the needy and with building affordable homes for sale. This agency has been developing a range of models. These include large apartments – with studio apartments attached – that facilitate mutual care and support by families. A more recent model consists of blocks of large flats, with studio apartments interspersed throughout the blocks. This model addresses the growing need to provide support, as well as independence, for all family members. Specialist housing blocks have been built in Tokyo, Japan, where two floors dedicated to older people with dementia provide a high level of nursing and support. Above these two floors are housed older people who are cognitively unimpaired, but might be physically frail. Above the flats for the physically impaired residents, there are flats for older people who simply want to live in an older person's community. Many of these active older people might have their parents living on the lower floors of the building.

Planners in Nanporo, in rural Hokkaido, have had to make major changes to master plans, as the anticipated growth of young households has not taken place. More than half of the designated land for housing lay undeveloped more than 25 years after the master plan was developed. A new master plan in 2001 shifted the focus on to the real growth areas of the population – older people – and placed them at the heart of the town. Under the so-called silver project, the town has developed day-care services, home-care service stations, and care homes, all located in the central area. Older people are thus literally at the hub of town services and shops, and they – metaphorically and economically – constitute the heart of the town.

Today's globalised world is increasingly characterised by financialisation and the neoliberal withdrawal of formerly state-provided services. An increasingly complex range of institutional actors engage in interactions that can either create opportunities for, or place restrictions on, older people seeking high-quality living in arenas of their choice. The institutional landscape is also increasingly fragmented, with some services being provided by the public sector, and others by the private or not-for-profit sectors. Funding for the latter might be by the public sector. From an older person's perspective, it is becoming more difficult to find a way through this increasing complexity, as **Table 2** illustrates.

Table 1 Institutional actors

Category	Agency	Role	Products and services
Public sector	Planning – national level	Determines national policy framework for development	Planning guidance from national level
	Planning – municipal level	Designates land at municipal level for development, including for housing	Local development framework at municipal level
	Housing	Provides housing for rent; provides telecare; provides repair services for older people – not tenure-specific	Family houses; apartments; sheltered housing or congregate living; extra-care grouped living; telecare services for all regardless of tenure; and 'handyperson' schemes
	Social services	Support those in need; commission and coordinate care packages from private and not-for-profit providers; and provide grants aid for adaptations	Social workers; care-home places and provision of financial assistance to those whose resources are too low to afford these; management of personalised budgets; and facilitation of moves to residential and nursing care
Private sector	Housing developers	Build housing for sale	Family homes and apartments; sheltered or congregate living; and retirement communities
	Individuals and companies	Develop and manage residential and nursing-care (assisted-living) units, including for those with dementia	Residential-care homes and nursing homes
Financial sector	Banks, building societies, and loan companies	Finance development and purchase by individuals	Loans for development; mortgages for purchase; and equity-release products for older owners
Not-for-profit sector	Housing companies	Develop and manage housing for rent and develop low-cost homeownership dwellings	Family homes; apartments; sheltered housing; assisted living; and extra-care or grouped living
	Home-improvement agencies	Coordinate major improvements or adaptations; provide repair services	Provision of bridging help for older householders by builders and funders and launching of 'handyperson' schemes
	Advice and campaigning groups	Provide conduit for older people's voice; and provide advisory services	Local and national groups; information shops; and web-based guidance
	Care providers	Provide services at home or at the neighbourhood level; run care homes and homes for dementia sufferers	Meals services, day centres, befriending services, care homes, and outreach services

Table 2 Range of services and providers in meeting the common needs of older people in the United Kingdom

Problem	Solution	Provider
Prone to falls	Telecare – call-alarm service and falls detector	Public-sector housing
Cannot get in the bath	Install walk-in shower	Local builder (private sector) supervised by a home-improvement agency (not-for-profit sector); work funded by Disabled Facilities Grant (public sector)
Cold house	Loft and cavity wall insulation, draught proofing of windows	Warm Front Grant: a partnership agency of the public sector (central and local governments) and the private sector (utility companies)
Concern about managing money	Council Tax Benefit; income maximisation	Advice from Age Concern (not-for-profit sector)
Broken stair-rail	Repair	'Handyperson' scheme (not-for-profit or public sector) with small charge to user, funded by Help the Aged (not-for-profit sector) or by the public–private sector regeneration partnership
Feeling isolated	Befriending service	Local voluntary organisation that is free to user, funded by Social Services Grant Aid (public sector) and National Lottery Charities Board (national charitable funder)

Drivers for Change: The New Older People

A significant driver has been the ageing of the postwar baby-boomer group. This cohort presents a number of significant challenges to the prevailing images of the life of older people. The idea of old age being a time of inactivity – as older adults cross the chronological demarcation line between working life and retirement – is blurring, as both individuals and societies question the waste of mature adults' experience and expertise. Old age and poverty used to be largely synonymous. In sharp contrast, however, the baby boomers enjoy significantly increased levels of material comfort over previous generations. How this influential group chooses to conceptualise old age and use its spending power is a challenge for all institutional actors.

In Japan, which has been described as the world's first hyperaged society, the baby-boomer generation or '*dankai*' constitutes 5% of the population. This group holds an estimated 110–113 trillion in savings and assets – approximately, 9% of Japan's wealth. All institutional actors have had to consider how they can put older people at the heart of their thinking. In Hokkaido, the northernmost of Japan's four main islands, depopulation has contributed to its strong ageing profile. Nearly a quarter of those who live in the rural areas are now 65 years or older. Instead of looking to balance the age profile, the regional prefecture has taken the bold step of seeing older people as an economic strength that can be exploited. Targeting the '*dankai*', particularly those living in the Tokyo metropolitan area, Hokkaido launched programmes to promote 'permanent residency'. Web-based questionnaires revealed that a majority of the Tokyo baby boomers were interested in living in Hokkaido either on a temporary or on a permanent basis. The regional prefecture estimated that if 3000 retired couples moved to Hokkaido and spent the rest of their lives there they would cost 120 billion in extra social-security provision but would bring up to 570 billion (£2.85 billion) of spending power to the region. Clearly by increasing the immigration of a wealthy cohort, opportunities to invest in housing, transport, shopping, and tourism can be created. Beyond these, health care and community activities can expand and improve the quality of life not only for older people but also for people of other age groups.

The other catalyst is the accelerated growth in numbers of the oldest among the older persons – the cohort that has members 85 years or older. This group is more likely to present with issues of frailty, both physical and cognitive. Forecasts for those suffering from dementia suggest that, by 2050, numbers in the United Kingdom will have grown by more than 150%. Similar figures are forecast worldwide. Contrary to popular view, most people with dementia are not in care establishments, but live in their own homes.

In the United Kingdom – New Choice Agendas

The election in the United Kingdom of the neoliberal Thatcher government in 1979 introduced choice in respect of public services, which included increasing opportunities for citizen participation. However the focus was on encouraging citizens to exit from services provided by the public sector, particularly local government. Among notable housing examples was the introduction of the public-sector tenants' 'Right to Buy' their homes.

New Labour, elected in 1997, has conceptualised a modern welfare state: providers and local people work together in partnership, with rights and duties on both sides. There is a commitment to make local government more relevant to the electorate and to improve public services. This is partly to be achieved by financial investment and partly through making shifts in the processes by which people access services. In consequence, instead of having choices made by experts, citizens may become decision makers in respect of their individual needs.

Part of the New Labour manifesto was a commitment to listening to older people. In 1998 the setting up of the 28 pilot projects of 'Better Government for Older People' created broad partnerships between the central government, the local government, and the not-for-profit sector with the aim of involving older people in interagency strategies that impacted on their quality-of-life indexes. Since then, the government agencies, which deal with pension and social-security entitlement, and the National Health Service, which delivers health care, have developed new ways of delivering services. This change is partly a result of working with older people's reference groups. The publication in 2000 of the green paper 'Quality and Choice: A Decent Home for All', and, subsequently in 2001, of 'Quality and Choice for Older People's Housing: A Strategic Framework' argued that the spectrum of actors must be broadened so that those seeking rental housing, as well as those seeking owner-occupied solutions, should be the framers of housing choices. Significantly the strategy, which focused on older people, was a product owned by the Ministries of both Housing and Health. This strategy emphasises the interdependency of housing and health and this is increasingly reflected in the greater integration of services, greater number of partnerships, and enhanced cross-disciplinary funding.

Table 3 Fresh approaches to housing, health, and welfare services

Provider-led or expert decisions	Service	Person-centred or choice
Social services (public sector) paid and delivered	Welfare and personal care	Individual budgets – choice of what, where, how, and from whom service is sourced
Experts fit people to property	Social housing	Choice-based leases – people choose what suits them (within limitations)
Patients wait to be fitted into the diary of the professional	Appointment with hospital consultant	Patients may choose dates and consultants that suit them

Access

The choice agenda is seen in three areas. These areas might not be targeted solely at older people; however, they can be seen as being potentially beneficial to them (**Table 3**).

In the arena of public-sector housing, among the many factors that impeded choice were allocation policies that focused on the bureaucratic matching of people and property. Social landlords are now encouraged to adopt a choice-based method, through which vacancies are advertised in the manner of estate agents (realtors), and prospective tenants 'bid' for the property using their points as currency. The bid with the highest points 'wins' the property. The policy is not targeted at older people, although retired people make up the largest group of social renters. Nevertheless, it is clear that choice-based letting might open up a broader range of options that were not known, in addition to the more generic feeling of being in greater control. However, do older people benefit in practice? Evidence from pilot evaluations demonstrated that vulnerable groups including older people were participating in the process but not bidding so much. This might indicate supply-side issues such as low availability of accessible and well-located properties. Equally likely, it may be that many older people lack the energy for a very demanding process. Evidence shows that support mechanisms for those who need help and advice to make a choice and to make a bid in person are not always available.

The interrelationship of home, health, and welfare means that, without appropriate care, many older people may have to consider a move to a different physical environment. The demands to decrease local government expenditure in England have led many local authorities to make cuts in social services expenditure. Eligibility criteria have been tightened, so that the majority of older people who need low-level support are ignored in favour of the minority with acute needs. More hours of home care are now being delivered but to far fewer people. Services that home care (once termed 'home help') previously delivered, such as shopping and housework, have been dropped and replaced with personal care, such as dressing and bathing. Those with less intense needs may have to look for support from the not-for-profit sector, where funding cuts make continuities of services less certain.

The choice agenda has impacted on the mode of community-welfare services. The introduction of individual budgets paid directly to individuals allows older people to have more control over the kinds of services they receive. Older people who are eligible for day care, personal care, respite care, or for equipment and adaptations to aid mobility in the home can elect to receive the money. They can then buy the service or equipment themselves, rather than accept the local-authority service. Potentially this is life enhancing. For example, instead of accepting a day-centre place, a man may pay to be accompanied to a football match that gives him much greater pleasure and is a 'normal' activity. However, the policy assumes that there is both quantity and quality of alternative services available in all localities and that this menu of choices is known to older people. A perverse outcome of this new person-centred approach is that lack of support for a traditional service may lead to its withdrawal. A warden in a sheltered housing scheme, for example, who provides both community development and a safety net, may be withdrawn if the demand for the service causes it to be uneconomical.

In evaluating the choice agenda and its impact on service access, while applauding the potential benefits, the issues for older people are more problematic. Some processes require energy that may be lacking. Paucity of information and a lack of independent advisers is a major stumbling block, which clearly has an impact on who does the choosing.

Sustainability

The 'ageing-in-place' agenda, which springs from the strong desire of a great majority of older people to remain in their own homes and neighbourhoods, demands intersectoral cooperation. Older people need a microenvironment in the home that will facilitate independence. This should be situated in a broader environment that provides good-quality services and community support.

They also need a sufficient income to allow them to maintain home and lifestyle choices. The problem of making choices and the lack of information are also a feature in the lives of those who want to remain at home with what is often referred to as 'a little bit of help'.

Those who need major adaptations to their homes to make them fit suitably with their mobility needs are dependent on external assessments not only of their physical health but also of their financial competence. The public sector (municipal authorities) may fund adaptations through the Disabled Facilities grants. Through this fund many older people who find difficulty in using stairs or getting into a bath have had adaptations such as ramps, stair-lifts, or a shower installed in their homes. Two institutional barriers may frustrate the needs of older people to make timely changes. The first is the length of time taken to assess individuals, owing to a shortage of occupational therapists in local authorities. The second is that the grant depends on the means of the beneficiaries; it is also under pressure from increasing numbers of older householders.

Those seeking to bridge the shortfall between the costs of these works and the grant, or those judged ineligible for the grant, need to find finance. Financial institutions have responded by creating new products variously known as equity releases, lifetime mortgages, or reverse mortgages. For older people in some developed countries such as the United States, the United Kingdom, and Australia, housing may be their most – or only significant – wealth asset while their income levels are low. The situation is most marked in Australia, where a sizeable majority of older people, both couples and single people, are dependent on the social-security payments, but more than three-quarters own their homes outright. A different example is presented by the United Kingdom, where a smaller proportion of homeowners are income poor but where house values have been characterised by sustained upward movements. The United Kingdom (and Spain) topped the Organisation for Economic Cooperation and Development (OECD) league table for average annual increases in real house prices between 1971 and 2002, giving the average homeowner more than £50 000 equity in their homes. Though housing markets are marked by volatility, estimates suggest that those who are 65 years or older in the United Kingdom, who are also generally outright owners, may have at least £460 billion unmortgaged equity in their dwellings. Research demonstrates that older people are very wary of these and have little product confidence. At present, the percentage of wealth released by older homeowners is small, although the trend is upward. Financial institutions are likely to increase the range of products but it may take government action and the provision of independent financial advice to raise public confidence. Given the new wealthy face of old age, it is increasingly likely that future cohorts of older people will be expected to fund all housing modifications themselves or will be assisted with loans but not grants.

Equity release works best for those with substantial property. In the United Kingdom homeownership has been driven down into the lower-income groups, who have also benefited from increasing house values. However, as in all market mechanisms, there is unequal access to financial rewards. Those at the high end of the housing-wealth spectrum, who are also likely to be in receipt of high incomes from multiple sources, are thus more likely to benefit than those at the lower end of housing wealth, who may not meet the thresholds set by financial institutions.

Planning and Design

As the proportion of older people increases, the needs of older people will become increasingly diversified: these could include retirement villages, extra-care schemes, sheltered housing, serviced-apartment blocks, co-housing developments that might embrace multidwelling parkland development, or commercial-building conversions. Those with large houses may wish to convert their dwelling into smaller units; families may seek granny-flat extensions. Minority ethnic communities might concern themselves with the provision of 'housing-plus-care schemes' in particular localities where elders may retain community support. Whatever the choice, these dwellings ideally need to be colocated with amenities and services and linked into transport routes. To enable these to happen, planners need to take full account of the numbers and circumstances of older people and to be able to respond to innovative solutions (**Figure 1**).

In practice, public-sector planners find that the needs and aspirations of older people clash with other planning priorities. Older people may aspire to move to an area of high environmental quality, believing perhaps that a better life in later life can be achieved in a less stressed location. The increasing demand for more rural housing in the United Kingdom is continually resisted by planning policies that severely restrict or prevent house building in villages. Instead housing development is designated primarily in market towns, which are seen as more sustainable in terms of amenities and services. This restriction on supply has contributed to house-price increases, which far outstrip those of urban areas.

Those seeking to live in age-targeted developments have new choices, one of which is the retirement village. These are more widely known in the United States, where purpose-built communities such as Sun City, Arizona, built in the 1980s, attract better-off retirees seeking a good climate and leisure facilities among their peers.

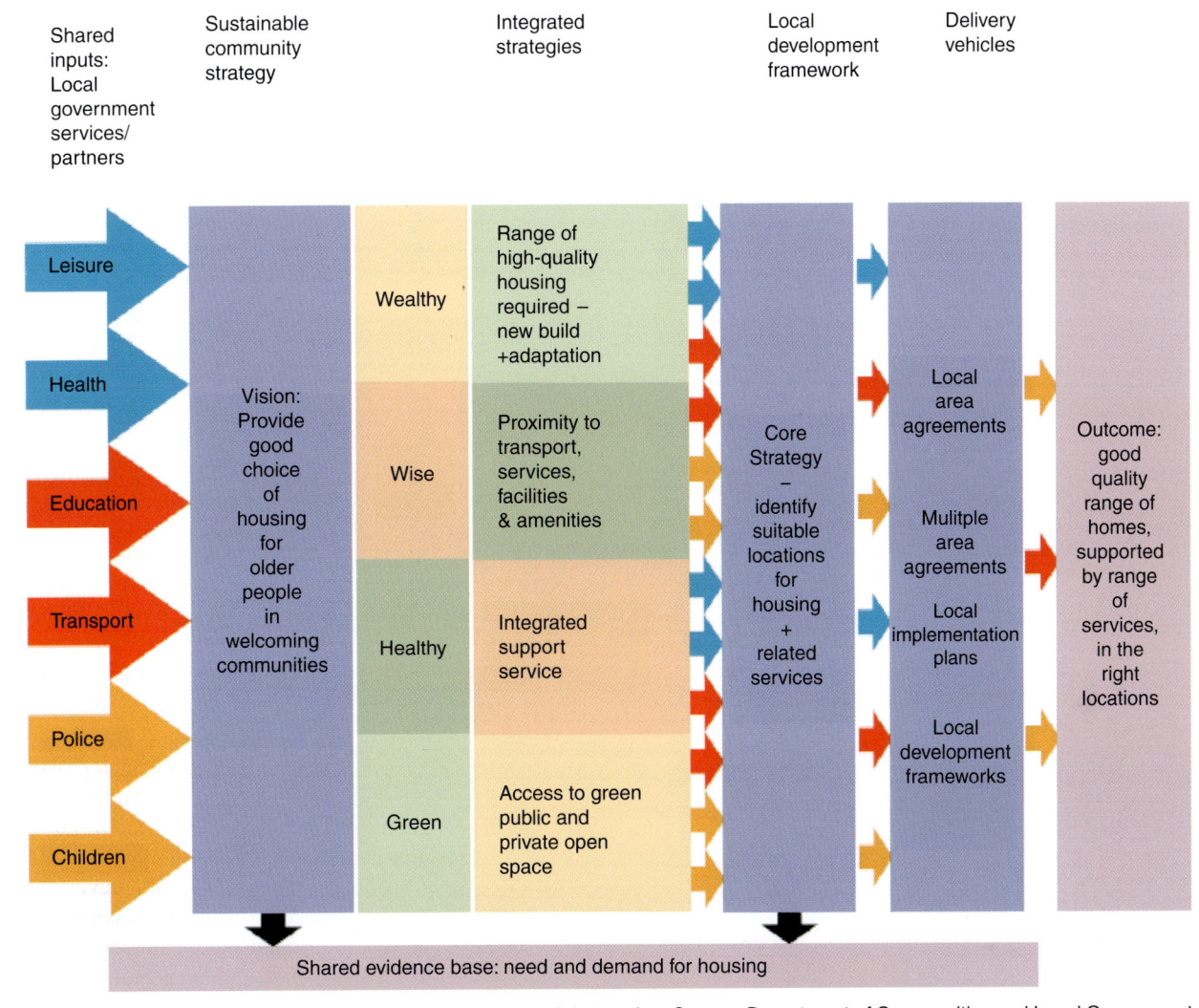

Figure 1 Joined-up approaches to planning for older people's housing. Source: Department of Communities and Local Government (DCLG) (2008) *Lifetime Homes, Lifetime Neighbourhoods: A National Strategy for Housing in an Ageing Society*, p. 112. London: DCLG.

The best-known and most-written-about development in the United Kingdom is Hartrigg Oaks in York, built and managed by the Joseph Rowntree Foundation.

Evidence from the planning applications made for retirement communities reveals planners' difficulties. First, the planners are not clear whether these are housing developments or health and welfare establishments that are judged by different planning criteria. The need for economies of scale and for a critical mass of dwellings to generate any sense of community means that developments may contain 100 units of accommodation or more. Hartrigg Oaks has 152 bungalows and a 42-room care home spread over a 21-acre site. The scale of such developments and the preference from developers and potential residents for greener locations can cause problems for planners. The latter are tasked with bringing forward brown field sites (that is, previously developed land, as opposed to green field sites) and to pay attention to issues of sustainability, particularly in terms of reducing reliance on private transport.

See also: Homeless People: Older People; Housing Equity Withdrawal in the United Kingdom; Housing Wealth Over the Life Course; Meanings of Home for Older People; Older People: Well-Being; Older People: Well-Being, Housing and Neighbourhoods; Place Attachment.

Further Reading

Clough R, Leamy M, Miller V, and Bright L (2004) *Housing Decisions in Later Life*. Basingstoke, UK: Palgrave.

Department of Communities and Local Government (2008) *Lifetime Homes, Lifetime Neighbourhoods: A National Strategy for Housing in an Ageing Society*. London: DCLG.

Department of Health and Department of Environment, Transport and the Regions (2001) *Quality and Choice for Older People's Housing: A Strategic Framework*. London: DETR.

Gilroy R (2003) Why can't more people have a say: Learning to work with older people. *Ageing and Society* 23(5): 659–674.

Gilroy R (2005) Meeting the information needs of older people: A challenge for local governance. *Local Government Studies* 31(1): 39–51.

Greater London Authority (2006) *Valuing Older People: The Mayor of London's Older People's Strategy*. London: GLA.

Huber J and Skidmore P (2003) *The New Old: Why Baby Boomers Won't Be Pensioned Off*. London: Demos.

Raynes N, Clark H, and Beecham J (eds.) (2006). *The Report of the Older People's Inquiry into 'That Bit of Help'*. York, UK: Joseph Rowntree Foundation.

Tetlow R (2006) *Continuing Care Retirement Communities*. York, UK: Joseph Rowntree Foundation in association with the Planning Officers Society.

Older People: Well-Being

D Olsberg, University of New South Wales, Sydney, NSW, Australia

© 2012 Elsevier Ltd. All rights reserved.

Glossary

Accessible A product, housing, or environment that is Accessible and meets prescribed government standards and regulations or agency requirements, for being physically accessible to people with disabilities.

Adaptable It refers to housing that has been designed so that it is Visitable, and can be modified easily and at minimal cost in the future, if a resident or visitor requires it in the future due to their disability or frailty.

Ageing in place It is used interchangeably with 'staying put' – a term that describes people remaining living in their own home in the community as they age, rather than having to move to institutionalised residential aged care.

Flexible housing Housing designed so that it can be easily reconfigured to accommodate a household's changing size, structure, and lifestyle.

Home modifications Custom structural changes made to a home so that the resident can continue to safely live and move around it, and are the traditional approach for making the home environment more accessible and safe for older people when required.

Older person Defined here as a person aged 55 years and over.

Universal The widely accepted definition of Universal Design is attributed to the Centre of Universal Design (1997): "The design of products and environments to be usable by all people, to the greatest extent possible, without the need for adaptation or specialised design."

Visitable A housing that is Visitable has three essential features which will allow a person in a wheelchair to visit. These are a path of travel that is without steps to enter the dwelling, an entrance doorway and internal doorways that are wide enough for a wheelchair to fit through, and a wheelchair-accessible toilet on the entrance level of the dwelling. In addition to these, other design features (not part of the definition) that increase the visitability of housing have been incorporated into various regulations, including having power outlets, thermostats, and light switches at a height that can be reached by a wheelchair user, having reinforcement in the bathroom walls so that grab bars can be installed, and having lever handles on doors.

Wayfinding The cognitive process whereby people find their way about the urban environment.

Demographic Changes and Ageing Populations

As Abraham Maslow argued, housing is a basic human need, and research demonstrates that having suitable and satisfactory housing becomes even more important for the welfare and well-being of people as they grow older. As almost all developed countries and most developing countries confront entirely unprecedented demographic changes as a consequence of the ageing of their populations, the availability of adequate, suitable, and satisfactory housing for older people is critical. The Organisation for Economic Co-operation and Development (OECD) reported in 2009 that in all OECD countries populations aged over 65 years have dramatically increased – both in absolute numbers and as a percentage of total populations. Canada, Australia, Ireland, Spain, and Italy are countries with the highest concentrations of elderly people, and already many countries spend more than 10% of their GDP on public pension expenditure. Health and welfare budgets are also expected to increase steeply as the large Baby Boomer populations, born in many countries between 1946 and 1964, reach retirement and constitute older age cohorts over the next 30 years.

Although older people are generally healthy and there has been an enhancement in the health and functioning of older populations, the absolute numbers of older people who are and will be at risk of disability and health decline are increasing. This is because of the pronounced increase in the number of individuals beyond the age of 85 years which represents the strongest growth dynamic in many societies. Three-fold increases in populations aged over 80 years will produce attendant increases in incidences of morbidity, disability, and dementia. The increasing numbers of older people over 80 who will be living alone, particularly single women, raise a new range of issues and, particularly, serious challenges. This persistent and increasing longevity of ageing populations and their enhanced expectations for welfare and well-being in later life demand increasing attention to the issue of housing by policy decision-makers in the government and by the private sector, as well as being fundamental to the future welfare and well-being of individual older men and women and their families.

Importance of Housing for Welfare and Well-Being of Older Persons

There is a wealth of research literature in the gerontological, gerosociological, geropsychological, architectural, planning, and design fields which attest to both the objective and subjective aspects of the vital importance of housing in old age in relation to health, welfare, and well-being-related outcomes. Objective functional housing aspects which are relevant include microenvironmental indicators, such as housing fittings, hazards and amenities, lighting, heating, insulation, and ventilation, and meso- and macroenvironmental indicators, such as housing and building type, neighbourhood conditions or urban/rural differences, and access to transport and general support services such as medical services, shopping, and recreational services. Subjective and behavioural aspects of housing for older people must also be considered. These include housing tenure, residential satisfaction, attitudes and aspirations for future housing, recognition of possible future morbidity, housing-related control beliefs particularly with regard to feelings of independence and autonomy, access to social interaction with family, friends, or relatives, and perceived levels of health and well-being as those feelings relate to people's domains. Such subjective and behavioural aspects are less often considered, yet they are central to the choices which older people make with regard to their housing. Such aspects have been shown to be highly relevant to health and well-being outcomes in terms of emotional and behavioural adjustment, social and personal identity, safety, privacy, feelings of belongingness, autonomy and well-being, personal independence, and control.

The fiscal sustainability of government provision for the welfare needs of ageing populations must, and will, continue to rest upon the range of choices which older people can and do make in their preparations for housing in later life. The desire to remain living independently in the community, 'staying put', or as it is generally referred to as 'ageing in place', is widely recognised in the research literature in many countries as the preferred choice of older people. Ageing in place is accepted as being in the interests of older people's independence, health, and well-being, and also reducing the economic burden on the governments of countries with ageing populations who are faced with the possible need for provision of institutionalised residential care for the aged. As a consequence, there has been a growing body of supporting policy research and programme development focused upon ageing in place over the last 25 years. If at all possible and practical, the priority has been to support the possibilities for older people to remain living independently in their own residences in the community for as long as possible, with assistance and community support as that becomes a necessity. Already in many countries, government policies related to housing and accommodation increasingly incorporate ageing-in-place programmes and enhanced community support for older people as a means of fiscal prudence. Such programmes are, at the same time, welcomed by home-owning older people who wish to remain living independently in the community. The policy concept 'ageing in place' is also likely to be made a priority by other governments and their service delivery departments seeking to control burgeoning welfare budgets for older populations. The success of ageing in place programmes depends upon the existence and continuity of high levels of homeownership of older people in most countries.

Homeownership among Older People

Ownership and attachment to the family home has had a particular place in most societies. Not only has the family home been the most significant family asset for the majority of older people, but homeownership has also been seen generally as central to personal identity and family values, and the capacity of older people to remain living independently in the community is particularly valued by them.

There are generally high levels of homeownership by older populations in most advanced developed countries, and homeownership has been a much-prized objective for large sectors of the populations in the past 50 years. Extended periods of economic growth and the housing boom following the Second World War, coupled with government housing policies which have historically focused upon facilitating homeownership, have led to the current high levels of homeownership among older people. In countries such as the United Kingdom, the United States, Canada, and Australia, more than 70% of older people are homeowners. Although homeownership is lower in European countries, homeownership among older people in general is over 50%, and the OECD reports a weighted average at 63% for homeownership in OECD countries among those aged over 65. Research also shows that most homes owned by older people are free of mortgage debt.

This may not always be the case. Baby Boomers, who constitute the major source of demographic changes in most countries, will have lower levels of debt-free housing in old age. Recent research in Australia reveals that one in four Baby Boomers aged over 50 years still has a home mortgage. Successive housing booms in advanced developed societies and increasing housing costs threaten housing affordability for many younger people who will be at risk of housing stress and threats to welfare and well-being as they age unless government policies address the housing affordability crises.

But the present predominance of homeownership among older people in most advanced developed countries suggests that ageing-in-place and community support policies will continue to dominate the housing and welfare policy agenda. The preference to remain living independently in the community by older people who are homeowners also supports the acceptance of ageing-in-place policies which incorporate community support programmes by a majority of older people.

Appropriate housing design, adequate community assistance and support programmes, and market responses are thus critical to support healthy, active, and productive ageing among those who remain living in their own home – whether it be to remain in their family home, to downsize to alternative abodes, or to move into cooperative housing communities, over-50s-assisted-living developments, or retirement villages – all domains where people retain personal private equity, independence, and personal control living in the community.

Housing Equity of the Elderly

Ageing-in-place policies and people's personal preferences do not, however, address the needs of older people who do not own their own home, who live either in private rental residences, or who live in rental residences publicly financed by governments or community and/or not-for-profit welfare organisations. The development of adequate housing for renters who are low-income earners or who are entirely dependent upon welfare support continues as a major challenge for ageing societies, affecting fiscal budgets, community organisations, and public and private renters. Older people in private rental sectors or in public or community housing often find themselves in desperate circumstances with untenable housing costs and minimal disposable income. Recent cuts in funding for public housing in many countries, which have occurred in the context of increasing housing affordability crises, have resulted in enormous hardship for those sections of the population who have never managed to access or who have lost access to homeownership and social housing.

The inconsistencies in levels of homeownership across older populations raise the issue of housing equity, as policies related to housing and accommodation have major consequences for older people's economic and health resources, social participation, personal functioning, and well-being. The stability or change of housing in old age reflects the individual's lifespan development, social and economic change, and relations between generations and successive cohorts as people age. Housing tenure also reflects legacies of employment and housing markets as well as current and past government policies regarding welfare housing and retirement income as these impact upon the individual's personal and household circumstances.

These disparities in access to homeownership are overlooked in the increasing dominance of ageing-in-place policies. Such policies are premised upon provision of community care for older people, programmes which can only be effective when people have a secure home base. Problems arise and ageing-in-place policies cannot be effective when increasing numbers of vulnerable people are stressed by high rents, face long waiting lists for public or community housing, or do not qualify for admission to residential care. The prospects for older people in private rental residences become even more of a threat as they grow older. Research demonstrates such issues currently gain scant recognition and can be expected to produce future policy and human crises.

Housing Preferences and Future Choices

A very salient factor in the success of welfare housing policies and the well-being of older people must be a recognition that there is a significant shift in the values and priorities of older men and women that is transforming the attitudes and expectations of people aged over 50 years about future housing tenure, lifestyle, and family relationships. Aspirations by older men and women for independence, flexibility, consumer, and lifestyle choices take precedence, challenging traditional notions of old age and family obligations. The main contributing factors, according to research findings, are increased longevity, changing family structures and family relationships, new forms of identity formation, and social expectations largely connected to the dominance of individualism and consumerist values. Greater social mobility and increasingly diverse life experiences and social backgrounds are also considered to be relevant.

There is a preference for housing in the general market, more than segregated and age-specific housing developments, and there is also a preference for housing that reinforces independence and autonomy. While there is a clear preference for older people to remain living independently in the community, this attachment is likely to be to location, not necessarily to the family home. Older people are now more accepting of change, with the Baby Boomers particularly comfortable with moving house. Problems of household and garden maintenance, divorce, death of a spouse, downsizing, and lifestyle preferences precipitate decisions to move. Confronted with options about their future prospects for housing as they age and experience morbidity or dependence, research demonstrates that some older people do accept the option of moving to a more suitable dwelling, either by downsizing or by moving to an assisted-living retirement village. However, by far, the most favoured option for older people is to stay in their own home with the support of community and professional care services.

There is considerable resistance to the possibility of moving into institutionalised residential care. Research in Australia, based on older people's experiences of family and friends, reveals that residential care facilities are often referred to as 'God's Waiting Room'. Other alternatives such as house sharing or living with family are not attractive options for most older homeowners. Research reveals that most of the older people are negative about having children live with them, living with their adult children, or renting out part of their house. The reasons given for not wanting to live with their children are mostly the desire for independence and autonomy (both for themselves and for their children), the potential for conflict because of different values and lifestyles, not wanting to be a burden to their children, and not wanting to be used for babysitting. Those who would have children live with them would do so mostly to help them out in an emergency, rather than to use their dwelling more efficiently.

Suitability of Current Housing Stock for Older People

There are questions concerning the capacity of the existing housing stock and urban environments to support older people in rapidly ageing societies, as existing housing stock in most advanced industrial societies presents significant problems for ageing inhabitants. Large proportions of homes built in the major building boom following the Second World War often lack modern conveniences, are poorly insulated, are unsuitable for anyone with mobility problems, and are often in need of significant repair and refurbishment. Most older homeowners live as couples or single persons in separate houses of three or more bedrooms. The number of single-person households continues to increase, and as would be expected, single-person households increase markedly with age. The numbers of single-person households in most advanced developed societies are expected to continue to increase as Baby Boomers age.

Seemingly, underoccupancy by older homeowners has increased substantially in most societies in the past 10 years, during which time the floor area of new dwellings has also increased significantly. However, research reveals that older people value the space in their home to accommodate regular visits from temporary residents. Also, older people spend more time in the home and are involved in more home-based activities, and as people age they are increasingly homebound. Those requiring assistance with core activities due to illness or disability can also place demands on space and fixtures and fittings in the home to assist with mobility and manoeuvrability or to allow for carer assistance. All these factors have a profound impact on space utilisation in the home among older people. This challenges often widespread notions of what may seem to be under-occupancy by older people, demonstrating that just because bedrooms are not used for sleeping, it does not mean that they are not used for other purposes that are important to people's lives and supportive of healthy and active ageing and well-being.

The most pressing questions are how to provide for possibilities that older people may continue to live independently in the community in existing or adapted housing stock, or how to provide housing for older people to move to and remain living independently. In general, older people do not plan ahead for changes to their home which may be required in order to cope with future morbidity or frailty. Research in Australia reveals that few older people have made modifications to their home, and there is a lack of understanding and underlying concerns about the requirements and costs of future modifications. More flexible housing design has a contribution to make, particularly around facilitating mutual support arrangements between household members and neighbours and catering to changing household needs as residents age in place.

Research in Australia has established that not only is the design of the dwelling important to the independence and well-being of older people, but neighbourhood design also has an important impact on their safety, independence, and social participation. Important aspects of neighbourhood design are found to include well-maintained and safe paths of travel and pedestrian crossings, age-friendly transport infrastructure design, accessibility to public and commercial premises, easy wayfinding, and crime prevention through environmental design.

Ways Forward for Housing for Older People

There are a number of important issues which are relevant for policy-makers, the housing industry, and consumers in all countries with ageing populations. The key implications for ageing, welfare, and housing policy are in the following four main areas.

Measuring Housing Utilisation and Efficiency among Older People

There is a need to review currently accepted measures of housing utilisation in order to gain a more accurate picture of how efficiently older people use space in their dwellings. This research must cover both older homeowners and older people living in public housing or community housing or renting privately. This would also require more systematic collection of data about temporary residents, floor area of dwellings, and the number and type of rooms in the dwelling. These data could be collected either as part of regular national census or via more regular inter-census sample surveys of older people's housing. Research reveals that there is a lack of knowledge among homeowners of the area measurement of their dwelling and the common unit of measurement varies with the location and age of the resident. Also, the different functions of designated 'bedrooms' such as bedroom, study, library, rumpus room, and so on, make the interpretation of the number of bedrooms in a dwelling ambiguous. These factors will need to be considered in future housing utilisation data collection in order to effectively gauge and plan for housing needs for older people in all ageing societies.

Improving Efficiency and Liveability for Older Homeowners

The strong preference for older people to remain in their own home for as long as possible with appropriate support suggests that the focus of policies for the future housing of ageing populations should be on appropriate housing in the community rather than increasing the provision of segregated and specialised age-specific housing developments, including retirement villages. Of course, there is also a pressing need for greater attention to the needs and desires of older people who do have to enter residential aged-care facilities, and governments in most developed countries are currently under pressure to review and improve these provisions as longevity continues to increase.

Although 'downsizing' may have appeal for some older people and those who see a benefit in releasing overly large land and dwellings to younger, larger households, the demand is not for very small dwellings or one-bedroom units, as might be suggested by the predominance of single and couple households. Future space-efficient dwelling types could include smaller three-bedroom dwellings; flexible dwellings with spaces that can convert to temporary bedrooms for guests at the times they are required; and multi-purpose rooms that can accommodate different uses, including hobbies, child care (grandchildren), fitness equipment, or private personal space, depending on the changing interests and life stages of the residents.

House sharing with family or boarders is not an attractive option to most older people, although some would be prepared to help their children out in an emergency by providing temporary accommodation. However, in research, many older people respond positively to living with children if self-contained accommodation is available. This supports further development of accessory dwellings, which would have the added benefit of providing a supply of affordable accommodation for lower-income older people, and facilitates multi-generational living arrangements important to some culturally and linguistically diverse populations.

Improving Housing Design to Support Ageing in Place

Supporting older people to age in place requires new attention to possibilities of making housing design more suitable and appropriate for whole of life occupation for people as they age or people with disabilities. Many governments have already introduced regulations requiring new homes to be constructed according to Visitable or sometimes Accessible Building Codes or Standards, which can and will make housing suitable for the needs and requirements of all of society, and particularly for ageing populations and the disabled. Many advocates argue the suitability of various design initiatives. These are generally seen to include the following:

- Visitable Design: Providing access features in all housing so that wheelchair users can visit the homes of their friends and family, and will have the most critical access features in their own home.
- Adaptable Design: Aimed at minimising the complexity and cost of future adaptations.
- Universal Design: Whereby the dwelling is designed in the first instance to provide for a wide range of abilities without any need for further modification.
- Home Modifications: Changes to conventional housing to provide modifications to suit the changing needs of residents.

Some design programmes require provision for assistive technologies or telehealth facilities, whereby vital health data can be collected, transmitted, and received by telehealth professionals, data assessed, and clients treated according to their needs. For those older people who choose, or are forced, to move, there is potentially a strong market demand for housing that already includes access features (whether basic Visitable features, or more comprehensive access features that have been provided through Adaptable or Universal Design). There is a preference for this housing being provided in the general community rather than a segregated age-specific development. Support most often comes from people who have had experience of a disability in the family or do presently see its value in an ageing society, or even to assist people with temporary injuries. Opposition is more ideological, based on concern about infringements to personal freedom and the unfairness of imposing additional costs on people who did not need those features.

Improving Neighbourhood Design for Ageing Societies

Design of the neighbourhood and provision of neighbourhood facilities can enhance or inhibit older people's social connectedness and community participation. The activities in which older people participate outside the home and the importance they place on having these within close proximity suggest that older people wish to live in areas that are well serviced by a range of commercial, retail, cultural, and community service facilities. This aligns with current urban design principles and guidelines that advocate higher density, transit-oriented, mixed-use neighbourhood, and town centres.

Research reveals that in most advanced industrial countries, older people are highly car-dependent and low users of public transport. This is partly due to the autonomy and freedom that the motor vehicle offers, but also to the often poor provision, convenience, and service of public transport in many metropolitan and regional areas.

While the quality of neighbourhood design and facilities varies considerably, research in many countries demonstrates that inadequate provision or poor quality of paths of travel, transport nodes, public open space, and access to public buildings, street furniture, local cafes, and public toilets can be a barrier to participation for some older people. While the needs of older people are covered to some extent in broader urban design, healthy city, sustainability, principles, and guidelines, more focused age-friendly guidelines for cities and neighbourhoods have yet to emerge.

Implications for the Housing and Development Industries

A range of issues are relevant to the housing construction and property development industries as the demand and a market for age-friendly housing develop. The question rests upon decisions either to produce specialised aged housing in enclaves (retirement villages or seniors living developments) designed around the needs of older people, or to increase the supply of mainstream housing designed to accommodate a wider range of ages and ability levels. Regulation of minimum access features in the United States and the United Kingdom; rapidly increasing demand for, and cost of, home modifications; and the overwhelming preference by the ageing population to remain living at home with the assistance of care services suggest that at least the minimum access features will be regulated.

Public Housing Policies for Aged Societies

Much public policy development depends upon changes in underlying perceptions of the importance of providing support to the elderly within the electorate and the ideologies of various governments. Fiscal austerity over the past 20 years and current retraction of government responsibilities more generally have impacted in particular upon the housing sector and the welfare needs of older people. Such needs are increasingly seen as the province of private responsibility. There remains a pressing need for the provision of stock of diverse and affordable housing for all older people. Older people vary enormously in their needs, circumstances, housing preferences, living arrangements, and financial capacities and so differing solutions are needed as a result. Of note also, differing cultural and social traditions across and between countries mean that it is unlikely that identical policy solutions are appropriate. Continuing national and regional research must be a priority to guide vitally important welfare and social policy development to improve the structures, availability, and affordability of housing for older people. The future welfare, health and well-being, quality of life, and liveability of older people and their families, together with the need to relieve the undoubted fiscal pressures to be borne by all levels of governments confronting ageing populations, mean that bold thinking is warranted and must be encouraged. For sure, the welfare of older citizens remains the measure of a just and equitable society.

See also: Homeless People: Older People; Impairment and Experience of Home; Meanings of Home for Older People; Older People: Housing Institutions; Older People: Well-Being, Housing and Neighbourhoods.

Further Reading

Australian Government (2007) *Intergenerational Report II 2007*. Canberra: AGPS. www.Treasury.gov.au

Beer A, Faulkner D, and Gabriel M (2006) 21st Century housing careers and Australia's future: Literature review. *National Research Venture 2 Research Paper 1*. Melbourne, VIC: Australian Housing and Urban Research Institute [AHURI]. www.ahuri.edu.au

Berry M (2007) Ageing in space: Transport, access and urban form. In: Borowski A, Encel S, and Ozanne E (eds.) *Longevity and Social Change in Australia*, pp. 239–264. Kensington: University of NSW Press.

Burton E and Mitchell L (2007) Neighbourhood Form and Layout Design, Findings and Recommendations. www.idgo.ac.uk/design_guidance/neighbourhood.htm (accessed 10 June 2011)

Harling E (2007) *Older People's Housing and Under-Occupancy: A Policy Brief*. London: International Longevity Centre. www.iluk.org.uk/record.jsp?ID=16&type=publication (accessed 10 June 2011).

Judd B, Olsberg D, Quinn J, Demirbilek O, and Groenhardt L (2010) Dwelling, land and neighbourhood use by older homeowners. *AHURI Final Report*. Melbourne, VIC: Australian Housing and Urban Research Institute. www.ahuri.edu.au

Kendig H and Catherine B (2007) Housing policy for a long-lived society. In: Borowski A, Encel S, and Ozanne E (eds.) *Longevity and Social Change in Australia*, pp. 219–238. Kensington: University of NSW Press.

Kendig H and Neutze M (1999) *Housing Implications of Population Ageing in Australia*. Canberra: Australian Government Publishing Service; Productivity Commission.

Morris A (2009) Contentment and suffering: The impact of Australia's housing policy and tenure on older Australians. *Australian Journal of Social Issues* 44(Summer): 363–377.

OECD (2001) *Territorial Outlook*, 2001 Edition. Paris: OECD.

OECD (2009) *Regions at a Glance*. Paris: OECD.

OECD (2009) *Factbook 2009: Economic, Environmental & Social Statistics*. Paris: OECD.

Olsberg D and Winters M (2005) Ageing in place: Intergenerational and intrafamilial housing transfers and shifts in later life. *Final Report*. Melbourne, VIC: Australian Housing and Urban Research Institute.

Olsberg D, Perry J, Encel S, and Adorjany L (2004) Ageing-in-place: Intergenerational and intra-familial housing transfers and shifts in later life. *Positioning Paper*. Melbourne, VIC: Australian Housing and Urban Research Institute. www.ahuri.edu.au

Oswald F and Wahl H-W (2004) Housing and health in later life. *Reviews on Environmental Health* 19(3–4): 223–252.

Quinn J, Judd B, Olsberg D, and Demirbilek O (2009) Dwelling, land and neighbourhood use by older home owners. *AHURI Positioning Paper*. Melbourne, VIC: Australian Housing and Urban Research Institute. www.ahuri.edu.au

Older People: Well-Being, Housing and Neighbourhoods

H Kendig, L Clemson, and L Mackenzie, University of Sydney, Lidcombe, NSW, Australia

© 2012 Elsevier Ltd. All rights reserved.

Glossary

Age-friendly city "An Age-friendly City is an inclusive and accessible urban environment that promotes active ageing."

Ageing in place 'Ageing in place' is the process by which people have the preferences and capacities to remain in their home of choice as they grow older.

Environmental press Environmental press consists of the demands and opportunities presented by physical and social environments and the consequences for individuals' competency and well-being.

Household A household is the group of people who share a dwelling and live together. The household head is the resident owner or person who signs the lease.

Land use Land use refers to the mix of residential, commercial, recreational and other uses of land.

Neighbourhood A neighbourhood is a geographically localised community that can be identified by a common usage or social connection.

Universal design Universal design is the process of designing and providing housing and communities that are accessible, usable, and adaptable by people of all ages and abilities.

Walkable neighbourhood A walkable neighbourhood is an area that one can easily walk over, often related to grocery shopping, restaurants, and visiting, and also refers to the type of land use and distances that encourage walking.

Ageing and Housing Perspectives

Individual and population ageing have profound influences on housing and neighbourhoods, while residential environments in turn have a major bearing on ageing experiences. The field of housing demography underscores how individuals and cohorts move through the housing stock as they progress through their lifespan in housing markets which are themselves changing over time. Households' decisions to move or stay in their homes form 'housing careers' that are fundamental to the operation of housing markets. Housing demand is influenced by changing patterns of family formation and employment patterns as they interact with the supply of housing and broader policy and market influences. Population ageing has been one of the major forces of change in housing markets over recent decades.

The influence of residential environments on older people can be conceptualised in the Person–Environment (P–E) Paradigm. The P–E Paradigm examines the functioning and well-being of individuals as an outcome of how well their capacities and preferences fit the demands and supports of their social and built environments. A good environmental fit will provide a balance of interests and challenges, reinforce a sense of identity and of control, and facilitate continued independence as people grow older. A poor environmental fit can overstress individuals and lead to a breakdown of competencies and well-being. The environmental fit approach provides key insights into changing residential needs and preferences, housing decision-making processes, and ways that environmental supports can compensate for disability and other vulnerabilities as people grow older.

This article brings together the housing demography and P–E perspectives to better understand the housing and neighbourhoods of older people and their importance for them. We begin by examining broad historical and lifespan forces that underlie the availability and usage of housing among older people today and in the future. We then move to the importance of housing for personal meanings, activities, and health before turning to neighbourhoods, financial considerations, and decision-making in terms of 'ageing in place' or moving. The article concludes by considering directions for policies and professional practice including environmental and home-based dimensions to maintaining independence and well-being.

Population Ageing and Housing Markets

Ageing and older people have a disproportionate influence on nearly all housing markets in Western countries because so many of them live in one-person or two-person households. For example, in the United States, it is estimated that more than 40% of dwellings are occupied by a household head who is aged 55 years or over. More than 90% of them live in single-family houses or apartments, while fewer than 10% live in any form of residential care or supportive housing. When they share households with younger people, it is usually the older person who owns or pays the rent. A relatively small and intensely disadvantaged group of older people live in rooming houses or boarding houses or are homeless. Over the post-Second World War era, the proportion of older people living alone (overwhelmingly widows) has risen greatly as a result of preferences for independent living and increasing incomes relative to housing costs.

Among older people today, their predominant housing career has been to leave the parental home and then to live in private rental housing before subsequently moving on to purchase and then pay off the mortgage on an owner-occupied home. The pace of this career is influenced by family formation and child bearing but, more importantly, by increased income and savings through dual-income households and career advancement. An alternative pathway, typically for those having fewer financial means, is to move to a public tenancy, either as a stepping stone to homeownership or as an alternative to it. A small, disadvantaged minority of individuals may never attain homeownership, remaining as permanent tenants, while others who have bought may subsequently relinquish homeownership as a result of marital dissolution or financial setbacks.

The current cohorts of older people have benefited greatly from the housing opportunities made available over the post-Second World War era by increasing real incomes, declining real costs of housing, readily available housing finance, and tax concessions and direct subsidies for home-buying. The financial rewards of homeownership have been accelerated over recent decades by general inflation and real rises of house prices along with continuing generous tax treatment of equity and capital gains in owner-occupied housing. By the time of retirement, the majority of Australians and Americans now in later life have paid off their homes completely (and some own second homes for amenity or investment purposes). Few have or will return to any form of tenancy during later life, and less than 40% will ever enter any kind of residential care.

The cohort momentum in housing tenure attainment will see increasing rates of homeownership in later life for baby boomers over decades ahead. However, while rising house prices are increasing wealth for those who have already bought or who are buying, it raises the financial barrier for subsequent cohorts to ever buy homes and it appears that life-long homeownership rates will be lower for those who entered the housing market in the 1990s or later and who will approach later life in the future. In an historic watershed, it seems likely that housing ownership rates and other dimensions of life-long economic well-being could be worse for later cohorts, adding to concerns for intergenerational inequalities. The consequences would fall heavily on those who also have modest financial means.

Cohort momentum and change also underlies the diversity of patterns in the location of older people. Massive suburbanisation from the 1950s through to the 1980s and home purchases by younger people at that time, then explains why, through ageing in place over subsequent decades, many older people are now located in postwar suburbs designed for cars, thus raising transport concerns for when they can no longer drive. Growing older in pockets of urban decline or in dying country towns can leave older people in areas of poor amenity with a shrinking asset that can be difficult to maintain or to sell. Post-retirement moves are relatively less common but those to urban infill housing, particularly high and medium density, are of significance for urban sustainability and infrastructure costs as well as for the mobility of individuals as they grow older. Moves to ex-urban living, for lifestyle or cost reasons, are another notable trend, although there can be reverse trends back to urban areas as people reach advanced old age and seek better access to family support and health and aged care services.

The housing situation of older people across Western countries has diversified substantially over recent decades along with increasing life expectancy and wealth in later life as well as major developments in housing markets. In addition to overall housing improvement and trends towards higher-density accommodation, new forms of supportive housing have emerged, including planned retirement and assisted living communities in the United States, sheltered housing in the United Kingdom, and retirement villages in Australia. Board and care homes and boarding or rooming houses, however, continue as pockets of disadvantage, particularly for life-long private tenants. The growth of public sector provision specifically for older people – and arguably its recent retraction due to fiscal austerity – is adding to the diversity of age-based housing provision.

In the United States, housing demographers are anticipating the possible consequences of the massive baby-boom cohort's eventual exit from the housing system from the 2020s onwards. This is a long-term trend, not a short-term adjustment over a few years, and hence the consequences for the economy and cities could be significant. While high levels of immigration may mitigate these pressures, there could be significant downward pressures on prices, opening opportunities for younger cohorts to enter the market, while the wealth of older homeowners could be eroded. Significant challenges could emerge in anticipating and responding to shortfalls of demand for the existing housing stock in particular geographical areas.

Meaning and Use of the Home

The home is a significant personal and social as well as financial resource for older people. Ideas and definitions of home involve notions of ownership, autonomy, independence, belonging, and privacy. The home can represent one's past self, symbolise a lifetime of memories and achievements, and provide personal continuity and for some a refuge through the transitions in later life.

The home can become increasingly significant as the base for daily activities as people have more time after retirement and eventually experience reduced mobility. Given the large amount of time, older people spend at home or in their gardens, it becomes highly problematic to argue that they are underoccupying their homes. Former bedrooms can be at the centre of recreational activities or home businesses or provide accommodation for relatives when they are visiting or need accommodation. Gardening can be an important activity for self-expression. Residence in a flat can be as much a locational or lifestyle choice as an adjustment to health or financial limitations. The visitability of the home can be central to social integration.

Overall, older people are as satisfied with their homes as any other age group of householders. While private tenants face potential insecurity, the housing concerns of older owners can include the age of their homes, repair and maintenance problems, and access limitations and safety. These factors can impact on independent functioning, physical activity, safety, and mobility as well as enjoyment of the home. Minor home upkeep and gardening are the most common housing-related needs, particularly for those who are in poor health or on low incomes.

The features of the home can represent a place of security and enable independence. Housing tenure and costs are crucial to standards of living and security. The home environment is a major contributor to the capacity of older people to successfully age in place.

Home and Health

The P–E relationship in the home can be significant for the health of older people. They can be more vulnerable than other age groups to environmental problems such as hypothermia in winter or hyperthermia on hot summer days. Virtually all older people report at least one long-term health condition that will need to be managed within the home and community context. Physical aspects of the home environment have also been linked with mental-health-related quality of life.

As the capacities of an older person decline, the home can increasingly become the setting for modest or even high levels of care. Home modifications or equipment can be introduced to the home in order to improve functioning and safety. Typically, privacy is decreased as carers enter the home, features of the home change, unfamiliar objects and people become part of the home, and the home may no longer reflect a personal identity. Relatively few older people modify their housing after retirement even when the home environment no longer accommodates changes in functional capacity that may go undetected. Frail older people face significant dilemmas when they are reluctant to have carers in their homes but are even more concerned about pressures from others to move to a relative's home or to residential care.

Falls are a significant risk for older people at home and they affect at least one in three people annually over the age of 65 in the community. They frequently cause injury, functional decline, loss of self-confidence, and increased risk of admission to residential care. Home environmental risk factors for falls include slippery or inadequate floor coverings, steps, and stairs, inadequate lighting, poorly designed furniture, poor access to bathrooms and toilets, inadequate footwear, the demands of pets, and features of the garden and garage. Many of these environmental hazards are potentially modifiable, for example, by adding grab rails, assistive equipment, architectural modifications, or behaviour change. The functional status of an older person, risk-taking behaviour, and level of exposure to environmental stressors combine to influence risk of falls in their home.

There is increasing evidence that assessing the risk of falls and modifying the home environment can reduce the risk of injury for older people. Falls prevention interventions are most effective when they target those at higher risk of falls, such as those aged 70 plus or those with an existing falls history. Programmes implemented by occupational therapists and other health professionals have added efficacy because they can tailor a range of interventions as most appropriate to each individual in his or her home.

Neighbourhood Environments

The neighbourhood environment can become important particularly for older people who no longer drive or have difficulties managing public transport. Research has shown that giving up driving is a major life event with serious implications for independence and well-being. Features of neighbourhood associated with independence and social participation include walkability, access to services, transport, connection with the community, and crime and fear of crime. Neighbourhoods of course differ greatly within and between different urban and rural areas, and they can change significantly as people grow older.

Neighbourhood quality has been found to have an effect on life satisfaction and self-rated health among older people. For example, green space and well-maintained neighbourhoods are associated with better health status, remaining independent for longer, and increased survival rates. The aesthetic appeal of the neighbourhood, having places to meet and interact, and seeing other older people outdoors may all contribute. Alternatively, deteriorating suburbs are associated with poorer perceptions of health and cognitive decline.

The neighbourhood environment can have a strong influence on the regular physical activity that is important for physical and mental health, maintaining functional capacities, and staying connected with community and being socially active. Significant factors include access to low-cost recreation facilities and services, quality sidewalks, manageable traffic flows, shops within walking distance, and higher residential densities. Street connectivity enables people to have many destinations directly available from their home and the walkability of the neighbourhood enables moderate physical activity and facilitates personal activities that are personally goal-orientated and self-generated.

Several interventions have shown that neighbourhood improvements can be beneficial for the social participation of older people. The ENABLE-AGE project (2007) in Sweden found that activity performance and togetherness-oriented participation were significantly related to good access to shops and services, good medical care in the vicinity, living close to friends and relatives, cultural opportunities in the vicinity and having good local transport. The MOBILATE project (2004) surveyed European elders about out-of-home mobility. The greatest risk levels of personal or environmental mobility limitations were found among women, those in rural areas, and those with the least health, social, and economic resources. The most common activities were shopping and accessing services, usually in the mornings, and visiting and recreational activities in the afternoon; few left home in the evening. They concluded that out-of-home mobility and its benefits can be improved through a variety of avenues, walking being the most common option and public transport least. The need for both user-friendly transport options and access to community transport programmes was supported by this and a number of other studies.

In assessing risk, older people tend to view themselves as living in an increasingly dangerous society. Further, the media is blamed for highlighting crime and victimisation of older people and thus creating higher perceptions of risk of crime. However, in reality, older people are less involved in street attacks and, despite some beliefs, are at much greater risk of a fall than a mugging in the vast majority of neighbourhoods. Physical signs such as graffiti, proliferation of rubbish, or damage to property are seen as evidence of the breakdown of social controls and thus indicators of criminal threat. Neighbourhood safety is perceived in terms of concerns such as the capacity to walk around at night, the intimidatory presence of groups of younger people, or the fear of the consequences of crime. People make adaptations and adjustments to risk by making behavioural changes such as restricting their spatial lifestyle or travelling at times and in ways that make them feel safe; for example, avoiding travelling at dusk or at school times when there are more likely groups of 'noisy, pushy' young people. The perception of risk alone can be sufficient to restrict mobility and social participation.

Housing and Financial Advantage

The quality and location of the home are crucially influenced by affordability and this in turn is one of the major factors in standards of living for older people. Older people who bought homes earlier in life and who own outright can have relatively low running costs, although home maintenance and property taxes can be expensive. Those who are renting privately are exposed to regular cost increases that can lead to housing poverty. Government tenants typically face costs intermediate between private tenants and outright owners. In Australia and the United States, rent assistance reduces some of the hardship, while the greater availability of public housing is significant in the United Kingdom.

For most older homeowners, the equity in their home is their major source of wealth. In Australia, for example, the value of their equity in the home substantially exceeds the value of any form of retirement or superannuation accounts. This housing equity yields ongoing returns in the form of low housing outlays, while appreciation of the home increases wealth, free of any capital gains or other taxes.

Housing assets can provide usable capital by trading down in the market and by sales that can fund moves into various forms of retirement housing and residential care. They can also provide security for Reverse Annuity mortgages that can finance modest ongoing cash drawdowns (e.g., to pay for home care) or occasional drawdowns to fund one-off expenditure such as home maintenance or other improvements. In Australia, owner-occupied housing assets are inherited tax free irrespective of the incomes of the deceased or their heirs, thus accentuating wealth inequalities between advantaged and disadvantaged families.

Ageing in Place and Moving Decisions

The vast majority of people age in-place in homes bought many years earlier when their family and financial positions were very different. This residential stability, notwithstanding many changes experienced by ageing individuals, is explained mainly by strong psychological and social attachments to home. Decisions to stay in homes of longstanding are enabled by the adaptability of housing to changing needs and by declining costs as mortgages are paid off. Decisions to move in later life can be motivated by positive 'pull' factors such as lifestyle moves typically soon after retirement or 'push' factors such as ill health, the loss of a spouse, or the inability to continue living independently in advanced old age.

Place attachment, defined as reflecting feelings about a geographic location and emotional binding of a person to places, grows steadily across the life course and culminates in very old age. Such attachment to home and comfort with familiarity leads to a propensity to age in place. With urban change over time, this can make the older people more vulnerable depending on whether they are in a deteriorating or a revitalising area. Price values of homes may have dropped yet increased in other areas.

Both staying and moving can have both positive and negative consequences. To remain in family homes in low-density suburban areas, when people can no longer drive, will limit access to amenities, shops, and activities, or else increase dependency on others for transport. When older people move to areas not planned for them – such as naturally occurring retirement communities (NORCs), the sea change phenomena, and the building of senior apartments along major arterial roads – these communities may not have the necessary social and health resources as they grow older unless there is commensurate public investment.

The process of moving may begin after many years of evaluating the positive and negative aspects or due to a sudden health-related crisis. There are important distinctions between voluntary and involuntary moves and an array of processes that occur in the 'push' away from the old location versus the 'pull' to the new location. Pro-active moves can anticipate future change and enable people to make changes and reestablish a sense of place attachment, while they still have substantial adaptability capacities. There is strong evidence to show that exercising choice, when deciding the timing or destination of moves, is crucial to continuing well-being.

Older adults today are increasingly mobile. It is anticipated that the number of moves of very old people will accelerate given their growing numbers and increasing range of housing options including purpose-built dwellings and assisted living arrangements. The most common moves by older people are to relocate to a more appropriate home within their familiar neighbourhoods, which is increasingly important at advanced ages. Lifestyle-induced migration and seasonable migration are increasing among relatively younger older people having substantial health and financial resources.

Future Directions

The future of housing and environments for older people will be heavily influenced by the ascendant baby-boom cohort that will be passing through later life from the present well into the 2040s. Their resources are greater and their aspirations have already proven to be more demanding and more varied than those who are currently in later life. However, there is much diversity among baby boomers, and their choices will be largely constrained to the existing stock of dwellings and neighbourhoods and their legacies. Opportunities for new directions will depend on society-wide economic developments, markets for existing housing, and ongoing reinvestment, changing uses, and new building and innovations. The response of housing markets and policies to the size and diversity of the baby-boom cohort will have major consequences for the housing and economic prospects of younger as well as older people.

New ideas and their implementation can steadily transform the livability of housing for all age groups. The World Health Organisation argues convincingly for Active Ageing strategies and Age-Friendly Cities that can enable continued participation, independence, and well-being notwithstanding disabilities. Universal design principles in housing and thoughtful urban planning can economically and effectively provide barrier-free environments enabling independence for generations to come. The rise of community care and client-centred care underscores the importance of enabling ageing in place as well as a variety of affordable home environments that provide choice and appropriate supports for frail older people. Ongoing research will be important to identify the most effective strategies in adjusting to the massive growth anticipated for older people in housing markets across developed countries.

See also: Asset-Based Welfare; Emotions at Home; Home as a Space of Care; Homeless People: Older People; Home Ownership: Economic Benefits; Housing and Sustainable Transport; Housing and the State in Australasia; Housing Equity Withdrawal in the United Kingdom; Housing Need in the United Kingdom; Housing Wealth Over the Life Course; Impairment and Experience of Home; Life Course; Meanings of Home for Older People; Neighbourhood Planning; Older People: Housing Institutions; Older People: Well-Being; Place Attachment;

Supported Housing; Vacancy Chains; Welfare Agencies and Assistance: United States.

Further Reading

Clemson L, Mackenzie L, Ballinger C, Close J, and Cumming R (2008) Environmental interventions to prevent falls in community dwelling older people: A meta-analysis. *Journal of Ageing and Health* 20: 954–971.

Haak M, Fange A, Horstmann V, and Iwarsson S (2008) Two dimensions of participation in very old age and their relations to home and neighborhood environments. *American Journal of Occupational Therapy* 62: 77–86.

Kendig H and Bridge C (2007) Housing policy for long-lived society. In: Borowski A, Encel S, and Ozanne E (eds.) *Longevity and Social Change in Australia*, pp. 219–238. Sydney: University of New South Wales Press.

Lang IA, Llewellyn DJ, Langa KM, Wallace R, and Melzer D (2008) Neighbourhood deprivation and incident mobility disability in older adults. *Age and Ageing* 37: 403–410.

Mackenzie L, Byles J, and D'Este C (2009) A longitudinal study of the Home Falls and Accidents Screening Tool (HOME FAST) to predict falls in older community dwelling people. *Australasian Journal on Ageing* 28: 64–69.

Mollenkopf H, Marcellini F, Ruoppila I, Szeman Z, Tacken M, and Wahl H (2004) Social and behavioural science perspectives on out-of-home mobility in later life: Findings from the European project MOBILATE. *European Journal of Ageing* 1: 45–53.

Myers D and Ryu SH (2007) Aging baby boomers and the generational housing bubble: Foresight and mitigation of an epic transition. *Journal of the American Planning Association* 74(1): 17–33.

Oswald F and Wahl HW (2005) Dimensions in the meaning of home in later life. In: Rowles GD and Chaudhury H (eds.) *Home and Identity in Late Life: International Perspectives*, pp. 21–45. New York: Springer.

Pynoos J, Kendig H, and Nishita C (2007) Housing. In: Birren J (ed.) *Encyclopedia of Gerontology*, 2nd edn., pp. 709–719. Oxford, UK: Elsevier.

Rubenstein L (1999) The importance of including the home environment in assessment of frail older persons. *Journal of the American Geriatrics Society* 47: 111–112.

Sugiyama T and Thompson CW (2007) Older people's health, outdoor activity and supportiveness of neighbourhood environments. *Landscape and Urban Planning* 83: 168–175.

Wahl HW and Gitlin L (2007) Environmental gerontology. In: Birren J (ed.) *Encyclopedia of Gerontology*, 2nd edn., pp. 494–501. Oxford, UK: Elsevier.

Wahl HW and Oswald F (2010) Environmental perspectives on aging. In: Dannefer D and Phillipson C (eds.) *International Handbook of Social Gerontology*, pp. 111–124. London: Sage.

World Health Organization, Ageing Life Course (2004) *Active ageing: A policy framework*.WHO/MNMH/NPH/04.8.

Wright F, Tinker A, Hanson J, Wojgani H, and Mayagoitia R (2009) Some social consequences of remodelling English sheltered housing and care homes to 'extra care'. *Ageing and Society* 29: 135–153.

Ontological Security

A Dupuis, Massey University, Auckland, New Zealand

© 2012 Elsevier Ltd. All rights reserved.

Introduction

Although the economic dimension of housing constitutes a dominant strand in housing research, a growing body of literature recognises housing's nonfinancial benefits, especially the deeper meaning and significance that housing and the home hold for many people. The concept of ontological security fits within this broader area of the meanings of home. The concept itself, and its obverse ontological insecurity, appeared initially in the work of psychiatrist R. D. Laing. According to Laing (1964: 40) people who are basically ontologically secure are able to face all the hazards of life from "a centrally firm sense" of their own "and other people's reality and identity". By contrast, those who have deep insecurities about their existence, manifested by various symptoms of mental illness, may be "utterly lacking in any unquestionable self-validating certainties". However, the connection between ontological security and housing has largely drawn on the treatment accorded to the concept by British sociologist Anthony Giddens. Understood broadly as a sense of trust in the world as it appears to be, Giddens described ontological security as the confidence that most people have in their ongoing sense of identity, a sense that others are reliable and constant, and their material environments secure. Put simply, ontological security involves a sense of the reliability of people and things.

Giddens on Ontological Security

Giddens argues that ontological security is a deep psychological need for individuals in all societies. It has to do with "... 'being' or, in the terms of phenomenology, 'being-in-the-world.' But it is an emotional, rather than a cognitive, phenomenon, and it is rooted in the unconscious" (Giddens, 1990: 92). It is a feeling of security that is based on a trust in the constancy of surroundings, the continuity of self-identity, and in the functional reliability of material objects used in the practice of the routines of daily life, and the pervasive and stable nature of habit. Giddens claims that ontological security develops from the trust relationships established in early childhood which act as an "emotional inoculation which protects against the ontological anxieties to which all human beings are potentially subject" (Giddens, 1990: 94).

According to Giddens, children learn to commit to trust in future events based on the patterning and reliability of their early routines and interactions. As trust is always formed in an absence, that is, one cannot know for certain that an event will occur at a particular time and at a particular place, one can only trust that it will or will not occur because of the evidence of the patterns of past experiences. This trust is based on a belief that people will act as they are expected to act and systems will operate with a patterned reliability. Ontological security therefore is not a calculative process of ascertaining the probabilities and risks of certain occurrences, but rather a response to the world as it has presented in the past and the anticipation that it will continue to present in the same way in the future.

In Giddens' depiction of the concept a distinction is made between the nature of ontological security in the premodern and the contemporary worlds, especially with respect to the systematic differences in the way day-to-day routines are carried out. Unlike premodern or traditional societies, where the daily routines were characterised by face-to-face interactions, especially within kinship systems, ontological security in the modern world is more fragile and tenuous. This is largely due to the changed nature of the modern world's trust mechanisms. Each of the four main foci of trust and ontological security of premodern times – kinship relations, place, religion, and tradition – play much less important roles in the modern world. Kinship relations have declined in intensity; the primacy of place has been largely destroyed as the local and global have become inextricably intertwined; religion has been displaced by scientific knowledge; and tradition and traditional practices have been undermined even more than religion by the "reflexivity of modern social life, which stands in direct opposition to [tradition]" (Giddens, 1990: 109).

Trust mechanisms too have changed, as trust is no longer embedded in face-to-face interactions. Instead, modernity requires a trust in expert systems and in symbolic tokens, both of which act as disembedding mechanisms in social interactions and exchanges. The acceptance of these mechanisms enables social interactions to be lifted out of space and time, referred to by Giddens as space–time distanciation, so that social exchanges and interactions can be reliably conducted at a distance and across time. Yet they maintain the power of interactions that in traditional societies could only occur between persons present at the same location and time. A simple example here is when an Internet purchase is made with a few clicks of a mouse, something that in times past would have likely required face-to-face interaction in a shop or other commercial premise and the physical exchange of money or a cheque – all of which would have taken considerable time.

The uncertainty associated with modernity is further heightened by the constant barrage of information disseminated through technologies. Given the vast amount of often contradictory information coming in, lay individuals often feel confused, not knowing what and who they should trust. As a consequence, people find they must constantly reexamine their rationales for actions and practices – a key characteristic of what Giddens calls reflexive modernity. This, however, is problematic as much of the knowledge upon which action and practice is based is itself uncertain and contingent, given not only the quantity of information available, but also the disagreement among experts.

In the face of such uncertainties Giddens asserts that ontological security has been undermined, which necessitates people working to establish a framework of ontological security in their everyday lives. Negotiating the modern world increasingly requires interactions between people who are strangers, who know little or nothing about one another. These exchanges, which must be facilitated with a degree of trust and confidence in order to ensure their effectiveness, now provide the services and assistance that would have previously been drawn from kinship and community networks. While recent information technologies have greatly enhanced the capacity to maintain contacts over large distances, these technologies cannot substitute for the intimacy provided by close personal contacts, and professional services do not provide the associative and affiliative bonds that mark meaningful relationships. It therefore falls to the relationships between friends, sexual partners, marriage partners, and children to supply the affective needs of individuals in modern society. These relationships have come to be marked by self-disclosure, trust, and intimacy, which in turn necessitate a sense of self-identity established on a process of self-enquiry and self-expression. The search for ontological security has thus resulted in a revolution in intimate ties between friends, partners, and spouses.

More broadly, these mechanisms of maintaining trust within modernity assist individuals to cope with the globalised and depersonalised nature of risk that has arisen out of modernity. Reminiscent of Ulrich Beck's risk society thesis, Giddens describes the risks associated with late modernity as having their basis in the application of human knowledge and technologies. Individuals have limited or no control over the miasma of risks that attend their daily lives, yet are still able to function. They may turn to: pragmatic responses to the problems they can deal with and disengagement from larger debates; cynicism; a reduction of the perception of threat through humour; or to active engagement through radical activity. Whatever the strategy, Giddens maintains that there is still a level of anxiety that attends these positions, suppressed or otherwise, which poses psychological consequences for individuals in the manner in which they shore up their sense of ontological security.

Connecting the Home to Ontological Security

In the 1980s and 1990s a number of scholars working in the area of the meanings of home made the connection between ontological security and housing, arguing that the home could provide the secure base through which people could achieve a sense of ontological security. A major catalyst for this work was the position developed by Peter Saunders, who, engaging with Giddens' concept of ontological security, argued that ontological security in the contemporary world could be attained through the home, and especially through homeownership. In particular, Saunders took issue with Giddens' view on the problems of attaining ontological security within the created or built environment.

While Saunders largely agreed with Giddens' analysis of change, he asked why the development of the created environment should result in ontological insecurity and anomie, and argued that Giddens was incorrect to stress the importance of natural rather than created environments for the maintenance of ontological security (Saunders, 1989a). Saunders also reminded us that Giddens' theory of structuration is premised on the recognition that modern life is routinised. The question Saunders posed was, why should routinised activities be seen differently in various epochs? What essentially was the difference between the routines of people in the modern world going to work every day, over the same route, on the train that left at the same time for the same destination, and the peasant of times past treading the same fields on a regular basis? Why should the latter routine maintain ontological security, while the former does not? Saunders argued that the important point was that day-to-day activity in both worlds is routinised and takes place through familiar space–time paths. Unlike Giddens, Saunders saw no necessity for these paths to be in a natural, rather than the built, environment. If we accept Saunders' argument that ontological security can be maintained in the built environment, it is only a small step further to accept Saunders' proposition that the home can be the key locale in modern society which can provide ontological security.

A key feature of Saunders' work was the argument that in modern societies, homeownership could influence people's sense of self and identity. His view was that if people felt secure in their homes, then homeownership represented a response to the contemporary problem of ontological insecurity. Summing up his earlier work Saunders claimed that "[t]he home is where people are off-stage, free from surveillance, in control of their immediate environment. It is their castle. It is where they belong" (Saunders, 1989b: 184). Saunders then went on to discuss whether ownership per se was a necessary condition for people to experience ontological security, or could tenants feel equally secure in their homes.

Subsequently Saunders supported his earlier somewhat speculative stance with more solid empirical material. Drawing on a household survey of participants from three English towns, Saunders found that owner-occupation was the preferred tenure for both homeowners and tenants. Owners saw the principal advantages of their tenure as autonomy and financial security. Tenants, similarly, saw the disadvantages of their tenure as lack of autonomy and lack of long-term financial security. Responses to questions on the meaning of and attachment to the home indicated that homeownership functioned as a source of ontological security for many people. While Saunders did not go so far as to suggest renters could not experience such sentiments, he argued that they must look elsewhere. Furthermore, Saunders claimed that the desire for homeownership appeared to be so strong for participants across all three towns that it could not be put down to financial considerations alone, but was at the core of most people's lives and at the centre of their aspirations and values (Saunders, 1989b).

Operationalising Ontological Security

Ontological security is not only a slippery concept to define, but also a difficult concept to operationalise. The previous section discussed Saunders' endeavour in this regard. A more systematic elaboration of the concept by Dupuis and Thorns (1998) broke down the concept into four operationalisable themes, which they then addressed through a set of empirical data drawn from interviews with older New Zealand homeowners. Basing their work closely on Giddens' discussions of ontological security, they argued that home as a source of ontological security is maintained when the following four conditions are met.

1. *Home as constancy in the social and material environment* Home can be conceptualised as an encompassing category that links together a material environment with a deeply emotional set of meanings to do with the permanence and continuity associated with home. While other facets of the built environment, like churches or familiar streets and neighbourhoods, might also offer some sense of ontological security, it is the home that provides the material environment most closely associated with permanence and continuity. The interview data Dupuis and Thorns drew on suggested that homeownership provided security and stability, whereas renting was viewed as a risky business with vulnerable tenants subject to the whims of the landlord and in constant fear of eviction. Home also meant the constancy of family, with almost all of the elderly participants associating home with bringing up children and being surrounded by family.

2. *Home as the spatial context for the establishment of routine* Many daily activities are routine actions which follow familiar space–time paths or courses of action. Perhaps the most salient characteristic of routine is familiarity. Dupuis and Thorns' interview data showed that of all the aspects of familiarity associated with home it was the familiar routines with family and children in particular that were most important, even when the children involved were married with homes of their own. Home was also strongly associated with the familiar rites and rituals of the collective life of a family and was seen as the gathering place for family celebrations. Rituals reinforce the family–home link, as they become a marker of who is included in 'family' by being invited into the home.

3. *Home as a site where people feel most in control of their lives because they feel free from the surveillance that is part of the contemporary world* A third aspect of ontological security focused on by Dupuis and Thorns was that of the home as a refuge from the outside world. A number of widows in their study commented on the comfort that their own home gave them following the death of their husband, providing them with a refuge where they could experience their grief in private, free from the disturbances of the outside world. Many respondents also commented on the sense of autonomy they had as homeowners. Frequent references were made to 'being able to do what you wanted, when you wanted, in your own home' and respondents spoke of adapting their homes in ways to suit themselves: of changing the colour of the decor, upgrading a garden, and keeping pets. Most felt that it was homeownership that let them 'do their own thing'.

4. *Home as a secure base around which people can construct their identities* Confidence in self-identity is an element in Giddens' depiction of ontological security. In the Dupuis and Thorns study being a homeowner provided a secure base around which participants' identities could be constructed. In New Zealand, becoming a homeowner has long been viewed as a rite of passage and looked on as an achievement and a source of pride. Homeownership is part of accomplishing an adult identity and offers owners the potential to modify their environment and thus stamp their personality on their home. The home also allows for the fashioning of gendered identities. The women interviewed tended strongly to fit the stereotypical gender role of the housewife and mother, were mostly the caretakers of wealth stored and displayed in the home, and were largely responsible for

the decor. The elderly men too tended to fit the stereotypical roles, both within and outside the home. They also tended to do the kinds of jobs that add value to the house such as handyman jobs, carpentry, and painting and papering.

Other writers too have attempted to treat the concept of ontological security systematically. For example, Kearns et al. (2000), while acknowledging that the concept is difficult to operationalise, concentrated on three psychosocial phenomena associated with the home: home as a haven; home as a site of autonomy; and home as a marker of social status. Home as a haven is related to the need to feel safe. The privatisation of the home has occurred at a time when life outside the home is more open to surveillance. A retreat from the public world to an autonomous site is therefore required, which the home provides. The authors also maintain that the positive regard of others (status) is required to maintain ontological security.

Ontological Security and Tenure

Early work connecting the home with ontological security focused on the ontological security afforded by homeownership. The subsequent debate has discussed the extent to which ontological security can be achieved in other tenures and a range of contexts. Contrary to the view that homeownership is the tenure most likely to confer ontological security, Kearns et al. (2000) showed that both renters and owners derived psychosocial benefits from the home. They also raised the question of the extent to which ontological security can be derived from sources outside the home. The same authors (Hiscock et al., 2001) also reported that ontological security is greater for social housing renters than renters in the private sector because of the lower rents. Elsewhere, ontological security has been associated with security of tenure, rather than the form of tenure. Both Marston (2004) and Mee (2007) commented on the benefits of ontological security for Australian public housing tenants, because that tenure was constant, affordable, and predictable.

Extending the debate to nonorthodox homes, Newton (2008) used the conceptual frame of ontological security to examine the emotional attachment to home and security among permanent residents of caravan parks. Caravan parks provide an interesting site through which to explore this connection in the light of the way they tend to be represented as locales of disadvantage replete with social problems on the one hand, and on the other as having a 'free and easy' lifestyle choice. Newton's findings were that many caravan park residents expressed feelings of safety, security, and happiness, all indicators of the concept of ontological security.

The extent to which people with mental illnesses can derive a sense of ontological security from their accommodation has also been researched. Padgett (2007), for example, argued that transitional housing for the mentally ill does not sustain the conditions outlined by Dupuis and Thorns above. Often stays in transitional housing are short term, turnover is high and, given the shared eating and sleeping arrangements and the constant surveillance and drug testing that occurs, the privacy associated with the home does not exist. However, Padgett referred to a study in which homeless, mentally ill adults were given access to independent housing, referred to as the housing first model. Typically it is the mental health condition and/or addiction of the homeless that are given priority, so this model is contrary to usual practice in the United States. Padgett showed that most participants in the study benefited materially and psychologically, which allowed her to argue that the experience of ontological security through housing can be extended to newly housed people with mental illnesses.

The connection between ontological security and the home raises questions of the extent to which ontological security is sought and can be achieved by the homeless. Kellett and Moore (2003) approached this issue through making a distinction between homelessness and homemaking. They showed that the notion of home can represent a goal and a route back into belonging in society and living an ordinary life, and contrasted this with the notion of homelessness as a situation of marginalisation and exclusion.

The Home and Ontological Insecurity

Another strand within the debate focuses on the home as a site that promotes ontological insecurity. Nettleton and Burrows (1998) made an important contribution to the debate by demonstrating that homeownership itself can be an insecure tenure. Writing at a time when homeownership rates in the United Kingdom had increased rapidly from 38 to 67% of households over an 18-year period, Nettleton and Burrows argued that this increase had also been accompanied by increased rates of mortgagee sales. A number of factors were implicated, including: the high costs of borrowing; the expansion of homeownership into groups at risk of unemployment; greater employment insecurity and increased rates of nonstandard work; an increase in unemployment and underemployment; and broader economic factors such as an economic downturn and restructuring. Just as successful homeownership may confer ontological security, instability in homeownership may create insecurity. Loss of a home may undermine identity, especially where homeownership is a marker of status, achievement, and adulthood. The difficulties that create problems in homeownership sustainability may therefore create the condition of insecurity for homeowners thus exposed.

The association of home with ontological security has also come into question from a number of writers who focus on the negative and darker side of home experiences. Just as home can be a haven, it can also be experienced as a place of brutality. For those who experience domestic violence or sexual abuse, the home offers little in the way of protection or contentment given that the home is the primary site where violence and abuse occur. The very fact that their homes are outside the surveillance of others offers the abuser free rein to operate. Similarly, the concept of home as a haven holds little resonance for those in weaker domestic power relationships (even when overt abuse does not occur), including children.

The home can offer little ontological security for those whose lives are home-centred in a negative or withdrawn way. For example, those unemployed who want to be engaged in work may come to experience home as a kind of prison rather than as a retreat or a haven. The same can apply to the ill or elderly who can feel trapped in their homes because of their physical or health condition. Imrie (2004), for example, showed how home, rather than being a haven and refuge, can be experienced as a place of confinement for disabled people, which can come to represent a loss of a former life, a lack of freedom, and deprivation. Imrie found that the interdependence of physical impairment and poor design meant that home could become a site of a loss of control and autonomy and intrusions on personal privacy. The reliance on others outside the home to assist with care also meant that the home was no longer perceived as a secure place, with diminished control over who had access.

This article has shown how the concept of ontological security has been taken up by writers interested in the meanings of home, and how homeownership, in particular, has been identified as a response to the contemporary problem of ontological insecurity – a condition where the sense of feeling 'at ease' and 'at home' has become increasingly tenuous and fragile. Various writers have argued that home as a source of ontological security can be maintained when certain conditions are met, including: when home is associated with permanence and constancy; when it is associated with routines, especially those of family life; when it is a site where people feel in control and free from outside surveillance; and when home provides a secure base from which people can construct their identities. There has been much debate as to whether ontological security can be attained in tenures other than homeownership, or in nonorthodox homes, such as caravan parks, and whether people with mental health issues or the homeless can attain ontological security in their patterns of life. A strong critical position suggests that homeownership itself can promote insecurity. The loss of a home due to an inability to continue mortgage payments can be calamitous both financially and emotionally. Similarly, the home can be a site of oppression and anything but a haven for those who, for various reasons, experience it as a confinement.

See also: Domicide; Experiencing Home; Illicit Drug Use and Homelessness; Meanings of Home; Meanings of Home for Older People; Mental Health and Homelessness; Philosophical Perspectives on Home; Policies to Address Homelessness: Housing First Approaches.

References

Dupuis A and Thorns D (1998) Home, home ownership and the search for ontological security. *Sociological Review* 46(1): 24–47.

Giddens A (1990) *The Consequences of Modernity*. Stanford, CA: Stanford University Press.

Hiscock R, Kearns A, Macintyre S, and Ellaway A (2001) Ontological security and psycho-social benefits from the home: Qualitative evidence on issues of tenure. *Housing, Theory and Society* 18(1): 50–66.

Imrie R (2004) Disability, embodiment and the meaning of home. *Housing Studies* 19(5): 745–763.

Kearns A, Hiscock R, Ellaway A, and Macintyre S (2000) 'Beyond four walls'. The psychosocial benefits of home: Evidence from West Central Scotland. *Housing Studies* 15(3): 387–410.

Kellett P and Moore J (2003) Routes to home: Homelessness and home-making in contrasting societies. *Habitat International* 27: 123–141.

Laing RD (1964) *The Divided Self: An Existential Study in Sanity and Madness*. Oxford, UK: Tavistock.

Marston G (2004) *Social Policy and Discourse Analysis: Policy Change in Public Housing*. Aldershot, UK: Ashgate.

Mee K (2007) 'I ain't been to heaven yet? Living here, this is heaven to me': Public housing and the making of home in inner Newcastle. *Housing, Theory and Society* 24(3): 207–228.

Nettleton S and Burrows R (1998) Mortgage debt, insecure home ownership and health: An exploratory analysis. *Sociology of Health and Illness* 20(5): 731–753.

Newton J (2008) Emotional attachment to home and security for permanent residents in caravan parks in Melbourne. *Journal of Sociology* 44(3): 219–232.

Padgett D (2007) There's no place like home: Ontological security among persons with serious mental illness in the United States. *Social Science & Medicine* 64: 1925–1936.

Saunders P (1989a) Space, urbanism and the created environment. In: Held D and Thompson J (eds.) *Social Theory of Modern Societies: Anthony Giddens and His Critics*. Cambridge, UK: Cambridge University Press.

Saunders P (1989b) The meaning of home in contemporary English culture. *Housing Studies* 4(3): 177–192.

Further Reading

Beck U (1992) *Risk Society: Towards a New Modernity*. London: Sage.

Path Dependency

B Bengtsson, Uppsala University, Uppsala, Sweden

© 2012 Elsevier Ltd. All rights reserved.

Glossary

Critical juncture A point in time when events take place from which the historical development continues in a direction which makes some alternatives easier to reach and others more difficult (or impossible) to reach at a later point.

Historical institutionalism A social science perspective that investigates the historical relation between previous events and the subsequent development of institutions and policy.

Efficiency mechanism A mechanism of path dependency based on the coordinating capacity of established institutions and the transactions costs of changing them.

Legitimacy mechanism A mechanism of path dependency based either on what political actors themselves come to see as legitimate or on their perceptions of what is seen as legitimate in society at large.

Political institution A set of rules, norms, and practices that regulate political action and interaction.

Path dependency A historical pattern where previous events set into motion self-reinforcing feedback mechanisms which considerably change the likelihood of subsequent events or outcomes.

Power mechanism A mechanism of path dependency based on the development of either political actors' own power or their perceptions of power relations in society at large.

Strong path dependency A historical pattern where contingent events set into motion historical processes with deterministic properties which make some, otherwise feasible, subsequent events or outcomes impossible.

Weak path dependency A historical pattern where events, which are more or less contingent, considerably changes the probability of subsequent alternative events or outcomes.

Welfare state retrenchment The dismantling or severe economic reduction of welfare state programmes, which typically meet with strong opposition from voters and vested interests.

Introduction

Path Dependency and Housing – General Conditions

The concept and perspective of path dependency has been given growing attention in the social sciences in the last decades. Path dependency is often seen as the basic causal pattern in historical versions of institutional theory. The general idea is that if, at a certain point in time, the historical development takes one direction instead of another, some, otherwise feasible, alternative paths will be closed – or at least difficult to reach – at a later point.

The general idea that history matters is certainly not new in housing studies. In particular the work by Peter Malpass on the history of British housing provision deserves to be mentioned here. However, explicit analyses in terms of path dependency have so far been rare. This is somewhat surprising; considering the specific conditions of housing provision, it should be particularly fruitful to analyse housing institutions and policy in those terms.

First, a well-known characteristic of housing provision is the longevity and physical sluggishness of the housing stock. Only a marginal percentage can be replaced by new production at a certain point in time, so political measures aimed at affecting new construction only have an impact on the urban structure and the supply of housing in the very long run. On the demand side the social importance of dwelling and the emotional, social, and cultural 'attachment costs' related to a household's transfer from one dwelling in one housing area to another have a stabilising effect. Social exclusion and norms of eligibility add to the continuity of the residential structure. These physical and social specificities of the housing market have institutional implications that may serve as obstacles to policy change.

Second, housing policy can be perceived as the state providing correctives to the housing market. Market contracts serve as the main mechanism for distributing housing, while state intervention has the form of correctives, defining the economic and institutional setting of those contracts. In a policy field based on market distribution the main institutions are those that define the rules of the game in that market, in housing crucially tenure forms and other types of regulations, including nonprofit organisations active in the market. Housing tenures help define the basic rights of possession and exchange that are fundamental to a capitalist economy, so political self-restraint may be expected, for example, avoiding to force major changes through without the support of a stable parliamentary majority.

Third, the fact that housing is ultimately distributed in the market may also in itself be a constraint to political change. For a new tenure form to be successful it is not enough that it is supported by politicians and voters; consumers must also be prepared to pay for it in the market, and producers to supply it.

These characteristics should make housing policy more path dependent than most other policy fields. Nevertheless applications have so far been scarce. The main exception is a recent Nordic project which compared the historical development of the housing regimes of Denmark, Sweden, Norway, Finland, and Iceland. In the following, this article is used to illustrate how a perspective of path dependence can be used in housing studies.

Path Dependency – the Strong and the Weak Version

Critics of path dependency often claim that the concept is rather empty and says nothing more than 'history matters'. To avoid this criticism some authors, like James Mahoney, claim that the concept should be defined rather strictly as something like 'historical sequences in which contingent events set into motion institutional patterns or event chains that have deterministic properties'. Such a strong definition, however, risks falling into another trap; since deterministic causation can seldom be claimed in the social sciences, the concept would be difficult to apply to analysis based on social action. A weaker definition would see path dependency as a historical pattern where one event, which is more or less contingent, considerably changes the probability of subsequent alternative events or outcomes. This weak concept of path dependency would transform the demarcation line between contingency and determinacy into a matter of degrees.

Would that mean that we are back to 'history matters'? The answer is yes, but that does not necessarily make the concept empty. In order to avoid this, path dependency in a social science context should be defined as an analytical perspective on history where a certain outcome can be traced back to a particular set of events on the basis of empirical observation and guided by some social theory. Path dependency would then be a particular form of analysis that focuses historical events and specifies in theoretical terms the elements that build up the path between those events. It assumes that history matters – but the empirical challenge is not to 'prove' this general assumption (which is probably always true) but to identify in what respect and via what type of mechanisms history matters in a certain context.

In an actor-based historical analysis the typical case of path dependency is where actors design institutions or make policy decisions at point (or points) A, which at a later point B, set the rules of the political game between the same or other actors. In retrospect, the historical development can be perceived as an ongoing and self-reinforcing chain of games between actors, institutional change, new games, new institutions, and so forth.

The mechanisms of path dependency that have been suggested in the literature may be summarised as efficiency, legitimacy, and power. This means that the (relatively) contingent events at point A would make some alternatives either more efficient, more legitimate, or more powerful at point B. The efficiency mechanism of path dependency has to do with the coordinating capacity of established institutions and the transaction costs of changing them. The legitimacy mechanism may influence either what political actors themselves see as legitimate or their perceptions of what is legitimate in society at large. Correspondingly the power mechanism may affect either actors' own power or their perceptions of power relations more generally. The power mechanism may also have an impact on which actors are allowed to take part in decision-making at point B.

The power mechanism can be fruitfully elaborated in relation to Steven Lukes' well-known faces of power. Earlier more contingent events at point A may at point B have an effect on either (1) decision-making: actors choose other alternatives due to what happened at point A; (2) agenda-setting: other alternatives come up on the political agenda due to what happened at point A; or (3) perceptions: other alternatives are conceivable to actors due to what happened at point A.

Tracing Path Dependency in Housing

Three central elements of actor-based path dependency analysis are (1) the event or events at point or points A, where one historical path is 'chosen' instead of another (the 'critical juncture'); (2) the decision-making process at point B, where the effects of the choice at point A become visible (the 'focus point'); and (3) the mechanism or mechanisms that explain the effects of the event at point A on the decision-making situation at point B. The logical way to identify these elements is to 'write history backwards' starting at point B, which would typically be an important and visible political decision-making process. If we find that some, otherwise plausible, alternatives were not chosen or even considered at this point, this would be an indication of where to find the previous point or points A. Comparing the situations at these two points should then give a clue to what type of mechanism has been at work between the two events.

Counterfactual analysis is an important element in a perspective of path dependency. What alternative development would have been possible at point B, if the event at point A had not occurred? The Nordic project included counterfactual analysis on two different levels. First, the individual links in the historical chains – the decision-making processes – were analysed making use of records of the political discourse and interaction in order to identify discarded alternatives. Second, the counterfactual analysis of the overall development of the housing regime in one country was carried out by using the development in the other countries as contrasting relief. When and why were alternative policies left aside, which might have led to a development closer to the housing regimes of the other countries? Did these alternatives at some point of time enter the political agenda or were they even perceived of? This combination of historical process tracing and counterfactual comparison proved to be a fruitful method to analyse path dependency in housing politics and policy.

Another methodological tool used in the Nordic comparison was a chronological model with four historical phases of housing provision: an 'establishment phase' with limited housing reforms in response to the early urbanisation; a 'construction phase' with comprehensive and institutionalised housing policies aimed at getting rid of housing shortage; a 'management phase' where the more urgent housing needs had been saturated; and a 'retrenchment phase' with diminishing state engagement in housing provision. This model was used to organise the material but, more importantly, it helped to identify structural challenges to the housing regimes in the transition from one phase to the next, which gives it some general validity for analysis of housing history. The same model was later used in a historical comparison between housing provision in four Nordic countries and the Baltic countries Estonia, Latvia, and Lithuania.

Why So Different? Five Nordic Housing Regimes

The point of departure for the Nordic project was the remarkable differences between the national systems of housing provision. Though housing policy in all the five countries has been 'social' in the meaning that an important goal has been to provide decent housing to households of lesser means, the institutional arrangements chosen to achieve this goal differ fundamentally.

In Denmark housing policy has been primarily directed towards rental housing, in particular in estates owned and managed by public housing associations, organised in small self-governed units where local tenants have a high degree of self-management, so-called resident democracy. In Sweden housing policy has also been implemented primarily by means of rental housing owned and managed by public housing companies, though, in contrast to their Danish counterparts, these companies are controlled by the local municipalities. Sweden also, together with Norway, has the largest share of cooperative housing in Europe. In Norway housing policy has been mainly based on individual and cooperative ownership, there are few professional landlords, and the social rental sector represents only a marginal percentage of the total stock. In Iceland too, owner-occupation has been used as a housing policy instrument, though in this case including strong elements of individual self-build. In Finland, finally, housing policy has not been directed at any particular form of tenure, and state support, combined with individual means-testing, has been given to both rented housing and owner-occupation. Swedish, Danish, and Norwegian housing policies have been described as 'universal' and directed towards all types of households and segments of the housing market. Finnish and Icelandic housing policies on the other hand are seen as 'selective' and oriented more directly towards households of lesser means and based to a large extent on individual means-testing.

The huge difference between the housing regimes of five countries that share a number of similarities in other respects – cultural, economic, and political – is truly a puzzle. We would rather expect some signs of convergence, in particular considering the collaboration and exchange of ideas that continuously take place between Nordic politicians, bureaucrats, and interest organisations. But the Nordic countries have retained their divergent housing regimes for at least 60 years by now.

What is the solution to the puzzle of 'why so different'? Very briefly, in the formative period of the Nordic housing regimes, between the turn of nineteenth century and World War II, different solutions – more or less contingent – were chosen in each country in order to deal with more or less specific housing problems that occurred at different points of time. When more comprehensive programmes of housing policy were introduced after the war, it was often seen as efficient (or even taken for granted) that the already existing, if still undeveloped, organisations and institutions should be utilised to implement the new programmes. With the massive production of new housing between 1950 and 1980, the respective national housing regimes were successively consolidated and institutionalised.

Housing provision in all Nordic countries has gone through the same historical phases of structural transformation due to industrialisation, wartime crises, mass construction, and subsequent market maturation and privatisation. Nevertheless, the differences have been remarkably persistent through the various challenges: the institutional changes that have taken place in each country have been incremental, and the new arrangements have retained distinct features of the preceding ones. This is true even when political actors have framed the reforms as 'system shifts'.

Counterfactual analysis gives further evidence of the strong path dependency. Not since 1946, at the time of the postwar housing reforms, has there been a plausible possibility in any of the five countries of 'importing' a housing regime similar to any of the other four. From that time the other Nordic regimes are still referred to in housing policy debates, but no serious import attempts have been made. Writing history backwards made it clear why apparently crucial housing policy reforms were so often seen as politically uncontroversial, except in details. It also helped explain why the occurring attempts to change fundamentally the housing regimes always have come up against strong resistance.

Analysing the processes in terms of the three mechanisms of efficiency, legitimacy, and power makes it possible to understand the basis of institutionalisation, and also the nature of the driving forces behind institutional change, as well as the obstacles to it. The analysis of the Nordic housing histories teaches us that the three mechanisms often work together and that it is not always easy to point out one of them as decisive. Hence, exploring further the relation between the mechanisms should be a fruitful way towards developing the theory of path dependency both in housing and more generally.

When it comes to the three Lukesian 'faces' of path dependency, the development over time is interesting. During the establishment phase, with its relatively *ad hoc* policy decisions and institutions, alternative solutions were often discussed explicitly. To some extent this was still done in the 'formative' decision-making after World War II, even though fewer alternatives were now conceived as feasible. When we move further into the construction phase, the form of path dependency changes from favouring one alternative over another towards limiting the political agenda, or even narrowing the perceptions of the decision-makers. This continues into the management phase, and even in the retrenchment phase; when Swedish and Danish nonsocialist governments go for 'system shifts', their proposals lean heavily on the existing institutions – and still they meet with dogged resistance.

This pattern implies that decision-making, agenda-setting, and perceptual path dependency may be used to construct a ladder or scale of institutionalisation, with 'not perceived' as the lowest level, via 'not on the agenda', 'on the agenda but decided against', 'decided in favour of', 'one and only alternative on the agenda' up to 'one and only alternative perceived'. The application of such a ladder should also be a fruitful contribution to theory development.

Path Dependency and Retrenchment – Other Studies of Housing Regimes

So far only a few studies have been published that claim to apply path dependency analysis on housing. Sometimes the term is used to indicate only a general perspective of 'history matters', where previous norms, institutions, or perceptions (or traces of them) have survived over long time. In contrast systematic analyses of critical junctures or discussions about the nature of different mechanisms of path dependency of the type attempted in the Nordic project are more seldom.

Walter Matznetter discusses social housing policy in Austria as an example of what Esping-Andersen defines as a conservative welfare state. He identifies the reconstruction after World War II as a window of opportunity for a unified housing policy. Instead 'the forces of tradition' – path dependency – led to a revitalisation of the selective social and housing policies from before the Austro-fascist takeover in 1934. While Matznetter, like the Nordic project, focuses on tenure and organisation, Julie Lawson in her comparison between limited profit housing in Vienna and Zurich highlights property rights, financial investment relations, and consumption patterns as path-dependent institutions.

Lévy-Vroelant et al. interpret the history of social housing in Austria, France, and the Netherlands 'through the combination of two complementary notions: path dependency and change'. However, their conclusions are mainly presented in terms of change: The population living in social housing and their social milieus have changed, and so have the standards, needs, and conceptions of good housing, as well as the relations between housing and the work force, the financing and the collective welfare or protection systems. Still some path dependency seems to be embedded in the legal and social construction of tenures and other institutions – as in the Nordic comparison. Path dependency perspectives on national housing regimes have also been used by Stuart Lowe (on Britain) and Mark Kleinman (on Britain, France and Germany).

One recurrent line of critique of path dependency analysis is that it has problems with explaining change. However, in the 'weak' and nondeterminist version, where actors are assumed to have some room of manoeuvre, change is not a paradox. Still continuity is what is normally expected, and observed change demands an explanation, once the development has set out on a certain path. The mechanisms that explained stability should also be in focus when discussing consequent change; when they lose their strength the path that was once self-reinforcing may turn into a *cul-de-sac*.

An interesting example of such 'path-dependent change' is the one exception to the relative stability of the Nordic housing regimes, that is, the decline in the 1970s of the Norwegian universal housing regime based on housing cooperatives. From that time the price control on cooperative dwellings was successively abolished due to strong market pressure from owner-occupation and the unregulated cooperative sector. This transformation, which finally undermined all possibilities for the cooperative tenure to serve as the mainstay of a universal housing regime, largely took place 'behind politicians' back' and was a consequence of inherent contradictions in the Norwegian housing regime.

In contrast, the Danish housing regime proved to be very resistant to the privatisation reforms launched in 2001 by a liberal-conservative government. Seven years after the introduction of a 'right to buy' as regards social rented dwellings such transactions had been carried out for only 40 dwellings. However, as Birgitta Gomez Nielsen shows, other policy reforms, less profiled than the sale of dwellings, have been slowly eroding the economic foundation of the social housing sector.

The tension between stability and change is the subject of the discourse on welfare state retrenchment (with Pierson as a leading name), which claims that dramatic reductions in welfare programmes are almost impossible to make due to opposition from citizens and strong client groups, that is, the legitimacy and power mechanisms of path dependency. Against this background Peter Kemp analyses how the ambition of the New Labour government to radically cut back and reform the housing benefit system in Britain ended up in rather modest amendments due to fear of electoral consequences and opposition from vested interests (mainly landlords who wanted to keep a system where benefits went directly into their bank accounts). Adrian Kay provides another example of why welfare state retrenchment should be examined in terms of individual programmes and not just welfare regimes as a whole. As an example of discrepancies in path dependency between levels he points out that while the share of households renting council home has diminished dramatically in the United Kingdom since the mid-1970s, central government has, consistently but in vain, tried to control rent setting in social housing but regularly comes up against institutionalised local policies for rent calculation.

The radical state budget cuts in Swedish housing policy in the 1990s, which met with surprisingly little resistance, confirm that change in housing provision is not impossible. Anders Lindbom explains this 'successful' retrenchment by the difficulty for citizens to observe financial cuts in a policy area that is so complex and nontransparent. Furthermore, the fact that housing policy is implemented via the market may facilitate financial cutbacks, because the political responsibility for the resulting rising housing costs is unclear. This finding, set against the results from the Nordic project, indicates that economic cutbacks may be easier to accomplish than institutional reform, for example, of tenure forms.

Applications on Other Levels

Path dependency perspectives in housing are not restricted to the national level. Housing policies are often implemented on the municipal level, and ultimately housing issues are very local. The constitutive sluggishness of urban structures and housing supply is first and foremost experienced by individuals and groups of residents. Nevertheless, applications of path dependency on micro levels are also scarce. An interesting exception is an investigation by Robertson et al. over 80 years of three neighbourhoods in the Scottish city of Stirling. The critical junctures identified here are the original planning of the estates, the introduction of the right to buy in the 1970s, and current plans to regenerate one neighbourhood. The relative social position of the estates, based on class and social attitudes, has not changed. The mechanism here is social identity, which of course could also be translated into efficiency, legitimacy, and power.

Another study of Scottish neighbourhood regeneration policy by Peter Matthews, based on critical discourse analysis of policy texts, reveals a 'mega discourse', where poor spatial communities have been continuously pathologised over the 40 years studied. This discourse has framed the policy options that have been discussed. Alternative perspectives have sometimes been launched, but never institutionalised. Here the main mechanism seems to be the discursive power of framing and social construction.

Bierre et al. analyse the path-dependent role of cultural norms and expectations from the 1930s and 1940s in today's low-cost housing in New Zealand. They conclude that while the socioeconomic and political contexts have changed, the institutions and ideas of the past linger and affect how today's policies are framed. For example, the ideas about morality and housing quality, that 'some were more deserving than others', which were expressed in early housing legislation are still common stereotypes.

The political and economic transition in Eastern Europe has often been discussed in terms of path dependency. To what extent can continuities from the old system be traced in the new institutions? Holt-Jensen and Pollock, who discuss housing policy in the Nordic and Baltic countries, see the decisions taken immediately after the collapse of the

Soviet Union, when state ownership and top-down management were discarded in the housing sector, as crucial to the following incremental and minor changes in the housing policy of the Baltic countries. In contrast Anneli Kährik, investigating the socio-spatial residential patterns in Tallinn and Tartu (Estonia), finds that even though transition to market economy had altered social stratification, the residential pattern in the late 1990s had considerable resemblance with the socialist structure. A vast majority of the population still resided in large high-rise housing estates from the Soviet period, and the socioeconomic residential status between these estates still largely reflected the old allocation principles. Thus, even after a complete breakdown of previous political institutions, the sluggishness of the physical urban structure and the housing market may in itself serve as a mechanism of path dependence.

Conclusions

Path dependency should be comparatively strong in housing provision, due to its social and physical specificities. Although recently some studies in the field have been framed in such terms, both on macro and micro levels, only a few of them (and in particular the Nordic comparison) explicitly identify and specify the nature of the critical junctures, or discuss what type of historical mechanisms have been at work. In most cases the concept is used primarily for saying that history matters.

Although the application of path dependency is mainly related to historical institutionalism, the crucial event at the critical juncture may also be ideas or policies. The mechanisms of efficiency, legitimacy, and power come in many forms, some of which are directly related to the social and physical characteristics of the sector, and it is not always easy to distinguish between them in empirical research. Weak path dependency does not rule out change, but far-reaching change still demands an explanation, so other dynamics must also be considered in the analysis.

Empirically the studies presented indicate that economic cutbacks may often be easier to accomplish than institutional reform, for example, of tenure forms.

See also: Comparative Housing Research; Housing and the State in Western Europe; Housing Policy: Agents and Regulators; Housing Policy Trends; Institutions for Housing Supply; Politics of Housing; Power; Social Housing Institutions in Europe; Tenure as an Institution; Welfare States and Housing.

Further Reading

Bengtsson B (2008) *Why So Different? Housing Regimes and Path Dependence in Five Nordic Countries*. Paper presented at the ENHR International Research Conference 'Shrinking Cities, Sprawling Suburbs, Changing Countrysides'. Dublin, 6–9 July 2008.

Bengtsson B (ed.), Annaniassen E, Jensen L, Ruonavaara H, and Sveinsson JR (2006) *Varför så olika? Nordisk bostadspolitik i jömförande historiskt ljus [Why So Different? Nordic Housing Policy in Comparative Historical Light]*. Malmö: Égalité.

Bierre S, Howden-Chapman P, Signal L, and Cunningham C (2007) Institutional challenges in addressing healthy low-cost housing for all: Learning from past policy. *Social Policy Journal of New Zealand* 30: 42–64.

Gomez Nielsen B (2010) Is breaking up still hard to do? Policy retrenchment and housing policy change in a path dependent context. *Housing, Theory and Society* 27.

Holt-Jensen A and Pollock E (eds.) (2009) *Urban Sustainability and Governance: New Challenges in Nordic-Baltic Housing Policies*. New York: Nova Science Publishers.

Kährik A (2006) *Socio-Spatial Residential Segregation in Post-Socialist Cities: The Case of Tallinn, Estonia*. Tartu: Dissertationes Geographicae Universitatis Tartuensis.

Kemp PE (2000) Housing benefit and welfare retrenchment in Britain. *Journal of Social Policy* 29: 263–279.

Kleinman M (1996) *Housing, Welfare and the State in Europe*. Cheltenham: Edward Elgar.

Lawson J (2010) Path dependency and emergent relations: explaining the different role of limited profit housing in the dynamic urban regimes of Vienna and Zurich. *Housing, Theory and Society* 27.

Lévy-Vroelant C, Reinprecht C, and Wassenberg F (2008) Learning from history: Changes and path dependency in the social housing sector in Austria, France and the Netherlands. In: Scanlon K and Whitehead C (eds.) *Social Housing in Europe II. A Review of Policies and Outcomes*. London: London School of Economics and Political Science.

Lindbom A (2001) Dismantling Swedish housing policy. *Governance* 14: 503–527.

Lowe S (2004) *Housing Policy Analysis. British Housing in Cultural and Comparative Context*. Basingstoke and New York: Palgrave MacMillan.

Lukes S (1974) *Power. A Radical View*. Basingstoke and London: MacMillan.

Mahoney J (2000) Path dependence in historical sociology. *Theory and Society* 29: 507–548.

Malpass P (2005) *Housing and the Welfare State. The Development of Housing Policy in Britain*. Basingstoke: Palgrave MacMillan.

Matthews P (2010) Mind the gap? The persistence of pathological discourses in urban regeneration policy. *Housing, Theory and Society* 27.

Matznetter W (2001) Social housing policy in a conservative welfare state: Austria as an example. *Urban Studies* 39: 265–282.

Pierson P (2004) *Politics in Time. History, Institutions and Social Analysis*. Princeton: Princeton University Press.

Robertson D, McIntosh I, and Smyth J (2010) Neighbourhood identity: The path dependency of class and place. *Housing, Theory and Society* 27.

Thelen K (1999) Historical institutionalism in comparative politics. *Annual Review of Political Science* 2: 369–404.

People and the Built Form

R Lawrence, University of Geneva, Carouge, Switzerland

© 2012 Elsevier Ltd. All rights reserved.

Glossary

Culture Refers to characteristics of human societies that involve the acquisition and transmission by nongenetic means (from one person to another, between human groups and societies, as well as over generations) of shared beliefs, customs, information, institutions, language, rules, symbols, technology, and values. Although culture was often interpreted by anthropologists to be a monolithic and static concept, today it increasingly designates a relativistic and pluralistic concept within and between human groups, societies, and nations.

Environment *The Oxford English Dictionary* defines environment as "the conditions under which any person or thing lives or is developed; the sum total of influences which modify and determine the development of life and character". Today the term human environment refers to not only those characteristics which people have constructed, modified, or perceived as components of human settlements but also interpersonal relations and social organisation which effect both physical and mental health and psychological well being. The environment of any living species is multidimensional and extremely complex.

Housing Refers to a physical structure that is meant to address basic human needs for shelter and security by providing protection against climatic conditions (excessive heat and cold) and unwanted intrusions from insects, rodents, and environmental nuisances such as noise that may be harmful for health and well being. Housing units can be reinterpreted in terms of not only their material components, but also according to the goals, priorities, and values of those who design and build, those who manage and maintain, and those who live in them.

Housing quality This is a complex concept because it is not an absolute or a static one. It is a relative concept, it is context dependent, and it varies over time. Housing quality has two interrelated sets of components: those physical, measurable components and the perceived meanings, values, and assessments of them. Hence it is necessary to account for the quantitative and qualitative dimensions. Not surprisingly, housing quality has been interpreted in many ways. This diversity reflects the rationale and objectives of those who conduct or sponsor research and policy formulation. For example, studies may be intended for the formulation and the implementation of government policies based on benchmarks or standards, or academic research that considers the relationship between objective measures and subjective assessments of them.

Identity This concept has also been interpreted as the qualities of sameness between an individual and others. The most common categories for comparisons are education, ethnicity, gender, nationality, place of residence, profession, and religion. Here identity refers to the common characteristics of individuals and groups in prescribed residential environments. An individual's housing environment, especially the social and cultural context of daily life, is a structured framework for the expression and transmission of personal and social identities.

People–environment studies Term that refers to a broad multidisciplinary field of theoretical and applied research stemming from a concern about the relations between people and their immediate surroundings. Contributions are from several disciplines and professions including anthropology, architecture, epidemiology, ergonomics, human ecology, environmental and social psychology, geography, sociology, and town/urban planning.

Residential environment Term that encompasses housing, neighbourhood, and community. This interpretation implies that the defining characteristics of residential environments include a composite set of natural and human-made components ranging from climate, topography, landscape, and vegetation to housing and building construction, infrastructure, community facilities, and services.

Introduction

Housing serves multiple functions some of which are explicit whereas others are implicit. First, a housing unit provides a physical structure that defines and delimits private domestic space of a household from communal and public space. Second, the envelope of the housing unit will act as a filter between the demarcated private spaces and their immediate surroundings and an efficient filter will sustain thermal, acoustic, and illumination levels within prescribed ranges of comfort that are culturally variable. Third, housing units are attributed meanings, that surpass those of a physical container and express the identity of residents. Fourth, housing has economic costs beyond the initial capital expenditure for their construction and including running costs and maintenance. Finally, houses not only have a monetary value but also nonmonetary values such as their ecological impact (the consumption of energy, construction, and land) as well as the generation of emissions and wastes. These multiple and complementary functions of housing have been studied from a wide range of technical, economic, and sociological perspectives.

People–environment studies is a term that refers to a broad multidisciplinary field of theoretical and applied research stemming from a concern about the relations between people and their immediate surroundings. In this article, the term immediate surroundings designates the internal and external conditions of housing units from the scale of rooms to residential neighbourhoods. During the 1960s, architects and psychologists played a crucial role working at the micro-scale of habitable rooms, buildings, and neighbourhoods. These contributions were labelled architectural psychology. In recent decades this term has largely been replaced by environmental psychology. However, this article shows that this term does not reflect the broad scope and diverse disciplinary concepts that have been applied especially to study housing and residential neighbourhoods. These contributions are from several disciplines and professions including anthropology, architecture, epidemiology, ergonomics, human ecology, environmental and social psychology, geography, sociology, and town/urban planning.

Definitions

Housing

Housing is a physical fabric that is meant to address basic human needs for shelter and security by providing protection against climatic conditions (excessive heat and cold) and unwanted intrusions from insects, rodents, and environmental nuisances such as noise that may be harmful for health and well being. Housing contains household activities and possessions. Housing can also be interpreted as a process by referring to the provision and maintenance of all kinds of residential buildings by either public authorities or private initiatives. The United Nations stresses that housing is a basic human right. It included the right to habitable and affordable shelter; legal security of tenure; and the availability of community services and infrastructure.

Dwelling

The physical unit of a house does not necessarily define the experience of home because other cultural, social, and psychological dimensions need to be considered. It is a process of cultivating one's personal place in the world by practices that reoccur daily.

Home

The terms house and home have different meanings in diverse languages. Home can refer to a house, a village (hometown), or a country (homeland). In contrast to common use in the English language these terms are not necessarily synonymous. It includes a symbolic association between an individual, her/his immediate surroundings, and the world. It implies an active relationship between a person and her/his physical and social environment.

Review of Research Findings

Housing units can be reinterpreted not only in terms of their material components, but also according to the goals, priorities, and values of those who design and build, those who manage and maintain, and those who live in them. Residential buildings and neighbourhoods should serve multiple functions and uses for an increasingly diverse population. However, requirements for visual and auditory privacy, or social contacts with neighbours, or gender differences in the use of collective and public spaces, or domestic practices for the preparation and eating of food may not be met in a large residential building or housing project with a standardised floor plan, kitchen equipment, and interior finishes. When these kinds of requirements prescribed by cultural conventions cannot be accommodated, then conflicts between the intended use of housing (by the architect, housing manager, or property owner) and the actual use of housing (by individuals, households, and specific population groups) can have several consequences. The possibilities offered or prohibited by the built form of housing to accommodate different kinds of household activities are largely related to the inherent/implicit or the structural/explicit adaptability of housing units. Certain ethnographic studies provide detailed information about why residents have made changes to housing. The reasons for changes extend beyond functional adjustments that are often made in order to accommodate new circumstances during the lifespan. Housing research shows that motives for change might include the wish to comply with new social trends (e.g., in house decorations) which indicate that the household adheres to a specific social group.

Statistics and household surveys in many countries show the increasing numbers of different types of households in specific urban neighbourhoods and large-scale housing estates. These households differ according to their ethnic origin, their nationality, their socio-professional status, and their culture, especially their domestic lifestyle. In-depth studies of the layout, furnishing, and use of housing units provide a large amount of information that contradicts generalisations that have often characterised the interpretation of housing by professional planners and policy makers.

The Architecture of Housing

The opportunity to construct housing offers two approaches for the analysis of people–environment studies. The first involves consulting the future residents (or their representatives) before or during the design and construction process. This approach can provide those responsible for the future housing project with point of view of the residents about different options for the physical fabric. It has been used to define behavioural criteria for the design of new housing units in a wide range of localities. The second approach involves the observation of a housing project during its use over an extended period of time. Repeated observations of occupied housing can enable those responsible for it to test assumptions about the interrelations between the residents and their domestic environment. Empirical studies of buildings in use are known as postoccupancy evaluations (POE). Often it has been argued that the findings of housing surveys can be reapplied in other localities but this kind of generalisation should be considered carefully. The first approach is proactive and relatively short compared with the second which involves in-depth empirical research.

A number of architectural research methods and design tools have been used to incorporate the needs of residents in housing design since the 1960s. These tools include:

1. Architectural checklists, standards, and specifications, usually descriptive texts, that present norms or regulations, sometimes linked to government housing loans or subsidies.
2. Design guidelines including principles, rules, or patterns presented often as texts and drawings (such as model floor plans).
3. Design games that present step-by-step decision making processes that lead to the selection of options between choices.

In these approaches aesthetic, functional, and ergonomic criteria are assessed in terms of client or user satisfaction sometimes in conjunction with cost/benefit analysis using monetary values.

Some research has considered the mismatch between the intended outcomes of housing designers and policy makers and the effective meaning and uses of residential environments and how the design and layout of housing units and urban neighbourhoods can enhance or impede social interaction between residents or prevent antisocial behaviour including criminal offences. There have been a small yet sustained number of contributions that have considered the health impacts of housing and residential environments on the health and well being of residents (see article Health and Housing).

It is increasingly recognised that the reciprocal relations between the design, meanings, and uses of housing units ought to be considered in terms of architectural, cultural, social, and psychological variables. This holistic and systemic framework ought to be applied bearing in mind the following principles. First, the specific characteristics of the location of housing including site orientation, microclimate, availability of construction materials, and the characteristics of the immediate surroundings. Second, these physical and material characteristics alone do not explain housing and domestic lifestyles; in addition social norms and conventions as well as personal preferences are transmitted in the layout, furnishing, and use of domestic space. Third, beyond economic and political factors that influence the availability and affordability of housing, an in-depth understanding of cultural, social, and psychological variables is necessary to analyse domestic processes including the cultivation of the private domestic domain, the residential biography of individuals and households, and residential satisfaction. Fourth, there is a nondeterministic dialectical relationship between people and the built form of housing owing to the influence of numerous implicit and explicit codes which act as mediators in dwelling processes.

Cultural Dimensions of Housing

Culture refers to characteristics of human societies that involve the acquisition and transmission by nongenetic means (from one person to another, between human groups and societies, as well as over generations) of shared beliefs, customs, information, institutions, language, rules, symbols, technology, and values. Although culture was often interpreted by anthropologists to be a monolithic and static concept, today it increasingly designates a relativistic and pluralistic concept within and between human groups, societies, and nations.

Housing cultures are complex and diverse but they are too often taken for granted. Housing, dwelling, and home are fundamental human constructs that are crucial components of human culture that partly define the condition and status of individuals and households in relation to others in their society. Cultures of domestic life explicitly concern the following three attributes: First, the artefacts and techniques of human groups (housing units, infrastructure, and services). This can be considered as the material culture of domestic life that may express and communicate cultural and social/group identities. The second attribute is the social organisation of human groups according to norms about kinship, household composition, and social relations. The residential environment expresses not only social conventions but also social differentiation by differences in architectural style, the size of housing units, and site location. It can also reinforce social exclusion instead of cohesion. The third attribute is the meanings attributed to the physical and nonmaterial components of human habitats and how these are expressed by language (e.g., a housing unit, a dwelling, a domicile, or home).

There are numerous theoretical and empirical studies that analyse the cultural conventions, rules, and values that are expressed in or attributed to the spatial layout, the furnishing and the use of housing units. These cultural dimensions of housing and everyday life are transmitted by the cultural predispositions of residents in the domicile. Ethnographies by cultural and social anthropologists and human ecologists in diverse countries confirm that although the internal organisation and use of housing units can be described according to orientation, climate, and the availability of construction materials, this description does not include the cultural meanings and values attributed to domestic space unless cultural dimensions are considered. These cultural dimensions are reflected in the preparation and consumption of food, the nomenclature of domestic space and household activities, customs about receiving family, friends, and neighbours, and rituals and religious practices for special occasions including birth, marriage, and death.

Other contributions in western countries show that several cultural variables ought to be considered if more than explicit and manifest functions of housing in urban areas are to be understood. Given the demographic diversity of contemporary urban societies in the larger capital cities of many countries, it is pertinent to identify which cultural variables influence the design, meaning, and uses of housing units in precise localities. Housing surveys have been completed in order to achieve this objective. They commonly rely on sociological survey methods which are applied to study a sample of the resident population. Other contributions have used the participant observation method in residential neighbourhoods, especially large-scale housing estates. In both cases follow-up studies have rarely been completed in order to identify constancy and change in the furnishing and use of housing units or in the meanings and lifestyles of the residents.

Social and Demographic Dimensions

People–environment studies focus on not only individuals but also social groups who comprise individuals that may share ideas, meanings, and values about housing and domestic life. A housing unit, specific rooms, and household objects can be attributed a number of functions and values which may be manifest and intentional, or latent and unintended. In general, manifest functions alone do not explain the furnishing, services, and appliances inside housing units. Many studies show how sociodemographic variables including age, gender, social class, household composition, and housing tenure can be related to the design, the meaning, and uses of housing units. For example, some studies show that the housing unit is a physical fabric that expresses social status and the identification of the residents with a social group. These values may be conservative and traditional, progressive and innovative, or a mixture of both. Some values may be expressed by residents in the decoration and use of some rooms whereas other rooms are quite different.

The preparation and eating of food is a common characteristic of housing in all societies, and the variability of how it is accommodated by domestic space provides an interesting case for the study of social and cultural diversity. A limited number of studies show that the domestic activities and routines in general, and those related to the preparation and eating of food in particular are prescribed by the significance of a specific meal in the total food system. Daily breakfast can have a different meaning to an evening meal, and this meal will not have the same significance if it is meant to celebrate a birthday of a household member. In principle, there are social and cultural codes that indicate what food is eaten, how it is embellished, when it is eaten, who is present, and where the meal is served.

Contributions in the field of people–environment studies show the interrelations between these dimensions of domestic life, how these dimensions are defined by different groups, and whether or not they evolve over time. Identity commonly refers to properties of individuality, the essential characteristics that make a person distinct from others (self-identity). Identity has also been interpreted as the qualities of sameness between an individual and others. The most common categories for comparisons are education, ethnicity, gender, place of residence, nationality, profession, and religion. In this article, identity refers to the common characteristics of individuals and groups in prescribed residential environments. An individual's housing environment, especially the social and cultural context of daily life, is a structured framework for the expression and transmission of personal and social identities.

Psychological Dimensions of Housing

Research shows that a housing unit and all its content is a medium for nonverbal communication between household members, family, friends, and strangers. Contributions by psychologists have confirmed that domestic space and household possessions have monetary and use values. In addition they become objects with psychological dimensions that express the self, because they convey information about the personal identity, group identity, and values of the resident. For example, domestic objects express private/personal and public/shared meanings and values because a housing unit is both a haven for withdrawal from the public realm of society and a stage for the expression of respect by members of the local community. Hence the concept of privacy can be interpreted not only in terms of the dialectical relations between spaces and activities inside the housing unit, but also in terms of individuality and communality. Studies show that residents prefer to have some personal control over the access that others have to them in their private domain by regulating the boundaries between the inside of the housing unit and the immediate environment.

Other contributions show that the design and furnishing of housing units is also related to past residential experience, known as the residential biography. Some of these contributions have adopted a phenomenological and developmental interpretation of housing conditions during the resident's life. These qualitative studies often use in-depth interviews with residents to decipher the meaning of housing and domestic life.

Cultivation is a multidimensional process in which implicit cognitive structures, individual and group practices, social rules and conventions, institutional structures, and human consciousness are purposely interrelated. The intentional use of space, time, and resources at any geographical scale implies that a part of the world is appropriated psychologically and physically. The term appropriation has etymological roots in the Latin word *appropriare*, which means 'to make one's own'. Cultivation processes may be conducted to express and communicate adherence to cultural traditions, or new social trends, or to express individualism rather than collectivism. Rituals, roles, and a wide range of conventional practices are commonly used during the construction of housing units, especially collective or communal housing types, in order to express and transmit cultural codes and social identities. The domestication of landscapes implies that geographical space, resources, and time are cultivated by people. Housing is one of the main forums for the application of cultivation during the life cycle.

Cultivation implies that researchers and practitioners should identify and understand the active, perhaps mobile, interrelations between individuals and their habitat. It can also account for the cognitive and symbolic interrelations between individuals, groups, and their past and present. Cultivation also stresses the importance of intentionality within the ongoing practices of domesticity, especially the way that individual, social, and cultural identities are expressed and communicated.

Acculturation involves the interaction between individuals and groups from different parent cultures. This collective process leads to the foundation of hybrid culture traits. Acculturation processes have been well illustrated in Australia during the first half of the nineteenth century and especially since the 1950s. One of the first outcomes of acculturation processes in the nineteenth century was the construction of vernacular houses with verandas and detached kitchens by migrants from England, Germany, and Scotland.

Critique of Contributions

When housing and the built environment are considered too narrowly then the interrelations between housing, health, and well being may not seem important. There is a growing recognition of a need for innovative approaches in the field of housing, as for many other problem-solving subjects. It is argued that current shortcomings are not simply the result of a lack of resources, or viable solutions, or political commitment. These shortcomings are above all the result of the narrow vision of academics, professionals, and policy makers who often isolate a variable and consider it in isolation from others. Interdisciplinary approaches can highlight the difference between a discipline-based interpretation of housing and an interdisciplinary one that combines the interpretation of biological, cultural, economic, political, psychological, and social factors in a new way following contributions in the field of people–environment studies.

The majority of housing research in the field of people–environment studies has presented the results of theoretical and empirical studies without explicitly addressing policy makers. There has been too little attention to methodological questions or the development of theory. This means that effective coordination between researchers and policy makers is still difficult to achieve. When collaboration is given a higher priority, then a number of interesting questions can be addressed. For example:

1. What is the pertinent unit of analysis? Typically, the researcher has defined the unit of analysis according to criteria that she/he consider appropriate. During the 1990s, this expert viewpoint was contested by those who have applied participatory approaches in which either the subjects or the end users of the research are involved in defining the terms of reference. For example, a key question today is 'What criteria does a human group consider to be crucial in order to establish, maintain, and transmit their identity from one generation to the next?' One response could be some specific components of the residential environment

that the group uses consciously to express and communicate their cultural and social identities.
2. How can housing researchers effectively combine quantitative and qualitative research methods in order to improve our understanding of the diversity of housing cultures? In general, housing research has been dominated by contributions that apply only one kind of method. For example, many empirical housing studies have considered the 'typical' household and house types. These contributions have ignored representative samples of different kinds of households and housing conditions. It is fair to claim that there has been too little concern for identifying and studying differences, even though households and housing conditions have become increasingly diverse. There is an urgent need to address diversity by using combinations of qualitative and quantitative research methods.
3. How can a temporal perspective be incorporated into housing research to overcome the static interpretation common to the majority of empirical studies? A temporal perspective is necessary in order to identify and explain change in the meaning and use of housing units, and household life. Although changes to the physical fabric of housing units may be few and infrequent, all residential processes may be interpreted as a means to communicate adherence to cultural traditions, or new societal trends, or individualism.
4. What are the strengths and limitations of case studies in housing research? A case study is meant to deal with the complexity of a contemporary subject (a single case). Each case is analysed in its naturally occurring setting using a combination of several research methods, data, and sources of information. A case study of collective housing, for example, can be defined either to consider only the intrinsic characteristics of the case, or to formulate generalisations that can be applied to other collective housing projects. How can generalisations from one case to another be made in terms of their typicality? How can one interpret results from different case studies? Do different results indicate subtle variations between cases, or is the methodology inappropriate in different localities? These questions have been debated, but there is no widely shared consensus about responses to them.
5. What methods are necessary to identify and interpret the logical, structural relations between cultural, social, and personal identities related to the design, meaning, and use of housing? In order to understand the cultural, social, and personal attributes of housing it is essential to analyse the meaning of specific components of housing units and the larger residential environment. It is also important to identify the mechanisms and the content of these different sets of attributes, to identify what they mean for different groups, and to understand whether they are specific to geographic locations and periods. This complex task raises fundamental issues that have not been well considered by mainstream contributions in the field of people–environment studies.

Conclusion

In the 1960s, housing issues were considered to be relatively simple because a rationalised, normative approach was commonly applied. It was assumed that investing resources in housing would generate innovative solutions by both the public and private sectors. Since then, and largely following the contributions in the field of people–environment studies, it has been increasingly recognised that there are no simple answers to housing issues because they are complex and multidimensional.

During the last four decades numerous academic and professional publications have shown that housing is attributed meanings not only in terms of the physical and material characteristics of residential buildings but also in relation to the socially derived conventions that vary between cultures, localities, and social groups. In addition, it has become more common to acknowledge how the characteristics of housing change over time. In principle, studies confirm that the meanings and uses of housing always involve an individual/personal relationship founded on processes of appropriation and personalisation. The contrast between the social and personal interpretations of housing has been illustrated by numerous studies.

The relations between residents and their housing, like housing design and housing policies, are multidimensional. Hence, these subjects are not structured within traditional disciplinary and professional boundaries. A broad integrated perspective recognises that architectural, behavioural, biological, cultural, economic, social, physical, and political factors need to be considered simultaneously if a comprehensive understanding of housing is to complement disciplinary and professional interpretations. Many contributions in the field of people–environment studies have helped to develop that understanding. Contributions from the multidisciplinary field of people–environment studies show that the spatial layout, the furnishing, and the use of housing units can be interpreted using cultural, social, and psychological concepts and methods. Moreover, the reciprocal relations between different variables can be studied using both a short-term and long-term perspective but this has not been common. This dual approach can relate the long-term architectural and social history of housing units in specific localities to the short-term processes of households in specific housing units. This innovative approach is a challenge for future contributions in this field.

See also: Cultural Analysis of Housing and Space; Domesticity; Ethnographies of Home and Homelessness; Health and Housing; Housing Need in the United Kingdom; Sustainable Housing Cultures.

Further Reading

Aragones J, Francescato G and Gärling T (eds.) (2002) *Residential Environments: Choice, Satisfaction and Behavior*. Westport, CT: Bergin and Garvey.

Altman I and Low S (eds.) (1992) *Place Attachment: Human Behavior and Environment*. New York: Plenum Press.

Altman I and Werner C (eds.) (1985) *Home Environments: Human Behavior and the Environment*. New York: Plenum Press.

Bechtel RB (1997) *Environment and Behavior: An Introduction*. Thousand Oaks, CA: Sage Publications.

Bechtel R and Churchman A (eds.) (2002) *Handbook of Environmental Psychology*. New York: John Wiley.

Clark W and Dieleman F (1996) *Households and Housing: Choice and Outcomes in the Housing Market*. New Brunswick NJ: Centre for Public Policy Research.

Després C and Piché D (eds.) (1995) *Housing Surveys: Advances in Theory and Methods*. Quebec: Laval University, CRAD.

Frank K and Ahrentzen S (eds.) (1989) *New Households, New Housing*. New York: Van Nostrand Reinhold.

Franklin B (1996) A new dimension to housing: context and meanings in the built form. *Environments by Design* 1: 163–184.

Kent S (ed.) (1990) *Domestic Architecture and the Use of Space: An Interdisciplinary Cross-Cultural Study*. Cambridge: Cambridge University Press.

Lawrence R (1987) *Housing, Dwellings and Home: Design Theory, Research and Practice*. Chichester: John Wiley.

Moore G and Marans R (eds.) (1997) *Advances in Environment, Behavior, and Design: Volume 4, Toward the Integration of Theory, Methods, Research, and Utilization*. New York: Plenum.

Newell PB (1998) A cross cultural comparison of privacy definitions and functions: A systems approach. *Journal of Environmental Psychology* 18: 357–371.

Sommerville P (1997) The social construction of home. *Journal of Architectural and Planning Research* 14: 226–239.

Stokols D and Altman I (eds.) (1987) *Handbook of Environmental Psychology, 2 Volumes*. New York: John Wiley.

Tognoli J (1987) Residential environments. In: Stokols D and Altman I (eds.) *Handbook of Environmental Psychology*, vol. 1, pp. 655–690. New York: John Wiley.

Relevant Website

www.iaps-association.org – International Association for People-Environment Studies (IAPS).

Peripheral Neighbourhoods

S Mugnano, University of Milano-Bicocca, Milan, Italy

© 2012 Elsevier Ltd. All rights reserved.

Glossary
Periphery Area of an urban settlement distant from the city centre.
Social periphery Area of the city characterised by a strong process of social exclusion of the residents.
Urbanisation Process of migration flow of population from rural to urban areas.

Definition

The notion of peripheral neighbourhood has drastically changed over the last century. The new millennium is starting by offering a new conceptualisation of the term. Generally speaking, periphery means the outside boundary or surface of something. In other words, it stresses the spatial dimension of a phenomenon and underlines that a place is distinctive with regard to a centre. In urban terms, the term periphery takes the shape of interrelation between the dichotomy on centre – periphery and the population social structure. The end of the last millennium was characterised by the shift from a vertical society to a horizontal one. As the Marxist approach has underlined, the industrial period was marked by a social class society where the population was divided into classes and the social structure was organised with an 'up' and a 'down'. The social economic transformation has moved toward a horizontal society where the population can be considered either included or excluded (in or out) from society. Talking of peripheral neighbourhoods means translating the notion of social exclusion into the spatial term, and looking at the condition of poverty from a social issue to an urban question. The cities of both developed and the developing world have their excluded population, and social inequality is generally associated with urban segregation (see article Residential Segregation). Being a peripheral neighbourhood has meant and still means different things depending on the geographical contents. So, while in the developing countries spatial segregation takes the name of a slum (see article Slums), in the United States of a ghetto (see article Ghetto), in European countries for a long time the phenomenon had overlapped with the term 'deprived areas' and neighbourhoods disadvantage (see article Neighbourhood Disadvantage).

The massive process of urbanisation has indeed produced enclaves in which poverty and deprivation have concentrated, and traditionally those zones were in the more decentralised part of the city. Recently, this axiom of rich centre versus poor periphery has partially changed. Some peripheral neighbourhoods have indeed become new strategic areas of the cities and places of social innovation (see article Gentrification and Neighbourhood Change). This work will look at the 'traditional' definition of peripheral neighbourhood and also at the new approach.

Mapping Poverty

Studies on the spatial concentration of impoverished individuals in particular areas has a somewhat long tradition. Spatial patterning of the residence of different class, income, employment, and ethnic groups has been a key theme of social investigation and analysis throughout its history. One of the first works studying the phenomenon of poverty in spatial dimension was carried out by Friedrich Engels as early as the 1840s. Engels was investigating the concentration of poverty, deprivation, and wealth in Manchester. Before the Industrial Revolution, the separation between residential and working-class areas was less developed. The massive migration toward the city and the appearance of a dangerous class in the city had produced a reaction of spatial distinction in the rich. Booth 1886 had carried out a long research fieldwork to draw a poverty map of London. By producing the first social cartography, even presented and awarded at the Universal Exposition in Paris in 1900, the author had attempted to relate the Londoners' socioeconomic profile with the different areas, zones, and neighbourhoods of the city. One of the most significant results of the work was the relationship between social class and urban space. For each neighbourhood/area, a dominant social feature could be identified. There were in fact some areas of the city with a higher concentration of lower class or poor people, and other parts of the city where the upper classes were located. For a long time geographers, sociologists, and anthropologists have questioned themselves how different social groups are distributed on a territory. In the sociological debate at the beginning of the last century, a major contribution was made by the neighbourhood studies promoted by the School of Chicago. Several scholars of the Chicago School (Park and Burgess, 1926) have argued that cities are generally formed by a mosaic of 'natural areas' which are distinctive from each other according to physical features and the lifestyle of their residents. More precisely, a natural area is a limited geographic area clearly characterised by physical and social homogeneity, which means having similar typologies of buildings, streets, arcades, structures of the public spaces, as well as the same sociodemographic and ethnic composition. Based on this assumption, a distinctive aspect was the development of ideal-type spatial organisation composed of three typologies of natural areas – centre, peripheral, and transitional zones. The question, then, is how an area of the city may be defined as central or peripheral. Is the distance from the focal point the basis of classification? Cities, villages, or any urban settlement have limited spaces and the different social groups are constantly competing with each other to gain the better positions. As in the animal world, where the strongest species are gaining the best places, according to the School of Chicago, stronger social groups are constantly trying to conquer the best places. In the urban hierarchy, the greater appeal of places depends on their geographical position, the ways of communications, and the value of the lands. For example, the morphology of a city, such as the presence of a river, the sea, or mountains, has certainly contributed to determining the focal point of the city. A few exceptions can be made, however. In the case where the natural element was also the local economy engine, the prestigious areas might have been located far away. This has happened in the development of the port towns (e.g., Barcelona, Marseilles, Genoa). The more productive the port was becoming, and the more intensified the trading, the more inadequate living conditions the neighbouring areas had (dust, smells, etc.) and therefore the less attractive they were for the better-off citizens. In the development of urban settlements, the presence of hills and valleys has also counted. Often the stronger social groups have occupied higher up areas of the cities, leaving the lower parts to the poor. Even in this case the exceptions prove the rule. La Paz, Bolivia, is one of the highest metropolises in the world (3800 m above sea level) and the local upper class and bourgeoisie have always lived in the lower part, a few hundred metres lower down, leaving the higher part to the poorer citizens.

Social Exclusion in a Spatial Perspective

An important step ahead in the debate on peripheral neighbourhood has been given by the notion of social exclusion. During the 1990s, there was a major shift in the discourse of disadvantage away from poverty and inequality to emphasis upon social exclusion. The issue cannot be reduced to a question of income. The emergence of the notion of social exclusion reflects an attempt to reconceptualise social disadvantage in the face of major economic and social transformation.

Although the morphological dimension might develop an urban hierarchy in a city, peripheral neighbours cannot be seen only as a spatial issue. Being far away from the city centre might not constitute being a marginalised and deprived area. There is in fact a distinction between being a geographical periphery and a social one. The current debate with the term social periphery identifies those areas/zones of the city with a high concentration of people living in social exclusion. Social peripheries are therefore areas where the condition of the residents goes beyond both the economic and social aspects of poverty to embrace lack of political rights and citizenship, and issues such as participation and social identity. Social peripheries are therefore areas characterised by people that are experiencing a process of social exclusion or social disqualification, which means labour market vulnerability, social welfare dependency, and lack of social networks. In addition, this process of social exclusion is reinforced by the special dimension (Forrest and Kearns, 1999). People living in a social periphery can face two different levels of social exclusion: on the one hand, the absence of individual or household resources, and on the other hand, a deficit in community facilities and services, such as remote shops, poor transport systems, and the absence of a supportive and cohesive social network. Indeed, concentrated poverty may have cumulative and qualitatively different effects on individuals, organisations, and infrastructures than less concentrated poverty. To some extent, the relationship between neighbourhood and cities follows the same pattern. Christaller (1933) has a hierarchical representation of the urban system where the rank of the city decreases according to the distance from the major economic and political centre. In the same way, the urban structure of European cities has had a centrally based development, and to some extent this is still maintained. The centre of the city hosts the major religious centres, the most important bureaucratic, civic or political activities, and the most famous cultural amenities. On the contrary, looking at social exclusion in a spatial dimension implies examining the complex chains of factors and constraints that people living in deprived neighbourhoods have in accessing urban opportunities In addition to social inequalities (gender, age, income, cultural resources, etc.), people living in a social periphery experience a different possibility/ability to negotiate space and time in everyday life in order to accomplish practices and maintain relations considered necessary for normal social participation. Living in places lacking in services forces people to move to other areas of the city to carry out their everyday activities (work, personal obligations, leisure, and institutional activities).

Therefore, it can be argued that the spatial pattern of deprivation can produce 'area effects' or better known as neighbourhood effect (see article Neighbourhood Effects: Approaches). This means that social periphery does not also mean deprived individuals but also poor assets of organisations and infrastructure. An additional aspect is that poor people are often trapped in their neighbourhoods. Households living in areas with limited resources are likely to be disproportionately dependent on local facilities – shops, schools, and health services. There is in fact a neighbourhood effect which we must take into account. Several researchers (Musterd and Murie, 2004) have stressed the fact that households in the same income, socioeconomic or poverty category, but with different local resources, perform differently. Where people live is therefore a key element in social exclusion.

Last but not least, there are methodological consequences. Looking at the deprived area from this multidimensional perspective implies developing appropriate research tools. Since the early 1980s in Europe, a new wave of area-based policies have been implemented to combat social exclusion. The necessity for each national government to detect the target areas has activated a rich methodological debate and different indices have been developed for measuring area deprivation. The British approach seems to have had the upper hand over the rest and leads the debate. Indeed, the first methodological attempt was the index of deprivation (DoE) developed in the United Kingdom in 1981. To stress the multidimensionality of the phenomenon, the index was composed of three main 'domains', economic activity, housing, and social groups. These three domains were indeed considered the indirect measures of deprivation. Several attempts have followed and different indexes have been produced; however, the most recent and commonly used is the index of multiple deprivation (IMD). Since 2000, this new index has broken new ground. The novelty of this research tool is the wide range of domains of deprivation covered. In specific terms, it includes income, employment, health and disability, education, skills and training, housing, and access to services. As may be noticed, it combines the two dimensions of social exclusion and spatial segregation.

Peripheral to the Centre? Peripheral Neighbourhoods Turning into Strategic Areas

However, the relationship between social exclusion and spatial segregation should not be misleading. Neighbourhoods which have high concentrations of disadvantaged households are highly differentiated in other ways. Contrary to expectations, deprived areas may be located in the inner city as well as on the edge of the city. Some may be older neighbourhoods and some are more modern peripheral estates. Not all deprived neighbourhoods have, for example, the same housing tenure. In other words, if we define peripheral neighbourhoods as those areas that are geographically on the edge of the city, we have to stress that those areas might not be deprived. On the other hand, if we define peripheral neighbourhood as a social periphery, this does not directly imply a geographical connotation. Historically most of the European cities have displayed a centre–periphery contrast. With some differences, both south and north European cities have a quiet significant presence of the upper- and middle-income classes in the inner city. For a long time, even despite a process of suburbanisation, several European cities have presented a broadly concentric social spatial structure with the rich in the centre and the social excluded population in the periphery. This common pattern has led to the interchange of the terms peripheral neighbourhood and deprived areas. Contemporary cities are presenting a new scenario where peripheral neighbourhoods might present different features. As recent debate has underlined, in European cities the spatial configuration might have varied, and three models can actually be identified, based on socio-spatial distribution. Until the 1970s, most of the cities were 'dramatic' in the sense that they were conceived as the arenas where social classes confronted each other and where demonstrations could develop in the full sense of the word. The spatial distribution between poor and rich was easily organised. This phase has been followed by a new social spatial configuration that Donzeot and Jaillet (1997) have called 'topologic city'. According to the authors the difference and confrontation between social classes has faded away. The gated community (see articles Gated Communities: Developed Countries; Gated Communities: Global South), on the one hand, and the ghettos, on the other hand, have produced a loss of interaction between different social classes and each social group is confined in its own place. Are the European cities so well defined? In reality the peripheries on most of the European cities are undergoing a process of transformation. Each urban context tends to develop its own unique pattern reflecting such aspects as the geography of the city and its history and culture. The present spatial inequalities are often the direct consequences of past political, economic, and social practices. In the process of deindustrialisation, substantial social and spatial changes have occurred in European cities. After the initial postwar rebuilding (1945–70), European cities experienced a long period of socioeconomic expansions, and the process of urbanisation was accompanied by an urban growth. In most of the European cities, in this period several geographically peripheral neighbourhoods were built. Since then, many European cities have experienced a radical restructuring of their economic base: traditional industries have declined or vanished from the urban scene while the services related to the creative and knowledge-intensive sector have grown. The process of deindustrialisation has particularly invested the edge of the cities. Therefore, the notion of peripheral neighbourhood has modified. While in the Fordist period, peripheral neighbourhoods were often related to a spatial dimension and usually connected to a negative perception such as stigmatisation and a form of total dependency regarding the city centre. In the peripheral neighbourhood of the postindustrial era, the spatial dimension has not completely disappeared but has slightly changed. The periphery is no longer exclusively determined by the spatial context but, as mentioned above, is related to its 'social' dimension. In addition, the peripheries of the cities are not a uniform and compact unit, but can vary drastically. Indeed, the peripheral neighbourhoods are becoming the new strategic areas of the city, hosting management centres of offices and services, large exhibition, and cultural and entertainment centres. Often the transformation of the peripheries has been marked by buildings with a high symbolic and evocative content with the aim of pushing away subjection to the centre of the city. The new competition process within the cities has restructured their spatial arrangement and equipped them with new infrastructure and amenities. Some peripheral neighbourhoods are therefore becoming places where private investors in partnership with the local authorities are working jointly to create a new image for the city.

Conclusion

The term peripheral neighbourhood changes depending on the perspectives of analysis. Taking in fact a sociological approach to the term, stress is placed particularly on the social segregation and social exclusion of households. On the contrary, in the case in which distance from the centre is used as a term for analysis, it is important to shift from a compact and uniform definition, moving towards an analysis of the different direction that the peripheries of the city are experiencing.

The axiom rich centre versus poor periphery has faded and most contemporary cities are experiencing a particularly jeopardising form of spatial segregation.

See also: Gated Communities: Developed Countries; Gated Communities: Global South; Gentrification and Neighbourhood Change; Ghetto; Neighbourhood Disadvantage; Neighbourhood Effects: Approaches; Residential Segregation; Slums.

References

Christaller W (1933) *Die zentralen Orten in Süddeutsch-Land*. Jena: Gustav Fischer.
Donzeot J and Jaillet MC (1997) *Deprived urban areas, summary report of the pilot study*. Brussels: North Atlantic Treaty Organisation, Committee on the Challenges of Modern Society, Report No. 215.
Forrest R and Kearns A (1999) *Joined up Places? Social Cohesion and Neighbourhood Regeneration*. York, UK: Joseph Rowntree Foundation.
Musterd J and Murie A (2004) Social exclusion and opportunity structures in European cities and neighbourhoods. *Urban Studies* 41(8): 1441–1459.
Park R and Burgess EW (1926) *The Urban Community*. Chicago, IL: University of Chicago Press.

Further Reading

Andersen HS (2003) *Urban Sores: On the Interaction between Segregation, Urban Decay and Deprived Neighbourhoods*. Aldershot, UK: Ashgate Urban and Regional Planning and Development.
Atkinson R and Kintrea K (2001) Disentangling area effects: Evidence from deprived and non-deprived neighbourhoods. *Urban Studies* 38: 2277–2298.
Engels F (1845) *Die Lage der arbeitenden Klasse in England*. United Kingdom: Stratford Books.
Kazepov Y (2005) *City of Europe*. Oxford, UK: Blackwell Publishing.
Lee P (1999) Where are the socially excluded? Continuing debates in the identification of poor neighbourhoods. *Regional Studies* 33: 483–486.
Touraine A (1991) Faceà l'exclusion. *Esprit* 169: 7–13.

Philosophical Perspectives on Home

K Jacobson, University of Maine, Orono, ME, USA

© 2012 Elsevier Ltd. All rights reserved.

Glossary

Phenomenology A philosophical method that describes the form of our experiences. The phenomenological method insists that human situations and experiences must be understood on the basis of what it is like for a person to live the situation or experience. Thus, phenomenology describes experiences as they appear to the first-person perspective rather than the way they appear to the third-person perspective of the scientific observer.

Polis An ancient Greek word commonly translated into English as 'city-state'. It is the root of our words 'politics', 'political', and 'polity'. To the modern ear, the translation 'city-state' may not capture fully enough the significance and character of the polis. The polis in ancient Greece was not merely a location or a population; it was, rather, a dynamic community of people united in the pursuit of their common good. Living in a polis – being political – was an active, dialogic practice in which persons came together to discuss the character and means of securing a good life. Aristotle argues that it is only in a polis that humans can adequately fulfill their nature as rational animals – that is, as beings who question what is good and bad, what is just and unjust, and what is, in other words, the right way to live; for it is only in the polis that there will be enough (but not too many) people to supply a healthy diversity of thought and a space for dialogue to stimulate such considerations. Insofar as the polis allows us the place to fulfill our human nature, it is, then, our highest good.

Ancient Conceptions of Home

The Jewish Bible (or Tanakh) contains many stories that suggest that the need to make a home is definitive of the human condition. Adam and Eve, originally given a place of their own in which they experience no need, are banished from this condition and must forever work to secure a home for themselves through their own efforts. In the story of Moses leading the Israelites, we see an entire people on the move to find a place where they can work on settling themselves. These stories emphasise the importance and difficulty that characterise our search for home. The Homeric epics are also stories of home. The *Iliad* tells the story of the Achaeans coming together as a nation to lay siege to Troy on the grounds that the Trojan Paris stole Helen from his host Menelaus, violating the principles of home and hospitality. The *Odyssey* in turn tells the tale of Odysseus's efforts to return to his own home from this siege, while his wife, Penelope, preserves the integrity of his home during his long absence. These stories emphasise the ways in which our homes establish our participation in human community – both family and nation – and the conflicts and responsibilities that emerge within and between such communities. The themes of these ancient stories are given philosophical expression in the writings of Aristotle.

Aristotle argues that natural things have a place where they belong and to which they will tend. For example, the rock's nature as full of earth is to tend towards the earth, downward with respect to the sky. Humans also have their natural place. We make our homes with our families in the *oikos* – the household. We begin, Aristotle argues, in the situation of an immediate family. Although the family is the necessary condition for our being in the first place, it is not, Aristotle argues, a sufficient sphere in which to live if we are to fulfil our proper human nature, because we are by nature *political*. Our proper place is in a world characterised by reflectivity and true choice, and thus is a place open to significant diversity and shaped by discourse and debate about matters of value and justice. In the face of our need to collectively determine and shape how we live, and to do so on grounds that are and will continue to be open, we experience the power of *making* a home for ourselves. We *develop* a home in and through the polis.

Socrates makes a similar point regarding the home-making character of human beings and particularly of their laws in the *Crito*. Faced with the option of escaping his sentence to death, Socrates chooses to abide by the laws that have brought him to this position. He argues that though the laws of his city were the ones that were leading him to his death, they were the same laws that made possible the way of being, that *is Socrates*. These laws shaped him; they were his home. In making this decision to abide by the laws, Socrates rejects motivations that arise out of merely personal concerns – such as wanting to protect one's own life or one's private family. Instead, Socrates is acknowledging that what he is – even as an "individual" – owes itself to something beyond this immediate personal realm – namely, to the city and its laws. He exists by means of the foundation provided by his political home. He is inherently a political being, not simply a private or familial one.

These philosophical views, expressed sometime after 400 BC, reflect a view that was significant in shaping Greek political culture in the preceding centuries. In his funeral oration in honour of those who died in the first year of the Peloponnesian War, the Athenian Pericles similarly identifies the source of what makes us who we are not in our private actions or our familial traditions, but rather in our political homeland. Each person is better described as a member of this homeland, as a citizen, rather than as a 'single' person or as an 'individual'. The strength or weakness of a person comes not from himself or herself, but rather from the strength or weakness of the homeland, and the homeland dies or thrives on the basis of the people that *it* makes possible and that in turn continue to contribute to shaping and carrying on this homeland. This patriotic nationalism was in fact coupled in Athenian politics with a focused political effort to cripple the powers of familial dynasties and to bring people to transfer their filial piety to their polis instead. This attempt to establish the polity above the family was even more pronounced in Sparta.

During the seventh century BC, Lycurgus made revolutionary changes to the governing of Sparta that in fact shifted the locus of human significance from the family to the state. Under Lycurgus's persuasion, the Spartans gave up their once privately held lands and possessions to the state, and these were then redistributed among the people by the state in such a way as to encourage equality among the people. Perhaps most stripping to the family's power over itself, authority over one's children no longer belonged to the family proper, but was given over to the citizenry. Lycurgus also disrupted the practices central to leading a private family life by providing and requiring common meals for the Spartans. Similar practices are discussed in book V of Plato's *Republic*. There Socrates and his interlocutors recognise that we are invested in what belongs to us, and that our care, when it comes down to making choices of how one's energy and resources will be expended, we will be directed towards what is our own before all else. The discussion suggests that the family may in fact get in the way of our fulfilment by maintaining in our lives unreflective emotions, favouritisms, and traditions that keep us from engaging with one another on the basis of reason and fair and open dialogue.

The political realm, unlike the private household, is that in which we distinguish ourselves as self-creating beings rather than as beings who follow in the inertial flow of what has been given to us from without, from the passively received, unquestioned realm of our heritage. Yet, this realm can also problematically overlook the importance of our familial traditions and the way in which they allow us implicitly to belong to something.

In Sophocles' *Antigone*, Antigone acknowledges the claim of the particular, of the private. We *do* live as particular people around particular hearths, the play reminds us, and, though the universality of law can serve to liberate us from the 'traps' of this particularity, this very universality can also fail *to see us*. Antigone's actions attempted to address a particular person in his particular relationship to her. In doing so, she reminds us of the family's importance as providing that realm in which we count in a particular way, in which we specifically belong here and have a unique and irreplaceable presence.

The Medieval Christian Conception of Home

In the New Testament and in many writings of the Middle Ages, we see a shift occurring around the issue of where human beings can find their proper home. As in the texts of Ancient Greece, there remains a sense that there *is* a home for us, but this home cannot be found here on earth during our own lifetime. Instead, the story of the birth, death, and incarnation of Jesus tells of a kingdom that is beyond this contingent, finite world: the eternal kingdom of God. It is to this eternal world that we properly belong and to which we can gain admittance if only we turn away from this present world as our ultimate home and convert ourselves to the one beyond. The way to our true home is through Jesus; we must take up his word and leave behind our own flesh and blood fathers (and mothers), and their finite laws and customs. In book IX of his *Confessions*, St. Augustine maintains that our proper place of rest is in the house of the Lord – a home that we cannot enter by ship, or chariots, or feet; it demands that we move towards it in a way that does not follow the motions or logic of this earthly world. Yet, we must somehow move towards it while within our state of being here. We must attempt to breathe in the air of Lord, while yet living in what Augustine describes as our 'house of grass' – a house of ongoing changes and impermanence that does not easily allow us to find that eternal, unchanging air to breathe. Christianity asks us to find our home in a place that, while ultimately our own, cannot be found in the immediacy of our lives. It is a deferral of our proper place to sometime and someplace beyond what we ourselves can secure for ourselves; it demands that we recognise that home is not something we can supply on our own, but rather owes itself to something beyond our personal or even our familial or political powers.

Modernity and Home: Locke and Marx

Locke focuses our attention on how we can secure a place for ourselves on this earth. In his *Second Treatise of*

Government, Locke argues that it is our responsibility and our prerogative to take the common world we encounter and to make it our own through our efforts. We make our world our own – proper to us, our property – through investing ourselves into the world. Locke argues, then, that our place on earth – our home – arises through our own efforts, and, not only this but also that these efforts secure us the *right* to call this our own and to protect it against the claims of others.

Locke's arguments regarding the nature of what belongs to us, how it comes to belong to us, and the rights surrounding this belonging proved to be massively influential in the shaping of the political structuring of much of the modern Western world. In both the Declaration of Independence of the American Revolution and in the Declaration of the Rights of Man of the French Revolution, we find a conception of the human being as an individual with rights to the property he has made his own. This conception of the appropriate way for humans – understood as liberal individual persons – to make their home was also the source of an aggressive colonialism. Locke's position offered an implicit support for the imperial practice that led to the seizing of North American lands by European people on the grounds that the native inhabitants of this land had never developed that land, and, therefore, did not have the right to lay proper claim to it. Because the natives' ways of engaging with the land showed little to no signs of 'improving' the land by marking it with visible signs of their labour, the European colonisation of this land was not, on Locke's model, a *taking away* of land that belonged first to the native inhabitants, but rather a laying claim to land that was lying in a state of waste. The natives, according to Locke's argument, had not yet made a home of this land through 'folding their labour into it'.

In his analysis of capitalism, Marx uses this same notion of investing ourselves in the products of our labour to show precisely how modern labour practices produce a situation of alienation rather than a situation of being at home in the world. Modern capitalism produces a situation in which individuals must sell their labour to be invested in the manufacture of products that are not their own. Marx argues that selling our labour in this way alienates us not only from the product of our labour and from our labour itself, but from our own bodies, other people, and nature as well. The wage labourers' work not only does not establish for themselves a place or belongings of their own and for which they possesses rights, but it also alienates them from themselves. They not only fail to make a home for themselves through their work but also are forced to live in such a way that their very potentiality for making themselves at home in the world becomes damaged. Whereas labour can be our way of making the world – our bodies, nature, our social environment – our own, in the modern capitalist setting, this resource for 'homemaking' has in fact become a source of alienation, of not-being-at-home.

Home in Contemporary Philosophy

Perhaps more than any other thinker in the history of Western philosophy, the phenomenological philosopher Martin Heidegger has taken up the issue of home as constitutive for understanding human existence. Heidegger argues that we are beings who *are* insofar as we dwell, that is, insofar as we are making a place for ourselves. In *Being and Time*, Heidegger describes us as 'being-in-the-world'. In describing us in this way, Heidegger indicates that we are always existing 'over there' in that to which we are attending. We are beings who *are* insofar as we are engaged with what, on the surface of it, may seem to be 'other than' us. We are 'in' the world, not as water is in a glass, but as beings who are thoroughly integrated with it in a relationship from which we could never be severed; the world, similarly, is only *as* being always already wrapped up with us. As being-in-the-world, we exist as a network of involvements and can never be reduced to a radically individual or solipsistic subject. We are always there in the world, or, said otherwise, always 'at home' in the world.

Yet, in spite of always being 'at home' in the world, we do not simply have our nature or situation settled for us. We are unlike a bird (or any other nonhuman animal), whose habitat and way of being are naturally set for it. In contrast to the bird, we are always involved in *making* ourselves what we are and in *making* ourselves at home in this world. In *Being and Time*, Heidegger describes the existential tension that arises from our nature as beings who must make ourselves a home. We live not only with the recognition (implicit or explicit) of our need to establish our daily affairs and actions for ourselves, but also with the deeper (typically only implicit) sense that the very source of giving these particular affairs and actions meanings and worth rests in us in the first place. We make ourselves a home in the deep sense that without us there is no home to be had. Because the meaningfulness of our world is not pregiven, in making a home for ourselves, we are also making a home for meaningfulness as such. Heidegger thus argues that our way of being is that of dwelling by 'safeguarding'. How we make a home – how we build – is thus always a matter of accommodating – more or less successfully, as the case may be – the fragile meaningfulness of our world. An act of building is, thus, not merely the objective raising of a physical structure, and is not merely important in how it satisfies instrumental needs but is more deeply existentially reflective of our way of being concerned with our being.

Ultimately, this recognition leads us to see that while we are always making ourselves at home in the world, we are never at home in an absolute sense, and this is true regardless of how diligent and successful we are at making ourselves at home. This project of making ourselves at home is, in other words, never finished, never gets us any closer to having secured a habitat for ourselves. While this structure of our way of being is what allows us to develop meaning, it is also the structure that means we are forever without a fixed essence. Because we can rely on no settled identity nor even a settled, absolute, given world, we live with a fundamental anxiety. This anxiety is the recognition of our way of being as being-in-the-world – that is, of our responsibility, so to speak, for the world as such and for ourselves. Though we typically try to evade this anxiety by living simply as 'they do', as 'one of them', conforming to familiar ways of inhabiting our world, there is ultimately no escaping this anxiety, just as there is no escaping the fact that we are beings who are always making ourselves at home and always such that we are never completely at home. We are forever becoming at home.

Heidegger's phenomenological explorations of the nature of home have been the inspiration for much contemporary work. We can see a parallel, for example, between Heidegger's recognition of the ways in which we are drawn to act simply as 'they do' and the work of artist, architect, and theorist Friedensreich Hundertwasser, who published many manifestos that criticised repressive and ultimately inhuman approaches to modern housing. Hundertwasser argues that current styles of building – especially track homes, massive apartment buildings, and standardised construction in general – deplete the expressive possibilities of the house. He argues that the house is our second skin – the outward expression of who we are – and that in modern approaches to building, this skin becomes standardised. We take on the attitude of being like any and every other person, like no specific person: we live, as Heidegger says, as 'one of them'. Hundertwasser saw this standardisation in excessive concerns with cleanliness and uniformity, and, as a counter to this, he championed the presence of moulds and other natural growths as a way to let go of the hypercontrol over the pristine and regular appearance of the structures in which we live and work. Hundertwasser actively attempted to break up people's tendency to 'move along as usual' through his use of non-right-angled architecture, and in arguing that tenants should have the right to alter the exterior face of their apartment. His goal was to get people to engage with their surroundings rather than simply to glide over them. His manipulations of architecture were rooted in his conviction that the shape of the structures in which we live are not incidental to how we exist. At the core, these structures are an embodiment of our way of living, and they in turn have a reflective shaping power over how we move about and express ourselves.

In his book *Poetics of Space*, French phenomenologist Gaston Bachelard argues that the ultimate importance of home (in its proper sense as a place of comfort, rest, and security) offers us a place where we are free to daydream. Home removes us from the demands of the external world, and particularly from the demands of approaching things objectively, enabling our ability to go beyond fixed ways of communicating, and to stretch the way in which we see. A home, then, is not merely a physical structure in which we spend significant bouts of time and that we call our own. Rather, home is that underlying existential structure that gives us our first orientation to the world; that gives us a certain refuge from what is beyond us (and thus allows us space for recuperating as well as daydreaming); and that provides a foundation from which we can venture once again into this beyond.

While home reflects back to us, whether explicitly or implicitly, what is our own, home cannot have this function without engaging with what is other or alien to us. Bachelard brings out the essential character of what is other in shaping the character of home by emphasising that the home cannot be protective and sheltering if there is nothing from which to protect or shelter us. Heidegger's reflections on Friedrich Hölderlin's poem 'Homecoming' similarly make the point that we cannot see what is ours or fully embrace it without having gone away from it and having been challenged by what is other than us. In their cross-cultural study of the ways home function in human experience, Mary Gauvain and Irwin Altman note that there are varying ways in which different people and different cultures have their homes, but they too point to a core element that seems to underlie these diverse determinacies – namely, the regulation of what is one's own and what is *other* to us. Home is, then, the experience of interpersonal *exchange*, where 'exchange' is understood as a necessary mediation with others in which we work to establish who we are with and through other people, with and through what is other to us. This conclusion drives Jacques Derrida's argument in *Of Hospitality*. Derrida argues that we can only become ourselves by opening ourselves to other people. There is a tension inherent to the experience of welcoming a guest into our homes. We want to accommodate the others, to give them what is proper to them. There is something inhospitable about imposing our way of living, our rules, on our guest; we should open ourselves to the ways that the guest desires and requires. Yet, a complete subservience to the guest's ways fails to provide for the guest *our* home. The tension, then, is the negotiation or exchange of ourselves with the other. It is in this exchange that we in fact learn not only who the guest is but also who we are. The guest, in other words, makes it possible for us to have *our* home in the first place. Derrida's argument carries a significant political implication. It is only through foreign exchange that we have a home and a homeland to begin with. We require the other to be self-same.

See also: Anthropological Perspectives on Home; Domicide; Emotions at Home; Ethnographies of Home and Homelessness; Experiencing Home; Feminist Perspectives on Home; Meanings of Home; Ontological Security; Political Ideologies; Politics of Housing; Rights, Citzenship, and Shelter; Social History; Social Justice; Social Movements and Housing; Social Theory and Housing.

Further Reading

Bachelard G (1964) *The Poetics of Space*, Jolas M (trans.). Boston, MA: Beacon Press. [Bachelard G (1958) *La poétique de l'espace*. Paris: Presses Universitaires de France.]

Casey ES (1993) *Getting Back into Place: Toward a Renewed Understanding of the Place-World*. Bloomington, IN; Indianapolis, IN: Indiana University Press.

Derrida J (2000) *Of Hospitality: Anne Doufourmantelle Invites Jacques Derrida to Respond*, Bowlby R (trans.). Stanford, CA: Stanford University Press. [Derrida J (1997) *De l'hospitalité: Anne Dufourmantelle invite Jacques Dérrida à répondre*. Paris: Calmann-Lévy.]

Gauvain M and Altman I (1982) A cross-cultural analysis of homes. *Architecture and Behaviour* 2: 27–46.

Heidegger M (1971) Building dwelling thinking. In: Hofstadter A (ed.) *Poetry, Language, Thought,* Hofstadter A (trans.), pp. 143–159. New York: Perennial Library.

Hundertwasser F (1997) *Hundertwasser Architecture: For a More Humane Architecture in Harmony with Nature*. Köln: Benedikt Taschen Verlag.

Jacobson K (2009) A developed nature: A phenomenological account of the experience of home. *Continental Philosophy Review* 42: 355–373.

Porteous DJ and Smith SE (2001) *Domicide: The Global Destruction of Home*. Montreal, QC: McGill-Queen's University Press.

Steinbock AJ (1995) *Home and Beyond: Generative Phenomenology After Husserl*. Evanston, IL: Northwestern University Press.

Place Attachment

BB Brown, I Altman, and CM Werner, University of Utah, Salt Lake City, UT, USA

© 2012 Elsevier Ltd. All rights reserved.

Glossary

Place attachment Positive bonds developed from behavioural, cognitive, and affective ties between individuals or groups and multiple levels of their sociophysical environment.

Place dependence How well a place satisfies needs relative to other alternatives.

Place identity Clusters of positive and negative cognitions or beliefs about a wide variety of places that help define self-identity.

Satisfaction with place The psychological state achieved when a place fulfils some needs, which does not necessarily require a positive bond to place.

Sense of place Place meanings, attachment, and satisfaction that derive from social construction as well as place properties.

Territoriality Perception that specific places or objects are owned by the person or group, with greater territoriality for psychologically central places of long-term occupancy.

Topophilia Vivid and concrete personal experiences of affective bonds with places, from fleeting to enduring.

Defining Place Attachment

Place attachments, first described in detail in a 1992 edited volume by Altman and Low, involve affective bonds to places across multiple geographic scales, with a variety of temporal qualities and social actors and processes contributing to the bonds. In that volume, after reviewing past conceptualisations of place attachment, Brown and Perkins concluded that attachments typically involve positively experienced bonds that individuals and groups form with sociophysical environments, which grow from behavioural, cognitive, and affective ties. Although people experience place attachments in many settings, this article highlights attachments to residences and neighbourhoods.

Typically, place attachments grow as people inhabit, use, and invest meaning in settings such as homes. For example, memories of pleasant social interactions at home enhance attachment and become inextricably woven into bonds with the home. Decorating the home, retreating to a bedroom, or hosting a party are practices that serve our needs, reflect who we are, and deepen attachment.

Place attachment offers a different emphasis than several allied concepts (see Glossary), although they are sometimes used interchangeably. For example, place identity focuses more on how place relates to self-identity. Sense of place involves a complex of attachment, meanings, and satisfaction. Place dependence refers to places that satisfy needs relative to alternative places. Satisfaction with place involves fulfilling needs, not necessarily forging bonds. Topophilia involves affective bonds from fleeting to enduring. Finally, human territoriality focuses more on perceived ownership. Thus, our definition of place attachment is a multifaceted phenomenon, somewhat different from other concepts used to understand people–place relationships.

History of Place Attachment Research

Place attachment research explicitly recognises the richness of positive bonds connecting humans with their homes and neighbourhoods. Place attachment researchers study, for example, how residents transform a house into a valued home by using it and investing it with meaning. Place attachment research thus provides a counterpoint to much research that had focused on housing solely as a commodity or an economic investment. In Fried's 1963 classic study of a Boston neighbourhood, residents were displaced when their homes, officially declared blighted, were razed for urban renewal. Expert outsiders thought residents would appreciate newer, better-quality housing, but residents resented the experts' claims to their neighbourhood and grieved over the destruction of their homes, despite their homes' physical deterioration. Those with stronger positive bonds to their former homes grieved most and many tried to secure new housing nearby, to remain close to the neighbourhood. Even decades later residents continued to publish a community newsletter, and families patronised a common summer camp in an effort to maintain community ties. In lower-income Baltimore neighbourhoods, Brower in 1980 described how routines of use and social connections with neighbours and kin established attachments to neighbourhoods and front yard areas. As in Boston, outsiders often viewed the residents' use of front yard areas as disreputable, thus failing to respect their place attachments.

These two early studies highlight a number of themes found in subsequent research. Place attachments are often profound; humans are so embedded in their environments that they do not always reflect on those bonds unless called to do so by outside threats, new situations, or turning points in life. Although individuals develop a sense of positive identity, security, and continuity in place attachments, the very foundations of those bonds are constantly changing, so place attachments also undergo change and transformation. Place attachments can be valued but contentious and residents still find their bonds to homes or lands at risk. Although early studies focused on threats to place attachment from urban neglect and renewal, subsequent studies reveal a wider range of place attachment changes, attributable to natural disasters, human-created disasters (war, political upheaval, and climate change), and normal lifespan events, such as ageing and relocation.

Levels of Analysis

Although the term 'place attachment' was first applied to homes and neighbourhoods, humans inhabit and use complex environments characterised by multiple levels of scale, from specific objects, to homes, neighbourhoods, cities, and nations. The nature of positive bonds to things and places can vary across these levels. For example, residents sometimes report stronger attachments to their cities and homes than to their neighbourhoods. Place attachments are also selective, with residents developing attachments to some neighbourhood settings, such as adult day care centres, coffee shops, or children's outdoor play areas, but not to others.

Temporal Processes

Place attachments also have temporal qualities. Longer durations of residence or engagement often relate to stronger attachments, although the salience and nature of bonds may transform over the life course. Place attachments to home may be especially important for those confined to home, such as youth, elders, and caregivers. On a day-to-day basis, places attachments are established through the temporal patterns of home life, with home providing a haven that allows for times of relaxation and private restoration as well as times of conviviality. Seasonally, holiday celebrations and gardening rituals may strengthen place attachment. In sum, place attachments are not static but involve complex daily, seasonal, and lifespan temporal processes that bond people to places.

Sociophysical and Psychological Processes

Place attachment necessarily involves a unity of psychological and social processes and physical settings. People and their relationships are embedded within physical contexts so that the very meaning of social processes cannot be abstracted from place, but is informed, constrained, and nourished by places. People actively cultivate place attachments with a home by selecting or building the home, arranging the furniture, tending the yard, hosting events, and enacting the routines of daily use and upkeep in the home. Attachment to home often extends beyond the immediate residents. For example, many societies have house-blessing rituals that help transform a house into a home that reflects individual and group identity, including in some societies the identities of family ancestors and house gods. These practices support a sense of security and continuity, identity, self-regulation, privacy regulation, self-esteem, and restoration. Place attachments are also informed by other social and physical dynamics. Power relationships, for example, are reflected in place attachments, such as when teens' bonds with their bedrooms are enhanced by the 'keep out' sign they erect on the door or when town officials use local parades to celebrate town identity but also decide who cannot participate.

Physical qualities of places contribute to but do not determine place attachments; instead, the sociophysical processes that create positive bonds are required. Nevertheless, some places are believed to be easier to bond with, such as high-quality housing and places with nature. The ancient Greeks even believed a 'genius loci' or guardian spirit imbued places with unique meanings that enabled attachments. The physical environment contributes to personal and social processes needed for effective functioning, which may account for positive bonds to places even when those places are of poor quality. Thus individuals can become attached to their homes regardless of social class and housing dilapidation.

Place Attachment and Aversive Experiences with Place

Restricting the definition of place attachment to positive bonds highlights their value and importance; however, a persistent theme in research has been the interplay of positively charged place attachments with more negative experiences. Although some researchers conceive of place attachment as encompassing negative feelings that serve to attach people to place, others reserve distinct terms for negative experiences that may prevent or undermine place attachments: alienation, placelessness, place aversion or topophobia, place ambivalence, place attachment disruption, and stigmatised places.

Negative emotions and thoughts about places can coexist with positive bonds, creating complex meanings of and ties to places. Homes can be the site of security, continuity, order, pride, and identity as well as violence, drudgery, chaos, shame, and alienation. As noted by Claire Cooper Marcus, home can be both a haven and a trap. Women in particular often say their homes are like prisons of unceasing work on behalf of unappreciative families, yet women also say they achieve personal pride and positive identity from their work in the home, which strengthens place attachment.

In sum, place attachment research varies in terms of the nature of the place attachment bond (cognitive or affective or both, positive or negative or both), temporal processes, and levels of analysis. These themes are explored further in the remaining sections that highlight attachments at different phases of life and in different kinds of places.

Place Attachment to Home for Youth and Adults

Place attachments among children often begin with the home, objects in the home, and nearby outdoor places. Children develop strong attachments to favourite toys, objects, bedrooms, and other areas that serve emotional needs and provide retreat and social spaces. Children forge and assert their identities partly by creating and transforming spaces into places of attachment, especially in places uninhabited by parents or other adults, such as forts or hiding places or small leftover spaces. In the teen years, a 13-country study showed that place attachments were associated with a sense of safety and the perception that neighbours were friendly; in addition, boys were more strongly attached to the home area than girls. Although homes often provide teens with a secure retreat, enhanced mobility allows teens to become attached to a wider variety of places.

Bonds children form may prove enduring. Temporary moves, such as to boarding school, may cause children to appreciate their bonds with home. As youth transition into adults and move away for longer periods they often report homesickness and a sense of having lost one's place. Even years after leaving a childhood home many remember fondly their special places from childhood. These childhood bonds are sometimes revealed when adults walk through neighbourhoods using a technique called emotional cartography. This technique tracks physiological responses and participants record psychological responses during a walk. Memories of childhood places and events become intermingled with contemporary feelings and events, revealing a rich map of past and present experiences with places.

As people age, many change residences for education, marriage, or other life events. Attachments to these new settings are intricately tied to the physical features, social relationships, and social and political contexts of the culture. A US study documented how newlyweds acquire favourite objects such as decorations or furniture that enable them to forge and enjoy their new marital identity. Even objects considered ugly by the couple may be prized and displayed nonetheless because the gift bespeaks a valued relationship or event. Couples also prominently display objects for others to see, such as wedding photographs. One study showed that couples who had such positively valued objects also had close and supportive relationships. As individuals continue to live in a place, their attachments and family-oriented symbolic associations often increase.

Place Attachments to Second Homes

Some have conceptualised bonds with temporary homes as deficient, based on inauthentic or superficial ties to aesthetically appealing places. But research shows that attachments to second homes can be strong, growing from appreciation of temporal rhythms of anticipation prior to the journey and regret upon leaving, enjoyment of sunsets and other natural events, and times with family and friends. Residents especially value their second homes as places that allow them to get away from civilisation and the commodification of life, connect to nature, and reflect upon or change identity. Positive bonds to a second home are appreciated despite negative experiences, such as maintenance responsibilities, vulnerability to burglary, or feeling alienated from year-round residents. On the other hand, some vacationers to South African beach towns felt that racial desegregation transformed their homely retreat into a place that highlighted distressing social change and upheaval, a phenomenon that likely happens in many full-time communities as well. In summary, psychological attachments to second homes can be complex and responsive to a variety of physical and social qualities.

Place Attachments to Homes in Old Age

Many elders prefer to 'age in place', even when diminished physical or financial abilities make it difficult to remain. Research shows that older age and more years in place predict greater place attachments, and that strong place attachments in old age relate to well-being. Elders may arrange a favourite 'control centre' at home, with easy access to good seating, a window view, the television and telephone, and other supports that help maintain independence and attachment, despite limited mobility. Compared to youth, elders may be more aware of how their home supports independence and may view future moves as threats to independence and autonomy. Indeed one study showed place attachments among ageing African Americans provided a reservoir of strength in the face of physical decline of ageing. Other research shows that women, who typically perform more domestic labour in their homes, often report place attachments based on everyday routines or their identities as family caregivers. Men, who typically spend more time outside their homes, often report place attachments based on the private retreat qualities of homes. Elders report that place attachments are supported by the beauty and solitude of places, safety from crime, historical ties, and symbolically important objects in homes.

Retirement communities sometimes offer a range of housing, from independent living apartments to skilled nursing units, so that, in theory, place attachments can be maintained despite the changes of residence dictated by health needs. In such communities stronger attachments are associated with more social bonds, close proximity to other residents and to a central activity building, and having shared enclosed garden spaces. New residents of assisted living facilities who report stronger attachments to the town and who are more socially involved with nonfamily members form stronger place attachments to their facility. In summary, attachments are important to elders and attachments to new places can be established through investments in the new people, activities, and places.

Home and Place Attachment Changes

Change is inherent in life, and many individuals create bonds to places that provide a sense of continuity and stability despite the reality of change. Changes may create problems depending on whether changes are positive or negative, or gradual or sudden. At times place attachments undergo positive and gradual changes, such as when residents personalise or expand a place to reflect their changing identity and needs; a vacation enables one to appreciate the home upon returning; a garden matures and flourishes; and a neighbourhood revitalises. Changes can be positive and sudden, like becoming a new homeowner or moving to a cherished place and feeling immediate attachment. Even when changes are positive, the disruption of bonds to a prior home can be disorienting. For example, even among students who desire to move to a university, their upended attachments feel disorienting and new ones can be slow to develop. Changes can also be negative and gradual, such as when a neighbourhood slowly declines or land gradually erodes under coastal homes; place attachment bonds may change or prove resilient in the face of such threats.

Of particular concern are sudden and negative changes that profoundly disrupt place attachments, such as abrupt and massive disasters. Unfortunately, as world population swells, global climate changes, and new migration patterns occur, place attachments may be increasingly subject to sudden and negative disruptions (see **Box 1**).

Sociopolitical Contexts and Consequences of Place Attachment

Place attachments can be strengthened or threatened by the sociopolitical contexts in which they are embedded. Sociopolitical forces can facilitate place attachments, such as when laws and policies protect private property, ease homeownership, maintain neighbourhood quality, and extend housing opportunities to diverse social groups. Sociopolitical forces can also prevent or threaten place attachments, such as when immigrants, women, minorities, or other groups are denied access to residential markets. For example, in the United States, it is legal in many areas for gay individuals to be denied or evicted from housing.

Place attachments have also been found to buffer individuals from sociopolitical threats or exclusions.

Box 1 Environmental Disasters Disrupt Place Attachments

In 2005 Hurricane Katrina destroyed parts of the Louisiana coast of the United States and rivers flooded the town of Carlisle in the United Kingdom. Katrina survivors longed for old and familiar places and reported increased family conflicts in the absence of their supportive community ties and places. At the same time, they had mixed feelings about returning home, given the enduring evidence of community destruction and the difficulties of starting over, perhaps in an emergency trailer that does not foster new attachment. Postdisaster destruction and looting can add to survivors' sense of loss, insecurity, and dislocation. The Carlisle flood victims similarly lamented the loss of their homes and valued possessions, such as one flood victim who found the print on her wedding certificate wiped clean. Although some postdisaster Carlisle homes were still liveable, survivors lost their customary supports for privacy, comfort, security, and routine; they felt housed, but not at home. These are just two global instances of place attachment disruption; many more occur without research documentation. Disruptions predicted to be associated with climate change suggest that millions of individuals will become environmental refugees, with their homes destroyed or uninhabitable. Place attachment disruption will be one psychologically devastating piece of a larger social and environmental crisis.

Residents of neighbourhood enclaves or ghettos, despite larger societal views of these places as stigmatising, often develop strong place attachments, perhaps in reaction to their low status and lack of welcome elsewhere. For example, experiences of racism within the broader society have been argued to intensify the positive qualities of attachments to home among racial minorities. In a neighbourhood affected by physical decline, Hispanic residents reported stronger attachments than their majority non-Hispanic white neighbours, which might reflect their exclusion from more affluent neighbourhoods. Residents of gay enclaves also reported feeling symbolic and emotional comfort and a sense of belonging in their neighbourhood, which contrasted with the censure and negativity outside their neighbourhood. Residents felt more acknowledged for their individual qualities and less stereotyped when in their neighbourhood. Finally, children confined close to home may develop especially strong home-based place attachments, albeit as a partial function of their exclusion from participation in other places.

Place Attachment and Negative Consequences

This article has noted how place attachments involve positive bonds. However, place attachments may also give rise to negative personal and societal consequences, topics of increasing research attention. At the individual level, place attachments to an immigrant enclave, for example, might over time become restrictive, preventing residents from exploiting educational or job opportunities outside the neighbourhood. Similarly, desires for place attachments motivate some to acquire costly home mortgages that result in economic stress and ruin. At the group level, place attachments can fuel conflict and xenophobia, by helping to define 'us' and 'our place' in contrast to the perception of 'them' and 'their place'.

Place attachments sometime commit us to dangerous places and practices by allowing us to minimise or deny the negative or risky qualities inherent in the objects, places, and practices central to attachment. For example, residents of a town that was periodically devastated by mudslides preferred rebuilding rather than resettling to safer areas; homeowners drawn to a town because it offered a rural retreat ignored the nearby toxic dump that eventually contaminated their homes and eroded their place attachments. Similarly, strong but false feelings of security in homes may blind residents to the need for protection from threats of burglary or natural disasters, and strong religious and home bonds motivate residents to remain in war zones despite threat of attack.

As consumers around the world are increasingly attached to the suburban consumption landscape as a way of showing individual achievement, social distinctiveness, and cultural taste, the negative environmental and social consequences of these forms of building attachment become more evident. Environmentally, suburban-style houses and their infrastructure may destroy lands. Residents' gardening and lawn care activities often build pride of place, commitment to neighbours, and display of family and neighbour identity, all of which foster place attachment. Yet when residents conceive of gardening practices in these positive ways, they may minimise the environmental damage and human health risks posed by toxic substances used to enhance the beauty of the home and landscape. Even holiday decorations, which normally support place attachments, sometimes expose residents to chemicals considered probable carcinogens, a danger we may be less alert to because of our focus on place attachment. Positive bonds to the important objects in our places of attachment may blind us to degrading labour practices and destructive environmental processes used in their creation.

Place Attachment and Preserving the Environment

Relph has claimed that strong bonds with places entail a sense of care and responsibility for them. Research has been mixed on the question of whether place attachments can motivate care for the people or places involved in attachments. Some studies connect place attachments to socially protective bonds, such as greater social capital, more nearby friends and neighbour relationships, and lower vulnerability to crime victimisation. Other studies connect place attachment to direct place protective actions, such as a willingness to pay, work, or take actions for preserving the environment or countering environmental threats, attending workshops focused on local place developments, or remaining in the place. However, in some cases, stronger place attachments are unrelated to civic engagements; or attachment to the block or apartment building relates to less investment in city-wide civic engagements; or strong attachments motivate some residents to resist societal benefits, such as hydropower plants, when sited near their homes. What is seen by outsiders as a NIMBY (not-in-my-backyard) reaction is seen by residents as place protective action.

Future Research

Both methodological and substantive advances could enrich our understanding of place attachments. Place attachment research is often based on surveys (see **Table 1**) but methodological and technological

Table 1 Place attachment survey questions

Survey Items and Response Options

1. On a 1–10 scale where 1 is not at all proud and 10 is extremely proud, how proud are you of:

	1	2	3	4	5	6	7	8	9	10	Don't know
a. Your neighborhood	O	O	O	O	O	O	O	O	O	O	O
b. Your block	O	O	O	O	O	O	O	O	O	O	O
c. Your house	O	O	O	O	O	O	O	O	O	O	O
d. The way your front yard looks	O	O	O	O	O	O	O	O	O	O	O
e. The way the outside of your house looks	O	O	O	O	O	O	O	O	O	O	O

2. How attached do you feel to the block you live on from 1 to 10, if 1 is not at all attached and 10 is strongly attached?

1	2	3	4	5	6	7	8	9	10	Don't know
O	O	O	O	O	O	O	O	O	O	O

3. If, for any reason, you had to move to another neighborhood would you be:

Very unhappy (4) A little unhappy (3) Happy to move (1) Doesn't make any difference (2)

Scoring

Place attachment $= (1c + 1d + 1e)/3 + (1a + 1b + 2 + 3)/4$, all variables z-transformed.

Note. Survey used for publication by Brown BB, Perkins DD, Brown G (2003) Place attachment in a revitalizing neighborhood: Individual and block levels of analysis. *Journal of Environmental Psychology* 23: 259–71.

---

advances can provide new ways to understand place attachments. Researchers can have participants report place attachment experiences and settings throughout the day (experience sampling), use tours to inquire about attachments ('go-along' interviews), employ participant photography and reflection upon places (photovoice), or provide maps that combine participant annotations with physiological monitoring (emotional cartography).

In terms of new substantive directions, in the face of ecological threats to our planet, future research should focus on how to prepare human populations for place detachment, increasingly needed as people are forced to migrate away from homes by environmental risk, erosion, destruction, or depletion. Future research will also be needed to understand how to engage place attachments to protect places. This issue is especially complicated given that the destruction of distant places can have far-reaching local consequences. Mobilising residents to protect against gangs menacing one's own neighbourhood may be easier than mobilising against distant threats, such as the destruction of rainforests across the globe, or mobilising against hidden threats, such as the toxic dangers present in our most cherished places and possessions. Finally, given increasing population mobility that brings diverse peoples together, research is needed regarding whether place attachments might be shared and appreciated in ways that bond diverse groups instead of dividing them.

See also: Home Objects; Neighbourhood Reputation; NIMBYism; Privacy, Sanctuary and Privatism; Restorative Housing Environments; Second Homes.

Further Reading

Altman I and Low SM (1992) *Place Attachment*. New York: Plenum.

Brower S (1980) Territory in urban settings. In: Altman I, Rapoport A, and Wohlwill JF (eds.) *Environment and Culture*, pp. 179–207. New York: Plenum.

Brown BB and Perkins DD (1992) Disruptions in place attachment. In: Altman I and Low S (eds.) *Place Attachment*, pp. 279–304. New York: Plenum.

Brown BB, Perkins DD, and Brown G (2003) Place attachment in a revitalizing neighborhood: Individual and block levels of analysis. *Journal of Environmental Psychology* 23: 259–71.

Brown BB, Perkins DD, and Brown G (2004) Incivilities, place attachment and crime: Block and individual effects. *Journal of Environmental Psychology* 24: 359–371.

Devine-Wright P (2009) Rethinking NIMBYism: The role of place attachment and place identity in explaining place-protective action. *Journal of Community and Applied Social Psychology* 19(6): 426–441.

Fried M (1963) Grieving for a lost home. In: Duhl L (ed.) *The Urban Condition*, pp. 151–171. New York: Basic Books.

Hidalgo MC and Hernandez B (2001) Place attachment: Conceptual and empirical questions. *Journal of Environmental Psychology* 21: 273–281.

Manzo LC (2003) Beyond house and haven: Toward a revisioning of emotional relationships with places. *Journal of Environmental Psychology* 23: 47–61.

Marcus CC (1995) *House as a Mirror of Self*. Berkeley, CA: Conari Press.

Proshansky HM, Fabian AK, and Kaminoff R (1983) Place-identity: Physical world socialization of the self. *Journal of Environmental Psychology* 3: 57–83.

Relph E (1976) *Place and Placelessness*. London: Pion.

Planning Institutions: Canada/United States

I Skelton, University of Manitoba, Winnipeg, MB, Canada

© 2012 Elsevier Ltd. All rights reserved.

Glossary

Planner An individual involved in collective processes of shaping or reshaping the built or social environment, on a paid or voluntary basis.

Planning activist A planner oriented towards reshaping planning processes and outcomes, usually towards socially progressive ends.

Planning institutions Organisations that represent a sector of planners, communicating their point of view and representing their interests.

Planning movement The assemblage of planners and planning institutions.

Professional planner A planner whose credentials have been certified by an institution of professional planners.

Introduction

This article examines planning institutions in Canada and the United States. The focus is on institutions that regulate or represent constituencies involved in planning (rather than the societal institutions through which planning takes place), and the national and international institutions listed later (by their current names) are considered. For reasons of space and focus, institutions operating below a national scale are not included.

1. Professional institutions
   Canadian Institute of Planners
   American Institute of Certified Planners
2. Planning movement institutions
   Community Planning Association of Canada
   American Planning Association
3. Planning activist institutions
   Planners Network

The article consists of four parts following this introduction. The first outlines the history of the various planning institutions. This material, in most instances, has been covered in the literature, and only an overview is provided here, with sources for further inquiry. Second, the current organisation and activities of the institutions are described, and third, membership issues are discussed. The article concludes with a brief summary.

Histories

Interpreting the history of planning institutions requires caution. Some authors have failed to distance themselves from the institutions, preventing their critical assessment of the historical record, and consequently have produced biased histories. Others have adopted lenses that identify particular groups as of secondary importance in the processes of planning institution formation and development, leading to histories in which the experience of, for example, women and racialised populations is unrepresented.

In Canada and the United States, planning institutions emerged in the early years of the twentieth century, when regulation and control were gaining some credibility in the context of widespread concern over urban development, social reform movements were working for collective provision of welfare, and environmentalists were already warning of the consequences of wanton use of resources. The year 1909 stands out as a turning point. In Canada, the Commission on Conservation was founded in that year under the leadership of Sir Clifford Sifton, a leading business promoter and politician, with funding from the federal government. The commission set important precedents for planning because it showed that when popular concern is high, planning can be accepted. It comprised the federal ministries of agriculture, mining, and the interior, provincial officials responsible for natural resources, and, anticipating an ongoing tension between the scholarly and practice sides of the profession, at least one academic from each province. The commission expressed antiurban sentiments, favouring decentralisation and access to the countryside over the congestion of the city. Its overall programme of environmental protection centrally involved the undermining of private property rights, which proved to overextend its base of support, and the commission was disbanded in 1921.

Also in 1909, the National Conference on City Planning (NCCP) in the United States initiated annual meetings to promote broad-based discussion on planning issues. Planning was taking shape as an organised activity and the NCCP involved many constituencies such as architecture, engineering, law, real estate, and social work. It stood independent of government, with funding from member dues, host city donations, and foundations, particularly the Russell Sage Foundation under the leadership of Margaret Olivia Sage. The NCCP had to deal with property rights, as did the commission in Canada; however, in this case the fissure between reformers, intending to undermine the status quo, and technicians, accepting of market rationality, led to a split in the movement and the technicians persevered.

Planners in both countries shared a concern to build up of a body of specialised planning knowledge. A knowledge base can facilitate claims to a scope of practice, which, in turn, is key to a profession's vitality. In 1917, the American City Planning Institute (ACPI) was formed to elaborate planning knowledge. The 68 ACPI founding members included architects, attorneys, developers, engineers, and landscape architects, as well as a scattering of other professionals, and its formation has been characterised as marking a methodological shift from urban design (underlain by aesthetic concerns) to rational analysis (underlain by emerging social sciences). Two years later the Town Planning Institute of Canada (TPIC) was formed. Smaller than the ACPI, it had only 18 founding members. Its orientation towards professionalism separated the new institute from the collectivist sentiments that had driven sections of the urban reform movement. Its orientation to property rights widened this rift and aligned the early TPIC with vested interests in real estate.

The planning institutions in both countries used publications to advance planning knowledge. With federal financial support, TPIC launched *Town Planning Journal* in 1920, and ACPI and NCCP sponsored *City Planning Quarterly* from 1925. A common trait of both the ACPI and the TPIC, beyond their publications and their orientation to technical and market rationalities, was the presence of Thomas Adams. Of rural Scottish origin and trained as a surveyor, Adams performed an "institutional hat trick" (Stein, 1994: 14) as founding member of these two organisations as well as the Royal Town Planning Institute in Britain. His widespread influence and his utilitarianism helped mark planning institutions with what is known in Canada as the Roebuck/Sifton/Adams Convention that "land can be efficiently managed for an identifiable public good through the effective application of scientific knowledge."

In 1932, in the economic climate of the Depression, the Canadian federal department of the interior cut funding for *Town Planning Journal*, and although the TPIC had grown to somewhat under 400 members, it suspended operation. While planning continued in relief projects, in resource management, and in social welfare work, the institution was not sustained during this period. In the United States, the Depression disrupted the ACPI, though public works under the New Deal led to a proliferation of civil servants involved in or interested in planning. This helped lead to a differentiation of institutions by 1934: the ACPI, the American Society of Planning Officials (ASPO), and the American Planning and Civic Association (APCA). As the names suggest, ASPO represented civil servants and APCA was a broad-based organisation for education and promotion. At this stage, while Canada's one planning institution was under suspension, the United States had three differentiated institutions.

In 1935 ACPI withdrew support from *City Planning Quarterly* and launched *Planner's Journal*, which continues today under a different name. By 1939 the technical orientation of the US institution was consolidated and the name changed to the American Institute of Planners (AIP), and the publication name thus became *Journal of the American Institute of Planners*.

In the boom following the Second World War, planning institutions in Canada and the United States prospered. In 1946 the Canadian federal government's Central Mortgage and Housing Corporation (now Canada Mortgage and Housing Corporation) provided funding for the foundation of the Community Planning Association of Canada (CPAC) and in 1952 for the revival of TPIC, which launched its publication *Plan Canada* in 1959. By 1970 TPIC had established a professional office in Ottawa, and in 1972 it adopted a federated structure, with seven regional affiliate institutions. In 1974 it assumed its current name, Canadian Institute of Planners (CIP).

The CPAC represented the education and reform interests of the planning movement and promoted public participation in planning. It published *Community Planning Review/Revue canadienne d'urbanisme* over the period 1951–73. The CPAC achieved a relatively balanced gender composition, partly because women were attracted to its orientation, though also because of barriers to participation in male-dominated associations. The organisation was short-lived, however, and when the federal government cut its funding, the CPAC, which had maintained a national office and staff, folded. Some provincial chapters persevered, the most active currently being in Alberta.

By the mid-1960s, the planning movement in the United States had become sufficiently robust that consolidation of its progressive wing emerged on the agenda. In 1964 Planners for Equal Opportunity (PEO) was launched at the AIP national conference. The PEO conducted advocacy, activism, and education on housing and planning issues, primarily in the northeastern regions of the United States, and it emphasised their highly racialised nature. It attempted to pull the AIP towards its progressive agenda by lobbying members, running for leadership positions, and promoting motions for adoption at AIP conferences. By the early 1970s, however, the PEO leadership acknowledged that under its current formulation, the organisation had not been able to foster sufficient activism among its members. Despite having a contact list of some 600 planners in support of its programme, PEO was disbanded.

Attempts to regroup the progressive wing of planning over the mid and late 1970s led to the formation of Planners Network (PN), which held its first conference near Washington, DC, in 1981. PN points out that it has maintained an independent focus for progressive planners as the political climate shifted from one of activism in the period following the war in Vietnam, to the more conservative contemporary period.

In 1978 the AIP was renamed the American Planning Association (APA), and ASPO joined it. At that time, *Journal of the American Institute of Planners* became *Journal of the American Planning Association*. At the same time the American Institute of Certified Planners (AICP) was formed as a national, professional body.

One aspect of the history of planning institutions is the level of their membership. (Although it is widely recognised that mainstream planning institutions have been white and male, data limitations preclude reporting on the *composition* of the membership in terms of diversity.) **Figures 1** and **2** show annual membership counts over the period 1967–2008, for the APA, AICP, and CIP, the latter differentiated between professional and nonprofessional members. Comparable data are not readily available for the other institutions. The CPAC membership numbered about 12 000 in the late 1970s, and its annual conferences were attended by up to 3000 delegates. The PN membership is currently about 500.

The figures show the strong growth of professional and nonprofessional members over the period. Total CIP membership increased from just over 600 to over 7600, more than 12 times. CIP growth was disrupted in the mid-1980s, possibly due to the recession early in the decade and uncertainty in relation to impending free trade with the United States. Over the 2000s CIP membership increased rapidly. APA membership grew over 1967–2008 from about 13 500 to 39 000, about three times. Growth rates for APA do not appear to be affected by economic cycles. Since the late 1980s, membership has increased rapidly for both CIP and APA. Differences between CIP and APA in the breakdown of the membership in terms of professional and nonprofessional status have shrunk. In 1967 the CIP membership was over 80% professional, and by 2008 it was about 55%; the APA moved in the opposite direction, from 4 to >40% professional. We should note that in CIP there is an expectation that many of the nonprofessional members will become certified, while this is not the case for APA.

Figure 3 shows total membership data standardised by national population. In 1967 both CIP and APA had fewer than one member per 10 000, CIP at 0.3 and APA at 0.7. In the mid-1970s the density of members in Canada surpassed that in the United States and growth remained stronger in Canada. By 2008, there were 2.3 CIP members and 1.3 APA members per 10 000 population. These figures show that the density of planning institution members is higher in Canada, but because planners may not be members, they do not reflect the densities of planners in the two countries.

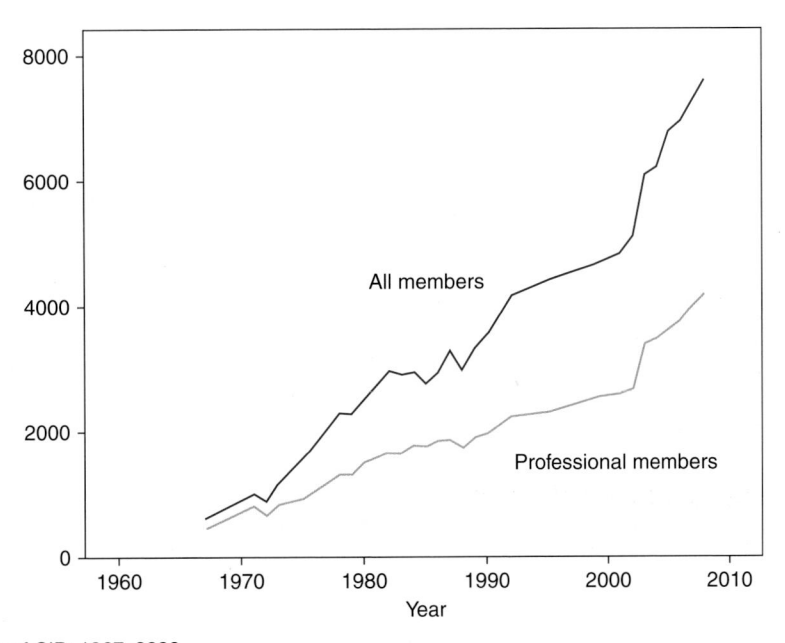

Figure 1 Membership of CIP: 1967–2008.
Source: special tabulation by CIP.

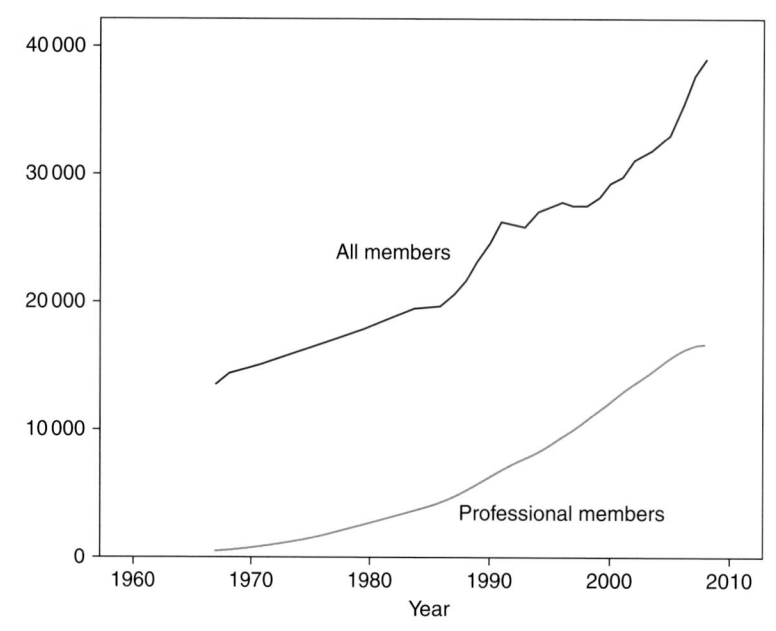

Figure 2 Membership of APA: 1967–2008.
Source: special tabulation by APA.

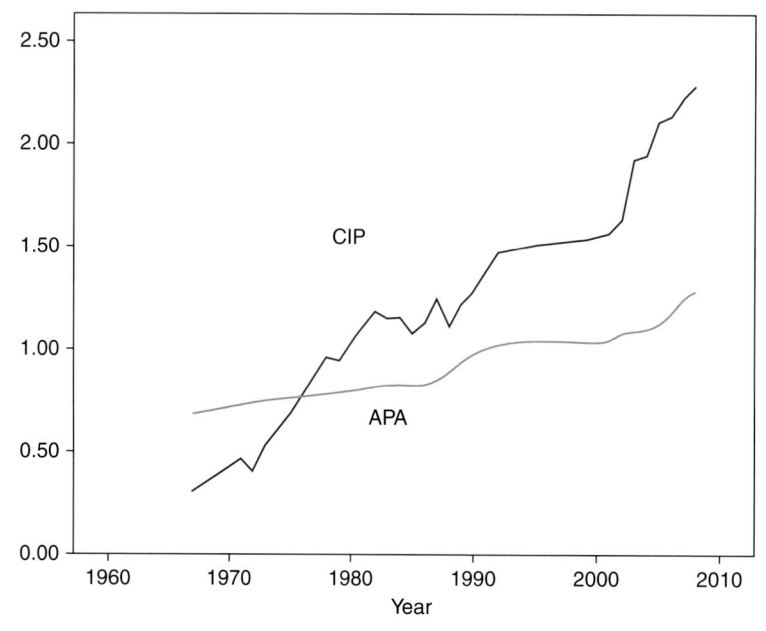

Figure 3 Members per 10 000 population: CIP and APA.
Sources for population data are as follows: Canada: Statistics Canada. Table 051-0005 – Estimates of population, Canada, provinces and territories.http://estat.statcan.gc.ca/cgi-win/cnsmcgi.exe?Lang=E&EST-Fi=EStat/English/CII_1-eng.htm (accessed 8 September 2008). United States: United States Census Bureau. *Statistical Abstract of the United States*.http://www.census.gov/prod/2005pubs/06statab/pop.pdf (accessed 2 September 2008).

Current Organisation and Activities of Planning Institutions

The seven affiliates of the CIP, listed west to east, are:

- Planning Institute of British Columbia – includes Yukon Territory;
- Alberta Association, Canadian Institute of Planners includes – Northwest Territories and Nunavut Territory;
- Association of Professional Community Planners of Saskatchewan;
- Manitoba Professional Planners Institute;

- Ontario Professional Planners Institute;
- Ordre des urbanistes du Québec; and
- Atlantic Planners Institute/Institut des urbanistes de l'Atlantique.

The APA maintains offices in Chicago and Washington, reflecting the office locations of its founding organisations AIP and ASPO. It has 47 chapters, generally one per state. The exceptions are:

- National Capital Area – includes Washington, DC and two counties of Maryland;
- New York Metro – includes New York City, Long Island, and the Hudson Valley;
- New York Upstate;
- Northern New England – includes Maine, New Hampshire, and Vermont; and
- West Central – includes Montana, North Dakota, South Dakota, and Wyoming.

AICP is a subsidiary of APA and operates at the national level. PN has 4 chapters in Canada and 14 in the United States. A chapter in the United Kingdom (PNUK) is emerging.

CIP and APA maintain a range of programmes for members, including annual conferences, employment services, insurance, and member networking. Both institutions are involved in publishing. CIP issues *Plan Canada* on a quarterly basis, with a mix of short peer-reviewed and nonreviewed articles. Since 2003, CIP has partnered with the Association of Canadian University Planning Programs and the Institute of Urban Studies at the University of Winnipeg to produce an annual volume of peer-reviewed planning papers. This appears under the name *Canadian Planning and Policy – Aménagement et politique au Canada* and is a supplement to *Canadian Journal of Urban Research*. APA publishes *Planning*, a monthly review of newsworthy planning initiatives, as well as several specialised publications for practitioners in areas such as law and zoning, and for groups such as planning commissioners, students, and youth. APA also publishes the peer-reviewed quarterly *Journal of the American Planning Association*.

Other activities of CIP flow through a series of committees at the national level. The Policy Advisory Committee has prompted the federal government to formulate explicit urban policy. The National Affairs Committee has led several initiatives. Its First Nations Subcommittee promotes planning in indigenous communities, and some CIP members have been inspired by the experience of the Indigenous Planning Division to establish a corresponding institution in Canada. Other initiatives of the National Affairs Committee include a Climate Change Adaptation Project and work in other environmental issues, infrastructure, and urban design. The International Affairs Committee coordinates CIP's work globally, building planning capacity in several countries, including China, Grenada, and Trinidad and Tobago. As cohost of the World Urban Forum in 2005 with the Planning Institution of British Columbia, CIP is a signatory to the Vancouver Declaration that puts planning in the centre of strategies for fulfilling Millennium Development Goals.

The APA has a highly articulated structure of divisions that link planners in interest areas through publications, conferences, and networking opportunities. Some divisions deal with population groups and others with thematic areas. The 20 divisions currently in place are as follows:

Population divisions	Thematic divisions
Gays and lesbians in planning	City planning and management
Indigenous planning	County planning
Latinos and planning	Economic development
Planning and the black community	Environment, natural resources, energy
Planning and women	Federal planning
	Housing and community development
	International
	New urbanism
	Planning and law
	Private practice
	Regional and intergovernmental planning
	Small town and rural planning
	Technology
	Transportation planning
	Urban design and preservation

The AICP is a subsidiary of the APA, with main activities in certifying professional planners, setting ethical standards, and developing the knowledge base. Its quarterly publication *Practicing Planner* is available to professionally certified planners.

PN focuses on linking and supporting members and fostering their communication, through the quarterly *Progressive Planning Magazine*, as well as maintaining information on its website and distributing an electronic newsletter and list serves. Local chapters engage in education work and activism on planning issues.

Membership Issues

Membership in CIP is accessed through the regional affiliates. As a professional institution, the main categories are provisional and full membership, with the expectation, as indicated, that members will progress from one to the other. Provisional members who have graduated from CIP-accredited university planning programmes intern for 2 years, maintain log books for review by a full member, and pass an oral exam for full membership. Without a recognised degree, a written exam or portfolio is required, and the internship period varies with education: 4 years for provisional members with degrees related to planning; 6 years if the degree is not related; and 15 years with no degree. Since 2007, full members have been required to participate in continuous professional learning. By the late 1990s, a public associate member category was introduced to allow nonprofessionals to join the institution.

Membership in APA and PN is acquired nationally, without restriction other than dues. For professionals, AICP holds written examinations semiannually. Only APA members are eligible to certify, and work experience is also required. For members with an accredited master's degree, the required period is 2 years; with an accredited bachelor's, 3 years; with a nonaccredited graduate degree in planning, 3 years; any other college degree, 4 years; and no college degree, 8 years. AICP membership must be maintained through continuing education.

Planning institutions define what is expected of members through formal statements, or codes. Contravention of the code can lead to cancellation of professional status, but there are other dimensions. As explained by Paul Farmer, executive director and CEO of APA and AICP, a code 'elevates' by setting value-laden standards. In 1994, CIP adopted a Statement of Values and a decade later revised its Code of Practice. The separation enabled CIP to communicate its underlying values and to define specific criteria for good practice. Values, nonenforceable, comprise eight points, including social and environmental responsibility. The code, which is enforceable, includes three areas of responsibility: to the public interest (4 points); to clients and employers (15 points); and to the profession (17 points).

CIP has updated the language of the Statement of Values and Code of Practice and at the time of writing intends that affiliate adoption will lead to a consistent standard nationally.

APA adopted a set of ethical principles in 1992. It does not include provisions for enforcement and is organised around three themes: the public interest (7 points); integrity and proficiency (13 points); and, in a section for practising planners, continuous improvement of their own competence and that of others in the field.

The AICP Code of Ethics and Professional Conduct was adopted in 2005. Like the CIP Code of Practice, it addresses the three areas of responsibility attended to by CIP: the public interest (8 points), clients and employers (3 points), and the profession (10 points). However, here these are phrased as 'principles to which we aspire' rather than as the potential basis for procedures against a professional planner. A further section of the AICP Code, 'Our rules of conduct', sets out 25 lines that professional planners must not cross, and a third section, 'Our code procedures', outlines the process for processing issues arising from the foregoing sections.

In their treatment of the public interest, the two professional codes reflect the utilitarian roots of the profession. Nevertheless, both institutions show they are moving away from this by including diversity issues in their professional codes. AICP prohibits unlawful discrimination (APA, 2009: Rule of Conduct 20), and CIP requires planners to respect the "diversity, needs, values and aspirations of the public" (CIP, 2008: Standard 1.1). PN shifts the social role of planning by advancing a Statement of Principles placing planning as a vehicle for social change, undermining the discrimination and inequalities of the status quo, and leading towards an equitable future.

Conclusions

A growing body of literature has been addressing how professionals write their history and construct their identity. Planning institutions in Canada and the United States perform a wide range of functions, including certifying and regulating professionals, influencing the development of planning knowledge through publications and the accreditation of planning education, promoting planning to government and in civil society, and providing services to members. In the United States, the APA provides a nonprofessional body for advancing planning. Although CIP introduced nonprofessional membership categories a few years ago, its membership consists overwhelmingly of certified and provisional members. During its life span, CPAC provided an independent voice for the planning movement in Canada. PN is an independent focus for progressive planners though its presence in Canada and the United States is small in comparison to the mainstream organisations.

See also: Architects; Civil Sector Institutions and Informal Settlements; Institutions that Represent Housing Professionals; Planning Institutions: China; Planning Institutions: Post-Socialist; Research Networks and Professional Institutions in Housing.

References

American Planning Association (2009) *AICP Code of Ethics and Professional Conduct.* http://www.planning.org/ethics/ethicscode.htm (accessed 21 July 2009).

Canadian Institute of Planners (2008) *Ethical Standards for the Planning Profession in Canada.* http://cip-icu.ca/_CMS/files/Ethical%20Standards.pdf (accessed 21 July 2009).

Stein DL (1994) Thomas Adams, 1871–1940. *Plan Canada* Special Issue, July: 14–15.

Further Reading

American Planning Association (2009) *Ethical Principles in Planning*. http://www.planning.org/ethics/ethical principles.htm (accessed 21 July 2009).

Armstrong AH (1959) Thomas Adams and the Commission on Conservation. *Plan Canada* 1(1): 14–32.

Artibise A and Stelter GA (eds.) (1979) *The Useable Urban Past: Planning and Politics in the Modern Canadian City*. Toronto, ON: Macmillan.

Birch EL (1980) Advancing the art and science of planning: Planners and their organizations 1909–1980. *Journal of the American Planning Association* 46(1): 22–49.

Birch EL and Silver C (2009) One hundred years of city planning's enduring and evolving connections. *Journal of the American Planning Association* 75(2): 113–122.

Black RVN (1967) *Planning and the Planning Profession: The Past Fifty Years*. Washington, DC: AIP.

Canadian Institute of Planners (2004) *Statement of Values and Code of Practice*. Ottawa, ON: CIP.

Hendler S and Harrison H (2000) Theorizing Canadian planning: Women, gender and feminist perspectives. In: Miranne KB and Young AH (eds.) *Gendering the City: Women, Boundaries and Visions of Urban Life*, pp. 139–156. Oxford: Rowman and Littlefield.

Krueckeberg DA (1980) The story of the Planner's Journal, 1915–1980. *Journal of the American Planning Association* 46(1): 5–21.

Peterson JA (2003) *The Birth of City Planning in the United States 1840–1917*. Baltimore, MD: Johns Hopkins University Press.

Planners Network (2009) History. http://www.plannersnetwork.org/about/history.html (accessed 2 September 2009).

Rutherford P (ed.) (1974) *Saving the Canadian City: The First Phase 1880–1920*. Toronto, ON; Buffalo, NY: University of Toronto Press.

Schaffer D (ed.) (1988) *Two Centuries of American Planning*. Baltimore, MD: John Hopkins University Press.

Sies MC and Silver C (1996) *Planning the Twentieth-Century American City*. Baltimore, MD: John Hopkins University Press.

Simpson M (1985) *Thomas Adams and the Modern Planning Movement: Britain, Canada and the United States, 1900–1940*. London; New York: Mansell Publishing Ltd.

Smith (1979) John Arthur Roebuck: A Canadian influence on the development of planning thought in the early nineteenth century. *Plan Canada* 19(3/4): 200–210.

Thabit W (1999) *A History of Planners for Equal Opportunity*. www.plannersnetwork.org/publications/pdfs/A_History_of_PEO.pdf (accessed 2 September 2009).

Wolfe JM (2003) A national urban policy for Canada? Prospects and challenges. *Canadian Journal of Urban Research* 12(1) (Supplement): 1–21.

Planning Institutions: China

Y Song, University of North Carolina, Chapel Hill, NC, USA

© 2012 Elsevier Ltd. All rights reserved.

Glossary

Coordination The act of coordinating, making different professionals and institutions work together for a goal or effect.

Infrastructure The basic physical and organisational structures needed for the operation of a society. The term typically refers to the technical structures, such as roads, water supply, sewers, power grids, telecommunications, and so forth.

Planning institutions The agencies representing the planning profession, with their work involving the development of policies affecting the natural and built environment and the specification of the standards of the planning profession.

Sustainable development A pattern of resource use that aims to meet human needs while preserving the environment.

Urbanisation The physical growth of urban areas as a result of global change, with movement of people from rural to urban areas with population growth equating to urban migration.

The Role of Planning Institutions in the Asia-Pacific Countries

Asia has unique and diverse urbanisation experiences compared to the other continents. It contains the largest number of urban dwellers, accounting for almost half of the world's urban population. It has also experienced fast urbanisation in a relatively short time; most Asian countries (except Japan, Kuwait, and Singapore) have urbanised very rapidly since the 1970s. For example, China's urban population increased from 18 to 56% and Indonesia's 16 to 31% in the same period. Needless to say, these increases in urban population have generated tremendous pressure in the urban infrastructure and housing sectors.

In the era of globalisation, many rapidly urbanising Asian cities aspire to become sustainable cities, with efficient governance, advanced technological and economic development, and enriching human, cultural, and environmental capital. It is important to note that there is no unifying model for Asia's growth. Diverse institutional settings in the Asia-Pacific countries have guaranteed property rights, made credible commitments and efforts to pursue efficient policy making, and limit corruption in a variety of ways. Asia proves that a variety of institutional arrangements can contribute to rapid urban growth. Planning institutions in these fast-urbanising countries are playing an important role in alleviating the pressure by fulfilling the following functions: the building and provision of urban infrastructure, the provision of social welfare, and the promotion of sustainable urbanisation. Specifically, planning institutions at all levels and in all sectors embrace different planning functions, including plan formulation and implementation, financial management, and coordination of planning with market economies. A typical set of plans includes economic and social plans, land resource plans, urban comprehensive plans, transportation plans, and environment protection plans.

Vertical Structure of Planning Institutions

In most Asian countries, planning functions are administrated by national level governments and their counterparts at the local levels. There is a general trend of decentralisation of power, similar to fiscal decentralisation that primarily devolves revenue sources and expenditures to lower tiers of government. The assumption is that by bringing the government closer to the people, decentralisation of service provision is expected to boost public sector efficiency, as well as accountability and transparency in service delivery and policy making. This implies the decentralisation of urban planning decisions to the urban level of government. For example, the Governor of Tokyo Metropolis has the overall control of metropolitan affairs and the authority and responsibility for maintaining the metropolitan services. In Taipei, elected city councillors have the power to pass and introduce bills and administer the city government for the public good.

Most Asian countries apply a top-down planning regime. In Singapore, the People's Action Party, which is in power, has deployed the state machinery in a highly interventionist manner to control politics, economy, and society. China, on the other hand, has a hierarchical structure of planning institutions. The People's Congress is an organisation form for state power. The main administrative system includes the central administrative organs, the State Council, and the local administrative organs at three levels: provinces, counties and cities, and townships and districts. At these local levels of governments, the people's congresses are the local organs of state power and have the capacity to elect members of the government. The local people's congresses also have the power to adopt local regulations and monitor government functions, including urban planning. The local governments usually follow the central government in developing different plans. For example, if the national government develops an economic and social development plan, every province, city, county, and township will follow up with its own plan.

We use the example of urban comprehensive plans to illustrate the institutional structure. As stated in China's City Planning Act, urban planning institutions at both national and local level, as representatives of State Council and local municipal governments, should be in charge of preparing urban comprehensive plans. Thus, the government of a city should deploy the urban planning process for its corresponding city, and county government should initiate the process for its town. These institutions should also coordinate with other governmental agencies or stakeholders and manage the implementation of the urban comprehensive plans.

The urban planning institutions at different levels (as shown in **Figure 1**) include the Ministry of Housing and Urban–Rural Development (MHURD) at the national level; the Department of Housing and Urban–Rural Development at the provincial level; and the construction commission, urban planning commission, or urban planning bureau at the city or town level. Planning institutions at different levels formulate urban plans for the corresponding city or town in two stages: the master plan and the detailed plan. In addition, planning institutions also play important roles in the plan approval process. For example, cities directly under the central government (Beijing, Tianjin, Shanghai, and Chongqing) should submit their urban plans to the State Council for approval. On the other hand, capital cities of provinces, cities with a population of more than 1 million, and certain designated cities need to submit their plans first to the provincial government and then to the State Council for approval.

Sectoral Structure of Planning Institutions

Most Asia-Pacific countries have urban planning departments at the local level. For example, in Korea, Japan, India, and China, functions of land development, transportation provision, economic growth, and environment protection are carried out by different institutions. To guide future urban development patterns, a wide range of plans, such as socioeconomic plans (or strategic plans), land resource plans, urban comprehensive plans, transportation plans, and environment protection plans, are formulated. Correspondingly, a variety of planning institutions are established to lead planning efforts in different sectors.

At the national level in China, for instance, comprehensive plans for land and resources and land use master plans are supervised by the Ministry of Land and Resources; comprehensive plans for river basins and flood control planning are supervised by the Ministry of Water Resources; transportation plans are supervised by the Ministry of Communication, the Ministry of Railway, and the General Administration of Civil Aviation; and regional (economic development) plans and national economic and social development plans are supervised by the National Development and Reform Commission. These institutions should coordinate with each other in plan formulation, implementation, and evaluation.

In Japan, the above planning functions are housed in Ministry of Economy, Trade and Industry, Ministry of Land, Infrastructure, Transport and Tourism, Ministry of Agriculture, Forestry and Fisheries, and Ministry of Environment.

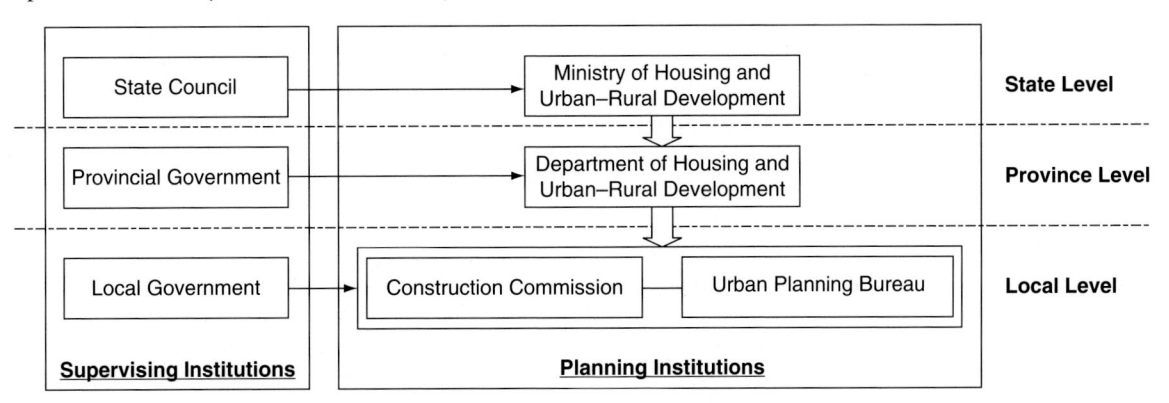

Figure 1 Planning institutions in China at different levels.
Source: Song Y and Pan X (2009) Toward better plans to guide smart development in Chinese cities. In Song Y and Ding C (eds.) *Smart Urban Growth for China*, ch. 10, pp. 193–214. Cambridge, MA: Lincoln Institute of Land Policy.

Table 1 Selected planning-related local institutions and their major functions

Bureau of urban planning
- Manage the urban planning process; inspect, approve, and file plans, as well as planning-related projects

Bureau of land and resources, or land and water bureau
- Manage the land use master plan and other land use-related activities; provide and inspect land use allocation to other agencies and stakeholders

Bureau of water resources, or river bureau
- Develop comprehensive plans for river basins and flood control

Bureau of transportation, or road transport bureau
- Participate in urban planning processes, especially those related to transportation planning; manage the traffic impact analysis for land use and construction development

Commission of development and reform, or policy bureau
- Establish the Economic and Social Development Plan, as well as regional development plans; guide the urban planning process

Bureau of public works, or infrastructure bureau
- Maintain the public infrastructure system, for example, sewage, sanitation, pipelines

Bureau of environmental protection
- Develop local environmental legislation; monitor the environmental protection of corresponding areas

Bureau of statistics
- Provide historical population and economic data to planning agencies

Source: Song Y and Pan X (2009) Toward better plans to guide smart development in Chinese cities. In Song Y and Ding C (eds.) *Smart Urban Growth for China*, ch. 10, pp. 193–214. Cambridge, MA: Lincoln Institute of Land Policy.

At the local level, preparing, establishing, implementing, and managing urban development plans generally involve many governmental agencies due to the complex institutional structure. Examples of planning-related local agencies and their roles and functions in the urban planning process in many Asian countries are listed in **Table 1**.

Functions of Different Planning Institutions

This section illustrates functions and contents of various plans administered by the planning agencies mentioned above.

Economic and Social Development Plans

In most Asian countries, where the promotion of economic growth is one of the major goals, the economic and social development plans play an important role in guiding subsequent urban and rural developments. The economic and social development plans generally guide decisions on capital investment projects and budgets, and provide overall development direction. Consequently, these plans play important roles in effecting infrastructure provision, economic growth, and urbanisation patterns. For example, Korea's long-range development strategic plans have profound impacts on urban growth trends and China's five-year plan on economic and social development provides guidance to draft many other policy documents and plans. Typically, these strategic plans cover key areas such as economic growth, settlement structure, population dynamics, management of natural resources, and environmental and public services. A general set of indicators is used to benchmark development goals and results such as GDP per capita, urbanisation level, ratio of R&D expenditure over GDP, population and employment growth, energy consumption, water consumption, water use efficiency, farmland protection, emission reduction, pension and health insurance coverage, and per capita disposable income for both urban and rural residents.

In China, the National Development and Reform Commission has been responsible for formulating the National Economic and Social Development Plan, commonly referred to as a five-year plan, every 5 years since 1949. The plan is based on inputs from all relevant ministries at the national level and the State Council and needs approval of the National People's Congress to be effective. The purpose of the five-year plan is to provide guidelines for economic reform, urban and rural development strategies, and social welfare development of the nation. All levels of local government, except townships, develop economic and social development plans after the national five-year plan is formulated. Local five-year planning is led by the Development and Reform Commission and the local government. Plans are reviewed and approved by the National People's Congress before they become effective. The local five-year plans are similar to the national five-year plan.

Land Use Plans

Land use plans generally concern the planning and drafting of policies regarding technology for the provision of infrastructures to use, develop, and conserve land resources. Almost all countries have established institutions for land management. The purpose of drafting land use plans is to specify land use and allocate land for different purposes, such as protected or preserved farmland, basic farmland, land development and conversion, land available for urban and economic growth, and farmland available for conversion to urban uses.

There are diverse institutional settings for drafting land use plans. In some countries, land use planning is a local task, while in others land preservation may be a top-down process. For example, in China, the land use planning process is administered by the Ministry of Land Resources (MLR) at the national level, the Department of Land Resources at provincial level, and then the land management bureaus at the local level. The amount of land to be protected or made available for development is largely determined by a higher level of government. Land use plans and their revisions for provinces, prefecture cities, and autonomous regions are reviewed and approved by the State Council. Plans and plan revisions for townships, cities, counties, and prefectures are reviewed and approved by the provincial government.

Urban Plans

There are different terms for urban plans – Comprehensive Physical Development Plan, Master Plan, Special Plan, Project Plan, or District Plan – in different countries. These urban plans aim to control urban spatial resources, guide the development and construction of cities and towns, provide sufficient public services, ensure public health, and protect public interests. In most countries, urban plans are required to ensure efficient consumption of natural resources, for the protection of ecological and cultural resources, to promote sustainable development, and to meet the needs of the general public, especially of disadvantaged members.

In China, the urban planning system is administered by the Ministry of Housing and Urban–Rural Development at the national level and planning commissions at the local level. The 1989 City Planning Act has been recognised as an important milestone in formalising China's urban planning system and outlining the explicit roles and functions of various institutions in the Chinese urban planning process. According to the Act, in the urban planning system, the planning institutions are responsible for drafting region-wide city-town system plans, master plans, district plans (optional), and detailed plans.

In the Chinese urban planning system, there are mainly two types of region-wide city-town system plans: one is the nationwide plan conducted by the State Council to coordinate developments in different provinces; the other is the province-wide plan prepared by each provincial commission to coordinate developments within different cities of a province. For those municipal cities and towns where county government offices are located, a city-town system plan should be included in the master plan and should be developed at the very beginning (even before the master plan) in order to guide in a consistent and conflict-free urban planning process. An important objective of these plans is to assist the rational allocation of production and population within the nation and the region. To be consistent with the goals in the corresponding economic development plans, these system plans determine the physical size and development hierarchy of the cities within the nation and the region. Generally, an urban plan should be prepared in at least two stages: the master plan (or comprehensive plan) at the first stage, and a detailed plan at the later stage. The master plan and the master plan guidelines are the most important steps in the city planning process. The master plan usually has a 20-year planning term. Long-term (such as 30-year) vision and growth strategies can also be discussed in the plan. The master plan is not only for the urban development area, but also for the whole region of a city's administrative zone. Moreover, large and medium-sized cities with more than 200 000 people can develop district plans if needed as a complementary document to the master plan. The district plan considers factors such as layout of urban growth, development of the city determined by the corresponding master plan, distinct characters of the district, natural or artificial boundaries (e.g., rivers and roads), and the city's subadministration zones. The detailed plan follows the master plan and the district plan and should contain the detailed layout designs for the proposed short-term construction projects. The detailed plan is further divided into the detailed development control plan and the detailed construction plan.

Transportation Plans

In most countries, regional transportation planning targets nonurban areas with the overarching purpose of building intercity, inter-region connections through different transportation modes. The regional railway system plans guide developments of national and local railways. The airport and related infrastructure plans formulate the national civil aviation networks. Urban transportation planning focuses specifically on areas within urban boundaries with the purpose of serving the transportation demands associated with developments within the city boundaries. The transportation plans include development of road networks, public transportation, transportation management, and transportation logistics.

In China, for example, transportation planning consists of regional transportation planning and urban transportation planning. The former is overseen by the Ministry of Communication, the Ministry of Railway, and the General Administration of Civil Aviation. These three institutions have different statutory responsibilities with corresponding focus on specific sectors. Urban transportation planning is in general a process under the urban planning system. Transportation planning activities are overseen by the urban planning institution in each city.

Cross-Institutional Coordination

The above section demonstrates that there are many plans and institutions involved in the planning process. Most countries would have at least institutions for economic, urban land use, transportation, and environment planning. This typically leads to a lack of coordination between planning and other line function departments. Therefore, integration of plans and coordination across institutions are essential for ensuring effective plans as well as effective implementation.

Figure 2 summarises recent efforts made by many cities in increasing coordination among institutions to bridge the tasks of social and economic development, urban development, transportation development, and environment protection. The planning agency responsible for evaluation of social and economic forecast shares evaluations of the population and economic conditions with other agencies to guide the planning of land uses, infrastructure, and environmental systems. The planning agencies responsible for land resource protection and urban land use allocation could be integrated so that decisions on new development location, and limitations and conservation of farmlands or open spaces are made simultaneously. The planning agency responsible for transportation planning needs to coordinate with land use and urban plan agencies so that the layout and capacity of transportation infrastructures and multimodal transportation systems (including road networks, rails, transit systems, and airports) respond to spatial allocation of land uses identified in land use and urban plans. In addition, the planning agency responsible for protection

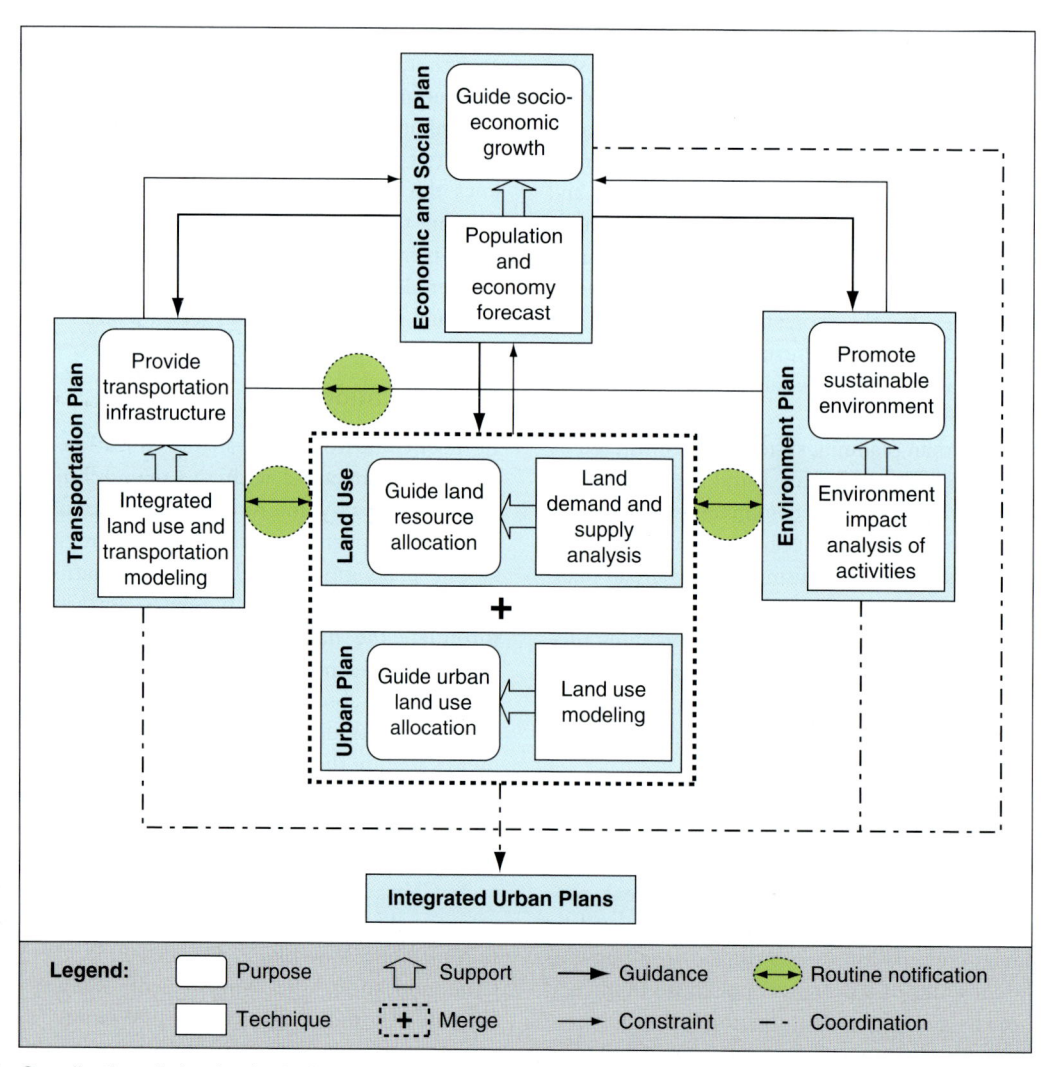

Figure 2 Coordination of planning institutions.

of sensitive ecological resources and environment needs to coordinate with urban planning and transportation planning agencies. In addition to monitoring traditional polluting sources such as industrial or agricultural wastes, better coordination with urban and transportation planning agencies can increase the environment planning agency's capacity for mitigating pollution caused by urban and transportation developments. As a result, recent reform efforts are characterised by a reduction in the number of institutions and consolidation of sectoral functions to streamline integration among agencies.

Implications of Institutional Structure on Housing Provision

In most large cities in Asian countries, scarcity of affordable housing is a major issue. This is due to insufficient supply, high rent or purchase costs, and lack of easy access to mortgage products. Affordable housing has become an important policy concern in the last two decades. Many cities aim to speed up the solution to the housing problems for low-income families. For example, China has made efforts to solve housing problems for 2.6 million families since 2009. It is important to note that the impact of affordable housing planning programmes will be modest unless local institutions form provincial and national coalitions to advocate systemic change. Programmes for building economic capacity and regulations for real estate developers are needed to support the actions taken at the local level. Without actions at higher levels of government, the positive impact of local affordable housing programmes is likely to be limited. In addition, coordination across planning institutions is essential to ensure access to land and infrastructure for affordable housing programmes. This implies setting up feasible goals of affordable housing provision in social and economic plans, by allocating land resources and sites for affordable housing units in land use and urban plans. Also, coordinating the provision of transportation infrastructure, especially multimodal options, and ensuring sustainable locations of housing developments in environmental plans can bring about more holistic implementation of affordable housing programmes.

See also: Central Government Institutions.

Further Reading

Berke PR, Godschalk DR, Kaiser E, and Rodriguez D (2006) *Urban Land Use Planning*. Urbana, IL; Chicago, IL: The University of Illinois Press.

Chow GC (2004) *Knowing China*. Singapore: World Scientific Publishers.

Ding C and Song Y (eds.) (2005) *Emerging Land and Housing Markets in China*. Cambridge, MA: Lincoln Institute of Land Policy.

Haggard SS (2004) Institutions and growth in East Asia. *Studies in Comparative International Development* 38(4): 53–81.

Knaap GJ and Song Y (2007) Compact urban form or business as usual? An examination of urban form in Orange County, Florida. In: Connerly C, Chapin T, and Higgins H (eds.) *Growth Management in Florida: Planning for Paradise*, ch. 9, pp. 141–154. Burlington, VT: Ashgate Publishing Limited.

Mello LR (2000) Fiscal decentralization and intergovernmental fiscal relations: A cross-country analysis. *World Development* 28(2): 365–380.

Ng MK and Hills P (2003) World cities or great cities? A comparative study of five Asian metropolises. *Cities* 20(3): 151–165.

Song Y and Ding C (eds.) (2007) *Urbanization in China: Critical Issues in an Era of Rapid Growth*. Cambridge, MA: Lincoln Institute of Land Policy.

Song Y and Pan X (2009) Toward better plans to guide smart development in Chinese cities. In: Song Y and Ding C (eds.) *Smart Urban Growth for China*, ch. 10, pp. 193–214. Cambridge, MA: Lincoln Institute of Land Policy.

Yeung YM (2000) *Globalization and Networked Societies: Urban-Regional Change in Pacific Asia*. Honolulu, HI: University of Hawaii Press.

Zhang Y, Song Y, and Ding C (2009) Plan integration for coordinated urban growth in China. In: Song Y and Ding C (eds.) *Smart Urban Growth for China*, ch. 9, pp. 175–192. Cambridge, MA: Lincoln Institute of Land Policy.

Planning Institutions: Post-Socialist

Z Nedović-Budić, University College Dublin, Dublin, Ireland

© 2012 Elsevier Ltd. All rights reserved.

Glossary

Governance Combined formal authority and procedures with informal practices and judgements by numerous entities that interact with the government.
Government Structure and function of public institutions with primary functions in the delivery of publicly supported goods and services.
Institutions Stable collection of rules and practices defining behaviour, reducing uncertainties, and increasing reliability of expectations in daily interactions and activities between all societal players in the private, public, and nonprofit sectors.
Market Interaction space for buyers and sellers to find each other, enter into joint contracts, coordinate the transfer of goods, agree on price and quantity for trade, ensure respect of property rights, hold in check the externalities, foster competition, and secure efficient flow of information.
Planning system Planning doctrine formalised and translated into laws and institutions with planning, urban development, and regulatory functions. Planning doctrine comprises the context-specific planning practices and approaches.
Privatisation Transfer of property from state/societal/communal ownership to private ownership through purchase or restitution of property rights.
Property rights The bundle of rights associated with a property; actual ownership of the property – usually divided between individuals and the government – and rights to use, build (or control building), sell, transfer, or inherit.

Institutional Embedding of Planning

City planning is a future-oriented activity for managing urban development and change. It is a social and political process among actors representing different public and private interests. As the societal activity, planning is dependent on a mix of cognitive, cultural, social, economic, and political institutions. Government and market provide the framework within which planning operates while cultural norms, mores, and practices comprise the context for planning. Spatial change occurs because of opportunities and restrictions created by forces such as state (government), market, and space. Although planning is institutionalised along the state–market continuum, the main difference between socialist and postsocialist planning is in their positioning towards the opposing ends of this continuum, with postsocialist systems drawing more strongly on market principles and institutions.

In almost two decades since the overthrow of state socialism (or communism) in Central, East and Southeast Europe (CESE), substantial changes have occurred in the nature, role, and functioning of government and other institutions involved in spatial development and urban planning. The transition of societies and cities from socialist to postsocialist involves – among other things – new systems of government (or governance); new legal, constitutional, and institutional frameworks; new economic order; new rules of social integration; and new policy choices for privatisation and redistribution of public assets. In addition to transition, the CESE countries have been caught in the concurrent processes of (re)Europeanisation and globalisation, but they are not alone in these dynamics. In fact throughout the 1990s and to the present, planning in capitalist regimes has undergone substantial transformations as well. Sorting out new local and global realities and finding planning modes and institutions that would most effectively deal with the evolving circumstances have been challenges common to transitional and other established market-based and democratic societies.

From Government to Governance

Regardless of the place of balance between government and market processes, in the majority of countries planning and policy-making is conducted as a government function. The varying of the styles of planning from fully bureaucratic and administrative to participatory and inclusive parallels the government–governance continuum but still does not diminish its government-centred nature. The government-planning powers are distributed among three levels – national, state, and local – and their balance affects the nature and scope of planning. Among the three levels, the state government tends to be the main collective actor in the public domain and the main potential locus of planning operating in the mode of social engineering, particularly prominent under the communist political regimes.

National-level planning is traditionally practised in the democratic countries, but with substantially varying emphasis placed on production of the actual national plan, its legal status, institutions in charge, preparation procedures, and modes of implementation and coordination. The CESE countries have departed from the national-level planning for the most part as a reaction to centralised planning during the communist political regime. In the same spirit of abandoning top–down socialist planning, the majority of the postsocialist countries have decentralised the authorities and powers from the state to the local level through new laws (**Table 1**).

The control and command role of the state has been substantially reduced as it has turned away from intervention towards coordination and regulation. Over the past 20 years, the newly empowered and increasingly fiscally independent local governments have learnt to take advantage of their freedom. They have also faced many internal and external pressures in terms of revenue sources, service provision, public scrutiny, local and regional competition, and globalisation.

Although the devolution of powers to the local level is pervasive across the CESE region, the regional level has been somewhat neglected, particularly in the initial stages of transformation. The important role of this intermediate-level government was recognised and subsequent legislative actions corrected for the early omission. However, the regional bodies have rarely received the full executive authority given to the local and state or national entities, and the relationships with these higher instances vary considerably. From early 2000s the countries applying for European Union (EU) membership have moved from centralised state systems to devolve power to local authorities (Hungary, Romania, Latvia, Slovenia, Estonia, and Lithuania), regions (Slovak Republic, Bulgaria, and the Czech Republic), or a mix of the two categories (Poland).

Finally, pan-European level has become an increasingly important framework for urban planning and policy at all levels – from state to local and multistate regions in particular. The framework has been developed with the establishment and subsequent enlargements of the EU and two major policy initiatives – agricultural and cohesion – that require harmonisation and integration across the EU territory. These initiatives also need to be translated in spatial terms and made coherent. European spatial planning is based on the European Spatial Development Perspective adopted in 1999, the INTERREG programme for stimulating transnational cooperation, the European Spatial Planning Observation Network (ESPON) for monitoring spatial development trends in member countries, and the Territorial Agenda adopted in 2007 aiming towards 'a more competitive and sustainable Europe of diverse regions'. European spatial planning is in the process of institutionalising but not without challenges and divergences from the common path. The concept of territorial cohesion succeeding the concepts of spatial planning and spatial development is intended to make pan-European development policy more spatially explicit. Territorial cohesion and equity

Table 1 Political decentralisation – sample of legislations and administrative structures

Country	Initial legislation[a]	Administrative structure[b]
The Czech Republic	1990 Municipalities Act 1992 Act on Local Self-Government 1997 Act on Establishment of Higher Territorial Self-Governing Units	6249 municipalities, 13 regions, and the capital city of Prague (also a region), 76 districts
Bulgaria	1991 The Local Self-Government and Local Administration Act The Administrative Division Act 1999 The Regional Development Act	263 municipalities, 28 districts (provinces), 6 planning economic regions
Hungary	1990 The Act on Local Self-Government 1996/1999 Law on Regions	251 towns, 22 cities, Budapest (county, subregion, capital with 23 districts), 19 counties, 173 administrative subregions; 7 statistical regions
Poland	1990 Act on Local Self-Government 1994 Act on the Local Self-government of Warsaw	16 voivodships, 373 counties including 65 urban counties, Warsaw with 11 districts; central district with 7 boroughs
Slovakia	1990 The Municipalities Act 1992 Local Government Act 2001 Act on Self-Government of Regions	2834 municipalities (Bratislava and Kosice with special status), 8 regions, 79 districts

[a]The table does not list additional legislative acts and amendments.
[b]The numbers reflect the recent, but not necessarily the most current, status.

in development are embedded in the European model of society, but these run against the conflicting aims of global competitiveness, sustainability, and territorial cohesion at the national scale.

Market

Planning has often been critiqued for its disregard of market forces and emphasis on government-driven regulation, particularly under the communist political regimes. It was primarily focused on achieving the national and regional economic growth objectives through implementation of sectoral and physical plans at detailed (urban block/area), citywide, and regional levels. However, rarely are the arguments one-sided. Planning is recognised as a necessary response to market failure, and underregulating urban development can be as detrimental as overregulating it.

The recent shift in CESE countries occurred from the socialist to postsocialist production regime, that is, from extensive accumulation through state-led industrialisation and redistributive state to intensive accumulation through commodification and spatial fix (export orientation, marketisation, and the entrepreneurial state), and from Fordism to post-Fordism, that is, from the economy of scale and Keynesian welfare state to the economy of scope and post-Keynesian workfare (the latter occurring throughout the developed world).

In the planning realm, it is the interface between the market and social rationalities that determines the public interest and urban development outcomes. The market forces are represented through increased participation of private sector stakeholders, for example, individual citizens, nonprofit organisations and groups, and real estate developers. However, the market institutions that affect urban planning and development most significantly are financial regulations and property rights. During the socialist period, the balance of ownership was tilted towards the state, particularly in urban areas, though substantial variation existed among the socialist countries. Reallocation of property rights between the public and private sectors has been happening on a massive scale in postsocialist countries since the end of the communist political regime. Privatisation and restitution of land and housing is probably the most radical aspect of the transition from state socialist to democratic and market-based systems. By the mid-1990s considerable housing stock was privatised in most countries as one of the first steps in the transition to capitalism and markets (**Table 2**).

Although some privatisation elements had been present before the 1990s, in most of the postsocialist CESE countries, major legislative changes were established soon after the fall of communism through constitutional or special legal provisions, for example, authorisation of sales to private entities, provision for management of property, restitution to former owners, facilitation of market transfers, judicial enforcement of property rights, regulatory land-use planning controls, and comprehensive housing policy. The legislation has produced a variety of results both expected and unexpected, including disincentives to assume ownership as a result of the financial burdens associated with it (maintenance in particular), and has also substantially reduced provision of social housing. It made housing more expensive, less secure, more segregated, and less socially equitable. The behaviour and interface between the development firms and planning and financial and property rights institutions (laws, cadastres, or courts) could be considered indicators of progress in the establishment of property markets and provision of urban housing.

Planning Systems and Laws

Planning systems are constituted on formalised planning laws and institutions. They are differentiated by variations in national legal and constitutional structures and administrative and professional cultures.

Table 2 Home ownership[a] and housing production[a] in selected cities/countries

City	Homeownership – % of housing stock	Country	1999 housing production as a % of 1990 housing production
Budapest, Hungary	76	Hungary	50
Ljubljana, Slovenia	77	Slovenia	96
Minsk, Belarus	44	Belarus	56
Riga, Latvia	25	Latvia	25
Tallinn, Estonia	92	Estonia	19
Tbilisi, Georgia	91	Georgia	17
Sofia, Bulgaria	92	Bulgaria	45

[a]Statistics based on United Nations Commission on Human Settlements 2000. Estimate by S. Tsenkova.
Source: Reproduced from Tsenkova S and Nedović-Budić Z (eds.) (2006) *Urban Mosaic of Post-Socialist Europe – Space, Institutions and Policy*. Heidelberg: Springer.

With some differences between the countries, from the mid-1940s through the 1980s, the socialist urban planning in CESE countries was characterised by the communist institutional and ideological framework that assumed a single-party political system; state ownership and distribution of the nationalised means of production and property; rejection of market principles and mechanisms; and general priority of public and collective interests and goals over the individual or private ones. During the communist regime, local governments had limited legislative powers and were largely dependent on income transferred from the state. However, planning was exercised with a substantial legal power. Legislation in support of urban planning was introduced with the first 5-year economic plans soon after the Second World War. Two distinct planning models were applied in those countries: (1) a Soviet-based centralised planning model, with hierarchical control mechanisms mostly exercised through intermediate regional agencies; and (2) a decentralised planning model, with centrally determined overall long-term goals, but with some planning and decision making exercised at the local level.

The formation of planning institutions and systems is a dynamic and complex process producing an idiosyncratic mix of old, new, and innovative practices, many of which display hybrid qualities, drawing on and influenced by many internal and external forces and actors, but also affected by the history, or 'pre-transitional situation' or 'path-dependency'. For example, in the case of the Czech Republic, Poland, and Hungary, one would expect that in the transitioning of legal and administrative systems, their common historic roots with Austria or Germany would re-emerge; similarly, Baltic states would take after a Scandinavian model. Legislative enactments, which are one of the fundamental elements in establishing a new planning system, have followed the transition from socialist to postsocialist regimes in the 1990s. The new acts prescribe the level of planning, the type of documents, and development control mechanisms (i.e., planning and building permits). Various institutions, ranging from the ministries of architecture and construction to urban and regional development, public works, environment, and housing, are in charge of planning. They are complemented by institutional setups at the national, regional, municipal, and detailed levels of planning. Most major CESE cities, capitals in particular, have produced new or updated existing master and strategic plans (**Tables 3** and **4**).

Postsocialist CESE countries vary substantially in the nature and speed of establishing their new institutional and urban development environments, including factors such as the speed of transition of the political and economic system, influx and placement of investments, public controls over land market and planning and building process, and privatisation of land and housing. Some examples are of East Germany moving and restructuring the fastest with intense investment activity; Hungary transitioning and privatising rapidly, but slower on the institutional change; the Czech Republic, Slovakia, and Poland advancing well but at a slower pace on all fronts and towards a mixed model with some remnants of state control; Bulgaria and Romania going ahead with a mix of action on privatisation and dissolution of old institutions and lagging in overall transition to a new system and the investments in private and public sectors; Albania being

Table 3 Legal and institutional planning framework – sample of countries

National legal and institutional framework for planning

Country	Main national institution in charge of planning	Basic urban (spatial) planning law and other planning-related legislation
Belarus	Ministry of Architecture and Construction	Law on the Fundamentals of Architecture and Town Planning Activities; Also, Building Normative Act.
Bulgaria	Ministry of Regional Development and Public Works	Spatial Planning Act; Also, Law of Self-government, Administrative and Territorial Organization Act, and Building Regulations and Land-use Codes.
Estonia	Ministry of the Environment	Planning and Building Act; Also, Building Law.
Latvia	Ministry of Environmental Protection and Regional Development	Law on Spatial Development Planning; Also, Building Regulations, Building Act, Regulations on Physical Plans, and Act on the Municipal Governments.
Lithuania	Ministry of the Environment	Law on Territorial Planning; Also, Code on Territorial Planning and Building Supervision, and Law on Assessment of Impact of Planned Economic Activity on Nature.
Poland	Housing and Urban Development Office	Physical Development Act; Also, Environmental Protection and Management Act, and Building and Land-use Codes.
Russia	Ministry for Regional Development	Urban Development Act; Also, Law on Architectural Activity, Law on Ecological Assessment, and Building, Housing and Land Codes.

Extracted from the Committee on Spatial Development in the Baltic Sea region (undated) and National Centre for Regional Development (undated).
Source: Reproduced from UN HABITAT, Hirt S and Stanilov K (2009) Revisiting urban planning in the transitional countries. *Background Study for Planning Sustainable Cities, Global Report on Human Settlements.* http://www.unhabitat.org/grhs/2009.

Table 4 Planning legislation and institutions at various levels – sample of countries

Country level	Czech Republic	Hungary	Poland	Slovenia	Germany
Planning legislation	Act on Physical Planning and Building Regulations (Building Act) (1976, last amendment 2000)	Act on Regional Development and Physical Planning (1996, 1999); Building Act (1996)	Building Code (1993); Spatial Planning Act (1994)	Building Act (2002); Spatial Planning Act (2002)	Federal Building Code; Federal Land Utilization Ordinance; sectoral planning low; building low
National level		National physical plan (2002 under consultation with Brussels)		Spatial development strategy; spatial regulation ordinance	Guidelines for regional planning
Regional level	Regional physical plan; strategic plan	Regional development plans; regional physical plans (not legally binding documents)		Regional development programme; regional concept of spatial development plan	Regional development programme; regional spatial plan
Local/municipality level	Master plan (land-use plan for all territory); municipal development programme (strategic plan)	Development concepts and programmes; master plan	Master plan	Spatial development strategy including concept of urban development and concept of landscape development and protection; spatial regulation ordinance	Land-use plan for cities (FNP); sectoral development plans (STEP); local development plan (Städtebauliche Rahuenplanung, Bebauungsplanung); development programmes (BEP)
Communes level (districts, boroughs)	Regulatory plan – detailed regulation plan for urban zone	Detailed local plans (land-use plan)	Detailed local plans (land-use plan/local taxation function)	Local plans (detailed regulation plans for urban zone)	Detailed plans

City level	Prague	Budapest	Warsaw	Ljubljana	Berlin
Formal planning documents	Master Plan (1986) (provisional plan, 1994; new zoning plan, 1999); Prague Strategic Plan (2000); Prague Regional Operational Programme (1999)	Master plan[a] (1988, 1993, 1998; new zoning regulation); Urban development concept	Master plan (1980, 1994, more suited to market conditions); Warsaw Development Strategy 2010 (2001); Spatial Development Plan (under preparation)	Master plan (1986, 1998, minor changes adopted, mainly traffic); new master plan, 1st phase: spatial development concept (2002)	Land Use Plan (FNP); general zoning framework; main transportation network; spatial distribution of public services
Informal/supplementary documents	Urban Study (area-specialised analytical study)	Sustainable development concept, programmes, and action plan; rehabilitation programme	Condition and Directions of Spatial Development of the Capital City of Warsaw Study (2001); development condition studies of the individual municipality	Strategy for Sustainable Development of the City (2002)	Development programme (BEP); urban development plans
Development control	Planning permits; building permits Plans certificate[b]	Planning permits; building permits	Planning permits; building permits (can be combined in construction permit)	Planning permits; building permits (can be combined) Plans certificate	Building permits

[a]Dual nature of municipal system: Municipality of Budapest and 23 district municipalities. Budapest districts have a large autonomy in the decision-making process, including the field of planning and development (e.g., development priorities and detailed zoning regulation).
[b]Certificate of approval for building use and occupation, after the completion of building.
Reproduced from Dimitrovska-Andrews, K. Article 6 in Hamilton IFE, Dimitrovska-Andrews K, and Pichler-Milanovic N (eds.) (2005) *Transformation of Cities in Central and Eastern Europe – Towards Globalization*, pp. 44–78. Tokyo: United Nations University.

quick to abandon or privatise the old but replacing it with an unregulated mostly illegal environment (e.g., unofficial housing market); former Yugoslavia making slow progress after being stalled by the ethnic unrest of the 1990s, but is in a somewhat chaotic and illegal regime; Baltic states picking up speed on all fronts – transition, investments, privatisation, and new controls, with some remaining elements of state control; and the Russian Federation and other former USSR states taking major steps in the direction of a market-based society but with emphasis on the local political control. The diversity of transitional paths is evident.

Conclusion

Planning is embedded in institutions and the two constantly change and evolve. Dating back to the 1970s, the planning paradigm shifted from bureaucratic and technocratic to facilitating, socially aware, and soft approaches; the 1980s brought economic globalisation, deregulation, and neoliberal politics, all contributing to augmenting regulatory planning with entrepreneurial tactics. In transitioning from socialist to postsocialist, urban planning responses have been quite diverse, reacting to specific and often dramatic conditions: political democratisation, reintroduction of market principles, the state's fiscal crisis, massive privatisation, commercialisation, discontinuation of 'welfare state' programmes, and intensified international financial transactions and investments in urban areas. The new circumstances have prompted not only new institutions but also a 'new notion of planning' that strives to regain its legitimacy, become more flexible, and adapt to the new economic and political circumstances. Although exacerbated by the transitional conditions, the challenges have been hardly unique to postsocialist countries. Globalisation, deregulation, and new competitiveness are faced by countries and regions worldwide, and the formation of postsocialist planning institutions has been caught in the ongoing current of changing nature of urban planning.

In the twenty-first century, urban planning deals with new complexities and interdependences and addresses competing spatial claims of inclusiveness, coordination, and ownership. From the institutional perspective, planning is moving from regulation and control to enabling, coordinative, and transformative roles. The emerging approaches to planning include entrepreneurial, strategic, collaborative, communicative, community-based, regionalism, and renewed forms of integrated and comprehensive planning. They tend to be at odds with institutional structures that support the traditional planning culture. They require more than the government as a player and instead need to include formal and informal relational networks of individuals, firms, pressure groups, trade unions, and social organisations.

The forces that affect planning institutions and urban development in Europe and across the globe are creating a convergence effect. The convergence is about globalising trends, international commons, hybrid planning approaches, and institutional isomorphism. Planning culture, on the other hand, creates a differentiating effect. The culture effect emanates from the values and attitudes held by professional planners regarding the role of the state, market forces, and civil society in the development at urban, regional, and national levels. Similarly, the institutionalisation of postsocialist planning proceeds in the same general direction but with many local varieties and different paths that counter the process of homogenisation. The postsocialist societal settings offer a rich laboratory for learning about urban planning as a collective action and the evolving formal and informal institutions that enable it, with culture being as important as political, economic, and social institutions and processes.

See also: House Building Industries: Post-Socialist; Housing and the State in the Soviet Union and Eastern Europe; Housing Finance Institutions: Transition Societies; Housing Policy: Agents and Regulators; Institutional Economics: New; Institutional Economics: Traditional; Institutions for Housing Supply; Private Sector Housing Management: Post-Socialist; Social Housing Institutions in Europe.

Further Reading

Albrechts L, Alden J, and da Rosa Pires A (2001) *The Changing Landscape of Planning*. Aldershot: Ashgate.
Alterman R (2001) *National-Level Planning in Democratic Countries*. Liverpool: Liverpool University Press.
Andrusz G, Harloe M, and Szelenyi I (eds.) (1996) *Cities after Socialism – Urban and Regional Change and Conflict in Post-Socialist Societies*. Oxford: Blackwell Publishers.
Balchin P, Sýkora L, and Bull G (1999) *Regional Policy and Planning in Europe*. London; New York: Routledge.
Booth P (1996) *Controlling Development: Certainty and Discretion in Europe, the U.S. and Hong Kong*. London: UCL Press.
Faludi A (ed.) (2007) *Territorial Cohesion and the European Model of Society*. Cambridge, MA: Lincoln Institute of Land Policy.
Friedmann J (1987) *Planning in the Public Domain: From Knowledge to Action*. Princeton, NJ: Princeton University Press.
Hamilton IFE, Dimitrovska-Andrews K, and Pichler-Milanovic N (eds.) (2005) *Transformation of Cities in Central and Eastern Europe – Towards Globalization*, pp. 44–78. Tokyo: United Nations University.
Hirt S and Stanilov K (2009) Revisiting urban planning in the transitional countries. *Background Study for Planning Sustainable Cities, Global Report on Human Settlements*. http://www.unhabitat.org/grhs/2009
Kettl DF (2002) *The Transformation of Governance – Public Administration for Twenty-First Century America*. Baltimore, MD: The Johns Hopkins University Press.
Nedovic-Budic Z (2001) Adjustment of planning practice to the new eastern and central European context. *Journal of the American Planning Association* 67: 38–52.

Newman P and Thornley A (1996) *Urban Planning in Europe*. London: Routledge.
Offe C (1997) *Varieties of transition – The East European and East German experience*. Cambridge, MA: The MIT Press.
Sanyal B (2005) *Comparative Planning Cultures*. New York and London: Routledge.
Scott JC (1998) *Seeing like a State – How Certain Schemes to Improve the Human Condition Have Failed*. New Haven, CT: Yale University Press.
Taşan-Kok T (2004) *Budapest, Istanbul, and Warsaw: Institutional and Spatial Change*. Delft: Eburon.
Tsenkova S and Nedović-Budić Z (eds.) (2006) *Urban Mosaic of Post-Socialist Europe – Space, Institutions and Policy*. Heidelberg: Springer.
Verma N (ed.) (2007) *Institutions and Planning*. Oxford; Amsterdam: Elsevier.
Waterhout B (2008) *The Institutionalization of European Spatial Planning*. Delft: Delft University of Technology.

Policies to Address Homelessness

P Flatau, Murdoch University, Perth, WA, Australia

© 2012 Elsevier Ltd. All rights reserved.

Glossary

Cost-effectiveness A form of economic evaluation in which an assessment is made of the differential impact a given homelessness intervention has on specified client outcomes relative to the cost of implementing a program. A cost–benefit evaluation converts all benefits to a monetary value and compares the differential dollar value of an intervention to the differential cost of the intervention.

Economic evaluation The analysis of the differential benefit of a homelessness program relative to the differential costs of implementing the program. Differential benefits and costs are evaluated on the basis of a comparison of outcomes under the program in question with a no-intervention case or against an alternative intervention scenario.

Evaluation An assessment of a homelessness program or strategy designed to determine whether the program was effective in achieving its goals.

Experimental study An evaluation study in which evidence on program effectiveness is derived from a randomised control trial in which eligible participants of a homelessness program are randomly assigned to the treatment group (program participation) or to a control group and an analysis is undertaken of outcomes achieved by the treatment group relative to the control group.

Homelessness intervention An action, strategy or program designed to assist those who are homeless or at risk of homelessness meet their housing and non-shelter needs.

Program effectiveness The extent to which a homelessness program improves specified client outcomes.

Quasi-experimental study An evaluation study in which evidence on program effectiveness is based on an analysis of outcomes achieved by the treatment group relative to the control group using statistical means to control for confounding effects.

Introduction

Homelessness interventions are actions, strategies, and programs undertaken by governments, community organisations, and local government councils designed to assist those who are homeless or at risk of homelessness meet their housing and nonshelter needs. Australian homelessness interventions are largely undertaken by governments (national and regional) in partnership with community organisations and local government councils. Governments fund and administer homelessness programs while nongovernment community organisations and local government councils deliver services to homeless people. In a small number of cases, community organisations and local government councils fund and undertake their own homeless services.

Evaluation of a homelessness intervention is an assessment of a homelessness program or strategy designed to determine whether it has been effective in achieving its goals. The evaluation may be commissioned or undertaken by the agency responsible for funding and administering the program or conducted independently by researchers. Evaluations seek to assess whether, and to what degree, the relevant program has followed appropriate processes and procedures, has addressed the needs of clients and secured positive change for them, and has been cost-effective. Evaluations use various methods and sources of data to examine these issues.

This article provides a brief overview of the existing range of Australian homelessness interventions, examines methodological issues related to the evaluation of homelessness interventions, and reviews selected Australian evaluations of homelessness interventions.

Australian Homelessness Interventions

Australian homelessness interventions fall into four main categories.

1. Crisis accommodation support for those who would otherwise be without safe and secure shelter, together with outreach services for those living 'on the streets'.
2. Strategies to improve homeless people's access to long-term housing and to provide them with support on entry into long-term housing.
3. Early intervention support for households at imminent risk of homelessness.
4. Homelessness prevention and structural programs designed to address the underlying causes of homelessness.

The largest homelessness intervention response in Australia involves the provision of supported crisis and transitional accommodation for those who would otherwise be without safe and secure housing. Complementing supported accommodation services are outreach and day centre services designed to assist homeless people with their health and personal needs while they remain 'on the streets'.

A key aim of homelessness interventions is to ensure that homeless people access and subsequently sustain long-term accommodation. In Australia, social housing authorities have increased the proportion of new allocations of housing to those in need, including homeless people, in recent years. 'Street-to-home' programs go one step further in that they not only assist homeless people access long-term housing but also help them to sustain their accommodation. These programs provide homeless people with support on an integrated basis, linking tenancy-related assistance with mental health, drug and alcohol, and other support services. Such programs have been introduced more widely in Australia in the last few years.

Another area of increased focus in Australia is the provision of early intervention support to those at risk of homelessness. Homelessness early intervention programs target individuals at immediate or imminent risk of homelessness. The most obvious examples are tenant support programs, which provide support to tenants facing the prospect of eviction from their tenancy and thereby becoming homeless. Tenant support programs have been implemented nationally, by most State/Territory social housing authorities, and in some private rental markets.

Homelessness early intervention programs are also evident in the justice, mental health, and drug and alcohol fields. A number of Australian States and Territories have provided transitional housing and support services to offenders eligible for bail, those exiting prisons and youth justice facilities, and people on drug treatment orders who are homeless or at risk of homelessness. Other programs provide long-term accommodation and social and health support to individuals with mental health conditions at risk of homelessness.

The final category of homelessness interventions encompasses programs which seek to address the underlying structural causes of homelessness. One structural cause of homelessness is the absence of accessible, affordable, and targeted housing exit points from homelessness. Dedicated building programs aimed at providing housing options for homeless people represent a critical structural homelessness program. Other examples of programs addressing the underlying causes of homelessness are those seeking to improve access to, and the effectiveness of, drug and alcohol rehabilitation services, those providing supported accommodation in the community for people with mental health conditions, and those focussed on severely disadvantaged job seekers, including homeless job seekers.

Homelessness prevention programs target groups of individuals who have a high statistical risk of future homelessness and seek to prevent that risk being realised for members of the groups. Children living in care arrangements – in which guardianship or custody of a child is transferred to a government department or community agency or other third party – represent one group with a high statistical future risk of homelessness. Interventions supporting children in care, particularly in their transition from care to independent living around the age of 18, represent one important homelessness prevention intervention.

The Australian Government's 2008 White Paper on homelessness, *The Road Home,* provides a new strategic framework for homelessness policy interventions in Australia. *The Road Home* committed Australian governments to the achievement of halving overall homelessness by 2020 and offering supported accommodation to all rough sleepers who need it by that time.

The White Paper details three key strategies:

- Placing increased emphasis on early intervention and prevention to stop homelessness from occurring in the first instance.
- Improving and expanding the work of homelessness services so that they are more "connected and responsive to achieve sustainable housing, improve economic and social participation and end homelessness for their clients" (Commonwealth of Australia, 2008: ix).
- Breaking the cycle of homelessness so that regular rough sleepers, those repeatedly homeless, and those who become homeless through crisis move into long-term stable housing with the support they need so that homelessness does not reoccur.

Evaluation Typologies and Methodologies

Evaluations of homelessness interventions can be classified on the basis of their objectives, the type of data they utilise, the methods of investigation adopted, and whether the evaluation has been commissioned by the funder of the program or has been undertaken independently.

Evaluations of homelessness interventions seek to assess whether appropriate processes and procedures have been followed by the intervention in question; whether the program addresses the needs of its clients; the extent to which the program has been able to deliver assistance to the intervention's target client group; and the extent to which the program has achieved positive outcomes for its clients.

Economic evaluations of homelessness interventions go one step further in comparing the effectiveness of the program in achieving improved outcomes for clients with the differential cost of undertaking the intervention. The aim of the economic evaluation is to determine whether, and to what extent, the intervention produces sufficiently improved outcomes for clients (against some specified counterfactual) per additional dollar spent.

Evaluations use a broad range of data sources. These include administrative data sources, survey-based client data, client and stakeholder interviews, and focus group sessions.

Evaluations of a homelessness intervention are often restricted to the analysis of outcomes achieved by clients immediately on exit from support. However, increasingly, attention is being directed – on the basis of evidence drawn from longitudinal surveys of clients – towards what outcomes are being achieved over time. An evaluation may have a narrow focus, whether clients access long-term housing as a result of the intervention, or a wider focus, examining a broad range of economic and social participation and health outcomes.

Evaluations may be based on descriptive analyses of the relevant data or follow a quasi-experimental or experimental research design. The distinguishing feature of experimental and quasi-experimental approaches is their attempt to compare outcomes for the client group in question with those of like nonparticipants. In other words, such approaches adopt a two-group comparison methodology.

In a quasi-experimental research design approach, differences between the 'treatment' group and those not receiving the homelessness intervention in question (but perhaps participating in some alternative program) are controlled for by statistical means; so only the independent effect of the homelessness program on client outcomes remains. In the experimental or randomised control trial approach, potential clients of a homelessness intervention are randomly allocated to the 'treatment' and 'nontreatment' categories. The estimated difference in mean outcomes between the 'treatment' and 'nontreatment' categories represents the differential impact of the program on client outcomes.

An important methodological issue in the evaluation arena is, Should an evaluation of an intervention follow a particular methodology if findings on program effectiveness are to be considered robust and of relevance to policy development?

In the health sciences, the randomised controlled trial or experimental approach is often viewed as *the* robust approach to the measurement of differential client outcomes. Indeed, health-based systematic reviews of the effectiveness of homelessness programs may require that a study is based on a randomised control trial methodology before it is selected for inclusion in the review (see Coldwell and Bender, 2007; Hwang et al., 2005). By implication, only studies that are based on a valid randomised control trial research design are accepted as being capable of producing robust evidence on program effectiveness.

A randomised control trial is certainly capable of producing robust evidence on program effectiveness. Nevertheless, the approach is not without its limitations (see Flatau and Zaretzky, 2008). If some homelessness agencies delivering support under the program decide not to be part of a trial on ethical or other grounds, while others do, there is potential for the study's findings to be unrepresentative of agencies and therefore clients as a whole. Some individuals may be reluctant to sign up to a randomised control trial because of fear of being assigned to the 'nontreatment' case. Moreover, some individuals in the 'nontreatment' group will, more than likely, participate in close substitutes for the program in question, perhaps without full recognition on the part of the researchers. This factor will affect the validity of findings tabled with respect to the mean differential impact of the intervention (see Heckman and Smith, 1995).

Furthermore, randomised control trials are typically structured to provide evidence on mean differential outcomes between the treatment group and the control group, but not for particular client subgroups. Modelling of the joint decision of the potential client to participate in the homelessness program and the homelessness agency to accept the participant is not captured in the randomised control trial. Finally, there are likely to be ethical concerns with randomised control trials in the homelessness field, related to the fact that the homelessness program or intervention in question will generally be presumed to be superior to the counterfactual, whether that is explicitly stated or not. That is, after all, why the program has been implemented. The assignment of homeless people to the nontreatment category then presents ethical dilemmas for homelessness agencies.

In the social sciences, particularly in economics, greater use is made of quasi-experimental approaches. However, this may be because of the ready availability of cross-sectional and longitudinal data sets which contain labour market and social program participation- and treatment-related variables among a raft of other relevant variables which allow the researcher to examine the impact of program participation on client outcomes, controlling for measured confounding influences. Implementation of a quasi-experimental design in the homelessness field is impeded by the fact that homeless people, including those in supported accommodation, are excluded from large-scale social science cross-sectional and longitudinal surveys on the grounds that they are not living in private residential dwellings.

A Profile of Australian Evaluations

It is common practice for Australian governments (Federal and State/Territory) to commission independent evaluations of homelessness interventions at the completion of programs' funding cycle. Results from the evaluation are used as an input into government decision-making on whether a particular program or broad homelessness strategy should be continued, and if so, in what form and with what level of funding.

Government-funded and -managed evaluations of homelessness interventions typically seek to address questions of both program accountability and program effectiveness. The issue of cost-effectiveness of a given homelessness intervention has not been the subject of detailed assessment in Australia due to both data availability problems and the absence of economic, financial, and accounting expertise in evaluation teams and commissioning agencies.

Evaluation studies commissioned by Australian governments have generally followed a one-group comparison design, in which the impact of the program is assessed on the basis of outcomes achieved by clients of the program alone. The adoption of a one-group comparison design leaves open the possibility that any improvement in client outcomes apparently associated with program participation could have occurred naturally in the absence of nonparticipation in the program.

Australian evaluation studies generally adopt a mixed methods approach, using a broad range of quantitative and qualitative sources. There is a focus on client administrative sources, which are used to analyse client outcomes arising from the homeless intervention. In a small number of cases, this has been augmented by a survey of clients conducted over a period of up to one year following entry to the program. Other sources used include relevant program and service documents; client, agency, and other stakeholder interviews; and focus group and feedback sessions.

The largest Australian homelessness intervention evaluation was the 2004 National SAAP Evaluation conducted in relation to the national co-ordinated program, the Supported Accommodation Assistance Program (SAAP) (Erebus Consulting Partners, 2004). SAAP has provided supported accommodation and outreach support to homeless people and women and children escaping domestic violence since 1985. (As part of the 2009 homelessness reform process, arising from the Australian Government's White Paper on homelessness, *The Road Home*, SAAP will be abolished. However, services previously provided under SAAP will continue to be funded and delivered under the broader umbrella of the *National Partnership Agreement on Homelessness*.) SAAP has been evaluated periodically since its inception.

The 2004 National SAAP Evaluation is a comprehensive assessment of SAAP accountability, effectiveness, and efficiency. It incorporates a large variety of data sources and analyses, including findings from the SAAP administrative unit record client data collections, client satisfaction surveys, results of public submissions, site visits to agencies and regional offices, interviews with program and agency staff and clients, a review of documents, and large-scale stakeholder feedback sessions and workshops.

Detailed information on the needs of clients and the support provided to clients is included in the SAAP administrative client data collection. The administrative data also includes a range of 'before-support' and 'immediately-on-exit-from support' indicators of client outcomes. On the basis of the SAAP administrative data client outcome measures, the 2004 National SAAP Evaluation suggested that program participation had led to improvements "for a significant number of clients who had specifically sought assistance in regards to employment, housing opportunities and income support. Young people who were undertaking education and training were also able to continue with their studies even though they were experiencing homelessness or at risk of being homeless. However, the data also suggests that the circumstances for the vast majority of SAAP clients had not changed" (p. 82). SAAP client satisfaction survey data suggested very high levels of satisfaction with the services provided by agencies, with support exceeding client expectations in the majority of cases.

Pre- and postintervention client outcome indicators provide one measure of program effectiveness. However, they need to be supplemented by long-term client outcome measures to provide a comprehensive account of client outcomes from program participation. Two-way comparisons of client outcomes from program participation would also enhance the ability of the SAAP evaluation to make stronger claims on the effectiveness of the program in improving client outcomes.

The 2004 National SAAP Evaluation provides estimates of the recurrent cost of providing support to SAAP clients. However, an assessment of the full net cost of providing assistance under SAAP is limited by the lack of data on capital costs, potential cost offsets from the provision of support (the reduction in nonhomelessness government expenditures that the program may generate), costs adjusted for the needs of clients, and costs broken down by service type. Given significant limitations on the information available on the costs of providing support and the relatively limited nature of client outcome information, the 2004 National SAAP Evaluation was not able to report on the overall cost-effectiveness of the program.

The 2008 Australian White Paper on homelessness, *The Road Home*, emphasises the role of early intervention homelessness programs in turning off the tap of homelessness. A number of innovative early intervention homelessness programs have been introduced in Australia in recent years and have been the subject of major evaluations. A feature of these evaluations has been the incorporation of a longitudinal client survey into the evaluation program together with the analysis of program effectiveness using a broad range of client outcome indicators. Three of these evaluations are briefly surveyed below.

The HOME Advice Program is designed to identify families at risk of homelessness before they reach crisis stage and provide tenancy and personal support services to these families. The key finding of the HOME Advice Program evaluation was that for every 10 families passing through the program, eight to nine avoided homelessness over the time they were in contact with the HOME Advice Program and receiving support (MacKenzie et al., 2007). Moreover, the follow-up survey of clients found that 72% of families did not experience a spell of homelessness in the year after receiving support. Preventing the occurrence of homelessness among families is potentially highly cost-effective, given the range of possible adverse consequences of family homelessness and the high cost of supports necessary for parents and children if homelessness were to be experienced.

The findings of tenancy sustainability of clients of the HOME Advice Program are consistent with those evident across a range of Australian public and private tenancy support programs designed to sustain at-risk tenancies (see Flatau et al., 2009). An at-risk tenancy is one in which households face significant difficulties in establishing and/or sustaining their tenancies due to immediate or long-standing social, health, or economic needs and/or are under threat of possible or actual eviction as a result of rent arrears, accumulated housing debt, or tenancy breaches, including property damage, inadequate property standards, and antisocial behaviour.

While there is limited information on client outcomes from Australian tenant support programs, it is clear that eviction and consequently homelessness is avoided for the vast majority of clients of tenant support programs (see Flatau et al., 2009). Tenant support programs lead to a reduction in rent arrears and tenant liabilities; improvement in property conditions and a reduction in charges related to property damage. They also result in increased linkage to services and improved access to counselling services, referrals to mental health and drug and alcohol services, financial counsellors; and, capacity building and increased self-esteem, confidence, and trust among tenants.

The Reconnect programme seeks to reconnect young people (aged 12–18 years) who are homeless or at risk of homelessness, with their families, with education, employment opportunities, and the community. As part of the Reconnect evaluation process, a *Longitudinal Survey of Reconnect Clients* was implemented which surveyed young people and parents entering and exiting Reconnect services and again 10 months later (Ryan, 2003). Results from the *Longitudinal Survey of Reconnect Clients* indicate that the incidence of unstable accommodation decreased following the provision of support, while the proportion of young people living with their parents increased. The provision of support appears to have led to a significant improvement in young people's and parents' reported ability to manage family conflict, and this improvement was sustained over time. Small improvements in engagement with education and employment were also evident as a result of participation in the Reconnect programme.

The Housing and Accommodation Support Initiative (HASI) is an early intervention partnership program between New South Wales Health and Housing authorities and nongovernment organisations (NGOs) which provides long-term accommodation, community participation support, and active mental health case management to those with mental health problems and disorders. A 2-year longitudinal study of HASI Stage One found that 85% of all HASI participants remained with the same housing provider over the 2-year period; community and labour market participation increased in the majority of cases, family connectedness and psychological wellness improved, and hospitalisation rates decreased (see Muir et al., 2007).

In their reviews of economic analyses of homelessness interventions, Berry et al. (2003) and Pinkney and Ewing (2006) point to the absence of Australian experimental and quasi-experimental research on the effectiveness of homelessness-specific interventions and of economic evaluations of homelessness programs. This stands in contrast to the relative availability of experimental studies examining the effectiveness and cost-effectiveness of health interventions, including studies focusing on mental health and drug and alcohol abuse interventions, many of which may disproportionately assist homeless people. The paucity of experimental and quasi-experimental research on the effectiveness of homelessness-specific interventions and of economic evaluations of homelessness programs also stands in sharp contrast to the existence of a relatively large number of Australian studies on the prevalence of psychological distress and psychiatric disorders, including substance use disorders, among homeless people.

One new piece of research which seeks to address this gap in the research evidence, and which is currently being undertaken, is an evaluation of the YP[4] trial of joined-up services (employment, housing, health, educational, and personal support services) for young homeless job seekers in Victoria. The trial was implemented as a random experiment with eligible homeless job seekers randomly assigned to 'treatment' and 'control' groups. An accompanying economic evaluation (cost–benefit analysis) of the YP[4] trial is being undertaken by researchers at Melbourne University (Borland, Tseng, Wilkins and Black). The evaluation will quantify the costs and benefits (in terms of dollars) of joined-up service delivery as compared with standard ('separate') service delivery.

The researchers involved in the evaluation report that the trial was not successfully implemented as a randomised controlled experiment and that limitations are apparent with regard to the base data on which benefits and costs will be calculated. Nevertheless, researchers should still be able to undertake a quasi-experimental analysis of the trial in which those in the treatment and control groups will be 'matched' with each other using proportional matching techniques and comparisons made on the basis of the matched samples.

Another preliminary economic evaluation of homelessness programs is that conducted by the Australian Housing and Urban Research Institute (AHURI) (see Flatau et al. (2008) and Zaretzky et al. (2008)). In their study, the authors compared the health and justice costs of homelessness program clients prior to the provision of support with those of the general population and examined the short-term impact of participation in programs in a one-group comparison. The authors also compared health and justice costs with the recurrent and capital costs of providing support under existing homelessness programs. Flatau et al. (2008) and Zaretzky et al. (2008) found that clients experienced immediate benefits from program participation and that the annual health and justice costs of the homeless population in the year prior not only exceeded those of the general population by a significant amount, but also were significantly higher than the costs of providing support under a range of existing homelessness programs. The potential therefore exists for homelessness programs to be highly cost-effective. Of course, it is highly unlikely that the full value of such potential cost offsets would be fully realised, but they give an indication of the cost of homelessness as compared with the cost of delivering services for the homeless.

Conclusion

Evaluations of homelessness interventions in Australia have consistently pointed to positive outcomes accruing to clients as a result of the intervention. This is particularly true of recent early intervention initiatives, evaluations of which have included longitudinal client surveys covering a broad range of client outcomes. A major gap in the Australian evaluation literature is the absence of experimental and quasi-experimental research on the effectiveness of homelessness-specific interventions and of economic evaluations of homelessness programs.

See also: Cost Analyses of Homelessness: Limits and Opportunities; Homelessness: Causation; Homelessness: Definitions; Homelessness: Measurement Questions; Homeless People: Indigenous/Aboriginal; Policies to Address Homelessness: Partnership-Based Approaches in Ireland; Policies to Address Homelessness: Prevention in the United Kingdom.

References

Berry M, Chamberlain C, Dalton T, Horn M, and Berman G (2003) *Counting the Cost of Homelessness: A Systematic Review of Cost Effectiveness and Cost Benefit Studies of Homelessness*. Melbourne, VIC: AHURI.

Coldwell CM and Bender WS (2007) The effectiveness of assertive community treatment for homeless populations with severe mental illness: A meta-analysis. *The American Journal of Psychiatry* 164(3): 393–399.

Commonwealth of Australia (2008) *The Road Home. A National Approach to Reducing Homelessness*. Canberra, ACT: Department of Families, Housing, Community Services and Indigenous Affairs.

Erebus Consulting Partners (2004) National evaluation of the supported accommodation assistance program (SAAP IV). *Final Report*. Commonwealth of Australia.

Flatau P, Coleman A, Memmott P, Baulderstone J, and Slatter M (2009) Sustaining at-risk indigenous tenancies: A review of Australian policy responses. *AHURI Final Report No. 138*. Melbourne, VIC: AHURI.

Flatau P and Zaretzky K (2008) The economic evaluation of homelessness programs. *The European Journal of Homelessness* 2: 305–320.

Flatau P, Zaretzky K, Brady M, Haigh Y, and Martin R (2008) The cost-effectiveness of homelessness programs: A first assessment, Vol. 1: Main report. *Australian Housing and Urban Research Institute (AHURI) Final Report No.119*. Melbourne, VIC: AHURI.

Heckman JJ and Smith JA (1995) Assessing the case for social experiments. *The Journal of Economic Perspectives* 9(2): 85–110.

Hwang SW, Tolomiczenko G, Kouyoumdjian FG, and Garner RE (2005) Interventions to improve the health of the homeless. A systematic review. *American Journal of Preventive Medicine* 29(4): 311–319.

MacKenzie D, Desmond K, and Steen A (2007) *Household Organisational Management Expenses (HOME) Advice Program Evaluation Report*. Canberra, ACT: Australian Government Department of Family and Community Services and Indigenous Affairs.

Muir K, Fisher K, Dadich A, Abelló D, and Bleasdale M (2007) *Stage 1 Evaluation Report Housing and Accommodation Support Initiative (HASI)*. New South Wales: NSW Department of Health.

Pinkney S and Ewing S (2006) *Costs and Pathways of Homelessness: Developing Policy-Relevant Economic Analyses for the Australian Homelessness Service System*. Canberra, ACT: Australian Government Department of Family and Community Services and Indigenous Affairs.

Ryan P (2003) *'I'm looking at the future': Evaluation report of reconnect*. RPR Consulting. Canberra, ACT: Australian Government Department of Family and Community Services.

Zaretzky K, Flatau PR, and Brady M (2008) What is the (net) cost to government of homelessness programs? *The Australian Journal of Social Issues* 43(2): 231–254.

Policies to Address Homelessness: Criminalisation and Control of Public Space

J Wardhaugh, Bangor University, Bangor, UK

© 2012 Elsevier Ltd. All rights reserved.

Glossary

Homelessness circuit The term 'homelessness circuit' is used in Britain to describe the provision of facilities and services for homeless people. Typically, these will be concentrated in a small area of a city centre, and include drop-in centres, hostels, and charities providing food, clothing, and other services.

Regulation of homelessness A combination of legal, criminal justice, planning, and social policies serve to regulate public aspects of homelessness. This can range from legislation to control begging to city ordinances designed to discourage rough sleeping, to periodic clearances of slum settlements.

Street homelessness The homelessness literature usually distinguishes between street homelessness and institutional homelessness. Street homelessness is also referred to as 'rooflessness' and 'rough sleeping', and describes those who have no access to any form of shelter.

Survival strategies Homeless people often engage in economic strategies of survival. These may be legitimate activities such as selling newspapers, or illegitimate or quasi-legitimate activities such as begging or prostitution.

Introduction

In 2008 the film *Slumdog Millionaire* received international acclaim (Beaufoy, 2008). Based on the novel *Q and A* by Vikas Swarup, it tells the story of young slum-dwellers as they make their way to fame and fortune. Many tourists now visit the newly famous Mumbai slum of Dharavi, reputedly the largest in Asia, in which the film was set (Sharma, 2003). In the early twenty-first century it would almost seem that homelessness and poverty have become cool. (The real-life irony is that two of the child stars – having found stardom – were later made homeless following demolition of their slum settlements (One India, 21 May 2009).)

There are extensive debates over the definitions of homelessness, and these will not be repeated here. For the purposes of this discussion, a broad definition will be adopted, including all those without permanent and secure accommodation which includes a minimum of essential facilities. Thus, slum-dwellers are included, on the grounds that their accommodation – while providing bare shelter – is not permanent, is often illegal or quasi-legal, and usually lacks one or more essential amenities, such as running water or sanitation. Often the dividing line between them and pavement-dwellers is thin and easily broken.

The *Slumdog* story is perhaps one of the oldest and most often told: poor people dream of riches and use their courage and resourcefulness in pursuit of the dream. The story of poverty and homelessness is also as old as human history, and – despite differences of society and culture – remains essentially the same across time and space. There may be one million pavement-dwellers in Mumbai, and many more homeless or poorly-housed people in its now famous slums, but there are also around 100 000 homeless people in Los Angeles, the "First World capital of homelessness" (Davis, 2006: 36). Globally, there are an estimated one billion people who are homeless or living in inadequate shelter, a staggering one in seven of the world's population (Glasser, 1994). Here, we are concerned with official and public responses to homelessness, the impulse to control, to demonise, and to criminalise the placeless person (Amster, 2008; Carlen, 1996; Doherty et al., 2008; Hermer and Mosher, 2002; Mitchell, 2003).

Regulating Homelessness

The earliest-known attempts to control what was then known as vagrancy are usually dated back to Britain in the fourteenth century (Beier, 1985), although in fact the earliest-known measure was a statute in 1274 restricting almsgiving by monasteries to itinerant people (Chambliss, 1964). The mid-fourteenth century saw the introduction of a series of measures designed to restrict people travelling in search of work, with levels of punishment increasing steadily with time. It is not until the sixteenth century, however, that we see the first real criminalisation of itinerancy. In 1530 the first statute was passed which defined beggars (usually associated with vagrancy or homelessness) as criminals, and various categories of unlawful behaviour and deviance were defined (Wardhaugh, 2000).

By 1535 vagrants were defined as felons, as enemies of the state, and the maximum punishment was the death penalty. Towards the end of this century, vagabondage was increasingly becoming associated with disorder and crime. Punishments were severe and often permanent. For example, branding of the person literally served to stigmatise them as deviant, whereas enslavement and banishment were responses with clear spatial dimensions (Beier, 1985).

The Law of Settlement and Removal was passed in 1662, providing for vagrants to be sent back to their places of origin (although in many cases this was difficult to establish among a largely illiterate and rootless population). This law remained in force for two centuries. Otherwise, there was little major change in the legislation until the passage of the 1824 Vagrancy Act. This served to rationalise and replace almost 30 previous vagrancy acts. Three categories of vagrant were retained – in increasing levels of seriousness – 'the idle and disorderly', 'rogues and vagabonds', and 'incorrigible rogues' – and the levels of punishment were reduced. This Act remains in force in Britain in the early twenty-first century and continues to be used to charge people with the offences of begging and sleeping rough, despite repeated calls for it to be abolished (Homeless Link, 19 April 2007).

The causes of homelessness – then and now – were often the push-pull factors of economic difficulties in home areas, along with the prospect of a better life elsewhere. This is as true for twenty-first-century Asia as it was in medieval Europe, and in both cases rapid urbanisation has been perhaps the single most important factor in creating social and economic upheaval and the consequent high levels of homelessness. The dilemma for the state is that – while it needs mobility of labour – it does not want large numbers of uncontained people without a fixed place of abode. Within this tension lies the explanation for many official attempts to legislate on – and against – homelessness.

Chambliss (1964) was one of the first commentators to note that homelessness is essentially a status offence. While specific activities are legislated against – such as begging and sleeping rough – in essence, it is about the *identity* of the person rather than what they *do*. The tramp and the vagrant of medieval and early modern Europe, the pavement-dwellers and migrant workers of modern Asia, the street children of Latin America – all have been subject to being labelled as the deviant and the outsider, and their subsistence activities criminalised. For example,

"a significant number of street children in Rio have been picked up by the police not for an infraction, but for simply being on the street" (Sanders (1987) cited in Glasser (1994: 74)).

British vagrancy legislation has had a global influence, first being exported to North America and later – by means of the establishment of the British Empire – becoming dispersed across the world. These laws remain in force today – virtually unchanged – in many countries across Asia and Africa. In India, for example, Davis (2006: 97) claims that more than 60 years of Independence have done little to alter the 'exclusionary geography of the Raj'. The case study of Goa below makes reference to some Indian legislation on begging which is close cousin to British vagrancy laws.

While there are of course many individual differences, there are also remarkable similarities in governmental attempts to control the poor and rootless. A very common tactic in countries as diverse as Brazil, Egypt, and Indonesia has been the clearance of slum settlements, ostensibly to 'clear up' city neighbourhoods, but – critics believe – in reality a cynical ploy to reclaim prime spaces for development for more affluent populations (Neuwirth, 2006). Davis (2006: 111) argues that "since the 1970s it has become commonplace for governments everywhere to justify slum clearance as an indispensable means of fighting crime". Similar 'clear up' campaigns are also waged periodically against pavement-dwellers, beggars, and street vendors. These procedures are conducted variously by the state police force and by private security firms, sometimes by hired gangsters. The justification is often based on city housing and planning policies, thus creating an alliance between social policy and criminal justice measures in order to regulate homelessness.

While much of the literature on the regulation of homelessness focuses on its repressive outcomes for homeless people, it is worth noting the recent arguments that, in certain circumstances, some degree of regulation may work in their favour. Arguably, a 'hands off' approach to street homelessness may simply leave many to continue to experience drugs and alcohol misuse, criminal victimisation, and other hazards of the street life. Conversely, some regulatory approaches which aim to take people away from the streets may have beneficial effects in terms of health and social welfare (Fitzpatrick and Jones, 2005; Johnsen and Fitzpatrick, 2007). Practical examples of regulatory measures with a moral dimension or welfare approach include the 'diverted giving' schemes in some British cities which encourage people to give to organised charities (which would then channel the money to 'deserving' individuals) rather than directly to people who beg on the streets (Hermer, 1999).

While academic arguments concerning the ethical dimensions of regulatory approaches to homelessness are being developed in countries like Britain, NGOs in the developing world are also engaging with these questions, and sharing an awareness of the moral dilemmas involved in, for example, giving money to people who beg. A worker with El Shaddai Street Child Rescue organisation in Goa (India) put it like this: "If someone makes one hundred rupees begging, someone else will take ten rupees. That's why it's better to give food to a child, so you know they will be fed, or else you don't know who's taking the money. And sometimes the parents ... [he mimes drinking from a bottle]". Coming from different perspectives, their conclusions are similar: that perhaps alternative responses need to be made to the social and economic needs of street homeless people.

The irony is that whether homeless people are treated as criminals or as people in need of welfare, in fact it is they who are at disproportionate risk of crime. They may experience physical and sexual abuse from members of the public or while staying in hostels and shelters; quite often they are preyed upon by gangs who control their sleeping spaces, begging pitches, and other economic activities, and – in some countries – street children have been victims of extreme violence, such as the notorious police killings in Brazil.

Case Studies of the Regulation of Homelessness

Two case studies are used here to explore some dimensions of the criminalisation of homelessness and the control of public spaces used by homeless people. In both cases, the observations are based on ethnographic research conducted by the author – the first in Manchester, a city in the north of England, conducted in the early 1990s, and the second in the Indian state of Goa, conducted in 2009.

Case Study 1: Manchester's Cardboard City, Early 1990s

In Britain the early 1990s was a period that saw an intensification of the trend towards the politicisation and criminalisation of street homelessness and its attendant urban incivilities (Amster, 2008). This political debate conflated begging with both street homelessness and crime, thereby serving to demonise all street people. At the same time, the academic argument was developed that the incivilities of 'aggressive' begging and street disorder contribute not only to an increased fear of crime but lead also to an increase in crime itself (Kelling, 1995).

At this time, the number of arrests and prosecutions for begging increased fourfold in London: around 80% of those begging were estimated to be homeless (Murdoch, 1994). The vast majority of the beggars in this study (some 80%) had had some contact with the police while begging, 78% had been moved on, 67% had been cautioned, and 55% had been arrested, usually under the 1824 Vagrancy Act.

The supposed dangers represented by the homeless, along with attempts to make secure ever-changing social and geographical boundaries, result in what Sibley has described as 'geographies of exclusion' (1995). Minority groups such as the street homeless are dangerous precisely because of their marginality, their lack of a place or group membership. Mary Douglas tells us that "all margins are dangerous ... Any structure of ideas is vulnerable at its margins" (1964: 121). A clear separation of groups, therefore, is essential to the maintenance of purity and safety and the elimination of impurity and danger.

Nevertheless, street homeless people do exist, and most cities make some provision for their needs. The range of shelters, drop-in centres, and other facilities is often referred to as the homelessness circuit. The location of this homelessness circuit within the city centre seems not to be consistent with the argument that the homeless are not welcome, nor indeed even tolerated, within prime urban space. During fieldwork, however, it emerged that venues on the homelessness circuit were invariably located in marginal places within prime city centre space. Thus, day centres were usually situated in back alleys or other inconspicuous locations (see **Figure 1**). Furthermore, if prime space was to be used, then this would take place predominantly at marginal times of the day, outside main business and shopping hours. The prime site of Piccadilly Gardens, for example, would often be avoided by the street homeless during the day for fear of being moved on by the police (see **Figure 2**). However, it could be used by voluntary agencies for the distribution of food and clothes in the evenings, once shoppers and workers had returned home (Wardhaugh, 2000).

The following account of daily subsistence on the homelessness circuit illustrates both the temporal and spatial nature of this ordering of daily routines:

> Well, I'd have to move anytime from eight o'clock onwards when the shops start to open, and then I go to the Salvation Army for my breakfast and a dinner. From 10 o'clock in a morning, till three o'clock anyone is welcome to have a free breakfast, free dinner. Then I go to St. Augustine's Church, get a butty, a brew there, then that takes us up to about four o'clock. Then we go Chinatown, have a few hours there. Then the handouts [in Piccadilly Gardens] come out about now, between

Figure 1 Drop-in centre for homeless people, Manchester city centre. This drop-in centre was provided by the probation service and offered a safe space for homeless people during the day and for those engaged in the sex trade by night. Homeless people were offered hot meals and showers, advice from staff, and company from other users of the centre. It was situated in the city centre, but was inconspicuous due to the lack of any sign indicating its presence, and the fact that it was located in a basement.

nine and half past.... It's just generally day centres we have to be in like, so as not to be on the streets, people just don't want you on the streets. But... from seven onwards [you've] just got to be on the street and just lie low, and if you don't know where the handouts are you have just got to find them. (Pete, aged 25) (All personal names used are pseudonyms, in order to protect confidentiality and anonymity.)

The repetitive, present-oriented, and often tedious nature of time on the streets is reminiscent of prisoners' accounts of 'doing time' (Cohen and Taylor, 1972). Indeed, the analogy between doing time on the streets and in prison is not a new one, but was made around 40 years ago by James Spradley (1970), with his description of men on Skid Row doing 'life-sentences on the instalment plan'.

Street homeless people and their paraphernalia of subsistence become 'matter out of place' (Douglas, 1964). Their daily routines and personal functions are perceived as both literally and symbolically polluting. This association between street people and dirt is often to be found in both popular and criminal justice discourses.

Street homeless people sometimes negotiate this transgressiveness by attempting to neutralise their perceived dangerousness, and they often achieve this by privatising public space (Lofland, 1973). For example, the

Figure 2 Piccadilly Gardens, Manchester city centre. Piccadilly Gardens is one of the few green spaces in Manchester city centre, and as such is highly valued by shoppers, workers, and others who use the city. It served homeless people in various ways, mainly as a location for a source of food and blankets in the evenings. Although completely redesigned in the twenty-first century, it continues to serve both domiciled and homeless citizens.

negotiation of space involved in the arrangement of blankets and cardboard on city streets is more than a random and purely physical activity. There is also a significant social dimension in that an individual's sleeping equipment is carefully placed so that it becomes a marker and a symbol of their territory, however temporary that may be (see **Figure 3**).

Terry (aged 20) gives an account of his successful attempt to privatise some public, albeit marginal, space for the private function of sleeping (see **Figure 4**):

[We've been] sleeping down in Chinatown, down a back alley in this shelter, under this set of stairs. It like had a cage round it and a door on the front of the cage, and we got blankets and put them all up [with] cardboard on the outside and cardboard on the floors and blankets on the floors, so it was quite warm. It was roughing it but it wasn't rough roughing it, if you know what I mean.

The police have a dual role in relation to the street homeless population: first, to regulate any illegal subsistence strategies and generally to maintain good order on the streets, and second to protect street people from harassment and criminal victimisation. With regard to policing as regulation, attention is more likely to be directed towards street people when, in pursuit of their daily routines of subsistence, they become too

Figure 3 Sleeping-bag by canal, Manchester city centre. Homeless people who sleep rough often choose locations which are least likely to attract unwelcome attention. Manchester has many canals and disused warehouse buildings, and these often serve as rough sleeping locations. In this case, the sleeping-bag has been left during the day, presumably to await its owner's return at night.

visible or too disorderly within prime space, fail to confine themselves to interstitial locales within prime space, or else fail to use such space at marginal times of the day. Arguably, it is the actual or perceived disruptiveness of such routines to mainstream communities that is the key factor in triggering a police response, rather than the legality or illegality of such activities (Wardhaugh, 2000).

Begging – a subsistence activity closely associated with street homelessness – is regularly practiced within most urban spaces. However, it is only periodically that police operations become focused on its regulation. Operation Cinderella took place during the first half of 1993, with the aim of reducing street begging in the centre of Manchester. This operation was widely believed by both agency staff and street homeless people to be linked to the city's Olympic bid, and the consequent felt need to project a 'clean' image to the international community. Whether they were accurate in this belief or not, many street homeless people did report having experienced an increase in police activity at around this time, both in relation to begging and, to a lesser extent, sleeping rough.

Many street homeless people held an ambivalent attitude towards the police. Kaz, for example, appreciated the protective role sometimes adopted by the police (see **Figure 5**):

Figure 4 Chinatown, Manchester city centre. Manchester's Chinatown is one of the largest outside of China itself. The picture shows the Imperial Chinese Arch which marks the entry to the district. For homeless people, Chinatown was often experienced as a 'safe space', especially for the evening and night-time hours. It was one of the few areas of the city where they reported feeling safe while sleeping rough.

> I sleep down on the canal basin, at the bottom of Deansgate... It's quiet, but there's loads of police around there as well... You're pretty safe there, except for when they're waking you up to make sure you're not dead (laughs).

Venues on the homelessness circuit are often liable to be omitted from the protective and regulatory gaze of the local police force, being left simply to 'look after their own'. This was the case with a day centre that was located within the homelessness circuit (see **Figure 1**):

> The police are fairly good at staying away from the day centre, in fact sometimes they're too good at staying away! It's been operating for about twenty years and they don't want to know what's going on. If there are any fights they leave it to us to deal with. It's as if they think that it's our fault for opening the centre, so therefore we should deal with any trouble that arises.
> (Jim, day centre co-ordinator)

Such benign neglect is illustrative of the ambiguous relationship that the police have in relation to the street homeless population: having a responsibility to protect Cardboard citizens, they are also official regulators of the contested space that they inhabit. In turn, street people perceive the police, either alternately or simultaneously, as repressive agents of control or as protectors and regulators of the dangerous streets.

Case Study 2: Goa – Slum-Dwellers and Migrant Workers, Early Twenty-First Century

Goa's rural and semi-rural slums provide a counterpoint to the traditional image of South Asian poverty. Small and secluded, often located in woods or by

Figure 5 Big Issue vendor, Gay Village, Manchester city centre. Big Issue vendors work throughout the city centre, as they do in towns and cities across Britain. The Gay Village was often a favoured location as vendors reported that people using the area were more often sympathetic to them than in other locations. Here, the vendor enjoys some friendly banter with a police officer.

Figure 6 Slum settlement, Anjuna, Goa. Small slum settlements are scattered throughout Goa and may be found in most towns and larger villages. They accommodate migrant workers and others who find themselves unable to gain access to adequate housing. In common with the better-known slums in urban India, these settlements generally lack electricity, running water, and adequate sanitation.

beaches, these slums seem to reflect a rustic idyll compared with the urban dystopias of Delhi or Mumbai (see **Figures 6** and **7**). Of course, this difference is superficial and the inhabitants – mostly migrant workers from the neighbouring states of Karnataka or Maharashtra – experience the same poverty, poor

Figure 7 Latrine in slum settlement, Arpora, Goa. Although often located in scenic locations, slums in Goa share the same problems as those in urban areas. Here, a latrine is placed directly on a small river, which is also the settlement's source of water for drinking, cooking, and bathing. This settlement is located in the village of Arpora, a tourist destination close to the larger town of Calangute.

facilities, and grinding struggle to survive as their urban counterparts. This homelessness is less obvious, yet it is commonplace: despite rapid urbanisation, India remains a predominantly rural country. Paradoxically, rural or semi-rural homelessness in India – although less well known than urban homelessness – may be less hidden than in the cities. Although it is on a smaller scale, slum settlements in states such as Goa tend to be integrated with other residential and commercial developments. These slum-dwellers are socially marginal, but tend to be located in, or next to, prime space. In urban areas slum settlements are often segregated from the rest of the city: in Delhi, for example, the slum areas are located on the other side of the Yamuna River than the city centre, and (although they accommodate many thousands of people) do not even appear on maps of the city (Dupont et al., 2000).

Goa is known to the Western world as a party place, a retreat for (often ageing) hippies, or as a package-tour destination (Tomory, 2000). For the 'new India' (the burgeoning middle classes), it is also a place of relaxation, hedonism, and escape. The migrant workers who reside in the slums come to Goa to service this economy: the men to work in construction, the women to work in the tourism industry, and both to provide goods and services to the tourists, often in the unregulated sector as beach vendors (see **Figure 8**). Others – including many of their children – work as rag-pickers and recyclers of glass and paper (De Venanzi, 2003) (see **Figures 9** and **10**). In this way the 'new India' of the affluent middle classes meets the 'old India' of poverty and homelessness. When international tourism is added to the mixture, then we can begin to understand homelessness in places like Goa as a global phenomenon.

Figure 8 Beach vendors, Baga beach, Goa. The beaches of Goa feature many vendors who offer for sale clothes, jewellery, and other items likely to appeal to tourists. They also offer services such as ear-cleaning and massage. Opinion is divided as to whether they offer useful services or are simply a nuisance. In any case, many tourists do purchase goods and services from them.

Figure 9 Migrant workers, Calangute, Goa. Common occupations for migrant workers include collecting paper, tin cans, and glass for recycling. Here, workers in Calangute load their goods onto a truck. Some of the workers were observed leaving a slum settlement nearby. Migrant workers generally occupy the lower strata of society and are often held responsible for a wide range of social problems.

Figure 10 Street children, Calangute market, Goa. These are the children of migrant workers, and they live in slum settlements scattered around the town of Calangute. Many of these children complete little formal education, instead working in a variety of occupations such as rag-pickers, beach vendors, and beggars. These two small boys were collecting paper from the Saturday market in Calangute for sale in the recycled paper market.

Here, homelessness is defined to encompass a wide range of populations, including slum-dwellers, itinerant groups, and residents of institutions such as hostels and beggars' colonies (Frank-Sharjah, 2006). Particular reference is made to the Lamanis, a tribal group from Maharashtra and Karnataka who often settle in Goa, becoming migrant workers and slum-dwellers. Lamanis are often referred to as a gypsy group, and the response to them is similar to that made to itinerant groups across the ages. They are commonly viewed as a troublesome and marginal population, and often it is asserted that Goa had no significant social problems such as poverty and homelessness until their fairly recent arrival (an arrival facilitated by the development of the Konkan railway, and encouraged by the burgeoning tourist industry). In fact, the establishment of slum areas to accommodate migrant workers may be dated to the late nineteenth century, when migrant workers from Uttar Pradesh arrived in the port town of Vasco to work on the Western India-Portuguese Railway (Faleiro, 2009). These slums still exist today.

As in medieval Europe and contemporary Britain, these itinerant groups tend to be marginalised and criminalised. Their often illegal settlements are highly insecure, and are subject to periodic clearance (Davis, 2006). Subsistence activities such as begging are illegal and often lead to unwelcome contact with the police. Slum-dwellers and migrant workers – especially the beach vendors – are periodically rounded up by the police for 'verification' of their status.

Figure 11 Child begging in Anjuna market, Goa. Many adults and children beg on the beaches and in the various markets of Goa. Begging is illegal in Goa, and both adults and children are vulnerable to being arrested or questioned by the police. Street children are also vulnerable to physical and sexual abuse, as well as to financial exploitation.

Not all beggars are homeless, nor all homeless people beggars, but begging is perhaps the single activity most closely associated with homelessness. For those with no skills or goods to trade, this remains the one economic activity with which they can engage (see **Figure 11**). However, it is not a risk-free activity. They may be vilified by the public (although many also provide donations of money and food), picked up by the police, and controlled by the beggar 'mafia'. Perhaps best described as pimps, there are those who control the streets and 'rent out' begging pitches (Dupont et al., 2000).

Agency staff who work with the children of migrant workers are aware of their dilemma: they must work to survive, but in doing so often engage in illegal activities. Little Acorns in Calangute is part of the El Shaddai charitable organisation and provides a night shelter and day care centre for street children, many of them from migrant worker families (see **Figure 12**).

One of their workers described it thus: "Begging is illegal in Goa. Children are quite often arrested by the police and taken to headquarters overnight, or sometimes they make them stay till the end of the season. Sometimes they bring the parents in also" (Fieldwork, March 2009).

Begging is indeed illegal in Goa, under the Goa, Daman and Diu Prevention of Begging Act, 1972. This legislation is similar to that in force elsewhere in India, perhaps most notably the Bombay Prevention of Begging Act, 1959, which served as a blueprint for subsequent forms of regulation elsewhere in India (Mukherjee, 2008). The Goan legislation provides penalties not only for the beggar but also for those 'wholly dependent on the beggar' (II:9) and those 'causing persons to beg' (II:11). In practice, however, it is much more likely that it is the beggars themselves – and in the case of children, sometimes their parents – who will be detained, rather than the beggar 'pimps'. In the

Figure 12 Little Acorns night shelter and day care centre, Calangute, Goa. This centre provides a night shelter for runaway children, as well as a day care centre for street children, many of them from migrant worker families. The agency provides food and shelter, as well as education and leisure activities for the children. For the parents, it provides a safe place where they can leave the children during the day while they are engaged in work activities.

latter case they are in a position to pay bribes to the police in order to evade criminal proceedings.

While itinerant groups have been subject to legal and social regulation for centuries, in recent times the reasons for regarding them with suspicion have changed. In Goa in 2008, for example, police took action against a number of slum-dwellers and migrant workers (Times of India, 4 December 2008). Following the terrorist attacks on Mumbai in November 2008, the neighbouring state of Goa experienced considerable fears of similar attacks, given the stated aim of targeting British and American tourists. Consequently, security was tightened, with, for example, some markets catering for tourists being closed for the 2008–09 season.

There would seem to be a clear connection between these fears and consequent heightened security and the identification of itinerant groups as a threat: "The Lamani women are often a nuisance along the coastal stretches and go very close to the foreign tourists to sell their wares ... [and] that can always be a tactic employed by those engaged in spying activities ... observed DySP [Deputy Superintendent of Police] Umesh Gaonkar" (Times of India, 4 December 2008). While many tourists do indeed experience the beach vendors as a nuisance (although others welcome or at least accept their attentions), the connection between this economic activity and engagement in spying or quasi-terrorist activities seems tenuous at best. Nevertheless, in Goa in December 2008 around 30 Lamanis (mostly women) were detained by the police for verification of their status, along with larger numbers of slum-dwellers and migrant workers from elsewhere in India, mostly Kashmiris (see **Figure 13**).

Conclusion

The story of poverty and homelessness is an old one: equally old is the chronicle of attempts to regulate the movement and behaviour of itinerant people. Legislation against activities such as begging and sleeping rough has existed across different times and societies, but the core 'offence' has arguably been the crime of being poor and homeless. The two case studies discussed here illustrate the various forms regulation may take, with the similarities perhaps outweighing differences of culture and society. For as long as available labour is surplus to economic requirements, while people migrate in search of work in the absence of adequate supplies of housing, and while others become homeless due to individual circumstance, there is likely to be regulation of various manifestations of homelessness.

Figure 13 Lamani woman, South Anjuna beach, Goa. Many Lamani women in Goa work as beach vendors, selling clothes, fruit, and other goods to both Indian and European tourists. Identified as one of India's gypsy groups, Lamani people are often perceived as a troublesome itinerant population. They have been subject to periodic police action, including detention and verification of their status.

See also: Ethnographies of Home and Homelessness; Homeless People: Refugees and Asylum Seekers; Shelter and Settlement for Forcibly Displaced People.

References

Amster R (2008) *Lost in Space: The Criminalization, Globalization and Urban Ecology of Homelessness.* El Paso, TX: LFB Scholarly Publishing.

Beaufoy S (2008) *Slumdog Millionaire: The Shooting Script.* New York: Newmarket Press.

Beier AL (1985) *Masterless Men: The Vagrancy Problem in England 1560–1640.* London: Methuen.

Carlen P (1996) *Jigsaw: A Political Criminology of Youth Homelessness.* Milton Keynes: Open University Press.

Chambliss W (1964) A sociological analysis of the law of vagrancy. *Social Problems* 12: 67–77.

Cohen S and Taylor L (1972) *Psychological Survival.* Harmondsworth: Penguin.

Davis M (2006) *Planet of Slums.* New York: Verso.

De Venanzi (2003) Street children and the excluded class. *International Journal of Comparative Sociology* 44(5): 472–494.

Doherty J, Busch-Geertsema V, Karpuskiene V, et al. (2008) Homelessness and exclusion: Regulating public space in European cities. *Surveillance and Inequality* 5(3): 290–314.

Douglas M (1964) *Purity and Danger: An Analysis of Concepts of Pollution and Taboo.* London: Routledge.

Dupont V, Tarlo E, and Vidal D (2000) *Delhi: Urban Space and Human Destinies.* New Delhi: Manohar.

Glasser I (1994) *Homelessness in Global Perspective.* New York: G. K. Hall.

Faleiro V (8 March 2009) Goa's slums. *Goa Herald.* http://www.mail-archive.com/goanet@lists.goanet.org/msg43359.html (accessed 21 May 2009).

Fitzpatrick S and Jones A (2005) Pursuing social justice or social cohesion?: Coercion in street homelessness policies in England. *Journal of Social Policy* 34(3): 389–406.

Frank-Sharjah N (2006) Beggar colony: Hell on earth.http://www.daijiworld.com/chan/exclusive_arch.asp?ex_id=311 (accessed 7 June 2009).

Government of Goa, *The Goa Daman and Diu Prevention of Begging Act, 1972.* Panaji, Goa, India.

Hermer J (1999) Policing compassion: 'Diverted giving' on the Winchester High Street. In: Dean H (ed.) *Begging Questions: Street-Level Economic Activity and Social Policy Failure.* Bristol: Policy Press.

Hermer J and Mosher J (eds.) (2002) *Disorderly People: Law and the Politics of Exclusion in Ontario*. Nova Scotia: Fernwood Press.

Homeless Link (19 April 2007) Homeless Link calls for Vagrancy Act to be scrapped. http://www.homeless.org.uk/db/20030313230517 (accessed 7 June 2009).

Johnsen S and Fitzpatrick S (2007) *The Impact of Enforcement on Street Users in England*. Bristol: Policy Press.

Kelling GL (1995) *Fixing 'Broken Windows': Order and Individualism in American Cities*. New York: Praeger.

Lofland L (1973) *A World of Strangers: Order and Action in Urban Public Space*. New York: Free Press.

Ministry of Home Affairs, *Bombay Prevention of Begging Act, 1959*. Delhi, India.

Mitchell D (2003) *The Right to the City: Social Justice and the Fight for Public Space*. New York, London: Guilford Press.

Mukherjee D (2008) Laws for beggars, justice for whom: critical review of the Bombay Prevention of Begging Act, 1959. *International Journal of Human Rights* 12(2): 279–288.

Murdoch A (1994) *We Are Human Too: A Study of People Who Beg*. London: Crisis.

Neuwirth R (2006) *Shadow Cities*. London: Routledge.

One India (21 May 2009) Slumdog Millionaire star Rubina Ali left homeless. http://entertainment.oneindia.in/bollywood/news/2009/rubina-azharuddin-homeless-210509.html (accessed 23 May 2009).

Sanders TG (1987) Brazilian street children: Part 1: Who they are. *UFSI Reports Indianapolis*. Universities Field Staff International.

Sharma K (2003) *Rediscovering Dharavi*. Australia: Penguin.

Sibley D (1995) *Geographies of Exclusion: Society and Difference in the West*. London: Routledge.

Spradley JP (1970) *You Owe Yourself a Drunk: An Ethnography of Urban Nomads*. Boston, MA: Little Brown and Company.

Swarup V (2005) *Q and A*. London: Doubleday.

Times of India (4 December 2008) More Lamanis rounded up for verification. http://timesofindia.indiatimes.com/articleshow/msid-3789880,prtpage-1.cms (accessed on 21 May 2009).

Tomory D (2000) *Hello Goodnight: A Life of Goa*. Melbourne, VIC: Lonely Planet Publications.

Wardhaugh J (2000) *Sub City: Young People, Homelessness and Crime*. Aldershot: Ashgate.

Relevant Websites

www.sananda.tripod.com/homeless – American Homeless Society
www.bigissue.com – Big Issue
www.crisis.org.uk – Crisis
http://childrescue.net/ – El Shaddai Street Child Rescue
www.homeless-international.org – Homeless International
www.homeless.org.uk – Homeless Link
www.homelessuk.org – Homeless UK
www.shelter.org.uk – Shelter

Policies to Address Homelessness: Housing First Approaches

V Stanhope, DK Padgett, and BF Henwood, New York University, New York, NY, USA

© 2012 Elsevier Ltd. All rights reserved.

Glossary

Assertive community treatment refers to a multidisciplinary team which shares a small caseload of consumers, providing intensive and continuous crisis intervention, treatment, and rehabilitation services in the community.

Chronic homelessness is defined by the U.S. federal government as being an unaccompanied homeless individual with a disabling condition who has either been continuously homeless for a year or more or has had at least four episodes of homelessness in the past 3 years.

Co-occurring disorders refers to a co-occurrence or co-morbidity of a severe mental illness and a substance use disorder. Substance use disorders are abuse or dependence on alcohol or other psychoactive drugs and severe mental illnesses are schizophrenia, bipolar disorder, and severe depression when accompanied by long-term disability.

Harm reduction is based upon a stages of change approach to substance use, meaning providers work with clients towards reducing use and the adverse consequences associated with use.

Housing First is an intervention based on consumer choice that serves people with psychiatric disabilities by providing immediate, independent apartments along with support services and does not require sobriety or treatment.

Linear housing is the residential system for people with severe mental illness in which clients typically start in communal facilities with intensive staff supervision and graduate through settings with declining levels of restrictiveness to independent apartments.

Recovery involves the development of new meaning and purpose in one's life as one grows beyond the catastrophic effects of psychiatric disability.

Supported housing refers to an empowerment/integration model which places consumers in independent housing coupled with flexible individualised services in order to facilitate community integration.

Homelessness among People with Severe Mental Illnesses

The extent of severe mental illnesses among the homeless has been well documented. Epidemiological studies conducted in the United States estimate that 20% of single adults who are sheltered or unsheltered homeless suffer from severe mental illnesses. Substance abuse disorders among the sheltered and unsheltered homeless range from 28 to 48%, and the majority of those with severe mental illnesses have co-occurring disorders. This population also constitutes a disproportionate number of the chronically homeless, which is defined by the federal government as "an unaccompanied homeless adult with a disabling condition who has either been continuously homeless for a year or more or has had at least four episodes of homelessness in the past three years". In the United States, approximately 120 000 individuals, who represent 18% of the total homeless, were chronically homeless on a single night, with male African Americans being overrepresented within this population.

Suffering from psychiatric and substance abuse problems may often hasten the descent into homelessness, but conditions on the street precipitate a level of depression and anxiety that often compound psychotic symptoms. Continued exposure to homelessness has profoundly adverse effects on every aspect of a person's physical, psychological, social, economic, legal, and spiritual well-being, where survival is not taken for granted but is instead an exhausting ordeal of seeking places to eat, sit and rest, and sleep. Being exposed to extremes of weather, dangerous or life-threatening situations, increased opportunities for infection, drug use, and arrest is associated with a manifold incidence of acute and chronic health problems and victimisation. As a result, people experiencing homelessness have a mortality rate up to four times higher than that of the general population. Many experience 'the institutional circuit' cycling between the streets, shelters, hospitals, and jails, with sporadic and uncoordinated encounters with care systems. Given the chaotic nature of this existence, social exclusion and isolation is another stressor in the lives of homeless people.

Policies Addressing Chronically Homeless

Along with a growing homeless industry of public and private shelters, the mental health system has been struggling to meet the housing needs of people with severe mental illnesses since deinstitutionalisation. But more recently the homelessness system has made this population a policy priority due to the realisation that, though a small group in relation to all people experiencing homelessness, they place a disproportionately high burden on social and medical services. Although homelessness in the United States can be attributed to the lack of affordable housing dating back to the Reagan era, the plight of the homeless has largely been understood in terms of individual pathologies. The focus on the individual rather than the structural has generated solutions that promote housing readiness among individuals rather than increasing the supply of housing. In turn, the research that has informed these solutions has also taken a demand perspective, focusing on the individual characteristics of the homeless, rather than the capacity of social service systems to provide housing.

The impetus for targeting services for the chronically homeless came from several landmark research studies that identified the service use patterns of this subgroup. Chronic users, as opposed to episodic or transitional, while only representing 11% of shelter users, account for 50% of the total shelter use. Contrary to popular belief, the costs incurred by people who live for long periods in shelters or on the streets are high. Studies estimated the average annual per person cost of incarceration, crisis services, emergency room visits, acute hospitalisation, and shelter use to be $40 500 (1999 dollars) in New York and as much as $150 000 in San Diego (1996 dollars). These findings garnered media attention and created an imperative among policymakers to address the problem of the chronic homeless.

In 2003, President Bush made ending chronic homelessness a top priority in his budget, and the U.S. Interagency Council on Homelessness launched the Collaborative Initiative to Help End Chronic Homelessness (CICH). The goal was to provide persons experiencing chronic homelessness with permanent housing funded by the following federal government agencies: Department of Housing and Urban Development, Health Resources Administration, Substance Abuse and Mental Health Services Administration, and Veterans Health Administration. With federal leadership and the prospect of funding, cities and states pledged to develop plans to end chronic homelessness in the next 10 years. Currently, 350 communities have implemented plans, which include improvements in discharge planning, outreach activities, and housing and community supports. The CICH facilitated access for 150 000 supported housing units and increased federal funds to develop additional housing units.

A Paradigm Shift in Housing

The plans to end chronic homelessness were significant not only in the extent to which they targeted resources towards a specific subgroup within the homeless population, but also because they represented a paradigm shift in services approaches for the homeless. Traditional services have been based on a linear approach which provided a sequence of housing types, from shelters to transitional to permanent housing. The goal of these programmes was to make clients housing ready, that is, to acquire the necessary skills to maintain housing. People would be expected to graduate through the system by engaging in services and maintaining sobriety with the end goal of attaining independent, permanent housing. This approach is predicated on the belief that homelessness arises from individual deficits in need of modification and that mental health services are pivotal to reaching the end goal of housing stability. However, despite increases in funding for linear approaches during the 1990s, there were no overall decreases in homelessness. In particular, these services were failing to meet the needs of long-term homeless persons suffering from co-occurring disorders.

Identifying and comparing housing models is challenging due to their diversity and the inconsistent use of terminology within the field. However, a markedly different approach to linear housing emerged in the early 1990s which was defined as supported housing (also labelled permanent supported housing, and more recently, permanent supportive housing). With an emphasis on community integration and consumer choice, supported housing provides immediate access to independent scatter-site apartments with flexible services depending on the resident's needs and preferences. The housing is made affordable by state and federal grants which allow the programme to subsidise rents for individuals with disabilities. The paradigm shift is reflected primarily in the fact that the housing is not conditional on participation in treatment or abstinence from substance use, with residents abiding by the usual tenancy requirements. As a result, residents are offered immediate access to stable housing, thereby avoiding the stress of frequent moves as they graduate through the continuum and the threat of eviction due to noncompliance.

The impetus for unbundling housing and services was driven by ethical concerns for human rights and dignity, by the failure of the status quo in reaching the chronically homeless, and by consumer preferences. The imposition of rules, particularly compliance with services and sobriety, in order to attain housing proved too much of a hurdle for many people living on the street with active addictions, resulting in service disengagement. As a result, linear approaches have shown modest results for housing stability with programme attrition rates of 50% and higher. Advocates also argue that such an approach is inherently coercive and violates federal law by placing people with psychiatric disabilities in an unnecessarily restrictive environment that is a barrier to community integration. Moreover, people experiencing homelessness have consistently expressed a preference for independent living over more structured settings, whatever their current living situation. The rise of the mental health recovery movement has provided additional support for the paradigm shift in housing by demanding client-driven services that are individualised, noncoercive, and foster community integration.

The Pathways Housing First Model

Pathways to Housing was the first site to provide Housing First for homeless adults with serious mental illness. Begun by Sam Tsemberis in New York City in 1992, Pathways to Housing reflected its founder's experience as a psychologist working in homeless outreach. Concluding that stable housing needed to be the priority in addressing the preferences of people living on the streets, Tsemberis created a programme that reversed the continuum by offering housing first (see **Table 1**). The programme was specifically targeted at the people who were hardest to reach, or as one staff member described it, "we are looking for people who are not looking for us". With this mission to engage those who had consistently resisted services, the model was congruent with later federal initiatives to end chronic homelessness. Philip Mangano, appointed during the Bush Administration to head the U.S. Inter-Agency Council on Homelessness, was quick to endorse Housing First and promote the programme to policymakers and service providers around the country.

As the first enactment of Housing First for single adults, the Pathways to Housing (PHF) model remains the best articulated and most empirically supported. This was affirmed by its classification as an Evidence-Based Practice by the Substance Abuse and Mental Health Services Administration in 2008. However, reflecting the overall lack of consensus on housing terminology, the term Housing First has been applied to programmes that vary from the Pathways Housing First (PHF) approach. The following sections describe the PHF approach with the understanding that some programmes do not conform to all aspects of PHF.

Values

Housing First is based on the premise that housing is a basic human right and that people who are homeless and suffer from psychiatric disabilities should not have to prove that they are ready for housing by first participating in treatment or being clean and sober. Housing is, therefore, separated from services, rather than being earned or used as enticement or coercion into treatment or sobriety. To reflect this separation, providers that acquire and coordinate housing are separate from the providers that deliver clinical services. Consumer choice shapes the Housing First approach with respect to both housing and services. Providers encourage clients to make choices about where they want to live and aspects or characteristics of their housing.

Enrolees are provided access to an array of treatment and social services, but it is programme policy that they choose their level of participation. Consistent with this approach, the programme adheres to the principles of harm reduction, that is, providers help to minimise adverse consequences of substance use if consumers

Table 1 A comparison of the linear approach to housing and the Pathways Housing First model

	Linear approach to housing	*Pathways housing first model*
Values	Housing to be earned and clinical expertise	Housing as a right and consumer choice
Eligibility/preconditions	Pre-conditions (no history of violence or incarceration; adherence to psychiatric and substance abuse treatment)	No pre-conditions
Housing		
Ownership	Provider/programme	Private landlord
Tenure	Transitional (graduation through continuum)	Permanent
Occupancy	Congregate and individual	Individual
Location	Concentrated in building or neighborhood and scatter-site	Scatter-site
Services		
Staff location	On-site and off-site	Off-site
Staff arrangement	Individual case managers	ACT team and individual case managers
Programme rules/expectations	Money management, curfew, no visitors and medication/treatment adherence	Money management no curfew, visitors allowed, meet with case manager and medication/treatment voluntary
Substance use policy	Abstinence only	Harm reduction

choose to continue using substances. Similarly, providers attempt to minimise the adverse consequences resulting from psychiatric symptoms if consumers choose not to take medication and find alternative ways to address symptoms. Services are consumer driven, with clients setting their own long-term goals. By structuring services that are individualised, nonlinear, and not time limited, the programme reflects a recovery orientation, working with clients for however long they may need.

Eligibility

To be eligible for Housing First, individuals must be homeless, have a psychiatric disability (including active symptoms or a history of psychiatric hospitalisation), and express an interest in receiving housing. Substance abuse and addiction, a history of violence, and/or history of incarceration do not disqualify the individual from entering the programme. Although Housing First does not demand medication adherence or sobriety, there are programme requirements. To be enrolled in the programme and receive an apartment, clients must agree to contact with clinical team and to apartment inspections. Depending on the level of support the clients are receiving, there are different required minimum levels of contact with providers, ranging from twice a month to six times a month. Clients with personal income must agree to contribute a portion to their rent so that the programme can assure the rent is paid in full and on time. Most programmes accept referrals from a variety of agencies that provide services to homeless individuals with psychiatric disabilities. In addition, Housing First providers may conduct their own outreach by directly approaching individuals living on the streets.

Housing

Housing First uses a scatter-site independent apartment model, renting affordable apartments from landlords in the community. This housing model is consistent with research that honours consumers' preferences for apartments of their own and provides consumers the option of living in the neighbourhood of their choosing whenever possible (housing and neighbourhood choices are restricted by the affordability and availability of units). To facilitate community integration, the programme does not rent more than 20% of the units in any given apartment building. Clients have the same rights and responsibilities as other tenants holding a standard lease, and they are required to pay 30% of their income towards rent (which typically consists of Supplemental Security Income or Social Security Disability Income). When necessary, the representative payee mechanism may be employed to ensure that rent and utilities are paid and to assist clients with money management.

Concerns about risks both to the client and the larger community from placing persons with active addiction in independent housing are addressed by the providers actively facilitating normative relationships with landlords, neighbours, family, and other natural support networks. Achieving housing stability is accepted as an ongoing task for many clients. Some are at risk of eviction due to relapse or incarceration. Providers work closely with clients to prevent housing loss, but in the event a client loses their housing, there is a strong commitment to rapid re-housing not contingent on client readiness. Housing loss only occurs for lease violations or long-term hospitalisation or incarceration (usually more than 90 days).

Support Services

Housing First clients have access to comprehensive services, which include evidence-based practices. In many programmes the service delivery method is Assertive Community Treatment (ACT), an evidence-based practice designed to be one of the most intensive outpatient mental health services provided in the community. The ACT team is an interdisciplinary team composed of the following staff members: team leader, psychiatrist, substance abuse specialist, peer specialist (a current or former recipient of mental health services), nurse or nurse practitioner, social workers, vocational rehabilitation specialist, and programme assistant. Services provided by the ACT team have no predetermined time limits and are available 24 hours per day, 7 days per week. The ACT team does not have individual caseloads. Instead, the entire team shares the caseload and visits with every client. Typically the participant to staff ratio is 10:1.

ACT team members, called service coordinators or case managers, provide participants with a number of comprehensive services in their home and community, including substance abuse treatment, mental health care, basic primary health care, medication assistance, vocational services, and family services. The services provided by the ACT team are flexible and participant determined. If the need or desire exists, members of the team can visit the participant several times a day, or only visit them the minimal two times per month. On a daily basis, the ACT team meets to review the entire caseload. ACT also provides an efficient platform to deliver other evidence-based practices, including supported employment, integrated dual disorder treatment, and wellness self-management.

Intensive case management can also be used as the service delivery model for PHF, with case managers having individual rather than shared caseloads. As the model evolves, there may be increased use of the intensive case management (ICM) model for clients with less intense service needs. The service delivery model may also be influenced by local funding streams and the need to secure reimbursement for services.

Programme Variation

There is variation in the type of housing and services offered under the rubric of Housing First. Whereas the PHF approach implies renting apartments from private landlords in the community, some agencies own and control their own housing, a variation from the original PHF model that views establishing landlord relationships as part of the programme's goal of community integration. Similarly, some Housing First programmes have opted for congregate living settings rather than a scattered-site model. For instance, Downtown Emergency Center in Seattle, WA, places clients in their own small congregate apartments within a limited geographic area and has staff onsite. Although onsite staff can more easily address housing problems, this arrangement does not uphold the functional separation between housing and services and precludes community integration. While some programmes maintain a housing department within the same agency and put in place adequate firewalls so as not to confound housing and services, other programmes use separate housing and service providers altogether, making the separation literal and functional. In either case, housing retention is not contingent on treatment-related matters, although relationship building between clients, landlords, housing providers, and treatment staff is often beneficial. The variation found among Housing First programmes raises some issues about fidelity, specifically what is essential and distinctive about the PHF model versus other housing models.

Programme Costs

Housing First programmes combine funds from federal, state, local, and private sources. Since public mental health services are the purview of state and local governments, contracts usually emanate from these sources. One appeal of Housing First for cities and localities is that they can leverage federal funds for the programme. The housing component may access federal government subsidies providing vouchers for clients, notably through the Shelter Plus Care and the Supportive Housing Program. Housing First programmes also assist clients in obtaining (or who already have) government vouchers provided to income-eligible persons. Treatment and services can be funded through Medicaid dollars (a state-federal cost-sharing source), with individual providers or ACT teams certified as providing Medicaid reimbursable services. Often programmes rely on state and local funds for start-up costs and then transition to federal funding sources. Overall, the programme is cost-effective, with Pathways to Housing spending approximately $22 000 on each client per year, versus the cost of $27 000 for shelter services and $40 500 for the collateral costs of living on the streets.

Empirical Support for Housing First

There continues to be a growing empirical base supporting the effectiveness of Housing First that includes both quantitative and qualitative research.

Pathways to Housing Studies

The New York Housing Study (NYHS) was a 4-year experiment in which 225 homeless mentally ill persons in New York City were randomly assigned to the Pathways to Housing or to linear programmes. Participants in Housing First spent 85% of their time stably housed, compared with less than 25% for participants in the linear programmes. After 2 years, Housing First participants still spent approximately 80% of their time stably housed, compared with only 30% for the control group. Reductions in homelessness were significantly lower for the linear group, who were homeless approximately 50% of the time at baseline, 27% at 1 year, and 25% after 2 years. Consumer choice was also greater among Housing First residents at 24 months and at 36 months. Utilisation of substance abuse treatment services was greater for the linear programmes but group differences for alcohol and drug use were not significant.

The New York Services Study (NYSS) was a qualitative study designed to elicit consumer perspectives regarding their service use and other dimensions of their lives. A total of 114 clients were interviewed across Pathways to Housing and three linear programmes. The higher rate of housing stability found in the NYHS was replicated in the NYSS with 54% of the linear group disengaging from their programmes compared with 11% of Housing First participants. Those in linear programmes disengaged due to substance relapse and/or a rejection of the restrictions associated with congregate living. Staying in treatment or engaged in services was related to provider empathy and assistance, to flexible rules and restrictions, and to imparting a sense of hope.

In terms of substance use, the study actually found that individuals in the Housing First programme were three times more likely to abstain from heavy drinking or illicit drug use than their linear group counterparts. For those in Housing First, living independently in one's own apartment gave participants a sense of independence and safety from outside intrusions that they did not have in congregate living. In describing their experience of living alone, participants often used 'loner talk' and invoked a need for privacy and social connectedness on their own terms.

Other Housing First Studies

Subsequent studies of Housing First programmes have confirmed the positive findings of the NYHS. Seven of the 11 cities funded by CICH used some variation of the Housing First model and achieved 85% housing retention rates after 12 months. The Department of Housing and Urban Development published the outcomes of their three city, 12-month study of Housing First programmes (one of which was Pathways to Housing), reporting an 84% housing retention rate for 12 months, with 43% spending the entire year in programme housing and 41% experiencing at least one departure but returning to the programme. In a suburban setting with long-term shelter residents, approximately 78% of Housing First participants remained stably housed over a 4-year period, demonstrating the model's application in a different setting. In Canada, 90% were in stable housing 1 year after being housed by a Housing First programme.

Reductions in service use have been consistent across Housing First programmes. In Chicago, Housing First clients were nearly two times less likely to be hospitalised or use emergency rooms as compared with a usual care group. In Denver, clients decreased emergency room use by 73%, inpatient stays by 66%, detoxification use by 82%, and incarceration by 76%. This reduction in service use results in significant cost savings, with one study finding that 95 Housing First clients reduced their service costs by a total of $4 million compared with their service costs for the year prior to their enrolment. In other domains, clients consistently expressed greater satisfaction with Housing First, particularly related to housing, but findings related to mental health outcomes and substance use have been mixed.

Future Directions

Housing First has become an essential component in initiatives to end chronic homelessness. In July 2008, the U.S. Department of Housing and Urban Development reported that the number of chronically homeless people living in the nation's streets and shelters had dropped by about 30% – to 123 833 from 175 914 – between 2005 and 2007, which policy makers attributed in part to the effectiveness of Housing First. The model has now been used in over 40 cities throughout the United States and is included in the large majority of city and county plans to end chronic homelessness. Globally, Canada has recently embarked upon a national multi-site replication study of Housing First, and several countries, including Australia, Japan, and Ireland, are considering implementing the model. As Housing First becomes more widely disseminated and implemented in diverse service systems, considerations related to fidelity become more prominent. In response, Pathways to Housing has developed a manual and a fidelity measure in order to promote consistent implementation across sites.

Despite its increasingly widespread adoption and evidence base, Housing First has not been without its critics. Ideologically, the harm reduction approach remains controversial due to concern that public funds may be used to support criminal activity and that abstinence is the only effective way to address substance abuse. Overall, a policy that prioritises allocating resources to adults with co-occurring disorders over other populations, such as woman and children experiencing homelessness, can create tension between competing interest groups. Also, some question the programme's ability to effectively treat people with active addictions, arguing that those with primary diagnoses of substance abuse are more difficult to house. While a small subset of more addicted persons might not be able to benefit from the Housing First approach, the overall success of the programme confirms that congregate or institutional care can be the last rather than the first resort.

While the aforementioned critiques reflect larger issues that have emerged as housing policy becomes increasingly intertwined with mental health policy, public health advocates have begun to conceptualise this issue more broadly in terms of how best to address individuals with 'complex service needs'. From this perspective, Housing First provides an intervention that not only helps those with co-occurring disorders but it can also improve health outcomes since many chronic health conditions such as diabetes, hypertension, and heart disease disproportionately affect the homeless. National and international efforts aimed at improving housing status and health outcomes, reducing costs, and increasing patient satisfaction have made service integration an urgent priority. These trends in various systems of care will dictate how Housing First evolves over the next decade.

See also: Ethnographies of Home and Homelessness; Home and Homelessness; Homelessness: Measurement Questions; Mental Health and Homelessness; NIMBYism; Policies to Address Homelessness: Partnership-Based Approaches in Ireland; Policies to Address Homelessness: Rights-Based Approaches; Policies to Address Homelessness; Policies to Address Homelessness: 'Staircase' Models; Shelter and Development; Social Psychological Perspectives on Homelessness.

Further Reading

Allen M (2003) Waking Rip van Winkle: Why developments in the last 20 years should teach the mental health system not to use housing as a tool of coercion. *Behavioural Sciences and the Law* 21(4): 503–521.

Carling PJ (1993) Housing and supports for persons with mental illness: Emerging approaches to research and practice. *Hospital & Community Psychiatry* 44(5): 439–449.

Culhane D, Metraux S, and Hadley T (2002) Public service reductions associated with placement of homeless persons with severe mental illness in supportive housing. *Housing Policy Debate* 13(1): 107–163.

Gladwell M (2006) Million dollar Murray. Why problems like homelessness may be easier to solve than to manage. *New Yorker (February 13):* 96–107.

Greenwood R, Shaefer-McDaniel N, Winkle G, and Tsemberis S (2005) Decreasing psychiatric symptoms by increasing choice in services for adults with histories of homelessness. *American Journal of Community Psychology* 36(3/4): 226–238.

Hopper K, Jost J, Hay T, Welber S, and Haugland G (1997) Homelessness, severe mental illness, and the institutional circuit. *Psychiatric Services* 48(5): 659–665.

Kertesz SG, Crouch K, Milby J, Cusimano RA, and Schumacher J (2009) Housing First for homeless persons with active addiction: Are we overreaching? *The Milbank Quarterly* 87(2): 1–52.

O'Hara (2007) Housing for people with mental illness: An update of a report to the New Freedom Commission. *Psychiatric Services* 58: 907–913.

Padgett DK (2007) There's no place like (a) home: Ontological security in the third decade of the 'homelessness crisis' in the United States. *Social Science & Medicine* 64(9): 1925–1936.

Padgett DK, Gulcur L, and Tsemberis S (2006) Housing First services for people who are homeless with co-occurring serious mental illness and substance abuse. *Research on Social Work Practice* 16(1): 74–83.

Ridgway P and Zipple A (1990) The paradigm shift in residential services: From the linear continuum to supported housing services. *Psychiatric Rehabilitation Journal* 13(1): 11–31.

Stanhope V, Henwood BF, and Padgett DK (2009) Understanding service disengagement from the perspective of case managers. *Psychiatric Services* 60(4): 459–464.

Tsemberis S and Eisenberg RF (2000) Pathways to housing: Supported housing for street-dwelling homeless individuals with psychiatric disabilities. *Psychiatric Services* 51(4): 487–493.

Tsemberis S, Gulcur L, and Nakae M (2004) Housing First, consumer choice, and harm reduction for homeless individuals with a co-occurring disorders. *American Journal of Public Health* 94(4): 651–656.

U.S. Department of Housing & Urban Development (2007, July). The Applicability of Housing First models to homeless persons with serious mental illness. *Final Report.* http://www.huduser.org/Publications/pdf/hsgfirst.pdf

Relevant Websites

http://aspe.hhs.gov/hsp/homelessness/CICH07/index.htm – Evaluation of the Collaborative Initiative to End Chronic Homelessness

http://www.endhomelessness.org/section/tools/housingfirst – Housing First by National Alliance to End Homelessness

http://pathwaystohousing.org/ – Pathways to Housing

http://www.nrepp.samhsa.gov/ programfulldetails.asp?PROGRAM_ID=195 – SAMSHA's National Registry of Evidence Based Programs and Practices

http://www.ich.gov/ – U.S. Interagency Council on Homelessness

Policies to Address Homelessness: Partnership-Based Approaches in Ireland

E O'Sullivan, Trinity College Dublin, Dublin, Ireland

© 2012 Elsevier Ltd. All rights reserved.

Introduction

This article provides an overview of the broad conceptual approach utilised to address homelessness in the Republic of Ireland from the mid-1990s to the present. The shorthand term for the institutional arrangements that have embraced government, employers, trade unions, and civil society, from the late 1980s, is 'social partnership'. From the mid-1990s, the Irish economy grew dramatically as evidenced by effective full employment and a substantial growth in net inward migration, earning Ireland the moniker 'the Celtic Tiger'. While, as Roche (2009: 184) notes, "commentators differ on the weighting social partnership should receive in accounting for Ireland's economic recovery and unprecedented performance .... few deny that its role was significant". Crucial to operation of social partnership was the process that brought together government, employers, unions, and NGOs (since 1996) every 3 years to negotiate a strategic consensus on the economic and social policy. These negotiations are underpinned by a review of the economic and social policy by the National Economic and Social Council (NESC), which incorporates all the key social partners. (Established in the early 1970s, the functions of the NESC are to analyse and report to the Taoiseach (prime minister) on strategic issues relating to the efficient development of the economy, the achievement of social justice, and the development of a strategic framework for the conduct of relations and the negotiation of agreements between the government and the social partners.) A voluminous literature now exists on conceptualising social partnership in Ireland, but as described by one of its key architects:

> [p]artnership involves the players in a process of deliberation that has the potential to shape and reshape their understanding, identity and preferences. This idea, that identity can be shaped in interaction, is important. It is implicit in NESC's description of the process as 'dependent on a shared understanding', and 'characterised by a problem-solving approach designed to produce consensus'. (O'Donnell, 2008: 20)

How these institutional arrangements should be conceptualised is contested. For some commentators, these arrangements were merely a variant on classical continental corporatism; and for others, a variant on neoliberalism (see O'Riain, 2006, for an overview of these debates). However, it can be argued that social partnership is distinctive from corporatism, in that it not only embraced national wage agreements, but also embraced a range of local as well as national issues, and the principles of deliberation and consensus building were applied to a host of problematic policy arenas, from drug misuse to urban regeneration. Thus, starting at a national level and dealing primarily with macro-economic issues, new forms of governance emerged from the late 1980s, which gradually filtered down to local areas and to a range of policy concerns. This emphasis on generating, through dialogue, a shared understanding of policy issues with a consequent focus on problem solving permeated the majority of policy areas, and homelessness was no exception. It is of note, however, that the initial national-level negotiated agreements rarely mentioned homelessness and that the adoption of a partnership-based approach to homelessness emerged within the context of social partnership, rather than being determined by social partnership. However, by the time of the most recent national partnership agreement in 2006, homelessness was firmly on the national agenda with commitments to ending long-term homelessness and developing new governance structures to oversee the process. This approach stands in contrast to more 'rights-based approaches' to tackling homelessness, in that the emphasis is on achieving a shared understanding of the issue and working through a process of deliberative democracy to achieve the desired outcomes; rather than imposing obligations on (usually) state agencies to provide accommodation and services via legislation as found, for example, in England and France (Loison-Leruste and Quilgars, 2009). This article provides an overview of this process of deliberation and consensus building in relation to homelessness in the Republic of Ireland and evaluates the robustness of this approach to policy-making in a context of substantial cuts in public services brought about by the general economic crisis in Ireland.

Developing a National Homeless Strategy

The Housing Act 1988 specified local authorities (the basic administrative unit of local government) as the statutory agency with responsibility for the homeless by obliging them to conduct periodic assessments of housing need and homelessness and identify their housing options. By the mid-1990s, it was increasingly recognised that homelessness was more than a question of housing supply;

rather, other services were required to successfully exit homelessness on a long-term basis. In a review of service provision for the homeless in Dublin, it was noted "that there are certain deficiencies both in the range of services provided and in the planning and co-ordination of service delivery" (Bardas Atha Cliath/Eastern Heath Board, 1995: 1).

To remedy the situation, the review recommended a new administrative structure to deliver homeless services. Called the Homeless Initiative, it was established in October 1996, with the objective of ensuring that services for homeless people were more effective, particularly by improving their planning, coordination, and delivery. (Homeless Initiative was replaced by the Homeless Agency in 2000.) This was to be achieved through analysis, planning, and the development of a strong partnership between all the agencies involved and was to replace the piecemeal and fragmented policy approach identified in the above review with the coordinated one. The Initiative was funded jointly by two central government departments (the Departments of Health and Environment – effectively the departments with responsibility for health, social services, and housing), operating under the direction of a management group, comprising two senior officials each from Dublin Corporation (the local authority agency for Dublin) and the Eastern Health Board (the health and social services authority for Dublin and the surrounding areas). In addition, a consultative forum consisting of representatives from the Eastern Health Board, all local authorities in the greater Dublin region, and from voluntary organisations providing services to homeless people was formed to aid the work of the Homeless Initiative.

The establishment of the Homeless Initiative was a crucial catalyst in devising new ways of responding to homelessness, particularly in developing a partnership-based approach, which in turn provided the stimulus for the development of a national strategic approach to homelessness. The beginning of this national strategic approach to homelessness was the establishment by the government, on the 19th of August 1998, of a Cross-Departmental Team on Homelessness under the auspices of the Cabinet Sub-Committee on Social Inclusion (Brownlee, 2008). In 2000, the team published a national policy document: *Homelessness – An Integrated Strategy* (Department of the Environment and Local Government, 2000). The broad principles enunciated by the strategy document were, that to bring enhanced coherence to the services available, what was required included: a continuum of care from the time someone becomes homeless, with sheltered and supported accommodation, and where appropriate, assistance back into independent living in the community; emergency accommodation should be short-term; settlement in the community to be an overriding priority through independent or supported housing; long-term supported accommodation should be available for those who need it; support services should be provided on an outreach basis as needed and preventative strategies for at-risk groups should be developed. To achieve these broad objectives, homeless forums were to be established in every local authority administrative area and 3-year action plans prepared. Both the homeless forums and the action plans were to include input from both the statutory and nonprofit sectors.

In early 2002, a *Homeless Preventative Strategy* was published with the key objective of ensuring that "no one is released or discharged from state care without the appropriate measures in place to ensure that they have a suitable place to live with the necessary supports, if needed" (Department of Environment and Local Government et al., 2002: 3). The implementation of these three strategy documents was monitored by the Cross-Departmental Team on Homelessness, which in turn reports to the Cabinet Sub-Committee on Social Inclusion, which is chaired by the Taoiseach (prime minister).

Reviewing the Strategy

In January 2005, the Department of Environment, Heritage and Local Government announced the undertaking of an independent review of the government's homeless strategies. This report was published in February 2006. The report systematically reviewed the 43 specific policy proposals identified in the two strategies and put forward 21 recommendations to aid the implementation of the strategies, and these were all accepted by the government. In relation to the 'integrated strategy', the consultants suggested that over 60% of the objectives outlined were either fully or significantly progressed. In relation to the 'preventative strategy', just under 30% were fully or significantly progressed (Fitzpatrick Associates, 2006). The report argued that in moving the homeless strategies forward, all agencies working in this area needed to refocus their energies to make "itself largely obsolete, which should, after all, be its overarching goal" (2006: 128). To aid achieving this objective, the report recommended that the two existing strategies need to be revised and amalgamated, a national homeless consultative committee be established, and all government policies should be proofed for any impact it might have on homelessness. These recommendations were signed up to by social partners in the next social partnership agreement, *Towards 2016* (Government of Ireland, 2006).

The Way Home – The Revised National Homeless Strategy

In 2006, a National Homeless Consultative Committee (NHCC) was established to provide input to the development of the revised Homeless Strategy and ongoing government policy on addressing homelessness. In August 2008, after some delay, the revised National Homeless Strategy, entitled *The Way Home: A Strategy to Address Adult Homelessness in Ireland, 2008–2013* was launched, and accepted the broad thrust of the recommendations in the review of the earlier strategies (Department of Environment, Heritage and Local Government, 2008).

The core objective of the strategy was that: "from 2010, long-term homelessness and the need for people to sleep rough will be eliminated throughout Ireland". This was to be achieved through six strategic aims that would (1) prevent homelessness, (2) eliminate the need to sleep rough, (3) eliminate long-term homelessness, (4) meet long-term housing needs, (5) ensure effective services for homeless people, and (6) better coordinate funding arrangements. In April 2009, an overview of the required inputs to ensure the successful implementation of the revised National Homeless Strategy was published (Department of Environment, Heritage and Local Government, 2009). Noting the changed economic environment in which Ireland found itself with the rapid deterioration of public finances, the plan stated that this "reinforces the critical need to maximize effectiveness and value for money in the planning, organization and delivery of quality homeless services" (2009: 5).

The Housing (Miscellaneous Provisions) Act 2009 gave legislative effect to many of the recommendations of the revised national homeless strategy by specifying that each housing authority adopt a homelessness action plan specifying the measures to be undertaken to address homelessness, and establishing homelessness consultative fora for each authority which must include voluntary homeless service providers in addition to the key statutory providers. This, in effect, replaces the previous administrative process with a new statutory basis for both the fora and the plans.

Measuring the Extent of Homelessness in Ireland during the Partnership Period

As noted earlier, following the Housing Act 1988, local authorities under section 9 of the Act are legally obliged to carry out assessments of housing need, with homelessness being one of the categories of need specified. The first assessment took place at the end of March 1989 and, to date, seven assessments have taken place. These data include only homeless households, which are registered and deemed eligible for housing by local authorities, and based on this measurement show a variable pattern (**Table 1**).

In recognition of the fact that not all homeless households are registered with local authorities for social housing, a more rigorous survey methodology was devised, commencing in Dublin in 1999 and three other major urban areas in 2008 (Cork, Limerick, and Galway), to ascertain the extent of homelessness in these areas. The methodology involved all homeless service providers, both voluntary and statutory, completing a standardised questionnaire in respect of each individual deemed to be homeless over a period of a week. Duplicates are removed and the data are analysed by an independent data analysis organisation. The results for 2008 show 2911 unique households utilising homeless services during the week 10–16 March 2008. It is not possible to identify trends in the case of Cork, Limerick, or Galway, as 2008 was the first year in which this survey was conducted. In the case of Dublin, in raw numbers, the number of households utilising homeless services was 2066 in 2005 and 2144 in 2008, but due to a substantial growth in the population of Dublin during that period, a slight decline in the number of homeless households on a per capita basis from 50.1 to 49.5 per 10 000 population is evident. In the case of Dublin and Cork (no data are available in respect of Galway and Limerick), 31 and 50%, respectively, of those utilising the services were in long-term supported accommodation or transitional accommodation. In Dublin, the numbers recorded as sleeping rough declined from 312 in 2002 to 185 in 2005 and to 110 in 2008. In broad terms, it would appear from the existing, albeit inadequate, data sources that the number of households experiencing homelessness and, in particular, those sleeping rough, have declined over the past number of years.

Table 1 Homeless households in Ireland, 1989–2008

	1989	1991	1993	1996	1999	2002	2005	2008
Number of homeless households assessed for housing	987	1507	1452	979	2219	2468	2399	1394

Source: Department of the Environment and Local Government. *Annual Housing Statistics Bulletin – Various Years*. Dublin: Department of the Environment and Local Government.

However, there has been a large increase in the number and proportion of foreign nationals reporting sleeping rough, from 9% of rough sleepers in 2005 to 38% in 2008. In addition, since the late 1990s, data on the number of homeless children (i.e., under 18 years of age), are collated by the Department of Health and Children and the Health Service Executive. The most recent data available suggest that, nationally, 234 children were identified as homeless in 2008. A total of 774 children were identified as homeless in 1999, suggesting a substantial decline in the number of children presenting as homeless over the past decade.

Partnership, the Demise of the Celtic Tiger, and Homelessness

As noted in the introduction to the article, the development of a partnership-based strategic approach to homelessness coincided and, indeed, was facilitated by Ireland's strong economic performance, which allowed for an unprecedented level of public expenditure on homeless services. Approximately €12 million was expended by the central government on homeless services in 1999, which grew to €90 million in 2007. Despite the rapid deterioration in the public finances in Ireland since 2008 and substantial retrenchment in virtually every area of public service provision, public expenditure on homeless services was largely protected from these cuts in 2009 and 2010. However, the ambitious target set and agreed on by all that by the end of 2010 no homeless person will spend longer than 6 months in an emergency accommodation – rather they would be provided with appropriate long-term accommodation – and that the need to sleep rough would be eliminated has become mired in operational and implementation difficulties. This should be set against the backdrop of a radical reduction in social housing provision due to a range of factors, but primarily a shift in policy and financing of all social housing in Ireland from building to leasing. The necessary reconfiguration of homeless service providers, particularly in Dublin, where the greatest concentration of homeless households is located, has proven difficult to achieve despite a series of detailed consensus-based implementation plans prepared under the auspices of the Homeless Agency (2007, 2009), which were largely based on a series of detailed evaluations of homeless services (see Rhodes and Brooke, 2010, for a detailed overview of these evaluations).

A key constraint has been the lack of progress in securing the units of long-term accommodation required to move the approximately 1200 households that are currently in costly private emergency accommodation. It was envisaged that these units would come from a mixture of units provided under leasing arrangements and managed by the not-for-profit sector, the private rented sector, and the local housing authority. Many not-for-profit agencies have been reluctant to provide housing units for households under the proposed leasing arrangements, primarily due to difficulties associated with the shift to a leasing model of funding from the previous capital funding model. Furthermore, many of the households currently in emergency accommodation express a preference for traditional local authority housing. Social housing in Ireland is currently undergoing a substantial reorientation, with a much greater involvement of the private sector and a decline in the role of the local authorities as housing providers (for further details, see Norris and Coates, 2010, and Norris and Fahey, 2009). The most recent policy statement in relation to social housing states that the "Construction/acquisition of social housing units is to be used only to replace units lost through tenant purchase (and) to meet needs where leased properties are unavailable and to meet special housing needs" (Department of Finance, 2010: 36). Despite these ongoing changes, many agencies and consumers have not taken full cognisance of these 'new realities' in Irish housing. It is unlikely that the level of funding secured for homeless services over the past 2 years will be maintained, with the government seeking a further cut in the order of €3 billion from public spending in 2011. Expenditure on homeless services has been relatively immune from these cutbacks to date, but both the macro-economic situation and the recent lack of progress in achieving the partnership-based objectives will make it difficult to maintain this level of funding. However, the minister with responsibility for the funding of homeless services, the leader of the minority Green Party in the current coalition government, has stated that he has made "it a priority during the three budgets that have taken place in the last 30 months that homelessness funding has been ringfenced against cuts" and that "protecting the homelessness budget will continue to be a priority for me" (Gormley, 2010).

Conclusion

The adoption of national and local homeless strategies represents a shift in the focus of Irish homeless policy in at least three ways. First, it adopts a more comprehensive approach than in the past and a key theme going through the documents is the responsibility and the need for a wide range of services to participate in reducing homelessness. Second, emphasising prevention and ending long-term homelessness demand a shift in service provision from temporary services to services addressing the causes of people becoming homeless and the need to sustain tenancies. Third, the scope of the homeless policy was geographically extended to become a national issue rather than one primarily for Dublin. The strategy addresses the responsibility of all local authorities to participate and to implement the objectives. A potential consequence of strengthening the responsibilities of the local authorities and turning the interventions from temporary accommodation to permanent housing is a reduction of the traditional roles occupied by NGOs.

The development of these strategies was underpinned by the concept of social partnership whereby a shared understanding of the issues was broadly achieved and a problem-solving approach adopted. This is most evident in the greater Dublin region where the Homeless Agency has responsibility for the planning, coordination, and administration of funding for homeless services. A shared understanding of the nature and consequences of homelessness, in addition to the need to provide homeless households with independent housing with support as required was achieved largely on the basis of robust research evidence. For example, of those households in contact with homeless services in the greater Dublin region during a week in March 2008, 19% were assessed as requiring long-term support, just over half requiring visiting support, and 29% requiring no support. Dissenting voices, of course, were also evident during this process, but by and large these voices pathologised the homeless and advocated the maintenance and extension of dependent services rather than services which would facilitate such households exiting homelessness. However, as the necessary reconfiguration of services for homeless households gathered pace, the level of enthusiasm for change diminished among certain service providers. This became increasingly apparent as voluntary organisations competitively tendered for new services for homeless households and the hitherto public display of unity among these organisations was placed under considerable strain. Social partnership allowed for the development of a shared understanding of homelessness, but also ensured, because it coincided with budget surpluses, that all organisations working with the homeless saw their revenue from the state increase.

As it became evident that substantial change was required to bring about a reconfiguration of services that would achieve the objective of ending long-term homelessness and reducing emergency services for the homeless, a 'stickiness' became evident in the pace of change. To date the permanent housing units required to move the 1200 households in private emergency accommodation to long-term housing have not materialised in any significant numbers, albeit that the process was initiated relatively recently; but unless these units of accommodation are provided, the impact of the reconfiguration of services will be limited and few financial efficiencies gained. The key obstacles to progress on implementing the objectives of the shared vision include:

- A view by approved housing bodies (i.e., nonprofit housing associations) that the financial model for the provision of housing units via a leasing scheme is not as favourable as earlier models has resulted in a reluctance by such bodies to deliver the necessary units.
- A reluctance by some agencies, particularly nonprofit housing service providers, to fully reconfigure their services and align them to a housing-based model due to a perception that many of their clients are incapable of independent living.
- An overemphasis on maintaining consensus among a diverse range of voluntary agencies rather than ensuring that the evidence-based policies were robustly implemented.

Rather than viewing these developments as an instance of neocorporatist governance underpinned by neoliberalism (Phelan and Norris, 2008), recent events have highlighted the limits of a social partnership approach, which emphasises consensus building and developing a shared understanding over problem solving and policy implementation. Social partnership was born out of the economic crisis of the 1980s and starting with national-level wage agreements, gradually filtered down to most areas of public policy. From the early 1990s, social partnership-based approaches to what appeared to be intractable social issues were established at the local and regional levels in addition to specific areas of public policy. The process of generating a shared understanding of issues was assisted by the fact that the statutory funding available to assist this process grew substantially, in the case of homelessness, particularly from 2000 onwards. As the process of consensus building deepened, funding continued to flow to aid the active engagement of all partners, but with little change in the organisation of service delivery.

The period in which the reconfiguration of services needed to implement the shared vision of ending long-term homelessness was planned coincided with the general economic downturn, and while the funding of homeless services was not reduced, neither did it grow. Thus, substantial change was now required from service providers in a much less benign economic environment and with much uncertainty about the future funding of services. The preservation of existing services and maintaining agencies' 'market share' became more pronounced in this context. Ideological divisions over how best to end homelessness such as the promotion of housing-led solutions over treatment-led initiatives partly resurfaced; no longer was the funding available to allow all agencies with varying ideologies to be simultaneously funded. The experience of developing a partnership-based approach to homelessness is, despite recent difficulties, a largely positive story. A shared understanding of both the causes and solutions to homelessness is largely evident among NGOs and statutory providers, in addition to policy-makers in central government, and should endure into the future. Timing is also important: a greater focus on policy implementation at an earlier stage, rather than continuing to negotiate a consensus on every detail, may have brought about more substantial benefits, but this is said with the benefit of hindsight. In conclusion, social partnership emerged in the context of a grave economic crisis in Ireland in the late 1980s. While the subsequent economic prosperity from the mid-1990s to 2006 generated economic surpluses that allowed for enhanced expenditure on a range of social services, including homelessness, these surpluses also resulted in less meaningful deliberative dialogue. A style of governance emerged from the centre of government, which attempted to smooth over debate with the promise of further funding. Ironically, as public funding for homelessness will inevitably decline in the forthcoming years, the necessity of maintaining a consensus on both the causes and solutions to homelessness will become all the more acute, but will need to focus on the implementation of evidence-based solutions to homelessness rather than the appeasement of all those who make up the 'homeless sector' in Ireland.

See also: Homelessness: Prevention in the United States; Policies to Address Homelessness; Policies to Address Homelessness: Housing First Approaches; Policies to Address Homelessness: Rights-Based Approaches; Policies to Address Homelessness: 'Staircase' Models.

References

Bardas Atha Cliath/Eastern Health Board (1995) *Review of Service Provision for the Homeless in the Dublin Region*. Report to the Department of the Environment and the Department of Health.

Brownlee A (2008) The changing homeless policy landscape: Paradise lost and found. In: Downey D (ed.) *Perspectives on Irish Homelessness: Past, Present and Future*. Dublin: Homeless Agency.

Department of Environment and Local Government, Department of Health and Children, and Department of Education and Science (2002) *Homeless Preventative Strategy: A Strategy to Prevent Homelessness: Patients Leaving Hospital and Mental Health Care, Adult Prisoners and Young Offenders Leaving Custody and Young People Leaving Care*. Dublin: Stationery Office.

Department of Finance (2010) *Infrastructure Investment Priorities 2010–2016: A Financial Framework*. Dublin: Department of Finance.

Department of the Environment and Local Government (2000) *Homelessness – An Integrated Strategy*. Dublin: Department of the Environment and Local Government.

Department of the Environment and Local Government *Annual Housing Statistics Bulletin – Various Years*. Dublin: Department of the Environment and Local Government.

Department of the Environment, Heritage and Local Government (2008) *The Way Home: A Strategy to Address Adult Homelessness in Ireland, 2008–2013*. Dublin: Department of the Environment, Heritage and Local Government.

Department of the Environment, Heritage and Local Government (2009) *Homeless Strategy: National Implementation Plan*. Dublin: Department of the Environment, Heritage and Local Government.

Gormley J (2010) Protecting homelessness budget will continue to be priority, says Environment Minister. Press release, 2 June 2010. http://www.greenparty.ie/news/latest_news/protecting_homelessness_budget_will_continue_to_be_priority_says_environment_minister (accessed 25 September 2010).

Homeless Agency (2007) *A Key to the Door: The Homeless Agency Partnership Action Plan on Homelessness in Dublin 2007–2010*. Dublin: Homeless Agency.

Homeless Agency (2009) *Pathway to Home*. Dublin: Homeless Agency.

Loison-Leruste M and Quilgars D (2009) Increasing access to housing: Implementing the right to housing in England and France. *European Journal of Homelessness* 3: 75–126.

Norris M and Coates D (2010) Private sector provision of social housing: An assessment of recent Irish experiments. *Public Money and Management* 30(1): 19–26.

Norris M and Fahey T (2009) From asset based welfare to welfare housing: The changing meaning of social housing in Ireland. *UCD School of Applied Social Science Working Paper WP09/5*.

O'Donnell R (2008) The partnership state: Building the ship at sea. In: Adshead M, Kirby P, and Millar M (eds.) *Contesting the State: Lessons from the Irish Case*. Manchester, UK: Manchester University Press.

O'Riain S (2006) Social partnership as a mode of governance: Introduction to the special issue. *The Economic and Social Review* 37(3): 311–318.

Phelan E and Norris M (2008) Neo-corporatist governance of homeless services in Dublin: Reconceptualization, incorporation and exclusion. *Critical Social Policy* 28(1): 51–73.

Rhodes ML and Brooke S (2010) How does evaluation 'work'? A case study of homeless services in Ireland. *Policy and Society* 29(2): 149–160.

Roche WK (2009) Social partnership: From Lemass to Cowen. *The Economic and Social Review* 40(2): 183–205.

Further Reading

Department of Health and Children (2001) *Youth Homelessness Strategy*. Dublin: Stationery Office.

Department of the Environment, Heritage and Local Government (2007) *Delivering Homes, Sustaining Communities – Statement on Housing Policy*. Dublin: Department of the Environment, Heritage and Local Government.

Policies to Address Homelessness: Prevention in the United Kingdom

H Pawson, Heriot-Watt University, Edinburgh, UK

© 2012 Elsevier Ltd. All rights reserved.

Glossary

Gatekeeping Procedures primarily designed to prevent homeless people from asserting their rights.
Homelessness prevention Action to help a household remain in their current accommodation or to help a household find alternative accommodation before they become homeless.
Homelessness strategy Analysis of homelessness causes and plans to address these.
Kitemarking A form of accreditation.
Legally homeless Person with no suitable accommodation he/she is legally entitled to occupy.
Local authority Local government unit with prescribed powers.

Introduction

Homelessness is an officially recognised problem in numerous countries, both rich and poor. Policy interventions aimed at addressing the issue are widely implemented across the developed world. Many such interventions might be seen by the countries concerned as constituting forms of 'homelessness prevention'.

In Britain, policies aimed at actively preventing homelessness have come to the fore in the first decade of the new millennium as an adjunct to the legal and institutional framework in place since the 1970s. Post-2002 homelessness prevention measures in Britain need to be seen within the context of this framework, which is internationally very unusual in its incorporation of legally enforceable individual rights to permanent housing – at least for certain homeless people. This contrasts with the norm elsewhere in Europe, North America, and Australasia, where any direct state assistance in accommodating homeless people is provided only on a discretionary and/or emergency basis.

Across Britain, the bodies charged with fulfilling state obligations to homeless people are local authorities. Hence, local authorities are also the prime movers in homelessness prevention.

A second contextual factor needing to be recognised here is that, within Britain, housing is a devolved policy domain under the 1999 devolution settlement. Important in relation to homelessness is the growing policy divergence between Scotland and other parts of the UK. Both via regulation and legislation Scotland has sought to build on the established rights-based approach. In England, by contrast, post-2002 policy development has incorporated greater emphasis on citizen empowerment and consumerism.

These distinctions have significant implications for the forms of prevention activity promoted and undertaken in different UK jurisdictions.

While this article does not deal with Wales in detail, it should be noted that recent homelessness policy developments in Wales have been fairly similar to those in England. For further information, see Clapham et al. (2009).

Defining Homelessness Prevention

To define homelessness prevention we must first define homelessness. Within the context of Britain's 'rights-based' policy framework, a person is formally homeless if there is no suitable accommodation he/she is legally entitled to occupy. A person is legally 'threatened with homelessness' if he/she faces the loss of accommodation within 28 days (2 months in Scotland). Against this backdrop, homelessness prevention is defined by the central government in England as encompassing local authority actions which

- help households to remain in their current accommodation;
- delay a household's need to move out of current accommodation so that a move into alternative accommodation can be planned;
- find a household alternative accommodation.

In Scotland, prevention is defined more simply as 'action to be taken by local authorities to prevent homelessness arising in the first place and then recurring'. Under both definitions, relevant actions by local authorities can aim to enable households to avoid 'primary' homelessness – initial loss of accommodation; or to preempt 'secondary' homelessness – the recurrent loss of accommodation.

Government Promotion of a Prevention-Focused Homelessness Practice

Legal Measures

Both in England and Wales and in Scotland, a more prevention-centred approach to homelessness emerged via new legislation enacted in 2002–03. This had been prefigured by the 1998 adoption of ambitious targets to reduce 'rough sleeping' or 'street homelessness' and by a variety of associated policy measures, including 'assertive outreach' and the expansion of hostel accommodation.

In England, the Homelessness Act 2002 formed a key foundation for the new policy direction. Critically, in common with 2001 legislation enacted by the Scottish Parliament, this placed a new duty on every local authority to develop and publish a strategy based on a review of homelessness in the local area. In drawing up homelessness strategies, local authorities must:

- assess the levels and likely future levels of homelessness in the district;
- catalogue existing services aimed at preventing homelessness, helping homeless people find accommodation, and providing other forms of support;
- analyse the resources available to the authority and to other agencies for providing these services.

Administrative Measures

Alongside the newly prescribed legal duty outlined above, the central government has used a variety of measures to encourage a local authority emphasis on proactively preventing homelessness, rather than operating in a purely 'responsive' mode. This has included the provision of central funding to underpin local 'prevention initiatives', and the publication of voluminous 'good practice' advice.

Particularly in England, prevention-focused local authority practice has also been promoted via quantified, time-specific, national targets set by the central government. The most important was the 2005 undertaking to halve, by 2010, the total number of temporary accommodation placements of homeless households in England. This was to be achieved by a combination of measures including the expanded supply of social housing as well as homelessness prevention measures.

Again in England, the central government has also used kitemarking to signify approval for authorities judged 'ahead of the field' on homelessness prevention. By conferring 'Beacon Council' (or, later, 'regional homelessness champion') status, the government also placed an obligation on designated 'elite' councils to disseminate to others favoured techniques and practices.

Grant funding for local prevention initiatives has provided government with substantial leverage over policy implementation – not only through the power to promote certain types of prevention model but also through the associated scope for scrutinising and influencing administrative practice at the local level. Here, a key role has been played by 'advisors' seconded from the ranks of local council homelessness managers to disseminate favoured prevention models and ways of working across the practitioner community. These advisors have played a crucial part in bridging the central–local divide, which has traditionally dogged the implementation of ministerial policy initiatives.

Linked with their function in helping local authorities 'interpret' ministerial aspirations in relation to homelessness prevention, the practitioner-adviser role has also included elaborating and promulgating government policy through authorship of good practice guidance. For example, a 2003 policy briefing identified three stages where local authority (or other agency) intervention can prevent homelessness:

- Early intervention: where those at risk are identified and services provided to support the person and their environment.
- Precrisis intervention: which can take the form of advice services, mediation services, negotiation with landlords to avoid imminent loss of a home, and services targeted at people at known risk points such as those leaving local authority care, prison, or the armed forces.
- Preventing recurring homelessness: Tenancy sustainment is seen as key to preventing recurring homelessness where there are problems that cannot be resolved by rehousing alone.

Homelessness Prevention Techniques

Overview

Table 1 sets out the most commonly implemented forms of homelessness prevention as identified by evaluative research in England and Scotland. Here, we distinguish between 'direct' and 'precautionary' measures. In the main, activities to preempt 'primary homelessness' (see above) are termed 'direct interventions' in the sense of being responses to specific anticipated events likely to result in homelessness (e.g., an eviction date). A distinct set of activities, mainly aimed at minimising 'secondary homelessness', involves 'precautionary interventions' targeted on groups 'at significant risk' of losing their home but where there is not (yet) a specific threat to a household's tenure of their accommodation.

Another way of classifying homelessness prevention activities is in relation to the groups on which these are targeted. In England, particularly in relation to 'direct' prevention activities, local authorities have tended to

Table 1 Main forms of prevention intervention: A typology

Initiative/activity	Target group	Typology category Direct	Precautionary
1. Housing advice	Primarily private tenants seeking to retain existing tenancies or access new ones	✓	✓
2. Facilitating access to private tenancies	Scotland: Mainly single homeless aged >25 England: As above, plus families at risk of homelessness but not yet formally assessed	✓	
3. Family mediation	Young people excluded from the family home	✓ (Eng)	✓ (Scot)
4. Domestic violence victim support	Women facing possible homelessness due to the threat of violence (usually from an ex-partner)	✓	
5. Tenancy sustainment support	Social sector tenants judged 'at risk' of being unable to sustain a tenancy		✓
6. Supported transitional housing	(a) Young people aged 16–18, and (b) former rough sleepers and others discharged from institutions		✓
7. Housing education	Secondary school children		✓

focus mainly on the family households liable to enjoy a statutory right to rehousing under the rights-based legal framework. In Scotland, by contrast, prevention activities targeted on this group have tended to be of the 'precautionary' form. In part, this reflects a much greater sensitivity to accusations of unacceptable 'gatekeeping' among Scottish local authorities. This refers to the potentially fine line between 'preventing homelessness' and denying the legal rights of homeless people (see below).

Housing Advice

Housing advice traditionally involves promoting rights of citizenship, improving access to services, and enhancing the effectiveness of the housing market. Usually provided mainly by local authorities, housing advice services have long been established in most areas of Britain. Many date from the 1970s and reflect the consumer rights ethic emerging at that time. Rising homelessness, together with official encouragement for local authorities to 'enable the consumer' in housing, led to expansion and refocusing of housing advice services through the 1980s and 1990s. The Housing Act 1996 (applicable in England) created a specific local authority obligation to "secure free advice about homelessness and its prevention in their area".

Improved or expanded housing advice services have featured widely as an aspect of local authorities' post-2002 homelessness prevention activities. In England, a key development here has been the emergence of the 'housing options' model. This involves a standard procedure whereby homeless people and other applicants for social housing participate in an initial interview to review their housing circumstances and prospects. The aim is to discuss, in detail, the feasibility of securing the applicant's existing accommodation or, failing that, to examine the full range of possible routes to accessing a new tenancy. Under the British legal framework, however, such discussions should be staged concurrently with local authority consideration of an applicant's homelessness status (rather than as a substitute for such an assessment).

Facilitating Access to Private Tenancies

Beyond simply 'enabling' individuals to look for private rented housing, many local authorities have also established more far-reaching measures to facilitate homeless households' access to private tenancies. Such schemes are characterised by the provision of financial and/or practical assistance to people at risk of homelessness. They are partly motivated by a recognition that – unlike social housing – the private rented sector has been expanding and that (in England) it generates twice the annual volume of lettings made by social landlords (albeit, tenancies with little legal security).

Rent deposit guarantee (RDG) or 'cashless bond' schemes are widely operated in both England and Scotland. The need for these arises from the fact that many landlords require new tenants to pay or lodge some form of bond as a security against the possibility of damage to the landlord's property or the abandonment of the property with rent unpaid. Where a departing tenant meets all the conditions laid down in the tenancy agreement any deposit paid should be repaid in full. Most RDG schemes do not involve an actual payment to the landlord. Instead, the local authority makes a formal commitment to the landlord to offer all or part of the deposit in the event of damage to the property, its furnishings, or equipment. Over and above the traditional RDG formula, some local authorities operate 'finder's fee' schemes, which feature the payment of nonreturnable 'premium' payments to landlords willing to provide a tenancy to a household nominated by the authority.

Complementing RDG and finder's fee arrangements, some authorities implement or commission other measures aimed at securing access to private tenancies for households at risk of homelessness. These include advice services specifically targeted on landlords (rather than aspiring tenants), the provision of property insurance, and guaranteed fast-tracking of housing benefit claims.

Family Mediation

For many local authorities a substantial proportion of the homelessness caseload involves young people reporting imminent or actual loss of accommodation due to ejection from the family home. In Scotland, for example, around a third of homelessness presentations tend to involve 'family/friend exclusions' (people being asked to leave the homes of friends, parents, or other relatives).

Family mediation schemes have been widely established to address the scenario described above. Associated with such activity, many authorities in England routinely undertake home visits as an initial component of their formal assessment of applications where the stated reason for homelessness is 'family/friend exclusion'. Family mediation aims to help parents and young people to discuss and reconcile the differences which have led to the threat of ejection.

Mediation may be provided in various ways. Under one scenario it is simply integrated within a home visit by a local authority staff member. A more formal approach involves cases being referred to specialist agencies or to a trained mediator employed by the authority independently of the homelessness service. In any event, as emphasised by official good practice guidance, it is important that an appropriate balance is struck between (a) ensuring that false claims of abuse are not made to secure a tenancy and (b) the need to consider whether encouraging a young person to return to their former host household might place them at risk of violence or abuse.

Domestic Violence Victim Support

For around one in eight households officially recorded as homeless in England, relationship breakdown involving domestic violence is the main reason for loss of settled home. In the vast majority of instances, the victims are women. Many authorities have attempted to address this scenario via measures to enable sufferers to remain in their own homes, to enable them to access crisis accommodation, or to support them in making planned moves into long-term tenancies.

Especially in England, a key focus of prevention activity aimed at homelessness due to domestic violence is the so-called 'sanctuary' model. Often run by local authorities in conjunction with the police, sanctuary schemes involve the installation of additional security measures to a woman's home to protect her and her family from the threat of violence from a former partner. Such measures can take the form of internal doors, mortise locks, safety glass, and personal and smoke alarms. In conjunction with physical security measures, a sanctuary scheme may involve the provision of legal advice, for example, to enable a woman to use the Family Law Act 1996 to remove a violent perpetrator, ban him from approaching the property, or to alter the tenancy such that the woman becomes the sole rather than the joint tenant.

Tenancy Sustainment Support

The 'precautionary' prevention measure most commonly operated by local authorities is the provision of support to help vulnerable tenants retain their tenancies. Typically, such services are focused on tenants of social housing, especially those who have been recently rehoused on the grounds of homelessness. The priority attached to activities under this heading is attributable to the recognition that an appreciable proportion of people making homelessness applications to local authorities are 'repeat homeless' cases. Likewise, research has demonstrated that up to a quarter of those moving into social housing give up their tenancies within a year and that some of these 'premature tenancy terminations' are potentially preventable via landlord action.

Tenancy sustainment services often involve provision of help in claiming benefits, budgeting and debt management, accessing community resources and services, furnishing accommodation, and helping individuals find meaningful occupation. As in all 'precautionary' approaches, tenancy sustainment support presents a major challenge for targeting such that services are – in the interests of efficiency – aimed narrowly at those households highly liable to the loss of their tenancy in the absence of assistance. Similarly, the effectiveness of tenancy sustainment support is particularly difficult to evidence in a credible way.

Referral Protocols and Supported Transitional Housing for High-Risk Groups

The recognition that people discharged from certain institutions are at high risk of homelessness influences prevention frameworks in England and Wales, as well as in Scotland. Of particular concern here are young people leaving care, ex-offenders being released from prison, and ex-service personnel leaving the armed forces. Research evidence has demonstrated that such groups are overrepresented among street homeless populations. Accordingly, it is standard practice for housing authorities to work closely with social services departments and with other relevant institutions in their locality in operating planned rehousing arrangements for individuals subject to discharge.

Particularly in relation to young people leaving care and vulnerable ex-offenders, planned discharge protocols are sometimes operated in conjunction with 'supported transitional housing' projects. This aims to equip residents with independent living skills to prepare them for taking on an independent tenancy. Assisting residents to access training and employment also forms part of the remit of some schemes of this kind.

Housing Education

Exemplifying the national commitment to precautionary forms of prevention, 'housing education' forms a standard component of the policy agenda in Scotland. In many areas, this involves disseminating basic information about housing options to all secondary school students.

Critical Perspectives on Homelessness Prevention

Concerns that 'homelessness prevention' could provide overzealous local authorities with cover for denial of applicants' legal rights have been voiced from some quarters. Acknowledging the dramatic reduction in homelessness numbers recorded in England since 2003 (see Conclusion), some sceptics have questioned whether this has resulted partly from undesirable 'gatekeeping' practices rather than entirely reflecting successful action to preempt individuals' housing crises.

Many of the misgivings around homelessness prevention have revolved around the 'informality' of the 'housing options' concept promoted in government guidance and the concern that this could have led in some areas to homeless people being systematically 'fobbed off' by local authorities. Nevertheless, official guidance for local authorities in England explicitly discourages the operation of 'housing options' arrangements in a spirit of 'gatekeeping' – defined as being 'where the process is seen primarily as a device to prevent or discourage people from seeking housing assistance'.

Measuring Homelessness Prevention Activity

Recording the scale and effectiveness of homelessness prevention activity presents a major challenge. Key issues include additionality (whether homelessness would, in fact, have occurred in the absence of the intervention) and sustainability (the durability of the 'solution' enabling an individual to avoid homelessness). In 2008–09, however, the central government in England introduced a monitoring regime requiring local authorities to record "the number of households for whom casework and positive action took place in order to prevent or relieve homelessness, either by the authority themselves or by a partner organisation".

Under this framework English authorities reported having prevented homelessness in respect of 130 000 households in the financial year 2008–09. To set this within context, authorities also reported that they made formal homelessness assessment decisions with respect to 113 000 households over this same time period, with 53 000 households being judged 'homeless and in priority need' (and, consequently, entitled to rehousing). As shown in **Table 2**, the majority of recorded prevention activity (61%) involved assisting people at risk of homelessness to find alternative accommodation, with action to facilitate access to a private tenancy being the single most common recorded intervention.

Conclusion

Particularly in England, the post-2002 shift to a prevention-focused approach ranks as a major development in official homelessness policy. That much is clear from the dramatic decline in homelessness numbers subsequently recorded. By 2008–09, 5 years after

Table 2 Type of homelessness prevention and relief recorded by local authorities, England, 2008–09

Case assisted to obtain alternative accommodation in the form of	No.	%
Private tenancy	37 820	31
Social housing	14 650	12
Hostel or house in multiple occupation	7 350	6
Supported accommodation	6 810	6
Accommodation with friends or relatives	3 170	3
Other	5 720	5
Total	75 520	61
Case able to remain in existing home, as a result of		
Assistance to sustain tenancy	8 340	7
Debt advice	4 690	4
Conciliation including via home visit	4 590	4
Negotiation with private landlord	4 290	3
Resolving housing benefit problems	3 850	3
Sanctuary scheme	3 820	3
Family mediation (using trained mediator)	2 950	2
Resolving rent arrears	2 740	2
Financial payments (e.g., to repay minor rent arrears)	1 960	2
Mortgage arrears interventions	1 680	1
Crisis intervention – emergency support	1 440	1
Other	7 500	6
Total	47 850	39
Grand total	**123 370**[a]	**100**

[a]Excluding incomplete returns.
Adapted with permission from: Pawson H and Davidson E (2008) Radically divergent? Homelessness policy and practice in post-devolution Scotland. *European Journal of Housing Policy* 8(1): 39–60.

its peak, the number of formal homelessness assessment decisions recorded by English authorities had fallen by more than 60%. In Wales, over the 4 years to 2008, households found to be 'unintentionally homeless and in priority need' fell by 38%. And even in Scotland, where prevention has been less aggressively promoted, rising homelessness presentations were reversed from 2005–06, falling back by 7% over the next 2 years.

At least in some English authorities, the interpretation of 'prevention' has incorporated elements of gatekeeping which appear to cross the boundary of strict compliance with statute. However, such practices have not proved susceptible to legal challenge.

See also: Cost Analyses of Homelessness: Limits and Opportunities; Homelessness: Definitions; Homelessness: Measurement Questions; Homelessness: Prevention in the United States; Homeless Families: United Kingdom; Policies to Address Homelessness.

Reference

Clapham D, Mackie P, and Pritchard J (2009) Homelessness policy in Wales: Which path will it take? In: Fitzpatrick S (ed.) *Homelessness in the UK: Problems and Solutions*. Coventry, UK: Chartered Institute of Housing.

Further Reading

Department for Communities & Local Government (2006) *Homelessness Prevention: A Guide to Good Practice*. London: DCLG.http://www.communities.gov.uk/publications/housing/homelessnessprevention

Department for Transport, Local Government and the Regions (2002) *More Than a Roof*. London: DTLR.http://www.communities.gov.uk/publications/housing/morethan

Fitzpatrick S and Stephens M (2007) *An International Review of Homelessness and Social Housing Policy*. London: Communities & Local Government.http://www.communities.gov.uk/publications/housing/internationalhomelessnessreview

Hawkey E (2004) Fobbed Off? *Roof* May/June: 20–23.

Pawson H (2007) Local authority homelessness prevention in England: Empowering consumers or denying rights? *Housing Studies* 22(6): 867–884.

Pawson H (2009) Homelessness policy in England: Promoting gatekeeping or effective prevention? In: Fitzpatrick S (ed.) *Homelessness Problems and Solutions*. Coventry, UK: Chartered Institute of Housing.

Pawson H and Davidson E (2006) Fit for purpose? Official measures of homelessness in the era of the activist state. *Radical Statistics* 93: 7–29.

Pawson H and Davidson E (2008) Radically divergent? Homelessness policy and practice in post-devolution Scotland. *European Journal of Housing Policy* 8(1): 39–60.

Pawson H, Davidson E, and Netto G (2007) *Evaluating Homelessness Prevention Activities in Scotland*. Edinburgh, UK: Scottish Executive.http://www.scotland.gov.uk/Publications/2007/03/26095144/0

Pawson H, Netto G, Jones C, Wager F, Fancy C, and Lomax D (2007) *Evaluating Homelessness Prevention*. London: CLG.http://www.communities.gov.uk/publications/housing/preventhomelessness

Randall G and Brown S (2002) *Helping Rough Sleepers Off the Streets: A Report to the Homelessness Directorate*. London: ODPM.

Policies to Address Homelessness: Rights-Based Approaches

I Anderson, University of Stirling, Stirling, UK

© 2012 Elsevier Ltd. All rights reserved.

Glossary

Homeless To be homeless: state of lacking adequate shelter; state of lacking a secure, adequate, affordable private space from which to conduct one's life. Note that definitions vary according to social and cultural context as well as national and international legal frameworks.

Homelessness Recognised social phenomenon of identifiable population lacking adequate housing; field for welfare policy intervention by state and non-state agencies in local, national, and international spheres.

Justiciable right to housing Right to housing which is enshrined in law and legally enforceable through the court system in a nation state by individuals or households lacking adequate accommodation.

Social right to housing Right to housing conveyed through a national constitution, a national welfare system, or an international treaty which acknowledges housing as a fundamental human right for those subject of such a constitution, welfare state, or international treaty, and where states seek to ensure housing as a human right but do not necessarily guarantee an individual right enforceable at law.

Introduction

While the term housing can have a somewhat technical definition referring mainly to adequacy of shelter from the elements, the English word 'home' conveys more than just a physical dwelling. The home is a social space from which to conduct life's activities, and from which occupants seek security and comfort in terms of both living accommodation and the surrounding environment. The costs of housing are crucial to households' ability to afford and maintain a home along with other aspects of desired standards of living. Consequently, even a literal interpretation of homelessness as 'being without a home' suggests that this implies more than just lacking adequate shelter, but that a person, family, or household does not have a secure, adequate, affordable, private space from which to conduct their life. The term homelessness is also subject to common-sense, cultural, and legal definitions ranging from absolute destitution to definitions which are relative to the norms of different nations and societies. Edgar and Meert (2005) developed an operational typology of homelessness based on four main conceptual categories: rooflessness, houselessness, insecure housing, and inadequate housing.

Across the globe, housing is provided and consumed through a combination of market mechanisms, state provision/intervention, third sector/nongovernment organisation (NGO) provision, and self-help/informal solutions. In responding to homelessness and the wider housing needs of the population, the housing policies of nation states reflect a range of influences such as demography, market forces, and intervention strategies. To an extent national policies and legal frameworks will reflect prevailing political ideologies although housing systems (e.g., in terms of the overall balance of tenure or finance mechanisms) take time to respond to political change. That said, state responses to homelessness can be influential and can range from 'rights-based' or legal approaches to 'softer' policy instruments such as offering financial incentives to local agencies to assist homeless households or otherwise encouraging 'enabling' approaches at the local level. Households may not explicitly consider the need to claim a 'right' to housing, especially if they are readily able to access suitable accommodation through a market mechanism. However, those who face severe constraints in the market sector or who face a homelessness crisis may well rely on the state to assist them in meeting their housing needs. In such circumstances the question of a right to housing becomes much more pertinent.

It is important to acknowledge that the concept of housing rights is a broad one, with varying potential interpretations of different possible types of 'rights' to housing. For example, Bengtsson (2001) distinguished between 'legalistic' rights to housing associated with more selective national housing policies and 'social' rights to housing associated with more universal housing and welfare policies. The two main examples explored in this chapter reflect the legalistic or 'justiciable' approach where housing rights can be enforced at law, which is quite different from the frameworks of rights contained in international treaties (also discussed below) which cannot necessarily be enforced at law within individual signatory states. Nonetheless, housing as a social or human right is important in that it recognises the basic need of human beings not just for shelter from the elements but also for accommodation which is safe, secure, affordable, and sufficient for the needs of the household. While international agreements, such as United Nations conventions and European treaties, will have some influence over the actions of nation states, it is important to examine the approaches of individual countries to uncover the existence (or otherwise) of rights-based responses to homelessness. Such an approach is advocated by the European Federation of National Homelessness Agencies (FEANTSA, 2008), which campaigns for a rights-based approach to tackling homelessness across the European Union (EU).

Rights-Based Responses to Homelessness: Examples from Europe

In Mandič's (2006) review of homelessness policies in the EU, France was identified as having introduced a right to housing in 1982, which was further enhanced in the Besson Act of 1990, although difficulties in implementation were acknowledged. Beyond this, Mandič concluded that the approaches of other EU member states to resolving homelessness appeared to demonstrate 'uniqueness' rather than identifiable patterns. Fitzpatrick and Stephens' (2007) study of 11 OECD countries also concluded that the United Kingdom was unusual in having a legislative basis for legally enforceable rights for homeless households. Notably, the UK system helped homeless people into settled/secure accommodation, compared to, say, Germany, where legal duties were only for the provision of temporary accommodation. In Sweden, Poland, and Hungary, limited rights for emergency accommodation for some homeless groups were identifiable and social welfare legislation assisted homeless people in other countries. Nevertheless, across the 11 countries, there was wide acknowledgement of the need for at least temporary accommodation and social support as part of responses to homelessness (Fitzpatrick and Stephens, 2007). Different strategies were evident in Central European states which had undergone post-1990 social, economic, and political transitions to EU membership, compared to those nations which had developed capitalist welfare states since the post-1945 period. Below, the examples of France and the Scottish jurisdiction within the United Kingdom are considered in more detail as both nations introduced enhanced, rights-based approaches to homelessness in the post-2000 period.

Scotland – Widening the Homelessness Safety Net

From 1977, a legal framework in place across England, Scotland, and Wales placed duties on local government (local authorities) to take action where individuals or households presented themselves as homeless or threatened with homelessness (extended to Northern Ireland in 1988). Homelessness was defined as lacking accommodation or being prevented from occupying accommodation, for example, because of a threat of violence (adapted from Fitzpatrick et al., 2009: xiii). The legislation did not, however, treat all households equally as local housing authorities were required to apply four 'tests' to applications for assistance:

1. Is the household 'homeless' as defined in the legislation?
2. Is at least one member of the household in 'priority need' of accommodation, defined as:
   a. Household with children of school age or an expectant mother?
   b. Households 'vulnerable' due to old age, health or disability, or other special reason?
   c. Household homeless because of an emergency such as a fire or flood?
3. Has the household become homeless 'intentionally' (by deliberate act or omission which led to homelessness)?
4. Does the household have a 'connection' with the local authority to which they have presented (through residence, employment, or family)?

If the authority judged that the household circumstances met all four tests (although a duty to accommodate arises irrespective of Test 4, local connection determined which local authority would have to provide long-term accommodation for the household), then a duty to provide accommodation would arise, and would generally be fulfilled by offering housing in the local authority's own rented housing stock (council housing) or by referral to an alternative social landlord (housing association or registered social landlord).

The process of political devolution instituted by the United Kingdom's New Labour Government elected in 1997 created a separate Scottish Parliament in 1999, enhancing the scope for differential housing policy and legislation in Scotland, compared to the rest of the United Kingdom. Recognising that the 1977 homelessness legislation was out of date, the New Labour-led coalition Executive set up the Homelessness Task Force to review the nature of homelessness in Scotland and to make recommendations for more effective responses. The task force published an interim report in 2000 and a final report and action plan in 2002 (Homelessness Task Force, 2000, 2002). Recommendations were incorporated into law in the Housing (Scotland) Act 2001 and the Homelessness, etc. (Scotland) Act 2003.

Essentially, the four tests of the 1977 legislation were to be reduced to one test – is the household homeless? Perhaps the most significant recommendation for legislative change was the phasing out of the differential treatment of households according to whether they were considered to have 'priority need' or not. In essence this recognised, after a long campaign that housing is a fundamental need of all households and that the distinction between priority and non-priority status was unfair and ultimately ineffective as separate policy initiatives (e.g., 'Rough Sleepers Initiatives') had been required for those not supported by the main safety net (Anderson, 2007). Although not explicitly announced as a 'right to housing', the new measures would mean that by 2012 there would effectively be a duty on local authorities to ensure that all households in Scotland had some form of accommodation. In 2003 the Centre on Housing Rights and Evictions (COHRE, an international human rights NGO) awarded the Housing Rights Protector Award to the Scottish Executive for this new homelessness legislation in recognition of its contribution to protecting human rights and safeguarding human dignity (Goodlad, 2005). Further, in 2009, the United Nations Committee on Economic, Social and Cultural Rights recommended that the Scottish homelessness framework be adopted throughout the United Kingdom (Bowcott, 2009).

After the 2007 Scottish Parliament elections, the Scottish National Party (SNP) formed a minority government. However, implementation of the new homelessness framework continued, irrespective of the changed political leadership in Scotland. By the end of the administrative year 2008–09, Scottish local authorities reported being more than 80% on the way to achieving the 2012 target of abolishing the priority/non-priority need distinction, albeit that there was variation in performance across the 32 authorities (Scottish Government, 2009).

Despite a public commitment to meeting the 2012 target to treat all homeless households equally, the SNP Government subsequently implemented measures to change the means by which local authorities could discharge their duties to some homeless households to include private, as well as public/social, sector tenancies (Scottish Government, 2010). While this private sector alternative represented a practical response to the evident pressure on the social housing sector, questions remained as to the suitability of the Scottish privately rented sector to provide adequate long-term solutions to homelessness. For example, Scottish social housing tenancies incorporated a wider package of 'tenants' rights' (e.g., on repairs, exchanging homes, tenancy succession, and, most importantly, protection from eviction) which did not apply in the private sector. Moreover, private sector tenancies remained generally more expensive than the social sector, but with less favourable housing allowance regulations (Anderson, 2009). Consequently, the effectiveness and sustainability of the Scottish private rented sector's potential contribution to the key policy goal of a right to housing for all by 2010 would require close scrutiny.

France – Introducing an Enforceable Right to Housing

In France, the long-standing legislative response to housing was also modernised in the post-2000 period as documented by Loison (2007). France recognised the right to housing as a social right enshrined in the Constitution of 1946 and reaffirmed in subsequent laws. Notably, the Besson Act of 1990 provided that guaranteeing the right to housing was a duty of solidarity incumbent upon the whole nation. The difficulty was that the right to housing was not legally enforceable as it gave no entitlement to relief through the courts for those who could not find somewhere to live (Loison, 2007). Rather, the phrase 'enforceable right to housing' (*droit au logement opposable*, abbreviated to DALO in the French language) dated from a 2002 report of the HCLPD (Haute Comité pour le Logement de Personnes Défavorisées, 'Homelessness Housing Committee'), which, as in Scotland, was the culmination of a period of substantial review. Loison characterised the enforceable right to housing as the difference between accepting the 'best efforts' of the state to respond to homelessness, and implementing a 'performance obligation' "under which central government's responsibility for guaranteeing the right to housing would be devolved to local authorities and homeless persons would have official forms of redress first by mediation and then through the courts" (2007: 186–187).

During this period of policy review, voluntary homelessness agencies were also campaigning for an enforceable right to housing. In 2005, public outrage at a series of fatal fires in multiple occupied buildings in Paris led to a private member's bill to introduce an enforceable right to housing, and, although it was not successful, a debate over the issue continued among the main political parties. Combined with the fire fatalities, in 2006 the emergence of 'tent cities' occupied by homeless people galvanised high-profile pressure group action by the voluntary organisation Les Enfants de Don Quichotte, resulting in a great deal of media attention and a campaign for action which spread from Paris to other French cities. Such media pressure was particularly effective in securing government action with plans to introduce an enforceable right to housing announced in President Chirac's New Year address, and passed into law in Bill No. 2007-290 (Loison, 2007). The key legislative measures of DALO included:

1. The state guaranteed the right to housing in the Besson Act.
2. From 1 December 2008, the DALO would cover the six highest-priority categories of applicants: roofless people, tenants facing eviction, people in temporary accommodation, people in substandard or unfit accommodation, people with at least one dependent child living in housing not regarded as decent, and people with a

disability or a disabled dependent whose housing is not regarded as decent.

3. From 1 January 2012, the DALO would be extended to all other people who qualify for social housing but had been waiting for an abnormally long time.

4. All groups could take their case to a mediation committee and then an administrative appeal tribunal and the court would be able to order the state to house the applicant.

The DALO was supplemented by measures to increase the supply of social housing and an enhanced plan of action on homelessness designed to ensure appropriate action to move people from temporary to settled accommodation and to provide required support for resettlement. Early evaluation of implementation of DALO (Loison-Leruste and Quilgars, 2009) suggested that the number of people helped was less than expected (just over 4000 by October 2008) but that it had raised the profile of homelessness on the policy agenda and provided better information to help ensure more effective practice in the future.

Housing Rights and the Effectiveness of Rights-Based Responses to Homelessness

A number of similarities are evident in the rights-based responses to homelessness in Scotland and France above. Both represented modernised frameworks which emerged from long-standing and evolving legislation influenced by civil society as well as the state. Both demonstrated socially inclusive approaches through a progressive widening of the characteristics of groups entitled to be housed in the event of homelessness, with the same target implementation date of 2012. The French approach was most explicitly introduced as an 'enforceable right to housing', while the rights-based approach was more implicit in the Scottish model. Ultimately, the effectiveness of both programmes will depend on the capacity of homeless households to claim or enforce these new legal entitlements to housing and the capacity of the national housing systems to adequately meet need.

In the Scottish case, legal provisions required local authorities to review cases where an applicant was not satisfied with the decision made. If the applicant was still not satisfied, the decision could be challenged in a court of law. Effectiveness was also being monitored through annual reporting to the central government of the progress towards the 2012 target. In France, a key component of the DALO was the right to apply to an administrative tribunal for legal relief against the authorities if homeless applicants had been waiting for housing for an abnormally long time and had not been offered suitable/affordable permanent housing. If the decision went against the state, it would have to compensate the complainant (Loison, 2007). However, whereas in Scotland the responsibility for implementation rested clearly with local government authorities, the French system was much more complex, with the involvement of government at central, regional, and departmental levels, as well as district associations and local authorities. This made the implementation of centralised policies extremely challenging in practice. Nonetheless, the DALO act also provided for annual monitoring and reporting, including quantifying the number of unsatisfied housing applications.

The two case studies can be further compared with the wider concept of housing rights as human rights (Kenna, 2005). The two principal instruments of the Council of Europe (47 member states) which relate to housing rights are the European Social Charter (and revised charter) and the European Convention on Human Rights and Fundamental Freedoms (Kenna, 2005: 31–54). The European Social Charter was established in 1961 and is gradually being replaced by the Revised European Social Charter (RESC) of 1996. Under Article 31 of the RESC everyone has a right to housing, requiring nation states to take measures to promote access to housing of an adequate standard, to prevent and reduce homelessness with a view to its gradual elimination, and to make the price of housing accessible to those without adequate resources. Regular national reports on compliance are submitted to the Council of Europe's Committee of Social Rights (CSR). The Committee of Ministers can make a recommendation to a state asking it to change the situation in law and/or practice and reports published by the committee offer benchmarks for national housing and homelessness policies. As at February 2009, however, only 25 of the 47 member states had fully ratified and implemented this charter (Council of Europe, 2009). Under the European Convention for the Protection of Human Rights and Fundamental Freedoms (ECHR), living conditions have been taken into account in cases concerning human dignity and the convention recognises that a home is more than a dwelling and that human rights and fundamental freedoms require respect for 'home' and private/family life. The ECHR has been ratified by all 47 member states of the Council of Europe, applies to all persons in a state (not just its citizens), and has strong enforcement mechanisms (Kenna, 2005).

In contrast, the EU approach (27 member states) has been to develop common governance arrangements for social protection, rather than legal rights, and housing has never been fully recognised as an area of competence at EU level. For example, instruments to support social inclusion such as national action plans (NAPs) make only superficial reference to housing (Kenna, 2005). Nevertheless, the 1990s and 2000s saw gradual recognition of the complex links between housing and other aspects of social exclusion/social protection which the EU sought to address. A 1997 resolution of the European Parliament expressed the desire for an EU housing policy, calling for the right to decent and affordable housing for all; in 1999 the Committee of the Regions raised the importance of homelessness issues; and EU texts on human dignity implicitly recognise the right to adequate accommodation as a fundamental human right. There are procedures for the discussion of housing issues through annual meetings of EU housing ministers. Homelessness tends to be discussed as a social inclusion issue whereas more general housing issues are held to be largely a market function, where concerns are more with consumer rights and property rights than with fundamental rights to housing (Kenna, 2005). Nevertheless, the EU does respect the United Nations Universal Declaration of Human Rights (see below) and EU members Belgium, Finland, the Netherlands, Portugal, Spain, and Sweden have all incorporated the right to housing into their national constitutions (even though it may not be explicitly legally enforceable as implemented in France).

At the global level, the most widely applicable human rights instruments are those under the auspices of the United Nations (150 member states), and nation states ratifying UN covenants must ensure compatibility between their national laws and their international duties. Article 25 of the 1948 Universal Declaration of Human Rights states that

> Everyone has the right to a standard of living adequate for the health and well-being of himself and of his family, including food, clothing, *housing* and medical care and necessary social services, and the right to security in the event of unemployment, sickness, disability, widowhood, old age or other lack of livelihood in circumstances beyond his control (Kenna, 2005: 14; emphasis added).

Kenna (2005) further documents that Article 11 of the International Covenant on Economic, Social and Cultural Rights (ICESCR, 1966) refers directly to the right to housing as part of the right to an adequate standard of living. This covenant has been ratified by 150 states and requires signatories to "take appropriate steps to ensure realisation of this right." General Comment 4 of the ICESCR further specifies required elements of housing policy, including

- legal security of tenure;
- availability of services, materials, and infrastructures;
- affordable housing (such that housing costs do not threaten other needs being met);
- habitable housing;
- accessible housing (including for groups with specific needs);
- location (environment and other services); and
- culturally adequate housing.

In theory, any person not enjoying these entitlements could claim that they do not enjoy the right to housing as enshrined in international human rights law (Kenna, 2005).

General Comment 7 requires that forced evictions are prohibited unless they are carried out fully in accordance with national law and international covenants on human rights. Finally, wider UN anti-discrimination instruments apply equally to housing as to other areas of policy.

Conclusion

Quality of housing outcomes reflects choice and constraint within any nation or society, and sometimes people may have no effective choice, resulting in their becoming homeless. For those facing the most difficult circumstances, a rights-based response to homelessness may offer an enforceable or justiciable procedure which actually empowers individual households to resolve their housing situation (Fitzpatrick, 2009). Housing rights as human rights conferred by the international conventions discussed above may be closer to a social form of housing rights, which, if effectively implemented, may well contribute to the prevention of homelessness and so avoid the need for a responsive solution. For example, DeDecker (2004) argued that Belgium's high degree of social protection resulted in it having among the lowest poverty levels in the world even though intervention in the housing market was weak. Of course the two approaches are not mutually exclusive. O'Sullivan (2008) has argued that the negotiated, consensual approach to developing a national strategy to combat homelessness in Ireland may prove more effective than an 'adversarial' (p. 229) legal rights approach. However, the extended rights-based legal framework in Scotland discussed in this chapter also emerged from a consensus approach through the Homelessness Task Force, and the DALO in France was implemented in conjunction with broader social inclusion measures.

As noted earlier, Bengtsson (2001) has argued that in more universalistic welfare states, social rights may be more appropriate and effective than justiciable rights. However, the introduction of social housing rights may be particularly challenging to secure in nation states where this would require fundamental shifts in national welfare provision. In such circumstances, enforceable housing rights may offer a short- to medium-term shift, which demonstrates some commitment to a rights-based response to homelessness and tackles the most urgent aspects of the problem. The direct transferability of the Scottish and French frameworks to other national contexts would not be straightforward, but they could perhaps be drawn upon as aspirational models, which demonstrate that policy can change and nation states can implement rights-based responses to homelessness.

At supra-national level, systems are in place to monitor states' performance in meeting housing rights obligations, for example, through the United Nations Committee on Economic, Social and Cultural Rights, the Council of

Europe's Committee of Social Rights, the European Union Social Protection Committee, and the European courts. These bodies provide at least some remedy against contraventions of international instruments, indicating that international human rights instruments can be used to address the development of human and housing rights within nation states. However, the question remains as to how accessible they are to individual households, as opposed to requiring substantial legal or advocacy support in order to successfully bring a complaint.

Although this article has argued for enforceable, rights-based responses to homelessness, the importance of broader housing and social policies to avoiding and alleviating homelessness is very much acknowledged. Neither universalistic social rights nor fully enforceable legal rights to housing may yet be achievable for all nation states, but the ideal of a well-developed rights-based approach to homelessness within a wider social system which promotes adequate housing and social protection for all is a goal worth setting.

See also: Cost Analyses of Homelessness: Limits and Opportunities; Ethnographies of Home and Homelessness; Homelessness: Causation; Homelessness: Definitions; Human Rights and Housing; Policies to Address Homelessness; Rights to Housing: International Instruments; Rights to Housing Tenure; Social Exclusion and Housing; Social Policy Approaches.

References

Anderson I (2007) Tackling street homelessness in Scotland: The evolution and impact of the Rough Sleepers Initiative. *Journal of Social Issues* 63(3): 623–640.

Anderson I (2009) Homelessness policy in Scotland: A complete safety net by 2012? In: Fitzpatrick S, Quilgars D, and Pleace N (eds.) *Homelessness in the UK: Problems and Solutions*, Ch. 7, pp. 107–124. Coventry, UK: Chartered Institute of Housing.

Bengtsson B (2001) Housing as a social right: Implications for welfare state theory. *Scandinavian Political Studies* 24(4): 255–275.

Bowcott O (2009) UK should adopt pioneering Scottish homelessness law, says UN. *The Guardian*, accessed online at Guardian.co.uk/society, Wednesday, 3 June 2009.

Council of Europe (2009) Information from website, http://www.coe.int/, accessed 4 February 2009.

DeDecker P (2004) Housing policy in Belgium: Reborn with a restyled welfare state. *European Journal of Housing Policy* 4(3): 261–281.

Edgar W and Meert H (2005) *Fourth Review of Statistics on Homelessness in Europe: The Ethos Definition of Homelessness*. Brussels, Belgium: FEANTSA.

FEANTSA (2008) *Homeless in Europe. The Right to Housing: The Way Forward*, Autumn issue. Brussels, Belgium: FEANTSA.

Fitzpatrick S (2009) Homelessness in the UK in an international context. In: Fitzpatrick S, Quilgars D, and Pleace N (eds.) *Homelessness in the UK: Problems and Solutions*, Ch. 10, pp. 158–174. Coventry, UK: Chartered Institute of Housing.

Fitzpatrick S, Quilgars D, and Pleace N (eds.) (2009) *Homelessness in the UK: Problems and Solutions*. Coventry, UK: Chartered Institute of Housing.

Fitzpatrick S and Stephens M (2007) *An International Review of Homelessness and Social Housing Policy*. London: Communities and Local Government Publications.

Goodlad R (2005) Scottish homelessness policy: Advancing social justice? *Scottish Affairs* 50 (winter): 86–105.

Homelessness Task Force (2000) *Helping Homeless People: Legislative Proposals on Homelessness*. Edinburgh, UK: Scottish Executive.

Homelessness Task Force (2002) An action plan for prevention and effective response. *Homelessness Task Force Final Report*. Edinburgh, UK: Scottish Executive.

Kenna P (2005) *Housing Rights and Human Rights*. Brussels, Belgium: FEANTSA.

Loison M (2007) The implementation of an enforceable right to housing in France. *European Journal of Homelessness* 1: 185–197.

Loison-Leruste M and Quilgars D (2009) Increasing access to housing – implementing the right to housing in England and France. *European Journal of Homelessness* 3: 75–100.

Mandič S (2006) *Fourth Review of Policies on Homelessness in Europe*. Brussels, Belgium: FEANTSA.

O'Sullivan E (2008) Sustainable solutions to homelessness: The Irish case. *European Journal of Homelessness* 2: 205–234.

Scottish Government (2009) *Operation of the Homeless Persons Legislation in Scotland: 2008–2009*. Edinburgh, UK: Scottish Government (web only http://www.scotland.gov.uk/Publications/2009/09/03122620/0).

Scottish Government (2010) *Scottish Statutory Instruments 2010, No. 2. Housing: The Homeless Persons (Provision of Non-Permanent Accommodation) (Scotland) Regulations 2010*. London: Office of Public Sector Information.

Policies to Address Homelessness: 'Staircase' Models

I Sahlin, University of Gothenburg, Gothenburg, Sweden

© 2012 Elsevier Ltd. All rights reserved.

Glossary

Staircase of transition/housing staircase A model to address homelessness, implying that homeless persons move stepwise from low-quality shelters, through various forms of supported housing, to next-to-normal rental flats. The higher the step, the more privacy, comfort, and tenure security is offered, while social control and rules of occupancy are eased. Each move upward requires good behaviour at a previous level in the staircase, while misbehaviour implies relocation to a lower step. The idea is to train the individual in independent living.

Secondary housing market Flats that local social authorities rent and sublease on special terms to homeless clients.

Transitional housing Flats subleased to homeless people with the intention of letting them take over the primary lease after a successful trial period, usually 12–24 months.

Public housing (Sweden) Housing owned by municipal housing companies, where rents are settled in negotiations with the tenants' association at a level considered to cover the company's costs and to reflect the use value of the dwelling. In this kind of public housing, the company is expected to be run in a businesslike manner, with no special responsibility for disadvantaged groups. Hence, applicants with rent arrears, uncertain or low income, unpaid debts, or previous neighbour complaints are rejected from private and public housing alike, while both kinds of rental housing try to attract well-off, stable tenants.

Introduction

Local authorities in charge of housing for the homeless in Sweden sometimes organise their supply of accommodation offers as a ladder or a staircase, where the bottom rung is communal living in a shelter while the highest one is a subleased, normal flat. Although higher levels in the stairs imply more space, privacy, and security, and less regulation and control by social workers, the client/tenant still does not have the same independence and tenure security as a regular tenant. Such an arrangement of homeless accommodation, consisting of at least three levels or ranks, where the intention is that the individual starts from a hostel or emergency shelter and then stepwise advances to almost ordinary housing, is sometimes called a 'staircase of transition', or simply a 'housing staircase'. A crucial feature of this model is that each move 'upwards' is conditioned upon good behaviour and rule compliance at lower steps, while failure to follow the rules implies dislocation to lower rungs. The staircase model requires – and is partly defined by the fact – that the tenants have no security of tenure, since the local social authorities (LSAs) keep the primary lease of the dwellings.

An ordinary, integrated dwelling rented directly by the property owner on the regular housing market with full tenure security is the ultimate goal of the staircase. Its top level usually consists of a subleased, self-contained flat, the contract on which can ultimately be converted into a regular tenancy. These transitional flats are often popular, but landlords are less willing to supply them and more particular in their selection of appropriate residents. In hostels and at lower steps in the staircase the hope for advancement and eventually a dwelling of one's own is supposed to give homeless people an incentive to behave well and comply with shelter rules and work plans. However, due to the facts that failure at one step results in displacement, and that the property owners often keep a right of veto to the conversion of tenancy agreements into regular tenure, many residents never succeed to leave the staircase for dwellings of their own.

The prospect of a housing career, implied in the staircase metaphor, affects the image of all steps as they become defined as being above or below another form of accommodation. In this way, it is similar to the general idea of promotion and career in work life, or to the education system. Unlike in the school, however, homeless residents in the staircase can quickly be relocated to lower levels, which implies that achievements at one level are easily lost, for example, in cases of trouble, conflicts, or relapses into drug abuse.

The staircase of transition should be regarded as an ideal type. Due to local differences in available accommodation resources and in target group differentiation according to homeless household composition, gender, age, or possible drug misuse, the local design and structure of the staircase vary considerably.

The Emergence of the Staircase Model

The staircase model emerged in Sweden in the late 1980s and became more common in the 1990s as a result of growing numbers of homeless people and of public housing becoming increasingly reluctant to let dwellings to homeless people with low or uncertain income, debts, bad records, or lack of housing references. In the early 1990s, housing allocation was deregulated and local housing assignment agencies closed. The LSAs, which in Sweden are municipal bodies, became responsible for providing housing for homeless people, while at the same time they lost their previous influence over the allocation of public housing. The solution was to rent houses or dwellings and sublease flats or rooms to homeless clients on special terms by making use of legislation originally designed for tenants subletting their private homes for a limited period of time. This enabled the LSAs to circumvent the tenure security established in the Tenant Law, and to tailor tenancy agreements to embrace behavioural aspects that are not possible to include in regular tenancies. In signing such an agreement, the tenant typically pledges to stay sober and consents to staff supervision through home visits, to detailed rules such as not having pets or guests staying overnight, and sometimes to an individual work plan, and additional rules can be tied to a specific unit of accommodation, depending on its target group, site, and property owner. Thus, a secondary housing market was established.

As the supply of such accommodation grew in scope and became more differentiated, many LSAs found it helpful to organise their resources in a way that would rationalise their allocation of housing and accommodation to homeless clients. The staircase model enabled them to make use of the differences through structuring accommodation options in a hierarchy. Making good behaviour in the less-popular hostels and shelters a condition for access to the more attractive, self-contained flats, with more privacy and less monitoring made each transfer upwards a reward. At the same time they could satisfy the property owners' higher demands on residents in housing integrated in the community.

Although the staircase is most developed and frequent in Sweden, there are tiered models with only two steps, for example, emergency shelter and transitional housing, in other countries, such as Canada, Australia, and the United States, which share some traits in common with the staircase. It is also akin to some interpretations of the system of 'continuum of care' that is frequent in the United States, for instance the linear residential treatment model sometimes used there. Here, the residents are expected to move from a shelter to some kind of congregate living and further on to transitional housing and finally independent housing. Like in the staircase model, advancement through access to a 'higher' level is dependent on the client's improvement and success at the current one. Like the continuum of care in some sites, the staircase of transition is frequently the only local model available, which means that all people who are assisted with accommodation by the LSAs are expected to go through it, even if they have no mental illness or substance abuse or other problems implied in the model. Unlike the continuum of care, however, the staircase does not include any treatment or therapy, although rules and supervision are supposed to support sobriety.

The Implications of the Staircase Model as a Solution to Homelessness

Embedded already in the staircase as metaphor is the idea of stepwise transition from homelessness to being permanently settled. This notion, in turn, presumes a whole theory of human needs, powers, motives, and interests. Furthermore, the model is based on a number of more or less explicit assumptions on homeless people's specific needs, problems, behaviour, and potential development, and by implication a theory on the causes of homelessness. Specifically, it constructs homeless people as incapable of independent living until they are taught and trained in housing skills.

Who will become and remain homeless (among people who cannot afford to buy their homes) is to a large extent determined by those controlling access to rental housing through evicting tenants and rejecting housing applicants. In most cases, Swedish landlords gather information on the home seekers' financial situation, regular income, work position, family size, and their possible misbehaving and rent arrears as tenants in the past. However, the staircase system is implicitly based on the notion of homeless persons in general having problems with substance abuse and with handling money and personal relationships. The long period of time that the clients are supposed to remain in the staircase presumes that it will take considerable time of training and control before a formerly homeless person is capable of independent living, and that waiting several years for permanent, independent housing will not harm the individual's life or motivation. It is further taken for granted that their everyday behaviour and interaction with neighbours need adjustment and improvement, and that this need outweighs possible wants of privacy, as it is often a condition for access to accommodation that the support staff can enter their homes without their consent. The use of sanctions in terms of dislocation to a lower step or promotion to a higher one implies a theory on human beings learning to behave through punishment and rewards.

On the other hand, the staircase idea is at odds with the general notion that problems like mental illness and substance abuse tend to appear in episodes, with months, years, or even decades between relapses. It is also at variance with the universal practice of young people moving from parental homes without any special training in 'housing skills', and it is neglecting the fact that many homeless people used to have homes of their own and became homeless because of family breakdown or job loss and because they, when looking for a new home, did not live up to the financial demands of local landlords.

Hence, the general assumption implied in the staircase model is that people become homeless because of substance abuse, mental illness, or misbehaviour and are incapable of independent living. Moreover, it is assumed that training in housing skills and good tenant behaviour under threat of eviction is a necessary and sufficient condition to make them acceptable on the regular housing market. Ironically, landlords may still not be convinced, and this is why municipal housing companies in several Swedish cities have begun to require an extra top step in the staircase, to ensure that the residents can behave in a normal flat without any support and control, before considering them as regular tenants with tenure security. Another irony is provided by findings in a nationwide Swedish study showing that municipalities that apply the staircase model, compared to municipalities that avoid it, consider a larger proportion of their population to be incapable of independent living and also tend to reject such people from accommodation in the staircase.

Advantages of the Staircase Model from the Point of View of the Main Parties

To assess the value of this kind of organising, structuring, and allocating homeless accommodation it is essential to take into account that the involved parties have different objectives, interests, and values. In what follows, I will distinguish between the functions of the staircase model for the landlords/property owners, the LSAs, and the homeless people themselves.

From the point of view of the LSAs, the staircase of transition enables social workers to use shelters and housing as resources to offer or withdraw in their work with clients. As homeless people can be transferred upwards and downwards in the staircase as a reward or punishment, respectively, with regard to not only their behaviour as tenants, but also their sobriety and their behaviour as clients, job seekers, workers, parents, and so forth, these options and risks are used as resources in motivation work, while the LSA staff's access to the subleased dwellings enables them to monitor their clients' behaviour and development. The staircase also provides a structure through which available housing and shelter resources can be distributed among homeless clients in a legitimate, almost meritocratic way. Hence, it serves as a tool for motivating homeless people to change, for supervising their ways of living, as well as for rationing various kinds of housing to homeless clients.

The staircase also justifies the use of hostels and shelters of bad quality. Since the social worker has a plan for the clients being transferred to better accommodation, and since the stay in a hostel is always *intended* to be short term, low quality can be excused. In relation to the staircase system, the hostel fulfils several functions: it serves a waiting room, as a place where the client's behaviour can be observed and assessed, and it keeps the client available for contacts. The hostel is also a place to put clients who are evicted from higher steps and have to start anew (and hence a means to deter them from misbehaviour). Finally, it may serve as an end station for people who after several failures are not considered fit for the staircase.

The advantages of the system for landlords/property owners are obvious. The conditions upon which the flat is let are partly designed by the property owners and often include, for instance, that the tenant be immediately removed if neighbours complain, irrespective of whether such complaints are validated or not. Because the homeless tenant does not have a regular contract, it is possible to circumvent prevailing legislation with regard to legal grounds for eviction and notice. Residents in the staircase, in contrast to regular tenants, can be told to move out within 24 hours or be given notice to leave within two days, and there is no formal procedure or possibility to appeal such decisions. Usually the LSAs implement such decisions, including changing locks, emptying the flat, and storing utilities. Since the landlords may deny access to subleased flats in the housing stock for homeless people who in the past caused complaints or had rent arrears, their usual exclusion strategies will not be hampered by inclusion attempts through the staircase.

Agreements between the social services and the landlords on when a resident in a transitional flat will be entitled to take over the lease are rarely formal or legally binding. This means that regardless of how well an individual behaved as tenant, the landlord may still not accept him or her as a regular tenant due to the usual rejection criteria, such as lack of income or a regular work position, or the existence of recorded debts. A statistical study of the municipalities in Sweden showed that in times and places where vacancy rates in public housing were high, the local homelessness rate did not decline, but more dwellings were rented by the LSAs. Arguably, the landlords did not mitigate their demands on new tenants to fill their vacant flats but preferred having the LSAs sublease them to homeless people. Due to the minimal tenure security in the staircase and the strict conditions of supervision and special rules of behaviour, landlords are ensured orderly tenant behaviour, while the LSA as formal tenant guarantees that rents and possible repair and eviction costs are paid in time.

From the perspective of the homeless residents, finally, the staircase of transition may have an initial appeal since it gives a vision that it is possible to reach the goal of a self-contained home within a few years. Those who are willing to change their lifestyles but unable to do it on their own might also feel safer with strict rules, control, and supervision. Some people do manage to climb the whole staircase and to finally get flats of their own; however, this is not the general experience.

The Actual Outcome of the Staircase Model with Regard to Homeless People and Homelessness

It is probably wise to distinguish between consequences for homeless individuals included in the staircase and those outside it, on the one hand, and how the staircase model may affect homelessness at large in the municipality and in the region/country, on the other.

On the individual level, people often get stuck at low or medium high steps in the staircase, without getting access to regular housing. Some residents are time and again downgraded to a lower step as a punishment for misbehaviour, which extends the time spent in the staircase, while others are expelled from the whole staircase system and referred to low-quality hostels. A survey by the National Board for Housing, Building and Planning of all LSAs in Sweden showed that only a tiny fraction of their tenants were allowed to take over the lease of a transitional home during 2008. This disquieting finding, which is consistent with previous local studies, reflects either that the average time spent in the staircase is very long or that the rate of success is very small.

Qualitative studies show that homeless people find it hard to settle down and make themselves at home in the housing staircase as they know that they will soon have to move on – they will be either downgraded or informally evicted due to misbehaviour, or encouraged to move to a higher housing level. Combined with the terms on which accommodation is offered at the lower steps, the extended waiting time, the growing uncertainty of future housing, and the risk to get stuck at a certain level, the staircase has proven hard to accept in the long run for a portion of the concerned people. Because of the rules, which often preclude pets and guests staying overnight, even in self-contained flats, some staircase dwellers also find it hard to maintain relationships with existing family members or to build new relationships. Couples are often not allowed to live together. Close supervision makes the risk for eviction due to rule-breaking high: having a beer or letting a guest in who is not sober may be sufficient for

an eviction. Although some residents feel that strict rules and supervision serve as protection from unwanted visits by acquaintances, boyfriends, and ex-mates, many who spent several years in the staircase do not want to give it another try if they fail and have to start all over again.

On the societal level, homelessness tends to remain or even grow locally where the staircase approach has been in use for several years. It is also observed that the number of places on the lower rungs increases more than the ones on the higher levels, while the number of homeless people totally outside the system is not reduced. This gradual distortion of the staircase may illustrate that homeless individuals on average spend longer periods of time on the lower steps than on the higher ones, or that many homeless people fail to climb more than half the stairs. The landlords' reluctance to accept that transitional contracts are transferred from the authorities to the tenants results in a bottleneck that contributes to blocking the through-flow in the system, and the residents' loss of confidence in the staircase makes it less useful as a motivation tool for social workers.

Statistically, rates of homelessness in a narrow, literal sense as well as in a broader one are higher in municipalities with a large secondary housing market, which is associated with the staircase model. This situation is explained, firstly, by the fact that this parallel system of housing allocation serves as an excuse for public housing landlords to reject homeless people, who are referred to the LSAs instead, and, secondly, by the fate of clients who have been evicted from the staircase. Those who are excluded even from the staircase lack any credibility as applicants for regular housing. Hence, for those outside the staircase it is more difficult to find housing than if no such model were applied in the town. A third factor is that landlords lack incentives to convert leaseholds to regular ones for well-behaving tenants on the top rung of the staircase. If the deal with the LSAs defines a certain number of flats that the landlords should supply as transitional housing, it is more convenient for the latter to have these dwellings occupied by people who have already proven to be good tenants, than to let new people in.

The pressure on the LSAs to house homeless people who cannot get access to regular housing makes it necessary for them to gain and keep the confidence of the landlords in order to convince them to supply more permanent and temporary housing. As a result, the authorities can become prone to creaming. A survey in the beginning of the 1990s showed that in municipalities applying the staircase model, homeless people regarded as incapable of independent living were to a high extent literally homeless and excluded from the staircase, which, instead, was occupied by people who according to the LSAs would be well suited for regular housing, if only the landlords had accepted them. This result not only falsifies the claim that the staircase succeeds in teaching people how to live independently, but also shows how this system undermines the tenure security in quite a share of the rental housing market.

Concluding Thoughts: The Staircase Paradox

Despite the absence of support in evaluations and research, the staircase model is surviving and being reproduced in Sweden. To resolve this paradox, it is necessary to recall the functions it fulfils for the LSAs and the landlords, and to understand that the model is by now being sustained by established routines, local traditions, agreements, and cooperation between these two parties. When a solution to a problem has been institutionalised, it takes more than proven failure to dismantle it. Even if it does not succeed in integrating homeless people in the housing market, its image of progress and reward appeals to decision makers and social workers alike, and the staircase is actively promoted by landlords and housing providers. In municipalities utilising the staircase model, there are often frequent and close cooperation between social workers and housing managers, and both parties may agree that the staircase serves some of their interests, regardless of its efficiency as a solution to homelessness.

The fact that the staircase model is still found attractive by a range of municipalities and also has been institutionalised in several sites may be partly due to isomorphism. It can also be suspected that the mere name and design as a 'model' has a convincing power. In Project Homeless in Norway, the staircase model was first considered but gave way to an alternative approach when it was presented as the 'normalisation model'.

The staircase has been the target of extensive and enduring criticism for almost two decades in Sweden. Recently, several big cities announced that they have abandoned the model, and the National Board for Health and Welfare has started to question its potential and does not recommend it anymore. Despite the absence of evidence that it works, however, many municipalities persist in using it and others have recently adopted it. There are also indications that the name is dropped but the practice sustained. An important reason for its survival in Sweden is that there is no social housing (i.e., housing which is allocated primarily on the basis of housing need), while public housing (owned by municipal housing companies) does not differ much from private rental housing with regard to rent levels, eligibility, and qualification demands. Housing applicants with rent arrears, low or uncertain income, or those who lack recent references from landlords are usually rejected from public housing. Hence, shelters, low-standard intermediate 'steps', as well as self-contained transitional dwellings remain the only housing resources at the LSAs' disposal, whether or not they are organised as a staircase, and a comprehensive model may be preferred to a scattered system of emergency shelters and transitional accommodation.

The staircase model's relative inertia towards criticism is also due to the general tendency to blame the individual if a treatment or training system does not work. Just like school failures may be blamed on the pupils, and poverty on the poor, homeless people are often seen as causing their homelessness. The staircase model with its focus on behaviour and promotion seems to reinforce this kind of account. People are not evicted unless they have misbehaved in one way or another, so from the perspective of the landlord and the social workers, those who are expelled from the staircase are themselves responsible for it. Such individual failures may even be regarded by landlords as a success for the staircase as a testing system that manages to identify people unfit for regular housing. On the other hand, if people after having climbed the whole staircase do succeed to obtain regular housing, such cases are viewed as an achievement of the model, even though these people might have managed equally well if they had been offered regular housing from the start. In this way, success is attributed to the staircase, and failures to the homeless tenants.

See also: Home and Homelessness; Home in Temporary Dwellings; Homelessness: Causation; Policy Instruments that Support Housing Supply: Social Housing; Policies to Address Homelessness: Housing First Approaches; Policies to Address Homelessness: Rights-Based Approaches; Rights to Housing: Marginalised Housing Groups; Supported Housing.

Further Reading

Benjaminsen L and Dyb E (2008) The effectiveness of homeless policies – variations among the Scandinavian countries. *European Journal of Homelessness* 2: 45–67.

Blid M (2008) *Ett folkhem för alla? – Kommunala insatser mot hemlöshet* [A people's home for all? – Municipal measures against homelessness]. Doctoral thesis. Östersund: Mittuniversitetet, Department of Social Work.

Knutagård M (2009) *Skälens fångar. Hemlöshetsarbetets organisering, kategoriseringar och förklaringar* [The Prisoners of Reasons. Homeless Work's Organisation, Categorisations and Accounts]. Doctoral thesis. Malmö: Égalité.

Löfstrand C (2005) *Hemlöshetens politik. Lokal policy och praktik* [The Politics of Homelessness. Local Policy and Practice]. Doctoral thesis. Malmö: Égalité.

National Board for Housing, Building and Planning (2009) *Hyreskontrakt via kommunen* [Leases through the Municipalities]. Karlskrona: Boverket.

Sahlin I (1996) *På gränsen till bostad. Avvisning, utvisning, specialkontrakt.* [*On the Border of Housing. Rejection, Expulsion, Special Contracts*]. Doctoral thesis. Lund: Arkiv.

Sahlin I (1998) *The Staircase of Transition.* National Report from Sweden to the European Observatory of Homelessness 1997. Brussels: FEANTSA.

Sahlin I (2005) The staircase of transition: Survival through failure. *Innovation* 18(2): 115–135.

Sahlin I (2006) *Homelessness and the Secondary Housing Market in Sweden 1990–2005.* Paper presented at the ENHR Conference in Ljubljana 2–5 July 2005.

Tsemberis S and Eisenberg RF (2000) Pathways to housing: Supported housing for street-dwelling homeless individuals with psychiatric disabilities. *Psychiatric Services* 51(4): 487–493.

Policies to Address Redlining

MB Aalbers, University of Amsterdam, Amsterdam, The Netherlands

© 2012 Elsevier Ltd. All rights reserved.

Glossary

Credit scoring Statistically based management tools for forecasting the outcome of extending credit to individuals. Credit scores are based on such common variables as occupation, length of employment, marital status, bank account, gender, and geographical address, which are analysed by computer systems and statistical methods in order to predict credit performance.
Predatory loan A subset of subprime lending. A form of price discrimination by unsuitable loans designed to exploit vulnerable and unsophisticated borrowers. If practiced place-based, it is a form of yellowlining.

Redlining The identification of an area, usually a neighbourhood or zip code area, where no financial services are provided. A form of place-based financial and social exclusion.
Subprime loan High-cost loan meant for borrowers with credit imperfections, but also sold to borrowers with a good credit history.
Yellowlining The identification of an area, usually a neighbourhood or zip code area, where financial services are provided only under uneven conditions, such as higher transaction costs and higher interest rates.

Introduction

Mortgage redlining is the policy of a mortgage lender to reject mortgage loan applications based on the neighbourhood. Many authors include uneven conditions such as higher transaction costs and higher interest rates than on other loans in their definition of redlining. For matters of clarity, we define such uneven home mortgage finance conditions as 'yellowlining' which is different from 'redlining' where a lender does not grant any mortgage loans at all. Redlining is a form of place-based financial and social exclusion (see article Social Exclusion and Housing). Through redlining, mortgage applicants are excluded 'from' obtaining housing by denying them mortgage loans. Homeowners are excluded 'through' housing because they are unable to sell their house, thereby becoming trapped in their home.

Lenders reject mortgage applications for neighbourhoods where they have no trust in the financial dependability of potential customers, or in the price development of houses in those neighbourhoods. The risk that a homeowner can only sell his/her home for a lower price than purchased, and as a result is unable to pay off the entire mortgage, is considered too high. Lenders assume that members of certain groups are on an average less able to fulfil their financial commitments. For example, if lenders believe that minority applicants are more likely than majority applicants in default, this creates an economic incentive to discriminate against minority applicants or minority neighbourhoods – whether this belief is founded on an empirical correlation or not (see articles Discrimination in Mortgage Markets; Discrimination in Housing Markets). This behaviour is illegal – a lender must base his/her decision on the observed credit characteristics of an applicant – but some lenders may respond more to economic incentives than to legal requirements. Mortgage redlining adversely impacts low-income neighbourhoods and ethnic-minority neighbourhoods in particular (see articles Ethnic Minorities and Housing; Neighbourhood Disadvantage). Yet, redlining strikes not only low-income families and ethnic minorities, but also everyone else applying for a mortgage in a redlined neighbourhood.

According to the sociologist Robert Merton, perception alone is sufficient for people to act; prejudices may come into play when excluding certain subjected groups from mortgage capital. If the exclusion is based on aggregate data, it is a matter of statistical discrimination: individual members of a group are excluded simply by the fact that their group on an average has a bad credit profile. By defining a situation where certain neighbourhoods come with a large depreciation risk or a large default risk and are therefore denied mortgage capital, lenders evoke a chain of events that eventually cause houses in these neighbourhoods to actually lose value. This may then increase default rates. Because mortgage loans are constrained, a majority of potential homeowners cannot buy a house in these neighbourhoods. Drops in demand lead to falling house prices. The circle is closed: house prices have dropped because it was impossible to get a mortgage loan in a redlined neighbourhood – and not so much because this neighbourhood was a high-risk investment. It became a high-risk investment because it was 'perceived' as a high-risk investment. This is a matter of a self-fulfilling prophecy: because prices are expected to fall, people act accordingly, which in fact causes prices to fall. The principle behind a self-fulfilling prophecy is that people not only react to objective circumstances in a situation, but also, and sometimes primarily, to the meaning that the situation has for them. As Merton has analysed, we see that public definitions of a situation, like expectations and prophecies, become an integral part of that situation and influence future developments.

So far, we have assumed that redlining is something that takes place at the level of the city, where mortgage lenders decide where to grant and where not to grant mortgages. And in fact, the actual decision to redline often takes place at this level. Yet, the decision taken at the city level by mortgage lenders depends on many factors, some of which are located at the city or neighbourhood level, while others are located at other levels. The practice of redlining cannot exist without a notion of internal differentiation of geographical space: no internal differentiation – or to put it differently, no submarkets – no redlining (see article Submarkets). The question of scale is central to any relevant explanation. We could say that redlining is a product of the uneven development of capitalism, of the application of credit scoring models, of prejudiced urban managers and gatekeepers, of the structure and regulation of the mortgage market, of statistical discrimination, or of neighbourhood decline and the de-valorisation of capital invested in the built environment. It is, of course, in some way, a product of all these forces. Rather than analysing the complex interplay between these factors, this article will focus on the origins and evidence of redlining.

Redlining Policies in Prewar United States

The origins of redlining policies are to be found in the development of modern mortgage markets in the United States. Initially the US mortgage market was modelled after European mortgage markets. But in 1913, the Federal Reserve Act allowed commercial banks to lend money on real estate, a credit function not permitted in most European countries until the second half of the twentieth century. The opening of the mortgage market to commercial banks coupled with the economic optimism of the 1920s led to a rapid growth of US mortgage markets. The boom of the 1920s was followed by the Wall Street Crash of 1929 and the crisis of the 1930s. During this crisis, homeowners lost their houses in two different ways. First, widespread unemployment made it impossible for many homeowners to pay off their mortgage loans, resulting in foreclosures and tax sales. Second, most mortgages in those days were of a fixed term of 5 years and most people typically refinanced their loan at the end of that period, but during the crisis people who retained their job were often unable to refinance their loan after 5 years because of the withdrawal of financial institutions from the mortgage market, and many homeowners therefore lost their homes. In the early 1930s, the average number of foreclosed mortgage loans was 250 000 per year and at some point exceeding a 1000 per day. At that time, half of all home mortgages in the United States were in default. Also financial institutions failed and went bankrupt along with their borrowers, partly as a result of the massive withdrawal of savings.

As a reaction to the depression, President Hoover organised a conference on home building and homeownership in 1931. The conference proceedings make four recommendations:

1. the creation of long-term, amortised mortgages;
2. the encouragement of low interest rates;
3. the introduction of government aid to assist private efforts to house low-income families; and
4. the reduction of home construction costs.

Hardly ever have any policy conference proceedings been implemented as actual policies so quickly and comprehensively. I will focus here on the creation of the Home Owners Loan Corporation (HOLC). The HOLC was designed to provide emergency relief to homeowners by refinancing or purchasing defaulted mortgages – in other words, to forestall foreclosures. Thanks to the HOLC 10 000 borrowers clung on to their homes in the mid- and late 1930s and, in addition, it refinanced more than one million mortgages, all on relatively low interest rates. The HOLC introduced the long-term self-amortising mortgage with uniform payments spread over the life of the debt, thereby replacing the 5-year nonamortising mortgage with a balloon payment at the end of the loan period. It set the standards for mortgage lending till this day and systematised appraisal methods across the United States.

The HOLC was instrumental not only in developing and applying uniform, standardised appraisals, but also in implementing and institutionalising redlining policies. The HOLC developed a neighbourhood rating and mapping system comprising four colours corresponding to four different numbers and four different letter codes: green, First-grade or A referring to "homogeneous neighborhoods... hot spots... in demand as residential locations in good times and bad... American business and professional men"; blue, Second-grade or B referring to "stable... still good... still desirable" areas that had 'reached their peak'; yellow, Third-grade or C referring to "definitely declining... heterogeneous" neighbourhoods that attract "undesirable element[s]" and are "infiltrated by a lower-grade population"; and lastly, red, Fourth-grade or D referring to neighbourhoods "in which the things taking place in C areas have already happened" as a result of "detrimental influences in a pronounced degree" and where houses have "little or no value today, having suffered a tremendous decline in values due to the colored element now controlling the district" cited in Jackson (1985: 197–200) *Crabgrass Frontier* and Hillier (2005: 216–217) *Residential Security Maps and Neighbourhood Appraisals*. According to the historian Kenneth Jackson, Jewish neighbourhoods, even the stable and affluent ones, would never be considered First-grade, while Black neighbourhoods were by nature considered unstable and declining or depressed and habitually coloured red (see article Neighbourhood Reputation). Crossney and Bartelt (2005), however, claim that the connection between ethnicity and lending is less strong, even though they admit it is clear that Black and mixed areas were more often redlined than homogeneous White areas.

Although the HOLC is often blamed for 'introducing' redlining policies and practices, it is important to note that the HOLC was simply following dominant ideas in real estate and mortgage markets, already practiced at the local level. However, the HOLC did 'implement' and 'institutionalise' redlining policies. As a government institution, it did institutionalise already-existing policies of redlining into government policies by designing redlining maps for more than 200 American cities. Fourth-grade, red-coloured neighbourhoods were no exception, but rarer on some city maps than on others. While the map of St. Louis County, for example, only shows a small number of neighbourhoods coloured red, the map of the city of Newark, NJ is full of redlined neighbourhoods and no single neighbourhood in Newark is coloured green. **Figure 1**, the map for the city of Baltimore, shows a classic pattern: inner-city neighbourhoods surrounding the central business district are coloured red, the next ring of neighbourhoods and the older suburbs are largely coloured yellow, while newer suburbs – albeit with a few exceptions – are coloured blue or, less common, green. In addition, in a few years time, the number and size of redlined areas could dramatically increase as Hillier's analysis of the HOLC Residential Security Maps for Philadelphia clearly shows: in 2 years time, the share of city-land redlined almost doubled to 34%.

Redlining policies were adopted not only by the HOLC and private mortgage lenders, but also by the Federal Housing Administration (FHA). The FHA, established in 1934 under the Roosevelt administration, was created to insure private mortgage loans. (The Veterans Administration (VA), created in 1930, started doing the same in the late 1930s.) A borrower pays a loan premium for an FHA- or VA-insured home mortgage loan; the premiums are used as reserves and would flow to the lender in case an insured borrower defaulted. Like the HOLC, the creation of the FHA changed the mortgage market and set standards and practices which are followed to this day. In 1972, the FHA had insured about 11 million loans for purchase and about 22 million loans for home improvement. The FHA's standardisation made it easier, less risky, and cheaper to buy a home, thereby fuelling the development of the mortgage market. The FHA helped to encourage suburbanisation, but also "hastened the decay of inner-city neighbourhoods by stripping them of their middle-class constituency", because "in practice, FHA insurance went to new residential developments on the edges of metropolitan areas, to the neglect of core cities" (Jackson, 1985: 206). The inner-city areas were overlooked partly because they had lower appraised values for housing and the FHA simply did not grant insurance in many of these areas. While FHA insurance was meant as a public back-up to ensure the provision of mortgage loans, the FHA, like the HOLC, redlined areas in which private lenders were also less likely to grant mortgages, or would only grant mortgages under less advantageous conditions, such as higher down payments and higher interest rates. Jackson concludes his groundbreaking work by claiming that the

> FHA also helped to turn the building industry against the minority and inner-city housing market, and its policies supported the income and racial segregation of suburbia. (. . .) FHA exhorted segregation and enshrined it as public policy. Whole areas of cities were declined ineligible for loan guarantees; as late as 1966, for example, FHA did not have a mortgage on a single home in Camden or Paterson, New Jersey, both declining industrial cities. This withdrawal of financing often resulted in an inability to sell houses in a neighborhood, so that vacant units often stood empty for months, producing a steep decline in value. (Jackson, 1985: 213)

Gotham in his study of uneven development in Kansas City throughout the twentieth century arrives at similar conclusions arguing that the FHA's "insurance system and home ownership subsidies established a racially dual home financing market by refusing to insure mortgages in areas not covered with a racially restrictive covenant, thus denying mortgages to Black families, and channeling capital into suburban housing construction" (Gotham, 2002: 63). Indeed, discussions on redlining have been connected to debates on the causes of segregation and forms of racial discrimination: redlining is often seen as a form of (institutionalised) discrimination and as one of the causes of segregation (see articles Residential Segregation; Ghetto). Together with many other mechanisms and policies, redlining is understood to be one of the causes of the erosion of cities, the decline of (inner-city) neighbourhoods and the mass exodus to the suburbs.

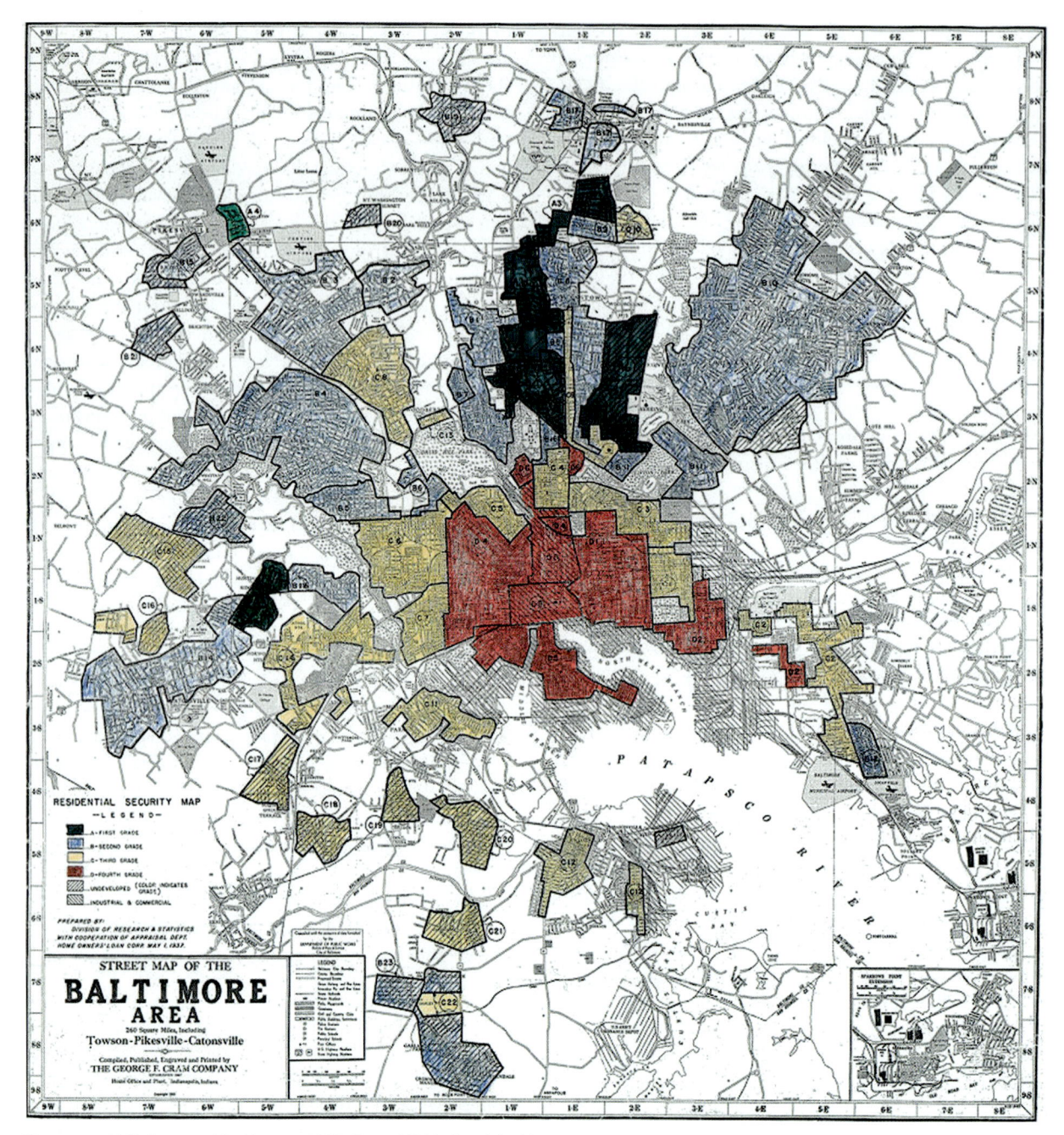

Figure 1 HOLC map of Baltimore, 1937. From US National Archives.

In the mid- and late 1960s, the FHA was forced to change its policies and make mortgage insurance available in formerly redlined and yellowlined areas. Today, FHA loans are actually responsible for increasing homeownership among Black households. However, as research by Wyly and Holloway shows, even if controlled for income, Black households significantly more often rely on FHA-insured loans. The assumption is that Black households rely on FHA-insured loans because it is more difficult for them to acquire loans in the non-insured mortgage market.

Redlining Policies in Postwar United States

In the wake of the social rights movement, redlining returned to the political and research agendas in the late 1960s and 1970s. Community-based organisations in particular claimed that lenders were redlining large parts of American inner cities (see article Community- and Neighbourhood-Based Organisations in the United States). In 1968, discrimination in housing – including mortgaging – became legally prohibited through the

Fair Housing Act. In addition, the US government responded by implementing the Home Mortgage Disclosure Act (HMDA) in 1975, and the Community Reinvestment Act (CRA) in 1977 (see article Discrimination in Housing Markets). These acts require lenders to report granted loans by census tract and to provide credit to the local communities within the states in which they are active. Despite these acts and the related move of the FHA to the inner city, research from the 1970s, 1980s, and early 1990s clearly shows the existence of redlining policies, mostly in inner-city areas. Some of the earliest studies from the 1970s found evidence of redlining, but have been criticised for omitting important variables and for the use of aggregate level data. Studies from the 1980s have demonstrated that minority and inner-city neighbourhoods receive less credit, but are susceptible to the criticism of preselection bias. Whatever the case may be, it is clear that community and legal struggles against redlining have been successful in diminishing redlining practices. The story of Atlanta, described superbly in an essay by Keating and colleagues, illustrates the potential impact which can be achieved through cooperation between community activism, university research (an MA thesis in city planning) and media investigations and reporting (the 1988 Pulitzer Prize-winning articles by Dedman).

Research often uses HMDA data to demonstrate the continuation of redlining, but recent evidence of de facto redlining is scarce. But like earlier studies, these studies are also open to criticism. Nevertheless, studies of discrimination in lending show that social groups as defined by race or area fare poorly in obtaining mortgage loans: for example, White neighbourhoods receive 3–4 times more loans per 1000 mortgageable structures when compared with minority neighbourhoods; even after controlling for factors such as income, a wide gap remains between different racial groups and between the neighbourhoods they inhabit. Although this does not necessarily prove the existence of redlining, it does show that disparate treatment on the basis of both race and place is indeed taking place. Or, in other words, recent research carried out in the United States shows that race-based exclusion clearly takes place, but that redlining (place-based exclusion) is often harder to prove and more contingent on the metropolitan area researched and on individual bank policies.

In conclusion, it is fair to say that while few would deny the existence of historic redlining in the United States, recent evidence of redlining is scarce. Today, redlining in the United States is less likely to take place because it is prohibited and banks have to make their lending data available for research. In addition, changes in financial markets have made it more likely that lenders will charge higher interest rates and closing fees in high-risk areas (yellowlining) rather than redlining those areas. Yet, we cannot simply conclude that redlining no longer exists in the United States. Indeed, researchers who demonstrate the existence of redlining policies can easily be accused of omitting variables. At the same time, researchers who demonstrate the nonexistence of redlining can be criticised on the same grounds, but also for not taking most of the lending process into account, for instance, by ignoring preapplication denials. Moreover, a great deal of research has overlooked the fact that lenders can easily adjust their spatial lending policies. Since redlining is measured on the district level, they can engage in cherry-picking behaviour by redlining part of a district as long as they grant mortgages in other parts.

More recently, authors have argued that redlining has been replaced by subprime lending and predatory lending (see article Subprime Mortgages). This is possible due to the increased use of credit scoring. Credit scoring enables lenders (often through credit agencies) to map the social characteristics of households, and by coupling those to financial characteristics and past financial behaviour, mortgage lenders try to predict the default risk of a borrower. Low-risk prospective borrowers can then be offered low-priced loans and while high-risk borrowers would have been denied a mortgage loan in the past, they can now get a high-priced loan. The problem is not only that some loans become too high-priced for households to handle, but also that several lenders in the subprime market offer mortgage loans with high prices that no longer hold any real correlation between risk and price. This segment of the subprime mortgage market – often referred to as 'predatory lending' or 'reversed redlining' – causes more harm to homeowners than it does benefit.

But how does this relate to redlining? It may seem that credit scoring systems are now so well developed to accurately predict borrower behaviour that lenders no longer need such crude methods as redlining to limit risk. Although this may very well be the case, this does not necessarily mean that redlining has in fact been completely displaced by credit scoring. First, redlining may still exist next to credit scoring: this way formal application procedures that generate the input for credit scoring systems have to make no mention of 'zip code policies', while lenders can still enact redlining policies. Second, lenders may use geographical location as an additional criterion, in particular when reassessing 'review cases'. Third, because geographical location may be included in credit scoring systems, redlining may take place through those credit scoring systems, as geographical location may be the decisive factor in turning down an application, in particular if geographical location gets a relatively large weight in a credit scoring system. Even though geographical location will not be the only factor predicting exclusion or inclusion, the result nonetheless is de facto or actual redlining.

Redlining Policies Outside the United States

Even though most research on redlining is carried out in the United States, there are also a number of studies documenting redlining processes in other, mostly Anglophone, countries. Research in the United Kingdom, South Africa, Australia, Canada, and the Netherlands has demonstrated the existence of redlining, whether in the 1970s and 1980s or in the 1990s and 2000s. In addition, recent research on Milan, Italy has demonstrated the existence of yellowlining, albeit not redlining. Redlining is sometimes mentioned in other countries, but we are not aware of any redlining research in the global South or elsewhere in Europe, though we should not conclude that redlining does not occur in these countries. In general, the existence of redlining is denied up until (and often beyond) the point when redlining is demonstrated. For example, redlining was thought not to take place in the Netherlands until recent research showed that it does. The most recent unambiguous example of redlining comes from the city of Rotterdam where at one point all the major banks (who together dominate the Dutch mortgage market) redlined large parts of the city. Typically, redlined neighbourhoods in Rotterdam are areas with relatively high percentages of low-income people, ethnic minorities, rental housing, and low-priced housing.

Redlining Research in the Twenty-First Century

Empirical research on redlining usually stops after a model has been constructed that shows the best possible fit between the independent variables and the dependent variable (i.e., lending behaviour). There are at least two serious shortcomings to this. First, it is not always clear how independent the so-called 'independent variables' are. Lending behaviour is often seen as a function of income, race, or housing values, but one can also hypothesise that these variables are a function of lending behaviour. Housing values, for example, will likely go down as a result of redlining. The point is that 'independent variables' can depend themselves on lending behaviour, and, thus, it is not appropriate to see lending behaviour as a unidirectional function of these variables. Second, the correlations between lending behaviour and other variables are usually presented as an explanation of redlining. Even if it would be possible to construct truly independent variables, not just in an econometric-theoretical model, but from empirical data, one cannot automatically assume that correlation equals causation.

We should not overlook the multilevel causation of social phenomena: the differences in lending behaviour between neighbourhoods depend not only on the differences between neighbourhoods within the city, but also on processes taking place at different scales. The production of space on the local level is not just dependent on local processes but is a result of the interrelationships between global, national, regional, and local processes. Redlining is not just a function of neighbourhood variables such as income, ethnicity, and housing value; it is also mediated through processes involving institutional frameworks at the national and city levels. One cannot conclude that a high concentration of ethnic minorities or a low average income per household 'explains' redlining. It is important to see how lending behaviour interacts with other processes at different levels and to show why redlining does not take place in neighbourhoods of other cities.

The geographical analysis of redlining has demonstrated that it is important to recognise that the occurrence of redlining is not of a structural nature, nor of an occasional nature, but rather of an endemic nature: it occurs under certain circumstances and conditions. Indeed, redlining is partly of a cyclical nature: it is influenced by the economic trends in the housing and mortgage markets as well as by the applicability of deliberate institutional control measures, whether they are laws or institutional structures such as private or public mortgage insurance. A decision to redline an area is made by lenders on a city level, but their decision is framed not only by the differences between neighbourhoods in the city, but also by processes and institutions at all scales. There is now limited evidence suggesting that the global financial crisis and the decline of subprime lending have given way to the return of redlining and yellowlining, not only in the United States but also in Europe.

Rational choice and neoclassical economics do not explain redlining; they merely assume that redlining is a rational decision taken to cut back risk and to increase profits. There is nothing wrong with this conclusion, but it tells us very little about the issue of where and when redlining takes place. It is only by looking at the processes and institutions located at different levels that we can begin to understand redlining. Future research would benefit not only from focusing on the different geographical levels or scales through which redlining is constituted but also from focusing on the search for actual or de facto redlining, because most of the recent literature has neglected this basic issue. It is incorrect to conclude that redlining does not exist as such merely because a local study has not found any evidence of redlining, just like it would be incorrect to suggest that redlining occurs everywhere because it occurs in one city. For the last three decades, neoclassical economists have dominated redlining research; it is up to human geographers and sociologists to re-place and re-socialise the inherently spatial and social nature of redlining.

See also: Community- and Neighbourhood-Based Organisations in the United States; Social Exclusion and Housing; Subprime Mortgages.

References

Gotham KF (2002) Beyond invasion and succession: School segregation, real estate blockbusting, and the political economy of neighborhood racial transition. *City and Community* 1: 83–111.

Hillier AE (2005) Residential security maps and neighbourhood appraisals: The home owners' loan corporation and the case of Philadelphia. *Social Science History* 29(2): 207–233.

Jackson KT (1985) *Crabgrass Frontier. The Suburbanization of the United States*. New York: Oxford University Press.

Further Reading

Aalbers MB (2011) *Place, Exclusion, and Mortgage Markets*. Oxford, UK: Wiley-Blackwell.

Crossney KB and Bartelt DW (2005) Residential security, risk, and race: The home owners' loan corporation and mortgage access in two cities. *Urban Geography* 26(8): 707–736.

Dedman B (1988) The color of money. Atlanta Journal-Constitution, 1988http://powerreporting.com/color/. (accessed 1 May 2011)

Harvey D and Chatterjee L (1974) Absolute rent and the structuring of space by governmental and financial institutions. *Antipode* 6: 22–36.

Immergluck D (2004) *Credit to the Community. Community Reinvestment and Fair Lending Policy in the United States*. Armonk, NY: Sharpe.

Keating LE, Brazen LM, and Fitterman SF (1992) Reluctant response to community pressure in Atlanta. In: Squires SD (ed.) *From Redlining to Reinvestment: Community Response to Urban Disinvestment*, pp. 170–193. Philadelphia, PA: Temple University Press.

Merton RK (1968) The self-fulfilling prophecy. In: Merton RK (ed.) *Social Theory and Social Structure*, pp. 475–490. New York: The Free Press.

Ross SL and Yinger J (2002) *The Color of Credit: Mortgage Discrimination, Research Methodology, and Fair-Lending Enforcement*. Cambridge, MA: MIT Press.

Squires GD (1992) *From Redlining to Reinvestment: Community Response to Urban Disinvestment*. Philadelphia, PA: Temple University Press.

Stuart G (2003) *Discriminating Risk: The U.S. Mortgage Lending Industry in the Twentieth Century*. Ithaca, NY: Cornell University Press.

Williams P (1978) Building societies and the inner city. *Transactions of the Institute of British Geographers* 3: 23–34.

Wyly EK and Holloway SR (1999) "The color of money" revisited. Racial lending patterns in Atlanta's neighborhoods. *Housing Policy Debate* 10: 555–600.

Policies to Address Social Mix in Communities

G Meen, University of Reading, Reading, UK

© 2012 Elsevier Ltd. All rights reserved.

Glossary

Dissimilarity index This shows the proportion of any minority group that would have to move across local boundaries to give a completely equal distribution of the minority over the city (or other spatial entity). The index ranges from zero (complete evenness) to one (complete segregation). The calculated value is sensitive to the choice of variable (e.g., ethnicity or income, or to spatial aggregate).

Hedonic house prices Hedonic house price models are a widely used regression-based method, whereby the prices of individual houses can be decomposed into the prices of the bundle of characteristics that make up each property. For example, each house has a certain number of bedrooms, lot size, garden, as well as neighbourhood characteristics, and hedonic analysis allows estimation of the prices of each of the attributes that make up the market price.

Monocentric model This is the basic model used in urban economics to explain the distribution of household types – notably the rich and the poor – over space. In the simplest version, all employment is located at the city centre and households have to choose between living close to the centre and, therefore, spend little time in commuting but face high housing costs and living in the suburbs where the reverse holds true.

Panel data Most empirical economic analysis is conducted either on aggregate time-series data – GDP and inflation are examples – or on cross-section samples of individuals or firms at particular points in time. Panel data combine the two approaches and follow a given sample of individuals or firms over time.

Thresholds Thresholds are an example of nonlinearity and in the natural sciences are sometimes used in complexity theory as an example of phases of transition. In economics, they imply that when an area reaches a particular point, the status changes dramatically. So, for example, when poverty falls to a certain level, the area takes off and investment in the area becomes profitable to the private sector. At that stage the area no longer needs government support.

Introduction

Attempts to improve social mix are not new and date back to, at least, the social reform movements in the nineteenth century. Although hard to believe, even the development of the now-exclusive Hampstead Garden Suburb in North London in the early years of the twentieth century was originally intended as a social experiment to provide good-quality housing to people of all social classes. Similarly, the expansion of public housing and the establishment of New Towns after the Second World War in the United Kingdom were seen as attempts to extend social mixing. But, whereas public housing estates were originally designed to contain households from different social backgrounds, including high-skilled workers, public housing now has disproportionate numbers of unskilled tenants living on benefits. These are examples of a general problem. It is extremely difficult for either philanthropists or governments, operating within a market economy, to encourage and maintain genuinely mixed communities. Residential sorting is the most likely outcome in a market economy. Throughout history, the evidence appears to suggest that segregated communities are the norm, with wealthier households being able to outbid the poor for the best locations. Furthermore, poorer households may seek out the areas with lower house prices and higher levels of social spending. Under this view of the world, the policies that are most likely to achieve mixing are those that encourage a narrowing of the income and wealth distributions.

Nevertheless, governments in both Europe and North America do continue to implement housing policies to improve mix as part of wider programmes to reduce the concentration of poverty. A number of potential benefits have been suggested, including the reduction in adverse neighbourhood effects and the promotion of social cohesion. In principle, segregated communities may contribute to worklessness through a spatial mismatch between residence and centres of employment, poor educational attainment among children, increases in crime, and poorer health. A key question, however, is the extent to which these problems are truly an outcome of location or are related to other factors, which are correlated with location. In fact, as discussed below, most of the evidence suggests that, even if the poverty of place is a factor, individual characteristics, including family background, exert an even bigger influence. Separating out the effects of location is one of the main problems for research in this area.

However, there are a number of prior questions to the examination of different policy initiatives. First, what is really meant by social mix? Second, why does theory suggest it is so difficult to achieve mix? Third, is social mix desirable? Each of these issues is discussed and provides perspective on current policies.

What Is Meant by Social Mix?

Social mix, or its opposite, segregation, includes a number of different elements; perhaps most commonly three aspects are considered – ethnicity, income, and housing tenure – although age, for example, is also sometimes taken into account. Of course, these are not independent; low-income households tend to be concentrated in public housing, or in the worst sections of the private rental sector in countries where there is a limited stock of public housing (e.g., parts of the United States and Australia), and ethnic minorities are disproportionately concentrated in low-income neighbourhoods.

Furthermore, mix and segregation are multidimensional. The literature identifies five dimensions: unevenness in the distribution of minorities; isolation from other social or economic groups; clustering into, for example, ghettos; concentration in high-density areas; and the centralisation of minorities within cities. In practice, empirical comparisons have concentrated on the first, using as a summary indicator, the dissimilarity index. The evidence suggests that changes in the index over time are small. In other words, patterns of segregation exhibit a high degree of persistence.

Furthermore, segregation is not the same concept as deprivation. For example, a city or local authority may exhibit a high score on standard measures of deprivation, but, typically, these scores represent an average across the city, whereas segregation (and social mix) refers to the distribution of deprivation (or other variable) within the city. In an extreme case, it is possible that all areas of a city have a high level of deprivation, but the deprivation is equally distributed across all areas. A further confusion in policy arises if the terms social mix, sustainability, and stability are used interchangeably. In policy circles, mixed communities are considered to be stable, but, in fact, as the next section discusses, there is no reason why mixed communities should be stable or sustainable. Indeed, economic models indicate that segregated communities are more likely to emerge as the stable structure. This is the difficult problem for policy, since mixing amounts to fighting against deeply rooted market processes.

Why Are Mixed Communities Difficult to Achieve?

A number of different strands of economic theory suggest that residential segregation is the most likely outcome to emerge over time in a market economy. The result emerges, for example, from the standard monocentric location model. A paradox to which the model provides one possible explanation is the observation that, in many countries, poor households tend to be concentrated together on more expensive inner-city land, whereas richer households are located in suburban areas with cheaper land. The result depends on the responsiveness of housing demand to a change in household income (the income elasticity of demand) relative to how households value travel time. If households want larger suburban homes as their incomes rise, but put a relatively low valuation on the time spent commuting to work (jobs are assumed to be located in the city centre), then the rich are more likely to live away from the city centre, leaving behind poorer households.

In practice, it is not the case that the rich always live in the suburbs. Paris is one example where richer households are concentrated towards the centre. Neighbourhood quality, or externalities, can provide one explanation for the diversity of outcomes. In the basic monocentric model, all areas are physically identical apart from distance to the centre, but neighbourhood quality in terms of area attributes has been found to be very important in hedonic house price studies. These attributes include the quality of schools, pollution levels, water frontages, and crime rates, for example. In Paris, these are of better quality in the centre than in the suburbs, but other cities exhibit the reverse pattern. However, it still remains the case that social mixing is not the norm, even if the location of the rich cannot necessarily be predicted. However, in general, where high-quality neighbourhood characteristics are in short supply, segregation is more likely to occur. One of the policy implications of this is that land-use regulations, by reducing the supply of good-quality housing and neighbourhoods, are more likely to encourage segregation.

Important recent work on segregation traces its foundations to the classic models of Thomas Schelling and concentrates on the effects of interactions in preferences between households. Schelling showed, originally by using coins on a checkerboard, that even if households have a weak preference favouring neighbours of the same type as themselves, high levels of segregation are likely to arise. Both the basic Schelling model and the subsequent developments, typically, assume only two household types, but demonstrate that completely integrated communities, where 50% of neighbours are of the same type, are unlikely to be a stable state. Even if a small number of households move, the whole structure of interrelationships breaks down and segregation emerges as the stable state. This is, clearly, important for policy. Politicians may wish to promote integrated communities (and the reasons are discussed in the next section), but segregation is the stable outcome.

A further strand of research considers the impact of spatial poverty traps, which hinder mixing, because poor households are unable to leave the worst areas and rich households have no wish to move in. Areas suffering from spatial poverty traps typically exhibit low population turnover. Poverty traps again may emerge from the interactions between individuals within an area. This research argues that an individual's behaviour depends not only on his or her own characteristics, but also on the position within a peer group. Under this view, the group has to reach a critical mass before it has any effect. This is sometimes known as a 'threshold'. But once the mass is achieved, the aggregate outcome is that the most deprived areas become locked in because of the disproportionate influence of the group behaviour. The role of peer groups has been discussed in quantitative models of criminal behaviour and schooling, for example. In such models, an individual's educational performance depends partly on the attitude towards education of the peer group. Poor performance by adolescent males is sometimes attributed to this source, and it is therefore unsurprising that it is difficult to attract higher-income households to areas which have a poor school reputation.

A further important feature of spatial poverty traps from the policy perspective is that regeneration expenditures may be effective for areas that experience only a modest level of poverty – government expenditures push areas to a take-off point above the threshold at which private investment becomes profitable. But, for areas with the highest levels of poverty, regeneration expenditures may be ineffective, unless the expenditures are very large indeed. But, given finite resources, the scope for action is limited. Furthermore, a threshold implies that the same policies are not appropriate for all areas. One policy does not fit all.

Spatial physical fixity, which hinders mixing, may also occur because of the development history of an area. Housing is often seen as a factor that contributes to a reduction in household mobility. The key characteristics of the housing stock are longevity and spatial fixity. Particularly, in a cyclical upswing, once the stock is in place, it is difficult to remove. These physical features are enhanced by the nature of property rights and the planning system. This implies that spatial structures in any area, typically, change only slowly – areas are locked into patterns that only vary significantly over decades or even centuries. Therefore, history matters. Furthermore, households often exhibit an attachment to their current location, because they are unwilling to disrupt ties with family and friends. Most household moves are, therefore, short distance. Given the combination of spatial fixity of area structures and household immobility, it is hardly surprising that patterns of wealth and deprivation are difficult to change through policy.

The Desirability of Mixed Communities

Despite the widespread international existence of segregation (this arises partly, but by no means exclusively, from immigration), the desirability of mixed communities is often taken as an article of faith in policy circles. But, even if achievable, the objective has been questioned. The case for government intervention to improve mixing depends on whether place, in itself, has an independent effect on economic and social outcomes – the so-called poverty of place. The standard reasons put forward by economists for government intervention surround market failure: place may have an effect on economic efficiency, there may be externalities that need to be corrected, or governments may wish to intervene on equity grounds. In fact, demonstrating that place unambiguously contributes to any of these is technically difficult.

There is a very large empirical literature that attempts to estimate the effects of neighbourhood on economic outcomes. The majority of this work is of US origin, but since the United States exhibits a higher level of segregation than Europe, it cannot necessarily be assumed that US evidence carries over. A summary of the recent work for both North America and Europe is presented in a special issue of *Housing Studies* in September 2007 (see Further Reading). The fundamental problem in this area is how to separate out spatial effects from other influences. For example, significant neighbourhood variables may be correlated with other omitted or unmeasurable individual characteristics. Neighbourhood may well be correlated with intergenerational factors because the economic or educational performance of children is likely to be determined by the economic status of parents. But, by no means do all data sets typically used to estimate neighbourhood effects include parental information. More generally, in any data set, there are likely to be relevant unmeasurable influences that are correlated with neighbourhood status, leading to biases in measures of the effects of neighbourhood on economic outcomes. Some of the technical problems can, however, be minimised where panel data sets are available. In addition, pseudo-experimental data, derived from the Moving to Opportunity (MTO) programme in the United States, have proved to be particularly fruitful (see Mobility Programmes for Disadvantaged Populations: The Moving to Opportunity Programme). A further problem for empirical research arises from the fact that neighbourhood influences are, by their nature, local, but few large-scale data sets provide local identifiers because of confidentiality issues.

Deconcentrating poverty, that is, moving low-income households from the worst neighbourhoods, does not necessarily lead to aggregate economic efficiency gains, because, in general, the benefits to those who move are offset by the losses to those already living in the better areas. An exception occurs where areas exhibit the thresholds described above. Moreover, for aggregate gains to occur, poor households have to be moved to much better areas, rather than to areas of only slightly lower poverty.

One justification for mixing owners into predominantly social housing areas lies in the potential externalities, arising from social capital. Owners have a greater incentive to maintain the overall quality of neighbourhoods, since the neighbourhood is capitalised into property prices. Therefore, promoting a higher proportion of owners may increase neighbourhood quality by reducing crime or improving educational performance, for example. However, it is not entirely clear whether ownership is simply proxying the time spent in the area. Owners move less frequently than renters and, therefore, have a longer time frame to establish the social ties in an area.

Finally, the sociology, rather than economics, literature has questioned whether mixing in terms of physical proximity truly establishes linkages between different social groups. There appears to be a consensus from the literature that (1) tenure diversification leads to improvements in the physical characteristics of homes and neighbourhoods; (2) there is evidence that insertion of owners has an indirect positive effect on areas through the behaviour of owners, independent of the characteristics of renters. In particular, their increased emphasis on maintenance and on the outlook of their immediate neighbourhood is argued to spill over to everyone's benefit; (3) there is some evidence that diversification may enhance the likelihood and effectiveness of collective action at the community level, and this may be linked to evidence that such policies do indeed reduce stigmatisation and enhance area reputation; (4) there is, however, evidence that social mix is in fact a relatively insignificant explanation of neighbourhood satisfaction – that is, it is more to do with environmental quality, privacy, and perceived safety. Furthermore, while bringing wealthier owners into relatively disadvantaged communities may widen social realms, it is less likely to bring different types of people into contact because relationships in communities are no longer the high-level interactions that they once were.

In summary, evidence remains conflicting on the importance of place, although, on balance, most research would suggest that individual and family circumstances have a stronger influence on the life chances of children, and housing mix is certainly not a panacea for neighbourhood problems. Nevertheless, given the state of play, it would be inappropriate to dismiss the potential importance of neighbourhood in policy.

Policies to Improve Social Mix

Despite the misgivings of academic research, housing policies to improve mix are undertaken in both North America and Europe, although approaches have differed on either side of the Atlantic. Programmes can be broadly classified into three types.

- Regeneration programmes designed to make neighbourhoods more attractive to middle-class households.
- Programmes designed to move low-income households to better-off neighbourhoods.
- Subsidies to moderate-income households in order to persuade them to live in the worst neighbourhoods.

European policy has tended to concentrate on the first of these categories with more emphasis in the United States on the second and third categories. UK approaches have included the use of (1) planning policies; (2) area-based regeneration initiatives; and (3) fiscal incentives. UK planning policy highlights the need to develop mixed tenure communities with priority for development being given to the reuse of urban land (60% of homes are required to be built on brownfield sites). A central element of English policy to promote mixed housing communities comes from Section 106 agreements. Arising from the 1990 Town and Country Planning Act, these allow planning authorities to enter into legally binding agreements with landowners or developers to support the provision of affordable housing, services, or infrastructure (see article Inclusionary Zoning to Support Affordable Housing).

In terms of regeneration, in 2005, the UK government set out a 5-year plan for neighbourhood revitalisation in *Sustainable Communities: People, Places and Prosperity*, which included the key objective:

> Faster progress to narrow the gap between the best and worst off to make sure opportunity and choice are for all, including a new more radical approach to renewal in a small number of very disadvantaged areas with the aim to create neighbourhoods with a more sustainable mix of tenures and incomes and address the problems of worklessness, skills, crime, poor environments and poor health.

In addition, in 2003, the Government created nine Market Renewal Pathfinders in the North of England and the Midlands, which exhibited high vacancy rates and low demand. The Housing Market Renewal schemes set out plans to replace obsolete housing, through demolition, refurbishment, and new building. The programmes' objectives are to close the gap in vacancy rates and house prices between pathfinders and their respective regions by a third by 2010 and to eradicate the problems caused by low demand by 2020 (see article Housing Policy and Regeneration).

Across Europe, a wide variety of area-based initiatives have been implemented, including:

- Physical neighbourhood improvement
- Active marketing and attempts to counteract bad reputations
- Change in tenure and tenure disposals
- Support for private service facilities
- Efforts to combat crime
- Empowerment of local residents and communities
- Direct support for socially weak groups, including immigrants
- Attempts to attract new firms
- Education and job training.

Evaluations have differed in their judgements on these programmes' achievements, but the balance appears to suggest only limited evidence of area improvement. This is, perhaps, unsurprising given the theoretical issues considered earlier, and the expected long time periods before success is likely to be observed, although a large number of case studies do provide some evidence of gains. Furthermore, it needs to be remembered that, even if it is possible to promote mixed tenure developments initially, mixed developments may not remain mixed over time in a market economy. As argued in the third section, theory suggests that segregation is the most likely long-term outcome. But few studies have followed the success of estates over long periods of time, although there is some evidence of permanent gains in those case studies that have been undertaken. Nevertheless, as noted above, broader analyses of patterns of segregation find little evidence that segregation has declined over the past 30 years.

In Europe, there are few examples of fiscal subsidies to attract high-skilled workers to the most deprived areas, despite the existence of incentives to attract industry. Among the few was the United Kingdom's 2001 introduction of Stamp Duty exemptions for properties valued at less than £150 000 in the most deprived wards of the country. In the United States, in the 1980s, a mortgage subsidy scheme was offered in Ohio to first-time buyers that moved to areas where their race was underrepresented. In the mid-1990s, Michigan introduced a 'Neighbourhood Renaissance Zone' where, for designated deprived areas, local property and income taxes were suspended for 12 years. However, perhaps, the most important fiscal subsidy in the United Kingdom was the introduction of the Right to Buy programme in 1980 (see article Privatisation of Social Housing). This provided price discounts to local authority tenants who wished to purchase their currently occupied home. As a result, public housing fell from approximately 30 to 20% of the current housing stock, with a corresponding increase in owner-occupation.

In contrast to Europe, the United States lacks a consistent policy commitment to creating mixed communities, although the decentralised system of US government has created many exceptions. Furthermore, the balance of policy has been designed to move low-income households to better-off neighbourhoods and to subsidise low- to moderate-income households in order to persuade them to live in the worst neighbourhoods. In the United States, vouchers have been an important tool to promote tenant mobility between areas.

The US Gautreaux and Moving to Opportunity Programmes are the best-known examples of attempts to move low-income households to better neighbourhoods through the use of Section 8 housing vouchers (see article Access and Affordability: Housing Vouchers). These programmes have generated a large volume of research designed to assess their success. Their popularity among researchers stems partly from the fact that the programmes approximate natural experiments (although the samples of participants are not entirely random) and provide one approach to overcoming the problems discussed above in identifying the effects of place on economic and social outcomes. By contrast, US Nehemiah developments are attempts to provide below-cost homes, in areas of high poverty, to moderate-income groups, who are becoming owners for the first time. Therefore, these groups gain from becoming owners, but suffer from greater exposure to areas of high crime and poor schooling.

Since 1992, the HOPE VI programme has been an ambitious attempt to redevelop inner-city, high-rise public housing, and to attract middle-income, economically active households to the redesigned areas (see article HOPE VI). The programme attempts to break up concentrations of poverty through the moves of existing tenants to higher-quality areas. The relocated tenants typically receive assistance on other public housing projects or receive vouchers to subsidise rents in the private sector. Given that redevelopment is at lower densities, there is no guarantee that tenants can return to their former areas. The evidence suggests that most tenants that leave with vouchers do end up in better locations.

In all countries, the success of policies to promote mixed communities depends not only on the supply of mixed-tenure dwellings and other initiatives, but also on the factors that influence household moving and location decisions. The evidence suggests that these are multifaceted. In addition to labour market influences, moving propensities depend heavily on age, tenure, housing costs, marital status, and presence of children in the household, for example. Particularly important is the finding that, internationally, moving falls sharply with age. Middle-aged households – especially those with school-aged children – have low moving propensities. Therefore, policies that attempt to attract middle-aged families, currently living in suburban locations, back to cities face problems, even if regeneration policies have improved the quality of the urban core. Internationally, growing cities have relied disproportionately on younger, high-skilled single or couple households without children, whose mobility is high. It may still be the case that, as the life cycles of these households progress, they will follow the traditional pattern of migration to the suburbs, particularly if city housing developments are not accompanied by schools and other infrastructure developments required by families. Nevertheless, there is evidence that improvements to the quality of the neighbourhood are important as a determinant of the location decisions of those who move. Therefore, it is possible that regeneration, planning, and fiscal policies could begin to mitigate future outflows from urban areas.

See also: Access and Affordability: Housing Vouchers; HOPE VI; Housing Policy and Regeneration; Inclusionary Zoning to Support Affordable Housing; Mobility Programmes for Disadvantaged Populations: The Moving to Opportunity Programme; Policies to Address Spatial Mismatch; Privatisation of Social Housing.

Further Reading

Beroube A (2005) *Mixed Communities in England: A US Perspective on Evidence and Policy Prospects*. York, UK: Joseph Rowntree Foundation.

Brueckner J, Thisse J-F, and Zenou Y (1999) Why is central Paris rich and downtown Detroit poor? An amenity-based theory. *European Economic Review* 43: 91–107.

Cheshire PC (2006) Resurgent cities, urban myths and policy hubris: What we need to know? *Urban Studies* 43: 1231–1246.

Galster GC (2002) An economic efficiency analysis of deconcentrating poverty populations. *Journal of Housing Economics* 11: 303–329.

Glaeser EL and Gyourko J (2005) Urban decline and durable housing. *Journal of Political Economy* 113: 345–375.

Glaeser EL, Sacredote B, and Scheinkman JA (1996) Crime and social interactions. *Quarterly Journal of Economics* 111: 507–548.

Kleinhans R (2004) Social implications of housing diversification in urban renewal: A review of recent literature. *Journal of Housing and the Built Environment* 19: 367–390.

Kling JR, Ludwig J, and Katz LF (2005) Neighbourhood effects on crime for female and male youth: Evidence from a randomized housing voucher experiment. *Quarterly Journal of Economics* 120: 87–130.

Massey D and Denton NA (1988) Suburbanization and segregation in US metropolitan areas. *American Journal of Sociology* 94: 592–626.

Schelling T (1971) Dynamic models of segregation. *Journal of Mathematical Sociology* 1: 143–186.

Skifter Andersen H (2002) Can deprived housing areas be revitalised? Efforts against segregation and neighbourhood decay in Denmark and Europe. *Urban Studies* 39: 767–790.

Whitehead CME (2007) Planning policies and affordable housing: England as a successful case study? *Housing Studies* 22: 25–44.

Policies to Address Spatial Mismatch

D Houston, University of St. Andrews, St. Andrews, UK

© 2012 Elsevier Ltd. All rights reserved.

Glossary

Area effects Effects disadvantaging residents of certain neighbourhoods. The main labour market effects are thought to stem from spatial concentrations of worklessness, leading to low aspirations and restricted access to information about employment opportunities.

Job accessibility The geographic proximity of jobs to residential areas.

Job search The process by which people seek jobs, including sources of information used, the role of social networks, and the spatial extent of search. The spatial outcomes of job search are also influenced by employers' hiring practices.

Key worker policies A set of policies aimed at attracting key workers to areas where housing is difficult to access, usually because of affordability. Key workers are usually those providing essential public services such as health professionals and teachers.

Labour market disadvantage A range of adverse outcomes in the labour market including low pay, unemployment, and involuntary economic inactivity.

Metropolitan core The high-density central part of a large metropolitan area, encompassing the city centre/downtown plus the inner/central-city neighbourhoods. The remainder of a metropolitan area is referred to as the ring.

Residential sorting Market forces and housing policies that combine to generate residential segregation within cities, for example, by race, ethnicity, class, or income.

Skills mismatch A mismatch between the skills of a workforce and those demanded by employers.

Social housing A term used in the United Kingdom to refer to rental housing subsidies by the state allocated according to housing need rather than on the open market.

Spatial mismatch A mismatch between the location of workers and jobs.

Spatial mismatch hypothesis The view that labour market disadvantage among African Americans in the United States is partly explained by racial segregation restricting access to suburban housing markets close to employment growth in the rings of metropolitan areas.

Spatial Mismatch

The term spatial mismatch refers to a mismatch between the location of workers and the location of jobs. This can occur at a variety of spatial scales, but the term usually refers to mismatches within metropolitan areas in developed countries. The spatial mismatch hypothesis was originally framed with respect to African Americans who are disproportionately found in central-city neighbourhoods, with residents dislocated from – and unable to commute to – low-skilled and manual employment, much of which has moved to metropolitan rings and beyond over the past 40–50 years.

Spatial mismatch is often presented as an alternative to skills mismatch and racial discrimination by employers in explaining labour market disadvantage in inner-city neighbourhoods, particularly among African Americans in the United States and ethnic minority groups more generally. The skills mismatch perspective sees metropolitan areas as relatively self-contained labour markets within which workers can commute freely. Consequently, according to the skills mismatch perspective, spatial concentrations of labour market disadvantage simply reflect the residential sorting of different racial, ethnic, and socioeconomic groups whose differential ability to compete for jobs explains spatial variation in labour market disadvantage, with neighbourhoods viewed merely as containers of individuals with certain labour market characteristics.

The spatial mismatch hypothesis originates from a seminal article by John Kain published in 1968, which stressed the impact of employment decentralisation on African Americans who were unable to follow the jobs moving to metropolitan rings because of residential segregation in housing markets. Since then, the spatial mismatch hypothesis has been broadened to consider other ethnic minority groups, as well as white central-city residents. Evidence is mixed but a degree of consensus has emerged – based on more robust methods that have been used since the 1990s – that there is a moderate spatial mismatch penalty in terms of labour market outcomes for African Americans and low-skilled central/inner-city residents. The spatial mismatch penalty varies between cities, with it tending to be strongest in larger metropolitan areas; in cities where employment decentralisation has been most marked; where residential segregation is at its greatest; in cities with less developed public transit systems; and for groups and neighbourhoods with the lowest auto/car ownership rates.

Since the late 1990s, the spatial mismatch hypothesis has been applied beyond the United States, mainly in European settings, particularly the United Kingdom (e.g., Fieldhouse and Gould, 1998). Although not explicitly using the spatial mismatch label, a number of Australian studies dating back to the early 1980s, and more recently, examine the impact of job accessibility on inner-city residents (e.g., Yates et al., 2005). Findings in Europe and Australia also point to a moderate spatial mismatch penalty on inner-city residents, particularly the ethnic minority groups, although the precise mechanisms producing segregation may differ slightly from country to country. For example, the role of UK social housing in restricting migration between districts – even within the same metropolitan county – has been noted, although this effect has also been detected in relation to public housing in the United States. Overall, it appears that some groups characterised by low residential and transport mobility – particularly unskilled workers, lone parents, part-time workers, women, and ethnic minorities – disproportionately suffer adverse labour market consequences due to spatial mismatch.

Methods to test the spatial mismatch hypothesis have had to contend with a number of issues. First, although conceptually simple, measuring job accessibility is complex with indices variously taking account of some or all of the following: road distance versus crow-path distance, travel time versus distance, mode of travel, car ownership, more distant jobs carrying less weight, and the level of competition for jobs from other residents and in-commuters. Second, ambiguity surrounds cause and effect with regard to, on the one hand, progression in the labour market and, on the other, moving to the suburbs. Some studies have attempted to circumvent this issue by focusing on youth who have not yet altered their residential location, and by assessing the labour market impacts of employer relocations and housing mobility programmes. Third, comparisons of commuting mobility across different racial, ethnic, and socioeconomic groups exclude the unemployed (because they do not commute), with the consequence that the commuting propensity of high-unemployment groups, such as ethnic minority groups, is overestimated. It has been argued that failure to adequately take account of these issues biases results systematically against finding evidence in support of the spatial mismatch hypothesis. For a review of these methodological issues and their implications for the spatial mismatch hypothesis, see Houston (2005).

The spatial mismatch hypothesis originally stressed the role of racial segregation in preventing residential adjustment through migration to areas of employment growth in the suburbs. In the United States, exclusionary zoning policies helped to create relatively homogeneous affluent suburbs by acting as a vehicle for racial discrimination in suburban housing markets that impeded the residential mobility of racial and ethnic minorities. However, this has been criticised as lacking theoretical underpinnings and offering a rather partial view of the spatial dynamics of metropolitan housing and labour markets. It is heavily influenced by neoclassical economics which sees migration as a mechanism through which labour demand and supply come into balance across space. Research by geographers has tended to give more emphasis to commuting constraints, while sociologists point to the restructuring of capitalism and urban development, as well as social networks, access to information about job vacancies, and spatial aspects of employers' hiring practices. In sum, what could be defined as spatial mismatch research has identified four broad mechanisms through which spatial mismatch can have adverse labour market impacts on certain groups: (1) employment decentralisation; (2) residential segregation/immobility; (3) commuting; and (4) job search and hiring.

Through time, spatial mismatch research has increasingly connected with other literatures on the welfare implications of residential segregation in general, and on the consequences of spatially concentrated social disadvantage in particular. For example, Kain, the pioneer of the spatial mismatch hypothesis, has argued in a 2004 article that today the most significant welfare implication of residential segregation for African Americans is low educational attainment associated with attendance at underperforming inner-city schools. Other research has emphasised that area effects resulting from spatially concentrated social disadvantage serve to limit social networks that can provide access to important labour market information and workforce intermediaries capable of linking people with jobs.

A feature of urban change in the twenty-first century has been some signs of economic recovery in a number of metropolitan cores in the United States and Europe. Although criticised for being characterised by large-scale commercial property development at one extreme and as soft initiatives such as cultural festivals at the other, there has nevertheless been some modest employment growth in metropolitan cores in recent years. A challenge has been in helping central/inner-city residents access the skilled jobs being created, for example, in financial services. Meanwhile, the bulk of other jobs being created in metropolitan cores are unattractive, low-paid, low-status positions servicing new high-paid professional elites. Many of the latter types of jobs are being filled by new waves of immigrants, for example, from the Asia Pacific into the United States and from Eastern Europe into the United Kingdom (see article Immigration and Housing Policy).

Policy Responses to Spatial Mismatch

Spatial mismatch is of policy concern for two reasons. First, labour surpluses in some locations contribute to the labour market disadvantage and resulting poverty and social exclusion experienced by some residents. For example, central- and inner-city locations can have concentrations of unemployment, low earnings, and social problems. Second, other locations may experience labour shortages which can serve to restrict economic efficiency and growth. For example, London relies on international immigration to fill both skilled and unskilled job vacancies, and has a Key Worker scheme to assist key public sector workers (mainly nurses and teachers) in securing affordable housing.

Four broad policy responses to spatial mismatch have been identified in the literature: (1) promote economic regeneration in central/inner-city locations; (2) encourage residential mobility; (3) improve transportation; and (4) enhance job search. Each of these is now considered in turn, reviewing evidence on the relative merits of each and drawing on examples from the United States and the United Kingdom by way of illustration.

Promote Economic Regeneration in Central/Inner-City Locations

Various policies have been put in place to combat the effects of economic decline in metropolitan cores, although few have the sole or even explicit aim of combating labour market disadvantage arising from employment decentralisation and the resulting spatial mismatch. The main concern has been with maintaining city centres as viable commercial, retail, and leisure hubs, particularly in Europe where the notion of the Compact City has been favoured on grounds of environmental protection and social cohesion. Less emphasis has been given to industrial development compared to commercial development within metropolitan cores. Indeed, many economic development policies encourage the movement of industry to out-of-town industrial parks including, in the UK context, New Towns built just beyond metropolitan areas. Nevertheless, some commercial developments in metropolitan cores in recent years have generated employment, although mostly in nonmanual occupations in services such as finance, retail, and leisure.

Policies to promote the economic regeneration of downtown areas and metropolitan cores more generally have been viewed with less enthusiasm in the United States than in Europe. In Europe, a number of factors come together to make stronger urban economic regeneration policies a slightly more appealing prospect than in the United States. First, most European states are ideologically comfortable with a strong role for the state in influencing patterns of economic development, not only for reasons of social protection, but also to help promote economic success, for example, through the creation of suitable land and infrastructure for industry. Second, European cities are historically of higher density and more mixed land use than their North American counterparts, and this balanced and compact urban structure is thought in Europe to be worth sustaining because it promotes social cohesion and environmental benefits, such as high levels of public transport/transit use. Third, land availability outside the existing built-up areas of many European cities is limited due to planning controls and the protection of prime agricultural land. For a review of these contrasts in urban development between Europe and the United States, see Downs (1999).

Although developments in inner-city areas tend to be retail or commercial rather than industrial, there have been substantial developments in some UK metropolitan cores throughout the 1980s and 1990s with large-scale state assistance through Urban Development Corporations (UDCs). One of the most conspicuous was perhaps the regeneration of the London Docklands with the creation of upmarket housing and commercial office space around Canary Wharf. Adjacent to London's greatest concentration of labour market disadvantage in the east end, the Docklands' redevelopment has been much criticised for not engaging with – or particularly benefiting – local communities. Although the UDCs were wound up in the early part of the twenty-first century, their legacy of land and infrastructure improvements endures and many British cities have followed them with various forms of partnerships between local government and private developers to help facilitate further development. For example, the Thames Gateway in London levering in substantial sums of public and private investment in housing and leisure developments, and Glasgow Harbour bringing new commercial developments and to a lesser extent housing to the north banks of the River Clyde, once the location of major shipyards. One limitation of UK UDCs has been their geographical concentration on city centre or downtown areas, with relatively little development effort in wider metropolitan cores encompassing inner-city neighbourhoods where concentrations of labour market disadvantage are found.

Evidence indicates that only a minority of jobs generated in recent years in metropolitan cores have gone to residents of adjacent inner-city neighbourhoods, with many of the jobs created being professional, skilled, and in the service sector. Furthermore, in the United Kingdom, increasing proportions of low-skilled jobs (such as cleaners and personal services) in these locations are now going to recent immigrants, particularly those from central and east European countries that have recently joined the European Union (EU) with its freedom of movement within the EU. Economic development strategies in US metropolitan areas have also been criticised for not delivering sufficient benefit to central-city residents.

Encourage Residential Mobility

In contrast to the United Kingdom, where the economic regeneration of key metropolitan cores has featured more strongly, the dominant policy response in the United States to spatial mismatch has been to encourage residential mobility to the suburbs, particularly of African Americans. This reflects the characterisation of central-city social problems in the United States as the result of racial segregation and immobility, rather than one of urban economic decline and skills mismatch, the more common perspective in the United Kingdom and the rest of Europe.

A number of large-scale residential mobility programmes have been introduced in recent decades, most notably the Gautreaux and Yonkers assisted housing programmes in the United States, and postwar slum-clearance programmes in the United Kingdom (although the latter predate significant employment loss in metropolitan cores and were primarily addressing housing squalor and overcrowding rather than labour market disadvantage). Following the apparent success of the Gautreaux and Yonkers programmes, the US Department of Housing and Urban Development (HUD) implemented a scheme of housing vouchers to promote residential mobility, and more recently established a number of Moving to Opportunity demonstration projects (see articles Access and Affordability: Housing Vouchers and Mobility Programmes for Disadvantaged Populations: The Moving to Opportunity Programme). In contrast, British slum-clearance projects are generally thought to have been less successful due to the negative impacts on community cohesion and social capital.

A number of studies have found evidence of improvements in labour market participation under the Gautreaux programme, the HUD housing voucher scheme, and Moving to Opportunity demonstration projects. However, the impact on educational attainment and on social networks (a potential source of information about jobs), in contrast, is generally more limited, with studies showing little or no improvement among those moved to suburbs as compared to those moved to central-city locations and as compared to those not relocated.

Improve Transportation

Most groups displaying high levels of worklessness also have a low propensity to commute, for example, the unskilled, ethnic minorities, and women. A policy response in both the United States and the United Kingdom has therefore been to subsidise or directly provide transport, although these are often locally based and have not been adopted as mainstream national policies. Travel schemes are often focused on welfare or benefit recipients as a means to encourage them to move into employment. For example, travel vouchers are given to people in some workfare programmes in the United States, and some local schemes in the United Kingdom provide the unemployed with time-limited allowances for travel costs, or loans to subsidise the purchase of motorised transport. The success of these schemes has been modest. Commuting may have to fit in with complex activity schedules which might include, for example, taking children to/from school, attending medical appointments, and caring for relatives. These schemes have also paid insufficient attention to the quality of public transport available, in particular its suitability for servicing the reverse commute from central city to suburb.

In other European countries, there has been much greater public expenditure on public transport infrastructure, with many European cities outside the United Kingdom having well-developed tram, light rail, or suburban railway networks. Employers themselves and consortia of employers also provide transport, for example, 'works buses' with central pick-up and drop-off points. Some large employers have dedicated public transport infrastructure, for example, IBM's production facility in Greenock, some 30 km from Greater Glasgow, has its own railway station.

Enhance Job Search

Proximity or good transport matter, but on their own are not always enough to bring workless people into contact with jobs. Vacancies, even for low-skilled work, and unemployment can exist cheek by jowl in and around the inner city. Poor job-vacancy information is related to the notion of 'area effects' whereby geographic concentrations of worklessness are thought to have a knock-on effect, for example, through restricted access to social networks that provide information about jobs and contacts with workforce intermediaries capable of linking people with jobs. Probabilities of entering employment are lower due to limited contact with people in employment, and restricted access to not only information about specific job vacancies but also wider information on pay, conditions, and security at different local employers.

A central thrust of workfare in the United States and welfare-to-work policies in the United Kingdom is to widen the spatial extent of welfare and benefit recipients' job search. As well as providing guidance and assistance in performing job search, sanctions are in place to compel welfare and benefit recipients to accept job offers at increasing distances from their place of residence. These supply-side policies have been criticised for downplaying the important role of the nature and attractiveness of entry-level jobs and the hiring preferences and practices of employers on the demand side. Specifically, the spatial outcomes of job search are also influenced by employers' preferences or prejudices, for example, preferring people who live close by or screening out applicants from stigmatised neighbourhoods.

Other schemes have been introduced to improve the matching of local people to local jobs more generally, particularly when a new development takes place. For example, the Braehead and Silvermile retail developments in Govan and Pollok, two high-unemployment neighbourhoods in Glasgow, were both set targets by local regeneration companies (which had played a role in securing the developments including financial pump-priming development sites) for recruiting workers from certain postcode areas within the surrounding area.

Conclusions

In the United Kingdom, spatial mismatch has not been recognised as a substantial part of the problem producing labour market disadvantage, or at least not one that politicians of any political colour have an appetite to tackle. Nevertheless, a more general concern for maintaining the economic viability of metropolitan cores motivated the activities of UDCs in the 1980s and 1990s that have ameliorated some of the effects of employment decentralisation.

In contrast, policy-makers in the United States have recognised spatial mismatch as requiring intervention. However, the dominant policy response has been to promote residential mobility, particularly of African Americans to suburban locations, rather than to alter the location of jobs. This strategy has not solely been about tackling spatial mismatch but also been about removing people from what are perceived to be socially dysfunctional communities with adverse 'area effects' on educational attainment, aspirations, and access to labour market information. The residential mobility strategy in the United States has had some benefit in labour market outcomes but less so in educational attainment and in providing access to social networks, although this may improve in the future as younger generations come of working age.

Schemes to improve transportation have tended to focus on individuals, through providing vouchers, subsidies, or loans to improve access to transportation. These schemes have not always taken sufficient account of the quality of public transport available, or the wider transport needs individuals have beyond commuting. Furthermore, these schemes tend to be local and have not been adopted as a key plank of national strategies to deal with labour market disadvantage or spatial mismatch.

Enhancing job search underpins initial interventions with participants in workfare programmes in the United States and in welfare-to-work policies in the United Kingdom. While producing some short-run improvements in labour market outcomes for individuals, these often result in the displacement of other workers from elsewhere in the labour market. Critics argue that policies aimed at improving matching of workless individuals to jobs need to engage more with employers and consider their hiring preferences and practices.

Spatial mismatch may be less important than neighbourhood skills profiles in explaining geographically uneven patterns of disadvantage in the labour market. However, the effects of spatial mismatch are nevertheless thought to be deep-seated and difficult to tackle. Although policy efforts can have modest impacts, individuals with poor access to transport and low residential mobility will surely require geographically proximate jobs if they are to participate in the labour market. These people may be beyond the reach of current policy settings.

See also: Access and Affordability: Housing Vouchers; Immigration and Housing Policy; Key Worker Housing Policies; Mobility Programmes for Disadvantaged Populations: The Moving to Opportunity Programme; Social Housing and Employment; Spatial Mismatch.

References

Downs A (1999) Contrasting strategies for the economic development of metropolitan areas in the United States and Western Europe. In: Summers AA, Chesire P, and Senn L (eds.) *Urban Change in the United States and Western Europe. Comparative Analysis and Policy*, pp. 15–54. Washington, DC: The Urban Institute Press.

Fieldhouse EA and Gould MI (1998) Ethnic minority unemployment and local labor market conditions in Great Britain. *Environment and Planning A* 30(5): 833–853.

Kain J (1968) Housing segregation, Negro unemployment and metropolitan segregation. *Quarterly Journal of Economics* 82: 175–197.

Kain J (2004) A pioneer's perspective on the spatial mismatch literature. *Urban Studies* 41(1): 7–32.

Houston D (2005) Methods to test the spatial mismatch hypothesis. *Economic Geography* 81(4): 407–434.

Yates J, Randolph B, Holloway D, and Murray D (2005) Housing affordability, occupation and location in Australian cities and regions. Positioning Paper. Australian Housing and Urban Research Institute. http://apo.org.au/research/housing-affordability-occupation-and-location-australian-cities-and-regions (accessed 1 October 2009).

Further Reading

Adams J, Greig M, and McQuaid R (2002) Mismatch in local labour markets in central Scotland: The neglected role of demand. *Urban Studies* 39(8): 1399–1416.

Blumenberg E and Manville M (2004) Beyond the spatial mismatch: Welfare recipients and transportation policy. *Journal of Planning Literature* 19(2): 182–205.

Chapple K (2006) Overcoming mismatch: Beyond dispersal, mobility and development strategies. *Journal of the American Planning Association* 72(3): 322–336.

Cooke TJ and Shumway JM (1991) Developing the spatial mismatch hypothesis: Problems of accessibility to employment for low-wage central city labor. *Urban Geography* 12: 310–323.

Ihlanfeldt KR and Sjoquist DL (1998) The spatial mismatch hypothesis: A review of recent studies and their implications for welfare reform. *Housing Policy Debate* 9(4): 849–892.

McLafferty S and Preston V (1996) Spatial mismatch and employment in a decade of restructuring. *Professional Geographer* 48(4): 420–431.

Morrison P (2005) Unemployment and urban labour markets. *Urban Studies* 42(12): 2261–2288.

Ong P (1998) Subsidised housing and work among welfare recipients. *Housing Policy Debate* 9(4): 775–794.

Rosenbaum JE and Harris LE (2001) Residential mobility and opportunities: Early impacts of the moving to opportunity demonstration program in Chicago. *Housing Policy Debate* 12(2): 321–346.

Policies to Promote Housing Choice in Transition Countries

M Lux, The Institute of Sociology, Prague, Czech Republic

© 2012 Elsevier Ltd. All rights reserved.

Glossary

Condominium A form of housing tenure in which parts (individual units) of an apartment building are privately owned, while the common areas, such as the hallways, the heating system, the elevators, the exterior, are owned in the form of ideal shares by all unit owners and thus jointly managed by the association of unit owners.

Demand-side subsidy Also called a 'subsidy per head', this is a public subsidy that encourages the demand for housing consumption by allocating cash allowances or grants directly to tenants and owner-occupiers. This subsidy most commonly comes in the form of a housing allowance (also housing benefit, housing voucher): a cash allowance paid to low-income households to cover a portion of their housing costs. An allowance increases housing affordability and the housing demand.

Housing tenure The legal arrangements governing a person's right to live in a particular house or flat; the legal terms of occupancy of a housing unit. The most common categories of housing tenure are rental housing, in which rent is paid to a landlord, and owner occupancy. There also exist mixed forms of tenure, such as cooperative housing. Tenure security refers to the level of security that the law grants the occupant of a housing unit, especially with regard to proprietary rights, the term of occupation, notice of eviction, and initial and subsequent rent setting in rental tenure.

Restitution of property The return of property, especially real estate that was expropriated by socialist regimes after the Second World War, to its previous owners or their descendants; in several transition countries legislation was introduced to enable this process.

Right-to-buy A central – governmental or parliamentary – policy, usually adopted in legislation, giving tenants in public housing the right to buy and obtain full ownership of the rental housing they are currently living in, and to do so under special conditions, usually at a preferential price.

Supply-side subsidy Also called a 'brick and mortar' subsidy; this is a public subsidy that directly promotes the supply (construction) of new housing and in particular the supply (construction) of new social rental housing. Such subsidies are distributed to municipalities, not-for-profit housing landlords, private landlords, and private owners, and they are provided in many different forms, most commonly as preferential loans and grants for new housing construction.

Transition country A post-socialist country in Europe or Asia that is going through extensive institutional, economic, social, and political reforms (transition) aimed at changing the country's former social system, based on a centrally planned economy and one-party political rule, into a system based on a market economy, democracy, and multipartyism. The term 'transition' is sometimes criticised as a universalistic linear concept. Owing to the diversity of real reform activities among transition countries, some scientists instead use the term 'transformation'.

Introduction

Tenure choice presupposes not just the formal existence of various legal housing options, but also a minimum stock in each housing tenure category, ensuring its accessibility and, in theory, a 'real', unbiased, free choice between housing tenures. The main housing tenure forms are owner-occupied housing and tenancy, and tenancy is often subdivided into social (public) and private tenancies.

In most post-socialist states, the mass 'give-away' privatisation of public housing into the hands of sitting tenants ate away at public rental housing so in the end it formed just a marginal share of the housing stock. The cuts in housing policy expenditures after 1990 left new social (public) housing construction marginal in scale and incapable of compensating for the loss of public housing due to privatisation. Private rental housing emerged most often from nothing, except in a few countries where specific restitution of residential properties was introduced. In some countries, the sector grew only gradually, often as a part of the grey economy; in other more developed states the supply of private rental housing has developed surprisingly rapidly. However, for several reasons, described in more detail below, rental housing never became a viable long-term alternative to owner-occupied housing up to now. While the socialist governments earlier had introduced explicit measures favouring one

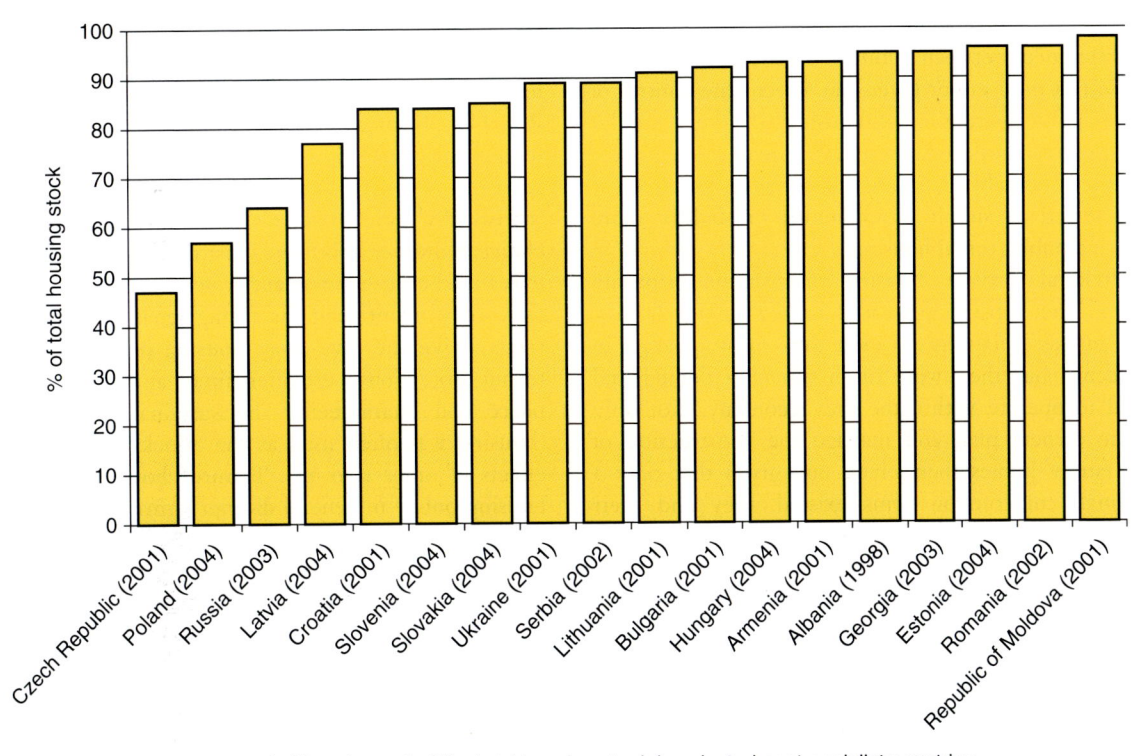

Figure 1 Share of owner-occupied housing out of the total housing stock in selected post-socialist countries.
Source: Data from Housing Statistics in the European Union 2005/2006, Bulletin of Housing Statistics for Europe and North America 2006 (UN/ECE), Dübel (2005).

tenure category, namely public rental housing, the post-socialist governments also maintained a biased tenure policy, this time favouring owner-occupied housing. The changes in the tenure structure, which favoured one form of housing tenure (**Figure 1**), left little room for the emergence of real tenure choice in transition societies.

Tenure Policy During Socialism

Even during the socialist period, several official forms of tenure existed that formally enabled the existence of housing tenure choice. The highest priority in public subsidisation went to public (semipublic) rental housing, the construction costs of which were fully covered by the state budget. In most countries the state (municipality) was the landlord of public housing, but there were several exceptions to this (such as in former Yugoslavia), where state enterprises functioned as public landlords. The principle of socialist housing policy was to allot people public (semipublic) flats for free 'according to their needs' and the rent was fixed at a low level. Tenants were given a 'deed' to the flat that granted them unlimited occupancy rights. No one spoke about 'renting' but about the 'personal use' of a flat. 'Personal use' became a form of tenure distinct from renting a flat: it could be inherited or transferred to relatives, or the deed-holders could exchange their deeds and flats with each other. Deed-holding tenants arrogated the right to renovate and repair the flat as they pleased, or even to sublease the flat without the owner's permission. When flats of different implicit value were exchanged deed-holding tenants in more valuable flats appropriated the right to request financial compensation for themselves to offset the difference in value. This specific form of tenure later came to be called 'quasi-homeownership'. Its resemblance to owner-occupied housing was further confirmed by the fact that this public rental sector exhibited an extremely low level of turnover. There are a number of rational explanations for the existence of this specific, 'unofficial' tenure: it represented a way of coping with the inadequacies of socialist housing (poor maintenance, an ineffective allocation system) and served as a substitute for the intergenerational exchange of housing wealth.

Cooperative housing tenure also emerged in several socialist states (Poland, former Czechoslovakia, and Russia). The costs of cooperative housing construction were covered by contributions from the cooperative members, state subsidies, and long-term, low-interest loans from state banks. However, socialist housing cooperatives differed from their counterparts in democratic countries. Housing development was undertaken by large co-ops, which over time ended up managing a stock of flats that sometimes numbered in the thousands. The differences between public and cooperative housing were in fact only minor given the direct state control of finance and construction of housing, the very similar tenant rights in both tenures, and the 'quasi-homeownership' status of public housing; co-op housing has often been viewed as simply synonymous to slightly more expensive public rental housing.

Individual (private) housing construction primarily involved the construction of detached family homes. What 'market' relations did exist were most apparent in this sector, but they were often officially denied and tended to operate within the grey economy. Not only did the owners plan and manage the construction of these family homes themselves, but, given that only a few small construction firms existed, they and their families also often had to perform a substantial amount of the actual construction work themselves. Official homeownership (often referred to as 'personal ownership' rather than the ideologically contentious 'private ownership') was thus legally restricted to detached housing – again with some exceptions, such as Bulgaria, where tenants allocated newly constructed, publicly financed flats were soon granted 'personal ownership' of them.

Tenures During Transition – Rental Housing

The de facto quasi-homeownership status of public rental housing had a substantial impact on people's expectations and led to the formation of powerful social norms that proved to be resistant to the political and economic changes after 1990: first, people expected that after briefly looking for a job they would obtain housing and that housing would remain their family home for life; second, the costs of housing, and rental housing especially, should not be too much of a burden on the household budget; and third, housing was supposed to give people a strong sense of personal security. From this point of view, the large-scale, give-away privatisations of public housing that after 1990 transformed transition societies from nations of tenants into nations of homeowners can be regarded as just the reconfirmation in a market environment of social norms and expectations inherited from the past. Moreover, if rental housing tenure was to compete with the owner-occupied alternative after 1990, it would also have to meet these norms and expectations, which even the new generation had inherited from their parents.

Owing to continuing rent controls and strong tenant protections, in a few transition countries rental housing continued to form a substantial share of the urban housing stock; this was either due to the voluntary decision of tenants not to become homeowners (Russia, Latvia) or to the absence of right-to-buy legislation (Poland). A few countries also applied 'in kind' property restitution to deal with the problem of the many apartment buildings that had been expropriated during the socialist period (Czech Republic, Estonia). This not only left rental housing tenure intact, but also formally created its private rental segment. The systems in these countries then were 'statistically' able to offer the population wider tenure choice. However, this formal distinction was less apparent in reality, because the tenant protections and rent controls were only maintained for sitting tenants (running contracts). Like the give-away housing privatisation, these tenant protections were often aimed at maintaining social peace and guaranteeing the sustainability of reforms (housing was often used as the 'shock absorber' for the effects of other reforms). Tenure choice policy or any housing policy in general did not figure among the priorities on the political agenda: no formal protections (except partially in Poland) were introduced for new tenancies (the term of contract, the initial rent setting, and subsequent rent reviews in contract extensions). The very weak tenure security and free market rent setting (initial and reviewed) for new tenancies thus contrasted sharply with the extremely strong tenure security and 'first-generation' rent controls applied to running tenancies.

There were some rational reasons for these circumstances. When the markets were immature and there were no price/rent statistics, it was almost impossible to determine the right type of regulation for new tenancies. Moreover, given existing gaps in the legislation, the weak power of law, and the increasing duration of judicial proceedings, both public and private landlords were already facing severe risks, and poorly implemented regulation would only have exacerbated those risks. Many private rental contracts were signed illegally or informally (e.g., the subletting of public housing, or private landlords' avoidance of written contracts to make eviction easier and to evade tax on rental income) and new regulations would have further increased the incentives for less-formal arrangements.

The absence of regulations governing new tenancies had two main consequences: the supply of private renting grew substantially in several transition states (the Baltic states, Central European countries, and Russia), but simultaneously there was a profound structural change in the demand for rental housing. These processes helped to clear the market, but also strengthened the one-way orientation of housing demand in favour of owner-occupied housing.

In countries with a high share of apartment housing, with condominium legislation, and with a relatively sufficient amount of housing (such as Lithuania, Estonia, Poland, Czech Republic, Slovakia), the number of flats rented by private landlords started to grow quickly, especially in the capital cities. The supply of private rental flats grew so fast that this market segment was soon larger than the amount of residual public rental housing remaining after privatisation. Most private landlords of 'market' rental housing operated on a small scale; they were families who through inheritance (or privatisation) had obtained ownership of a flat that they did not need for their own use and decided to keep it as an investment. Professional investors also quickly emerged, but small-scale property owners remained the most common type of landlord in private residential real estate in transition countries. These landlords offered housing to managers, working migrants, people who had just become divorced or separated, young people who had just left home, and students. The availability of this housing helped to support labour mobility and tenure choice, especially among young people.

However, the perceived role of private rental tenure was shaped by the absence of regulation, the existence of a large illegal rental segment (oral, informal contracts), and 'high' level of market rents ('high' either objectively, as a result of the initial shortage, or subjectively, in relation to inherited expectations). When confronted with the social norms of high security and low rent that people continue to attach to housing, private rental tenure, although it afforded more choice and greater mobility, failed to gain a popularity and came to be viewed as just a transitional and residual form of housing. Rental housing on the whole lost its former standing as a form of life-long housing, and, except for public (social) housing, it came to represent just a short stop on the way towards owing one's housing; in super-homeownership countries this form of tenure even came to be stigmatised. It retained character of more permanent 'residual' housing only for foreign migrants flowing into the country from abroad or for people with insufficient or unstable incomes who are unable to get mortgage finance, even with the help of public subsidies.

This perception (demand structure) did not change even when markets were stabilised by additional supply and when written legal contracts came into standard use (Poland, Estonia, Lithuania, Slovakia, and Czech Republic). The insecurity involved in renting a flat related to the term of the contract (most landlords continued to offer just short-term contracts) and the subsequent rent reviews (the need to renegotiate almost every year) put an unbearable amount of risk on the shoulders of tenants, especially when compared to the security provided by owner-occupied housing. It is sometimes argued that the insecurity and unaffordability of housing for young couples has dramatically shifted demographic trends, causing a record decrease in the fertility rate and rapid ageing of the population of transition societies. Owing to constraints on demand, in some countries the supply of private rental housing already exceeded demand at the end of the first decade of the new century, and private rental yields significantly dropped (Lithuania, Czech Republic, to some extent also Poland and Estonia).

In transition countries the municipalities (and in a few countries later also not-for-profit housing associations) continued to offer secure tenancy and preferential rents to low-income or priority households, but the number of flats newly allocated was extremely low because of the small size of the sector, the slump in public housing construction, and the low turnover of tenants. The residual public housing was not privatised usually because of its poor quality and bad location, that is, its low property value. Even two decades after the change in regimes, social rental housing remained only an opened challenge rather than an existing alternative: in every transition country only a very small portion of the rental housing stock explicitly serves those in housing and social need. Some transition states have introduced or recovered supply-side subsidies for the construction of social rental housing and routed them to the municipalities (Czech Republic, Slovakia, later also Hungary and Romania); other states have instead passed not-for-profit housing legislation and established grant systems to encourage the construction of not-for-profit social rental housing by private social landlords (Poland and Slovenia) or have established other forms of private–public partnership in this field (Russia). However, up to 2010 only a negligible amount of new social housing had been built in most transition countries (except in Russia, Poland, and the Czech Republic) and policy measures are constantly changing (see more in article Social Housing Landlords: Post-Socialist).

Rental housing tenure has suffered an additional disadvantage as a result of the poor effect that housing allowances had on rental housing demand. Many countries introduced housing allowances only recently, while in others, where they were introduced in the 1990s (e.g., Estonia, Poland, Romania, Czech Republic, Slovakia, and Hungary), housing allowances served rather as additional social support for low-income families living in rent-controlled housing than as a real demand-side subsidy that respects the market reality of new tenancies. The formulae used to calculate housing allowances failed to take into account the higher, market rents of new tenancies, so their main goal was not to stimulate demand but rather to maintain the current housing standards of already-existing tenant households.

Tenures During Transition – Owner-Occupied Housing

Since most voters in transition countries became homeowners, public housing became residualised, and private renting failed to establish itself as a viable alternative in the public eye, most governments focused their support on owner-occupied housing. The bias in policy measures also influenced the freedom of tenure choice, which itself was reformulated as a choice between different types of owner-occupied housing and different types of housing finance. Instead of a neutral choice between different types of housing tenure and a tenure-neutral public policy, there appeared a typically steep, socially constructed housing ladder in post-socialist countries and policy that explicitly favoured one form of tenure – private homeownership.

Transition countries introduced a number of measures to make it easier to acquire owner-occupied housing: down-payment grants (Hungary, Romania, and Slovakia), preferential loans, often granted through specialised state housing funds/agencies (Romania, Czech Republic, Slovakia, Albania, Slovenia, Lithuania, and others), interest subsidies on mortgage loans (Czech Republic, Poland, Lithuania, Hungary, and Slovakia), interest subsidies on mortgage bonds (Hungary), tax credits on housing savings (Poland), tax credits on housing loan repayments (Hungary), tax relief on interest on housing loans (Czech Republic, Russia, Romania, Serbia, Armenia, and others), tax deductions for the costs of purchasing/building a housing unit (Russia, a lump-sum deduction in Poland), tax exemptions for profits from mortgage banking (Czech Republic and Slovakia), premiums on housing savings (Czech Republic, Slovakia, Hungary, Latvia, Croatia, and Slovenia), and other measures. In many cases, these subsidies were limited to new housing construction; some of these measures were later redesigned or abolished.

Despite the preferential support given to owner-occupied housing acquisition, it took at least 10 years for market-based housing finance to actually develop (since the year 2000). The delay was caused by the unstable macroeconomic situation in the transition countries in the 1990s, and by the banking crises, high inflation, high unemployment rate, legislative gaps, unreliable property registration, and a lack of competition among mortgage lenders. However, since 2000 mortgage financing has spread especially quickly in Estonia, Hungary, Latvia, Lithuania, Poland, Czech Republic, Slovenia, and Slovakia; in many of these countries, foreign currency denominated loans or special mortgage loans (dual-indexed mortgages in Poland or deferred payment mortgages in Hungary) became popular. Competition in this sector grew rapidly and just a few years after full macroeconomic stability was achieved in these countries (around the year 2005) market-based housing finance systems were already offering not only classic mortgages with acceptable interest rates but also almost the same range of products as systems in the West (including flexible mortgages, 100% loan-to-value ratios, equity withdrawal mortgages, and others – see article Housing Finance Institutions: Transition Societies). In other transition states with a less stable macroeconomic situation, the development of housing finance systems progressed more slowly (e.g., Russia, Belarus, Albania, Romania, Bulgaria, and Armenia).

The private construction of detached family homes continued after 1990 and featured the same patterns established under socialism with people continuing to build their homes by themselves, with physical and financial assistance from family members and help from wider social networks, and paying informally for contracted services; small construction firms and later on professional developers gradually also became involved in the construction of family homes. In some countries the demand for detached housing and the increase in migration to urban centres from rural areas led to large areas of illegal settlement (Albania and Armenia) and more generally to urban sprawl.

The conditions for the private development of apartment housing were initially poor and accompanied by an unprecedented level of uncertainty. The home-building industry and the building materials industry were technologically underdeveloped, inefficiently managed, over-staffed, and dependent on (accustomed to) state finance. However, as access to mortgage and project finance improved and once condominium legislation was introduced, development projects for private apartment housing began to emerge in Central European transition countries, starting with the high end of the market and gradually scaling down to mid-level market segments. New private housing development in this region is almost exclusively directed at owner-occupied housing, but some signs of institutional investment into new rental housing have appeared (Poland) and some small investors have also been buying new flats for the purpose of letting.

Owing to the incomplete privatisation of the housing stock and the growing number of small residential investors, homeownership and both public and private rental housing tenures can be sometimes found within a single apartment building. This helps maintain socially mixed settlement patterns in localities. However, in many countries condominium legislation (homeowners' associations) either has yet to be passed or has proved to be incomplete – the ownership of common areas in privatised apartment houses is often unclear (Albania, Armenia, Belarus, Serbia, and Russia) and so they are still managed by the municipalities or their designated management companies. This leads to the physical deterioration of the property and increases the management debt. It also constitutes a further subsidy to owner-occupied housing, which again makes it look much like the earlier quasi-home-ownership tenure (public rental housing under socialism).

Conclusion

The picture of tenure structure changes and tenure choice development in transition countries shows how substantially formal provisions can differ from real conditions. Under socialism, public rental housing in practice resembled owner-occupied housing, and in the post-socialist period in many countries owner-occupied housing obtained through the large-scale privatisation of public housing de facto resembles public rental housing owing to the absence of legally established condominium responsibilities. The give-away privatisation of public housing greatly diminished the size of the public housing stock. Though not always was it residualised, tenure choice in countries that formally have a larger share of public rental housing is in practice constrained by the very low (tenant) turnover and by continued privatisation. Despite the fact that private 'market' rental housing emerged as a new option and in some countries the supply of such housing grew quickly, it never became a real alternative to owner-occupied housing, and owing to the extreme lack of tenure security for new tenancies it was soon perceived as a transitional and residual form of housing. Owing to biased housing policies, the negligible amount of rental housing construction, and the inherited social norms and expectations, real housing choice is seen only within one form of housing tenure – that is the choice between different forms of owner-occupied housing and housing finance. However, several transition states, especially those in Central Europe, have already launched more diversified policies and introduced new programmes aimed at widening tenure choice in the future.

See also: Housing Finance Institutions: Transition Societies; Policy Instruments that Support Housing Supply: Social Housing; Social Housing Landlords: Post-Socialist.

Reference

Dübel A (2005) *Rental Choice and Housing Policy Realignment in Transition: Post-Privatization Challenges in the Europe and Central Asia Region*. Washington, DC: World Bank.

Further Reading

Donner Ch (2006) *Housing Policies in Central Eastern Europe*. Vienna: Donner.
Kemp P (2007) *Housing Allowances in Comparative Perspective*. Bristol, UK: Policy Press.
Lowe S and Tsenkova S (eds.) (2003) *Housing Change in East and Central Europe: Integration or Fragmentation?* London, New York: Ashgate.
Lux M (ed.) (2003) *Housing Policy: An End or a New Beginning*. Budapest: LGI/OSI.
UNECE (various years) *Country Profiles on the Housing Sector*. New York, Genéve: UN/ECE.

Policies to Promote the Environmental Efficiency of Housing

RE Horne, RMIT University, Melbourne, VIC, Australia

© 2012 Elsevier Ltd. All rights reserved.

Glossary

Climate change This refers to the increase in the Earth's atmospheric temperature since the mid-twentieth century. The IPCC has attributed this change to human activity and predicts it is causing rising sea levels, species extinctions, and more extreme weather events, and that these trends will continue with ongoing emissions through the twenty-first century.

Demand-side management (energy demand management) Financial or other incentives aimed at making it worthwhile for energy suppliers to assist their customers to engage in energy-saving activities. Incentives include regulating energy tariffs, subsidies, or organising efficiency competition between suppliers.

Energy efficiency labelling schemes A requirement to display on various products an energy rating (often in the form of a letter or a number of stars) together with other information which indicates the typical level of resources used by the product. The information is aimed at assisting customers in making decisions about purchases.

Greenhouse gases Greenhouse gases are those gases in the Earth's atmosphere which absorb heat energy and raise the surface temperature of the Earth. These include carbon dioxide and other gases whose concentrations have increased dramatically since the beginning of the Industrial Revolution. Data for these gases are often quoted in terms of 'equivalent number of tonnes of carbon dioxide' shown as tCO_{2eq}.

Intergovernmental Panel on Climate Change (IPCC) An expert panel established in 1988 by the World Meteorological Organisation (WMO) and the United Nations Environment Programme (UNEP). The stated aims of the IPCC are to assess scientific information relevant to human-induced climate change, the impacts of human-induced climate change, and options for adaptation and mitigation.

Kyoto Protocol An international treaty produced under the auspices of the United Nations which established legally binding commitments to reduce greenhouse gases by signatory nations.

Passive house design A built form which is designed to minimise the need for mechanical heating, cooling, or lighting in order to provide indoor comfort to occupants.

'White' or energy-saving certificates Documents certifying deemed or actual reductions in energy consumption, usually tradable to energy producers or suppliers who are required to meet certain mandated energy reduction targets.

White goods A generic term applied to domestic appliances used for cooking, cleaning, and food preservation, such as refrigerators, washing machines, and cookers.

Introduction

The modern era of policy initiatives to promote the environmental efficiency of housing has its origins in the reemergence of environmental concern in the 1960s. In popularising these concerns, authors such as Rachel Carson and later the Club of Rome set out a new challenge for policy-makers to address pollution and unsustainable resource use associated with modern Western lifestyles. Further impetus was provided through the oil crises of the early 1970s. Subsequently, major campaigns began targeting 'behaviour' (such as the United Kingdom's 'save it' campaign) along with a range of initiatives designed to encourage retrofitting of products such as insulation to improve energy efficiency of housing. Given this history, much of the focus of this article is on the developed world.

The resurgence of neoliberal economic policies in the late 1970s led to extensive privatisation of energy supply systems and increasing efforts to promote homeownership. Energy efficiency was invariably seen as a minor factor in cost-benefit equations, leaving consumers to compare prices among options for energy provision and efficiency within the more-or-less competitive marketplaces of energy providers. However, the rising evidence for climate change has led to an imperative to reduce greenhouse gas production, including in response to commitments made as part of the Kyoto Protocol and subsequent agreements. In addition, rising concerns regarding the ability of low-income or vulnerable households to secure habitable indoor environments during extreme cold or hot weather spells led to initiatives to tackle 'fuel poverty'. As a result, alongside local initiatives to manage demand in the face of limited supply, a steadily rising set of regulatory interventions has emerged since the 1980s, designed to improve the energy efficiency of housing. These policies have so far mainly been introduced in developed countries, such as the members of the OECD, which have the highest per capita energy consumption.

The housing sector is seen as an area which can provide significant greenhouse gas savings because it consumes a significant proportion of energy and established knowledge and techniques exist to improve thermal performance. It has been estimated that the building sector accounts for 30–40% of total energy consumption worldwide. This has also been rising worldwide; both across the developed world as well as in developing countries across Asia, the Middle East and North Africa. While it is noted that housing constitutes only a proportion of building energy use, there is widespread acceptance that significant savings are achievable in this area. Material produced for the Intergovernmental Panel on Climate Change (IPCC) Fourth Report on climate change concludes that at least 29% savings could be achieved in residential and commercial buildings at relatively modest or even negative cost – this is the highest level of reduction predicted for any of the sectors investigated.

Despite the fact that policies have increased in number, type, and sophistication, energy efficiency policies have not led to widespread reductions in energy demand. Indeed, global greenhouse gas emissions resulting from energy use in residential buildings have continued to rise. In the developed world, this rise has occurred for a number of reasons, including expansion of the housing stock, increases in floor area occupied per person, and changes in household technologies and use patterns. The situation in the developing world is more variable. For example, policies have recently been introduced in many developing economies across Asia, whereas in the poorest countries, little has currently been implemented. The remainder of this article outlines the types of policies which have been introduced so far, offers an assessment of their effectiveness, and suggests possible directions for developments in this area.

Policy Approaches To Date

A number of reviews of relevant policy approaches to date have been undertaken, including in the context of the IPCC Fourth Report, as part of the OECD's Sustainable Buildings Project and for the United Nations Environment Programme (UNEP) Buildings and Climate Change Initiative. In common, these works indicate the complexity and variation in policy detail which has developed from legislature to legislature. Policy approaches vary from 'command and control' regulations in the form of binding standards, to financial incentives and other market mechanisms, to education campaigns seeking to influence and empower civil society, and to a range of combinations thereof. This complexity is partly a reflection of the fact that there are variations between different areas in terms of climate, level of development, and economic and political structure. On top of these factors, the building sector is itself a complex entity which largely consists of small concerns dealing with separate, one-off projects delivered for individual clients.

The first response of many countries was to regulate energy use via building codes with the aim of reducing energy demand for heating and/or cooling through improving thermal efficiency and passive thermal performance. By 2005, 19 out of 20 OECD countries had regulations, typically through setting standards for overall (modelled) building performance and/or by setting 'deemed to satisfy' regulations for specific items such as the level of insulation required in different building elements. The former provides for more flexibility in design and suits a market-based policy environment. Here, the overall performance of buildings is often achieved through rating schemes such as those implemented following the European Directive on the Energy Performance of Buildings, or the Green Star program in the United States. These have tended to specify such items as insulation requirements, window size and performance, and the efficiency of boilers. It is important to note that both approaches rely on well-trained inspectors and a compliant, supportive, and well-equipped industry, while in addition, the former relies on appropriate software for modelling, training, and assessment purposes. Difficulties have been encountered locally in enforcing energy efficiency codes, and in many countries, a building certificate system has been introduced either on a voluntary (e.g., United States) or a compulsory basis (e.g., European Union (EU)).

These regulations and standards have been introduced at varying levels of government. Some have been introduced across a group of countries as in EU regulations. Others have been introduced at a national level, such as the Japanese Comprehensive Assessment System for Building Environmental Efficiency (CASBEE) scheme. In some cases, particularly where the national government has been seen to be reluctant to become involved in energy reduction schemes, such as in United States and Australia, individual states or even local governments have introduced their own schemes and have then been seen to be the leaders of developments in the country.

A second type of policy approach to encourage energy efficiency is by taxation policy, subsidies, or other financial incentives. Based on a rationalisation discourse which assumes actors seek utility maximisation, various mechanisms have targeted the market either from the point of view of the suppliers or consumers of energy:

> The purpose of economic instruments and incentives is also to change the market conditions in a way that makes energy-efficient buildings more financially attractive than ordinary buildings (UNEP, Building and Climate Change report, p. 38).

On the supply side, a fundamental problem for energy efficiency is that many energy supply systems have been set up to reward suppliers on the basis of the amount of energy supplied, rather than the energy services delivered or the efficiency of services delivered. The problem is particularly marked when environmental impacts such as those arising from human-induced climate change are not included in industry costs and are instead treated as an externality. This encourages suppliers to use fossil, nuclear, or other 'undercosted', high environmental impact energy sources rather than more environmentally benign sources such as renewables. To overcome this, a number of demand-side management schemes have been introduced, usually starting by regulating the tariff charged by the energy suppliers at a higher level than the unregulated market value. Suppliers are then rewarded for introducing energy efficiency schemes and fined if specified targets are not achieved. Subsequently, various options to assist low-income households pay the higher resultant fuel bills have been introduced; for example, the US government introduced compensation for low-income families, which spend a proportionately larger amount of money on energy than other families.

Another market-based approach involves directing energy suppliers/generators to reduce net pollution by prescribed amounts, through instituting a system of tradeable permits or certificates. To comply they must purchase certificates commensurate with the pollution caused (often known as 'white' certificates). These may originate through energy-efficiency-related activities; for example, certificates may be awarded for installing insulation or replacing appliances with more efficient alternatives.

A further market-based approach to encourage energy efficiency involves providing direct incentives on the demand side. These include payments, rebates, subsidies, and/or tax or other financial incentives to consumers who take actions to improve the overall performance of the dwelling, such as by installing insulation, or switching to energy-efficient appliances, or switching to renewable energy sources.

Energy efficiency incentives targeting householders also extend beyond the 'heating and cooling' aspects of energy demand. These often take a different approach to those aimed at the building shell, for example, programmes designed to encourage replacement of energy-using devices with more energy-efficient alternatives, on the assumption that lower overall energy demand will result. For example, energy efficiency labelling schemes for household appliances are now widespread and aim to provide a simple and clear indication of energy implications of given items, to assist consumers making purchases. These information-based schemes may be adopted in conjunction with rebates and/or with minimum energy performance standards, which set mandatory minimum levels of performance for appliances such as refrigerators or air conditioners while they are in use (and sometimes also on standby power). By 2004, 57 countries had introduced legislation in this area covering some 46 products, including lighting, electrical goods such as computers and televisions, heating and cooling devices, and kitchen and laundry-related 'white goods'.

Appliance labelling and related policies have proved generally cost-effective – for example, in the United States, costs of US$2 per household have produced savings of up to US$1270 per household, while in the EU, related policies have encouraged a significant uptake of energy-efficient refrigerators, with an estimated net saving of between US$65 and US$191 per tCO_{2eq}. A program has recently been instituted in China which it has been estimated could save the equivalent of the total current residential electricity program over a 10-year period. It is important to note that these schemes are effective only if standards are regularly reviewed and improved.

Regarding developing countries, two initiatives were developed under the auspices of the Kyoto Protocol to allow developed countries to promote energy schemes in developing countries as a way of offsetting their own targets (the 'Clean Development Mechanism' and 'Joint Implementation' policies). Significant potential exists, with around one-half of potential savings in buildings being low cost (below US$20/$tCO_{2eq}$). However, the initial schemes were somewhat restrictive. In response, the UNEP Sustainable Construction and Building Initiative provides assistance in dealing with a number of identified restricting factors.

The third type of approach in promoting household energy efficiency involves education or awareness-raising programmes, often termed 'behaviour change' and often introduced alongside regulatory, voluntary, or market-based interventions. Indeed, a combination of a mandatory approach and an information-based vehicle has emerged in recent years in the form of policies requiring the mandatory disclosure of residential energy use at the point of sale and/or change of lease of dwellings. Ostensibly marking an extension of energy labelling from white goods into whole dwellings, this approach is now becoming common across the Western world, with a European Directive and various legislation enacted or on the statute books across North America and Asia-Pacific.

One underlying assumption with mandatory disclosure is that prospective buyers or renters of properties will factor energy efficiency into their considerations, thus driving a market in energy-efficient homes, and establishing a 'price premium' on residential energy efficiency. A wider assumption with education and information programmes is that, when provided with both information about the need for energy efficiency and 'action competence' about how to improve energy efficiency in the home, householders can and will change their behaviour and more energy-efficient outcomes will result. These and other assumptions underlying market-based initiatives have been questioned, as discussed further in the following section.

Success of Policies To Date

There are indications that existing policies are having some effect. The overall rate of increase in energy use in buildings across the OECD countries is 0.1% per annum on the latest available data (1999–2004). This rate of increase has decreased substantially from the average growth rate for the previous 30 years which was 1.4%. However, given the wide range of policy approaches attempted to date, it is perhaps surprising that the inroads into housing energy efficiency have not prevented further growth given that there have been predictions that substantial reductions are possible. Two questions provide the focus for consideration of the overall success of policies to date:

- To what extent have the appropriate aspects of household energy use been targeted in policy attempts to promote energy efficiency? and
- How effective have policies been in delivering energy efficiency in terms of cost-benefit and demand reduction?

In assessing the appropriateness of the targeting of policies to promote energy efficiency in housing, the following starting observations can be made:

- Policies to date have tended to target thermal efficiency in preference to other aspects of building lifecycle energy demand;
- An initial emphasis on new housing has now been superceded by widespread acceptance that existing housing invariably requires retrofitting as part of any systematic attempt to significantly improve energy efficiency by 2050; and
- The focus to date has been across the so-called developed world rather than the developing world.

Focus on Thermal Efficiency

Residential buildings result in energy use across all three phases of their life: 'during construction', while they are 'in use', and during 'demolition'. Across the countries of the OECD, 80–85% of total energy use is attributed to operation, indicating that policy emphasis on this area is essential. However, this broad generalisation risks concealing important issues linked to the diversity of housing types, household needs, and climates – which in turn indicate large variations in the sources of residential energy demand.

The largest proportion of operational energy demand in developed countries is usually consumed in providing space heating and cooling (typically 50% in cool or hot climates) followed by appliances (20–26%) and water heating (11–19%). By comparison in developing countries, energy for water heating typically outstrips both appliances and domestic refrigeration and air conditioning. In warmer regions, the heating demand is reduced although this may be offset by a rise in the energy used in cooling. Both heating and cooling requirements can be reduced by elements of passive solar design and encouraging building practices such as improving insulation levels of walls, windows, and doors, although the particular effectiveness of different design or technical options varies according to both diurnal and seasonal fluctuations in outside temperatures and humidity, and occupational factors.

From New to Existing

As building envelope requirements are enhanced, the proportion of total housing energy demand taken up by thermal conditioning may be expected to decline, while relative energy demand in other areas increases, for example, from the use of appliances. In turn, policy interventions to improve energy efficiency of these appliances are justified, and have begun to appear. Another important consideration for policy in this area is the balance between old and new buildings in the housing stock. Policy attention to date on new buildings reflects the relative ease associated with upgrading new-build regulations in comparison to retrospectively seeking to upgrade homes which are owned and/or occupied by households.

Upgrades in the existing housing stock may potentially be relatively intrusive, expensive, and less effective than upgrades during initial construction. However, because of the low turnover in building stock, the majority of the potential for improvement in the short term lies in modifying the existing stock. Even in Western countries which have increasing populations, such as Australia, the housing stock is only being added to in the order of 1–2% per annum, leaving over 98% of the stock as 'existing' housing. In order to deliver significant energy efficiency improvements in the next few decades, it is inevitable that existing housing must also be tackled.

Focus on Developed Countries

The focus of housing energy efficiency on the developed world is broadly appropriate, given that in much of the developing world the energy use is comparatively low and in some countries, mainly sub-Saharan Africa, at a subsistence level. The reasons for seeking energy efficiency also play out, given that the paramount policy question in the West is climate change mitigation, while in the developing world meeting basic housing energy needs is the primary concern. Moreover, more diverse nonfossil fuel energy sources are used across the developing world; about 2.4 billion people obtain their energy for heating and cooking from biomass (plant material and animal dung). Policy initiatives to assist developing countries in introducing more efficient stoves are therefore appropriate in this context.

Turning to the question of policy effectiveness to date, the IPCC assessed 20 policy tools through a working group study. All the instruments reviewed in this qualitative and quantitative assessment showed potentially significant energy and CO_2 savings; however, the costs per tonne of CO_2 saved diverged considerably. Appliance standard, building code, labelling, and tax exemption policies achieved the highest CO_2 emission reductions. Appliance standards, energy efficiency obligations, demand-side management programmes, public benefit charges, and mandatory labelling were among the most cost-effective policy tools in the sample, all achieving significant energy savings at negative costs. Investment subsidies (as opposed to rebates for purchases of energy-efficient appliances) were revealed as the least cost-effective instrument. Tax reductions for investments in energy efficiency appeared more effective than taxation. Labelling and voluntary programmes were indicated as sources of potentially large savings at low costs if they are combined with other policy instruments. Similarly, information, education, and social capital programmes can also achieve significant savings and effectively accompany most other policy measures.

Directions for Future Policy Development

As mentioned previously, there has been some improvement in the trend of energy use in houses. However, the consumption level still appears to be increasing – as does the evidence of adverse environmental, economic, and social consequences of not achieving major reductions in energy and water use. Given the resultant rising urgency for effective policies to mitigate climate change through more significant savings, three broad implications can be drawn for future policy development in this area:

- The dynamics of climate and demand reduction will necessitate regular revisions to policy direction and focus over coming decades;
- Expectations of dwellings as sources of shelter and comfort and as sites of food preparation and consumption, cleansing and leisure, are dynamic, and various policies to limit energy demand are required; and
- Significant changes are required in the infrastructures, skill sets, and organisations of housing provision, retrofitting, and maintenance, and these in turn require policy interventions.

Since climate change is already detectable and is affecting the comfort and condition of residential property, changes in the utility value, energy demand, and adaptation needs of these buildings are inevitable. Also, as building shells are improved, so policy attention should properly turn to reducing embodied energy demand and to other sources of energy demand across the housing life cycle. Policies designed to effect retrofitting for energy efficiency should take account of these factors – and of the large body of evidence that householders are not driven solely by rational economic behaviour as implied in many programmes to date.

Managing the dynamics of household standards and service expectations is perhaps the most significant policy challenge, and the example of recent trends is illustrative. The overall energy use per household dropped in the years from 1971 to 2001 and this was a result largely of a reduction in building heat losses. However, energy demand across the residential sector rose by 32% because of two countertrends. The first was that people chose to live alone or in smaller households, and the number of households increased by 36%. An even more significant impact was that the energy consumption related to lighting and appliances rose by a total of 70%. Even though more energy-efficient lighting is in use, the total number of lights increased as lighting service expectations changed, leading to higher levels of illumination and the rise of particular lighting technologies. An equivalent effect has occurred in relation to heating and cooling; it has now become the norm in many buildings to have a strictly controlled climate as people's expectations of 'comfort' have altered.

Similar trends are occurring in the emerging economies. The Chinese Research Academy for Environmental Sciences reports that the living space of the average Chinese is likely to double in the next few years. If this is taken into account together with a growing demand for appliances, particularly in urban China, any energy reduction due to more efficient appliances and building practices will be more than negated. It can be expected that rising levels of environmental concern will be insufficient in themselves to counter these disturbing trends in energy consumption. As noted in the UNEP report, 'Building and Climate Change', p. 23, "People often do not behave consistently with their level of concern about environmental problems. In fact, environmental considerations are probably only to a smaller extent determining human behavior." Any significant reduction in energy use will require shifts in social practices – and 'normalised' pro-environmental behaviours are only likely to occur hand-in-hand with particular changes to the infrastructures, institutional arrangements, and systems of governance associated with housing and households.

While policy interventions to fix market externalities and initiatives to provide information, examples, and demonstrations are important, in a world shaped by consumption and characterised by rapidly changing household practices and standards, these will be insufficient in themselves to deliver significant demand-side reductions. For example, in addition to examples of viable energy-efficient housing structures, there is a need to develop significant, widespread models of possible ways to live in them – and to conduct household practices – in ways which avoid high consumption and are socially and culturally coherent. In turn, reconfigurations of institutional relations are needed which enable communities to develop action competences and networks within which new or modified practices can flourish. New policy initiatives must therefore draw on knowledge of social practices and consumption beyond the dominant rationalisation discourses, which have produced limited responses to regulations, rebates, and other market mechanisms to date.

Significant interventions are also required on the supply side – both in energy supply and in the housing construction and retrofitting industries. Reconfiguring these in order to shape logical shifts to energy-efficient configurations requires both changes to the rules by which markets driving energy demand operate and changes to the industries which provide the materiality of housing. Many studies have shown that there are not many builders able to build passive houses; it requires knowledge which builders do not have the resources to obtain, nor are the markets and institutional contexts within which they operate suited to system-level innovation and change. Housing industries invariably exhibit a blend of innovation and tradition. On the one hand, research has established the basic principles of effective, economic, low-energy design as well as developing new products and materials to further reduce energy and emission outputs. On the other hand, investigations like the Egan report in the United Kingdom have shown these industries to be conservative in nature, implying a need for extensive and concerted policy change.

In conclusion, policies to create energy-efficient homes are well established across the developed world. Drawing upon both traditional standard-setting regulation and market-based approaches, they are characterised by underpinning market rationalisation discourses, and they have failed to deliver significant reductions in energy demand. New policy approaches are required to address enduring obduracy within both households on the demand side and industries on the supply side. Moreover, in the attempt to 'steer' a transition towards 'energy-efficient households', there is a need for policy to set long-term goals and to map clear pathways towards these goals, constantly reviewing interventions along the way.

See also: Building Regulations for Energy Conservation; Climate Change; Climate Change: Adaptations; Community Energy Systems; Eco-Communities; Eco-Renovation; Ecological Footprint; Energy Saving; Housing Dynamics: Environmental Aspects; Housing Policy: Agents and Regulators; Housing Standards: Regulation; Sustainable Lifestyles; Sustainable Urban Development.

Further Reading

Boardman B (2005) *Policy Packages to Achieve Demand Reduction in ECEEE SummerStudy: What Works and Who Delivers?* Mandelieu, France: ECEEE.

Carson R (2002) *Silent Spring: 40th Anniversary Edition*. New York: Mariner Books.

Cheng C, Pouffray S, Svenningsen N, and Callaway M (2008) *The Kyoto Protocol: The Clean Development Mechanism and the Building and Construction Sector. A Report for the UNEP Sustainable Buildings and Construction Initiative*. Paris: UNEP.

Club of Rome (2004) *The Limits to Growth: The 30 Year Update*. White River Junction, VT: Chelsea Green Publishing Company.

Crosbie T, Stokes M, and Guy S (2008) Illuminating household energy demand and the policies for its reduction. *Energy and Environment* 19(7): 979–993.

Egan J (1998) *Rethinking Construction*. Office of the Deputy Prime Minister, UK: London.

Guy S (2006) Designing urban knowledge: Competing perspectives on energy and buildings. *Environment and Planning C: Government and Policy* 24: 645–659.

IEA/OECD (2003) *Cool Appliances: Strategies for Energy-Efficient Homes*. Paris: OECD.

IEA (2005) *Key World Energy Statistics: 2005*. Paris: IEA.

OECD (2003) *Environmentally Sustainable Buildings: Challenges and Policies*. Paris: OECD.

Shove E (2003) *Comfort, Cleanliness and Convenience: The Social Organisation of Normality*. Oxford, UK and New York: Berg Publishers.

Shove E, Chappells H, Lutzenhiser L, and Hackett B (2008) Comfort in a low carbon society. *Editorial of the Special Issue of Building Research and Information* 36(4): 307–311.

Stern N (2007) *Stern Review on the Economics of Climate Change*. London: HM Treasury. http://www.hm-treasury.gov.uk/sternreview_index.htm (accessed 20 October 2011).

UNEP (2007) *Buildings and Climate Change: Status, Challenges and Opportunities*. Paris: UNEP.

Urge-Vorsatz D, Mirasgedis S, Harvey D, and Levine M (2007) Mitigating CO_2 emissions from energy use in the world's buildings. *Building Research and Information* 35(4): 458–477.

Relevant Websites

www.aceee.org – American Council for an Energy Efficient Economy.

www.ibec.or.jp – Comprehensive Assessment System for Building Environmental Efficiency (CASBEE).

www.eceee.org – European Council for an Energy Efficient Economy.

http://europa.eu/legislation_summaries/energy/energy_efficiency/l27042_en.htm – European Directive on the Energy Performance of Buildings.

www.greenstarusa.com – Green Star Program.

www.ipcc.ch – Intergovernmental Panel on Climate Change.

www.iea.org – International Energy Agency.

www.passiv.de – Passive House Institute.

www.unepsbci.org – UNEP Sustainable Buildings and Climate Initiative.

Policies to Support Access and Affordability of Housing

J Yates, University of Sydney, Sydney, NSW, Australia
V Milligan, University of New South Wales, Sydney, NSW, Australia

© 2012 Elsevier Ltd. All rights reserved.

Glossary

Accessibility Accessibility relates to the impediments that must be overcome if a household is to acquire housing of a satisfactory standard. It is typically associated with home buyers and, in this article, relates to the capacity of first-home buyers to meet lender's repayment and deposit requirements on the mortgage loan needed to finance dwelling purchase.

Affordability Housing affordability relates to ongoing/recurrent housing costs in relation to income and typically implies that housing costs do not exceed 30% of income for households in the bottom 40% of the income distribution. However, it cannot be defined, precisely because housing needs vary by household type and circumstances and because the capacity to meet those needs varies by income. Affordability problems arise when households are unable to maintain an adequate standard of living after they have met their housing costs.

Demand-side subsidies Demand-side subsidies (sometimes described as subject or consumption subsidies) provide assistance directed to the individual to increase their purchasing capacity.

Supply-side subsidies Supply-side subsidies (sometimes described as object, production, or 'bricks-and-mortar' subsidies) provide assistance directed to reducing the cost of providing housing.

Introduction

As developed countries have become wealthier, much of the focus of housing policy has shifted from addressing housing shortages and housing quality to dealing with housing affordability and access to housing. The motivation behind such a shift was never clearer than in the early part of the twenty-first century when a cocktail of factors contributed to rapid increases in house prices and rents in most Organisation for Economic Co-operation and Development (OECD) countries. These outcomes, in turn, were associated with significant declines in housing affordability for many households. In the decade to 2006, housing costs as a share of household disposable income tended to increase. By the mid-2000s, for example, average expenditure on housing accounted for more than one-fifth of household disposable income in most OECD countries. Because housing is the largest component of household consumption, increases in housing costs as a proportion of disposable income can have a deleterious influence on household living standards. This provides a key reason for policy concerns with housing affordability and with access to housing. Housing affordability relates to ongoing/recurrent housing costs in relation to income. Accessibility relates to the impediments that must be overcome if a household is to acquire housing of a satisfactory standard.

Housing costs have increased and housing affordability has declined generally because house prices have risen faster than incomes. House price inflation affects households differently depending on whether they are established owners, recent purchasers, or renters. For existing owners, increases in house prices can be beneficial in that they increase housing equity and, by increasing total household wealth, provide additional security, particularly for indebted households. In most countries, housing wealth is the largest component of total household net worth, and in many OECD countries, owner-occupied housing accounts for as much as two-thirds of total household assets. The possibility that declining housing affordability excludes aspiring homeowners from access to this important contributor to household wealth provides a further reason for policy concerns with access to owner-occupied housing.

On the other hand, for recent purchasers, house price falls have the reverse effect and can be problematic for those with relatively low initial equity in housing (typically, lower-income buyers). In such instances, policy may seek to ensure that such households remain in homeownership. This is particularly so because risks of foreclosure increase and risks to the real economy increase as a result.

For private renters, sustained increases in house prices eventually are likely to result in increases in rents and declines in rental affordability. Affordability problems are exacerbated for low-income renters by chronic shortages of low-rent housing in a number of countries. This is particularly so if they face problems of access to a limited existing supply of affordable rental housing, because the stock that is available is not appropriate to their needs, because of discrimination, or because they are unable to compete with those better able to pay.

Renters in public or social housing can be protected from affordability problems since their rents typically are less affected by market trends. However, the share of social housing has been static or declining in most countries over the last two decades, and hence eligible households have more limited access to this tenure.

In summary, housing affordability problems and problems of access to housing are not issues that affect all households equally. Indeed, many households benefit from the house price increases that render housing unaffordable for others. Those most at risk of facing problems beyond their control tend to be lower-income households, the young, the old, and the disadvantaged.

Determinants of Access and Affordability Problems

In most OECD countries, housing provision is dominated by the market, primarily through owner-occupied housing but supplemented to a greater or lesser extent by private rental housing. Social housing generally has declined in importance. In most markets, increases in real prices or rents tend to be a clear signal that demand has outstripped supply. Housing markets are different only in that they are more complex. Because house prices and rents are key factors affecting affordability, ultimately the key drivers of affordability outcomes are the multitude of factors that influence the supply of and demand for both owner-occupied and rental housing.

On the supply-side, the cost of housing is affected by the availability and cost of materials and skilled labour; land development processes and policies; infrastructure costs (including development charges); property-related taxes; and, above all, the availability of land. Supply of developable land, in turn, is determined by land release policies and by land-use zoning policies. The less responsive is the supply of land, the greater will be the impact of any increase in demand. The more urbanised is any particular region, the more likely are land supply restrictions to result in upward pressures on prices with the result that affordability outcomes can vary significantly, both between cities and regions and between suburbs within the same metropolitan region.

On the demand-side, key factors include household growth (in turn, affected by natural increase, immigration, and household formation); real incomes, real household wealth, and the distribution of both income and wealth; tax concessions for both owner-occupied and rental housing; concessions for first-home buyers; returns on alternative investments; availability of finance for housing; interest rates (or, more generally, the real user cost of housing capital); and the institutional structure affecting housing-finance provision. Any of these drivers in the housing market can change affordability outcomes. Some have direct impacts on housing costs, while others have indirect impacts through tenure outcomes.

Some of these demand and supply factors are cyclical in their impact and, consequently, the fortunes of many households aspiring to access homeownership ebb and flow with the rise and fall of house prices and/or interest rates. The boom and bust of house prices around the turn of the twenty-first century provides a good example of this cyclicality. Other factors, however, have contributed to underlying structural pressures. For example, rising real incomes have contributed to rising housing standards and to rising land prices in regions where land supply is constrained. Together, these pressures have resulted in numerous lower-income households (many of whom are single-income) being unable to find affordable housing. Overall, effective policies to redress housing affordability problems will be those that are based on a sound understanding of the key drivers in housing markets.

Because there are multiple drivers of affordability outcomes, many of the most influential levers that affect affordability lie outside of the range of what are conventionally described as housing policies. Fiscal and monetary policies, transport planning and infrastructure provision, population distribution and settlement planning, income support, and encouragement of urban and regional sustainability are all ways in which governments can, and do, intervene to affect housing outcomes. These broader policy challenges are not addressed specifically in this article, but it is important to recognise that they can be significant contributors to affordability and access problems through the impact they have on housing demand and housing supply.

Why is Policy Concerned with Access to Housing and Housing Affordability?

Concerns about access to housing and housing affordability have been central to housing policy for two sets of reasons: first, because of their impacts on individual households, and second, because of their impacts on the economy as a whole.

Concerns with the impacts on individual households derive from a desire to ensure that living standards are maintained and that households are not pushed into poverty because of the cost of their housing. In the absence of adequate housing assistance, after-housing-cost poverty can be particularly severe for lower-income private renters. Affordability problems also can be severe for some marginal purchasers, who tend to be better off than lower-income renters but who are stretched by their decision to buy rather than rent. Competition in mortgage markets in the post-1980s era of financial liberalisation resulted in a general relaxation of lending standards, and a number of less scrupulous lenders began to offer riskier loan products to increasingly marginal borrowers. With many of these loans, borrowers were unable both to meet their nonhousing needs and to sustain their mortgage repayments when interest rates increased, or when anticipated future income streams were not realised.

Housing affordability also becomes a policy issue when those who aspire to become home purchasers are unable to access homeownership. Again, those most likely to be affected are low- to moderate-income households with insufficient borrowing capacity to purchase even the lowest priced of dwellings. Although there is some debate over the economic benefits or otherwise of low-income households being assisted into homeownership (often because of the risks associated with such ownership), there is increasing evidence that households who become homeowners have greater household net wealth than do renters with similar socioeconomic and demographic characteristics. There is also evidence that homeowners benefit socially as well as financially from homeownership. In some of the literature on the social benefits of homeownership, however, there is uncertainty as to whether it is homeownership per se, the unobservable characteristics of those who attain homeownership, or simply the security provided by homeownership but not necessarily only by homeownership that are the key drivers of the social benefits observed.

The importance of owner-occupied housing in contributing to economic and social well-being provides a rationale for policies that support access to homeownership, and policies that safeguard homeowners facing adverse circumstances. Uncertainty surrounding the basis of homeownership's social benefits suggests that such policies might also support and sustain access to any secure form of housing tenure.

The second set of reasons why housing affordability has been central to housing policy concerns arise from its impacts on the economy as a whole and, in particular, its impact on economic activity, efficiency, and distributional outcomes (see article Housing Markets and Macroeconomic Policy). The fallout from the subprime crisis has highlighted the ways in which housing and mortgage markets are inextricably linked to broader financial markets and to the economic system as a whole. Weak housing markets contributed to significant declines in economic activity. In turn, this reduced demand for housing and led to a further weakening of housing and mortgage markets.

A lack of affordable housing also can affect the efficiency with which national and regional labour markets operate, particularly in large metropolitan areas (see article Housing and Labour Markets). There are a number of ways in which such outcomes might arise. High housing costs, for example, may be reflected in rising wage levels that feed back into rising housing prices in a region, although the precise nature of the causal processes is unclear. If pronounced, this can undercut the competitive advantage of firms locating in the region. Differentials in affordability between areas may create labour market impediments by inhibiting migration to high-employment, high-cost locations and, conversely, encouraging migration to low-employment, low-cost areas.

High housing costs and low affordability have their corollary in substantial increases in the wealth levels of residential property owners. This results in a widening gap between them and the sizeable minority of households who do not own residential property. Increasing disparities in wealth add to the risks of a loss of social cohesion. In addition, intergenerational equity is compromised by the increasing disparities between those who gain access to homeownership and those who do not.

Policies to Improve Affordability and Access

Policies to improve affordability generally, but not exclusively, have been targeted at renter households. Policies to improve access generally, but not exclusively, have been targeted at home buyers. A wide range of approaches have been employed in each case. In broad terms, these can be categorised into three distinct approaches: demand-side subsidies, supply-side subsidies, and regulation.

Demand-side subsidies (sometimes described as subject or consumption subsidies) provide assistance directed to the individual to increase their purchasing capacity. Supply-side subsidies (sometimes described as object, production, or 'bricks and mortar' subsidies) provide assistance directed to reducing the cost of providing housing. Each of these forms of assistance can be provided either directly, appearing explicitly as an item in the relevant government's budget, or indirectly, occurring implicitly as a concession or exemption for particular activities from taxes or charges. Regulation covers a wide range of levers ranging from explicit rent regulation, eligibility criteria defining who can access subsidised housing, or restrictions on the use of publicly provided funds to planning or zoning laws affecting land-use and building codes. **Table 1** provides a comprehensive (UK-oriented) list of the many fiscal and planning instruments used in these broad categories. **Table 2** indicates which of these fiscal instruments are employed or have recently been employed in many OECD countries.

Table 1 Taxonomy of instruments used to improve affordability and access to housing

	Tax	*Subsidy*	*Regulation*
Demand	**Category 1** 1.1 Mortgage interest tax deductible 1.2 Owner-occupiers can claim depreciation 1.3 Preferential tax treatment of home-savings plans 1.4 Rent payments tax deductible 1.5 Tax credits for low-income tenants 1.6 Exemption from transfer tax for first-time buyers 1.7 Tax relief for employee on employer-run house savings schemes 1.8 Property tax relief for low-income households 1.9 Exemption from transfer tax for new homes	**Category 2** 2.1 Housing allowance 2.2 Subsidies to savings for house purchase (interest subsidies or one-off grants on house purchase) 2.3 Subsidised mortgages for low-income households 2.4 Grants and other assistance to first-time buyers 2.5 Grants for low-income buyers (not tied to savings) 2.6 Right-to-buy and other discounts for council tenants 2.7 Improvement grants for low-income owners	**Category 3** 3.1 Government assigns housing to low-income households
Supply	**Category 4** *Income tax* 4.1 Providers of social housing exempt from income tax 4.2 Tax relief on investment in construction of affordable housing for rent or sale 4.3 Depreciation for rental units 4.4 Landlords can deduct interest on loans and operating expenses 4.5 Landlords can set rental losses against other income 4.6 Lower tax rate for landlords' capital gains 4.7 Tax relief for interest from mortgage-backed securities used to fund low-interest mortgages or low-income housing 4.8 Allow capital outlays on construction/conversion of rental property to be offset against rental income 4.9 Preferential treatment for housing-finance institutions *Land/property tax* 4.11 Taxation of empty land to encourage housebuilding 4.12 Taxation of empty property to bring back into use 4.13 Discount for new/renovated houses, or abatement for specified period *Sales tax* 4.14 Reduced rate on conversions, new build 4.15 Housing associations pay lower sales tax	**Category 5** 5.1 Grants for construction or renovation of affordable housing 5.2 Subsidised loans for developers of affordable housing 5.3 Provision of land for affordable housing at below market value or free 5.4 Grants to bring empty homes back into use with allocation attachments 5.5 Government guarantees for housing association loans 5.6 Government guarantees of rent or mortgage payments from low-income households	**Category 6** 6.1 Require developers to include certain percentage of affordable housing 6.2 Rent control 6.3 Require employers to provide housing 6.4 Prohibit move of rental flats to owner occupation

Reproduced from Holmans A, Scanlon K, and Whitehead C, with Shilling J and Hills J (2002) *Policy Options to Promote Affordable Housing*. Cambridge: Cambridge Centre for Housing and Planning Research.

Table 2 International affordable housing policies (followed now or recently)

Category	Policy description	UK	USA	F	SP	N	DK	B	IT	IR	G	FI	AU	SW	CA
1.1	Mortgage interest tax deductible	•	•												
1.2	Owner-occupiers can claim depreciation														•
1.3	Preferential tax treatment of home-savings plans			•							•				
1.4	Rent payments tax deductible			•											
1.5	Tax credits for low-income tenants		•												
1.6	Exemption from transfer tax for first-time buyers									•					
1.7	Tax relief for employee on employer-run house saving schemes					•									
1.8	Property tax relief for low-income households	•								•					
1.9	Exemption from transfer tax for new homes	•													
2.1	Housing allowance	•	•	•		•	•	•		•	•	•	•	•	
2.2	Subsidies to savings for house purchase			•	•										
2.3	Subsidised mortgages for low-income households	•		•	•	•									
2.4	Grants to first-time buyers	•													
2.5	Grants for low-income buyers	•													
2.6	Right-to-buy discounts for council tenants	•													
2.7	Improvement grants for low-income owners	•													
4.1	Providers of social housing exempt from income tax						•				•				
4.2	Tax relief on investment in construction of affordable housing		•												•
4.3	Depreciation for rental units		•								•				•
4.4	Landlords can deduct interest on loans and operating expenses	•									•				•
4.5	Landlords can set rental losses against other income		•										•		
4.6	Lower tax rate for landlords' capital gains										•				
4.7	Tax relief for interest from mortgage-backed securities for housing		•									•			
4.8	Landlords can set capital outlays against rental income	•													
4.9	Preferential tax treatment for housing-finance institutions									•					
4.10	Preferential tax treatment for employer-provided housing														
4.11	Taxation of empty land to encourage house building			•											
4.12	Taxation of empty property to bring back into use			•											
4.13	Property tax discount for new/renovated houses, or abatement	•													
4.14	Reduced rate of sales tax on conversions, new build			•											
4.15	Housing associations pay lower sales tax			•											
5.1	Grants for construction or renovation of affordable housing	•		•	•							•		•	
5.2	Subsidised loans for developers of affordable housing			•	•									•	
5.3	Land provided for affordable housing at below market value	•													
5.4	Grants to refurbish empty homes						•		•						
5.5	Government guarantees housing association loans										•				
5.6	Government guarantees rent/mortgage payment of low-income households	•	•												

F = France; SP = Spain; N = Netherlands; DK = Denmark; B = Belgium; IT = Italy; IR = Ireland; G = Germany; FI = Finland; AU = Australia; SW = Sweden; CA = Canada.
Reproduced from Holmans A, Scanlon K, and Whitehead C, with Shilling J and Hills J (2002) *Policy Options to Promote Affordable Housing.* Cambridge: Cambridge Centre for Housing and Planning Research.

Demand-Side Subsidies for Renters

Most countries provide housing assistance that is explicitly targeted at low- to moderate-income households with the intent of improving housing affordability. The most common examples are demand-side subsidies targeted at renters and described generically as housing benefits, housing vouchers, housing certificates, rent or accommodation assistance, rent rebates, or rent supplements. In Finland, Denmark, and France more than 20% of households receive housing allowances, in Spain, Estonia, the United Kingdom, and the Netherlands between 10 and 15% do, while generally less than 5% do in other European countries. With the exception of the United States, which falls into the third of these groups, the remaining Anglophone countries fall within the middle category. Although there are many approaches to providing this form of demand-side assistance, all are based on payments paid to an individual or household in order to reduce the financial burden of their recurrent housing costs. They vary, however, in terms of coverage, in terms of the level of assistance, and in the way in which this is provided.

For example, some assistance (e.g., housing benefit in the United Kingdom) is provided on an 'as of right' basis to all eligible households; other assistance (e.g., Housing Choice Vouchers or Section 8 vouchers in the United States) is budget-constrained with the number of eligible households assisted limited by the funds available (see article Access and Affordability: Housing Vouchers). Some fully meet the gap between the actual rent charged for the dwelling and an amount that is deemed to be affordable (e.g., rent rebates in public housing in Australia and housing benefit in the United Kingdom); some only meet the gap up to a 'standard' rent (defined by needs and location as in France and in some provinces in Canada); others require the recipient household to pay a proportion of the rent charged (e.g., in the Netherlands).

Kemp (2007) provides a useful comparative overview and points to some of the problems associated with income-related housing allowances in a number of countries, especially in relation to housing consumption and work incentives (see article Access and Affordability: Housing Allowances).

Demand-Side Subsidies for Purchasers

As well as providing assistance for renters, a few countries provide as much or more demand-side support to assist lower-income first-home buyers into homeownership. This is particularly so in the Anglophone countries. Low- or moderate-income households often rent not by choice but because purchase is impossible given their low borrowing capacity, their low saving capacity, and the cost of reasonably priced homes. Demand-side policies to improve access to housing tend to address the first two of these constraints. The third constraint tends to be addressed by supply-side subsidies and regulation (see article Policy Instruments that Support Housing Supply: Supply-Side Subsidies).

Part of the rationale for such assistance has been given earlier. However, assistance to low-cost homeownership is also favoured because it often makes less demand on government budgets per assisted household than assistance to renters does. Home purchase assistance is provided because of the income and wealth constraints that lower-income households face.

Income constraints arise when loans are limited by a maximum repayment to income ratio. In some countries, this is replaced by a maximum loan to income ratio but the maximum loan is likely to vary according to the financial environment. Repayment to income ratios are also likely to vary according to household income and possibly household size when capacity to pay is assessed on the basis of residual income (i.e., after housing costs are met). Income constraints are exacerbated when interest rates are high. They can be made less restrictive if interest rates are directly subsidised or, more commonly, when mortgage interest is tax deductible. Direct interest rate subsidies usually are only available for mortgage lending provided by state-owned or state-regulated institutions. However, many countries provide indirect assistance through tax deductibility for mortgage repayments (see article Access and Affordability: Homeowner Taxation).

Indirect assistance is also provided by guarantees or default insurance, which reduce credit risk for lenders and allow them to lend with higher loan to value ratios or at lower rates of interest. Government-guaranteed mortgage schemes exist in a number of European countries, the United States, and Canada. These can be explicit, as in the case of the Dutch Homeownership Guarantee Fund (WEW), or implicit, as in the case of the US Federal National Mortgage Association (FNMA or Fannie Mae) and Federal Home Loan Mortgage Corporation (FHLMC or Freddie Mac). Until the first of the Fannie Mae and Freddie Mac rescue packages passed by US Congress in July 2008, there were no explicit state subsidies or guarantees provided to Fannie Mae or Freddie Mac. However, a perception that they were supported by government guarantees has provided a considerable implicit subsidy, which has allowed them to borrow more cheaply than would otherwise have been the case. Since the subprime crisis, there has been a resurgence of housing-assistance schemes that focus on keeping households in homeownership rather than on assisting them with access to homeownership. Such guarantees can be provided as mortgage insurance, which focuses on lenders (see article Access and Affordability: Mortgage Guarantees), or mortgage protection insurance, which focuses on borrowers (see article Foreclosure Prevention Measures). In general, there is indirect assistance only when such guarantees or insurance are automatic, as is the case of the National Mortgage Guarantee provided by the Homeownership Guarantee Fund Foundation, which protects the lender. In most cases, there is a cost rather than a subsidy involved when insurance is voluntary, as is the case with the Mortgage Payment Protection Insurance (MPPI) in the United Kingdom (that covers the borrower for debt repayments in the event of unavoidable loss of income such as from illness or unemployment) or when it is required (e.g., compulsory insurance when loan to valuation ratios exceed a certain limit).

Wealth constraints arise both when financial institutions impose down payment or deposit constraints on borrowers and when there is a gap between household borrowing capacity and the cost of a reasonably priced home. This gap is increased by transaction costs such as stamp duties. One example of direct assistance is a deposit assistance scheme, such as first-home owner capital grants in Australia (see article First Home Owner Grants). A more generous example is the discount of up to 50% of the dwelling price that has been provided to long-term council housing tenants under the Right to Buy scheme in the United Kingdom (see article Privatisation of Social Housing). Exemptions and concessions from costs such as stamp duties are examples of indirect assistance.

In many countries, a wealth constraint is addressed by subsidy schemes that assist households saving for a deposit. The Bauspar savings scheme in Germany, along with similar schemes in Austria and France, are typical. Such schemes generally subsidise household savings for a number of years, and then may provide households with a subsidised second mortgage. Tax-assisted savings (in which the interest return on savings is either exempt from income tax, taxed at a concessional rate, or subsidised with a matching contribution) are a further example. In some countries, such savings may be intended to provide for superannuation payouts after retirement but are made available to assist access to homeownership. The use of compulsory savings accumulated in the Central Provident Fund in Singapore is one of the longest standing examples of such an approach. A general concern with many of these schemes is their inability to target assistance to those who are most in need of it (see article Contract Saving Schemes).

In times of high inflation, additional constraints on borrowing capacity arise from the so-called front-loading problem associated with conventional self-amortising mortgage instruments that are based on a constant repayment stream over the life of the loan. A solution to this problem is offered by index-linked loans where initial repayments are lower but increase over time in the expectation that incomes increase at the same rate. Indexed loans were introduced in some countries during the 1970s and 1980s, when inflation was high. In many cases, they were introduced by governments, presumably because private lenders were unable or unwilling to assess the risks associated with such loans. Iceland is one of the few countries where significant use is still made of such loans. The state-owned Housing Finance Fund issues 25-year and 40-year CPI-linked bonds. These are covered by a government guarantee and are traded on the stock exchange.

An alternative approach to addressing front-loading problems has been to use shared equity schemes, such as those introduced in the United Kingdom during the 1970s. Early schemes were funded by the central government purchasing half the dwelling. As incomes increased, households could buy out the government share and staircase to outright ownership. Similar products have been proposed more recently by both private and public sectors as a solution to the deposit gap faced by potential homeowners in the high house price era of the early 2000s. Public sector schemes generally have subsidies that operate through below-market returns on the publicly funded component of the dwelling and through the implicit protection that the public funding provides for borrowers reliant on private finance (see article Shared Equity). Despite differences in the way in which direct demand-side assistance for housing is provided, all demand-side subsidies suffer from the same potential weaknesses. If they add to housing demand or there is a limited supply of affordable housing, they may put upward pressures on house prices or rents. Their success also depends on the household's ability to find appropriate housing. It is partly for these reasons that complementary supply-side subsidies have been used to increase the supply of affordable housing for lower-income households. The term 'affordable housing' is used generally to describe any housing that is provided at a below-market rent or price to households whose needs are not being met in the market.

Supply-Side Subsidies for Renters

Supply-side subsidies for rental housing have been used when the private market has not been able to produce housing at rents low enough to be affordable for the lowest income households and when demand-side subsidies have been ineffective in achieving affordability outcomes. The most common examples of explicit supply-side subsidies are grants for the direct provision of public or social housing, or use of grants to private or nonprofit providers of affordable housing to lower-income households. For a considerable part of the twentieth century, government-funded social rental housing was the mainstay of rental housing provision in many countries. Much of the past emphasis on such publicly subsidised and provided housing arose from the need to respond rapidly to severe shortages of housing at the time.

Affordability for tenants generally was achieved by some form of cost-based rents, which ensured protection from increases in house and land values over time (see articles Policy Instruments that Support Housing Supply: Social Housing, and Rent Policies For Social Housing).

In principle, supply subsidies reduce the cost of providing affordable housing and increase its supply. If this housing is retained in public or not-for-profit ownership, such subsidies also can ensure housing remains affordable in perpetuity. However, subsidising the dwelling rather than the tenant requires administrative rules that govern rent setting and allocation policies to ensure affordability outcomes are achieved and sustained. Historically, attempts to meet supplementary goals, such as security of tenure, can result in poor targeting of subsidies, with some households receiving assistance when this was no longer needed. However, such an outcome can also result in greater social mix in such housing than is achieved by tighter targeting.

The high inflationary era of the 1970s meant that the goal of achieving specific affordability goals through use of supply-side subsidies had high upfront costs, and a given outlay resulted in considerably fewer households being assisted in the short term than was possible through use of demand-side subsidies. At the same time, crude shortages of housing had been overcome and supply-side subsidies (particularly those that were used to fund direct provision of affordable housing by the public sector) were seen as being ineffective because of a concern that they crowded out private provision of affordable housing. All of these factors contributed to a general decline in direct supply-side subsidies and to a contraction in the supply of public or social rental housing in most Western economies in the past few decades. Other factors (e.g., a desire to increase tenant choice) also have contributed to the move away from direct provision of social housing. This change in direction has also been associated with a desire to develop a so-called intermediate market where housing is priced below a full market rate but not subsidised as deeply as social housing.

The decline in social housing, the failure of private rental markets to provide and retain low-cost stock and the rising cost of demand-side subsidies, has contributed to a renewed interest in indirect supply-side subsidies targeted at not-for-profit and/or for-profit providers of affordable rental housing (see article Affordable Housing Strategies). Many of these subsidies have been provided indirectly as tax concessions, the precise nature of which depends on the institutional environment in the country in which they are employed. An example is the Low Income Housing Tax Credit (LIHTC), the single largest support for affordable rental housing in the United States (see article Low-Income Housing Tax Credits). Austria's use of housing construction convertible bonds is another.

Other examples of supply-side subsidies to assist provision of affordable rental housing are those directed at investors or developers through the finance system (e.g., use of tax-exempt bonds to finance affordable housing development or rehabilitation), and tax concessions allowing investors to deduct depreciation and interest costs against nonrental income (see article Social Housing: Measures to Attract Private Finance).

Supply-Side Subsidies for Purchasers

Some of the mechanisms described earlier are also used to subsidise affordable housing for purchasers. A common form of direct supply subsidy is provision of publicly owned land for affordable housing at no cost or at below-market value. Supply-side assistance is also provided when direct grants are provided for nonhousing purposes (e.g., community development or urban renewal) in areas where significant numbers of affordable dwellings are to be built.

Indirect supply-side subsidies arise whenever housing developers are not charged for the provision of public infrastructure needed to convert greenfield land to serviced land ready for development. When infrastructure is funded directly by the government (either through capital outlays or by borrowing paid for out of future taxation revenue) or by private sector funding with costs recouped on a user-pays or fee-for-service basis, there is little scope for directing such indirect supply subsidies to affordable housing. However, when infrastructure is funded by planning contributions from the uplift in land values following the rezoning of land for housing and the granting of planning permission, governments (e.g., in the United Kingdom and United States) have sought to negotiate the inclusion of affordable housing commitments from developers (see article Inclusionary Zoning to Support Affordable Housing). Such policies need to be implemented through the planning or regulatory process to ensure the intended outcome is achieved. A number of mechanisms (e.g., covenants that prevent speculative resale) can be used for this purpose (see below).

By the start of the twenty-first century, there was a widespread consensus that, for a number of reasons, existing supply-side and demand-side subsidies had been insufficient to generate affordable housing outcomes for an increasing number of households, and particularly renter households. This led to a renewed focus on regulation and planning.

Regulation through Planning

Planning policies explicitly recognise the importance of the location of housing and can be used to meet a variety of affordability goals. For example, they can encourage the provision of affordable housing in socially mixed communities, and they can improve access to jobs and services for lower-income households by locating affordable housing in well-serviced and job-rich areas. This can lower living costs by reducing travel costs.

Different planning strategies and mechanisms can be used to promote, provide, or protect affordable housing. Residential land supply levers enable the steady release of new land and stabilise the land market. They can operate through land audits and active identification or creation of new development opportunities by assisting in the assembly of potential development sites, or by acquiring or dedicating existing land for affordable housing. Barrier-reduction strategies remove constraints on development of low-cost housing. They can operate, for example, by speeding up approval processes for preferred developments. Preservation strategies counteract processes of urban change. They can control demolition of existing low-cost stock or prevent change of use (e.g., by protecting boarding houses or caravan parks from redevelopment). Incentives for new affordable housing reduce the cost of development. They can operate through density bonuses or increased floor space entitlements for projects providing affordable housing units. Finally, securing dedicated affordable contributions directly increases the supply of affordable housing. These can be voluntary negotiated agreements or mandatory controls imposing legal obligations on developers to contribute affordable housing as a condition of development approval.

In the United Kingdom, for example, the use of the land-use planning system (through Section 106 Agreements whereby local authorities can negotiate with developers seeking planning permission for new private housing) is becoming the most important instrument for adding to the stock of affordable housing in the United Kingdom.

The use of planning instruments is not universally accepted as a means of facilitating affordable housing provision, particularly when these are imposed at a local level and when developer charges differ across localities. Critics are concerned that they inhibit local economic development, drive jobs to regions where less use is made of these instruments, and increase the price of housing. However, there is no clear evidence of whether or not such effects occur and, in any case, any assessment of the costs must be offset against the potential economic and social benefits of increasing the supply of affordable housing.

An entirely different kind of regulatory approach to the use of planning mechanisms to affect affordability outcomes has been through controls on rents charged to tenants, or interest rates charged to purchasers.

Rent Regulation

In many countries, rent controls on private rental housing were introduced in the postwar period in the form of ceilings on nominal rents, as a means of ensuring that landlords were not able to benefit from the extreme housing shortages of the period. Many countries still maintain some form of rent control although the forms have changed over time to mitigate some of the negative effects of the earlier regulations (see article Access and Affordability: Rent Regulation). Most rent controls currently in place are more flexible. These rent stabilisation policies or second-generation rent controls either curb rent increases (e.g., by tying these to inflation) or limit the rate of return that can be obtained from rental property. They are designed to protect tenants but are typically accompanied by vacancy decontrol. Because of this, additional controls are often needed to ensure security of tenure and to protect tenants from eviction (see article Security of Tenure Legislation in Private Rental Housing).

Financial Regulation

Regulations that operate through the financial system typically affect providers of, or investors in, rental housing. These can operate in a number of ways. For example, finance provided by the private sector for social housing is often supported by state guarantees or insurance on long-term loans. In the Netherlands, for example, the Social Housing Guarantee Fund is a not-for-profit foundation that provides guarantees and government-backed counter guarantees that enable registered housing associations to attract loans at relatively favourable terms for specified purposes.

Social housing providers also can receive support by accessing loans at below-market rates of interest that are the result of requirements placed on financial institutions to channel funds to them. This practice was widespread before the general deregulation of financial systems that occurred in the mid-1980s but is still in place in many countries. In France, for example, social housing agencies (HLM – *organisme d'habitations a loyer modéré*) have access to cheaper loans funded from deposits managed by a special state-owned financial institution. These agencies also benefit from state subsidies on interest rates.

Another form of financial regulation that has played a significant role in contributing to affordability outcomes in the past is the regulation of mortgage interest rates. In the main, interest-rate regulation served as a means of keeping interest payments for home purchasers below what they otherwise would have been, particularly when it was combined with a policy of preferential lending to first-home buyers (see article Mortgage Interest Rate Regulation).

Factors Affecting the Effectiveness of Different Types of Policies

In the past 30–40 years or so there have been a number of shifts in the focus of housing policies and in the instruments used to achieve access and affordability objectives. In relation to housing affordability, housing subsidies have been redirected away from supply-side subsidies towards demand-side subsidies. There has also been a change in focus from policies supporting rental housing to those supporting access to homeownership. The first of these shifts has led to considerable debate over the question of whether demand- or supply-side subsidies are more effective in promoting affordability in rental housing. The second remained largely unquestioned until the subprime crisis and its aftermath.

Rental Policies

On the basis of evidence from their relatively recent review of US literature, Khadduri et al. (2003) outline the conditions under which demand- or supply-side subsidies might be expected to be most and least effective. This evidence suggests demand-side subsidies are generally more effective in meeting affordability objectives than are supply-side subsidies because they can be well targeted and are more cost effective for government budgets than are supply-side subsidies. However, they are less effective in tight housing markets (where vacancy rates are low) and in housing markets where the price elasticity of affordable housing supply is low. In such cases, they could increase the cost of housing in the affordable segment of the housing market and result in a net loss to low-income households.

Supply-side subsidies are more effective in curbing rent escalation in markets where the private market supply response is not adequate to meet increasing demand. They are also more effective in supporting comprehensive neighbourhood revitalisation efforts and in providing opportunities for low-income people to live in neighbourhoods in which they would have difficulty using a demand-side subsidy.

This evidence suggests that much of the debate on the relative merits of demand-side versus supply-side policies in achieving an affordability objective has been misplaced. It points to the value of both approaches and to the need for flexibility and responsiveness to local conditions.

Homeownership Policies

Although there is an emerging consensus that both demand-side and supply-side subsidies, along with appropriate regulatory policies, are all likely to be needed to achieve sustainable affordability outcomes in the rental sector, the issue of subsidies for owner-occupation is more problematic. Demand-side subsidies that facilitate access are often seen as inequitable because they provide support to households with fewer affordability problems and more choices than many of those in the rental market, inefficient because they add to price pressures in the housing market, and ineffective since they merely bring forward purchases that would have occurred in any case. There are also concerns that encouraging vulnerable households into homeownership and exposing them to the associated risks may not be in their best interests. The subprime crisis and subsequent global financial crisis suggest that it also might not be in the best interest of the economy as a whole.

Indirect tax subsidies lower the housing cost burden on existing homeowners but typically have a perverse impact on access to homeownership (see also articles Access and Affordability: Homeowner Taxation and Taxation). In the main, they are distortionary and both horizontally and vertically inequitable. As outlined at the start of this article, the case for supporting access to homeownership relies on broader objectives than those of affordability.

Conclusions

Recognition of the importance of a wider range of objectives than that implied by a narrow focus on ability to pay underpins much of the recent assessment of the appropriate role for housing policy and, in particular, underpins much of the assessment of policy mechanisms that support access and affordability.

Policies directed towards one objective often have had unintended consequences on other objectives. Thus, for example, policies that supported homeownership at the expense of social rental housing have had unintended consequences that include residualisation of the social rental system, concentration of poverty, and exclusion. It is important, therefore, not to assess the effectiveness of specific policies against a narrow objective, such as housing affordability, when other objectives may be equally important.

Table 3 presents a matrix of the effectiveness of various programmes in meeting seven policy goals that offer a more comprehensive framework against which affordability and access policies could be assessed. These findings reflect an evidence-based review of 70 years of policy and practice (in the United States). Because the effects of policy are inherently local and because policy objectives are likely to vary according to national circumstances, the assessments provided in **Table 3** may need to be revisited for specific programmes in other countries.

Despite the caution about assessing policies against a narrow range of objectives, however, it is possible to draw a number of broad conclusions on the basis of recent and past experiences. Rental assistance programmes require deep subsidies if they are to reach the neediest

Table 3 Potential effects of housing programmes on policy goals

	Rental housing assistance		Homeownership assistance				Land use regulations
	Supply-side production	Demand-side vouchers	Supply-side mortgage credit	Homebuyers tax policies and assistance	Supply-side production		

	Supply-side production	Demand-side vouchers	Supply-side mortgage credit	Homebuyers tax policies and assistance	Supply-side production	Land use regulations
Preserve and expand the supply of good-quality housing units	Yes – rental stock has been expanded, though more units need to be produced	Somewhat – may encourage landlords to maintain existing housing	Maybe – but impact is indirect	Maybe – but impact is indirect	Yes – primary goal of these programmes is expanding owner-occupied stock	Mixed – some programmes expand supply while others limit new affordable construction
Make housing more affordable and more readily available	Yes – but affordability depends on size and duration of subsidies	Yes – primary goal is affordability; success depends on households' ability to find units	Yes – but impact is indirect	Yes – enhances buying power, but depends on price of housing stock	Yes – primary goal of these programmes is affordability and access	Maybe – rent control may moderate rent increases in tight markets
Promote racial and economic diversity in residential neighbourhoods	Rarely – depends on where new units are located, and who is eligible to occupy them	Possibly – if recipients can find units in diverse neighbourhoods	Possibly – depends on locational decisions of buyers	Possibly – if recipients can find units in diverse neighbourhoods	Possibly – depends on the location of units produced and local economy	Mixed – some reforms can expand affordable housing in affluent communities
Help households build wealth	Generally not – though lower rents may lead to increased family assets	Generally not – though lower rents may lead to increased family assets	Yes – but depends on house price appreciation and individual borrower circumstances	Yes – but depends on house price appreciation and individual borrower circumstances	Yes – but depends on house price appreciation and individual borrower circumstances	Mixed – some programmes provide wealth-building opportunities while others do not
Strengthen families	Possibly – but little literature exists to confirm programmes' ability to strengthen families	Possibly – but less impact if units are located in distressed neighbourhoods or occupancy rules discourage family unification	Yes – but less impact if units are located in distressed neighbourhoods	Yes – but less impact if units are located in distressed neighbourhoods	Yes – but less impact if units are located in distressed neighbourhoods	No

(Continued)

Table 3 (Continued)

	Rental housing assistance		Homeownership assistance				
	Supply-side production	Demand-side vouchers	Supply-side mortgage credit	Homebuyers tax policies and assistance	Supply-side production	Land use regulations
Link housing with essential supportive services	Sometimes – when units are designed in conjunction with effective supportive services	Generally not	No	Probably not – unless services are explicitly linked with assistance	Probably not – unless services are explicitly linked with assistance	No
Promote balanced metropolitan growth	Rarely – depends on where the new units are built	Possibly – depends on recipients' ability to find units in suburban areas and close to job opportunities	Unclear – depends on general population's locational choices	Unlikely – though possible if recipients can find units in suburban areas and close to job opportunities	Rarely – the location of units thus far has generally not promoted balanced growth; however, neighbourhoods have benefited from homeownership	Mixed – zoning and regulatory reforms can promote affordable development in all jurisdictions, though some do not

Reproduced from Katz B and Turner M (2003) Rethinking local affordable housing strategies: Lessons from 70 years of policy and practice. *Discussion Paper Prepared for the Brookings Institute Center on Urban and Metropolitan Policy and the Urban Institute.* http://www.brookings.edu (accessed 26 January 2004).

households; affordable housing should not be clustered in low-income neighbourhoods; efforts to further expand homeownership to underserved minorities should proceed cautiously; and, finally, land-use and other regulatory policies can have profound effects on the location and supply of affordable housing.

The overview provided by this article highlights the diverse range of instruments that has been employed over time and place to address access and affordability problems and suggests there has been a changing emphasis on demand-side, supply-side, and regulatory policies in response to changing ideologies as much as to changing needs. Increasingly, evidence on the effectiveness of these policies suggests that use of multiple instruments through a mix of demand, supply, and regulatory policies provides a more robust approach to addressing affordability problems than reliance on one dominant instrument, as has occurred in past approaches to policy. Flexible and responsive mixing of these instruments should also provide a robust approach to the changing economic and social environment in which housing policy operates.

Access to housing and housing affordability has been a key challenge facing policymakers for many decades. Recent trends suggest it is likely to remain so into the foreseeable future.

See also: Access and Affordability: Homeowner Taxation; Access and Affordability: Housing Allowances; Access and Affordability: Housing Vouchers; Access and Affordability: Mortgage Guarantees; Access and Affordability: Rent Regulation; Affordable Housing Strategies; Contract Saving Schemes; First Home Owner Grants; Foreclosure Prevention Measures; Housing and Labour Markets; Housing Markets and Macroeconomic Policy; Inclusionary Zoning to Support Affordable Housing; Low-Income Housing Tax Credits; Mortgage Interest Rate Regulation; Policy Instruments that Support Housing Supply: Social Housing; Policy Instruments that Support Housing Supply: Supply-Side Subsidies; Privatisation of Social Housing; Rent Policies For Social Housing; Security of Tenure Legislation in Private Rental Housing; Shared Equity; Social Housing: Measures to Attract Private Finance; Taxation.

References

Kemp P (ed.) (2007). *Housing Allowances in Comparative Perspective*. Bristol: The Policy Press.
Khadduri J, Burnett K, and Rodda D (2003) Targeting housing production subsidies: Literature review. *Paper Prepared for U.S. Department of Housing and Urban Development Office of Policy Development and Research, Abt Associates, Inc.* http://www.huduser.org/Publications/pdf/TargetingLitReview.pdf (accessed 20 November 2008).

Further Reading

Elsinga M, Priemus H, and Cao L (2009) The government mortgage guarantee as an instrument in housing policy: Self-supporting instrument or subsidy? *Housing Studies* 24(1): 67–80.
Forrest R and Kearns A (2001) Social cohesion, social capital and the neighbourhood. *Urban Studies* 38(12): 2125–2143.
Gurran N, Milligan V, Baker D, Bugg L, and Christensen S (2008) New directions in planning for affordable housing: Australian and international evidence and implications. *Australian Housing and Urban Research Institute Final Report No. 120.* http://www.ahuri.edu.au (accessed 29 January 2009).
Hoek-Smit M and Diamond D (2003) The design and implementation of subsidies for housing finance. *Paper Prepared for the World Bank Seminar on Housing Finance*, 10–13 March. http://housingfinance.wharton.upenn.edu/Documents/design%20and%20implementation%20of%20subsidies%20for%20housing%20finance.pdf (accessed 1 March 2009).
Holmans A, Scanlon K, and Whitehead C with, Shilling J, and Hills J (2002) *Policy Options to Promote Affordable Housing.* Cambridge: Cambridge Centre for Housing and Planning Research. http://www.communities.gov.uk/documents/housing/pdf/141134.pdf (accessed 20 April 2009).
Jacobus R and Lubell J (2007) *Preservation of Affordable Homeownership: A Continuum of Strategies.* Center for Housing Policy Brief. http://www.ncbcapitalimpact.org/uploadedFiles/downloads/JacobusLubelloptions4-07.pdf (accessed 8 January 2008).
Katz B and Turner M (2003) Rethinking local affordable housing strategies: Lessons from 70 years of policy and practice. *Discussion Paper Prepared for the Brookings Institute Center on Urban and Metropolitan Policy and the Urban Institute.* http://www.brookings.edu (accessed 26 January 2004).
Kemp P (ed.) (2007) *Housing Allowances in Comparative Perspective* Bristol: The Policy Press.
Khadduri J and Wilkins C (2007) Designing subsidized rental housing programs: What have we learned? *Paper Prepared for Revisiting Rental Housing: A National Policy Summit, November 2006, Joint Center for Housing Studies.* http://www.jchs.harvard.edu/publications/rental/revisiting_rental_symposium/papers/rr07-5_khadduri.pdf (accessed 20 November 2008).
Lawson J and Milligan V (2007) International trends in housing and policy responses. *Australian Housing and Urban Research Institute Final Report No. 110.* http://www.ahuri.edu.au (accessed 12 November).
Quigley J and Raphael S (2004) Is housing unaffordable? Why isn't it more affordable. *Journal of Economic Perspectives* 18(1): 191–214.
Rohe W, van Zandt S, and McCarthy G (2002) Social benefits and costs of homeownership. In: Retsinas N and Belsky E (eds.) *Low-Income Homeownership: Examining the Unexamined Goal*, pp. 381–406. Washington, DC: The Brookings Institution.
Stephens M, Whitehead C, and Munro M (2005) *Lessons From the Past, Challenges for the Future for Housing Policy. An Evaluation of English Housing Policy 1975–2000.* London: Office of the Deputy Prime Minister. http://www.communities.gov.uk/documents/housing/pdf/138130.pdf (accessed 1 March 2009).
Yates J and Whitehead C (1998) In defence of greater agnosticism. *Housing Studies* 13(3): 415–423.

Policy Instruments that Support Housing Supply: Social Housing

M Berry, RMIT University, Melbourne, VIC, Australia

© 2012 Elsevier Ltd. All rights reserved.

Glossary

Demand-side subsidy Any benefit paid to the housing consumer/resident that reduces the price of housing to that consumer; it can be delivered in the form of cash (e.g., a grant) or a reduced taxation liability (e.g., exemption from tax on imputed rent accruing to home owners) or submarket interest rate.

Negative gearing Offsetting the excess of (for example) rental expenses, including mortgage interest costs, over rental income against the (rental) investor's other taxable income.

Not-for-profit housing Dwellings provided and managed by not-for-profit organisations, funded by some combination of government, private, and charitable sources.

Public housing Dwellings directly provided and managed by government, financed through taxation or public borrowing, though not necessarily constructed by government agencies.

Supply-side subsidy A benefit accruing to the housing producer/provider in order to lower the cost of housing provision to the consumer/resident.

Tax credit A rebate on the tax liability of a qualifying investor.

Rationale for Social Housing

Social housing has three key characteristics: rents are set at below-market levels, dwellings are allocated according to need rather than ability and willingness to pay, the scale and reach of social housing is dependent on the political and financial commitment of the government.

Housing in the developed nations is primarily provided through the market. However, housing markets are imperfect and incomplete; market failure leads to chronic undersupply and poor housing conditions, especially for many lower-income households in capitalist economies. Decent housing has positive externalities, like good health outcomes, stable family relations, and sustainable access to employment. Housing markets do not adequately 'internalise' these effects and so undersupply adequate housing. Similarly, information asymmetries limit the capacity of consumers to accurately judge the quality of housing on offer. Finally, inequalities in the distribution of income and wealth are reflected in and reinforced by the provision and location of housing. The consequences include homelessness, overcrowding, insecure tenure, health problems, educational disruption, and spatial mismatch between housing access and employment opportunities. Governments, therefore, intervene in various ways to ameliorate the social and economic costs of housing market failure. Social housing provision – that is, the provision of housing by government and not-for-profit agencies at submarket rents – is one of the major forms of intervention.

Historical Emergence of Social Housing

Social housing emerged from the late nineteenth century onwards, in the countries first undergoing industrialisation and urbanisation. Rapid urbanisation in countries like Britain resulted in significant migration from the countryside to the city and the growth of unhealthy, overcrowded 'slums'. Poor housing conditions were seen to threaten both public health and middle-class welfare and morals, while also undermining the productivity of urban workers. Government legislation in areas of public health, building controls, sanitation, and town planning aimed at ameliorating the worst of these problems. After the First World War many countries engaged in more direct forms of intervention in order to expand the supply of good quality housing at affordable cost to low-income and otherwise disadvantaged households. After a century of public housing provision, the proportion of houses owned and managed by government agencies varies widely between countries.

Sweden, while building a large public housing sector, also supported the growth of not-for-profit housing associations, partly financed by government subsidies and trade union engagement. The Netherlands developed a large housing association sector, initially supported by central government subsidies and loans which were eventually capitalised into a one-off act of debt forgiveness, backed by government guarantees, allowing the sector to maintain itself and expand through leveraging private mortgage finance. Swiss and Austrian policy initiatives in the post-Second World War period also facilitated not-for-profit organisations accessing private investment to provide housing to lower-income households at sub-market rents.

Housing policy reforms in England from the early 1980s onward shifted away from public housing towards encouraging the growth of both owner-occupation and the housing association sector. The main policy interventions here were the right-to-buy (RTB) accorded to public tenants and the transfer of public housing from local government to the housing associations (see below).

Germany and Australia, on the other hand, saw the development of a robust private residential rental sector, supported by regulatory protection in the former case and taxation incentives in the latter (e.g., mortgage interest deductibility, investment allowances, and negative gearing).

In the United States, the low income housing tax credit (LIHTC) scheme was introduced in the 1980s to attract private equity investment into the provision of rental housing to lower-income households at submarket rents. This programme effectively stopped further expansion in the small state government–provided public housing sector, as federal funds for these schemes were cut back.

It is also the case that countries vary in the balance of social housing provided by government and not-for-profit agencies. Cultural and historical differences may account for the greater reliance placed on one or other of these delivery approaches. Thus, countries with a strong social democratic tradition may lean more towards direct government provision, while countries with a stronger individualistic culture prefer to rely on the not-for-profit sector.

In most countries, especially over the past 30 years, social housing has assumed a residual role. Perhaps only in periods of sharp economic downturn, as has arisen globally in the wake of the 2008 global credit crisis, does social housing investment expand significantly. But the policy motivation can be its important macroeconomic role, helping to stabilise the economy at large, rather than housing policy goals.

The Main Policy Instruments

This section focuses, albeit selectively, on the fiscal instruments and regulatory/legislative frameworks utilised in particular countries in the postwar period to boost the supply of affordable social housing. The use of land use planning instruments, including impact or linkage fees and inclusionary zoning, is covered elsewhere in the encyclopedia.

United States

Public housing has declined in the United States over the past three decades. Policy attention has focused on attracting private equity investment into the low-rent end of the private rental market. The LIHTC scheme was introduced by the federal government in the Tax Reform Act of 1986. Under this programme, made permanent in 1993, federal tax credits are allocated to housing developers to assist in financing the construction of dwellings to be rented to low-income households. These credits are passed onto private, corporate, or institutional investors in return for equity contributed up-front to construct the dwellings. This reduces the cost of finance to developers, allowing them to house eligible households at submarket rents. The credits are allocated to state government housing finance agencies on a per capita basis. These agencies then call for bids by developers and allocate the credits on a competitive basis aimed at maximising the supply of affordable dwellings.

To date, more than two million dwellings have been provided to low-income tenants under this programme, accounting for about a quarter of all new rental dwellings constructed annually, making it the largest rental assistance scheme in the United States and probably the largest private equity financed affordable rental housing intervention globally. The earliest developments have now used up their tax credits and this raises major policy concerns about preserving stock in low-cost rental beyond this period. Recent research has found that the risk of losing LIHTC stock from low-income tenancy is lowest when not-for-profit organisations are involved in the development and state agencies have imposed affordability restrictions on developers in addition to those entailed in the LIHTC programme itself. As the stock ages and requires major upgrading, state agencies and not-for-profits have the opportunity to buy out original investors wishing to exit ownership. The latter may be willing to sell at reasonable prices in order to liquidate their investments and avoid investment in necessary dwelling improvements.

England

The Housing Act of 1974 marked the beginning of the policy switch away from municipal public housing towards the housing association sector. The Housing Corporation (HC), established in 1964, became the key regulatory and funding agency. Financial arrangements changed from a focus on supply-side capital and recurrent subsidies to local government towards a mix of supply-side capital grants (actually, subordinated government loans) to housing associations and a (demand-side) housing benefit payable to all eligible low-income tenants. The Housing Act of 1988 entrenched this policy trajectory and established a regulatory regime that would encourage the large-scale flow of private mortgage finance into the expansion of housing association stock over the next 20 years. This entailed regulatory HC oversight in the areas of housing association expenditure practices, accounting and reporting standards, and maintenance and management practices. Mortgage lenders were given further comfort by HC arrangements to deal with individual housing associations that experienced serious financial or operational difficulties.

Initially, housing associations relied heavily on Social Housing Grant from the HC, modestly leveraged by private mortgage finance in order to grow their housing stock. As this market matured and lenders became more familiar and comfortable with the sector and regulatory environment, the rate of leverage increased to around 50%. Given the apparent stability of a government-guaranteed revenue stream, in the form of housing benefits, the robust regulatory structure, the absence of housing association mortgage defaults, and continuing central government commitment to the Social Housing Grant for new stock, lenders reduced the interest rate spread on housing association mortgage loans to around 40 basis points above the rate at which banks lent to each other prior to the credit crunch of 2008–09.

The second major boost to the housing association sector, from the late 1980s onwards, came in the form of the large-scale voluntary transfer (LVST) of public housing stock from local government to the housing associations, since rebadged (in the mid-1990s) as registered social landlords. This programme entailed the equivalent of a 100% private-debt financed management buyout, transferring ownership and control of public housing estates to housing associations (when a majority of sitting tenants so voted). The transfer price was determined by the central government taking into account factors like quality of the stock, the projected income stream and operating costs, and reinvestment requirements to meet acceptable housing standards. In some cases this price was negative, requiring a one-off payment by Treasury to recipient housing associations to satisfy lenders as to continuing viability. Increasingly the LSVT mechanism came to be a vehicle for the government's urban regeneration programme, as has occurred with respect to housing association activities in other countries like France and the Netherlands.

Almost one million dwellings had been transferred from local government to the housing associations by 2005. The social housing stock (including public housing) has fallen to around 18% of the total housing stock in England (down from 33%), with the housing associations now accounting for 45% of the sector. Although, at one level, this transfer represents a zero-sum arrangement, it could be argued that the total English social housing stock would have been even lower in its absence. In the first place, the central government placed increasingly stringent loan and other financial constraints on local authorities, limiting their capacity to maintain and operate their existing stock, still less expand it. Second, the stock transfer process encouraged the growth of larger, more efficiently run housing associations able to access the deregulated financial markets. The need to access private loan finance also encouraged a process of concentration, through merger and acquisition, in the housing association sector. One consequence was the ability of large associations and syndicates of associations to finance stock expansion by selling investment-grade bonds, a route explicitly denied to local authorities. Finally, by increasing the asset base of housing associations, the risk to lenders was further reduced, placing downward pressure on the former's cost of finance.

Nevertheless, some disquiet as to the sustainability of this policy regime surfaced in England in the early years of the new millennium, even before the US-triggered global financial crisis. First, increasing regional inequalities in income and land values threatened the rental streams and asset backing of social housing in declining regions. Second, and conversely, high land values in some areas made it difficult for housing associations to acquire sites for new dwellings; recent experience suggests that access to appropriate sites is increasingly dependent on the application of land use planning instruments. Third, uncertainty about future housing benefit provisions, social rent-setting regimes, and other regulatory arrangements increased policy risk for private lenders. In each of these cases, lenders may need to price risk in more discriminating ways.

In the wake of the global credit crisis and the financial state of the banks, including the country's major mortgage lenders, it is not clear whether the social housing sector can continue to rely on a growing supply of relatively cheap loan finance to further expand the sector to meet growing social need. Credit rationing, as the banks reduce their appetite for housing loans, is likely to severely constrain housing association activity. Finally, rising land values in some regions is both limiting the growth of the social housing stock and placing pressure on rising rents, with adverse long-term consequences for housing affordability.

The Netherlands

Over the past 20 years Dutch social housing policy has shifted even more radically than England's away from the provision of supply-side subsidies to a reliance on regulation, demand-side rental subsidies, and private loan finance. Housing associations now own 34%, and local government 1%, of the total housing stock. In 1995, the 'grossing and balancing' process resulted in the national government transferring the present value of future capital and operating subsidies to the housing associations, by writing-off the latter's outstanding debt to government. This provided the associations with a large unencumbered asset base on which to borrow from private lenders in order to maintain and expand their stock.

Access to mortgage finance was enhanced by a number of regulatory provisions. First, a private guarantee fund for social housing (WSW) effectively insures mortgage lenders against default. The guarantees provided through the fund by both local and national governments allow mortgage loans to be made to the housing associations at below-market rates. Second, the central housing fund (CFV) is a nongovernment public statutory agency responsible for oversight of the financial viability of the housing association sector and for intervention, when required, to rescue or restructure individual associations in financial difficulty. Since 2001, the CFV has also been able to provide equity funds to associations for specific purposes by levying the whole sector. The levy is split into two parts. The first is based on the number of dwellings and the second is based on the value of the dwellings (upon which local taxes are based), on a 50/50 basis. The amount per dwelling was 26.50 Euros and 0.18 Euros for every 1000 Euros value in 2008.

The large footprint of the housing associations in the Dutch housing system is testament to the relative success of the sector in financial and operational terms. The average size of associations has increased and their number has decreased from around 900 to 500 in the past 15 years, suggesting significant gains from economies of scale. However, it is far from clear that the sector is meeting the full range of housing needs of households unable to access appropriate and affordable housing in the private market. Social rents have been increasing faster than inflation and average earnings. Rents are based on both the utility value of the dwelling and tenant income. Very-low-income and other disadvantaged households are increasingly dependent on the tiny remnant public housing stock and charitable organisations, in spite of the rental assistance programme.

As is occurring in England, France, and Germany, the Dutch government is relying on the housing associations as key agents of change in large area-based urban regeneration programmes. There is, however, evidence of significant tension between the increasingly professional and commercial orientation of the associations and the broader social goals of government. Changes in taxation laws after 2006 have removed corporation income tax exemptions for the housing associations. This limits the extent to which an association can cross-subsidise low-rent housing targeted at low-income tenants by profitable developments at higher rents to higher-income tenants. Tightening land supply constraints and rising construction costs, added to the upward drift in rents, have seen growth in the social housing stock decline sharply and the problems of providing affordable housing to the most vulnerable households intensify. These developments run against the long-established role of the housing association sector in meeting a broad range of housing needs, by location, dwelling type, and client groups, and its strong past contribution to social inclusion.

Austria

Austrian housing policy has a long tradition of providing supply-side subsidies to mass-produced municipal public housing and the limited profit housing association sector. Unlike developments in the Netherlands and other European countries, Austrian social housing continues to rely primarily on these funding sources to meet the needs of households unable to access affordable private housing. In addition, the federal and state governments have introduced new policy instruments to access private finance to boost social housing provision. The housing association sector accounts for 15% of the total housing stock with local government public housing making up a further 10%. The nine state governments allocate and monitor social housing outcomes within their jurisdictions. Thus, actual outcomes reflect their varying policy priorities and ideologies, with affordable rental provision highlighted in urbanised, social democrat–controlled electorates and home ownership encouraged in more conservative rural regions.

Housing associations have access to low–interest rate government loans to partly finance new house construction. Interest rates start at zero for the first 5 years and then increase slowly over the next 20–25 years to a maximum that is 1.5% below market mortgage rates. This low-cost source of finance funds up to 40% of a housing development. Private market rate loans can leverage a further 40–60%. An equity contribution of 10% is required by the developer, which can be a for-profit provider or a housing association. Rents must be set to cover operating and financing costs, including a return on owner equity, allowing a 2% premium for risk management purposes. Rental adjustments move in line with inflation and interest rate movements. All returns must be reinvested in social housing provided at cost-based rents. Eligibility is wider than in most countries with a broad section of the population accessing social housing at some stage in the life course.

Government legislation in the 1990s initiated a new market for tax-privileged Housing Construction Convertible Bonds that further expanded the supply of submarket rate private loan finance to social housing providers. Bonds are issued for terms of 10–20 years, at fixed or variable rates. To make this form of investment attractive, the housing bonds have two tax advantages: first, exemption from the capital gains tax is granted for the first 4% of returns, and second, the purchase of the bonds is classified as a special expense which can be deducted from income tax. Five new savings banks have been established by the major private banks to grow this market. Neighbouring Switzerland has introduced a similar bond issuing agency, backed by government guarantee. These tax benefits are only available to persons. By the end of 2006, the total volume of bonds had reached approximately € 11 billion, of which € 9–10 billion has been directed towards the financing of housing construction.

In short, Austrian social housing policy relies on a mix of traditional supply-side public housing provision and provision by housing associations and private developers utilising new financial instruments, in part engineered by deliberate government policy. Rents are kept affordable by limiting costs through low-cost loans, modest-sized dwellings, discounted land acquisition prices, efficient scale and management, and an equity contribution by the provider. Austria does not seem to be experiencing problems caused by rising rents and declining stock growth, by comparison, for example, with the Netherlands.

Policy Trends

In spite of the immense historical, cultural, political, and institutional variations across the advanced industrial societies, some recent common trends in policy approaches aimed at supporting the supply of social housing can be observed.

First, with few exceptions (e.g., Austria), national governments are seeking to move from supply-side towards demand-side subsidies related to housing consumers' incomes.

Second, private investors, especially lenders, are seen as an increasingly important source of debt finance for new social housing. This development has required appropriate regulatory arrangements and/or guarantee structures and changing subsidy regimes. Social rents in some countries have progressively increased to meet an increasing cost of finance and other investor concerns, creating significant affordability and crowding issues for vulnerable households, especially where the traditional public housing sector is in decline.

Third, the role of housing associations, already predominant in some countries, has strengthened considerably as key agents for delivering housing and other policy outcomes. The contribution of social housing providers to urban regeneration and poverty alleviation programmes in declining regions and urban subregions is a case in point.

Fourth, there has been increasing interest in attracting private equity finance into expanding the supply of social housing. However, to date, only the United States has succeeded in achieving large-scale flows in this context.

Finally, in rapidly growing regions, constraints on both land for new housing and greater dwelling density are increasing the cost of providing social housing, reinforcing the upward drift in social rents and the slowdown in stock growth.

See also: Housing Supply; Impact Fees; Inclusionary Zoning to Support Affordable Housing; Low-Income Housing Tax Credits; Privatisation of Social Housing.

Further Reading

Boelhouwer P (2007) The future of Dutch housing associations. *Journal of Housing and the Built Environment* 22(4): 383–391.
Czerny M and Weingärtler M (2007) *Housing Construction and Renovation as a Tool of Economic Prosperity*. Vienna, Austria: Federal Ministry of Economics and Labour.
Czischke D and Pattini A (2007) *Housing Europe 2007, Review of Social Cooperatives and Public Housing in the 27 EU Member States*. Brussels: Cecodhas.
Gibb K and Whitehead C (2007) Towards the more effective use of housing finance and subsidy. *Housing Studies* 22(2): 183–200.
Lawson J (2010) Path Dependency and Emergent Relations: Explaining the Different Role of Limited Profit Housing in the Dynamic Urban Regimes of Vienna and Zurich. *Housing and Theory Society* 27: 204–220.
Lawson J and Milligan V (2007) *International Trends in Housing and Policy Responses*. Melbourne, VIC: Australian Housing and Urban Research Institute.
Malpezzi S and Vandell K (2002) Does the low-income housing tax credit increase the supply of housing? *Journal of Housing Economics* 11: 360–380.
Nygaard C, Gibb K, and Berry M (2007) Ownership transfer of social housing in the UK: A property rights approach. *Housing, Theory and Society* 24(2): 89–110.
Scanlon K and Whitehead C (eds.) (2008) *Social Housing in Europe II: A Review of Policies and Outcomes*. London: London School of Economics and Political Science.

Relevant Websites

www.ahuri.edu.au – Australian Housing and Urban Research Institute
www.cchpr.landecon.cam.ac.uk – Cambridge Centre for Housing and Planning Research
www.facsia.gov.au – Department of Families, Housing, Community Services and Indigenous Affairs
http://en.wikipedia.org/wiki/Affordable_housing – Affordable Housing
www.hud.gov/offices/fheo/lihtcmou.cfm – Homes and Communities
www.otb.tudelft.nl – Delft University of Technology

Policy Instruments that Support Housing Supply: Supply-Side Subsidies

M Cigdem, RMIT University, Melbourne, VIC, Australia

© 2012 Elsevier Ltd. All rights reserved.

Glossary

Demand-side subsidy Government assistance to improve the ability of households to pay for housing.

Displacement Occurs when lower-income residents or public/social housing tenants are forced to move out of their neighbourhood, either through formal relocation programmes or through rising housing costs.

Elasticity of demand A measure of the relative change in the amount purchased in response to a change in price.

Head leasing A scheme whereby a public or social agency leases housing from a private landlord and sublets to eligible tenants.

Inclusionary zoning A mandatory or incentive-based programme that requires affordable units to be built as part of a housing development.

Low-income housing tax credit A tax credit that gives incentives for the development of housing and is targeted at low-income Americans.

Public housing A form of housing tenure that is built, operated, and owned by government and that is typically provided at below-market rents to low-income households.

Social housing A form of housing tenure that is supplied by voluntary or not-for-profit providers, but typically subsidised by government.

Supply-side subsidy Government assistance aimed at reducing the costs of producing or maintaining housing units so that they are affordable to low- or moderate-income households.

Introduction

Supply-side housing subsidies are designed to increase the availability of affordable housing for low-income households. They are utilised by governments to lower the costs of constructing or maintaining housing units. Governments of industrialised countries in particular have a long-standing tradition of employing supply-oriented policies to tackle the issue of housing shortages. Such programmes typically take the form of cash grants, low-interest loans, land use interventions, tax incentives, and the relaxation of regulatory barriers. These initiatives can add to the housing stock either directly or indirectly. Direct methods involve governments taking responsibility for the construction or rehabilitation of dwelling units for eligible low-income households. Indirect methods offer incentives to private developers who produce more affordable homes.

The purpose of this article is to outline supply-side policy instruments that are most commonly used by governments of developed countries, and discuss their effectiveness by drawing on the experience of Western governments. The structure of this article is as follows: section 'Subsidies to Housing Supply: An Economic Analysis' provides an economic analysis of supply-side subsidies and their impact on the housing market. It examines the circumstances in which they will be most effective; section 'Types of Supply-Side Subsidies' describes the various supply-side policies adopted by developed countries; and section 'Concluding Remarks' focuses on new reform directions.

Subsidies to Housing Supply: An Economic Analysis

Supply-oriented housing subsidy programmes have been used by Western governments to expand the stock of decent and affordable housing. But, how is this achieved? As the subsidy is attached to building structures or bricks and mortar, rather than to the household, it lowers the cost of production for not-for-profit or for-profit owners, or public bodies of various sorts. In turn, these reduced production costs will be reflected in lower house prices to buyers or rents to tenants.

In **Figure 1**, we consider how a supply-side subsidy that reduces the costs of production will affect the rent charged and quantities bought and sold of rental dwellings. The horizontal axis measures the quantity of rented housing units where all housing units are assumed to be homogeneous. The vertical axis represents the rental price of these housing units. The demand curve plots the quantity of housing services consumers are willing to purchase at a particular rent. As it is sloping

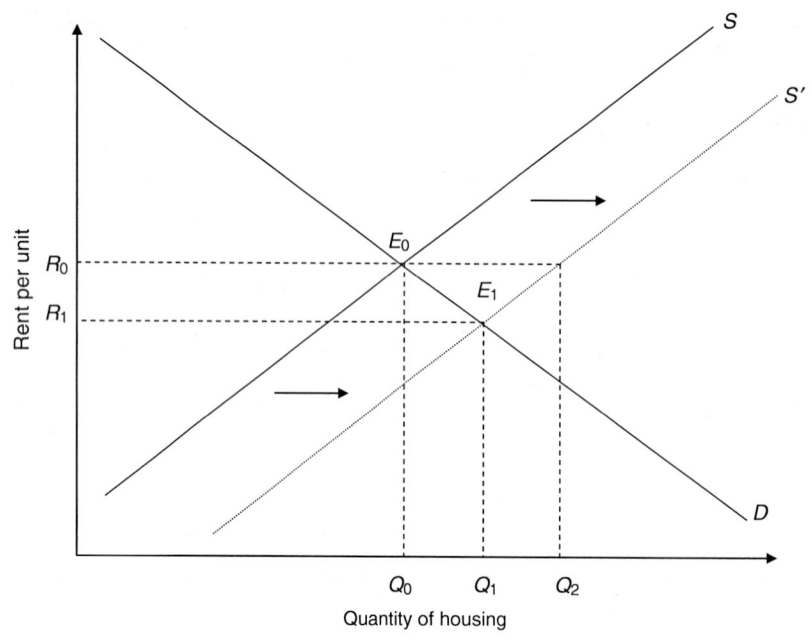

Figure 1 Effect of a supply-side subsidy in the housing market.

downwards, it assumes that a lower rental price will encourage an increase in the quantity of housing services demanded, holding all else fixed. The supply curve, on the other hand, slopes upwards in the long run. It assumes that the incremental cost of supplying additional rental housing is increasing. The intersection of these two curves at E_0 determines the equilibrium rent.

So how does a supply-side subsidy affect housing markets? From the producer's perspective, a housing subsidy that reduces production costs will motivate landlords to increase the supply of rental housing at any given rent, as represented by a shift in the supply curve from S to S'. At the original equilibrium rent, R_0, however, there is now excess supply ($Q_0 < Q_2$) and vacancy rates will increase. Landlords are compelled to lower rents from R_0 to the new postsubsidy equilibrium rent R_1, and the amount of housing consumed by tenants will increase from Q_0 to Q_1.

Price Elasticity of Demand and the Effectiveness of Supply-Side Subsidies

This analysis of demand and supply has established the way in which a supply-side housing subsidy influences both the equilibrium rental price for housing services and the corresponding quantity of housing units that landlords are willing to offer. Of equal importance, however, is the magnitude of these changes that can range from small to large, conditional on the responsiveness of the quantity of housing demanded to changes in rents. In economics, such a measure is called the price elasticity of demand (PED). It can be defined using the following formula:

$$\text{PED} = \frac{\text{Percentage change in quantity demanded}}{\text{Percentage change in price}}$$

For example, if a 10% fall in the price of rental housing results in a 20% increase in quantity of housing services demanded, the PED can be calculated as

$$\text{PED} = \frac{20\%}{-10\%} = -2$$

In the above example, the PED is $->1$ in absolute value as the percentage change in quantity demanded is greater than the percentage change in price. When this is the case, the PED is said to be 'elastic'. Conversely, if the PED is <1, it is said to be 'inelastic'.

Figure 2 illustrates the importance of price elasticity by placing elastic and inelastic demand curves such that they both pass through an initial housing market equilibrium at E_0. At this presubsidy equilibrium, rents are equal to R_0 and quantity demanded equals Q_0. After the introduction of the supply-side subsidy, the supply curve shifts out to S'. So what happens to the housing stock? The answer to this depends on whether demand for housing is price elastic or inelastic. In the case of an inelastic demand curve ($D_{\text{inelastic}}$), there is a reduction in rents from R_0 to R_1 but a relatively small increase in the quantity of housing consumed (Q_0 to Q_1). In the case where demand is more responsive to rent changes (from Q_0 to Q_2), rents only fall from R_0 to R_2, but there is a relatively large increase in the quantity of housing consumed. The analysis shows that if housing is a necessity such that the amount of housing demanded changes little if rents fall, the main impact of supply-side subsidies is to improve the affordability of existing housing. There will be relatively little impact on new supply.

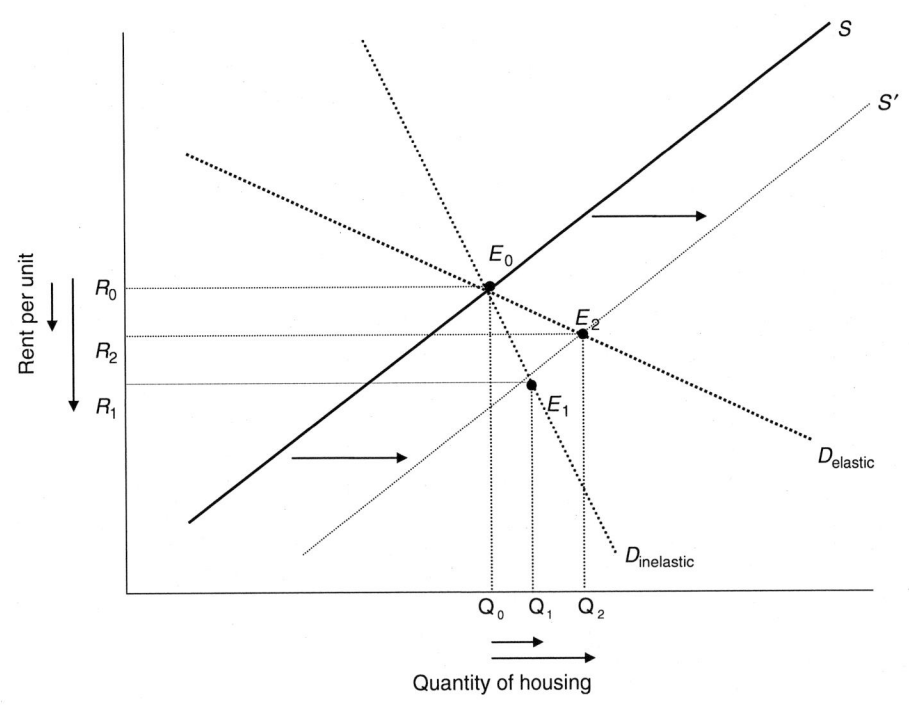

Figure 2 Elastic and inelastic demand curves.

Types of Supply-Side Subsidies

There are three main ways that governments utilise subsidy programmes to promote increases in housing supply:

1. Increasing supply directly through the construction of public/social housing or indirectly through offering incentives that promote private provision of housing opportunities;
2. Rehabilitation or upgrading of existing substandard dwellings to an acceptable standard; and
3. Relaxing the regulatory barriers that might impede private developers in the delivery/production of housing; or through the 'positive' use of the planning system via programmes such as density bonuses and inclusionary zoning. While these interventions involve no cash transfers to housing providers, they offer preferential treatment that can promote the supply of affordable housing by reducing costs of production.

These are discussed in detail below.

New Construction

One of the main strengths of supply-oriented housing subsidies is that they can directly bring about an increase in the stock of affordable housing through stimulating new construction. Supply-side subsidies around the world are typically targeted on rental housing. The subsidies can be either direct assistance to the government construction and subsequent management of public/social housing, or indirect assistance targeted on private suppliers of rental housing.

Public/social housing

Governments may directly add to the existing housing stock through the provision of public/social housing. Public housing is a housing tenure that is financed, owned, and managed by government agencies. Social housing is a broader category that also includes housing that is owned and administered by voluntary or not-for-profit providers (for a discussion on this topic within this encyclopaedia, see article Policy Instruments that Support Housing Supply: Social Housing).

A cogent argument in favour of the direct provision of affordable housing by government bodies is that it is a more targeted approach to meeting the housing needs of disadvantaged tenants as compared to indirect subsidy programmes that seek to achieve the same outcome but by incentivising private supply. Through guaranteeing increases in the housing stock, direct public provision bypasses many of the uncertainties posed when relying on market forces. Critics, however, argue that the construction of public housing may lead to displacement. As low-cost public housing increases, demand for private housing units falls, leading to the displacement of private, nonsubsidised production. We discuss the issue of displacement further in the next section.

Subsidies to private providers

Indirect supply-oriented programmes use subsidies targeted at the private sector and designed to encourage private investors or developers to increase the new construction of rental housing. Encouraging private sector provision of affordable rental housing has gained considerable popularity in developed countries in recent times. There is a range of mechanisms that can be used to incentivise private developers to provide housing. Such subsidy programmes include project-based rent subsidies, favourable tax treatments, guarantee schemes, and head-leasing programmes. These are discussed below.

Project-based rent subsidies: Landlords may receive project-based rent subsidies for serving low-income tenants. An example of such a programme is the Project-Based Voucher (PBV) programme, which is a component of the Section 8 Housing Choice Voucher Program (HCVP) implemented in the United States. Unlike the demand-side component of HCVP, which is a 'tenant-based' programme offered to the renter and therefore 'portable', the PBV programme subsidy is attached to the building itself. The subsidy therefore remains with the housing development even after the exit of individual tenants, and so it benefits incoming low-income tenants. Under the programme, the US Department of Housing and Urban Development (HUD) enters into a contract with for-profit owners of private multifamily housing over a fixed period of time, who in turn provide housing to low-income households in accordance with the local rent levels and related guidelines established by HUD. In a typical case scenario, the subsidy, paid by HUD to the landlord, will cover the difference between 30% of the household's income and the contract rent.

Favourable tax treatment: This is another popular supply-side approach that promotes new construction by offering tax preferences often geared to the supply of affordable rental housing. The UK's Business Expansion Scheme (BES) was one such programme implemented between 1989 and 1993. This incentive scheme provided up-front tax relief to individuals investing in companies letting residential properties on assured tenancies. The programme was essentially designed to encourage the supply of privately rented housing in the United Kingdom and to foster the emergence of more landlords. In the United States, the Low-Income Housing Tax Credit (LIHTC) programme offers a dollar-for-dollar tax credit for investments in affordable housing. The programme offers funding for the construction costs of new or rehabilitated affordable housing by allowing the investor to take a federal tax credit that is equivalent to a large portion of the cost incurred in developing low-income housing units in a rental project (see article Low-Income Housing Tax Credits).

Guarantee schemes: Several developed countries favour the use of guarantee systems as an effective way to enhance the supply of affordable housing. These schemes are designed to appeal to housing providers who, rather than assuming the entire risk of a housing investment, can utilise guarantee schemes to share some of the investment risks with government. One such risk is household capacity to meet their financial obligations, whether it be paying rents or making mortgage interest payments. In offering guarantee schemes, governments take on some of the financial risk by securing some portion of the commercial loans taken out by investors in affordable housing. Guarantee schemes in developed countries offer a range of risk cover, with some schemes offering a 100% guarantee which encompasses both loan and transaction costs, while others cover only a portion of the total loan amount.

Head-leasing programmes: Head leasing is where a public or social agency leases housing from a private landlord and sublets that housing to tenants who satisfy eligibility criteria for public or social housing. An example in Australia is the Sale and Leaseback Program introduced in 1996 by Defence Housing Australia (DHA), a government enterprise that provides a range of housing services for defence force members. Under the Sale and Leaseback Program, private investors acquire DHA-owned properties and then lease them back to DHA who manage the lease of the housing. The DHA therefore becomes contractually responsible for the provision of property management and maintenance services. Furthermore, the lease guarantees rents for the term of the lease, regardless of whether or not the property is occupied, at rent levels that never fall below the initial rent, and ensures zero vacancy risks. These types of properties account for over 60% of all residences that accommodate defence force members.

Rehabilitation or Upgrading of Existing Dwellings

An alternative to subsidy programmes that encourage new construction are programmes supporting the rehabilitation and/or upgrading of existing dwellings (see articles Housing and Neighbourhood Quality: Home Improvement Grants and Housing and Neighbourhood Quality: Urban Regeneration). These programmes typically seek to reverse the physical decay of dwellings in rundown neighbourhoods. Since the residents invariably have relatively low incomes, they usually need assistance from publicly financed programmes or subsidies. Such improvements can entail either the demolition or redevelopment of dwellings, often as part of a slum clearance scheme, or the rehabilitation of housing by means of repair, improvement, conversion, or modernisation. Rehabilitation programmes can generate positive spillover effects whose scope often extends beyond the boundaries of project sites to include the wider neighbourhood community. Some of these benefits include:

- improving local private property values by revitalising or replacing existing public housing and removing neighbourhood eyesores in the process;
- enhancing the housing options available to households with low or moderate incomes;
- eliminating or ameliorating the adverse effects of discrimination; and
- breaking up concentrations of poverty by encouraging mixed-income and mixed-tenure communities.

An often-studied rehabilitation programme is the HOPE VI project introduced in the United States (see article HOPE VI). The programme aims to improve communities by removing physically deteriorating public housing sites and replacing them with mixed-income housing. The main criticism of such rehabilitation programmes is displacement concerns that threaten low-income tenants and are caused by the upward filtering of low-income housing units to higher-income households. Displacement effects can take on two dimensions. The first is the immediate dislocation experienced by low-income households as a result of increases in real occupancy costs and property taxes in revitalised areas. The second dimension refers to concerns about long-run reductions in the housing stock for low-income tenants created by the upgrading of formerly declining neighbourhoods which, by attracting higher-income occupants, drives out lower-income tenants. To negate the adverse effects of neighbourhood rehabilitation, governments often couple such programmes with new construction of affordable housing that is designed to offset the loss of affordable housing units through the upgrade of previously low-income housing.

Relaxing Regulatory Barriers and 'Proactive' Use of Planning

In the housing context, regulatory barriers can be described as interventions, either deliberate or de facto, which either prohibit or discourage the construction of affordable housing by increasing its cost of production, or curbing revenue. They can come in various forms including strict building, planning, and subdivision standards, rent control, land use controls, taxes, and licence fees. Some of these regulations directly affect the cost of constructing new housing or the rehabilitation of existing dwellings and can therefore raise costs and cause lengthy development delays. For instance, programmes that set low maximum density requirements ultimately result in higher housing costs as they require more land per dwelling, and the cost of these larger lots becomes capitalised into the selling price of the dwelling. The removal or relaxation of these barriers could bring about positive changes at relatively low cost to the government, particularly in instances where they hinder the construction of low-income housing. State and local governments could, for example, allow speedy planning approval of medium- to high-density developments, or other types of housing aimed at low-income households, as the resulting reduction in delay, fees, and charges is likely to have a significant impact on housing supply. Another example is the 'anti-snob' laws that have been implemented in several states in the United States and allow developers of affordable housing to bypass cumbersome local planning laws if the local jurisdiction does not currently provide sufficient opportunities for affordable housing development.

An alternative approach that is also exploited by some local and state governments is the proactive or 'positive' use of planning schemes to encourage the development of affordable housing. The most high profile of these approaches is inclusionary zoning schemes (see article Inclusionary Zoning to Support Affordable Housing) and density bonuses (see article Housing Supply: Urban Growth Boundaries). With inclusionary zoning ordinances municipalities require developers to set aside a fixed percentage of new construction in designated areas for affordable housing. They are often used in conjunction with density bonuses, which are grants offered to developers who, for every unit of affordable housing developed, are allowed to construct a greater number of market rate units than would be otherwise permitted. The main appeal with inclusionary zoning is that they contribute directly to the new housing stock, and thus offer an uncomplicated means of ensuring growth in housing supply. Density bonuses are advantageous for the developer because they permit the developer to build additional units on a site, thus generating more income. Sites without density bonuses are restricted by zoning codes to a lower number of units.

Concluding Remarks

In the past, supply-side subsidies were regarded as the main form of housing assistance, and were particularly prominent in regions like North America and Europe.

From around the 1970s, however, Western governments have gradually steered away from traditional supply-side assistance and relied increasingly on more demand-oriented policy instruments. Programmes like Rent Assistance in Australia and housing vouchers in the United States have gained greater momentum as they have proven to be significantly less costly than new construction programmes, and may offer low-income households more housing choice. Such options are not provided by supply-oriented subsidies, which are generally attached to the building, making them distinguishable from housing occupied by higher-income households and can therefore stigmatise the surrounding community. Another drawback of supply-side subsidies is their tendency to distort markets. This is particularly evident when governments assume roles that could be carried out more efficiently by the market.

For these reasons, there is a general trend away from direct government-funded provision towards a more enabling role that focuses more on the demand side of housing markets. That is, governments are placing greater emphasis on deregulation of the planning system that relaxes cumbersome constraints hindering housing supply. Also, many countries are encouraging the private finance of social housing and a greater involvement from the private sector in housing supply through, for example, transfer of public housing to social housing agencies.

See also: HOPE VI; Housing and Neighbourhood Quality: Home Improvement Grants; Housing and Neighbourhood Quality: Urban Regeneration; Housing Supply: Urban Growth Boundaries; Housing Supply; Inclusionary Zoning to Support Affordable Housing; Low-Income Housing Tax Credits; Policy Instruments that Support Housing Supply: Social Housing.

Further Reading

Apgar WC, Jr. (1990) Which housing policy is best. *Housing Policy Debate* 1: 1–32.

DiPasquale D (1999) Why don't we know more about housing supply? *The Journal of Real Estate Finance and Economics* 18(1): 9–23.

Dodson J (2006) Rolling the state: Government, neoliberalism and housing assistance in four advanced economies. *Urban Research Program Research Paper 7*. Brisbane, QLD: Griffith University.

Flood J and Yates J (1989) Housing subsidies and income distribution. *Urban Studies* 26: 193–210.

Galster G (1997) Comparing demand-side and supply-side housing policies: Sub-market and spatial perspectives. *Housing Studies* 12(4): 561–577.

Golland A (1996) Housing supply, profit and housing production: The case of the United Kingdom, the Netherlands and Germany. *Netherlands Journal of Housing and the Built Environment* 11(1): 5–30.

Haffner M and Oxley M (1999) Housing subsidies: Definitions and comparisons. *Housing Studies* 14: 145–162.

Hulse K (2002) *Demand Subsidies for Private Renters: A Comparative Review*. Melbourne, VIC: Australian Housing and Urban Research Institute.

Malpezzi S and Mayo SK (1997) Getting housing incentives right: A case study of the effects of regulation, taxes, and subsidies on housing supply in Malaysia. *Land Economics* 73(3): 372–391.

Malpezzi S and Vandell K (2002) Does the low-income housing tax credit increase the supply of housing? *Journal of Housing Economics* 11(4): 360–380.

Milligan VR, Dieleman FM, and Kempen R (2006) Impacts of contrasting housing policies on low-income households in Australia and the Netherlands. *Journal of Housing and the Built Environment* 21: 237–255.

Quigley JM (1979) What have we learned about urban housing markets? In: Mieszkowski P and Straszheim M (eds.) *Current Issues in Urban Economics*, pp. 391–429. Baltimore, MD: Johns Hopkins University Press.

Turner B and Whitehead M (2002) Reducing housing subsidy: Swedish housing policy in an international context. *Urban Studies* 39(2): 201–217.

Political Ideologies

P King, De Montfort University, Leicester, UK

© 2012 Elsevier Ltd. All rights reserved.

Glossary

Hegemony The 'common sense' worldview of the dominant class that is successfully imposed on a society.

Political ideology A set of political beliefs about how society ought to be and how to improve it, irrespective of whether those ideas are true or false or good or bad.

Introduction

The end of the twentieth century has been said to have brought with it the end of ideology. According to Francis Fukuyama the end of history has been reached, with liberal democracy being the optimum form of social organisation. In the 1990s politicians such as Blair and Clinton stressed that they concentrated on 'what worked' and were not concerned with what they saw as the outdated ideologies of the left and right. A new 'Third Way' between socialism and conservatism had been found, which would allow for the pragmatic coupling of social justice with entrepreneurship. The collapse of Soviet communism in Eastern Europe and the adoption of a form of capitalism by China indicated an end to ideological hostilities. In terms of housing, policies in most developed countries shifted away from direct provision and towards supporting individual households. Owner occupation came to dominate housing systems and social provision increasing became seen as an outdated anachronism, justified at best as a safety net for those unable to gain access to housing through markets.

Yet the financial crisis of 2007–08, precipitated by a collapse in the US housing market, has shown that history did not end in the 1990s. In what must be one of the most unexpected political developments of the postwar period, governments throughout the developed world, including the United States of America and the United Kingdom, have nationalised banks and financial institutions to protect them from the harsh winds of global capitalism. The clarion call of the old hard left – to nationalise the banks – has actually happened and in the very countries where leaders such as Reagan and Thatcher had proclaimed the death of socialism. In some countries, such as New Zealand, owner occupation is in decline, and more generally there is a reassertion of the need for social provision.

So the end of ideology was merely an illusion, and we still live in interesting times. We appear to be back to a situation where politics is not settled and where there are genuine debates about the direction economies can and ought to take. Of course, in the academy ideology never went away and debates on the nature of housing tenure and the role of housing subsidies were long and heated. What is perhaps different now is that more people are prepared to listen and engage in the debate.

This article explores political ideology in relation to housing. It begins with a definition of political ideology and then looks briefly at the various types of ideology that have been applied to housing. It then explores some of the problems with regard to using political ideologies to explore housing. In particular, two problems are discussed: first, the discrepancy between what might be called 'pure' ideology in its academic setting and the use of ideology in an actual political setting; second, the problem of overgeneralisation, where labels are used too glibly to attach a particular significance to an idea or policy usually with the aim of discrediting it by association.

What Is a Political Ideology?

It is only slightly facetious to define an ideology as something somebody else has, but to which we are immune. In the history of political thought ideology has been seen as a pejorative, as a means of describing those who are deluded (according to Marxists), prone to irrationality (as seen by classical liberals), or dependent on theory instead of real life (according to traditional conservatives). This distrust of ideology carries through to conventional political discourse, in that most politicians would decry policies based on preconceived ideals, insisting instead that they concentrate on the practical and workable. Ideology, therefore, has historically been seen as a form of false thinking and accordingly it is something we should seek to rid ourselves of.

However, as Ian Adams has argued, recent years have seen a change of attitude, amongst academics and commentators at least. The word now tends to be used

> in a non-partisan, non-pejorative way, so that it means simply a set of political beliefs about how society ought to be and how to improve it, irrespective of whether those ideas are true or false or good or bad. (1993: 3)

An ideology can therefore be seen as a set of beliefs that we accept and use to justify our actions. These beliefs rest on some normative principles which cannot be gainsaid or further underpinned. Our ideological position can therefore be seen to be the bedrock of our opinions and attitudes. We cannot, as it were, go any further down than these ideas to base our actions. Put another way, we cannot defend our ideology with noncircular argument – it is where no further justification is possible.

We can therefore argue that it is a part of certain ideologies, such as Marxism and classical liberalism, to hold a particular attitude towards ideology. Having said this, ideologies do operate differently. In particular we can distinguish between those ideologies that are concerned with societal outcomes and those more concerned with the processes by which outcomes are determined. Both Marxism and classical liberalism can be seen as normative social theories seeking to justify a particular form of social organisation. The former is concerned with the establishment of a society based on principles of equality, whilst the latter is based on the maximisation of personal freedom. Yet both take a particular form of social organisation as being optimal. These ideologies seek to describe what the desired form of society will look like and how it will operate.

However, conservatism, at least in its more traditional varieties, is somewhat different. Conservatism is an ideology concerned with means. It does not have a particular end, other than that of 'good government'. Conservatism is concerned more with procedure than particular ends. It therefore has no universal principles and tends to reject abstract theorising. Conservative ideology therefore presents no model for how society should look, rather it is concerned with the means by which both change occurs and can be managed. The key distinction of conservative ideology is that it is dispositional rather than patterning. It is a concern for processes rather than specifying outcomes.

The Uses of Ideology

So there are different forms of political ideology, but of what use are they? As stated above, to call someone ideological is frequently to insult them and accuse them of acting out of prejudice or an ulterior motive.

Despite this, it can be suggested that there are at least three reasons why we should see political ideology as important in the study of housing and other phenomena. First, ideology provides us with a way into the political. It gives us a jargon or vocabulary to help us understand phenomena. Hence the use of basic oppositional terms such as 'rights and responsibilities' and 'equality and freedom' can be used to frame important debates on the distribution of resources such as housing.

In particular, debates within housing have tended to focus on tenure. The right to private property ownership can be countered by an emphasis on meeting need and showing solidarity to those without adequate resources. Hence since the late 1970s there has been much academic debate over the extension of owner occupation and the residualisation of social provision.

Second, political ideologies, precisely because they are oppositional and based on distinct normative positions, help us to distinguish between arguments and to create category distinctions. We can again see this in arguments over the nature of property rights and the importance of owner occupation for views based on socialist and conservative principles.

But, third, we can use political ideology to link housing phenomena to broader social ideas and movements, such as the legitimate role of the state and the market, and so help us to understand how housing fits into a broader context. Political ideologies have a wide resonance that connects the present to the past and across cultural boundaries.

There is then some purpose to using distinct political ideologies to elucidate housing phenomena and we can point to a few examples in the literature. Many have used social democratic ideas of active government and scepticism of markets to inform this study of housing as a part of the postwar British welfare state. This ideology is used to support social provision and an active state which subsidies the provision of housing. Social democrats have argued that an overemphasis on market individualism has led to a residualisation of social housing and an overreliance on private property as a source of household welfare. These writers will critique owner occupation and the manner in which successive governments have promoted owner occupation, often at the expense of social housing. A particularly relevant example here is the controversy over the right to buy in the United Kingdom, introduced in 1981 to allow sitting tenants to buy their dwelling at a discount.

In contrast to this, conservative thinkers have extolled the virtues of property ownership, albeit in different ways. Some tend to emphasise the notions of stability and security that property rights bring. It encourages an acceptance of the status quo, as well as a sense of security and complacency at the personal level. More abstractly, there are conservative thinkers who contend that property rights are the basis of social relations in that rights determine the use of things and our ability to include and exclude others. Some conservatives argue that conservatism is the dominant ideology within the political culture of many Western countries, but particularly the United States and the United Kingdom. Accordingly the ideology transcends what might be called the tribal divisions of political debate: Therefore, all UK political parties operate within a conservative milieu. This is, needless to say, a controversial argument which is contested by the left of centre consensus in housing studies.

Also on the right we can see a number of what might be called libertarian positions, which, for example, criticise the imposition of planning restrictions on housing development and worry about the incentives that accrue from the direct state provision of housing. Whilst conservatives might accept social provision, libertarians will tend to argue against all forms of state involvement in housing and seek to promote markets as the principal means of accessing housing.

Of course, the arguments in support of markets gained considerable currency in the 1980s and 1990s with the election of right of centre governments in countries such as Germany, the United States, and the United Kingdom. Housing policy tended to follow this more liberal approach, in terms of both a shift in focus towards owner occupation and a reduction in social provision. A further aspect of this rightward shift was a greater emphasis given to market and commercial disciplines in the operation and management of public services. This took the form of an increased use of private operators to run state-run facilities, the use of private finance as well as outright privatisation. In terms of housing this was manifested not merely by an increase in owner occupation but also by the use of private finance and a general shift away from object or supply side subsidies and towards support to individuals aimed at bolstering demand. The 'housing problem' in many countries was recast as a problem of access and choice at the individual level rather than a matter of structural inequalities and diverging class interests.

This latter view was most associated with a Marxist analysis of society. There is a considerable Marxist literature on owner occupation, which sees property as a form of false consciousness aimed to further the interest of a dominant class and to ensure the reproduction of labour in advanced capitalist societies. Much of this literature dates from before 1990 and indeed can be seen as a reaction against the shift to the right in policy. However, many of these ideas still hold considerable currency in the literature. In particular, the view that owner occupation is illegitimate and an imposition for the benefit of certain interests still carries some weight.

Whilst Marxist ideas have tended to disappear from the mainstream of housing studies over the last couple of decades we can see an increasing use of discourse analysis, which makes use of the idea of hegemony. Hegemony can be seen as the 'common sense' worldview of the dominant class that is successfully imposed on a society. However, the notion need not carry with it any of the essentialist arguments that plagued Marxist ideas in the 1960s and 1970s associated with thinkers such as Louis Althusser and Manuel Castells. Instead hegemony can be linked to poststructuralist concepts of the self and identity to explore the manner in which ideology is embedded within all social relations. These ideas have recently been used by a number of housing researchers interested in new and emerging social theories.

This discussion has only pointed to a few examples of the use made of political ideology, but it is clear that certain notions feature strongly, particularly the role of the state and the capability of individuals as decision makers within markets. What also comes to the fore in the literature is controversy over the role of property rights and owner occupation. In many ways this ought not to be surprising in the light of the retrenchment of state provision, privatisation, and the move towards personal subsidies that have occurred in many developed countries since the late 1970s. Political ideologies, therefore, can be seen as a useful tool in the development of debates on housing and help us to understand the transformations that have made and broken housing policies over the last generation.

However, there are some problems with the use of political ideology with regard to housing, and indeed more generally. Two of them are mainly discussed here: The problems of purity and labelling. In the former case this points to the limits of ideologies to inform policy debates, and in the latter case the dangers of overusing ideology to detract from debate.

Purity and Policy

There is an obvious difference between the positions taken by academics and those adopted by practical policy makers. Those of us who live by ideas and concepts see a virtue in stating these ideas and concepts as clearly, accurately, and precisely as possible. We seek exact definitions and hone concepts so that we can be absolutely clear about their use and their purpose. We seek a rigour and a consistency – a purity – in our positions.

However, to coin a phrase, politics is the art of the possible and so it involves compromise and ambiguity, to the extent that a concept might be drained of much of its import. Politicians might seek to enhance personal choice in housing, but do so without changing the basic structures of provision: Landlords might be encouraged to adopt choice-based lettings, but without foregoing their positions as gatekeepers and managers of scarce resources (Brown and King, 2005). Accordingly, applicants have some more choice, but only within the confines of unchanged structures of provision that retain landlords as the key decision makers.

Of course, it might be that we would not want absolute purity and intellectual rigour in policy making. A good example of this is the libertarianism position of Robert Nozick. Nozick can be said to have reenergised libertarian thought with his book Anarchy, State and Utopia, and indeed it is a deeply influential book that has created an enormous critical literature. Yet Nozick's position is an extremely rigorous and abstract one. He argues for the ultraminimal state, which provides only basic protection from external threats and nothing more. Nozick undertakes a very detailed philosophical defence of this position and concludes that no other form of state provision is morally consistent with the preservation of individual rights.

This view found some support amongst policy makers, particularly in the Reagan administration after 1980. Nozick's arguments against state intervention were seen to be useful in the Reagan crusade against big government. However, on finding that Nozick's vision of libertarianism extended beyond the economic sphere to include the abandonment of immigration controls, the legalisation of all drugs, and complete sexual freedom, the policy makers took fright and left Nozick to his ivory tower in Harvard.

The problem with Nozick's position was precisely its consistency and rigour – the very things that academics would take as crucial to the development of an argument. Yet this purity does not necessarily translate well into political action. Hence conservatives like Reagan might be critical of state intervention, but they do not rid themselves of the powers of government. Rather they make extensive use of it to achieve their ends. Many supposedly free market reforms include top-down impositions, such as the Thatcherite programme of privatisation and the Right to Buy. The second Bush administration, perhaps the most right-wing US administration since the 1920s, increased government spending massively just as the supposedly left of centre New Labour government did in the United Kingdom.

For politicians and policy makers it is never a matter of taking an absolute position. When they take office politicians must continue to run the great offices of state and maintain basic services, even as they seek to carry out their election pledges. Accordingly, they must compromise and prioritise and cannot afford to take a fundamental or pure position on policy; or at least, not whilst retaining reasonably frequent elections and allow for dissent and opposition. Hence, parties ostensibly of the left in the United States, the United Kingdom, Australia, and so on find they have no alternative but to support owner occupation because this is what their electorate expects.

Where Nozick is useful is precisely that he takes an idea – the basis of a coherent political ideology, in this case libertarianism – and tests it to destruction. His work is an example of taking an ideal to its logical conclusions. But, in doing so, he also shows the limits of any political ideology to practical policy making.

Labelling

A different problem is where a particular political ideology is used as a form of shorthand to express a criticism without actually engaging with the specifics of an argument. This process involves the identification of an argument with a particular ideology or political position and then using a general critique of that ideology to dismiss the argument. The critic here seeks to diminish a position not by arguing against it, or by engaging with the particular arguments of its author, but by assuming that as it adopts, say, a Marxist or libertarian position, it is guilty of the general faults of that position. Political ideology is here being used as a label by which arguments can be conveniently categorised without the need to engage with it in detail.

An important part of this process is the use of particular words that are deemed to take on a particular meaning. As an example we might point to the word 'market' as one such label which is then associated with a particular set of ideals. If an argument can be categorised as being 'market-based' its critics can then contain it by the use of standard criticisms of such arguments.

But, of course, these words used as labels can tell us as much about the critics as the arguments they are ostensibly addressing. In this sense the use of terminology is itself significant. So, to use the concept discussed above, those who use 'hegemony' as a significant concept will tend to adopt a particular view determined by poststructuralist ideologies. Similarly, the use of the term 'neoliberal' as a catch-all for the supposed supporters of capitalist globalisation and free markets actually says as much of the users of the label. Indeed, no actual supporter of international free markets would refer to themselves as a 'neoliberal'; the term is almost exclusively used in a critical sense.

Conclusions

What this discussion shows is that we cannot separate ourselves from our own ideology, even as we seek to understand the ideologies of others. We cannot free ourselves from the bondage of ideology even as we criticise others for being bound. Indeed we will frequently use ideologically charged notions to comment on and critique the ideological positions of others.

This suggests that we need to be cautious and remain aware about ideology in all its forms. But this does not suggest that we should be afraid of ideological positions or seek to divorce ourselves from them. Not only will this be a vain attempt, but it will also drain much of the significance of our arguments and our endeavours. An ideology is our bedrock position; it is our fundamental belief system which we use to make sense of the world. It therefore helps us to come to terms with why certain things matter, with why we hold onto certain things and flee from others.

See also: Politics of Housing; Property Rights Approaches; Social Class and Housing; Social Movements and Housing.

Further Reading

Adams I (1993) *Political Ideology Today*. Manchester: Manchester University Press.
Ball M (1983) *Housing and Economic Power: The Political Economy of Owner Occupation*. London: Methuen.
Brown T and King P (2005) The power to choose: Effective choice and housing policy. *European Journal of Housing Policy* 5(1): 59–75.
Fukuyama F (1992) *The End of History and the Last Man*. London: Hamish Hamilton.
Hayek F (1960) *The Constitution of Liberty*. London: Routledge.
Honderich T (1990) *Conservatism*. London: Hamish Hamilton.
Jacobs K and Manzi T (1996) Discourse and policy change: The significance of language for housing research. *Housing Studies* 11(4): 543–560.
Kemeny J (1981) *The Myth of Home Ownership: Public Versus Private Choices in Housing Tenure*. London: Routledge.
King P (1996) *A Conservative Consensus?: Housing Policy Before 1997 and After*. Exeter. Imprint: Academic.
King P (2003) *A Social Philosophy of Housing*. Aldershot: Ashgate.
King P (2009) *Understanding Housing Finance: Meeting Needs and Making Choices*, 2nd edn. London: Routledge.
Malpass P (2005) *Housing and the Welfare State*. Basingstoke: Palgrave.
Nozick R (1974) *Anarchy, State and Utopia*. Oxford: Blackwell.
Quinton A (1993) Conservatism. In: Goodin P and Pettit P (eds.). *A Companion to Contemporary Political Philosophy*, pp. 244–268. Oxford: Blackwell.
Ronald R (2008) *The Ideology of Home Ownership: Homeownership Societies and the Role of Housing*. Basingstoke. Palgrave: Macmillan.
Saunders P (1990) *A Nation of Home Owners*. London: Allen & Unwin.
Scruton R (2001) *The Meaning of Conservatism*, 3rd edn. Basingstoke: Palgrave.

Politics of Housing

B Bengtsson, Uppsala University, Uppsala, Sweden

© 2012 Elsevier Ltd. All rights reserved.

Glossary

Corporatism A system of interest representation in which organisations are granted influence on political outcomes via institutionalised representation, accepted by the state, in politically relevant decision-making processes.

Housing policy The goals, means, and social and material outcomes of political decision-making directed towards housing provision.

Housing politics Political decision-making processes related to housing provision, including their political and institutional prerequisites and effects.

Housing tenures Institutions and sets of practices that regulate how the consumption of housing is organised in a society, and in consequence, influence action and interaction more generally in the field of housing.

Hybrid organisation An organisation with both economic and noneconomic goals.

Middle-range theory A theory with limited scope, which explains a specific set of phenomena in relation to a certain type of context.

Path dependency A historical pattern where previous events set into motion self-reinforcing feedback mechanisms which considerably change the likelihood of some subsequent events or outcomes.

Policy theory The total of normative and causal assumptions underlying a policy.

Political institution A set of formal rules, norms, and practices that regulate political action and interaction.

Urban governance The political process by which a city or neighbourhood is actually ruled, typically in cooperation between several formally independent units including local state authorities, building contractors, housing companies, local businesses, and residents' organisations.

Policy and Politics in Housing Studies

It has often been claimed that the academic field of housing studies is dominated by a policy perspective, including an ambition to make relevant and useful contributions to political, administrative, and professional decision-making. More seldom, researchers in the field take a perspective of politics and power on housing provision, analysing the political institutions of relevance and the political games and processes of decision-making on housing issues. Moreover, the few exceptions are mainly case studies with limited theoretical ambitions. To some extent this sparse interest in housing politics may be seen as an expression of the comparatively modest role played by political science in housing studies.

This article focuses on housing politics and reviews research efforts and results on housing institutions (state and nonstate) and on the processes of interaction either between elite actors in the housing sector or between elite actors and citizens and households in general. The argument is related to three societal levels: (1) national housing systems; (2) local urban governance; and (3) estate management and resident participation. The concluding section discusses some of the main accomplishments in research on housing politics, and points out some promising ways forward.

The concept of politics is best defined in contrast to policy. While policy is related to the social and material outcomes of political decision-making, politics is about conflict and cooperation between actors with diverging interests, and the effects of such interaction in terms of policy, implementation, institutional design, power, and legitimacy. The demarcation line between housing policy and housing politics is not clear-cut, and a lot of empirical work in the field actually includes both. However, a focus on housing politics means emphasising process rather than outcome; action, interaction, and social relations rather than structure; formulation and application of policy rather than its contents. Most importantly, a politics perspective emphasises strategic interaction between political actors, and the institutional rules and consequences of such interaction, rather than the social and material results of political decision-making in society at large. The study of politics often implies an interest in what Robert Merton has termed 'middle-range theorising' and in the intentional, more or less rationalistic, social mechanisms of political games and power relations.

A Political Perspective on Housing Provision

What distinguishes the politics of housing provision from the politics of other welfare state sectors – and from welfare state politics in general? The answer is related to the academic discussion about the 'policy theory of housing provision'. The socially and politically dominant policy theory of housing provision as welfare state policy defines housing as being at the same time an individual market commodity and a public good demanding state involvement. This makes analogies with other welfare sectors, in which state allocation is the main distributive mechanism, misleading. Since housing should, as far as possible, be distributed in accordance with consumer preferences, the politically defined 'needs' cannot be fulfilled by direct state allocation. Instead, voluntary market contracts between buyer and seller or between landlord and tenant serve as the main mechanism for distributing housing, while state intervention typically has the form of correctives, defining the economic and institutional setting of those market contracts.

The Norwegian political scientist, Ulf Torgersen, has described housing as 'the wobbly pillar of the welfare state'. In other welfare sectors, for example, pensions, schooling, and health, fairly clear standards have been extracted from the vague concept of need, standards that define when the institutions in charge are responsible for taking action. Those responsible for implementing the policies are typically trained bodies of professionals, within a fairly unified institutional complex with well-defined borders, a certain esprit de corps, and a national director. In housing, such bureaucratic modes of implementation would be seen as an intrusion on consumer sovereignty, and instead the policy is implemented via markets, sometimes amended by political correctives. In consequence, politically defined 'needs' of housing must include manifest or latent consumer preferences as an important ingredient. Although recent changes, including ideas of new public management, have made other welfare state sectors more market oriented than before, the policy theory of market correctives is still a distinguishing characteristic of housing provision.

This specific policy theory has important, although somewhat different, implications for housing provision and politics at different societal levels. At the macro level of national politics, the policy theory of state correctives to the market gives a crucial role to political decisions on tenure forms and market regulations. At the meso level of policy implementation, the parallel to the bureaucratic arrangements of other policy fields is typically informal coalitions between a number of independent actors and institutions: local authorities, contractors, housing companies, nongovernment organisations, and so on. At the micro level of final delivery of the housing counterpart to the encounters between 'street-level bureaucrats' and clients/citizens is typically market transactions between landlords and tenants.

The Macro Level – Tenure Politics

Political games over housing policy and provision are to a large extent about tenure forms and other types of market regulations. Such market regulations place legal restraints on the bargaining room for sellers and buyers, landlords, and tenants. Tenure politics and policy may also provide economic support (or obstacles) to certain types and forms of housing by means of subsidisation, financial security, or tax relieves (or their opposites). While the policy theory of market correctives means that, in principle, it is not for the state to decide how citizens should be housed, it may still be for the state to give citizens a real opportunity of finding decent housing at a reasonable cost in the market.

This is why housing tenures are the most important political institutions of housing provision as welfare state policy. The Finnish sociologist, Hannu Ruonavaara, has defined housing tenures as "institutions, sets of practices and rules that regulate a particular field of human action and interaction". Thus, political decision-making on housing tenures, including how social housing is organised, sets the rules of housing politics at the micro and meso levels – and, through institutionalisation, at the macro level as well.

There is a rich, almost abundant, literature on housing provision at the national level, and tenure policy regularly has a central position in the accounts and analyses. However, most work on housing regimes and housing systems, whether single country or comparative, has the focus on policy and only considers politics in brief, without theorising. Often, this type of literature describes the historical development of housing in the country or countries that are studied, the main institutions in terms of tenure forms, the systems of finance, land, and estate regulation, the characteristics of the existing stock and the quantity and quality of recent production. If power and politics are discussed it is often in relation to particular actors and institutions rather than in universal terms.

As pointed out by Kemeny and Lowe, there is actually an unexplicated theoretical perspective informing this type of descriptive policy-centred analysis, one in which the central government has important formative influence, almost a capacity to pick and choose between different housing systems. The other side of this implicit government omnipotence is that institutional context is downplayed, and the role of actors other than the government and political parties tends to be disregarded. What we get in terms of housing politics is often non-theoretical narratives about what policies specific governments, commissions, parties, and political leaders have supported. Also, the institutions are often rather myopically presented in terms of formal organisation, official functions, and so on, and without the theoretical relief necessary to allow any general conclusions.

In contrast, the challenge for academic students of housing politics is to analyse the roles played by political actors, institutions, and discourses in more general terms by replacing proper names and specific characteristics with theoretical concepts and perspectives that make some form of general conclusions possible beyond the empirical cases studied. In the tradition of middle-range theorising, the aim should be to identify and analyse logics, patterns, and mechanisms in one empirical context that may also be recognisable in other similar contexts.

Some early comparative work relates differences in housing policy to elite ideology and politics. Often the analysis is rather voluntary without adding much to the historical accounts. In a more ambitious exploration along similar lines, Lennart Lundqvist compares housing and privatisation in four European countries, applying a perspective of policy networks and power resources to explain the continued economic support to mortgaged owner-occupation in a period of general cutbacks. He analyses how political parties were prepared to change their ideological stance on housing provision in order to gain or retain support from the voters in that sector. In a more recent study of retrenchment in housing, Anders Lindbom explains how the radical state budget cuts of the 1990s in Swedish housing policy came up against remarkably weak resistance due to the difficulty the political actors, as well as the general public, had in discovering and reacting against financial cuts in a policy area that is so complex and nontransparent as housing provision. The difficulty to get a comprehensive overview of the social and economic outcomes of housing provision can be seen as another aspect of the policy theory of market correctives.

Other investigations focus on how housing politics relate to the social and economic structures in society. One ambitious empirical study in this tradition is a comparison from the 1980s between housing provisions in Britain and Sweden by Peter Dickens and his colleagues. Differences in the relation between capital, labour, and landownership are seen as crucial to understanding the variability over time and between the two countries, with a generally more speculative and commodified house building in Britain. Notwithstanding its open-ended Marxian perspective, the study identifies interesting patterns of interaction between elite and mass actors.

Another seminal work along similar lines is a comprehensive book by Michael Harloe about the historical development of social rented housing in six countries, which is based on the concept of 'structure of housing provision'. This study encompasses both politics and policy, and social structures as well as political actors and institutions. The main strength of the book is how the development of social housing is placed in the context of the general social and political evolution in each country, and Harloe identifies a universal trend towards residualisation of social housing. Although his analyses are more structural than political, his rich material also lends itself to more actor-oriented and open-ended discussions of the politics and institutions of social housing.

Jim Kemeny has taken up a similar theme from a more institutional viewpoint. He highlights the crucial distinction between an 'Anglo-Saxon' dualist rental market, with a residual public rental sector directed at households of modest economic means, and a 'European' unitary model, without individual means-testing and based on the integration of profit and nonprofit rental systems. This distinction has important implications both for market outcomes and for the conditions of housing politics, and the historical development of the different systems is analysed in terms of interaction between the political actors, state and market institutions, economic development, and housing discourse.

In the 1980s, a number of studies were published that applied a perspective of corporatism to housing provision. The literature on corporatism in general often investigates the tripartite relation between the state, business organisations, and labour unions. In housing politics, with its policy theory of market correctives and its orientation towards consumption, other organised interests may also sometimes acquire a corporatist bargaining relation to the state, for example, housing companies, mortgage lenders, and consumer organisations. With the growing impact of European Union (EU) institutions on housing provision and policies and the growth of internationally active NGOs, we may be witnessing a revival of housing corporatist perspectives – although this time at the European level.

Recently, historical institutionalism and path dependency represent what seems to be a fruitful perspective for studying the interplay between political action and institutional conditions in housing. Stuart Lowe applies a politics-oriented variation of path-dependency analysis when he explores the dramatic historical development of the British housing tenure structure in the twentieth century. He identifies some critical junctures in the historical development and highlights in particular the impact of the two world wars. A more comprehensive attempt along similar lines is a comparison between the development of the – surprisingly different – housing regimes of five Nordic countries. In the formative period, between the turn of the nineteenth century and the Second World War, different solutions were chosen in each country in order to deal with specific housing problems that occurred at different points of time. When more comprehensive housing programmes were introduced after the war, already existing, if still undeveloped, organisations and institutions were utilised to implement them. With the massive production of new housing between 1950 and 1980, the diverging regimes were successively consolidated and institutionalised.

The Meso Level – Urban Governance

In contrast to some other welfare state sectors, housing provision is implemented entirely at the local level – in regions, cities, and neighbourhoods. At these levels too, conditions of politics and power are largely determined by the policy theory of state correctives to the market. The political meso level of housing provision is typically not a governmental office but a network of interdependent actors and institutions: local authorities, building contractors, housing companies, local business, residents' organisations, and so on. The function of the local state institutions is not primarily to guarantee direct allocation to citizens, but rather to organise and carry through physical, economic, and social planning with the aim of fulfilling, in the long run, citizens' housing needs. In consequence, at the meso level housing provision is only one element among others in urban planning and urban politics – though arguably the most basic one – with housing actors typically positioned outside the public sector.

To some extent Britain has been an exception to this, since the management of social rented housing has been entrusted to local authorities. Several interesting and revealing investigations have been published on housing bureaucracies and in particular social housing management in Britain. Lately, with the ongoing residualisation of council housing and the expansion of housing associations, the institutional conditions of housing politics at the meso level in Britain seem to be converging towards those of other European countries with single-purpose independent landlords responsible for social housing provision. One aspect of this model of implementation is exploited in the relatively new academic discourse on hybrid organisations in housing, that is, organisations with both economic and noneconomic goals.

Urban planning and urban governance certainly represent a vast and dynamic field of practice and research, and a perspective limited to housing provision is not always fruitful in this broader context. There is, however, at least one important aspect that makes housing critical in urban governance and assigns a special role to housing actors in the local games of planning and negotiation. In a perspective of democracy the residents of an urban neighbourhood can be seen as a local 'demos' – a collective of citizens who are directly affected by the 'interdependent and autonomous' negotiations, networks, and partnerships where political and professional stakeholders are involved. Tenure policy at the national level has an important impact on the conditions of local governance and planning, since owner-occupants typically can be expected to have stronger veto power than rental tenants – provided that they can agree on strategies, as in the NIMBY cases where opposing groups of homeowners have succeeded in blocking the development of local infrastructure and care centres. (This is also an illustration of the links between housing provision and other aspects of urban politics.)

There is certainly no lack of sociological and geographical studies of housing and living conditions in poor and deprived housing estates, but the academic interest in the local games of politics in these contexts has been weaker. One interesting exception, which has a distinct perspective of housing politics, is Nils Hertting's investigation of local governance networks in area renewal in a Stockholm district, in which he analyses how key actors hold on to their preference for mutual cooperation over many years, although they are repeatedly frustrated both by the collaborative process and its outcomes.

The Micro Level – Resident Participation and Housing Democracy

The political micro level is where citizens ultimately receive the public good, and the policy theory of market correctives has an impact on housing politics at this very local level as well. As mentioned, the final delivery of the public good of housing is normally not executed by state (or state-regulated) officials but by market actors following a completely different logic of implementation. In owner-occupation this is typically a one-time transaction – though of long-lasting importance to the individual household. In the rental sector the contract relation is more permanent, and thus the role of the 'street-level bureaucrat' of housing policy is played by the public or private landlord. Here the potential market power of landlords due to tenants' attachment to their dwelling and neighbourhood gives the local games a dimension of justice and equality – and thus provides the justification for different forms of market regulations.

Microlevel housing politics has to do with micro power and collective action on the individual estate, that is, questions related to tenant participation and other forms of very local cooperation. In a study from the late 1980s and early 1990s, Liz Cairncross, David Clapham, and Robina Goodlad identified three different models of participation based on the roles taken by the local authorities: traditionalism, consumerism, and citizenship. The authors found that the construction of the 'political' interaction between tenants, housing managers, councillors, and tenants' associations is related to the differing prerequisites inherent in these models. The citizenship model, with its focus on tenants both as individuals and as a collective, gave tenants the opportunity to organise and, to some extent, exert pressure on other players in the local housing games.

With a more elaborate game-theoretical approach the author of this article analyses collective action in housing estates applying a model of a self-reinforcing 'cooperative circle', from (1) shared norms of cooperation, via (2) active participation, and (3) residents' power resources to (4) real collective influence, which then feeds back into norms of cooperation. He finds that each link is sensitive to disturbance, and that the crucial social mechanism at work in the cases where local collective action has been institutionalised is the development of a norm of 'local utilitarianism' which can be formulated as 'I take part if it is needed and if I can contribute to the collective good in my estate.'

These studies, with their focus on actors and institutions, have a perspective of housing politics at a very local level. Another aspect of the sociogeographic concentration of local residents (and residents' organisations) and the shared interest in a rather well-defined territory is that it makes 'very local' housing politics an empirical field well suited for the study of mechanisms of small-scale democratic interaction. Some good illustrations of this are Johnston Birchall's investigation of housing cooperatives in Britain and Lotte Jensen's study of Danish social housing governance and 'housing democracy'.

Studies of urban protest and urban social movements, which embrace both the meso and micro levels, are also of relevance to housing politics. One early and exemplary work in this genre is Michael Lipsky's studies of protest in American cities, in particular rent strikes in New York, in the 1960s. Lipsky's conclusions about the probability of success when powerless groups go out in protest point out a number of both tangible and symbolic aspects, which should still be of relevance today. One important strategy in such cases is appealing to other actors with more political power; however, this dependency on the responsiveness of other groups tends to make actions vulnerable and short-lived.

Concluding Discussion – Accomplishments and Ways Forward

A perspective of politics, institutions, and power seems to offer interesting and valuable insights into the political conditions of housing provision at the macro, meso, and micro levels. However, the commendably prudent ambitions of middle-range theorising make it difficult to summarise the 'state of the art' in a few brief and concise sentences. The research results presented in this article shed considerable light on several different types of social and political mechanisms at work at the different levels of housing politics. Together, scientific findings about mechanisms provide a tool box for the analysis of other similar situations in other national and local contexts. But they do not provide any universal answers as to how housing politics functions or what types of politics have which types of effects.

Which are the most promising ways forward in research on housing politics? The social and political construction of the policy theory of housing provision as state correctives to the market has not been much debated in recent years, although housing policies and institutions have gone through considerable change in most countries. The increasing de facto interventionism in the national systems of housing provision from the EU indicates that this may be a discourse worth revisiting. The sociopolitical construction of housing policy in different national and international contexts may be investigated both at citizen and political elite levels and using both qualitative and quantitative methods.

At the macro level we may be witnessing a revival of perspectives of corporatism in the study of EU housing politics. This can be combined with historical institutionalism and path dependency, which appears to be a particularly promising approach to housing provision with its generally high degree of physical and social sluggishness. Framing or frame analysis is another topical theoretical perspective which has so far been applied to housing provision mainly in the study of homelessness and affordable housing. This approach offers a promising combination of agency and discourse analysis, which should be fruitful in the study of the performative aspects of housing politics, for example, the framing, reframing, and social effects of symbolic discourses about 'the right to housing' or 'the homeowning society'. Such subjects have been fruitfully covered by housing sociologists, but the more actor-related aspects, including the impact of this type of ideas on political institutions, have so far been less investigated.

Approaches of historical institutionalism and framing analysis could also be used to shed more light on the complexities of housing politics at the micro and meso levels, and some interesting work has been produced here, for example, the investigation by Douglas Robertson and his colleagues of the development of divergent neighbourhood identities over 80 years in three housing estates in the Scottish city of Stirling. A renewed interest in urban protest and urban movements can also be predicted in the wake of recent uprisings in impoverished metropolitan districts. As pointed out by Chris Pickvance, housing studies in this field should relate more to the general social movement discourse and its theoretical frameworks such as resource mobilisation and political opportunity structures.

The analysis of hybrid organisations as political actors and institutions should also be of high relevance to our understanding of the conditions of housing politics, policy, and implementation. In contrast to what is the case with hybrid organisations in other sectors, the geographical concentration of the residents brings to the fore issues of participative and deliberative democracy, which further complicates the internal goal conflicts of such organisations.

See also: Central Government Institutions; Comparative Housing Research; Housing Governance; Housing Policy: Agents and Regulators; Path Dependency; Power; Social Movements and Housing; Social Theory and Housing; Tenure as an Institution.

Further Reading

Bengtsson B (2000) Solving the tenants' dilemma: Collective action and norms of co-operation in housing. *Housing, Theory and Society* 17: 175–187.
Bengtsson B (2001) Housing as a social right: Implications for welfare state theory. *Scandinavian Political Studies* 24: 255–275.
Bengtsson B (ed.), Annaniassen E, Jensen L, Ruonavaara H, and Sveinsson JR (2006) *Varför så olika? Nordisk bostadspolitik i jämförande historiskt ljus* [Why So Different? Nordic Housing Policy in Comparative Historical Light]. Malmö: Égalité.
Birchall J (1988) *Building Communities the Co-Operative Way*. London: Routledge & Kegan Paul.
Cairncross L, Clapham D, and Goodlad R (1997) *Housing Management, Consumers and Citizens*. London; New York: Routledge.
Dickens P, Duncan S, Goodwin M, and Gray F (1985) *Housing, States and Localities*. London; New York: Methuen.
Harloe M (1995) *The People's Home? Social Rented Housing in Europe and America*. Oxford, UK; Cambridge, MA: Blackwell.
Hertting N (2007) Mechanisms of governance network formation – A contextual rational choice perspective. In: Torfing J and Sorensen E (eds.) *Theories of Democratic Network Governance*, pp. 43–60. Basingstoke, UK; New York: Palgrave Macmillan.
Jensen L (1995) Challenges to citizenship. *Scandinavian Housing and Planning Research* 12: 177–194.
Kemeny J (1995) *From Public Housing to the Social Market. Rental Policy Strategies in Comparative Perspective*. London: Routledge.
Kemeny J and Lowe S (1998) Schools of comparative housing research: From convergence to divergence. *Housing Studies* 13: 161–176.
Lindbom A (2001) Dismantling Swedish housing policy. *Governance* 14: 503–527.
Lipsky M (1970) *Protest in City Politics: Rent Strikes, Housing and the Power of the Poor*. Chicago, IL: Rand McNally and Company.
Lowe S (2004) *Housing Policy Analysis. British Housing in Cultural and Comparative Context*. Basingstoke; New York: Palgrave MacMillan.
Lundqvist LJ (1992) *Dislodging the Welfare State? Housing and Privatization in Four European Nations*. Delft, The Netherlands: Delft University Press.
Robertson D, McIntosh I, and Smyth J (2010) Neighbourhood identity: The path dependency of class and place. *Housing, Theory and Society* 27: 258–273.
Torgersen U (1987) Housing: The wobbly pillar of the welfare state. In: Turner B, Kemeny J, and Lundqvist LJ (eds.) *Between State and Market: Housing in the Post-Industrial Era*. Scandinavian Housing and Planning Research, Suppl. 1. Stockholm: Almqvist and Wiksell.

Post-Bubble Housing in Japan

Y Hirayama, Kobe University, Kobe, Japan

© 2012 Elsevier Ltd. All rights reserved.

Glossary

Bubble economy An economic situation in which an abnormal rise in the values of assets often involving housing and land assets is accelerated by debt financing.

Government Housing Loan Corporation An agency of the Japanese government, which was established in 1951 to provide middle-class households with low-interest mortgages for their access to owner-occupied housing. The corporation was abolished in 2007.

Hot spot A metaphor for districts where the real estate market is increasingly active due to an increase in property investments.

Negative equity A situation where the market value of a house is insufficient to cover the cost of repayment of the mortgage taken on to acquire the property.

Property ladder A metaphor to describe households' moves from a rented house to an owner-occupied house and to a house with a higher property value.

After the Bubble Burst

The housing system in postwar Japan has consistently driven the expansion of the owner-occupied housing sector. Because the private ownership of housing has provided a material and symbolic basis for securing homes, accumulating assets, and maintaining membership in mainstream society, a large majority of households have successively ascended the housing ladder towards attaining homeownership. This has underpinned the maintenance of a 'homeowner society'. Since the bubble economy collapsed in early 1990s, however, prolonged economic stagnation has aided in restructuring the circumstances of property ownership, which has led to declining effectiveness in the homeownership-oriented housing system. In an increasingly globalised economic environment, various countries have undergone the sustained expansion of owner-occupation along with a more volatile economy. The impact of economic changes on homeownership has thus drawn increasing attention. Japan constitutes one of the most mature homeowner societies in industrial and postindustrial countries with concerted development of the owner-occupied housing sector even while experiencing radical economic transformations that have seen a decline in the system of promoting homeownership. Japan thus provides an acute case in relation to how economic instability affects the structure of property-owning societies. This article looks at post-bubble housing in Japan with particular reference to transformations in homeownership.

The Japanese bubble economy appeared in the latter half of the 1980s. The abnormal upsurge in land and housing prices started in Tokyo and spread to Osaka, Nagoya, and the rest of the country. With the Japan–US trade friction as a background, the Japanese yen immediately appreciated, and interest rates were rapidly slashed after the Plaza Agreement in September 1985. The easing of monetary control, along with the government's policy to promote urban redevelopment, resulted in the excessive flow of capital into real estate. Measured against the previous year, the price rise of residential land was 68.6% in the Tokyo region in 1988 and 56.1% in Osaka in 1990. Between 1980 and 1990, price–income ratios in the Tokyo region increased 5–8 times for a condominium and 6.2–8.5 times for a ready-built single-family house.

The collapse of the bubble at the beginning of the 1990s marked a turning point, and Japan entered a noticeably prolonged period of enduring recession characterised by minimal or negative real growth in GDP, rising unemployment rates, and reduced incomes. The overall economy became deflationary, and the real prices of land and housing dropped sharply. The security of residential properties as assets was thus undermined. Although the Japanese economy eventually began to recover in 2002, the economic upturn was not particularly strong and did not translate into improving the household economy. Rises in real estate prices were only seen in Tokyo and a few other large cities during the short period from 2006 to mid-2008. Land and housing prices continued to drop throughout the rest of the country even after the post-bubble recession ended (see **Figure 1**). Moreover, Japan again began entering a severe recession in 2008, having become involved in the global financial crisis triggered by the US subprime mortgage meltdown. This has provoked sharp drops in housing new starts, property transactions, and house prices.

Post-bubble stagnation has not only unravelled the economic pillar of homeownership but also encouraged the reorientation of housing policy. The Japanese

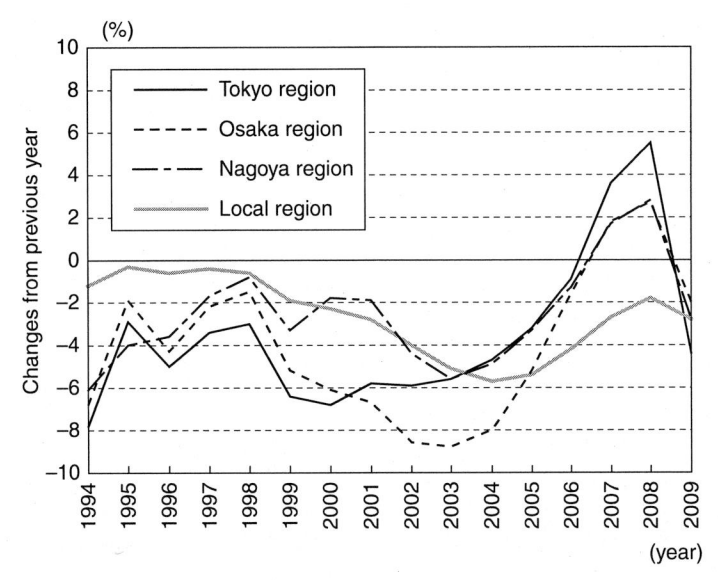

Figure 1 Trends in residential land prices.
Reproduced from official announcement of land prices.

government took the initiative in promulgating a housing system oriented towards middle-class homeownership from the 1950s. The Government Housing Loan Corporation (GHLC), established as a state agency in 1951, provided many households with low-interest mortgages for their access to owner-occupied housing. Of the various measures available in housing policy, the supply of GHLC mortgages was especially emphasised to promote middle-class homeownership. Along with the policy of facilitating housing acquisition, the level of owner-occupied housing has been maintained at ~60%, representing its position as the dominant housing tenure. In response to the post-bubble recession, however, and within the context of pervasive neoliberalism, the government has moved towards accentuating the role of the market in providing and financing housing since the mid-1990s. In line with this new policy to expand the sphere of the market economy, the GHLC was abolished in 2007, signifying an important shift in the postwar history of Japanese housing policy. Although the Japan Housing Finance Agency was established as the successor to the GHLC, it withdrew from the primary mortgage market and has since only dealt with the secondary market of mortgage securities. The reorganisation of housing policy, combined with prolonged economic stagnation, has thus disintegrated the traditional system of expanding homeownership.

Decline in the Property Ladder System

In Japan, as well as in many other homeownership-based societies, the housing system has successively guided younger generations to follow older generations into a conventional life course involving home purchase. However, economic changes have differentiated housing conditions between different generations. Since the bubble burst, younger cohorts have been faced with economic barriers preventing them from entering the homeownership market. As **Figure 2** clearly indicates, the level of homeownership has dropped significantly among younger households. Between 1983 and 2008, the percentage of owner-occupied housing decreased from 24.9 to 11.7% for households with a head aged 25–29 years, and from 60.1 to 46.5% for those aged 35–39 years. Despite the drop in the level of homeownership for younger households, the average level of homeownership for all households has largely been stationary. This is due to an increase in the proportion of the older population having higher homeownership levels.

The 'casualisation' of the labour force with a substantial decline in wages has been responsible for the tendency by younger cohorts to delay entering the homeownership sector. Neoliberal policy has involved the deregulation of the labour market, and major amendments to the Dispatched Labour Law in 1999 and 2003 played a key role in drastically promoting casual employment. The labour market has thus been reoriented around declining stability in employment with associated rapid increases in the number of short-term contracts, part-time workers, and temporary employees. The impact of labour-market reorganisation has concentrated on younger generations. According to the Employment Status Survey, of all employees, the average percentage of nonregular employees (part-time, temporary, and dispatched employees) rose from 15.8% in 1982 to 33.0% in 2007. During the same period, the percentage

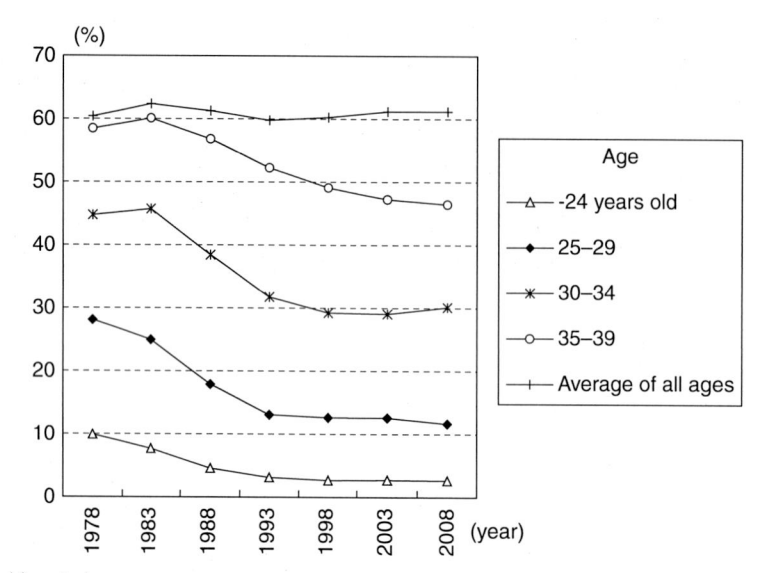

Figure 2 Home ownership rate by age.
Reproduced from Housing Survey of Japan and Housing and Land Survey of Japan.

of nonregular employees aged 20–24 years increased more sharply from 11.4 to 43.1%.

It is also important to look at a noticeable increase in younger people who have delayed marriage and their establishment of independent families. In Japan where acquiring an owner-occupied home is strongly linked to establishing a family, most people do not purchase a house until marriage. The increase in unmarried individuals has thus meant a decline in housing purchases. According to the population census, between 1980 and 2005, the percentage of unmarried people for the 30–34 age group rose from 21.5 to 47.1% for men and from 9.1 to 32.0% for women. Moreover, worsening economic conditions have increasingly deprived young individuals the opportunities of getting married and establishing their own families. There has been a clear correlation between the unmarried rate and economic status. The Employment Status Survey in 2002 revealed that the percentage of unmarried men aged 30–34 years in regular employment was 41%, while the figure for those in nonregular employment was notably high at 70%.

In addition, the economic burdens imposed by accessing and maintaining homeownership have become heavier, accelerating the decline in the level of owner-occupation for younger cohorts. The collapse of the bubble led to the deflation of housing prices. However, the decrease in incomes has translated into smaller deposits and therefore larger mortgage liabilities. The supply of GHLC mortgages was expanded to a record high level in the first half of the 1990s, and interest rates since the 1990s have remained at extraordinarily low levels because of policies to stimulate economic recovery. This has effectively encouraged housing purchasers to take out larger housing loans. Consequently, despite the drop in house prices, the burdens of mortgage repayments have increased. Younger households with lower incomes have been plunged into particularly disadvantageous economic conditions in terms of purchasing a house. According to the National Survey of Family Income and Expenditure, of owner-occupier households with a head aged ≤34 years, the percentage of those whose mortgage repayments to disposable income was ≥20% increased from 14.8% in 1989 to 33.0% in 2004.

A new phenomenon for younger generations has been a rapid increase in parental home dwellers or 'parasite singles' – young unmarried adults who continue to live in parents' houses. According to the Population Census, between 1980 and 2005, the percentages of parental home dwellers rose from 24.0 to 41.3% for the 25–29-year age group, and from 8.2 to 24.8% for the 30–34-year age group. Until the mid-1990s, the aftermath of the bubble economy generated an image that young adults living in parental homes indulged themselves by consuming luxury goods without having to incur housing costs or food expenses. This provoked a 'parasite bashing' phenomenon in popular discourses, where the dependent behaviours of young adults were explicitly criticised. Since the late 1990s, however, along with the post-bubble recession as a backdrop, many researchers have begun to argue for the economic instability of younger cohorts, and various surveys on young individuals have found that many parental home dwellers are nonregular employees who do not have sufficient income to leave home to establish an independent household. It is thus reasonable to regard the increase in parental home dwellers not as a phenomenon reflecting young people's dependent attitudes but as a consequence of their economically rational behaviours in relation to securing places to live.

Devaluation of Residential Properties

Before the bubble burst, the system of homeownership expansion was implicated in the capital gain–based economy where owning a house was a primary mechanism of accumulating assets. Renters entering the homeownership market as first-time buyers were able to expect an appreciation in the real value of properties they were acquiring, while those possessing a house could have prospects of moving to a better house using the property as a stepping stone. Indeed, capital gains fuelled the system of propelling people towards the top of the property ladder. Since the bubble collapsed, however, most residential properties have continued to fall in value with an increase in capital losses. This has meant a substantial shift in the economic aspects of homeownership, where the tendency for owner-occupied housing to generate capital losses has come to be perceived as 'normal' rather than 'abnormal'. An owner-occupied home in today's Japan is of a new type with no promise of capital gain.

Almost all households that have purchased a dwelling within at least the past two decades have experienced devaluation of their properties. However, the extent of housing depreciation has been strongly differentiated between different types of dwelling, and the drop in housing values has especially affected households that purchased condominiums during the peak of the bubble. The rate at which housing prices have fallen has been greater in second-hand housing than in newly built housing, and in condominiums rather than in single-family dwellings. The scale of capital losses generated on condominiums has thus been substantial.

As illustrated in **Figure 3**, the average price of a newly built condominium with a floor area of 70 m^2 was ¥67.2 million (£448 000 [£1 = ¥150, November 2009]) in the Tokyo region in 1991. This fell to ¥20.3 million (£135 000) by 2008, generating a capital loss of ¥46.9 million (£313 000). Similarly, newly built condominiums with a floor area of 70 m^2 in the Osaka region in 1991 cost ¥54.5 million (£363 000) on average, and their value dropped to ¥15.5 million (£103 000) in 2008, which generated a capital loss of ¥39.0 million (£260 000). In other words, the value of condominiums purchased during the peak in the bubble has fallen very sharply by some 70%.

The asset conditions of homeowners have worsened with an increase in outstanding mortgage debts and a decrease in gross residential property assets. This has led to an increase in homeowners trapped in negative equity. According to the National Survey of Family Income and Expenditure, from 1989 to 2004, the percentage of owner-occupier households with negative housing equities rose from 8.0 to 23.6% for the ≤34-year age group, and from 3.6 to 24.0% for the 35–44-year age group. There has been an increase in owner-occupiers with heavier mortgage liabilities who have retained properties whose values have continued to drop.

Economic changes have also led to an increase in mortgage defaults. This signifies the beginning of a new era characterised by higher risks pertaining to the maintenance of homeownership. As mortgage defaults increased, the GHLC was pressed to launch a series of new schemes to assist borrowers who could not repay their housing loans. As a result, increasing numbers of

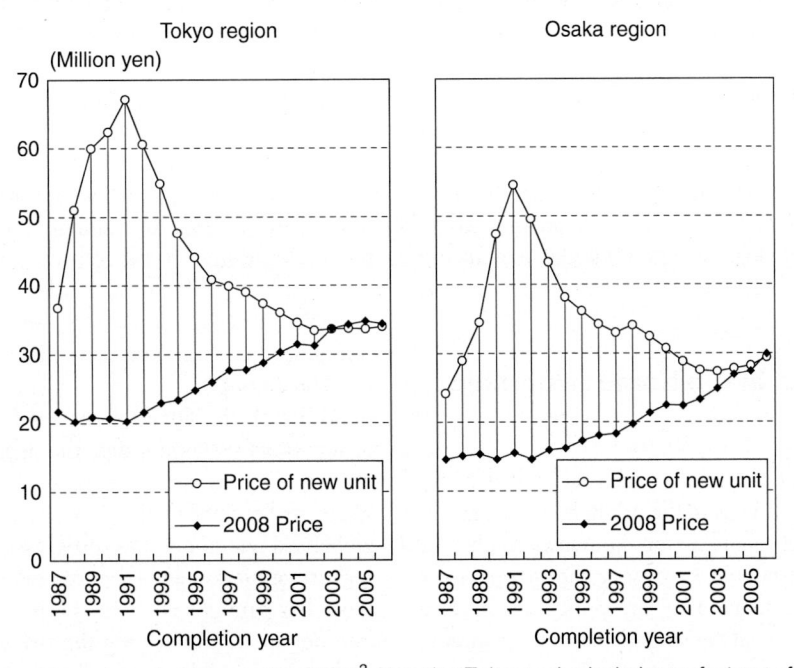

Figure 3 Capital losses on typical condominium units of 70 m^2. Note that Tokyo region includes prefectures of Saitama, Chiba, Tokyo, and Kanagawa. Osaka includes prefectures of Shiga, Kyoto, Osaka, Hyogo, Nara, and Wakayama. Reproduced from Tokyo Kantei.

borrowers were permitted to extend mortgage repayment periods. The Japan Housing Finance Agency (formerly GHLC) reported that of the total amount of outstanding GHLC mortgages, the percentage of defaulted mortgages, plus those with a possibility of default rose from 1.8% in 2000 to 8.4% in 2007. According to data provided by the Supreme Court, the number of auctions on foreclosed real estate properties increased from 44 048 in 1991 to 73 537 in 1998 and remained at high levels until the early 2000s. The figure then decreased to 54 920 in 2007 because of the short economic upturn but again rose to 67 201 in 2008 when the global financial crisis began to affect Japan as well as many other countries. Foreclosures of residential properties with negative equity have brought about particularly troubling situations where the former owners have lost their houses but continued to service remaining debt liabilities.

The liberalisation of housing policy involving the abolition of the GHLC has imposed more risks relating to mortgages on individual housing purchasers, particularly those with lower incomes. This has been responsible, at least partly, for the increase in mortgage defaults. The GHLC provided long-term, fixed-interest loans to mitigate the influence the volatile financial market had on borrowers. The dissolution of the corporation in turn increased the exposure of mortgage borrowers to economic volatility. Unlike the GHLC that provided all borrowers with mortgages under homogenous conditions in terms of interest rates, loan limits, and guarantee fees, private banks have supplied more diverse mortgage commodities under varied lending conditions. This has encouraged lower-income housing purchasers to take out riskier housing loans. As some surveys on mortgage borrowers have revealed, loan-to-value ratios have been higher for lower-income borrowers than for those on higher incomes. Borrowers on lower incomes have also tended to choose a variable-rate mortgage rather than a fixed-rate one. The initial interest on a variable-rate mortgage is lower than that on a fixed-rate mortgage. However, variable-rate loans are riskier because of uncertain interest levels in the future.

Spatial Divisions in the Homeownership Market

Since the mid-1990s, the spatial fragmentation caused by differentiated ups and downs in the urban housing market has created a novel context for homeownership. In response to the post-bubble recession, the government launched urban renaissance as a key policy in the late 1990s, with the aim of regalvanising the nation's economy. A series of measures to promote urban redevelopment has been vigorously put into practice. The combination of the prolonged recession and the government's response to it has led to the division of urban space into 'hot spots', where the housing market is increasingly active, and 'cold spots', where the market is persistently inactive.

In the central and waterfront areas of large cities, particularly Tokyo, a construction boom of condominium towers of over 20 stories has reflected and reinforced the appearance of new hot spots (see **Figure 4**). According to a survey by the Real Estate Economic Institute, in the greater Tokyo region, which includes the prefectures of Tokyo, Kanagawa, Chiba, and Saitama, 491 condominium towers or 139 457 units were completed by 2008. New starts of high-rise housing are expected to increase further. Hot spots were not born naturally but artificially created by the urban renaissance policy to facilitate urban redevelopment. The public sector invited private investors to participate in the redevelopment by selling them large tracts of public land. The wide-ranging deregulation of urban planning enabled the construction of tower-type condominium blocks. Various public corporations at both national and local levels joined redevelopment projects to support the private developers by taking responsibility for the construction of roads, waterworks, and parks. The boom in the condominium market was produced by the policy of accelerating housing acquisition.

A condominium tower block forms a fortresslike 'vertical enclave'. Not only does it create an economic and social differentiation of space but it is also symbolic of the fragmentation of urban space. A large-scale building complex is horizontally cut off from its neighbourhood, and its higher floors are vertically segregated from the ground level. The complex produces a closed and self-contained space in itself. Within the complex, residents are provided with hotel-like services and have access to various facilities such as a fitness room, a relaxation room, a party room, and retail shops. The security systems to protect the complex are tight, and each building is equipped with many surveillance cameras. Common-use areas, such as stairs and corridors, which were open to the outside air in traditional multifamily residential buildings, are enclosed within buildings in the newer towered condominium blocks. The architectural profile of the 'vertical enclave' is totally alien to its vicinity, and those dwelling in it rarely have contact with the residents of the surrounding neighbourhood.

Although the government has fuelled the production of hot spots in large cities, the aggressive urban renaissance policy to stimulate real estate investment is not likely to be sustainable. The increased volatility of the globalised economy has progressively affected Japan's real estate market and the outbreak of the global financial crisis has brought about a sharp decline in investments into hot spots. Underlying the rise of hot spots in Tokyo was an increase in transnational real estate investment. The post-bubble decrease in land prices combined with continued low interests encouraged overseas investors to

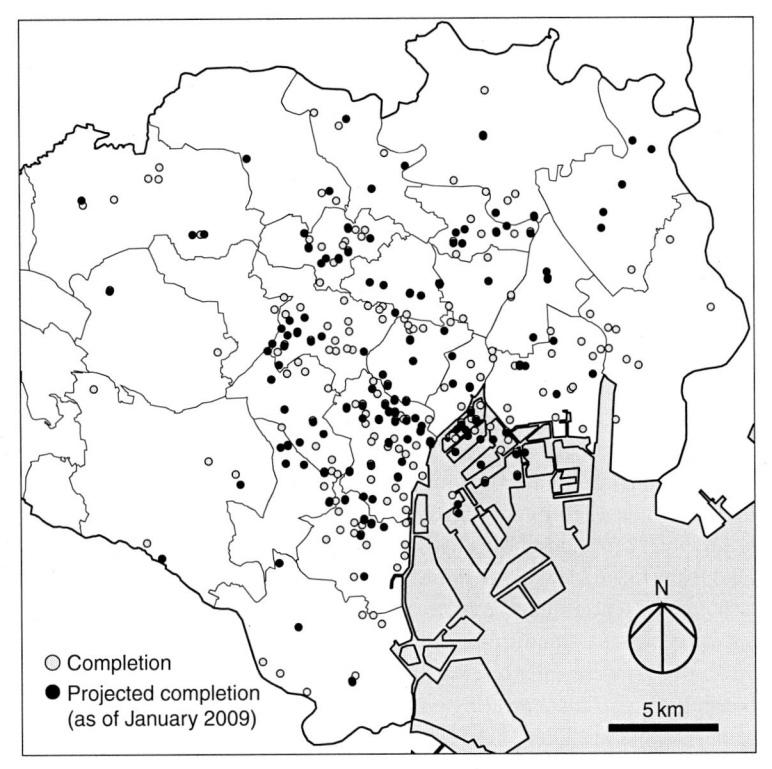

Figure 4 Location of tower-type condominium blocks, Tokyo ward-districts. Reproduced from Real Estate Economic Institute Co., Ltd.

acquire real estate properties in Tokyo. Immediately after the occurrence of the subprime crisis, however, investors from overseas swiftly retreated from Tokyo's real estate market. There were also increasing numbers of luxurious and expensive rented housing blocks mainly occupied by rich business people from overseas. However, the subprime crisis has led to a sharp increase in vacancies in the blocks. With the globalised financial crisis, real estate markets in Tokyo and other large cities have entered a period of apparent decline.

Cold spots have been formed mainly in the suburbs and the outskirts of cities, where housing prices have been continuously declining and the housing market has remained stagnant. It was not only the bursting of the bubble but also the formation of the hot spots themselves that produced the cold spots. The urban renaissance policy stimulated the construction of condominium blocks in city centres that led to an inevitable decline in demand for housing in the suburbs and the urban peripheries. Households that purchased a suburban condominium in the bubble period have suffered the continued devaluation of residential property. Those who move to the suburbs generally desire single-family houses. During the bubble period, however, families with moderate and middle incomes purchased condominiums in the suburbs, as housing prices had risen so dramatically. The marketability of a condominium unit of this type nose-dived in the post-bubble period. Households that acquired a suburban condominium are now repaying massive amounts on the loans for their housing that is further declining in value.

Changes in the Rented Housing Sector

In Japan's postwar homeowner society where housing policy has been focussed on promoting middle-class homeownership, the direct supply of rented housing by the public sector has been positioned as a residual measure. Public housing has been allocated to low-income households and public corporations have constructed rental housing for urban middle-income households. However, according to the 2008 Housing and Land Survey, the proportions of low-income public housing and public corporation housing were low, at 4.1 and 1.8%, respectively. Furthermore, since the mid-1990s the liberalisation of housing policy has further marginalised the provision of public rented housing. In terms of low-income public housing policy, the existing stock could be reconstructed or renovated but almost no new housing will be constructed. The income criteria for moving into public housing have also been narrowed. Many local governments, which have suffered from financial burdens in managing low-income public housing, are now beginning to unload some rental properties. The Japan Housing Corporation, which was founded as a national public corporation in 1955, was reorganised into the Housing and Urban Development Corporation in 1981, and into the Urban Development Corporation in 1999, and then into the Urban Renaissance Agency in 2004. The new agency withdrew from the construction of new housing and laid out plans to dispose of a number of rental properties.

As the supply of public rented housing has been residual in Japan, private rented housing has occupied the main position in the rental market, accounting for around a quarter of all housing. Since the bubble collapsed, the economic burdens imposed by purchasing a house have become heavier while the value of most residential properties has continued to decline. Therefore, increasing numbers of households, particularly younger households have increasingly relied on the private rented sector. Between 1983 and 2008, the percentage of private rented housing increased from 33.5 to 56.2% for households with a head aged 30–34 years, and from 18.4 to 31.0% for those aged 40–44 years. However, many renters have experienced disadvantages in terms of physical conditions and housing costs. The government has traditionally operated a tenure-discriminatory housing system, concentrating on expanding middle-class home-ownership. There has been little assistance for the construction of private rented housing and absolutely no provision of rental subsidies. This has been based on the assumption that private rented housing provides a temporary foothold on the lower rungs of the housing ladder and that many households move out of private rented dwellings after a short period and acquire their own domiciles. With transformations in the housing economy, however, an increasing number of households have begun to live in private rented housing for longer periods, meaning an increase in those who are living under disadvantageous housing conditions.

The post-bubble deflationary economy is likely to promote a drop in market rents. Nevertheless, real rent levels have risen. The main factor behind this is the reduced availability of low-rent housing. In Japan, many 'nonprofessional' property owners have managed rented dwellings. Although providing private rental housing has not been particularly profitable, many individuals or families who hold land have constructed rented housing as a sideline without having to invest in site acquisition. This has made the supply of low-rent housing possible. The rent levels of multifamily housing in wooden structures have particularly been set at low levels. Although dwellings of this type have mostly been substandard in terms of floor area and amenities, they have functioned as low-cost shelters for low-income renters to live in. However, the number of existing low-rent private rental dwellings has substantially decreased as a result of structural aging or dilapidation.

In addition, in the late 1990s, the government began to restructure the private rented housing market in alignment with neoliberal policy. The intention was to 'modernise' the system of providing and financing rental housing while establishing a more 'professional' and profitable market for investments in private rented housing. This led to major amendments to the Housing Lease Act in 1999. Before this amendment, tenants' security of tenure was protected and hence landlords could not easily evict them. However, with this amendment, it is now possible for owners to rent their houses for more limited periods and hence more accurately calculate their prospects of making profits. As a consequence of the new policy to 'modernise' the private rented housing sector, low-rent dwellings provided by nonprofessional landlords are declining while higher-rent dwellings financed by more professional investors are on the increase.

Towards a Post-Homeowner Society?

Japan's contemporary housing situation has raised questions as to the extent to which homeownership-based societies can be maintained and whether a 'post-homeowner society' will emerge or not. Private ownership in Japan continues to occupy the main position as the dominant housing tenure. In this sense, Japan's homeowning society will be likely to be maintained in the foreseeable future. However, homeownership in today's Japan is completely different from before. Since the early 1990s, most owner-occupied houses have consistently generated capital losses and an increasing number of homeowners have been trapped in negative equity. Many households are now increasingly being excluded from routes that could take them into the homeownership sector. There is no doubt that the effectiveness of the traditional homeownership-oriented housing system has progressively been undermined. With the decline in the property ladder system, it is likely to become more necessary for the government to reconsider the organisation of housing policy and improve the conditions of not only owner-occupied housing but also rented housing. Many developed countries, which underwent prolonged periods of unprecedented housing inflation, have now begun to enter a new period with a more precarious economy. It is not certain at present how the current global financial crisis will affect societies oriented around homeownership. However, an examination of Japan's experience suggests the importance of questioning the extent to which homeowner societies are sustainable.

See also: Financial Deregulation; Government/Public Lending Institutions: Asia-Pacific; Housing and the Macroeconomy; Housing Demand; Housing Finance Institutions: Asia; Housing Markets and Macroeconomic Policy; Mortgage Market, Character and Trends: Japan; Price Dynamics in Housing Markets; Risk in Housing Markets.

Further Reading

Forrest R and Hirayama Y (2009) The uneven impact of neo-liberalism on housing opportunities. *International Journal of Urban and Regional Research* 33(4): 998–1013.

Forrest R, Kennett P, and Izuhara M (2003) Home ownership and economic change in Japan. *Housing Studies* 18(3): 277–293.

Hayakawa K (2002) Japan. In: Agus MA, Doling J, and Lee D (eds.) *Housing Policy Systems in South and East Asia*, pp. 20–37. Houndmills: Palgrave Macmillan.

Hirayama Y (2003) Housing and social inequality in Japan. In: Izuhara M (ed.) *Comparing Social Policies: Exploring New Perspectives in Britain and Japan*, pp. 151–171. Bristol: Polity Press.

Hirayama Y (2005) Running hot and cold in the urban home ownership market: The experience of Japan's major cities. *Journal of Housing and the Built Environment* 20(1): 1–20.

Hirayama Y (2007) Housing and state strategy in post-war Japan. In: Groves R, Murie A, and Watson C (eds.) *Housing and the New Welfare State: Perspectives from East Asia and Europe*, pp. 101–126. Aldershot: Ashgate.

Hirayama Y (2010) The role of home ownership in Japan's aged society. *Journal of Housing and the Built Environment* doi: 10.1007/s10901-010-9183-8.

Hirayama Y and Izuhara M (2008) Women and housing assets in the context of Japan's home-owning democracy. *Journal of Social Policy* 37(4): 641–660.

Hirayama Y and Ronald R (eds.) (2007) *Housing and Social Transition in Japan*. London: Routledge.

Hirayama Y and Ronald R (2008) Baby-boomers, baby-busters and the lost generation: Generational fractures in Japan's homeowner society. *Urban Policy and Research* 26(3): 325–342.

Izuhara M (2000) *Family Change and Housing in Post-war Japanese Society: The Experiences of Older Women*. Aldershot: Ashgate.

Oizumi E (1994) Property finance in Japan: Expansion and collapse of the bubble economy. *Environment and Planning A* 26(2): 199–213.

Ronald R (2004) Home ownership, ideology and diversity: Re-evaluating concepts of housing ideology in the case of Japan. *Housing, Theory and Society* 21(2): 49–64.

Ronald R and Hirayama Y (2006) Housing commodities, context and meanings: Transformations in Japan's urban condominium sector. *Urban Studies* 43(13): 2467–2483.

Saito A and Thornley A (2003) Shifts in Tokyo's world city status and the urban planning response. *Urban Studies* 40(4): 665–685.

Post-Conflict Housing Restitutions

A Buyse, Utrecht University, Utrecht, The Netherlands

© 2012 Elsevier Ltd. All rights reserved.

Glossary

Compensation Legal alternative when restitution is not possible, taking the form of monetary compensation or compensation in kind.

Ethnic cleansing The killing or forced displacement of all groups perceived to be of a different ethnicity than the majority in a certain area.

Housing restitution Recognition of legal title over a dwelling, in the sense of ownership or tenancy or any mixed forms, and actual repossession of the house for a person who had been forced to abandon such dwelling.

Refugee Person displaced across state borders and recognised as having to flee for fear of persecution.

Restitutio in integrum The principle which requires the violator of a legal obligation to restore a situation to its original condition.

Postconflict Challenges

Housing restitution for refugees and displaced persons is one of the many challenges faced by postconflict societies. It consists of the process of returning houses to the former inhabitants who had been forced to leave as a consequence of armed conflict. Restitution is an essential prerequisite for the return home of these groups and helps to prevent renewed conflict. Processes of restitution are seen as a way of redressing past injustices for large groups of displaced persons. At the same time, the restitution of housing can provide an economic and psychological starting point for people trying to rebuild their lives after the end of armed conflict. Housing restitution in a postconflict context is particularly difficult for many reasons. Others, often themselves displaced persons, may have taken possession of the housing in question. Local authorities may obstruct restitution to minority groups – especially when ethnic cleansing has taken place during the preceding conflict. Finally, implementation systems are often weak. Restitution and return are closely connected, but separate issues. For sustainable returns, security and nondiscriminatory access to work, education, and social services are equally necessary.

Housing Restitution as a Right

For many centuries housing restitution was rather a question of power than of rights. Ethnic cleansing and other forms of forced population transfer occurred during many armed conflicts and the return of the displaced depended entirely on the political will of the conflict's victors. With the advent of the international human rights movement in the twentieth century, and especially after 1945, this changed. The right to respect for the home, to adequate housing, to nondiscrimination, and to a certain extent to the protection of one's possessions were included in human rights treaties, such as the International Covenant on Civil and Political Rights, the International Covenant on Economic, Social and Cultural Rights, and, on a regional level, the European Convention on Human Rights. Until the present day, a right to housing restitution as such has not been recognised in such universal or general treaties. Nevertheless, it can be considered as an emerging norm under customary international law. An increasing number of resolutions of UN bodies and peace treaties contain restitution rights for housing and property lost during war. Such a right could also be construed as a corollary to the right to return and as a part of an emerging individual right to reparations for violations of human rights law. The apex of the development of a right to housing restitution is the Principles on Housing and Property Restitution for Refugees and Displaced Persons (often called the Pinheiro principles after their drafter, the Brazilian expert Paulo Sérgio Pinheiro). These principles were developed and adopted by the United Nations Sub-Commission on the Promotion and Protection of Human Rights in 2005. The document as such is not legally binding upon states, but some of its provisions reflect current international human rights law. The principles also contain guidelines for postconflict states based on best practices in the field. They represent the most extensive and authoritative legal overview of the issue of housing restitution.

As the above shows, the right is difficult to construe conclusively from the primary sources of international law – treaties and international custom. Although present to greater detail in 'soft law' texts (such as the Pinheiro principles), these are *ipso facto* weaker from a legal perspective and thus tend to yield less compliance.

Therefore, in the absence of a generally binding international human right to housing restitution, the incorporation of such a right in national legal systems, by way of a peace treaty, constitution, or other legal regulation, has proved to be particularly essential to ensure effective processes of restitution.

Institutional Matters

Housing restitution may in some cases occur outside any institutional structures. This is the case when the houses of refugees or displaced persons have not been destroyed or occupied by others, or when restitution can be negotiated in good faith with the temporary new inhabitants. In all other instances, institutions can help to structure and ease the process of restitution.

There are no specific institutions for housing restitution on the international or regional level. Within the context of the European Convention on Human Rights, however, the European Court of Human Rights has indicated in some cases that restitution was the most appropriate remedy for certain forms of housing rights violations, such as forced evictions. This happened, for example, in the *Brumărescu v. Romania* judgment, which concerned the deprivation of an apartment building in violation of the right to protection of property. In other judgments, such as the *Akdivar v. Turkey* judgment, the Court ordered compensation to be paid to the former inhabitants of a house which had been destroyed in violation of the Convention. The Court's case law reflects the international legal principle that *restitutio in integrum* is the most preferred remedy for a violation of an international obligation and that compensation should be given if restitution is impossible. The Court's judgments are legally binding.

Especially after the end of the Cold War in the early 1990s, housing restitution institutions were created in postconflict states. Often this was part of either a peace treaty or a new constitutional structure, in which such institutions were given a mandate which was in principle temporary, but in practice often open-ended. In some countries, such as South Africa, restitution institutions were part of a purely national structure, whereas in others, especially those in which UN's peacekeeping and reconstruction efforts were undertaken, the institutions were internationalised in either their legal basis or their composition or both. Bosnia and Herzegovina and Kosovo are examples of the latter. Such an international component was intended to ensure independence, impartiality, and respect for human rights in highly antagonised societies. National courts and administrative authorities were often perceived, both by the international community and large parts of the population, as tainted by the armed conflict and as representing only one of the various ethnic or religious groups in a society.

Two kinds of restitution mechanisms can be distinguished: judicial and administrative. Judicial institutions should abide by the highest standards of impartiality and independence and generally offer more procedural safeguards for claimants. They also generally apply higher standards of proof which may make it more difficult for applicants to submit successful restitution requests. As a result of these factors, judicial proceedings can be much more time-consuming and less accessible than administrative ones. However, in cases in which the applicable rules or legislation do not provide clarity or where the balancing of interests is particularly complex, a judicial process may be the only way to secure fair outcomes in restitution procedures.

However, the experience with postconflict housing restitution schemes shows that an administrative mechanism is often necessary in order to deal with the very high amount of claims. An administrative mechanism can function more quickly and efficiently than a judicial one by applying standardised decision-making procedures and lowered requirements of proof. A refugee trying to reclaim his house will, for example, only have to show some kind of proof of former habitation, such as paid bills for electricity or rent, instead of a full contract or ownership papers – items often forcibly left behind when being displaced during armed conflict. The trade-off between precise, fully balanced decision making and these forms of faster processing of claims is difficult, but often needs to be made in order to avoid extremely long delays.

Bosnia and Herzegovina

The process of housing restitution in Bosnia and Herzegovina after the end of the armed conflict in 1995 is one of the large-scale examples of such processes in the world. It has also been considered as one of the most successful efforts undertaken. The Dayton Peace Treaty explicitly contained a right to housing restitution for all those displaced during the war. A range of international human rights treaties was declared directly applicable in Bosnia. To sustain the restitution process and restore human rights protection, a number of semi-internationalised institutions were set up alongside existing national and local mechanisms. They were semi-international in three ways: their legal basis was an international peace treaty, their main normative points of reference were international rules and principles, and their membership consisted partly of non-Bosnians. A Commission on Real Property Claims was mandated to adjudicate claims. A Human Rights Ombudsperson could investigate postconflict human rights violations, which included property issues, and make recommendations. A Human Rights Chamber functioned as a judicial mechanism to decide through binding decisions on claims of alleged postconflict human rights violations. In parallel, displaced persons could claim at the local level through administrative and judicial procedures. Finally, the Constitutional Court could also decide on human rights issues, which again included property restitution matters.

In the first postwar years, restitution efforts were severely hampered. There were several reasons for this. The most important one was the unwillingness of local authorities to allow the return of refugees and other displaced persons of a different ethnicity than their own ruling group. This unwillingness was reflected both in discriminatory property laws and practical obstruction. The myriad of institutions where applicants could claim caused both confusion and unnecessary overlap. The international community in Bosnia initially perceived restitution as purely a necessary condition for the overall goal of the return of refugees instead of a goal in itself. Progress was made haphazardly by negotiating on the local level with municipalities on the return of groups of people. In practice, refugees became a political bargaining chip rather than claimants with an enforceable right to housing restitution.

Reacting to slow progress, the international organisations active in Bosnia and Herzegovina, led by the specially appointed High Representative with quasiconstitutional powers, started to act in a more concerted way. Discriminatory laws were abolished and restitution was finally implemented as an individual right. Pressure was put on local authorities to speed up the processing of claims and especially to implement them. The result was that 10 years after the end of the war, the very large majority of claims (over 90%) had been decided upon and implemented. Although no official figures exist, it is estimated that about half of the displaced persons who had successfully reclaimed their homes actually returned. The rest opted for de facto compensation by selling or letting their houses. These outcomes made the Bosnian restitution process one of the most successful rights-based processes in contemporary history.

Other Instances of Housing Restitution

In non-European contexts the restitution of housing has often been conducted under the broader heading 'land and property restitution'. Specifically, in developing countries, the main asset of refugees in terms of economic value is land rather than housing as such. Very often, restitution efforts in developing states are hampered by a lack of clear property registration and generations of overlapping land claims. Rwanda is an example of the latter, where a series of displacements have led to competing land claims. In some countries, restitution efforts are geared towards indigenous peoples who have traditionally had little access to the justice system in their societies. In Guatemala, for example, following the 1996 Peace Agreement which ended long years of civil war, it has been very difficult to reclaim land. Even a process of compensation by providing alternative land was only partially successful. The weak commitments undertaken by the Guatemalan state have led to a minimal solution, in which the negative effects of the war have not been undone for large groups of people.

Often, the lack of any strong international involvement has meant that little progress in restitution was made or that displaced persons were forcibly resettled. This happened, for example, with the Kurdish population in Eastern Turkey in the 1990s. In other cases the state actively blocked the return of refugees. The case of Palestinians unable to return to their former homes in Israel is an example of the longevity of such a blockade. In other instances, such as Georgia, the antagonisms between the central state and breakaway entities have been so great that effective restitution for minority groups is not possible.

In Kosovo, with the start of the mission of the United Nations after the 1999 war, efforts have been undertaken to set up a similar system to the Bosnian one, but with considerably less success. A Housing and Property Directorate was set up to receive claims and to mediate. In addition, a Housing and Property Claims Commission was established to decide on claims when mediation had failed. Although many people were able to return to their original houses, this overwhelmingly benefited Kosovars. Restitution and subsequent returns of minority groups such as Serbs has remained an elusive prospect due to lack of safety and political circumstances.

The very diverging results of the various restitution efforts show how difficult it is to achieve success in practice. To achieve a fair process of restitution, it is of paramount importance to ensure equal access in practice to all victims of the loss of housing, including disadvantaged minorities and other vulnerable groups. Restitution processes should also include a gender-sensitive approach. In many instances, such processes have failed on these points. Since corruption or lack of knowledge within administrative institutions can directly affect restitution, a parallel approach to develop good governance practices should be adopted. Finally, and probably most importantly, restitution issues have very often been at the mercy of political forces. As long as housing restitution is not conceived as a human right, but rather as a political bargaining chip, efforts to attain restitution will remain severely flawed.

Conclusions

Housing restitution has increasingly become an important element in the reconstruction of postconflict states. Since restitution is often very closely connected to the return of refugees and displaced persons, it is a very sensitive issue. This especially holds true when the armed conflict was to a large extent construed as an identity conflict between various groups. In those instances, the return of minorities is often opposed by local authorities. The larger the involvement of international organisations and other outsiders, the better the chances usually are for housing restitution. But even in those instances in which specific housing restitution institutions were created, success has often remained elusive. Institutions constantly have to balance requirements of efficiency and respect for human rights and the rule of law. This balancing act has to occur in an often challenging environment of antagonising political forces and a lack of resources and security. A complicating factor is that restitution of preconflict property may restore certain social inequalities which endanger a society's stability. In that context, it is important to give precedence to residential justice (the restitution of housing) rather than property restitution in the broadest sense. A final issue is the sheer size of the problem in most postconflict regions: the number of refugees and displaced persons is often high, which in turn affects the number of applications for restitution and thereby the feasibility of the whole housing restitution process.

Restitution of housing and property can only function effectively if it is part of a broader peace process. Returns of refugees and other displaced persons are not possible without minimum safeguards for security. More structurally, restitution and subsequent returns are viable only if and when there are economic opportunities, such as employment, for returnees. In addition, nondiscriminatory access to education and social services is essential to ensure the returns are successful in the long run. In order to be feasible, restitution processes should thus be part and parcel of a broader and integrated approach to rebuilding postconflict societies.

See also: Human Rights and Housing; Shelter and Settlement for Forcibly Displaced People; Slum Clearance.

Further Reading

Bassiouni MC (ed.) (2002) *Post-Conflict Justice*. Ardsley: Transnational Publishers.

Buyse AC (2008) *Post-Conflict Housing Restitution. The European Human Rights Perspective, with a Case Study on Bosnia and Herzegovina*. Antwerp/Oxford: Intersentia.

COHRE (2001) *Housing and Property Restitution for Refugees and Internally Displaced Persons: International, Regional and National Legal Resources*. Geneva: COHRE.

Cornell T and Salisbury L (2002) The importance of civil law in the transition to peace: lessons from the Human Rights Chamber for Bosnia and Herzegovina. *Cornell International Law Journal* 35: 389–426.

European Court of Human Rights, 23 January (2001), *Brumărescu v Romania* (just satisfaction), Application number 28342/95.

European Court of Human Rights, 1 April (1998), *Akdivar v. Turkey* (just satisfaction), Application number 21893/93.

FAO, Norwegian Refugee Council, OCHA, UNHCHR, UN-Habitat and UNHCR. (2007) *Handbook on Housing and Property Restitution for Refugees and Displaced Persons*. Geneva: FAO a.o.

Garlick M (2000) Protection for property rights: a partial solution? The Commission for Real Property Claims of Displaced Persons and Refugees (CRPC) in Bosnia and Herzegovina. *Refugee Survey Quarterly* 19: 64–85.

Hastings L (2001) Implementation of the property legislation in Bosnia Herzegovina. *Stanford Journal of International Law* 37: 221–254.

Kälin W (2006) Internal displacement and the protection of property. De Soto H and Cheneval F (eds.) *Realizing Property Rights. Swiss Human Rights Book*, Vol. 1 pp. 175–185. Zürich: Rueffer + Rub Sachbuchver.

Karadjova M (2004) Property restitution in Eastern Europe: domestic and international human rights responses. *Review of Central and Eastern European Law* 29–3: 325–363.

Leckie S (ed.) (2003) *Returning Home: Housing and Property Restitution Rights of Refugees and Displaced Persons*. Ardsley: Transnational Publishers.

McBride J (2000) Compensation, restitution and human rights in post-communist Europe. In: Meisel F and Cook PJ (eds.) *Property and Protection. Legal Rights and Restrictions*, pp. 87–105. Oxford: Hart Publishing.

Nowak M, Parmentier S and Bossuyt M (2005) Reparation by the Human Rights Chamber for Bosnia and Herzegovina. In: De Feyter K, et al. (eds.) *Out of the Ashes. Reparation for Victims of Gross and Systematic Violations*, pp. 245–288. Antwerp: Intersentia.

Sub-Commission on the Promotion and Protection of Human Rights (2005) Housing and Property Restitution in the Context of the Return of Refugees and Internally Displaced Persons. Final Report of the Special Rapporteur, Paulo Sérgio Pinheiro, UN Doc. E/CN.4/Sub.2/2005/17.

Von Carlowitz L (2004) Settling property issues in complex peace operations: the CRPC in Bosnia and Herzegovina and the HPD/CC in Kosovo. *Leiden Journal of International Law* 17: 599–614.

Williams R (2007) The contemporary right to property restitution in the context of transitional justice. *Report for the International Center for Transitional Justice*.

Post-Disaster Housing and Reconstruction

C Johnson, University College London, London, UK
G Lizarralde, Université de Montréal, Montréal, QC, Canada

© 2012 Elsevier Ltd. All rights reserved.

Glossary

Disaster A serious disruption of the functioning of a community or a society causing widespread human, material, economic, or environmental losses which exceed the ability of the affected community or society to cope using its own resources.

Hazard A dangerous phenomenon, substance, human activity, or condition that may cause loss of life, injury, or other health impacts; property damage; loss of livelihoods and services; social and economic disruption; or environmental damage.

Recovery The restoration, and improvement where appropriate, of facilities, livelihoods, and living conditions of disaster-affected communities, including efforts to reduce disaster risk factors.

Resilience The ability of a system, community, or society exposed to hazards to resist, absorb, accommodate, and to recover from the effects of a hazard in a timely and efficient manner, including through the preservation and restoration of its essential basic structures and functions.

Systems approach Scientific approach to the study of complex phenomena or complex problems. In this approach, the investigator studies the system (a set of elements having relations between them and their attributes) within its own environment, allowing for a holistic understanding of the problem and its own complexity.

Vulnerability The characteristics and circumstances of a community, system, or asset that make it susceptible to the damaging effects of a hazard.

Disasters and Vulnerability

The United Nations International Strategy for Disaster Reduction (UNISDR) defines a disaster as: "A serious disruption of the functioning of a community or a society causing widespread human, material, economic or environmental losses which exceed the ability of the affected community or society to cope using its own resources." There are many different types of disasters that can cause damage to the built environment, and damage may be inflicted to housing, businesses, and schools and also to critical infrastructure, such as roads, airports, and hospitals, as well as to people and natural ecosystems.

It is usually the poor who are more vulnerable to the devastating effects of a disaster and may have more difficulties recovering from it. Poor communities in low- and middle-income nations build informal housing where they can access land informally (and often illegally). These locations often include unstable sloping land vulnerable to landslides, riversides vulnerable to flooding, and low-lying areas vulnerable to inundation. Informal settlements often lack proper infrastructure for drainage or for flood protection and informally built houses may be more susceptible to damage. In terms of means for recovery, the poor are more likely to have fewer savings, less opportunities for employment after the disaster, and less access to government programmes, financing and subsidies. For example, while homeowners may have access to insurance claims and government subsidies for reconstruction, housing for renters or squatters is not included in most reconstruction programmes. For poor families, a disaster may wipe out all of their assets.

Characteristics of Post-Disaster Housing and Reconstruction

In the immediate aftermath of a disaster, shelter can be provided quickly, and this fulfils the most basic needs, however, it is recovery that people want. The reinstatement of a private and secure place to live and the continuation of work and other livelihood activities are key to this recovery. Decisions must be made quickly on where to rebuild, how to rebuild, and how to finance everything. Sometimes national- or local-level policies and plans may exist to guide development, but these all need to be updated based on the current situation. Disaster-induced housing damage is a telltale sign that there are systemic problems in housing production, location, or inequalities in development. Ideally, these problems need to be addressed in a proactive manner in reconstruction.

Figure 1 Post-disaster reconstruction project in Nueva Choluteca, Honduras. After hurricane Mitch, much effort in Nueva Choluteca was placed on the reconstruction of about 2000 housing units. However, insufficient efforts were made in the construction of infrastructure (Photo: Lizarralde).

Post-disaster reconstruction is affected by the fact that building houses is one of the most evident ways for agencies, organisations, and governments to show that resources are being spent and aid is being delivered. Houses are tangible proof of actions being taken in order to help affected households. It is therefore not surprising to find that less attention is often given to other – not so tangible or visible – needs related with recovery. Such is the case of the reconstruction of infrastructure for public services and financial or housing solutions for renters. It is therefore common to find post-disaster reconstruction projects in which houses are built more quickly than sewage systems or electricity networks (see **Figure 1**). It is also common to find reconstruction programmes that do not address the needs of landless families that rent space and that must endure the increasing rents that come with the typically reduced offer of residential space after disasters.

Common Stages of Post-Disaster Housing Recovery

People whose homes are damaged or destroyed in a disaster go through different stages of housing recovery. Not all disaster-affected people will pass through all stages of post-disaster housing and achieving full housing recovery may take several months to several years. The length of recovery may depend on several factors, such as the family's housing situation before the disaster, the extent of damage to the house, the scale of destruction in the area, and access to financing, materials, and labour. Quarantelli (1995) defines four different stages in housing recovery:

1. 'Emergency sheltering' is used during the height of the emergency and in the immediate aftermath; it may be as simple as a plastic tarp, refuge at a neighbour's house, or in a purpose-built shelter, such as those built for cyclones.
2. 'Temporary sheltering' is generally used after the emergency and for several days to several weeks. These may be tent camps, or public buildings commandeered as collective shelters. Usually, these facilities also provide meals, medical, and psychological support services for the disaster-affected families.
3. In the 'temporary housing' stage, families are able to reinstate their daily activities, such as school, work, meal preparation, and other social functions, however, in a temporary locale, such as a small prefabricated house or a rented apartment (**Figure 2**).
4. 'Permanent housing' is the final stage in housing recovery, when families have replaced their pre-disaster housing conditions with a long-lasting solution that is similar or, hopefully, of better quality.

Figure 2 Temporary settlement in Armenia, Colombia after the 1999 earthquake. Wood structures were erected by the National University of Colombia with the contribution of users.

The Need for Decentralised Decision-Making for Post-Disaster Housing and Reconstruction

Unfortunately, post-disaster reconstruction tends to be considered just as a technical problem. That is, as a problem of delivering quickly and cheaply the greatest number of houses. This approach underestimates the complexity of the real challenge that disasters pose to vulnerable communities. In reality, interventions in post-disaster housing and reconstruction must confront important challenges such as the identification of appropriate locations (which often leads to a problem of land management), the development of efficient financial schemes, the development of sustainable sources of income generation for affected families, and so on. A great number of project actors are thus confronted with the problem of working with limited and dynamic information and often without clear leadership. These actors might include agencies of the regional and national governments; the local government; international agencies; nongovernmental organisations (NGOs); local, national, and international banks; professionals in the building industry (architects, planners, contractors, and engineers); community-based organisations; and the affected population.

Following the Humanitarian Response Review in 2005, the international humanitarian community has developed a cluster approach to response, which allows multiple outside organisations to coordinate their actions and to allow for clearer leadership and a more accountable and professional system of response. The Global Shelter Cluster deals with issues of sheltering and transitional housing and is convened by the International Federation of Red Cross and Red Crescent Societies in disaster situations.

The tendency in post-disaster situations is often to concentrate decision-making in order to speed up procedures and the delivery of solutions. However, this concentration of decision-making only aggravates the problem of acting with limited information. Research in this area has shown that successful approaches to reconstruction require a systems approach to the complexity of the challenges that must be faced (Lizarralde et al., 2010). Reductionist approaches that concentrate exclusively on the technical aspects of construction or the speed of aid delivery or the physical aspects of construction rarely produce positive results. Instead, integrated approaches that consider reconstruction and housing as a complex system largely affected by its environment produce better results.

Too often, organisations tend to centralise decision-making. National or local governments, for instance, often assume centralised project planning and management. While these programmes may be successful in terms of numbers of houses produced, there are many problems that stem from the lack of people's participation in the rebuilding process (**Figure 3**). Frequently, this implies that end users (who really hold the information required about their own needs, expectations, and desires) may not be directly involved in the design, financing, and planning

Figure 3 Mass housing approach to reconstruction by the central government in Turkey after the 1999 earthquake led towards standardisation in designs (Photo: Johnson).

of their own housing solutions. In addition, the responses made by centralised processes usually rely on the repetition of a housing model – a model that is considered the most appropriate response to the equal distribution of limited resources among the majority of beneficiaries. As repetitive housing units rarely respond to the individual needs and conditions of families (which are by nature different), lower levels of users' satisfaction characterise reconstruction projects. Many post-disaster housing projects suffer from dysfunctional design of the units, inappropriate materials, and remote locations. This can be an insurmountable problem, and at worst, result in a huge waste of resources when people refuse to occupy the housing units.

Decentralised decision-making and distribution of risks between project actors tend to produce better results. This can, for example, include approaches in which end users assume (or are given) individual responsibility of their own recovery. This presupposes the need to provide aid and support to end users in the making of their own decisions regarding technical, financial, design, management, or construction issues. However, it also implies that decisions are made at the level in which information is really available: at the level of individual households who know their own needs, their own expectations, their own constraints, and their own potential.

Innovative approaches based on a redistribution of risks and decentralisation of decision-making include 'people-driven' procurement and entails people in key decision-making roles during all the project phases, including project initiation, planning, design, construction, and post-occupancy management. In people-driven reconstruction (particularly in rural reconstruction and reconstruction of affected houses in urban areas), end users determine how their house is rebuilt, choosing the materials, the construction technology, and the design. Construction may be done by the family, or the family or community may choose to hire a builder. In cases in which urban reconstruction requires higher levels of coordination of collective services (infrastructure, public services, and collective spaces), other approaches such as incremental construction provide positive results. In incremental construction, basic services, infrastructure, and core units are provided to users, who can later enlarge their units and finish them according to their own priorities, needs, and expectations.

Overall, end users are usually part of a government programme or NGO project from which they obtain financing and often guidance or technical support. People-driven programmes, for example, the one instituted in Gujarat after the 2001 earthquake, have been found to produce better results than contractor-driven approaches and have produced housing that is responsive to people's needs.

Informal and Formal Post-Disaster Reconstruction

Before conducting a reconstruction initiative, it is of prime importance to recognise the functioning of the building sector. In most low-income and many middle-income countries, the building industry is composed of two parallel and complementary sectors: the formal and the informal. Conceptually, the formal sector comprises registered professionals and companies that are part of the official, legal, financial, and taxing systems. It is traditionally represented by architects, engineers, designers, and urban planners who are registered with professional associations and who work with formally established companies or not-for-profit organisations. The formal sector also comprises construction companies and subcontractors that are legally registered and that comply with existing regulations and norms. By contrast, the informal sector is composed of non-registered construction companies and small industries that are not legally registered, and individuals who work in construction without permits and without necessarily complying to industry standards (see **Figure 4**). The informal sector usually accompanies or conducts self-build constructions and is particularly active in informal settlements and slums. However, in practice, this distinction is sometimes inaccurate as companies in the building sector in low- and middle-income countries might combine characteristics and behaviours that are conceptually attached to one or the other sector. More generally, the boundaries between the formal and the informal sector are blurred and dynamic.

Nevertheless, what is certainly important is to consider the complexity of the industry and the complementary characteristics of all its components (formal and informal). The informal sector tends to be neglected or ignored by most housing initiatives created by the formal sector. However, decision-makers should not forget that it is precisely the informal sector that is responsible for building the majority of housing for the poor. It is the same industry that holds the most valuable information about the successful strategies and mechanisms that permit building solutions for the poorest sectors of the society.

It is therefore important to recognise that the informal sector of the building industry can neither be ignored nor be neglected. If anything is needed, it has to be supported through special programmes to educate about hazard-resistant building and by addressing the underlying drivers of informality.

Land Management

Conflicts over land, and determining who has the right to occupy it, occur in many post-disaster situations. Disasters such as those caused by earthquakes, floods,

Figure 4 Prefabricated units built by informal construction companies in the townships of Cape Town, South Africa. Post-disaster reconstruction initiatives require a comprehensive understanding of the building industry, including its formal and informal components (Photo: Lizarralde).

landslides, or tsunamis destroy large tracts of the built environment and thus force people to leave their homes and communities in the immediate aftermath of the event. Many of them are not able to return. Described as 'disaster capitalism' by Naomi Klein in *The Shock Doctrine*, the crisis situation brought on by the disaster allows for new policies to be ushered in quickly, and these policies typically concern deregulation, privatisation, and the reduction in funding for social programmes. Thus, people and organisations in power are able to use the disaster to change the status quo for their benefit. Nowhere is this more striking than over the issue of access to land in the wake of a disaster.

In many cases, decision-makers consider it inappropriate to rebuild the housing stock in the affected area. This decision might respond to the fact that the area is at high risk of future disasters or that the area should assume a different vocation or use. Often, both arguments are exposed simultaneously, for instance, slum eradications are usually justified by risk assessment, whereas economic interests or political preferences push the decisions to change the use of the occupied land.

Conflicts over access to land are manifested through a variety of policies and practices. These may be through legal disputes, such as those that arise when public authorities use the destruction as a means to enforce existing laws against habitation in protected areas. A land-use planning response in Sri Lanka and Indonesia after the South Asian tsunami was to set up 'buffer zones' of a few hundred metres between the shoreline and areas for rebuilding. Traditional fishing communities, which relied on being near the coast, were to be forced to rebuild away from the coastline, whereas commercial hotels were being given the ability to build on the valuable land next to the water.

The resolution of the conflict over land, the right to it, is a central issue for the recovery process. Without access to land, the recovery of both housing and employment become problematic, if not impossible. Very often, the permanent rebuilding process cannot begin until outstanding land disputes are resolved.

In many cases, decision-makers offer relocation to a new house or new land, as a form of compensation for people whose land is under dispute. However, when large amounts of 'new houses' are required, mass construction of units is favoured (economies of scale are often intended). Large plots of land must thus be identified. However, large portions of land are scarce and expensive in areas where jobs, transportation, and services are available (i.e., in areas of high demand). The common response to this problem is often building in remote areas or in pieces of land that are not in high demand for residential use. The consequence is that relocated families must often confront the disadvantages of being far from jobs, public transportation means, services, and infrastructure. In many cases, relocated families resort to refusal to relocate in the new settlements or the abandonment of housing units in favour of settling informally in better-located areas.

Technology for Post-Disaster Housing

As previously discussed, design for post-disaster housing is most successful when the decision-making is decentralised, and affected families can choose the designs and technology that best suit their needs. Post-disaster housing projects may also spark an interest in traditional building technologies, which sometimes are found to be more hazard-resistant. Often as part of a recovery initiative, organisations may try to introduce a new building technology, or a modification or rediscovery of the existing local technology that is more resilient to disasters. The difficulty here is that even when people are trained to use the new technology, or to relearn traditional technologies, they rarely will adopt the new methods in post-project modifications. The problem with new technologies is that the materials may not be readily available, may be too expensive or too difficult to work with.

Many disasters destroy neither all the houses in a settlement nor all parts of a house. A great number of doors, windows, sinks, toilets, tiles, and so on can be recuperated after most earthquakes, floods, and landslides. Surprisingly, most common approaches to reconstruction are based on construction of complete units. Research in this area demonstrates that common approaches to housing delivery rarely allow for recycling of existing (recoverable) components. This demonstrates common lack of flexibility in project management, architectural design, and project planning. It has been identified that more efforts are required in reconstruction practices to optimise the advantages of recycling of construction components.

Financing for Reconstruction

Financing for reconstruction projects and programmes comes from a variety of sources. In high-income nations, financing for reconstruction is met through a combination of private insurance and government subsidies. In low- and middle-income nations, reconstruction funding is highly driven by donors (of all kinds) and by international agencies and development banks. In countries with strong socialist-communist regimes, or countries with strong central government control, the government may finance most of the reconstruction of people's homes and infrastructure (although some of this money may come in the form of loans from development banks).

In order to qualify for reconstruction financing, families may have to meet certain criteria, which may vary from funder to funder. For example, funding for reconstruction by an NGO may include all families living in a given area, or the poorest families (**Figure 5**). In some situations, groups of people may come together to form communities, in which they are able to access financing for housing and land as a group. This was a system encouraged by the Asian Coalition for Housing Rights after the South Asian Tsunami. In Turkey, after the 1999 earthquakes, only families who were homeowners before the disaster were included in the government's permanent reconstruction programmes and thus tenants or squatters were not included. The sporadic and uncoordinated nature of the financing for reconstruction often leaves gaps in funding, where some families do not qualify for reconstruction funding, or they do not have enough money to rebuild their entire house. Money and goods received varies widely from family to family across a disaster-affected region.

Figure 5 'Beyciler' housing reconstruction project in Turkey, produced by an NGO in partnership with the beneficiary families, was meant to target the poorest families in the region who did not qualify for government assistance (Photo: Johnson).

In high-income nations, homeowners' insurance frequently plays a large role in paying for the costs of reconstruction. This may be topped-up by the government, or private donors may come to the assistance of those without insurance coverage. However, the same problems of lack of financing or patchy financing may leave the poorest sectors of the society still without adequate post-disaster housing assistance. This has been the case in Japan and in the United States after recent disasters.

Conclusion

Post-disaster housing and reconstruction is a complex political process in which various state and non-state actors need to consider the availability of land, financing, multiple scales of building, and equal distribution of resources especially for the poor or landless. At its best, reconstruction involves transferring of decision-making power to end users. This implies facilitating individual (or communal) responsibility over financing, construction, design, and management of individual projects, and it may also imply facilitating collective responsibility over community needs and expectations. This process requires support on legal, administrative, and financial issues and regulatory frameworks and planning systems at urban, regional, and national levels that allow the decentralisation of decision-making to happen. Projects, therefore, require a systems approach to management (particularly to integrate project stakeholders) and interdisciplinary planning.

See also: Homeless People: Disasters and Displacement; Housing Policies in Developing Countries; Housing Subsidies in the Developing World; Rights to Housing: Developing Societies; Rights to Housing: Marginalised Housing Groups; Self-Help: Policy Assistance; Shelter and Settlement for Forcibly Displaced People; Slum Clearance.

References

Lizarralde G, Johnson C, and Davidson CH (eds.) (2010) *Rebuilding after Disasters: From Emergency to Sustainability*. London: Spon Press.

Quarantelli EL (1995) Patterns of shelter and housing in US disasters. *Disaster Prevention and Management* 4(3): 43–53.

Further Reading

Alexander D, Davidson CH, Fox A, Johnson C, and Lizarralde G (eds.) (2007) *Post-Disaster Reconstruction: Meeting Stakeholder Interests Proceedings of a conference held at the Scuola di Sanità Militare*, Florence, Italy, 17–19 May 2006. Firenze: Firenze University Press. http://www.grif.umontreal.ca/pages/irecpublicns.html (accessed 25 September 2009).

Barakat S (2003) *Housing reconstruction after conflict and disaster. Humanitarian Practice Network Paper Number 43*. London: Overseas Development Institute.

Barenstein JD (2006) Housing reconstruction in post-earthquake Gujarat: A comparative analysis. *Humanitarian Practice Network Paper Number 54*. London: Overseas Development Institute.

Comerio M (1998) *Disaster Hits Home: New Policy for Urban Housing Recovery*. Berkeley, CA: University of California Press.

Information and Research for Reconstruction (i-Rec) (2002) *Proceedings from the International Conference on Post-Disaster Reconstruction: Improving Post-Disaster Reconstruction in Developing Countries*, Montreal, Canada, 23–25 April. Montreal: i-Rec. http://www.grif.umontreal.ca/pages/irecpublicns.html (accessed 25 September 2009).

Information and Research for Reconstruction (i-Rec) (2004) *Proceedings from the Second International i-Rec Conference on Post-disaster Reconstruction: Planning for Reconstruction, Coventry University, England*, England, 22–23 April. Montreal: i-Rec. http://www.grif.umontreal.ca/pages/irecpublicns.html (accessed 25 September 2009).

Information and Research for Reconstruction (i-Rec) (2008) *4th International i-Rec Conference on Post-Disaster Reconstruction: Building Resilience, Achieving Effective Post-Disaster Reconstruction*, Christchurch, New Zealand, 30 April–2 May. Montreal: i-Rec. http://www.grif.umontreal.ca/i-Rec.htm (accessed 10 August 2008).

Lloyd-Jones T (2007) *Mind the Gap! – Post-Disaster Reconstruction and the Transition from Humanitarian Relief*. London: RICS Publications.

Lyons M, Schilderman T, and Boano C (eds.) (2010) *Building Back Better. Delivering People-Centred Housing Reconstruction at Scale*. London: Practical Action.

United Nations Disaster Relief Organization – UNDRO (1982) *Shelter After Disaster: Guidelines for Assistance*. New York: UNDRO.

Relevant Websites

www.grif.umontreal.ca/i-Rec.htm – I-Rec Information and Research for Reconstruction.

www.preventionweb.net/english – PreventionWeb.

www.shelterproject.org – shelterproject.org.

www.unisdr.org – UN International Strategy for Disaster Reduction.

Power

P King, De Montfort University, Leicester, UK

© 2012 Elsevier Ltd. All rights reserved.

Glossary

Authority An influence exerted over others that is accepted as legitimate.
Hegemony A position of leadership or dominance, particularly within a state.
Legitimacy Justified according to law or precedence and conforming to the standard or expected type.

Introduction

In 2010, the UK government announced a string of proposals aimed at reforming welfare benefits and reducing the large public deficit that has arisen under the previous government. Part of these changes involved the capping of housing benefit payments to prevent households living in excessively expensive housing. Unsurprisingly, these proposals proved to be controversial and led to a heated, and sometimes, hysterical debate. The opponents of these proposals argued that the changes would lead to higher levels of homelessness and even create a form of social cleansing whereby the poor would be excluded from certain high-cost cities such as London and Oxford. It was seen as an attack on a powerless group of individuals by an uncaring government seeking to prosecute an ideological agenda of small government.

However, the supporters of capping benefit payments argued that a key problem with the UK system was that it allowed landlords a considerable degree of control over the market, in that they could set high rents secure in the knowledge that housing benefit would cover the cost on behalf of their tenants. Therefore, we can suggest that the problem with the private rented market was that landlords were able to exercise power at the expense of tenants and the taxpayer. The aim of the caps was to redress that power relationship back towards a more favourable position for the taxpayer.

This debate shows something of the nature of power and power relations. On the one hand, we can describe an apparently strong government imposing its will on a powerless group, but on the other hand, we can suggest a legitimate authority is seeking to rebalance the relations between different sections of the community. Not only does it show that power can be exerted on housing systems from the outside, by government in particular, but also that the relationships within housing systems – between landlord and tenant for instance – are also important.

Power is both ubiquitous and amorphous: it is always there, but it is often hard to locate or pin down exactly. Of course, power can sometimes be brutal when it is exercised in war, violence, and argument. On these occasions, it is all too clear where the power lies and what impact it has. But power need not be so forcefully exercised: most UK citizens will defer to a police officer even though they will usually be unarmed. Power therefore often involves a level of acceptance, which in turn rests on a sense of authority and proper legitimacy. How this authority develops, becomes, and remains acceptable is therefore an important, if extremely complex and contested question. But this need for it to be accepted also demonstrates that power is a matter of relationships: it is not just a one-way relation where the powerful control or manipulate the powerless. What matters is the manner in which the powerless address those with power and how they respond. These relationships will inevitably be unequal, and so what will matter is how power is distributed and what ability the weaker party has to resist and mitigate the effects of the power exerted by the other.

These issues will be considered in this article, although they cannot be dealt with comprehensively and completely. It will rather be a case of opening up some of the issues and providing pointers for further study and analysis. The discussion begins with an attempt to define power relying on the ideas of Lukes and Foucault. This is followed by a discussion of housing and power relations. The second half of the article considers some criticisms of theories of power, concentrating particularly on the issues of self-restraint and authority.

Defining Power

It is not possible to provide a complete overview of the compendious literature on power that ranges from the Greeks through Machiavelli, Marx, and onto the poststructuralists, and so in this section only two of the main thinkers on the subject will be discussed. These are Lukes and Foucault, and they are chosen because their work is the most influential in recent times. Lukes' argument is also useful, in that he builds his argument out of a critique of older notions of power.

All theories of power, however, concur that it is a relational state. It is concerned with the relationships between individuals and groups. Power is an important concept because these relationships are unequal such that one party is capable of influencing, controlling, or manipulating the other. This provides us with a very simple view of what power might be: it is where a stronger force is able to influence a weaker one. However, Lukes argued that this is an insufficient definition, and using the work of thinkers such as Gramsci and Althusser, he sought to devise a more nuanced, yet radical, view of power.

Lukes posits three dimensions of power. The first is similar to the simplistic notion we have just described. Power is about decision making which is measurable in terms of outcomes. In this sense, it is a zero-sum game, where the more influence one player has the less can be held by others. This form of power is seen as being exercised by formal institutions and is one-dimensional because it is apparent and relates only to observable conflict within political structures.

Lukes describes two-dimensional power as a development from this earlier view. It takes the formal aspects of power described above but adds to them the informal and considers a wider range of measures beyond the formal. So those in power might not use overt coercion and direct force, but might instead use influence, persuasion, and inducement. This notion of power is concerned with how groups are able to exert informal influence over others through their control of elements within society. This conception of power might be seen as similar to the classical Marxist conception of power relations.

The three-dimensional view that Lukes prefers is again additive, taking elements of the first and second view but adding in a further range of elements. So not only is power a result of formal and informal structures and influences, but it is also concerned with how preferences are shaped by values, norms, and ideologies. It acknowledges that power is vested in all forms of social relationships including language. However, this ubiquity means that power cannot always be measured in any quantifiable manner, but can only be inferred.

The importance of this three-dimensional view is that norms and values are things that individuals and societies accept as taken-for-granted parts of their lives. They do not question these but rather are part of the ordinary routines of daily life. They are not things that are thought about consciously and so power is effectively hidden. Lukes therefore does not see power as a zero-sum game but as ubiquitous and intrinsic to the nature of social relations. This means it is a rather more amorphous concept, but it does make it more nuanced and complete.

There are similarities between Lukes' view and that of Foucault who was developing his theories at roughly the same time (the 1970s). Foucault in his studies on medicine and prisons discussed the so-called technologies of power, which serve to discipline and regulate the actions of individuals. For Foucault, power is not a matter of brute force or open coercion. Indeed in his seminal book *Discipline and Punish*, he contrasts the premodern notion of power as represented by the public execution of an attempted regicide in all its gruesome detail with the ordered prison regimes of the nineteenth century which sought to control individuals through rules and regulations and the imposition of order. An important element in Foucault's thought is the fact that power is exercised through the choices and actions that individuals make themselves. Power operates through self-discipline and by the way in which individuals can be made to act ostensibly out of their own volition.

According to Foucault, power does not act on people so much as through them. In this sense, power is linked to knowledge and how people come to accept commonsense views of the world. Power operates because of belief systems and common knowledge that create a sense of the normal and abnormal, and the acceptable and the unacceptable. Certain forms of discourse become 'normalised' as apparently immutable truths. As with Lukes' view, Foucault sees power as amorphous and ubiquitous. Properly speaking, there can be no absence of power, and it can merely be resisted or opposed by other discourses, which would themselves, if successful, become hegemonic.

Power is therefore not always open or obviously brutal, but is intrinsic to normal social relations. This does not mean that it is any less invidious, rather that power, so to speak, mutates according to the development of social relations.

Housing and Power Relations

There are a number of ways in which we can consider power relations within a housing context. Perhaps the most obvious way, and the one that relates to a more traditional view of power, is to look at the relations between different levels within housing systems and see the nature of control between them. So, for example, in Britain, since the 1970s, there has been a consistent drive towards the centralisation of decision-making. Central government seeks to control local spending, the quality of provision, and the means in which housing is allocated. Despite the history of the development of social housing in Britain, which has been essentially one of local provisions for local people, by the late 1990s government was openly discussing social housing as a national asset.

This sense of power is important because it introduces the notion of legitimacy. In the British political tradition, the state is considered to be unitary taking the form of the Crown in Parliament (the elected House of Commons acting as the will of the Monarch). Accordingly, local authorities and other agencies are given permissive powers by Parliament, which, of course, can be changed only at the centre. Local government may only act if given express permission, and so its actions are also only legitimate with the sanction of Parliament. Legitimacy therefore implies particular accepted roles within a state, which suggests that power can be circumscribed through a sense of appropriate application. An example of this is the manner in which the UK government was forced into repealing a form of flat-rate local taxation popularly known as the Poll Tax in 1991 after it was commonly seen as unfair. Even though this policy had been included in an election manifesto, it was considered illegitimate for it to be implemented. Power, therefore, needs to be backed by a sense of what is proper and accepted.

While the above discussion is concerned with power in a rather overt way, we need to consider how power might operate in the more covert manner considered by Lukes and Foucault. One interesting example of this is the development of the concept of antisocial behaviour (ASB) in the United Kingdom. The concept of ASB can be said to have been 'invented' as a distinct offense in the 1990s where previously social landlords and the police had dealt with 'noise and nuisance'. ASB included many forms of behaviour, including the playing of loud music, vandalism, and graffiti, but quickly developed into an entity in itself which allowed certain groups – hoodie-wearing teenagers, for instance – to be pathologised. Within barely a decade, the notion of ASB had become institutionalised as a normal part of the discourse of housing management and so can be seen as a means of disciplining certain forms of behaviour seen as abnormal.

One of the main aims of the New Labour government in the United Kingdom between 1997 and 2010 was the 'empowerment' of socially excluded groups. In housing this was to be achieved through the extension of choice. Households were to be given choice in terms of bidding for properties that became vacant instead of waiting to be allocated a property at the discretion of the landlords. In addition, private sector tenants were to be empowered by having Housing Benefit paid to them instead of directly to their landlord. This, it was argued, would inculcate a sense of responsibility and allow households control over their own affairs.

Part of this empowerment of households was the intention to rebalance the power relations between landlord and tenant. This relation is a classic example of asymmetrical power, where one party that controls the access to housing is able to exert influence over the other. Of course, it is precisely this power that makes the means of dealing with ASB anywhere near effective: landlords have the power to evict badly behaving tenants. However, in other contexts, government has sought to equalise this relationship by altering the manner in which benefits are paid and dwellings are allocated.

A final example with regard to housing that we might consider is the power relations within the dwelling itself. Housing might be a locale for conflict based on unequal power relations between genders and between adults and children. Housing is used and perceived differently according to gender and to age, but there may not be an equal ability to fully use the dwelling according to these particular perceptions. Where men are the principal earners and where parents take decisions without consulting their children, we can suggest that unequal power relations exist. Many of these conflicts may remain hidden because of the nature of private dwelling and so the significance of power relations might be hard to define. However, this example shows that power relations affect housing at all levels, from national decision-making down to relationships with the home.

Power and Self-Restraint

Power, as have seen, is about the ability to control, influence, or manipulate a situation or other people. It is often seen as being vested in one person or body that is then able to exert this control or influence over others in order to achieve their ends. This implies that those who are being manipulated are powerless, being exploited, and used for the ends of others. Defined as such, power is clearly something to be avoided or curtailed. Yet, should power always be seen as a negative?

Without power there can be no social order, in that decisions cannot be enforced or laws implemented. As Hegel has shown, without order, social relations would not be possible. Individual freedom, for Hegel, can only derive out of a social structure that permits individuals the liberty to act through constraints placed on others. This puts a dramatically different gloss on the issue from that of Lukes and Foucault. Power is therefore not something necessarily invidious or the tool of hegemonous forces, but rather a necessary means of lubricating social relations in order to allow individuals to fulfil their ends. So without tenure regulations there could be no means of either landlord or tenant exercising their rights of a property.

Moreover, the idea of self-discipline and restraint need not necessarily be seen in the manner described by Lukes and Foucault. As an example, Nozick has shown how side-constraints on the actions of individuals are the basic requirement for the exercising of individual rights. Nozick argues that individual rights are enabled through constraints placed on each individual, which then prevents them from coercing others into doing anything against their express will and intention. In this regard, self-restraint is not an example of power but actually the means by which power is restrained to allow individuals to develop their own ends free from coercion.

So, the issue is not really whether there is power or not, but who has it, how it is used, and whether the possibility of countermanding unreasonable power exists. Hegel sees power as an essential prerequisite for social action, while Nozick argues that self-discipline is the means by which power is limited to further individual freedom. This returns us to the idea of legitimacy. Hegel sees power as legitimate, but Nozick seeks to develop the limits of this legitimacy. The advantage that these normative views have over the more structural critics of power such as Lukes and Foucault is that both the Hegelian and Nozikean view of power are dynamic and capable of development: we can see how power might operate with social relations to create change and so alter the nature of power relations themselves. The problem of Foucault's view in particular (although it applies to many theories of discourse) is that it is merely descriptive of a particular set of social conditions without being capable of explaining those conditions or the means by which any development might occur. Foucault can infer that change occurs, but only comparatively through looking at different examples over time. This rather static view of power is therefore ultimately a limited one as compared to the arguments of Hegel and Nozick who see power as enabling and so as a potential means for social development.

Authority

There is one further point that needs considering with regard to power. In the conservative political tradition, in particular, it is recognised that the manner in which power is connected to legitimacy is through the notion of authority. Authority, according to Scruton, is what is prior to any possibility of choice or contract. It is the established and unquestioned patterns within which we operate. This is clearly related to the Hegelian notion of order, in that it is authority – the established means of acceptance – that creates the parameters for individual action.

Conservatives would argue that power without authority lacks a proper legitimacy and becomes little more than brute force. When institutions are imbued with authority, they are accepted and deferred to. Indeed, it might be the case that certain institutions retain authority while lacking any real power. One example of this is the British monarchy, which lacks any real political power, but the Queen is still taken to be head of state, is deferred to, and is seen as an essential part of the Constitution.

Authority is important because it helps further in dealing with the issue of self-restraint. Why is it that individuals act in particular ways, apparently voluntarily, even though it is clearly not in their interest to do so? If we see a neighbour's door left open after they have gone out, we are more likely to close it or guard it rather than take advantage of the situation to take whatever we can carry. We do this because we respect our neighbours and their property. But it is also because of a certain moral code laid down in law. We know that certain sanctions are applied in order to police that moral code and we, by and large, stick to the code even though we might very often not be punished for any transgression. We accept the authority of the law of the land and the institutions that enforce that law. Property rights are respected out of a duty to others and because of laws that seek to protect them as well as us.

Likewise, in electoral systems such as the United Kingdom and the United States, we accept the outcome of elections even though a majority might not have voted for the victorious party. The government has authority because of what it represents and because of the traditions that are embodied within the institutions of government.

But if there can be authority without power, there can also clearly be power without authority. There are governments which are considered to be illegitimate, either because of the means by which they have come to power or because of certain actions they have taken while in power. Likewise, there might be laws that are considered to be illegitimate and lacking in authority because they do not form part of the established political traditions of the country, as was the case with the poll tax discussed earlier. The elected government certainly had the right to enact this legislation that had formed part of its election manifesto. Yet, it was not considered acceptable. Many individuals and groups actively resisted the poll tax and achieved its repeal, effectively ending the career of Margaret Thatcher as Prime Minister despite her landslide electoral victory 3 years before.

This returns us to discussion at the start of this article on the capping of housing benefit. The government elected in 2010 clearly has the power to enact the changes. It has the majority in Parliament to do as it wishes. It has the apparent authority, in that the people of the United Kingdom accept it as their government. This, however, does not end the debate about these proposals and we can suggest that much of the controversy is over the legitimacy of proposals which, its critics claim, will lead to the poor being excluded from certain parts of the country. So what matters here is not merely that government has the power to act, or that it wishes to remake the power relations between landlords and tenants, but whether it is legitimate for government to exercise its power in this manner and whether ultimately the members of this society believe it has the authority to do so.

Conclusion

In this article, we have considered some of the issues relating to power. Of necessity, we have been brief in dealing with what power is and how it operates. However, it is clear that the notion of power has some explanatory force in terms of housing. However, the nature of power as a concept is contested and we need to be aware that it used to express diametrically different conceptions of the social order. We should therefore treat the concept with care and ensure that we can define precisely what we are considering and then use it accordingly.

See also: Housing Governance; Politics of Housing; Social Justice.

Further Reading

Bachrach P and Baratz M (1970) *Power and Poverty: Theory and Practice*. New York: Oxford University Press.
Clapham D (2005) *The Meaning of Housing: A Pathways Approach*. Bristol, UK: Policy Press.
Foucault M (1977) *Discipline and Punish: The Birth of the Prison*. London: Penguin.
Foucault M (1980) *Power/Knowledge*. Harlow, UK: Pearson Education.
Hegel G (1991) *Elements of the Philosophy of Right*. Cambridge, UK: Cambridge University Press.
Jouvenel B de (1990) *On Power: The Natural History of its Grounds*. Indianapolis, IN: Liberty Press.
Lukes S (1974) *Power: A Radical View*. Basingstoke, UK: Macmillan.
Lukes S (ed.) (1986) *Power*. Oxford, UK: Blackwell.
Nozick R (1974) *Anarchy, State and Utopia*. Oxford, UK: Blackwell.
Richardson J (2006) *The Gypsy Debate: Can Discourse Control?* Exeter, UK: Imprint Academic.
Scruton R (2001) *The Meaning of Conservatism*, 3rd edn. Basingstoke, UK: Palgrave.

Price Determination in Housing Markets

G Meen, University of Reading, Reading, UK

© 2012 Elsevier Ltd. All rights reserved.

Introduction

This article concentrates on the factors that determine the time-series properties of house prices at different spatial scales across different countries. Although there is considerable agreement in the literature on the basic theory, in practice, international empirical studies adopt a wide variety of approaches and, consequently, reach different conclusions on the key drivers. An example is the debate on whether the international increase in prices from the second half of the 1990s to 2007 represented a bubble or was, simply, a consequence of movements in fundamentals. Conclusions depend strongly on the model specification. Similarly, different econometric methods are used in the literature. In early studies, relatively little attention was paid to time-series properties, but increasingly issues of dynamic specification, unit root tests, and cointegration play a central role. A further set of issues arise from spatial heterogeneity. Despite the large number of national studies, the United States or even the United Kingdom cannot be considered as a single housing market. It would be remarkable if the key elasticities did not vary between different parts of the country. For example, areas that face the strongest zoning controls are likely to experience greatest price volatility.

This article is, therefore, concerned with a number of issues:

(1) The theory of house price determination
(2) Econometric technique
(3) Empirical implementation
(4) Bubbles and fundamentals
(5) Spatial variation.

The Theory of House Price Determination

At the simplest level, house prices can be derived as a reduced form from structural housing stock demand and supply functions, given by eqns [1]–[4], which exclude, at this stage, any form of dynamic adjustment. Equation [1] includes generic versions of most of the variables typically found to be important in empirical studies – a combination of economic and demographic variables. Notice that (1) for the moment, the cost of finance is simply captured by the (nominal) market interest rate and excludes expectations and taxation; this is generalised through the user cost of capital below: (2) credit availability, which was particularly important in the credit crunch from 2007, is captured through the mortgage stock; again this is made more formal below: (3) the restriction $\alpha_2 = -\alpha_7$ is expected so that demand is a function of real prices: (4) the supply eqn [2] is related to prices, construction, and finance costs, and $(1-\beta_3)$ represents the depreciation rate on the existing stock. Note that some of the literature on new housing supply stresses the importance of the changes in prices rather than the level as a key determinant. Consequently, eqn [2] can be interpreted as a flow, new housing supply equation: (5) in the reduced form, eqn [4], the effect of interest rates could, in principle, be either positive or negative, depending on the relative strengths of α_5 and β_5. However, in a stock framework, there are good reasons for believing that the demand effect will dominate, since new supply is a small percentage of the existing stock: (6) similarly, although construction costs appear in eqn [4] – and in many empirical studies – there are good reasons for believing that, particularly in the short run, they have little effect on prices. If so, this implies prices can be conditioned on the existing stock and current period new supply will have little influence. In the longer run, however, if the supply of housing is perfectly elastic, then prices should be determined by costs alone, that is, $\gamma_2 = \gamma_3 = \gamma_4 = \gamma_5 = \gamma_6 = \gamma_7 = 0$. However, there is little empirical evidence that these restrictions hold, suggesting that land-use planning or zoning regulations limit supply responses even in the long run (see article Supply Elasticity of Housing).

$$h_t^d = \alpha_1 + \alpha_2(ph)_t + \alpha_3(ry)_t + \alpha_4(pop)_t + \alpha_5(i)_t + \alpha_6(m)_t + \alpha_7(pc)_t + \varepsilon_{1t} \quad [1]$$

$$h_t^s = \beta_1 + \beta_2(ph)_t + \beta_3(h)_{t-1} + \beta_4(cc)_t + \beta_5(i)_t + \varepsilon_{2t} \quad [2]$$

$$h_t^d = h_t^s \quad [3]$$

$$ph_t = \gamma_1 + \gamma_2(ry)_t + \gamma_3(pop)_t + \gamma_4(i)_t + \gamma_5(m)_t + \gamma_6(pc)_t + \gamma_7(h)_{t-1} + \gamma_8(cc)_t + \varepsilon_{3t} \quad [4]$$

where $H^{d,s}$ is housing stock demand and supply, PH is nominal house prices, RY is real incomes, POP is population, i is market interest rate, M is mortgage debt outstanding, PC is consumers' expenditure deflator, CC is construction costs, and ε is the error term. Lower case denotes logarithms (except for the interest rate (i)).

Although eqn [4] forms the basis of many empirical studies, an alternative can be derived from the standard life-cycle consumption model, extended to housing. In this context, the user cost of capital is central. In the intertemporal utility maximising model, there are two goods, housing services and a composite consumption good (C). If the flow of housing services is proportional to the housing stock (H) and, given a real discount rate (r), lifetime utility is described by eqn [5]:

$$\int_0^\infty e^{-rt}\mu(H(t),C(t))dt \quad [5]$$

Equation [5] is maximised with respect to the period-to-period budget constraint, eqn [6], and technical constraints, eqns [7] and [8], which describe the evolution of asset stocks (housing and financial) over time.

$$g(t)X(t)+S(t)+C(t)=(1-\theta)RY(t)+(1-\theta)i(t)A(t) \quad [6]$$

$$\dot{H}(t)=X(t)-\delta H(t) \quad [7]$$

$$\dot{A}(t)=S(t)-\pi A(t) \quad [8]$$

where $g(t)$ is real purchase price of dwellings (PH/PC above), $X(t)$ is new purchases of dwellings, $S(t)$ is real savings net of real new loans, θ is household marginal tax rate, $RY(t)$ is real household income, $i(t)$ is market interest rate, $A(t)$ is real net nonhousing assets, δ is depreciation rate on housing, π is general inflation rate, (.) is time derivative, and δ, π, and θ are assumed to be time invariant.

From the first-order conditions, the marginal rate of substitution between housing and the composite consumption good, (μ_b/μ_c), is given by eqn [9]:

$$\mu_b/\mu_c = g(t)[(1-\theta)i(t)-\pi+\delta-\dot{g}^e/g(t)] \quad [9]$$

This is the widely used standard definition of the real housing user cost of capital and represents the real price of housing services, where $(\dot{g}^e/g(t))$ is the expected real capital gain. The definition may be extended to include such elements as property taxes, maintenance expenditures, and transactions costs but, at least in time-series models, movements in eqn [9] are dominated by changes in the interest rate and in capital gains on housing.

However, the user cost of capital has to be amended if credit constraints are binding. If there is an absolute constraint on the amount of borrowing, $M(t) < \bar{M}(t)$, then the user cost is defined by eqn [10], where the expression takes into account the shadow price of the rationing constraint, $\lambda(t)$.

$$\mu_b/\mu_c = g(t)[(1-\theta)i(t)-\pi+\delta-\dot{g}^e/g(t)+\lambda(t)/\mu_c] \quad [10]$$

Equation [10] captures the investment (through the capital gains term) as well as the consumption aspect of housing decisions and, in a slightly different form, can be expressed as a market efficiency condition or an arbitrage relationship. If $R(t)$ represents the real imputed rental price of housing services, arbitrage requires

$$g(t)=R(t)/[(1-\theta)i(t)-\pi+\delta-\dot{g}^e/g(t)+\lambda(t)/\mu_c] \quad [11]$$

Equation [11] implies that the return on housing, represented by the imputed rental plus any capital gain on housing net of depreciation, equals the post-tax return on alternative assets, allowing for any credit constraints. Furthermore, the equation implies that only real interest rates have any effect on real house prices, whereas the empirical literature suggests that nominal interest rates can also have an independent influence, due to front-end loading. To test this, eqn [11] can be rewritten as follows:

$$g(t)=R(t)/[(1-\theta)i(t)+\delta-\gamma(\pi+\dot{g}^e/g(t))+\lambda(t)/\mu_c] \quad [12]$$

The term $\gamma(\pi+\dot{g}^e/g(t))$ represents the nominal capital gain on housing and γ may take a value between zero and unity. If only real rates affect prices, then $\gamma = 1.0$. A value of less than unity implies that nominal as well as real interest rates are a determinant of prices.

Equation [12] is simply a discounting equation, and if all the variables are measurable, it could be used as the basis of market efficiency tests. However, in practice, the presence of transactions and search costs, for example, make it unlikely that eqn [12] is adequate without the addition of lags. All empirical studies suggest that adjustment to any equilibrium is slow – certainly much slower than in purely financial markets. Also, for many countries, all the variables in eqn [12] are not available. For example, in the United Kingdom, until recently rent control was commonplace and long time series on market rents were not published. Furthermore, measuring credit constraints is problematic. Consequently, there are relatively few direct tests of eqn [12].

Nevertheless, eqn [12] is particularly important as a possible basis for discriminating between fundamentals and bubbles from the mid-1990s, whereas neither the commonly used house price-to-rent ratio nor the price-to-income ratio are valid indicators of bubbles. Equation [12] shows that the price-to-rent ratio is the inverse of the user cost, and unless the user cost is constant, there is no fixed ratio between prices and rents.

Note that eqn [12] can be used to investigate the effects of the credit crunch, since credit restrictions raise housing costs faced by households. The equation also indicates that monetary policy is likely to be less effective as a way of stimulating the housing market, when constraints are binding, because any increase in housing demand from lower interest rates may be offset by increased rationing as mortgage demand expands. Again in the context of the credit crunch, lowering nominal interest rates has little effect without the accompanying increase in credit availability. Operationally, however, the problem is how to measure $\lambda(t)$.

A further issue relates to leveraging, which raises returns in housing booms and increases the losses in a slump. For example, US cities where a high percentage of individuals are heavily leveraged appear to be more responsive to city-wide shocks. Although eqn [12] does not take account of leveraging, as Muellbauer and Murphy (1997) show, the closely related leveraged excess return to housing is given by eqn [13]. Conceptually, the excess return measures the total percentage gains from investing in housing (capital gains and imputed rental) minus the costs (here mortgage costs and depreciation) relative to the return on an alternative risk-free asset.

$$ER(t) = \frac{\{[\pi + \dot{g}^e/g(t)] + R(t)/g(t) - lvr(t)i_m(t)(1-\theta) - \delta\}}{(1 - lvr(t))} - (1-\theta)i_f(t) \quad [13]$$

where i_m is mortgage interest rate, i_f is risk-free interest rate, and lvr is mortgage loan-to-house value ratio.

The term in {.} represents the return to housing net of borrowing costs. The gross return is equal to the capital gain, [.], plus the imputed rental expressed as a percentage of the asset price, $R(t)/g(t)$. The costs incorporate depreciation, (δ), and mortgage costs net of tax, $i_m(t)(1-\theta)$. Since most households borrow less than 100% of the house value, mortgage costs are multiplied by the loan-to-value ratio. For the outright owner, $lvr = 0$ and the mortgage interest rate disappears from the expression. This net return is compared with the post-tax return on alternative investments, $(1-\theta)i_f$. The excess return on housing was positive in the United Kingdom for most of the period from the 1950s until the early 1990s, although the calculations make no allowance for credit restrictions. Excess returns can be used as a basis of market efficiency tests, since excess returns should not be autocorrelated in an efficient market. But surveys confirm that, over a wide range of US studies (Case and Shiller, 1989), covering different spatial areas, both house price inflation and excess returns are highly autocorrelated and investors can make persistent excess returns. One view is that autocorrelation arises from the existence of transactions costs, both financial and in terms of search costs, which limit the spatial range of the search. Therefore, although excess returns exist, exploitable trading rules are not necessarily available.

As noted above, eqn [12] is rarely estimated directly, due to data measurement problems and adjustment lags. Particularly in the European literature, the former problem is typically overcome by the substitution of the expected determinants of $R(t)$, for example, income, demographic variables, and the housing stock. However, this has two disadvantages; first, this is no longer a direct test of market efficiency, but a joint test with the factors that determine rents. Second, the substitution implies that it is difficult to distinguish empirically between the life-cycle and reduced form models, since both contain similar regressor sets. Again in the European literature, lags are frequently captured through error correction specifications. This is discussed further in the next section, which deals with econometric issues.

Nevertheless, either the reduced form or life-cycle models provide the basis of nearly all empirical house price models. Given the agreement over the basic theory, it is perhaps surprising that a wide variety of results is found in the empirical literature – even on the most basic parameters. As shown in sections 'Econometric Issues and Data Properties' and 'Empirical Implementation', this occurs primarily from the choice of variables reflecting demand and supply and from differences in econometric technique.

Econometric Issues and Data Properties

In the United Kingdom, time-series models of house prices were used as one of the early applications for testing new ideas on dynamic specification. Prior to this line of research, dynamics or lagged adjustment tended to be treated in a rudimentary manner, despite the fact that lags arising from transactions and search costs are a fundamental feature of the market. The use of autoregressive error processes to 'correct' for autocorrelation was frequently employed, despite the fact that these represent a restricted form of lag structure, which, in practice, is rarely validated by the data. Nevertheless, even in modern quantitative housing research, it is not uncommon to find the application of these error models. However, more general models of dynamic specification led to the widespread adoption of autoregressive distributed lag models and to the development of error correction models and to cointegration. A key element of these methods is that greater attention is paid to the time-series properties of the data. At least in the European house price literature, error correction models and cointegration have dominated research. In the United States, approaches are more diverse, although the error correction approach is frequently used (Malpezzi, 1999).

In order to demonstrate key issues, **Figure 1** plots house prices for the United States and United Kingdom as examples, although many other advanced economies excepting Germany and Japan share broadly similar time-series properties. The first frame graphs real house prices in levels, the second gives the ratio of house prices to income, and the third shows real price growth. The period covers 1975Q1–2007Q4. The first and second frames are indexed to 2001 = 100. A number of features stand out. First, from the third frame, prices have been consistently more volatile in the United Kingdom, although the US average is misleading, since the coastal regions exhibit greater volatility than the country average. Second, particularly in the United Kingdom, neither real house prices nor the price-to-income ratio are stationary, that is, untrended. Third,

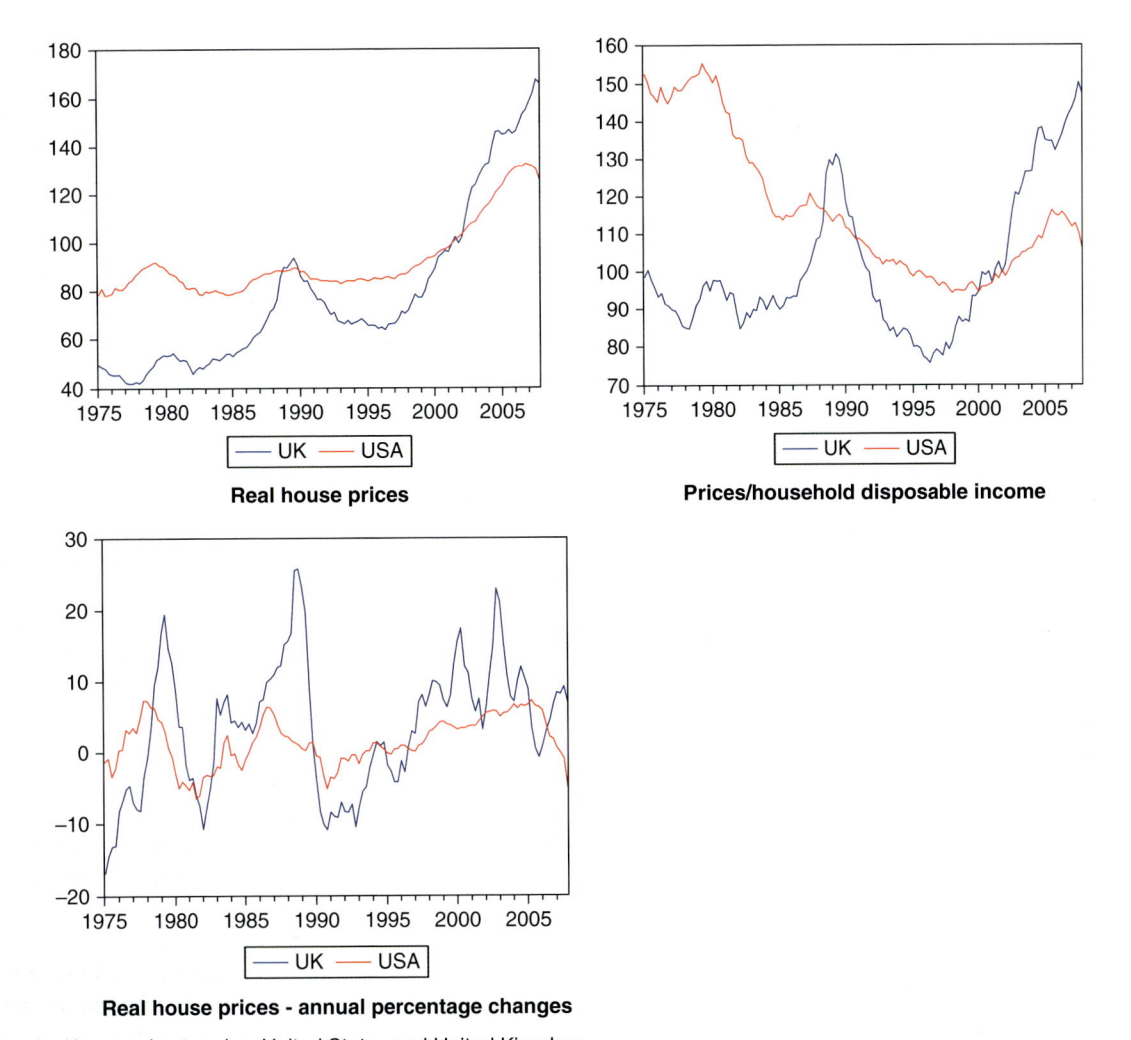

Figure 1 House price trends – United States and United Kingdom.

the differenced annual real price changes are closer to stationarity.

The annual growth in real prices can be used as the basis of market efficiency tests. The test involves whether real house price inflation exhibits short-run positive autocorrelation, but longer-term mean reversion and is defined by eqn [14]:

$$\Delta(g_t) = \phi_0 + \sum_{j=1}^{n} \phi_j \Delta g_{t-j} + \varepsilon_{4t} \qquad [14]$$

where g_t is real house prices at time (t), ε_t is error term, Δ is first difference operator, and lower case denotes logarithms.

The parameters of interest are (ϕ_j), but the variables are tested entirely in terms of differences. If housing markets are fully efficient, then no autocorrelation in price inflation is expected, (ϕ_j) = 0, for all (j) so that house prices follow a random walk. In most studies, strong positive autocorrelation is found at the first (annual) lag, with some evidence of mean reversion, that is, negative coefficients, at longer lags. Overall, the similarity of autocorrelation structures, across countries, is striking, even though the trends in price levels may be very different (the autocorrelation structures for the United Kingdom and United States, using the data in **Figure 1**, are also very similar).

However, similar autocorrelation structures do not imply a consensus about the factors that cause changes in house prices – empirical models used in the United States differ considerably from those used in the United Kingdom. Furthermore, since the variables are in differences, the long-run level of house prices is undetermined. The specification eliminates any form of error correction or cointegration. In Abraham and Hendershott (1996), a version of eqn [14] is nested within a broader framework, summarised in eqn [15]. In the equation, φ_5 is the autoregressive parameter and is interpreted as a 'bubble-builder', whereas φ_6 is the 'bubble-burster' and implies that prices fall if they are above equilibrium. Notice that the included variables are similar to those in eqn [4], although there are possible omissions.

$$\Delta(g)_t = \varphi_1 + \varphi_2\Delta(cc)_t + \varphi_3\Delta(ry)_t + \varphi_4\Delta(i)_t + \varphi_5\Delta(g)_{t-1} + \varphi_6[g^*-g]_{t-1} + \varepsilon_{5t}$$
[15]

where g^* is equilibrium house prices.

Equation [15] is similar to an error correction model (ECM), which, as noted above, has dominated the European house price literature. In general, the ECM can be written as eqn [16], where θ_3 is the error correction coefficient determining the speed of adjustment to the long-run equilibrium. The variables in the X vector represent eqn [4] with the addition of house price expected capital gains, $(p\dot{h}^e)$, which are part of the user cost in eqn [12]. The equation can be generalised to higher order lags in the dynamics:

$$\Delta(g)_t = \theta_1\Delta(g)_{t-1} + \theta_2\Delta(x) + \theta_3[(g)-\theta_4(x)]_{t-1} + \varepsilon_6 \quad [16]$$

where $X' = [RY, POP, H, M, i, p\dot{h}^e, CC]$.

In addition to allowing for autocorrelation through θ_1, [.] captures any market deviation from fundamentals. The term also captures possible cointegration between prices and the regressor set and determines the long-run elasticities. Note that if the dependent variable is stationary in differences, then cointegration is required if the adjustment parameter is to be significantly different from zero. However, the set of regressors in X is broad; in particular, house prices are unlikely to be cointegrated with income alone. **Figure 1** showed that the price-to-income ratio in the United Kingdom is trended. This is important since it implies that income is not the only fundamental determinant of house prices. Therefore, policy rules based on simple price-to-income ratios are likely to be seriously misleading. This issue is considered further below.

Equation [16] is a single equation and, indeed, a considerable number of studies in the literature are estimated in this way. But since eqns [1]–[4] represent a system, the question arises under what conditions can the price equation be estimated independently without bias to the coefficients If eqns [1] and [2] are both seen as flow equations, then joint estimation would appear appropriate. But this is less evident in a stock-adjustment model, where eqn [1] represents the demand for the stock and eqn [2] is the new flow supply. Since new supply has little effect on the existing stock, prices can be estimated conditional on the stock. The key features of the theory underlying the stock-adjustment model are set out in Poterba (1984). In eqn [17], the return on the housing stock is made up of the rental, $R(.)$, plus any capital gain and is equal to the return on alternative assets, represented by (a_1g). In terms of eqn [12], $a_1 = (1-\theta)i - \pi + \delta + \lambda/\mu_c$. The rental is determined by conditions in the market for housing services and, hence, is expected to be related to the size of the housing stock, population, and income. Therefore, eqn [17] is directly related to the derivation of the price equations above.

Equation [18] represents flow housing supply and is positively related to the real house price (as a proxy for profitability) and negatively to the size of the existing stock through depreciation.

$$\dot{g} = a_1 g - a_2 R(H, POP, RY) \quad [17]$$
$$\dot{H} = b_1 g - \delta H \quad [18]$$

In empirical work, the validity of estimating prices as a single equation can be tested through weak exogeneity restrictions in a vector error correction model (VECM), which is a generalisation of the single equation ECM.

Empirical Implementation

Increases and falls in house prices have become a national obsession in many parts of the world. This is scarcely surprising given (1) the high proportions of wealth held in housing and (2) the possible effects of housing on national economies. Until recently, most studies were either carried out in North America or the United Kingdom, with additional contributions from Scandinavia, the Netherlands, Ireland, Spain, and the Pacific Rim, for example. However, because of factor (2), increasingly, international comparisons have been undertaken of the factors affecting prices by international agencies such as the OECD. But such studies are difficult, because of the problems of compiling internationally comparable data and because of the very different institutional frameworks in which they operate, notably in terms of mortgage markets.

The aim of all empirical, time-series studies of house prices is to explain (and possibly forecast) the cycles and/or trends, such as those shown in **Figure 1**. Of course, models specified in differences cannot explain the latter. Within this overall aim, the emphasis of studies differs. Perhaps, the most common themes are as follows:

(1) The relative importance of fundamentals versus bubbles.
(2) The effectiveness of monetary policy (both through interest rates and credit conditions).
(3) Demographic change.
(4) The effect of zoning or land-use regulations.
(5) The impact of taxation.

Equations [4] or [16] set out a typical selection of variables that have been included in price studies, but **Table 1** gives a more generic classification. Although not distinct, the table divides variables into cyclical and trend influences. For example, income and wealth fluctuate over the economic cycle, but also exhibit a long-run upward trend in line with productivity gains. However, in the second column, population, headship rates, and the housing stock (although not new supply) vary only to a

Table 1 Factors affecting real house prices

Cycle	Trend
Income	Population size and structure
Interest rates (real and nominal)	Headship rates
	Migration
Credit availability	Housing stock and planning regulations
Wealth	
Expected capital gains	Housing taxation
Construction costs	
Employment/ unemployment	

limited extent over the cycle. Migration and the tax structure probably have both trend and cyclical elements.

As suggested in section 'The Theory of House Price Determination', although there is agreement in the literature on the theoretical structure of price models, there is considerable variation in the precise regressor set. Few include all the variables in **Table 1**. Local house price studies, in particular, are limited by the unavailability of many of the relevant factors at a fine spatial scale.

Omission of relevant variables is likely to lead to biases and it is noticeable that there are greater differences in results between countries than within countries. Although this could reflect true structural differences, it is likely that part of the difference is due to omitted variables. Standardising on a common model structure, differences between the United States and United Kingdom are smaller than might be expected from an initial reading of the literature (see Meen, 2002). In particular, UK results generally find that the long-run elasticity of house prices with respect to income (which is equal to the income elasticity of demand divided by the price elasticity of demand) is greater than 1, but US results find much lower values. However, the difference depends on whether the equations are conditioned on the housing stock. Of course, some US studies, although not all, do include the housing stock. In the UK case, since the price elasticity of housing supply is very low, income increases have almost permanent effects on prices.

High-income elasticities are important in the debate over the relative roles of fundamentals and bubbles in explaining the post-1996 international house price boom, since income is considered in many studies as the main fundamental. Although this debate is considered in more detail in the next section, if the income elasticity is low, it seems unlikely that much of the boom could be attributed to fundamentals and any downward biases in the elasticity will incorrectly attribute the boom to a bubble. Similarly, assuming that only real interest rates and not nominal rates affect prices will lead to an overestimate of any bubble. Therefore, conclusions about bubbles are difficult to draw, since they are heavily dependent on the specification of the underlying model.

Since prices provide a key transmission mechanism between housing and the economy, the response of house prices to interest rates and credit availability is important for policy. However, in terms of modelling, two issues arise: (1) the relative importance of nominal and real rates and (2) the structural mortgage market change and the impact of credit rationing. Although the discount rate in eqn [11] is defined in terms of real rates, eqn [12] argues that nominal rates are equally important because of front-end loading. Early UK research, including credit rationing variables, added either the outstanding mortgage stock or the supply of new mortgages; since credit was rationed and exogenous to the household, this was a valid procedure until the liberalisation of mortgage markets in the early 1980s. In terms of eqn [12], at this point the shadow price becomes no longer binding, mortgages are determined by demand and have no valid role in a price equation. This form of market switch is difficult to incorporate, since the shadow price is not directly observable. However, the most important feature of the ending of rationing is that prices are expected to become more sensitive to market interest rate changes. US price studies have, typically, not included credit availability variables, since the country has not faced the same form of institutional restrictions as other countries. However, deposits or down payments are still required even in an unrationed system, because of potential moral hazard.

Few would dispute that population and household formation are key determinants of housing demand and, therefore, prices. Declining average household size has meant that the total number of households is continuing to expand, despite slower rates of population growth as the baby-boom generation ages. In England, household projections are the basis of national, regional, and local housing construction plans. The US study by Mankiw and Weil (1989) of the effects of demographics on price trends proved particularly controversial, because of its prediction of a 47% real house price fall by 2007, arising from population age trends. But important technical criticisms of the study were made at the time and, of course, the fall did not occur.

Zoning and land-use regulations can affect prices indirectly through housing supply since they reduce the price elasticity of supply; however, some US studies include measures of regulatory stringency directly as a determinant of the price. Uniformly, regulation is found to raise prices. Furthermore, in unregulated cities, house prices are close to construction costs, but, in heavily controlled areas, prices are well above costs. Also, price bubbles are more prevalent where the price elasticity of supply is low. These areas are particularly concentrated on the US East and West coasts where controls are strongest.

The effects on prices of taxation and subsidies to owner-occupation have long been a field for research. An important early branch examined the interaction of high rates of inflation during the 1970s with a tax system that conferred benefits to owner-occupation that other forms of investment did not enjoy. The interaction implies that real house prices and the housing capital stock are nonneutral with respect to the rate of inflation. Studies were both partial in nature and more general, concentrating on either rental versus owner-occupancy decisions or on the differential return to owner-occupation as opposed to nonresidential investment where tax provisions differ. Since the United Kingdom had similar rates of inflation and tax provisions at that time, the conclusions of the US literature carried over to the United Kingdom. The literature, however, became less topical with the reduction in general inflation, the cut back in owner-occupation subsidies and, indeed, the fall in US house price inflation in the 1980s. More recently, however, the capitalisation of tax subsidies into house prices has reemerged as an issue and support for the capitalisation hypothesis appears to hold.

A further US area of research concentrates on impact fees – local charges imposed on developers to finance the provision of infrastructure. Importantly, studies have to take into account not only the direct effect of the fee as a form of excise duty, but also the total effects, which allow for the improvement in public capital services financed by the fees and the capitalisation of the services into house prices.

In the United Kingdom, the distortionary impacts on prices of the property taxation system, notably council tax, have received particular attention because of its regressive nature and the implications for relative house prices around the country.

Bubbles and Fundamentals

The causes of the international post-1996 price boom have received considerable attention. The central issue is whether the boom is primarily due to fundamentals or represents a bubble. Media commentators have tended to assume the latter, but this is based on limited analysis, hampered by the difficulty of agreeing on the appropriate definition.

In contrast to the media, academic research is more cautious in claiming the existence of bubbles. Simply because strong price growth and volatility are observed, this provides no evidence of bubbles. At the most basic level, the demand and supply model in eqns [1]–[4] generates strong price growth in response to demand shocks, if the price elasticity of supply is low in the short run. The popular view that prices are out-of-line with fundamentals rests on three observations. First, the ratio of house prices to incomes is above the long-run trend. Second, the ratio of prices to rents is above trend. Third, conventional house price models underestimate the strength of the boom. All of these can be challenged.

The importance of the price-to-income ratio rests on the view that income represents a measure of fundamentals. But, although income is almost universally found to be an important determinant of house prices – as noted above, UK results find an elasticity well in excess of unity – it is, by no means, the only factor influencing prices, which can be construed as fundamental. From **Table 1**, variations in wealth, demographics, housing supply, and interest rates can also be considered as fundamental and shift the relationship between prices and income. Alternatively, in the United Kingdom, prices and income alone are not cointegrated, but the wider set of variables does form a cointegrating vector. Similarly, US studies find contradictory evidence on cointegration between prices and income, but this does not rule out cointegration with a broader set of variables.

Equation [11] is also a measure of fundamental value – prices are the discounted stream of rents – but the price-to-rent ratio is the inverse of the discount rate. However, unless the discount rate is constant, there is no reason why the price-to-rent ratio should be time invariant. Since the discount rate has fallen sharply in recent years internationally, it is unsurprising that the price-to-rent ratio has risen. Furthermore, it is equally unsurprising that prices should fall from 2007, because the credit crunch effectively raises the discount rate through (λ).

As argued in the last section, misspecified models tend to ascribe more of the boom to bubbles than to fundamentals. Misspecified models also, typically, exhibit coefficient variability in recursive tests. Therefore, structural or reduced form models that can explain the post-1996 periods provide strong evidence in favour of fundamentals. In fact, if the main countries that have experienced rapid rates of house price inflation are considered, it is not unambiguously clear from the literature that models do underestimate house price inflation. Overvaluation appears to be limited to a small number of countries. But findings depend strongly on the form of the model employed. Models that support fundamentals place particular emphasis on the low levels of nominal interest rates in a low inflation world. Furthermore, the simple fact that house prices have fallen since 2007 does not provide evidence of the bursting of a bubble. From the user cost definition, the drying up of mortgage finance would be predicted to cause a fall in prices, even in an equation for fundamental value.

At least in the United Kingdom, recursive tests (see Meen, 2008) suggest a considerable degree of coefficient stability between 1997 and 2005 consistent with a fundamentals interpretation. Subsequent unpublished work extending the data sample to 2007 suggests a limited degree of market overvaluation, but not on the same scale as the estimates of 20–30% produced by some commentators. By contrast, in the United States (see Case and Shiller, 2003), price models do not appear to fully explain the boom and, furthermore, surveys find evidence of an expectations-fuelled boom.

Spatial Variation

It is commonplace to suggest that countries do not consist of a single housing market, since spatial fixity means that dwellings (except mobile homes) cannot easily be transported around the country in response to disequilibrium in demand and supply. Instead, housing is usually considered as a set of interrelated submarkets, which vary by location and product type. A large literature, which is not the subject of this article, is concerned with the appropriate definition of submarkets.

But even aggregate house price studies benefit from the availability of spatially disaggregated data. At one level, the spatial dimension implies that panel data sets can be constructed across both time and space, increasing the number of available observations. However, it needs to be borne in mind that spatial data sets are usually structured according to administrative boundaries – for example, states or Metropolitan Statistical Areas in the United States or regions in the United Kingdom – which rarely correspond to housing market areas. In estimation, inappropriate aggregation may lead to aggregation biases and requires the use of spatial econometric techniques to capture spatial lags and spatial error correlation.

However, spatially disaggregated data also allow the richer testing of economic hypotheses. Different areas of any country may respond in different ways to external shocks. For example, spatial data allow the testing of the importance of zoning regulations, because the strength of controls varies across the US states. As noted earlier, speculative bubbles are more likely to occur in the coastal regions of the United States, because of stronger zoning regulation and greater price volatility are expected if the price elasticity of supply is weak. Spatially disaggregated data can be used to examine variations in supply elasticities.

A further strand of research examines spatial differences in response to national shocks, notably changes in monetary policy. In the spatial econometrics literature, this is an example of spatial coefficient heterogeneity. Random coefficient variation is, perhaps, to be expected, but the more important question is whether coefficients exhibit distinct spatially related patterns. For example, variations in levels of debt gearing across cities, states, or regions may imply that locations differ in their responsiveness to national interest rate changes.

Spatial coefficient heterogeneity is one of the central concerns of the spatial econometrics literature, but a second is the nature of spatial lags, that is, the interconnectedness of movements in prices. It is unsurprising to find common movements and, because of search costs, it might be expected that the prices of near neighbours would change almost contemporaneously, whereas locations that are far apart would exhibit time lags. There is a large literature that attempts to capture these relationships.

Expanding on the efficiency literature discussed above, arguably, arbitrage should take place over space to eliminate differences in returns. If markets are spatially efficient, then the returns in one spatial market should not be useable to predict the returns in another. The US literature suggests that this is not the case and finds evidence that house price changes in a given submarket are related to changes in contiguous markets. This might be considered as evidence of a 'positive feedback effect', whereby recent strength in one local submarket feeds into other submarkets, as new information becomes available.

Regional price interactions have been a central concern of the UK house price literature. The most commonly observed feature of regional house prices in England is the so-called ripple effect and is typified by an initial increase in house prices in the South of the country during the early stages of a cyclical upswing, with the other regions catching up at a later stage. Consequently, although short-term price dynamics differ between the North and South, there appear to be processes operating that ensure long-run relativities are restored. In fact, whether regional prices do rise in line with each other is still considered controversial. A second set of patterns is typified by the fact that prices in the four southern regions of England have risen and fallen at a similar rate contemporaneously, that is, there is little evidence of the lag implicit in the ripple effect between the southern and northern regions.

The literature has adopted two broad approaches to the modelling of regional price dynamics. The first is concerned with statistical tests of the nature of regional spatial interactions between house prices. Much of this literature attempts to establish the nature of long-run, cointegrating relationships between the regions and the extent to which London is a leading indicator for the remaining regions. Recent advances in this direction have been the introduction of tests for asymmetric adjustment between periods of upswing and downswing. Tests of the ripple effect or, more generally, spatially lagged relationships have spread to other European countries. Recent studies have been conducted for Ireland, where there is evidence of spatial diffusion originating in Dublin with further studies for Helsinki and Madrid. In summary, the most recent international evidence suggests that London, as a capital, is not alone as being a lead region.

However, this strand of the literature has less to say about the economic processes that generate the similarities and differences in regional house price movements. The second strand is concerned with the drivers of change. There is a danger that the ripple is treated as a mechanical process that always occurs over successive cycles. But, the price relationship between London/South East and the remaining regions has not been constant in the United Kingdom, but has changed over time. Therefore, it is important to understand the nature of the housing market changes. A number of potential transmission mechanisms have been put forward. First, the roles of information diffusion, search costs and arbitrage are discussed above. Second, migration and commuting flows are likely to be an important part of the story. Third, the observed positive correlation between house sales and prices may be related to credit conditions. If, on moving between regions, existing owners have to make a down payment, then sales and prices depend on the value of the house in the previous location. Fourth, the observed pattern can, in fact, occur even if there are no spatial links between housing markets, if the determinants follow similar patterns. If the elasticity of house prices with respect to earnings is high, changing spatial earnings patterns have an even larger effect on the spatial house price distribution. In the United Kingdom, cyclical changes in the economy have often begun in the South with other regions catching up later. Similarly, the economic slump of the early 1990s was primarily concentrated in the South. However, there is still little direct evidence that regional earnings trends are consistent with those in house prices. A final possibility is that the regions may have differential responses to national shocks. As noted above, the most obvious example is the responsiveness to interest rate changes. These can give the impression of spatial lags even if adjustment is really intraregional.

Conclusions

Over the last 30 years, internationally, there have been very large numbers of empirical time-series house price studies and the expansion shows no signs of slackening. Economists are not immune from national obsessions with house prices and the availability of long house price data series in some countries has been a spur to empirical work. However, this article discusses neither the methods used to construct price indices nor the quality of the data.

Furthermore, the article does not attempt to catalogue the full range of studies, but instead concentrates on the central themes of the literature and the techniques employed. These themes cover (1) market efficiency, (2) price volatility and the role of bubbles and fundamentals, (3) monetary policy and credit rationing, (4) demographics, (5) fiscal policy, (6) zoning and land-use regulations, and (7) spatial variation.

There is considerable agreement on the appropriate theoretical framework, based on extensions to the standard life-cycle consumption model. But despite this, there is wide variation between empirical results found for the United Kingdom and United States – the countries which account for the majority of price studies. The differences arise primarily from technique and choice of variables used to explain prices.

See also: Forecasting in Housing Research; House Price Expectations; House Price Indexes; Price Dynamics in Housing Markets; Simulation Models for Housing Analysis; Supply Elasticity of Housing.

References

Abraham JM and Hendershott PH (1996) Bubbles in metropolitan housing markets. *Journal of Housing Research* 7: 191–207.
Case KE and Shiller RJ (1989) The efficiency of the market for single family homes. *American Economic Review* 79: 125–137.
Case KE and Shiller RJ (2003) Is there a bubble in the housing market? *Brooking Papers on Economic Activity* 2: 229–362.
Malpezzi S (1999) A simple error correction model of house prices. *Journal of Housing Economics* 8: 27–62.
Mankiw NG and Weil DN (1989) Baby boom, baby bust and the housing market. *Regional Science and Urban Economics* 19: 235–258.
Meen GP (2002) The time-series properties of house prices: A transatlantic divide? *Journal of Housing Economics* 11: 1–23.
Meen GP (2008) Ten new propositions in UK housing macroeconomics: An overview of the first years of the century. *Urban Studies* 45: 2759–2781.
Muellbauer J and Murphy A (1997) Booms and busts in the UK housing market. *Economic Journal* 107: 1701–1727.
Poterba JM (1984) Tax subsidies to owner-occupied housing: An asset market approach. *Quarterly Journal of Economics* 99: 729–752.

Further Reading

DiPasquale D and Wheaton W (1994) Housing market dynamics and the future of house prices. *Journal of Urban Economics* 35: 1–27.
Englund P and Ioannides Y (1997) House price dynamics: An international empirical perspective. *Journal of Housing Economics* 6: 119–136.
Hendry DF (1984) Econometric modelling of house prices in the United Kingdom. In: Hendry DF and Wallis KF (eds.) *Econometrics and Quantitative Economics*. Oxford, UK: Basil Blackwell.
Himmelberg C, Mayer C, and Sinai T (2005) Assessing high house prices: Bubbles, fundamentals and misperceptions. *Journal of Economic Perspectives* 19: 67–92.
Meen GP (2001) *Modelling Spatial Housing Markets: Theory, Analysis and Policy*. Boston, MA: Kluwer Academic Publishers.

Price Dynamics in Housing Markets

M Cho, The KDI School of Public Policy and Management, Seoul, South Korea
K-H Kim, Sogang University, Seoul, The Republic of Korea, and Singapore Management University, Singapore

© 2012 Elsevier Ltd. All rights reserved.

Introduction

Housing is an asset whose fair market value is not transparent. That is, unlike the stock of a company whose shares are traded in an organised exchange, price discovery of a house is in general, based on infrequent transactions (usually with a 4–5-year time interval), asymmetric information between the buyer and the seller, and a lengthy search and bargaining, rather than a competitive bidding, process. In consequence, its value conclusion is prone to various measurement errors, which further impacts policy and business applications of value prediction.

Housing price dynamics is a key element of housing market analysis. Housing price volatility, defined as the variance of the unpredictable component of house price appreciation (Miller and Peng, 2006), has important implications for the wider economy through its impact on private consumption and new residential construction, as well as affecting mortgage markets and capital markets through securitisation of mortgages.

This article examines several aspects of housing price dynamics, focusing on both explained and unexplained price changes along with their policy implications. This article is a complement to the article Price Determination in Housing Markets, which focuses mostly on the explained component of housing prices. Our contribution pays more attention to volatility, or the unexplained part of housing price. It also expands on an earlier survey paper on the subject by Cho (1996) which discusses housing price indexes and testing for housing bubbles and the efficient market hypothesis (EMH). To that end, we first provide a conceptual framework by discussing the key determinants of housing price variability with a simple demand–supply model. We then present alternative models of housing price processes that can be used in performing historical mark-to-market analysis, as well as in forming forward-looking home price distributions. Next, we present data and modelling issues related to some applications of dynamic home price models, such as testing for speculative bubbles, automated (or model-based) property appraisal, and assessment of mortgage credit risk. The article ends with concluding remarks on future research agenda.

Conceptual Underpinning

A Simple Model of Determinants of Housing Price Variability

A simple demand–supply diagram can be used to illustrate how the price elasticity of demand or supply influences the magnitude of the price change following a demand shock. First, consider an outward shift of the demand curve against two supply curves with different slopes. The consequent increase in housing price will be the larger for the less elastic supply curve (Malpezzi and Wachter, 2005). The price elasticity of housing supply is conditioned by the availability of developable land as well as land-use and building regulations. Cities with more stringent regulations tend to have less elastic housing supply and thus larger volatility of housing price, other things being equal. Glaeser et al. (2008) found that this was the case during both the 1980s boom and the post 1996 boom, but that there were a large number of highly elastic cities that had temporary price explosions in the years since 1996.

Next, take two demand curves with different slopes against a given supply. If the demand curve shifts to the right horizontally by the same amount, housing price will rise more when the demand curve is less elastic (van den Noord, 2005). Tax breaks to owner-occupied housing can make housing demand less sensitive to price changes, making housing price more volatile, other things being equal. Using a very small sample of European countries, van den Noord (2005) has found that there is a positive correlation between the tax wedge (the difference between the before-tax and after-tax real interest rate on mortgage loans) and the variability of real housing price (the root mean square deviation of real housing price from trend).

Historical Mark-to-Market

Suppose that one attempts to predict the current price of a particular house, $P_{i,t}$, based on two factors – its prior sale value k periods ago, $P_{i,t-k}$, and the estimated area-wide average housing price change between $t-k$ and t, $\hat{h}_{t,t-k}$ (a log growth rate of area-wide average housing price between two time periods, $h_{t,t-k} = Log(P_t/P_{t-k})$). The prediction is a straightforward mark-to-market application:

$$P_{i,t} = P_{i,t-k} \cdot \hat{b}_{t,t-k} \qquad [1]$$

In this exercise, the prediction is made based on at least one stochastic variable $\hat{b}_{t,t-k}$ with its own error process (assuming that the prior transaction price is arms-length and unbiased estimate of true value, and hence, error-free). The intuition behind this is that, whatever geography we choose to compute b over, there is a chance that the price process of a particular house (property i in this case) deviates from the area-wide average price change, due mainly to a high degree of heterogeneity in neighbourhood and structural attributes of individual houses therein. This type of error is referred to as cross-sectional dispersion.

The area-wide price change b can be measured using the estimated indices covering the time period in question:

$$\hat{b}_{t,t-k} = \hat{I}_{t,t-k} + e_{t,t-k} \qquad [2]$$

There are competing methods for estimating I, such as hedonic model, repeat sales model (RSM), neural network or other nonparametric model, and even tax assessment model. Whatever the underlying model is, ideal conditions for the best unbiased value prediction should ensure an independently identically distributed residual (e) with zero mean and constant minimum error variance (σ_e^2), that is, $e \sim iid(0, \sigma_e^2)$.

In the United States, RSM is established as the best practice for measuring area-wide dynamic housing price changes, due mainly to the parsimonious data requirement. All that is needed to fit the model is a sample of properties transacted multiple times along with their transaction prices in different time periods. Cho's (1996) survey of early studies on RSM discusses different RSMs, along with potential biases in obtained parameters, important ones being renovation bias, trading frequency bias, sample selection bias, and aggregation bias. Estimating RSM produces the cross-sectional dispersion, e in eqn [2], with the following specification:

$$\hat{e}_{t,t-k}^2 = \hat{a} \cdot (t-k) + \hat{b} \cdot (t-k)^2 \qquad [3]$$

where a and b are parameters to be estimated by using residuals from the first stage of the RSM estimation. It is assumed that $a \geq 0$ and $b \leq 0$. The implication is that the dispersion (e in eqn [2]) increases with time interval between two sales, $t-k$ in our case, but at a decreasing rate. Using the fitted residual from eqn [3], one can construct a confidence interval around the predicted mean value from eqn [1]. For example, a 95% confidence band under a normality assumption is shown as, $P_{i,t-k} \cdot \hat{I}_{t-k} \pm 1.96 \cdot \hat{e}_{t-k}$. Case and Shiller (1989) assumed a linear error process, with no quadratic term in eqn [3]. Ahraham and Schaumann (1991) extended the specification by adding the quadratic terms, and Goetzmann (1992) raised the issue of transformation bias and suggested an adjustment factor.

In the United States, cross-sectional dispersion is public information, as the Federal Housing Finance Board updates and publishes the parameters a and b for different states on a quarterly basis. Both I (mean growth rates) and e (cross-sectional dispersions) tend to vary widely across geographical areas.

Forward-Looking Housing Price Distribution

Forward-looking housing price prediction is a critical input to various policy and business applications. In the context of the individual property valuation (as in eqn [1]), predicting housing price l-periods ahead from today (time t) can be expressed as:

$$P_{i,t+l} = P_{i,t-k} \cdot (\hat{I}_{t-k} + \hat{I}_{t+l}) + \hat{e}_{t-k} + \hat{\xi}_{t+l} \qquad [4]$$

where $\hat{I}_{t+l}$ and $\hat{\xi}_{t+l}$ represent predicted future index growth rate (between t and $t+l$) and its forecasting error, respectively. For now, assume $\xi \sim iid(0, \sigma_\xi^2)$.

Obtaining the two forward-looking variables in eqn [4] requires further assumptions on housing price dynamics. At the theoretical level, as in the case of any financial asset, the optimal housing price at a particular point in time (under no arbitrage condition) can be expressed as a sum of two components: the market fundamental value, or the discounted present value of forward-looking cash flows generated from the asset (e.g., rent per period in the case of housing) and a deviation from the fundamental value, often termed as a bubble representing an economic agent's expectation that he/she will sell the asset with capital gain in a future time period (i.e., the component in home price reflecting a pure demand for future capital gain):

$$P_t = \sum_{\mathcal{J}=1}^{\infty} \left(\prod_{j=1}^{\mathcal{J}} \frac{E_t[R_{t+j}]}{(1+E_t[r_{t+j}])} \right) + B_t = P_t^* + B_t \qquad [5]$$

Assuming a time-varying risk-free short rate, r_t, and permanent holding, the optimal value of residential property, P_t, under this definition is specified as a discounted present value of forward-looking rents, R_{t+j}, and the bubble term, B_t.

In empirically fitting a market level housing price process, there are two broad approaches one can think of. First, one can assume a random walk process of location-wide housing price changes (with a drift, or an intercept, term):

$$P_t = \alpha + \beta \cdot P_{t-1} + \xi_t \qquad [6]$$

The null hypothesis to test is $H_0: \beta - 1 = 0$, under which $P_t - P_{t-1} = \alpha + \xi_t$. In this approach, all that is needed in forming future housing price distribution is 'appropriate' constant mean growth rate (α) and standard deviation (σ_ξ)

computed from historical data. Due to its simplicity, this approach has a potential appeal in various industrial applications. For example, one can apply a stochastic differential equation (or a diffusion model) in projecting future housing price changes with the historical long-term mean and volatility.

However, starting from Case and Shiller (1989), a series of studies rejected the random walk hypothesis based on home price indices estimated from RSM (Cho, 1996). These studies generally reject the weak-form efficiency in the housing markets in the United States, that is, households systematically failed to incorporate the information on past price appreciation into their expectations on current price changes. Similar tests were conducted using data from other countries as well. For example, Larsen and Weum (2008) tested for and rejected a weak-form efficiency using the 1991–2002 quarterly data on transactions of co-ops in Oslo, Norway.

Second, as a more reasonable and conceptually sound approach, a serially correlated housing price model can be used. There are a wide array of models to choose from under this approach, including a vector autoregressive (VAR) model (e.g., Sutton, 2002), and an error correction model (ECM) (e.g., Capozza et al. 2004; Malpezzi, 1999; Meen and Andrew, 1998). It is fair to say that there is no universally best housing price model, and that the selection tends to be sample-, location-, and time-specific.

Nonetheless, ECM is emerging as a reasonable model framework in analysing housing price dynamics. Following Capozza et al., a typical ECM is specified as:

$$\Delta P_t = \alpha \cdot \Delta P_{t-1} + \beta \cdot [P_{t-1} - P^*_{t-1}] + \gamma \Delta P^*_t + \xi_t \quad [7]$$

where P^* is the long-run equilibrium price that reflects a set of market fundamentals (at a particular time period), and α, β, and γ are parameters to be estimated. Usually, P^* comes from another time series model, for example, the value fitted from a linear equation such as:

$$P_t = \sum_{k=1}^{l} \delta^k X_t^k + \nu_t \quad [8]$$

The vector of market fundamentals (X) typically includes the user cost of capital for owning, household income (area-wide trend), construction cost, and measures of various natural and man-made constraints on land and housing supply.

In this setting, any deviation between equilibrium and realised price levels (the second, right-hand side variable in eqn [7]) will be corrected over time so that the actual price will revert to its long-term equilibrium level as long as $\beta < 0$. The autocorrelation parameter, α, shows the level of price rigidity (i.e., positive growth being followed by another positive growth for a more prolonged time period, and vice versa), while the third right-hand side term in eqn [7] represents a contemporaneous change in the fundamental price levels. Under an efficient market hypothesis, there should be no serial correlation ($\alpha = 0$) nor any contemporaneous adjustment of fundamental values that explain changes in actual price ($\gamma = 0$) because the fundamental values already reflect all relevant information to the price dynamics.

The ECM equation can be used to empirically calibrate the correction process for non-zero B_t, the smaller the mean reversion parameter in absolute term (and $\beta < 0$), the longer it takes B_t to dissipate. Furthermore, Capozza et al. suggest conditions $\alpha < 1$ and $(1-\alpha)^2 < 4\beta$ for the correction process to be a convergent cycle (as opposed to an explosive noncyclical one) (see Capozza et al. (2004) for the derivation of the above conditions). Empirical evidences on α and β based on metropolitan-level housing price data from the United States indicate that only a small number of cities in the coastal regions (e.g., Los Angeles, San Jose, San Francisco, Boston, and Washington DC) exhibit cyclical and convergent housing price dynamics and, hence, satisfying the above conditions, while most other MSAs show no pronounced cyclical pattern. At a more micro level, Hwang and Quigley (2009) have investigated the issue of spatial diffusion in home price process. Using a property-level data set, they not only reject a random walk in home price movement but also find supporting evidence of mean reversion and diffusion of innovations over space.

An example of study of Capozza et al. (2004) type using non-US data is Glindro et al. (2008). They estimated the fundamental housing value as a function of demand-side variables (real GDP, population, real mortgage rate, and the mortgage credit to GDP ratio), supply-side variables (building permits and real construction costs), prices of other assets (equity prices and exchange rate), and a composite index of institutional factors using a 1993–2006 panel data set on nine Asia-Pacific countries. They then estimated eqn [7] above for country data as well as the city-level data. Four countries were associated with damped oscillation of housing prices whereas five countries as convergence to the fundamental values. Also, housing prices were found to be more volatile in markets with smaller supply responses.

Model Specification Issues

There are several modelling issues in fitting a dynamic area-wide housing price equation. First, the mean reversion term in the ECM specified in eqn [7], that is, $[P_{t-1} - P^*_{t-1}]$ may be caused by model specification error rather than by speculative forces to be corrected. A good example of such specification problem is the omission of the hard-to-capture supply-side constraints (e.g., zoning and other land-use regulations) in most empirical studies (exceptions include Glaeser and Gyourko, 2005; Glaeser and Ward, 2009; Glaeser et al. 2005, 2008). Measuring time- and location-varying regulatory restrictiveness is difficult, but it is a key driver of housing price dynamics. Its omission will lead to a classic case of bias caused by the exclusion of a relevant variable.

Second, most estimated housing price equations are reduced-form models that include various demand- and supply-side market fundamentals. Nonetheless, there are several sources of simultaneity bias between housing price dynamics and mortgage finance variables (Pavlov and Wachter, 2004, 2009), and between price changes and macroeconomic variables (Case and Quigley, 2008; Leamer, 2006). For example, user cost is the conventional measure to capture mortgage market conditions, but the volume of lending and mortgage product types also influence housing price dynamics, as shown in the explosive housing price appreciation in the United States between 2003 and 2006 boosted by subprime mortgage lending. Yet, mortgage lending volume is also influenced by housing price movement, driven both by fundamentals and by speculative bubbles.

Third, there are other sources of bias in projecting future home prices, such as time-varying volatility (i.e., the variance of ξ in eqn [4] being nonconstant), which requires fitting a GARCH-type model (Chinloy et al. 1997; Crawford and Fratantoni, 2003). There are index-related biases as well, for example, the geographical and intertemporal aggregation biases as tested by Calhoun, Chinloy, and Megbolugbe (1996).

Applications and Policy Implications

Human-Based vs Model-Based Property Appraisal

It has long been argued in the literature that human-based property appraisals are biased in both mean and volatility, that is, a systematically deflated second moment (the appraisal smoothing) and a systematically inflated first moment (the incentive-driven appraisal bias). As surveyed by Geltner et al. (2003), there have been a large number of studies since the late 1980s on the phenomenon of appraisal smoothing. These studies model the behaviour of human appraisers as a partial adjustment process in that they rely on two reference values in their assessment – an estimate of contemporaneous fair market value and a lagged appraised value of the property observed from a prior time period. As long as the weight to the latter is nonzero, there is a possibility of intertemporal smoothing such that the variance of appraised values over time is likely to be biased downward from its market-driven level (i.e., $E[e'e]$ from eqn [2] being smaller than it should be).

It is also well-documented that the appraisal outcome in the residential mortgage lending is likely to be skewed towards over-appraisals, that is, $E[e] > 0$, which can result in an underprediction of credit risks borne by mortgage applications (see Chinloy et al., 1996; Cho and Megbolugbe, 1996; Leventis, 2005, among others). These studies demonstrate that it is extremely rare that appraisers put lower value estimates than observed sale values, less than 5% of all cases examined by Cho and Megbolugbe, for example. Given the fact that mortgage lenders generally use the minimum of appraised value and reported sale value in underwriting loans, the implication is that the appraisal does not add much additional information in the process of credit assessment.

During the last decade or so, the use of Automated (Property) Valuation Models (AVMs) rapidly expanded in the United States, not only in the mortgage finance industry but also in mass property appraisals by local governments. An unbiased valuation model with minimum error variance can greatly improve historical mark-to-market valuations of residential properties and, hence, subsequent credit risk assessment in mortgage lending. (Refer to Kelly, 2006; LaCour-Little and Malpezzi, 2003; Noordewier et al. 2001 for the correlation between biased appraisals and the likelihood of mortgage default or delinquency.) Although RSM generally yields the best prediction outcomes (over hedonic and other models), combining multiple models to obtain unbiased value prediction will minimise error variance. Nonetheless, this does not necessarily mean that AVM is a perfect substitute for human-based property appraisal. Given the fact that the former generally suffers from lagged data, in some cases from nonavailability of data (e.g., extensive property characteristics), the two should be supplementary to each other.

Assessing Mortgage Default Risk

Forward-looking housing price distribution is the critical input to mortgage credit risk assessment, usually via a Monte Carlo simulation (see Lin et al. 2008 for three correlated state variables used in the mortgage pricing). Although there are complexities involved with a portfolio-level property analysis (e.g., diversification benefits), this application is essentially an extension of the property-level valuation as shown in eqn [4]. Related to that topic, Yang et al. (2008) demonstrated that incorporating different sources of home price volatility is critical in performing a portfolio-level mortgage credit risk analysis. Specifically, omitting the cross-sectional dispersion produces a large downward bias in estimated default indicators such as probability of default or probability of negative equity, much more so than omitting the forecasting error. Hence, excluding the cross-sectional or other volatility component in assessing mortgage credit risk can generate biased outcomes in mortgage pricing as well as in estimation of capital reserve.

Although forming a forward-looking housing price distribution is critical in measuring and managing the mortgage default risk, there is growing evidence that the subprime mortgage industry did not have the industry best practice in this regard until its demise. Unlike interest rate modelling, which has a long tradition since the 1970s, conceptual guidance for projecting housing prices still has a number of loose ends. They include what forecasting model to use (e.g., an autocorrelated one vs a random walk model), how to segment geography (metropolitan areas vs states vs whole country), how to measure and reflect diversification benefits (across geographical areas vs across mortgage products), as well as correlation between housing prices and interest rates, what volatility specification to be used (e.g., the top-down vs bottom-up approaches), and so on. It is fair to say that the literature on this subject is in its infancy in offering theories and guiding industry practices.

Testing for Speculative Bubbles

Econometric testing of asset price bubble boils down to testing statistical significance of B in eqn [5] assuming a 'correct' specification of P^* based on an appropriate set of market fundamentals. For example, Gurkaynak (2008) surveys various empirical methods for testing the bubble primarily focusing on the equity market. In most studies surveyed, the bubble term, B, is assumed to be independent of market fundamentals (hence, to P^*). However, this assumption is relaxed by Froot and Obstfeld (1991) and Driffill and Sola (1998), who tested the intrinsic bubble, that is, the type of bubble that is correlated with market fundamentals. Overall, this strand of empirical studies generally fails to offer a definitive answer as to whether a bubble exists, because testing for its existence is a joint test of specification of the market fundamental price, P^*, and the bubble, B (see West, 1987).

In the light of this, Glaeser et al. (2008) examine the nature of housing price bubbles, should they exist, instead of testing for their existence. They have developed a model showing that rational bubbles can exist when the supply of housing is fixed but not when it is elastic and when there are a finite number of home-buyers. They also show that, under the assumption of adaptive expectations by households, more inelastic places might have bigger and longer bubbles.

Future Research Agenda

During the last two decades, there has been a significant advancement in measuring dynamic home price changes, in both national and subnational levels, with indices from RSM models, and in fitting time-series models with those indices along with demand- and supply-side market fundamentals. Furthermore, empirical housing price models are being more widely used in various policy and business applications, ranging from a property-level micro market-to-market analysis to testing speculative bubble in a macro housing market context. We expect this trend of advancement to continue, in particular, due to the observed failure of the subprime mortgage industry in properly projecting future home prices with appropriate mean and volatility specifications.

As specific areas for future research, we suggest a short list including: explicitly modelling the interaction between price and quantity cycles; more clear modelling of linkages between housing market fundamentals and macroeconomic variables; further advancement in modelling and applying expected (or mean) and unexpected (or volatility) parts of home price dynamics in forming forward-looking price distributions. Another area of future research is predicting turning points, that is, peak or trough, in housing price cycles (see Shiller (2007) for a discussion of difficulties in predicting turning points), for which several recent studies utilise a discrete model such as a logistic regression model to estimate the probability of downturn or upturn. Related to this is the asymmetric role of supply elasticity between upturns and downturns (see Glaeser et al., 2008). Last but not least, co-movement of home prices, either nationally or globally, and indentifying common drivers of price dynamics (Kim and Renaud (2009) document the global housing price boom and its underlying forces.) will also be a fruitful avenue of future research.

See also: House Price Expectations; House Price Indexes; Price Determination in Housing Markets.

References

Abraham J and Schaumann W (1991) New evidence on house prices from Freddie Mac repeat sales. *Journal of the American Real Estate and Urban Economics Association* 19(3): 333–352.

Calhoun C, Chinloy P, and Megbolugbe I (1995) Temporal aggregation and house price index construction. *Journal of Housing Research* 6(3): 419–438.

Capozza DR, Hendershott PH, and Mack C (2004) An anatomy of price dynamics in illiquid markets: Analysis and evidence from local housing markets. *Real Estate Economics* 32(1): 1–32.

Case KE and Quigley JM (2008) How housing booms unwind: Income effects, wealth effects, and feedbacks through financial markets. *European Journal of Housing Policy* 8(2): 161–180.

Case KE and Shiller RJ (1989) The efficiency of the market for single family homes. *American Economic Review* 79(1): 125–137.

Chinloy P, Cho M, and Megbolugbe I (1996) Appraisals, transaction incentives, and smoothing. *Journal of Real Estate Finance and Economics* 14: 89–112.

Cho M (1996) Housing price dynamics: A survey of theoretical and empirical issues. *Journal of Housing Research* 7(2): 145–172.

Cho M and Megbolugbe I (1996) An empirical analysis of property appraisal and mortgage redlining. *Journal of Real Estate Finance and Economics* 13(1): 45–55.

Crawford G and Fratantoni M (2003) Assessing the forecasting performance of regime-switching, ARIMA and GARCH models of house prices. *Real Estate Economics* 31(2): 223–243.

Driffill J and Sola M (1998) Intrinsic bubbles and regime switching. *Journal of Monetary Economics* 42: 357–373.

Froot K and Obstfeld M (1991) Intrinsic bubbles: The case of stock prices. *American Economic Review* 81: 1189–1214.

Geltner D, MacGregor B, and Schwann G (2003) Appraisal smoothing and price discovery in real estate markets. *Urban Studies* 40: 1047–1064.

Glaeser EL and Gyourko J (2005) The impact of zoning on housing affordability. *Harvard Institute of Economic Research Discussion Paper Number 1948*. Cambridge, MA: Harvard University.

Glaeser E, Gyourko J, and Saks R (2005) Why have house prices gone up? *Journal of Economic Geography* 6: 71–89.

Glaeser EL, Gyourko J, and Saiz A (2008) Housing supply and housing bubbles. *Journal of Urban Economics* 64: 198–217.

Glaeser E and Ward B (2009) The causes and consequences of land use regulations: Evidence from Greater Boston. *Journal of Urban Economics* 65(3): 265–278.

Glindro ET, Subhanij T, Szeto J, and Zhu H (2008) Determinants of housing prices in nine Asia-Pacific countries. *BIS Working Papers No 263*. Bank of International Settlements.

Goetzmann W (1992) The accuracy of real estate indices: Repeat sales estimators. *Journal of Real Estate Finance and Economics* 5(1): 5–54.

Gurkaynak R (2008) Econometric tests of asset price bubbles: Taking stock. *Journal of Economic Surveys* 22(1): 166–186.

Hwang M and Quigley JM (2009) Housing price dynamics in time and space: Predictability, liquidity and investor returns. *Journal of Real Estate Finance and Economics* 41: 3–23.

Kelly A (2006) Appraisals, automated valuation models, and mortgage default. *Manuscript*. General Accounting Office.

Kim K-H and Renaud B (2009) Global house price boom and its unwinding: An analysis and a commentary. *Housing Studies* 24(1): 7–24.

LaCour-Little M and Malpezzi S (2003) Appraisal quality and residential mortgage default: Evidence from Alaska. *The Journal of Real Estate Finance and Economics* 27(2): 211–233.

Larsen RE and Weum S (2008) Testing the efficiency of the Norwegian housing market. *Journal of Urban Economics* 64: 510–517.

Leamer E (2006) Homes and Jobs and Bonds. *UCLA Anderson Forecast,* June 2006.

Leventis A (2006). Removing appraisal bias from a repeat-transactions house price index: A basic approach. *OFHEO Working Paper 06-1*.

Lin CC, Cho M, and Yang TT (2008) Default risk and relative values of ''exotic'' mortgage products: A multi-factor simulation approach. *Paper Presented at 2008AREUEA Annual Meeting*.

Malpezzi S (1999) A simple error correction model of house prices. *Journal of Housing Economics* 8(1): 27–62.

Malpezzi S and Wachter SM (2005) The role of speculation in real estate markets. *Journal of Real Estate Literature* 13(2): 143–164.

Meen GP and Andrew M (1998) On the aggregate housing market implications of labour market change. *Scottish Journal of Political Economy* 45(4): 393–419.

Miller N and Peng L (2006) Exploring metropolitan housing price volatility. *Journal of Real Estate Finance and Economics* 33: 5–18.

Noordewier T, Harrison D, and Ramagopal K (2001) Semivariance of property value estimates as a determinant of default risk. *Real Estate Economics* 29(1): 127–159.

Pavlov A and Wachter S (2004) Robbing the bank: Non-recourse lending and asset prices. *Journal of Real Estate Finance and Economics* 28: 147–160.

Pavlov A and Wachter S (2009) Mortgage put options and real estate markets. *Journal of Real Estate Finance and Economics* 38(1): 86–103.

Shiller RJ (2007) Historic turning points in real estate. *Cowles Foundation Discussion Paper No. 1610*.

Sutton G (2002) Explaining changes in house prices. *BIS Quarterly Review*: 46–55.

Van den Noord P (2005) Tax Incentives and housing price volatility in the euro area: Theory and evidenc. *Economie Internationale* 101: 29–45.

West KD (1987) A specification test for speculative bubbles. *Quarterly Journal of Economics* 102(3): 553–580.

Yang T, Lin C and Cho M (2009) Collateral risk in residential mortgage defaults. Journal of Real Estate Finance and Economics (forthcoming)

Privacy, Sanctuary and Privatism

R Dowling, Macquarie University, Sydney, NSW, Australia

© 2012 Elsevier Ltd. All rights reserved.

Glossary

Privacy Situation in which individuals have freedom and control, often associated with intimate, caring relationships.

Privatism Situation in which people withdraw from collective/public life and reorient their activities around home.

Separate spheres A set of ideas that emerged in the late eighteenth century in which a spatial moral and gendered separation of the world into collective life (public) and personal life (private) is prescribed.

Privacy and Home

That home is a private space or realm is one of the key meanings of home. In defining the privacy of home, comparisons are often made as to what home is not. Home is not the state/government, home is not work, home is not the church, home is not the realm of politics, and home does not encompass commercial activities. The contrast with public is hence central to the definition of private. Essentially, home as private denotes that it is separate from, indeed outside of, the collective institutions of public life. The contours of home as private can be usefully delineated through reference to definitions of private. According to Australia's *Macquarie Dictionary*, for example, private means (1) one's own, (2) individual, (3) confidential, (4) not holding public office, (5) out-of-public view, and (6) not open or accessible to people in general. Each of these subtle definitional differences is inflected in home as private: (1) a site to own; (2) a site for the individual rather than the collective; (3) a space for intimate, confidential relationships; (4) a space that is not politics; (5) a space secluded behind fences, walls, hedges, and hence away from the gaze of others; and (6) a space with restricted entry without invitation. In broad terms, then, home is a site, and a set of relationships, that fosters the individual and his/her interests rather than those of the collective. As summarised in a much-cited overview paper by Shelly Mallett, home as private denotes that it is a familial realm, removed from public scrutiny and surveillance. Home offers a space of freedom and control for the individual, and for intimate, caring relationships.

Home as private is a modern invention. Medieval homes, for example, were public spaces in myriad senses: full of people and used as public meeting places. Privacy for individuals within the home in that era was also nonexistent, with up to 25 people living in one or two rooms within a dwelling. As Davidoff and Hall's (1987) pioneering account shows, home as private was a product of a realignment of economic, political, moral, and spatial orders through the later parts of the eighteenth century. Here, for the middle class, home and dwelling were reinterpreted through the lens of separate spheres: a spatial moral and gendered separation of the world into collective life (public) and personal life (private). As a "territory of the mind" (p. 319), the distinction between public and private was reproduced in rules of etiquette, the regulation of social interaction, and, importantly for understanding home, in bricks and mortar. Here, family relations were played out in private homes physically distinct from the market place, and productive work was banished from the dwelling or was restricted to domestic servants hidden at the back. Family and home life for the English middle classes was created according to the ideal that the home should be a place enclosed from the intrusion of people who were neither family nor friends. The late eighteenth century hence saw the parameters of home as private and established it as a sanctuary and haven for the family but with specific class and gender characteristics.

Home as haven or sanctuary is a central idea in the privacy of home. While public space outside the home is seen as imposing and dangerous, home space is inside, enclosed, and safe. It is a sanctuary, a place to retreat into, that provides a respite from the uncertainties of commerce and the messiness of politics. Home is also a respite from work, a place of relaxation, a haven. There are debates around what conditions produce and maintain home as a secure sanctuary. One of these is private property. It is argued that the ability to maintain the home as a sanctuary is greater with homeownership. When individuals own, or are buying, their home, it is easier to monitor entry of others as well as bolster feelings of security. Indeed, Saunders argues that homeownership guarantees a form of ontological security unavailable to those who rent. Notwithstanding the thorough and well-founded critiques of Saunders' claims, it remains that the case of homeownership underpins a more attainable home as sanctuary.

There is considerable debate, however, about the social and geographical specificity of home as sanctuary. Feminists ask whether home as sanctuary is pertinent to the lives of many women. Primary responsibility for domestic labour and childcare means that home is a space of work for many women and cannot, by definition, be a sanctuary or respite from work. In the context of domestic violence and emotional abuse, for many women home is certainly not a haven, but a site and source of alienation and upheaval. Indeed, the presumed sanctity and privacy of the home, in legal and cultural terms, can lead to an underreporting of domestic violence and work to exacerbate these situations.

The class specificity of home as sanctuary is equally important. Home as sanctuary is more readily available to, and sometimes confined to, the middle class. For example, the discourses of separate spheres that underpinned the emergence of home as private in the late nineteenth century were class specific. These discourses were mobilised to help an emerging and rapidly growing middle class in Europe and North America distinguish itself in part through its domestic expectations and aspirations. Such a vision of middle-class domesticity served to elevate the privileged position of white, middle-class women over and above those women who were, and always had been, employed both inside and outside the home. The privacy of home is similarly never completely available to those who rely on state-provided housing. In jurisdictions such as Australia and the United Kingdom, for example, state housing authorities established standards of cleanliness and occupancy and often enforced them by entering an individual's home without warning. Home as sanctuary is hence an ideal and practice connected to both class and social differentiation.

Intimacy, care, and family are also important correlates of privacy in the home. The activities of caring for family members, care for the self (washing, dressing, grooming), intimacy with others, and the related 'private' emotions such as love and desire occur within, and are associated with, home spaces. Indeed, the emergence and consolidation of the nuclear family as the idealised family formation coincided with the delineation of home as a private space. The notion of home as private implies that all members of a family do not desire privacy from each other; indeed the ideal of 'familial togetherness' requires family members to embrace sharing space within the home. This is not always the case. Family members seek sanctuary from each other, a respite within the home. Thus, we see separate areas for children (rumpus rooms, playrooms) and parents (parents' retreats), multiple bathrooms to accommodate individual desires for privacy, and multiple electronic devices (televisions, computers) scattered throughout the home to facilitate the fulfilment of each family member's individual aspirations. Privacy in the private sphere is both sought and achieved.

Home as a site just for private nuclear families is far from universal. In cultures outside the West, the sharing of domestic space across generations and family networks is far more widespread. The New Zealand Maori 'marae', for example, is a home not just for the individual nuclear family but is by definition a community space in which extended families reside. How, and the extent to which, home is a private space in this context is thus quite different. Even in the West there are strong movements towards collective dwellings, using nomenclature such as shared housing, communes, cohousing, cooperative housing, or intentional communities. Here, dwellings are deliberately constructed to facilitate both individual privacy and collective activities. Some may include shared kitchens, others may involve shared open spaces and gardens, while still others may be completely communal in which there is no private space. Across this spectrum of collective residential arrangements, the association between home and the private nuclear family is questioned, although to varying degrees.

A final element to consider is the materiality of privacy in the home. Feelings of home as a private space are both created and reproduced materially. In the eighteenth century, for example, maintaining a home that was not publicly accessible to all was partially achieved by building fences, planting hedges, and installing gates. In the twenty-first century, installation of camera surveillance at dwelling entrances achieves a similar outcome. Materialities of privacy are not confined to external borders of home. Domestic architecture often codifies a transition from public to private. The formal room, or parlour, is situated at the front and used for receiving guests, while the informal living spaces inhabited by family members are at the back of the dwelling. Home as a sanctuary for family is announced through photographs and other wall decorations, as well as the provision of enclosed outdoor space, typically at the back of the dwelling. Privacy in the private sphere also has material and architectural dimensions. Whereas open plan design is associated with ideals of familial togetherness, privacy within the home may be facilitated by the building of walls, strategic placement of furniture, or even organised sequencing of activities and occupants in a shared space. Across these diverse practices, an ideal of privacy for individuals and households remains.

Privatism

Interest in the links between home and privacy has waned somewhat in recent scholarship. The concept of privatism has garnered increasing attention. Privatism refers to the preference for, and process of, withdrawing away from collective or public life and reorienting activities around home (Saunders and Williams, 1988). Certainly, a focus and prioritisation of the private realms of home and family is implicit in longstanding discourses of home and privacy. Contemporary descriptions of privatism, however, imply that a significant historical shift has occurred. This shift was partially identified in Christopher Lasch's 1995 reflections in his 1977 book *Haven in a Heartless World*. According to Lasch (1995: xxiv):

> The same historical developments that have made it necessary to set up private life – the family in particular – as a refuge from the cruel world of politics and work, an emotional sanctuary, have invaded this sanctuary and subjected it to outside controls. Relatedly, the domestic sphere stretched into and through other scales like the nation and the city.

For Lasch, the sanctity of the home and the privacy of the private sphere are being invaded and eroded. For others, the contemporary world is characterised by an increasingly dangerous, oppressive, and unpredictable public sphere: increasing crime rates, social unrest, unsafe public spaces, and ethnically and religiously diverse nations. This retreat into the home results from an understanding of these phenomena as dangerous and to be fearful of, alongside more generalised social anxieties. Home hence becomes as much a fortress as a sanctuary, a space, and an ideal to be fortified and defended. Materially we can see this in the astoundingly quick and global spread of gated communities. Fortification of individual homes also occurs through various means, often supported by legal and popular discourse. In the United Kingdom, for example, there has been debate about the type and extent of force homeowners may use to protect their home from robbery and invasion. In this sense, privatism refers to a general discourse of fear of the public realm and is manifest in more extreme forms of defending the sanctity of home.

There is a second, related sense of privatism that is also important in understanding home. Here, privatism is less a reaction to outside forces and more a positive embracing of home life, popularly called cocooning. The changing nature of lifestyles in the West has meant that daily routines have become more home-centred. Children's play, for example, is more likely to occur indoors or in private backyards and less likely to involve neighbourhood parks and front yards. The declining cost and increasing availability of electronic forms of home entertainment – televisions, pay-per-view movies, DVDs, computers, games, home theatres – further enhance the viability of children's and adults' recreation needs being met within the home. The popularity and spread of domestic lifestyle television, with its emphasis on the home chef and home renovations, is both a symptom and a perpetrator of privatism. Seemingly ubiquitous programmes on home cooking, do-it-yourself renovations, architectural showpieces, for example, are watched within the home and also encourage home-based recreation. In this variant of privatism, privacy is neither simply defensive (the fortified home), nor a retreat (home as sanctuary). Rather, it is home as focus or control centre, the heart through which the individual and family desires are achieved and interaction with the public sphere coordinated.

Beyond Privacy: Porosity and Interdependence of Public and Private Spheres

Although it is one of the most frequently identified meanings of home, and with strong purchase in ideal homes (including its associated referents to haven, sanctuary, security, safety, and intimacy), the associations between home and privacy have been subject to thorough critique. These critiques have been theoretical and empirical, and raise significant questions about the strength and clarity of associations between home and privacy. Centrally, the criticisms relate to issues with the conceptual and empirical bases of the notion of separate spheres. Foundationally, the point is made that public and private are not separate but linked and, more importantly, create each other. Empirically, the point is made that the separation of public and private and the ascription of unique characteristics to each do not even apply to the period from which the ideal of separate spheres emerged. Even in this time and place, home was never simply private, but both public and private. For the English middle class of the eighteenth century, for example, men and women occupied both public and private life, such as women's involvement in the family business. Similarly, in nineteenth-century America, domestic intimacy was subject to significant societal evaluation and moral codes; the private sphere was governed by public norms. The home, in sum, is never purely private.

A second line of critique of thinking about the home in relation to separate spheres is primarily theoretical: that public and private are interdependent. Indeed, what is public has been defined through the exclusion of the private (Pateman, 1989). What happens in and definitions of the domestic sphere are influenced by processes and characteristics of the public sphere and vice versa. These critiques of the distinction between the public and the private have important implications for scholarship on home. They suggest that home is best understood as a site of intersecting spheres, constituted through both public and private. Since home is not simply domestic, an understanding of what home means, and how it is created and reproduced, requires as much attention to processes of commerce, imperialism, and politics as to household negotiations.

Home is neither public nor private but both. Home is not separated from public and political worlds but is constituted through them: The domestic is created through the extradomestic and vice versa. There are various ways in which the fluid boundaries of public and private are constituted through home, and some key examples are given here. In terms of politics, scholarship has been directed towards the home as a site of politics. For example, Lesley Johnson (1996) compellingly shows that modernity is also constituted through home. Experiences within the home – such as caring for children or older relatives, and relations with neighbours – are actually about creating citizens and modern subjects. Similarly, Marston uses the example of the domestic sphere in nineteenth-century United States. The security and sanctity of the domestic sphere was justified materially and metaphorically to engage in national political debates. Furthermore, in relation to the state, the 'intrusion' of state policies and practices is historically and geographically widespread. House design, hygiene, and safety standards are subject to considerable state regulation. Most recently, in the West is the example of environmental regulations that specify the extent of, and means through which, the carbon footprints of dwellings should be reduced.

A material, or architectural, continuum between public and private is also evident. Parisian apartments, for example, were influenced by contemporary practices in commercial architecture, including the use of iron, steel, and glass. In the twentieth century, Dutch windows served the purpose of bringing together public and private in Dutch domestic life. In Dutch domestic architecture, windows have performed complicated functions. One of these has been to enable monitoring of the outside by those inside, using large windows, without or with minimal curtains or blinds, to see what was going on outside. In the postwar period, windows became linked to a 'showcase mentality' in which outsiders could see what was inside. In a slightly different context, ethnographic research by Daniel Miller, in a council estate in North London, showed that for some residents these dwellings were experienced as inhospitable, and they felt alienated from them. For other residents, however, a potentially alienating environment became a site of belonging, evidenced by kitchen decorating and remodelling. Some would place colourful decorations such as tea towels, ornaments, and curtains throughout the kitchen to draw attention away from the alienating features of the flat. Yet others completely remodelled and individualised their kitchens. Privacy in this sense is never fully secured.

An important corollary of this argument that home is by definition both public and private is that the public can be private, or that privacy exists in the public sphere. For example, the concept of mobile privatism was coined to describe the ways in which privacy can be achieved while a person is on the move (and therefore away from home). Mobile telephones, portable sound systems, mobile internet, and smart phones all facilitate the carrying out of individualised activities that had previously been carried out at home. As such, they create privacy in public. Even more specifically in relation to home, recognition of intersections of public and private alerts us to the ways in which public homes – prisons, student housing, homeless shelters, refuges for victims of domestic violence – are also private. They are, within limits, individualised through practices of dwelling.

Conclusions

Privacy is a contested concept in relation to understanding home, with contradictory contours in the contemporary world. Home is certainly culturally, socially, and materially constructed and idealised, as a form of sanctuary and haven and as a private realm. This is a socially differentiated phenomenon, especially in terms of gender and class. Yet, rather than a simple acknowledgement of the home as a private sphere, the accepted position in contemporary scholarship is that home is an amalgam of public and private. What is characterised as public, and characterised as private, is theorised as constructing each other, such that home is simultaneously public and private, and privacy can be achieved in public spaces (such as hospitals, prisons, and parks). In other words, the sanctity of home is created through engagement with the public. Moreover, there are important ways in which home is just as much public as private, including work and politics. Correspondingly, domestic senses of privacy are not confined to the home. This co-constitution of public and private in contemporary homes is challenged somewhat by recent work on privatism. This research emphasises the less permeable and more hostile material and symbolic boundaries placed around home to maintain it as a private space. Even there, however, the socio-legal and economic foundations of privatism nonetheless highlight the infusion of the public and private realms of home, and it is to be expected that future research on home and privacy will more richly excavate these connections.

See also: Domestic Violence; Domesticity; Feminist Perspectives on Home; Gender Divisions in the Home; Meanings of Home; Technology and Surveillance in the Home.

References

Davidoff L and Hall C (1987) *Family Fortunes: Men and Women of the English Middle Class 1780–1850*. London: Hutchinson.

Johnson L (1996) 'As housewives we are worms': women, modernity and the home question. *Cultural Studies* 10(3): 449–463.

Lasch C (1977 [1995]) *Haven in a Heartless World: The Family Besieged*. New York: Basic Books.

Pateman C (1989) *The Disorder of Women. Democracy, Feminism and Political Theory*. Cambridge, UK: Polity Press.

Saunders P and Williams P (1988) The constitution of the home: Towards a research agenda. *Housing Studies* 3: 81–93.

Further Reading

Atkinson R and Blandy S (2007) Panic rooms: The rise of defensive homeownership. *Housing Studies* 22(4): 443–458.

Blunt A and Dowling R (2006) *Home*. London; New York: Routledge.

Cieraad I (1999) *At Home: An Anthropology of Domestic Space*. Syracuse, NY: Syracuse University Press.

Mallett S (2004) Understanding home: A critical review of the literature. *The Sociological Review* 52(1): 62–89.

Munro M and Madigan R (1993) Privacy in the private sphere. *Housing Studies* 8(1): 29–45.

Rybczynski W (1988) *Home: A Short History of an Idea*. London: Heinemann.

Waghorn K (2009) Home invasion. *Home Cultures* 8(3): 261–296.

Relevant Websites

http://www.communities.org.au – Cohousing Australia.
http://www.ic.org – Intentional Communities.

Private Protection and Housing Property Insurers in the United States

RW Klein, Georgia State University, Atlanta, GA, USA

© 2012 Elsevier Ltd. All rights reserved.

Glossary

Habitational policy A habitational policy is any policy that covers a residential dwelling and is issued as a homeowners or dwelling fire policy. Habitational policies are distinguished from commercial policies that are purchased by owners of firms and other properties that are considered commercial in nature (e.g., apartment buildings, condominium buildings, etc.).

Homeowners multiperil insurance A form of insurance for residential properties that bundles several different coverages for various perils (e.g., causes of loss). These coverages encompass the dwelling, detached structures, personal property or contents, loss of use, and liability.

National flood insurance program A programme sponsored by the US government that provides flood insurance for residential and commercial properties.

Peril A cause of loss such as fire, windstorm, flooding, explosions, earthquakes, and theft, among others.

Policy deductible An amount that the insured retains on any claim. The insurer covers any remaining amount up to the policy limit. The typical deductible ranges from $500 to $1000.

Residual market mechanism A government-sponsored arrangement to provide home insurance to owners unable to purchase coverage from a private insurance company. The typical mechanisms used in the United States are Fair Access to Insurance Requirements (FAIR Plans) and state-sponsored insurance companies (less common).

Voluntary market The private market for home insurance in which insurance companies voluntarily choose whether to offer coverage to applicants unless they are mandated to offer coverage under government regulations.

Characteristics of Residential Property Insurance

If housing is viewed as a necessity for most people, then managing and financing the risk associated with owning or occupying a home becomes important. Insurance is one of several devices used to finance such risk. This article reviews the market for residential property insurance, with the primary emphasis on homeowners multiperil insurance. Other forms of residential property insurance also are described. While the markets for home insurance are mature and appear to function relatively well in developed countries, they are plagued by certain problems that are discussed in this article.

This article is written primarily from a US perspective where most property insurance is supplied by private companies. There are numerous differences between markets for home insurance in different countries due to variations in circumstances. An exception is Canada where homeowners insurance is very similar in how it is structured relative to how it is structured in the United States. It is reasonable to presume that some form of private property insurance is available to households in most if not all developed, market-based economies. In transitional and developing economies, the supply and use of private property insurance is more sporadic. Higher-income households may tend to procure insurance but this is less likely to be the case for low-income households. The latter may rely more heavily on family and government resources to cover property losses to the extent they are available. The relative roles of private versus public financing of losses from natural disasters such as earthquakes, windstorms, and floods vary among countries (OECD, 2009).

Homeowners multiperil insurance is the type of insurance most commonly used to cover owner-occupied residential properties. Homeowners multiperil insurance packages several different coverages for residential structures, their contents, and their inhabitants (Rejda, 2004). The perils covered typically include fire, windstorm, hail, riot, lightning, explosion, theft, and malicious mischief, as well as personal liability. Homeowners multiperil coverage is confined to residential structures, including multiunit structures (2–4 units), where the owner occupies one of the units.

There are several forms of homeowners multiperil insurance that differ in terms of the perils insured and

Box 1 Homeowners multiperil policy provisions and options

Coverage	Form			
	HO-2	HO-3	HO-5	HO-8
Dwelling (A)	Minimum varies by company	Minimum varies by company	Minimum varies by company	Minimum varies by company
Other structures (B)	10% of A	10% of A	10% of A	10% of A
Personal property (C)	50% of A	50% of A	50% of A	50% of A
Loss of use (D)	30% of A	30% of A	30% of A	10% of A
Personal liability (E)	$100 000	$100 000	$100 000	$100 000
Medical payments (F)	$1000 per person	$1000 per person	$1000 per person	$1000 per person
Perils	Named	Open-dwelling Named-contents	Open	Named, Limited
Loss settlement	RC – Dwelling ACV – Contents	RC – Dwelling ACV – Contents	RC – Dwelling ACV – Contents	RC – Dwelling ACV – Contents

From Rejda GE (2004) *Principles of Risk Management and Insurance*. Boston, MA: Pearson.

the types of losses that are covered. See **Box 1** for a summary of the coverages provided under the standard Insurance Services Office (ISO) policy forms. The HO-3 policy is the typical contract sold. It has coverages for the home and attached structures, detached structures, personal property (i.e., contents), loss of use, personal liability, and medical payments for others. Other policy forms offer more or less coverage as detailed in **Box 1**.

Some standard policy provisions may be modified and consumers typically have several options in tailoring their coverage to meet their needs. These options include: (1) the policy deductible; (2) the basis of loss settlement on personal property (replacement cost (RC) or actual cash value (ACV)); (3) named or open perils coverage; and (4) alternative coverage limits. The traditional homeowner's policy carries an overall deductible that applies to all property coverages and perils. This is typically a fixed dollar amount, ranging from $100 to $1000 or more, with $250–$500 being the most common. Some insurers also offer deductibles that are a stated percentage of the Coverage A (dwelling) limit for all perils. Most recently, insurers have begun to offer separate wind deductibles in areas subject to tropical storms and hurricanes.

Homeowners policies typically provide RC coverage on the dwelling and other structures and ACV coverage on personal property (i.e., contents). However, homeowners may purchase RC coverage on contents through a special endorsement. The standard policy covers the dwelling on an 'open-perils' basis and contents on a 'named-perils' basis. Under open-perils coverage, a peril is covered unless it is specifically excluded in the policy provisions. Under named-perils coverage, a specific peril must be listed to be covered. The different policy forms vary as to the application of named and open perils coverage.

There are also options available to cover personal property at a greater value than the standard limits, or to cover liability at a greater level than the standard limit ($100 000). Also, depending on the state and company, certain coverages may be included or excluded in a specific contract, and special endorsements may be added to provide supplemental coverage, modify standard coverage provisions, or exclude other coverages. Some of these options are discussed further below.

The standard homeowner's insurance policy excludes damage caused by flood (surface water) and earth movement (e.g., earthquakes, sinkholes, landslides, etc.). In the United States, the flood peril (including flooding associated with hurricanes) must be insured through a separate policy through the federal National Flood Insurance Program. Damage due to earth movement can be covered through a special endorsement or a separate policy. Some insurers also exclude coverage for wind in certain coastal areas of the United States. In such instances, homeowners generally can obtain wind coverage from a government-sponsored plan.

It is also possible to purchase a more limited dwelling fire policy to cover a residential structure or its contents against certain property perils, with or without extended coverage for other perils, including windstorm (Rejda, 2004). Dwelling fire policies are less common than homeowners multiperil policies, and generally represent a very small portion of insured homes. Insurance policies also have been designed for renters (tenants) and condominium unit owners. These policies mainly cover personal property and also provide liability coverage.

Homeowners Insurance Markets

Market Structure

Market concentration

Market concentration is an important aspect of insurance market structure, both in terms of its potential effect on competition and market performance, and its implications for insurers' vulnerability to severe losses from a catastrophe or series of catastrophes. On the one hand, less concentration may be advantageous in promoting greater competition as well as greater risk diversification. On the other hand, greater concentration can facilitate increased economic efficiency if low-cost insurers are able to write a larger share of the market and also reap administrative savings from servicing a greater number of policies in a given geographic area.

Market concentration is typically measured using concentration ratios (the combined market share of some number of the leading firms) and the Herfindahl–Hirschman Index (HHI). The HHI is equal to the sum of the squared market shares of all firms in the market and can range from near zero to 10 000 (the HHI value when there is only one firm in the market with a 100% market share).

Higher values of these indices indicate higher market concentration. These measures reflect the potential market power possessed by the largest firms in a market as well as their share of the risk covered by insurance. Note that concentration is principally measured using insurer groups plus nonaffiliated insurers, which better reflects the implications of concentration for competition.

Table 1 shows the top 10 homeowners insurers in the United States in 2007 and their market shares. State Farm was the leading insurer group with a 23% market share followed by Allstate with an 11.8% market share. In most states, State Farm and Allstate account for 30–50% of the market. The combined market share for the top 10 insurers was 66.8%. Many homeowners insurers also provide auto insurance, which increases their economies of scope and strengthens their market positions.

Table 2 compares market concentration levels in homeowners' insurance in 2006 with other selected lines. In 2006, 438 insurance companies sold homeowners insurance which represented 12.3% of the premiums written in all property-casualty lines. The top 10 companies accounted for 64.2% of market premiums and the HHI was 784. This level of market concentration would

Table 1 Top 10 homeowners insurers: 2007 (based on Direct Premiums Written (DPW))

Rank	Group	DPW ($000)	Market share (%)
1	State Farm Group	28 114 716	23.0
2	Allstate Ins. Group	14 379 336	11.8
3	Zurich Ins. Group	9 202 814	7.5
4	Nationwide Corp. Group	5 765 026	4.7
5	Travelers Group	5 642 572	4.6
6	USAA Group	5 311 636	4.3
7	Liberty Mutual Group	4 457 264	3.6
8	Chubb & Son Group	3 674 595	3.0
9	American Family Ins. Group	2 852 100	2.3
10	Hartford F&C Ins. Group	2 229 415	1.8

Source: Data from NAIC Financial Database, author's calculations.

Table 2 Property-casualty insurance market structure: 2006

					Since 1997	
Line	Number of insurers	Pct. of sector DPW (%)	CR10 (%)	HHI	Entries (%)	Exits (%)
Personal auto	389	33.2	64.1	651	29.4	48.9
Commercial auto	389	6.2	44.4	272	33.4	46.2
Fire & Allied	438	12.3	64.2	782	27.9	41.2
Commercial MP	544	4.2	53.7	502	24.8	41.6
Medial malpractice	365	7.4	49.0	318	24.1	45.6
General liability	697	12.2	57.7	595	36.8	42.8
Medical malpractice	225	2.5	45.8	295	112.4	57.2
Workers' compensation	312	9.5	54.2	487	32.1	48.0
Other	715	20.0	43.1	255	26.2	45.8
All lines combined	1,270	100.0	48.6	318	43.5	43.4

Source: Data from National Association of Insurance Commissioners (NAIC) and author's calculations.

typically not be considered high enough to raise concerns about the competitiveness of the market or the ability of insurers to flex any market power.

Entry and exit

Some further insight into market structure can be gained by looking at the market entry and exit conditions for insurers. Low entry and exit barriers are an important factor in the competitive structure of a market. Ease of entry allows new firms to enter a market and impose competitive pressure on incumbent firms. Indeed, even in a highly concentrated market, the threat of entry can discipline firms in the market. The cost of exit is also important because it can discourage firms from entering a market. Further, the flow of insurers in and out of catastrophe-prone markets can facilitate a broader diversification of this risk.

It is difficult to quantify entry and exit barriers, but it is possible to offer some qualitative observations as well as to analyse data on actual entries and exits. Regulatory capital requirements in the United States are relatively low and do not appear to be high enough to be a substantial entry deterrent (Klein, 2005). Also, new and growing insurers can use reinsurance to boost their capacity. Information, expertise, distribution outlets, reputation, and customer relationships probably have a greater effect on entry. Information and expertise can be particularly important for proper pricing and underwriting in markets subject to catastrophe risk or that present other special circumstances. Personal lines insurers employ an array of distribution systems, some involving higher fixed costs (e.g., exclusive agents) and others involving higher variable costs (e.g., independent agents). Some insurers have invested heavily in marketing and developing a reputation with consumers. The significance of these entry costs or barriers probably depends on the segment of a market that an entrant is seeking to penetrate. For example, competing against well-known, direct writers for preferred risks could be a more challenging proposition than marketing to high-risk insurers served by nonstandard carriers or government facilities.

With respect to the actual frequency of entries and exits, we would expect to see at least a small number of insurers both entering and exiting a workably competitive market over time. Insurers that fail to respond to buyer needs efficiently and earn reasonable profits would be expected to leave the market. New insurers entering the market can help respond to growing demand, promote innovation, lower prices, and pressure incumbent firms to improve. However, markets subject to a high level of catastrophe risk present a special challenge. Entry can be discouraged by restrictive regulation and exit impeded by exit barriers. On the other hand, some entrants may be encouraged by the opportunity to write to homeowners who have been terminated by other insurers, which helps to maintain the availability of insurance.

In **Table 2**, we can see that exits have outpaced entries at the national level. Since 1997, entries constituted 27.9% and exits accounted for 41.2% of the insurers writing homeowners insurance in 1997. This reflects some consolidation in home insurance and other lines nationwide. This consolidation is due to insurers' efforts to increase their sales in saturated markets as well as increase their economies of scale. Further, some insurers have dropped home insurance to concentrate on other lines where they believe they have a greater comparative advantage. Florida is an exception to this general trend as approximately 60 companies have entered its market to assume policies dropped by other insurers. Most of these entrants are newly formed, single-state companies (Klein, 2009).

Market Performance

Insurers' conduct and ultimately market performance or outcomes are of the greatest interest to various stakeholders. The key market outcomes include the price of insurance, the availability of coverage, policy terms, and profitability. For obvious reasons, property owners are most interested in the price of insurance as this can have a significant effect on their housing costs and budget. They are also interested in the availability of coverage and policy terms as they can affect how much insurance they can purchase, the insurers they can purchase insurance from, and whether they will need to obtain coverage in the residual market. Insurers have a stake in these outcomes, but their profits (or losses) and financial viability are of particular concern to them. If insurers are unable to recover all of their costs, including their cost of capital (at least in the long run), it becomes difficult for them to justify and sustain operations in a market. Also, continuing operations under such conditions can ultimately threaten their financial strength and solvency, with adverse consequences for their owners and all of their policyholders. Here the focus is primarily on the price and availability of insurance as well as insurers' profitability.

Price of insurance

The US Bureau of Labor Statistics includes tenants and household insurance in its Consumer Price Index (CPI). **Figure 1** compares percentage changes in the price indices for home insurance, the repair of household items, and the median price of existing single-family homes for the period 1999–2008. As can be seen from the figure, the price of home insurance increased only 17.2% compared to 58.6% for household repairs and 43.5% for single-family homes. Recognising that the housing bubble contributed to unsustainable increases in

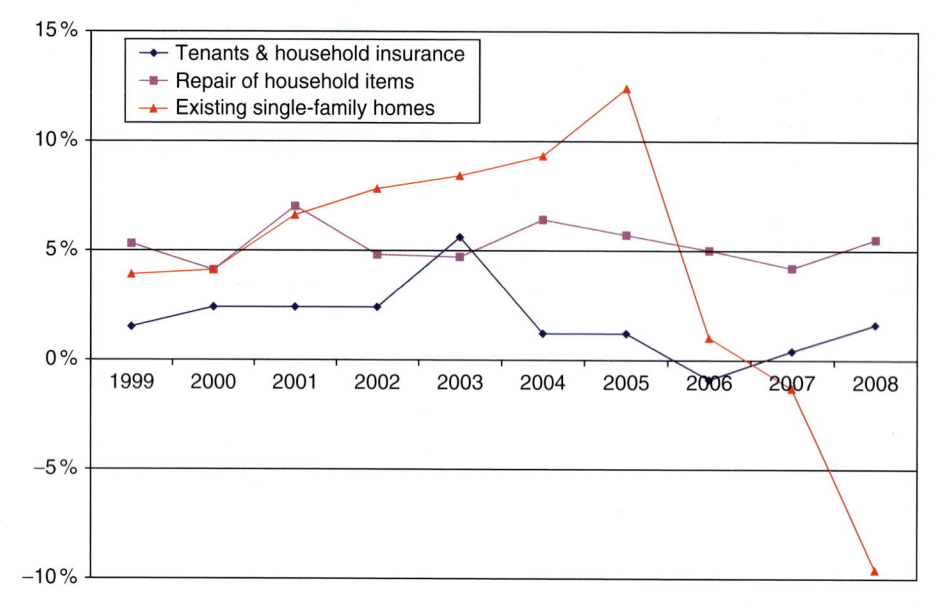

Figure 1 Percent change in consumer price index household insurance and related items. Source: Data from Bureau of Labor Statistics and National Association of Realtors.

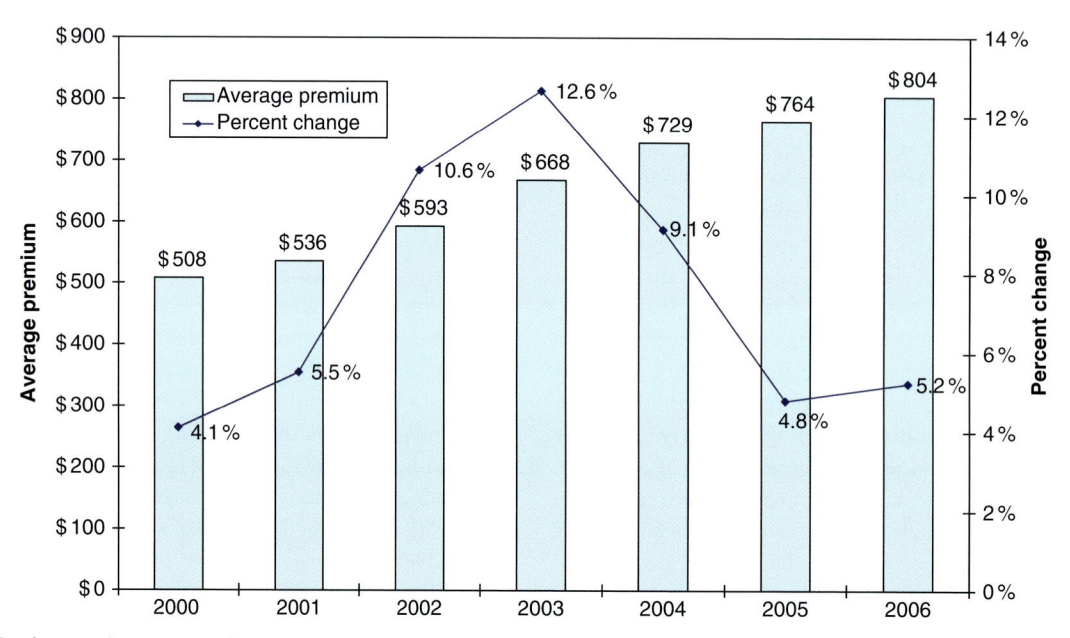

Figure 2 Average homeowners insurance premiums 2000–2006. Source: Data from National Association of Insurance Commissioners.

home prices (which began falling in 2007–08), the data suggest that the cost of home insurance has risen at a relatively modest pace consistent with the general rate of inflation.

Another way of looking at the price of home insurance is to plot the average homeowners' premium paid as shown in **Figure 2** for the period 2000–06. In this figure we can see that the average premium increased from $508 in 2000 to $804 in 2006. This constitutes a 58.3% increase over the entire period. A number of factors affect the average premium that are not controlled in the manner used to compute the CPI for home insurance. Obviously, as the replacement value of homes increased (including the building of bigger and better houses), the premiums paid by homeowners also rose.

It should be stressed that the price of home insurance can vary greatly among homeowners and homes. Many factors affect this variation including the location of a home. All other things being equal, homeowners insurance prices are significantly higher in urban areas and areas subject to significant weather risks, including hurricanes.

Availability of coverage

The availability of insurance coverage is also an important performance outcome and an area of attention and concern to property owners, government officials, and other stakeholders. 'Availability' is a somewhat elusive phenomenon to measure or quantify and can mean different things to different people. The preferred definition might be how easy or difficult it is for homeowners to obtain the coverage they want in the 'voluntary market' from the insurers they prefer but acquiring information on this or even measuring availability so defined is difficult.

Hence, economists tend to use other insurance availability indicators such as the proportion of uninsured homes or the size of the residual market. However, there are problems with, and caveats to, these measures. It is difficult to obtain data on the proportion or number of uninsured homes, and the lack of insurance on a home may be at least partly a matter of choice on the part of the homeowner. Also, a home may have insurance, but the amount or breadth of coverage may be considerably less than what the homeowner would prefer. Similarly, the number and proportion of homes/policies in the residual market are affected by a number of factors of which insurers' willingness to supply insurance is only one. Finally, this measure can confound prices with the 'availability' of coverage – some homeowners may be able to choose to obtain insurance in the residual market because it costs less than what they would be required to pay in the voluntary market and there are no eligibility requirements that would prevent them from doing so.

With these caveats and limitations in mind, we can look at the size of the residual market over time to gain some perspective on availability. Understanding that this measure is affected by several factors, it is generally conceded that the supply or availability of insurance in the voluntary market is a major driver of the size of the residual market. **Figure 3** shows figures on the number of habitational policies in state Fair Access to Insurance Requirements (FAIR) plans and state 'wind pools' or 'beach plans'. FAIR plans generally provide full coverage similar to but not necessarily identical to insurance coverage provided in the private market. Wind pools or beach plans provide only wind coverage in designated coastal areas. We can see from this figure that there has been a significant increase in the number of policies in state FAIR plans from 1992 to 2007. Some (perhaps much) of this increase is likely attributable to an overall increase in the number of homes. Still, some of the increase is likely due to the diminished availability of private insurance in some states. This is especially true in states subject to significant catastrophe risk arising primarily from hurricanes and tropical storms.

Generally, with a few exceptions, the proportion of homes that are insured through residual market mechanisms (RMMs) represents only a small portion (in the area of 1–2% or less) of the total homes insured in a state. Two exceptions are Florida and Louisiana where the RMMs account for approximately 20% and 7% of the total markets respectively in those states. While the availability of coverage can be a significant problem in

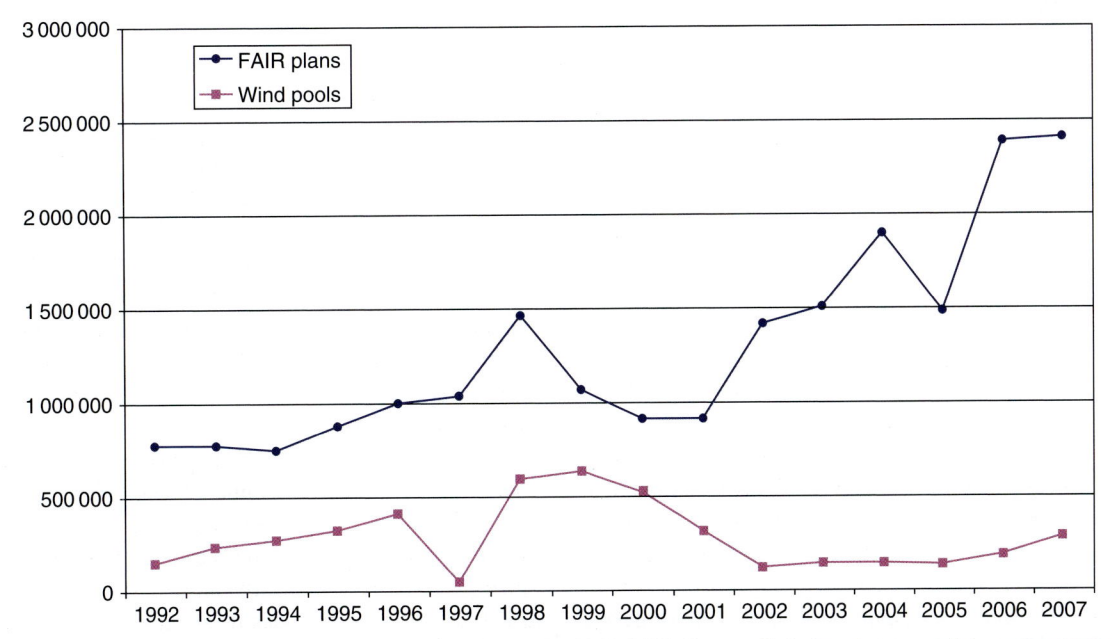

Figure 3 Insurance policies issued by FAIR Plan and wind pools, 1992–2007. Source: Data from Insurance Information Institute.

certain areas, most RMMs do not impose a substantial burden on a state in relative terms, Florida and Louisiana excepted.

Profitability

The final measure of market performance examined is insurers' profitability. Firms' profitability is an important market performance outcome. In an efficient, competitive market, long-run profits would be expected to provide firms a 'fair' rate of return equal to their risk-adjusted cost of capital. If firms' profits are too low and they are unable to remedy the deficiency, it will encourage market exit or retrenchment that could have adverse effects on consumers. On the other hand, if firms sustain high profits over the long term, it would raise questions about the competitiveness of the market.

The problem in insurance markets, especially in lines like homeowners' insurance, is that profits can be highly volatile from year to year. In other words, insurers can earn low or negative profits in some years and what appear to be high profits in other years. Still, over the long run, profits would be expected to 'average out' near what would be considered a fair rate of return. This is closer to being the case in homeowners' insurance markets that are subject to 'normal' weather-related perils, but hurricane-prone markets are subject to much greater volatility and much longer 'return periods'.

Figure 4 plots insurers' annual rate of return on equity (ROE) for homeowners insurance and all lines for the period 1998–2007. As can be seen from this figure, insurers earned positive profits in all but two of the years for homeowner's insurance during this period, but their ROE fell below what would be considered adequate in terms of meeting their cost of capital. For the entire period, the average ROE was only 4%. We can also see that profits were fairly volatile with a standard deviation of 4.7%. By comparison, the average ROE for all lines was 7.1% and the standard deviation was 3.6%. This indicates that homeowners' profits were lower but more volatile than profits for all lines.

The low and volatile profits for homeowners' insurance can be attributed to several factors but weather-related losses are likely to be a significant factor. Insurers' prices also lagged behind their claim costs in the late 1990s and early 2000s and did not catch up until 2003. This was true for some inland states (subject to tornadoes and other storms) as well as coastal states. Some insurers have retrenched from coastal areas as noted above, in part because of low profits. Klein (2009) estimates that insurers' cumulative profits for southeastern states were −7.2% as of 2007 for the period 1985–2007. Hence, it is not surprising that insurers have soured on writing more business in the southeastern states.

Issues in Homeowners Insurance

Natural Disasters

Insurers' exposure to and losses from natural disasters has been a significant issue. The predominant causes of natural disasters are earthquakes, tsunamis, wildfires, tropical storms/hurricanes, and floods. Many insurers

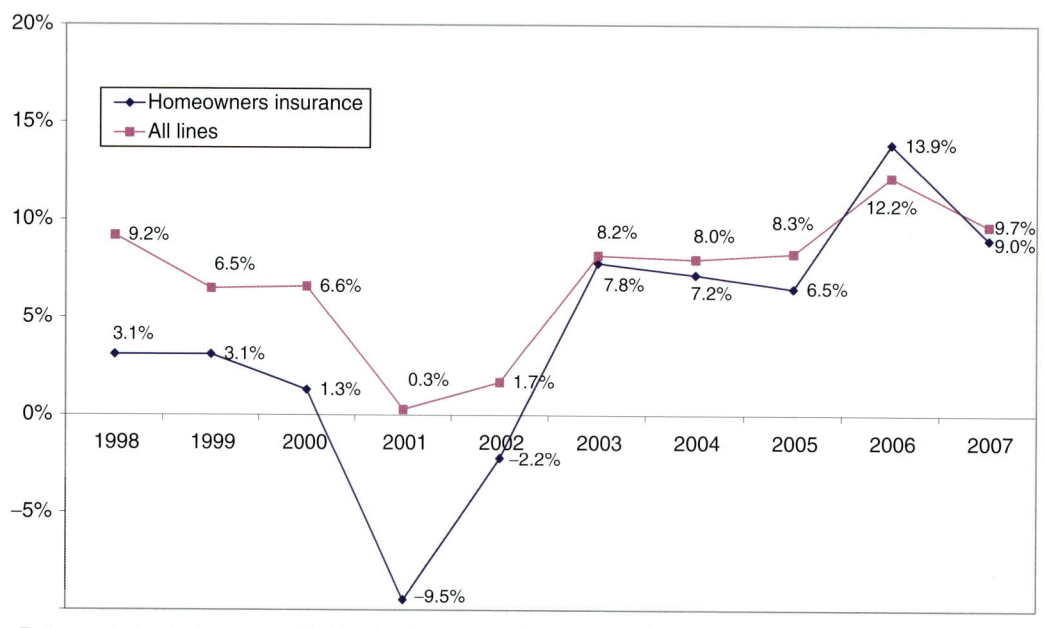

Figure 4 Estimated rate of return on equity (ROE). Homeowners insurance and all lines: 1998–2007. Source: Data from National Association of Insurance Commissioners.

have raised their prices and decreased their exposures in areas exposed to these kinds of perils. This has significantly increased the cost and reduced the availability of insurance for some homeowners. In most of the affected states, regulators have sought to preserve the availability of coverage to the extent possible by allowing insurers considerable discretion with respect to their prices. Florida is an exception where regulators have clamped down on rates. This has inevitably worsened availability.

Many states are also subject to tornadoes, hail storms, and so on, and these perils have contributed to higher insurance prices and possibly diminished availability of coverage. Wildfires in places like California have also caused problems. Still, these problems appear to be much less significant than the problems caused by hurricane risk. In fact, there are reports that homeowners' insurers have sought to increase their business in inland states since 2005 as they have retrenched from coastal areas.

Unfortunately, there is no silver bullet that will fix the problems caused by catastrophe risk. Allowing insurers to charge higher rates would help to remedy but not fully resolve availability problems. Another partial solution lies in greater hazard mitigation. Mitigation can take several forms including discouraging development in high-risk areas and making homes more storm-resistant. Affected states are encouraging greater mitigation and have made significant strides in this area, but they have much farther to go. Legislative proposals have been introduced in Congress that would establish some form of national catastrophe insurance/reinsurance programme that would ease the pressure on coastal states. However, there is not a strong appetite among noncoastal legislators for such a programme and its prospects are dim in the current climate.

Urban Insurance Problems

The cost and availability of homeowners insurance has also plagued some urban areas. These problems date back at least to the 1960s and remain unresolved. The areas most severely affected are older, inner-city neighbourhoods, especially low-income areas. Consumer and housing advocates have contended that insurers engage in explicit or implicit 'redlining', that is, arbitrarily refusing to offer insurance and/or charging excessive prices in these areas. Most recently, these advocates have promoted the concept of 'disparate impact' and have sued insurers on this basis. Insurers have rejected redlining claims and the applicability of disparate impact standards to home insurance.

The problems faced by these urban areas are also difficult to fix. Indeed, they may be worsening in light of the decline in house prices and the rise in foreclosures. The challenges posed by theft, vandalism, fires, and so on do not have easy remedies. Insurers have participated in pilot programmes designed to mitigate these problems but there is not good information on how successful they have been. If they have been successful, they may offer a guide for broader programmes. Still, their expansion is likely to be costly and to ultimately involve a trade-off between insurance costs and the cost of mitigation measures.

Mould Contamination

The problem of toxic mould struck a number of states in the late 1990s and early 2000s, effectively compounding the problems caused by other perils. Affected homeowners filed claims for damages from mould contamination that were rejected or tempered by insurance companies. The fundamental issue was the source of the contamination. Homeowners policies (at that time) covered losses from the 'sudden' discharge of water (e.g., pipes breaking) but excluded losses from other causes, such as excessive moisture, slow leaks, defective building materials, and so on. Because of lawsuits and regulatory sanctions, insurers took several routes to address the risk of mould contamination. These routes included adding an endorsement for mould contamination (regardless of its source) and higher rates, among others. It appears that the problems associated with mould contamination have subsided but it still remains a threat.

Summary and Conclusions

Insurance is a necessity for many homeowners and, hence, its cost and availability are important issues. While the evidence suggests that homeowners insurance markets are generally competitive, this does not prevent high costs or the reduced supply of coverage due to the nature of the underlying risks that insurers cover. Consequently, many of the problems discussed in this article are unlikely to go away in the near term. At the same time, it is reasonable to hope that these problems can be diminished over time through enlightened public policies, insurer innovations, and a rebound of housing markets.

See also: Economics of Housing Choice; Environmental Risks: Earthquakes; Environmental Risks: Flooding; Health and Housing; Mortgage Insurance; Mortgage Payment Protection Insurance; Policies to Address Redlining; Post-Disaster Housing and Reconstruction.

References

Klein RW (2005) *A Regulator's Introduction to the Insurance Industry*. Kansas City, MO: National Association of Insurance Commissioners.

Klein RW (2009) *Hurricane Risk and Insurance Markets: An Update and Extension*. Atlanta, GA: Georgia State University.

Organisation for Economic Co-operation and Development (2009) *Innovation in Country Risk Management*. Paris: OECD.

Rejda GE (2004) *Principles of Risk Management and Insurance*. Boston, MA: Pearson.

Squires GW (1997) *Insurance Redlining: Disinvestment, Reinvestment and the Evolving Role of Financial Institutions*. Washington, DC: Urban Institute Press.

Further Reading

Harrington SE and Neihaus GR (2004) *Risk Management and Insurance*. Boston, MA: Irwin McGraw-Hill.

Skipper HD (1998) *International Risk and Insurance: An Environmental Approach*. Boston, MA: Irwin McGraw-Hill.

Relevant Websites

http://rmictr.gsu.edu – Center for Risk Management and Insurance Research.

http://www.iii.org – Insurance Information Institute.

http://www.disastersafety.org – Institute for Business and Home Safety.

http://www.fema.gov – National Flood Insurance Program.

http://www.oecd.org – Organisation for Economic Cooperation and Development.

Private Rental Landlords: Developing Countries

A Gilbert, University College London, London, UK

© 2012 Published by Elsevier Ltd.

Glossary

Landlord Someone who rents out property to a tenant. The term includes landlady, a word only being used when it is clear that the latter is the landlord, for example, in the case of a widow without adult sons. In many cases, the sex of the landlord is irrelevant because the householders are a couple. In some places, the man will manage the tenants; elsewhere it will be the woman. The inclusion of women under the term landlord is not meant to be sexist and is used in the same way that most actresses, these days, prefer to be called actors.

Secure tenure "[T]he right of all individuals and groups to effective protection by the State against unlawful evictions" (UNHABITAT, 2002d: 6).

Tenants Households paying a prearranged rent for the exclusive occupation of all or part of a dwelling unit. This tenure also includes both formal and informal situations. That is to say, the term renting embraces households who pay a regular sum of money to a landlord whether the landlord is a government institution, a cooperative, or a private individual, and irrespective of whether a formal contract has been issued. A landlord in a self-help settlement who has established a verbal contract with the tenant is still a landlord. So long as the tenant recognises that there is a contractual relationship with another individual who has ownership rights over the property and a regular payment is being made, the distinction between owners and tenants is a real one.

The Business of Renting

Until the middle of the twentieth century, most urban families throughout the world lived in rented accommodation. Whereas rural people owned their homes or built their shelter either on communal land or on the land they farmed, most urban families rented. This included families from every social class – it was not just the tenure of the poor. Most rental housing was supplied by those with money to invest and/or land on which to build. Private enterprise produced most of the housing, mainly small-scale investment but with some cases of large-scale development including sometimes major institutional investors like the church.

Gradually, the sources of rental housing changed. Private investment became less profitable and increasingly problematic. In developed countries, the growth of stock markets and other opportunities for investment transformed the commercial calculus. Many former landlords moved into real estate development for sale, especially when governments began to encourage owner-occupation. In places, increasing state intervention also discouraged landlords from continuing to invest in rental housing. Where rents were held down and it was difficult to evict tenants, rental housing ceased to be a profitable investment. Only in a handful of countries did commercial investment continue; in Germany and Switzerland it remains important to this day.

In poorer countries, the transition from renting to ownership came later because cities began to grow rapidly much later than in most developed countries and because governments did not intervene much in the housing market until the widespread adoption of some kind of rent control legislation in the 1940s. Up to 1950, most urban households in Africa, Asia, and Latin America continued to rent their homes.

After 1950, the situation changed dramatically. In Latin America, where many cities were growing very rapidly during the 1950s and 1960s, there was increasing pressure on the housing stock. In response, governments encouraged the better-off to buy homes through subsidised mortgages and in some instances built housing to let to the homeless. But the most important form of governmental action was to encourage, or at least not to prohibit, the growth of shantytowns. Millions of poor people took advantage of the opportunity to obtain free plots of land on which they could construct a shelter and avoid the need to pay rent. Modern transport in the form of the bus and train encouraged suburban development for both the rich and the poor. In some cities home ownership grew rapidly – in Mexico City from 27% in 1950 to 64% in 1980.

With new opportunities for real estate investment opening up, together with other kinds of outlets for capital like stocks and shares, many commercial and institutional investors ceased building for rent. After 1960, few commercial landlords in Chile, India, Mexico, Nigeria, or South Africa increased their holdings and many investors sold out. In many developed countries, public investment attempted to fill the gap created and built large numbers of housing units. For other reasons, communist governments also followed this route and built state housing on a massive scale. While many governments in poorer countries sought to replicate that example, it was seldom taken up on a large scale, partly because of a lack of resources and partly because the state proved to be an inefficient and highly politicised landlord (see article Rental Market and Rental Policies in Less Developed Countries). Nor did the social housing sector attempt to step in (see below).

Despite the lack of large-scale investors, the absolute number of tenants increased in most cities in Africa, Asia, and Latin America and, in a few, even the proportion grew. If someone was building rental housing, in general it proved to be the small-scale landlord. While some of these investors were middle class, who created space in the formal housing stock, the majority of the new landlords were humbler people living in the growing self-help settlements. Indeed, without the efforts of the world's self-help settlers, there would be very little rental housing in most cities today.

Who Are the Landlords?

One of the problems involved in describing private landlords in developing countries is that until the 1980s, there was very little research on private landlords in poor countries. This reflected governmental obsession with encouraging home ownership and academic obsession with the growth of self-help ownership. Even today only a handful of governments in poor countries have developed some kind of rental housing policy. Unlike the ordinary home owner, applauded as heroes in most societies and subsidised by most governments, private landlords have occupied a netherworld – clearly present but to a large extent invisible.

Landlords have seldom hit the headlines partly because they preferred it that way, tax evasion was not uncommon, and because few tenants protested or mounted rent strikes against private landlords. But it was also a result of the fact that few landlords had many outstanding features. The research published over the last 25 years has shown that most landlords operate on a small scale, don't make much money, and are rather like most other people. Unlike the situation in the nineteenth and early twentieth centuries, landlords no longer come from the ranks of the elite and, generally, they have little political influence. Only in a handful of countries, such as Kenya, have powerful people decided to invest in rental property. In Nairobi, for example, Mugo (2000) reports "that out of a sample of 120 landlords interviewed 57% were public officials (government officers and politicians)".

Small-Scale Landlordism

Most recent research suggests that most landlords in poor cities operate on a small scale and that very few are rich. In Latin America, although there is often a substantial middle-class rental market where the landlords are themselves middle class, the typical landlord is now a former self-help builder. A majority of landlords are now to be found in the self-help settlements renting out rooms in their modest homes. As self-help settlers, they tend to have similar backgrounds and incomes to their tenants and most live in the same building.

These small-scale or 'petty commodity' landlords are interested in making money from their 'investment' but they generally lack the professional skills of the large commercial operators. They do not understand balance sheets or more sophisticated forms of marketing and neither their turnover nor their profits would impress most business managers. They tend to invest in a piece-meal way, when money is available, but, because there are so many of them, the rental housing stock expands. They may be invisible to governments, who do nothing whatsoever to help them and whose rhetoric often seeks to disparage them, but small investors have been responsible for most of the expansion of rental housing in Africa, Asia, and Latin America.

In Africa, most landlords share the same kinds of backgrounds with their tenants. They all tend to be migrants and the landlords differ only insofar as they have usually lived in the city longer and are a little better-off. While wealthy landlords have been noted in Mali and in Kenya, they are very much the exception.

In Asia, large-scale landlordism has developed in a few cities, including Bangkok and several Indian cities, and in Kathmandu, Nepal, civil servants, businessmen, industrialists, and large farmers have become landlords. But the general rule seems to be that most investors are small-scale operators.

In Latin America, the large-scale landlord who once dominated the rental housing scene has virtually disappeared.

Age

Landlords tend to be older than other owners and much older than their tenants. Because of their age, landlords are much more likely to be retired people, to live in larger properties than other families, and to have lived longer in their current home. Even in South Africa where many council house dwellers rent out accommodation in their backyards, they are much older than their tenants.

Male or Female?

Both men and women act as landlords. Most male landlords have a female partner, who often handles the tenants, but many widows and separated women rent out property on their own. Whether men or women dominate the business varies from country to country and depends on local custom and on the demographic structure of the cities.

In some societies, as in much of West Africa and India, most landlords are men because only they are permitted to inherit property. Elsewhere other factors tend to be more important. In Nairobi, most landlords are men because they dominate the political and administrative classes that control access to land in that city. Patterns of migration and ageing also have an influence. Where migration streams to the cities contain more women, as in the Philippines and Latin America, there tend to be more landladies. Where migrant flows are male dominated, the opposite is true. Ageing is also increasingly important. Because women tend to survive longer than men, the older the urban population, the more female landlords there are.

Resident or Absentee Landlords

Most landlords tend to live on the premises. This is nothing new in the history of landlordism even in developed countries where the taking in of 'lodgers' is a long-established strategy among both owners struggling to maintain an income and aspirant property developers. Contemporary landlords in most poor cities are very similar, renting rooms to individuals and families and sharing the facilities. The main exceptions are where large-scale landlordism has developed and where the tenants or new owners of subsidised state housing illegally let or sublet the whole of their property, for example, in Kingston, Jamaica, in Santiago, Chile, or in Mexico City.

Race, Ethnicity, and Discrimination

In many countries, housing tenure is influenced by race and ethnicity. In the United States of America, for example, 70% of non-Hispanic white households owned their home in 1991 but only 43% of black households. Insofar as home owners in the formal sector tend to be more affluent than tenants and income is inversely related to ethnicity, landlords tend to be drawn from certain racial or ethnic groups. But equally important is migration. Insofar as migrants come from a different racial or ethnic group than that of the resident urban population, landlords and tenants are likely to have different ethnic backgrounds.

Sometimes ethnic differences between landlords and tenants lead to discrimination. Certain ethnic groups may be refused accommodation because of the prejudices of the landlord. Landlords in Surat, India, are reported to be reluctant to accept migrants from Orissa who have a reputation for drunkenness and for being 'difficult'.

But there is also plenty of evidence to suggest that many landlords are happy to take in strangers and outsiders, sometimes because they are perceived to be less troublesome. In Mushin, Lagos, "private owners prefer to rent to members of ethnic groups other than their own because, as they report, it is easier to collect rents from those to whom one is not close" (Barnes 1982: 16). Outsiders are also more likely to vacate the premises when requested, unlike certain members of the family.

Other nonracial or ethnic characteristics can also lead to discrimination against tenants. Age, sex, and marital status clearly influence landlords. In Kenya, many landlords are reluctant to rent to single women, although they like widows with children who "pay rent in time and take good care of the structures" (Syagga et al. 2002: 33). In India and Mexico, landlords dislike letting to single men; in Bangalore, it is women-headed households, whether widows or single women, who are less welcome. And, landlords all over the world have always been reluctant to take in large families; in nineteenth-century Britain landlords considered children to be the "worst despoilers of property" (Englander 1983: 10).

Temporary and Casual Landlordism

Why do some home owners let property and others not? For some it is something that they drift into, often starting when a household finds it has extra space. When older children leave home, the parents may rent out the space they have vacated. Sometimes this is a temporary arrangement, when the children need to return home or a member of the extended family needs shelter the tenants may be asked to leave.

Letting property also provides a partial solution to the problem of what to do with a house if it cannot be sold. Some people inherit homes that they do not wish to live in but which they cannot sell. For example, "... there are cultural factors in West African societies which make the sale of personal houses a taboo.... if there is a market for 'ready-made' houses, the size of such a market is immeasurably small" (Arimah, 1997: 110). Elsewhere some owner-occupiers need to move house but are unable to sell it. In Johannesburg, as crime and civil violence increased, many former white tenants who had bought their homes in the central areas fled to the safer northern suburbs. When financial institutions redlined large parts of the inner city, they were unable to sell and became "reluctant absentee landlords" (Morris, 1999: 106).

Profitability

All landlords let property in order to obtain an income but the strategies they follow are highly diverse. Clearly, some landlords carefully calculate the return on their capital, take any incentives that may be on offer from the government, minimise their taxable income, and employ professional accountants and agents. Such 'commercial' landlords are mainly concentrated in the high- or middle-income sectors. However, it is clear that the creation of rental accommodation in some low-income areas has also been perceived to be highly profitable. Such landlords may not follow every facet of real professional practice, but there is no denying their commercial acumen. Landlords in the 'slums' of Nairobi, Bangkok, Benin City, and Bombay have all been reported to operate in a business-like way.

However, most self-help landlords seem much less 'professional' in their behaviour. Unlike the more commercially minded they will not compare their housing investment with the potential returns from other activities. There are exceptions but few small landlords know much about accounting practices or the law. Some even have trouble reading and writing. Some landlords do not seem to be greatly concerned about maximising their income. The rents may be low but they still have the house. Investing in property is vital in providing parents with something to leave the children; something that many owners claim to be one of the key virtues of ownership. Under such circumstances, rents may be a lesser consideration.

While every landlord wants some kind of return from his or her investment, the precise motivation for renting is highly variable. As Kumar (2002: 3) points out renting serves as "a safety net against precarious employment, meeting household expenditure, housing improvements, a regular source of income when moving from waged employment to own account forms of employment, capital investment and rotation in business, as a form of pension after retirement and old age and as investment for the next generation". Most landlords rent out rooms or apartments because they need to supplement a meagre income; indeed, for some, it is their only income. Few are going to get very rich on what they receive from tenants. They let accommodation because they know no other way to make money. Being a landlord means investing in something they broadly understand – bricks and mortar. They do not understand, or indeed trust, most kinds of financial institution, let alone stock exchanges and hedge funds. The virtue of being a landlord lies in the security it offers for the future. After all, large numbers of landlords are old and are living either on their pension or entirely from their rent. But renting out property also helps guard against sudden, unexpected financial difficulties. Unemployment and economic recession are likely to increase potential landlords' willingness to rent.

Tenants often complain that rents are too high, while many landlords say that they are too low. There is no question that some tenants are paying more than they can afford and, over the years, many landlords have no doubt exploited tenants. At the same time, it is equally clear that rents are sometimes too low to attract more investment – a situation particularly likely when rent controls are operating. In practice, research shows that when rents are wholly determined by market forces, they tend to rise and fall in line with real incomes. After all, landlords cannot raise the rent too high without the risk of leaving their property empty. Faced with generalised poverty, most landlords set low rents because their tenants cannot afford to pay more. But because they are receiving relatively little in rent landlords cut back on maintenance and investment. In such circumstances rents are simultaneously too low and too high. Landlords do not receive enough to provide adequate accommodation or to keep their own families out of poverty. At the same time, tenants earning very low incomes are forced to pay a high proportion of their earnings in rent. The problem lies not in rent levels or exploitation by landlords but with urban poverty.

Of course, in exceptional times, this generalisation may not hold up so well. Should a 'natural' disaster destroy some of the housing stock or should rural people be forced to flee in large numbers to the city, rents may rise to levels which the poorest simply cannot pay. The result will be a rise in homelessness and overcrowding. Poor households will either sleep in the streets or rent less space at a lower cost.

Is Renting Socially Polarising?

Today, powerful landlords dominate the rental housing stock only in a few cities in Africa, Asia, or Latin America. The world has changed and most landlords operate on a small scale and tend to let property to people from the same social class. Under such circumstances, the rich cannot easily be accused of exploiting the poor. In any case, many landlords are themselves poor and are reliant on their rents to survive, particularly in the case of older landlords and even more so in the case of widows. Many tenants sympathise with their landlords because they recognise that the latter are similar to themselves. And, of course, most tenants plan to become home owners one day and perhaps build extra rooms which they will rent out.

The main source of housing inequity today is not caused by poor tenants paying too much rent to rich landlords. Much more important is the growth of home ownership and the perverse incentives which encourage the better-off to seek capital gains from buying more expensive property. In the process, rising housing prices exclude the poor from access to home ownership. Social polarisation is even produced among home owners by the differential rates at which the prices of different kinds of homes rise. Property values soar in affluent areas whereas prices in deprived areas tend to rise more slowly and, of course, fall dramatically in times of recession. The current subprime crisis has drawn our attention to the inequities of home ownership and the problems of negative equity and foreclosure. In some former communist cities, such as Hanoi, Vietnam, privatisation of the public housing stock has also contributed to growing inequality.

Informality Versus the Law

Rental-housing practice in poor cities tends to cover the whole spectrum from total legality to total illegality and it is virtually impossible to draw a neat dividing line. Some landlords do not have a formal title to their property, many do not pay for infrastructure and services, and in many cities formal rental contracts are rare. Sometimes landlord–tenant relations obey certain parts of the law but not others – agreements are frequently made orally. But even if every landlord and tenant were to sign a written contract it would help little because of the slowness and expense of the judicial system; the courts in most poor countries serve landlords and tenants badly. Landlords and tenants also ignore the law because they do not understand its complexities and because they cannot afford the legal costs involved.

At times, informality leads to tension between landlords and tenants. Some landlords lock tenants out of the property if they have not paid the rent. Some tenants make too much noise or damage the property. However, research suggests that the large majority of landlord–tenant relationships are relatively amicable. And, given the ineffectiveness and often corrupt nature of state intervention in many poor cities, any attempt to legalise landlord–tenant relationships would arguably make matters worse.

Indeed, the very success of the small landlord suggests that it has been the very absence of government involvement that has provided the opportunity. Unlike those in the formal sector, small landlords have been largely unhampered by rent control, tax, or planning regulations. But a price has to be paid for this informality, in terms of poor living conditions, lack of services, and overcrowding. At the very least the case should be examined of how small landlords might be helped by governments anxious to foster a tenure-neutral policy and to stimulate both expansion and improvement in housing conditions.

The Social Housing Sector

Faced with the reluctance of commercial landlords to create more rental accommodation, many governments in developed countries have increasingly looked towards the social housing sector. But in most poor countries, nonprofit making organisations which provide housing for the poor are scarce. While, cooperatives and associations of squatters and tenants have proliferated in many parts of India and to a degree in South Africa, their development has been limited. In any case, few cooperatives have ever created much accommodation for rent; their main interest has been to defend their tenant members against the landlords and to turn their members into home owners.

Conclusion

Today, rental housing may accommodate up to one billion people across the globe, mainly in urban areas. While formal and informal home ownership is rising in importance in most poor cities, the magnitude of urban growth means that the numbers of tenants are usually increasing. Little of their accommodation is provided by the state or by social housing associations; the main generator of rental housing is the small-scale private landlord. Because letting accommodation has not proved to be particularly profitable, most commercial organisations have left the field open to smaller scale operators. Increasingly the self-help builders in informal settlements have created space – either they have rooms to spare in their own house or they have been prepared to extend their properties. Their main motivation has been to supplement the household income and they regard renting as a safe business, one that they understand. Some of these landlords exploit their tenants but generally landlord–tenant relations are harmonious. The real problem is the poor quality of the accommodation and services available. Arguably, this is less the fault of the landlords than a consequence of the high incidence of urban poverty. If the amount of poverty could be reduced, the quality of most rental accommodation would improve and overcrowding would be reduced.

See also: Home Ownership: Economic Benefits; Housing and the State in China; Housing and the State in Latin America; Housing and the State in South Africa; Housing and the State in South Asia; Housing and the State in the Middle East; Housing Policies in Developing Countries; Housing Subsidies in the Developing World; Migration and Population Mobility; Submarkets; Urbanisation and Housing the Poor: Overview.

References

Arimah BC (1997) The determinants of housing tenure choice in Ibadan, Nigeria. *Urban Studies* 34: 105–124.

Englander D (1983) *Landlord and Tenant in Urban Britain, 1834–1918*, Oxford: Clarendon Press.

Kumar S (2002) Room for manoeuvre: Tenure and the urban poor in India. http://www.worldbank.org/urban/symposium2003/docs/presentations/kumar.pdf

Morris A (1999) *Bleakness and Light: Inner-City Transition in Hillbrow*. Johannesburg: Wits University Press.

Mugo PN (2000) An analysis of the real estate market in the slums: A case study of Kibera slums – Nairobi, Department of Land Development, University of Nairobi.

Further Reading

Amis P (1996) Long-run trends in Nairobi's informal housing market. *Third World Planning Review* 18: 271–285.

Ball M (2002) *RICS European Housing Review 2002*, The Royal Institution of Chartered Surveyors Policy Unit, London.

Barnes ST (1982) Public and private housing in urban West Africa: The social implications. In: Morrison MKC and Gutkind PCW (eds.) *Housing the Urban Poor in Africa*, pp. 5–29. New York: Maxwell School, Syracuse University.

Cadstedt J (2006) *Influence and Invisibility: Tenant in Housing Provision in Mwanza City, Tanzania, Department of Human Geography*, Stockholm: Stockholm University.

Coulomb R (1985) La vivienda de alquiler en las areas de reciente urbanizacion. *Revista de Ciencias Sociales y Humanidades* 6(15): 43–70.

Crankshaw O, Gilbert AG, and Morris A (2000) Backyard Soweto. *International Journal of Urban and Regional Research* 24: 841–857.

Dubel HJ, Brzeski WJ, and Hamilton E (2006) Rental choice and housing policy realignment in transition: Post-privatization challenges in Europe and Central Asia region, *World Bank Policy Research Working Paper* 3884.

Gilbert AG (1983) The tenants of self-help housing: Choice and constraint in the housing markets of less developed countries. *Development and Change* 14: 449–477.

Gilbert AG (1993) *In Search of a Home*, London: UCL Press.

Grant M (2007) Lodging as a migrant economic strategy in urban Zimbabwe. *Development Southern Africa* 24: 77–90.

Ha S-K (2004) Housing poverty and the role of urban governance in Korea. *Environment and Urbanization* 16: 139–155.

Huchzermeyer M (2007) Tenement city: The emergence of multi-storey districts through large-scale private landlordism in Nairobi. *International Journal of Urban and Regional Research* 31: 714–732.

Karki TK (2002) Policies to improve the quality of life in the private rental housing of Kathmandu Metropolitan city, mimeo, Kathmandu.

Kumar S (1996) Landlordism in Third World urban low-income settlements: A case for further research. *Urban Studies* 33: 753–782.

Kumar S (2002) Room for manoeuvre: tenure and the urban poor in India, http://www.worldbank.org/urban/symposium2003/docs/presentations/kumar.pdf

Martin SM and Nell M Associates (2002) *An Assessment of Rental Housing in South Africa*, Report for USAID, Johannesburg.

Morange M (2002) Backyard shacks: The relative success of this housing option in Port Elisabeth. *Urban Forum* 13: 3–25.

Park, S-Y. (2007) Housing and the new welfare state: Perspectives from East Asia and Europe. In: Groves R, Murie A, and Watson C (eds.), *The State and Housing Policy in Korea.* pp. 75–100. Surrey: Ashgate.

Syagga P, Mitullah W, and Karirah-Gitau S (2002) Nairobi situation analysis supplementary study: A rapid appraisal of rents in slums and informal settlements, report prepared for the Government of Kenya and UN-HABITAT Collaborative Nairobi Slum Upgrading Initiative, mimeo

Tipple AG (1988) *The history and practice of rent controls in Kumasi, Ghana.* World Bank, Water Supply and Urban Development Dept. Working paper No. 88-1.

Tran HA and Dalholm E (2005) Favoured owners, neglected tenants: Privatisation of state owned housing in Hanoi. *Housing Studies* 20: 897–929.

UNCHS (1989) *Strategies for Low-Income Shelter and Services Development: The Rental Housing Option,* UNCHS: Nairobi.

UNCHS (2003) *Rental Housing: An essential option for the urban poor in developing countries,* UNCHS: Nairobi.

UNCHS/ILO (1995) *Shelter Provision and Employment Generation,* UNCHS: Geneva.

Private Rental Landlords: Europe

J Hoekstra, M Haffner, H van der Heijden, and M Oxley, Delft University of Technology, Delft, The Netherlands

© 2012 Elsevier Ltd. All rights reserved.

Glossary

Private rental sector Dwellings that are let by private individuals or firms that have a profit objective. Depending on the particular context, private rental dwellings may have market or submarket rents, and they may be subject to more or less government intervention. In general, private rental dwellings are allocated on the basis of supply and demand.

Introduction

For a long time, the private rental sector has been a somewhat forgotten tenure. Both policy makers and house seekers perceived it as a last resort. Tenants would consider private rental housing only if they urgently needed a dwelling and could not find suitable accommodation in the social rental or the owner-occupancy sector. Policy makers who wanted to promote rental housing tended to turn to the social rental sector. Moreover, many governments imposed strict rent regulation and tenant security, which limited the profitability for private rental landlords and hampered new investments. The private rental sector also suffered from a bad image. For many people, it was associated with bad quality housing and profiteering landlords.

In the last two decades, this situation has changed somewhat. In several countries, the decline of the private rental sector has stopped and new policy initiatives, such as the fiscal incentives for private rental landlords in France, have led to renewed interest in investments in private rental housing. Policy makers have also rediscovered the potential of the private rental sector. Increasingly, the sector is seen as a good alternative for social housing, and private rental landlords may sometimes receive subsidies or other forms of government support if they provide rental housing with moderated rents for lower income groups.

This article describes and analyses the developments in the private rental sector in Europe, illustrated with the help of examples from a selected number of mainly Western European countries. It starts by defining the concept. After that, the historical development of the private rental sector is discussed and some international comparative figures are presented. Subsequently, the policies that are relevant for the private rental sector are outlined; with a particular focus on new policy developments that stimulate private rental landlords to provide social housing in exchange for financial support. Finally, the future of the sector is discussed.

Defining Private Rental Housing

The private rental sector, sometimes also called the market or commercial rental sector, can be defined in many different ways. The social and private rental sectors are usually seen as two tenures that exclude each other, each having completely different characteristics on aspects such as ownership, orientation, rent levels, degree of government intervention, and housing allocation (see **Table 1**). However, the reality is often more complicated than the dichotomy as **Table 1** suggests. In practice, the two rental sectors may not differ from each other on all the aspects that are mentioned in the table. For example, private individuals or firms may well provide housing at submarket rents, either stimulated to do so by means of government subsidies, or forced to do so by government-imposed rent regulation. At the same time, public landlords or housing associations may let part of their dwelling stock with an explicit profit objective, for market rents.

Which exact definition of the private rental sector applies depends on the particular context; different countries can apply very different definitions. This is best illustrated by the case of Germany. In this country, the distinction between the private rental sector and the social rental sector is not based on ownership or orientation but on the subsidy system. Any type of German landlord can obtain a time-limited government subsidy as long as the landlord agrees to let the property under a special allocation system and with an agreement on initial rent and rent rises.

Two main types of private rental landlords can be distinguished. First of all, there are the individual private rental landlords. These households typically possess only

Table 1 Aspects defining private rental and social rental housing

	Private rental sector	*Social rental sector*
Ownership	Private individuals or private commercial organisations (firms)	Public organisations or private organisations that are approved by the government (e.g., housing associations)
Orientation	Profit oriented	Nonprofit oriented
Rent levels	Market rents	Submarket rents
Degree of government intervention	No or limited government intervention	Heavily regulated by the government
Housing allocation	On the basis of supply and demand	On the basis of need

one or a few dwellings that they let in order to get a supplement on their income. After 1945 the role of individuals as investors in the private rental sector gradually diminished. In many cases, private persons were not able anymore to raise the financial resources that are needed for the construction of new rental dwellings. Moreover, improvements in the social security and pension system made small-scale landlording less necessary for financial reasons. Second, there are the organisational private rental landlords. This concerns firms that specialise in private renting. In some countries, for example The Netherlands, these firms tend to be tied to financial institutions such as pension funds or insurance companies. Organisational private rental landlords often transfer the responsibility for the letting process to intermediary institutions such as real estate brokers.

Characteristics of Dwellings and Tenants

In most countries, the housing quality of the private rental dwelling stock is less than the housing quality in the social rental sector and the owner-occupancy sector. Furthermore, in several countries the private rental sector can be split up into two subsectors. On the one hand, there is a sector with older, often prewar, dwellings that are mainly in the possession of individual landlords. Housing quality problems are relatively common here because the landlords may not have the resources for, or are not interested in, investments in maintenance and renovation. On the other hand, there often is a segment with postwar dwellings in which organisational private rental landlords play a relatively important role as owners. In the latter segment, which is considerable in size in some countries and fairly small in others, the dwellings are generally relatively expensive and of good quality.

The profile of tenants in the private rented sector differs between countries and is more or less in line with the function of the sector within the different housing systems. But in general, at least in most West European countries, the socio-economic profile of tenants in the private rented sector on average is higher than that of tenants in the social rented sector and lower compared to the owner-occupied sector. Compared to the social rented sector, tenants of private rented dwellings on average have a higher income, a lower level of welfare dependency, and are younger. Behind these averages, the variation in the characteristics of tenants is larger within the private rented sector than within the social rented sector in most countries. Within the private rented sector, various segments can be distinguished: from low-income groups living in low quality, substandard dwellings to high-income groups in high quality, upmarket housing.

The Historical Development of the Private Rental Sector in Europe

After the Second World War the proportion of private rented dwellings in the housing stock of the Western European countries varied from more than 40% (Western Germany) to nearly 60% (The Netherlands). In the postwar period great shifts have occurred in the proportion of various tenure categories. The owner-occupied sector and the social rented sector have increased at the expense of the private rental sector. The decline of the private rental sector was the result of demolition of existing, poor quality private rented dwellings, conversion of private rented dwellings into owner-occupied ones, and relatively little new construction of private rental dwellings. The consequence of this development is that in most countries, a large part of the present private rental sector (often more than half of all private rental dwellings) dates from before 1950.

The strict rent regulation and tenant security that characterised many European countries till the 1980s are often seen as the major culprits behind the decline of the private rental sector. However, political factors play a very important role as well. In the 1950s and 1960s many governments invested heavily in the development of the social rental sector, although the task of this sector was not the same in all countries. As a result the size and role of the social rented sector developed differently in the Western European housing systems. In some countries (particularly Sweden, Denmark, and The Netherlands), the social rental sector developed into a major tenure that accommodated broad sections of the population and offered an attractive alternative to the private rental sector. In other countries (such as Ireland, Belgium, and since the 1970s also the United Kingdom), the social rented sector is smaller and mainly targeted at low-income groups.

Recently, governments in many European countries have withdrawn from the housing market in order to give more room to the market sector. Financial support for social rental landlords has been diminished or sometimes even completely abolished. This often leads to a decline in the size of the social rental sector as well as to a residualisation; lower income groups are increasingly concentrated in social rental dwellings. In many countries, the financial support for the owner-occupancy sector (e.g., fiscal aid) has been diminished as well, although the share of this sector generally keeps on increasing. However, as a result of a big increase in house price, the accessibility of the owner-occupancy sector is often a problem for low-income households and starters on the housing ladder.

If the social rental sector is closed off to middle income groups and the owner-occupied sector becomes financially unattainable or unacceptably risky to some households, a vacuum may come into being on the housing market. In such a situation, new investments in the private rental might offer a way out. Whether such investment really takes place depends among other things on the possibilities of making a sufficient return. In some countries, the government attempts to enhance the investment conditions for private rental landlords by means of deregulation of rents, or subsidies and tax concessions to private rental landlords. In a number of European countries (England, Ireland, Belgium, Germany, France) governments also try to get the private sector involved in social provision.

Reliable international comparative data on the current size of the private rental sector are scarce. Statistics on this topic are not systematically collected on an international level and each country applies its own definition. For example, some countries include dwellings that are provided rent-free in the private rental dwelling stock, whereas others do not. Under these restrictions, **Table 2** provides an indicative overview of the current share of the private rental sector in a selected number of European countries, based on various data sources. Most countries in the table have a private rental sector that consists of between 10 and 25% of the total housing stock. The only exception to this is Germany, where more than half of the dwelling stock is let without government subsidies, thus complying with the German definition of the private rental sector.

As far as the recent development (since 1990) of the private rental sector is concerned, the pattern is mixed. In Finland, Germany, Ireland, Sweden, and the United Kingdom, the share of the private rental has increased since the 1990s. The exact reason for this will differ between countries but it can be expected that deregulation of rents and tenant security, as well as financial incentives by the government, have facilitated this process. Especially in Finland, Ireland, and the United Kingdom, the rent regulation and tenant security were significantly liberalised in the 1980s and 1990s.

In the Southern European countries on the other hand, the share of the private rental sector keeps on decreasing. This might be due to the fact that households in these countries tend to have a strong preference for homeownership, not only to solve their housing needs but also for

Table 2 Share and development of the private rental sector around 2002 in a number of European countries

Country	Share private rental sector	Development since 1990
Finland	15–17%	Increasing
Germany	49–51%	Increasing
Ireland	11–13%	Increasing
Sweden	24–27%	Increasing
United Kingdom	9–11%	Increasing
France	20–23%	Constant
Netherlands	10–12%	Constant
Austria	17–20%	Decreasing
Belgium	25%	Decreasing
Denmark	17–19%	Decreasing
Greece	20%	Decreasing
Italy	14–16%	Decreasing
Portugal	15–21%	Decreasing
Spain	10%	Decreasing

Source: Norris M and Shiels P (2004) *Regular National Report on Housing Developments in European Countries. Synthesis Report*. Dublin: The Housing Unit; Ministry of Infrastructure of the Italian Republic/Federcasa (2006) *Housing Statistics in the European Union 2005/2006*, Rome: Federcasa; and Scanlon K and Whitehead C (2004) *International Trends in Housing Tenure and Mortgage Finance*, London: The Council of Mortgage Lenders.

investment reasons. Moreover, the tenant security is strict in most Southern European countries, which makes landlords reluctant to invest in private rental housing.

Policies towards the Private Rented Sector

Even though the private rental sector is often regarded as a sector in which market forces dominate, government intervention is far from absent. Government policies that are specifically relevant for private renting include: rent control, tenant security, housing allowances, tax concessions, and housing quality policy (**Table 3**).

With the exception of the United Kingdom, in most countries the private rental sector is subject to some form of rent control. Usually a difference is made between rent setting for new contracts and rent adjustment for ongoing contracts. Sweden and The Netherlands are the countries with the strictest rent regulation. In Sweden rents that are negotiated between social landlords and their tenants form the guidelines for rents set in the private rental sector in a locality. In The Netherlands, about 85% of the private rental dwelling stock is subject to rent regulation. Within the Dutch rent-regulated private rental sector, a normative system of quality points is used. The higher the number of quality points, the higher the maximum rent that may be set. As far as rent adjustment is concerned, the Dutch government decides each year on the maximum annual rent increase that is permitted, usually linking this increase to the inflation. In countries like Belgium, France, Germany, Ireland, and Spain the rents for new contracts may be set freely. The annual rent increase is based either on some kind of index (Belgium, France, and Spain) or on market conditions (Germany and Ireland).

Rent regulation of ongoing rental contracts will have an effect only if there is sufficient tenant security. The strongest tenant security can be found in Germany, The Netherlands, and Sweden, where rental contracts in the private rental sector have an indefinite term. In most other countries, rental contracts in the private rental sector have a limited term, varying from one month (England) to several years (Belgium, France, Ireland, and Spain).

For households in the private rental sector housing allowances usually are available. Typically, the amount of allowance that a household receives is largely based on the actual rent that a household pays (The Netherlands, Flanders in Belgium, Sweden). In a few countries (England, Germany), however, some kind of norm or notional rent is used to determine the amount of subsidy. This implies that there is no direct relationship between the actual rent and the amount of housing allowance that a household receives so that consumers may be more interested to search for the 'best deal' (shopping incentive). In most countries mentioned, the housing allowance system is an open-ended system allowing any low-income household (up to the income limit) to apply. The exception is Flanders, where the system has been specifically designed for households which move from a bad quality rental dwelling to a private rental dwelling of standard quality.

One way of subsidising the supply of private rental dwellings is via the income tax system. Some countries

Table 3 Policies for private renting, around 2007

Rent regulation	
New contract	
Free rent setting	Belgium, France, Germany, Ireland, Spain
Regulated rent setting	The Netherlands, Sweden
Annual rent increase	
Based on market developments	Germany, Ireland
Regulated by an index	Belgium, France, Spain, Sweden, The Netherlands
Term of rental contract	
Indefinite	Germany, The Netherlands, Sweden
Limited	Belgium, England, France, Ireland, Spain
Housing allowances	
Based on actual rent	Belgium[a], Ireland, Sweden, The Netherlands
Based on notional rent	England, Germany
Income taxation	
Concession(s) available	France, Germany, Ireland, The Netherlands
Concession(s) not available	Belgium, England
Regulation/subsidisation of housing quality	
Specific	Belgium[a], England, France, Ireland
Not specific	Germany, The Netherlands

[a]Known for Flanders, one of the three federal regions of Belgium.

provide tax concessions to particular private rental landlords. In The Netherlands for instance this is the case for pension funds which are exempt from paying corporate tax on their profits from renting. In Germany a time-limited depreciation deduction is available for any rental property. In Ireland a proportion of the cost of capital expenditures can be deducted from the rental income. In France there are several tax concessions for individual households that invest in the construction or refurbishment of private rental dwellings.

Concerns about the bad quality of dwellings or unsafe dwellings have stimulated governments to either regulate or subsidise investments in quality improvements, usually next to regulation of housing quality in general. England is an example where selective licensing for English private landlords owning houses in multiple occupation (where households in the same building share a kitchen, bathroom or toilet) has been introduced. Flanders and Ireland are also examples of countries using regulation, but with a possibility to penalise (money and/or prison) landlords for offences relating to standards. In France, specific subsidies are available for private rental landlords who invest in improving the quality of their dwellings.

Social Housing Provided through Private Rental Landlords

Housing that is owned privately and rented to tenants, and thus deemed part of the private rented sector, can be used by governments to meet housing needs and thus effectively be a form of social housing. There are several means by which governments use the private sector to supply social housing, as shown by the following examples. In Germany where, as explained above, the standard division of the housing stock into social and private rented sectors on the basis of ownership does not apply, subsidies are provided for dwellings, whether they are new-build or existing dwellings regardless of the type of landlord. This subsidy system, the principles of which were set out after the Second World War, requires that rents are held below prescribed levels for several years while the subsidy is paid. After the subsidy expires, rents can gradually be brought into line with market rents. In France, special loans are available to both social and private rental landlords that wish to provide rented dwellings in the 'intermediate sector'. This sector aims to house tenants with income levels above those for social tenants but below those who can afford to rent in the private market. Around a quarter of such loans go to individual or organisational private rental landlords. They sign a contract with the state for a period of 15 to 30 years and during this period they keep rents below market levels.

In England, private firms are eligible to bid for social housing grants and to manage social housing. Since 2004 the grants have in principle been available to private contractors and developers as well as nonprofit providers.

In Flanders, Belgium, a small number of private landlords let their properties through 'social rental agencies' or letting offices. This gives the landlord a guaranteed rent, although below the market rent, and reduced management costs as a result of the service provided by the agencies. Social rental agencies aim to create an alternative market for vulnerable tenants who are unable to find a social rental dwelling. They allocate dwellings on the basis of needs and some receive subsidies from the government.

In Ireland, through the Rental Accommodation Scheme (RAS) local authorities set up contracts with private landlords who agree to provide accommodation that meets minimum standards. The RAS is expected to expand the amount of private rented accommodation available on a long-term basis to low-income tenants who are unable to access local authority housing. The scheme is also expected to improve the quality of the accommodation provided and increase tenant choice. The local authority makes direct payments to the provider and the tenant makes an income-related contribution to the costs by a payment to the local authority. Landlords benefit from long-term guaranteed rental streams.

The Future of the Private Rental Sector

After several decades of decline, the private rented sector is now expanding in some countries (see **Table 2**). This is due to a combination of increased support by governments and increased demands from certain groups of households. The future growth of the sector will depend on the extent to which such support and demand continues. Favourable polices towards the sector are important in countries where the sector is expanding. Government policies will continue to have, in all countries, important impacts on the size and quality of the sector and the terms on which dwellings are occupied, especially rent levels and security of tenure. Support for investors through grants, fiscal concessions, and market rents are likely to induce positive supply responses. Continuing incentives for improvements to the stock and the implementation of regulations that penalise poor quality are likely to result in more decent homes in the private rented sector. Policies that promote enhanced security of tenure are likely to increase the relative attractiveness of the sector to households seeking accommodation, and demand can be assisted by favourable housing allowance regimes.

Examples have been provided of cases where government support helps to provide a bridge between the social and private rented sectors. This means that the market rented sector is being used for a social purpose and is directly contributing to meeting the needs of households who cannot afford market rents. In some countries, this bridging of the gap is likely to increasingly blur the boundaries between the sectors. Where the relative advantages of owner occupation are limited and private renting provides good security of tenure (e.g., Germany), the demand for private renting is likely to remain strong. In some countries (e.g., England) the restricted ability of potential first-time buyers to become owner occupiers, as a consequence of credit restrictions and less confidence in the investment prospects of home ownership, may, for a while at least, be a source of additional demand. In alternative scenarios, under which home ownership becomes more popular and/or there is an expansion of social housing, the sector will decline as it did in several countries for many years. In short, the fortunes of the private rented sector are inevitably linked to that of the other tenures. In this context government policies that influence the relative desirability of private renting to investors and households will have an important impact on the size and role of the sector.

See also: Access and Affordability: Rent Regulation; Private Rental Landlords: North America; Private Sector Housing Management: Europe; Security of Tenure Legislation in Private Rental Housing; Supply-Side Subsidies for Affordable Rental Housing.

References

Norris M and Shiels P (2004) *Regular National Report on Housing Developments in European Countries. Synthesis Report*. Dublin: The Housing Unit.

Ministry of Infrastructure of the Italian Republic/Federcasa (2006) *Housing Statistics in the European Union 2005/2006*, Rome: Federcasa.

Scanlon K and Whitehead C (2004) *International Trends in Housing Tenure and Mortgage Finance*, London: The Council of Mortgage Lenders.

Further Reading

Boelhouwer PJ and van der Heijden HMH (1992) *Housing systems in Europe: Part I. A Comparative Study of Housing Policy*, Delft: Delft University Press.

Donner C (2000). *Housing Policies in the European Union*, Vienna: Christian Donner.

Haffner M, Hoekstra J, Oxley M, and van der Heijden H (2009) Bridging the gap between social and market rental housing in six European countries? *Housing and Urban Policy Studies 33*, Amsterdam: IOS Press.

Harloe M (1995) The People's Home? *Social Rented Housing in Europe & America*, Oxford UK and Cambridge USA: Blackwell.

Kemeny J (1995) From Public Housing to the Social Market. *Rental Policy Strategies in Comparative Perspective*, London/New York: Routledge.

O'Sullivan E and De Decker P (2007) Regulating the private rental housing market in Europe. *European Journal of Homelessness* 1(December 2007): 95–117.

Oxley M and Smith J (1996) *Housing Policy and Rented Housing in Europe*, London: E & FN SPON.

Priemus H and Maclennan D (eds.) (1998) Private rented housing, special issue for the Netherlands. *Journal of Housing and the Built Environment* 13(3): 197–409.

Whitehead C and Scanlon K (eds.) (2007) *Social Housing in Europe*, London: London School of Economics and Political Science.

Private Rental Landlords: North America

A Mallach, The Brookings Institution, Roosevelt, NJ, USA

© 2012 Elsevier Ltd. All rights reserved.

Glossary

Core housing need An official term used in Canada to measure the number of households with severe housing deficiencies and limited incomes.

Exclusionary zoning The use of municipal land use regulations, particularly zoning, as a means of excluding certain types of housing, and by extension, certain 'undesirable' populations.

Overcrowding A larger number of individuals in a dwelling unit than is appropriate from a health or safety standpoint relative to the size or number of bedrooms in that unit.

Property owners and managers survey (POMS) A detailed survey of a sample of rental housing property owners and managers conducted by the US Bureau of Census in 1995, which offers the most comprehensive picture of the private rental housing industry in the United States.

Rent control A state or local law or ordinance regulating the amount to which landlords can increase the rent of their units and the circumstances under which increases are permitted.

Vacancy rate The number of housing units in a geographic area that are vacant and available for rent, expressed as a percentage of the total rental housing stock in that area.

Key Features of the Private Rental Housing Market

The Role of the Private Rental Sector

Although the United States and Canada are widely seen as nations of home owners, this is not really true. The private rental sector is an important part of both countries' housing markets, with a larger share of their total housing stock than in any EU country except for Germany. Although this is partially attributable to their smaller social housing sector, it also reflects the relative ease with which until recently investors have been able to obtain financing for rental housing.

The private rental market represents roughly 28% of the housing stock in the United States and 25% in Canada. In contrast to the widely held image of rental housing as multiple-unit apartment buildings, half of all rental housing in the United States is in one to four unit structures, with most of those being single-family homes. Many inner cities or inner-ring suburbs contain neighbourhoods in which over half of the single-family homes are rental housing owned by absentee investors. While Canadian data are hard to compare with that from the United States, a substantial – but smaller – share of that country's rental stock is also in single-family or detached duplex structures.

A significant percentage of two to four unit rental properties are owner-occupied structures, where the owner occupies one unit and rents out the others. This housing type, often known as 'duplex' or 'triple-decker' housing, is particularly widespread in the Northeast, where two and three unit mixed-tenure properties make up a large share of the housing stock in many urban areas. Housing of this sort is less common in Canada, where two-thirds of all rental units are in apartment buildings (**Table 1**).

Changing Demand Patterns in the Rental Sector

During the past few decades, the rental market in the United States has changed dramatically. In the 1950s and 1960s, tenure was as often defined by demographics and life cycle as by income. Today, homeownership rates are substantially higher, and single people and minorities who may have been blocked in the past can access home ownership; as a result, in most of the United States tenure is largely a function of income, although single individuals are still more likely to be renters than home owners. The median income of tenants dropped from 83% of the homeowner median in 1950 to 69% in 1960, and to 51% in 2000 (**Table 2**) (the equivalent figure in Canada is 60%). In the 1995 Property Owners and Managers Survey, 38% of multifamily owners characterised their tenants as 'low income'.

This change has major implications for rental property ownership. The steady relative decline in renter incomes has acted as a curb on rent levels, and in some markets led to reduced property maintenance, and in extreme cases, abandonment of rental properties. In the absence of a

Table 1 Distribution of rental housing stock in the United States and Canada by property type in 2000

US classification	United States	Canada	Canadian classification
1 unit, detached	25.5%	13.1%	Single detached house
1 unit, attached	5.8	10.7	Semi-detached or row house
2 units	9.2	8.5	Apartment duplex
3 to 4 units	11.8	67.1	Apartment building
5 to 9 units	13.4		
10 to 19 units	12.0		
20 to 49 units	9.0		
50 or more units	9.0		
Mobile home, recreational vehicle, or boat	4.2	0.6	Movable dwelling

Source: US Annual Housing Survey 2007; Statistics Canada.

Table 2 Median income of renters and home owners in the United States and selected metropolitan areas in 2000

	Median renter income	Median owner income	Renter income as % of owner income
United States	$51 323	$27 362	51%
Boston	$67 659	$32 348	48%
Chicago	$63 438	$31 319	49%
Denver	$62 647	$31 595	50%
Detroit	$59 056	$27 775	47%
Houston	$58 822	$29 969	51%
Los Angeles	$62 118	$30 840	50%
New York	$70 843	$32 293	46%

Source: US Census 2000.

strong social housing sector, moreover, the great majority of low-income renter households in both the United States and Canada depend on the private rental sector for shelter. They are not only subject to serious cost burdens, but often suffer from poor quality housing or overcrowding as well.

This has led to a more sharply bifurcated rental market. While a large share of the rental industry targets lower-income households, a small but growing share aims at satisfying demand for high-quality rental accommodations from affluent young single individuals and couples. This market is closely associated with resurgent demand for downtown living, not only in traditionally mixed-use downtowns like Philadelphia, but in Sunbelt cities and even in otherwise distressed Rustbelt cities. The same pattern can be seen in Canada, most notably in cities like Toronto and Vancouver.

Price, Condition, and Occupancy Trends

Over the past decades, rental housing conditions in the United States have changed dramatically. While in 1950 only 20% of renters spent more than 30% of their income on rent, by 2007 that percentage had increased to nearly 50% of all renters. 25% of renters spent more than 50% of their income for rent. The physical condition of rental housing has improved; nearly all housing in the United States offers complete plumbing, heating, and kitchen facilities, although substandard conditions are still not uncommon in inner-city and rural areas. Overcrowding remains a serious problem, particularly in areas with heavy immigration and high housing costs, such as California and the New York metropolitan area (**Figure 1**).

Canada characterises housing conditions from the perspective of 'core housing need', the number of households with problems of affordability, overcrowding, or housing condition. Rental housing deficiencies closely resemble those in the United States. Excluding those households whose incomes would permit them to access acceptable housing, 28% of all Canadian renters, or roughly 1 million households, had core housing needs in 2001. Of these, nearly three-quarters experienced affordability problems alone; among the rest, renters in overcrowded conditions outnumbered those in substandard housing by roughly two to one.

The Aging of the Rental Stock

For both economic reasons and the effects of public policy, private rental housing in both the United States and Canada tends to be considerably older than owner-occupied housing. New rental housing is not being produced and older, obsolete units are not being replaced at rates commensurate with their share of the housing stock, or the marketplace need for rental housing. In 2006, 13%

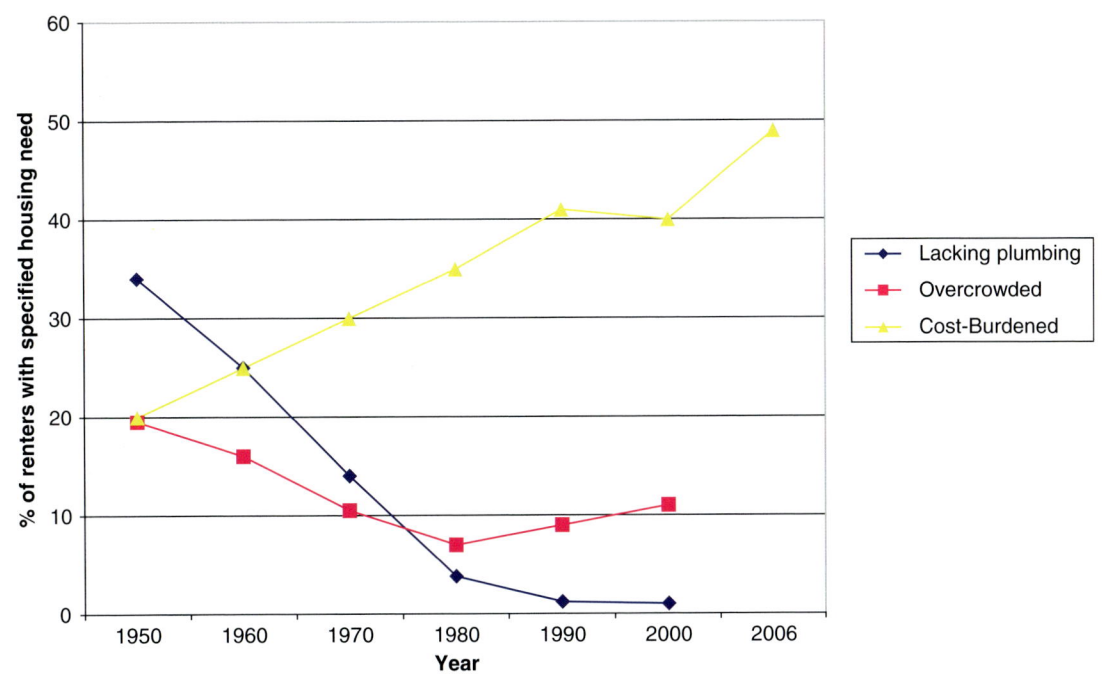

Figure 1 Trends in rental housing needs 1950–2006.
Source: US Census of Housing; American Community Survey.

of the rental stock in Canada was 15 years old or less, compared to 26% of the owner-occupied stock.

The overall trend is similar in the United States but less pronounced. During the 1990s, rental completions accounted for 16% of all housing units in the United States compared to only 9% in Canada (**Table 3**). New rental construction in the United States, however, is heavily concentrated at the extremes – means-tested housing constructed with public sector assistance and upscale housing for affluent young households. Erosion of the rental stock is greatest among 'middle-market' rentals in small multifamily buildings with 10 to 49 units.

This trend carries with it serious implications for the future of the private rental sector. With production of new rental units significantly below demand, economic theory would suggest that rents are likely to increase to reflect a supply/demand imbalance. While that is true in some areas, the ability of landlords to raise rents is often constrained either by low renter incomes or by public sector regulation. Rent control, which may further depress rental housing production, is widespread in Canada (six provinces have some form of rent control) and in some key regions of the United States, such as California and the New York metropolitan region.

Moreover, other means exist to expand rental supply where regulatory barriers or economic conditions make it unfeasible to build new rental housing. In many areas, supply is created by investors buying formerly owner-occupied housing and converting it to rental occupancy, a practice which in some cases can hasten destabilisation of the neighbourhoods where it is taking place. Acquisition of condominium units by investors is another common way of expanding rental housing stock, although its incidence has recently been reduced by lender reluctance to

Table 3 Production of rental and owner-occupied housing in Canada

	Owner-occupied housing	Rental housing	Rental share of housing stock	Rental share of production during period	Share of owner stock added during period	Share of rental stock added during period
TOTAL	8 509 780	3 878 500	31.3%			
1991–1996	682 990	203 240		22.9%	8.0%	5.2%
1996–2001	679 780	132 515		16.3%	8.0%	3.4%
2001–2006	875 045	173 820		16.6%	10.3%	4.4%
TOTAL 1991–2006	2 237 815	509 575		18.5%	26.3%	13.0%

Source: Canada Mortgage and Housing Corporation (CMHC).

finance purchase of condominium units in which more than a modest share of the units are investor-owned.

Elsewhere, particularly in suburban areas where construction of multifamily housing is often impeded by exclusionary zoning, additional rental supply is provided through the informal sector through the often-illegal conversion of single-family houses into multifamily occupancy. These means of augmenting rental supply are also significant in Canada, where they are referred to as the 'secondary rental sector'. Including rental of single-family houses, this sector represents roughly one-third of the Canadian private market rental sector.

Reflecting the availability of these means of augmenting the rental supply, rental housing vacancy rates have steadily risen over the past few decades in the United States, averaging close to 10% since the middle of 2003 (**Figure 2**). In Canada, in marked contrast, rental vacancy rates over the same period have been much lower, falling to 2.2% in the fall of 2008.

The Private Rental Housing Industry

Ownership

Ownership of private rental housing is highly diversified in both the United States and Canada. The majority of units are owned by small investors in the United States, while the Canadian rental stock is roughly evenly divided between small owners and medium/large-scale owners.

The great majority of single-family rental properties in the United States are owned by individuals, often by a husband and wife. The typical owner is in his or her late fifties and has a job unrelated to property ownership; of those who do not, however, most have retirement or other income, since few earn all of their income from their properties. While historically most small owners have been long-term investors, the 1998–2006 housing bubble attracted large numbers of short-term speculators into the industry – the share of home purchase loans for one to four family properties in Nevada made to absentee owners tripled from 9% in 1999 to 27% in 2005. As prices have come back down in 2008 and 2009, the ranks of investor-buyers in the United States have begun to grow once again.

Ownership is highly dispersed. Nearly half of all owners of single-family detached rental properties own only one property, with another quarter owning two to four properties, while 70% of the owners of two-family rental properties own either one or two properties. By contrast, ownership of large multifamily buildings is usually in the hands of partnerships or corporations (**Table 4**). Real Estate Investment Trusts (REITs) play a relatively small role in rental property ownership, representing less than 5% of the stock in Canada and less than 1% (in 1995) in the United States.

This bifurcation carries over into management and maintenance practices. Property maintenance of one to four unit properties tends to be carried out by the owner himself, in sharp contrast to the professionalised

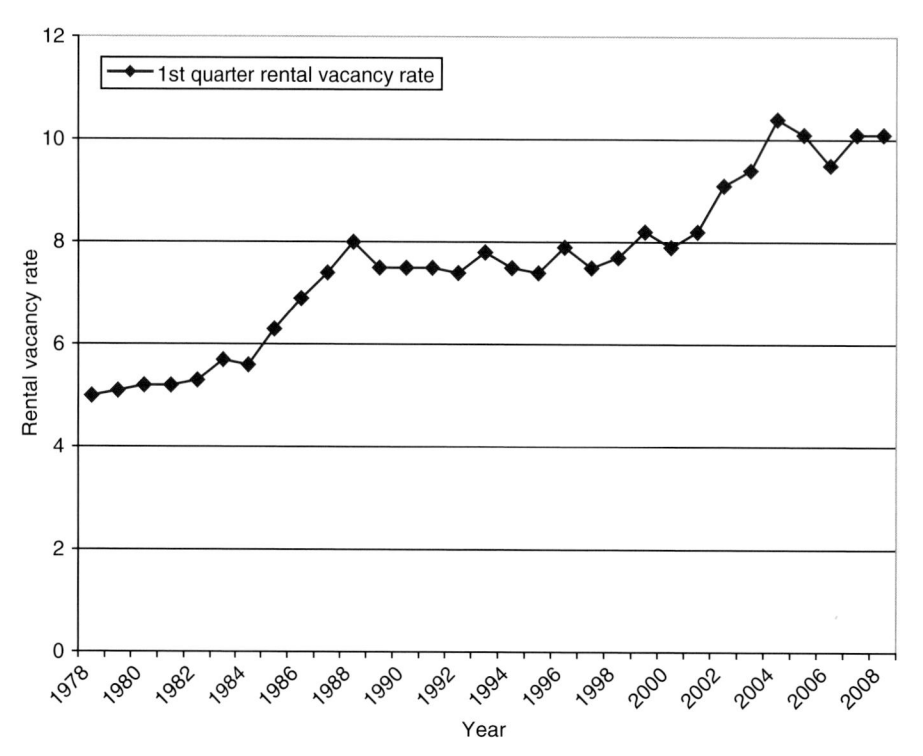

Figure 2 Rental vacancy rate trend in the United States 1978–2008.
Source: Housing Vacancy Survey, U.S. Bureau of the Census.

Table 4 Ownership of rental housing in the United States by property size in 1995

	Total	<5 units	5–49 units	50+ units
Individual investor, husband/wife	86.3%	89.9%	74.4%	30.6%
Partnership	5.7	3.9	10.7	38.3
Real Estate Investment Trust	0.7	0.6	1.2	2.6
Corporation	2.9	1.9	6.7	16.6
Other (including nonprofit entities)	2.7	2.2	4.6	7.1

Source: Property Owners and Managers Survey (POMS).

maintenance and management systems employed by large corporate rental property owners. This difference in approach has powerful implications for the economics of rental property ownership.

Financing

The availability of financing for acquisition or development of rental property has been critical to the vitality of the private rental industry in the United States. Until the onset of the 2007 financial crisis, investors seeking to acquire single-family properties found it nearly as easy to obtain mortgage financing as homebuyers. While paying a somewhat higher interest rate they were able to obtain financing with modest down payments, or finance the entire acquisition by combining a first and a second mortgage, a practice known as 80:20 or 'piggyback' financing. Easy financing helped fuel an explosion in speculative buying of single-family properties in both inner cities and new Sunbelt subdivisions in the late 1990s.

A sophisticated multifamily housing finance system has emerged in the United States, combining public markets, private markets, and credit supplied or insured by government-sponsored enterprises (GSEs) or insured by government agencies, primarily the Federal Housing Administration (FHA). Despite its depth, the system has two significant limitations. First, it is highly reliant on support by public and quasi-public entities; since 2007, the FHA and the GSEs have been the sole vehicles through which multifamily financing remains available. Second, it strongly favours large-scale projects by well-capitalised entities over small projects. Multifamily projects under 50 units often have great difficulty finding capital, and where they do, it is available only at greater cost and on less-favourable terms. Specialised lending entities, such as the Community Preservation Corporation in New York, have emerged to fill this gap.

The Canadian system for multifamily finance is more limited, which may contribute to the lower levels of private rental housing production in Canada. Canadian lenders are more conservative, and tend to impose strict underwriting and loan-to-value standards on multifamily lending. While the Canada Mortgage and Housing Corporation (CMHC) supplements private lending activities, neither its resources nor the scope of its activities are comparable to the combined efforts of the GSEs and the FHA. The CMHC's programmes for rental housing renovation are limited to housing built to serve low-income tenants, and do not benefit the private rental industry generally. Some cities, such as Montreal, offer programmes to increase renovation of the rental housing stock.

Economic Issues

Despite the availability of financing, operating private rental housing in many parts of the United States is far from a lucrative proposition. According to the Property Owners and Managers Survey (POMS), large numbers of landlords do not make an operating profit, and roughly one-third of the owners of one to four unit properties lose money (**Table 5**). The profitability of rental operations reflects a sharp difference between the different housing types that make up the rental stock. While mortgage payments typically eat up only 38% of the rent receipts in large multifamily properties, they take 77% of the rental receipts from single-family rentals (**Table 6**).

Operating cost profiles vary sharply by building size and type. The owners of large properties, who are rarely involved in day-to-day management, usually maintain highly professionalised operations with significantly higher

Table 5 Profitability of rental housing operations by building size

	1 unit	2–4 units	5–19 units	20+ units
Made profit	45%	46%	58%	70%
Broke even	21%	20%	16%	9%
Lost money	34%	34%	26%	21%

Source: POMS.

Table 6 Costs and net operating income as percentage of rental receipts by building size (buildings with mortgages)

	1 unit	2–4 units	5–49 units	50+ units
Mortgage payments	77%	65%	51%	38%
Real estate taxes	12%	13%	10%	8%
Net operating income	11%	22%	39%	54%

Source: Residential Finance Survey 2001.

operating costs than smaller buildings. The difference is multiplied by building type, with high-rise buildings having much higher operating costs than low-rise buildings with similar numbers of units, reflecting such features as elevators, structured parking, and greater ratios of common space to dwelling unit space. The Institute of Real Estate Management reported in 2004 that total operating expenses for high-rise buildings in the United States were $6.27 per square foot of rentable area, or $500 per month for a modest 950-square-feet apartment.

By contrast, owners of small buildings, particularly one to four family units, are more likely to be hands-on managers, who perform much of the maintenance themselves, and typically do not budget their time and that of family members as a cost against rent receipts. This also reflects a major difference between the two groups' expectations. While large corporate or partnership owners expect a positive cash flow on a regular basis – and are likely to unload properties that fail to deliver – small owners more often buy and hold properties for appreciation and are less dependent on cash flow. Thirty per cent of the owners of single-family rental properties reported to the Residential Finance Survey in 2001 that their mortgage payments alone exceeded their rental income.

Private Rental Housing and Public Policy

As in any developed country, many public policies and practices have emerged that affect the private rental housing industry. While some of these may be designed explicitly to support the industry, others may have hostile intent, while still others may have inadvertent effects on the industry.

Neither the United States nor Canada can be said to have a clear rental housing strategy or a coherent sense of how rental housing fits into larger housing policy. In the United States, in particular, housing policy in recent decades has been a de facto homeownership policy, an often-irresponsible effort to increase the homeownership rate among lower-income households and people of colour. Rental housing has been at most an afterthought.

The sole area where private landlords frequently intersect with the federal government is the Housing Choice Voucher programme (initially known as Section 8), under which low-income families receive rent vouchers to enable them to afford housing in the private rental market. The programme is similar to European housing allowance programmes; it is not an entitlement programme, however, but rather one in which large numbers of eligible households compete for a much smaller supply. As of 2009, some 2 million vouchers are in use, representing roughly 6% of the total rental market. Although designed to foster the deconcentration of low-income families, vouchers tend to be geographically concentrated, particularly in high-cost coastal metropolitan regions, tending to magnify the market distortion and social effects of the programme. While Canada has had some demand-side programmes since the 1980s, they grew significantly as a result of the federal 2001 Affordable Housing Initiative, which provided funds for a Rent Supplement Program administered by the nation's provinces under agreements with the federal government.

Regulation of the Rental Industry

The rental housing industry is most powerfully affected by state (or provincial) and local regulation. State and local governments impose often-stringent housing code standards, landlord registration requirements, rent controls, and more, which affect the quality and economic viability of the existing rental stock and the attractiveness of future residential investment. Local land use regulations often impede and only rarely encourage the construction of new private market rental housing. Some local governments with large rental stocks, however, offer landlords training, technical support, and financial assistance, usually in the form of low-interest or deferred loans for property improvement.

While large multifamily landlords tend to deal with regulation in their stride, for most small landlords, government is a problematic, even punitive force. The legal system is widely seen as insensitive to the realities of the low-margin business in which small landlords are engaged, both in the proliferation of different regulations problematic in themselves, and second, in the manner in which they are administered and the burden they place on the landlord (**Table 7**). Even facially reasonable regulations can become burdensome if administered arbitrarily, or where the political climate is hostile to small landlords.

Table 7 Regulations and restrictions affecting rental housing operation

Category	1 Family detached	1 Family attached	2–4 Family	5+ Family
Percentage responding that regulations or restrictions make it difficult to operate the rental unit:				
	22.5%	29.2%	47.5%	53.3%
Which restrictions or regulations (% of those responding affirmatively above)?				
High property taxes	73.1	62.2%	50.3%	38.4%
Lead-based paint	17.3	25.8	13.3	10.3
Waste disposal	15.5	15.0	10.4	13.0
Asbestos	15.0	14.6	8.2	8.9
Parking restrictions	12.0	29.0	18.8	21.2
Americans with Disabilities Act	11.7	14.8	6.1	11.6
Zoning/use of property	11.2	11.2	8.2	7.1
Water quality	9.2	8.5	4.9	5.2
Radon	8.2	10.3	3.8	3.5
Rent control	6.8	13.2	7.7	12.3
Utility hookup limits	6.7	9.3	5.6	5.7
Historic preservation	2.8	9.5	4.6	2.4

Source: POMS.

Code enforcement, particularly where enforced stringently or insensitively, can easily conflict with the 'good enough' approach of many landlords in lower-income areas, an approach on which the continued existence of a stock of adequate, if not outstanding, older housing at affordable prices depends. Strict code enforcement has often been linked to owners in lower-income areas abandoning their rental properties, a link that, although yet to be rigorously tested, appears plausible.

Rent control is less widespread but still fairly common in areas with large rental property inventories, where it is often enacted through pressure from organised tenant groups concerned about uncontrolled rent increases. In recent years, there has been some backlash at the state level, often reflecting pressure from landlords or development interests. Massachusetts has banned local rent control outright, while other states have exempted newly constructed rental housing from rent control, either entirely or for some fixed number of years. While there is widespread sentiment among economists that rent controls are an inefficient and arguably counter-productive public policy, this view has been challenged, particularly where the rent control machinery offers a variety of 'safety valves', allowing landlords increases to cover the cost of tax increases or capital improvements, or mitigate hardship conditions.

More pernicious is the practice of using local land use regulation to place barriers in the path of constructing new rental housing, whether subsidised or through the private market. Such practices, a form of exclusionary zoning, are widespread in many suburban areas, despite a number of state court decisions over the years seeking to curb their use. Regulations routinely limit the amount of land zoned for multifamily housing 'as of right'; that is, where approval does not require discretionary action by a municipal board. This reflects hostility to higher-density housing and to renters as well as fear that property tax revenues from such developments will not cover public, particularly school, costs. Where multifamily housing is permitted, it is often under conditions designed to limit the number of school children, or to ensure that it is expensive, upscale housing.

Conclusion

Both the United States and Canada are fortunate to have substantial private rental housing industries which accommodate – for the most part in adequate quality – much of each nation's population, particularly their lower-income households. This industry has grown largely without public sector support, in the face of public sector policies that have strongly favoured home ownership and single-family homebuilding over rental construction.

The subprime mortgage debacle and the collapse of the 1998–2006 housing bubble made clear the dangers of a one-sided homeownership policy. With homeownership rates in the United States dropping, the importance of a vital rental industry was more widely recognised. By 2008, policy makers were calling for greater emphasis on the rental sector, although it remained unclear how this would translate into specific programmes or policy initiatives.

Much of the vitality of the private rental industry, however, stems from its nature as a dispersed, localised industry with millions of separate players operating largely under the public policy radar screen. The critical task for public policy in the future will be how to nurture this decentralised industry, avoiding excessive involvement while setting a minimum floor for quality and responsible ownership in the industry.

See also: Private Rental Landlords: Developing Countries; Private Sector Housing Management: North America; Social Housing Landlords: North America.

Further Reading

Arnott R (1995) Time for revisionism on rent control? *Journal of Economic Perspectives* 9: 99–120.

Belsky ES, Goodman J, and Drew R (2004) *Middle Market Rentals: Hiding in Plain Sight*. Cambridge, MA: Joint Center for Housing Studies of Harvard University.

DiPasquale D and Cummings JL (1992) Financing multifamily rental housing: the changing role of lenders and investors. *Housing Policy Debate* 3: 77–116.

Housing Supply Working Group (2001) *Affordable Rental Housing Supply: The Dynamics of the Market and Recommendations for Increasing Supply*. Toronto, ON: Ontario Ministry of Municipal Affairs and Housing.

Gilderbloom JI and Appelbaum RP (1987) *Rethinking Rental Housing*. Philadelphia, PA: Temple University Press.

Goodman J (1999) The changing demography of multifamily rental housing. *Housing Policy Debate* 10: 31–57.

Katz B and Turner MA (2007) *Rethinking U.S. Rental Policy: Building on State and Local Innovations*. Washington, DC: The Brookings Institution.

Mallach A (2007) *Landlords at the Margins: Exploring the Dynamics of the One To Four Unit Rental Housing Industry*. Cambridge, MA: Joint Center for Housing Studies of Harvard University.

Malpezzi S (1998) Private rental markets in the United States. *Journal of Housing and the Built Environment* 13: 353–386.

Miron JR (1995) Private rental housing: The Canadian experience. *Urban Studies* 32: 579–604.

Newman SJ (2005) *Low-End Rental Housing: The Forgotten Story in Baltimore's Housing Boom*. Washington, DC: The Urban Institute.

Retsinas NP and Belsky ES (eds.) (2007) *Revisiting Rental Housing: Policies, Programs and Priorities*. Washington, DC: Brookings Institution Press.

Retsinas NP and Belsky ES (2008) *America's Rental Housing: The Key to a Balanced National Policy*. Cambridge, MA: Joint Center for Housing Studies of Harvard University.

Relevant Websites

www.cmhc-schl.gc.ca – Canada Housing and Mortgage Corporation library
www.jchs.harvard.edu – Joint Center for Housing Studies of Harvard University
www.macfound.org – MacArthur Foundation
www.census.gov – Property owners and managers survey
rhol.org/rental/homepage.asp – Rental housing on line
www.urban.org – The Urban Institute

Private Sector Housing Management: Asia Pacific

EC-M Hui, The Hong Kong Polytechnic University, Hong Kong SAR, P R China
TH Khan, University Technology Malaysia (UTM), Skudai, Johor, Malaysia

© 2012 Elsevier Ltd. All rights reserved.

Glossary

Common property Real property in a multiple ownership (MO) situation, where each co-owner has an undivided interest. In an MO situation, it usually refers to common areas shared by co-owners inside or outside the building, such as lobby, corridor, gardens, and so on.

Management companies A professional organisation that can be hired by owners or owners' committees to manage a property. In multiple ownership situations, such companies are usually hired to manage the common properties.

Multiple ownership A property where there is more than one owner. By property, it can denote piece of land, buildings on the land, flats and other spaces inside the buildings, and spaces on the land outside the buildings.

Owners (or co-owners) A person who has the right on a property by virtue of legal possession.

Owners' committee A central authoritative body of owners (co-owners). One form of it is to include all (co-) owners of a property, while the other is to systematically elect a body that is made up of some of the owners who can represent all of them.

Private sector housing Housing built by individuals or private sector developers for sale or rent.

Property Land, buildings, flats, and premises including common areas inside and outside buildings and on land.

Property management Maintenance of the value of property by creating and preserving a well-ordered environment.

Property manager A professional who, either as a freelancer or as an employee in a property management company, contributes professional knowledge in order to manage a property.

Public sector housing Housing built by the state.

Strata title system A system in multiple ownership situations where each co-owner owns the common property as well.

Introduction

Property management refers to the maintenance of the value of a property by creating and preserving a comfortable, safe, as well as well-ordered living, working, and shopping environment. It also involves the arrangement of advice and support, and working with other agencies to achieve this goal. Managing property has been a prominent service in Asian countries such as Singapore, Hong Kong, Japan, and China. These countries were chosen for this article because they have their own significant elements regarding the property management issues within the region. China represents a developing country, Japan has one of the most prosperous economies in the world, whereas Hong Kong and Singapore represent two of the most developed 'newly industrialised' countries. In terms of property management, each has its own distinctive characteristics in terms of style, organisation, and corporate structure.

The Development of Property Management Industry in Private Sector Housing

Rapid urbanisation associated with high density of population has brought about a phenomenal growth of residential buildings in this region in the form of high-rise building blocks consisting of numerous flats. It has become a popular solution for quick supply of housing stock. Here, the term high-rise refers to building blocks ranging from six storeys to even 50 or 60 storeys, which are common in this region. Both public and private sectors are involved in developing these building blocks as a means to supply housing stock. The supply can come in the form of individual blocks or a group of blocks popularly termed as a housing estate. The term property is used to denote not just land, but also the individual flats and the surrounding areas. The vastness of these properties has brought with it a new kind of concern, which is the management of these properties. However, the term 'property management' essentially deals only with the elements of properties on which all users have common rights such as entrance to the housing estate, entrance to the individual blocks, lobbies, lifts, landscapes, internal streets, building facades, roofs, service pipes, and so on, which can be termed as common property. Thus, 'common property' can be defined as real property owned by tenants in common, who have undivided interests in that property.

In the case of public housing, where the state or some other form of organisation is responsible for developing the building blocks and where the users are only tenants, the problem associated with property management is less severe because such a developer retains ownership of the whole property and is the sole regulator in case of any dispute in property management issues. However, the situation gets complicated in cases of private housing, where there are numerous co-owners in a single building block, and many more in the whole housing estate; this demands strong statutory control to solve concerns related to property management.

This situation, referred to as a multiple ownership (MO) situation, varies in definition from country to country, and thus the statutory controls also have different forms in different countries in this region. In some countries, such as Hong Kong, co-owners are given a specific number of shares of exclusive rights over their own flat, but an undivided share over the common property. In some other countries, such as Singapore, each co-owner is also entitled to share common property in proportion to the share values of his/her own flat, and the share values are based on the total area of the owned flat or its capital value or a combination of both.

The first one is known as common law system and the latter as strata title or condominium system. In the strata title system, each co-owner has an interest in the common property, and therefore can have a veto action against the others regarding any dispute in its usage. This can cause difficulties in common properties, in a situation popularly described as the 'tragedy of commons'; the common properties can suffer from over-usage with the co-owners becoming over-active. This ultimately creates the necessity to engage a third party with the help of necessary statutory controls in order to take care of the common property so that the common properties can be effectively used by all co-owners. On the other hand, in the common law system, the landlord retains the ownership of the common properties but allows the co-owners to use them only with a limited right, an act defined as 'easement'. However, when any dispute arises in the usage of common property, for example, unauthorised dumping, illegal building works, and so on, co-owners usually prefer nonaction, a situation popularly described as the 'tragedy of anti-commons'. Therefore the common properties are likely to suffer from under-usage and hence the need for external intervention to take care of that situation.

If the number of co-owners is few, both situations could historically be solved by the owners themselves as it was done historically. However, in this region, the current MO system in building blocks brings a huge number of co-owners together, and therefore professional intervention has become a popular solution for property management. This has given rise to many professional property management companies in the region.

However, there is a need to create a central authority in the MO situation, which has the power to hire the property management companies. This is a challenge as huge numbers of co-owners need to be united. Different countries have adopted different systems for that. Some of them have strong statutory bases (e.g., Singapore), while some other countries suggest voluntary participation (e.g., Hong Kong) to create that central authority. In either situation, the similarity lies in the fact that once that authority is formed, it has the legal power to hire and give the contract to property management companies.

As property management companies have proved effective in managing the common properties in these buildings, their demand is on the rise, and the competition between companies has become higher with each of them trying to raise the standard in order to attract more contracts. This has opened up a market for a newer category of professionals termed 'property managers', who get institutional training in tertiary institutions along these lines before starting a career in this field. Many universities in this region now offer related disciplines and attract young achievers in the field of professional property management. This eventually enhances the benchmark of the service quality provided by property managers and the property management companies they work for.

The benchmarks of property management companies in this region have reached certain levels and two major aspects have been a standard in most countries. The first one involves the duties for property management companies which include (but are not limited to) the following:

- Maintaining safety and security of the premises (engaging staff at the reception or entrance to protect the premises from intruders, CCTV monitoring in lobbies, lifts, deep corners in alleys or corridors, etc.)
- Maintaining cleanliness and overall hygiene of the premises ('regular' such as cleaning of premises, lifts, and landscapes, and 'on demand' such as upgrading facade outlook, pesticide usage, landscape treatment, and gardening)
- Protecting unauthorised development inside the common property (storage in common places, unauthorised

building works such as billboards and advertisements, etc.)
- Promotional activities to encourage social interaction among users (decoration of the premises, organise activities on special occasions, arrange free newspapers, distribute advertising on occasions in the neighbourhood, shuttle bus service for users to strategic locations in the city, etc.)
- Legal actions (take part in contractual agreements, show empty flats to potential users, advertise for rentable or saleable flats, etc.)
- Self-enhancing activities (arrange feedback questionnaires from users for self-improvement studies or research purposes, staff training for their professional development, etc.)

The second one involves the qualitatively assessable professional attitude of property management companies based on which the central authorities can hire, renew, or terminate contracts. These may include (but are not limited to) the following:

- Inefficient action to solve particular problems (not being able to maintain desirable hygienic conditions in the premises, inefficient handling of security, etc.)
- Lack of communication with owners (irregular meetings, failure to respond to the central authority on particular occasions, etc.)
- Lack of managerial action (failure to create an overall desired environment in the premises, etc.)

Property Management across Asia-Pacific

The following briefly describes the existing systems in property management based on their style, organisation, and corporate structure in four countries in the Asia-Pacific region. To conclude, a comparative analysis will show the different relative merits and demerits of the respective systems.

Singapore

In Singapore, the number of strata developments is significant and is constantly increasing due to land scarcity. There are different types of strata developments such as single use and simple and complex mixed use. The fundamental features of strata title are the separation and differentiation between the ownership of common property and the ownership of individual units. Improper management of common property often affects the depreciation in the value of the property.

Management corporations (MCs) are responsible for maintaining and managing the common property in multiple property developments. Common property includes common facilities such as lifts and car parks, which unit owners own shares in as tenants-in-common. MCs work closely with all unit owners in order to make sure that the latter have a say in the management of their individual units and its common property.

Such management of common property can work either through an 'in-house management team' or through a managing agent appointed by the MC. There is no difference in superiority between the two systems. This depends on the given MC's approach to management. For instance, in order to achieve efficiency, they can enjoy cost savings by directly engaging a professional management agent. However, MCs typically employ in-house teams when they want to exercise direct control over the daily and long-term functions of the strata development.

Hong Kong

The enforcement of a 'deed of mutual covenant' (DMC) defines the rights and responsibilities of the owners and tenants. Additionally, the government has introduced a series of ordinances/regulations relating to building management, such as the Building Management Ordinance (BMO), the Fire Safety Ordinance, and the Electrical Worker Registration Scheme.

In Hong Kong, the organisational structure takes the form of an owners' incorporation (OI). Owners are encouraged to elect their representatives to represent themselves on a management committee, which is involved in the daily operations of a building. Under the administration of this committee, owners can supervise and terminate the services of a property management company that does not perform satisfactorily. It can also buy third-party risk insurance.

Formation of OI is voluntary and commonly there are a number of OIs in older Chinese buildings where the number of owners is limited (usually less than 10), and thus the absence of property management companies as well. However, nowadays, major property developers such as Cheung Kong (Holdings) Limited, Henderson Land Development, and Sun Hung Kai Properties Limited encourage the formation of OIs and engage professional property management services during the initial periods of handover (e.g., the first year) according to the building's use, quality, size, location and age, ownership profile, and the capability and strategy of that property management company itself. For instance, a high-standard management service can be reflected in high-rent locations. Moreover, the management fee is charged largely based on the actual expenditure, including staff salaries, administrative expenses, equipment maintenance, cleaning costs, and gas costs.

The government lets private management companies manage the common properties inside public housing estates as well (e.g., Link REIT). However, the quality of the service is lower than that in the case of private housing as the users in such housing have comparatively lower earnings and may not be able to afford a higher management fee.

Japan

Japan has established the rules of property management within the context of complex legal relationships between owners, between owners and owners' committees, and between owners and property management companies.

The government has emphasised the role of intermediaries in providing training for the property management staff, supervising them, giving market information to property management companies, and so on. Members of these associations, such as 'senior housing management associations', 'elevators management associations', and 'residential management associations', have a close relationship with property management companies.

In some smaller residential areas, owners can achieve self-management through this highly specialised division of work. Moreover, under the law in Japan, the property management professionals should be registered and have passed the relevant professional examinations. Similarly, the property management companies should have a licence from the relevant government departments before operating their businesses.

China

At present, there are two kinds of management patterns in China. The reason is because there are differences in the speed of the economic development and economic reforms in different parts of the country. In those big cities where market economies develop faster, people typically enjoy professional property management services that provide comprehensive management services. However, most cities in China still lag behind and continue to follow a traditional administrative pattern that lacks integrated services and concentrates only on the maintenance of houses.

Property management companies first appeared in the southern city of Shenzhen in the 1980s. The numbers of such companies have dramatically increased since then because of the reform of public housing management offices. However, the setting up of the owners' committees usually does not quite follow democratic rules. For instance, property management companies occasionally appoint their own staff to the owners' committees to act as representatives.

The Chinese government has recognised that a unified approach to property management is essential.

In 1994, the 'Regulation of Property Management in Residential Estates in Shenzhen Special Economic Zone' was first established for local regulation concerning homeowners' organisations. Not long after, the name of 'owners' management committee' was changed into 'owners' committee'. Similar owners' organisations were also introduced in other provinces and cities. In 2003, the State Council issued 'State Ordinance of Property Management', stating that the owners' representatives and developers should have the owners' assembly conducted under the guidance of the relevant property management authority. In order to put forth the policy, 'Rules for the Owner's Assemblies and Owners' Committees in Shenzhen' were taken into effect in 2005. A 'residents' committee' was introduced to have control over owners' organisations. Two years later, the Chinese central government released the 'Real Right Act of People's Republic of China', stating that the owners may have an owners' assembly whereby they vote for an owners' committee.

Recently, a 'zero-fee' policy has sometimes been adopted in different forms in the property management industry. In one of its forms, some property developers use rental income to pay for the management services they provide. In another form, in some areas, management fees are paid for mainly by subsidies from government, authorities, or state-owned companies. Hence, it is hard for the property manager to judge accurately the quality of service to be provided and to establish an effective regulatory mechanism.

Conclusion

To sum up, the property management industry plays an important role in Asian countries, particularly Singapore, Hong Kong, Japan, and China. Their own culture and economic development determine the types of property management models that have been adopted. Based on the three distinctive characteristics, that is, style, organisations, and corporate structure, **Table 1** summarises the models in these four economies.

Several interesting points can be derived from the comparison. The first one relates to the amount of state intervention. In Singapore, the government has intervened in the property management industry through the Private Residential Management Council. In Japan, standardisation can be achieved through giving the information to the Central Management Union. In China, the central government started to put forward some general principles for regulating property services in the mid-1990s. By

Table 1 Comparison in Property Management models across Asia-Pacific

	Singapore	Japan	Hong Kong	China
Property management style	Co-manage style	Legal relationship	Contractual relationship	Nonsystematic pattern
Property management organizations	–Subsidiary proprietors –Management corporation	Professional institutions	–Owners' incorporation –Management committee	Property management companies alone
Property management companies	–Managing agent –In house management team	High degree of professionalism	Conventional property management services	Existing two kinds of property management patterns: administrative and professional

contrast, in Hong Kong, the government policy has been regarded as relatively noninterventionist.

The second point relates to competition among property management companies. Although China currently has more than 20 000 property management companies, they are still noncompetitive under the existing socialist market economic system. The Chinese government is slowly going through a learning curve about how to regulate the property management industry in an emerging economy. In contrast, other countries such as Japan, Singapore, and Hong Kong are all striving to provide quality property management services and standardisation within their own economies. They all stress the promotion of safety, convenience, comfort, cost saving, and effort saving.

The third point relates to property legislation. In China, for example, the legal system for property management is still lagging behind the speed of change in this sector. This is hampering development in the professional management industry. On the other hand, the Japanese stress self-management in the organisation and running of private sector property through a high division of labour. In contrast, Singapore and Hong Kong have clearer legislation to regulate relations between different agents for responsibilities, rights, and interests.

The fourth point concerns the property management fees. They are mostly market driven in Hong Kong, Japan, and Singapore. Combined with their own property management model conditions, the fee is consistent with their respective features. In contrast, in the case of China, nonstandardised or zero management fees may allow property agents to grow quickly in numbers.

Among all the mentioned economies, property management in China is the most immature. The Chinese government has gradually taken steps to spread a unified and professional management across the provinces and cities. However, due to its own culture and relatively low standard of living, it is unlikely that a systematic pattern of management will be implemented very soon.

See also: Private Sector Housing Management: Europe; Private Sector Housing Management: North America; Private Sector Housing Management: Post-Socialist.

Further Reading

Baldwin G (1994) Property management in Hong Kong (an overview). *Journal of Property Management* 12(4): 18–23.

Chan O, Lau P, and Fung PY (2001) *The Best Management Practices for the Estates Management Industry in Hong Kong*. Hong Kong: City University of Hong Kong.

Chen LM (2008). Challenges of governing urban commons: Evidence from privatized housing in China. *Proceedings of the 12th Biennial Conference of the International Association for the Study of Commons*. Cheltenham, UK, 14–18 July.

Chen SCY and Webster CJ (2005) Homeowners association, collective action and the costs of private governance. *Housing Studies* 20(2): 205–220.

Christudason A (2008a) Choice of property management system for residential strata developments in Singapore. *Journal of Property Management* 26: 97–111.

Christudason A (2008b) Legislation affecting common property management in Singapore. *Journal of Property Management* 26: 207–219.

Gilleard JD and Pan YQ (1999) Challenge and opportunity: Facility management in Shanghai. *Journal of Facilities* 17: 105–111.

Hastings EM, Wong SK, and Walters M (2006) The management of multiple ownership property in Hong Kong. *Journal of Property Management* 24(3): 293–308.

Heller MA (1998) Tragedy of the anti-commons: Property in transition from Marx to markets. *Harvard Law Review* 1(11): 621–688.

Khamkongkaew W (2005) Managing property in Hong Kong, travel guide and information. *Asia News Update.com*. http://www.asianewsupdate.com/article/managing_property_hk.html (accessed 12 April 2010).

Khublall N (1993) *Strata Titles*. Singapore: Butterworths Asia.

Li LH (1997) Property management in China: Opportunities and problems. *Journal of Property Management* 15(1): 6–11.

Tang BS, Wong SW, and Liu SC (2006) Property agents, housing markets and housing services in transitional urban China. *Housing Studies* 21(6): 799–823.

TelferYoung (2006) Changing forms of property ownership. *Telfer Young Newsletter*. http://www.telferyoung.co.nz/news/newsletter/ty1163114876.html (accessed 10 November 2010).

The Link REIT (2009) http://www.thelinkreit.com/ (accessed 12 April 2010).

Walker A and Flanagan R (1991) *Property and Construction in Asia Pacific: Hong Kong, Japan, Singapore*. Oxford: BSP Professional Books.

Walter M and Kent P (2000) Institutional economics and property strata title – A survey and case study. *Journal of Property Research* 17(3): 221–240. 2000 http://www.informaworld.com/smpp/title~content=t713735323~db=all~tab=issueslist~branches= 17–v17.

Wuguan (2006a) Korea and Japan property management perspective. *CNREALITY.* www.robroad.com/data/2006/0718/article_50736_1.htm (accessed 12 April 2010).

Wuguan (2006b) US and Hong Kong property management model. *CNREALITY.* www.robroad.com/data/2006/0718/article_42838_1.htm (accessed 12 April 2010).

Wuguan (2006c) Property management 'zero fee' inappropriate. *CNREALITY.* www.robroad.com/data/2006/0718/article_48321_1.htm (accessed 12 April 2010).

Wuguan (2006d) China Property Management Association. *CNREALTY.* www.robroad.com/data/2006/0718/article_43003_1.htm (accessed 12 April 2010).

Xu JF and Fang ZD (1996) Management of urban residential districts in China. *Property Management* 14(2): 40–44.

Yiu CY (2005) Institutional arrangement and unauthorized building works in Hong Kong. *Structural Survey* 23(1): 22–29.

Private Sector Housing Management: Europe

N Nieboer, Delft University of Technology, Delft, The Netherlands

© 2012 Elsevier Ltd. All rights reserved.

Glossary

Commercial landlord Owner or manager of one or more homes, who lets these properties for commercial purposes.

Neoliberalism A recent political view on society, advocating room for market forces and a modest role for government.

Portfolio development Quantitative and/or qualitative development of an organisation's portfolio (i.e., the housing stock) or (the formulation of) a set of policy principles regarding this development.

Social landlord Owner or manager of one or more homes, who lets these properties for social purposes.

Introduction

'Housing management' is a broad term, and is not well delineated in literature. Pearl stated in 1997 that there was little clear consensus as to what the term actually means. Franklin argued in 1998 that "the pursuit of housing management is beset by the fact that it is far from prescriptive, that it lacks clearly defined boundaries, and that those who perform it are unsure of its aims and objectives". Traditionally, housing management was (and still is) associated with practical, operational issues such as rent collecting, allocation, and maintenance, but later on other, less operational tasks and activities were also included, such as promoting liveability and community involvement, and even portfolio development. In this article we follow the broad definition of Priemus, Dieleman, and Clapham, who define social housing management as "all activities to produce and allocate housing services from the existing social housing stock". Although this definition is related to 'social' housing, we can also use this definition for the management of all housing, irrespective of the tenure, namely by simply leaving out the word 'social'. According to Priemus, Dieleman, and Clapham, housing management consists of a variety of activities, which can be divided into several categories, including technical management (maintenance, renovation, etc.), social management (housing allocation, marketing, etc.), financial management (treasury, rent policy), and tenure management (letting, buying, selling).

Owner-Occupied Sector and Rented Sector

The definition given above entails some restrictions on the actors who carry out housing management. Although it is an option to regard anyone who is responsible for a home as a housing manager, the use of the term is generally related to 'professional' housing managers. This means that we concentrate on housing management organisations and not on, for instance, individual homeowners. As the vast majority of housing management organisations are active in the rented sector, we have chosen to focus on the rented sector.

Private and Public, Social and Commercial

In the rental sector in many countries, the private housing sector coincides with the commercial housing sector. Because of this coincidence both sectors are sometimes treated as synonymous. However, we reject this conflation of terms for two reasons. First, it is analytically incorrect to confuse a dimension related to the ownership of the properties (either in the hands of a public body or not) with a dimension related to the purposes for which these properties are held (social or commercial). Second, in a number of countries private housing organisations are not only commercial landlords, but also social landlords. These private, not-for-profit organisations can be seen as a third sector, next to the public landlords and the private commercial landlords. The size of this private, non-profit housing sector can be considerable, as is the case in, for instance, the Netherlands, Austria and, increasingly, the United Kingdom. Using the distinction between public and private and between social and commercial, a matrix can be created, which is depicted in **Table 1**. This matrix also shows a fourth sector, namely the public commercial sector, which is a theoretically possible category, but nonexistent in reality. This article focuses on the two private subsectors, in the middle column, namely the private social landlords and the private commercial landlords.

Table 1 Classification of rental housing sectors on the basis of ownership and general management purposes

	Private	Public
Social	Private social landlords	Public social landlords
Commercial	Private commercial landlords	(Nonexistent)

As for the private commercial landlords, it is relevant to distinguish between small landlords, owning one or a few homes, and professional housing organisations, which manage a larger number of homes. The latter subsector is dominated by institutional real estate investors, such as pension funds and insurance companies. As has been indicated above, this article focuses on professional housing organisations.

Distinction between Portfolio Management, Asset Management, and Property Management

A common distinction in real estate management is that between portfolio management, asset management, and property management. **Figure 1** contains a list of activities performed and output produced at each of these levels. Traditionally a pyramid or a triangle is used to indicate both the hierarchical relationship between the three levels and the relative size of the activities in each type of management.

'Portfolio management' concentrates on the allocation of investments among several asset options. Within the real estate sector, the main options are housing, offices, and retail. Within housing, dwelling types or regions can be distinguished. Formulating goals about the desired size and the desired mix of the housing portfolio is an essential activity in portfolio management.

'Asset management' concerns the assessment of individual projects (estates). On the basis of these assessments, it is decided what type of investment will be made in each of these projects (e.g., refurbishment, sale, small improvement, consolidation), and which allocation (target groups) and pricing (rent) policy has to be applied.

'Property management', finally, is concerned with 'daily' administrative, technical, and commercial management as well as maintenance activities.

Some authors describe portfolio management as a strategic activity and property management as an operational activity. They state that portfolio management takes place at the strategic level of the organisation, asset management at the tactical level, and property management at the operational level. We do not follow this line of thinking, because each of the activities in **Figure 1** has strategic as well as operational aspects. Maintenance activities, for example, can be carried out following strategic guidelines about what and what not to do. Conversely, portfolio strategies are usually supported by several, partly operational analyses of the housing stock. Although portfolio management is relatively more an issue at the strategic level, we argue that the difference between the levels of real estate management is gradual in this respect.

Although the three types of management apply to both the commercial and the social rented sector, there are considerable differences between the two sectors.

The first difference is in the content of housing management. In commercial housing management the emphasis is on financial performance. Assets are evaluated on the basis of yields and discounted cash flow. It is not true that commercial landlords always strive for maximal

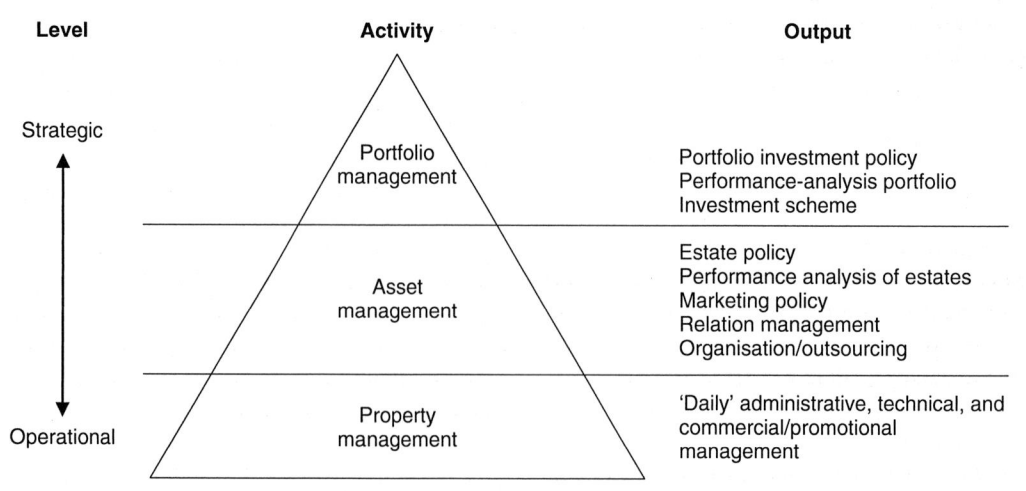

Figure 1 Organisational levels of real estate management. Adapted from Miles ME, Haney RL, and Berens G (1996) *Real Estate Development: Principles and Process*, 2nd edn. Washington, DC: Urban Land Institute.

return; in some cases, stable returns are regarded as more important. Nevertheless, the emphasis is still on risk and return. In the social rented sector, management decisions involve a balancing of different, incomparable objectives, such as providing housing to those in need, improving social sustainability, improving the energy performance of the housing stock, and keeping a sound financial position. Financial performance is 'only' one of the criteria for management decisions, and mostly not a leading but a conditional one. This difference between the commercial and the social landlords has profound consequences for housing management. Investments that cannot be earned back (by an increase of the rent or the market value) are usually not made by commercial landlords, but could be a valuable option for social landlords if they fulfil social purposes. As for the larger commercial real estate investors, the relatively short exploitation period exacerbates this difference in management, because the period to earn back the investment is also shorter.

The second difference between the social and the commercial sector concerns the relative weight of each of the three types of management. Compared to social landlords, commercial landlords (especially the larger organisations among them) put a relatively strong emphasis on portfolio management. Outsourcing of property management activities to professional management companies is a common phenomenon, whereas in the social sector property management activities are relatively dominant. The latter is especially true for social housing sectors in which parts of the portfolio management and asset management tasks are the responsibility of the government. One of the consequences is that technical considerations prevail in the social housing organisations, whereas market considerations prevail in the commercial real estate sector. It must be stated, however, that government dominance over the private social housing sector has considerably declined in almost all European countries. As a consequence, the necessity for housing management organisations to develop their own portfolio and asset management policies has increased. We will have a closer look at this development in the following section.

Shift from Government to Market

The rise of neoliberalism in the 1980s and 1990s entailed a shift of responsibilities from government to market in many Western countries. This development was particularly visible in the social housing sector, where government influence is, almost by definition, larger than in the commercial housing sector, although it must be noted that there are also countries (e.g., the United Kingdom) in which the commercial private sectors are less regulated than they were before. The shift away from government control and towards market forces was often coupled with reduced levels of government support, a growth of the owner-occupied sector, and greater independence of social landlords from the government. In many Eastern European countries, the abolition of the communist system was followed by a large-scale privatisation of the housing stock. Because this has taken place mostly through sales to occupiers, it has not led to a considerable growth of the private rental sector. The changes in Western Europe have been less radical, but there too the predominantly neoliberal politics has imposed a greater requirement on landlords to consider financial risks and the associated present and future market position of their dwellings.

It can be assumed that reduced government intervention leads to an increased market and financial pressure on the social housing sector. Consequently, a higher degree of market orientation and businesslike behaviour in the sector could be expected. However, Gruis and Nieboer conclude from a study carried out in several European countries that, despite the neoliberal policies, market orientation has been weakly developed among social landlords. It appears that market forces alone are not enough for them to become market-oriented. In several countries, not market forces, but government or government agencies press social landlords to adopt a more market-based policy. In England, regulations give this pressure visible form, for example in requirements for a wide range of public service providers, including housing associations, to publish efficiency statements. In France, eligibility for subsidies is conditional on stock planning. In Belgium, the Flemish umbrella organisation stimulates professionalisation of the housing associations by offering businesslike management tools. Thus, in these countries, a businesslike approach in the sector is more likely to result from government discipline than from market discipline.

Distinction on the Basis of Product Diversification

Another dimension of housing management concerns product diversification and entry into new markets. This is frequently discussed in literature on strategic (business) management. Ansoff distinguishes between entering or not entering new market segments, and between developing and not developing new products. Miles and Snow depict these decisions as relating to essential characteristics of different types of organisations, distinguishing 'defenders', 'analyzers', 'prospectors', and 'reactors', which are described as follows:

- 'defenders' concentrate on a small market: strong emphasis on improvement of efficiency, weak interest in innovation;

- 'prospectors' constantly look for new markets: strong emphasis on innovation, weak interest in improvement of efficiency;
- 'analyzers' operate in both stable and dynamic markets, according to their analyses;
- 'reactors' do not anticipate market developments but adapt themselves to changed circumstances if they are forced to.

Gruis has applied this classification to social housing, in which, generally speaking, 'prospectors' diversify their products and 'defenders' do not. He argues that diversification involves not only commercial activities of social landlords, but also their social activities. These can be nonhousing activities (e.g., community development, care, and other welfare activities), and also housing activities (e.g., exploring new housing markets), which are relevant for this article. Gruis presents a typology of four categories, crossing the social–commercial division with the division between 'defenders' and 'prospectors'.

Distinction between Taken-for-Granted Assumptions and Rational Calculation

A striking result from Gruis' study is that the 'prospectors' are leading the way in both social and commercial diversification. This underlines the importance of the prospector–defender dimension, but questions the nature of the social–commercial division. This distinction is further put in perspective when we take into account the organisations, notably nonprofit landlords, which generate commercial surpluses in order to be able to invest for social purposes. It appears that the social–commercial distinction was a good concept in the past to distinguish the nonprofit and the profit subsector within the private sector, but this dimension has become blurred in the previous two decades. For this reason, Mullins and Nieboer suggest a new dimension, namely the distinction between taken-for-granted assumptions and rational calculation, which cuts across the abovementioned dimensions of government–market, social–commercial, and prospector–defender. Mullins and Nieboer argue that the process of rationalisation of housing management organisations is not confined to commercial activities, but stretches out to social activities as well. Examples are methods to measure social impact or 'social return' (as opposed to commercial return) and the application of business strategic models in the development of portfolio or asset management strategies. Such examples, however, are not widespread in Europe. Most examples mentioned in international literature can be found in the United Kingdom, France, the Netherlands and, to a lesser extent, Germany and Austria, but even in these countries they are exceptions rather than the rule. We expand on this later in this article.

Other Distinctions in Housing Management

Besides these relatively general approaches to housing management, distinctions in housing management can be made related to management activities mentioned earlier in this article, such as investment planning, allocation, and pricing. These typologies can be applied not only at the portfolio level, but also at the level of estates or individual properties. Examples of aspects on the basis of which housing management decisions can be classified as such are:

- target group (according to income, household size, age, and other population or household characteristics);
- location aspects, such as preferred location type (inner city, suburb, countryside, etc.), region(s), and geographical concentration/dispersion;
- price segment (rent level or sale price);
- quality standard.

Expressions of Rationalisation – The Concept of Strategic Asset Management

A useful concept to clarify the extent to which housing management can be called rationalised is that of 'strategic asset management'. The native equivalent of the term 'strategic asset management' has its origins in Dutch social housing, but its features can be observed in various European countries. The aim of this type of management is generally to structure investment decisions of housing management organisations and, consequently, to be better prepared for any anticipated market risks. So, strategic asset management combines both market orientation and a rationalised, systematic way of investment decision-making. It also combines principles of (commercial) asset management and strategic planning to develop methods and tools for management of the housing stock. Strategic asset management can be typified further on the basis of three interrelated characteristics that can be found in literature on strategic business planning, namely market-oriented, systematic, and comprehensive. **Table 2** gives a summarised description of these characteristics, followed by a more detailed description.

Market-Oriented

Housing management can be seen as market-oriented by definition in the sense that it is always concerned

Table 2 Characteristics and summarised descriptions of strategic asset management

Characteristic of strategic asset management	Summarised description
Market-oriented	Renting, allocation, sale, maintenance, and improvement are related to occupiers' preferences, market forces, and financial returns
Systematic	Structured frameworks are used for the decision-making and planning process
Comprehensive	Objectives for the development of the entire stock of housing are formulated, and individual complexes are analysed in relation to one another

with fulfilling a housing demand by offering a housing supply. However, because this definition would be meaningless, we prefer to follow literature on strategic planning, which emphasises the need for an analysis of a company's own strengths and weaknesses in relation to the opportunities and threats in their (market) environment in support of strategy formulation. Among commercial real estate investors, strategies are based on an analysis of the market position of the products, market prospects and – in general – opportunities to earn money. In the 'classic' portfolio analysis, designed by the Boston Consultancy Group, cash performance is crucial in the analysis of business units. In analogy with commercial practice, a market-oriented landlord can be expected to place more emphasis on analysing market demand and opportunities. Important decision-making factors in strategy formulation will be current lettability, future market expectations, financial return, and opportunities for sale. A wide range of strategies will be considered and applied: diversification of the price and quality of dwellings within the portfolio according to housing demand will be a central theme in asset management.

The occurrence of market orientation can be reflected in the various housing management decisions: rent (increases) will be related to the quality and market position; allocations, maintenance, and renewal activities will take market demand and tenants' preferences into account; and landlords will have an active sale policy to generate financial income and meet housing preferences.

Systematic

Many books on strategic business planning suggest the use of systematic planning procedures and rational frameworks for decision-making. Thus, within strategic asset management, a landlord will put effort into rational and transparent decision-making. The process of formulating asset management strategies will be well structured. Decision-making factors will be clearly marked and the way in which decisions are reached will be reported. Asset management decisions have a large influence on the quality, affordability, and availability of dwellings – the key objectives of social housing everywhere. This impact on social housing objectives places a demand on the quality of the decision-making process. Tenants and (other) parties working with social landlords (governments, care and welfare organisations, etc.) may expect a 'justifiable' policy, which is supported by rational arguments as part of a transparent decision-making process. In fact, it can be argued that social landlords should strive towards such a transparent policy as part of their social objectives. This means that investment options are selected in accordance with one or more fixed principles, or with a previously established pattern.

The occurrence of a systematic approach towards asset management can be reflected in the application of decision-making frameworks – comparable, for example, with private sector portfolio analyses – and structured processes – comparable, for example, with strategic business planning as described by Kotler (see **Figure 2**), Aaker, and Bryson.

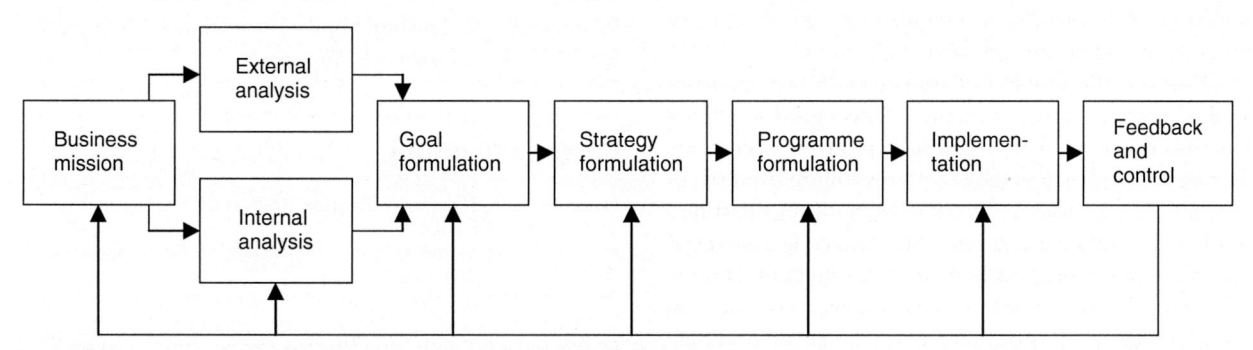

Figure 2 The business strategic planning process according to Kotler.

Comprehensive

A major characteristic of strategic business planning is that it deals with the objectives of the organisation as a whole, at top-management level. Comprehensive housing management will focus not only on individual dwellings or estates, but will also reflect on the composition of the stock as a whole. In this respect, it is opposed to a more partial approach, in which specific areas or homes are considered without taking into account the overall (portfolio) context. A comprehensive (portfolio) approach helps social landlords to determine which part of the stock should be given priority for investment and intensive management. Furthermore, reflection on the desired growth direction of the portfolio as a whole, in relation to housing needs, allows them to put decisions about individual estates in a wider perspective.

Tendencies towards Strategic Asset Management?

A study published in 2004 deals with the extent to which the abovementioned features of strategic asset management can be found in practice. The European countries under review in this publication are Austria, Belgium, Denmark, England, France, Germany, Latvia, and the Netherlands. In several of these countries, in particular in England, France, and the Netherlands, social landlords carry out initiatives for the structured development of a housing stock policy. The examples include well-structured procedures including the formulation of portfolio goals, analysis, option assessment, and option appraisal, and classifications of dwellings or estates on the basis of structural, residential, and/or financial criteria. Partly on the basis of these criteria, decisions are reached concerning whether to renovate, demolish, sell, consolidate, and suchlike. In addition, in England, Austria, the Netherlands, and Belgium, we see the rise of national benchmarking systems, which may indicate a move towards the professionalisation of the sector. In Denmark, a benchmark showing administrative and other expenditures per landlord is already in force. In this country, investment budget planning is highly systematised by mandatory regulations on budgetary procedures and onsite technical evaluations.

However, the number of initiatives in the countries studied is rare. To date, structured housing stock policies have been restricted to a few leaders in the sector. So, despite the tendency to move towards a more fixed structure for the appraisal of investments, most organisations' housing portfolio policies cannot be defined as systematic according to the previously given definition of this term. This may be illustrated by characterisations, such as: "activities are performed very much on an *ad hoc* basis" (Latvia), "several [housing companies] have not formalised their methods and their procedures have remained tacit" (France), and "performances are not systematically and periodically evaluated and decisions on asset management are mostly taken on an *ad hoc* basis" (Belgium).

In most of the countries studied, the market orientation of housing stock policy has increased, but only to a modest extent. In most of the countries (Austria, England, France, Germany, and the Netherlands), the research has found the introduction of asset management practices in which the quality and market position of the housing stock play a much more clear-cut role than was previously the case. The practices include the introduction of market analyses, decision-support systems, or rating systems calculating property's yields and earning capacity in the investment decisions. Lettability and financial return play an important role in these initiatives, thus 'challenging' the traditional dominance of technical considerations. Especially in areas of low demand, there seems to be an increased attention to analysing lettability, turnover rates, and general market developments. At the same time, however, there is insufficient evidence to state that a market-oriented approach has been commonly adopted. Each of the countries studied shows that signs of a more traditional task-oriented approach is still very much alive, due to a traditional attitude within the social housing sector and/or the regulatory framework. For instance, initiatives by landlords to develop a rent policy in which quality and price are more in accordance with each other are severely hampered by tight rent regulations.

In none of the countries studied did the characteristic 'comprehensive' really live up to its promise. When it comes to investment decisions, aspects on the levels of homes, buildings, or neighbourhoods, such as technical condition, maintenance costs, and lettability, are dominant; portfolio considerations usually play a subordinate role.

See also: Housing and the State in the Soviet Union and Eastern Europe; Private Rental Landlords: Europe; Private Sector Housing Management: North America; Private Sector Housing Management: Post-Socialist; Privatisation of Housing: Implications for Well-Being; Social Housing Landlords: Europe.

Further Reading

Aaker DA (1998) *Developing Business Strategies*, 5th edn. New York: John Wiley & Sons.
Ansoff HI (1984) *Implanting Strategic Management*. Upper Saddle River, NJ: Prentice Hall International.
Bryson J (2004) *Strategic Planning for Public and Non-Profit Organisations*, 3rd edn. San Francisco, CA: Josey-Bass.
Franklin B (1998) Constructing a service: Context and discourse in housing management. *Housing Studies* 13: 201–216.

Gruis V (2008) Organisational archetypes for Dutch housing associations. *Environment & Planning C: Government and Policy* 26: 1077–1092.

Gruis V and Nieboer N (eds.) (2004) *Asset Management in the Social Rented Sector: Policy and Practice in Europe and Australia*. Dordrecht: Kluwer Academic Publishers (now: Springer).

Kotler P (1997) *Marketing Management*, 9th edn. Upper Saddle River, NJ: Prentice Hall International.

Miles ME, Haney RL, and Berens G (1996) *Real Estate Development: Principles and Process*, 2nd edn. Washington, DC: Urban Land Institute.

Miles RE and Snow CC (1978) *Organisational Strategy, Structure and Process*. New York: McGraw Hill.

Montezuma J (2006) A survey of institutional investors' attitudes and perceptions of residential property: The Swiss, Dutch and Swedish cases. *Housing Studies* 21: 883–908.

Mullins D and Nieboer N (2008) Comparing Dutch and English housing associations: Rational calculations and taken for granted assumptions. In: Norris M and Silke D (eds.) *Shrinking Cities, Sprawling Suburbs, Changing Countrysides*, pp. 1–23. Dublin: University College of Dublin; Centre for Housing Research.

Pearl M (1997) *Social Housing Management: A Critical Appraisal of Housing Practice*. Basingstoke, UK; London: Macmillan.

Priemus H, Dieleman F, and Clapham D (1999) Current developments in social housing management. *Netherlands Journal of Housing and the Built Environment* 14: 211–224.

Private Sector Housing Management: North America

J Londerville, University of Guelph, Guelph, ON, Canada

© 2012 Elsevier Ltd. All rights reserved.

Glossary

Common area expenses Expenses of maintaining the commonly owned areas of a condominium, shared among the owners usually in relation to unit size. These are paid monthly to the condo corporation; the property manager ensures that they are collected and uses the proceeds to pay common area expenses. Part of the condo fee is put into a reserve for future capital expenses.

Condominium Form of tenure in which the dwelling unit itself is individually owned and other parts of the development (land, hallways, recreation facilities, etc.) are jointly owned by all residents in the complex.

Co-op Housing owned by a legal entity, typically a corporation. The shareholders in the corporation have the right to occupy one unit; the rules governing the co-op are spelled out in an occupancy agreement.

Effective gross income The gross potential income for a rental property minus any losses due to vacancies or bad debts.

Gross potential income The income a rental property could earn if it were full, taking into account existing lease terms and assuming vacant units are rented at market rents.

HVAC Heating, ventilating, and air conditioning systems in large buildings.

Net operating income The effective gross income of a rental property minus the operating costs (utilities, property taxes, maintenance, etc.) paid by the owner.

Property Management

Owners of rental properties or condominiums can manage the properties themselves, hire third party companies to complete the tasks associated with managing the property, or make use of a mixture of the two, keeping some responsibilities and outsourcing others. This article addresses the tasks involved in managing property, discusses the pros and cons of outsourcing management, and describes the management process in North America. Typical compensation structures for property managers are also covered.

The Role of the Property Manager

The third party property manager acts as an agent for the owner of the property in his absence. As such the property manager is almost always responsible for collecting rent or common area expenses from condominium owners plus handling the day-to-day maintenance of the building (grass cutting, minor repairs, etc.). Other duties assigned to an external property manager can include any or all of the following: financial management (rents, financial reporting to the owner, contractor payments, etc.), marketing and leasing, physical maintenance (daily repairs and preventive maintenance), financing/refinancing, renovation (plans, obtaining permits, tendering, hiring contractors), insurance, and purchase and sale of assets.

If the external manager is responsible for several properties for the same owner and has the full range of allocated tasks mentioned above, he is commonly referred to as an asset manager. The asset manager plays a much more strategic role in management of the property. In addition to ensuring that day-to-day maintenance and financial issues are taken care of, the asset manager will also advise the owner on when and how to refinance, disposition of underperforming assets, renovations and energy retrofits as well as strategic acquisitions of additional properties. The asset manager provides tactical advice designed to maximise the overall value of the owner's real estate portfolio.

Size of the Property Management Industry in North America

The size of the third party property management sector is difficult to measure in North America, since there is no official tracking of whether units are managed by the owner or by an outside property management firm. It is not uncommon for small rental buildings to be managed by the owner but the trend is towards more concentrated ownership, especially of larger buildings.

Some real estate investment trusts (REITs) target ownership of residential multifamily properties. For example, Equity Residential is a publicly traded REIT and a member of the S&P 500. They currently own

147 000 apartment units in 23 states, although they have owned as many as 225 000 units. CAPREIT in Canada owns over 27 000 apartment and townhouse units in 6 of the 10 Canadian provinces. Most REITs manage their own properties internally in order to maintain tight control over operating and marketing costs and so that the property management fees accrue to the managers of the REIT. In a sense this is part of the third party management system since the owners of the properties are technically the unit holders in the REIT. While REITs tend to self-manage their portfolios, pension funds, insurance companies, and foreign investors are more likely to rely on third party full service property/asset managers.

In the United States, dwelling units are categorised by tenure in the census as owned, condominium/co-op, or rented. According to the 2007 American Housing Survey (see US Census Bureau website), 9.2 million units were either condominium or co-op tenure, nearly 7.2% of the 128.2 million housing units. In Canada, the corresponding percentage of condominiums is 7.5% or 913 000 of the total 12.2 million units (see Statistics Canada website). Although it is possible for condominiums to be self-managed, it is not common, so it can be anticipated that most of these units would be managed by third parties.

Rental units (unsubsidised) comprise 30% (38.3 million units) of the total units in the United States. In Canada, the rental stock is 31.5% (3.9 million units) of the total housing stock. It is not possible to determine how many of these units are managed by the owner and what percentage are managed by third party managers. The National Apartment Association in the United States is an industry organisation representing landlords and property managers. Of their 51 000 members, 44% are property management firms; although there is no indication of the size of these companies, clearly it is a major sector in the real estate industry.

There are 21.4 million units (condo and rental) in buildings greater than five units in the United States according to the American Housing Survey 2007. Canadian apartment buildings of five storeys or more represent 1.1 million units or 9% of the stock.

In-House Versus Outsourcing of Property Management Functions

Owners of rental properties can manage their own buildings or hire a third party company to act as their agent in management of the property. Some owners use a mixture of the two – retaining some responsibilities and hiring a third party to do some of the management tasks. There are several reasons why hiring a professional property manager may be optimal for a rental or condominium property.

The HVAC (heating, ventilating, and air conditioning) systems in modern buildings have become more and more complex as owners have become more concerned with energy efficiency, operating costs, and comfort in buildings. Computerised systems monitor temperatures and energy use. The owner of the property generally does not have the technical expertise to manage and maintain this sophisticated equipment himself. The building systems are frequently monitored with the reporting system having a feed to a computer at the firm that installed or maintains the equipment. Security systems have also become highly technical in recent years. As the technical and computerised aspects of property management grow, professional expertise in these areas is an important skill that the manager of the property should possess. Hiring a property manager with experience in dealing with the technical experts is clearly advantageous to the owner.

Most residential property is subject to significant government legislation in North America. This can include (among many other restrictions) rent control legislation requiring notice of rent increases delivered in a prescribed manner and limits on the size and timing of rent increases. Rent control legislation varies significantly from one geographic area to another. Failure to recognise the differences in the regulations affecting each property can lead to violation of the legislation and fines or other penalties affecting the economic viability of the property. There can also be legislation that restricts the owner's right to discriminate against tenants on the basis of family status (number of children), pets, race, and so on. Managers need to be fully aware of these when vetting new tenants. For buildings that have received low-income housing tax credits (LIHTC), the reporting and operating requirements are very restrictive; not complying with the requirements can lead to a loss of the credits. This has a significant effect on the value of the property and its operating cash flow. Property managers who deal with this legislation on a daily basis will be more up-to-date than a property owner who has only one or two properties in a given jurisdiction.

Legislation for condominiums is also complex in certain geographic areas. For example, in the province of Ontario in Canada, condos must have an expert review the condition of the building every 5 years and an assessment made of any physical improvements that the building will need over time. The expert then needs to ascertain whether the capital reserve fund for the condo is sufficient to cover any expected improvements needed for the coming years. If not, the monthly maintenance fee is raised to amortise the expected costs of covering the deficiency. This regular review is a critical aspect of maintaining the financial health of the complex. Any prospective purchaser can request a report on the sufficiency of the reserve fund; this makes it easier for the vendor to sell his or her unit.

In condos that do not have this type of legislation requiring monitoring of the adequacy of the reserve fund, any major unexpected capital expenditure can require an assessment of the individual unit holder in order to cover the capital cost of the repair, for example if the roof needs replacing. These special assessments can be thousands of dollars and can create financial hardship for the condo unit owner. Uncertainty about these types of costs can greatly affect the ability of the owner to sell his unit in a timely fashion for an adequate price.

It is important for those managing a property to have a thorough knowledge of the market affecting the property – vacancy rates, rent levels, target market, and types of tenants likely to be interested in leasing a unit. This is critical for a rental property but also important for condo properties to assist owners with marketing their units. A local property manager is likely to have a much better assessment of the market than an owner who is not familiar with the local area. Particularly when the owner has properties in a far location, or has only one or two properties in a particular city, hiring a third party property manager with strong local market knowledge is generally a shrewd decision.

The owner, when deciding to hire a third party manager, is trading off cost, control, and time commitments. If a building is self-managed, the owner has complete control over all decisions made regarding the property. Using a third party manager requires relinquishing some of this control. The owner can still set limits on the manager's judgments but some actions will necessarily be left to the manager's discretion. However, hiring a manager does free up the owner's time to concentrate on more strategic elements of his investment portfolio.

Hiring a third party manager can be either more or less expensive than self-managing a property. If the owner has only one or two properties in a city, management of the properties is often less expensively done through fees paid to a third party. On the other hand, if the owner has a group of properties in one location, it may be more efficient to hire in-house property managers. These managers can be paid a set salary, which can be less expensive than the fees paid to a third party manager if there are a sufficient number of properties in the portfolio to make it economic.

Issues Specific to Condominium Management

Management of condominium properties shares some similarities with management of residential rental properties in terms of the physical management of the property and collection of monthly condo fees/rent. However, there are significant differences as well.

Owners of condominium units live in the building and are strongly interested in the quality of management in the building. A well-managed building will add to the value to their individual unit when they wish to sell it. The Board of Directors of the complex is elected from among the residents; the board hires the property manager and sets criteria for standards of management (with approval at an annual meeting of residents). The property manager is thus dealing with multiple owners rather than just one.

Residents of the building are typically much more likely to criticise actions of the onsite staff than are rental tenants in a similar building. They know the manager is paid from the proceeds of their monthly common area fee and they feel they have the right to monitor and comment on the actions of the manager. Management of the relationship with occupants of each unit and in particular the Board of Directors is critical if the manager wants to retain the contract.

The property management company is responsible for managing only the common areas of the complex. Owners are responsible for any maintenance issues within their own units. This reduces the overall scope of the property manager's job but again his work is subject to much greater scrutiny by residents.

Turnover rates tend to be much lower in condo complexes than in rental properties. Renters tend to move more frequently than owners, who will live in their units longer. As well, when owners do leave the building, they are responsible for fixing up and selling their own units. In a rental building, the property manager is responsible for cleaning and repairing any deficiencies in the vacant unit and for ensuring that it is rented as soon as possible to an appropriate tenant. Reducing turnover is often a significant responsibility of the rental building manager, since the costs of 'churn' are high.

Although the responsibilities of the condo property manager seem on the surface to be much less time consuming than those of the rental building manager, the significant interaction with owners in the building and the generally higher standards of maintenance for condos tend to offset much of this apparent time saving.

Fee Structure and Contracts for Property Managers

Because property managers act for the owner and their activities are not supervised on a day-to-day basis (particularly if the owner is in another city), their relationship is an example of the principal–agent problem. The principal–agent problem results from the premise that any agent will act in his or her own best interests. For example, if the property manager's fee is based on a percentage of rents received, he may attempt to fill the building with tenants without a thorough check to ascertain whether they are appropriate for the property and likely to be good long-term prospects. This will maximise his fee for the year but is not in the best long-term interests of the owner. It is important that the owner set up the contract and fee structure for the manager in a way that motivates the manager to act in the best interests of the owner, while also maximising the manager's own profit from the arrangement. The owner needs to motivate the manager to find good quality tenants at reasonable rents and maintain the property in an efficient way while making sure the asset maintains its value.

The principal–agent problem occurs in many settings. For property management, the trouble arises because the agent works independently. The owner of the property cannot observe on a daily basis what the manager is doing; he has no way of observing the level of effort the agent is expending. As an example, an ongoing vacancy problem can be the result of a very soft rental market or because the manager is not spending sufficient time and resources finding a tenant for the unit. The owner cannot observe which situation is reality without further investigation. This is particularly important where the property is in another city where the owner cannot visit the property frequently. In order to compensate for this, the owner must structure the contract with the agent, the fee structure for compensating the agent, and the reporting requirements in such a way as to provide as much incentive as possible for the agent to act in the best interest of the owner.

Typically a manager of a rental property is rewarded based on the percentage of gross potential income (GPI) or on effective gross income (EGI). Neither of these is a perfect incentive. If the compensation is based on GPI, the manager has no particular incentive to fill units – he receives his fee whether the unit is occupied or not. He also has no particular incentive to manage costs since the net operating income of the property earned after operating expenses are paid does not influence his earnings. As a result of these potential disincentives for the manager to act in the owner's best interests, the owner will need to put further checks into place to monitor the manager's activities.

A manager rewarded based on EGI does have an incentive to fill any vacant space. However, there is no particular incentive to fill the unit with high-quality tenants. The owner needs to set criteria for the quality of tenants he is looking for in order to lay down boundaries for the property manager. This may include minimum household income levels, maximum number of residents relative to size of units, minimum acceptable credit scores, and any other features upon which the owner is legally entitled to discriminate. Some owners require that they view the tenant application before a unit is rented. Limits on the rent the property manager may charge for the unit can also be required.

In addition to carefully constructing the contract and fee structure, the owner needs to find other ways to monitor the performance of the manager. An overall annual financial budget for the building should be prepared by the manager. Detailed monthly financial statements should be required to be submitted in a timely manner. Any deviation of the building's performance from the budget should be explained in detail. The owner may also want to schedule regular telephone conferences with the manager to go over any ongoing problems identified in the reports and discuss appropriate measures to be taken.

The owner may want an annual marketing plan for the building and a monthly report from the manager on leasing activities with reasons for any variation from the annual plan. A similar annual plan and monthly reports regarding maintenance and capital improvements for the building will be necessary. Any maintenance or capital repair issues identified should be passed on to the owner in a timely manner.

The owner may want to physically inspect the building annually at least to ensure that it is being properly maintained; he may also want to hire an engineer or other third party professional to review the quality of maintenance on the building. A survey of or interviews with residents to ask about their service experience with the property manager can also reveal useful information to the owner, including such items as availability and responsiveness of onsite staff. A log of maintenance requests and resolution is also a valuable tool.

The fee structure for condominium managers is necessarily different. Owners of units are responsible for their condominium fees whether they occupy the unit or not, so vacancy within the complex is not an issue for the property manager. A fee based on EGI would therefore be meaningless in a condo situation. Generally, condominium property management companies are compensated on a 'per door' basis; their fee is a flat amount per unit. Although there are no firm guidelines, the larger the complex is, the lower the per unit fee will be in general, since there are some economies of scale for the manager. The more amenities the building has, such as swimming pools and other recreation facilities, the higher the per-unit fee will be.

Accreditation of Housing Management Professionals

There are several professional accreditation systems for managers of residential properties in North America. The Institute of Real Estate Management (IREM) is an affiliate of the National Association of Realtors®. It is an association of professional real estate managers, both multi-residential and commercial, in the United States and

Canada (as well as other countries around the world). It provides real estate education and certification to its members. Entire organisations can be certified with the Accredited Management Organization designation. Individual members can earn an Accredited Residential Manager (ARM) designation. There are various routes to the ARM depending on the candidate's background education but the designation requires a combination of courses related to property maintenance, human resources management, finance, marketing and leasing, and ethics. There is a final cumulative exam at the end of the coursework. As well, the candidate must have at least 1 year's relevant work experience, three letters of reference, and is interviewed and recommended by their local IREM chapter.

Condo managers in the United States can become Certified Managers of Community Associations® (CMCA®) through the National Board of Certification for Community Association Managers. This requires successfully completing a course and a cumulative exam that covers

- governance and legal matters,
- operating budgets, reserves, and property assessment,
- risk management and insurance,
- maintenance and contracting,
- management of meetings of the board and the entire condo, and
- management of people.

The CMCA must be recertified every 2 years through providing evidence of at least 16 hours of continuing education.

In Canada, accreditation is at the provincial level. For example, the Association of Condominium Managers of Ontario accredits members through two college programmes in the province. Members earn the Condominium Management and Administration certificate through taking five required courses in condominium law (two courses), human resources management, physical building management, and financial management. There is also a sixth elective course. Each of these is 15 weeks long with one 3-hour class a week. Once the courses are complete, candidates must write a cumulative exam and achieve a grade of 75%. They must also have 2 years of relevant work experience.

Clearly the education and accreditation processes differ widely for different types of property managers, depending on the accrediting body and their location.

Challenges Facing Property Managers

Property managers of residential buildings face considerable challenges. In order to maintain revenue, they need to keep units full with tenants able to pay rents. This requires close attention to rental arrears and a firm policy for ensuring these are resolved quickly. The cost of churn (turnover of a unit to a new tenant) is high. It includes marketing costs, credit checks, preparing and showing the unit for prospective tenants, and vacancy while the preparation work is being done. It is far cheaper in most cases to keep an existing tenant than to look for a new one. The property manager also needs to closely monitor the market in the area of his building to ensure that rents remain at market levels and to evaluate the necessity for tenant incentives to maintain occupancy. The rental of units needs to always conform to any rent control or human rights legislation in place in the jurisdiction of the unit.

Maintenance of a building is also critical for a manager. Both emergency and preventive maintenance are important to ensure that the capital value of the asset is maintained. Frequently vandalism is an issue in rental buildings; if it is not dealt with promptly, the problem tends to escalate. However, it is also important to provide maintenance in as cost-effective a manner as possible. Some property managers will have maintenance staff in-house; others will contract this responsibility out. In the latter case, a detailed mechanism for soliciting competitive bids for major projects and evaluating the quality of the work done is essential.

Capital improvements are another source of risk for the property manager. These need to be projected over a 5-year time frame to allow for financing of any major expenses to be in place before the improvement is required. Insurance is another aspect of property management that requires significant attention to ensure that the property is adequately covered against risk. Environmental issues have become more significant in recent years and legislation places the responsibility for clean-up of environmental problems with the owner.

Conclusion

Property management of residential buildings, both rental and condominium, is becoming more complex as sophisticated HVAC systems are installed by owners and as legislation governing such properties becomes more complex. It is also essential to have a strong knowledge of local market conditions to effectively manage such properties. Frequently, the optimal choice for an owner of this type of property is to hire an accredited professional property manager to maximise his returns from his investment.

See also: Collective Ownership; High Rise; Low-Income Housing Tax Credits; Maintenance and Repair; Private Rental Landlords: North America; Private Sector Housing Management: Asia Pacific; Private Sector Housing Management: Europe; Residential Real Estate Investment Trusts.

Further Reading

Becher-Smead A (1996) Tax-credit essentials. *Journal of Property Management* 61(2): 16–19.

Farncombe M and Waller A (2005) Outsourcing for corporate real estate managers: How can real estate learn from other industries? *Journal of Corporate Real Estate* 7(3): 258–270.

Jensen MC and Meckling WH (1976) Theory of the firm: Managerial behavior, agency costs and ownership structure. *Journal of Financial Economics* 3: 305–360.

Kipnis B (2001) Technology: A glimpse to the future. *National Real Estate Investor* 43(1): 107.

Klingenberg B and Brown RJ (2006a) Optimization of residential property management. *Property Management* 24(4): 397–414.

Klingenberg B and Brown RJ (2006b) Rent control revisited: Effects on property management. *Property Management* 26(1): 56–65.

Kyle RC (2005) *Property Management*, 7th edn. Chicago, IL: Dearborn Real Estate Education.

National Apartment Association (2009) *Annual Report*. http://www.naahq.org

Novogradac MJ and Krabbenschmidt JE (1992) Managing low-income housing tax credit properties. *Journal of Property Management* 57(4): 6–7.

Robinson WL (1999) Winning a large condominium account. *Journal of Property Management* 64(5): 72–75.

Shockman C and Piette MA (2000) Innovation adoption processes for third party property management companies, working paper. *Proceedings of the ACEEE 2000 Summer Study on Energy Efficiency in Buildings: Efficiency and Sustainability.* 20–25 August. Pacific Grove, CA: Asilomar Conference Center.

Wong JKW, Li H, and Wang SW (2005) Intelligent building research: A review. *Automation in Construction* 14: 143–159.

Relevant Websites

www.statcan.gc.ca – Statistics Canada

www.census.gov – US Census Bureau

Private Sector Housing Management: Post-Socialist

S Tsenkova, University of Calgary, Calgary, AB, Canada

© 2012 Elsevier Ltd. All rights reserved.

Glossary

Arrears Unpaid, overdue debt owed by homeowners or tenants to the management company, the utility providers, or the condominium association. Arrears are typically the maintenance fee but can also include unpaid utility costs.

Bylaws or rules Written document(s) that outline the rules and regulations that condominium members, the board, and staff must follow typically in compliance with national legislation regarding housing management and ownership. The bylaws outline the obligations of the condominium members and act as a contract between them and the board.

Capital repairs Refer to restoration and improvement of housing, including all construction work performed to extend the normal economic life and/or to improve the quality of existing structures and technical engineering systems.

Emergency repairs A repair to remedy any defect which puts the health, safety, and security of a tenant or a third party at immediate risk or which affects the structure of the building adversely, which is not planned as part of the preventative maintenance plan.

Homeowners' association Institutional entity which manages multi-apartment housing, meets financial obligations, and initiates contracts and renewal projects in condominium type housing.

Planned repairs Include planned and cyclical repairs and improvements to maintain the current standard and value of the housing.

Reserve fund Money set aside by the condominium owners' associations for special circumstances, capital repairs, and contingencies.

Special resolution A resolution that is submitted to a meeting of the condominium members and approved by more than a simple majority of members. The percentage of required votes is different for each country, but in case of major repairs and investments a majority of at least two-third of the votes cast is usually required.

Structural repairs Major repair works that are essential to maintain the basic functions of stability and weather resistance in the main structural elements of a dwelling, that is, in floors, walls, or roofs. Major works to these elements will involve replacement or substantial reconstruction of the component or element.

Introduction

This article provides an overview of housing reforms and their impact on the existing housing with a particular emphasis on progress towards the establishment of a competitive system of housing management. This is one of the critical areas for policy intervention due to the high share of multi-apartment housing in urban areas across the region. The argument advanced here is that housing management has been particularly slow in adjusting to the new market reality, both in the private and public housing stock. The challenges are multidimensional – technical, social, and financial – making the task difficult. The comparative analysis explores the changes in housing management systems and some of the constraints for their efficient operation in the housing sector.

Housing Management and Privatisation: A Troubled Relationship

In Eastern Europe the 1990s have marked a departure from a 'command system' of housing provision, with deregulation of housing markets and privatisation of public housing being the flagship of the reform process. Privatisation of public, enterprise, and cooperative housing has fuelled the expansion of homeownership, creating 'nations of homeowners'. In the context of the shift away from direct state intervention to market-based provision of housing services, new owners were expected to assume major responsibilities for housing maintenance and management. In recent years, postsocialist countries have chosen different strategies to address major issues related to the management of privatised housing. Whereas these strategies have not been explored in a systematic manner, there seems to be a consensus that most countries face multiple challenges – technical, organisational, and social. First, a significant share of the housing stock in the region is in the form of multi-apartment housing with substantial needs for investment in technical improvements of engineering systems and building envelope. Second, the absence of efficient intermediaries (condominium and homeowners associations), along with the uncertain legal framework, makes it difficult to mobilise funds for routine investment in maintenance, leading to further deterioration of the stock. Third, affordability constraints faced by households and their strategies to cope with the escalating price of utilities reduce their ability to invest in maintenance and renovation. The cumulative impact has led to significant decline in the quality of multifamily housing, particularly in housing estates across the region.

The most recent data indicate that the tenure structure in the postsocialist countries is quite polarised. Homeownership has grown steadily in most countries, particularly in those belonging to the former Soviet Union, where owner occupation exceeds 90%, which is well above the 65% average in western Europe (**Figures 1** and **2**). In fact, some of the poorest countries in the region have the highest rates of homeownership.

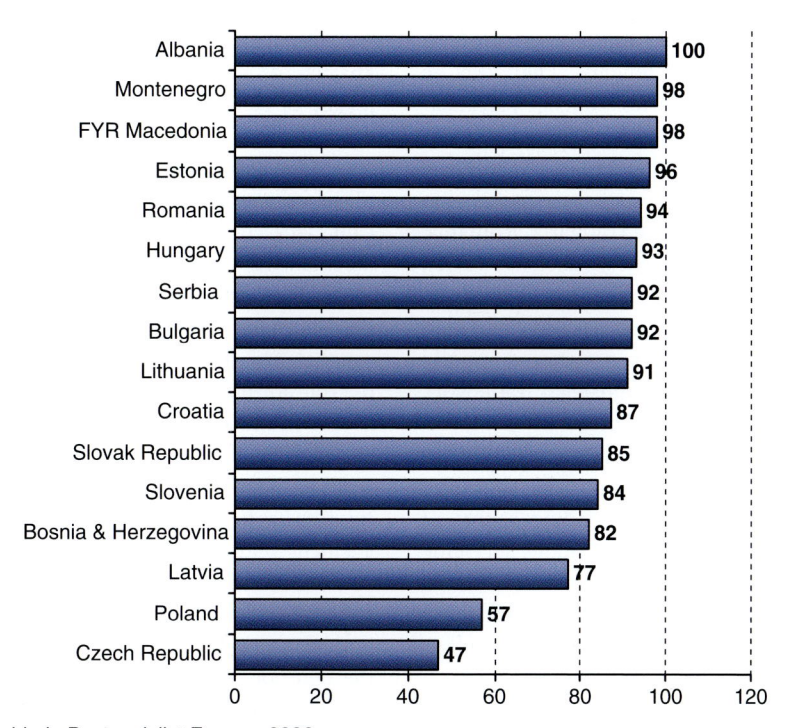

Figure 1 Homeownership in Postsocialist Europe, 2006.
Source: Author's estimates based on data from national statistical institutes.

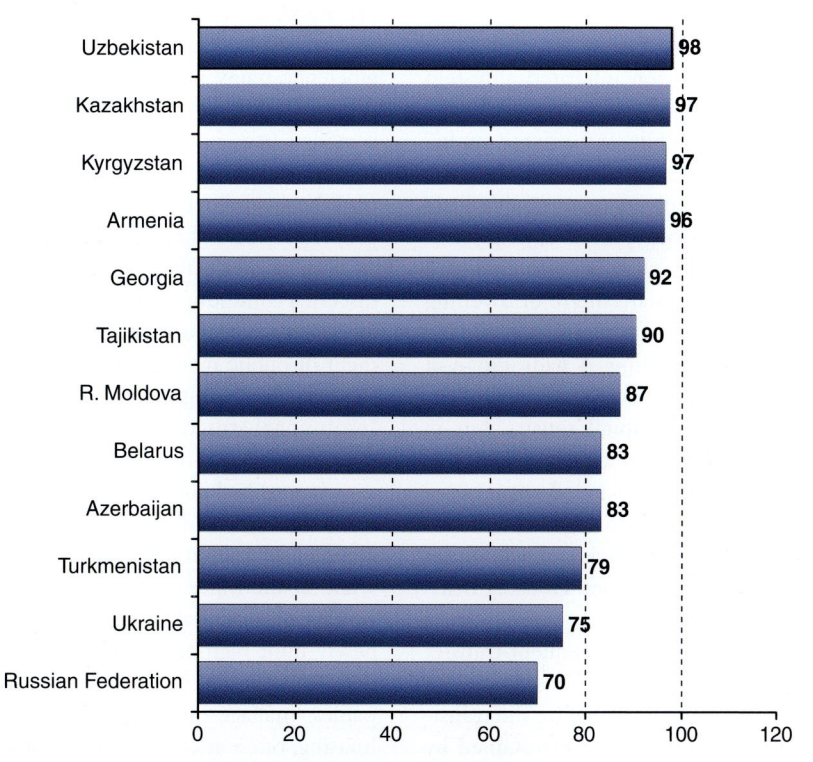

Figure 2 Homeownership in the Commonwealth of Independent States, 2006.
Source: Author's estimates based on data from national statistical institutes.

Poland, the Czech Republic, and Russia are notable exceptions with rates of homeownership below 70%. Mass housing *privatisation* was the flagship of the reform process, leading to significant transfers of public housing since 1990 – Russia (22.3 million dwellings), Poland (1.4 million), Latvia (0.4 million), and the Slovak Republic (0.3 million). Reform strategies in postsocialist countries mainly differ with respect to the price at which dwellings were sold to existing tenants. They can be grouped into the following categories: voucher privatisation (Bosnia and Herzegovina, Latvia, Lithuania), privatisation free of charge (Albania, Armenia, Moldova, Georgia, Kazakhstan, Russia), and low-price privatisation typically at 10–15% of market value (Bulgaria, Romania, Serbia, and Montenegro). The extent of sales has varied considerably both within and between countries. Notwithstanding these differences, several common problems emerged: (1) privatisation progressed rapidly without the necessary institutional and legal framework for the effective management of multifamily housing; (2) the transfer of ownership rights in most countries was limited to the dwelling itself without the necessary provisions for the transfer of corresponding shares of common areas – land, building envelope, stairs, servicing areas; (3) privatisation policies transferred substantial public assets to low-income owners without the necessary resources to deal with the renovation backlog as well as with rapidly escalating maintenance costs.

The Institutional Framework for Housing Management

Most of the countries in the region inherited a system where municipal- and state-owned maintenance companies were managing both the public and private multi-apartment housing stock. The fees for day-to-day repairs and improvements were nationally regulated with little differentiation with respect to quality, location, or price of the dwelling. Typically, monthly charges were collected on the basis of a fixed rate per square metre of dwelling space with some adjustment for the type of construction and number of storeys in the building. A wide range of detailed regulations established lifecycle assessment rules and schedules for investment in capital repairs, but in practice little work in that regard was carried out.

Maintenance companies typically carried out a range of construction, utility repair, and housing maintenance work. These public companies were large and economies of scale were essential for their operations. Housing management and maintenance was not the core of their business; the activity was subsidised by frequent transfer of funds from other operations such as construction of buildings and infrastructure. In Croatia, before the transition, 70% of the total housing stock was maintained by publicly owned companies, while in Russia this share was close to 90%. In other countries, such as Bulgaria and Romania, if owners' associations existed they had no real control over management decisions and/or funding. The public maintenance companies collected the user charges for utilities from the owners and/or tenants for common areas as well as for the buildings where individual metering devices for water and electricity in individual apartments did not exist (Moldova and Albania). The legacy of centralised and extensively subsidised housing management had important consequences: (1) there was no competition in the provision of maintenance services; (2) maintenance was deferred; and (3) there was a significant lack of financial discipline and cost recovery mechanisms.

Housing reforms in the last 15 years have created new conditions for housing management. A series of legal, institutional, and financial reforms have been carried out, but the transformation process has failed to define a system that is efficient. Essentially the transition from a centralised and excessively subsidised system to one based on market competition, private ownership, and cost recovery for housing services has been particularly difficult. The municipal management and maintenance companies faced a different situation. Without state or enterprise subsidies, and poor collection of regular maintenance charges from owners, the typical reaction was 'low fee–no service' which accelerated the deterioration process in multi-apartment buildings as the examples from Tirana and Podgorica illustrate (see **Figure 3(a) and 3(b)**). In some countries municipal maintenance companies were divided into smaller units, privatised, or restructured in accordance with construction sector policies. This forced the institutions to seek internal efficiency gains in order to operate exclusively without subsidies, although reportedly some emergency grants are provided (e.g., in Moldova, Russia, and Latvia). Housing maintenance is significantly underfunded; in some countries the tariffs cover only 20–40% of the costs required for proper service and barely cover emergency repairs.

Twenty years after the reforms were initiated, one can discern a continuum of housing management arrangements in postsocialist countries. Despite the significant involvement of public management and maintenance companies, the typology highlights a diversity of experiences. Institutional structures range from public to private with the option of self-management exercised by homeowners' associations and cooperatives. At one end of the spectrum is management and maintenance carried out by municipal companies (a slight variation from the old socialist model), while at the other is the delegation/contracting out to a private professional management company, a practice in newly built high-end condominiums. Housing profiles of Belarus, Georgia, and Moldova indicate that public companies manage and maintain most of the privatised housing, often at centrally or locally controlled prices. By

Figure 3 The lack of management has accelerated the deterioration process in multi-apartment buildings in Tirana (a) and Podgorica (b).

contrast, in the Czech Republic and Poland, even the sizeable share of public housing is often managed by private firms contracted by local municipalities. Self-management is a viable alternative that is likely to become more important in the future with the institutionalisation of homeowners' associations (HOAs), offering residents more control over negotiation of service agreements and potential cost savings. In Bulgaria, Albania, Romania, and to some extent in Croatia, HOAs have the right to contract any company or private person to carry out maintenance. In these cases, competition has had a positive effect on the performance of the maintenance companies (public and private) with respect to prices and quality. In countries where the market has been liberalised, there is an overall lack of professional management companies which are licensed to carry out technical assessment and asset management. The process is also challenged by the high cost for their services as well as the lack of organisational and managerial experience of the newly established HOAs.

The Legal Framework for Housing Management

Most countries in the region have introduced condominium ownership or its equivalent based on historical interpretation of multi-apartment ownership models in existing property legislation. While there are some variations, in general, condominium ownership is based on the unit owner having absolute ownership of a unit, plus an undivided interest in the ownership of the common elements owned jointly with the other condominium unit owners (e.g., roof, elevator, and building land). Each owner may have a separate mortgage for his or her individual unit and is individually responsible for making the payments and real estate taxes on it. In addition, owners contribute to the funding of common expenses for repair of structural elements, building installations, and utility charges for common areas.

The new legislation, adopted after the reforms in 1990, typically defines HOAs or Condominium Owners Association as the institutional entity which manages multi-apartment housing, meets financial obligations, and initiates contracts and renewal projects (see **Box 1**). Most HOAs are not registered as legal entities; thus, behind every contract there are individual owners. Although the new condominium legislation in Albania, Moldova, and Romania stipulates mandatory HOAs, only 20% of the condominiums in Romania and 15% of those in Moldova have established such associations as legal entities. In Albania, Lithuania, and Latvia research indicates that progress in this regard has been very limited.

> **Box 1 Housing management in Croatia, Romania, and Serbia.**
>
> In **Croatia**, the management and maintenance of apartments, including regular operation, improvements and other works, is regulated by the *Ordinance on Buildings Maintenance*. Maintenance of apartments is financed by the co-owners on the basis of contracts with public or private firms registered for house management and maintenance. Only registered companies can provide services for large buildings.
>
> According to the *Housing Act of 1996*, in **Romania**, the management of multi-unit buildings is the responsibility of the association of owners (HOA). The associations' rights and obligations are: approving and amending the budget, collecting financial contributions, imposing penalties in case of late payments, concluding contracts and most importantly, managing, maintaining, repairing, replacing and modifying the common parts of the buildings. The HOA also approves or amends decisions on rules and regulations, monitors the condition of the building and keeps the building's technical logbook updated. Legal or natural persons, associations, public agencies or specialised companies appointed by HOA can manage the condominium.
>
> In **Serbia**, the 'Owners Assembly/Council' can contract public or other companies for housing management and maintenance. If no maintenance is provided, the municipality will appoint a public municipal company directly charging its tenants/owners for public services such as land rent, central heating, water, sewerage and electricity in common areas. The supervision is delegated to municipal housing departments.
>
> Source: Tsenkova (2009).

While costs are expected to be borne by the owners, it is important to state that the new Condominium Laws, bylaws, and special resolutions in countries across the region typically differentiate between decisions with low-cost consequences and decisions on higher investments, such as renovations and structural repairs. The first normally requires a simple majority of votes, the latter a higher share of support (e.g., 67% of owners in Romania, 75% in Albania).

Recent experience across the region indicates that a fair amount of effort has been directed at the improvement of the legal framework, but without an efficient enforcement system its effects may be questionable. The new laws defined with various degrees of detail rights and responsibilities of ownership as well as the procedures for contributions to maintenance costs of common areas. Several barriers to the implementation of these laws exist: (1) individual owners have been reluctant to establish new organisations and to assume a wide range of responsibilities; (2) multiple changes to the legal framework provided inconsistent guidelines regarding cost-sharing mechanisms and enforcement possibilities. Albania, Moldova, Georgia, and Montenegro are prime examples where ambiguity in the legislation, coupled with economic difficulties of the owners, has created cumulative debts and no action to resolve housing management problems.

The Triple Challenge for Housing Management

Technical Challenges

The collective form of privatised housing from the past has a critical effect on housing management, not only in terms of institutional and legal challenges, but more importantly related to the quality of existing housing. Nearly every observer in the region concludes that the deterioration process in parts of the urban stock has reached a critical stage. Most of the buildings were constructed in the 1970s and 1980s in response to rapid urban growth and migration to the cities. Panel technologies, which featured prominently in Russia, Lithuania, Bulgaria, the Czech Republic, Moldova, and Romania, resulted in large-scale developments with demanding requirements for their housing management. The life expectancy of multifamily panel housing is approximately 50 years and a significant portion of the older stock no longer complies with technical standards. In addition, the region is exposed to earthquake risk, so the physical condition of panel housing raises concerns over its capacity to withstand natural disasters. Even in the new multi-apartment housing that is less than 30 years old, the initial quality was not very high. Subsequently, inadequate investment in maintenance as well as deferred structural repairs have aggravated the technical problems with leaking roofs, obsolete installations, elevators, and poor wall insulation. Furthermore, the accelerated privatisation of the housing stock often transferred ownership of the apartments while municipalities were left with the ownership of buildings, land, and common areas. Mixed ownership is an issue in countries such as Latvia, Russia, and the Czech Republic where owners and tenants live in the same building. The lack of clarity with respect to responsibilities in the maintenance and management of common areas as well as some of the financial difficulties experienced by tenants pose frequent challenges for the efficient management of the housing stock and its renovation.

In addition, the level of housing-related services (water, energy services, district heating, garbage collection, and waste management) has declined because of subsidy cuts, rapidly escalating costs, and massive arrears with respect to utility costs. As a result of these processes not only have public services deteriorated, but the normal maintenance of the housing stock has also accumulated a huge backlog. The quality of multi-apartment housing in the region is mixed; assessments indicate that renovation investment needed in central European countries alone is EUR 227 000 million. The refurbishment of high-rise housing estates in postsocialist Europe may well be the single most important housing issue facing the European Union today.

Social Challenges

In most of the cases multi-apartment buildings have a social mix inherited from the previous system of housing allocation. Income and labour market inequalities in recent years have led to an impoverishment of the home-owners, which is one of the reasons for the poor maintenance of multi-apartment buildings. The cost of housing-related services and utilities has increased in real terms, but quite unevenly: Energy costs and central heating costs have increased the most, crowding out other expenditures. The rapid growth in utility costs in many countries has resulted in accumulated arrears. In the absence of support for housing and utility services, more affluent owners have continued to subsidise their neighbours by paying the cost of utilities and maintenance of common areas, roofs, and technical infrastructure as well as financing urgent repairs. Others have just cut back on individual consumption, such as central heating. A few countries (Poland, the Czech Republic, Latvia, and Estonia) have introduced a system of housing allowances, while others (Bulgaria, Russia) have experimented with energy allowances to provide 'affordable warmth', but systematic attempts to address the impact of growing social inequality and poverty in the housing sector through wider social welfare and redistribution policies is nonexistent.

It is not surprising that despite different coping mechanisms, arrears are widespread and a lack of payment discipline common. Studies have reported lack of respect for the law as well as 'free rider' problems and refusal to pay regular contributions for the maintenance and modernisation of common areas in multi-apartment buildings. In cases where municipal maintenance companies still manage privatised housing under contractual obligations at locally controlled prices, tariffs are inadequate to cover the true cost for services, while the government lacks sufficient funding to make up the difference (see **Box 2**).

Box 2   Multi-apartment housing in Azerbaijan.

Reforms in housing and communal services remain incomplete. In the early transition years, privatization of apartments created a new group of owners, who acquired the benefits of apartment ownership without fully assuming the responsibilities. State-set maintenance tariffs are too low, and are not augmented with other funds, so apartment buildings continue to deteriorate. The current institutional framework requires both maintenance and structural repairs to be provided by the state through its Housing and Communal Services Departments (ZhEKs). Without adequate financing, ZhEKs cannot provide routine maintenance, but instead provide a form of catastrophic insurance. If the roof falls in, for example, then the ZhEKs will repair or replace it at no charge.

Source: World Bank (2006).

The outcome is inadequate investment to sustain the quality of privatised housing assets.

Financial Challenges

Lack of adequate financing is considered a major constraint for housing management. While in recent years budgetary discipline and more transparent and accountable budgetary processes have been introduced, chronic underinvestment in maintenance has left owners with major technical challenges. The requirements for structural repairs and improvements after 20 years grow exponentially. In most cases multi-apartment buildings have reached the critical stage in the lifecycle assessment where a major infusion of capital will be needed to bring them back to standards. Buildings have poor quality and the current stream of revenue does not ensure sufficient funds for renovation and improvement of the building envelope (roof, foundations, elevation, etc). Renovation planning is also problematic within the context of unclear financial and management responsibilities. Furthermore, in addition to the traditional technical and organisational challenges, it is difficult to borrow funds for major improvements. Banks often request individual owners to sign a mortgage or a loan contract, which makes the process extremely cumbersome and costly. Lending institutions have not developed any products for renovation of multi-apartment housing and the high interest rates certainly discourage borrowing.

The financing of rehabilitation requires specially designed credit lines and some incentives (tax exemptions, rebates, etc.) to facilitate the process. Very few countries have launched programmes to assist this process, mostly targeting energy efficiency retrofits. The Czech Republic, Lithuania, Latvia, and Slovakia have secured lines of credit from international financial institutions which, coupled with government assistance, leverage much-needed long-term investment for the rehabilitation of multi-apartment housing. A precondition for access to these lines of credit and grants is the formation of HOAs and a system of housing management. In Slovakia approximately 11 000 apartments have been renovated and measures range from insulation of walls and roofs to installation of efficient heat pumps, boilers, and solar heaters. In the Czech Republic the programme for repairs of prefabricated housing (PANEL) provides an interest subsidy of EUR10 per sq m plus state guarantee on 70% of the loan. Despite the small outreach, PANEL encourages a more proactive housing management style and has delivered tangible results (see **Box 3**).

The key issue is mobilisation of funds, savings (including intergenerational savings), loans, and mortgages to pay for rehabilitation and renewal. Various mechanisms can be used to encourage financial institutions to develop competitive products (state guarantees, shallow subsidies,

> **Box 3   Housing rehabilitation programmes in the Czech Republic.**
>
> The Czech Republic has launched two programs since 2001 aiming at the rehabilitation of multi-apartment panel housing, which makes up 57 percent of the housing stock. The programs support individual projects as well as regeneration of panel housing estates. Low-cost credits and subsidies fund up to 70 percent of the costs, while homeowners, cooperatives and municipalities provide matching funds. Most of the borrowers (85–90%) are housing cooperatives and homeowners' associations. So far the programs have assisted the rehabilitation and energy efficient retrofitting of less than 8 percent of the panel housing.
> Source: Ministry of Regional Development of the Czech Republic, 2007.

insurance). This needs to be complemented by targeted subsidies and reversed mortgages for low-income owners to allow renovation measures to proceed at a large scale for the whole building.

Conclusion

In the aftermath of privatisation, the management and rehabilitation of multi-apartment housing in postsocialist countries is potentially one of the largest problems facing governments and homeowners. Failure to establish homeowners' associations and efficient private management systems to carry out preventive maintenance and repairs may result in massive structural problems in more than half of the urban housing stock. Recently, most countries have introduced laws to regulate the operation of homeowners' associations and have established the framework for competitive provision of maintenance services, but the implementation has been slow and inadequate. Incremental policies through 'trial and error' continue to reshape the legal framework and organisational structures for housing management, focusing on problems to be remedied rather than strategic options. In the spirit of incrementalism, the policy evolution emphasises less government involvement, fiscally conservative programmes, and limited experimentation with assistance to low-income households. While in the high-end condominium market a fairly competitive system has emerged, the management of privatised multifamily housing has three significant challenges – technical, social, and financial – which need to be systematically addressed.

See also: Collective Ownership; Private Sector Housing Management: Europe; Private Sector Housing Management: North America; Privatisation of Housing: Implications for Well-Being.

References

Tsenkova S (2009) *Housing Reforms in Post-socialist Europe. Lost in Transition*. Heidelberg: Springer-Verlag.
World Bank (2006) *Multi-apartment Housing in Azerbaijan: Issues Note*. Washington, DC: Infrastructure Department, Europe and Central Asia Region.

Further Reading

Gruis V, Tsenkova S, and Niebor N (2009) *Managing Privatised Housing: International Perspectives*. Oxford: Wiley-Blackwell.
Struyk R (ed.) (2000) *Homeownership and Housing Finance Policy in the Former Soviet Bloc: Costly Populism*. Washington, DC: Urban Institute Press.
Tsenkova S (2004) The limits of housing reforms: Implications for housing management. *Open House International* 29(3): 12–22.
United Nations Economic Commission for Europe (2003) *Guidelines on Condominium Ownership of Housing for Countries in Transition*. Geneva: United Nations Economic Commission for Europe.

Relevant Websites

www.unece.org – Housing Profiles

Privatisation of Housing: Implications for Well-Being

P Malpass, University of the West of England, Bristol, UK

© 2012 Elsevier Ltd. All rights reserved.

Glossary

Housing associations The term used in some countries to describe nonmunicipal social landlord organisations.

Public housing (social housing) Housing provided by the state, municipalities, not-for-profit organisations, and sometimes by profit-seeking landlords, at affordable rents and usually allocated on needs criteria rather than strict ability to pay.

Rent controls Measures adopted by governments to set rents at less than open market levels; sometimes introduced for ideological reasons and sometimes as temporary expedients during times of great shortage.

Right to buy Statutory right introduced in a number of countries for tenants of public housing to buy their existing homes at less than the open market valuation.

Subsidies Tax expenditures that reduce housing costs borne by consumers below open market levels.

Tax reliefs Arrangements allowing consumers and/or providers to offset some or all of their housing expenditures against tax liabilities.

Introduction

Privatisation of housing has become a global phenomenon, adopted more or less enthusiastically in one form or another in many different countries, for a variety of reasons. In some countries it has been the defining narrative of housing over the last 20 or 30 years. Places as diverse as the United Kingdom, Romania, and China have pursued a wide variety of privatisation policies. In the space available here, it is only possible to provide an outline sketch of the sorts of measures that have been implemented around the world, and to identify in broad terms the implications for well-being. Part of the difficulty inherent in writing about privatisation of housing is that the concept itself is not only multifaceted but also contested. Moreover, each country started from a different position and proceeded in its own way, at its own pace.

The Context of Privatisation

The privatisation of housing in recent decades is an aspect of the much wider debate about the appropriate role of the state in the economy as a whole, associated with social, economic, and political change embracing the production, distribution, and consumption of a range of goods and services. In capitalist countries this has taken the form of a neoliberal ascendancy which is itself at least partly a reaction to the previous period in which collectivist policies flourished and as such, it represents a retreat from or outright repudiation of attempts to manage or replace markets. In the countries of the former Soviet Union and those of Central and Eastern Europe previously in the Soviet bloc, the collapse of communism in the late 1980s was generally followed by large-scale privatisation (Clapham et al., 1996; Lowe and Tsenkova, 2003), while in China an equally dramatic transformation has been achieved.

Housing systems generally reveal a mix of public and private activity. The extent to which market forces are free to operate varies from place to place and time to time. During the twentieth century, and particularly in the three decades after 1945, there was a widespread tendency for governments to increase intervention in housing systems, sometimes for positive ideological reasons and sometimes despite an enduring ideological preference for private markets. Market forces and private property rights were never completely removed from housing in socialist countries, but neither were they unrestrained in capitalist countries that were committed to the private ownership of property. Everywhere the free flow of market forces was restricted in various ways, often without going so far as to prevent continuing market activity: rent controls, subsidies, tax reliefs, and planning restrictions on property development rights were widely adopted, at different times and to varying degrees. In addition, many governments moved further towards the decommodification of housing by developing forms of public housing in which it was normally the case that key decisions about the volume of new building, the allocation of dwellings, and the rents to be charged were based on political and/or administrative criteria rather than market-based supply and demand. In some cases, notably in Russia, it was the state that built and owned this sort of housing, and in China state-owned work units provided housing for their workers; elsewhere, for example in the United Kingdom and

Sweden, the task was undertaken by the local government while in the Netherlands and Denmark, independent not-for-profit housing associations took the lead. In centrally planned economies, the production, management, and maintenance of public housing was generally undertaken by state-owned organisations, whereas in other countries production was often carried out by private contractors commissioned by social landlords. Privatisation also had an impact in the United States (but see Rohe and Stegman, 1992) although the market has never been seriously challenged and public housing has never been more than a tiny sector for the least well off, whose incomes have meant little take-up of opportunities to buy.

Privatisation can be seen as a historically specific secular tendency to rebalance the mix of public and private in favour of market forces, removing or reducing regulations, controls, and subsidies that had been developed in the previous period. The most eye-catching aspect of privatisation, the transfer of ownership of public housing to new owners, often sitting tenants, on attractive financial terms, highlights the historical specificity because these transfers presupposed the prior construction of public housing. While it is the disposal of such housing that grabs the headlines and focuses debate, privatisation is in fact a much broader phenomenon referring to the overall direction of travel as market forces become more prevalent and pervasive in housing systems. It is about the normalisation of (unregulated) markets and as such it is about establishing a different set of taken-for-granted perceptions and expectations about how, and on what terms, housing is to be provided and consumed. On this view privatisation is a characteristic of the housing system as a whole, and it is possible to refer to a national system undergoing privatisation even where there is no attempt to sell off state-owned assets.

Forms of Privatisation

It has been suggested that privatisation proposals come in two general forms: load shedding and empowerment (Linneman and Megbolugbe, 1994). Load shedding means that governments distance themselves from the financing and production of goods and services, while empowerment here refers to situations where governments remain involved in providing finance but rely on private organisations for delivery of goods and services. This is not inconsistent with the more detailed set of categories in **Table 1** (based on Murie, 1993), which lists seven forms of privatisation identified in research in the United Kingdom. The United Kingdom has often been seen as a pioneer in this area, adopting in the early 1980s a more wide-ranging programme of privatisation than other European countries up to that time. These

Table 1 Forms of privatisation

Deregulation	Reducing or removing state regulation of private activity, in areas such as private renting and mortgage lending
Commercialisation	Increasing user charges and reducing subsidy and tax finance of state activity, thereby strengthening market signals across the housing system
Demunicipalisation	Reducing municipal ownership by disposal to sitting tenants and new landlords, and reducing development activity
Encouragement of private provision	Creating a climate within which private enterprise can flourish. Removing competition from subsidised state agencies. Increased subsidy, tax finance, and legislative provision for private production and consumption
Contracting out	Arrangements for an increased private role in areas which remain the responsibility of state agencies. Subjecting certain housing activities to market testing, making state agencies compete with the private sector
Incorporation	Embracing quasi-public agencies in the private sector
Preparing for privatisation	Preparing the ground for other forms of privatisation by, for example, reforming regulatory regimes to encourage private sector involvement in the provision of public housing, or legislation to permit state (or quasi-state) agencies to convert to private status

different measures overlap to some extent and are mutually supportive.

This list is not exhaustive and not all forms of privatisation will be found everywhere. Additional activities might include developing mortgage lending industries in contexts where there has not been a tradition of debt-financed homeownership and only limited capacity for household saving. To the extent that privatisation is about enabling markets to work more effectively and efficiently, it is not necessarily about the state doing or spending less, but just operating differently.

There is a certain pick and mix quality to privatisation, in the sense that it is possible, for example, to privatise aspects of the supply side of public housing without necessarily altering the consumption side terms and conditions enjoyed by tenants. The UK government in the 1990s introduced (largely ineffective) legislation, which requires municipal housing authorities to subject their housing management to regular competitive tendering, but without privatising the consumption side. In principle at least it would be possible to privatise consumption, charging market rents on a first-come first-served basis, while leaving supply in the hands of public sector bodies.

Housing Privatisation in Western Europe

Governments in Western Europe have generally worked on the assumption that the private market would provide housing for most people, most of the time. In this sense the growth of interventionist policies after 1945 can be seen as a contingent response to the particular circumstances of the time: rent controls reflected gross shortages and construction subsidies were designed to achieve high volumes of new building. Once the worst shortages were removed it was to be expected that the underlying preference for market forces would lead to reduced intervention, thereby reprivatising housing systems. As it happened, this process was accelerated by the economic crisis of the mid-1970s, which caused governments to review commitments to public expenditure. It has been suggested (Doherty, 2004) that an accumulation of evidence during the 1990s demonstrated a common European experience of a tendency towards state withdrawal from direct involvement in housing, and that this stemmed from the 1970s' economic crisis which had ended the postwar boom and challenged the idea of interventionist government. By the same time the housing shortages of the postwar period had eased and living standards had risen significantly, making it easier to argue that there was no longer a need for the state to regulate the market, nor to involve itself in the provision of housing (except for the least well off and most vulnerable households).

Comparative analysis of housing policies in the United Kingdom, France, and Germany has shown that in all three countries, policy has shifted towards the market, with signs of privatisation as early as the 1960s, when the Federal Republic of Germany phased out rent controls (Kleinman, 1996). In 1986 the West German government removed federal subsidies to social housing, and 2 years later social housing companies were privatised as a result of removal of their tax privileges. In France the decisive shift towards a more market-oriented policy was the Housing Act of 1977 which set out to allow market forces to operate more freely, to raise rents towards market levels, to reduce state aid by targeting it on aid to low-income families rather than the promotion of new construction, and to simplify the housing finance system. In the United Kingdom high output policy was effectively abandoned in 1968 (in the context of an economic crisis), and in 1972 the first steps were taken to raise public sector rents on a par with regulated private sector rents. This can be seen as a key development in the British version of the wider trend towards subsidising people rather than buildings. In the mid-1980s, legislation was passed to open up the mortgage lending industry to the full effects of market forces and in 1988 steps were taken to deregulate the private rental market.

Public housing has been on the defensive since the 1970s and the rapid growth seen in earlier years seems to have disappeared virtually everywhere. Not all countries, however, have followed the pioneering British policy of privatisation by subsidised sales to sitting tenants of local authorities (but not charitable housing associations) through a statutory right to buy (Forrest and Murie, 1990; Jones and Murie, 2006). The impact of the right to buy in Britain was immediate and substantial, resulting in the sale of 2.5 million dwellings between 1980 and 2008; over the same period the combined effect of sales and low levels of new building was that the public rented sector fell from 32 to 18% of the total stock. Although other countries did not adopt the British approach, in France and the Netherlands, for example, government policy has been in place to support the growth of homeownership and to favour sales without going so far as to insist on a right to buy. As a result the level of sales in these countries has been very low by comparison. In Britain the fact that over 90% of public housing in 1980 was owned by municipalities made it particularly vulnerable to a government that was determined to pursue privatisation. The right to buy has generated fewer sales in recent years and can now be seen as a spent force in British housing policy, but local authorities have continued to lose stock through transfers to housing associations. This process, which has involved over 1 million homes since 1988, is interpreted by some as a form of privatisation, and in one sense it is because housing associations are defined as private sector bodies, but at the same time they remain committed to the provision of housing at rents affordable by people on low incomes.

In the Netherlands, which has the largest social housing sector in Western Europe (35% in 2007), social housing provision has always been dominated by independent housing associations which could not be so easily steered by government. In fact the Netherlands governments have not sought to press privatisation through sales to individual tenants, but in the 1990s there was a significant privatising move when housing associations agreed to forego subsidy in future years in return for having their existing debts written off. This process, known as grossing and balancing, increased the financial independence of Dutch social housing organisations although they remain subject to regulation. Social housing in the former Federal Republic of Germany was defined not by tenure or ownership but by receipt of financial assistance; once that assistance expired the dwellings passed into the open market sector. As a result of high levels of building in earlier years but lower levels more recently the social housing sector has been rapidly unravelling, and is now down to less than 5%. This sort of privatisation was always implicit in the way that social housing was defined and funded, although its impact reflects the declining rates of investment to replace dwellings transferred to the private sector. In 2006 the Federal Government of the united Germany withdrew from involvement in housing policy (Stephens et al., 2008).

Privatisation in Central and Eastern Europe

Privatisation of housing in Central and Eastern Europe may resemble the equivalent process in the West, especially in the way that large numbers of dwellings have been transferred to sitting tenants, but there are important differences. Whereas in the affluent democracies of Western Europe, privatisation can be seen as a reassertion of faith in capitalism and the prevailing private market economy, further east in the countries of the former Soviet bloc, privatisation represented a rejection of communism and the command economy. And whereas privatisation in the West took place in the context of reasonably stable political and economic conditions, in the East it was part of a rapid political and economic transformation. Moreover, in the West there were already established mortgage markets and legal procedures for buying and selling properties with proper title.

The model of housing provision in countries that made up the Soviet bloc from the late 1940s until 1990 has been defined in these terms:

> Exclusion of the market, the omission of housing costs from incomes, and the centralisation of all important investment decisions were preconditions of a system in which all important aspects of housing were meant to be under the control of state institutions. Housing was intended to be a form of public service, in which the private sector should not have a role either in production or distribution. (Hegedus and Tosics, 1996)

However, as Hegedus and Tosics point out, the model was never realised in its pure form. There remained significant amounts of privately owned housing, even within Russia itself, although active housing markets were effectively suppressed by, among other things, strict rent controls. However, in Bulgaria there was a long-established preference for homeownership and a form of right to buy, so that over 80% of households were homeowners even before 1990, although housing production remained in the hands of state-run organisations. In Hungary public sector tenants had a right to exchange for another tenancy or for owner-occupation and a market existed in which money changed hands. In Russia, where two-thirds of housing was provided by the state, rents had not been raised since 1928, and in the German Democratic Republic, rents in the late 1980s were still at levels set in 1936. This meant that throughout the period of Soviet domination after 1945 no one was paying anything like a true market rent, and management and maintenance were neglected, facts that had serious implications after the adoption of market principles in the 1990s.

After the collapse of the Soviet Union, promarket governments came into power, encouraged to press ahead with reform by Western governments and international agencies such as the World Bank and USAID. Privatisation of housing was a universally adopted policy. Amidst the turmoil of transformation the transfer of dwellings to their occupants at highly discounted prices, or in some cases at nil cost, has been seen as a shock absorber (Struyk, 1996), providing people with a degree of security and stability in an uncertain and rapidly changing world. Not all countries privatised the ownership of state housing to the same extent, at the same pace, or on the same terms, and there were different arrangements for the restitution of property to former owners. Estonia, Romania, and Slovakia undertook large-scale transfers through right to buy, but in the Czech Republic and Poland the scale and speed of privatisation was more modest. In Russia dwellings were effectively given away and in Hungary dwellings were being sold from the mid-1980s for as little as 15% of their value.

Transferring dwellings to individual homeowners is only one part of a privatisation strategy, and it is the easy part. The more difficult tasks include the establishment of a savings and loans industry as a necessary prerequisite of a dynamic housing market, and the provision of housing allowance schemes to protect low-income households from the full impact of market prices. It has been claimed that governments have been more enthusiastic about transferring ownership than pursuing less popular policies such as cost recovery rents and deregulation of management and maintenance (Tsenkova, 2008).

Privatisation in China

The Communist victory in China in 1949 led to nationalisation of all urban land, and in due course to a largely decommodified housing system. Existing owner-occupiers retained title to their homes but over time the properties of private landlords were taken over by the state (Wang and Murie, 1999). The great majority came to rely on flats provided by the state or work units, in a context in which housing was, in effect, treated as part of the social wage. As in the Soviet bloc, rents were very low, usually only about 2% of incomes. The first experiments with a revived housing market began in 1979, which resulted in small numbers of newly built dwellings for open market sale. From 1983 some workers were able to buy their flats at heavily discounted prices, but they did not acquire full ownership rights at that stage. In the early 1990s the pace was stepped up and the aim was to have two-thirds of urban couples in homeownership by 2000, paying five times their annual salary to buy their state rental apartments. It was only in 1999 that the full bundle of property rights was privatised and commodified (Davis, 2003), but according to the census of 2000 approximately three-quarters of the urban population were homeowners. From this point market rents were to prevail and public housing programmes were more clearly targeted on lower-income and vulnerable groups; transition to a market-based system was virtually complete. To facilitate home purchase, the central government reformed the banking sector to ensure that mortgage finance was available (Li and Huang, 2006).

Implications for Well-being

Assessing the implications of privatisation for well-being is both necessary and very difficult, not least because of the great diversity of contexts and approaches in different places. In general the economic argument for privatisation is that it increases the efficiency of housing systems. However, efficiency gains tend to come at the expense of equity, and inequalities in the labour market are generally mapped onto housing markets. To the extent that privatisation of housing accompanies a wider economic transformation incorporating greater income differentials, then the implication is more rather than less inequality in housing well-being.

In the United Kingdom, where a considerable amount of research has been carried out on the impact of privatisation, the picture is reasonably clear: the right to buy rewarded an already privileged cohort of tenants, those who occupied the best and most desirable homes, and whose life cycle position meant that they not only qualified for the highest discounts but had incomes that made buying affordable. There is evidence that experience has been similar in other countries too: in the Soviet bloc, members of the Communist Party and 'nomenklatura' were more likely to occupy desirable dwellings and be able to buy them at advantageous prices. Reporting research in six East European countries, Lux (2003) observed that

> Housing privatisation, often recommended by international organisations, was shown to have many drawbacks and intensified the social tensions between those who were able to take advantage of house purchase subsidies and those who were not.

Even where tenants are able to take up the chance to buy, some have found that they have acquired a liability rather than an asset, and to some extent privatisation in the Soviet bloc in particular gave the authorities an opportunity to offload problematic rundown and poorly maintained blocks of flats. In addition to looking at those who buy under privatisation schemes, it is necessary to consider the implications for those left behind, and who find themselves paying higher rents to local authorities that still lack the resources to provide adequate repair and maintenance services. In the United Kingdom, and to a lesser extent other countries in Western Europe and also countries further east, the evidence suggests that privatisation disproportionately involved the sale of better properties and had a residualising effect, moving towards a situation where social housing is seen as a safety net service for the least well-off. As such, it can have a stigmatising effect on tenants in a way that was not evident when a broader cross-section of the population was housed there.

Privatisation through transfer of full property rights to sitting tenants is an unrepeatable offer and so there is a need to look at the implications for the well-being of those who were already waiting for public housing and others who come along later. Their interests would not be harmed if levels of new building were maintained, but the evidence from both Western and Eastern Europe is that privatisation has been accompanied by falling levels of construction. In the former Soviet bloc countries, the decline in new building might be interpreted as partly a product of the economic disruption of the transformation and the difficulties of establishing sustainable housing markets. However, the evidence from Western Europe does not suggest a return to the building of high levels of affordable housing once economic stability is achieved.

In Central and Eastern Europe the outcomes of privatisation can be summed up in these terms:

> It is readily apparent that the liberalisation of the housing systems across all these countries has not been a panacea bringing in its wake easy solutions or greater quantity of more affordable housing. Indeed, it is only too clear that despite progress the rapid privatisation of the state housing stock, leading to half the countries becoming 'super' owner occupied nations, there are major social problems and diseconomies arising from these new marketplaces for housing. (Lowe, 2003)

The implications for the well-being of ordinary workers in these countries are clear. Elsewhere it is perhaps possible to be rather more optimistic, but it is inescapable that markets in general work best for those who have the most money and privatisation can only exacerbate existing inequalities.

See also: Gentrification and Well-Being; Home Ownership: Economic Benefits; Housing and the State in China; Housing and the State in the Soviet Union and Eastern Europe; Housing and the State in Western Europe; Policies to Promote Housing Choice in Transition Countries; Social Housing in the United States: Overview.

References

Clapham D, Hegedus J, Kintrea K, and Tosics I, with Kay H (1996) *Housing Privatisation in Eastern Europe*. Westport, CT: Greenwood Press.

Davis D (2003) Housing and social change. In: Forrest R and Lee J (eds.) *From Welfare Benefit to Capitalised Asset: The Recommodification of Residential Space in China*. London: Routledge.

Doherty J (2004) European housing policies: Bringing the state back in? *European Journal of Housing Policy* 4(3): 283–302.

Forrest R and Murie A (1990) *Selling the Welfare State*. London: Routledge.

Hegedus J and Tosics I (1996) Housing privatisation in Eastern Europe. In: Clapham D, Hegedus J, Kintrea K, and Tosics I (eds.) *The Disintegration of the East European Housing Model*. Westport, CT: Greenwood Press.

Jones C and Murie A (2006) *The Right to Buy*. Oxford, UK: Blackwell.

Kleinman M (1996) *Housing, Welfare and the State in Europe*. Cheltenham, UK: Edward Elgar.

Li S-M and Huang Y (2006) Urban housing in China. *Housing Studies* 21(5): 613–624.

Linneman P and Megbolugbe I (1994) Privatisation and housing policy. *Urban Studies* 31(4/5): 635–651.

Lowe S (2003) Introduction. In: Lowe S and Tsenkova S (eds.) *Housing Change in East and Central Europe*. Aldershot, UK: Ashgate.

Lowe S and Tsenkova S (eds.) (2003). *Housing Change in East and Central Europe*. Aldershot, UK: Ashgate.

Lux M (2003) Efficiency and effectiveness in housing policies in the Central and Eastern European countries. *European Journal of Housing Policy* 3(3): 243–265.

Murie A (1993) Privatisation and restructuring public involvement in housing provision in Britain. *Scandinavian Housing and Planning Research* 10: 145–157.

Rohe WM and Stegman MA (1992) Public housing home ownership. *Journal of the American Planning Association* 58(2): 144–158.

Stephens M, Elsinga M, and Knorr-Siedow T (2008) The privatisation of social housing: Three different pathways. In: Scanlon K and Whitehead C (eds.) *Social Housing in Europe II*. London: London School of Economics.

Struyk R (ed.) (1996). *Economic Restructuring of the Former Soviet Bloc*. Washington, DC: Urban Institute Press.

Tsenkova S (2008) The future of social housing in the EU: Reform challenges in the Czech Republic, Latvia and Lithuania. In: Czischke D (ed.) *Welfare Transformation and Demographic Change in Europe: Challenges for the Social Housing Sector*. Brussels: CECODHAS.

Wang YP and Murie A (1999) *Housing Policy and Practice in China*. London: Macmillan.

Further Reading

Murie A, Tosics I, Aalbers M, Sendl R, and Mali BC (2005) Privatisation and after. In: Hall S, van Kempen R, and Dekker K (eds.) *Restructuring Large Housing Estates in Europe*. Bristol, UK: Policy Press.

Privatisation of Social Housing

MB Aalbers, University of Amsterdam, Amsterdam, The Netherlands

© 2012 Elsevier Ltd. All rights reserved.

Glossary

Condominium A form of housing tenure where a specified part of a piece of real estate (usually an apartment) is individually owned while use of and access to common facilities is controlled by the association of owners that jointly represent ownership of the whole building.

Housing association A private, not-for-profit body that provides low-cost social housing for people in housing need.

Housing privatisation The transfer of ownership from a social housing landlord to sitting tenants, other individual owners and/or investors.

Restituted dwellings People who have previous claims on land or property that have been seized by earlier regimes can reclaim it.

Right to Buy A policy in the United Kingdom which gives tenants of council housing the right to buy the home they are living in.

Social housing An umbrella term referring to rental housing which may be owned and managed by the state, nonprofit organisations or a combination of the two, usually with the aim of providing affordable housing.

Introduction

Housing policy, characterised by public or social housing projects, was for a long time central to social welfare orientation in most European and some other countries (see article Housing and the State in Western Europe). During the past 20 years, a trend towards deregulation, privatisation, and liberalisation became generally accepted throughout many countries. In particular, the privatisation of the social housing stock has changed both the housing market and urban governance constellations. Housing privatisation is here both an effect of local political decisions and a challenge for the local actors affected by or determining urban policy. Privatisation itself has taken different forms, and discussions of privatisation policies have referred to the movement of rents towards market levels, contracting out of various services to private sector agencies, and the transfer of ownership in various forms. It can be considered ironic that nonprofit social housing programmes were considered to be more efficient and effective for large parts of the population than private, for-profit provision of housing, while housing privatisation is currently, at least in part, justified on the same grounds. This article concentrates on the transfer of ownership to sitting tenants, other individual owners and/or international financial investors.

In the international literature, two approaches to housing privatisation are widely discussed: the 'Right to Buy' policy in the United Kingdom and the wholesale selling off of social housing in many Central and Eastern European (CEE) countries. The introduction of the Right to Buy in the United Kingdom grew out of ideological and electoral considerations and a desire to encourage homeownership for its own sake. The sales in CEE countries are associated with changes in political regimes in the late 1980s (see article Policies to Promote Housing Choice in Transition Countries). The privatisations in CEE countries are widely presented as political shock absorbers, demonstrating that changes in political regimes have direct, tangible effects on individual households and citizens. It is also argued that privatisation in these circumstances allowed new systems of local government to avoid the high maintenance and repair costs associated with ownership of properties that could be in poor condition. In other words, housing privatisation in the United Kingdom in the 1980s was a consequence of the neoliberal agenda promoted by the British government, while the wholesale selling off of social housing in many CEE countries was associated with changes in political regimes in the late 1980s, and the reestablishment of market economy principles.

But there are many other privatisation experiences, and by means of example we will focus on two of them: Germany and the Netherlands. Along with some other European countries, the Netherlands has avoided a wholesale commitment to privatisation. Although the approach can be characterised as 'cautious', locally significant privatisation measures have been introduced, in particular in the bigger cities such as Amsterdam where homeownership rates were traditionally very low. The second example is Germany as illustrated by the City of Berlin, half of which was, of course, part of a former socialist state. The purchasers of the housing stock in Berlin are predominantly international financial investors such as Private Equity Funds. The approach is far from 'cautious' and can be described as a 'massive sell off' of public housing.

Outside Europe, there are of course other countries where social housing has been privatised. There are case studies from socialist states outside CEE such as China, where privatisation has a great deal to do with changing state–employer–employee relationships, but also from Hong Kong, where privatisation has taken place since the late 1970s. In the latter case, the quantity and quality of social housing have actually increased despite large sales programmes, partly because the state has kept control of most of the city's land and has been committed to building new social housing. In numerous developed countries outside Europe, such as the United States, Canada, Australia, New Zealand, and various East Asian states, as well as in many developing counties, social housing has historically played a small, residual welfare role and wholesale sell offs have not been feasible.

Privatisation Policies and Practices

The earliest mass privatisation is associated with the United Kingdom where significant numbers of council houses (public housing) were sold to sitting tenants who became homeowners well before the introduction of the Right to Buy in 1980. However, the Right to Buy introduced a uniform national scheme entitling almost all sitting tenants in local authority housing and the tenants of some housing associations, to buy the property that they lived in. It gave them formula-driven claims to a discount on the price at which they could purchase. These discounts were very substantial and were increased so that they could reach 70% of the market value in some cases. Although there have subsequently been some modifications which reduce the maximum discount that can be obtained in some places, the Right to Buy provides an unambiguous entitlement to tenants. This entitlement cannot be blocked by the landlord, although the transfer of council housing to not-for-profit housing organisations does affect entitlement. Where this stock transfer has taken place, existing tenants have a 'preserved' Right to Buy, but any new tenants do not have the Right to Buy. Leaving this aside, the process is activated by the tenant. Although there have been some surges in sales activity associated with changes in the detail of the Right to Buy programme design, or rumours that it was to be more dramatically modified, in general sales under the Right to Buy have fluctuated with housing market and economic changes.

In contrast to the United Kingdom, CEE countries like Hungary and Slovenia have been characterised by short-term explosions of activity. In these countries, a Right to Buy was introduced following political changes and motivated by political ideology. It was introduced as a short-term scheme, which was subsequently replaced by locally determined schemes with different provisions. The unified national schemes operated for 2 years in each country. These short windows of opportunity, as well as the much higher levels of discount, explain the much higher numbers of sales occurring in a short time period in these two countries when compared with the United Kingdom.

In Hungary, the Law on Housing that took effect in January 1994 introduced a Right to Buy under which local government could only resist the sale of flats in a building if the conditions of the building were very bad, if an earlier decision had been taken to rehabilitate the area, or if the building was a listed monument. If none of these circumstances prevailed, the local government had to turn the whole building into a condominium and offer all the flats for sale, even if only one of the tenants announced her/his wish to buy. The prices paid were very low. In most cases, 15% of the market value; 30% of the market value if the building had been substantially renovated in the last 15 years. In each case, a further 40% discount was given if the tenant paid in cash. (If not, the tenant paid by instalments over 35 years, on a fixed 3% interest rate – at that time inflation was around 30% per year.) The Right to Buy in 1993 was endorsed by the elections in 1994. (No political party opposed the Right to Buy.) Providing real estate ownership to the citizens was also in line with the philosophy of the transition. Finally, tenants wanted to buy their flats as they feared soaring rents.

In Slovenia, the main reasons for privatisation of the public stock included:

- removing the burden of high maintenance and renewal costs from the state budget;
- generating a considerable amount of cash to assist the state budget during the critical period of establishing an independent economic base;
- redistributing the wealth accumulated as 'public property' during the period of socialist rule; and
- establishing better housing management and maintenance and refurbishment of multifamily housing.

The 1991, Housing Act transferred the entire public housing stock into the ownership of municipalities who were obliged to sell dwellings to their sitting tenants if they, or any of their immediate family, expressed a willingness to purchase. The buyer was entitled to a 30% discount on the total value of the dwelling, a further deduction of the amount the tenant had paid during the period of tenancy as a 'contribution' to the social housing fund, and a discount equivalent to personal investments in the housing unit in the form of improvement. The tenant purchaser could either pay 10% of the total amount within 60 days of signing the purchase contract with the rest to be paid in equal monthly instalments for the next 20 years or pay the total amount within 60 days of signing the purchase contract. This latter method of payment attracted a 60% discount on the cost of the dwelling. This privatisation model applied uniformly to all public rental dwellings throughout the country, with the major exception of 'restituted' housing, that is, housing given back to the people who originally owned it before it was nationalised. Taking into account all the discounts and deductions, it is estimated that the average selling price for dwellings sold off under the Right to Buy was a mere €100 per square metre, which was approximately 10% of the then average market value in Slovenia.

In both Hungary and Slovenia, the transfer of all housing to local authorities and the establishment of condominiums for all dwellings in buildings where even one sale was completed, meant that the whole stock was affected by privatisation, not just the stock purchased by tenants. But the proportion of tenants who bought was also high, and the short window of opportunity during which they could take advantage of more generous Right to Buy discounts was a key influence. While tenants initiated action – as in the United Kingdom – the costs of delay for tenants created pressure to take up the offer quickly and signalled governments desire to drive the process as strongly as feasible.

In the reunited Germany of 1994, almost 3 million housing units (i.e., 8% of the total housing stock) were in possession of either municipalities or community-based housing associations (see article Social Housing Landlords: Europe). The quota in Eastern Germany was considerably higher: in 1990, more than 3 million housing units (41% of the Eastern German housing stock) were held in public ownership. More than 1.1 million housing units were returned to their former private owners (restitution) or were privatised by a special law on adoption of housing market principals in East Germany (*Altschuldenhilfegesetz*) in the years after the reunification. Public housing in East Germany plummeted to 30% of the housing stock in 1999. In the first 5 years of the twenty-first century, more than 500 000 public housing units had been privatised to international financial investors.

In the City of Berlin, the share of public housing was close to 30% in 1990, but as a result of privatisation politics it has fallen to about 15% today. Since 1990 we have witnessed the privatisation of 200 000 public housing units in Berlin, with 125 000 units sold by the City between 2000 and 2005. We have to differentiate here between two kinds of privatisation: a stock transfer on the one hand (when public housing associations sell a part of their stock), and on the other hand, the privatisation of public housing corporations themselves, which occurs when local government sells its share in a housing association to private owners. The main argument justifying housing associations' privatisation of the housing stock is the weak budget position of associations and the high cost of renovation and modernising the public housing stock. More than 120 000 housing units were privatised in this way. The core argument for local government to privatise housing associations is the fundamental crisis of the public budget. Berlin's debts are estimated at approximately 50 billion euros. Around 88 000 housing units were privatised by selling two housing associations (Gehag and GSW (Gemeinnutzige Siedlungs- und Wohnungsbaugesellshaft Berlin)) for approximately 1 billion euros. With the sales of 212 000 dwellings, the City of Berlin has altogether taken in only 4 billion euros since 1990. This implies an average price of less than 20 000 euros per housing unit.

Finally, in the Netherlands, the Right to Buy has never existed and the approach to the sale of social housing has been more cautious. This is partly because most political parties have not been entirely convinced by the case for privatisation. In addition, the relationship between the state and the main providers of social rented housing has been different from elsewhere. The most important social housing providers, the housing associations, are not public but private not-for-profit organisations. Until the early 1990s, the idea of selling social housing was virtually unthinkable in Dutch politics. The few attempts that had been made were rather halfhearted. Because so many conditions were attached to the sale, there were very few sales. With the policy document *Housing in the Nineties* (1989), the national government took its first steps towards a withdrawal from the housing market, and privatisation became more common, but only since the late 1990s has privatisation been a real issue. After much discussion, a Right to Buy idea was abandoned as many members of parliament were afraid that a Right to Buy would lead to marginalisation and residualisation of the social housing stock – the British situation was sometimes referred to as a 'worst case scenario' – while other members of parliament indicated that they did not have the power to force the housing associations into a Right-to-Buy-like scheme. The alternative was a more moderate Stimulation-to-Buy scheme that would offer subsidies to help low-income households with purchases. This proposal was included in the *Promotion of Home Ownership Act* (BEW) of 2000. What has emerged from this is managed sales schemes in which the landlord chooses what to sell. Although there has periodically been pressure from national government to adopt a more general approach to privatisation, the process has remained firmly within the control of housing associations. The volume of sales under these schemes has been very much lower than in the other countries, although it has risen in recent years.

Who Benefits?

Much of the research literature associated with housing privatisation has focused on who benefits from the process. There are major differences in this respect. Perhaps the most substantial body of evidence relates to the sale of council houses in the United Kingdom where the better, more attractive properties have been sold (especially houses with gardens), and purchasers tend to be the more affluent households among those who were council tenants (middle- to lower-income groups in relation to the population as a whole, but not including the highest income groups or the lowest) in the middle of the family cycle. Properties in blocks of flats and particularly in those blocks which were built in the 1960s and 1970s are less likely to have been bought. To some extent, the Right to Buy in the United Kingdom has creamed off the best properties and the most affluent tenants from the state housing and housing association sectors, leaving a social rented sector which is more residual both in terms of property and in terms of the narrower social profile of tenants.

In contrast, in Hungary and Slovenia, the scale of uptake of the Right to Buy is much higher. All tenants except the very poorest have participated in the Right to Buy. The process has been less socially selective than in the United Kingdom and less selective in terms of property types. This is partly because these countries with large postwar mass housing estates provided some of the best-quality and best-condition housing, especially when compared with rundown, older properties in cities. Consequently, the attractiveness of these properties is generally higher than that in the United Kingdom where its market position is much more ambiguous, and would often be regarded as comprising the bottom end of the housing market and hence a less attractive purchase. Even so, give-away privatisation in Hungary generates a huge equity problem because of the difference between market values and the discounted selling prices. Taking into account that the best public housing units were allocated according to merit in the socialist period, estimates show that 40% of asset value went to households in the top quarter of the income distribution, while only 17% went to the lowest quarter.

In Slovenia, two major groups benefited from public housing privatisation: the sitting tenants who were given the opportunity to become homeowners at minimum cost; and the state, which acquired substantial financial resources in the process, and also succeeded in ridding itself of the burden of housing management and maintenance. Households living in apartments with a high market value (in the centres or in other favourable locations of major cities) were the ones that benefited the most. On the other hand, the losers were the households that lived in restituted dwellings, whose Right to Buy was strongly restricted. Most of them continue to live under a constant threat of being evicted.

In Berlin, the number of privatised social housing units in West Berlin (108 000) is only a little higher than that in East Berlin (104 000), while the share of public housing in East Berlin (17%) is somewhat higher than that in West Berlin (13%). The majority of sold units are relatively small, with most of the rents below average and with relatively large shares of older people and of households who depend on social benefits. More than half of all privatised housing was sold to financial investors such as Private Equity Funds. Only 5% of housing was privatised directly to sitting tenants or to other social housing tenants. While housing corporations have a long-term interest in their properties and in the rents coming in, the financial investors have a short-term interest and have mostly purchased with a view of reaping a capital gain. Cerberus, the purchaser of 65 000 dwellings from the public housing corporation GSW is an impressive example of this new housing economy. Apart from the GSW deal, Cerberus has been involved in at least nine housing transactions (with around 30 000 dwellings) in Berlin since 2004.

The pattern of benefit in the Netherlands is not so clear because of the selective process of sale orchestrated by landlords. Because landlords are intent upon selling properties in order to achieve other objectives, and more importantly, because many tenants have declined the offer to buy their home (to a large degree because monthly mortgage payments would be much higher than the monthly rent), there is also sale to other owner-occupants in the Netherlands, and this means that the beneficiaries of privatisation are not restricted to sitting tenants.

Conclusions

The impact and the outcomes of the privatisation process are very diverse across the different countries referred to in this article. Privatisation has had a very limited impact in the Netherlands and those that have eventuated were generally intended. The remaining social housing estates are still predominantly rented; in several cases, privatisation has taken place alongside active restructuring both in terms of dwelling types and tenures (see article Rights to Housing Tenure). Though the impact in the Netherlands is limited, the outcomes in the United Kingdom have been substantial. Nevertheless, there have been varied consequences across the United Kingdom's regions, as well as by type of property and tenant characteristics. Twenty-five years on from the introduction of the Right to Buy virtually all parts of the council housing stock have been touched by privatisation. Although the proportions of properties sold may be low, there are some sales in almost all parts of the stock. In the large estates, there is mixed tenure and in blocks of flats there are leasehold management problems. Perhaps just as important is the increased concentration of deprived households in these estates.

In the big-bang privatisations illustrated in this article by Hungary, Slovenia, and also Germany, the impact of privatisation has been more dramatic. Before 1990, public rental housing was almost exclusively in buildings that were wholly state owned and this changed dramatically. It could be argued that housing privatisation was executed too quickly without giving sufficient consideration to all the possible outcomes. In Slovenia, those who were unable to exploit the Right to Buy (nonpublic housing sitting tenants) contend that the measure was unfair since it benefited only some, while everybody participated through monthly contributions in the creation of the public housing stock. Disputes still continue regarding the rights of the sitting tenants and those of the new landlords of restituted dwellings, and there are no serious indications that any viable solution to the problem will be found in the near future. Coupled with the condominium arrangements and economic restructuring which has left many households with very low incomes, privatisation of housing has transformed ownership and management processes, but offers no general prospect of responding to problems associated with dwelling quality, maintenance and repair, or improvement and renewal. The Berlin privatisation politics do not incorporate the sitting tenants into the privatisation process and a majority of privatised housing was en-bloc sold off to financial investors.

The nature, extent, and legacies of privatisation are very different and present different problems in relation to the future of these estates in different countries. In the Netherlands, the framework for renewal and restructuring is stable – but could face serious challenges when major investment activity is needed. In the United Kingdom, the process is much more complicated and winning consent and support for major policy initiatives now involves negotiation with a much more diverse group of interests and stakeholders. Some situations have arisen where the Right to Buy significantly increases the costs and delays associated with renewal. In Berlin, we see a dramatic reduction of the public housing stock and selective upgrading activities. In consequence, the local government lost an important instrument of political regulation and intervention in the housing market. On the other hand, increasing rents in privatised housing stock limits marginal groups' access to housing. The short-term financial relief for the City of Berlin may be more than welcome, but the long-term effects may be very costly, not just for tenants faced with rising rents and evictions, but also for the city at large as affordable housing is easier to lose than to re-create. Finally in the cases of Hungary and Slovenia, the changed legal and ownership situations present an entirely new challenge for policy-makers and without significant funding from elsewhere the problems of winning consent to major initiatives may prove insurmountable.

Acknowledgement

This entry largely draws on Murie et al. (2005) and Aalbers and Holm (2008).

See also: Housing and the State in Western Europe; Policies to Promote Housing Choice in Transition Countries; Rights to Housing Tenure; Social Housing Landlords: Europe.

References

Aalbers MB and Holm A (2008) Privatising social housing in Europe: The cases of Amsterdam and Berlin. In: Adelhof K, Glock B, Lossau J, and Schulz M (eds.) *Urban Trends in Berlin and Amsterdam*, pp. 12–23. Berlin: Berliner Geographische Arbeiten, Humboldt Universität zu Berlin.
Murie A, Tosics I, Aalbers MB, Sendi R, and Černič Mali B (2005) Privatisation and after. In: Van Kempen R, K Dekker, S Hall, and I Tosics (eds.) *Restructuring Large-Scale Housing Estates in European Cities*, pp. 85–104. Bristol, UK: Policy Press.

Further Reading

Aalbers MB (2004) Promoting home ownership in a social-rented city: Policies, practices and pitfalls. *Housing Studies* 19(3): 483–495.
Boelhouwer PJ (1988) *De verkoop van woningwetwoningen. De overdracht van woningwetwoningen aan bewoners en de gevolgen voor de volkshuisvesting*. Delft, The Netherlands: Delft University Press.
Borst R (1996) Volkswohnungsbestand in Spekulantenhand? Zu den möglichen Folgen der Privatisierung von ehemals volkseigenen Wohnungen in den neuen Bundesländern. In: Häußermann H and Neef R (eds.) *Stadtentwicklung in Ostdeutschland. Soziale und räumliche Tendenzen*, pp. 107–128. Opladen, Germany: Westdeutscher Verlag.
Forrest R and Murie A (1990) *Selling the Welfare State*. London: Routledge.
Glock B and Keller C (2003) The impact of property restitution on housing development in East Germany. In: Lowe S and Tsenkova S (eds.) *Housing Change in East and Central Europe*, pp. 105–112. Aldershot, UK: Ashgate.
Hegedüs J and Tosics I (1994) Privatisation and rehabilitation in the Budapest Inner districts. *Housing Studies* 9: 39–54.
Holm A (2006) Der Ausstieg des Staates aus der Wohnungspolitik. In: Altrock U, et al. (eds.) *Planungsrundschau: Sparsamer Staat – Schwache Stadt?*, pp. 103–113. Berlin: Verlag Uwe Altrock.
Jones C and Murie A (2006) *The Right to Buy: Analysis & Evaluation of a Housing Policy*. Oxford, UK: Blackwell.
Lowe S and Tsenkova S (eds.) (2003) *Housing Change in East and Central Europe: Integration or Fragmentation?* Aldershot, UK: Ashgate.
Priemus H and Mandič S (2000) Rental housing in Central and Eastern Europe as no man's land. Special issue: Rented housing in Eastern

and Central Europe. *Journal of Housing and the Built Environment* 15(3): 205–215.

Sendi R (1995) Housing reform and housing conflict: The privatisation and denationalisation of public housing in the Republic of Slovenia in practice. *International Journal of Urban and Regional Research* 19: 435–446.

Struyk RJ (ed.) (1996) *Economic Restructuring of the Former Soviet Block. The Case of Housing*. Washington, DC: The Urban Institute Press.

Turner B, Hegedüs J, and Tosics I (eds.) (1992) *The Reform of Housing in Eastern Europe and the Soviet Union*. New York: Routledge.

Property Rights Approaches

CA Nygaard, University of Reading, Reading, UK

© 2012 Elsevier Ltd. All rights reserved.

Glossary

De facto rights The ability to control, affect, and derive the user value or income stream generated by an asset or asset attributes – also referred to as economic rights.

De jure rights Legal rights or title rights that are recognised and enforced by legal institutions and by the government – also referred to as nominal rights.

Delineation The separation and recognition of individual asset attributes and their specific user value or income stream.

Property rights bundle Assets (objects) are conceptualised as consisting of a bundle of attributes. Ownership confers property rights to part or the entire bundle of attributes.

Public domain Where the transaction cost of delineation exceeds the user value or income stream of specific attributes these are said to remain in the public domain, i.e. no exclusionary mechanism exists.

Residual claimant The de facto (economic) owner or owners of any noncontractually determined or captured net income or welfare generated by assets or specific asset attributes.

Transaction costs The costs of establishing, monitoring, and enforcing property rights associated with a specific attribute or bundle of attributes.

Introduction

Property rights theory (PRT) is a field of New Institutional Economics (NIE). As with other fields in NIE, PRT analyses governance structures of economic coordination and behaviour in light of positive and non-negligible transaction costs. The welfare experienced by individuals and households is affected by numerable aspects of the urban economy and housing markets. Decisions made by public and private actors regarding the urban economy, spatial organisation, land use, and housing markets affect individuals' present and future welfare.

Neoclassical economic models assume that price signals suffice to allocate resource to their highest-value use. However, the significant transaction costs associated with land use, spatial organisation, and real estate markets pose major analytical barriers to conceptualising the urban economy in a neoclassical framework in which property rights are fully delineated and assigned and transaction costs are zero. PRT focuses on the delineation and assignment of property rights under positive transaction costs and shows that the content and distribution of property rights affect the allocation and use of resources.

This article sets out an introduction to the property rights methodology and briefly applies the property rights methodology in two market economies and a transition (emerging) market economy context.

Property Rights Theory and Conceptual Tools

According to PRT, commodities have multiple attributes; that is, they consist of a bundle of attributes that, in principle, are separable. For instance, owner-occupation gives the owner the right to use the premises for residential purposes. All premises are associated with certain levels of comfort, amenities, and security that constitute part of what is being purchased. If the house appreciates in value over time the individual owns the right to this capital increase as well as any income stream generated by the asset, for instance, rental income. If the house is located at a place of scenic beauty the property confers ownership of the view as well as access to local (private and public) amenities and neighbourhood characteristics. Less obvious attributes of the house are its fire risk, flooding risk, pollution emitted by the property, or neighbourhood visual or environmental impact. Finally, the house may be part of a nonexclusionary estate where members informally try to decide the parameters of conduct and maintain a common green area. The price that the individual is willing to pay for this particular house reflects his or her valuation of the entire bundle of attributes. However, ownership is seldom unrestricted. A real estate developer might block the view, the local planning authorities might decide to build a new road in the area, or government policies to encourage mixed communities may result in the introduction of housing for low-income families – all of which may change the type of local amenities available in the area. Although the residential attribute remains the same, the individual's valuation of the entire bundle may now substantially change as a result of his or her valuation of the remaining bundle of attributes.

An individual's valuation of an attribute thus reflects the individual's ability to secure an expected level of value or welfare. For many types of goods this depends to an extent on the ability to exclude others from consuming all, or parts of, the value or welfare. The emphasis of PRT in the social sciences is, in other words, on the economic value, or welfare, derived from ownership. PRT defines ownership as an individual's right to utilise, earn, and extract income and welfare from an asset and asset attributes; change its form; or dispose of these rights through transfer or exchange to another party (right to alienate). In practice, full ownership of this kind is rare and many urban policy and economic issues, such as urban regeneration, pollution, externalities and changes in land use, reflect the distribution of various aspects of ownership amongst different actors. PRT therefore distinguishes between de facto and de jure property rights.

De jure (or legal) rights are rights that are recognised and enforced, in part, by government and legal institutions. De facto (or economic) rights involve the ability to control, consume, and appropriate the value and welfare generated by assets. De facto rights may stem from the efforts by individuals to capture parts of the income stream or welfare, contractual arrangements and cultural and social traditions. In capitalist and market societies de jure rights enhanced de facto rights to the extent that they involve third-party recognition of the rights to the income stream or welfare and the right to alienate and may thus reduce transaction cost and uncertainty in the case of dispute resolution. However, legal recognition is not sufficient, or indeed necessary, for economic rights to exist and remains a diffuse concept in many transition economies in which the delineation and distribution of property rights may be unclear. The extensiveness and completeness of de jure property rights differ between jurisdictions. Thus, the mere existence of legal rights does not necessarily ensure that economic rights cannot be captured by another party.

Property rights are closely related to residual claimancy, that is, the owner(s) of any noncontractually determined or captured net value or welfare. In the illustration above, the individual (as a de facto owner) is the residual claimant in that he or she benefits (incurs a loss) from any increase (decrease) in the value of the house. Being the economic owner of any change in value is an incentive, net of costs, to improve asset value. However, residual claimancy is frequently shared with other individuals (Barzel, 1997; e.g., insurers, utility firms, neighbours) who also stand to benefit or lose from a change in attribute value and whose actions might affect the asset's value. In PRT, an individual's share in the residual should increase in accordance with his/her contribution to the average income or welfare an asset can generate (Barzel, 1997). Where the marginal contribution of individuals' actions to attribute valuation is variable, unpredictable, and difficult to measure, it is costly to determine whether the welfare or income flow from any specific action (e.g., capital improvements) is what it should have been. Incomplete contracting resulting from bounded rationality, asymmetric information, exchange parties acting with guile, and/or costliness of establishing delineable and enforceable rights thus leaves part of the welfare or income stream in the public domain and subject to wealth-consuming capture activity.

The value of asset or attribute property rights depends on the security of rights. When exchange parties or nonowners are able to affect or appropriate a share of the expected income or welfare flow from an action, there is a disincentive to invest or capitalise income or welfare through an exchange of rights. Transaction costs associated with contracting and exchange thus determine the extensiveness of contracting and the security of rights. Where all the de jure and de facto property rights of a bundle of attributes are completely aligned with one individual (a special, and for urban economics unrealistic, case with only one residual claimant), the value of rights (to the owner) has been maximised by minimising uncompensated exploitation. However, while this removes contracting and exchange-specific transaction costs, it may be subject to other transaction costs that lower the total potential value of the asset. First, the property rights holder's human capital may not match that which is necessary to generate the full potential income or welfare, and second, full concentration of property rights inhibits specialisation and economies of scale (Barzel, 1997). Maximisation of net asset value, then, is achieved when property rights are delineated and distributed so as to minimise uncompensated exploitation and, where existing, allow specialisation and economies of scale.

Separation of attributes can occur where the expected value of attribute ownership exceeds transaction costs (monitoring and enforcement costs) associated with establishing and enforcing property rights. The degree and type of property right that is exchanged is a function of the ex ante cost of contracting and the ex post cost of monitoring and enforcing contracts. A redistribution of property rights can enable the redirection of parts of an asset's value or welfare to 'another' use – for example, to a use more highly valued than its ex ante use or a user able to extract a higher value or welfare. The delineation of property rights along attributes allows for specialisation and economies of scale. In the illustration above, the individual can invest time resources in the efficient functioning of the informal governance arrangements, or seek to outsource this service to a third party. By taking out an insurance against fire, flooding, and burglary the individual is transferring some of the property rights in these attributes to another (specialist) party. PRT thus posits that different individuals have comparative advantages in owning different attributes.

Property rights may be left in the public domain (not to be equated with public ownership), where the transaction costs of delineating rights are prohibitive. An attribute is in the public domain if its use is not charged for at the margin. In the illustration above, the visual impact of the house is difficult to establish with any degree of certainty and, although the very attribute may have been instrumental in the individual's valuation of the house, the cost of establishing the precise value of its visual impact on the neighbourhood is prohibitive and hence left in the public domain. For instance, adjacent homeowners are not charged or compensated for the value impact on their property. The public domain can be defined spatially or otherwise, and it is the domain in which competition for the consumption of income or welfare occurs. Where such competition leads to congestion, the distribution of property rights is inefficient to the extent that the resources individuals expend on capturing public domain rights accrue to no one and thus by definition are wasteful. Importantly, the public domain is not simply an extension of public property or ownership. A number of public goods or local public goods are, in effect, exclusionary due to cost-access considerations and the spatial extent of the attribute (Webster, 2002). Cities thus comprise a number of smaller publics that each enjoy de facto ownership secured by cost-access considerations. Moreover, private property may exhibit public domain problems for those individuals who have bought the right to access. For instance, if all the members of a private golf club want to play golf simultaneously, the golf course would be congested and some individuals would have to wait – expending time resource.

Where property rights are costly to delineate, transacting gives rise to a notion of implicit and explicit bundling of attributes. In the illustration above, access to neighbourhood characteristics or the scenic view is implicitly bundled (though this need not be the case), whereas property-specific amenities and rights are explicitly bundled. Transacting, then, is the reallocation of de jure and de facto property rights amongst the transacting parties and involves the transfer of right to income or welfare from a bundle of property rights from one party to another.

The antecedents of a dynamic element of PRT come from Coase's (1937) analysis of market and firm organisation of economic activity where nonnegligible transaction costs give rise to competing forms of governance of economic activity. Similarly, Coase (1960) argues that the presence of nonnegligible transaction costs inhibits the delineation of property rights. The distribution of property rights, which in a zero transaction cost world would be inconsequential, thus determines the subsequent allocation of resources and economic efficiency. Moreover, different distributions of property rights arise in response to different allocative problems or challenges and affect the incentive structure of economic behaviour. A comparative assessment of the income and welfare stream generated by different distributions of property rights enables us to assess the economic efficiency of institutional and organisational evolution.

What then is efficient? PRT views the delineation of property rights and bundling of attributes assigned to the party most capable of extracting the inherent (or potential) value or welfare as efficient. As such, property 'rights' provide decentralised incentives to maximise existing assets and, through trade, allocative efficiency. PRT here differs from other NIE disciplines in which, in the case of agency theory, the focus is on an alignment of the incentives of the agent with the principal (enforced through monitoring mechanisms) or, in the case of transaction costs economics, a choice of market or hierarchical structures of governance (Kim and Mahoney, 2005).

Transfers of property rights occur in response to relative changes in asset attribute valuation. The relative value of attributes is likely to change over time as societal preferences, technology, and institutional and organisational arrangements change. In this dynamic sense the trade in property rights enables the allocation of resources to their highest-value use by allowing alternative agents to maximise the implicit value or welfare, in response to these changes, by establishing exclusionary mechanisms that constrain uncompensated use. A static distribution of property rights may, on the other hand, result in the over- or underconsumption of resources. This, then, implies that the allocation of property rights determines the boundaries of the public and private domains and, by implication, the boundaries of public and private governance structures of economic activity. (While PRT envisages that trade in property rights allows resources to be directed to their highest-value use, a related issue in PRT is the intimate relationship between the existing distribution of property rights and the existing distribution of wealth and power. Therefore changes in property rights also reflect the maximisation of political power. This endogeneity in the demand for property rights and modification of property rights gives rise to the endogeneity in demand for institutions that may cause the persistence of inefficient property rights regimes.) The notion of changing boundaries of the private and public domains and private and public structures of governances has important implications for the analysis of urban policy and economics.

The governance structure of economic activity reflects the mode by which owners capitalise the value of their respective property rights (i.e., convert value into political and/or economic gain). The redistribution of property rights is therefore an essential element of public policy reform and the governance of economic activity. As in the illustration above, ownership confers property rights to positive and negative externalities alike. Government intervention in private markets is often targeted at perceived market failure arising from the uncompensated existence of such externalities. However, government policy that realigns property rights (redistribution and residual claimancy) to deal with public domain or externality issues changes the incentive structure of agents and the relative value of assets and income streams, which can result in intended 'and' unintended market outcomes.

Applied Property Rights Theory
Direct Public Provision of Social Housing

Welfare state systems in industrialised countries differ in their degree of universality and extent of service provision. In the United Kingdom and the United States the emergence of not-for-profit (NfP) organisations since the 1960s has accompanied an overall reduction in welfare services, a shift towards more means-tested eligibility, and a drive to decentralise service responsibilities. The increased financial and political support for the NfP sector, to some extent reflects efficiency concerns with the mode of service delivery, but cannot be separated entirely from the NfP sector's strategic potential in a struggle between central and local governments over the control and use of public resources (Wolch, 1990). Moreover, the interaction between public organs and the NfP sector became increasingly formalised with increased regulatory oversight and monitoring requirements. Standardisation of interaction reduced the transaction costs of expanding the use of NfPs, but also constrained the autonomy of the NfP sector.

From a PRT perspective, social housing consists of a number of attributes of which the actual de jure and de facto property rights bundling reflects the organisational and institutional mode of governance. Changes in the value of attributes lead to the rebundling of property rights, allowing greater value or welfare to be derived and the emergence of a new organisational structure. The growing financial and political support for NfPs and the transfer of social housing in the United Kingdom, first to sitting tenants and subsequently to NfPs as going concerns, reflect the unbundling and rebundling of property rights in public housing. Ownership of social housing confers de jure and de facto property rights to social housing attributes. The value and cost of different attributes determine the value of these property rights; attribute value may change in response to political, economic, and technological circumstances. Nygaard et al. (2007, 2008) therefore argue that ownership transfer might be seen as the spin-off of property rights to which the transaction costs of delineation declined and/or the (perceived or real) dissipation of income and welfare was sufficient for a specialised owner to extract a surplus. In other words, the transfer of property rights in social housing allows an alternative owner to establish exclusionary mechanisms to capture income or welfare.

The analysis of transfer of property rights in social housing is a comparative analysis of property rights ownership ex ante and ex post transfer. The transfer of social housing in the UK as going concerns involves the sale of the physical housing stock from the Local Authority (or additionally Scottish Homes in the case of Scotland) to an NfP organisation. (Note that property rights analysis of social housing reform varies according to type of transfer or management organisation.) However, Nygaard et al. (2007) argue the typical delineation and transfer of property rights in social housing substantially increases the central government's de jure and de facto property rights. The NfP organisation assumes the de jure and de facto ownership of the management and housing delivery attributes, but attributes related to the social policy implementation agenda are de facto transferred to the central government's regulator. The distribution of property rights that ensues following a transfer thus primarily reflects Local Authority and central government value extraction strategies and constraints. Moreover, Nygaard et al. (2007) argue that such a redistribution of property rights constitutes a significant redistribution of property rights 'within' the public sector and is essential to a recentralisation of social housing policy and power incentive structure.

The 'specialised' buyer, in a number of transfers, is simply the previous housing management personnel (Gibb and Nygaard, 2006). However, the specialised buyer's ability to generate additional income and welfare remains dependent on local and central funding incentive structures, maintaining the regulator of the latter's residual claimants to the income and welfare stream. The ability of the regulators to financially and organisationally penalise the NfP organisation ensures the alignment of the NfP's behaviour with policy objectives and enables the central government to derive value from (de facto property right) the managerial or housing delivery attribute as well. In some cases the specialised buyer's reliance on central government funding opportunities is sufficiently strong for the specialised buyer to perceive incentives as fiat.

In Australia, the Commonwealth State Housing Agreement (CSHA) was the principal vehicle for the provision of below-market housing – a CSHA priority was public housing provision. However, since the end of the 1980s the Commonwealth has placed increased emphasis on Commonwealth Rent Assistance (CRA) as the vehicle for assisting private rental households in meeting their housing expenditure. These changes and the emphasis on Community Housing Organisations (CHO), if continued, entail a significant redistribution of property rights 'within' the public sector. In Australia, the Commonwealth State Housing Agreement (CSHA) was the principal vehicle for the provision of below-market housing, predominantly in the form of public housing. However, reforms since the 1990s are affecting the value of property rights (and shares in any residual) in publicly

(State and Territory owned) and nonpublicly-owned social housing. First, the increased expenditure on Commonwealth Rent Assistance (CRA) to assist households meeting below-market (private) rental costs, and second, greater regulatory oversight of social housing provision and increased financial support for NfP organisations since the mid-2000.

These trends are embedded in the National Affordable Housing Agreement (NAHA) that superseded the CSHAs in 2009, and ongoing reform objectives. The reform agenda for social housing considers greater regulatory standardisation and growth of the CHO/NfP sector – from some 11% in 2010 to 35% of the social housing stock in 2014 (FaHCSIA, 2010). A combination of public housing stock transfer and tax incentives for new build available to NfP providers under the National Rental Affordability Scheme, in conjunction with CRA, underpins these aims. The systemic trend embedded in the NAHA and the ongoing reform agenda thus reflect additional delineation of property rights in social housing and a redistribution of property rights and residual claimancy within the public (Commonwealth, States, and regulatory bodies), NfP, and private sectors. Thus, specialisation and standardisation (of regulation and funding) potentially enhance the value of social housing property rights by reducing the transaction costs of ownership, contracting, and investment.

Changes in funding and monitoring arrangements will affect the relative value of social housing attributes in Australia and, likely, the organisational structure of social housing delivery.

Land Reallocation and Urbanisation in China

Following China's communist revolution in 1949 private property was abolished and property rights over resources were nationalised. A dual system of land ownership emerged in which de jure property rights to urban and rural land was entrusted to the various administrative layers and rural collectives, respectively. However, the absence of private property in the socialist tradition renders the concept and delineation of property rights ambiguous. Multiple actors in the collective and urban hierarchies jointly exercise property rights, but the delineation and distribution of rights is frequently unclear and rights are incomplete (Tian, 2008; Zhu and Hu, 2009). For instance, rural collectives do not have the formal right to convert land to nonagricultural uses without approval from the administrative hierarchy, and income rights are formally restricted to agricultural uses (Tian, 2008).

Prior to economic reforms in 1978 and fiscal decentralisation in the 1980s land was allocated administratively and free of economic rent (an important element of rent extraction and contestation in socialist economies, however, concerned the extraction of political rent) where the centralised nature of production sought to align land users' (de facto owners') incentives with those of the central planning apparatus in that the state acted as principal 'and' agent. Once allocated, however, land was difficult to retrieve (or reassign) and land use right became a distinct socialist institution (Zhu, 2004). The resulting pattern of land use in Chinese (and many transition economy) cities therefore significantly differed from those in market economies. With economic decentralisation in 1978 and the formalisation of a land lease system and marketisation of 'land user rights' in 1988 a land-rent gradient emerged. Urban land can, after payment to the state, be leased for a fixed period (depending on use) through tender, auction, and negotiation. However, ambiguously delineated property rights meant that a substantial part of the land-rent differential between current use and potential use value is left in the public domain. While the dual system of land ownership formally remains in place, de jure and de facto property rights holders at different levels in the collective and urban hierarchies have become significant residual claimants. Conditioned by political, fiscal, and social constraints and obligations these actors have developed a range of strategies to capture public domain value. Competition for public domain value has shaped the processes of brownfield redevelopment in cities and conversion of rural land.

In urban areas local growth coalitions (Zhu, 2005), consisting of public and private sector agents, emerged that are able to extract the existing land capital value rent. Both 'danwei' rights holders (state enterprises/existing users, de facto rights holders) and de jure property rights holders, in the form of municipal- and district-level administrative authorities, have acted as agents for redevelopment in this process. 'Danwei' property rights holders transfer 'land use rights' to investors in order to capitalise de facto property rights (Zhu, 2004). 'Land development right' is established (negotiated) between the 'danwei' and the local government, which reflects the 'danwei's' 'land use rights'. Given that 'land development rights' are only informally recognised, 'danwei' rights holders have an incentive to realise redevelopment projects quickly since the land-rent differential can only be secured once a building is ready for sale or lease (thus capitalising the land-rent differential in the redevelopment's market value). The municipal government is paid a fee to certify the land transfer (Zhu, 2004). De facto and de jure (at local government levels) rights holders were thus able to capture public domain value at the expense of the state (also a de jure rights holder). Due to the ambiguous delineation of property rights the tacit acceptance by de jure property rights holders (the state and the various administrative levels as agents of the state) of 'danwei' 'land use right' holders' ability to share in the land capital value gap was essential to ensure that 'danwei' holders relinquish 'land use rights'. While purposeful in the early period of transition (Zhu, 2005), the central state has since 2002 sought to curtail inefficiencies (oversupply, low-quality development) and irregularities (corruption) arising from competition in the public domain by enhancing its de jure rights. However, legal and political ambiguity in transition may have been instrumental to social stability (Ho and Spoor, 2006).

Competition for public domain value is also evident in the conversion of rural into urban land. The conversion of rural land constitutes the main source of land for urban development through land lease. Urban authorities can expropriate agricultural land by paying a compensation fee. The formal compensation stipulated by the Land Administration Law is based on the land value under agricultural use and does not reflect the potential use value (land-rent gradient). Therefore, under formal conversion the land value gap is primarily capitalised by urban authorities (making urban authorities a key residual claimant) while the various de jure collective property rights holders share the compensation. However, a conversion process can also be initiated by collective de jure property rights holders. In these cases informal land development projects are carried out by the various de jure property rights holders (e.g., townships and villages). Ambiguously delineated de jure property rights, however, mean that townships and villages rights holders compete between themselves and with urban authorities for the capitalisation of the land rent gap in the public domain (Zhu and Hu 2009). Hybrid conversion processes, in which land is expropriated but a small portion of the reclassified land is returned to collective ownership, have also emerged that allow the de jure collective owners to formally appropriate a fraction of the land value gap.

A property rights analysis highlights the unlocking of economic growth arising from reallocation of property rights amongst existing urban land users and from agricultural land users to urban land users. On the other hand, ambiguous and incomplete property rights lead to competition for land-rent differentials (value) in the public domain and capitalisation of the value gap through development. The ensuing oversupply of developable land leads to rapid urbanisation, shrinking agricultural land, and weakly coordinated conversion of agricultural land at the urban fringe, which potentially exacerbates negative externalities (overcrowding, pollution, 'land encircling', etc.), infringes on the rights and values of other property rights holders, and does not adequately reflect the scarcity of agricultural land in some areas. Moreover, strategies for preempting formal conversion of agricultural land, or minimising formal compensation costs, can also result in the concentration of such externalities within the built-up area of some cities (Tian, 2008).

Conclusions

This article has introduced PRT and its application to important housing and urban economics issues. PRT views assets as consisting of bundles of rights, where the delineation and redistribution of de jure and de facto property rights are viewed in terms of their ability to generate additional income or welfare. Transaction costs determine the extent to which property rights are delineated and exclusionary mechanisms can be enforced. The application of PRT analyses the extent to which the alignment of de jure and de facto property rights of multiple property rights holders enables the maximisation of net asset value. The application of PRT analyses 'who owns what' and the extent to which the distribution of de jure and de facto property rights (and shares in any residual) enable the maximisation of net asset value. A distribution of property rights that minimises uncompensated exploitation is regarded as economically efficient as it incentivises the most productive use of assets and efficient allocation of economic resources. Conceptualising assets as bundles of attributes enables specialisation and economies of scale. Incomplete contracting, however, may render income and welfare in the public domain and subject to wealth-dissipating capture activity, while institutional factors and high transaction costs may perpetuate inefficient property rights allocations.

This article has focused on the understanding of key PRT principles and an application of some of these principles to the institutional evolution of urban policy, illustrated by social housing reform and the delineation and reallocation of land-related property rights in China. However, this is not meant to play down very important normative aspects of PRT and the delineation of rights. PRT is concerned with the distribution of property rights and the ensuing behavioural incentive structure that shapes urban economies and systems. This contains important equity and welfare state concerns as well as political economy considerations. The exclusionary mechanisms that raise the value of property rights can also lead to disenfranchisement, social exclusion, or perceptions of inequity, which also shape the urban landscape and economy. While PRT provides conceptual tools that enable detailed and fruitful analysis of many housing and urban economics issues – this article has examined but a few – a complete analysis of the individual issues requires an assessment of how to compensate those who are excluded through property rights redistribution. Moreover, a complete evaluation of the welfare and income gains from property rights delineation and trade ought to consider the total, that is, not just to the eventual holders of rights, welfare or income gain from property rights delineation.

See also: Collective Ownership; Economics of Housing Externalities; Economics of Social Housing; Housing and the State in China; Housing Policy: Agents and Regulators; Institutional Economics: New; Politics of Housing; Privatisation of Social Housing; Transaction Costs in Housing Markets.

References

Barzel Y (1997) *Economic Analysis of Property Rights*, 2nd edn. Cambridge, UK: Cambridge University Press.

Coase R (1937) The nature of the firm. *Economica* 4: 386–405.

Coase R (1960) The problem of social cost. *Journal of Law and Economics* 3: 1–44.

FaHCSIA (Australian Government Department of Families, Housing, Community Services, and Indigenous Affairs) (2010) *Regulation and Growth of the Not-For-Profit Housing Sector*. Discussion Paper. Canberra: FaHCSIA.

Gibb K and Nygaard C (2006) Transfers, contracts and regulation: A new institutional economics perspective on the changing provision of social housing in Britain. *Housing Studies* 21: 825–850.

Ho P and Spoor M (2006) Whose land? The political economy of land titling in transition economies. *Land Use Policy* 23: 580–587.

Kim J and Mahoney J (2005) Property rights theory, transaction costs theory, and agency theory: An organizational economics approach to strategic management. *Managerial and Decision Economics* 26: 223–242.

Nygaard C, Gibb K, and Berry M (2007) Ownership transfer of social housing in the UK: A property rights approach. *Housing, Theory and Society* 24: 89–110.

Nygaard C, Berry M, and Gibb K (2008) The political economy of social housing reform – a framework for considering decentralized ownership, management and service delivery in Australia. *Urban Policy and Research* 26: 5–21.

Tian L (2008) The Chengzhongcun land market in China: Boon or bane? – A perspective on property rights. *International Journal of Urban Regional Research* 32: 282–304.

Webster C (2002) Property rights and the public real: Gates, green belts, and gemeinschaft. *Environment and Planning B* 29: 397–412.

Wolch J (1990) *The Shadow State: Government and the Voluntary Sector in Transition*. New York: Foundation Centre.

Zhu J (2004) From land use right to land development right: Institutional change in China's urban development. *Urban Studies* 41: 1249–1267.

Zhu J (2005) A transitional institution for the emerging land market in urban China. *Urban Studies* 42: 1369–1390.

Zhu J and Hu T (2009) Disordered land-rent competition in China's periurbanization: Case study of Beiqija township, Beijing. *Environment and Planning A* 41: 1629–1646.

Further Reading

Alchian A and Demsetz H (1973) The property right paradigm. *Journal of Economic History* 33: 16–27.

Eggertsson T (1990) *Economic Behaviour and Institutions*. Cambridge, UK: Cambridge University Press.

Furubotn E and Richter R (2005) *Institutions and Economic Theory: The Contribution of the New Institutional Economics*, 2nd edn. Ann Arbor, MI: University of Michigan Press.

Grossman S and Hart O (1986) The cost and benefits of ownership: a theory of vertical and lateral integration. *Journal of Political Economy* 94: 691–719.

Libecap G (1989) Distributional issues in contracting for property rights. *Journal of Institutional and Theoretical Economics* 145: 6–24.

Webster C and Lai L (2003) *Property Rights, Planning and Markets: Managing Spontaneous Cities*. Cheltenham, UK: Edward Elgar.

Public-Private Housing Partnerships

T Brown, De Montfort University, Leicester, UK

N Yates, Kingston upon Hull City Council, Kingston upon Hull, UK

© 2012 Elsevier Ltd. All rights reserved.

Glossary

Design, build, finance, operate (DBFO) A private-sector consortium responsible for the design, construction, financing, and operation of a scheme with the public sector taking the lead on the initial procurement and the monitoring of performance.

Design, build, operate (DBO) The public sector provides the finance and a consortium of private-sector agencies are responsible for the design, construction, and delivery.

General government financial deficit (GGFD) Unlike PSBR (see below), it does not include borrowing by public corporations.

Local delivery vehicles (LDVs) These are partnerships that bring together public- and private-sector organisations to deliver joint projects through a single agency. Local authorities might provide land while developers and investment institutions could contribute finance and skills.

Private finance initiative (PFI) An arrangement whereby a consortium of private-sector partners comes together to provide an asset-based public service.

Public private partnerships (PPPs) A risk sharing arrangement based on a shared vision between public and private organisations to achieve specific outcomes.

Public sector borrowing requirement (PSBR) PSBR (which is also referred to as public sector net cash requirement – PSNCR) is the quantity of money a government has to borrow in order to finance its annual expenditure. The PSBR covers the gap between the government's income and expenditure.

Transfer of undertakings protection of employment (TUPE) Regulations aimed at safeguarding the rights of employees on their transfer to a different employer.

Introduction

The aim of this section is to highlight issues on public private partnerships (PPPs). More specifically, the objectives are to:

- outline the international dimension;
- draw attention to the rhetoric underpinning the use of PPPs and the theoretical benefits of inter-organisational working;
- highlight the rise of PPPs as part of the shift in governance from hierarchies and markets to networks;
- clarify the confusion on definitions through the use of an approach based on a series of questions, that is, 'the what, who, why, how, and when?';
- analyse the challenges in adopting PPPs; and
- comment on the future of PPPs.

Much of the literature on PPPs focuses on generic issues such as governance and collaborative working. Case studies frequently centre on capital investment projects covering hospitals, schools, and transport. With a few notable exceptions, there has been relatively little in-depth coverage of the housing sector.

Nevertheless, the term 'partnership' has become so common that it has no clear meaning apart from being an alternative to traditional state- and market-orientated approaches. Partnerships, PPPs, and PFIs are terms that are often used interchangeably.

The International Dimension

The OECD comments on PPPs that

> The early trend setters include Australia and the United Kingdom, but by 2004 the list also included countries such as France, Germany, Ireland, Italy, Japan, Korea, Portugal, Spain, Turkey, Argentina, Brazil, South Africa and several others. (OECD [2008] Public-Private Partnerships. Paris: OECD Publishing, p. 11)

By the middle of the last decade, the United Kingdom remained dominant with between 33 and 57% of all of the largest PPP/PFI project finance deals. South Korea had between 12 and 24%, Australia between 3 and 12%, and Spain between 6 and 13%. Nevertheless, despite this widespread phenomenon not all countries have embraced PPPs. The Danish government, for example, has considered their use but there has been only limited engagement because of regulatory issues and strong public finances.

Because of the domination of PPPs and PFIs by the United Kingdom, much of the focus of this contribution draws on the literature and case studies from this country.

The Rhetoric of Public Private Partnerships

The British deputy prime minister in 2002 stated,

> Partnership is about bringing additional investment into public services, helping to develop new ways of working, helping to bring in new expertise, ingenuity and rigour, and helping to meet the rising expectations of the public ... It would be absolutely crazy for a government to depart from a policy that has brought so much benefit to so many people, and that has begun to tackle the massive disinvestment after decades of neglect. This government has no intention of doing so and will carry out the promise it has made to provide first-class public services through the combined benefits of public and private capital in a truly public private partnership for the public good. (Prescott J [2002]: Delivery – The Partnership Approach: Speech to the UK Government Conference on Public-Private Partnerships on 16th October 2002)

This quotation summaries an impressive list of the assumed benefits of PPPs. This can be illustrated using examples from housing policy in England. Firstly, they bring in additional private funding. Since the late 1980s, housing associations have collaborated with local authorities, private developers, and financial institutions on new development and modernising existing social housing. In total, over £25 billion of private finance was levered in by housing associations between 1990 and 2005. This was slightly more than the amount of government expenditure for housing associations. In other words, private finance enabled a doubling of housing association activity. Secondly, PPPs bring in new ways of working. This can be illustrated through the multiplicity of acronyms associated with the commissioning and procurement process. For example, DBFO (design, build, finance, and operate) and DBO (design, build, and operate) are frequently used. The former involves a private-sector consortium being responsible for the design, construction, financing, and operation of a scheme with the public sector taking the lead on the initial procurement and the monitoring of performance. The latter centres on the public sector providing the finance and a consortium of private-sector agencies being responsible for the design, construction, and delivery. These approaches can be contrasted with traditional procurement systems where major refurbishment and new build would be undertaken through a competitive contract initiated by the local authority as a client. Thirdly, PPPs encourage new expertise, ingenuity, and rigour. Local delivery vehicles (LDVs) are partnerships that bring together public- and private-sector organisations in a single hybrid organisation. Examples include economic development companies, local housing companies, urban development corporations, and urban regeneration companies. Local authorities might provide land while housing developers and investment institutions could contribute finance and skills to the 'new' organisation. Finally, PPPs help to meet the rising expectations of customers and communities. The public want better services at less cost. The utilisation of private rather than public finance limits the initial requirement for government funding, while the outcomes will be 'state of the art' schools, hospitals, and transport infrastructure as well as new and refurbished homes.

The plausibility of PPPs is reinforced by a myriad of sound bites such as 'there is no alternative', 'the delivery instrument of choice', 'collaborative advantage', 'neither market nor the state', and 'a near-compulsory model'. Governments frequently mandate public-sector organisation to work in partnership with the private sector through a 'carrot and stick' approach. Additional incentives are made available often through competitive bidding programmes. Organisations are penalised through regulatory regimes for not adopting PPPs.

In addition, the theoretical benefits of inter-organisational collaborations are alluded to in many studies and these can be summarised as:

- Better decision making by the inclusion of a range of stakeholders with different skills.
- Accessing new and additional resources, for example finance and land.
- Tackling cross-cutting 'wicked problems' such as the regeneration of socially excluded neighbourhoods.

The Rise of Public Private Partnerships

The growth of PPPs in recent decades can be located within the broader debate on modes of governance and coordination. Partnerships (and networks) can be seen as an alternative to hierarchies and markets. They are linked to the third way, which was the political philosophy of many left-of-centre governments in North America and Western Europe in the 1990s.

Hierarchy is associated with a public-sector bureaucratic mode of operation and the rise of the welfare state in the postwar period. It gives preeminence to the role of governments and other public-sector agencies as enablers and providers of services including social housing. It has been referred to as the 'golden age of public housing'. There was the 10-year million homes programme in

Sweden between 1965 and 1974 to meet the goal of an affordable home for everyone. In France, the number of social housing units increased from 0.27 m in 1945 to 4.2 m by 1991, while in Denmark it increased from 0.07m to 0.43 m over the same period.

A market approach is associated with the Thatcher and Reagan governments in the 1980s in Britain and the USA respectively. Key features included privatisation through the mandatory right to buy in Britain. Between 1980 and 1997, over 1.3 million council properties were sold. Urban regeneration was primarily led by private developers rather than the state in the regeneration of rundown inner-city areas.

Left-of-centre governments in North America and Western Europe in the 1990s argued they were shifting direction from the first way (hierarchies and bureaucracies) and the second way (markets) to a third way. From a PPP perspective, a key feature was the commitment to move away from a command and control approach associated with hierarchies and the competition scenario associated with markets. In their place, the emphasis was one of cooperation and collaboration between public, private, and voluntary sectors. The benefits of networks for governance were highlighted. They were seen as potentially bridging the gap between elected politicians, stakeholders, and members of the public through community empowerment.

There has, thus, been the rise of a diverse range of overlapping partnerships. In the late 1990s, research showed that there was a plethora of at least 700 urban partnerships in Britain with as many as 75 operating in a single city. They have continued to proliferate. In 2005, the Audit Commission calculated that there were 5500 partnerships in the United Kingdom and they accounted for £4 billion of public expenditure. There are, for instance, local strategic partnerships, urban regeneration companies, local housing companies, development trusts, and economic development companies.

It is, however, important to appreciate that partnerships are not a new invention of the twenty-first century. In the nineteenth century in cities, such as London, charitable housing trusts worked with private landowners and the emerging local government sector to provide housing for the working classes. In the period after the Second World War, many city centres in Western Europe were redeveloped through partnership between the public and private sectors. During the Thatcher government in Britain, urban development corporations were established to redevelop rundown areas such as London Docklands. These were partnerships between central government and the private sector and marginalised the role of local authorities and communities. The striking feature of the first decade of the twenty-first century has been the proliferation and establishment of many different types of partnerships.

Defining Partnerships

There are a plethora of acronyms including generic examples such as PPPs (public private partnerships), as well as specific programmes including PFIs (private finance initiatives). They have multiplied at national, regional, subregional, local, and neighbourhood levels and cover, for instance, the housing, health and social care, education, transport, and regeneration sectors.

There are as many definitions as there are books and articles on partnerships. These range from straightforward approaches such as

> … an agreement between two or more independent bodies to work collectively to achieve an objective. (Audit Commission, 2005)

through to a study for the British government that stated,

> A…partnership is a process in which a local authority works together with partners to achieve better outcomes for the local community, as measured by the needs of the local stakeholders, and involves bringing together or making better use of resources. This working together requires the development of a commitment to a shared agenda, effective leadership, a respect for the needs of the partners, and a plan for the contributions and benefits of all the partners. The dynamic aspect of the process requires specific goals of partnership working to be identified, performance to be evaluated, and the assessment of the continuing fit between partnership activities and community needs and priorities. (Newchurch & Company and DETR, 2000)

The Commission on Public Private Partnerships commented in 2001 that debates on PPPs 'generate more heat than light because there is little agreement as to what constitutes a partnership or the types of problem that they might help to solve'. It further stated that a relatively straightforward working definition would be

> … a PPP is a risk sharing relationship between the public and private sectors based upon a shared aspiration to bring about a desired public policy outcome. (Commission on Public Private Partnerships, 2001, p. 40)

These definitions focus on improved outcomes for local communities, more effective use of scarce resources, the importance of the process of developing a partnership, sharing costs and benefits, the need for clear aims and objectives, and the involvement of a wide range of stakeholders. It distinguishes PPPs from more traditional approaches such as a contractual situation between a client and a provider.

Nevertheless, while such generalisations are useful normative expressions of what should happen, they fail to provide an adequate framework for understanding the diversity and variety of PPPs. The complexity has been tackled in definitions that centre on the 'what', 'who', 'why', 'when', and 'how' questions. 'What' relates to the different types of partnerships. These include strategic partnerships that focus on policy, service delivery partnerships, and programme partnerships such as LDVs. The 'who' question centres on the members of the partnership, while the 'why' query considers the rationale for joint working. This may centre on, for instance, a moral imperative to tackle a complex cross-cutting problem. The 'how' question focuses on facilitating collaboration and making partnerships work effectively. As has been already noted, governments may step in and encourage joint ventures through financial incentives. 'When' relates to the life cycle model of a partnership especially the changing governance and organisational arrangements during the duration of a project. This 'question-based' framework can, therefore, be adopted in scoping the nature of housing-related PPPs. For example, there is use of the PFI to redevelop poor-quality social housing estates in England. The 'question-based definition' helps to reveal the complex realities.

- 'What?': The clearance, redevelopment, refurbishment, and future management of a social housing estate including the creation of mixed tenure through shared ownership and owner occupation. They are likely to be linked but separate PFIs for new schools and health centres.
- 'Who?': Organisations involved include councils (e.g., housing and planning departments), housing associations, the third sector, developers, construction companies, private-sector funders, and local community groups.
- 'Why?': Government policy promotes the use of the PFI to tackle the redevelopment of social housing estates. It earmarks funding through competitive bidding programmes to help to promote innovation in provision and service delivery. There is a lack of alternative funding sources.
- 'How?': In order to secure government approval, effective collaboration between the public, private, and voluntary sectors is essential. Councils set the overall strategy and work with private-sector consortiums (including housing associations) to put together detailed proposals.
- 'When?': The development and delivery depend on the government timetable. This usually involves the submission of an outline bid by the local project partnership for government approval as part of a competitive process. Successful bidders are required to submit a detailed business plan for second-stage approval. If this meets government requirements, councils as the lead partner are provided with PFI 'credits', that is, access to private-sector funding.

Challenges for Public Private Partnerships

The rhetoric supporting PPPs together with the theoretical benefits should not be accepted in an uncritical manner. A useful starting point is the vagueness over the use of concepts such as partnership, collaboration, and networks, as well as the tendency to use terms, such as PPPs and PFIs, interchangeably. As has already been pointed out, there are also many specific types of partnerships such as local housing companies and development trusts. Much greater care is needed over terminology and a helpful approach is to adopt the definitional stance outlined in the previous section. This addresses important issues such as the relative role and power of public and private organisations in partnerships, as well as the status of third-sector agencies and community groups, which are often marginalised in debates on PPPs. It also tackles the reality of partnership working. The life cycle of PPPs includes stages where a hierarchical mode of operation is dominant. For example, the monitoring of PFI contracts is little different from that for traditional procurement arrangements. At other times, a more market-centred approach may be in the ascendancy when the private sector arm of the partnership uses subcontractors to carry out specific tasks. A collaborative phase may exist when, for instance, the public and private sector are liaising with users over the implementation of a scheme.

The specific example of the PFI highlights the challenges. Criticisms have focussed on seven grounds. Firstly, it is argued that service delivery is adversely affected. Schemes may take many years to reach fruition, while residents continue to live in poor conditions and face long periods of uncertainty. A proposed housing PFI project in a city in England for the regeneration of a small part of an estate was initially discussed in 2008. There was a substantial period of consultation with residents and the local authority will be submitting a proposal for government approval at the end of 2010. Assuming the bid is successful, the tendering process to set up a PFI will then take place and work may commence in 2013. Meanwhile, a number of tower blocks are gradually being emptied of tenants in anticipation that the PFI project will proceed. There are, thus, continuing issues for local residents including uncertainty on the timetable for the project and the deteriorating quality of the housing and neighbourhood. But the local authority is faced with the situation that a housing PFI is the only realistic source of funding for estate regeneration over the next few years.

Secondly, it is suggested that projects are distorted in the development and design stages to reflect the priorities of the private sector rather than the customers. Partnership schemes may involve a larger proportion of private sector and shared ownership housing and less social rented accommodation. It, of course, might be argued that this might help to create mixed tenure communities rather than monolithic public estates, which were associated with the golden age of public housing. A more telling concern, however, is likely to be the phasing of development that will be geared to market conditions. Social housing is likely to be provided either when the owner-occupied sector is less buoyant or at the end of the development period.

Thirdly, it is argued that the PFI does not necessarily transfer risk from the public to the private sectors. Indeed, it is worth noting that in the United Kingdom, the economic recession has resulted in the government acting as lender of the last resort on some PFI schemes due to the reluctance of the banks to provide funding for consortiums (see below). In 2009, only 35 PFI schemes in total worth £4.24 billion were signed off, which was the worst performance for a decade. Between 1997 and 2004, over 600 PFI deals were agreed.

This links to the fourth consideration of funding that was outlined in the first section. In accounting terminology, PFI contracts are 'off-balance sheet', that is, they are not part of the public sector borrowing requirement (PSBR). Nevertheless, the public sector has to provide a stream of revenue payments over an extended period of time. This raises interesting challenges if, for example, the nature and form of schemes need to change to reflect new ideas. There have been demands that the United Kingdom should switch its system of accounting in a phased manner to the general government financial deficit (GGFD) approach that is used throughout much of Western Europe. This would result in public-sector capital expenditure not being counted as part of the national debt. It would weaken one of the rationales for PPPs and PFIs as private finance would not be required. Nevertheless, it is important to highlight that many Western European countries do use PPPs as a way of increasing capital expenditure.

A fifth issue is whether projects come in on time and within budget. The overall evidence in the United Kingdom is that the majority of schemes in health, transport, and education meet these requirements but there are notorious and frequently quoted examples of failure. For example, the Isle of Skye bridge project in Scotland cost £93 million against a budget of £15 million.

A sixth aspect is whether PPPs and PFIs deliver both value for money and additional investment in neglected public assets. These must be carefully scrutinised as it is argued that they reconcile two competing demands – the desire for increased capital spending while also maintaining a prudent fiscal strategy. Additional finance from the private sector together with market disciplines is seen as the solution. But the reality is that the public sector is committed to a stream of revenue payments over the life of the project (which could be in excess of 30 years) to a private-sector consortium operating, say, a DBFO scheme. This has been neatly summarised as 'paying tomorrow for what we get today i.e. apparent savings now could be countered by the formidable commitment on revenue expenditure in years to come'.

The final consideration is the impact on employment. Under the PFI, many staff have their contracts of employment transferred to a new employer through a process known as TUPE (transfer of undertakings protection of employment). Trades unions have argued that this can lead to worsening conditions for the workforce. For example, pension rights are not subject to TUPE.

From a political perspective, PPPs have been criticised from both the right and left of politics. Supporters of a market approach have argued for 'smaller' government with public provision transferred to the private sector through a process involving, for example, more support for developers and housebuilders. On the other hand, left-of-centre adherents view PPPs as a backdoor measure leading to privatisation. They have called for a greater role for the state. But, as we have seen, there is a danger of over-simplification. Partnerships for the redevelopment of city centres were part of post-Second World War approach for regeneration, while urban development corporations were set up by the Thatcher government. It is the relative power of the public- and private-sector organisations that needs to be considered rather than assuming that PPPs can be abandoned.

Evaluating Public Private Partnerships and Moving Forward

Evaluating PPPs is a challenging issue. Governments' agendas for improving services, such as housing, are orientated to the use of partnerships. But the assessment of partnerships is skewed towards developing good practice on effective collaboration. This has resulted in a significant literature on making partnership working more successful. However, there is the assumption that underpins most of this work that partnerships are better able to deliver public services than bureaucratic hierarchies and markets. The difficulties with assessing the future of PPPs and addressing the challenges, especially for PFIs, are the lack of robust research on their impact. This was summed up by a former government health minister in England, who commented in relation to building new hospitals that PPPs and PFIs have always been 'plan A', and there never was a 'plan B'. If it is assumed that the same principle applies to housing capital investment, the ability to compare outcomes under hierarchies, markets, and partnerships is problematic.

Reference has already been made to the impact of the credit crunch on PPPs. In Britain, because financial institutions have been increasingly unwilling to lend to private-sector consortiums, the Treasury announced in 2009 that it was providing temporary funding for some PFI projects.

It was argued that this would prevent schemes being delayed or cancelled. This represented a significant transfer of risk back to the public sector and went against one of the principles of PPPs. A further challenge over the next decade will arise because of changing international accounting standards. There are moves to require the financial costs to be included 'on balance sheet' rather than 'off balance sheet'. This will create a level playing field with other financing sources. Commentators have argued that these two factors could lead either to a return to traditional commissioning or procurement (a hierarchy approach) or a greater reliance on the market and privatisation.

See also: Social Housing: Finance.

Further Reading

Audit Commission (2005) *Governing Partnerships – Bridging the Accountability Gap*. London: Audit Commission.

Ball M and Maginn P (2005) Urban change and conflict: Evaluating the role of partnerships in urban regeneration in the UK. *Housing Studies* 20(1): 9–28.

Bult-Spiering M and Dewulf G (2006) *Strategic Issues in Public-Private Partnerships – An International Perspective*. Oxford, UK: Blackwell Publishing.

Carley M (2000) Urban partnerships, governance and the regeneration of Britain's cities. *International Planning Studies* 5(3): 273–297.

Commission on Public Private Partnerships (2001) *Building Better Partnerships*. London: Institute for Public Policy Research.

Entwhistle T, Bristow G, Hines F, Donaldson S, and Martin S (2007) The dysfunctions of markets, hierarchies and networks in the meta-governance of partnerships. *Urban Studies* 44(1): 63–79.

Glendinning C, Powell M, and Rummery K (eds.) (2002) *Partnerships, New Labour and the Governance of Welfare*. Bristol, UK: Policy Press.

Huxham C (ed.) (1996) *Creating Collaborative Advantage*. London: Sage.

Koppenjan J, Charles M, and Ryan N (2009) Managing competing public values in infrastructure projects. *Public Money and Management* 28(3): 131–135.

McQuaid R and Scherrer W (2010) Changing reasons for public-private partnerships (PPPs). *Public Money and Management* 30(1): 27–34.

OECD (2008) *Public-Private Partnerships – In Pursuit of Risk Sharing and Value for Money*. Paris: OECD Publishing.

Osborne S (ed.) (2000) *Public-Private Partnerships – Theory and Practice in International Perspective*. London: Routledge.

Parker D (2009) Public private partnerships. *Journal of the Institute of Economic Affairs* 29(1).

Pollitt C (2003) *The Essential Public Manager,* ch. 3. Buckingham, UK: Open University Press.

van Boxmeer B and van Beckhoven E (2005) Public-private partnerships in urban regeneration. *European Journal of Housing Policy* 5(1): 1–16.